D0094588

Staying True

Staying True

JENNY SANFORD

BALLANTINE BOOKS TRADE PAPERBACKS / NEW YORK

Book design by Susan Turner

For Marshall, Landon, Bolton, and Blake with all my love to you, my greatest gifts from above

PROLOGUE

◇

I SEE NOW THAT JUNE 24, 2009, WAS A DAY THAT CHANGED FOR-
ever the trajectory of my life, but it did not change me.

I woke up early that day, as I have always done during our
summers at the beach. The boys and I were at our house on
Sullivan's Island, where we had moved when the school year
ended a few weeks earlier. My mornings there began with a
sunrise cup of coffee in the hour before the boys woke. I sa-
vored that quiet time alone as the kitchen filled with light and
I wrote in my journal. I jotted thoughts, rarely a narrative of
events, and usually reflected on a passage of scripture. My de-
votions had become more urgent and searching in the six
months since I discovered that my husband, Mark Sanford,

the governor of South Carolina, was having an affair with a woman in Argentina.

As I sat on a stool at the kitchen island writing, I knew Mark's flight from Buenos Aires was about to touch down. He had been out of the state (though the world didn't yet know how far he'd wandered) for several days. The media and his political opponents were asking pointed questions about where he was, but only a few reporters had called me. Being on Sullivan's—two hours away from the state capital, Columbia—was a blessing on that front. I'd found out only the day before that Mark was in South America. Within hours, the world would know, and the press would be hovering at the end of our driveway.

The truth was that Mark and I had been quietly separated and had not spoken for two weeks, at my request, with clear restrictions on contact with the Argentinean woman he had started an affair with a year earlier. If he and I were to have a chance at reconciliation, he agreed not to contact her or the boys and me while he sorted things out. Cut off this way, I hoped, Mark might understand what it would be like to lose his family in the form he'd always known it. I wanted Mark to ache for what he'd always said mattered most to him. I thought he got it. Before he left to "get his head right," as he'd explained it to the boys, he looked me straight in the eye and said, "I will not see her." That morning I knew he had broken that promise.

My prayers were brief but pointed: "Lord give me strength. Lord let Mark find you. Lord protect our boys." So many times, I had prayed for the patience to wait this out, or for understanding for him and for me. I felt the full weight of the day ahead on my shoulders. This time when I clasped my hands and shut my eyes, I prayed that the Lord would grant me the strength to protect our children in the ugly time ahead, and I prayed for Mark who was clearly lost.

The only one of the four boys at home that morning was thirteen-year-old Bolton, who was about to leave for a day of fishing with his uncle and cousin. As he gobbled down his breakfast, I pictured our dear friend and Mark's long-time aide, Chris Allen, picking up Mark at the Atlanta airport. A loyal young man who had recently tied his business goals to Mark's political future, Chris had driven through the night to be there when Mark landed. By now, they were on the road to Columbia. I wondered if Mark understood that the whole country, it seemed, wanted a full description of his "hiking the Appalachian Trail."

The phone rang. It was Mark calling from the car. "Hey, how are you?" he asked quietly.

"How am I? How do you think I am?" I sighed.

"Jenny, be gentle with me," he said in a tired voice.

"Gentle?" I asked incredulously. "Do you know what kind of a storm you are returning to? And where do we stand?"

"The good news is it's over now," he said of his affair, and then added, "I've already met a reporter at the airport and told her of my love of adventure travel and so on. I'll call you after I get to Columbia."

I asked again, "What about us?"

"I told you it's all behind us . . . everything's good."

Good?! What part of this did he think was good? I wondered.

I had been anticipating this call, searching for the right way to respond, but everything about his manner caught me off guard, beginning with his blasé tone. I don't know what he could have said to soothe me, but at least I expected an apology and some expression of regret. I hadn't detected a note of that in his voice. He was riding down the highway with Chris arranging for a press conference later that morning and I was one of a number of things he was dealing with. By the time we hung up, I hoped it was slowly dawning on him that this story about his "adventure" wasn't going to hold.

There had been many a morning in the six months since I discovered his affair when I had cried about the state of my marriage, and just as many evenings spent praying with my two girlfriends Frannie and Lalla Lee. This morning, at least, I wasn't going to cry. I was the one who needed to get my head right. I grabbed my iPod, smeared on some sunblock, and headed out the back gate to the beach, some two hundred yards away.

The sun was moving quickly higher in the slate blue sky and the air was hot and sticky, but that thickness didn't dim the sparkle of the sea. My spirit lifted as soon as I set my flip-flops in the sand. Orange and yellow wildflowers lined the path behind our house that leads to the shore. "His Strength Is Perfect" was the first tune on my iPod, which helped my spirits too, as I emerged from the corridor of low dunes and saw the broad beach before me.

This was not in my control, not in my hands, I thought, as the song changed to "I Can Only Imagine." What my future held was something I, the woman who always thought years ahead, now couldn't imagine. Could I imagine a life without Mark, the man whose ambitions had been the center of all that we had done as a family for twenty years? Without him, what was our direction? And how did he feel about me now that he had seen her? Once we got through this day, both of us had life-changing decisions to make. I walked more quickly along the shore, smiling when I saw dolphins playing in the surf. At the beach, I feel wondrously small; my problems are insignificant in this big, beautiful world. This would all sort itself out, and at some point, I would know what to do next. I felt certain of that and that only. I breathed steadily, more deeply, and drank in the peace the sea affords, a tremendous luxury in a world and life otherwise very public.

When I returned, I found that Lalla Lee Campsen, one of my oldest friends in South Carolina, had let herself in. Of course she was there. I could have guessed that she would be from the moment I turned up the path home. She sat at the kitchen island with a notepad and a pen, fielding calls. Petite, bright-eyed, and always smiling, Lalla Lee was the first of Mark's childhood friends to embrace me when this Midwestern Catholic girl found herself living in the Deep South. In those carefree days before politics consumed my time, we'd boated together and played many sets of tennis. Our boys had become good friends, almost as close as Lalla Lee and I had. I was grateful for her steady presence. Whatever this day brought me, we would face it together.

I heard the door to the carport slam and went to the top of the stairs to see Frannie Reese, my closest friend on the island, sprinting upstairs toward me, a bundle of energy in her shorts and bathing suit. She had two cups from Starbucks and handed me one. When we first moved to Sullivan's Island back in 1998, Frannie's husband, Tim, was away almost as much as Mark had been during his years serving in Congress. She and I started out as carpool pals, but within months we were picking up each other's kids after school, taking them to appointments and to practices and eating dinner frequently at each other's homes, herding our kids around like one big mob. Recently, when my sister Kathy moved to Charleston and had a baby of her own, she fell seamlessly into Frannie's generosity. Frannie came to see how I was doing that morning. She said she'd be back before Mark's press conference. I retreated to shower and freshen up.

As I finished getting dressed, I heard Kathy's boisterous voice filling the main room as she came through the front door. She's an artist with a wicked sense of humor who, like our mom, knows how to make an entrance. "He wasn't hiking the Appalachian Trail," she announced. "He was getting Argentine tail!" I laughed. How good it felt to laugh!

Unbidden, my local sisterhood had assembled itself at my house, and my sister Gier was on the plane here from Chicago. So, too, was my dad, who would be arriving within an hour or two. I thought of Blake and Landon, ages ten and fifteen, four miles off the coast deep-sea fishing with Lalla Lee's sons and a friend, and Marshall, our oldest, in the Caribbean, for a two-week summer job. I paused next to the bed that Mark and I shared, to appreciate how truly I loved and was loved and how nothing that happened that day could take any of that from me.

Out in the kitchen, Kathy and Lalla Lee urged me to eat, but I had no appetite. We picked at the salads that Kathy thought to bring. The phone continued to ring, but we were screening the calls. It seemed we were hunkered down in a safe zone, in our cinder-block fortress by the sea, waiting for the next shoe to drop.

"So, Jenny, while you were in the shower Mark called again," Lalla Lee told me reluctantly.

"Are you kidding?" Kathy said, grinning at me. "I gave him a piece of my mind when I answered Jenny's cell. Of course, he thought I was her for a while."

I shook my head, imagining what Kathy had let loose on Mark. Kathy and I have had our sisterly spats, but we are fiercely protective of each other. I felt safer with her around.

After lunch, Chris Allen patched through Mark, who was polling those he trusted on how much he should reveal.

"Should I tell everything?" he asked, businesslike still.

"Whatever you think is right," I said. "What does Lerner say?" I asked, referring to our longtime media adviser and friend in DC.

"He says not to get into too much detail," Mark sighed.

"I agree with that. But you have to be honest about where you were and why."

This was Mark at the mansion and in work mode. I had long ago come to understand that private talk would have to wait.

The day before, when I knew for certain that Mark was in Argentina, I reached out to my family in Chicago, and my dad volunteered to fly to Charleston to be at my side, as had Gier. In the coming weeks, there would be a time when I would need my mom's lively spirit and take-charge attitude, but that day I needed Dad and his calm. I was folding laundry mindlessly, trying to keep busy, when he pulled into the driveway. Just the sight of him, tidy in his pressed khakis and golf shirt, made me feel more firmly anchored to the ground. Yet all I could manage was a weak smile when he walked through the door. Since Mark confessed his affair to him a few weeks earlier, Dad and I had spoken many times. Now we hugged, not saying much. Up close, I saw the pain he carried in his eyes. I was not sure what there was to say.

Mark called again, first announcing that the press conference would be later in the afternoon.

"*The State* has some of our emails," he admitted. I understood that the "our" of that statement did not refer to me, but to his correspondence with his lover. If they were anything like the racy letter I'd discovered in Mark's desk that January, I needed to brace myself for another public humiliation.

"How many do they have? How long have they had them?"

"I don't know."

So, my best political, if not spousal, advice: "Well, be honest and get it over with. Whatever you do, don't talk about your heart."

Then Gier arrived with her boys and mimicked how she had waved as they drove past the reporters and photographers who slumped, bored, in the driveway. It was time for Mark's press conference, and we all crammed into my bedroom, some holding hands as we watched Mark enter the Capitol rotunda. He walked, distracted and guilty, to the podium, squirming, not knowing how to begin. Frannie is the type who likes to ask questions and she started up. I had to caution her that I wanted to hear every word. We were somber and a little frightened as Mark started to ramble. He spent considerable time—it seemed like an eternity—apologizing to everyone in his life, every citizen of the state, people of faith all over the world. Then he revealed the state of his heart. He described days spent crying in Argentina with his lover.

I still don't quite know why I wanted to hear every syllable, but it felt important to bear witness to this in real time, to hear what the watching public was hearing. That said, I am grateful to this day that I can't remember much of it. While it was going on, I was in such shock, it felt as though this was happening to someone else. I wished that were true. Out the bedroom window, I saw a bright orange container ship heading out to sea on its way to Turkey or China. What I wouldn't have given to be on it!

Finally, no longer able to stand the sight of Mark pining

away with tears streaming down his face, Kathy looked at Lalla Lee and said exactly what all of us were thinking, "Will you call someone and tell them to please pull him away from that camera?" Lalla Lee called Chris Allen to suggest this, but the press conference did not end.

As Mark carried on, Kathy moaned, "Let's just end this!"

As if taking a cue from his vocal sister-in-law, Mark did finally finish, but then the commentators began talking about "another politician who cheated on his wife." Wronged Political Spouses is a list no one wants to be on, but now my name would be featured there. Immediately my cell phone rang. It was Mark. Lalla returned to the kitchen to handle the house phone and Frannie went too, to make dinner. I took the call on the porch.

"How'd I do?" he asked.

"Are you kidding me? You cried for her and said little of me or of the boys." I guess he'd forgotten I was not the one to praise this performance.

We hung up, and I went to the study above my bedroom for some privacy. I wanted to say something, to respond, to react, even though I knew that was not the usual protocol followed by betrayed political wives. I'd already missed the part in this ritual where I would stand with head bowed next to him in front of hundreds of cameras as he made his shameful admission. (If I'd been there, perhaps he'd have gotten off the stage sooner.) I had never considered myself a traditional political spouse, though, and this wasn't the moment to start being one. I had been working on a statement.

The night before, over dinner at the Campsens, we had discussed what I could say. Once home, I wrote a formal one-page statement. Now I reviewed what I'd written to see if it still reflected what I felt. It did. I wasn't ashamed and I wanted no one's pity. I asked my dad to read my statement and he suggested a few minor adjustments. Those done, I sent it to my assistant in the First Lady's Office, who emailed it to the local and national press. I also walked down the driveway and handed it to the reporters gathered there. Handing over my statement gave me a wonderful sense of release. I knew there would be endless requests for interviews in the coming days and weeks, and Mark and I would engage in more painful conversations. For that moment, though, my thinking was complete. I truly believed I would be able to enjoy a relaxed dinner with my family, and I really couldn't wait to hug the boys as they returned home. I knew in my heart that whether I reconciled with my husband or not, saying what I truly felt at this time of personal crisis would begin a new chapter in my life. I did what seemed reasonable to me and it seems to have opened new doors: doors to sharing, doors to friendship, doors to some kind of peace.

STATEMENT FROM FIRST LADY JENNY SANFORD
(RELEASED 5:19 P.M., JUNE 24, 2009)

I would like to start by saying I love my husband and I believe I have put forth every effort possible to be the best wife I can be during our almost twenty years of marriage. As well, for the last fifteen years my husband has been fully engaged in public service to the citizens and taxpayers of this state and I have faithfully supported him in those efforts to the best of my ability. I have been and remain proud of his accomplishments and his service to this state.

I personally believe that the greatest legacy I will leave behind in this world is not the job I held on Wall Street, or the campaigns I managed for Mark, or the work I have done as First Lady or even the philanthropic activities in which I have been routinely engaged. Instead, the greatest legacy I will leave in this world is the character of the children I, or we, leave behind. It is for that reason that I deeply regret the recent actions of my husband Mark and their potential damage to our children.

I believe wholeheartedly in the sanctity, dignity, and importance of the institution of marriage. I believe that has been consistently reflected in my actions. When I found out about my husband's infidelity I worked immediately to first seek reconciliation through forgiveness, and then to work diligently to repair our marriage. We reached a point where I felt it was important to look my sons in the eyes and maintain my dignity, self-respect, and my basic sense of right and wrong. I therefore asked my husband to leave two weeks ago.

This trial separation was agreed to with the goal

of ultimately strengthening our marriage. During this short separation it was agreed that Mark would not contact us. I kept this separation quiet out of respect of his public office and reputation, and in hopes of keeping our children from just this type of public exposure. Because of this separation, I did not know where he was in the past week.

I believe enduring love is primarily a commitment and an act of will and for a marriage to be successful, that commitment must be reciprocal. I believe Mark has earned a chance to resurrect our marriage.

Psalm 127 states that sons are a gift from the Lord and children a reward from Him. I will continue to pour my energy into raising our sons to be honorable young men. I remain willing to forgive Mark completely for his indiscretions and to welcome him back, in time, if he continues to work toward reconciliation with a true spirit of humility and repentance.

This is a very painful time for us and I would humbly request now that members of the media respect the privacy of my boys and me as we struggle together to continue on with our lives and as I seek the wisdom of Solomon, the strength and patience of Job, and the grace of God in helping to heal my family.

Staying
True

ONE

As I maneuvered the unfamiliar Honda hatchback through the foggy roads of South Carolina's lowcountry, I wondered why I was making this torturous journey to see Mark Sanford. It was 1987, and I'd only been on a handful of dates with him, dates that were not overwhelmingly romantic. One such date was brunch with my parents (not exactly a recipe for romance) in New York around Thanksgiving. Shortly thereafter, he'd invited me to spend New Year's Eve weekend with him and his family at their farm on the South Carolina coast. I had found the invitation intriguing because it was unexpected and because Mark was different from the men I'd dated before. I asked my mom for her two cents.

"He seems like a nice young man and you should go see

him," she said. "Go to South Carolina, it will be fun no matter what. And I'll bet he has nice friends!"

I certainly agreed with her that it would be an adventure either way. Little did I know . . .

Mark had told me where to look for the car in the Charleston airport parking lot and that the directions for the fifty-mile drive to Coosaw, the family farm, would be on a clipboard on the passenger seat. I hadn't anticipated the car would be a stick shift. Though I'd tried before, I didn't really know how to drive a stick.

When I was a teenager, my friend Julie and I had tried to teach ourselves to drive a manual transmission truck on untraveled back roads and small-town streets in northern Wisconsin. We laughed as we stalled and stalled, hardly able to go a few feet without having to start the truck again. We got around a bit, but we'd never taken the truck out in traffic and only drove in daylight. All these years later, I remembered the general idea and, with some bucking and stalling and squealing of wheels—and some out-loud questioning what I'd gotten myself into—I made it out of the airport as directed.

I had first met Mark seven months earlier, on Memorial Day weekend in the Hamptons, a summer destination for many young New Yorkers. My friend Moira and I had taken the train from Manhattan out to a house we were renting with a few other women, and we needed a ride to meet up with some friends at a party. Mark had driven to Long Island from Manhattan, where he had a summer job at Goldman Sachs. He and his friend Bob were dispatched to pick us up, arriving in this same beat-up two-door hatchback. The car seemed way too small for Mark's tall, lanky frame, and with all of us packed in, it was a very tight fit indeed.

There was something attractive to me about Mark right from the start. I was used to Wall Street's suspender-snapping braggarts, the kind of men I met often in the mergers and acquisitions department at the investment banking firm, Lazard Frères and Co., where I worked. Mark was pleasant and soft-spoken. We exchanged phone numbers and I remember hoping this southern gentleman would someday call. But I have to admit that I met other men that summer who inspired that hope in me. We were all young—I was 24—that summer and I didn't think that this would turn into something long-term.

I tried to picture that charming southern man as I continued on my frustrating journey to see him. The Honda stalled out twice before I got onto Highway 17 and headed south. The road was narrow with innumerable potholes and obscured by thick lowcountry fog. I charted my progress by the few signs I saw along the way, noting towns with names such as Red Top, Ravenel, and Edisto. My knuckles turned white as I gripped the stick, keeping the car in third gear the whole way. I was afraid to shift gears, slow down, or stop, terrified of hitting a deer or alligator or one of the other creatures Mark had told me might be around these parts. This was a long way from Manhattan, and a longer way still from where I grew up in Chicago.

As I drove, I had plenty of time to consider Mark's intentions in inviting me to meet his family and ring in the New

Year. It wasn't entirely clear if he was interested in me romantically; making me drive myself didn't suggest that I was someone he was dying to see. Our time together in New York had been fun and engaging and, by this point, there was a flirtatious attraction between us, but things hadn't progressed to true romance. I still wasn't thinking long-term about him. What was he doing? What was I doing? After about forty-five minutes, I carefully pulled over when I saw a phone booth in Jacksonboro, then scarcely a town, with only a gas station and a closed-down restaurant. I tried to call Mark, but no one answered at Coosaw. I was thankful I also had the phone number of the home in Yemassee, where the New Year's Eve pig roast was being held. I got the hostess, Evie Chace, on the phone and explained my situation.

"Good God, you're by yourself in Jacksonboro!" she exclaimed. Evie told me that Mark was already at the party—he'd left Coosaw without waiting for me. She gave me directions to her house and said she would let Mark know I was on my way.

I arrived to the party well underway. Evie—wearing a necklace of blinking Christmas lights (how could I not love her immediately?)—welcomed me warmly and began to introduce me around conspiratorily: "This is Jenny, Mark's date. Can you believe he left his car for her at the airport and she made it here on her own on a night like this?!"

Gradually I found my way around the room to Mark and his family. Mark gave me a peck on the cheek and coolly said, "Hey. Glad you made it" as though I'd just stopped in from down the street. He was completely relaxed and enjoying the party, not particularly focused on me or my comfort. Truth to tell, I started looking around for those cute friends Mom thought he might have.

Another handsome young man greeted me. He offered his hand politely, "Bill Sanford. Nice to meet you. You must be Jenny."

"I am," I responded, "and I am so glad to be here and not in that Honda."

"Can I get you some wine?" asked Mark.

It's about time! I thought. "Yes, thanks, that would be nice."

Mark disappeared momentarily to get me a glass, and I began to look around the crowded dining room. As I scanned the room, I saw a woman who looked a lot like me, but dressed in tweedy hunting attire. She introduced herself.

"You muuust be Jenny!" she said, with dramatic emphasis. She continued: "I cannot believe Mark left a car for you. I'm *Saah*rah Sanford and we are all so excited to meet you."

"That wasn't a problem," I said. "I just wish I knew how to drive stick!"

"John Sanford. Nice to meet you. You mean you really don't know how to drive stick? What did you do?" asked another Sanford clone.

"I just drove," I said, matter-of-factly.

"Our brother can be such a piiig!" said Sarah.

Mark and his siblings looked so much alike with their dark brown hair, warm hazel eyes, and just the right amount of freckles. What a good-looking family, I thought. As the wine hit my system and the warmth of the room and the people swept over me, I began to unwind from the harrowing drive, leaving my New York intensity behind. Mark started to introduce me around with pride, showing genuine interest in me. I was glad I had not complained about the drive or drawn attention to the strain I left behind when I entered the party. I felt I had just passed some test with Mark, and not complaining about what I'd endured was part of it.

After cocktails, Mark found me a jacket to wear when we went outside to sit around picnic tables draped in red-and-white checkered cloths. Dinner was roast pig and slaw, a delicious traditional South Carolinian feast that I would come to eat my fair share of in the years ahead. Mark said he had been celebrating New Year's Eve at Evie's with these folks as long as he could remember. This was just the type of familial gathering that was missing in my New York banking life, so far from my own family and home. Mark and I held hands by the open fire as fireworks exploded over the rice fields just beyond.

After leaving the party, we drove a short distance to Coosaw; blessedly, Mark took the wheel. He had described the farm as rough and tumble, yet beautiful. By the time we arrived, however, I could barely see anything in the pitch-black night. We formally welcomed the New Year with a sweet midnight kiss alone on a dock overlooking the river, the fog hovering close over the water.

As I fell asleep that night in a small cabin not far from the main house, the pride I felt from having passed the test fell away a bit and I began to wonder why I had to be tested at all. Tonight it seemed Mark was actively testing my mettle, assessing my tolerance for what exactly I didn't know. There still seemed to be a lot I didn't know about him. But even as I was uncertain about him, I certainly was interested and wanted to know more.

I knew that Mark's father, a surgeon, had died after a long battle with Lou Gehrig's disease (ALS) when Mark was still in college. He was buried at Coosaw, sacred ground for the Sanford family. Mark was now in his last year of the graduate business program at the University of Virginia, and I could tell he was driven; he talked about a big future for himself in real estate. But I didn't have a sense of his dreams beyond his ambitions; yet knowing about those dreams suddenly seemed of interest to me.

I have always thought of love as more than just a feeling. To me love is a verb, an action that you engage in every day through the things you do for those you cherish. I had had a serious relationship in college and thought I was really in love. In time, that feeling faded, and my commitment wore thin. In my first years on Wall Street, I'd had a few brief relationships, some more intense than others. As a result, I knew what it felt like to look one day at a man I had strong feelings for and realize I couldn't possibly spend my life with him. I didn't want that kind of relationship anymore.

Mark's even-keeled nature was part of the intrigue for me. Perhaps developing a friendship with Mark before the sparks began to fly was part of his appeal. Gradually getting to know each other, slowly opening our hearts was novel to me personally and suggested the kind of old-fashioned love I'd heard about from my parents and grandparents.

I had long witnessed my parent's complete dedication to one another. Theirs still is a steady, solid love, and they've stayed committed to each other through fifty years and my mother's long battle with melanoma. My grandparents were fiercely committed to each other, too. In my Gramps, Bolton Sullivan, I saw a passionate love of his wife, literally until his death.

Gramps lived the last ten years of his life in a great deal of pain from damage to the nerve endings in his feet. He would spend hours in his chair by the window at their home in Florida and often, when I visited, he would tell me of his love for Nana. Even as he felt his body deteriorating, he repeatedly said he wanted to live because he didn't want to leave his beloved wife. Not one for sentimentality in the same way, and to diffuse the inherent sadness in what Gramps said, Nana quipped: "I'd go today if the good Lord would have me, but I'm not sure He wants a grumpy old woman like me."

By the time my grandfather was ninety-four, he had become quite frail. Nana's health had also deteriorated after she broke her hip and she developed congestive heart failure. She was sick enough that a priest was called in to bless her and read her last rites. As the priest prayed over Nana with family nearby, Gramps quietly closed his eyes in the next room and died. Incredibly sweet love. Thinking she had gone, he had clearly decided peacefully to join her; he just couldn't fathom being separated. Just as Gramps was absolutely true to his love until the end, Nana was true to her loveable, cantankerous self, too: She recovered and lived many more months happily playing bridge in a nursing home!

I hadn't yet found the man who had inspired that kind of devotion, the kind of man worthy of the kind of love I knew I was capable of giving. Honestly, I hadn't been looking too hard. Although I hadn't experienced it yet myself, I expected that the platitudes about true love were absolutely true. I imagined that it would involve understanding, patience, sacrifice, selflessness, and commitment. If I was going to commit, I would give it my all. I wanted to pledge loyalty to another person, to a set of values, goals, and dreams, and to a family. I realize that to some this might seem the opposite of romantic. But I saw from watching and talking to my parents that passion and romance come and go through the seasons of life; what sustains you are shared values and common goals. I found *that* incredibly romantic.

Just a few hours later, Mark came to the small cabin where I slept and handed me old hunting gear so we could hike to a freshwater pond in the woods to watch the sun rise. The sun was coming up as I slipped my feet into the rubber boots and donned a thread-worn jacket. Mark held my hand as we worked our way in silence to a spot in the reeds at the side of the pond where dozens of mallards and buffleheads flew in to feed. As the daylight grew brighter, I slowly became aware of the beauty of this place. Egrets and blue herons soared gracefully over the still water. Mark named the creatures as if they were old friends and wasn't at all anxious about the alligators he spotted nestled in the pluff mud for warmth. City girl that I was — and largely still am — I thought they were logs at the water's edge.

As the sun rose, I soaked in the magical beauty of Coosaw, a large tract along a tidal basin just past the mouth of the Combahee River. The sparkling waters of the river served as a backdrop for palmettos and large live oak trees draped with clumps of gently swinging Spanish moss that surrounded us. This was a place outside of time, a world that filled me with peace. But I was seduced by more than the natural beauty of the landscape. I could see that this was where Mark's heart resided, and as it became clear what the place had meant to him over the years, I began to see it in the same way.

Mark was a junior in high school when his father was diagnosed with ALS and the family — Mark, his two brothers, sister, and their mother — moved from Florida to their summer home on Coosaw, the place they thought he'd be happiest in his final days. Although the doctors had given his father only six months to live, his dad died almost six years later when Mark was finishing his undergraduate degree. The eldest of his siblings, Mark went to great effort to save this family home. As his father declined, his focus on spending all his time with the family kept him from preparing financially for what would happen after he died. When his father passed, Mark discovered how expensive it was to maintain the farm and understood that he needed to raise money immediately to pay ongoing farm expenses and the inheritance taxes.

The estate advisers told him he would have to sell the farm to meet the family's obligations, but Mark refused. Although he was only a young man, Mark stepped into the role of head of the family and made some difficult decisions to save the farm. He sold the herd of cattle that had grazed the land for years, and reluctantly let the seven full-time employees go. Much of the maintenance of the farm had to be deferred, unless Mark and his siblings could do it themselves. This was a painful time for the family, a time of stress and hardship when every day Mark feared that he might make a choice that would result in them losing this precious homestead. Yet he kept his vision clearly focused on what mattered to him and the family and, through his discipline and their collective effort, they managed to keep Coosaw.

When the sun was higher on the horizon, I walked with Mark back to the main house, a lovely but worn old brick structure. Though technically a plantation, in the light of day I could see why Mark and his siblings referred to Coosaw as a farm. To me the word "plantation" conjures an image of a grand old antebellum home with servants bringing trays of mint juleps to the veranda for men dressed in seersucker and women in cotton dresses. Coosaw certainly wasn't that. But it also didn't fit my Midwestern idea of a farm with rows of corn and barns and cows and chickens.

Scattered around the main house were several falling-down red-roofed barns with faded and chipped white paint. Old tractors and farm equipment in various states of disrepair dotted the landscape, along with a few small hunting cabins.

The Sanfords had a homemade fix for everything. They had replaced the rusted-out floor of a jeep with a sheet of plywood. Sure, Coosaw was tumbledown, but I was completely charmed.

We entered the incredibly comfortable and lived-in main house. The décor was tired, the upholstery faded and tattered, and generally the place was a mess, with dirty boots and shotguns heaped in the entryway and clothes drying by the fire. Mark's family and a few friends had congregated in the kitchen. Everyone was pitching in to prepare a big breakfast, swapping stories of hunts from the weekend, or catching up on each other's lives. When the meal was set out, we all paused, holding hands in a circle for the blessing. As soon as the meal was done, everyone was up, cleaning the kitchen or setting off to tackle one of the many chores that had been discussed over breakfast: tending the dikes, grading the dirt road, moving the tractor, fixing the dirt bike, or cleaning the guns.

I was put on the kitchen crew. While tidying the kitchen, surrounded by family photos of Sanfords at Coosaw or at the old home in Florida, I got the chance to chat at length with Mark's mother, Peg. She spoke of how delighted she was to have all of her children home. I was flooded with a sense of Mark, of his tight-knit family, of *Sanfordness*. Even though we came from very different backgrounds and parts of the country, it became clear to me there that we had a great number of things in common.

My big Catholic Midwestern family was, in its way, as close knit and fiercely loyal as Mark's Southern Protestant clan. I was raised in Winnetka, Illinois, a well-to-do suburb of Chicago. Both my parents grew up there as well, and my siblings and I all attended the same grade school, Saints Faith, Hope & Charity. I was the second child of five and the oldest of three girls in a row. It sure seemed that the girls dominated the Sullivan household, despite the presence of our brothers Bolton and John. (Perhaps that is just how I wistfully see it now, looking back from this world of mine that is so completely populated by men and boys.)

Our childhood was a happy one, safe and secure. We walked or rode our bikes to school, came home for lunch daily, and even in the dead of the winter, Mom routinely sent us out to play, warning us not to come in until dinner. There were always kids everywhere. In addition to my siblings, within just a few blocks we had *two* sets of nine first cousins. Our family gatherings never had fewer than twenty people and frequently as many as fifty. While I was studious and a bit shy, I was never lonely. The family just opposite our home had ten children, including the youngest one, who had bells attached to his shoes so his family could find him when he wandered away, often ending up lost in our house. I now can see this setting as wonderfully old-fashioned and simple; it was in many ways idyllic. I considered us blessed.

We Sullivans were certainly comfortable, but I never thought of us as wealthy. My great grandfather had founded the Skil Corporation, which manufactured the world's first portable circular saw, a Skilsaw. He started from nothing, raising enough money to make one Skilsaw, selling it, and raising enough to make another. Great Grandpa wasn't the one with business sense. That was my Gramps, who, as a very young man, took over the management of the company from his dad and made it into a national brand and a real business. My father's goal when he assumed a leadership role was to make the company international, which he did in the early 1960s; he then managed the company right through the tough business cycle in the late 1970s, when the company was eventually sold. Our family never wanted for anything, but Mom taught us to hunt for bargains. If we found something we liked, she often told us not to mention it to our father so he wouldn't worry about the cost, leading us to believe we had real financial concerns. (Her code to us, "DTF," meant "Don't Tell Father!") In fact, that may have been the case. Or it might have been part of Mom's strategy to raise appreciative and thrifty children.

We spent summers at the local country club or away at summer camp, and we vacationed yearly in Florida, visiting our grandparents. These were surely luxuries, but we otherwise lived modestly. Our house was not air-conditioned (not a big hardship in Chicago except for a couple of weeks in the summer). During heat waves, we would all sleep together in the screened porch. Once my little brother tried to cool down by dunking his head in the toilet!

Dad traveled often for business and usually played golf while home weekends spring through fall. He had then and still has a gentle spirit, a steady, diligent work ethic, and an excellent head for business, all qualities I now saw I used every day in my banking job. I consider my dad a man of great integrity. These were the same qualities I saw in Mark and his family throughout the weekend at Coosaw. Certainly no family is perfect—I had had many epiphanies about my own family's imperfections over the years, as surely most teenagers and young adults do, but I think I understood even then that looking for perfection in a partner was folly. Still, what I saw in the Sanfords that first weekend at Coosaw made me think that his family was close to perfection and a lot of that impression had to do with Mark and the courageous way he worked to save the family farm.

The gentle and thoughtful nature that had first drawn me to Mark seemed even more precious to me at Coosaw. The men I knew in finance bragged about the smallest triumphs. Here was a man who had, after the debilitating death of his father, done some of the hardest work of his life to save this beautiful land, yet had hardly mentioned a word of this to me during all the months I'd known him. For the first time, I started to think very seriously about this man: so different, sweet, and yet a challenge in so many ways.

TWO

◇

SOON AFTER I RETURNED FROM SOUTH CAROLINA, MARK VISITED New York for a job interview and left flowers with my apartment doorman with a cute note asking me out for dinner that evening. Surprises can backfire! I already had dinner plans with another man that night, so Mark and I didn't connect on that visit. Thereafter, Mark became more focused in his efforts to woo me, sending regular notes and calling to pin my schedule down before he arrived in the city.

As we grew closer, I started visiting him on weekends at the University of Virginia, where he was finishing his MBA. I was touched when he asked me to be among his family when he graduated in May. As his graduation approached, we began to speak about the future. By the fall of 1988, Mark had moved to New York to work full-time in commercial real estate. The night he proposed the following spring, he made me a candlelight dinner and placed a beautiful family heirloom ring on my finger. We planned the wedding for November at my parents' place in Florida.

Although I had just been named a vice president at Lazard, a rarity for a woman in her twenties, I knew I could walk away without regret if we decided to move to South Carolina. I had pursued a job in investment banking but my long-term ambition had always been business in general. In my senior undergraduate year at Georgetown, one of my professors suggested I send a resume to Lazard, a top-drawer firm with no female partners and a notorious "sink-or-swim" mentality. I didn't think I had a chance, but I dutifully sent it off. As luck would have it, I was one of four analysts hired that year, and the only female. Shortly after graduation, I moved to New York to begin the job. I hoped to learn a great deal from it, but planned to eventually return to the Midwest for a less crazed corporate position.

Every day I walked down Fifth Avenue past the huge gleaming gold statue of Prometheus in front of 1 Rockefeller Center on my way to work. When the elevator doors opened on Lazard's headquarters, however, the atmosphere was surprisingly shabby. The carpet was soiled, and the desks were old and mismatched. These tattered conditions were part of the company's philosophy. The partners prided themselves on producing the most reliable advice, rewarding themselves handsomely with the profits and leaving little left over for decorations or the latest technology. My first office was in a small room I shared with two associates and three bulky computers. Yet despite the threadbare infrastructure, the atmosphere was electric.

I started there in the "greed is good" era of the 1980s, when huge corporations were taking over smaller companies, splitting off deadwood business interests and turning around to combine forces again and again. Lazard was in the thick of everything. My job in mergers and acquisitions was to help with the process of valuing the companies to be acquired, merged, or sold. I worked with an intensity that amazes me now.

As a deal was coming together, the partner in charge had his team of associates scrambling. Though market conditions seemed favorable at that moment, we all knew that opportunities could disappear in a flash, taking fortunes with them. We had to get our part exactly right. If just one number was off, millions could be lost. Partners shared in the enormous profits of the firm, an incredible motivation for them and all the ambitious young people, like me, who crunched numbers long into the night and through most every weekend. Too many mornings I went home only to shower and change my clothes before heading back.

One winter afternoon in the early months of my time at Lazard, I was in the company library searching for documents. I heard a loud whoosh and jerked my head up from the files to see a dark blur streak past the library window. I pressed my face to the window to see what had just fallen and trembled when I saw a figure imprinted on the roof of a car. Later I found out that this was a stock trader who had jumped out the window of the floor directly above me. I cried and shook again when I learned he had left behind a wife and young family.

Often in the years that followed while I worked at Lazard, I would think of that dark imprint far below and speculate about what had driven the man to jump. Was it some personal demon? Or was it this life all of us were leading? This work demanded everything you had. We lived on a scale and at a pace where few could survive for long. Looking at some of the partners, I could see how the endless pursuit of today's opportunity throws life off balance. In time, the same thing began to happen to me. I was burning out.

It wasn't a straight line from seeing that suicide to changing the pace of my own life, but a few years after the death of that trader, despite promotions and solidly increasing pay for my work, I asked to be re-assigned to a job with steadier hours for a year. The powers that be agreed it was time for me to broaden my knowledge of the business, so they moved me to the bond desk in capital markets. The new assignment was dull by comparison and didn't use the best of my skills, but I was happy because the new schedule was predictable. I could make plans—and keep them! I could see more of my friends and have good visits with my family. And it was during this time that I met Mark.

There is a chance that if he had crossed my path a few months earlier, I wouldn't have noticed the charm of that soft-spoken Southerner. The fact that I was not driving myself so hard gave me the biggest luxury of all: time. With more time on my hands, I was noticing different things, or at least I had more time to consider what I was really seeing. I looked up from my frenzy and there was Mark, humble, hardworking, whip smart, stunningly handsome, with a clever but subtle sense of humor.

Before we were engaged, I returned to the banking side of things. One night while eating take-out food over work at the office, a manila envelope arrived at my desk via courier. I opened it to find a formal legal document with a handwritten note from Mark attached by a paper clip. "Dearest Jenny, I know we haven't discussed this so why don't you just sign the attached and return to me and we can move quietly on from here."

The document looked legitimate; I began to fume as I read:

"This **PRENUPTIAL AGREEMENT** is made this ____ day of May, 1989, between the undersigned parties, Jennifer C. Sullivan (hereinafter referred to as "Wife"), of New York, New York, and Marshall C. Sanford, Jr. (hereinafter referred to as "Husband") of Dale, South Carolina.

WHEREAS, both parties are above the age of eighteen (18) years and, notwithstanding the sagacious counsel of their parents, peers and true inner selves, wish to become husband and wife; and

WHEREAS, both parties wish to establish an efficient mechanism for resolving the innumerable differences which they anticipate will arise throughout their married lives; and

WHEREAS, the parties desire to set forth their agreements and understandings herein;

NOW, THEREFORE, in consideration of the foregoing, of the mutual promises herein set forth, of the invaluable loss of personal freedom and dignity, and of other good and sufficient consideration, the receipt of which is hereby acknowledged, the parties agree as follows:

1. **Purposes.** The purpose of this marriage are manifolded to provide companionship during two drab and uneventful lives; to pool resources in order to forestall the inevitable effects of an erratic and ruinous economy; to provide a convenient source of blame for whatever tragedies, short of nuclear attack, befall the parties together or individually; and not incidentally, to vent either party's wanton, shameful and animalistic desires.

2. **Term.** The marriage shall be solemnified on November 4, 1989, and shall seem to last a lifetime whether it does or not.

In skimming those first clauses it dawned on me that this must be a joke. But as I read on, I wasn't so sure because there were shades of the Mark I knew in the demands he was making. Still, I hoped he was poking fun at himself.

3. **Expenses.** Wife agrees to share equally the expenses of maintaining the household. Additionally, Wife agrees to limit her expenditures for all her personal items and usages (including but not limited to, clothes, panty hose, make-up, jewelry, perfume, automobiles, entertainment, medical bills and medicines) to ONE HUNDRED DOLLARS ($100) per month, which amount may be increased only by the written agreement of parties. Any amount not spent in any given month shall lapse.

4. **Decisions.** The parties recognize that numerous decisions must be made each day which affect the parties together or individually, and recognize, too, the necessity for a decisionmaker in the event of their inability to agree on the proper solution to any particular problem. In deference to Husband's gender-related superior intellect and judgment, Wife hereby agrees that Husband will be the final arbiter in all matters. . . .

"Gender-related superior intellect" must have been the tip-off for me. I was laughing out loud when I called Mark to "thank" him for the thoughtful "delivery." I was impressed with the time and creativity he had put into this hoax. He had pulled a fast one on me, a hard person to fool. This fake prenup was filled with outlandish things a chauvinistic, selfish, and single-minded husband might desire of a wife and

Mark was none of those things. Today I do wonder at some of the clauses that have proven true over time, despite the fact that we never signed the silly thing. Mark is notoriously frugal so his fake demands about spending and accountability foreshadowed one aspect of our life together. But it is Clause 9, having to do with children, that I find most prescient: "In the event of pregnancy, Wife hereby agrees to make male children." I couldn't have known then that I would have only sons, even if I did learn that it was one of Mark's dearest wishes that he have them.

Every individual within a couple brings differences of perspective and experience to a marriage, and Mark and I were no different in that regard. Whereas I tend to trust in what the future will bring and live very much in the here and now, Mark needs goals to focus his future and by which he can assess his progress. Once during our engagement he asked me to meet him at a restaurant for dinner and told me to bring a list of my lifetime goals for us to discuss. I chuckled when I saw he had brought a notepad with pages of goals, dreams, and hoped-for adventures. I carried a blank piece of paper. He was astonished at what he took to be my lack of ambitions, but I explained that my goals were pretty straightforward and writing them down wouldn't clarify them for me. I had thought long and hard about his request. In the end, I really only wanted to be remembered as a good mother and grandmother; a life well-lived by me would leave behind genera-tions of well-adjusted and happy children, each productive in their own way.

Needless to say our conversation continued for a very long while that evening and, in fact, it was a conversation we revisited almost annually for many years to come. Once en-couraged to put pencil to paper, my list grew and included becoming involved in something I considered a worthy cause (as opposed to making money just for the sake of it), running my own business one day, and being a good wife to Mark. Also, because I was determined to get good enough to keep up with Mark and the other Sanfords, I added that I wanted to learn to hunt and be able to shoot just one quail in my life-time.

To be fair, I admired that Mark had thought so seriously and carefully about the benchmarks of his success, but I can see now that this was an early inkling of an aspect of his char-acter that was just under his gentle, thoughtful manner: his profound restlessness.

Mark's goals were divided into several categories includ-ing physical, career, financial, mental, spiritual, family, and values. On his "physical" list were the goals to climb Mt. Rainier, bike across America, and consistently beat his broth-ers in tennis. He also wanted to take an "adventure" trip an-nually. For his career and financial goals, he set the bar high as well: He wanted to be an articulate spokesman and moti-vator of men, make a good deal of money, and own his own company by the time he was 30, and he aspired to one day be a U.S. Senator. I couldn't argue with his ambition and I loved his many ideas for adventure travel. Later Mark would keep an adventure resume in addition to a work resume; seeing the exotic and far-flung corners of the world has provided us both with many wonderful memories and experiences, though because of our children, it was often Mark who traveled on these adventures alone.

He even had spiritual goals. He shaped those by memorizing and aspiring to "live by" Bible verses that best encapsulated his thinking. He cherished Galatians 5:22: "The fruit of the Spirit is love, joy, peace, patience, kindness, goodness, faithfulness, gentleness and self-control." He also wanted to follow Matthew 5:16: "Let your light so shine before men, that they may see your good works and praise your Father in heaven."

Faith has been a constant in my life ever since I was a small child comforted by watching my parents pray, saying blessings at meals, and being tucked into bed with a prayer. Faith in our extended family wasn't just something you had, it was something you lived. I saw my dad pray nightly on his knees before his cross. Though he rarely preached to us, when I saw my father, such a huge figure to me, praying in this humble position, I felt the serenity of knowing that someone was always watching from above. Sunday mass at the Catholic church down the street was an unquestioned part of the family routine, and for my parents, it was often a daily practice. Faith and family was a constant mix and a steady presence.

While I had learned all about the Bible in church and school, we were never taught to commit a verse to memory. I was impressed at how lightly these powerful words tripped off Mark's tongue. He knew these verses so well that they had become part of how he saw the world. When I got home, I looked them up so that I could think more about what Mark wanted to "personify and live." The more I thought about these, the more I agreed that they described worthy spiritual goals, albeit coming at me in an unfamiliar way.

Although Mark's family and mine worshipped in different ways, I believed we shared the same values. Mark reinforced this in my mind when he agreed that we could do our religious preparation for marriage in the Catholic church I was attending in New York City. A very close friend of my family's was a Jesuit priest, Fr. Leo O'Donovan, and he agreed, after meeting Mark and thoroughly discussing his faith, to marry us in a Catholic ceremony in a nondenominational church. Nothing about this in any way felt like relinquishing my own faith. Mark and I were bringing our respective traditions together and the blend seemed then—and turned out to remain—effortless.

A short while before the wedding, when Mark and I were picking readings and vows, Mark told me that he didn't want to use a wedding vow that included the promise to be faithful. He was worried in some odd nagging way, he said, that he might not be able to remain true to that vow. In retrospect, I suppose I might have seen this as a sign that Mark wasn't fully committed to me, and with the benefit of the knowledge I have about Mark now, I could point to this moment as a clear sign of things to come.

At the time, though, I thought his honesty was brave and sweet, and I suppose I also thought it was a classic case of pre-wedding cold feet. But I took his concern seriously. I told him that I had unshakable faith in him and thought that his values and moral principles matched up—and would continue to match up—with his actions in the world. As often as I have replayed this moment from our young relationship in my memory, I can't see it any other way. Being unfaithful was not inevitable. I know that many men doubt that they can remain faithful to their wives for life, but I believed that Mark was among those who would be able to do so.

Nonetheless, he had raised the issue and we needed to talk it through. I explained to Mark that I believed marriage was so much more than words spoken in a vow and that I was marrying him because I was deeply in love with him as a whole and even flawed human being. More than that, it seemed fundamental to a happy marriage that one would have a partner who had unwavering faith in you and thought better of you than you thought of yourself. To me marriage was a lifetime commitment made to one another in front of God, family, and friends. The specifics of what we *said* weren't important to me, but rather the spirit of the ceremony. And I pointed out that fidelity was implied no matter how we phrased it—it was one of the fundamental commandments!

I tried to explain to Mark that I felt that marriage was in many ways a leap of faith. I put my faith in his goodness more than anything else, and he needed to do the same with me. We would be two people holding hands and leaping into an uncertain future. How could we know what that future would hold for us? We had to trust that we could make it together no matter what fate threw our way. So long as our commitment remained our priority, I told him I knew we could weather any storm. I can see now how this might sound like I was *convincing* Mark to be faithful to me, but that's not how the conversation unfolded. Instead, my clear conviction about what marriage meant and my faith in his ability to live up to it seemed to calm him. He said he wholeheartedly agreed.

In Fr. Leo's homily at the ceremony he spoke of the privilege family and friends felt to be present as "You begin the journey of lives shared together completely. Perhaps the notion of journey, or pilgrimage, is as fitting an image as we can find for human life in general—and certainly for marriage." He also said, "I can promise you that what you will discover about each other will amaze and comfort and, yes, perhaps occasionally trouble you. The joy of it is that you set off on the journey together. . . . Jesus is united to us as a symbol of God's everlasting covenant, and the marriage of this young man and woman symbolizes that union for us. It is in each other's faces that they will see God and show God to us. It is in their goodness to the men and women around them, but above all in their goodness to each other that they will learn how the love of neighbor is indeed a single commandment with the love of God." He concluded, "If you ever doubt that you are the face of God for each other, remember that we today, with enormous joy and confidence, see God radiant in both of you."

THREE

◇

I CAN ONLY BEST DESCRIBE OUR NEWLY MARRIED LIFE AS BLISSFUL. We were young and healthy (or soon to be in his case—he battled a serious case of mono when we returned from our honeymoon and for many weeks he could do little more than sleep). We were deeply in love and had a world of possibilities in front of us both. We were beginning the satisfying and happy work of building a life together.

Mark moved into my Manhattan apartment and I continued working while he tried to get a new real estate company off the ground, one with a goal of investing in properties in the Southeast. I knew his heart wouldn't stay engaged in New York City living as long as his focus continued to point south, and I knew all along that a move was in order.

During one of Mark's business trips south, he found an

historic house—called a tenement because it shared a wall with the house next door—on Wentworth Street, in downtown Charleston. It had lost its roof in the big hurricane of 1989, Hugo. The extensive repairs the house needed made it affordable for us, and it was in the heart of Charleston, which promised activity for me and an office for Mark within walking distance of our home. Another advantage was that we would be only about an hour from Coosaw.

I can still remember seeing the house for the first time. Even in all its disrepair, it was charming; it would be ours. The original builder had brought his maritime experience to bear on the entrance: The entrances to both sides of the building were flanked with lights—red and green—like the ones marking the channel into the Charleston harbor. The exterior was old brick and the inside had high ceilings and random-width heart-of-pine floors, quite common in old Charleston homes, but exotic to me at the time.

From New York we supervised repairs to make the home safe and comfortable. Mark hired an old friend who was a contractor to put up new Sheetrock on the damaged walls and replace broken glass, as well as make some minor upgrades in the kitchen and bathrooms. Mark questioned his friend about every expenditure and negotiated ways to bring the work in at the price he wanted to pay. Miraculously, everything got done without them coming to blows.

Although we were both committed to this move, when we talked about Charleston, Mark worried out loud that I would miss the fast pace of the big city.

I knew he was wrong about that. Truth be told I could hardly wait to begin our life there.

As it happened, on one of my last days at Lazard, I shared an elevator with the formidable head of the firm, Michel David-Weill, a diminutive man who reportedly earned about $50 million each year. Ruddy-faced and white-haired, Michel looked up at me over his spectacles and asked in his thick French accent, "But Jen-ni-fer, what weel you do in zeez South Caroliiiina? Who weel you talk to?"

I didn't worry about having people to talk with. South Carolina had a tremendous amount to offer and fascinating people. I hoped we would be blessed with children, and I knew that investment banking did not mix well with having a family. Michel was right about one thing, though. I would need to keep my mind busy and remain involved in something that would balance time with the kids, should we be lucky enough to have them. But beyond that, I knew I wanted to be home for our children as much as I could be while they were young. I had no confidence whatsoever that I would get the child-rearing right. Time would be the judge of that. I did know that I had only one real chance—while they were young—to make a mark on their lives and I took that seriously.

Before we moved to Charleston in early December we had the old floors refinished. The weather was so damp, however, that the floors took longer than expected to dry. We redirected the moving truck to Coosaw for an extra few days. Mark convinced the drivers not to charge us for the delay in exchange for giving them a cabin to stay in at Coosaw and plenty of time to spend with a gun in a deer stand. There is no doubt a lot of backroom negotiating and compromise involved in getting things done in New York and in many other places in this country, too, but this particular barter system—move us in tomorrow and welcome yourself to some hunting on my land while you wait—struck me as wonderfully southern.

Of course, there were many "we're not in Kansas anymore, Toto" moments in those early days in Charleston. Ever used to walking briskly down New York City's streets with my eyes down, tightly clutching my purse, I loved the pleasant greetings we received from strangers as we walked the streets of this genteel and more relaxed city, my purse swinging freely and my head and shoulders focused happily ahead.

Homemaking was also a revelation. Mark and I decided we could make the cosmetic improvements on the house ourselves. I painted some of the rooms and the kitchen floor, made curtains, and even learned to hang wallpaper by myself. We didn't have a dining table, so Mark dragged a musty drop-leaf one out of the barn at Coosaw, along with a few old chairs, which I cleaned and then covered with fresh fabric. He also found a set of twin beds for the guest bedroom that I painted so they wouldn't look so dingy. There was no telling what had lived in the mattresses he found in the barn to put on those beds, but we used them anyway.

It was in living together in a space new to both of us—sharing my apartment had still been sharing *my* apartment—

that we began to rub up against each other and start to work out a complementary way to be. Living together for the first time was one thing: Getting used to someone's habits and quirks can test your patience. But for us, it was the traditions and expectations that we had each inherited from our families that started to highlight our differences. I know this is common—I think I must have known this even then—and see now that this is the real task of the beginning of a shared life. Discovering these things about another person and learning to love and honor the differences were our next tasks.

While living in our house on Wentworth, however, I quickly learned firsthand of Mark's frugality and how it would now impact my every move. After getting a South Carolina driver's license, I wanted a car so I would not have to depend on Mark if I needed to go somewhere outside the neighborhood. He was against buying a new car so he went with his friend Ozzie, a used-car dealer, to an auction to make sure he got the most for his money. I didn't gripe—I needed a mode of transportation, not a seat of luxury—but Mark's frugality quickly showed itself to be his badge of honor and something I had to get used to.

As careful as he was with our money, however, it was a little ironic that he wasn't terrific at keeping track of things, at least in any way that another person could make sense of. Mark wrote down on scraps of paper important transactions such as swapping a tract of land with one of his brothers. Later, even though he remembered to the letter the deal they'd made, he'd struggle to find the note that backed it up.

It wasn't long before I took over the family checkbook. Mark agreed happily because he knew that I could tend to the minutiae, but would always keep him informed of the bigger picture. I made a balance sheet with our overall financial position, marital assets combined, and he seemed to breathe easier. Still he wanted to watch and approve every dime I spent, which drove me mad. Eventually I learned we could peacefully coexist if I kept overall expenses to an agreed-upon level, but was free to choose where to save or to spend. This arrangement helped us both avoid petty disagreements.

Little did I realize as a young woman in love that there would be many moments when these same qualities, particularly his frugality, would cost me. I remember the first birthday I celebrated after we moved south. Mark gave me a hand-made birthday card with a picture of him holding birthday balloons on the front. I thought it was sweet that he drew a picture for me himself. But inside the card, strangely, was a picture of half a bike. I didn't quite understand the picture. Mark explained I would get the other half in the future. Well, that Christmas he drew me a picture of the other half of the bike, and months later, he delivered the gift to me, a used purple bike he had purchased for $25! My reaction at first was disbelief; he had given me nicer gifts while engaged. In time, however, I came to know this was just part of who he was. And I could play along: A few years ago, we were trying to put aside some money for repairs on a small cottage at Coosaw, so for Christmas I drew Mark a picture of half a house!

In addition to the more common compromises on finances and blending our faith traditions, our marriage brought unexpected challenges as I grew to know more deeply what made Mark tick. If one of the primary tasks in a young marriage is for both of the new partners to separate completely from their families so that they can form traditions of their own, that first Thanksgiving, less than four weeks into our married life, I saw how difficult that task would be for Mark.

When all of the Sanford siblings arrived at the farm for the holiday weekend, Mark promptly took our bags upstairs where there are two bedrooms and one shared bathroom. Mark's mother's bedroom was on the first floor and traditionally one of the rooms upstairs had always been his sister Sarah's. The other large bedroom (with bunk beds, trundles, desks, and even surfboards hanging from the ceiling) was for Mark and his brothers. I was confused. Were we displacing Sarah? I thought surely we'd be sleeping in one of the small cabins, perhaps even the one I'd stayed in alone when I first came here for New Year's Eve. Instead, Mark explained, I would be sleeping with his sister while he slept across the hall with his brothers.

"You've got to be kidding!" I said.

"I've always slept with my brothers and I don't see why that has to change now that we're married," he replied matter-of-factly. This was no big deal for him—it just was what it was. I thought it was absurd. In the end, we didn't have to stand in that hall (that oddly doubles as a closet) disagreeing for long. Mark had just been diagnosed with mono and that made him an undesirable bunkmate. His brothers voted him out. We stayed in one of the small cottages after all.

It was also in our first year of our marriage that my sweet grandfather closed his eyes, thinking he was off to join his wife, who he was sure had died in the next room. When the news of his death came to me I relayed it tearfully to Mark and told him I'd set about making reservations for us to fly to Chicago for the funeral. Mark, however, said he wouldn't be going. He explained that he had hardly known my grandfather. Having only met him a handful of times, he didn't think he needed to be at the funeral.

I was hurt, even angry, and I cried then for both my grandfather and Mark's lack of sensitivity. This seemed so out of character for his thoughtful and gentle nature. I explained that I wanted Mark to travel to Chicago to support me in mourning for a person I had adored. I explained how it was something I needed, and that it was expected of him; my family might also feel hurt by his absence. But Mark held firm that he didn't need to go with me to the funeral.

Somewhere in the tears (mine) and the stoicism (his), I realized that Mark and I had never talked about funerals in relation to our respective faiths and traditions. I took a deep breath and asked Mark to tell me of the services he had been to in his life and to describe what funerals meant to him. I learned then that Mark had only been to one funeral in his life: his father's.

Dr. Sanford had died surrounded by his family on

Thanksgiving Day in 1982. Mark and a family friend built a cypress casket, and then brothers Billy and John dug a deep grave beneath their Dad's favorite oak tree with a backhoe. After a service at church in Beaufort the family drove to the gravesite on Coosaw with a very small group of friends. There was a short burial blessing and then the few guests and Peg departed, followed by Sarah, who wanted to walk home alone along the river. Then Mark and his brothers used three shovels to carefully cover their Dad's coffin with dirt, working until the top was made smooth and neat again. This was his experience with the end of life and with marking someone's passing. It started to make sense to me that he didn't feel it would be appropriate to be part of the service for my grandfather. To him, a funeral was a deeply personal and private affair. My pleading and my explanation that my tradition was very different—my grandfather's funeral would be a big Irish Catholic Celebration of Life—didn't change Mark's mind. I traveled to Chicago alone.

As disappointing as it was to not have Mark's support, learning the full story of his father's funeral helped me understand my husband better. A father's death is a huge event in any life, but Mark's father's was extraordinary in the way it shaped Mark's worldview.

When his father fell ill, Mark felt responsible to his father and his family. In a way, from the moment that his father was diagnosed, Mark's youth ended. After his father died, the tough decisions Mark had to make to save Coosaw made him the embodiment of someone who had lived through an experience like the Great Depression, almost like someone from another time. This was at the heart of his deep-seated frugality and his constant sense of his own mortality. I knew he would always wonder what he missed out on in life because of taking on so much at a young age.

In understanding this, I learned not to take personally Mark's thrifty ways, but I also started to appreciate in a deeper way the different loads we each carried into our shared emotional space. It became clear why Mark had asked me to have that discussion about goals, and why his many different goals had to be listed on pages and pages. He needed to accomplish as much as he could in whatever time God granted him. This also helps explain why Mark could be restless and impulsive.

After we finished renovating our house, Mark began agitating for the next big project. Our house came with an adjacent vacant lot. After less than a year, we sold the house we renovated and rented a house nearby so that we could design and build a new home on that vacant lot. We wanted our new home to be one we would own forever and yet one that was uncomplicated and easy to leave for weekends spent at Coosaw or for longer breaks in the summer. City living was fine for Mark, but he was adamant that he never wanted to feel closed in, so we made having a view of the harbor an important part of the design.

Building a house from the ground up is exhilarating. You watch your ideas, your creation, your hopes and dreams start to blossom with each new wall put up and floor laid down. But I don't recommend it for the faint of heart. Even the best of teams have faltered under the pressure of so many large and so many petty decisions. And the way money seems to hemorrhage, even the most careful accounting can make your head spin.

I had, of course, learned with our first home renovation how important sticking to a budget was for Mark. I also learned how much I disliked having his fingers in every little decision I made. Unless we divided our areas of decision making, I knew we'd end up arguing about the cost of door-knobs, and I didn't want him micromanaging the nonfinancial decisions such as paint color either. We avoided conflict in our second home the same way we had over our check-book. We came up with an overall budget and design for the house and then split responsibilities, with each of us having complete control of specific areas with attached budgets.

Mark dealt with the outside of the house and the garage, yard, roof, and deck, while I dealt with all details of the interior. If I wanted expensive curtains, then I would need to skimp on cabinets or vice versa. I trusted him with the choice of brick or with shutters and he trusted my choice of paint colors and fabrics, all within the original boundaries we had agreed to. This turned out to be an incredibly effective way to survive the project, and I'm not a little proud to be able to look back at that time and see that two controlling personalities (one who was also a penny-pincher, and the other who realized she was pregnant) worked as a real team through it all.

Yes, too true. Shortly after settling into the rental home I discovered I was pregnant. This was a real surprise to both of us; starting a family was a few years off on both of our lists of goals. I was immediately excited nonetheless. Mark, however, was quite anxious at first. He thought he would be better suited to be a father if he was a bit older (his father was 45 when Mark was born) and he worried too what he would do, how he would react, the way he would play and interact, if this baby was a girl. At first his mumblings seemed funny. I couldn't quite believe that the idea of a baby girl would cause him so much fear. But I soon realized that his anxiety was real. Even as he started to get excited about the idea of a baby—and he did; we both embraced it pretty quickly—he imagined boys, sons. His sister was always "one of the boys" in his childhood household. I often think that a girl would have been great for Mark. She might have softened him up a bit, and I know he would have been a wonderful father to her. But somehow God gives you only what you can handle. Maybe sons are what Mark could handle. Little did either of us know there would be four!

Mark and I worked together on plans for the new house and then watched it being built as my belly grew. Friends held a baby shower for me, and I prepared a small nursery in the house while Mark continued to keep his fingers crossed for a boy. I was able to continue playing golf and tennis and even worked planting fields at Coosaw while pregnant, though I did tire more easily as I grew quite large. Mark joined me at one Lamaze class before deeming it a waste of his time since, as he explained, "I've spent many long nights helping cows give birth and I know what to do when the baby gets stuck." Of course, many fathers still didn't attend births in those days, so Mark didn't really feel he needed to know too much about the human birthing process. Instead, my sister Kathy came to be with me for the birth. We spent lots of time taking bike rides on the cobblestone streets in Charleston hoping to help nudge delivery along, to no avail.

When I was almost two weeks overdue, my labor was induced. Delivered at 10 pounds, 5 ounces, on June 23, our first son, Marshall, was a healthy, very content baby whom Mark delightfully began to refer to as the "little man." Mark was instantly a very proud and very doting father. He called his family and mine to brag of this fine baby boy and to tell them all how healthy and handsome he was. Mark's mother, Peg, came to stay with us for a few days and I was thankful for the help since I was not all that nimble after the delivery.

Mark's enthusiasm for Marshall was wonderful to witness, but I could see changing diapers would not be his strong suit. He had planned a trip to climb Mt. Rainier with a few friends and, as the baby had been late in coming, his trip would begin when Marshall was only two weeks old. Marshall took to nursing right away, and he usually slept well between feedings. I was comfortable and confident in my mothering instincts. I didn't really see any reason for Mark not to go off and enjoy his adventure.

Actually, taking care of a newborn alone while Mark traveled turned out to be much easier in many ways than assimi-

lating to life at Coosaw with Mark and his siblings while raising Marshall.

I remember waking up with Marshall as the sun rose one
morning on a family-filled holiday weekend and having a difficult time keeping him safe in the kitchen while I heated his
bottle. He was crawling around the floor, which was, as usual,
littered with farm dirt and dead cockroaches, and I saw scattered shotgun shells too. If that wasn't enough, that morning
there were also beer bottles left by Mark's younger siblings
who had likely gone to bed just hours before. I happen to love
the abandon with which the Sanfords look at cleanliness at
Coosaw, but throwing a baby into the mix and then adding
his siblings and their habits made it all quite a challenge at
times.

Pulling a shotgun shell from my baby's tight grasp was all
the more ironic given my mother's involvement in gun control. Mom has long had a can-do attitude, and when I was
about eight, she became particularly frustrated reading about
so many shooting deaths in Chicago. She decided to do
something about it and worked with a few fellow moms to
create an organization that soon became one of the first national efforts toward handgun control. They started a campaign to "Ban the Bullet" with slogans like "We need guns
like we need a hole in the head!"

This brought her all sorts of good attention and some un-
welcome as well. We had to unlist our home phone number
due to the many threats we received from outraged gun owners, and a national hardware store chain even refused to do

business with Skil as a result of mom's gun-control lobby. She was invited to appear on the *Today* show in the early 1970s, and my sister Gier and I were lucky enough to travel with her to New York. I remember being excited about flying to the big city for the first time, staying in a hotel, and eating at a fancy restaurant, not the important work our mother was doing there.

I now fully understand the many people — in South Carolina and elsewhere — who take seriously the right to bear arms, but remain amazed that my mom's gun-control efforts were not brought to light and used against Mark in our campaigns. I also remain amazed that our babies survived those early days pioneering at Coosaw.

FOUR

———◇———

Y FALL OF 1992 I WAS ENCHANTED WITH THE NEWFOUND JOYS
of motherhood and enjoying every minute of life in this
historic, eclectic, and sophisticated little town. We had a
beautiful baby, were building a dream house, and shared an
exquisite farm nearby. Also, I had developed many new and
dear friendships with such women as Virginia Lane, an architect down the street, and Sally Coen, then my across-the-
street neighbor, who had recently had her first son, too. I had
also become close with Lalla Lee Campsen, who wasn't anything like my traditionally Irish Catholic New York and
Chicago friends. Lalla Lee is sweet and very Southern, and
she is a great shot, drives a boat well, and doesn't drink. Lalla
Lee's family has a hunting spot near Coosaw, and she and her
husband Chip met through Mark. Together she and I shared

time outdoors with our boys and our tennis games, but we also shared our spiritual sides.

With good girlfriends to complete the picture, Mark and I had such a wonderful quality of life, unlike anything I had experienced while in New York. We had enough money, but this wasn't about riches. For lack of a better way to say it, I was so *pleased* by all Mark and I had accomplished in the few years we had been married. I knew every compromise I'd made to bring this about had been wise and I didn't think of any of the choices I had made as sacrifices. For all of the pieces of my identity—my work, most importantly—and my family traditions that I'd surrendered, I'd received blessings that were so much stronger and more precious to me: my husband, our child, our home, and our rich life in Charleston.

Mark and I were smiling one hot, sticky evening as we watched Marshall sleeping peacefully in his crib when Mark said, "Jenny, with the exception of that little man, I'm bored with life. I want to be stretched and pushed to the point of exhaustion. I want to be consumed. I don't want to just exist."

A little taken aback, I noted that this was ironic, since he had been so concerned about whether I would be bored when we moved here. It now seemed our roles were reversed. He acknowledged this irony, but he brushed it aside. His restlessness was awake again and apparent on his face.

I understood Mark's need to travel and to seek adventure, and all along I encouraged that, while hoping he would find what he needed to settle his spirit. Now, as his wife, I sensed his frustration and shared it in a way, absorbing what I could for him but unable to cure whatever it was that lay at the heart of his angst.

Shortly after announcing the need for something new to do, Mark considered some more significant real estate ventures, and his angst began to take a more specific direction. As he looked at the local and regional markets and the economy, he also considered the national climate that affected his ability to accomplish his goals. This was during Bill Clinton's first administration, and Mark began to worry about the big-spending ways of our federal government and what that meant for our young and growing family if spending was not brought under control. On many occasions, we talked at length and deeply about his frustrations. As a way to focus his thinking, he wrote a thirty-page paper on the national debt and the problems with our Social Security system. I engaged in the policy talk over countless dinners, though I have to admit that the paper made my eyes glaze over. What was exciting, however, was that it ignited a passion in Mark, and I was happy to see him energized and focused.

Mark began to pay attention when the congressional seat for our coastal district, which runs from just south of Charleston up the coast to the North Carolina border, opened up when the incumbent retired. The race for the seat had already attracted a number of people who were actively campaigning. There were two well-financed candidates running (the favorite, Van Hipp, had run the state Republican Party) and a third who had very high name recognition because his father, who had the same name, was a long-time Congressman for the district in years prior. Mark met with local business and political leaders to discuss what they wanted from the next person who would represent that district in Congress. I saw how interested Mark was in getting the right person in that position, but I didn't think he imagined *he* might be the right person. Aside from Mark's exploring candidate positions, we had talked very little of party politics. In South Carolina, you don't register to vote with a party affiliation, so I actually had to ask Mark which party he considered himself to be a part of. While unwavering in his conservative principles, he considered his answer before declaring he was a Republican.

While Mark was pondering deficits and Social Security, I found myself pregnant again. This time, neither of us was much surprised. We both wanted several children and had wasted no time working toward that goal after Marshall was born. Soon after settling into our new house, we welcomed our next son. My labor was induced before the due date because Marshall had been so big. On September 28, 1993, John Landon was born easily, weighing in at a mild 7 pounds, 10 ounces. Mark was wild with joy at having a second son. He was tender and sweet with both Marshall and Landon from the very first moment he held them. As one of my favorite Psalms, Psalm 127, puts it: "Like arrows in the hands of a fighting man are sons born to a man in his youth. Happy is he who has his quiver full." Mark was well on his way to enjoying a quiver full.

Still, he was restless.

I was in the hospital recovering from Landon's delivery when Mark formalized something that by then I'd known he was seriously considering. He announced he'd decided to run for Congress. He said that the decision felt right and that he felt compelled to run in this particular race. Then, he dropped another bombshell:

"And, Jenny, you are going to run my campaign."

"Me? You have got to be kidding! I've never even volunteered on anyone's campaign!"

"But you're free," he continued.

"Free? I think my plate is pretty full right now!" I said. I was still in the hospital bed, after all. Clearly he meant a different kind of free.

"You can do this with the babies at home," he explained "and we can just put a phone line in the kitchen. The only way this will even possibly work is if we keep our expenses incredibly low and that's why I really need you. You are free. I know why I am running and have my ideas all mapped out but I need someone to keep the trains running on time, and you are great with that kind of stuff."

I wish I could say that I threw my head back and laughed at Mark's logic or that I was wildly enthusiastic at the prospect of working hard for no pay. Instead, my honest reaction was that Mark had devised a plan that was textbook blind leading the blind. But I did know a sparkle in Mark's eye when I saw one. This decision might be the thing that would still his restlessness. Even though this work was really about achieving Mark's dream and not my own, I felt it was worthy and I thought it would be something we could do together while raising our family in the midst of it all. I think I waited until I was home from the hospital with Landon, but I accepted Mark's challenge. I signed on to help him to achieve a goal. I was excited, and at the time it didn't seem like much of a sacrifice.

I suppose you could say that women are built for sacrifice. After all, we "sacrifice" a youthful, firm body to childbearing. Imagining holding that sweet baby in your arms can make the discomforts of pregnancy endurable. Over the nine months of sharing space with a growing child, a woman can find the joy that comes from physical generosity. As the baby grows, you give him life, your life: nutrients, oxygen, protection and, bit by bit, your heart. Then you launch him into the world and experience a wrenching release—emotional and physical to be sure—and then the joy that this new little person brings to you and all around you. You'd give anything to keep that child safe and to make his life good. Sacrifice? By any definition, it becomes a part of everyday life.

When Mark announced his candidacy on November 16, 1993, shortly after Landon was born, he said, "I am running because I believe that unless we do something about the debt and the deficit, it has the capacity to undermine the financial foundation on which all of our businesses, jobs, and savings rest." The local paper noted the next day that "[Sanford] has no previous experience in elected office, no name recognition and little backing" (*Post and Courier*, November 17, 1993). The paper continued, "'What's wrong with regular folks who don't have name recognition going out and getting involved in politics?' he [Mark] asked. Will it work? Not too often in South Carolina politics will an unknown step in and win a race for Congress."

I told Mark that I would put all my efforts toward helping him get elected this one time, but if he did not win, I was not willing to do it again and again as so many others seem to do. One shot. Thus I agreed, quite naïvely, to run Mark's race for U.S. Congress. Never once, to my recollection, did either one of us question or discuss what would happen if he were to win.

FIVE

◇

As a child in Chicago, we Sullivans were fans of the Cubs, but when push came to shove, we were Braves fans through and through. My father, mom's brother (my Uncle Tom), and a few of their friends owned the Milwaukee Braves long before owning baseball teams was profitable. When the team became the Atlanta Braves and even after the team was sold, we continued to think of them as our home team; we cheered for them over the Cubs any time they were in town.

We Sullivans also, of course, had brand loyalty to Skil products. We steered clear of all things Black & Decker.

As I got older, I understood loyalty to be the intangible thing on display between siblings and cousins—I had so many living nearby that it seemed we were one big mutual fan club. What an incredible gift it was to have such a supportive family clan, a ready and reliable cheering squad for any and all of us. I think I also understood that loyalty was at the root of good marriages. I could see that my parents were unfailingly loyal to one another, as were both sets of grandparents. This was not blind loyalty, but the kind of support that comes from knowing another person deeply, having committed to helping them succeed in life, and loving them warts and all.

It was not until Mark decided to enter politics, however, that I felt profound loyalty in my own bones and recognized it would be essential to our marriage and our goals.

That first intense congressional campaign was such an uphill challenge that it seemed to others, and sometimes to me, that the effort was hopeless, a pointless quest that could never end in victory. In many ways, the hopelessness of his quest was irrelevant to him. Mark was an ideologue with strong beliefs and a sense of urgency for change that would not be stilled. He saw this run at government office as a chance to inform others of the risks of debt and deficits. Whether he won or not, he hoped to change the public discourse on these issues. This, he felt, was an undertaking that would satisfy his need to be challenged intellectually and that would give him the exhausted thrill that comes with a job well done and a battle well fought. Simply put: The prospect of running a different kind of campaign, one based on principles and values, energized him. When Mark put his real estate business in the hands of a partner so he could focus full-time on the campaign, I knew he was serious.

Mark and I understood that as a complete political unknown, he would have trouble raising money. To get started, however, we needed some base capital. We decided to loan our campaign $100,000 of our own money—money we had earned and saved and some I had inherited—so we could compete with the better-financed opponents.

Our strategy was to raise as much money as possible and spend very little of it until the end of the race when most regular folks were deciding who would get their votes. Our first big expense was campaign stationery, which we used to write to anyone we had ever known asking for contributions. This included old friends and people we had worked with. My father showed his support by writing his friends as well. Many sent us money despite our slim chance of success, and we were grateful for every dime we received. Others honestly told us why they could not support us. We were surprised that some ignored our requests altogether. At least, we thought, we had discovered who our real friends were.

Mark created his campaign headquarters—my office— by building a wall to partition off part of our garage. He dragged an old carpet and a few folding tables from the barn at Coosaw to furnish the windowless space. It is an understatement to say that this office was not glamorous! I think we had two phones, and it seemed terribly sophisticated that I could answer the lines from phones upstairs in the house as well.

Mark's sister Sarah was our sole volunteer in charge of signs (often homemade), and she walked any parade Mark and I could not make on our own. We had a few loyal volunteers who came to help lick envelopes or map neighborhood routes for Mark to knock on doors. Mark ordered a whopping two hundred bumper stickers and six large road signs, a meager amount, of course, to cover any congressional district. He treated those bumper stickers as if they were made of gold. He would only let someone have one if Mark was permitted to follow that person to their car to make sure the sticker made it onto the bumper.

Mark traveled the district (still in that stick-shift hatchback), meeting with Republicans, speaking to rotary groups and church groups, and attending fish frys and candidate forums whenever he could. I learned his positions on the issues and spent lots of time writing out answers to the questions each newspaper and interest group sent to us. Mark would then review the answers and tweak them if needed. I would ultimately type out the final responses on Mark's little Apple Macintosh computer and fax or mail them out to the world. In addition to learning of Mark's beliefs in depth, I respected the fact that he wanted to share his thoughts on an issue honestly and earnestly instead of giving the standard political sound-bite answer we were accustomed to hearing. We used this same careful attention when fielding questions on the phone.

On the weekends and many weekdays, Mark set out from our home early in the morning to knock on doors. We decided that he should focus his attention on mostly conservative, Republican districts with people who were more likely to be sympathetic to his message of cutting back government spending and government intrusion in our lives.

Mark wasn't just a deficit hawk on the stump; he also lived that message in the running of the campaign. By February 1994 we had added $19,100 of contributions to our account book yet had spent only $786. Mark's opponents had spent more than $100,000 by that point in the campaign. Though penny-pinching was his nature, Mark seemed to understand that unless we paid attention to every precious dollar, we would easily and quickly be bled dry. There was constant pressure to purchase ads in Republican newsletters or in the local newspaper to keep up with what other candidates were doing. Mark impressed upon me the importance of remaining disciplined, and I followed his lead by managing expenses carefully in the office.

The press pays very little attention to those they think are fringe candidates, and they had lumped Mark in with that crowd. If people think you can't win, many won't show up to volunteer or give you money, even if they warm to your message. This forced us to think more creatively about ways to draw attention. Free press was all we could afford. As he walked door-to-door, Mark started handing out fake billion-dollar bills and told the voters he believed Congress was spending our hard-earned tax dollars as if they were "funny money." This clever stunt brought a bit of welcome and free media attention, but not enough to gain the notice of power players within the Republican Party.

As it happens, even if you are on the same Republican

team, sometimes you are not the right kind of Republican or perhaps you have not paid your dues within the party establishment. This seemed to be the case with Mark—no one within the party thought he had yet earned the right to this competition. He repeatedly drove two hours to speak to a monthly gathering of Republicans in Myrtle Beach, only to be told by the same woman in charge that she couldn't find time to fit him into the agenda. Mark's ideas were part of the Republican Party's stated ideals, and yet somehow the establishment considered him an outsider, not loyal enough to represent the party or its cause.

Mark's message encompassed term limits, too. He didn't want to become a career politician and was wary of those who did. He believed that we should return to the model our country was founded on: a citizen legislature where ordinary people served for a while and then went back to being regular citizens who had to live under the laws they helped to create. He announced he would limit his own tenure, if elected, to just three terms or a total of six years. He also thought that political action committees gave incumbents an unfair advantage, so he refused to take any money from them. If all candidates restricted themselves in these ways, he believed, we'd get more common-sense decisions from our representatives about taxes and the spending of our money. In standing up and offering to limit his own term, Mark set himself apart from the other candidates who may have pledged to support term limits in general, but would not commit to limiting their own.

I think anyone following this congressional race would have been impressed by Mark's integrity, even if they didn't share his political views. I was fully immersed in the day-to-day running of the campaign and of caring for our two young sons (while Marshall had been a very content baby and a good sleeper, Landon had terrible colic and his restless sleep made both Mark and I exhausted in a not very satisfying way!), but even I found time to be impressed. Mark seemed to be hitting his adult stride, and it was an amazing thing to witness.

After spending seven-and-a-half months knocking on doors, driving to every event in the district, handing out fake money, speaking at forums, putting up signs, and handing out bumper stickers, we got hard numbers on how difficult it is to become known without spending money to get out a message. The local paper did a poll of likely voters six weeks before the primary, and Mark Sanford came in fifth out of a field of seven with only two percent support. We found this incredibly disheartening, though not unexpected. I remember asking Mark if all this effort really was futile, but he remained steadfast. Our media campaign was about to begin over July 4 weekend, and that was when we hoped our message could really begin to penetrate.

I continued to draw strength from an increasingly clear sense of Mark's positions on all the issues and also from that elusive thing called loyalty. I had Mark's back, and I got my back up when I found something had been said or written about him that I felt was wrong. If a reporter twisted the truth,

I couldn't sleep until I had set the record straight. In response to an article I found completely misleading, for instance, I sent this rather scathing letter to the editor of the *Post and Courier*. It was printed on July 20, 1994:

No Campaign Deficit

The word "deficit," as defined in the dictionary, means the amount by which a sum of money falls short of the required amount. Deficit spending refers to the practice of spending funds in excess of income, something our federal government does every day. My husband, Mark Sanford, is running for Congress because he is frustrated with the way our government is spending money and the way it is not making common-sense decisions on a variety of fronts. His bumper stickers, signs and stationery all have a "reduce the deficit" logo on them. I was shocked, then, to read an incorrect report in your paper today that Mark had "rung-up" a "deficit" in his campaign.

Mark's campaign has never run a deficit and never will. To date, it has taken in $203,740 and spent $127,885, leaving a cash surplus of $75,854. Maybe your reporter studied accounting at the same school as most of our politicians. Mark has never run for office before, but he decided to run for Congress because he feels so strongly that regular folks, not people closely tied to the political system, need to get involved in government. It is crucial to our future and to that of our children to change the way things are done in our federal government and to start getting decisions from Congress that make sense again.

Mark strongly feels that we all need to stand up for what we believe in. That's why Mark—a "political newcomer," as your paper calls him—has invested money in his own campaign as he would do in any business transaction as well. In addition, he's raised more than $103,000 from individuals who agree with his message of change, more than a dollar for every dollar he's invested himself, hardly "financing most" himself as your paper states. What's wrong with standing up and doing what you believe is right?

Mark believes in campaign finance reform, and instead of just saying he favors legislation that does away with PACs, he has himself refused to take a dime from any political action committee. Mark doesn't just support term limits; he has taken the first step by limiting his own.

Mark is a man of honesty and integrity who doesn't believe in politics as usual or in political rhetoric. I am proud of Mark and of everything he has done in his campaign to date. We need lots of Mark Sanfords in our government and maybe in journalism too.

Jenny Sanford
16 Wentworth Street

As I re-read that letter now, I can remember the visceral feeling, the buzz, that the campaign gave to those close to it. I can also remember well the exciting momentum that started to build once we went on the air with ads. Many seemed to like Mark's fresh face on television, and some recalled reading of his term limits pledge or meeting him when he knocked on their door. When the paper ran another poll on July 31, just over a week before the primary, Mark had jumped to fourth place with fourteen percent in the polls, an incredible jump in a very short time. Mark's candidacy started to really take off, and our garage campaign office finally had a real group of volunteers.

Although Mark began this campaign with his thirty-page paper on debt and Social Security, we learned all too soon how the press can take long, thoughtful answers to questions on issues and reduce them to sound bites, often twisting their meaning, intentionally or otherwise. We also learned that there will always be some reporters against whom we never had a chance: For whatever reason, they were intently against Mark and his candidacy. This phenomenon became abundantly clear when Mark answered a question for the newspaper in Myrtle Beach, one that is distributed in a significant part of the district he sought to represent in Congress. The issue was about roads.

In the historic city of Charleston, there are many who would like to close off the city and keep tourists from entering, the feeling being that if we were to build more interstates heading here we might as well make them one-way as no one will want to leave once they get here. Myrtle Beach could not be more different. They want more roads built to bring more tourists and more revenue.

Mark answered the Myrtle Beach paper's question: If there was a huge federal bill filled with billions of wasteful spending and dozens of bridges to nowhere, but it had a small sliver of money for building roads in Horry County and Myrtle Beach, would he vote for it? Staunchly against unnecessary spending, Mark said he would have to vote against that bill. The reporter printed that Sanford "would vote against roads" in the area, implying Mark was against any road funding.

This created a firestorm so large that we had to spend precious resources defending Mark's position. When Mark personally confronted the reporter about why Mark had been quoted out of context, the writer looked at Mark and replied "life is out of context." It was as though he was as astounded at Mark's and my ire as we were with his journalism. He seemed jaded. Mark and I were much less so back then.

As the primary election drew closer and we started rising in the polls, we experienced the ugly underside of politics more specifically. I had heard of dirty tricks before in our state, but nothing prepared me for just how downright mean the sport of politics could be here. We became the subject of mystery calls to voters, otherwise known as push polls, in which a phony group such as "Citizens on Behalf of Fairness in the Media" calls and asks the innocent voter a question that implies something about a candidate that simply isn't true.

The push poll call is designed to plant damaging associations in a voter's mind that will cause him or her not to vote for the candidate who is the subject of the call. South Carolina is famous for this particular dirty trick. Our state was the place where unknown operatives helped to derail John McCain's 2000 effort to become president by asking unsuspecting voters if they knew McCain had an illegitimate black child. The McCains had adopted an orphan from Sri Lanka, an act of pure generosity of spirit, but the push poll made him sound like a philanderer. For Mark, the implied accusation was a lot milder, but still very damaging to Mark's candidacy if it were true, which it was not. The caller asked: "If you learned that Mark Sanford was a good friend of Bill Clinton . . . would you support him?" (Needless to say, being a friend of Bill Clinton's was not a good thing in a Republican primary.) We also experienced the impact of special interest groups who send out voter guides, sometimes entirely honest and other times crafted in a manner to highlight a specific favorite candidate over others with similar views on the issues.

Looking back now, I see how this was just the first taste of something we would be forced to swallow again and again in each of Mark's campaigns. I look around at the political landscape today and I can still see dirty politics on display at every turn. It was a great place to be in life and in our lives together that we could still be outraged and baffled by these things. I am no less outraged today, but I am no longer at all surprised.

I was personally exhausted as the primary drew to a close, but I have to admit we were also having fun. We had great new friends in our volunteers; we shared enthusiasm and a mission. Doing more with less was part of every aspect of the campaign. Volunteers would color large stickers to attach to our six road signs with short messages that would make them come alive, messages like "Just Three Terms" or "No PAC Money." We also had our small team of volunteers shake signs at the base of the Ravenel Bridge or at busy intersections, all designed to give the illusion of widespread excitement and energy. Whether Mark won or not, we both believed we had run a campaign to be proud of. We shared a sense of purpose and that was exhilarating. For the first time since I had known him, Mark was completely and fully absorbed in something that seemed to satisfy his restlessness, which made me happy to see.

Life as a mom, however, was quite a juggle during this time. Thankfully Landon's colic had passed and he was sleeping full nights, but nonetheless I was stretched thin. I was in the campaign office most of the day while someone watched the boys so I could oversee all activities in the basement office. I would break for lunch with the boys and would somehow squeeze in grocery shopping or time for a well-check at the pediatrician or some other such family necessity.

The boys were now two and almost one years old, and they were able to travel with me to campaign events or to TV stations. They were a draw when we shook hands in the parade at the Hell Hole Swamp Festival or when we went to the

Chicken Bog Fest in Loris. But they were still very small, they needed their sleep, they needed routine, and they needed their parents' attention. Truth to tell, my loyalties were torn as the campaign heated up. I wanted to do a good job with the campaign, but I also wanted to raise my boys well and to love them fully, and there was not enough time in the day to do both. However, my belief that God always seems to put the right people in your life at the right time was soon rewarded. Our house was down the street from the College of Charleston, where my favorite sitter (one who didn't mind Landon's screams) was a student. She moved in with us as the primary neared, which allowed me to work long into the evenings after I'd put the boys to sleep. Having someone I trusted to keep them safe and to be on call for them helped put my mind at ease as we carried on.

As the August 9 primary date approached, I felt as if we were running on adrenaline. Even though I was swept up in the momentum and excitement, I was ready for this endeavor to be behind us. There are many times in life when one feels completely out of balance and this was one of them. I had a purpose then, and it was to fully support Mark's candidacy while balancing the needs of our young family. Fulfilling this purpose was satisfying but doing this well left no time for me, no quiet time for personal growth or reflection or to recharge my batteries. I know I was growing as a person through the testing of our values and through my deepening knowledge of my husband but I couldn't keep this frenetic pace indefinitely. As with so many difficult things in life, I found this time was made easier because I knew there was an end that was clearly in sight.

On primary night, we gathered joyfully with close friends, family, and campaign volunteers at a local cafe. I was dressed in my red-white-and-blue campaigning attire from that day, with Landon on my hip in onesie pajamas and a pacifier in his mouth. Marshall sported Barney pajamas and red tennis shoes. He waved flags and ate cake, all way past his normal bedtime.

We watched the results come in on television, knowing that it would be close. If no candidate earned more than fifty percent, there would be a runoff election in two weeks for the first- and second-place candidates. We expected Van Hipp to come in first, as he was the frontrunner and the political establishment candidate. Our focus was on the pack of candidates vying for second place. We knew we were outspent by more than two to one by two or three of the candidates, yet we believed our disciplined and incredibly focused campaign still stood a hair of a chance. We were quite literally in shock when, with ninety-nine percent of the votes counted, the results were as follows:

Van Hipp	31%
Mark Sanford	19%
Bob Harrell	17%
Mike Rose	17%
Mendel Rivers	12%
Sarah King	3%
John Henry Whitmire	1%

The news reports that night and the following morning described "an electoral Cinderella story" and talked of Mark as a "giant killer," likening him to David from the David and Goliath story. The press was suddenly enchanted with Mark, describing how he "came from nowhere" to win his spot in this runoff. Clearly, they had missed all our hard work! We were exhausted and elated, tired but victorious. And the battle had somehow just begun.

Swept up in a tornado of our own making, we realized that we had to raise more money immediately, film new ads, and work even harder, smarter, and somehow faster to get our message out. Mark was still very much the underdog, but the momentum was on our side. As this was a very conservative district, the odds were good that if he won this runoff election he would be able to win the seat in the general election. Having said that, if he won, we would have yet another exhausting campaign for the election in November. I got tired just thinking of it.

This part of the campaign was different because it was so intense, being squeezed into just two weeks. Van Hipp came out swinging. He described Mark as liberal, a real taboo in a conservative primary. We suspected that Van Hipp was financing more push polls. Implying it was Mark's position on the issue, callers asked voters things such as, "Would you vote for Mark Sanford if you knew he favored legalization of drugs?"

Mark got so riled up by this that he went to Hipp's house in the middle of the night to confront him. When Van opened the door clad only in his boxers, Mark stuck a tape recorder in his face and demanded that he state whether he was behind the calls or not. Van was undaunted by this confrontation. He denied funding the polls, and we couldn't prove that he was doing so. And misinformation-filled mailings to voters continued: literature saying that Mark Sanford was "pro-abortion" and that he was "for universal health care" though neither was true.

Mark and I found these tactics colossally discouraging, and we vowed we would always run our campaign honorably, never saying something through the campaign medium we were not comfortable saying directly to the opponent. We wanted to change the terms of the debate, to actually have a debate of ideas without getting into the politics of personal destruction. At the end of the day, we believed, people liked honorable men and women in government and if we remained loyal to our values, voters would see Mark in this light. At this moment in the campaign, I understood my value to Mark was much higher than just the fact that I was "free." If Mark had spent money to hire a campaign manager, not only would he have used precious resources, but he would likely have been strongly advised to respond to negative attacks in kind, thus compromising those values that I knew were so important to us both.

Unbelievably—to many, even to us—Mark won fifty-two percent of the vote in the runoff primary. What an upset! It seemed to us that the stars were aligning, and the shot in the arm that this win gave both Mark and his campaign staff would be the fuel for most of our future confidence. We celebrated heartily with volunteers and friends and family on election night and my happiness and my pride and my excitement was real. Yet I couldn't wait for the festivities to end so that I could get to sleep. But of course, the activity never stopped. We were immediately swept into the next race for the general election.

This time the Republican Party was united behind Mark. We were one of the hopefuls that would be part of a Republican takeover of the U.S. House of Representatives, and all eyes were focused on winning against our Democratic opponent, Robert Barber. Fundraising was much easier as the national party sent other politicians such as Dick Armey and Jack Kemp down to star at events and help raise more money. People came out of the woodwork to volunteer or to offer their advice or their services. Suddenly the campaign had outgrown the space we had available in our garage, so when a supporter offered to provide us with an office down the street from our house, we moved to more professional environs.

As the campaign expanded rapidly, I tried to step down as campaign manager. The general election felt quite different from our grass roots, ideological efforts at home. More was at stake and the effort was bigger and less personal than when we were working just to get Mark through the primary. I wanted to return to being a mom, but our media consultant pleaded with me not to, as he didn't want us to fix what wasn't broken. Mark understood that I wanted to step back and he understood why, but he begged me to stay on. We had made it this far together, he reasoned, and we had been a winning formula.

I struck a deal of sorts. I agreed to stay, but we would engage others to lighten my load. I know we actually hired one person but there were quite a few people with serious campaign experience who joined us as volunteers, too, and their combined support helped relieve me of the exhausting full-time detail. Nevertheless, we didn't fully trust the agendas of all our new "friends" in this campaign, especially after the day we discovered two volunteers rifling through files they didn't need to be looking through. When they couldn't really explain what they were up to, we asked them to leave. From then on we kept an eye on all unknown newcomers. Mark and I continued to keep the real decision making between ourselves and our media adviser.

Late in September, Mark and I traveled to Washington, DC, so that he could sign Newt Gingrich's famed Contract with America. It was on this trip that we began to feel like we were on a much larger team: We met so many other Republican candidates and U.S. Representatives who all wanted to help us win. As collegial as that began to make us feel, we learned that with these higher stakes came dirtier tricks, and we were naïve enough to take real offense, to be bothered by it. As we arrived at a Republican fundraising dinner that evening, there were picketers outside the entrance. Mark saw a few holding signs with his name on them that said things like "Sanford you're eating the heart of the lowcountry." Mark, honestly wanting to know what he had done that upset these picketers, went up to one to ask him directly. After tapping the man with the sign on the shoulder, he discovered the man had clearly been hired to hold the sign: He had no clue who Mark Sanford was and could barely speak a word of English.

During this brief trip, we also discovered how deeply the opposition would be willing to dig to oppose Mark's candidacy. A reporter we met there showed Mark a full-page ad printed in *Roll Call* magazine and paid for by the Democratic Congressional Campaign Committee that listed ten Republican candidates for Congress, including Mark. On the other column was a list of things these ten had done. The idea of the ad was to match the name of the candidate with their past. The list had all sorts of outlandish credentials like "claims that white, Anglo-Saxon men are an endangered species" or this candidate "claims Greeks and Romans were homosexuals" and so on. I looked at the list and had no clue which act was attributed to the man I was married to. After eliminating the ones I knew could not have been Mark's doing, I narrowed it down to Mark having been a "goose exterminator." I asked him if he'd ever been one. It turned out one summer during college he worked to control the goose population in New Zealand by shooting geese and injecting poison into unhatched eggs, something I'd never known, yet the press had managed to find out before me.

Goose exterminator or not, the contrast between Mark and his Democratic opponent Robert Barber was clear, no more so on display than when Barber falsely claimed Mark opposed hiring more police and that he advocated legalization of prostitution. When asked if he would support a specific bill on crime, Mark responded that he would not because of the wasteful spending in the bill. Barber used Mark's stance, absurdly, to label him as "pro-crime."

When Barber's attacks on Mark's positions on the issues didn't cause him to gain any ground, he went after Mark's personal life. He tried to paint Mark as a wealthy tourist from out-of-state, although in fact the Sanfords had moved to South Carolina from Florida fifteen years earlier and had spent every summer there before that. His tone implied that if you are successful or of means, you are unfit to represent a congressional district. Then he picked on Mark for not voting in every election, as he had not registered to vote during the year and a half he lived in New York City.

In my mind, this just meant he was a normal citizen; when he had moved away he hadn't bothered to change a lot of things, including his driver's license. He had known the move north would be temporary. That "normal guy" image was what we emphasized in our ads. The style was friendly and direct, with Mark speaking to the voters about the issues he cared about, no gimmicks or sleazy attacks. Perhaps that was what made people believe that they knew him. After just a few weeks of running our ads, Mark went from a virtual unknown to someone who was recognized on the street. Suddenly when he knocked on doors, he was greeted warmly. He relished it when someone gave him a thumbs-up or told him they agreed with his positions and would likely vote for him in the upcoming election. I think that even with all the perks and parties and praise that comes with political success, there is nothing quite as empowering in all of politics as the unsolicited thanks of someone on the street.

On election night, almost exactly one year after beginning our stitched-together campaign, we held our celebration at Calder's Pub on King Street in Charleston. Mark won the election with sixty-seven percent of the vote, almost 95,000 votes: a very healthy total. We had run an almost flawless campaign—rising from two percent in the polls in just four months. We won despite spending much less money than our opponents in each of the three elections. By focusing exclusively on the issues Mark cared about, we ran an honorable and effective campaign, never once taking our eye off the ball. Republicans were elected in many districts all across the nation that same night as control of the House was transferred from the Democrats to the Republicans for the first time in decades. Through our victory we were joining up with a movement that pledged to take the country in a bold, new direction.

For me, however, that election victory was not as exciting as the primary had been. In such a heavily Republican and conservative district, Mark's chances had been very good once he became the party candidate. My excitement was at the prospect of getting back to a more normal life. Marshall was now speaking in full sentences and potty training while Landon had just taken his first steps. They were swept up in the activity too but I yearned for more time with them, time when we could enjoy being instead of doing.

In an interview I gave to our local paper the next day about the election and my expectations, I said boldly that I'd never liked politics, didn't want to be involved in politics, and, "now that this campaign is over, I'm finished with politics." The story went on:

"I was exhausted," she said. "I couldn't answer one more stupid question. I couldn't smile at one more person. I missed being with my children."

Mrs. Sanford isn't sure what comes next— whether she'll stay in her Wentworth Street house or move to Washington.

Right now, she says, she's focused on something more immediate. After the ten houseguests leave and the pillows are put away, she's going to spend a night at home with her family. No one else. She'll wear blue jeans and eat popcorn. She won't answer the phone. Better yet, the phone won't even ring.

After that, she wants to see her friends, read something beside political treatises, and play some tennis or golf. (*Post and Courier*, November 10, 1994)

Little did I know then that the busyness was far from over, the houseguests would linger, and my desire for time alone with my family would become the fight of my life thereafter.

Looking back I now realize this was the beginning of Mark's unyielding loyalty to the conservative principles of fiscal stewardship and limited government. It is this unyielding loyalty to principle that is so rare in politics and yet it is perhaps this same unyielding focus on these conservative principles that caused Mark to lose sight, over time, of his personal values that I think matter more. It is one thing to campaign on the issues but I was soon to learn that in elected office one's adherence to the issues is challenged continually. Mark's loyalty to the issues from then on would be seriously tested and so would his loyalty to me and to himself.

SIX

At the moment when Mark won his seat in Congress, we were the closest we'd ever been, victorious in something that we started from just a table in a chilly garage. My commitment to manage his campaign was one of those here and now choices. Mark had a dream and working with him to achieve it was a way to help him feel more fully alive. When I said I'd do it, I was taking the long view, imagining we would reminisce some day about what great fun we had that crazy time he decided to run for Congress. I gave it my all, and improbably, I became the wife of a politician.

We made another quick series of decisions about what seemed to make sense in the day to day. A congressional salary is nothing compared to Wall Street standards, or of one in real estate, so we had to think carefully about how we were going to live within our means. The first decision was whether our family would move with Mark to DC or remain in Charleston.

The House of Representatives' two-year term makes it the elected body most responsive to the people. What this meant for a political newcomer like Mark is that he had to be home in the district as often as he could on weekends to remind the voters who he was and what he was doing for them. The government will cover the cost for a congressman to travel home if his time home includes official business. The government will not, however, cover the cost of flights to DC for visits by the representative's spouse and children. We decided we would see more of Mark if we remained in South Carolina and saw him on trips home. Logical, yes, but amazing to me now, how naïve I was to agree to being a single mother four or more days a week. In my own defense, I know now that raising the boys didn't give me much time to think!

Shortly after he was elected, I traveled to DC with Mark for orientation and to help him look at apartments. Of course, he was only looking at cheap places in neighborhoods that seemed very dangerous to me. When he decided to sleep in his office on a futon, my mother called me, alarmed.

"You can't let him sleep in his office!" she said.

"Why not?" I responded. As if I could somehow get Mark to change his mind!

"Well that's just not okay for anyone to live that way, and what will he do when you visit?"

"Mom, I think it's just fine." I said. "I saw the awful apartments he wanted to rent and I would be worried for his safety in them, and mine as well. If I were to visit him there, I would likely find myself cleaning the place. If he sleeps in his office, when I visit once or twice a year, I can stay in a hotel for a nice break and he can visit me," I explained.

She saw immediately where I was coming from and agreed we had a good plan.

When I think back to the two of us at that time in our lives, I marvel at how wonderfully naïve and idealistic we were. We saw the world as black or white and were dismissive of those who saw it in shades of gray. Through the campaign for Congress, my love for my husband deepened as I saw him refuse to be swayed from his beliefs in order to pick up a few votes or an endorsement. He would rather lose the campaign than win it through sleazy compromises, and my idealistic young heart swelled with pride to be married to such a principled man.

But after our principled campaign, we took a crash course in the reality of rules-to-live-by for elected officials. It became immediately apparent to me that campaigns never end; they are a constant part of public life, and public officials follow an entirely different set of standards. I didn't believe that Mark would get caught in these traps because of his loyalty to his core beliefs.

We've all seen many times how a candidate promises to lead courageously and follow ideals, then the endless horse trading of being an elected official causes those ideals to slip. In the crude reality that exists behind the scenes, every issue has a history, constituencies on differing sides, as well as lobbyists for or against flattering the legislators and offering them trips and lavish meals to curry favor. In order to get anything done, representatives trade a vote on a bill they don't really believe in for promises of support on another bill. Bit by bit, those initial ideals and goals get chipped away. All the more reason, Mark and I believed, to keep them in focus and make every decision guided by a conscious appreciation of them. Mark's constant struggle to hew to his own standards of frugality, for instance, was not just a virtue he would promote in government, but one that he would demonstrate in his daily life in Congress.

From the very first day, he closely watched expenses in the office, requiring the staff to save paperclips and copy on the reverse side of used paper. As long as the federal budget remained unbalanced, Mark refused to take a pay increase, instead donating the raise the representatives voted themselves to charity. (In his first year in office, with what he saved on administrative costs, Mark also returned more than $200,000 in funds to the U.S. Treasury.) Plus, on principle, he refused the franking privileges, which allow representatives to send mail for free. Mark believed this amounted to a campaign subsidy that protected incumbents at the expense of citizen legislators like himself.

Once he got to Congress, Mark's Cinderella story captivated the national media, which was charmed too by the fact that Mark wasn't just a deficit hawk on the stump. He caught the first possible plane home when voting ended, bringing his dirty laundry back each weekend. He bragged about how he could survive two weeks on a $20 bill by grazing at lobbyist-funded receptions and being driven by staff to required events. When the press found out where he was living, images of the futon in the middle of his grand congressional office space made great television. Mark found the attention difficult to refuse. In truth, he relished every bit of the glare and soon grew to seek it.

As the media lavished attention on him, the people in our district became more aware of his budding national presence. They called or wrote to tell Mark how proud they were of his election, and how hopeful they were that he would succeed. Where fundraising had been nearly impossible during our first campaign, suddenly unsolicited checks filled the mailbox, along with offers from complete strangers who wanted to host fundraisers for Mark's reelection.

I learned immediately of "the almighty schedule" and of the importance of fighting for open time for our family. The scheduler booked Mark's time in five-minute increments throughout each day and into the evening. If Mark allowed it (and he largely did), he could fully book each evening and weekend with speeches, dinners, parades, or even with travel to spots around the world to learn more about the issues being debated and discussed in Congress. There were many weekends when Mark was home in name only. He'd show up, hand me his laundry, spend a few precious hours with the boys and me, then be off to an all-day marathon of public events and fundraisers.

In the meantime, I was just as busy with our little constituents, to whom I was connected in a way that no one but they and I could see or appreciate. Mark's connection was necessarily diffuse and to a broad public. Mine was intimate. I was wholly and completely engaged as I held down the fort in Charleston with my pack of babies, another of which, Bolton, arrived in the second year of Mark's first term. One night in particular reminds me of the very different kinds of lives my husband and I were leading.

When Marshall was three and a half and Landon was two and a half, both had a violent stomach bug, and I found myself running around cleaning up after each one, repeatedly changing sheets and pajamas while trying to comfort them both and nursing baby Bolton as well. At one point, I got Landon back down in his crib and had Marshall with me in my bathroom. I pleaded with Marshall to wear a pull-up diaper because I just couldn't keep up with all the mess. He insisted he was a big boy and didn't need a diaper anymore. During a moment of clarity, I realized I would not win a negotiation with a stubborn toddler, so I got Marshall a pillow and blanket and placed them in the tub, and said, "Well then son, you are just going to have to sleep in the tub!" At the prospect of sleeping uncomfortably and alone in the bathroom, Marshall gave in and agreed to wear the diaper "just for one night." Whatever you might say about the maturity of his colleagues, these were not the kinds of negotiations Mark was having in Congress!

The boys and I had our own pleasures and routines. I treasured my time with them. We loved sitting together with take-out pizza and watching movies while just a few channels away their dad cast his vote on an important bill on C-SPAN. Mark had a rare opportunity to serve the country, and all of us were pitching in. I reminded myself that my lot was no different than the wife of a busy salesman and a lot better than the spouse of a solider serving in one of our wars. And at least I could see my husband on C-SPAN if I really wanted to tune in. Job asked: "Shall we indeed accept good from God and not accept adversity?" We had been richly blessed. Doing my small part to accommodate Mark's busy life while focusing on the blessings underfoot was minimal on the adversity scale; it was not too much to ask.

Knowing Mark's extremely frugal habits, I knew not to expect much from Mark for birthdays or for Christmas, even if I felt it was surely nice to be remembered every now and again. After our first big primary and run-off wins in 1994, Mark surprised me over a romantic dinner one evening with a beautiful gold pin, a laughing elephant I have worn plenty over the years he has served as a Republican. Once in office, however, his habits deteriorated and he even forgot my birthday once. Thereafter, I nudged the scheduler to remind him. (My birthday is on September 11, and since 2001 Mark has learned to remember it without a reminder.)

One birthday during the later congressional years, Mark decided to do something very nice for me. He had a friend pick out a diamond necklace and he had a staff member hide it in my closet. Then he faxed clues to the campaign office in our basement as to where I should look to find my birthday gift. I had the boys join me in the scavenger hunt and, working together, we found it. I loved it! Not only did I love the necklace, but this reminded me of what I loved about Mark Sanford. The scavenger hunt was clever and his notes and clues were ever so boyishly sweet.

A few days later, he arrived home from DC. We had dinner guests, and I was proudly wearing my lovely new necklace. As soon as he saw me wearing it, he said *"That* is what I spent all that money on?! I hope you kept the box!"

He returned the necklace the next day, thinking it was not worth the money he had spent. He could see I was disappointed, but he promised to make it up to me. In truth, once I knew he thought he had overspent, I also knew it would pain him to see me wear the necklace had I insisted on keeping it. I wouldn't have felt comfortable wearing it in his presence, so what was the point? I had married him, after all, knowing he was not a big-spending Wall Street type. I remained thankful for the thought and the sweet scavenger hunt nonetheless.

I wasn't the only one to bear the brunt of Mark's frugality. Mark had a standing weekly movie night with fellow congressmen Lindsey Graham and Steve Largent and they would rotate who was responsible for the movie tickets and snacks. When it was Mark's turn to get the popcorn and soda, Mark chose the best deal. He bought one large bag of popcorn and a jumbo-sized Coke with three straws. I'm not sure if Lindsey and Steve thought Mark's decision was stingy or hilarious. But his explanation was simple and true to form: The Coke had free refills.

In all fairness, I realize that seriously caring about saving money is an admirable (and rare) quality in a politician. Mark's frugality isn't for show. It is in his core. Spending money gets his attention. I learned to use this to my advantage.

We arrived home late one Sunday evening in January 1997 from a congressional retreat in Hershey, Pennsylvania, with Marshall and Landon. We'd left baby Bolton at home with a sitter, Zetta Brown. Upon return, Zetta told us Bolton was sleeping soundly upstairs, but she thought she had heard a bird in the house.

When I went upstairs to unpack and get ready for bed, I discovered two bats sleeping peacefully in my sink. I called for Mark, who calmly got the bats snug in a t-shirt. The older boys were enthralled as he gently released the bats out the front door. We proceeded to unpack and tucked Marshall and Landon into their beds. Then I went to bed too, only to find bats swooping through my bedroom as soon as I turned out the lights.

This time I called frantically for Mark, and he got a tennis racket and started whacking at bats throughout the house as the boys slept. (I later learned it is against the law to kill bats, a federal law Mark called worthless once I informed him of it.) Nine bats later, we went to bed, though I lay awake and kept one eye open for bats for too long.

Though Mark thought doing so was a waste of money, the next morning, I called a pest control man named John to make sure the bats were gone. John discovered that a cap on the chimney had been torn back, allowing space for the bats to enter the house through the fireplace. He did what he felt was needed and told me once the bats left to feed that evening, they would not be able to return. But at dusk, the bats were swooping through the kitchen, and I was a nervous wreck! Bats in the house seem to swoop right at your face, making you want to dive for the floor. Mark killed a few more that evening and then chuckled at my fright as he departed for DC the next morning.

I couldn't take another night of them. I vacated the house before dusk and took the boys to sleep at a friend's down the street, while giving the keys to the house to my new friend John.

It turns out bats can hibernate inside. We needed to be patient a bit longer as he enticed them all to leave. Not a job for me. I felt I was wearing out my welcome with the three little boys at my friend's house and also felt little empathy from Mark, safe in his batless office in DC.

So, on Thursday I moved with the three boys to a suite in a local hotel and called Mark to tell him that I was not moving back in until he had slept in the house for at least two nights without seeing a bat. Facing the prospect of paying for an extended hotel stay, Mark sprang into action, effectively dealing with every last bat. We happily returned to live together as a family Sunday night.

Mark described his time in Congress as similar to being a member of a fraternity, bantering about ideas with colleagues and remaining friendly despite disagreements. He also enjoyed standing on principle to nudge change in one direction or to keep change from happening too fast in another direction. As engaged and happy as he seemed, I began to wonder if remaining true to what he believed was making him a very lonely or unsatisfied man.

As a staunch fiscal conservative, Mark was on the fringe of his party in Congress. He was one of a handful who opposed the relaxing of our nation's mortgage rules in the 90s, for example, when few could conceive of being against a law that claimed it would encourage home ownership for everyone. He made many lonely votes against large military bills too, because of the tendency to bloat military spending with unnecessary earmarks. His principles required him to oppose things—opposition that later would be used to portray him as heartless. He was one of the sole votes against a breast-cancer stamp because it cost money and he thought it was merely feel-good legislation that would ultimately lead to more government creep. In some cases, it was he and just one or two others voting together on an issue.

At one point in the middle of his second term, we rented a house on the South Carolina coast for a much-needed vacation and the differences in our pace and lack of connection caught up to us. I was feeling the strain of living apart, and I was also exhausted by my time alone juggling the demands of the boys. On a walk together alone along the shore, I tried to explain my frustration. I didn't begrudge Mark his time away from the doctor's appointments, the school events, and later the homework, because I saw Mark's career as a family effort. But his work protected him from the ordinary, day-in, day-out connection with the boys, I explained, and as a result I felt he was becoming out of touch with us. My job was tapping into the most tender parts of my heart and soul. His job demanded that he be calculating and sometimes manipulative. I was growing more vulnerable, and he was forming a hardened shell.

For his part, Mark complained that I didn't understand the stress and pressure he was under. We didn't say it in so many words, but it was clear that while both of us were rarely alone, in our own distinct ways, we were lonely.

What we did say led to tears — mine — and to a soul search about whether we should even stay married. I know many marriages weather similar discussions, sometimes with one spouse threatening to leave. Neither Mark nor I threatened to leave, but we were both working hard to be understood and falling short. Our geographic distance was yielding a real emotional distance as well. I questioned then whether he really understood me. I assume he questioned that about me as well. His seeming inability to understand my needs and my worries also made me question if he truly loved me. I don't know if he could say the same, but in many ways I think we were discovering things about our marriage that made us each afraid for the future of it.

At the same time, this heart-to-heart served as a wake-up call of sorts. We were acknowledging that life had become hard, but we still loved each other and also had a family that we both dearly wanted to hold together. We both hoped that life would get easier, that we would enter into a new and more manageable "season" once his time in Congress was through. In the meantime, we agreed that his career was an important part of both of us, and that we didn't want to upend it by continuing to move apart. Divorce just wasn't an option. We wanted to stay together and we would. Besides, I believed him when he said he would end his service in Congress after six years. At the moment of this painful argument, we were about halfway through.

SEVEN

E VEN WITH A RENEWED AND EXPLICIT COMMITMENT AFTER OUR argument on the beach, Mark and I spent less and less time together during his last term in Congress. By then our home was on Sullivan's Island. We had sold our house in Charleston and bought an informal and seemingly indestructible cinder-block one near the beach on Sullivan's, an island at the mouth of the Charleston harbor. I had instantly fallen in love with life on Sullivan's. The pace, the proximity to the sea, and the simplicity of the home itself suited me and gave me great happiness, even with Mark gone so much. This still-cherished year-round beach retreat has given us all some needed space — indoors and out — though Mark has taken refuge in its walls less than the rest of us. Indeed, at that point he was returning home infrequently on the weekends, traveling more often, expanding his knowledge of the issues in South America, Khazakstan, Bosnia, India, you name it. I got used to having him gone and justified it by his need for adventure and travel and, yet again, reminding myself of that finish line that I could see coming toward me in the distance. This was a fairly lonely existence for me all the same. Mark was seeing the world, but I wanted him to see that this world that he and I created was just as interesting. I worried that so much of it was slipping away from him unnoticed, never to be reclaimed. That restlessness and drive I had admired so much when we were courting was causing him to look outside the home for adventure, while I believed the adventure of my life was nestled in my arms.

I now have some perspective on how this snuck up on us. Our entry into this unreal world started quickly and, at first, we were both caught up in the excitement of it all. As soon as we won that first campaign for Congress, the phones were ringing with other politicians congratulating Mark on his win and suggesting one course of action or another. The press wanted interviews and sound bites for the evening news. Congressional tabloids asked for photos and bios to profile the newest members of this exclusive club. Lobbyists called to flatter Mark as they pitched their causes and successful businessmen wanted to meet him for lunch or dinner to ensure their interests were protected. The accumulation of this special treatment was no doubt a big part of what disconnected Mark and me from each other and what disconnected Mark from the values and priorities he once held dear. On

Wall Street, I saw many a man whose ego grew as his income rose and he got more attention from those around him, but nothing I saw there compares to the immediate and transformational ego-stroking of politics.

I can see now that it was naïve to think that marriage and family would take the edge off Mark's frenetic hunger. After all, right at the moment when I had achieved a lifelong goal—the birth of our first son Marshall—Mark said he was bored. He wanted to be stretched to the limit, and as much as he loved me and our growing family, domestic life didn't do that for him. Motherhood was stretching me physically and emotionally in ways he couldn't share and that he didn't appreciate.

Many marriages suffer when the partners start to prioritize differently and then grow apart from one another. The more I saw Mark pack his schedule, the more I tried to become the antidote; I worked to balance the frenzy. I supported his campaigning and entertained with him as much as possible when he was home on weekends, but I also would regroup and slow down during the week when he was away. When he pulled us into his freneticism, I pulled the other way, trying to carve out time for us to recharge instead of deplete our batteries.

This push-pull was probably futile. I grew to see I couldn't fix him and he didn't want me to slow him down. I couldn't find his happiness, but I could make the effort to connect with my own.

Though I admired the way Mark persevered in the aftermath of his father's death, over time I less charitably saw the mirror trait of that perseverance: stubbornness. He did things his way, and his way only, on a host of fronts. Still, I knew the stresses Mark was under and the challenges he faced so I had to pick my battles with him carefully. We had our shared goals, our family, and our focus on his career to bind us together. My feeling was that anything that distracted from those things was something I could let go of since there were so many pressing responsibilities that needed our full attention. As a modus operandi, this more or less worked because our basic values remained shared.

Call it perseverance or stubbornness, Mark didn't make it easy for himself to succeed in Congress. He would regularly return from DC frustrated that he had "nothing to show" for his valiant efforts; at least, he said, I had the babies to show for my hard work. His popularity was sky high with the voters in our district because he took a stand against wasteful government spending. This made him a maverick among his peers. Fighting so many majority-supported big bills made it hard to champion laws of his own; he wouldn't support other representatives' bills so they had little motivation to support his. Opposing legislation often did succeed in keeping federal spending lower than it would have been but it wasn't like a notch on the belt of success to be remembered for. He also wanted to enact laws he believed in, including some that would further restrict rampant government growth, and on that front, he frequently faced defeat.

I tried to help Mark see that success—as he was coming to define it in his day-to-day work—didn't correlate to self-worth. Through the highs and lows of his own life, my father has demonstrated that success is a personal thing defined by the way you live your life every day, and by what you do with the skills you have and the blessings you have bestowed on you. I praised Mark for his hard work. I praised him for the hard work of opposition. My praise was never quite enough. Like many men, his personal bar for success is satisfied by more tangible things. On the weekends at home when not campaigning, I would often find Mark on a track hoe at Coosaw from dawn till dusk creating a pond or even digging a giant pit for the boys to play in (and, possibly, risk their lives!), complete with a PVC pipe for chicken fights and a zip line. He explained he loved seeing his progress "one scoop at a time" and knew at the end of the day just what he had succeeded in creating. In this—building something—he could feel satisfied.

One brilliant fall Sunday at Coosaw, we took the boys deep into the woods for a picnic. I spread a blanket under the bright blue skies in a large clearing, while Mark got the boys to help him start a fire in a grand stack of logs left by a crew that had been logging timber there. Shortly after the fire was lit, the wind began to pick up. After finishing our simple lunch, I had to pack away the blanket and leftovers as the breeze strengthened. In no time whatsoever, the flames were two stories tall and the wind was blowing some of the flames in the direction of the neighboring stand of pines. I was terrified watching our little boys trying to beat back the flames with skimpy branches. Alarmed, I drove with the baby to a local store to ask the old men gathered there to help while the storekeeper called the fire tower. Eventually a small plane dropping water from above helped get everything under control. As we left for Charleston and the airport so that Mark could catch his flight to DC, a passing fireman asked him if he was related to Congressman Mark Sanford. Neither denying nor confirming his identity, Mark just smiled and moved along.

This was the first time I witnessed Mark communicate something less than the truth, an episode that I have considered and reconsidered in different lights over time. Had knowledge of this gotten out, who knows what the media would have done with it?

The longer we stayed in politics, the more contemptuous I became of this media circus and its carnival atmosphere complete with barkers and stunts and people who are trying to trick you. This battle over who controls the image affects everything the politician and his family do. It felt to me as if they were always looking for the slightest mistake or for something they could twist and sensationalize. As a result, we all found ourselves calculating how whatever we did might look to an unsympathetic audience, even if we had done nothing wrong.

Mark had made a mistake building a fire in those conditions, but it's the kind of mistake that happens all the time and the wind had shifted and strengthened. Would political pundits weigh in, using it as a metaphor for Mark's judgment? Perhaps a future opponent would use the story to blame Mark for taking advantage of the same state resources whose budgets he cut back. In that way, it is understandable that he wanted to keep this quiet. On the other hand, his fear that the story might show him in a poor light caused him to sacrifice a piece of his own integrity. The same Latin words that mean "not" and "touch" are behind the word integrity. A person of integrity is whole, complete, untouched. People of integrity are the same in the dark as in the light. The fear of how this would look caused him to withhold the truth then, and in time he would do so to the press, and to me, again.

One of Mark's trips during his last term in office was to India, something that incited a mundane crisis, but one that made me wonder again about our future together. We were flying to Seattle over Memorial Day weekend for my brother's wedding. Mark thought this would be a good time to pick up some extra income and a way to put into practice something he'd learned watching so many poor in India: Don't be so attached to things. From his distant perch in DC, he rented our house to some Citadel grads. He didn't consult with me about this, and then he got the dates wrong, renting it two days before the boys and I were supposed to leave. I was suddenly, frantically, cleaning the house so that it would be presentable to the renters, then we had to move somewhere for two days (an expense in and of itself—the net gain on this weekend was not much!) so that I could attend Landon's kindergarten graduation before we flew west.

Mark flew directly from DC to Seattle, so I flew with all four boys (all under the age of eight at the time) and met up with Mark there. On the long flight, Blake (one and a half) conveniently got sick and I was more than happy to pass him to Mark's clean arms upon arrival. My nerves were frazzled from the trip and I was fuming.

Our relationship was chilly that weekend, to say the least. Once alone, I told him I thought he was incredibly self-absorbed and disconnected from reality and from me. I reminded him that the special privilege of marriage is that the two partners get to know each other in a deeper way than the rest of the world, in fact, one hopes, almost better than they know themselves. I thought the world that Mark lived in illuminated the image, the superficial, a part of him that was calculated to be unknowable. It wasn't the first time I thought it, but it might have been the first time I articulated it: The more he succeeded politically, the more time he spent living in that persona, and none of it served our marriage well.

Mark knew he was still in the dog house even after we returned from the wedding. He sought help by calling the leaders of a fellowship he and several other political figures attended when in Congress and asking them to speak with me. I wasn't pleased to do so. I figured that Mark had portrayed me as an irrationally angry wife and that they would gang up on me to convince me to drop this issue. They did anything but. All three of the men comforted me by telling me that I was right to be angry with Mark. But a member of the group, whom I'll call Jack, advised me that staying angry with Mark was not an option. If I wanted to heal the relationship, I had to open my heart and be kind, even if Mark was in the wrong. *They* would work on Mark. We even went so far as to talk about sex, and he told me not to withhold it as punishment as that would make everything worse. The marriage and family mattered more than this one issue, he advised. I was buoyed up by this support and all the new things I had to consider when looking at Mark and the pressures he was under, the strange way public figures live their lives and are with their families. My meeting with these men from the fellowship was the first time I heard an explicit description of the term "disconnect" in reference to politicians, and it seemed apt. I think one even called it "the Congressional Disconnect." Move on and let go of the anger I did.

I had become pregnant with baby number four just as Mark's final campaign for Congress began. Mark was so popular in his district that he had no major party opponent so our campaign was fun, consisting mainly of public appearances in front of friendly crowds. But Congress doesn't stop for childbirth. I was scheduled to have my labor induced so that Mark could arrange to be present for the birth. Right up until that day, however, we worked. Two days before we were scheduled to be at the hospital, Mark and I spent hours on the tarmac at the military base in Charleston shaking hands with folks at the air show as our boys climbed in and out of military helicopters, planes, and tanks. It was hot and humid, and I gripped my hands tightly beneath my giant belly, fearful the baby I was carrying might drop flat on the steaming airstrip if I let go.

Mark's friend Senator John McCain, who was quietly beginning his run for president, visited our home the next day, a Sunday. Mark had a group of about thirty men for lunch to meet him. I served sub sandwiches from the deli on paper plates, about all I could handle at that stage in my pregnancy. Mark prompted McCain to tell stories from his time as a POW and gathered our boys to listen. The hubbub of boisterous political talk died down as the whole group leaned in to hear his tales from the Hanoi Hilton.

One story that particularly moved Mark and me was about McCain's cellmate, Mike Christian. Every day, no matter what horrors he and the other prisoners had endured, they rose to pledge allegiance to the flag. Mike Christian had sewn a replica of the flag onto his shirt for the soldiers to look at when they pledged. When the guards discovered it, they ripped the flag off his shirt and beat him severely. Upon return to his cell, he quietly began sewing on another flag. He was, quite literally, willing to die for his flag and his country.

Mark and I drove to the hospital the next morning and Blake arrived easily, another healthy baby. Mark and I decided to give him the middle name of Christian, in honor of the patriot-soldier in McCain's story. From the first, Blake seemed calm and steady, something that still serves him well as the youngest of this brood. Mark then caught the midmorning flight to DC in time to vote in Congress. Having these kids was so easy for Mark, I think he would have been happy with ten sons, but the pregnancy and birthing of them all was clearly less easy on me, and we had decided that these four healthy blessings were just enough. The next day I was scheduled to get my tubes tied.

As I was wheeled in for surgery, the nurse asked me why I didn't have anyone with me for support. I was surprised at her question. It hadn't really occurred to me that I would need Mark there for the surgery. What would have been his role? He could wring his hands and worry about my progress from Washington just as well as he might have from the waiting room. In any event, I told her my husband had been with me the day before, but he'd gone back to work. Maybe her question was perfunctory, or maybe she truly was surprised to find me alone. Either way, I can see now that our circumstances were unusual. Somehow, I had become perfectly accustomed to managing alone. My independence gave Mark tacit permission to leave that day, and, I can't help but wondering, later as well.

Late in the 1990s, Mark was nearing his last term in Congress and his anxiety about what would come next in his life was active on all fronts. Impressed by the dedication and professionalism of the military he saw through his activities on the Hill, he began to regret that he had never served. He lamented the increasing disconnect between the rights that go with being an American and the responsibilities of citizenship. So, during his last term in Congress, he enlisted in the Air Force Reserves. In addition to seeing this as a responsibility of citizenship to participate, he also wanted to set a good example for our boys. By the time the military accepted Mark, he was already running for governor, but he decided to honor his commitment, and I was proud of him for that decision, even as I understood that he would now have even fewer weekends at home for the family.

Perhaps part of Mark's anxiousness was also because he was approaching forty, and he wasn't taking it very well. By that point, ten years into our marriage, I was accustomed to his restlessness and list making, but the confluence of passing that age marker and ending his time in an important job made this transition more fraught than others had been.

Mark's zest for living life to the fullest comes, I think, from his fear of dying, and of dying young in particular. I think this feeling overcame him as a young man when he quite literally put his father in the ground. He often spoke about how short life is and how he needed to fill every minute. Mark is not alone in his point of view, of course, but the worry that stuck most in my mind was his sad feeling that past the age of forty he would have "no more good summers." As someone who treasures every day, every season, this statement was and is unimaginable to me. On the brevity of life, we both agree. The difference is how we chose to spend our time. I wanted to savor each moment while the boys were young and he clearly wanted not a moment to sit still.

As a result, the small signs that he was starting the inevitable process of slowing down unnerved him. When his back hurt or his sore knees kept him from running ten miles at the same pace he had when he was younger, he took this as evidence of his approaching death. He brushed aside my suggestions that he adjust his exercise pattern to suit his age. He was going to fight this at every turn, never giving in to the inevitable.

He's not alone in this fruitless struggle. Our culture celebrates the hardness and vigor of youth, the edge that comes with it, and seemingly has no time for its opposite. But I believe in what Marcus Aurelius said: "There is change in all things. You yourself are subject to continual change and some decay, and this is common to the entire universe." I feel strongly that the best way to age is not to fight it and the change that comes with it. Rather, I try to embrace it and grow through it.

Whatever our differences though, his concerns were genuine and, I have to admit, the inspiration for a great fortieth birthday party.

Naturally, I threw him a surprise party. He thought he was going to give a formal speech at Middleton Plantation but on his way to the building in which he expected to speak, his friends and family emerged from the gardens all dressed in funeral wear. Everyone wore black, the women were handed lace veils, and someone even came dressed as the grim reaper. The special feature of this celebration wasn't presents. Nearly everyone there had written a eulogy for Mark. His worst nightmare—that he would die at forty—

became the inspiration for a memorable celebration that, I hoped, showed him how much he was loved.

Mark was a good sport about the party, though perhaps the rest of us thought it was a lot funnier than he did. In trying to gently—or not so gently as the case may have been—rib him about his worry, I hoped to relieve him of it. I wanted to show him that life was not anywhere near over and that he was not now on the path to decline. I wanted him to see that there was much fun to be had then and ahead.

EIGHT

———◇———

I EXPECTED THAT IN 2000, WHEN MARK KEPT HIS CAMPAIGN PROM-
ise not to run for a fourth congressional term, he would return to a smaller-scale life with me and the boys. I believed
Mark would be ready to return to working in real estate and
be even more successful for all the knowledge he gained in
Congress and all the powerful and important contacts he had
made while serving there. All of this, combined with more
time with me and the boys, would give him, I hoped, many
more ways to quantify his accomplishments, to feel successful
and finally appreciate that his life had meaning.

We never really had the time to find out. It wasn't very
long before people from across our state started to urge Mark
to consider a run for governor, probably one of the hardest
jobs in politics. As with his first run at Congress, Mark's ap-

petite for a challenge was whet at the prospect of seeking a job where it would be difficult to get elected. He would yet again have to win a tough primary against six other Republicans and after that, he would face a well-funded Democratic incumbent, Jim Hodges. He was also energized by the idea that if elected, it would also be a challenge for him to succeed.

South Carolina state government operates under a truly archaic system. After the Civil War, politicians worried that a heavily black constituency would some day elect a black man as governor. With that in mind, then-governor Ben Tillman led the effort to change the state constitution dramatically, stripping the governor of most of his powers. The legislature, a variety of constitutional officeholders, and various unelected boards and commissions have largely run the state ever since. The governor is often the first to be blamed when he can't fulfill his promises, even though the mechanism of state government is arranged in a way to block him at almost every turn.

Mark spoke with advisers and consultants and friends about whether or not to run. The more people he talked to, the more excited he became about the possibility of making real change. Instead of accepting the idea that he would be working within a highly restricted environment, he wanted to run on a pledge to reform the government and to bring fiscal responsibility, common sense, and a businesslike approach to all the affairs of our state. He saw the need for a governor to look out for the interests of the state as a whole, as a chief executive should. Just as important to him was preserving the

Our wedding day,
November 4, 1989

Past bedtime, primary night, 2002

Campaigning was always a family affair.

Boyhood fun at Coosaw, the Sanford family farm

Blake meets President George W. Bush.

Mark's swearing-in for his second term as a U.S. Congressman, January 1997

Fun at the Governor's Mansion

More fun with friends, celebrating my fortieth birthday at the Mansion

The boys with my father, Christmas 1999.

Sisters Kathy and Gier with me and Mom before Mark's inaugural in 2006.

Gubernatorial inaugural ceremonies, January 2007

Mark's third and final term as a U.S. congressman, summer 1999

Our maturing family, May 2009

aesthetic look and feel of the state. He had strong feelings about protecting open space, keeping rivers pristine, and saving forests. He wanted to avoid the kind of overdevelopment seen in South Florida. This was and still is a rather rare stance for a Republican. With these as his issues, we calculated that there was a slim chance he would win.

Mark also consulted the boys and me about his decision, and we all were unified in our support. The way I saw it was not so dissimilar to when Mark decided to run for Congress. The prospect of running for the state's highest political office energized Mark; the intense focus and his ideas for new possibilities for the state clearly would make him happy. I also figured that this would be a fifteen-month undertaking from the day he decided until what might well be a primary defeat. If Mark happened to win, I would at the very least look forward to all of us living together under the same roof, unlike his time in Congress.

He wanted to go for it; I pledged my support. But this time, I was adamant that I would not serve as campaign manager.

Mark hired a young woman to handle his schedule and another to manage incoming money and plan fundraisers. Next he hired a press secretary who, though worth his weight in gold, came cheap (which Mark liked) because his most recent job had been playing in a rock band. Many others showed up to volunteer through that first summer and the momentum started to build, but Mark was frustrated having to manage the staff and seemed unable to find a manager to his liking. As the summer wore on, he began his push to get me to change my mind and return again as campaign manager.

Although I was proud of running his successful congressional campaigns, I knew from experience the toll the job would take on the boys. I also knew it would likely unhealthily shape the kind of time I would have with Mark. These were reasons enough to refuse the role, but there was another big reason I worried about. If I took the job, ours would be the only statewide campaign in South Carolina ever led by a woman, much less a wife. There were—and still are—many in the political and power base in the state who sneered openly at me and suggested it was not my place to do this work. I have come to love South Carolina deeply, but I'm not blind to the challenges still in place for women there. There still exists an old-fashioned chauvinism that would have women stay out of positions of power or strength. Perhaps they forget that South Carolina has plenty of strong and successful women in its history.

One such famous trailblazer (and a personal hero) was Eliza Lucas, who, in 1738, was left in charge—at the age of sixteen—of her family's three plantations in the lowcountry. In addition to overseeing the plantations, she educated her younger sister and some of the slave children, pursued her own courses in French and English, and did legal work for poor neighbors. All the while she experimented with a new crop called indigo. By the age of nineteen, Eliza Lucas became the first in South Carolina to successfully produce blue dye from indigo, ultimately leading to great wealth for the area. After marrying Charles Pinckney, Eliza had four children, including two who were key players in the move toward our nation's independence and the war that followed. Not only did Eliza Pinckney accomplish great things when facing life's challenges, she also *gave back* to the world. She was a loyal wife, she raised successful children, and she left an indelible mark in more ways than one.

Mark knew that these were my standards of personal success and he worked on me—sometimes playfully, sometimes seriously—to see that in coming back on as campaign manager I would have the opportunity to meet them. He continued to plead his case, and six and a half months into his campaign I gave in, plain and simple. As fall began and the older boys returned to a school routine, I secured help for the little ones and started to pitch in formally with the campaign.

Win or lose, I knew that for me, the standard of success in this campaign wouldn't be measured by the simple metric of whether Mark won. As the boys were older, their needs were more complex. I felt my efforts would be a success if I ran a well-organized, ethical campaign while never feeling that I had neglected my children.

Toward this end, I tried to stay close to home. The ground floor of our Sullivan's Island home has a concrete slab floor and exposed heating/AC ducts. Until Mark announced his candidacy for governor, we used it as the boys' playroom, a place where they could do whatever they wanted, and we also had one room there that served as Mark's office. Thereafter, we rearranged the entire space for the campaign office, bringing down folding tables as desks and adding computers and phones as needed. By closing off a corner near the bathroom, we created a bedroom for campaign workers, bringing two sets of bunk beds from the barn at Coosaw, and putting the boys' old dinosaur sheets on them. It became known as Jurassic Park. We also used the old garage area and divided that space into more campaign offices.

The average age of the group downstairs was about twenty-two, which gave me, at age thirty-nine, the right to refer to my "little kids" upstairs and my "big kids" downstairs. Before long it was anybody's guess as to what or who I would find when I went down the steps. I felt sometimes as if I were in charge of a large group of animals at a zoo.

When the boys returned from school—Marshall in fourth grade and Landon in second were in school until three o'clock and Bolton and Blake were home all afternoon—they added an entirely new flavor to the campaign. At any given moment, we'd have big and little kids jumping or wrestling together on the trampoline or shooting hoops in the driveway. The boys made a game out of catching the press secretary on breaks outside for a smoke. We had a bunny, Sully, who came downstairs with Bolton to visit often. Our kids charged through the offices dressed in armor with swords, or they might swap football cards with one of the campaign workers, or ride bikes to get snacks together down the street. We had a cat then named Spot who did not take kindly to the new routine at the house. He randomly threw up on the computer keyboards and sometimes would disgust us further by presenting a creature caught on his hunt.

Things downstairs were active into the evening most nights. I would cook dinner upstairs and soon was cooking for extras, happy to have others so dedicated to our new mission. I did my best to juggle it all and usually enjoyed all the activity in the house. There were certainly times, though, that I wanted to close my eyes and wish it all away. I reminded myself again and again that this pace and this activity would not, could not, last forever.

A campaign is an intense affair and a statewide race has so many overlapping facets that it becomes a big boiling pot that needs to be kept bubbling without spilling over. While we all had a great deal of fun in the campaign, and some of the daily volunteers or employees are now lifelong friends, it would be a lie to say that I never lost my cool. I understood that loose talk, loose finances, or shaky attention to detail can all unravel a campaign. There was a place at the bottom of the stairs where we hung beach hats and baseball caps. I would bring a worker to this spot if I needed to have a stern or serious discussion about an issue in a semiprivate location. Not surprisingly, the gang began to speak of getting in trouble as being "taken to the hats."

Fundraising in politics is also a 24/7 job—not something I ever enjoyed, but it seems a necessary evil throughout the political process. We raised and spent more than $7 million in small increments through mail or events in South Carolina and beyond during that campaign. We had stacks of shoeboxes filled with checks around the office and systematically made sure that every donor received a letter signed and personalized by Mark.

I tend to think of the ability to raise money as an indication of the strength of one's ideas and of one's ability to communicate those ideas. Mark was good at it; I was not. I chose to abstain. On most evenings Mark was off raising money, while I focused on keeping things going at home. As we got closer to the election, I attended fundraisers if they were large ones or appeared with Mark when needed, but I held off as long as possible so I could stay at home with the boys. I know Mark gave back to the country and to the state through his service as a congressman, governor, and in the Air Force Reserves, work of which we can all be proud. Yet I wonder what it cost him to continually be at functions with his hand out asking for money. I have long believed that it "is in giving that we receive" and that generosity helps keep a person focused on important things in life outside of the self. The constant take, take, take is one of those things that serves as another way to isolate a politician. In this way, the easier it got for him to ask others for money, the more he moved away from our youthful idea of a citizen legislator and toward the identity of a career politician.

Even though fundraisers weren't my thing, the boys and I did need to be on the road with Mark for appearances. While I care about being generally well-groomed, on the campaign trail in a high-profile race the idea of "appearances" gets ratcheted up several notches. I always needed to be aware of how I looked or how our children looked or acted in public. The public pays close attention to adorable little boys, but unfortunately, little boys are hard to control, especially when one or more of them is potty training. I had always encouraged the boys to simply go outside discreetly if they couldn't hold it. This saved many a pair of pants during potty training. But in the early stages of the campaign, Blake, then aged two, dropped his short pants to relieve himself unceremoniously on a gravestone in an old churchyard as we were leaving a crowded church service. I had all the boys dressed in matching outfits, so I couldn't pretend this boy wasn't my own—tempting as that might have been at the time—so when a woman there called Blake to my attention, I grabbed him up and hurried to the bathroom hoping not to make a scene.

On another occasion, I had all the boys on stage in Columbia as we awaited the arrival of President Bush, coming in to campaign for the party. I had given them clear expectations for their behavior: They could run around onstage until I told them it was time to stop and then they were expected to sit very quietly through the president's speech. One of the secret service men was getting anxious about Blake, who was dancing on the stage in his cowboy boots waving an American flag in one hand and his blankie in the other. I didn't see much harm in Blake entertaining the crowd as they waited in the heat, and I promised him the boys would behave when told. On cue, when President Bush arrived they quieted down and sat patiently through the speech. The next morning, however, there was a photo in the paper with the president at the podium and just behind him to the side was Bolton (maybe five) with his head in his hands looking incredibly bored! Mark was disappointed in me for not coaching the boys to look interested, but I myself was proud of their good behavior. There's only so much you can ask of a child, and sitting quietly through a political speech was the limit!

One time we traveled from city to city campaigning over a weekend, ending up at a fundraising event. After the event we loaded the boys in the car and headed to a friend's house in the country near a town called Estill. We arrived past midnight and moved the boys to beds while they were asleep, something that had become a common occurrence on the campaign trail. We were staying in a private cabin and in the morning awoke in a room full of large stuffed game on the walls. When we asked if the boys knew what city we were in, one responded "Africa!" Sometimes I, too, felt like we were lost on safari.

In the weeks leading up to the primary the boys, out of school for the summer, joined us on a tour of the state in a Winnebago we dubbed the Caravan for Change but that they referred to as the Win-a-Bagel. We did our best to make things fun for the boys—they played GameBoys, tic-tac-toe, or cards, watched movies, and ate fast food. It was pretty clear that they often had a blast with all the campaign volunteers along the way. Certainly that is my hope. Surely they missed out on fun with friends during that time, but it was a family adventure all the same.

The boys did journal on occasion during the campaign so

I do have a way to test my impression against their own experiences. Marshall's journal says, "We went in the caravan and it was huge! We went around the state to different places shaking signs and screaming vote for Mark Sanford. . . . It was crazy but it was worth it for dad." Landon felt a little differently: "I went in a win a bagel and a van. It was very boring. It felt like we were in there for a month." And later: "My mom is mostly on the computer and has lots of calls. My dad has a lot of calls to." He was right about that. We were nothing if not busy and constantly on the phone but I hope that they will have a generally—if not specifically—positive memory of their political experience in time.

When we won the primary and the campaign for governor moved to an office outside the house (in addition to needing more space, it was hurricane season and our beach house was thought to be vulnerable), I more or less moved with it. I had a great young girl who helped to care for the boys during this crunch time, and I trusted that they were okay, but I missed them terribly. I missed seeing them every day after school, and I hated not knowing what they were doing for homework or eating for dinner on the many nights I wasn't home to join them.

But I was also very proud of them then, and I remain so now. I know they were as tired of the campaign as we were and yet I asked them to persevere for just a few more months and to do their best in school in the meantime. They did beautifully. It's amazing what kids can do when you have faith in them.

As soon as Mark won the Republican nomination, he became the immediate enemy of the incumbent governor and the existing political establishment. I learned to live with the knowledge that a good portion of the state disliked Mark because of his party affiliation and that they disliked me by extension. If nothing else, the campaign process and then life in the public eye taught me that you can't really live to make others happy. You also simply can't correct all the misperceptions about you or your spouse or your intentions on any given event or statement. Mark understood before me that it is much easier to let things go, than to try to right every wrong. This is, in fact, one of the best things Mark has taught me: to let God be responsible for righting any wrongs.

By the time Mark ran for governor, I had learned this lesson well. When I think back to how incensed I could become when Mark was misrepresented in the newspaper or by his opponents, I marvel at the energy I put into fighting back, writing that impassioned letter to the editor, for instance, to correct the record on what I now see as merely a slight. I suppose the world of politics had toughened my skin, but with four children to be responsible for during Mark's run at governor, I had less time and energy to fight back than when I had had only two. In addition, people now knew what Mark stood for and what he had tried to accomplish when he was in Congress. We didn't have to work so hard to create a good identity for him and craft his positive message. Much of that work was already done.

And then there's the simple truth that I had come to understand and that I wanted to model for our kids: What matters most is how you live your life, not what you have to show for it. I ask myself if I have tried my best to love my family, to improve my character, to make a positive impact on the world in some small way. I know who I love and I know who loves me, and if I have made a positive impression on others, that's great. But if someone out there doesn't like me or Mark because of something they read in the paper or heard on TV, then that is okay with me too. I had come to understand by then and live by it still today: At the end of the day I need to be happy with myself and my own behavior in light of the person I know I can be and in light of the person I want to be in the eyes of our Lord, the ultimate judge, the only one that matters.

Although the pace was hectic and I went to bed exhausted nearly every day, I didn't pray for relief from the challenges in my life. I was fully committed to this new quest, and I wanted to meet the challenges that came my way. Instead my prayers were for discernment in setting priorities, protection for us and our boys, and strength to proceed. Then, and during other trying times of my life, I found meaning in an old Jewish proverb: "I ask not for a lighter burden, but for broader shoulders."

Incredibly, we won the election. At the celebration at a local restaurant there was more media than I had ever seen and homemade signs in the crowd saying things like "Thanks for running an honorable campaign!" We were thrilled and exhausted and Blake fell asleep in my arms as the night wore on. As it was a school night, I wanted to get the boys home. I tried to cut out early, carrying Blake and leading the other boys through the kitchen instead of working my way through the crowds. A policeman with a gun and wide-brimmed hat came up to me and said "I'll take him Mrs. Sanford. The car is right outside." Policeman or not, I wasn't about to pass my sleeping child over to a stranger with a gun, and so I thanked him quickly and told him I had my own car and was happy to take the kids home myself. Then it occurred to me to ask "Do you even know where we live?" "Yes ma'am," he replied. "We've been watching you there for two weeks."

That was my first clue about how significantly our life was about to change. Once again, we had achieved success at the polls by focusing on the campaign tasks at hand and juggling our family, hoping to make a difference. We had not spent one minute thinking of or planning for the future in the event we were to win.

We looked upon Mark's new job as quite an honor and a time to truly serve and to make a positive difference for our boys and the future of our state. We were tired but enthusiastic, exhausted and yet energized, hopeful and yet realistic, and encouraged too because this time, we would all be living in the same house, sharing the journey together. I was about to find out all that would come with this "free" house and the full price we would ultimately come to pay.

NINE

◇

I NAUGURATION DAY WAS COLD AND CRISP WITH A BRIGHT BLUE SKY, picture perfect and a bit surreal. As I helped our sons, then ages ten, nine, six and four, get dressed for the formal inaugural ceremony, I thought about how these four little boys would be walking out of the house and into state history.

Yet there I was doing the ordinary things that every mother does: making sure their clothes looked just right, that they had enough socks and underwear in their overnight bags to last until our things arrived from Charleston in a week, and checking that their book bags held what they needed for school. The ordinary and the extraordinary collided when we opened the front door and the security detail whisked us into the state SUVs to begin our first day as the First Family of South Carolina.

The Sullivan family motto, learned from my grand-mother Nana when we were children, was A.Y.T.C.—adapt yourself to circumstances. My aunt Gier, my dad's sister, a mother of nine, lived just a few houses away when I was grow-ing up. She was the reigning authority on adapting to what-ever was thrown her way. I took up the mantle for a new generation when my family moved into the governor's man-sion. From the day of the election forward, all circumstances were new: finding a new school, moving, and learning how to oversee the mansion.

A few weeks after Mark was elected, the curator led me on a tour of the mansion, one of three historic homes on nine acres in a secluded complex. We walked past an emerald green lawn and blooming camellias as the curator described the gardens in summer, bountiful with incredible roses, irises, daffodils, and hydrangea. Built in 1855 to house offi-cers from a nearby military academy, the state turned it into the governor's mansion after the Civil War, when much of Columbia was destroyed by fire.

Mark and I thought of the mansion as the people's house, and we took our responsibilities as custodians seriously. As we walked inside I saw how the house was in great shape after the previous administration had spent millions on renovations. The curator ushered me into the grand, gleaming marble Hall of Governors, past somber portraits of Mark's predeces-sors. Everywhere she pointed out exquisite museum-quality antiques, some upholstered in vibrant silks and pristine cot-tons, many that had been donated by prominent families. As we walked the hallways, I noted the fragile light fixtures, historic paintings, and exquisite battleship silver with growing alarm. We were moving four bulls into this china shop!

The day of the inauguration, the security team seemed as nervous about meeting our brood as our boys were excited about discovering where they hid their guns. They drove us directly to Mark's new office at the Capitol and then escorted us as we walked behind the procession of the cross, mace, and legislators to the inaugural prayer service while bagpipes played. For the first time, I truly felt "handled" and I was quite thankful. After the chaos of crisscrossing the state with four boys during the campaign, I could relax and enjoy every moment. Then we made our way through the waiting crowds, past dozens of cameras and blinding flashes, and back to the Capitol where Mark was sworn in.

I was awed. So many people had put their faith in Mark, and we wanted to live up to their expectations. Being First Lady and living in the governor's mansion was an honor, something to be lived fully and absorbed wholly. I knew I would struggle to keep in focus the fact that I was Jenny, a wife and mother, long before I was First Lady of South Carolina. Throughout Inauguration Day, the boys constantly offered reminders of where my focus should be.

After Mark was sworn in, we hosted a luncheon for all the constitutional officeholders at the Lace House, adjacent to the mansion. Then we held the traditional governor's open house. We stood in the Hall of Governors, greeting people who had waited in the cold for hours to meet Mark and me, warmed by hot cider and cookies provided by the mansion staff. I remember Bolton, then age six, running in from the other side of the hall screaming with glee, "Dad, this place is *incwedible* and you ought to see the kitchen!? They have bwownies, Little Debbie cakes, evewything, and its all FWEE!"

Together he and his brothers already had covered every inch of this grand house, while Mark and I had yet to get above the main floor. As we stood shaking hundreds of hands, the boys were running all over the mansion, finding secret staircases and alternate routes between the floors that allowed them to avoid the formal rooms and the waiting public. When they tired of that, they snuck their friends past security to join them on the lawn.

There were moments when I just wanted to dash off and find out what they were up to, but I couldn't budge. I was so delighted when I heard a familiar voice yell out, "Oh my goodness! What is the fastest-talking girl in the Midwest doing married to the governor of South Carolina and living in a house like this?" It was Julie Joyce Kenary from Winnetka, the friend with whom I lurched around Wisconsin back roads on a summer afternoon trying to master the stick shift. She'd traveled all the way from Boston to surprise me! Comforted to have someone there who "knew me when," I too felt I needed to pinch myself to make sure this was really happening.

After that and the inaugural barbecue, I could hardly stand any longer. We'd smiled until our cheeks hurt. When

Mark and I finally went upstairs to get ready for bed, we were exhausted, yet filled with pride and great hope in our grand new home. I was pleased I had worked with the staff to give the mansion some personal touches for our first night there. I'd sent ahead family photos and favorite paintings of the low-country, which they hung around the family quarters and the public rooms. We'd also sent a bunk bed to add to the beds already in the mansion. Marshall wanted his own room, and there were plenty of bedrooms in the mansion, but Mark believed in carrying on as he and his brothers had, and I agreed that sharing a room was yet another way they might learn adaptability.

We tucked them into their beds and made our way, weary but joyful, into our new bedroom. Our family was beginning another exciting journey through unknown territory. I myself stumbled looking for light switches during the night. The learning curve would be steep.

As First Lady Iris Campbell told me, living in the mansion was "like living above the shop" and she was so right. Our rooms were at the top of the long staircase in the entrance hall and they were not fully closed off. We could hear the events and tours below, and they likely could hear us too. When guests often exclaimed, "This house is beautiful! Don't you just love living here?" I would smile and politely respond, "It is a beautiful home and there *is* so much that comes with this house!" Yes, and even more than I expected on that first day as First Lady.

In the first week, I discovered that the boys required a new set of rules. I found myself yelling, "Boys, don't throw those balls! You might break the chandelier!"

Marshall's pragmatic response: "Whoever heard of a chandelier in a playroom?"

Balls, swords, and toy guns had to remain outside or in the pool house. Running in the house or sliding down the banister was discouraged, rather ineffectively. At first, I said no scooters in the house. I relented when the boys showed me how well the wheels glided on the marble floors and in the kitchen without leaving any scuff marks. We had great wheelbarrow races in the marble hallway and even whirled each other around in the wheelchair we kept for elderly or disabled guests. Thankfully no one went through the glass doors.

The boys also played manhunt or hide and seek with the aid of the mansion's security cameras. I'd hear one of them at the bank of security monitors yelling to another outside, "He's under the big oak tree!" Once, the boys were playing hide and seek with friends inside the mansion, and security called me in to look at one boy who was hiding in the industrial dryer in the basement. The guard was worried for his safety. I chuckled at this clever hiding spot. I was only worried about the dryer.

I realized quickly that each time the boys had friends over, I needed to line up the newcomers outside the front door and explain the rules before entering, including, you break it, you pay for it. Our only mishap was a science experiment with fire and wax conducted in the dining room. Needless to say, the boys soon found out how much it cost to refinish a table.

When we had been in the governor's mansion just a few months, Blake decided to take the elevator to go upstairs for bed. The elevator got stuck, and he was trapped inside for forty-five minutes, a long time for a small child. The security team called me down to watch Blake on the elevator camera recording his every move. First we turned the power on and off, trying to reboot the system. That didn't work. Next we called the elevator company, but the representative who had the right key was three hours away. I went to the elevator door to keep Blake comforted while the staff tried to solve this problem. Finally we had to take the option everyone wanted to avoid: a 911 call to the fire department, which also had a key.

As soon as the firefighters left, a reporter called asking why fire trucks had been at the governor's mansion. On the front page of the paper the next day was a photo of Blake under the headline "4-Year-Old Survives Elevator Scare." Ever adapting, we used the experience as a lesson to the boys that actions have consequences. They should think, we explained, before getting ideas about pouring suds into the mansion's fountain or pulling a false fire alarm, anything that might alert emergency authorities and thus the press. Learning to be on guard for the press has thus far helped keep the boys from embarrassment, but all the same, I regret the loss of innocence and boyishness that accompanies the grown-up-too-soon requirement to be ever conscious of one's public image.

In these unique surroundings and with this schedule, I constantly struggled to give the boys normal responsibilities, such as regular chores. I didn't want them getting used to living a life of luxury. I asked that they make their beds daily, feed the dogs, and clear the table. But even that last simple request had to be modified for mansion living. I would have liked them to clear the dishes to the industrial kitchen and rinse and stack them at the sink. One sink, however, featured a hose with a nozzle that hung from the ceiling, a tempting weapon if there ever was one. After several epic water fights, I asked them only to clear the plates and dishes from the table, no rinsing required.

In addition to managing the boys, managing the mansion took more time than I had expected. The mansion was broke. Most of the funds appropriated for that fiscal year were gone, and we still had six months to go. I had to somehow find the money to continue the events that "the First Lady *always* hosts" and more. I worked to make sure that we didn't have to close the mansion, as Mark had suggested to the press. I'm a believer in leaving things better than you found them, and I certainly didn't want to allow this grand old complex to deteriorate on my watch. I raised money privately to help finish out the year and set out immediately to cut costs and reorganize the staff.

First, I eliminated the high-paid position of mansion director, and I took over those duties myself for free, learning on the go. Then the new chef discovered that the outgoing administration had burned most of the kitchen files, including financial records, event details, recipes, grocery information, and items to guide us on how to keep the mansion running. Suddenly I was managing a large staff with well-defined, though limited, duties without a guidebook. Some people just washed dishes while others only helped in the kitchen. After the first week, a staff member told me about a new crisis. We needed to hire an additional person to help the woman whose sole duty was keeping up with the cleaning, as she needed help with the ironing.

"The ironing?" I asked, amazed. "Please tell me what, exactly, requires so much ironing?"

She had been taught that the First Family must always look pressed and perfect, and thus she routinely ironed every shirt, all shorts and pants, even underwear. The sheets were washed and ironed every week. Now that there was laundry for six people in the First Family, the ironing responsibilities would surely be too much for just one person who also was charged with doing the cleaning.

"You've got to be kidding me!" I laughed. She obviously had no clue about Mark Sanford, a guy who prided himself on saving money on dry cleaning by making a starched white shirt last ten days. The notion of taxpayers funding someone to iron his underwear was absurd!

I chuckled as I led the woman to the dryer and showed her how we Sanfords "iron" polo shirts, shorts, pants, and underwear: we removed them from a dryer while hot and shook out the wrinkles before folding and placing the clothes in a drawer. Changing the linen every two weeks was sufficient for me, and my kids wouldn't notice, I assured her, if they were ironed. I told her not to bother. Crisis solved.

After that, I instituted a team approach with adaptability as the new mode for everyone. I asked the staff to have an open mind and to think on their feet. Someone doing laundry might be expected to serve when the governor entertained guests and someone helping the chef would also be expected to load the dishwasher when needed, and so on. It was not long before the chef and I figured out who worked well in this type of setup and scaled down the staff accordingly. This reorganization saved the taxpayers more than $1.5 million over the years and has allowed us to operate without further private funds.

In addition to reorganizing operations at the mansion itself, I knew we had to attack the long-term problem of maintenance on the historic property. There was a nonprofit Governor's Mansion Foundation, and I decided to raise money to modestly renovate the empty Lace House so it could be rented for events and generate income for the complex. Mark's mother is a concert pianist who had studied at Juilliard, and she performed beautifully there to help us raise funds. When the renovation was complete, the Lace House soon became one of the top places in Columbia to host a wedding. The house ultimately netted hundreds of thousands of dollars in profits, which is in turn used for upkeep on the property.

The boys and I also wrote a children's history book called *Mischief in the Mansion* to raise money for the Foundation. I'd been giving the boys a daily business lesson on the way to school. Driven there in a state vehicle, I'd read them highlights from the *Wall Street Journal* and quiz them on how the news affected stocks. "The price of oil is way up today boys. What does that mean?" Mark had opened each of them an account with five hundred dollars so they could trade. They began watching the market carefully. As a result, they didn't like the fact that they didn't profit from the sale of the books, but we learned about producing a book and marketing it all the same. By combining the small profit from the book, fees from the rentals, and Foundation funds, we then renovated the historic gardens. This further increased rentals there and improved access and use by the public.

Living a life with so many formal ceremonies offered us other great parenting opportunities. We could teach the kids how to be polite young men who knew how to conduct themselves with our company. If we had formal dinners or receptions, we would encourage the boys to join us in welcoming visitors. We chose carefully which dinners we wanted them to attend, only requiring them to be there when we hoped they might learn something from the guest. When the dinner was just for adults, we asked them to come downstairs to shake hands around the formal dining table and then return to do their homework upstairs. If the English cut-crystal chandelier shook, we knew a game of tag was taking precedence over their studies. This was wonderful boy noise to me. I didn't want to sanitize their home experience too much. Yes, they were greeting formal guests who sat around a table under a majestic chandelier, but sometimes they were barefoot and sometimes in mismatched pajamas. However they were dressed, they made me smile and helped keep my perspective grounded.

The boys weren't the only ones learning about protocol and etiquette. We entertained Madame Wu Yi, a vice premier and at the time the highest-ranking woman in China. The staff and I studied the rules of Chinese decorum and how they acknowledge a respected visitor, rules that were very different than the way honored guests are entertained in the west. The guest of honor had to sit facing a certain direction, we used red and yellow flowers arranged in numbers favorable to the Chinese, and we avoided anything white so as not to offend. Guests had to be arranged for a predinner meeting specifically according to rank, and we had to figure out the pecking order exactly. Mark was away on military duty for that event, and thus I adapted and was intent on making a good showing all on my own. I was proud that we made no mistakes.

With Mark as governor, things for us as a family changed in some ways for the better and in some not quite so. Living again under the same roof, Mark was often there to put the boys to bed and out of that grew his cherished routine of telling them a Bible story or lesson for the day. Yet we were still at the mercy of the almighty schedule. Mark was back into the life of five-minute meetings and thirty-second sound bites. For his schedulers, the public came first. This was a constant battle, and it was easy to get worn down. There were many nights when he was out giving speeches, being the featured speaker at fundraisers, or traveling the country and the globe for state business. Even nights at home were often booked for receptions and other official events. Still we had more family time than we had had when he was in Congress. On the nights when Mark was home, he attended many of the boys' sports events, and he truly delighted in riding bikes with them or playing sports on the lawn. We grew to savor the occasional evening we had when it was just the boys and us.

There were extraordinary occasions for the boys too. Once we had an event at the mansion where there were NASCAR cars in the driveway and Tony Stewart landed on the lawn in a helicopter. (Blake conveniently had a cold and had skipped school that day.) They loved it when Steve Spurrier, coach of the Carolina Gamecocks, would come by or Dave Odom, the basketball coach. The boys became avid fans of the USC teams and so I tried to get used to the notion that four sons wearing hats that said "COCKS" was something of which a mother should be proud.

When we returned from a ten-day trip in August 2003, we discovered the mansion had developed a different kind of life of its own: black mold that was growing up the walls in the hall outside our bedroom and on every item of clothing and every pair of shoes in our closet. This was despite the fact that the air conditioner had been running the entire time we were gone. The arm of the bureaucracy that governed expenses at the house—the Budget and Control Board (BCB)—said that all we had was a tiny humidity problem and that everything in the house was fine. If it was *my* house, I said, and I had just spent all that money renovating it, I would get everyone who had had anything to do with the air system in to figure out why this happened.

Alas, it was not my house and clearly, governor or not, we were not in charge. The BCB worked to reduce the humidity but ignored the possible cause of the mold—government housing and bureaucracy at its best. Mark wouldn't let me pay someone to look into the problem, so I asked an engineer to volunteer his time. He concluded that there was, indeed, a problem in the house. No surprise to me. Still the BCB stonewalled me until I literally had to threaten in June 2004 to sue a bureaucrat over our own health and safety. The threat worked and soon efforts began to fix the problem. We decided the safest course was for us to all move into the one-room pool house. Getting permission to sleep in the pool house took some doing too as we needed approval from a number of state and federal agencies to do so, but it was surely safer than breathing the toxic mold.

Despite the six of us being crammed into that one room for weeks on end, I have a fondness for that pool house. One of my cherished memories of our time at the mansion took place there, and it has nothing to do with mold and is unrelated to swimming in the pool.

Near the end of Mark's first term, Bobby McNair, the son of former governor Robert McNair, asked if he could have a reunion of sorts in the mansion with other sons—most now grown men—of South Carolina governors.

Bobby arrived with five other sons of governors on a weekday evening when it was pouring buckets of rain. Mark was away for military service again, but the boys and I showed the group around the house so that they could take a look around their old home once more. We ended up relaxing in the pool house where everyone told stories of the hijinks from their time there.

Jim Edwards told of an inmate who chased another with a knife from the kitchen before disappearing on Jim's bicycle, never to be seen again. During our tenure, inmates from the Department of Corrections worked almost exclusively outside on the grounds, but in earlier years the house was staffed inside and out with inmates, often then referred to as trustees. We heard about inmates picking locks on the refrigerator for a governor who was hungry and of inmates actually teaching some of these boys how to shoot guns. Imagine that!

One man remembered when there were goats on the property and others told of getting drunk in the pool house or with the security detail when they were teenagers living there. One told of a faux pas he made in front of the press, cameras rolling, when he mistakenly ate the fancy pat of butter, thinking it was a mint. They all recalled sliding wildly down the banister and attending parades and festivals all over the state. Michael Hollings recounted his mother's request that a trustee bring in his new baby brother to show to the dinner guests at the formal dining table. When the trustee arrived, he presented baby brother Fritz to the guests on a silver platter.

Like veterans of the same battles, the men and boys at the gathering also compared notes on their time spent in the shadow of a father who was governor.

Bobby McNair had called for this reunion, and it was becoming clear why he had done so. Bobby was in a serious battle with cancer, and perhaps also in the process of evaluating his life. At the end of the evening, he looked at our young boys and summed things up. "I want each one of you to know that there has not been a day in my life when I didn't walk down the aisle of a church or the aisle of a crowded auditorium when I didn't feel the eyes of those in the room looking at me while they whispered, 'There goes the son of the governor.' Well I want you to know that while you will always be the son of Governor Sanford, much more importantly, each one of you are who you are all on your own first. Each of you is special and unique and has survived life in this place and you will go on to live lives of your own independent of your dad or who he has been and what he has done. Yes you'll always be the son of a governor but you will always be *you* first."

In light of Mark's recent actions, I can appreciate what a gift Bobby's perspective was to me and an even more important gift for our boys. The challenge for any child is to develop a true sense of who he is. The child who develops a solid sense of self-worth independent of his parents, his siblings, or his circumstances is best equipped to face the world. Many of us try to live up to the expectations of those who precede us, which shades our sense of independence or worth. I can only imagine how difficult it is to be raised as the son of a successful governor, and then as a son of a man known for something less reputable altogether. I hope as the boys go forward they can remember Bobby's caution to be themselves first.

TEN

IN THE SUMMER OF 2004, THE BLACK MOLD IN THE GOVERNOR'S mansion drove the boys and me to the beach house the minute school was over. Mark stayed in Columbia during the week, sleeping in the pool house while the workmen attacked the mansion. He joined us at the beach on weekends. After the hothouse of the capital, the summer was blissfully uncomplicated. We spent our days by the water with my girlfriends and their families. As the children played, we read books, we barbecued, we gossiped, we relaxed. For the first time in a while, I could breathe fresh air. Best of all Mark and I were in a pretty good place. Though we were both incredibly busy, we'd been living under the same roof at last, and with that proximity, I'd fallen in love with Mark all over again.

One sign of our reconnection was that when I had a hysterectomy that August, Mark was at my side for one long, sleepless night in the hospital. After I was discharged, he took the boys back to Columbia, giving me ten days by myself at the beach to rest up before accompanying him to New York for the Republican National Convention.

I luxuriated in this time alone. The surgery had rendered me pretty immobile, but every day I walked to the beach at least once. I read lots of books and reflected on where I was in life. I felt myself aging, and the changes in my mind and body felt good. I yearned to soften into a slower kind of life, something more tender, and with less conflict. My childbearing years were definitively over, but instead of feeling that as a loss, I was filled with hopefulness about what was to come for me and Mark in time. However long he would remain governor, I knew there would be an end to the busy political life ahead. I found myself thinking again about Galatians 5:22, the same scripture Mark had listed as a spiritual goal when we discussed them nearly fifteen years earlier in New York: "The fruit of the Spirit is love, joy, peace, patience, kindness, goodness, faithfulness, gentleness and self-control." We had, in fact, lived that Galatians verse, except for peace. I could see that peace on the horizon. Peace would come to us when Mark stepped out of the limelight.

By that summer, we had lived together as a family for almost four years, but it wasn't until we moved into the mansion that Mark truly came into his own as a father. There I could rely on him to help me discipline the children, which was a huge relief after the congressional years. Gradually he started taking over their spiritual guidance too. As governor, he had an "Open Door After Four" one day a month when any South Carolinian could speak directly to him. People of all backgrounds came seeking assistance. Their stories were often heartbreaking to hear, and Mark was a spellbinding storyteller as he retold them. The boys listened over dinner, drinking in his stories from those afternoons. Often Mark would end on a lesson from a Bible verse, and they'd discuss it for a while or continue with the lesson as he tucked them into bed. Mark seemed to enjoy this too. He expanded his repertoire to tell stories from politics, or from his day at the Capitol. These sessions filled a great hunger the boys had for more time with their dad.

During this time Mark took it upon himself to create what he called the Sanford Family Constitution. When he read it to us over dinner one evening, I nodded in agreement. Everything in it described my own belief system as well. I was impressed that Mark had found time to create the statement, but I shouldn't really have been: The process of quantifying his beliefs and goals was reminiscent of the goal itemization he'd introduced to me all those years before. This document described a vision for our family in which "God is glorified and the communities each of our lives touches are better because of the lives we live. Toward that end, our mission is to be a nurturing, loving and fun safe harbor and home place—where each member is loved unconditionally for who they are, where values are instilled, and where each person is encouraged to develop their talents, find their passion and pursue it with excellence to indeed glorify God and make the world a better place." The family constitution also talked about the things we value: love, faith, passion and excellence, hard work, appreciation, honor and integrity, fun and stewardship and responsibility.

I have a difficult time now looking at this family doctrine in light of Mark's recent actions. That summer, though, I wanted to think of the good times we had and the better times that were to come. The demands on all of our time were significant, but we were settling into a routine as a family and enjoying respite and time together as best we could. I was learning how to seriously prioritize my time, and once again, I focused on the fact that the busy life wouldn't last forever. I was even feeling content.

George Orwell says, "To see what is in front of one's nose needs a constant struggle." In relaxing into my optimistic vision for the future, I now see that I wasn't acknowledging how disconnected Mark was becoming from his stated Sanford Family values.

A governor necessarily has to have a team of people to schedule his every move. If Mark agreed to attend a meeting or to make a speech, he had someone at his elbow jotting down that commitment. At the end of each day, he'd receive a schedule for the next one so detailed it would even advise him what to wear. He no longer had to think about how to get places. His security detail drove him. People everywhere wanted to have their picture taken with him or just shake his hand. I, too, had staff to help coordinate my days, but I wasn't surrounded by "yes" folks, ready to jump to attend to every need.

During the campaign, Mark had promised a lot to his constituents, a very ambitious agenda, and many voters admired his willingness to take it all on. He didn't just want to govern the state, he wanted to reform it, cutting spending and growing the economy instead of the government. This rookie governor, a stranger to the ways of the Capitol, picked a fight with the old boy network, asking them to abolish entire programs and dramatically cut services or merge longstanding agencies.

Mark railed against the legislators who campaigned as deficit-conscious conservatives but stuffed the budget with questionable projects for their districts. As part of his campaign to reform the way government does business, he challenged the legislators to repay a state deficit (the existence of which was unconstitutional) before adding new programs. They paid some off but proposed new spending before finishing the job. That spring, Mark captured the public eye and the national spotlight by carrying two squealing piglets he named Pork and Barrel to the floor of the legislature. The legislators hated how this made them look, and they blustered about lack of decorum in the hall of the legislature. But it worked. They adopted Mark's policies, fully repaying the debt. I was proud of him, but he wasn't making any friends; in pushing so hard for his fiscal principles, he was attacking many within his own party.

With so much underway, Mark was never off duty. He

was besieged from many sides during his day job and simultaneously raising money already for reelection. I was frankly amazed by how he survived. I had experienced the pressures of Wall Street, but they were nothing like what a governor faces. He was elected to serve *all* the people, not just the shareholders, or the company bottom line. Plus he had determined enemies within who were wily in blocking his agenda and frequently planted spurious rumors about him in the media. Witnessing the incredible demands on his time inspired profound empathy in me. With his growing involvement with the boys and the principled battle he was waging, I felt a richer admiration for his abilities and the strain than I had during the congressional years.

That admiration and appreciation fueled my thinking about our future during my recuperation at the beach, looking forward to the easy way we could be with the boys, and with each other, once this time in politics was done and he could focus more of his heart and mind on our family. I guess I conveniently edited out of this vision how, as the pressures on him never let up, I saw him gradually detaching again. Mark was gone speaking or fundraising many evenings while I turned down most evening requests for the First Lady's presence so I could be with the boys. Evenings when he was in Columbia, it was routine for the staff to call to advise me where he was on his schedule. It wasn't uncommon for a staffer to call saying, "The governor wanted me to call to let you know that he has scheduled dinner for nine P.M. instead of seven because he needs time to work out before he sees the boys." I would then ask her to relay the message that dinner would be no later than eight because of bedtimes and home-work. Incidents like this infuriated me. He didn't call me himself, but had an aide issuing an order from the governor's office, an order that the aide had no authority to change. Pre-sumably neither did I.

I could see it happening again if I was honest with myself, that feeling I sometimes had when he was home from Con-gress that he was here, but not here. He might, in fact, already have his eye on the next goal. I could see it sometimes in the way he treated his staff. Like many people drawn to politics, most on Mark's staff believed in his mission and were willing to put up with rough treatment to serve the cause. He could be very short with the staff if he thought they'd been sloppy, wasted his time, or gone "off message."

And he was beginning to be short with me too. After the election he found himself at a disadvantage without clear continuity between the issues he campaigned on and the re-alities of carrying those out in office. He convinced me he needed me to help bridge that gap by helping to manage his office mornings while the boys were at school. I saw in time that my role as a sounding board and adviser had taken some of the romance out of our relationship. When he was home, I got the brunt of his complaints and his worries because I un-derstood all the issues, and not enough of the fun-loving and patient man the public saw. Indeed, he was never short with constituents or with the man on the street, and this contrast was increasingly hard for me to endure. I tried sometimes to talk to Mark about the madness of his schedule and the damage that it was doing to us. I asked for time away, time without a political conference or family. Mark wholeheartedly agreed that we needed that time, but somehow those plans always got squeezed out by the all-important demands of his overburdened schedule.

As I recuperated at the beach that summer, I was torn between hoping Mark wouldn't run for reelection and worrying if he would be happy with the slower pace that would come with choosing to leave office. I knew in the end it would be his decision, not mine. But did he really want another four demoralizing years fighting to enact his agenda? Because of the checks and balances setup in South Carolina, he really had very little control, and it seemed he had few allies as well. Despite his high popularity statewide, the press rarely acknowledged how he stuck to his campaign principles while governing. The headlines were all, "Governor Wants Cuts in Spending" or "Sanford Bad for Public Schools." These were much more dramatic ways of phrasing what Mark was doing than "Governor does exactly what he promised to do while campaigning"!

If he decided to run again, I knew that this time I would refuse to run his campaign and stand strong against any cajoling on his part to get me to reconsider. He couldn't claim he didn't have the money to hire anyone this time. I would help out with the campaign but remove myself from any duties in his office. If we were in the governor's mansion for another four years, I decided, I would spend my time enjoying this unique life, raising our sons and instilling character, focusing on my own causes and quiet volunteer work, and planning for our family's future.

My dear friend Sally Coen joined us in New York for the convention. In our unmarked security car, we glided down Eighth Avenue, using the designated dignitary lane to pass easily through block after block of congested traffic as we made our way toward Madison Square Garden. Out the window, we could see hundreds of New Yorkers staring as the sleek black cars whisked past. As we got close to Madison Square Garden, we saw protestors and the sounds outside our windows grew louder, even if their words were indistinct. We didn't have to stop for them. We took a private route underground and pulled into a special area for VIPs.

From there, we were ushered up to a private box overlooking the convention floor, which was jammed with delegates waving flags and brightly colored banners. Sally joined us for the parties and stood with me at press events while the media hung on Mark's every word. His reputation as a man who lived by his word and didn't shrink from a fight made him a hero to some outside the state. There was some talk in the run-up to the convention about how this handsome, principled young governor might have a place on the national political stage. We knew there was a long distance between that kind of chatter and running as part of a presidential ticket, but the attention was flattering to Mark all the same. Sally was more than a little starstruck. "Wow!" she said. "I could really get used to a life like this!" I didn't want to burst her bubble by explaining how quickly it gets tiresome.

Or maybe I was just exhausted. Because of my recent surgery, I couldn't keep up with the normal frenetic schedule. Most evenings I cut out early to sleep. I now know that while I was at our friend's house resting one evening, Mark had the opportunity—and took it—to meet privately with the Argentinean woman he had met a few years earlier while in Punta del Este, Uruguay. Their reconnection, I was to learn when Mark gave an interview to the Associated Press about his affair, generated all kinds of sparks, and yet I detected nothing when he returned to me later that night.

He was able to make it all happen without me knowing and certainly without any immediate consequences from me or to his job. It's ironic that I was more deeply in love with him than I had been in a decade while he was feeling powerful, independent, and righteous in his growing success. Everything about the world around him told him he could remain immune from the consequences of meeting up with an appealing stranger for a romantic meal in a secluded New York bistro.

After the trip to New York, Mark began to consider seriously whether or not he was going to run again. He expressed real uncertainty about his strength to fight for and then serve a second term and we talked through the pros and cons at great length. We discussed carefully what would happen if he were to run and win or to run and lose, or to choose not to run and thus, in effect, hand victory over to the status quo. We also talked about the boys and what would be best for them. They wanted him to run again, both because they didn't want to see him give in and because they were enjoying their school and no longer wanted to return to Charleston. Mark decided to run this one last time.

Of course, from the moment Mark was elected in the first place his political opponents constantly called the media pushing one story or another designed to turn public opinion against him, even in tiny ways. I began to feel this political reality more once we were officially in reelection mode. I remember one particularly distasteful occasion when I agreed to help sell a new line of state pottery that had just arrived in our state gift shops. The pottery was elegant in its simplicity, made in Italy and decorated with the state logo. I allowed the state agency to include a postage-stamp-size photo of me in the sales brochure in which I was pictured drinking tea from one of the cups.

Soon after the brochure was released, a statehouse reporter called. He wanted my reaction to those who were criticizing me for my part in using state money to sell china that was not from South Carolina. I thought surely he must be kidding. I explained that I had nothing to do with the decision on where to manufacture or how to sell the china. I was merely trying to help the state make some money. He said others noted that we needed more jobs in our state and sell-

ing expensive foreign china—the cup and saucer cost $34—
didn't do so.

Backed against the wall by this surprising turn of events
and with Mark in a reelection campaign, I had to defend myself. I responded that the former administration used a good
deal of state money to buy china and French flatware for use
in the mansion. That hadn't created jobs in our state either.
We even told this reporter of copies of the purchase logs for
more than $100,000 worth of china and Christofle flatware.
None of what we told him was in his story.

As with so many reporters, he knew the angle he wanted
to take and the story would run as he wanted it to, whether
honest and ethical in my view or not. This is exactly the kind
of thing Mark had to deal with constantly, and I certainly
didn't envy him that. It's amazing to me what sort of contor-
tions we needed to go through to rebut this ridiculous phan-
tom of a story. It didn't feel good to feed information to the
press that might be damning to someone else's character, especially when they too had done nothing wrong. Yet I knew
there were likely plenty in our state who might read such an
article on the china and take their reaction to the polls against
Mark.

That's the press, though: Frequently there when you
don't want them around and rarely there when you do. I wish
I had had the presence of mind to ask the press camped out at
the end of my drive after Mark's return from Argentina where
they had been for my many speeches, press conferences, or
events on health, the cause I have promoted as First Lady. As

a family, we did runs and walks and biked across the state and kayaked rivers to highlight the need for more regular exercise in our sedentary state, often with little notice. On one such bike ride in Aiken with a pack of other bicycle enthusiasts, I was saddened that there was almost no press to help us highlight this obvious social problem. Sadly, this is not unique to me or to South Carolina; it is all too common everywhere.

On Sunday of our last weekend before the gubernatorial re-election in November 2006, we attended the groundbreaking for the City of Light, a large Christian evangelical center that Mark had helped bring to South Carolina. Mark was on a stage adjacent to a big dirt pit full of bulldozers with other speakers and performers, some wearing sunglasses because of the bright industrial lights focused on them. The boys and I sat in the second row watching Mark give a speech that was broadcast across the globe.

Afterward, Mark said his face felt sunburned. In the middle of the night, I woke up to him sobbing next to me, his body shaking from pain. He said he couldn't open his eyes. I called an ophthalmologist friend in Charleston, even though it was two in the morning. He said it was likely that faulty lights at the event that afternoon had burned Mark's corneas. He found an all-night pharmacy in Columbia that carried the drops Mark needed. I sent security to get them and stayed up all night putting drops in Mark's eyes each hour to help soothe the pain.

In the morning Mark was taken by his security detail to the doctor. I had arranged for the boys to skip school so we could fly around the state on our last media tour before election day. We did so without Mark. Thus we entered our final election day with Mark out of commission because he had been blinded at an event about faith!

Mark met the boys and me on Sullivan's Island Monday night. He could see, but his eyes were quite swollen. I continued to put drops in his eyes through the night. Tuesday morning we all went together to cast our votes for Mark at our home precinct, but because Mark had with him only his driver's license, which had a Columbia address, and no registration card, a woman in charge there wouldn't let Mark vote. Clearly either she was not his biggest fan or she was a real stickler for rules. By this time I was thinking *Lord, what are you telling us? Is this a sign of things to come?* But any foreboding I might have felt passed quickly. Off we went to North Charleston, half an hour away, to get the appropriate documents before returning to vote and then heading to Greenville and finally Columbia to meet more family, friends, employees, and volunteers for what would turn out to be a celebration of Mark's having won another four years in office.

Mark again decided not to have a formal Inaugural Ball because the state was still in tight times, but the Republican Party paid for one as a fundraiser. In keeping with the austerity of the times, Mark chose not to wear a tuxedo, ever mindful of the image presented on camera to the general public. To match him in style and in spirit, I wore a pretty dress I borrowed from my sister-in-law Julia and a few pieces of my sister Kathy's jewelry. Even with these pared-back events, every bedroom in the mansion was filled with family, and overflow family and close friends were all in nearby hotels. There was activity everywhere and excitement in the air.

I woke on the morning of the reception to find that our dogs Jeep and Julius had discovered the packages of linens for the event that night and for the brunch the following morning and had chewed them up and strewn the remnants all across the great lawn. Surely life in this house was never dull! The party had to go on regardless of the dogs and their antics. I gathered the linens and hurried back into the house to see if we could quickly wash and press the ones the dogs had not torn and perhaps find others to make up the difference. We did, and the parties went on, with the rescued linen for the next morning safely locked away overnight.

At the second inaugural morning prayer service, our friend and pastor Greg Surratt's sermon was more than prescient in light of what has happened in the last year. Greg remarked that we will all be remembered for something and the only question that remains to be answered is, for what? He counseled Mark to remain focused in his last years of public service, as did the Old Testament character Joshua, who concentrated on serving the Lord. He urged Mark to "be strong and courageous" (Joshua 1:6) and to finish strong by remaining humble and listening to others while continuing to act on his convictions. He reminded us all that while Joshua wasn't perfect (and none of us are), Joshua didn't succumb to the selfishness and scandals of other leaders of his time. Joshua had finished well.

Mark's inaugural address was about a time for vision, and he spoke of the struggles he had faced in his first term, saying, "I stand before you a little grayer, a little wiser and tempered by reality, but nevertheless affirmed by my conviction that we can, together as South Carolinians, make a change for the better." After he took the oath, four Air National Guard F-16s flew overhead, leaving a trail of noise and smoke in the clear blue sky.

Once again we shook hands for hours as the public visited the mansion and the boys played with friends and cousins on the lawn. This time when we prepared for the barbeque at the fairgrounds we knew our way around a house that was now almost our real home. It was a joyous and happy occasion on so many levels. Instead of worrying about things to coordinate and organize, this time, I remember thinking that I should enjoy every minute I could.

ELEVEN

WHILE I HAD EXPECTED MARK TO SLOW DOWN IN HIS SECOND term (at the very least the fundraising would taper off) his pace quickened instead. I suppose he didn't really take in Pastor Greg's sermon advising him to make sure every action he undertook reflected the legacy he wanted to leave. I knew, of course, that his days would be packed with state responsibilities, but I didn't expect him to take on even more. Almost from the moment of his inaugural, I saw him committing to fundraisers for the Republican Party, if not for himself, to help enact his agenda for reform. Mark began to give speeches around the country and to be courted by national conservative organizations and the national press. His restlessness was evident again. What would he do when *this* term was up?

Could he be satisfied returning to real estate? Should he run for another office?

Perhaps this is how our lives together started to twist out of balance. Our fundamental differences in pace probably should have worried me years before when I saw the lists of his goals. Instead, I believed the difference between Mark's desire for immediate success and my sense of the story of our lives spooling out over time would balance each other out. I could take the long view, and he would specialize in the here and now.

For a very long time, my marriage to Mark and our commitment to our family has allowed me to work toward my goals daily, even as true balance often eludes us. A woman's life is a juggling act, to be sure, and I'm not the only mother who feels that whatever you devote your time to this moment cheats someone else. Every day requires recalibration. Today it is Landon's turn for attention because he is graduating, while tomorrow it might be Marshall because of his tennis match. Whoever gets sick gets my time, but next week might take me away from the boys to travel with Mark or this evening might find me away from all of them for a First Lady event.

In that way, our life is kind of like a seesaw: The up and down is the only predictable part, and each one of us clusters on one side to bring some equilibrium back to the one who is flying high. What keeps me sane is the knowledge that over time the attention we all get will even out. The fact that no two days are ever the same with kids in tow has stretched me to my limits, most times happily so, but I've had faith that the priority I've given our boys will pay dividends through *their* good character and their happiness. I've trusted that Mark and I would one day have time alone again together and have drawn strength and a sense of calm from having this long-term sense of achieving goals and shared values.

I think it's fair to say that Mark has not felt this peace or this calm. Mark has always scanned the horizon for fresh opportunities and grander ways to achieve his goals. Honestly, when we met, I loved him for this too. I had lived briefly in that world of short-term goals and immediate gratification at Lazard. I understood the attraction of creating a rare opportunity and running at it with everything you had. Mark's unrelenting drive was attractive to me, given that it was married with what I thought of as a more soulful and humble character.

But Mark's anxiousness was even evident when he scheduled vacations. After Mark won reelection, we realized that we had spent so many years campaigning in some manner or another, we had never taken the boys on a spring break vacation. Mark set about making up for lost time, making plans for a one-week family adventure out West. After surfing on Laguna Beach, we toured the sights in LA and then traveled east to the Kelso Dunes and the Hoover Dam before the highlight, hiking the Grand Canyon. This was one of the prettiest hikes and one of the most enjoyable adventures we had ever shared together. In true Mark Sanford form, however, it wasn't just a mild hike. We hiked to the bottom to spend the night, then swam in the cold river before hiking back out the next morning. Then we drove to Las Vegas for an overnight and early departure the next morning. In Vegas, Mark and the boys went out on the town, touring the sights of the strip. I chose to have a glass of wine at the bar and went to bed.

That glass of wine and time alone were essential for me after all we had jammed into the previous days together, just as continuing to go, go, go was what Mark and the boys needed. I knew that if I had tried to keep them in the hotel room for some quiet time with me, it would have been Five Bulls In A Hotel Room. A boy's balance, and Mark's balance as well I supposed, is like a gyroscope; he has to keep spinning to feel calm at the center. My hope was that over time I could help my sons see that there is also value in a quieter life, the one that I was yearning for daily.

I began the summer of 2008 at the beach with the boys, as usual, while Mark finished off state business in Columbia. In late June, he went on a business trip to South America with the state's commerce department, and as I later came to learn, he completed the trip with a rendezvous with the woman he knew in Argentina. After his return, we spent a busy two weeks of work and fun at Coosaw, though I shiver when I think that while I was cleaning up after a delicious family meal with the boys and their cousins, he was emailing his "soul mate" with visions of her tan lines.

Mark had booked the entire summer with not a moment to rest. We traveled to New York City and then to Philadelphia with other governors and their families, taking a detour to visit Gettysburg. Then we were off to the Far East with the boys. In China, we met with dignitaries, including a formal Chinese lunch with our old friend Madame Wu Yi. We toured the sights in Beijing before heading west by train to visit Tibet and the base camp of Mt. Everest, followed by two days in India, a day in Bangkok, and a day in Hong Kong. We packed plenty into this whirlwind trip, and the boys returned with all sorts of rocks from their visits, but Blake somehow left his beloved Blankie Bear in Beijing. Aside from the frenetic pace, nothing Mark did during that trip hinted that his heart and mind were elsewhere engaged.

But when home that fall, I began to notice changes in Mark, a distracted quality; he didn't slow down. He began to travel to hunt on any free day, even during the week. He stopped reprimanding the boys when they acted out of line or spoke rudely to me or to others. This was a break from his previous stern approach to everything from dishonesty to back talk. As I watched him pull back from this practice, the boys took more liberties as they saw their boundaries disappear.

I found this incredibly frustrating, but he ignored me when I pointed out the change and he ignored my pleas for assistance. Instead, he began to advocate a much softer approach. "Let's just love them," he might say, as he continued to indulge their limit-pushing. He also scaled back his devotion time with the boys. This, too, frustrated me, as he was becoming in many ways as detached from the family as he had been while he was away in Congress.

I decided not to call him too harshly on the changes I saw in him, thinking he was going through another period of searching. I knew that the approaching big birthday—when he would turn fifty—was weighing on his mind and that things would return to normal as he came to terms with that milestone.

They did not. We hosted receptions for supporters at the mansion but sadly, he still sometimes asked, "Who are my friends?" I pointed out the friends we had hosted as guests at football games, invited for overnights at the mansion or weekends at Coosaw. These were people who were truly fond of him as a person as well as supportive of his agenda. But he was right to notice that he didn't have a group of close friends—at least not that he had kept up with or met with regularly—that would keep him accountable and down to earth. As rich as our life may have seemed to an outsider, in some ways, Mark's life in politics has made for a lonely existence for all of us, especially given the isolated nature of the compound on which we lived in Columbia. I understand how he had become so compartmentalized and walled off from real understanding of his friendships and their value. With Mark as governor, we were often so busy that we saw very little of the kind of people who knew us well and would always be brave enough to hold us accountable for our actions. Friends share a healthy respect for one another and their similarities, differences, strengths, and weaknesses. In this crush of people who wanted to be friends with us for their own reasons, many valid, I found myself starved for real friendship. Many of our true friends were reluctant to call us because they assumed we were busy. I would often learn, after the fact, that they had been in Columbia for, say, a child's soccer game and stayed in a hotel, not wanting to bother me. All I wanted was the company of real friends instead of the tiresome busyness and loneliness that came with the job and the house. I began to encourage friends to please call when they were in Columbia. I told them I would honestly let them know if we were busy or not. Some were better at staying in touch when in town than others, but all had great intentions and remain close today. In time, I also made great friends in Columbia for all the right reasons, as did our boys. But for Mark it has seemed loneliest.

Indeed, he spent most of his time asking others for help with his campaign or pushing an issue and seemed to spend little time reassessing himself and whether he was living life according to the goals and values he held dear. Though always for good causes, charity dinners and political events can't replace casual, unstructured, let-down-your-guard time with old and dear friends.

Though I wouldn't have thought anyone could take much more than Mark was already juggling, in the fall, the pressures on him increased dramatically. The economy in our state soured, and then the national markets collapsed. Mark traveled to hearings on Capitol Hill to speak. He stood firmly against the stimulus package that President Obama and others promoted as the solution to our financial crisis. When he was fighting to reject federal stimulus money in early 2009, the bulk of the political class and the media and a large majority in the public couldn't conceive of someone being against so-called "free" money, even as his popularity with conservatives was incredibly high.

From late 2008 to June 2009 Mark did somewhere close to eighty national interviews on the stimulus and government spending, an astonishing number. The more outspoken he was, the more the press wanted him on air. People began to call or write from all over the country urging Mark to consider running for president in 2012 and, regardless, to continue to fight Obama and the huge increase in spending. Our country needed him, they said, and he was eager to rise to the occasion. Whether with adulation or criticism, the media attention that came with his position and notoriety fueled both his belief in his convictions and, I now see, his ability to compartmentalize his emotional response to it all. Wrapped up in staying true to his message, he became empty of connection to almost everything else.

Mark and I traveled to Miami for a Republican Governors Association conference in November 2008, where he was elected chairman of that organization. Shortly thereafter, he traveled to Ireland to shoot birds with other RGA contacts. At the end of the trip to Ireland, he disappeared. He had stopped calling home, and I called his staff to find out what was going on. They said he had flown to New York, but they were unclear on the purpose of the visit. I didn't know either, but I would soon come to know that this trip to New York was for a rendezvous with his mistress. When he finally called, I asked him what he was doing in New York and who he was with. He told me he was alone. I said that I didn't believe him. The pressure had been getting to him, he said, and, unbelievably, he was also upset about the bald spot that was forming at the back of his head. He just needed some time away from all of the stress and his worries. I cut him some slack. I can't say I completely bought the line he was selling me, but I put the unaccounted-for time out of my head. I chose to ignore my doubts.

In any event, I had plenty of reasons to appreciate the pressures he was under, pressures that seemed to mount every day. In December 2008, Mark and his staff worked long hours trying to finish the budget for the next fiscal year. The state revenues were down substantially. Mark came home drained every night, telling me of the awful choices he had to make on the budget, where each proposed cut was as difficult as the next and every one of them slashed at something that had already been cut to the bone. Though the legislators held the power, the governor led with his budget, and he would take most of the blame. Every possible moment he was not needed at the office, he seemed to be on the television or away at a new hunting spot or traveling to give a speech or raising RGA funds or money for his own cause. When he was home, he was often speaking on the local or national news before dinner, sometimes returning to a television studio to appear again on the late-night news cycle. His frantic schedule coupled with his frenetic drive to fill every minute as well as his unquenchable ambition were all tearing him apart. He looked exhausted and had bags under his eyes; he had lost weight and his eyes appeared glazed. It seemed to me that Mark had become the empty-eyed politician he used to abhor.

All of these dramatic changes in him suggested a deep emptiness inside, too. Even a young body needs time to rest, to recharge, but all Mark did was charge ahead, ignoring how his worst fears about aging were manifesting in his body. Mark has long had trouble with his back and has suffered a sore shoulder from time to time, but that fall it seemed as though his body was completely falling apart as he clung desperately to the desires of youth. It was apparent that he was suffering. The yogis refer to suffering, or dhukha, as the resistance or reaction to pain. When I looked at Mark, I saw a man in so much pain: physical, intellectual, and emotional. Somewhere inside of me I knew he was in moral conflict as well, but that was honestly something I chose not to explore. My concern and my pleas for him to slow down, to soften, went unheard. There was so much on the surface that seemed to need my attention, that the idea of scratching that surface and confronting Mark with what I saw was just not tenable.

On one level, you might say that Mark was having a classic midlife crisis. Yet to label it as such, pack it neatly in a box, and place it on a shelf denies the way his adherence to political principle, the public acclaim, government pressure, and media attention aided and abetted this episode. Of course, he had the tendency to view his life as a quest that was never completed, and this would have existed within him even if he had never been elected. In a way that is just what drives him. I can see Mark's break with his values now as probably a combination of these forces: the unreal way in which being a public figure distorted his sense of self compounded by the coming crisis that was turning fifty.

Mark had long lived in a world where he never had to perform the normal tasks of life nor suffer the consequences of his lapses of decorum in the office or spikes of bad temper, albeit often with a gentle voice. No matter his private failings, his staff protected him from exposure. But now, the media, the hated media, was lavishing positive attention on him, and he found it irresistible. He was the man of the moment, the stalwart hero who was standing on principle and refusing to accept money from the federal government. In all ways, he was a man who stood apart from the quotidian world. He was lauded, celebrated for his constant seeking of new ideas, new horizons, and, unbeknownst to me, new sensations. Was it so much of a stretch then for him to think that if he worked hard enough at it, he might beat this aging thing too?

Here again, our difference in approach is profound. I have always looked forward to getting older. As someone who has dozens of things to do on any given day, or at a particular moment, I expect that when I reach my senior years all of that will gracefully, gently subside. As each year passes, I feel more and more content with who I am and how I have lived my life. As my body began to slowly age (I too have had health and age-related issues, including many skin cancer scares and many minor surgeries to remove them), I was more and more awake to the precious gifts surrounding me each day, but Mark's angst was growing about what was to come. Where I was learning to accept gracefully the challenges that have come with aging, he had tried to deny them. As he faced the prospect of turning fifty and his time as governor was coming to an end, Mark continued to live in an increased frenzy, as if something were missing and he had to find it before he died.

Perhaps the foundation for the differences in Mark and my approaches to aging is the fact that all four of my grandparents were still alive when I was a child. Mark briefly knew two of his grandparents, but perhaps he never saw the beauty or wisdom in their age. My mom's parents, Honey and Bumpa, were full of fun and energetic almost until they died. Bumpa was tall and bright and could make me laugh. I remember sitting on his lap as he blew smoke rings from his pipe. His other classic grandfather trick was making a silver dollar magically appear from behind my ear. Naturally, he let me keep the silver dollar, making it that much more special. Honey, my grandmother, is my real model for aging well. In many ways, she blossomed as she aged. She was soft-spoken, petite, and graceful, and her grace increased in her later years. She walked daily, stretched her mind by reading, and even took up painting late in life.

My father's parents showed me a different advantage to the later stages of life. My Gramps awed me with his wisdom about business and his insights into character. Older people have so much time—time to listen, reflect, and share magical memories. All my grandparents had experienced great joys and successes, as well as tribulations, but they had reached a state of contentment and enjoyment. With them as my examples, I had never been fearful about aging, recalling John Greenleaf Whittier's lines: "Strike when thou wilt the hour of rest,/But let my last days be my best." The family did our part to make the elders feel as if their last days were indeed their best. We celebrated milestones in our grandparents' lives, such as birthdays and fiftieth anniversaries, and we always welcomed opportunities to be with them.

Anne Morrow Lindbergh said, "only in growth, reform, and change, paradoxically enough is true security to be found." When I think of those words, I recall how gracefully Honey lived after Bumpa died. She could have withered at the prospect of living her last years alone. Her security came from living in the present. I see the same quality in my mother as I have watched her play tennis, paint, and enjoy time with her grandchildren, living far longer than any doctor projected. I am reminded of how special each day of life is and how important it is to seek to enjoy each step along the way. As with meditation in yoga, I am mindful that I need to learn to become present and familiar with myself so I can feel my experiences and not just react to them.

As I felt myself happily relaxing into my age, I was pulling away from Mark's world. Weekends at Coosaw and time at our beach house have helped balance the demands on our time while in Columbia, and we have all cherished these getaways. I think the boys and Mark have been most happy at Coosaw, where they could just be boys, kayaking the rivers or creeks or swimming to the banks of pluff mud at low tide. Mark is the Pied Piper there, able to round up all the children and get them working on some big project.

Some weekends he rented a track hoe, and he and the boys replaced a floodgate or repaired dikes. Other times all of them, even the little guys, took to the woods to set a big fire — a controlled burn — to cut back the underbrush. I didn't fully partake of these manly events but I often watched for a while. I enjoyed the peace of walking at Coosaw, finding balance on the shifting terrain. Uncluttered time in nature has been my personal time to recharge, and then I rejoin the noisy men. I relish the delight on the boys' faces as they return covered in soot or mud, hungry for a hearty meal I have cooked, followed by discussion around the fire after dinner or a Jeep ride under the stars to spot deer in the woods. My eyes were trained on the horizon too, but my vision of it was us at the beach, Mark at home, while we as a couple cherished the launching of our four fine young men into the world. As Henri Bergson said, "To exist is to change, to change is to mature, to mature is to go on creating oneself endlessly." As I faced the realities of my aging and dealt with my various health crises, I wanted to grow to understand them, to deal with them, to learn from them, and to live wholly with them.

We had lived our time in the public eye, but my vision of our future as we grew older was one where we could be as vital to the world around us in a much more private context. I was moving inward, slowing down, reveling in these changes and the changes to come. Little did I understand, as I started to draw more strongly on my inner life and look toward my goals, that January would bring me a revelation that would derail that strong vision I had of my years to come with my family as I knew it.

TWELVE

———◇———

I ALWAYS BELIEVED THAT MARK AND I HAD NO SECRETS. AFTER ALL of these years in the public eye, our lives were open books to one another, let alone to the public. Though we drifted apart a bit during his time as governor, we were partners in parenting, and we were still intimate. The physical space we shared even remained close: In the office adjacent to our bedroom in the governor's mansion, our desks were next to each other. So it was not at all odd on an afternoon back in January for me to be looking in his desk.

The beginning of the year is the time I put things to right after the holidays. Mark's State of the State speech and the Obama inauguration had already taken up catch-up time but with Mark away hunting Thursday and Friday that week, I had the time to tackle a few lingering issues. One of them was to search for some documents I thought would settle a question about Coosaw that had come up between Mark and his siblings. While the boys were at school on Friday, I searched the files we kept in storage but didn't find what I was looking for there. Later that day, it occurred to me that Mark's desk might hold the needed paperwork. If what I was looking for wasn't there, I told myself, I'd call it quits and let Mark search further himself when he got home.

I walked into the tall office with long windows overlooking the mansion driveway and went to Mark's desk. Ignoring the scattered papers on top and the stacks of books on the floor that Mark planned to read, I went straight for the drawer on the left side, where I knew Mark kept files about current issues. In random order, one labeled simply "B" caught my eye. I opened it and saw quickly that this was not a file dedicated, as I thought, to correspondence with Mark's brother Bill—often called just B by his siblings. Instead, a letter, an article clipped from a magazine, and a printed email exchange inside told me that B stood for Belen, a woman, I learned sitting there, Mark had slept with and whom he believed to be his eternal love.

I suppose it's cliché to say that I felt as if I had been punched in the gut. But that's the best description I can muster for what this surprise felt like. I was short of breath. I began to shake. Stunned, I wasn't sure of what to do next. I had so many questions. How could I not have known? Had I really known, on some level? When and where had he been seeing her? How had he found time for an affair? Did he really love her? How could he do this to me and to the boys? I read the letter again and saw the depth of what he professed to be his feeling. I looked at the article, but it didn't mean anything to me; for all I know even today, it may have been misfiled.

The email made things still more clear. It showed Mark had arranged to use a friend's apartment in New York City for a visit he had scheduled in the coming weeks. I knew that the ostensible reason for the trip was to meet with publishers interested in his idea for a book on conservative values, but I could only assume he was also planning to see his lover then. He had been gone so much recently . . . where had he actually been? I don't know how long I sat in his chair. Eventually I got up and moved to my side of the office and sat motionless at my desk a bit longer, the thin file in my lap. I tried to think of what I should do. Should I call him? Should I call a friend? A lawyer? Should I cry? Was this even happening? I was shocked into stillness, until I heard Mark's voice downstairs.

I put the file on my desk and stood up when he walked into our office. Fresh from the hunt, he was disheveled, and his plaid shirt was untucked. He looked as if he hadn't slept all night. He kissed me hello and then went to his desk. Still dumbstruck, I calmly handed him the letter and confronted him very simply with what I'd discovered: "Please tell me about this."

Mark glanced down at the letter, and his shoulders slumped immediately. Again I noticed that he looked very tired. "Jenny, I'm sorry. I'll end it," he said.

The next thing I said had been looping endlessly through my mind and seemed to be what mattered most of all: "Well, do you love her?"

"No," he said emphatically. Despite his declaration of love in the letter, I believed him. "She doesn't mean anything. In fact I was up really late last night telling Jim Kuyk that this was crazy and that I had to end it." Jim is an old friend—he was in our wedding, in fact—and Mark's lawyer. I didn't think there was any legal significance in Mark's having confided in him, but I wondered immediately how many people knew about this affair before I did.

We heard the sound of a few of the boys running up the stairs to greet Mark.

"Let's finish this discussion downstairs," Mark said and then turned to his sons and tousled heads and caught them up on his successful hunt. I would have given anything for this to be a discussion that had an end point, but I suspected it wasn't something we could dispense with simply "downstairs." Still, downstairs I went.

A few minutes later, boys scattered to other parts of the house, Mark and I sat together on a couch in the library. I sobbed softly—still unable or unwilling, I'm not sure which, to rant and rave with the hurt I was feeling—as Mark tried to explain himself. I was hoping it was just a one-time event, an act of passion, but Mark admitted that he had seen this woman in Argentina and then twice in New York. I asked if there had been other affairs and he insisted that this was his only transgression, the only one. Insisting Belen didn't mean anything to him and avoiding any real details of the logistics of their time together, Mark promised to end the affair. His voice was kind and apologetic but he didn't reach out to comfort me. A profound sadness came over me sitting there. A fundamental part of what I believed about my husband and about our life together had just died and it seemed as though I might never get it back.

My mind raced, looking for an explanation better than the one he was providing. Mark had abstained from sex and drinking during college while his dad was so sick. Having gotten a few things out of my own system in college, I could appreciate that he had long wondered what, if anything, he had missed by not experimenting in those years. I knew that he was under almost impossible pressure on the job. I understood how something like this might have happened theoretically, though I couldn't wrap my head around how Mark—this man of his word and of faith—could have made such terrible choices. Still, I knew that I could and would forgive him. It might have been my survival instinct kicking in, a willingness to forgive and move on, perhaps even the hope that in forgiving quickly I could eradicate the ugly knowledge I'd gained that day. But my immediate impulse to forgive Mark has not proven to be only that. I can see now that forgiving him was an essential part of healing for myself as well.

Through tears, I told Mark that I wanted to forgive him and to believe that this was it, that it wouldn't ever happen again. My simple condition was that he had to fully commit to the marriage in a way that he had not done in the past. It had to be better, not just a return to the same. Still sitting apart from me—perhaps a posture that should have worried me—he agreed.

At dinner that night, I tried to keep up the normal patter for the boys' sake, but I left the table early, explaining that I simply wasn't feeling well. I sobbed upstairs in my bathroom. I don't know how long I sat there, but at some point in the evening Mark came in, hugged me gently, and assured me everything was going to be okay. How I wanted to believe that! What a wonderful thing it would have been to just believe that and try to move on. But as anyone who has ever been betrayed knows, we can't really outsmart or overrule the part of the brain that has registered that betrayal.

Forgiveness, too, is a willful and deliberate act and it takes such effort. I made the effort, but I lost sleep over it. For many nights—and many months—I often had trouble getting to sleep and had a terrible time staying that way. I often got up in the wee hours of the morning, read my Bible, and stared into space. I began to keep a journal of my thoughts and some of Mark's comments and found that doing so helped me focus on what mattered. I was beat down, exhausted, and deeply sad, but the first thing I wrote in that journal shows me that even in that dark hour I was determined to continue to see my glass as half full. I started with Psalm 118:24 "This is the day the Lord has made, let us rejoice and be glad in it."

The next day, Saturday, Mark and I were scheduled to attend a black-tie dinner in Charleston. Ostensibly to get ready, but really just to clear my head, I went out for a pedicure and a massage, soaking up every minute of the solitude. Discovering Mark's affair had somehow made me feel ugly, unwanted, and even dirty. For just a little while, the pampering and the fancy dress I put on that evening made me feel good.

I asked Mark to drive instead of taking a security detail to the event so we could speak frankly during the hours in the car. As we talked, it became clear to me that, contrary to what he'd said the day before, Mark had real feelings for this woman. He touted her wealth, bristled when I asked questions, and defended her when I referred to her plainly as his "whore." "She is not a whore!" he protested. He seemed to be oblivious to his ability to pierce my heart.

We also spoke of the trip to the world economic forum in Davos, Switzerland, where we were scheduled to go the next day. I told Mark that I didn't see how going to Davos could be a priority at this time. Instead, I thought we should stay home and we should be together without other people, or dinners or speeches. Mark resisted upending our plans, but he ultimately agreed we would stay home and even go away together for a weekend.

A few days later, I asked Mark if he had told Belen that their affair was over. He said that doing so wouldn't be quite that easy. Though I had understood that they had got together while Mark was on a commerce department trip to Argentina in June 2008, their relationship, he explained, had actually started—albeit platonically—seven years earlier via email. She had been a friend, and he didn't think he could just cut her off so quickly. He still hoped he could travel to New York in a few weeks to see her. He promised he would end it there in person. I wouldn't have it—he had to end it immediately on the phone.

It was Wednesday before Mark emailed Belen to ask her to call so they could talk about ending the affair. He spoke to her from his office for I don't know how long. I didn't want to know; I also didn't need to know that he had found the call difficult, but he told me it was. But difficult or not, tears or no tears, afterward he told me unequivocally that the affair was over. I felt relieved, to be sure. But I knew that the flesh and the spirit can lust against one another and I worried that what he had originally said might be true: It might not be so easy to end this thing.

I had long since realized that marriage to Mark was not going to be all roses or romance. Certainly I didn't always feel loved by him or have that "in-love" feeling for him as often as I would have liked, but that, I rationalized—and believed— was real marriage. I had faith that we had a *real* marriage, one that could weather the periods of distance and come back again to connection. Our stresses were real but were focused in an honorable direction. My daily prayers had always included prayers for my marriage. After finding that letter, I needed God's love and grace even more powerfully.

As we'd planned when we cancelled the trip to Switzerland, we traveled that weekend to the mountains around Asheville without the boys. This was meant to be a time to reconnect but it'd been such a long time since we'd made this space for each other that it was more surreal than relaxing. Plus, the circumstances surrounding our decision to be alone now hung over us the whole time. At some point over that weekend I realized that I had just begun an emotional roller-coaster ride, one that would last far longer than I could ever have imagined. Just because we agreed we would put Mark's affair behind us didn't mean we could do so quickly. That recognition was a blow as well.

And, of course, it wasn't yet over. That weekend, Mark broke down and cried, but not for what I expected might bring him to tears. He explained that he had always been so *good*, so dutiful. He had led his siblings through a tough time after their father died. He had remained true to his conservative principles in his political career although doing so meant going against a considerable tide. It became clear to me this romantic relationship he had was a way of doing something for himself—it felt good and he didn't really want to give it up. Though on that weekend away he didn't spell it out explicitly, it was becoming clear that he intended to see her again in New York.

How could he possibly think I would let him go through with the plan I had seen him make in that email, a plan to spend two nights in New York with her? I asked incredulously. I told him repeatedly that I felt it was one thing to forgive adultery but in no way could I condone it, especially in my own marriage. I wrestled with this very thing in my journal that night: "I trust his intentions are good—he says it is over—but how can I trust the result when faced with such temptation? And what of the lack of humility? The lack of respect for me? Is he not putting her feelings over mine? Does he really love me?" I felt so sad and misunderstood. Though forgiveness might be possible, it dawned on me that reconciliation would be a harder thing to manage. I wondered constantly, frantically searching my heart to know if the right reaction was to leave him.

Faith requires prayer and time, and I suspected Mark's prayers had been neglected given the demands on his time. The world around us conspires to make finding time for prayer difficult. A well-known Psalm says "Be still and know that I am God." In A *Gift from the Sea*, Anne Morrow Lindbergh also talks of the importance of seeking solitude amidst our multitasking lives. She speaks of the importance of finding empty space— because, as she puts it, our time is all used up or scribbled on. It is in this empty space, or when we can be still, that we find God and reconnect with our true inner self. My sense of security for our marriage came from a deep well of understanding of ebb and flow, a concept that honored commitment over the long haul and was founded in my faith. In accepting our distance as an inevitable part of eventually coming back together, I had settled into a peace with our life and lifestyle with the help of my prayers.

In retrospect, I might have been learning to justify Mark's lack of empathy, his travels and schedule, or other imperfections. I now wonder if he took our stated certainty of a future together as a license to stray without consequence. But all this is even still just speculation on my part, and in those early days it was far too much for me to even begin to consider. The questions that dogged me were ones that would ultimately break the commitment from my side as well: At what point are children ill-served by the example set by their parents and their marriage? And what of my personal dignity and self-respect if Mark continued to see his lover?

Later in the year, when I'd confided in friends about what was happening and what Mark was asking to do, I better understood that allowing him to see Belen in New York—which is what I eventually agreed to let him do—was ludicrous. Of course, it was ludicrous of him to continue to ask me to let him go, but he wore me down, asking again and again and insisting that the way for this to be over was to allow him the closure he needed. Even stranger—though a lifeline to me at the time—was our agreement that we would ask for a friend's help in keeping Mark in line.

Every minute of Mark's two days in New York—including meetings with publishers—he would have a friend of ours, Cubby Culbertson, by his side. Mark could see Belen for dinner with Cubby as their escort. Cubby had been and still is a dear friend to both of us, and he was helping Mark regain his moral focus from the moment I learned of the infidelity. He stepped up and into this odd request, dropping his own plans to help an old friend stay the course and save his marriage. His willingness to help Mark and me discreetly was a tremendously generous and selfless act, but I wasn't at peace with the decision before or even after the arrangements were made.

Indeed, before Cubby agreed to accompany Mark I wrote in my journal, "I cannot condone this future act because A) it is wrong in God's eyes B) it would cause me to lose my self-respect, dignity etc—esp as we look to the boys as example going forward. . . . Perhaps he needs to be thinking of how he gets back his dignity in God's eyes—by His grace."

My arm twisted into this strange position, however, Mark went to New York and Cubby went too. The first night, I received a text from Cubby that read "Sleep well. He played by the rules." I went to sleep but once again could not sleep long. Instead, I thought long and hard about whether Mark had ever loved me and about whether I should leave him. Again, I turned to my journal. I wrote: "Is M's suffering now/future because A) he will not have/see his "eternal love" or B) he hurt his wife, whom he truly loves? Can I stay in marriage if the answer is A? I know I can stay if the answer truly is B." I thought about what it would do to our boys if I left yet I also wondered if I could stay much longer if Mark didn't show real effort toward making the marriage stronger.

While Mark was gone I prayed for strength and shed many tears. I also began to be more fully aware of how out of touch I was with the demons Mark was wrestling with and that I could not really help him.

I expected or hoped that Mark would be a new man when he returned from New York but in time I saw that was not at all the case. After a few good weeks he became distant again, and before long he was pestering me for permission to see his lover that summer so he could find "the key to his heart." That he would consider asking me repeatedly for permission to see his lover again was unfathomable. It was one thing for me to forgive his indiscretions and move toward reconciliation, but to condone it further meant for me to compromise my own morals and integrity. That was a bridge too far for me and cut deeply against my faith. I have committed plenty of moral sins in my past, but in each case I have grown in the aftermath, begging forgiveness from the Lord or from others and moving on as a better person, learning from past mistakes. But this was missing with Mark. He seemed to be traveling a path of his own making, seeking his own comfort, no longer guided by a power above. I began to see him as lost, disconnected from his basic values, and I began to pray differently.

Now I prayed for His will to be done and for me to bear the future with grace and peace. I asked for calm for my boys and acceptance of the future. I sought understanding of Mark's actions and prayed that the Lord would wake him to the error of his ways. I praised more and asked less. A verse I contemplated was Nehemiah 8:10: "for this day is holy to our Lord. Do not sorrow, for the joy of the Lord is your strength." I tried over and over to put joy in my head and heart and to remain strong. I focused on the love from God, the blessings in my life—boys, family, faith, and friends.

I began to think differently about the marriage than I had

in years past too. I thought of the lies and the deception and questioned how I would know when it had all ended. I pondered humility and remorse. I read of Paul in 1 Timothy and considered how he had acknowledged his sins and become humble in that knowledge. As he matured he grew into a great leader by tapping into that humbleness. Mark's star had been rising in the political world, but I was not seeing or feeling any humility.

Even as I wrestled with what I might have seen or what I should have understood earlier, I refused to beat myself up over my past choices. I forgave myself my long-standing belief that Mark and I would be together alone again after the *next* political position. I was proud to conclude that giving and doing more for our marriage than I had received in return had been the right thing to do for our family. But, I also finally understood that our relationship couldn't be so lopsided going forward. I had told him as much that first day I confronted him: My simple condition for staying together was just that. But I seemed to reach something much more clearly identifiable as a decision, beginning while Mark was gone in New York: I could stay in the marriage if Mark found a true and humble spirit of remorse and if he recognized that he loved me and that he had deeply hurt me. What Mark did had changed the dynamics. I was committed to doing my part but I could not be the only one doing so.

I was under no illusion that Mark would change overnight, so I steeled myself to be gentle and patient. I prayed for the strength to be so. Throughout, I reminded myself that no matter what, I was loved by my God, my friends, and my family, that I was being the best I could be. This knowledge gave me some peace. I felt sanguine about my future, whatever it might turn out to hold for me.

THIRTEEN

———◇———

THE WEEKEND MARK TRAVELED TO ARGENTINA, A REPORTER
called to ask if I knew where my husband was, and I had
a choice to make. The choice was not whether to tell the
truth. Like everyone in my family, I always pretty much say
what I think and move on. In the world of politics, that's not
always the best policy, despite my strong impulse to do so.
The goal with a reporter was to reveal enough of the truth to
satisfy his curiosity while saying as little of substance as possible.

Consider what I could have said. Mark was a man who
spoke often about living according to principles and values,
and our family was part of his appeal, evidence of character.
Revealing that I had kicked him out would allow his political
enemies to gleefully advance any number of agendas. Even

in my heartbreak, I considered his public image almost as often as I plumbed the impulses of my heart.

Truth was, I had wanted to leave him almost as soon as he returned from his farewell trip to New York with Cubby, even if it would serve to wake him up and ultimately save the marriage and family. The begging to be allowed to see his mistress again in Argentina began shortly thereafter, and I had had about all I could take.

Mark still saw me as his sounding board. Over those months, he wondered aloud to me if he shouldn't just follow his heart. What if he could find true happiness only in Argentina? Would he always live his life in regret, in wonder, because he didn't take this chance? Clearly, these were thoughts I wished he'd kept to himself. He was in a daze, though, a dreamy state similar to the way he appeared at points in the now-famous press conference after Father's Day. Indeed, when I'd reminded him later of the hurtful things he'd said in those intervening months, he couldn't remember most of them.

There was many a time I pictured just packing up the boys and letting Mark sort it out on his own. Most in the small circle who knew my situation recommended I do just that. But that would have put the burden of halting his rising star on me, and I wasn't ready to shoulder that responsibility.

In the beginning the circle of people I confided in was indeed small. It included two friends, my sister, and Jack, who had advised me well and cooled me down after Mark rented our house out without consulting me. The day after I discovered the letter, it was actually Mark who suggested I call Jack in DC. I wanted help, I needed counsel, and I trusted Jack. As before, he was ever kind and patient, telling me emphatically not to beat myself up. He also gave me two excellent pieces of advice on that first phone call.

He knew that my instinct would be to keep this to myself. "Jenny don't do this alone," he said, urging me to confide in just one or two very close friends.

I took his advice, but I didn't feel comfortable just picking up the phone and telling this shattering news to the two women I chose to confide in: Frannie and Lalla Lee, my close friends in Charleston. Instead, I texted them, asking them to call when they could do so privately. Both called right away. We cried together and they vowed to help me through, as good friends do.

We set up time to pray together as well. Days later, when I joined them in Charleston for that purpose, I gave them the love letter I'd found. I had considered destroying it, but something told me I might need it one day as proof of the affair. I hoped that day would never come but, in the meantime, I didn't want it around our house where I might read it again. Those were emotions I was trying to move beyond. I trusted them to keep that document safe. A few weeks later, I shared the secret with my sister Gier too, and she joined in this sisterhood of support. For many long and difficult months, I was thankful to have these women ready to listen whenever I called.

Jack's other piece of advice was how to handle Mark. Jack

understood men in power well. He counseled that seeking revenge would erode any chance of reconciliation. I needed to resist the urge to rant or get back at Mark. If Mark said things that hurt or upset me, I was not to respond. Easier said than done, he agreed, but he was offering to take the burden off my shoulders. I should hand these hurts to Jack, who would confront Mark in a way that my tears might derail. This method would allow me, Jack said, to be like "the Bride of Christ." I could work on forgiveness and kindness, while he worked with Mark to make amends.

I needed Jack's tag-team support very quickly thereafter. Just a few days later, Mark was angry at me for convincing him not to go to Davos, though it was also clear that he was just plain angry with me for catching him in this entanglement in the first place. Holding my tongue and then tattling on Mark to a third party was difficult. My instinct at a moment like this was to stand up for *myself.* But I followed Jack's plan and he backed me up, explaining to Mark that traveling to Davos at a critical time like this was absolutely the wrong thing to do.

There were times when I wanted to scream and rant at Mark, and I'm sure I was snide on occasion or hurt him with the truth. For the most part, however, discussions between us did not spiral into spiteful words. I was quite disciplined. I don't think I ever said anything I felt I couldn't take back. With Jack's wise counsel, I left the punishment to someone else.

Yet Mark was unrelenting, in time escalating pressure to

get me to condone his foreign adventure. Once I realized we were going in the wrong direction, I was ready to move out. In April and early May, Jack was of the same mind. He suggested that I'd put up with too much and urged me to leave Mark as a way to wake him up and perhaps save the marriage. My female friends agreed that the shock of us gone was the best chance I had to knock some sense into Mark. But Marshall was just about to take his exams for junior year, the ones that really count for college. If I could avoid pulling the rug out from underneath him just long enough to help him get through this critical educational moment, I would.

In early May I wrote in my journal, "Allowing my husband to see his lover for whatever reason goes against who I am and my entire sense of right and wrong. I explained this over and over to Mark but he thought I was not hearing or understanding him. I understand him—he loves someone else and he wants to have one final fling with her to see if it brings 'true happiness' before he settles with me and puts his 'heart to rest' over her. What he does not see is how morally offensive it is to me to even listen to this. It is ripping my heart up and I told him so."

I was at a real crossroads. And I was very tense. I wasn't so worried about going it alone. I was worried about direction. Because of his position, I didn't want to make a rash decision that would bring down Mark's career, and he knew I cared about helping him avoid that. And I was thinking of the boys, who didn't deserve this in the least. In retrospect, I know I was probably too respectful of his work responsibilities and was letting him too much off the hook of his home responsibilities.

So we came up with a plan. The plan I favored was to throw the kids into the car on the last day of school and leave with them for the summer to a place unknown to Mark. Jack found us a house in Annapolis, where Marshall was enrolled in a one-week session at the Naval Academy. From there we would find a place somewhere on Cape Cod, and Mark would not know where to find us. Jack said this plan was what a guy like Mark really needed, some real shock to his tightly controlled self-wound world. I felt as though I was still trying to give back sight to the blinded soul.

Before school ended and we could depart in surprise, Mark continued wearing me down. I didn't like negotiating with him. He wanted my permission to go, but I was never going to grant it. Why did he persist? I explained that I thought the decision before him was if he could commit wholly to me in a way he hadn't done before. Give it a year. Give it two years. And if it doesn't work out between us, then go see her, I said. She's not going anywhere.

"What if she does?" he'd ask. "Do you want to wake up when you are eighty and know you never had a heart connection?" Fast-talking, straight-shooting me, I was largely speechless. Of course, I believed I'd had a "heart connection" with him!

Anyway, Mark got wind of my plans for leaving town and it did *not* wake him up, so I instantly changed plans. We would head to the beach on Sullivan's Island, and instead of deserting Mark, we would welcome him to come and be with us, spending time with us with no schedule whatsoever. He said he would join us at the beach during that largely unscheduled three-week period soon to come. I thought we would slowly settle into something that was better during his visit and that our open time as a family would be a salve for us all. Mark, however, did not seem happy about it all.

Instead, his yearnings for his distant lover intensified as soon as he arrived at the beach. I'd never seen him like this. He was just in a tizzy, an internal tizzy, and he couldn't sit still. He was sometimes sleepless, and I knew I didn't understand the demons he was wrestling. His requests to see his lover now were almost frantic in tone. He even asked if we could formally separate for one week so his visit would be legally permissible. Needless to say, that was not even a bit okay with me. When I wouldn't budge, he began calling friends seeking their permission. Why permission from a friend would have mattered, I don't know. But none of his friends told him that they thought this was a good idea.

On Mark's second night with us at the beach, we went to a good friend's house for dinner. I found it too much for me to bear being there as the married couple managing our children with smiles on our faces when there was so much roiling beneath the surface. I left early on my bike.

Once home alone, I sat on the porch looking at the sea, waiting for some kind of an answer to come to me. For months, I had been holding this secret for him. Although I had called a lawyer shortly after I learned of the affair to see how one prepared for divorce, I had not filed any formal documents or successfully used legal leverage out of respect for him and his position. In early May, however, I had tried: I had had my lawyer draw up a contract saying I would not tell anyone else of the affair out of respect for his political career if he would agree not to see Belen. He would not sign the contract. Later in May, I had told our political adviser of the situation, shocking him completely. He wrote Mark an impassioned email warning him that if he didn't reverse course, "you will lose your wife, your children, and your career." I also told my assistant of the affair and of my struggles to wake him up. As more people learned of the affair, the likelihood it would become publicly known also increased.

I was up at three in the morning sitting on the porch looking out at the ocean when Mark came to sit with me.

"What's wrong?" he asked.

"What do you think is wrong? I'm married to a guy who is in love with someone else," I said. "I'm not going to stay in a marriage like that."

"No, no, I love you," he said.

"Then why do you want to go see her?" I asked.

"It's my heart. I've got to figure this thing out."

Once again, the inanity and insensitivity of his remark left me reeling. No one has the key to your heart, I explained. *You* have the key to your heart. Yet again I was clear: "I will not allow you to go see her," I said.

In his continued misery, I heard his decision. I had had enough. I told him he had to leave the house that day and not contact me or the boys. My hope was that starving him of daily contact with me and the boys might bring him around to appreciate what he might lose.

About nine later that morning, we called the boys into the family room and sat them down. "You know your mom and I have been having some problems," Mark began. "You've seen our strains and you've seen your mom crying. I haven't been good to her. I'm mixed up right now and I've got to get myself right. I'm going to be leaving for a month. I'm not going to talk to you for thirty days, until July 10. I'm just going to go write my book and get my head right." The boys were upset and started to object, but ultimately they accepted that we were serious.

I walked with Mark out to the driveway. I told him, "You look me in the eye and tell me you will not see her."

"I will not see her," he said. He had always prided himself on his honesty.

"You mean it?"

"I will not see her," he said, before departing with security for Columbia.

Apparently, within a few hours, he bought his ticket to Argentina.

Although I had been running the household alone for more than a decade, the space left by Mark's departure was unsettling. Before, I always had a sense of Mark as the vital missing piece. During my days with the boys when he was traveling and working, I thought often about where he was and the important work he was doing for the state or nation. Thinking about what he was doing filled my mind with purpose, somehow making my loneliness easier. Now, without him calling frequently to make plans or consult with me about news of the day, the world shifted. I started to understand what life would be like without Mark, and it was amazing how quickly I became comfortable with the idea of it.

I knew he was in the Capitol the week after he left us at the beach, and I also know a few of his close friends went to be with him to berate him for thinking of going to see his mistress. Mark's old friends Jim Wheeler and Chad Walldorf went straight to Columbia to spend the night with Mark and to try to convince him not to see Belen again. Jim lives in Florida, and he flew to meet Mark, and Chad drove two hours to do so. Each loyal friend acted out of wanting to see Mark make the right decisions. They were trying, as had I, to hold him accountable to the values he had espoused and to the man they knew him to be. They thought they'd made some headway: Each called to tell me that they believed Mark understood the pain and problems he had caused and that they believed him when he said he wouldn't see her again.

Cubby Culbertson—the old friend who left his own family and work for two days to babysit Mark in New York—also proved to be a dear friend to Mark during this time as he repeatedly counseled him to follow the moral code outlined in the Bible and to get his heart pointed in the right direction.

In the fateful June press conference, Mark would refer to Cubby as a "spiritual giant," and I know that Mark regretted letting these friends down. Mark had people in his camp willing to go to great lengths to keep him focused in the right direction, and he didn't listen to a single one. I'm still a little awestruck at Mark's inability to listen to all these good, honest, and devoted friends. Moreover, that Mark seemed to have lost track of their worth to him shows how disconnected he had become.

But when he went missing, thoughts that he was with his lover in Argentina or elsewhere dominated my mind. Those suspicions were the subject of phone calls with friends and members of his staff who had scraps of information that suggested he'd traveled to the Appalachian Trail. As a gut response, I worried otherwise or that if he was there, perhaps he was not alone. And while I had an impulse to cover for him, to perpetuate his lies to protect our children, in truth, I didn't know for certain what he was doing.

So, when the reporter asked me if I knew where my husband was, I answered truthfully that I had no idea. I have heard since from people who read that quote, which was published in newspapers all over the country, that they wondered what my tone of voice was when I delivered that remark. In my memory, my tone was even, unremarkable. I didn't want to set off any alarms. One of my favorite Bible verses is Colossians 4:6, "Let your speech always be with grace, seasoned with salt." I said that Mark had a book contract and that he had been distracted. I didn't tell the reporter the *nature* of that distraction, of course. I simply said Mark and I had agreed he needed time to get his head straight and that he hoped to write. I so wish he actually had been writing.

I have always told the boys that lies come from fear, from cowardice. During the campaigns when they would be upset because Mark's political opponents were trying anything they could to knock Mark down, Mark and I would tell them that the truth gives you a backbone, a reason to stand tall and the means to do so. This was a message I felt deeply. Perhaps the only thing dealt with less than honestly and openly in my childhood was fear. When Mom was sick, our parents tried to make it seem like her cancer was not a big deal. We all knew her sister had just died of the same cancer. Despite what our parents told us, we kids were all afraid. That denial, and the fear underneath it, distorted our family in ways I think none of us appreciated until much later.

I recently asked my sister Gier why she never stood up for me or took my side in a certain disagreement I had with my mother during our turbulent teen years. Ever the peacemaker, Gier explained that she wanted to take my side, but she was afraid Mom was going to die and she didn't want to do anything to upset her.

Her logic makes perfect sense to me now, as a woman who has matured to appreciate the many shades of gray that come with conflicting loyalties. I adore Gier in a way that is only deepened by understanding that childhood struggle she was engaged in to keep her mom alive. We were not raised in a way or in a time or place where we could sit together and express our fears about losing our mom. If Mom was going to deny her illness with a big smile on her face, a splash of lipstick, and a pretty silk scarf, who were we to drag her into the living room and force her to confront it? We were children, children who carried so much inside that we didn't know how to express. I know how uncomfortable it made all of us to hold what was essentially a lie inside our hearts and to cover over that fear with all sorts of justifications and fantasies that were as extreme as the reality.

My mother never let the challenges of life divert her from her main goals. As children, we had no idea how she suffered and what terrors kept her awake at night. Now that I am an adult who has dealt repeatedly with comparatively minor skin cancers of my own, I have such profound admiration for my mother's persevering spirit. As the only survivor of an experimental cancer treatment program twenty years ago, she is an inspiration to me today because of her positive spirit. She was a warrior in the face of certain death. Mom wants to do the things that make her feel alive and give her days meaning. She never wanted to appear as if she was just about to die. She has her sights set on living as long as she can and enjoying every minute. I can see now how she didn't want to worry us, and as an adult I can respect that approach.

When the crisis of Mark's infidelity hit our family, however, without question I knew I would handle it in a different way for our children. I would face it head on, openly and honestly.

When Mark left the beach to "get his head straight" we

had still not told the boys any specifics about the nature of the tension between Mark and me. Before he went missing I knew I needed to reveal more to them about our circumstances, despite the advice of many who admonished me not to talk to the boys, not to burden them. My goal was honesty, but not brutal honesty. The message was brutal enough without me adding my pain. Was it possible, given everything I was feeling, to be both truthful and kind? Of course I would be kind to the boys and respectful of their love for their father. I had to find a way to explain things to them that would allow them to continue to love their dad and not force them to hate him out of loyalty to me or a desire to protect me.

When I sat the boys down, I explained to them that I had discovered in January that their dad was having an affair.

"Did they have sex?" asked Bolton.

"Yes, that's what an affair is about," I said.

I told them they didn't know the woman and they had nothing to do with causing the affair nor could they have prevented it. It was not their fault. I also told them that I loved their dad and was hopeful that he would keep his word as he had looked me in the eyes and said "I will not see her" when he left.

"Mom, that would be a pretty big lie if he sees her," Blake said.

"Yes," I agreed, "it would be a very big lie."

I assured the boys that I would never leave them and that they shouldn't worry about a thing because I would work to provide whatever they might need in the future. I was a little teary when discussing this painful personal subject with them, but I also felt as if a weight had been lifted after I shared this secret with my precious sons. No child should have to learn such things, but I wanted them to be well prepared in case the story got out; I didn't want them to learn about Mark's affair from the television or the public. We prayed together for Mark, for the choices he would make.

A few days later when I had reason to believe Mark was with his lover, I decided to sit down with the boys again and to tell them her name was Belen Chapur and that she lived in Argentina. The children thought of the notes Mark had recently sent each of them.

"That's it. His notes were good-bye," Blake said.

I was crushed by the hurt they must have felt at learning of his betrayal, and also by their thinking he might abandon them. Then with such clairvoyance Bolton exclaimed, "Oh my gosh. This is going to be worse than Eliot Spitzer!"

Yes, I thought, *unfortunately it will be.*

It broke my heart to call Marshall in the Turks and Caicos, where he was working a brief summer job, and to tell him the same things over the phone, just before his seventeenth birthday. I wanted to be with him to give him a big hug, but I made sure someone there kept a close eye on him. I was thankful in a way that he would miss the coming circus at home. In another way, though, I missed him deeply and I know his brothers did too. We were facing this as a family and taking strength from each other as we confronted our situation and our feelings honestly. What a mix of feelings we had. We had the shame of the betrayal and the coming public humiliation, but we also had our faith, our love of Mark and our family. I could see the gray of the confusion of conflicting emotions as clearly as I could see some part of it as black and white.

If there is any overriding message from this summer that I wanted our boys to remember it was that you may choose your sin but you cannot choose the consequences. Actions and sin do have consequences. The full consequences of the choices Mark made are still being discovered. I hope, though, that my boys have learned that dishonesty rarely serves one well, and it is always better to "walk in the truth."

I have long understood the concept that things may not be right with my circumstances but "it is well with my soul." Horatio Spafford, the man who wrote that song, had an even greater challenge to face than I did. All four of his daughters drowned in the Atlantic Ocean on a ship coming home from France. One of the lines in that song is "When sorrows like sea billows roll; Whatever my lot, Thou has taught me to say, 'It is well, it is well, with my soul.'" My circumstances were less tragic, but obviously not great. But I too had a peace in my soul. With Mark gone, with him no longer beseeching me for permission to betray me further, I could listen without disturbances to the strong voice of my true spirit. I felt a peace that came from knowing that I had acted in the best manner I knew possible in this marriage, I had loved to the best of my ability. It is well with my soul. But I would be completely well if I could forgive Mark fully and move on freely. If he was with her again after this clear restriction, could I?

In the governor's mansion, Landon occasionally dressed the bust of Ibra Blackwood in a blue wig, swim goggles, and a hat for the amusement of our visitors. Governor Blackwood is beloved for pardoning all the inmates on his mansion staff one Christmas long ago. So the story goes, he hung small envelopes with certificates of pardon bearing the name of each of the inmates on the Christmas tree in the large drawing room. How I wish the simple act of forgiveness in everyday life was as easy as hanging an ornament on a tree.

Of course, it was easy for Governor Blackwood to pardon those inmates; whatever they had done had happened to someone else, a family or an individual who even years later might still be struggling to forgive the person who caused that crime. When someone errs against us or causes harm, it is in our basic nature to fight back or to right a wrong. Watch any two children at play together long enough and you are bound to see one snatch a toy or stick from the other. The response is immediate. The wronged child grabs the toy back or screams and bops the other child over the head. Rarely is forgiveness instinctive. Forgiveness has to be learned, and even practiced, until it is easier to be truly and fully given. I had practiced it plenty, and if Mark was with his mistress again, my ability to do so would be tested further.

In a way, being in the political life has helped. Holding a

grudge takes time and energy. When I thought back to that letter to the editor I wrote during Mark's first campaign for Congress, I marveled at the amount of energy I expended on something that, if it were to happen today, wouldn't inspire a response at all. I've grown to ignore the lies printed about my husband or about me and I no longer try to right such perceived wrongs. I found that if I kept matters unresolved or bottled up, I was more engaged with that person than if I had forgiven them. I didn't want to spend the little time I had engaged in grudges. The more I let go, the freer I felt.

Yet I was not at all free from the kind of hurt Mark had inflicted. He had lied right to my face and gone to see his lover. He had deceived me, disregarded my emotions, my needs, my desires, my basic integrity. And this lie hurt the boys immensely, in ways unfathomable to me on so many levels. I walked the beach and reminded myself daily and joyfully of who I was and how I had been blessed. Yes I was truly blessed. I could feel that part. While I felt a genuine impulse to forgive, this time I knew it would not be easy and would take time and effort.

Every time I attend mass, the congregation asks aloud to be forgiven as we recite the Lord's Prayer, "forgive us our trespasses as we forgive others who trespass against us." We seek forgiveness from above, while we simultaneously are grantors of forgiveness to those around us. Matthew 7:4–5 says, "How can you say to your brother, 'Let me take the speck out of your eye' when all the time there is a plank in your own eye?

You hypocrite, first take the plank out of your own eye, and then you will see clearly to remove the speck from your brother's eye." I would be a hypocrite in my own eyes and in the eyes of the Lord for asking for forgiveness for my sins while judging Mark as unforgivable. The ultimate judgment is not mine; it is in the Lord's hands.

So too, it is the Lord who is responsible for making things right in this world. Mark had become so self-absorbed that he was lost. He had become so focused on his will and his desire that he was blinded to his actions and their consequences in a connected world. I understood that if Mark acted sinfully, it was not up to me to make him right or to punish him for his behavior. Mark was in charge of his behavior and, though I understood many of the trials he has faced, I reminded myself that I couldn't presume to know the challenges he has within.

Still, I continued to struggle with the concept. If I didn't forgive him, it would be as if I were saying that what he had done was too painful, too humiliating for anyone to say to him in any form that what he had done was okay. As much as that is true, I reminded myself that it was not my responsibility to mete out judgment. Saying "I forgive you" is not the same as saying "what you have done is okay." If I continued to deny Mark my forgiveness, I would remain entangled in his emotions. I knew that I couldn't force myself into his heart by refusing to forgive him. He was supremely self-absorbed, involved in his own tragedy, the tragedy of his lost chance of happiness with his one true soul mate, or however he might characterize it. He was not concerned about my feelings. I had become an abstraction to him, an obstacle, and whether I forgave him or not was irrelevant to what he would do next. Forgiveness, then, was for me.

As I walked the beach on those mornings of profound struggle, I thought again and again of the substance behind a favorite quote from Desmond Tutu, "forgiveness is the grace by which you enable the other person to get up, and get up with dignity, to begin anew." Forgiveness really is a gift for each of us. It gave us the freedom to move forward happily, free from our unfortunate situation.

Mark and I had long ago planned to go to Coosaw for July 4 so our house at the beach had been rented for that week, soon after Mark had returned from Argentina. I didn't want to spend a week at Coosaw given what was going on between Mark and me. My Mom and Dad were in Chicago for the summer and offered to let me use their house in Florida. Wanting to make this week special for the boys, and needing the strength and support of friends for me, we headed to Florida with Frannie and her four kids and two extra kids in tow.

We loaded the cars with surfboards, golf clubs, and tennis rackets and off we went. Denise, an old roommate from my time in New York, flew to meet me from her home in DC as did another friend from New York, Melissa. My sister Gier and her oldest son Fitz traveled from Chicago. The eleven kids kept us busy cooking big meals between all of the activities. My sister and girlfriends kept me laughing whenever possible.

We were all together the day Mark called to tell me that he had more explaining to do. Another woman, it seemed, had come forward and suggested to a member of the press that she had also had relations with Mark, which meant he would likely have to address the accusation with an AP reporter who would be interviewing him later in the day. I was gut-punched all over again. Mark had sworn to me when I'd discovered his secret back in January that Belen was the only "other" woman. Now he explained that there had been nothing much at all with this new woman, nothing he had felt I needed to know about before. Ever businesslike, he wanted to know what I thought he should reveal in the interview. Here again he was asking for *my advice* instead of first considering how the news might make me feel. Here again he was only really admitting his indiscretions because the woman had come forward, forcing him to come clean. I would soon learn—secondhand from the AP interview—that Mark had had yet more dalliances over the years, but that in his opinion he had not "crossed the line" as he'd done with Belen. When I pressed him for details when I saw him a few days later, I understood fully that his and my definition of an appropriate line were not at all the same.

Discovering that he had flirted with the idea of other affairs and perhaps even acted on some of his impulses was in a way more devastating than the public humiliation of the press conference when he returned from Argentina. How long, I wondered, had I had my head in the sand? I couldn't help but think I had been deceived through the entire marriage, and for the first time in all that painful year I felt duped. Mark had handled me the way he'd tried to handle the press. He'd given me just enough information when he had to, but clearly he hadn't given me the whole story. Not back in January. And maybe not even now. How could I know? How would I ever really know? I despaired about being able to forgive this bigger, broader hurt. I was about as close to breaking as one can be. I was testy, grumpy, teary, and exhausted.

My sister and girlfriends put up with me and supported me every step of the way. They made sure I took care of myself and that I remained focused on the kids and on deciding what was to come next with the kids and the marriage. Denise even made sure I started thinking about my future. Emails and letters poured in from around the country. We heard about people forming Jenny Sanford support groups and some organization began hawking t-shirts and mugs with "Team Jenny" on them. Denise registered web sites in my name and applied for a trademark so I would be protected from people exploiting my name and my image. I don't know what I would have done in this time without these and other friends and their loyal and loving support. I needed them desperately and they came through brilliantly.

Mark joined us in Florida at the end of the week to help drive home, and I found him to be surprisingly devoid of true remorse, only regret for the outcomes. Needless to say, I was incredibly disappointed and our drive home was tolerable for me because I had Mark drive with Frannie, who remained mostly silent except for the boys in her car roughhousing and harassing each other in the back.

After we returned from Florida, feeling spent by Mark and simultaneously recharged by my friends, Mark and I went to an intense five-day marriage counseling session. I got a lot out of this marathon session—I learned a lot about Mark's psychology and a lot about my own as well. Day after day of talking about yourself and probing your motivations was helpful to me. I came home from the counseling hopeful for my future, whether with Mark or without, but also had a renewed willingness to work one last time to improve things, for the sake of our kids. Mark seemed distant still, but promised me that the trip to Europe we had planned for the next week near the end of that summer would be great for the two of us and the kids. I didn't really want to go to Europe, but I didn't want to disappoint the boys; they had been earning money to help pay for the trip and their dedicated efforts should, I felt, be rewarded. (Bolton had walked the beach selling lemonade and water from a cart and Blake sold lemonade and performed magic tricks [!] from a stand on the street while Landon painted part of the house.) At that point, I was committed to reconciliation, though not much in Mark's actions gave me reason to be hopeful for it. But Mark repeatedly promised he would *show me* how committed he was, and this family trip to Europe, I reasoned, would give him a chance to start doing so.

But there wasn't much time for him to demonstrate his professed new resolve. This was another jam-packed Sanford family vacation with a cruise from Venice to the Greek isles along with time in London, Paris, and the beaches of Normandy, all in less than two weeks. Mark was considerate and sweet to me the first two days, and then he was hot and cold for the rest of the vacation. All in all, I think he was wallowing in his self-pity and still pining for his girl, while also trying to go through the motions to keep the marriage together. By the end of the trip, I couldn't wait to get home.

Before heading to Europe, in anticipation of a possible more permanent move to the beach, I had hired a contractor to add some bookshelves and closets and to paint and restore the interior of the house after its years of summer rentals. My Mom came through like a superstar and made sure the workmen did as promised while we were away. She got the house put back in shape with new computer lines and freshened up bedrooms for the boys. This was no small task in a short time and I was so thankful to have her there in charge.

The boys each said Europe was the highlight of their summer, so I guess Mark and I were able to keep it together in their eyes. On the last day, however, we took the Chunnel from Paris to London and were recognized by a member of the press on the train. On arrival in London, there was a small pack of paparazzi waiting for us, and it broke my heart to have the boys see Mark hounded like a criminal.

One thing was clear to me when we got back. Mark hadn't yet convinced me that he would be the least bit different in our marriage going forward. As soon as we got back to Columbia, therefore, I told the boys that we were moving back to the beach for the foreseeable future and that they would be changing schools. My not-so-secret hope was that Mark would be lonely in the big mansion by himself and that he'd glimpse the future that would be his if he continued to be so remote and unrepentant. Mark wasn't keen on the idea of us moving—he would miss us, he said, and he thought the move punished him too much—but he backed me up in order to present a united front to the boys. The boys were not wild about the move either, but with their parents in agreement, we started to prep for it.

I didn't look forward to having to move, but as it turned out, I had pleasant surprises in store for me. All I had to do was tell a few girlfriends of my planned move and they went into action. Some put fresh flowers in the pots at the beach so the house would feel lived in. Others showed up with garbage bags to help move things from the mansion, and another crew met us at the beach as we arrived. Mom smiled at me in the kitchen as the camera trucks waited for a tidbit of news at the end of the driveway. Mark had taken the boys to Coosaw for two days so that they wouldn't have to be a part of the chaos of the move, and so they too were pleasantly surprised to find peace, calm, and, to top it all off, private bedrooms at long last (and for the first time in their lives!) for Marshall and Landon.

If nothing else, this crisis has taught me never to take my friends for granted. Not that I ever have taken them for granted, but it reminded me that there are times in life when we absolutely need friends. We need to love them and we need to listen to them. Likewise there are times when we need our family. We can easily get into a position where we think we can do so much on our own, and often we can, but we are not meant to live alone. I can only imagine where I would be this very moment and what our family and future would be like if Mark had listened to and respected the advice of his dear friends instead of following his "heart."

FOURTEEN

NOTHING REJUVENATES MY SPIRIT MORE THAN A WALK ALONG the shore. Watching the willets scamper at the edge of the water as the tide ebbs calms me and makes me feel closer to God. In the quiet, unstructured time that comes when I can be still and soak up the wonders of His creation, it is difficult to feel anger or to wallow in my suffering. My daily walks there help me put my life in perspective, all of its insignificance, and all of His goodness.

Now that the boys and I have settled at the beach, we have relaxed into a comfortable rhythm. I am up early reading and then getting their breakfast. Then they race through their meals, and Marshall herds them into his truck. A few minutes later, they are peeling out of the driveway, gravel spraying, as they dash off to school. Then lovely peace, and hours ahead where I can think, or write, grocery shop or see a friend. But first, I can hear the beach calling to me as I open the gate to the path there. With each step I take away from the house, I release. Release from the bills to be paid, laundry to be folded, scraped knees to be kissed, and dreams, dreams yet to dream, let alone fulfill. And what of the dreams for our marriage that the house once contained? Who was I to Mark and who was he to me?

Daily chores mix with questions, images, and memories that sometimes distract me from what really matters and how I truly feel. Near the end of the path, my steps quicken with eagerness for the sea and the sense of order it can give to a disordered mind. And then I am there, with the Atlantic stretched wide before me. The sense of timelessness and the beauty I feel in this space helps me cultivate my faith.

There are days when I feel supported by its peace, charmed by the brightness as the foamy edges of waves timidly advance across the sand. Other days the sea is violent, tumultuous, aggressive with gritty wind and cold spray. Sometimes I look out across its peaceful and unruffled surface and wonder what turmoil remains below. The sea allows a world of contradictions. Tossed around by contradictions, I am steadied by my faith.

Faith is waking up every day with an attitude of gratitude, knowing that, as I once wrote in my journal, "This is the day the Lord has made, let us rejoice and be glad in it!" These were the thoughts that steadied me in this tumultuous year when my world fell to pieces. My pain was so intense and the future horribly uncertain, I took my faith from watching the sun set and knowing it surely would rise again, or watching the tides rush out, knowing the waters would flow back in. At that moment, faith needed to be just that simple for me to receive comfort from it, as everything I believed had suddenly shown itself to be untrue.

There were times when I walked with swift determination, in a heart-pounding frenzy, to shake these feelings out of me. Other walks, I went slowly, pausing to absorb the vastness. On days filled with turmoil and doubt, I wanted to know, to feel, that these problems were insignificant spread out across this calm expanse. I didn't always find peace there quickly, but my faith kept me searching until I did.

In July, just a few weeks after Mark's visit to Argentina, I was returning from a long walk on the beach when I saw a young woman helped to shore and saw the Sullivan's Island rescue squad speed out in search of another. The sea had stripped the woman of her clothes, and another woman had wrapped her in a t-shirt and towel. I hurried over to help comfort her. She said the friend she had been swimming with was not from the area, and had thought she knew how to handle the strong currents but proved not to be as strong a swimmer. The other woman and I prayed for her and for her lost friend. When it became clear that she was in good hands, I hurried home to make sure my boys were safe.

I called Marshall, who was with his brothers, and all were accounted for and safe at a nearby park. I began to cook dinner, watching the rescue helicopters as they circled in vain, searching for a young life. I thought, Lord I am listening. . . . what are you telling me? I began to sing happily while I made spaghetti. I have a beautiful home, a good life, and wonderful, happy, bright children. I have great friends and a loving family. I am fine and I am blessed beyond belief. In my journal the next day I wrote of joy: "Find joy every day. My problems are insignificant." I prayed, Psalm 139: "Search me, O God and know my heart; test me and know my anxious thoughts. See if there is any offensive way in me and lead me in the way everlasting." My heart has been pained but it is clean and I have peace. I have so much gratitude, there is no space, even in this vastness, for one drop of bitterness or regret.

I have many good girlfriends on the island, as well as my sister and friends nearby. On weekends, we often sit together while the kids tumble around. There are often communal dinners where someone brings a salad and someone else gets something on the grill. There seems now to be enough time for everything and yet each of these moments is too precious to waste. It is not perfect, but we have found balance.

I have been unwavering in my quest for understanding—for growth, knowledge, wisdom, and discernment. This has been true throughout my life and my marriage and certainly through these trying personal times. I have been patient and worked hard not to judge rashly or quickly but rather to understand, to learn. And I have learned. I learned that I need others to help and support me in trying times. I am vulnerable. I have learned just how loved I am. My family and friends have been incredible. My faith has remained strong and my God ever loving. I have also learned just how great and resilient our boys are and how undeserving of this crisis they truly are.

I have loved and will love again. I have lived these married years as loyally, as honestly, as lovingly and as committed as I could. I have worked hard and enjoyed our successes. I have given of myself, have been blessed with incredible friendships, and have worked on building character—mine and our children's. With the strength of my faith and the blessings in my midst I am ready for the next chapter of my life where I hope to fully live each day, love each moment, and find joy along the way. I have known that character, self-respect, and integrity are so difficult to develop and earn and so easy to lose. I have tried my best to act responsibly, patiently, and fairly and will freely welcome the next chapter with no regrets from the past and no fears for the future. I will persevere with my feet firmly planted—preferably with some sand between my toes—focused on my priorities and looking onward and ever upward.

AFTERWORD

My morning beach walks these days still begin with the dogs barreling past me as I open the gate to the path crowded with wild beach rose. But I have pep in my step now and more often than not, I've got upbeat music playing on my iPod. I'm able to smile happily, genuinely, at neighbors on the path.

This time last year, things were very different. My walks were anxiety-filled and much less happy; I had very little pep in my step, to say the least. Writing this book in the elapsed time has been incredibly cathartic. I in no way set out or wanted to "tell all" and I was conscious of how venturing into the unkind would hurt Mark, hurt our children, and hurt me, too; vengefulness was not an option. Rather I wanted to share my thoughts on faith, relationships, attitude, and priorities in life. I had a sense that there were many who could benefit from my perspective and I knew that if I could give of myself in this small way I would be better for it. The response I have received from readers everywhere proves the point: their comments and encouragement have been extraordinary and truly gratifying.

Some people have thanked me for the inspiration or helpful advice this book has somehow imparted to them. Many have shared their own tales of betrayal or loss and speak of what they gained from the book. Others told me the book helped them to repair their marriages or inspired them to make positive changes in their lives. Still more sent along encouraging verses or thoughts and warmed my heart by telling me that they continued to lift me and the boys up in prayer.

Hearing from so many about the trials in their lives or in their own marriages has confirmed my belief that facing challenges and heartache is universal; no one is totally immune. It also helped me put my own situation in perspective: there are so many people who bear far more serious burdens each and every day. But the letters and emails and phone calls and outreach have also reinforced my belief that leaning on our faith and our relationships with loving family and friends is the sure way to nurture inner strength, and it is the way to remain true to your best self.

Of course, a handful of people have also written to me less in support of what I've put to the page than with questions and comments about what I can best categorize as my "judgment," either in writing the book or in my decision to marry Mark in the first place. No question has been put to me more by pundits and the press (and it was put to me in almost every interview I gave in promoting this book) than one that has to do with a conversation I had with Mark before we were married, the one we had about Mark's vague concern over including the vow to be faithful in our wedding ceremony. "Didn't you see this as a sign that Mark might cheat?" some have asked. "Shouldn't that have been a red flag from the start?"

My response to this line of questioning was initially, both publically and privately, more than a little exasperated. I made it clear in the book, I'd point out to interviewers, that I never gave Mark a "pass" on the subject of faithfulness. Mark hadn't made a big deal of this issue and we didn't have a big, memorable argument about it, either. I tried to remind everyone who asked me about it that Mark and I talked his worry through to our mutual satisfaction. And anyway, I'd tack on, how could I have known then what would come to pass? Mark's being unfaithful was *not* inevitable; it was his choice, just as choosing to remain faithful was within his power as well.

Now that I've had more time to consider the question—and to think about how best to describe my train of thought all those years ago—I am less exasperated yet also *more* confident in the way I handled Mark's "concern." I'm no less sure today that Mark did have what it takes to be true and I still believe that we wanted the same things from our marriage. I still don't think I was wrong to try to really listen to his concern and reassure him of what I saw to be his inherent goodness and trustworthiness. I didn't browbeat him or force him to include specific language in the ceremony (indeed, not unlike so many who use their own language or who choose other vows from the menu of options, we did not include that particular phrase), but rather I made sure he agreed and understood fully that marriage was in and of itself a commitment to each other and a vow of fidelity, regardless of the words spoken. My love for him may have clouded my thinking, as some have said, but even if that's true, I am happy to report that even knowing what I know now, I wouldn't change a thing about our wedding, our vows, or our promises to each other. Indeed, I was joyful at the prospect of marrying Mark, and I was happy being married to him for a good, long time. I am profoundly grateful that four wonderful sons came of our union. I can only imagine what it would be like to live one's life with such doubt and so little ability to trust, but I see nothing positive in doubting my part in a long-dead conversation. I see nothing gained from trying to ferret out the first inkling that Mark might stray.

Even as I am a firm believer in marriage—and in my decision to get married to Mark—it is now public knowledge that I ultimately decided to walk away from my own. Coincidentally, my divorce was made final shortly after the initial publication of *Staying True*. An unfortunate chapter in my story, to be sure, but not the last.

In an essay for *Reader's Digest* in the late 1980s called "Requiem for a Marriage," the novelist and fellow South Carolinian Pat Conroy wrote that "each divorce is the death of a small civilization. Two people declare war on each other, and their screams and tears infect their entire world with the bacilli of their pain. The greatest fury comes from the wound where love once issued forth." There is no question that when a marriage unravels there is a great deal of pain, hurt, and anguish involved. Our boys certainly understand the role their dad's actions played in the demise of our marriage, and yet like all children, they just wanted the family to stay together and for us to remain married. On this subject Pat Conroy went on, eloquently: "Divorces without children are minor-league divorces. To look into the eyes of your children and to tell them that you are mutilating their family and changing all their tomorrows is an act of desperate courage that I never want to repeat." I made the decision to divorce and I have felt the pain it has caused the children, their dad's actions notwithstanding. Nevertheless, the boys are adjusting as well as can be expected and have all flourished in the first year of their new school now that we are home on the coast. Time will truly tell the impact of their parents' divorce, but in the meantime I will continue to do the best that I can to nurture and love them as we all digest the many real changes in our lives. Regardless of what comes next for me, they remain my first priority and the time I have invested with them will ultimately yield my greatest legacy.

In the final analysis, I know I gave Mark more chances than he probably deserved to start to make things right between us, but he repeatedly chose not to rise to the challenge. However badly he might have wanted to, he wasn't able to come back to me, to our life, and to our commitment. Coming to terms with this was tough and terrible at times. I grieved for our past, for our future, for the happiness we once had and couldn't seem to find again. The grief came in great waves and I wondered if it would ever stop. But ultimately, I have found great peace and have no regrets. By acting carefully and prayerfully I was spared the kind of protracted hand-wringing and angst people assume of my situation. The grief passes. I can say with some little pride that I have survived the process of getting a divorce and am getting on with the process of adjusting to life without a marriage.

The result, so far, has been not only liberating and gratifying, but it has opened up new possibilities and opportunities for a successful and fulfilling future. I now face new challenges as a single mother and with sons whose world was also turned upside down, but I am experiencing the joys of being back in a home of my own, in a real neighborhood, void of politics and the press for the most part. The boys, too, are learning what it is like to live like normal boys, mostly outside of the fishbowl.

I've found another silver lining in terms of work, too. When Mark and I were married, I always figured that when our kids were old enough, I would go back to work in some form that would really challenge and satisfy me. I can now see, however, that my willingness (indeed my choice) to play "second fiddle" to Mark's career aspirations had become entrenched. I'm not so sure I could have reinvented myself professionally in his shadow and found true satisfaction. Now I can look at employment opportunities in a whole different light.

Last but certainly not least, I can now look at romance differently, too. I have the mature knowledge of how difficult relationships can be and I understand how to humbly work through differences—after all, I was able to make it twenty years with someone! Instead of looking at a long-term relationship as one that might include raising a family, I can look—if I choose—for someone to enjoy the opportunities that come with experience and maturity, to relish watching those same gains in my sons, and to share the possible blessings of grandparenthood. I can seek someone to grow old with, respectfully, peacefully, and happily. My expectations for a relationship are different, more open, more accepting, and yet I have the comforting, underlying, and fundamental knowledge that I don't need a romantic relationship at all. I have long known that my happiness comes from within, with God's help, and it is something I choose daily.

I have also come to know fully that I am not in control of anything but my own daily choices. I have done my best to live well and will continue to do so. I have loved fully and have loved well—there is no reason I cannot do so again. I have been successful as an independent woman and as a married woman and see no reason why I cannot be successful as a mature but divorced woman, too. I have lived a full and mostly happy life and as I approach fifty I truly believe that, for me, the best is yet to come.

—JENNY SANFORD, July 2010

ACKNOWLEDGMENTS

One of the incredible blessings of life in the public eye has been, for me, the outpouring of support from people of all walks of life across South Carolina and even from some across the nation. These are people who have helped us and our family in different ways throughout the various campaigns we have endured or through Mark's time in office or trials along the way. Some licked envelopes or volunteered their time, others raised or donated money, some sent notes of support or said encouraging words on the street, and countless told us they were praying for us. In all the years of public service, I never felt as if we walked alone. For that I will remain forever grateful. This book would not be possible without your collective support.

Of course, this book would not be on shelves without the

able help of my editor, Marnie Cochran; my publisher, Libby McGuire; my collaborator, Danelle Morton; and my agent, Joy Tutela. A fine team of strong women. We worked together beautifully, happily, and in record time—a real accomplishment. My thanks to you all.

The people who have helped me on this incredible journey of life are too numerous to mention by name but I would not be where I am today without your constant love and support. My family, especially my parents, have been unfailing cheerleaders and a great safety net. My girlfriends, from all the various stages and places in my life, have been so loyal and always there to laugh together, give a hug, share a smile, or lend a shoulder to cry on. I appreciate you all more than you know.

My boys have been a constant source of love and joy, and they are my greatest legacy. I am grateful for each one of them.

And finally I am thankful for the many blessings I have received from my God, and most of all for His unfailing love.

Staying True

———◆———

JENNY SANFORD

A Reader's Guide

QUESTIONS AND TOPICS FOR DISCUSSION

1. Many people feel that memoir is a compelling genre because real life is sometimes stranger than fiction. Were you interested in Jenny Sanford's memoir because of the well-publicized events it chronicles? Did the book satisfy your hope for details about how she dealt with this difficult time in her life?

2. *Staying True* chronicles the long span of the Sanford marriage—more than twenty years from the day they met—yet Jenny Sanford chose to begin and end the book with events from the summer of 2009. Do you feel this drew you into the story? Kept you in suspense? Or dealt up-front with what many people already knew about Mrs. Sanford? How did the author's storytelling decisions affect your reading experience?

3. Jenny Sanford has said that she hopes that telling her story will help other readers who are in the throes of a difficult time in their lives, and that the book will help others stay true to their deepest-held values in order to make decisions that are right *for them*; it is not meant to be prescriptive. Still, did you learn anything from Mrs. Sanford? Do you feel that you might better be able to weather your personal storms for having read about the way she dealt with her own?

4. Deep religious faith gave Jenny Sanford great comfort throughout the marital ordeal described in this book and has been a guiding force throughout her life. Has your own faith provided you similar comfort in trying times? How do you think Jenny's experience would have been different without this central anchor in her life?

5. When faced with the decision to stay or to leave after discovering a husband's infidelity, so many women feel trapped by their circumstances. For some it's a financial issue, for others, the needs of their children or families complicate their decision. What do you think trapped Jenny Sanford in place?

6. In late 2009, Jenny Sanford filed for divorce and in early 2010, the divorce was granted. Because she felt that she had given Mark Sanford every opportunity to do right by their marriage and because she did not act rashly when she first

learned of his betrayal, she felt great peace in making the decision to divorce. Does the news of the Sanford divorce surprise you? Do you think you would have ultimately come to the same decision?

7. Being a mother has made Jenny Sanford's life richer than she could have imagined, but being a mother also complicated things when she was forced to confront the problems in her marriage; she very much wanted to teach her children about both forgiveness and acting with dignity, two things that were, at times, hard to reconcile. Do you think she has provided a good role model for her sons in this regard?

8. If you are a mother, do you think that role colors your ability to make decisions and/or complicates your idea of right and wrong?

9. Consider the different ways that the Sanfords nurtured or deflected friendships in their lives and the way that they then leaned on or isolated themselves from friends during this difficult time. Do their experiences help you see your own friendships more clearly and/or encourage you to be more or less appreciative of your friends?

10. Jenny Sanford provides an up-close perspective on gubernatorial and congressional politics. What do you think of politics and politicians in light of what she reveals?

11. Do you feel that the ego stroking and lack of privacy that come with being a political figure contributed to Mark Sanford's actions? How do you think political stresses affected Jenny and the marriage in general?

12. Which aspects of Jenny Sanford's personality do you identify with most? With which do you identify with the least?

13. How has *Staying True* impacted you? Do Jenny Sanford's choices and decisions change the way you think about your own life story?

ABOUT THE AUTHOR

JENNY SULLIVAN SANFORD was born and raised in Winnetka, Illinois. A graduate of Georgetown University, she now lives on Sullivan's Island, South Carolina, with her four sons.

Join the Random House Reader's Circle to enhance your book club or personal reading experience.

Our FREE monthly e-newsletter gives you:

- Sneak-peek excerpts from our newest titles

- Exclusive interviews with your favorite authors

- Special offers and promotions giving you access to advance copies of books

- Fun ideas to spice up your book club meetings: creative activities, outings, and discussion topics

- Opportunities to invite an author to chat with your book group on the phone

- Anecdotes and pearls of wisdom from other book group members . . . and the opportunity to share your own!

To sign up, visit our website at
www.RandomHouseReadersCircle.com

When you see this seal on the outside, there's a great book club read inside.

de Smith and Brazier

Constitutional and Administrative Law

Sixth Edition by
Rodney Brazier

Penguin Books

PENGUIN BOOKS

Published by the Penguin Group
Penguin Books Ltd, 27 Wrights Lane, London W8 5TZ, England
Penguin Books USA Inc., 375 Hudson Street, New York, New York 10014, USA
Penguin Books Australia Ltd, Ringwood, Victoria, Australia
Penguin Books Canada Ltd, 10 Alcorn Avenue, Toronto, Ontario, Canada M4V 3B2
Penguin Books (NZ) Ltd, 182–190 Wairau Road, Auckland 10, New Zealand

Penguin Books Ltd, Registered Offices: Harmondsworth, Middlesex, England

First published 1971
Second edition 1973
Reprinted with minor revisions 1974
Third edition 1977
Fourth edition 1981
Fifth edition, published in Pelican Books, 1985
Reprinted with minor revisions 1986
Sixth edition 1989
Reprinted in Penguin Books, 1990
10 9 8 7 6 5

Printed in England by Clays Ltd, St Ives plc
Filmset in 9/11 pt Monophoto Times

Contents

Preface

More structural changes have been made to this edition than to any previous one. The chapter on the Crown and the royal prerogative had become rather unwieldy, and so the material on the prerogative in relation to external affairs has been used as the basis for a new chapter 7. More importantly, a new chapter has been written on the protection of human rights. This has been done in order to set Part Five on Civil Rights and Freedoms into perspective, to expand greatly the space devoted to the European Convention on Human Rights, and to evaluate more fully the case for a new, home-grown bill of rights. The discussion of the legislation on racial and sexual discrimination has been incorporated into this chapter. Other rearrangements of material have also been made. For example, the chapter on tribunals and inquiries has been put back so that the reader now proceeds from the introductory chapter on administrative law straight into the two chapters on judicial review, without having to make an excursion into tribunals and inquiries. Again, I have relocated the pages on ministerial responsibility from the chapter on the Prime Minister and the Cabinet (the words in the title of which are now transposed to reflect its contents more accurately) to the chapter on Ministers, departments and civil servants so as to stress the fact that the concept does not vary according to whether a Minister is or is not a member of the Cabinet. Two other chapters, 5 and 12, have been slightly retitled.

It would be difficult to list even the most important changes in constitutional and administrative law which have taken place in the last four years and which are reflected in this new edition. Some may, however, be cited by way of example. In chapter 3 on the United Kingdom a full account is given of attempts at further devolution in Northern Ireland, and of the Anglo-Irish Agreement. Chapter 5 on the

United Kingdom and the European Community has been considerably expanded to give a fuller description and assessment of the institutions of the Community and of Community law, particularly as the latter affects United Kingdom law and practice. In Part Two on the Executive the available evidence is presented about Mrs Thatcher's use of Cabinet committees and of informal groups of Ministers in arriving at decisions; inevitably in doing so Mrs Thatcher's style of government is considered. A new section has been added on the confidentiality of Cabinet proceedings and papers. The use of leaks by Ministers is further described, as are the effects of the Westland affair in that regard, as well as in others. In the chapter on public boards and the economy, a full account is given of the massive privatization programme. In Part Three on Parliament and Legislation the explanation of the principal rules of electoral law has been amplified, and the changes made by the Representation of the People Act 1985 have been incorporated. Further modest and useful reforms suggested by the Select Committee on Procedure are noted, although few have been adopted by the House of Commons. Much more detail is entered into on the work of the departmental select committees; there again the Westland affair has proved instructive. Part Four on Justice, Police and Local Government contains much new writing. Chapter 19 on the administration of justice gives a full account of the Crown Prosecution Service and of the Lord Chancellor's principles and policies in relation to judicial appointments and promotions. Chapter 21 on local government records the many alterations to local authority power made by Mrs Thatcher's Government – the most radical since the nineteenth century, but in this case so as to decrease rather than to enhance local government powers. Parliament has affected the content of Part Five on Civil Rights and Freedoms with legislation such as the Interception of Communications Act 1985, the Public Order Act 1986, the Immigration Act 1988 and the Criminal Justice Act 1988 (as it affects extradition law); the courts have influenced Part Six on Administrative Law in such areas as the availability of judicial review, the doctrine of legitimate expectation, public interest immunity and several others.

I have excised outdated material which no longer helps us to understand the modern constitution, but the new material added has produced by far the longest of all the six editions of the book. In preparing it, I happily record my thanks to my regular correspondent Mr Geoffrey Lock, Assistant Librarian of the House of Commons Library, for his generous help on many detailed points. I have included cross-references to my *Constitutional Practice* in which there is a much fuller treatment of a number of topics.

The change in the title of the book reflects my association with it since 1977. I am well aware, however, that this book is nowhere near as good as it would have been had Stanley de Smith lived.

I have sought to state the law and describe constitutional developments down to January 1989.

Rodney Brazier

Part One

General Foundations

The first chapter asks some elementary questions and indicates answers. What do we mean by a constitution? What matters are dealt with in the constitutions of other countries? Why have we no written constitution in Britain? In what circumstances (if any) might we adopt one? How can constitutions be classified?

Chapter 2 outlines the main features of the British constitution today. It touches very briefly on the theory of the rule of law and the doctrine of separation of powers. It reviews the sources of British constitutional law. And then it goes on to deal at some length with conventions of the constitution, those rules of political practice which have played such an important part in the British system of government. How do they differ from rules of strict law? In what sense are conventions 'rules'? How does one identify conventions? It is easier to ask some of these questions than to answer them. A number of individual conventional rules will be examined in later chapters. In this chapter we give a preliminary indication of the impact of European Community law on the constitutional law of this country.

The integral parts of the United Kingdom and of the British Islands (two quite separate concepts in our law) are examined in chapter 3. The continued attempts to provide a satisfactory constitutional framework for Northern Ireland are described, including the important Anglo-Irish Agreement of 1985. And unsuccessful attempts to provide for legislative devolution to Scotland and Wales are noted.

In chapter 4 still more awkward questions are asked. In other countries the constitution is the supreme law. In this country Parliament is traditionally supposed to be entitled to pass any law whatsoever on any subject whatsoever. What makes a constitution valid and supreme? Why is (or was) Parliament sovereign? How do judges behave in other countries when a revolutionary change of government takes place and the new rulers act in ways unauthorized by the constitution? This is a basic question about the foundations of a legal system. Can Parliament's law-making authority ever be restricted? If so, how? Is it really entitled to legislate for any part of the world? Can it effectively limit its own powers in any way? Have its powers been limited by Britain's accession to the European Communities and the enactment of the European Communities Act 1972? Here we take a closer look at Community law doctrine and its repercussions on the legal concept of parliamentary sovereignty. We do not yet know whether or when United Kingdom courts will change their attitude towards Acts of Parliament. The suggested answers to quite a lot of the questions posed in this chapter are somewhat speculative. Students may find parts of it difficult. They should not be despondent. The subject-matter of later chapters will be more down-to-earth. Anyone who feels so inclined can read chapter 4 again, and more closely, at a later stage. But what is said about Community law needs to be noted.

Chapter 5 examines in more detail the relationship between the United Kingdom and the European Community. The chapter has been expanded; the political background, purposes and institutions, and the law of the Community are surveyed and the effect of the Single European Act is explained.

Chapter 1

Constitutions[1]

What are constitutions?

When de Tocqueville observed that the British constitution did not exist, few people took his remark at its face value. Lawyers have not been deterred from writing books about constitutional law, nor are books by non-lawyers on the British constitution in short supply. Dicey's assertion that we had no administrative law in Britain was a more serious matter; it frightened writers away from the subject for many decades, and only in the last thirty years or so has the practising side of the legal profession come to regard administrative law (or the law relating to public administration) as a living reality, wholly worthy of study. But the study of the law of the constitution earned respectability long ago.

In the vast majority of modern states or political societies there exists an identifiable document, or a group of documents, called the constitution, embodying a selection of the most important rules about the government of the country. Books on constitutional law in these countries are usually commentaries on this special document or group of documents – on the historical circumstances in which a constitution came to be adopted, on the political and philosophical assumptions underlying it, on the special position of authority enjoyed by the constitution within the legal order, on the individual provisions of the constitution and their implications, on their amendment, interpretation and practical operation. In so far as these commentaries stray beyond the bare text of the constitution, they show that the terms 'constitution' and 'constitutional law' can be and often are used in a wider sense, to describe matters which are thought to be of 'constitutional' importance

[1] Several of the points made in this chapter are set out with exemplary lucidity by Sir Kenneth Wheare in his *Modern Constitutions* (2nd edn, 1966).

– importance, that is to say, in understanding what lies behind and beyond the 'constitution', so that the constitution can be understood as a central feature, but not the sole feature, of the rules regulating the system of government. If the term 'constitution' thus acquires a penumbra of ambiguity, this is not a matter of any great consequence.

And so studies of constitutional law are likely to range into history, political and legal theory, political science, and legislative and political practice. In those countries where courts have power to inquire into the compatibility of legislative and administrative action with the constitution, books and lecture courses on constitutional law will include a lot of material about judicial review. This is the position in, for example, the United States, Canada, Australia and India. In the United States today it would be absurd to consider the meaning of constitutional expressions such as 'freedom of speech', 'due process of law', and 'the equal protection of the laws', except by scrutinizing recent judicial interpretation, which happens to be far more significant than what the framers of the constitution and its amendments meant or thought they meant by those expressions. Similarly, in Canada the general power of the Federal Parliament to make laws for the 'peace, order and good government of Canada'[2] loses its deceptive simplicity when viewed in the context of restrictive judicial decisions. In Australia the meaning of the important constitutional guarantee of absolute freedom of inter-state trade and commerce has been moulded by the High Court in a series of leading cases by a process of unavowed judicial legislation.

Quite often the text, or much of the text, of a constitution is not intended to be taken literally. It sets out the framework of government, postulates how it ought to operate, and makes declarations about the purposes of the State and society and the rights and duties of citizens; but no real sanction is provided against violation of particular provisions of the constitution. Much of the constitution is 'programmatic', an affirmation of dogma or of objectives to be realized one fine day.[3] In such countries the study of constitutional law may be hardly distinguishable from jurisprudence or political theory; the books on the subject can still be bulky and verbose.

Although written constitutions differ widely in their purposes, form and content, they will normally be found to have two characteristics in common. They will be the fundamental law of the land; and they will be a kind of higher law. They will be fundamental law in so far as they

[2] Constitution Act 1867, s. 91.
[3] See, for example, J. F. Triska (ed.), *Constitutions of the Communist Party States* (1968).

designate the principal organs of government and invest them with authority; thus, they will constitute and define the Legislature, and state what is the scope of its law-making power and the procedure for exercising that power. In other words, they will be the law behind the law – the legal source of legitimate authority. They will also, as a rule, be a higher form of law, in that the law (or some of the law) set out in the constitution will be hierarchically superior to other laws and will not be alterable except by a specially prescribed procedure for amendment. In a number of countries, courts have jurisdiction to pronounce laws inconsistent with the constitution to be invalid.[4] In order to escape such a fate, a law will have to be properly adopted as a constitutional amendment; and the same procedure will normally apply to a measure designed to 'amend' the constitution by way of addition without subtraction. Procedures for constitutional amendment differ widely from one another, but they usually require the amending measure to be passed by special majorities in the Legislature, or to be submitted to the people voting at a referendum, or both. It is perfectly possible, and is indeed not uncommon nowadays, for various provisions of a constitution to be alterable in different ways; some may be alterable by an ordinary legislative enactment, and others 'entrenched' at various levels against legislative encroachments, depending on the degree of importance originally attached to particular parts of the constitution. In West Germany and Cyprus, certain constitutional provisions were expressed to be unalterable by any means. To this extent the constitutions of those countries were, of course, rigid. But the rigidity or flexibility of written constitutions cannot be ascertained merely by comparing procedures for constitutional amendment. A constitution containing a cumbersome procedure for its own amendment may in fact be very flexible if there is no effective opposition to the party in power; and the majority of modern states have authoritarian régimes. The constitution of Sri Lanka (formerly Ceylon),[5] on the other hand, remained remarkably stable for nearly twenty-five years, although most or all of it could be changed, quite simply, by a bill commanding the support of two-thirds of the members of the House of

---

[4] Judicial review of the constitutionality of legislation is not accepted in a number of other countries (for example, France). Unconstitutional legislation may consequently be deemed to be valid for the purposes of application and enforcement in the courts. The only remedy against this usurpation of legislative power will be political.

[5] A republican constitution was adopted in 1972, by a Constituent Assembly, not following the procedure for amendment prescribed by the independence constitution. This was a deliberately contrived 'breach of legal continuity', designed to give Sri Lanka an 'autochtchonous', or home-grown, constitution. See p. 66.

Representatives. The main reason for its durability was the existence of a volatile multi-party system, in which governments were preoccupied with sustaining their own position in a usually unsuccessful attempt to avoid defeat at the next election.

As every beginner knows, the United Kingdom has no 'constitution' in the narrower sense of the term. There is no document or group of documents called the British constitution. But since Britain has a regular system of government, with a complex of rules defining the composition, functions and interrelationship of the institutions of government, and delineating the rights and duties of the governed, Britain does have a constitution and a body of constitutional law, if these terms are used in a broader sense. Even if Britain did have a formal written constitution, this would not necessarily determine the boundaries of the study of British constitutional law, for many rules of constitutional interest would not be found in the written document itself. In the absence of such a document, an author's selection of topics has to be conditioned by what he personally regards as relevant or instructive.

Why, then, have we no 'constitution'? Why does nearly every other country in the world have one? What topics would probably be dealt with in a constitution for Britain, and why? Before trying to offer answers to these questions, one must touch upon a preliminary problem. Some English lawyers will say that to adopt a written constitution would be pointless. It would be pointless because such a constitution would have no higher sanctity than an ordinary Act of Parliament; it could be amended or repealed the next day by another Act of Parliament, just as if it were an Act for the licensing of rat-catchers. For it is (or has been) a fundamental rule of British constitutional law that the United Kingdom Parliament is incapable of restricting its own omnipotence.

Now, the question of parliamentary sovereignty raises some extremely difficult issues, which we shall examine in chapter 4. For example, how 'fundamental' are the rules about the omnipotence of Parliament? For the moment it is enough to say that an orthodox opinion does not become unassailable merely because it is widely held by distinguished authorities.

What goes into constitutions?

Constitutions are primarily about political authority and power – the location, conferment, distribution, exercise and limitation of authority and power among the organs of a State. They are concerned with matters of procedure as well as substance. More often than not they also include explicit guarantees of the rights and freedoms of individuals. And sometimes, as we have noted, they incorporate ideological pronouncements – principles by which the State ought to be guided or to which it ought to aspire, and statements of the citizens' duties.

There is no pre-ordained stereotype of an ideal constitution. The form and content of a constitution will depend first on the forces at work when the constitution is established and amended, secondly on common-sense considerations of practical convenience, and thirdly on the precedents available to the politicians and their advisers who draw up the constitution. The first and third points may be particularly important. For instance, there was a very big difference between Ghana's independence constitution of 1957 and its republican constitution of 1960. The 1957 constitution was incorporated in an Order in Council drafted in London after an Independence Conference. The 1960 constitution was drafted in Ghana. The former was a 'Westminster model' type of constitution, an agreed compromise package-deal[6] embodying a parliamentary executive and various safeguards for individual and minority group interests. The latter was made to suit the requirements of Dr Nkrumah alone; it provided for a presidential form of government and included no significant safeguard for the interests of individuals or groups which might have resisted the pretensions of the Convention People's Party. In 1964 the constitution was further amended to make Ghana a single-party state. Clearly the changes made in 1960 and 1964 were strongly influenced by constitutional precedents set in neighbouring French-speaking African states. After the fall of Nkrumah in 1966, local opinion swung away from single-party authoritarianism, and the constitution adopted in 1969 included a wide range of devices designed to prevent serious abuses of legislative and executive power. To put the matter in another way, Ghana had reverted, at least for the time being, to 'constitutionalism' or the idea of limited government. But in less than three years the régime was overturned by a military *coup*. Constitutions in developing countries are apt to prove frail structures, mainly because so much value is attached to the acquisition and retention of political power. Changes of government are likely to be usurpations of power, followed by the suspension or supersession of the constitution.

[6] See generally, Y. P. Ghai and J.P.W.B. McAuslan, *Public Law and Political Change in Kenya* (1970), chs 5, 13.

A written constitution for Britain?

Every independent Commonwealth country has a written constitution, with the exception of Britain itself, Israel[7] and a few countries which are in the process of reconstructing new constitutions in place of old ones that have been overturned. All British colonies have had a written constitution. Indeed, so has nearly every country in the world.[8] Why does Britain stand out as an anomaly?

The answer lies above all in the facts of history. In other countries constitutions have been granted or adopted to mark stages in a progression towards (or a regression from) self-government, to establish the foundations of the machinery of government in a newly independent State (for example, the United States, Cyprus) or a reconstituted State (for example, Malaysia, Tanzania), or to rebuild the machinery of government following the wreckage caused by defeat in war, or to start afresh after a revolutionary upheaval or because of widespread dis-illusionment with the existing régime, or even to signify a change in ideological attitudes. With very few exceptions, governments in the modern world feel it necessary to point to a constitution as the source of their authority – if only as a badge of legitimacy or respectability.

In Britain none of these factors has been effectively at work. England has not been unambiguously defeated in war, or at least has not been successfully invaded (save by special invitation) since 1066. There were, it is true, two revolutions in England during the seventeenth century. The Civil War of 1642–8 ended with the execution of Charles I in 1649 and the establishment of a republican Commonwealth. From the ferment of political ideas there emerged in 1653 an authentic written constitution, skeletal but readily identifiable, the Instrument of Government. But in the welter of controversy this document (which was to be influential in the North American colonies) was soon reduced to the status of a scrap of paper; the revolution petered out and Charles II was restored in 1660. In 1688 James II was deposed after a reign of three years; the Crown was offered to a usurper, William of Orange, who accepted it jointly with his wife Mary, James II's daughter, and the Glorious Revolution triumphed. The revolutionaries, however, were insistent that they were nothing more than the conservators of the ancient rights and liberties of the people, which James had been seeking

---

[7] See E. Likhovski, *Israel's Parliament: The Law of the Knesset* (1971). New Zealand had no written constitution until 1987: her constitution now consists of a consolidation of previously scattered enactments, together with some new law. See Constitution Act 1986 (New Zealand).

[8] See A. Blaustein and G. Flanz, *Constitutions of the Countries of the World.*

to subvert. James, moreover, was deemed to have abdicated. Apart from changing the line of succession to the throne, and enacting, in the Bill of Rights 1689, some fairly important limitations on the royal prerogative, Parliament attempted no fundamental restatement of the constitution. To have made such an attempt would have been politically imprudent,[9] and in any event this was not a time when constitutions had become fashionable. And, indeed, instead of laying the foundations of a written constitution, it formed a base for the concept of untrammelled parliamentary sovereignty. Since then the serenity of historical continuity has survived Jacobite revolts, the French Revolutionary and Napoleonic Wars, riots at home and some bloodied noses in far-away encounters; and the two World Wars of the twentieth century have ended in victory. In modern times Britain has known neither the humiliation of conquest nor the turmoil of full-scale revolution.

Since England was a sovereign State for many centuries, the question of adopting a constitution on the attainment of independence did not arise. But in 1707 England ceased to be an independent State. It entered into union with the independent State of Scotland. This union was founded on Articles of Union negotiated by commissioners representing the two Parliaments, and it was consummated by separate Acts of Union merging the two Parliaments into a new Parliament of the United Kingdom of Great Britain. The Articles of Union, incorporated with the Scottish Act in the English Act of Union, were expressed to be fundamental and unalterable conditions of the Union. They provided a rudimentary framework of a written constitution. Yet south of the border the Act of Union has not been regarded as enjoying any greater binding force in strict law than other statutes of major constitutional importance.[10]

There are other reasons why the question of adopting a written constitution has seldom been seriously agitated – insularity, a lack of interest in political philosophy, a dearth of enthusiasm among politicians for restraints that might impede their freedom of action when in office, a relatively high degree of homogeneity, a latitudinarian and pragmatic approach to religious and political differences, and a widely

[9] Immediately after the Revolution, when the conditions under which the throne should be offered to William and Mary were being discussed, more radical views were canvassed, but they were shelved because an ensuing controversy would have delayed the settlement; see T. P. Taswell-Langmead's *English Constitutional History* (11th edn, 1960), p. 447; J. R. Western, *Monarchy and Revolution* (1972), ch. 9.

[10] See further, p. 73. The legal effect of the Act of Union with Ireland 1800 has also been a matter of controversy.

diffused acceptance of traditional forms, gradualism and parliamentary methods. Britain's one intractable political (and religious) problem was Ireland; and it is significant that it was in relation to Ireland, in 1885, that fundamental thinking about the restructuring of the British constitution came to the surface. Only after the First World War, with the partitioning of Ireland and the creation of a separate Irish Free State (later Eire, and now the Republic of Ireland), was it possible to sweep this embarrassing problem under the carpet – till 1969.

Has there been any recent development important enough to warrant serious speculation about the prospects of adopting a written constitution for the United Kingdom?

1   A number of factors have tended to undermine social stability or to depress national morale in Britain. From time to time there is disillusionment with the main political parties, a 'credibility gap' between promise and achievement; a more sober awareness that any British Government's freedom of action in international and economic affairs is severely circumscribed; a realization that Britain has become less prosperous than several other industrial countries, that the individual citizen and his parliamentary representative count for little in public affairs, that ancient faiths and habits of deference to authority rest on insecure foundations. But if there are widely diffused feelings of malaise and pessimism, they have yet to crystallize in any general demand for basic constitutional change, although the Alliance parties, and latterly the Democrats, have campaigned for parliamentary elections to be based on a system of proportional representation, and the enactment of a new Bill of Rights.

2   By acceding to the European Communities on 1 January 1973, the United Kingdom accepted obligations entailing profound changes in our constitutional law. But it is perfectly possible to be a member of the Communities without having a written constitution. If, however, the Communities were to develop into a federal super-State – and that is still a remote prospect – we should probably need to have a written constitution so as to define the limited competence of our domestic organs of government.

If, however, it were legally possible – and we shall beg this question for the time being – to create a federal constitution, hierarchically superior to any parliamentary body in the United Kingdom, then the study of constitutional law in this country would attain new dimensions. We should have to consider judicial review of the constitutionality of legislation – a matter which up to now has affected only Northern

Ireland. And then there would be other questions to ask. Apart from restrictions on the *territorial* competence of the Legislature, should there not be introduced restrictions on the *type* of legislation it was competent to pass? For instance, might it not be a good thing to have a constitutionally entrenched Bill of Rights, preventing the Legislature and the Executive from, say, authorizing or taking any retrospective penal measures, or making unreasonable encroachments on freedom of movement or expression, or taking away property rights without compensation? There has been much debate about whether, and if so in what form, a new bill of rights should be enacted.[11] To embark upon it would be to enshrine the principle of limited government in an institutional form, common enough in other lands but novel in Britain. Naturally one would have to work out satisfactory procedures for the amendment of entrenched provisions, and the procedures might differ according to the context.

This having been said, such an idea has not proved attractive to the traditional parties of government (but it has been advocated by the Alliance parties and the Democrats). Certainly, governing the country would become more difficult. And imagine what the position would have been in 1972 if the United Kingdom Government and Parliament had been *legally debarred* from encroaching on the autonomy of Northern Ireland.[12]

A written constitution for Britain would have to be justified by reference to an overwhelming political need for restricting Parliament's powers. If this justification were established, it would be sensible to include in the constitution a selection of the most important rules about the organs and machinery of government.

Aspects of classification[13]

Written and unwritten

This mode of classifying constitutions has already been discussed. Among liberal democracies, only the United Kingdom and Israel lack a

[11] Sir Leslie Scarman, *English Law – the New Dimension* (1974); Anthony Lester, *Democracy and Individual Rights* (1969); Hood Phillips, *Reform of the Constitution* (1970); Michael Zander, *A Bill of Rights?* (3rd edn, 1985); *Legislation on Human Rights with particular reference to the European Convention* (Home Office, 1976): *Report of the Select Committee on a Bill of Rights*, H.L. 176 (1978); Lord Hailsham, *Elective Dictatorship* (1976); Joseph Jaconelli, *Enacting a Bill of Rights: the Legal Problems* (1980). See also below, p. 430.

[12] See ch. 3.

[13] For a more elaborate classification see Leslie Wolf-Phillips, *Comparative Constitutions* (1972). See also Leslie Wolf-Phillips, *Constitutions of Modern States* (1968), Introduction.

written constitution in the narrower sense of the term. But the law of the constitution in those countries can be found in writing – in statutes, law reports, parliamentary standing orders, works of authority, and so on, although an authoritative and reasonably comprehensive document called the 'Constitution' is lacking.

Flexible and inflexible

Constitutions for which no special procedure for amendment is prescribed are *prima facie* more flexible than others. But flexibility is a matter of degree, and will not necessarily be predetermined by the formal procedure for constitutional amendment. And some constitutional rules will in practice be more flexible than others. In the United Kingdom the 'constitution' is, in theory, entirely flexible, but legislation to abolish the monarchy or to extend the maximum duration of a Parliament could only be passed in very extraordinary circumstances. In Ghana under Nkrumah the superior judges (other than the Chief Justice) enjoyed security of tenure against the Executive, and their tenure was entrenched by the constitution; but in the political situation existing in 1964 the President had no difficulty in first procuring a constitutional amendment rendering the judges dismissible at his pleasure and then going on to dismiss some of them for incurring his displeasure.

Monarchical and republican

This is no longer a difference of any general importance, because it tells us nothing worth knowing about the form or substance of government. One can have an absolute monarch or one with extensive personal discretionary powers (as in Nepal), or one with very limited personal powers (as in the United Kingdom and several Commonwealth and Western European countries). One can have a President who is head of State but is not the effective executive head of Government (as in India and West Germany), or one who is both head of State and head of Government (as in the United States and a great many other countries).

Presidential and parliamentary

This method of classification is concerned with the executive branch of government and its relationship with the Legislature. Under a 'presidential' system the head of the executive branch is also head of State, and is not a member of or directly responsible to the Legislature. In a parliamentary system the chief executive is a Prime Minister who is a member of and is responsible to the Legislature. Thus the American system and its imitators are distinguishable from the Westminster model of responsible government. But this kind of classification is not very illuminating, because of the wide variations within each type of system. For example, in Kenya there is an executive President, but he has to be a member of the Legislature; in Tanzania and several of the other presidential régimes in Africa, the President cannot be a member of the Legislature but (in contrast to the United States) his Ministers must be members of the Legislature, though they are not fully responsible to it. Again, whereas the President of the United States has no power to dissolve Congress, the power of dissolution is vested in Commonwealth executive presidents; and whereas the constitutional powers of the American President are hedged about by checks and balances, presidential heads of governments in new states are usually freer from restraints. And the constitution of the fifth French Republic is both presidential and parliamentary.

Single-party and other constitutions

Obviously a constitution under which only one party can legitimately operate tends to differ from one in which, at least ostensibly, freedom of political association is permitted. A constitution for a single-party State is apt to be something of a political manifesto. In such a constitution, lip-service may still be paid to the basic freedoms of the individual. Again, however, constitutional forms may give little indication of what happens in practice. In some states with single-party constitutions there is more freedom of expression than in near-by countries with impeccably liberal constitutions.

Federal and unitary

The difference between a federal and non-federal constitution will often be clear-cut; sometimes it will be only one of degree; sometimes it will be positively misleading. The United States, Australia, Canada, West Germany and Switzerland are manifestly federal States. The relationship between the United Kingdom and Northern Ireland under the Act of 1920 was strictly non-federal, since Northern Ireland had no exclusive field of competence, but in practice the degree of regional autonomy till 1970 was substantially greater than that of the republics of the Soviet

Union or even the states of Malaysia, both of which countries have nominally federal constitutions. Tanzania is a part-federation, since Zanzibar has exclusive fields of competence both in theory and in practice; but for political reasons the term 'federal' does not appear in the constitution inasmuch as it implies a degree of disunity as well as diversity.

Diarchical and other constitutions

A diarchical constitution can be defined as one in which there is a division of governmental competence between two or more authorities in the State otherwise than on a regional basis. For instance, law-making powers may be divided between the Legislature and the Executive, the former having power to pass laws within a defined field and the latter having an autonomous and exclusive power, derived directly from the constitution, to issue decrees, ordinances or regulations within a defined field; this, broadly speaking, is the position under the French constitution.[14] Such divisions of competence have certain affinities with the separation of powers doctrine, of which more will be said later; they also indicate that the concept of unitary, as distinct from federal, constitutions is not particularly illuminating in some political systems.

[14] Nicholas (1970) *Public Law* 251.

Chapter 2

The British Constitution

Characteristics

Here will be stated, or restated, very briefly the main features of the British constitutional system. All the characteristics to be listed differentiate the British constitution from *some* other constitutions.

Unwritten character. The British constitution is not written in a basic document or group of documents.

Continuity of development. It has evolved over the centuries with but few sudden or dramatic changes, and a high degree of historical continuity has been maintained as the constitution has been brought up to date. Of the modern institutions of government, some are still rooted in medieval origins. Among the existing rules of British constitutional law, quite a number were laid down in the seventeenth century or earlier. Our history is still with us. But the constitution is not a museum piece. The greater part of our constitutional law has been made this century.

Parliamentary sovereignty. Parliament as a legislative body can enact any law whatsoever on any subject whatsoever in the eyes of United Kingdom courts, according to the generally held view.[1] Changes in rules of constitutional law can be effected by ordinary legislation.

Law and convention. Particularly in the working of the executive branch of government and its relationship with the Legislature, the constitution is regulated to a large extent by rules which do not belong to the normal legal categories. These rules are called constitutional

[1] For possible exceptions to this basic rule, see ch. 4.

conventions. They are rules of political conduct or binding usages, most of which are capable of being varied or of simply disappearing as political conditions and ideas change. If conventions are to be classified as rules of constitutional law, then the term 'law' must be given a very broad meaning. To use the term 'law' in more than one sense is not in itself unusual. Sometimes it is convenient to contrast convention with 'strict law'. Thus, in strict law (by virtue of the royal prerogative) the Queen can dismiss her Ministers at pleasure. By convention this legal power is exercisable only in very extraordinary circumstances. And because it is well understood that, save in exceptional situations, the Queen must act in accordance with ministerial advice, Parliament still adopts the form of conferring discretionary powers on Her Majesty. This dichotomy of law and convention pervades much of our constitutional law.

Flexibility. The absence of a cumbersome procedure for altering rules of constitutional importance, the omnicompetence of Parliament and the pliability of many constitutional conventions tend to make the British constitution flexible and easily adaptable. But, as has been pointed out, flexibility is a question of degree. It would be easier in practice to enact legislation to abolish the House of Lords or the hereditary peerage or the Privy Council than, say, to abolish the remedy of habeas corpus. Moreover, not every constitutional convention is flexible in practice; some conventions are very rigid.

Unitary nature. The United Kingdom is a unitary, not a federal, State at the present time. If it were a federal State, Parliament would not be omnicompetent.

Freedom of political activity. The legitimacy of organized dissent and opposition to the Government is recognized by convention; and nowadays there are few oppressive legal restrictions on freedom of expression and associations in political controversy. Elections are freely conducted (although whether through a fair electoral system is another matter).

Limited monarchy. Succession to the throne is hereditary. The functions of the head of State are primarily ceremonial, and despite their amplitude in strict law they are now of little or no political significance in normal times.

Bicameralism. The upper House of Parliament, the House of Lords, still constituted mainly on a hereditary basis, is of minor importance; the lower House, the elected House of Commons, is the focus of political attention.

Parliamentary Executive. The political arm of the executive branch of government is recruited from and located within Parliament, and the Cabinet is collectively 'responsible' to Parliament in general and the House of Commons in particular. A Government would either have to go to the country or resign if it were to lose a vote of confidence in the Commons.

Executive dominance in the Legislature. Because of the structure of modern British parties, and the operation of the electoral system and certain constitutional rules, the Government in office is normally able to command parliamentary support for the implementation of almost any policy that it is in practice likely to adopt. The Government has indeed to be *responsive* to parliamentary opinion, as well as to the weight of opinion in the electorate at large, but one must not imagine that it is in any real sense a delegate or agent of Parliament. Parliamentary government is not government by Parliament. The Government governs in and through Parliament. At the same time, it would be erroneous to speak in terms of 'Cabinet dictatorship'. A Government operates within a complex network of constraints, restricting its freedom of manoeuvre.

Impartial public service. The civil service is non-partisan except in so far as it serves the Government in office. Its insulation from political involvement, and the security of tenure enjoyed by its members, have been the product of convention, not of strict law.

Judicial independence. The Judiciary is appointed by the Executive, but it is conspicuously independent both of the Executive and of the Legislature, partly because of rules of strict law but mainly because of extra-legal factors. The prestige of the superior judges in Britain is exceptionally high by any international standard. Whether this fact is related to the self-imposed rule that judges cannot question the constitutionality of duly enacted statutes is a matter for speculation.

Constitutionalism. Despite the absence of constitutionally entrenched guarantees and prohibitions or impregnable institutional bulwarks against the abuse of power, serious encroachments on basic individual freedoms are rare in times of peace,[2] and the protection of dissenting minorities in Britain is more efficacious than in many states which enjoy a superabundance of devices designed to achieve this end. Those rules and practices which do restrain abuses of public power under the British constitutional system are generally observed. The formal restraints are not always as effective as in some other liberal democracies – for instance, Parliament is a less formidable body than the United States Congress; the powers of the courts are significantly narrower than in America; civil liberties are not buttressed by a bill of rights – but there is a widely diffused acceptance of the principle that the restrictive rules of the political game are more important than the retention of power, or the pressing of legal power to the ultimate limit at the expense of individual liberty. In this sense we can say that constitutionalism, or limited government, or the rule of law – the meanings of these expressions overlap – exists in Britain.[3]

The rule of law and the separation of powers

Dicey[4] saw the rule of law as a central feature of the British constitution. He had his own idiosyncratic ideas of what the concept of the rule of law implied. His ideas, rooted in Whiggish libertarianism, were very influential for two generations;[5] today they no longer warrant detailed analysis. Nor would it be justifiable to examine the general concept of the rule of law at length in this book. The concept is one of open texture; it lends itself to an extremely wide range of interpretations. One can at least say that the concept is usually intended to imply (i) that the powers exercised by politicians and officials must have a legitimate foundation; they must be based on authority conferred by law; and (ii) that the law should conform to certain minimum standards of justice, both substantive and procedural. Thus,

[2] But note the anti-terrorist legislation which has been in force since 1974. See below, p. 465.

[3] The readers who feel that these assertions show an establishmentarian bias may wish to consult as correctives Harold Laski, *Parliamentary Government in England* (1938); Ralph Miliband, *The State in Capitalist Society* (1973); Paul O'Higgins, *Censorship in Britain* (1972); D. N. Pritt, *Law, Class and Society* (1970).

[4] A. V. Dicey, *Introduction to the Study of the Law of the Constitution* (10th edn, 1959), pt 2, especially ch. 4. The first edition was published in 1885. See R. A. Cosgrave, *The Rule of Law: Albert Venn Dicey* (1981).

[5] Sir Ivor Jenning's *The Law and the Constitution* included a sustained critique of Dicey's views, moderated, however, in the later editions. See Appendix 2 to the 5th edn. For more sympathetic assessments, see E. C. S. Wade, Introduction to the 10th edn of Dicey, pp. xcvi-cli (1959); Lawson (1959) 7 *Political Studies* 109, 207, cf. Ford (1970) 18 *Political Studies* 220; and All Souls – *Public Law* seminar, 'Dicey and the Constitution' [1985] *Public Law* 583. For further comment see below, pp. 533–7.

the law affecting individual liberty ought to be reasonably certain or predictable; where the law confers wide discretionary powers there should be adequate safeguards against their abuse; like should be treated alike, and unfair discrimination must not be sanctioned by law; a person ought not to be deprived of his liberty, status or any other substantial interest unless he is given the opportunity of a fair hearing before an impartial tribunal; and so forth. The concept has an interesting characteristic: everyone who tries to redefine it begins with the assumption that it is a good thing, like justice or courage. When Communist theoreticians extol the merits of 'socialist legality', they could simply substitute the term 'rule of law', though their conceptions of what is connoted would differ from those of liberal democratic ideologists.

The doctrine of the separation of powers, like the rule of law, has usually been discussed as one which *ought* to be embodied in a system of government. But whereas commentators are almost unanimous that the rule of law (whatever it may mean) is splendid, the virtues of the separation of powers do not evoke so enthusiastic a chorus. Perhaps this is partly because the doctrine has acquired a harder core of generally accepted meaning, and because some constitutions survive adequately without relying on it for sustenance.

This is not to say that the quintessence of the separation of powers is easy to distil. The doctrine has emerged in several forms at different periods and in different contexts.[6] It is traceable back to Aristotle; it was developed by Locke; its best-known formulation, by the French political philosopher Montesquieu, was based on an analysis of the English constitution of the early eighteenth century, but an idealized rather than a real English constitution; the disciples of Montesquieu, particularly numerous in the North American colonies, added their own refinements; and today the doctrine survives in a number of curious manifestations. No writer of repute would claim that it is a central feature of the modern British constitution. However, a brief survey of the doctrine brings out more clearly some features of the British system of government.

The doctrine, as propounded by Montesquieu and his followers, may be stated briefly as follows.

1   There are three main classes of governmental functions: the legislative, the executive and the judicial.
2   There are (or should be) three main organs of government in a State: the Legislature, the Executive and the Judiciary.

[6] For the fullest recent analysis, see M. J. C. Vile, *Constitutionalism and the Separation of Powers* (1967).

3   To concentrate more than one *class* of function in any one person
    or organ of government is a threat to individual liberty. For
    example, the Executive should not be allowed to make laws or
    adjudicate on alleged breaches of the law; it should be confined to
    the executive functions of making and applying policy and general
    administration.

Even if one accepts the first two propositions, one is not obliged to
accept the third. To concentrate a large *quantity* of power in the hands
of one person, in the absence of proper safeguards, is surely more
dangerous than to combine a few powers analytically different in
quality in the same hands, if adequate safeguards exist. And a rigorous
segregation of functions may be highly inconvenient. In many countries
subscribing to versions of the separation of powers doctrine, rule-
making powers have been vested in the Executive because it is manifestly impracticable to repose such powers exclusively in the Legislature.
The third proposition stated above is therefore both extreme and
doctrinaire, and is not taken literally by all proponents of the theory.

One of the implications commonly read into the separation of
powers doctrine is that the three branches of government ought to be
composed of different *persons*. In the United States for instance, the
President and his Cabinet cannot be members of Congress (although
the Vice-President presides over the Senate). It does not inevitably
follow that the one branch of government should not be in a position
to dominate the others. Matters may be so designed that each branch
operates as a check on the others. Again we can use the United States
as an illustration. The President may veto legislation but has no power
to dissolve Congress; although he holds office for a fixed term and is
not dependent on the support of a Congressional majority, he can be
impeached by Congress,[7] he appoints federal judges but his appointments need to be confirmed by the Senate,[8] the courts can determine
the constitutionality of legislative enactments and administrative action,
but judges cannot validly be given powers totally alien to the judicial
office; federal judges cannot be removed by the Executive but they can
be impeached by Congress. In France, on the other hand, the separation

[7] Impeachment of a President is, however, rarely embarked upon. President Andrew
Johnson was impeached in 1868 but escaped conviction by one vote; impeachment
proceedings were started against President Nixon but were pre-empted by his resignation
in 1974 in the aftermath of the Watergate scandal, on which see Philip Kurland,
Watergate and the Constitution (1978).

[8] President Lyndon Johnson's choice for Chief Justice, Justice Fortas, two consecutive
nominations to the Supreme Court, of Judges Haynsworth and Carswell, by President
Nixon and one by President Reagan, of Judge Bork, were rejected by the Senate.

of powers has been understood to preclude the ordinary courts from determining the constitutionality of legislation; yet judicial and administrative functions are commingled in the *Conseil d'État*, and legislative and executive powers in the Presidency.

In Britain we have Cabinet government with a parliamentary Executive; the Law Lords act both as judges and as legislators; the Lord Chancellor is a Minister as well as head of the Judiciary and an active member of the House of Lords in its legislative capacity. Legislative powers are delegated by Parliament to members of the Executive (the Queen in Council, and Ministers); powers to determine justiciable controversies are also confided in Ministers and other non-judicial agencies. Indeed, there never was a time in English constitutional history when the functions of government were neatly compartmentalized. The medieval *Curia Regis*, the King's Council, exercised all three classes of functions. Parliament was a High Court as well as a legislative body. For several centuries the local government authorities in the counties were judicial officers, the justices of the peace. But the modern Judiciary does stand in a special position. Professional full-time judges are disqualified from membership of the House of Commons because any other arrangement would hardly be compatible with the judicial office; the Law Lords generally abstain from politically controversial debate in the upper House, and only the Lord Chancellor and former occupants of that office have a free rein. Moreover, a number of rules and practices insulate judges in office from political pressure.

If we had a written constitution, this insulation of the Judiciary might be more complete. Two examples bring out this point. In the Commonwealth of Australia the constitution allocates the legislative, executive and judicial powers to the corresponding organs of government. There is a parliamentary Executive, as in Britain, and the Australian courts have declined to hold that parliamentary delegation of legislative powers to the Executive is unconstitutional; but they have held that the judicial power of the Commonwealth can be vested only in 'courts' within the meaning of the constitution, and that powers wholly alien to the judicial cannot be vested in those courts.[9] In Sri Lanka (Ceylon)[10] the constitution did not allocate judicial powers in

---

[9] See *Att.-Gen. for Australia* v. *R. and the Boilermakers' Society of Australia* [1957] A.C. 288 (P.C.) affirming the decision of the High Court of Australia *sub nom. R.* v. *Kirby, ex p. Boilermakers' Society* (1956) 94 C.L.R. 254. See also *Hinds* v. *R.* [1977] A.C. 195. The *Boilermakers'* case was followed (with some reluctance) by the Australian High Court in *R.* v. *Joske and Others* (1974) 130 C.L.R. 87.

[10] For a general commentary on the 1972 constitution, see J. Cooray, *Constitutional and Administrative Law of Sri Lanka* (1973).

the same form, and it would be reasonable to infer that the separation of powers doctrine had no place in the constitutional jurisprudence of the island. But in a famous case the Judicial Committee of the Privy Council held that implicit in the constitution lay the principle that the province of the Judiciary was immune from the grosser kinds of encroachment by the Executive and the Legislature; hence, retroactive legislation designed to secure the conviction and punishment of particular persons for specified conduct was declared unconstitutional, for it approximated to a non-judicial judgment.[11] One wonders how the War Damage Act 1965, which reversed a judicial decision of the House of Lords[12] with retroactive effect, would have fared if it had been measured against a written British constitution in which judicial review of the constitutionality of legislation was accepted.

It is easy to see, therefore, that the immunity of the Judiciary from interference by the political organs of government could be fortified by a written constitution; and such a constitution would certainly entrench the judges' security of tenure. To that extent the doctrine of the separation of powers, and the climate of thought of which it is a part, has practical value. Whether it would be helpful, as a means of restoring the vitality of Parliament, to separate the Executive from the Legislature in Britain is an interesting but academic speculation. The blending of Executive and Legislature is a fundamental characteristic of the British system of government. To discard it would be a more startling change than the introduction of federalism and entrenched civil liberties in a written constitution.

Sources of British constitutional law

The law of the constitution, though in one sense unwritten, is traceable to written sources, some of which are recognized as authoritative lawmaking agencies.

Legislation

This is by far the most important single source of constitutional law. In the first place, there are Acts of Parliament such as the Bill of Rights 1689, the Act of Settlement 1701, the Act of Union with Scotland 1707,

---

[11] *Liyanage* v. *R.* [1967] 1 A.C. 259; cf. *Kariapper* v. *Wijesinha* [1968] A.C. 717 (*Liyanage's* case distinguished).
[12] *Burmah Oil Co.* v. *Lord Advocate* [1965] A.C. 75.

and the European Communities Act 1972, embodying rules of major importance in the history of the constitution. There are numerous Acts dealing with the electoral system and the composition and functioning of Parliament (for example, the Representation of the People Acts, the Parliamentary Constituencies Act 1986, the House of Commons Disqualification Act 1975, the Life Peerages Act 1958, the Peerage Act 1963 (permitting the disclaimer of hereditary peerages), the Parliament Acts of 1911 and 1949 (asserting the primacy of the House of Commons in conflicts between the two Houses), and the Royal Assent Act 1967). There are statutes relating to the monarchy, regulating the succession to the throne, authorizing the adoption of new forms of the royal style and titles, and providing for a regency; but there are not many statutes of general importance defining the authority of the political executive branch. Acts of Parliament have made big changes in the law relating to civil liberties (for example, the Habeas Corpus Act 1679, the Administration of Justice Act 1960, the Public Order Acts, the Defamation Act 1952, the Obscene Publications Acts, the Race Relations Act 1976, the Theatres Act 1968 and the Police and Criminal Evidence Act 1984). We have legislation relating to British nationality, the status of aliens, and immigration and deportation; regulating the conditions under which fugitive offenders may be extradited; conferring diplomatic and kindred privileges and immunities. In the general area of administrative law we have major enactments such as the Crown Proceedings Act 1947, the Parliamentary Commissioner Act 1967, and the Tribunals and Inquiries Act 1971, and a host of statutes regulating particular fields of administrative action. And then there are numerous Acts concerning Commonwealth relations, such as the Statute of Westminster 1931 (setting the seal on the concept of Dominion status) and independence Acts. One has only to glance through the statute book for any year since the late 1960s to appreciate how much legislation of constitutional interest is enacted by Parliament. The overwhelming bulk of this legislation has been introduced by Ministers.

Subordinate legislative instruments are also a source of constitutional law. For example, Orders in Council are made under the Ministers of the Crown Act 1975 to transfer functions between Ministers and to alter their titles; Orders in Council and regulations of constitutional importance can be made under the European Communities Act 1972. Orders in Council (made by the Queen in her Privy Council) and rules and regulations made by Ministers under statutory authority are called statutory instruments within the meaning of the Statutory Instruments

Act 1946. In a narrow field, the Crown has an inherent law-making power exercisable by virtue of the royal prerogative; examples of the use of this non-statutory power are Orders regulating the civil service.

Common-law sources

Beneath this general rubric are subsumed rules widely different in character from one another.

(*a*) There is a small group of customary rules, now partly modified by statute, determining what is an Act of Parliament and enunciating the principle of parliamentary sovereignty. Clearly these rules are of fundamental importance in our legal system. Their origins and present status will be examined in chapter 4.

(*b*) The royal prerogative is the gradually diminishing residuum of customary authority, privilege and immunity, recognized at common law as belonging to the Crown, and the Crown alone. In the great *Case of Proclamations* (1611)[13] the judges of the common-law courts emphatically asserted their right to determine the limits of the prerogative; and since the Revolution of 1688 this claim has not been contested by the Crown. Among the prerogatives still exercised by or in the name of the Crown are the appointment of Ministers, the dissolution of Parliament, the power of pardon and the award of honours and dignities; these powers must, as a matter of constitutional convention, normally be exercised on ministerial advice. The immunity of the monarch from prosecution in the courts is another aspect of the royal prerogative.

(*c*) Judicial decisions are also a significant source of constitutional law. Indeed, Dicey went so far as to assert that the British constitution was 'a judge-made constitution'.[14] He was thinking particularly of the rules relating to the liberty of the person, freedom of expression and freedom of association, which had been demarcated largely by binding precedents set by the superior courts. The law of civil liberties is still to a large extent judge-made, though statutory restatement has become increasingly important in recent years. The law relating to judicial review of administrative action is predominantly judge-made, and it has probably developed faster since 1963 than in any comparable period. Again, judicial decisions have set limits not only to the royal prerogative but also to the ambit of parliamentary privilege.

[13] 12 Co. Rep. 74.
[14] Dicey, op. cit., p. 196.

(*d*) Legislation of constitutional importance may be moulded by judicial interpretation; and there are common-law presumptions of legislative intent (for example, that major constitutional innovations cannot be introduced,[15] and taxation cannot be imposed,[16] save by virtue of clear and express statutory language) which conserve what are understood to be constitutional principles against casual erosion.

Conventions of the constitution

In order to avoid tedious repetition, and in an attempt to do justice to the complexity of the topic, we shall consign to a separate section the role of conventions as a source of law.[17] Here it is enough to say that if conventions are regarded as a source of law, then it is inappropriate to affirm that the law of the British constitution is part of the ordinary law of the land; for it has at least one source which is extraordinary inasmuch as it begets rules unaccompanied by judicial sanctions or relief.

The law and custom of Parliament

This comprises the rules relating to the functions, procedures, privileges and immunities of each House of Parliament. To a small extent it is statutory, and to a still smaller extent judge-made. For the rest, it is either to be found in resolutions of each House (recorded in the official Journals, in *Hansard*, and on some important matters in standing orders) or not to be found in any authoritative source because it rests on informal understandings or practices. For example, the functions of the Leaders of the two Houses and the party whips, the duty of impartiality cast on the Speaker of the House of Commons and the convention that the chairman of the Public Accounts Committee shall be a member of the Opposition, are not formally recorded, though they can be elicited from a reading of parliamentary debates. In any event,

---

[15] See, for example, *Nairn* v. *University of St Andrews* [1909] A.C. 147 (votes for women could be conferred only by a direct grant); *Re Parliamentary Privilege Act 1770* (1958) A.C. 331 (important provision of Bill of Rights 1689 not impliedly repealed by generally worded subsequent Act).

[16] See, for example, *Att.-Gen* v. *Wilts United Daries Ltd* (1921) 37 T.L.R. 884, though see now pp. 282–3. The courts also adopt presumptions against so construing legislation as to oust the supervisory jurisdiction of the superior courts to determine the rights and liabilities of individuals, or to authorize deprivation of private property without compensation; see generally D. L. Keir and F. H. Lawson, *Cases in Constitutional Law* (6th edn, 1979), pp. 15–22. The force of the last-mentioned presumption has been weakened: *Westminster Bank Ltd* v. *Beverley B.C.* [1971] A.C. 508.

[17] See pp. 28–47.

the internal proceedings of the two Houses are not cognizable by the courts. For this reason, large tracts of the law relating to parliamentary privilege have never been subject to judicial appraisal. And so a great deal of the law and custom of Parliament lies outside the scope of the *ordinary* law of the land.

Community law

With the accession of the United Kingdom to membership of the European Communities on 1 January 1973, Community law became a source of the constitutional law of Britain.

Community law[18] is to be found in the Community treaties;[19] in regulations, directives and decisions of Community organs (the Council of Ministers, a political body composed of Foreign Ministers; or the European Commission, a supranational body composed of top Community officials); and in rulings and decisions of the Court of the Communities (the European Court). It is applied *mainly* by courts of the member States, but authoritative rulings are given by the European Court. According to that Court, Community law is distinct from national law but exists alongside it; and where Community law is in conflict with national law, Community law prevails. By section 3 of the European Communities Act 1972, the United Kingdom accepted the binding authority of the rulings and principles laid down by the European Court. The Court has stated quite clearly several times that no Parliament of a member State can legislate inconsistently with Community law. Hence our acceptance of Community law *seems* to involve a rejection of the doctrine of parliamentary sovereignty. We shall consider this matter more fully in chapter 4. But potentially, at least, the importation of Community law brings with it a constitutional innovation of the highest importance.

At various points in the book we shall note the actual or likely impact of Community law on the law of this country. In fact the content of Community law has up to now been fairly remote from the subject-matter of constitutional law; for Community law is largely about agriculture, free trade, fair competition, transport regulations, social security and so on. But on certain matters – for example, immigration

---

[18] For a good and concise outline, see P.S.R.F. Mathijsen, *A Guide to European Community Law* (4th edn, 1985). See below, ch. 5.

[19] A shorthand expression covering the three original treaties establishing the three Communities (ECSC, EEC and EURATOM), the instruments by which the United Kingdom acceded to the Communities, and various other Community agreements. See the European Communities Act 1972, s. 1.

and aspects of public finance – it bears directly on specific areas of constitutional law.

One very important point needs to be made at this stage. Some rules of Community law are (according to Community doctrine) 'directly applicable' in the sense that they confer rights or impose duties on individuals, rights and duties which are enforceable in national courts without being re-enacted by the governmental organs of member States. These rules are, in the main, *regulations* made by the Council of Ministers or the Commission. Section 2(1) and part of section 2(4) of the European Communities Act give effect to the concept of 'direct applicability'. The relevant Community rules are to be applied by the courts of this country 'without further enactment', as if they were Acts of Parliament. This was a major constitutional innovation. These regulations are made in Brussels in consequence of decisions taken in Brussels. And they are *primary* rather than delegated legislation.

Community law will be considered further in chapter 5.

Authoritative works

Literature on the constitution has only persuasive authority. Sometimes unusual and abstruse questions of constitutional law arise before a court – for instance, peerage law,[20] or aspects of the royal prerogative,[21] or the law of treason,[22] or the definition of an act of State,[23] or the jurisdiction of the English courts in British protectorates[24] – and reference may then be had to the views of writers of repute for the purposes of guidance. When a particularly awkward question relating to the scope of parliamentary privilege was referred to the Judicial Committee of the Privy Council for an advisory opinion, the opinions of constitutional historians in the eighteenth and nineteenth centuries were copiously cited in order to explain the mischief which an obscure and ambiguous Act of 1770 was designed to cure.[25] In controversies about the existence and scope of individual constitutional conventions – controversies which usually take place outside the courts of law – the views of modern writers such as Jennings, Anson, Dicey, Maitland, Keith, E. C. S. Wade, Hood Phillips, Amery, Mackintosh and others are frequently prayed in aid. On issues of parliamentary privilege,

[20] *Re Parliamentary Election for Bristol South-East* [1964] 2 Q.B. 257.
[21] For example, *Burmah Oil Co.* v. *Lord Advocate* [1965] A.C. 75.
[22] *Joyce* v. *D.P.P.* [1946] A.C. 347.
[23] *Nissan* v. *Att.-Gen.* [1970] A.C. 179.
[24] *Ex p. Mwenya* [1960] 1 Q.B. 241.
[25] *Re Parliamentary Privilege Act 1770* [1958] A.C. 331.

Erskine May[26] is regarded as an exceptionally persuasive authority. It is fair to say that in the diffuse field of constitutional law the opinions of authorities are resorted to more often than in other branches of English law. They are a useful subsidiary source of constitutional law in the broad sense of the term. In administrative law cases the opinions of modern writers – especially those of the late Professor de Smith – have come to be quoted in argument and are occasionally cited in judgments. In cases involving points of Community law, on which few British judges would regard themselves as experts, recourse is occasionally made to the opinions of specialist writers.

Conventions of the constitution[27]

There is no rule of statute or common law to the effect that there must be a Prime Minister and a Cabinet, though legislation providing for the payment of ministerial salaries rests on the assumption that these institutions do exist. But clearly the Prime Minister and the Cabinet are cardinal features of the British constitution. They are creatures of convention, not of strict law.

Again, as we have noted, the Queen has enormously wide powers, prerogative and statutory, but she is obliged by convention to exercise these powers on and in accordance with ministerial advice, save in a few very special situations. This is the most important convention of the British constitution. The main exceptions to the general rule will be considered in chapter 6.

There are many other major conventions of the constitution, dealing with relations between the Executive and the Legislature (for example, the rules about ministerial responsibility to Parliament), relations between the two Houses of Parliament (for example, the rule that money bills have to be introduced into the House of Commons), the working of each House (for example, the rule that the Speaker of the House of Commons shall behave impartially), the civil service and the Judiciary.

It is obvious that *some* constitutional conventions are far more important than most of the statutory and common-law rules connected with the British system of government. The convention that the Queen must assent to bills duly passed is overwhelmingly more important than

---

[26] Sir Thomas Erskine May, *Parliamentary Practice* (20th edn, 1983).
[27] See generally Dicey, op. cit., chs 14 and 15; Sir Ivor Jennings, *The Law and the Constitution* (5th edn, 1959), ch. 3; Geoffrey Marshall, *Constitutional Conventions* (1984); Colin Munro, *Studies in Constitutional Law* (1987), ch. 3.

her strictly legal prerogative power to withhold her assent. Since the rules of strict law, in this context and many others, give a grotesquely misleading picture of the rules actually observed, and observed on the assumption that they are binding, constitutional conventions ought to be treated as part of constitutional law.

At once we are in terminological difficulties. In one aspect conventions are law; in other aspects they are not. Dicey was quite clear that they were not '"laws" in the true sense of that word, for if any or all of them were broken no court would take notice of their violation'.[28] In other passages he observed that laws were 'rules enforced or recognized by the courts', whereas conventions were 'a body not of laws, but of constitutional or political ethics', the 'constitutional morality of the day', 'not enforced or recognized by the courts'.[29]

Dicey's distinctions between strict law[30] and constitutional convention were too clear-cut and have been severely criticized,[31] but they have substance.[32] For instance, if the Queen were to refuse her assent to a bill of which she disapproved, no court would deem the bill to be an authentic Act of Parliament. If a Government, defeated on a vote of confidence in the House of Commons, neither resigned nor advised a dissolution of Parliament, no court would take cognizance of this gross breach of convention by granting a declaration that any of the Ministers was not legally entitled to exercise his office. No form of judicial redress is obtainable purely for a breach of convention. And in the eyes of the courts, Parliament is competent to legislate in unequivocal disregard of conventional limitations on the exercise of its powers.[33]

Distinctions of substance between constitutional conventions and rules of strict law are well illustrated by the evolution of Dominion status within the Commonwealth. By 1926 most of the self-governing Dominions were in effect independent States, equal in status, for most purposes, to the United Kingdom. They had achieved this status not by legislation but by the development of conventions, many of which were

---

[28] Dicey, op. cit., p. 27.

[29] ibid., pp. 417, 422. See also Hood Phillips (1966) 29 *Mod. L. Rev.* 137.

[30] The term aptly employed by Sir Kenneth Wheare in *The Statute of Westminster and Dominion Status* (5th edn, 1953), ch. 1.

[31] Notably by Sir Ivor Jennings, op. cit., ch. 3. See also J. D. B. Mitchell, *Constitutional Law* (2nd edn, 1968), pp. 26–39.

[32] For a subtle defence of the basis of the distinction, see Hood Phillips (1964) 8 *Journal of the Society of Public Teachers of Law* (N.S.) 60. For an attempt to say the last word, see Munro (1975) 91 *L.Q.R.* 218.

[33] *Madzimbamuto* v. *Lardner-Burke* [1969] 1 A.C. 645 at 722–3 (legislation dealing with internal affairs of Southern Rhodesia).

formally recorded (or created) in resolutions of Imperial Conferences. There remained a few elements of formal inequality. Some of those (for example, the procedure for appointing a Governor-General) could be and were removed by the formulation of new constitutional conventions. Others could not be removed by convention. In strict law the Dominions were still colonies. They were prohibited by section 2 of the Colonial Laws Validity Act 1865 from legislating repugnantly to United Kingdom enactments extending to them as part of their own law. Among these enactments were the Judicial Committee Acts 1833 and 1844, under which the prerogative power of the Crown to grant special leave to appeal from colonial courts to the Privy Council was placed on a statutory footing. This power to give leave to appeal and to hear appeals was not expunged by convention; and in 1926 the Judicial Committee of the Privy Council held[34] that the Canadian Parliament was incompetent to abolish the appeal by special leave from Canadian courts in criminal matters. The necessary legal authority could be conferred only by United Kingdom legislation. Some of the Dominions pressed for the enactment of enabling legislation, and Parliament passed the Statute of Westminster 1931. This excluded the Dominions from the definition of 'colony', abolished the repugnancy rule and empowered Dominion Parliaments to legislate inconsistently with United Kingdom legislation extending to their countries.[35] Thereafter the Canadian Parliament was able to pass legislation abolishing criminal appeals to the Privy Council.[36]

The distinction blurred

These examples suggest that the distinction between law and convention is reasonably clear. But in a number of contexts the distinction is blurred. In particular, Dicey was exaggerating when he said that conventions were 'not recognized' by the courts. The courts do sometimes take cognizance of conventions;[37] sometimes they use them

---

[34] *Nadan* v. *R.* [1926] A.C. 482.

[35] ss. 1, 2, 11; see generally, Wheare, op. cit., and R. McG. Dawson, *The Development of Dominion Status 1900–1936* (1937); and ch. 34, below.

[36] *British Coal Corporation* v. *R.* [1935] A.C. 500. See also *Att.-Gen. for Ontario* v. *Att.-Gen. for Canada* [1947] A.C. 127 (abolition of appeals in civil matters; see below).

[37] In *Att.-Gen.* v. *Jonathan Cape Ltd.* [1976] Q.B. 752 Lord Widgery L.C.J. referred extensively to the convention of collective ministerial responsibility (on which see below, p. 181); in *Air Canada* v. *Secretary of State for Trade* [1983] A.C. 394 reference was made to the convention that Ministers do not see certain papers of a previous Administration of a different political party without the agreement of its Prime Minister (on which see below, p. 174).

as aids to interpretation. Thus, English courts have occasionally supported their refusal to review the grounds on which executive discretionary powers have been exercised by pointing out that a Minister is responsible to Parliament for the exercise of the power.[38] In one Privy Council appeal, Canada's accession to independence, and the convention of equality of status recited in the preamble to the Statute of Westminster, were primary reasons for so interpreting an ambiguous section of the Canadian constitution as to empower the Federal Parliament to abolish appeals to the Privy Council from all Canadian courts in civil cases.[39] In another, more recent, appeal it was contended that appeals from Ceylon courts had been impliedly abrogated by the grant of independence, because the report of the Judicial Committee on such an appeal was issued in the form of an Order in Council affecting the law of Ceylon. The Judicial Committee held[40] that although a *legislative* Order in Council purporting to alter the law of Ceylon would have been invalidated by the Ceylon Independence Act 1947, a *judicial* Order in Council was, by convention, no more than the formal promulgation of a determination by a court of law which had not yet been deprived of jurisdiction by the Parliament of Ceylon. Again, the High Court of Australia has used constitutional conventions as an aid to statutory interpretation, holding that United Kingdom amendments to copyright legislation in 1928 and 1956 did not alter Australian law in the absence of any indication that they purported to extend to Australia with Australian concurrence; the original legislation passed by the United Kingdom Parliament in 1911 had undoubtedly extended to Australia as part of its law, but conventional limitations on the territorial competence of the United Kingdom Parliament and Government had evolved since that time.[41]

A striking illustration of a constitutional convention having as much

---

[38] See, for example, *Liversidge* v. *Anderson* [1942] A.C. 206 (where the Home Secretary was expressly required by regulations to make reports to Parliament); *Carltona Ltd* v. *Commissioners of Works* [1943] 2 All E.R. 560; *Robinson* v. *Minister of Town and Country Planning* [1947] K.B. 702.

[39] *Att.-Gen. for Ontario* v. *Att.-Gen. for Canada* [1947] A.C. 127.

[40] *Ibralebbe* v. *R.* [1964] A.C. 900. Appeals from Sri Lanka (Ceylon) were terminated in 1972.

[41] *Copyright Owners Reproduction Society Ltd* v. *E.M.I. (Australia) Pty Ltd* (1958) 100 C.L.R. 597; see Gray (1960) 23 *Mod L. Rev.* 647; Bennion (1961) 24 *Mod. L. Rev.* 355. The amendment made in 1956, after Australia had adopted the Statute of Westminster, was held moreover to be inoperative in Australia because it was not *expressed* to have been made at the request and with the consent of the Commonwealth of Australia, as was required by section 4 of the Statute. See further pp. 76–8. The power of the United Kingdom Parliament to legislate for Australia was finally ended at Australia's request by the Australia Act 1986, s. 1: see further below, pp. 663–4.

effect in practice as strict law comes from Canada. The Canadian Government sought patriation of the constitution in the early 1980s, but agreement on the new settlement could not be reached with the provinces. When the Government decided to proceed without it some of the provinces challenged the legality of the Government's actions in the courts. The Supreme Court held that, although no rule of law existed which established provincial consent as a prerequisite to any constitutional amendment, there was a convention that such consent would be obtained.[42] The Government thereupon delayed its plans and held further negotiations in which nine of the ten provinces agreed to revised Federal proposals which formed the basis of Canada's 1983 constitution.[43]

These examples[44] show how constitutional conventions may materially influence judicial decisions. In this sense they may be compared with recitals in the preamble to an Act of Parliament. The terms of preambles are not directly enforceable in court, but the facts and purposes (and occasionally conventions[45]) there set out may be used as aids to the interpretation of ambiguous provisions in the main body of the Act. Alternatively conventions may be compared with the Directive Principles of State Policy, which are an integral part of the constitution of India but are expressed not to be 'enforceable by any court';[46] they are nevertheless used as guides to constitutional interpretation.

Some conventions, then, may be indirectly justiciable. And some rules of strict law may be non-justiciable. The latter point can be illustrated in constitutional and administrative law.

1   General duties to provide efficient services are cast by statute on public corporations administering nationalized industries. These duties may be formulated in terms so broad that no person would be able to obtain a judicial pronouncement that the corporation had failed to carry out its duty.[47] Sometimes the nationalization Act will state explicitly that these general duties are not enforceable in any court of law.

---

[42] *Reference re Amendment of the Constitution of Canada* (1982) 125 D.L.R. (3d) 1.

[43] See Canada Act 1982, and Laskin [1982] *Public Law* 549; Sharpe [1987] *Public Law* 48.

[44] See further, *Ryder* v. *Foley* (1906) 4 C.L.R. 422; *Commercial Cable Co* v. *Government of Newfoundland* [1916] 2 A.C. 610.

[45] Notably in the preamble to the Statute of Westminster 1931, reciting basic conventions about equality of status in the Commonwealth. A preamble is part of an Act and can be debated and amended during the passage of the bill. Each clause will begin 'Whereas . . .'

[46] Constitution, art. 37.

[47] cf. *Watt* v. *Kesteven C.C.* [1955] 1 Q.B. 408 (duty of local education authorities to have regard to the general principle that as far as possible children are to be educated in accordance with parental wishes (Education Act 1944, s. 76) unenforceable by aggrieved parents in legal proceedings).

2 Under the Parliament Act 1911, a money bill passed by the Commons can be presented for the royal assent after one month although it has not been passed by the Lords. The Act defines a money bill and provides that a certificate given by the Speaker of the House of Commons that the bill is a money bill shall not be questioned in any court. If the Speaker's certificate were based on an erroneous interpretation of the statutory definition, no way of raising the issue before a court would be feasible, unless possibly the error was so flagrant as to raise doubts as to the Speaker's good faith.

Examples could be multiplied. It is enough to say that non-compliance with statutory norms is not necessarily coupled with the possibility of judicial sanctions, even the sanction of nullity.

3 There is the curious case of section 1 of the Northern Ireland Constitution Act 1973: '. . . it is hereby affirmed that in no event will Northern Ireland . . . cease to be part of . . . the United Kingdom without the consent of the majority of the people of Northern Ireland voting in a poll held for the purposes of this section . . .' This reads like a particularly solemn affirmation of a constitutional convention,[48] binding on the United Kingdom Parliament and Government but placed in the main body of an Act instead of in the preamble. Here the distinction between strict law and convention not only lacks substance but is tenuous in the matter of form.

4 Written constitutions in other countries often embody non-justiciable rules. Some are non-justiciable because the constitution says so. To this category belong those provisions in a number of Commonwealth constitutions requiring the Governor-General to act on ministerial advice. In the constitution of Ceylon, British conventions concerning the exercise of discretionary functions by the Queen's representative were incorporated by general reference; and it was expressly stated that the question whether these conventions had been observed was not to be inquired into by any

---

[48] See also Cmd 534 (1969) (N.I.), referring to the 'clear pledges made by successive United Kingdom Governments that Northern Ireland should not cease to be a part of the United Kingdom without the consent of the people of Northern Ireland' (§56(1)). Section 1 of the 1973 Act replaced section 1(2) of the Ireland Act 1949 which had referred to 'the Parliament of Northern Ireland'; that Parliament was abolished by section 31 of the 1973 Act and the formula cited in the text was enacted. For an argument that section 1(2) of the 1949 Act was in law a redefinition of the meaning of the United Kingdom Parliament, see Harry Calvert, *Constitutional Law in Northern Ireland* (1968), pp. 23–33.

court.[49] Was this constitutional provision not 'law'? Are the Directive Principles of State Policy in the Indian constitution (which are only indirectly justiciable) and the corresponding statements of principle in the constitutions of the Republics of Ireland and Malta not part of the law of constitution? And what is one to make of those constitutional provisions, common enough in non-Commonwealth countries (for example, France), which impose limitations on legislative competence but cannot be the subject of adjudication because judicial review of the constitutionality of legislation is not an acceptable doctrine?

Why not codify conventions?

One may argue that the illustrations cited above are marginal or anomalous cases which do not significantly weaken the general proposition that conventions are not directly enforceable in courts whereas obedience to rules of strict law is directly enforceable through courts. This is broadly correct. But why is a distinction between strict law and convention maintained at all in the United Kingdom? Why not codify conventions in a strictly legal form? After all, conventions and rules of strict law alike are binding rules.

The answers to these questions are not simple. The reasons for retaining the distinction are various. In the first place, there is the constitutional role of the monarch. Most of the main conventions of the constitution were originally evolved in order to ensure that the monarch exercised his prerogative powers on the advice of Ministers responsible to Parliament. This end could be and was achieved by a gradual process in which royal discretion was quietly eroded. Abrupt changes in the law should, it was felt, be avoided unless the monarch behaved like James II. As long as the monarch played, or thought he was entitled to play, a significant role in the making of policy decisions, it might have been politically imprudent to urge that his dwindling personal influence should be attenuated by statutory restrictions, for example, by requiring him to act on the advice of the Privy Council or the incipient Cabinet or a named Minister. No obvious harm was done by leaving the monarch with wide prerogative powers exercisable in strict law in his personal discretion; and unnecessary friction could have been caused by trying to take them away, particularly as long as a

---

[49] Jennings, op. cit., pp. 120–21; see also his *Constitution of Ceylon* (3rd edn, 1949). Sir Ivor Jennings was the main architect of the Ceylon constitution. See generally de Smith, *The New Commonwealth and its Constitutions* (1964), ch. 3, on methods of incorporating 'conventional' rules into Commonwealth constitutions.

large section of the general public thought of the monarch as the executive head of government. A prerogative power might be converted into a statutory power or duty exercisable under prescribed conditions, but these conditions would not include an obligation to act on ministerial advice. *New* statutory powers and duties could be vested in the monarch, the Crown in Council or a named Minister without breaking away too blatantly from historical tradition. And the tradition was not valueless. To involve the monarch personally in the making of important decisions on matters of State lent greater dignity to the business of government; and there were exceptional situations, not easily definable, where the monarch's personal views ought to be taken into account, or even to prevail in a time of constitutional crisis. Even today, time-honoured formal tradition is not easily eradicated unless there are obvious reasons why it should be. If there is urgent pressure for clarification or change (for example, in Commonwealth affairs), conventions may be explicitly set down as conventions in their existing or a modified form, or rules of strict law may replace them.

Secondly, it would be difficult or even harmful to define a number of important conventions. For example, some of the conventions about ministerial responsibility or the working of the Cabinet system are blurred. Codification would purchase certainty at the expense of flexibility; informal modifications to keep the constitution in touch with contemporary political thinking or needs would be inhibited.[50] Evolution by conventions is still needed in countries with written constitutions. In some contexts the rules ought *not* to be crystal clear. Clarification would tend to stultify one purpose of conventions – keeping the constitution up to date. Again, a situation may arise in which a convention ought, in the public interest, to be waived; waiver would be more difficult if the convention were set down in unambiguous language. These are, of course, admissions that many conventions are significantly different from typical rules of law.

Thirdly, as long as a conventional rule is regularly observed, there is no apparent reason for codifying it.[51] Lay peers regularly comply with their conventional obligation not to present themselves to sit with the

---

[50] This was one of the reasons why the Radcliffe Committee on Ministerial Memoirs (Cmnd 6386 (1976)) rejected the proposition that the rules concerning the publication of former Ministers' autobiographies or diaries should be put into statutory form. Instead it recommended that the rules should be drawn to Ministers' attention, and amended as needs be, by the Prime Minister. See further below pp. 190–92.

[51] One could equally say that there is no sound reason for not codifying it. The reasons, sound or unsound, are characteristic inertia masquerading as veneration for unwritten constitutional tradition, and the absence of political pressure for change.

Law Lords to hear an appeal in the House of Lords; the Speaker of the House of Commons regularly behaves impartially.[52] If these conventional rules were to be broken, they could simply be restated in formal terms or superseded by statutory rules. In 1909 the House of Lords disregarded its somewhat vague conventional duty to defer in the last resort to the will of the Commons; the sequel was the Parliament Act 1911, redefining relationships between the two Houses on a statutory basis.

Nevertheless, it is unsatisfactory that the content, and indeed the very existence, of some of the most important conventions should be indeterminate. There is no consensus of opinion on the *conventional* powers of the Queen to remove a Prime Minister, to require a dissolution of Parliament or to refuse a request for dissolution. Clarification may be brought about by the march of events in a time of political turbulence; but the Queen may then be criticized for having acted 'unconstitutionally' or for having failed to discharge her constitutional duty to act; she will be unable to answer back, and those who will speak for her may have to rely on dubious precedents, debatable opinions of writers, and principles deduced from a concept of the constitutional system with which some are bound to disagree. An authoritative statement, prepared by an expert body, of the conventions regulating the constitutional functions of the monarch might therefore be useful, difficult though it would be to formulate.[53] But if such conventions were to be codified, they ought not to be made directly justiciable,[54] even if they were written into an Act of Parliament or a new British constitution. Experience in new Commonwealth countries has shown that whilst the embodiment of such rules in the texts of constitutions makes for greater certainty, so that people have a clearer idea of what may, must or cannot be done, the burden thrust upon the courts when they are called upon to determine whether prescribed rules have been complied with in a politically sensitive situation is liable to be excessive. Whatever the outcome, the prestige of the Judiciary will probably suffer. If the rules of the game are to be set down, they do not

[52] There are customary rules of the House of Commons directing the manner in which he is to use his casting vote in the event of a tie.

[53] The Australian Constitutional Convention, for example, seeks to do this at regular meetings. It is made up of delegates from the Commonwealth and State Parliaments, and in 1983 formally declared 34 conventions. Not surprisingly it could not agree on the Governor-General's power to dismiss Ministers (on which see below, p. 116). See C. Sampford and D. Wood [1987] *Public Law* 231.

[54] For discussion of this matter, see H. V. Evatt, *The King and his Dominion Governors* (2nd edn, 1967), chs 29–33; Geoffrey Marshall and G. C. Moodie, *Some Problems of the Constitution* (5th edn, 1971), pp. 34–6; de Smith, op. cit., pp. 86–7; Keith (1967) 16 *I.C.L.Q.* 542.

require the courts to decide whether, for example, a Prime Minister has been validly dismissed. This is pre-eminently a question about the reins of power. If the constitutionality of such an act is disputed, the controversy is unlikely to be resolved by the pronouncement of a court.[55] However, clarification of the rules by codification may reduce the area of potential conflict.

One point must be made to avoid misunderstandings. Some rules of political behaviour, or standards of conduct in public affairs, have in fact been 'codified', or promulgated in an authoritative form. For instance, the principles governing the private financial interests that a Minister of the Crown can properly retain after appointment can be found in a statement by Sir Winston Churchill published in 1952.[56] These principles embody constitutional conventions because they state rules that ought to be followed by Ministers; and enforced resignation would be the sanction for breaking them. Each incoming Prime Minister gives his new team written guidelines, entitled *Questions of Procedure for Ministers*. Some other assertions about what is right and proper in public affairs do not enjoy the same degree of importance; or the standards of conduct they lay down may be more elastic; or their original or continuing authority may be disputed; or the consequence of deviating from them may be no more than adverse criticism from political opponents. It may, therefore, be doubtful whether such statements are to be regarded as embodying conventions (or rules) at all. Nearly all discussions about the existence and scope of the *lesser* constitutional conventions include arguments of dubious authenticity.

Interrelationship between law and convention

Law and convention are closely interlocked. To quote Jennings, constitutional conventions 'provide the flesh which clothes the dry bones of the law; they make the legal constitution work; they keep in touch with the growth of ideas'.[57] Conventions presuppose the existence

---

[55] Dismissals were held valid in *Adegbenro* v. *Akintola* [1963] A.C. 614 (Western Nigeria) and invalid in *Ningkan's* case [1966] 2 *Malayan L.J.* 187 (Sarawak). See, on the latter case, Thio (1966) 8 *Malaya L. Rev.* 283; Keith (1967) 16 *I.C.L.Q.* 542. The decision in the former case was reversed locally by a constitutional amendment having retroactive effect, followed by the abolition of appeals from Nigerian courts to the Judicial Committee. The decision in the latter case was accepted, but a state of emergency was proclaimed, the constitution amended (validity upheld in *Ningkan* v. *Government of Malaysia* [1970] A.C. 379) and the Chief Minister dismissed.

[56] 496 H. C. Deb. 701-3 (25 February 1952); reproduced as Appendix 2 to the Report from the Select Committee on Members' Interests (H.C. 57 (1969–70)). See also p. 181 and 910 H.C. Deb. 58–9 (written answers 27 April 1976), 94 H.C. Deb. 781 (25 March 1986).

[57] *The Law and the Constitution* (5th edn, 1959), pp. 81–2.

of a framework of strict law; they do not exist in a legal vacuum. For example, conventional rules about the functions of the Cabinet Office presuppose the existence of a Cabinet, which presupposes the existence of a Privy Council and Ministers appointed by the Crown. In turn, some rules of strict law presuppose conventions. Statutes dealing with ministerial salaries presuppose the existence of a Prime Minister, a Cabinet, Leaders of the Opposition and party whips, though they do not define their functions.[58] And when Parliament gives Her Majesty powers of appointment to offices of State and other statutory discretions, it acts on the tacit assumption that she will use her powers only on ministerial advice.

Again, as we have seen, the line between strict law and convention is sometimes uncertain. Legal duties are not always justiciable, and conventions may be justiciable in so far as the courts use them as aids to construction.

None of these comments is likely to be regarded as controversial. If, however, one asks the question: Are rules of strict law and constitutional conventions obeyed for similar reasons? problems at once arise.

1 Dicey contended that 'the sanction which constrains the boldest political adventurer' to obey a convention he might feel inclined to break was his fear that breach would almost immediately bring him into conflict with the courts and the law of the land.[59] Thus, if the convention that Parliament be summoned each year, or that a Government which has lost a vote of confidence in the House of Commons must go to the country or resign, were to be broken, legal authority for collecting the most productive taxes, for spending money and for maintaining and disciplining a standing army would soon expire, for such authority is granted by Parliament only for a year at a time. Since the Government would have to perform acts devoid of legal authority, Ministers and officials would soon find themselves in the dock or mulcted in damages. Obedience to conventions was therefore buttressed by the sanctions of strict law.

The weaknesses of Dicey's argument are familiar. Some political adventurers may indeed have been deterred from breaking certain conventions for fear of indirectly incurring legal sanctions; but who knows? The boldest adventurer will (as Dicey himself conceded) carry out a *coup d'état* and defy the law. The not so bold is far more

---

[58] See especially the Parliamentary and other Pensions Act 1972; Ministerial and other Salaries Act 1975; Parliamentary and other Pensions and Salaries Act 1976; Parliamentary and other Pensions Act 1987.

[59] Dicey, op cit., pp. 445–6.

likely to be deterred by fear of the *political* consequences – justified charges of unconstitutional conduct, public ridicule or odium, loss of office or even the precipitation of revolution. Moreover, many conventions are not buttressed by the threat of legal sanctions. If the Queen were to refuse her assent to a bill because she disapproved of it, this could not entail breach of any legal rule; but it might lead to *changes* in the law – the abolition of the power to refuse assent, and imposition of statutory duties to exercise other royal discretionary powers on ministerial advice; or enforced abdication, or abolition of the monarchy. If the majority of the House of Commons voted to expel the Opposition, or if a lay peer were to insist on sitting with the Law Lords, or if the Speaker were to make a party political speech in the Commons, conventions would be broken and the consequences might be very unpleasant for those concerned; but obedience to the existing conventions is not explicable in terms of legal sanctions.

2 Conventions are normally observed for a variety of mundane reasons – force of habit, inertia, desire to 'conform', belief that it is 'right' to obey them and wrong to disobey them because they are reasonable rules or because they are part of a reasonable structure of rules which ought to be preserved and upheld. In so far as they are observed by persons involved in politics who feel inclined to break them, obedience can usually be attributed to fear of disrepute and its political implications. Now, most of us obey the criminal law for much the same set of reasons.[60] If, for example, one finds a purse containing a large sum of money in the street, one is likely to resist any temptation to appropriate and keep it because one feels one *ought* not to behave in such a way. If one's decision to hand it in to the police station is materially influenced by fear of being prosecuted and convicted for theft, the probability is that one will be more concerned with the *social* disgrace involved in a publicized conviction than with the prospect of being fined or sent to prison. The sense of obligation and the fear of disagreeable consequences which tend to induce people to comply with conventions are broadly similar to the corresponding feelings which conduce to observance of the criminal law. There are, of course, many people who will not feel any sense of obligation to return the purse, who will be deterred from dishonesty only by the prospect of detection, and who will fear imprisonment but not loss of social esteem. And some politicians will cheerfully break a hallowed convention (for

[60] cf. Jennings, ibid., Appendix 4.

example, about ministerial responsibility to Parliament) if they think they can carry if off without adverse personal repercussions. Again, some of us will break certain rules of strict law, for example, speed limits on a clear road in a built-up area, without compunction provided that a police patrol car is not in the vicinity, because we do not feel a sense of obligation to obey the rule to the letter. Awareness that a patrol car is close behind us will slow us down, not because we are overcome by a sense of moral obligation but because we do not want to be stopped and perhaps have to pay a fine.

This is not a jurisprudential essay and these points will not be elaborated. It is enough to repeat that the sense of legal obligation is often much the same as the sense of obligation to obey constitutional conventions. One difference between strict law and conventions is that legal obligations are on the whole more complex, technical and exactly defined; another is that where there are direct sanctions for breach, strictly legal sanctions tend to be more specific and can be imposed by authoritative tribunals endowed with powers of interpretation. These differences are not trivial. But are they really fundamental?

Identification of constitutional conventions

If one can borrow from the vocabulary of H. L. A. Hart, constitutional conventions, in so far as they impose duties,[61] are primary rules of obligation unaccompanied by an adequate apparatus of secondary rules of recognition, interpretation (or adjudication) and change.[62] And the tests for the ascertainment of conventions are neither universally agreed nor, when agreed, easily applied in a large number of marginal cases. Some conventions are clear-cut; some are flexible; some are so elusive that one is left wonderng whether in fact the 'convention' is an ethereal will-o'-the-wisp. It is often particularly hard to say whether a political practice has crystallized into a constitutional convention and, if so, what is its scope.[63]

1   Most of the conventions of the constitution are binding usages,

---

[61] Some confer powers – for example, the special powers of a Prime Minister.

[62] *The Concept of Law* (1961), ch. 5. Hart does not himself characterize conventions in this manner. For him, a system of 'primary rules' unaccompanied by the 'secondary rules' referred to above is exemplified (p. 99) by the customary law of some simple (or primitive) societies.

[63] See Sir Kenneth Wheare, *Modern Constitutions* (2nd edn, 1966), ch. 8, cf. Marshall and Moodie, op. cit., pp. 26–31.

understandings or practices.⁶⁴ They are forms of political behaviour regarded as obligatory. When or how does a non-binding *usage* become binding? General acceptance by everybody whom the usage affects (the Queen, Ministers, members of Parliament, civil servants or judges) and by authorities on the constitution that there is an *obligation* to continue to behave in that way is, of course, the most satisfactory answer. Such an answer is not always forthcoming. The difficulty can be illustrated by reference to two major conventions. The first is that the Queen is obliged to assent to a bill of which she personally disapproves, unless presumably she is advised by the Cabinet to withhold her assent. The last time the royal assent was refused was in 1708: Queen Anne was not prepared to agree to the creation of a Scottish Militia. But a century later it was still thought imprudent to support bills for the removal of the disabilities attaching to Roman Catholics, on account of George III's personal objections. In 1829 George IV grudgingly gave his assent to such a bill; this can be regarded as an unequivocal normative (or rule-constitutive) precedent, the balance of the constitution having shifted away from independent royal discretion; but in the years between, who can say when usage had hardened into convention? Secondly, it is a convention that the Prime Minister should be chosen from the House of Commons (or from among persons elected to the House if a change of Prime Minister becomes necessary as a result of a General Election). The last Prime Minister to sit in the Lords was Lord Salisbury in 1902. In 1911 the powers of the Lords in money matters were reduced to vanishing point and their right to reject other Commons' bills was confined to a suspensory veto. It was, therefore, arguable that thereafter the Prime Minister had to be chosen from the ranks of the Commons. The question did not arise till 1923, because the most suitable candidates were all members of the Commons. But in that year a vacancy arose because of Bonar Law's resignation on grounds of grave ill-health; the most eligible candidate appeared to be Lord Curzon, but Stanley Baldwin was appointed by the King instead, ostensibly on the ground that since the Labour Party, which was by then the main Opposition party, was almost unrepresented in the Lords, the office ought to go to a commoner.⁶⁵ This appeared to be a normative precedent: the King had passed over Curzon because

⁶⁴ See, for example, the discussion of the conventions on ministerial responsibility (pp. 181–94).

⁶⁵ See Sir Harold Nicolson, *King George V* (1952), pp. 375–9.

he thought he was *obliged* to do so, and there were good reasons for his choice. If the King had not thought himself obliged so to act – if, for example, he was influenced in his choice of Baldwin by his awareness of Curzon's unpopularity among sections of the Conservative Party,[66] or if a memorandum of advice, heavily emphasizing the unsuitability of Curzon, was thought by the King to be an accurate statement of Bonar Law's views, although the memorandum was in fact composed by another and had put the case far more strongly than Bonar Law would ever have put it[67] – this could still have been cited as a persuasive precedent for the existence of such a convention, given the shift in the balance of the constitution since 1902. But there would have been more room for argument; for the establishment of a new convention would then have to be inferred mainly from propositions about what was necessary for the proper working of the constitution.[68]

2   What if there is substantial disagreement as to the existence or content of a convention? In 1940 both George VI and Neville Chamberlain would have preferred Lord Halifax to Winston Churchill as Chamberlain's successor. Here it is possible to assert that they were mistaken in thinking that such an appointment would have been constitutionally proper, even if Churchill had been compliant – and fortunately he was not. But if such a view could be seriously entertained on a point which by that time was clearly covered by convention, one must accept that divided counsel may be heard on a great many other, more controversial issues; and that personal inclination and political expediency may well be determining factors. Academic authorities on the constitution enjoy no immunity from partisan sentiment; in the Irish home rule crisis in 1913 both Dicey and Anson, active opponents of the Liberal Government, expressed manifestly unacceptable views on the conventional powers of the King to override his ministers.[69] And even when an authority on the constitution is able to adopt a more detached attitude, the materials available to him about the precedents may be inadequate – political and royal biographies are the

---

[66] As L. S. Amery indicated in his *Thoughts on the Constitution* (2nd edn, 1953), pp. 21–2. See also Kenneth Rose, *Superior Person* (1969).

[67] See Robert Blake, *The Unknown Prime Minister* (1955), pp. 517–27; Thomas Jones, *Whitehall Diary* (1969), vol. 1, pp. 235–6. See further, on this difficult issue, Robert Rhodes James, *Memoirs of a Conservative* (1969), pp. 150–66; Keith Middlemas and John Barnes, *Baldwin* (1969), pp. 158–69. Probably the truth of the matter will never be known; there are discrepancies in the accounts revealed.

[68] See further Marshall and Moodie, op. cit., pp. 30–34.

[69] See Jennings, *Cabinet Government* (3rd edn, 1959), Appendix 3.

best sources but are not always timely or comprehensive – and opinions on what rules are necessary for the working of the contemporary constitution can reasonably differ. Differences of opinion among practising politicians as to the scope and very existence of the conventions they ought to observe are, of course, both frequent and unreasonable.

3 A convention can be created without any background of pre-existing usage. It can come into being (a) by express agreement, or (b) by a unilateral undertaking, or (c) within a limited field, by a decision imposed by the Prime Minister or adopted by the Cabinet for its own regulation. For example, (a) it was agreed at an Imperial Conference in 1930 that in future the Governor-General of a Dominion should be appointed by the Crown exclusively on the advice of the Dominion Government concerned and that the United Kingdom Government would not even have a formal part to play in such an appointment. (b) In 1949, when Eire left the Commonwealth and became the Republic of Ireland, the United Kingdom Government and Parliament undertook not to exclude Northern Ireland from the United Kingdom without the consent of the Northern Ireland Parliament. (c) Under Mrs Margaret Thatcher fewer decisions are taken by the full Cabinet and more by informal meetings of Ministers.[70] This development was designed mainly to streamline decision-making by restricting the range of matters which individual Ministers could bring before the full Cabinet, and no doubt partly so as to keep more decision-making in the Prime Minister's own hands. Ministers were obliged to accept the new procedures if they wished to remain in the Government.

4 Conventions may lose their binding force or change in content. So, of course, may rules of strict law. But conventions tend to change in different, and sometimes mysterious, ways.

A convention established by express agreement may be superseded or modified by agreement. Constitutional conventions share this characteristic with conventional rules of international law. For example, the convention relating to the appointment of Governors-General of Dominions on local advice was understood to extend, by necessary implication, to the removal of Governors-General, and to the appointment and removal of Governors-General of newly independent Commonwealth countries; but at the Mauritius Constitutional Conference in 1965 it was agreed that when Mauritius became independent, the

[70] See below, p. 172–4.

Government of Mauritius would not advise Her Majesty to remove the Governor-General (in whom the constitution would repose a number of unusual and important personal discretionary powers) except on grounds of medical incapacity upon the report of an independent tribunal appointed by the Chief Justice.[71] In this instance the general convention remained, subject to an exception.

Again, decisions by the Prime Minister or the Cabinet about the manner in which the Cabinet is to operate may be superseded by new decisions. But perhaps conventions of this sort ought to be put into a special category in that (like some of the sessional orders of the House of Commons) they are understood to be experimental, though undoubtedly binding until they are altered or discarded in the accepted manner. Judicial precedents are also binding till they are authoritatively reversed, overruled or disapproved. We do not regard them as non-binding merely because their authority may be ephemeral, unless it is clear that they are based on a wrong principle.

A convention may, alternatively, lose binding force because of a major change in circumstances. In 1961 the United Kingdom Government agreed that it would be contrary to convention for Parliament to legislate for Southern Rhodesia on any matter within the competence of the Southern Rhodesian Legislature without the consent of the Southern Rhodesian Government.[72] In 1965 the Government of Southern Rhodesia made a unilateral (and unlawful) declaration of the colony's independence. The United Kingdom Parliament immediately reasserted plenary legislative authority in relation to Southern Rhodesia.[73] This could not reasonably be construed as a breach of convention; the survival of the convention presupposed the continuance of a constitutional relationship which the Government of Southern Rhodesia had repudiated.[74] Problems of interpretation may arise where changes in circumstances are less dramatic. For example, on Harold Macmillan's resignation from the office of Prime Minister on grounds of ill-health in 1963, the Queen invited Lord Home to form a Government as his successor. Home was known to be the most acceptable candidate to the Conservative Party; but what of the convention that the Prime Minister could not be a member of the Lords?[75] A few months previously, Parliament had passed an Act

---

[71] Cmnd 2797 (1965), p. 8. This convention was not written into the constitution.
[72] Cmnd 1399 (1961), p. 3. See further below, ch. 34.
[73] Southern Rhodesia Act 1965; see also the Southern Rhodesia Constitution Order 1965 (S.I. 1965, No. 1952). For Northern Ireland, see pp. 50–57.
[74] cf. de Smith, op. cit., p. 42.
[75] See pp. 41–2, 161.

under which it had become possible for Lord Home to disclaim his hereditary peerages.[76] He promptly disclaimed them, became Sir Alec Douglas-Home, and obtained a seat in the Commons at a by-election shortly afterwards. Presumably this change in the law was understood to have modified the convention to the extent that a peer could become Prime Minister if he agreed to disclaim his title and to try to obtain a seat in the Commons forthwith. If at the time of Home's appointment no such undertaking was offered or extracted, his appointment would probably have been unconstitutional.

Conventions have also disappeared or been varied because they have been disregarded with impunity and with general acquiescence. In this respect they differ from all rules of strict law in this country except local or mercantile customary rules. For example, before 1918 the decision when to advise the monarch to dissolve Parliament had been taken by the Cabinet as a whole. In November 1918 Lloyd George decided to advise a dissolution on his own initiative. Cabinet colleagues not merely acquiesced in this step but erroneously justified it by reference to nonexistent precedents.[77] Thus arose the modern convention that the decision to advise a dissolution was for the Prime Minister alone, though it was still open to the Prime Minister to discuss the matter with his colleagues, privately or in a Cabinet meeting.[78] Doubtless all conventions are binding, but some are more binding than others. (The obvious retort is that the conventions about advice to dissolve Parliament are of major importance.) The disappearance of a convention in these circumstances might alternatively be rationalized on the ground that it had atrophied unobserved, or had dwindled to the status of a non-binding usage, compliance or deviation being equally permissible. Whether a convention retains its binding force, and if so, how much, is often demonstrable only by the empirical test of 'break it and see'. The outcome of such an experiment may still be equivocal; breach may be represented, or interpreted after the event, as a mere *ad hoc* waiver;[79] allegations of unconstitutional behaviour are frequently made in the cut and thrust of day-to-day politics and are as often

---

[76] Peerage Act 1963, passed in consequence of the campaign waged by Lord Stansgate (Mr Tony Benn). All peers by inheritance could disclaim within a year after the Act became law; thereafter only *new* peers by inheritance (or peers who had inherited subject to infancy or another disability) could disclaim (s. 1). See further pp. 299–300.

[77] Jennings, *Cabinet Government* (3rd edn, 1959), pp. 417–19.

[78] Such discussions were certainly held by Mr Wilson, Mr Heath, Mr Callaghan and Mrs Thatcher, and probably by other post-war Prime Ministers. See Rodney Brazier, *Constitutional Practice* (1988), pp. 83–4.

[79] See below, pp. 188–9.

shrugged off, sometimes on the spurious ground that no binding convention on the matter had ever existed;[80] adverse pronouncements by constitutional experts and editorial writers in the better informed daily and weekly journals are not endowed with the aura of prestige that surrounds the judgments of the superior courts.

We arrive at a position where there is a clear case for differentiating some conventions from most rules of strict law. When there are serious doubts as to the scope, even the very existence, of a conventional rule, and no adequate means of allaying those doubts, one cannot expect to find a widespread sense of obligation to obey that rule. Appeals to the voices of authority may evoke a Tower of Babel or the inscrutable muteness of the sphinx. Appeals to precedents may be less convincing than appeals to principle. Perhaps the most persuasive summing up is that 'the crucial questions must always be whether or not a particular class of action is likely to destroy respect for the established distribution of authority and whether or not it is likely to maintain respect for the constitutional system by changing (or sustaining) the distribution of authority'.[81] This distribution of authority implies the maintenance of limited monarchy, representative government, responsible government and efficient government; it implies also that constitutional rules must be compatible with the realities of practical politics. Given the vagueness of these criteria, it is not surprising that no attempt to list the conventions of the constitution would command universal assent. If half a dozen constitutional lawyers were separately to set down the conventions governing collective ministerial responsibility, it would be astonishing if six identical sets of answers were to be produced.

Replacement of conventions by statutory rules: a footnote

We have noted that many conventions could be codified in a statutory or non-statutory form; and that Commonwealth constitutions often include provisions on matters which in this country are regulated solely by convention. We also observed that a loose convention about legislative relations between the Lords and the Commons was replaced in 1911 by a precise set of statutory rules. Writers occasionally misstate the effect of the Parliament Act by describing it as an enactment of constitutional conventions. On the contrary, it was a partial

---

[80] cf. Dicey, op. cit., p. 441. This is the main single reason why identification of conventions is so difficult. People who ought to be *obeying* conventions deny their existence or unmake them by their disobedience.

[81] Marshall and Moodie, op. cit., p. 32. See also Jennings, *Cabinet Government* (3rd edn, 1959), ch. 1.

supersession of constitutional conventions by rules of strict law. The other favourite example of the 'enactment' of constitutional conventions is the Statute of Westminster 1931. What this Act did was

1　to recite, in the *preamble*, certain conventions about Dominion status;
2　to relieve the Dominions of legal incapacities attributable to the fact that, before the Statute, they were colonies in strict law; and
3　to provide, in section 4 of the Statute, that no future Act of the United Kingdom Parliament was to extend, or be deemed to extend, to a Dominion as part of its law unless the request and consent of that Dominion were *expressly declared* in such an Act.

The exact legal effect of section 4 is still disputable.[82] But alone among the sections of the Statute of Westminster can it be compared to the enactment of a convention. The corresponding *convention* was set out in the preamble. It records 'the established constitutional position' that no law made by the United Kingdom Parliament 'shall extend to a Dominion as part of its law otherwise than at the request and with the consent of that Dominion'. Even section 4, therefore, does not precisely reproduce constitutional convention; it embodies the substance of the convention but adds something to it.

[82] See pp. 76–7. The Court of Appeal has discussed some limited questions about s. 4: in particular, it has held that provided there is an express declaration in any Act under consideration that the Dominion had so requested and consented, then the courts will not inquire into whether that request and consent had actually been given: *Manuel* v. *Att.-Gen.* [1983] 1 Ch. 77 at 106.

Chapter 3

The United Kingdom

The United Kingdom[1]

The United Kingdom means the United Kingdom of Great Britain and Northern Ireland and its territorial waters. It is a unitary sovereign State.

In 1284 Wales was annexed by the Crown. Effective integration with England was deferred till 1536, when Welshmen were placed in the same legal position as Englishmen, Welsh constituencies were given representation in the English Parliament and the English system of local government was extended to Wales. From 1746 till 1967 the word 'England' in an Act of Parliament was deemed to include Wales; for Acts passed since then this slur on the principality has been removed.[2] There is an annual debate on Welsh affairs at Westminster. The Welsh Grand Committee is a deliberative body and considers bills and other matters relating exclusively to Wales which are referred to it. If it recommends that a bill should receive a second reading the House does so without debate. Not much use is made of the committee for legislative purposes, however, partly because few bills relate exclusively to Wales and partly because there is a permanent anti-Conservative majority in Wales, so that a Conservative Government's controversial legislation might flounder in that committee.[3] Administrative devolution is more important. In 1951 the office of Minister for Welsh Affairs

---

[1] See D. G. T. Williams, 'The Constitution of the United Kingdom' [1972B] *Camb. L.J.* 266.

[2] Welsh Language Act 1967, s. 4. Does Wales include Monmouthshire? There is no all-inclusive answer to this question, but under the Local Government Act 1972, s. 20(7), Sched. 4, it does geographically, though Monmouthshire ceased to exist as a local government unit.

[3] House of Commons S.O. No. 98; see below, pp. 292–6, for the Select Committee on Welsh Affairs set up in 1979.

was created; at first the office was combined with another departmental responsibility,[4] but in 1964 the Welsh Office became a separate Department headed by a Secretary of State with a seat in the Cabinet. He has responsibility for primary and secondary education in Wales and a number of other local and regional services; most of the Office's work is done in Cardiff. There are also Welsh departments of some Whitehall ministries – for example the Ministry of Agriculture, Fisheries and Food. Provision has been made for the use of the Welsh language in courts sitting in Wales, and for certain official purposes.[5] Welsh nationalism, nurtured on a distinctive culture, emerged as a political force of some consequence in the late 1960s. The response to it of the Government, Parliament and of the people of Wales will be considered later in this chapter.[6]

In 1603 James VI of Scotland became James I of England; this was a *personal* union and did not make Scotland and England one. In 1707 the Acts of Union created a United Kingdom of Great Britain, merging the Scottish and English Parliaments in pursuance of negotiated Articles of Union.[7] Scotland[8] has its own Established Church,[9] judicial system, criminal and civil law[10] (rooted in Roman concepts but now substantially influenced by the common law and United Kingdom legislation), local government and educational systems. Accordingly, a substantial measure of responsibility for Scotland's internal affairs rests in Scottish hands, though by no means enough to satisfy separatists in the Scottish National Party. At Westminster a large majority of Scottish bills go to the Scottish Grand Committee and a Scottish standing committee, the part played by the House of Commons as a whole being little more than formal.[11] There has been a Secretary for Scotland since 1885 and a Secretary of State since 1926; he is always a member of a peace-time Cabinet. St Andrew's House, Edinburgh, is the

---

[4] The first Minister for Welsh Affairs was the then Home Secretary, Sir David Maxwell Fyfe. He was known in Wales as 'Dai Bananas'.

[5] Welsh Courts Act 1942; Welsh Language Act 1967.

[6] See below pp. 62–3.

[7] A. V. Dicey and R. S. Rait, *Thoughts on the Union* (1920).

[8] Including Rockall: Island of Rockall Act 1972.

[9] The Presbyterian Church of Scotland. The Church of Ireland was severed from the Church of England in 1869 and the Church of Wales was disestablished in 1914.

[10] See T. B. Smith, *Scotland: The Development of its Laws and Constitution* (1962); D. M. Walker, *The Scottish Legal System* (5th edn, 1981). There is a separate Law Commission for Scotland and a Scottish Committee of the Council on Tribunals.

[11] See Edwards (1972) 25 *Parliamentary Affairs* 303; H.C.S.O. Nos 86, 93–7; pp. 292–6 below for the Select Committee on Scottish Affairs established in 1979. The Scottish Grand Committee also considers the Scottish estimates. Peers of Scotland sit in the House of Lords.

home of the five sub-departments of the Scottish Office – the Department of Agriculture and Fisheries for Scotland, the Scottish Development Department, the Scottish Economic Planning Department, the Scottish Education Department and the Scottish Home and Health Department. The Secretary of State also has responsibility for a number of minor Departments (for example, the General Register Office for Scotland, the Scottish Record Office), and for public corporations operating only in Scotland (such as the two electricity Boards and the Highlands and Islands Development Board). He also has joint responsibility for the Forestry Commission and the Crown Estate Commissioners. A number of United Kingdom Departments have regional organizations in Scotland with Scottish directors or controllers; the Secretary of State has a miscellany of coordinating functions. There are Scottish boards, councils or committees for some of the nationalized industries and other quasi-government bodies.[12] The Lord Advocate has a unique blend of responsibilities for the Scottish legal system, particularly on the criminal side.

In the Plantagenet period Ireland was subjected to the overlordship of the Kings of England. Attempts to subdue its turbulent people were seldom sustained or efficacious. After the Reformation, Protestant settlement and discrimination against the Roman Catholic populace provoked insurrection followed by repression, more thoroughgoing in the times of Cromwell and William III than in earlier years. In 1783 the British Parliament purported to relinquish jurisdiction over Ireland; and for 'eighteen years Ireland was no more subject to England than was England to Ireland'.[13] In 1801 Ireland, which then had a separate Parliament, entered into union with Great Britain, and the Irish question entered into British politics. A hundred members of Parliament were elected for Irish constituencies.[14] Irish nationalism grew, and eventually Gladstone, at seventy-six, was converted to the cause of Irish home rule; but his party split on the issue – Dicey and Anson were among the more prominent Liberal Unionists – and his first Home Rule Bill was defeated in the Commons. The second was thrown out by

---

[12] See, for example, J. D. B. Mitchell, *Constitutional Law* (2nd edn, 1968); J. N. Wolfe (ed.), Government and Nationalism in Scotland (1969); Mitchell in Andrews (ed.), *Welsh Studies in Public Law* (1970), ch. 5; J. P. Mackintosh, *The Devolution of Power* (1968), ch. 6; Royal Commission on the Constitution, Written Evidence 2 – the Scottish Office, the Lord Advocate's Department and the Crown Office; J. G. Kellas, *The Scottish Political System* (2nd edn, 1975); M. Keating and A. Midwinter, *The Government of Scotland* (1983).

[13] F. W. Maitland, *Constitutional History of England* (1908), p. 335.

[14] There were also twenty-eight representative peers of Ireland in the Lords. See p. 298, note 8.

the Lords. In August 1914 the Government of Ireland Act was passed under the Parliament Act procedure, providing for an internally self-governing, undivided Ireland, with its own Parliament subject to the overriding paramountcy of the United Kingdom Parliament. This measure, bitterly opposed by the Protestant majority in the province of Ulster and their sympathizers across the water, never came into effect. It was superseded by the Government of Ireland Act 1920, which provided for two separate (and subordinate) Parliaments, one for Northern Ireland and one for Southern Ireland. Because of an armed uprising in the South, only part of this Act became operative. In 1922 the Irish Free State (now the Republic of Ireland) was created and given Dominion status.[15] From then on,[16] the United Kingdom meant Great Britain and Northern Ireland.[17]

The constitution of Northern Ireland and the powers of its Government and Parliament were set out in the 1920 Act as amended by subsequent legislation of the United Kingdom Parliament.[18] Under the 1920 Act Northern Ireland had some of the trappings of an independent State – a Prime Minister, Cabinet and Privy Council, a bicameral Parliament (composed of a Senate and a House of Commons), responsible self-government, a Supreme Court with a Lord Chief Justice, and so on. The Northern Ireland Parliament had a general power to make laws for the peace, order and good government of the six counties. Appearances were not entirely deceptive. Various aspects of public law have been regulated differently in Northern Ireland. For instance, gas was never nationalized; there are no lay magistrates. In their own house the Northern Ireland authorities were, to a large extent, masters, till law and order broke down.

The United Kingdom Parliament retained plenary legislative powers in Northern Ireland (section 75 of the 1920 Act) and the powers of the

[15] In United Kingdom law by virtue of the Irish Free State (Agreement) Act 1922 and the Irish Free State Constitution Act 1922. For the constitutional problems arising out of the legislation, see Sir Kenneth Wheare, *The Constitutional Structure of the Commonwealth* (1960), pp. 90–94.

[16] The exact date of the Free State's departure from the United Kingdom within the legal meaning of the latter term is not altogether clear. See Sir Kenneth Roberts-Wray, *Commonwealth and Colonial Law* (1966), pp. 32–5.

[17] Northern Ireland comprises six of the nine counties formerly comprised within the province of Ulster. The terms 'Northern Ireland' and 'Ulster' are, however, often used interchangeably.

[18] The leading commentary, written from the standpoint of a moderate Unionist, is Harry Calvert's *Constitutional Law in Northern Ireland* (1968). For an informative and close critique, see Claire Palley, *The Evolution, Disintegration and Possible Reconstruction of the Northern Ireland Constitution* (1972), reprinted from (1972) 1 *Anglo-American Law Review* 368–476.

United Kingdom Government were potentially unrestricted; but in relation to 'transferred matters' (i.e. matters assigned to Northern Ireland competence) the practice was for the United Kingdom to intervene only at the request or with the concurrence or acquiescence of the Northern Ireland Government. Nevertheless, even before orderly civil government began to collapse, the United Kingdom was able to exert some influence over Northern Ireland's policies within the transferred field because of Stormont's financial dependence.

In the period from October 1968, when communal disturbances broke out in Londonderry, till the time of writing, more constitutional and administrative reforms in Northern Ireland were introduced than in the preceding sixty years. The basic problem was simple to state, perhaps impossible to solve. Public life (and often private life) in Northern Ireland was dominated by sectarian faction and the problem of the border with the south. A million Protestants were overwhelmingly unionist; half a million Catholics were predominantly separatist and republican. Of the twelve M.P.s returned from Northern Ireland constituencies to Westminster, at least nine would be Protestant Unionists. The Unionist Party was permanently in office at Stormont; the minority had no prospect of attaining political power by constitutional means. In such circumstances the Westminster model of responsible government would not work in the manner familiar in Great Britain. By 1972 at the latest, as attitudes on both sides polarized amid mounting terrorism, repression and hatred, it had ceased to work at all.

In 1969 the main specific grievances of Catholics were found to be[19] the allegedly discriminatory allocation of public housing; discrimination in local government appointments; distortion of local government boundaries (and restriction of the franchise to ratepayers) to perpetuate local unionist dominance; failure by the Government properly to investigate complaints of unfair discrimination; resentment of the existence and conduct of the Ulster Special Constabulary (the 'B Specials'), a paramilitary force; the existence and use of the Civil Authorities (Special Powers) Act (N.I.) 1922, a kind of permanent Emergency Powers Act.[20] A series of reforms followed, mainly prompted by Westminster, the United Kingdom having been obliged to send large

[19] Report of the Cameron Commission on Disturbances in Northern Ireland (Cmnd 532 (N.I.1969), § 229). For a fuller study, see the Report of the Scarman Tribunal of Inquiry on Violence and Civil Disturbances in Northern Ireland in 1969 (Cmnd 566 (N.I. 1972)). See also the Report of the Hunt Committee on the Police in Northern Ireland (Cmnd 534 (N.I. 1969)).

[20] For the invocation of powers under this Act before disturbances began, see *McEldowney* v. *Forde* [1971] A.C. 632.

reinforcements of troops to Northern Ireland in an attempt to restore order. Local government reforms, already under way, were expedited.[21] Universal suffrage for local electors was introduced and the 'business premises' vote for Stormont electors was abolished.[22] The 'B Specials' were stood down and the Royal Ulster Constabulary was (for the time being) disarmed; a new part-time local military force, the Ulster Defence Regiment, was formed;[23] the G.O.C. Northern Ireland was placed in control of the R.U.C. for security operations, with direct responsibility to United Kingdom Ministers. An interesting and potentially important innovation was the establishment of the office of Commissioner for Complaints,[24] who has power to investigate complaints of injustice caused by maladministration by local and other public bodies lying outside the jurisdiction of the Parliamentary Commissioner for Administration; he can receive complaints direct from members of the public, and if a complaint is upheld the person aggrieved can apply to a county court for damages and an injunction. Other reforms included the establishment of an independent Community Relations Commission[25] and the vesting of responsibility for prosecutions in an independent Director of Public Prosecutions subject only to the English Attorney-General.[26]

Reform came too late to satisfy the republicans, who had been brought increasingly under the sway of the Provisional wing of the Irish Republican Army. The situation was exacerbated by the introduction in August 1971 of the large-scale internment of security suspects under the Civil Authorities (Special Powers) Act (N.I.) 1922;[27] and far-reaching proposals for internal constitutional reform in Northern Ireland[28] met with little overt response among the more moderate nationalists. In March 1972 the United Kingdom imposed direct rule on Northern Ireland; the functions of the Parliament and Government

[21] See p. 397. In 1969, moreover, the unionist-biased system of local government in Londonderry had been replaced by a Development Commission.

[22] Electoral Law Acts (N.I.) 1968 and 1969.

[23] Ulster Defence Regiment Act 1969; Cmnd 4188 (1969); Police Act 1969.

[24] Commissioner for Complaints Act (N.I.) 1969. For description and evaluation, see Poole [1972] *Public Law* 131; Garner (1970) 21 *N.I.L.Q.* 353; Elcock (1972) 50 *Public Administration* 87; Claire Palley, op. cit., pp. 422–5. The P.C.A. has only a very limited jurisdiction in relation to Northern Ireland: see Parliamentary Commissioner Act 1967, s. 13.

[25] Palley, op. cit., pp. 425–6.

[26] S.I. 1972, No. 538 (agreed before direct rule was imposed).

[27] For inquiries into complaints about the conduct of the security forces in connection with this operation, and in the shooting in Londonderry in January 1972, see Cmnd 4832 (1971) (the Compton Report), Cmnd 4901 (1971) (the Parker Report), and H.C. 220 (1971–72) (the Widgery Report).

[28] See especially Cmnd 560 (N.I. 1971), Cmnd 568 (N.I. 1972).

of the province were vested in the Secretary of State for Northern Ireland. Westminster placed it on record that nothing done under the Act imposing direct rule (the Northern Ireland (Temporary Provisions) Act 1972) was to derogate or authorize derogation from the status of Northern Ireland as part of the United Kingdom,[29] and a plebiscite on the border issue was held in March 1973.[30] Nearly sixty per cent of the electorate voted in favour of the province remaining a part of the United Kingdom. Troops re-occupied the Catholic 'no-go' areas in Belfast and Londonderry and Her Majesty's Government governed again. Internment by executive order, bereft of procedural safeguards,[31] had been phased out and replaced by detention in pursuance of a determination by judicial commissioners subject to appeal to a judicial tribunal.[32] Imaginative suggestions for the constitutional future of Northern Ireland were canvassed.[33]

A succession of constitutional experiments was tried subsequently. A sequel to the 1972 discussion paper was published in March 1973.[34] In order to hold the ring, direct rule under the 1972 Act was renewed for a further year. Under the Northern Ireland Assembly Act 1973 and the Northern Ireland Constitution Act 1973 the Northern Ireland Assembly and Executive, based on power-sharing between the two communities, were established, and the Stormont Parliament was abolished.[35] The paramount legislative sovereignty of the United Kingdom Parliament was retained.[36] On that basis direct rule was ended on 1 January 1974. But the implementation of the new constitution met a severe setback in May 1974 following the collapse of the Executive after two weeks of a politically motivated strike in the province by so-called 'loyalists'. Direct rule was re-imposed the following day. The Assembly was prorogued and later dissolved.[37] Next came the election of a Constitutional Convention under the Northern Ireland Act 1974,[38] to deliberate for one year. As

[29] ibid., s. 2; see also Cmnd 534 (N.I. 1969), para. 56(1); Cmnd 4154 (1969), para 1.

[30] Northern Ireland (Border Poll) Act 1972.

[31] cf. (1972) 23 *N.I.L.Q.* 331.

[32] S.I. 1972, No. 1632.

[33] *The Future of Northern Ireland*; a paper for discussion (Northern Ireland Office, HMSO, October 1972).

[34] Northern Ireland Constitutional Proposals, Cmnd 5259 (1973).

[35] Northern Ireland Constitution Act 1973, s. 31. The Act also contains anti-discrimination provisions, and established the Standing Advisory Commission on Human Rights: ibid., s. 20. The Commission reported in 1987 that 'serious and substantial' inequalities of opportunity persisted for Catholics: see Cm 237 (1987). A White Paper on fair employment has also been published: see Cm 380 (1988).

[36] ibid., s. 4(4).

[37] S.I. 1974, No. 926; S.I. 1975, No. 422.

[38] The Act also made continued provision for direct rule: s 1 and sched. 1.

was generally anticipated it failed to agree and was, in turn, dissolved.[39]

At the time of writing, therefore, Northern Ireland is still subject to direct rule by virtue of the Northern Ireland Act 1974, section 1 and schedule 1.[40] Broadly, that statute puts the Constitution Act 1973 on ice and allows Her Majesty in Council to make laws for Northern Ireland; any executive functions may be carried out by the Secretary of State for Northern Ireland. Emergency powers are exercised mainly under the Northern Ireland (Emergency Provisions) Act 1978. This Act consolidated most of the Northern Ireland (Emergency Provisions) Act 1973 (which repealed the Civil Authorities (Special Powers) Act (N.I.) 1922 and which substantially implemented the Diplock Commission recommendations on legal procedures to deal with terrorist activities[41]), the Northern Ireland (Young Persons) Act 1975 and the Northern Ireland (Emergency Provisions) (Amendment) Act 1975. The duration of the powers in the 1978 Act may be extended by Orders in Council from time to time. It has been amended by the Northern Ireland (Emergency Provisions) Act 1987. The 1978 Act will automatically lapse in 1992 (but no doubt will be extended before then).

From 1974 to 1979 next to no overt political initiatives were forthcoming from Westminster: the maintenance of security was given priority. True, the number of Northern Irish M.P.s was increased from twelve to seventeen,[42] but it was not until the Conservatives regained power in May 1979 that two successive initiatives were made and two White Papers published, in 1980 and 1982.[43] On the basis of the 1982 White Paper a new Northern Ireland Assembly was elected.[44] Under the Northern Ireland Act 1982[45] a flexible approach to the ending of direct rule and to the devolution of power to the province was envisaged.[46] First, the Assembly was to meet and, while direct rule continued, was in effect to have deliberative and consultative functions.[47] Secondly, if agreement could be reached in the Assembly on proposals for full or partial devolution, then they would be

[39] S.I. 1976, No. 349.
[40] Orders in Council are made at six-monthly intervals continuing the 1974 Act in force.
[41] Cmnd 5185 (1972). 'Diplock courts', consisting of a judge without a jury, were set up: see the 1978 Act, ss 7, 30 and sched. 4. The 1978 Act was reviewed by Sir George Baker: see Cmnd 9222 (1984), and comment by Bonner [1984] *Public Law* 348.
[42] House of Commons (Redistribution of Seats) Act 1979.
[43] The Government of Northern Ireland: proposals for further discussion, Cmnd 7950 (1980); Northern Ireland: a framework for devolution, Cmnd 8541 (1982).
[44] By virtue of the Northern Ireland Assembly Act 1973, s. 2 and the Northern Ireland Constitution Act 1973, s 27(7).
[45] See Gearty [1982] *Public Law* 518.
[46] Northern Ireland Act 1982, ss. 1, 2.
[47] ibid., s. 3.

submitted to the Secretary of State for Northern Ireland. The Assembly was elected in 1982: the mainly Catholic Social Democratic and Labour Party contested the elections and won fourteen seats, but announced that it would take no part in Assembly affairs. No real progress was made in the Assembly on devolution, but many debates on Northern Irish affairs took place.

There can be no significant improvement in the problems of Northern Ireland without some cooperation with the Republic of Ireland. For that reason a major initiative by Mrs Thatcher's Government and the Irish Government led to the conclusion of the Anglo-Irish Agreement at Hillsborough in 1985.[48] While affirming that any change in the province's status can only come about with the consent of a majority of its people, the Agreement established an Inter-governmental Conference. This Conference, with representatives from Northern Ireland and the Republic, meets regularly at ministerial or civil service level as appropriate, the joint chairmen of ministerial meetings being the Secretary of State for Northern Ireland and an Irish Minister. Other Ministers, and the chief constable of Northern Ireland and the commissioner of the Irish Garda, hold separate meetings as required. The Agreement sets out in some detail the topics to be discussed: in summary they include North–South relations, political matters, and security and legal affairs (including the administration of justice, and whether the province should have a new bill of rights). Many meetings have been held at various levels and some progress has been made, but the Agreement has been bitterly resisted by Northern Irish Unionists. The Unionist majority in the Northern Ireland Assembly had formed a one-party committee to analyse the Agreement, so prompting the Alliance Party to join the Social Democratic and Labour Party in boycotting it. It having become pointless – and not inexpensive – to continue the Assembly's life, it was dissolved in 1986.[49] The Unionists launched a hopeless legal challenge to the Agreement;[50] all fifteen Unionist M.P.s resigned their Westminster seats to fight simultaneous by-elections to demonstrate the strength of feeling against Irish 'interference' in the affairs of the province.[51] Any long-term constitutional change which might flow from the Anglo-Irish Agreement cannot be achieved in defiance of Unionist views, but equally further legal and

[48] See Cmnd 9657 (1985).
[49] S.I. 1986, No. 1036.
[50] See *Ex p. Molyneaux* [1986] 1 W.L.R. 331.
[51] One seat was lost to the S.D.L.P.; the other 14 Unionists were returned – although with only a slightly higher total vote than they had achieved at the 1983 General Election. See Boulton [1986] *Public Law* 211.

administrative devolution to Northern Ireland remains the policy of all the main British political parties.

The Channel Islands and the Isle of Man[52]

The Channel Islands and the Isle of Man are not parts of the United Kingdom, though in some legal contexts the term 'United Kingdom' is deemed to include them. With the United Kingdom they constitute the British Islands.[53] They are dependencies of the Crown, and belong to Her Majesty's dominions. Although they fall within the definition of a 'British possession',[54] they are not colonies. Their status is unique.

The islands have other points of similarity. They have ancient institutions. Their affairs are subject to a degree of superintendence by the Home Office, acting on the recommendation of the Committees of the Privy Council for the affairs of Jersey and Guernsey and for the Isle of Man, and petitions relating to matters arising in the islands may be directed to the Privy Council. The principal channel of communication between the islands and the United Kingdom Government is the Home Office, and the Home Secretary is the dominant figure in the Privy Council Committees, which today never meet as deliberative bodies. Assent to local legislation is given by Order in Council and is not a mere formality. Modifications to measures passed by the States of Jersey and Guernsey are still sometimes made after representations by or through the Home Office. Control over Isle of Man legislation has been more freely exercised; bills have been dropped under Home Office pressure and in 1962 the royal assent was withheld from a Manx bill on wireless telegraphy. Public administration in each of the principal islands is conducted mainly through committees or boards of the legislatures; in this respect the pattern resembles that of a British local authority, and particularly in the Channel Islands there is no clear-cut separation of powers between Executive and Legislature. The customary law, on which the local law was once based, is now being replaced by more modern legislation. Appeals lie from the highest courts of the islands to the Judicial Committee of the Privy Council.[55] The United

[52] See Report of the Royal Commission on the Constitution, Cmnd 5460 (1973), Part XI.
[53] Interpretation Act 1978, s. 5 and sched. 1.
[54] ibid.
[55] Appeals are infrequent. There are differences in judicial structure. In both Jersey and Guernsey there is a Royal Court, composed of the Bailiff (a lawyer and the principal insular officer) and elected jurats who can be laymen. There is a separate Court of Appeal composed of barristers from the mainland. In the Isle of Man there are Deemsters who sit as judges, and a Judge of Appeal, an English barrister, who sits with a Deemster. See further Robilliard [1979] *Crim. L. Rev.* 566.

Kingdom Government is responsible for the defence and international relations of all the islands.[56]

There are also important points of dissimilarity in status and internal constitutional structure. In particular, Jersey and Guernsey have full internal self-government and financial autonomy whereas the Isle of Man has not; the Lieutenant-Governor of the Isle of Man has active executive responsibilities as an agent of the United Kingdom Government,[57] unlike the Lieutenant-Governors of Jersey and Guernsey. In 1967 the United Kingdom Parliament and Government imposed on the Isle of Man the Marine etc. Broadcasting (Offences) Act,[58] outlawing broadcasting from 'marine structures' within the British Islands and the contiguous sea area. No similar imposition has been made upon Jersey or Guernsey in recent years.

The Channel Islands

When the Duke of Normandy became King of England in 1066, the Channel Islands were already part of the Dukedom; and when King John lost the mainland of Normandy, they remained as possessions of the Crown. These islands off the French coast now comprise the bailiwicks of Jersey and Guernsey. Within the bailiwick of Gurnsey lie the only two other Channel Islands having a sizeable population, Alderney and Sark. Alderney has its own representative legislature, the States, and provides certain local services, but in 1948 responsibility for

---

[56] As far as practicable, the United Kingdom procures the insertion of a territorial application clause into treaties to which it becomes a party so that its obligations under the treaty shall not extend to matters lying ordinarily within the area of internal self-government of territories (including the Islands) for whose international obligations it is responsible. The treaty obligations will then only be extended to those territories with their concurrence. Today this is seldom practicable. Under international pressure and for reasons of self-interest, the United Kingdom often incurs international obligations (particularly under multilateral conventions) extending of their own force to such territories but dealing primarily with local domestic matters. The United Kingdom Government may then be impaled on the horns of a dilemma; either it becomes an international defaulter by failing to secure the *implementation* of the treaty obligations in local law; or it infringes the canons of constitutional propriety by insisting on implementation, if necessary encroaching on the field of local autonomy. The European Convention on Human Rights has recently presented problems for the enforcement of Guernsey housing laws and has also led the European Court of Human Rights to pronounce against birching on the Isle of Man. See further p. 429.

[57] In the words of the Joint Evidence submitted in 1970 by the Home Office and Tynwald (the Isle of Man Parliament) to the Royal Commission on the Constitution, 'he is the head of the insular administration, his powers resemble those of an archetypal colonial governor, and he is subject only to the control of the Secretary of State' (Part B, s. 7).

[58] Extended to the Isle of Man by S.I. 1967, No. 1276, in fulfilment of a multilateral international convention; see note 56 above.

all the main services was vested in Guernsey. Sark, though nominally a dependency of Guernsey, is substantially autonomous. Owned by a feudal lord with anachronistic institutions, Sark ('where time stands still') is an anomalous survival of an age long past.[59]

The status of Guernsey[60] in relation to the United Kingdom, and its institutions of government, closely resembles that of Jersey.

Jersey[61] has a Lieutenant-Governor appointed by the Crown, and insular officers (the Bailiff, who occupies a position comparable to that of the Lord Chancellor or possibly the Lord Chief Justice, the Deputy Bailiff and the Law Officers) appointed by the Crown from among Jerseymen after local consultations. Administrative decisions are made by committees of the States, the unicameral Legislature. The closest approximation to an executive branch of government is an informal meeting of the insular officers and the presidents of the principal committees. The States are composed of the Bailiff, who presides – he acts as an impartial Speaker and has a power of 'dissent' – the Law Officers and the Dean of Jersey (who may speak but not vote), twelve senators elected for six years, twenty-eight deputies elected every three years, and twelve constables elected from the parishes. (Guernsey has two separate bodies, the States of Deliberation, a legislative body, and the States of Election, which elects certain members of the States of Deliberation as well as the jurats and court officers.) There is universal suffrage. In 1969 allowances for the less affluent members were introduced. Legislation by the States falls into two main classes: Laws, which have effect only when assented to by Her Majesty in Council,[62] and regulations, of a more limited scope; the latter do not require the royal assent. The insular constitution is not contained in a single instrument, but much of it can be pieced together from Laws of the States.

The Crown used to legislate for Jersey by prerogative Order in Council, but as the island has acquired a Legislature with an elected

---

[59] Sark (with a population of over 600) has no motor cars (though five of its residents are reputed to own private aircraft), no income tax, no divorce law and a prison for two. The Seigneur of Sark, Michael Beaumont, continues to levy customary feudal dues from the populace and to exercise a formidable influence over local affairs.

[60] *Vaudin* v. *Hamon* [1974] A.C. 569 is an instructive case on the sources of law in Guernsey.

[61] See F. de L. Bois, *Constitutional History of Jersey* (1969) (Appx 1 to the Submission of the States of Jersey to the Royal Commission on the Constitution, 1970). See also *In re a Debtor, ex p. Viscount of the Royal Court of Jersey* [1981] Ch. 384; de L. Bois [1983] *Public Law* 385.

[62] The Lieutenant-Governor also has a power, no longer exercised, to veto a bill encroaching on the prerogative. Bills are called *projets de loi*. Transactions (including bills and regulations) passed by the States are also called 'Acts' of the States.

majority an attempt to do so today would probably be improper.[63] Parliament retains, in strict law, plenary legislative authority for all those parts of Her Majesty's dominions which have not attained independence or over which Parliament has not renounced its sovereignty. Acts of Parliament extend to Jersey only by express words or necessary implication. The Act is accompanied by an Order in Council directing that it be registered in the Royal Court.[64] The insular authorities may suspend but not refuse registration; in any event, it would appear that such an Act is operative in the island of its own force. In practice, Parliament hardly ever legislates directly for the island; an Act intended to alter the law of the island will provide for its extension to the island by Order in Council made under the Act with such modifications of the Act as may be specified in the Order. Consultation with the insular authorities will then take place and an accommodation will be reached.

It would be contrary to constitutional practice for Parliament so to legislate for the island as to impose taxation or regulate matters of purely domestic concern or derogate from the island's constitutional autonomy without the consent of the States.

Under ancient royal grants, the island has been given immunity from United Kingdom taxation – it has its own fiscal laws – and the right to duty-free entry of its produce into the United Kingdom. Guernsey and Jersey now make voluntary contributions towards United Kingdom defence – some £700,000 each in 1987–8.

The entry of the United Kingdom into the EEC could have posed a serious threat to the island's domestic autonomy. Under article 227(4) of the Rome Treaty, the terms of the Treaty apply to all European territories for whose external relations a member state is responsible. Unqualified accession by the United Kingdom would have entailed the economic integration of Jersey with the United Kingdom if the terms of the Treaty had been implemented in Jersey by the United Kingdom Parliament. As this would have been unacceptable, especially to Jersey, a special Protocol was negotiated by the United Kingdom Government, whereby the Channel Islands and the Isle of Man were brought within the Communities for most purposes but exempted from the Treaty provisions relating to value added tax and fiscal harmonization.[65]

---

[63] Under the rule in *Campbell* v. *Hall* (1774) 1 Cowp. 774, formulated in relation to colonies. See p. 659. An Order in Council establishing a Court of Appeal was made in reliance on the prerogative in 1949 but it never came into operation. Appeal courts were finally set up in 1961 after legislation had been passed in the usual way.

[64] See note 58 above. A similar procedure applies in Guernsey.

[65] See Cmnd 4862–I (1972), pp. 16, 17, 82–4. The islands had to accept the common

The Isle of Man

The island is situated in the Irish Sea. In the early 1970s the islanders, like the Jerseymen, were seeking a redefinition of their constitutional position *vis-à-vis* the United Kingdom. However, the changes they sought in the existing relationship were larger; for the Isle of Man lacked a full measure of internal self-government. Apart from legislative controls exercised through Parliament and the Privy Council,[66] the Crown asserts an ultimate responsibility through the Lieutenant-Governor for the good government of the island in respect of such matters as financial proposals, the disposition of the police, the direction of the civil service and the nomination of members of public bodies. The Lieutenant-Governor is advised by an Executive Council composed mainly of chairmen of boards of Tynwald; but he is not obliged to act on the advice tendered. Tynwald, one of the most ancient legislative bodies in the world – originally it was a court – consists of two chambers, a directly elected House of Keys, and an indirectly elected Legislative Council with a very small number of *ex officio* members. Since 1981 the Lieutenant-Governor has had the power of royal assent for bills passed by Tynwald, except for any measure which the Privy Council might reserve to itself: formerly all bills had to go for royal assent to the Queen in Council. The island has its own system of internal taxation. Even before accession to the EEC the island was in customs union with the United Kingdom under the Isle of Man Act 1958 and received a share of the duties thus collected for the island; it paid $2\frac{1}{2}$ per cent of this revenue as a contribution to the United Kingdom in respect of defence and common services (for example, overseas representation).[67] Insular produce was exported to the United Kingdom free of duty. The Isle of Man Act 1979 (which repealed and re-enacted, with amendments, the 1958 Act) continued the customs union but established, from 1 April 1980, an Isle of Man Customs and Excise service. Officials of the United Kingdom service no longer collect customs and excise duties or other indirect taxes in the island on behalf of the island.

The constitutional history of the island is convoluted. Till 1266 it was under Norse rule; then it was ceded to the King of Scotland; early in

---

external tariff, internal free trade and common agricultural policy. Community rules on freedom of movement of persons and services extended to the islands but the islanders were not accorded reciprocal treatment in that sphere.

[66] See Report of the Joint Working Party on the Constitutional Relationship between Isle of Man and the United Kingdom (Home Office, HMSO, 1969).

[67] For a synopsis of the position, see references cited in notes 60 and 66 above.

the fourteenth century it passed, somewhat obscurely, to the King of England, who granted it to subjects, styled Lords of Man. In 1765 it was revested in the Crown by Act of Parliament.[68] The doubts still entertained by some Channel Islanders as to the legal omnicompetence of the United Kingdom Parliament over those islands are not shared by Manxmen.

Devolution[69]

Attempts since 1969 – made entirely by Labour Governments – to devolve substantial legislative, administrative and executive responsibilities to Scotland and (to a lesser extent) to Wales have thus far come to nought.

Partly – some say largely – as a means of assuaging Scottish and Welsh nationalist feeling in the mid-1960s the Wilson Government set up the Royal Commission on the Constitution in 1969 (the Kilbrandon Commission). Its task was 'to examine the present functions of the central legislature and government in relation to the several countries, nations and regions in the United Kingdom'. The Commission reported in 1973.[70] The Labour Government which returned to office in 1974 introduced the Scotland and Wales Bill.[71] It received a second reading in December 1976. As a major constitutional measure, its committee stage was taken on the floor of the Commons, where disaster for the Government struck. So determined were the supporters and opponents of the measure fully to debate it or utterly to destroy it – or, for various motives, to achieve some intermediate result – that parliamentary progress was made agonizingly slow. In February 1977, therefore, the Government sought to introduce a 'guillotine' motion[72] to curtail debate. But this was ignominiously defeated:[73] twenty-two Labour M.P.s voted against it and another twenty-one abstained. The bill was, in effect, abandoned but with the promise of new proposals for the following session.

[68] Isle of Man Purchase Act 1765. There is no corresponding or analogous legislation for the Channel Islands.

[69] For a good short account see Colin Munro, *Studies in Constitutional Law* (1987), pp. 21–34.

[70] Vol. I, Report, Cmnd 5460; Vol. II, Memorandum of Dissent, Cmnd 5460–I (1973).

[71] This was partly based on the Kilbrandon Report; Devolution within the United Kingdom; some alternatives for discussion (1974); Democracy and Devolution: proposals for Scotland and Wales, Cmnd 5732 (1974); Our Changing Democracy: devolution to Scotland and Wales, Cmnd 6348 (1975); Supplementary Statement, Cmnd 6585 (1976); and on the Government's decisions subsequent to those publications: see 912 H.C. Deb. 270–84 (25 May 1976); 916 H.C. Deb. 1455–71 (3 August 1976).

[72] For the meaning of this term, see below p. 269).

[73] 926 H.C. Deb. 1234–1367 (22 February 1977).

The new scheme[74] among other things involved two bills, for Scotland and Wales respectively. Fortified by the parliamentary strength which it had acquired through the Labour–Liberal arrangement[75] the Government introduced the Scotland Bill and the Wales Bill, which received their second readings in November 1977 by substantial majorities.[76] Guillotine motions were speedily approved. Although several defeats were inflicted on parts of the measures, the most damaging for the devolutionists was the inclusion of a clause in the Scotland Bill against the Government's wishes which would require that if less than 40 per cent of the Scottish electorate voted 'yes' in the proposed referendum, an Order in Council would have to be laid before Parliament to allow for the repeal of the legislation.[77] (A similar clause was inserted in the Wales Bill.[78]) The Scotland Act and Wales Act of 1978 duly received royal assent. On 1 March 1979 referendums were held in Scotland and Wales. In Scotland, failure to achieve the '40 per cent requirement' meant that the implementation of the Act was not approved; in Wales, the people decisively rejected the Wales Act regardless of that requirement.[79] Following these defeats the minority Labour Government appealed for brief inter-party discussions. The Conservative Party saw this as an attempt to play for time and (not only for that reason) put down a motion of no confidence. It carried against the Government by one vote – the first successful vote of no confidence since 1924. Parliament, at the Prime Minister's request, was dissolved, and the Conservatives won the General Election. The new Administration introduced the repeal orders, which were carried without a vote.[80]

The present Government continues to oppose any legislative devolution, partly because it remains politically weak in Scotland and Wales. The Labour Party is committed to try again to set up a Scottish Assembly when it returns to power; the S.D.P./Liberal Alliance has advocated major devolution of power to Scotland, Wales and the English regions, a policy continued by the Democrats.

---

[74] For a detailed description, see 936 H.C. Deb. 313–28 (26 July 1977).

[75] See below p. 187.

[76] See 939 H.C. Deb. 51–213 (14 November 1977) and 939 H.C. Deb. 357–512 (15 November 1977).

[77] See 942 H.C. Deb. 1460–1548 (25 January 1978). This became s. 85 of the Scotland Act.

[78] This became s. 80 of the Wales Act

[79] In Scotland, 32.5 per cent of eligible electors voted 'yes', 30.4 per cent voted 'no' and 37.1 per cent abstained. In Wales the equivalent figures were 46.5 per cent 'no', only 11.8 per cent 'yes' and 41.7 per cent abstained.

[80] S.I. 1979, No. 928; S.I. 1979, No. 933.

Chapter 4

Ultimate Authority
in Constitutional Law

Parliamentary sovereignty

The Queen in Parliament is competent, according to United Kingdom law, to make or unmake any law whatsoever on any matter whatsoever; and no United Kingdom court is competent to question the validity of an Act of Parliament. Every other law-making body within the realm either derives its authority from Parliament or exercises it at the sufferance of Parliament; it cannot be superior to or even coordinate with, but must be subordinate to Parliament. So has run the most fundamental rule, the 'very keystone', as Dicey put it, of constitutional law in this country.[1] It is usually called the concept of parliamentary sovereignty. In this chapter we shall have to consider how far this doctrine is affected by the United Kingdom's accession to the European Communities. For the moment, let us assume that it remains intact.

Some writers dislike the term parliamentary 'sovereignty', and prefer to use the word 'supremacy'. 'Sovereign' and 'sovereignty' are words of many meanings.[2] We sometimes speak of the Queen as the Sovereign without attributing to her unlimited authority. We speak of sovereignty in international law when we mean independence, or freedom from external control; in this sense Australia is a sovereign State, but it does not have a 'sovereign' Parliament, because the powers of that Parliament are subject to the constitution. Is the constitution, then, 'sovereign' in Australia? To John Austin, the best-known British writer on sovereignty,[3] every developed State had to have a 'sovereign', who made laws in the form of commands which were habitually obeyed, and whose legal authority was absolute, indivisible and illimitable. Obvi-

---

[1] *Introduction to the Study of the Law of the Constitution* (10th edn, 1959), p. 70.
[2] See F. H. Hinsley, *Sovereignty* (1966).
[3] *The Province of Jurisprudence Determined* (H. L. A. Hart ed., 1954).

ously the location of sovereignty within a federal constitutional system is, by this token, an unrewarding pursuit.[4] Others have defined the concept of sovereignty in different ways at different periods and in different contexts. Dicey, for instance, referred to the Queen in Parliament as the legal sovereign and the electorate as the political sovereign.[5] Clearly the concepts of national sovereignty, parliamentary sovereignty and popular sovereignty have little in common with one another.[6] Hence there is a case for jettisoning the word 'sovereignty' altogether as being too ambiguous. But to discard the term in favour of the doctrine of 'supremacy' of Parliament is not particularly helpful, if only because the latter term conveys the suggestion that the House of Commons, or the Lords and Commons, as a matter of political or sociological fact, are supreme within the State; and manifestly they are not. And so we shall use the phrase 'parliamentary sovereignty', but to denote a legal concept or group of concepts which do not necessarily carry any implication about the effective seat of political power within the State.

How and when was this principle of the unlimited legislative competence of Parliament established? Was it established by Parliament itself; or by the courts; or by whom? And whence was derived the authority to lay down such a principle? Such questions about the ultimate foundations of constitutional law are not peculiar to the United Kingdom. They arise in countries where the central legislature lacks an unbounded sweep of legislative competence. What are the sources of authority for the validity of the supreme constitutions in those countries?

Foundations of the constitutional order

A written constitution is regarded as the primary source of legal authority within a State. In it lies the explanation of the Legislature's power to make laws, the Executive's power to govern and administer, the Judiciary's power to adjudicate. But if we take one step farther, what is it that confers this legitimating quality on the constitution? This question produces some convoluted answers.

Take the constitution of the Commonwealth of Australia. Here the answer seems fairly simple. The constitution is valid because it was duly

[4] For a subtle analysis, see Geoffrey Sawer, *Modern Federalism* (2nd edn, 1978), ch. 7.
[5] Dicey, op. cit., p. 73.
[6] But see pp. 81–2 on the relationship between national sovereignty and parliamentary sovereignty in the EEC context.

enacted by the United Kingdom Parliament, which had power to enact it. Subsequent amendments to the constitution are valid because they have been made in the manner and form prescribed by the constitution. In other words, legal continuity has been preserved.

The case of Australia, however, is exceptional in the modern world. In the large majority of independent states there has been, at one time or another, a breach of legal continuity, and a constitution has been adopted or changed in a manner unauthorized by the pre-existing legal order. This is true of a high proportion of the African states which have become independent. Since independence they have had revolutions and *coups d'état*; often the constitutional instrument has itself been abrogated and replaced, or suspended and modified, in a manner precluded by the independence constitution. And a few countries have deliberately chosen to adopt a new constitution peacefully but in a manner unauthorized by the pre-existing constitution. This is an assertion of legal nationalism, of what is called 'constitutional autochthony',[7] designed to demonstrate that the authority of the constitution is rooted in native soil, not derived from an imperial predecessor. Such a course has been followed in Eire (the Republic of Ireland), India and Sri Lanka. A constitution is adopted by a Constituent Assembly in the name of the people, or presented to the people for their approval; it will not receive the royal assent like normal constitutional amendments.

Take again the constitution of the United States of America. Since its adoption in 1787 it has remained intact, apart from amendments duly made in terms of the constitution. But was the constitution valid in the first place, and if so, why? In 1776 the Thirteen Colonies had unlawfully declared their independence of Britain, and had repudiated the sovereignty of the United Kingdom Parliament.[8] 'We, the People of the United States', proceeded to 'ordain and establish a constitution'. In fact it was formulated at a convention consisting of delegates from the several states and then ratified by the Congress. The name of the 'sovereign' People was invoked to confer upon the constitution moral authority and binding force.

The vague concept that ultimate 'sovereignty' resides in the 'people' is widely acceptable because of its political overtones. Even where a constitution has been overturned from above or below by manifestly

---

[7] Sir Kenneth Wheare, *Constitutional Structure of the Commonwealth* (1960), ch. 4.

[8] The United Kingdom Government recognized the independence of the United States in 1783, but the American Colonies Act 1766 (the Declaratory Act), reiterating the paramount sovereignty of the United Kingdom Parliament, remained on our statute book till 1964.

illegitimate means, it is commonplace for the *de facto* holders of power to assert that they derive their mandate from the people, because it is awkward to be stigmatized as an undemocratic usurper. And by producing a constitution approved by or on behalf of the people, the accolade of legitimacy is achieved. Or is it?

It is one thing to say that government should rest on the consent of the governed; it is another thing to proclaim that a constitution has acquired the force of supreme law merely because it has obtained the approval of an irregularly convened Constituent Assembly or of a majority of the electorate or both. Yet to assert that all constitutions (or constitutional amendments) procured in a manner inconsistent with the pre-existing legal order are legally invalid will land one in a morass of absurd and insoluble difficulties. If the constitution of the United States is a nullity, then presumably only the United Kingdom can validate (with retroactive effect) the millions of governmental measures and judicial decisions taken in that country since independence. This is plainly,ridiculous, for nobody doubts that the United States became an independent State in international law before the end of the eighteenth century. In any case, whence did the United Kingdom Parliament derive its omnicompetence? In July 1688 James II dissolved his Parliament. In December he fled the country, having dropped the Great Seal of the Realm in the Thames a few days earlier. William of Orange, having reached London, met groups of peers, former members of Parliament and other notables; they advised him that elections should be held in the boroughs and counties. The Convention of Lords and 'Commons' met in January 1689, and next month offered the Crown to William and Mary jointly, subject to conditions set out in a Declaration of Right. The offer having been accepted, the Convention passed an Act asserting that it *was* Parliament,[9] and then enacted the Bill of Rights, incorporating the Declaration of Right. Clearly the Convention 'Parliament' had been irregularly summoned; its affirmation of its own legal authority carried the matter no farther; there had been no King from December 1688 (assuming that James II was deemed to have abdicated or to have forfeited the Crown) till February 1689; William III had no hereditary legal title to the throne and therefore had no authority to assent to bills.[10] Has every purported Act of Parliament since 1688 been a nullity? Is a Stuart still the rightful King?

[9] Crown and Parliament Act 1689.
[10] cf. F. W. Maitland, *Constitutional History of England* (1908), pp. 283–5; T. P. Taswell-Langmead's *English Constitutional History* (11th edn, 1960), pp. 445–59.

Once questions such as these are asked,[11] one must acknowledge that in certain circumstances a breach of legal continuity, be it peaceful or accompanied by coercion and violence, may have to be treated as superseding the constitutional and legal order and replacing it by a new one. Legal theorists have no option but to accommodate their concepts to the facts of political life. Successful revolution sooner or later begets its own legality. If, as Hans Kelsen has postulated, the basic norm or ultimate principle underlying a constitutional order is that the constitution ought to be obeyed,[12] then the disappearance of that order, followed by acquiescence on the part of officials, judges and the general public in laws, rules and orders issued by the new holders of power, will displace the old basic norm or ultimate principle and give rise to a new one.[13] Thus, might becomes right in the eye of the law.

This is a persuasive rationalization of the legal consequences of a successful revolution, like the rebellion of the American colonists or the English Revolution of 1688. It does not, however, answer all questions. It offers a description, not a prescription. It does not dictate what attitude judges and officials *ought* to adopt when the purported breach of legal continuity takes place. However, in recent years judges in Pakistan,[14] Uganda[15] and Rhodesia (now Zimbabwe)[16] seem to have proceeded on the assumption that they have to accept a successful revolution as a law-constitutive fact if they remain in office.[17]

Here we are beginning to stray far afield. The argument can be summarized in this way: sooner or later a breach of legal continuity will be treated as laying down legitimate foundations for a new constitutional order, provided that the 'revolution' is successful; there is, however, no neat rule of thumb available to judges during or immediately after the 'revolution' for the purpose of determining

---

[11] One possible answer, deducible from rationalizations of later medieval practice when usurpations of the throne were not uncommon, is that William became King *de jure* after he had dissolved the Convention 'Parliament' and the *new* Parliament of 1690 had validated the legislation passed by the Convention. As a matter of State necessity (see p. 69) a *de facto* King had been regarded as competent to summon a lawful Parliament.

[12] *Pure Theory of Law* (2nd edn, transl.), p. 201; *General Theory of Law and State*, p. 115.

[13] *General Theory of Law and State*, p. 118. See also H. L. A. Hart, *The Concept of Law* (1961), pp. 114–16, 118–19, for a similar but not identical formulation.

[14] *The State* v. *Dosso* P.L.D. 1958 S.C. 533. But in 1972 the courts held that the case had been wrongly decided: *Jilani* v. *State of Punjab* P.L.D. 1972 S.C. 139.

[15] *Uganda* v. *Prison Commissioner, ex p Matovu* [1966] E.A. 514.

[16] *R.* v. *Ndhlovu* 1968 (4) S.A. 515.

[17] There is now a substantial body of legal literature on the problems arising from these and similar cases. Most of the articles are referred to in Dennis Lloyd, *Introduction to Jurisprudence* (5th edn, 1985), ch. 4; A. W. B. Simpson (ed.), *Oxford Essays in Jurisprudence* (1973), chs 2 (Eekelaar), 3 (Finnis); Bundu (1978) *I.C.L.Q.* 18.

whether the old order survives wholly, in part or not at all. It so happened that the Revolution of 1688 gave a clear pointer to the Judiciary. There was a suspension of business in the courts, and after the throne had become vacant new judges had to be appointed because of a 'demise of the Crown'. These appointees were not at all likely to call the validity of the régime in question.[18] After a while (at the latest, after the failure of the Jacobite revolt in 1715) it would have been merely silly for a judge or commentator to deny that the Bill of Rights 1689 and other legislation passed after the Revolution were valid. Efficacy and acquiescence had established a new basis for legality. The particular circumstances in which the Revolution of 1688 took place, and its immediate practical consequences, laid a secure foundation, moreover, for judicial acceptance of the doctrine of absolute parliamentary sovereignty. The doctrine grew out of a particular state of affairs. A fundamental change of a political nature may bring about a fundamental change in legal doctrine.

The concept of necessity

One other comment must be made. In some situations where unconstitutional action has been taken by persons wielding effective political power, it is open to a judge to steer a middle course. He may find it possible to assert that the framework of the pre-existing order still survives, but that deviations from its norms can be justified on grounds of *necessity*. The principle of necessity, rendering lawful what would otherwise be unlawful,[19] is not unknown to English law; there is a defence of necessity (albeit of uncertain scope) in criminal law,[20] and in constitutional law the application of martial law is but an extended application of this concept. But the necessity must be proportionate to the evil to be averted, and acceptance of the principle does not normally imply total abdication from judicial review or acquiescence in the supersession of the legal order; it is essentially a transient phenomenon. State necessity has been judicially accepted in recent years as a legal justification for ostensibly unconstitutional action to

[18] And in 1689 the Commons committed two former King's Bench judges, Pemberton and Jones JJ., to prison for a decision prior to the Revolution (see *Jay* v. *Topham* (1689) 12 St. Tr. 821), in which they had overruled a plea to the jurisdiction and given judgment against the Sergeant at Arms for an arrest carried out on the orders of the House. This was held to be a breach of the House's privileges.

[19] See generally Glanville Williams (1953) 6 *Current Legal Problems* 216.

[20] cf J. C. Smith and Brian Hogan, *Criminal Law* (6th edn, 1988), pp. 222–9; Glazebrook [1972A] *Camb L.J.* 87; Law Commission, Report No. 83 (1977), which recommended that 'any defence of necessity at common law' be abolished.

fill a vacuum arising within the constitutional order in Pakistan,[21] Cyprus,[22] Rhodesia[23] and Nigeria.[24] To this extent it has been recognized as an implied exception to the letter of the constitution. And perhaps it can be stretched far enough to bridge the gap between the old legal order and its successor.[25]

Parliamentary sovereignty surveyed

In its early days Parliament was a judicial as well as a law-making body. It was the High Court of Parliament, supreme over other courts. But it did not follow that its law-making competence was unlimited or unrivalled.

In the first place the supremacy of the Crown in Parliament was rivalled by the Crown acting outside Parliament. The Crown claimed and exercised an autonomous prerogative power to make laws by ordinance or proclamation. Not until James I's time do we find an unequivocal pronouncement by the courts that the King could not change the general law of the land by virtue of the prerogative.[26] The King, moreover, claimed power to impose taxation incidentally to the exercise of prerogative powers (such as the power to regulate foreign affairs including external trade, and the power to take emergency measures for the defence of the realm) recognized as being vested in

---

[21] *Special Reference No. 1 of 1955* [1955] 1 F.C.R. 439; Sir Ivor Jennings, *Constitutional Problems in Pakistan*. For a somewhat different approach to this principle, see *Jilani's* case (note 14, above).

[22] *Att.-Gen. of the Republic* v. *Mustafa Ibrahim* (1964) Cyprus Law Reports 195; de Smith in *Annual Survey of Commonwealth Law 1965* (ed. Wade), pp. 3, 76–8.

[23] *Madzimbamuto* v. *Lardner-Burke* 1968 (2) S.A. 284, a decision of the Rhodesian Appellate Division given before the court was prepared to recognize the success of the rebellion as fully legitimating the *de facto* Government; cf. note 16 above. On appeal the Privy Council (Lord Pearce dissenting) rejected the principle of necessity as applied by the Rhodesian judges [1969] 1 A.C. 645. However, it should not be inferred that the principle has no application at all in constitutional jurisprudence. Notwithstanding Lord Camden C.J.'s famous dictum in *Entick* v. *Carrington* (1765) 19 St. Tr. 1030 at 1073, that 'with respect to the argument of State necessity . . . the common law does not understand that kind of reasoning', such a principle was applied a few years later by Lord Mansfield in *R.* v. *Stratton* (1779) 21 St. Tr. 1045 at 1224; see also *Sabally and N'Jie* v. *Att.-Gen.* [1965] 1 Q.B. 273 at 293, *per* Lord Denning M.R.

[24] *Lakanmi and Ola* v. *Att.-Gen.* (*West*), 24 April 1970, where the Supreme Court of Nigeria, rejecting the Government's arguments, held that the military take-over in January 1966 had been a manifestation of necessity, not a revolutionary breach of legal continuity; and that fundamental rights under the pre-existing constitution were still in force save in so far as they were modified by the operation of necessity. This analysis of the facts may be regarded as courageous but far-fetched.

[25] See, for example, note 11. Necessity here becomes a 'supra-constitutional' principle.

[26] *Case of Proclamations* (1611) 12 Co. Rep. 74. This is perhaps the leading case in English constitutional law.

him; and in two great constitutional cases of the seventeenth century, the *Case of Impositions* (1606)[27] and the *Case of Ship Money* (1637)[28] – the latter decided after the *Case of Proclamations* – the courts upheld the validity of this ancillary taxing power. But the Bill of Rights 1689 laid it down that the raising of money for the use of the Crown by pretence of prerogative was unlawful. Again, the Crown had claimed – and the courts upheld the claim within certain limits in cases decided in 1674[29] and 1686[30] – a prerogative power to dispense with the operation of a statute for the benefit of an individual; but the Bill of Rights declared that in future dispensations would be invalid.[31] The Bill of Rights also declared that the 'pretended power of suspending of laws' by prerogative was unlawful; this was a reference to James II's disastrous attempt to enforce the suspension of the statutes which discriminated against Dissenters and Roman Catholics[32] – a premature experiment in religious toleration, albeit toleration with an ulterior motive, which precipitated a Glorious Revolution against royal tyranny. Thus did Parliament effectively dispose of the pretensions of the Crown to rival or subordinate its authority.

Since the Bill of Rights also changed the succession to the throne, so that title to the Crown was itself dependent on parliamentary authority, it would have been very difficult thereafter to contend that there were legal bounds to the powers of Parliament. Earlier in the seventeenth century there had been no dearth of juristic pronouncements on the limitations on Parliament's competence, though they jostled with others proclaiming the transcendent and absolute authority of Parliament.[33] In James I's time there were dicta to the effect that Acts of Parliament contrary to common right and reason,[34] or making a man a judge in

[27] *Bate's Case* (1606) 2 St. Tr. 371.
[28] *R.* v. *Hampden* (1637) 3 St. Tr. 825.
[29] *Thomas* v. *Sorrell* (1674) Vaughan 330.
[30] *Godden* v. *Hales* (1686) 11 St. Tr. 1165.
[31] Inland Revenue extra-statutory concessions to taxpayers may be contrary to the Bill of Rights. See *Vestey* v. *I.R.C.* (*No. 2*) [1980] A.C. 1148 at 1195 *per* Lord Edmund-Davies; Dawn Oliver [1984] *Public Law* 389; but cf. Alder (1980) 130 *N.L.J.* 180.
[32] See *Trial of the Seven Bishops* (1688) 12 St. Tr. 183. For a startling modern analogy, see *Fitzgerald* v. *Muldoon and Others* [1976] 2 N.Z.L.R. 615 (New Zealand Prime Minister purported to abolish by a press notice a superannuation scheme established by statute; held invalid as being in breach of article 1 of the Bill of Rights 1689 and contrary to the undoubted principle that only Parliament has the power to make and unmake law, no other person having the ability to set aside legislation).
[33] Dicta, extra-judicial and other, are collected together and discussed in Geoffrey Marshall's *Parliamentary Sovereignty and the Commonwealth* (1957), ch. 5.
[34] *Dr Bonham's* case (1610) 8 Co. Rep. 114 at 118, *per* Coke C.J. Contrast Coke's extra-judicial comment in vol. 4 of his *Institutes*, p. 36: 'of the power and jurisdiction of Parliament, for making of laws in proceedings by Bill, it is so transcendent and absolute, as it cannot be confined either for causes or persons within any bounds.'

his own cause,[35] were void. That there were prerogatives inseparable from the King's person, so that no Act of Parliament could deprive him of them, was generally conceded;[36] but one of those 'inseparable' prerogatives was the dispensing power. After the Revolution of 1688 and the Bill of Rights – the product of an alliance between parliamentarians and common lawyers – these were but empty phrases. Faintly re-echoed by the words of Blackstone in 1765, paying lip-service to the primacy of natural law,[37] they had long since ceased to have legal significance; for the judges had tacitly accepted a rule of obligation to give effect to every Act of Parliament, no matter how preposterous its content.

The omnicompetence of Parliament, at least in respect of persons, matters and territory under the jurisdiction of the Crown, in the eyes of the courts can be supported by numerous dicta and some decisions squarely in point, and is illustrated by legislative practice. Attempts to impugn the validity of Acts of Parliament because of inconsistency with rules of international law have been rejected.[38] When a taxpayer challenged the validity of assessments made under a Finance Act on the ground that they were directed partly to an unlawful purpose (the manufacture of nuclear weapons with a view to their possible use) it was held that even if such a purpose were contrary to international law:

What the statute itself enacts cannot be unlawful, because [it] is the highest form of law that is known to this country. It is the law which prevails over every other form of law, and it is not for the court to say that a parliamentary enactment . . . is illegal.[39]

---

[35] *Day* v. *Savadge* (1614) Hob. 85 at 86, 87, *per* Hobart C.J.; see also the surprising dicta by Holt C.J., in *City of London* v. *Wood* (1701) 12 Mod. 669 at 686–8. The modern view of Parliament's authority to make a man a judge in his own cause is stated by Willes J., in *Lee* v. *Bude and Torrington Junction Rly* (1871) L.R. 6 C.P. 576 at 582.

[36] D. L. Keir and F. H. Lawson, *Cases in Constitutional Law* (6th edn, 1979), pp. 73, 74, 83, 89, 91–2.

[37] *Commentaries*, i. p. 41 (laws are invalid if contrary to the law of nature). Blackstone's words were taken seriously in the North American colonies.

[38] See, for example, *Mortensen* v. *Peters* (1906) 14 S.L.T. 227; *Cheney* v. *Conn* [1968] 1 W.L.R. 242. Similarly, the Crown in the exercise of its prerogative power to delimit the extent of territorial water was not bound by international law: *Post Office* v. *Estuary Radio Ltd* [1968] 2 Q.B. 740 at 757. Statute has since replaced this prerogative power: see Territorial Sea Act 1987, s. 1. But there is a rebuttable presumption that neither Parliament nor the Crown intended to violate a treaty or other rule of international law (ibid.). See also p. 145.

[39] *Cheney* v. *Conn* [1968] 1 W.L.R. 242 at 247, *per* Ungoed-Thomas J. See also *R.* v. *Jordan* [1967] *Crim. L. Rev.* 483 (an unsuccessful attack by Colin Jordan on the constitutional validity of the Race Relations Act 1965); *Madzimbamuto* v. *Lardner-Burke* [1969] 1 A.C. 645 at 723; *Blackburn* v. *Att.-Gen.* [1971] 1 W.L.R. 1037 at 1041, *per* Salmon L.J.

Parliament has in fact passed retroactive penal legislation,[40] prolonged its own existence, transformed itself into a new body by the Acts of Union with Scotland and Ireland, repealed and amended provisions of those Acts which were to have permanent effect,[41] altered the procedure for making laws (under the Parliament Acts) and followed the new procedure, and changed the succession to the throne (by the Bill of Rights, the Act of Settlement 1701, and His Majesty's Declaration of Abdication Act 1936). The courts will endeavour to construe Acts of Parliament so as to avoid a preposterous result, but if a statute clearly evinces an intention to achieve the preposterous, the courts are under an obligation to give effect to its plain words.[42] The safeguards against the enactment of such legislation are political and conventional, not strictly legal.

Possible legal limitations on parliamentary sovereignty[43]

Acts of Union

It can reasonably be argued that the Acts of Union with Scotland and Ireland were constituent Acts, establishing a new United Kingdom Parliament and setting limits to its powers.[44] The case for still regarding the Act of Union with Ireland 1800 in this light has been undermined by a series of basic legislative changes.[45] The case for so regarding the Act of Union with Scotland 1707 is not so weak. Much water has indeed flowed under the bridges since that time, but the position of the Established Church in Scotland and the Scottish system of judicature, entrenched as fundamental and unalterable in the

[40] An Act of 1541 enabled Lady Rocheford, an accessory to Catherine Howard's adultery, to be tried and executed for treason although she had become insane after arrest: Nigel Walker, *Crime and Insanity in England* (1973), pp. 183–4.

[41] An attempt to impugn the Irish Church Act 1869, which had changed an unalterable provision of the Act of Union with Ireland by disestablishing the Church of Ireland, failed in *ex p. Canon Selwyn* (1872) 36 J.P. 54. This decision is criticized, on the ground that the Act of Union with Ireland was a constituent Act, limiting the competence of the United Kingdom Parliament, by Harry Calvert, *Constitutional Law in Northern Ireland*, pp. 27–33. cf. J.D.B. Mitchell, *Constitutional Law* (2nd edn, 1968), pp. 69–74.

[42] See, however, the anomalous decision in *Green* v. *Mortimer* (1861) 3 L.T. 642 (private Act of Parliament treated as void because the court thought its provisions were absurd).

[43] See A. W. Bradley in J. Jowell and D. Oliver (eds), *The Changing Constitution* (1985), ch. 2.

[44] See p. 9, above.

[45] cf. note 41; the biggest changes up to the time of writing were the establishment of the Irish Free State (now the Republic of Ireland) and a subordinate Northern Ireland Parliament (abolished by the United Kingdom Parliament in 1973). Moreover, at the time of the Union, Ireland was not unambiguously an independent State.

Articles of Union, remains largely intact.[46] Although the immunity of the surviving fundamental principles of the Union from legislative encroachment by the United Kingdom Parliament without Scottish consent[47] is probably to be regarded now as a matter of convention rather than of strict law, one cannot be certain that Scottish courts would take this view. In *MacCormick* v. *Lord Advocate* (1953) Lord Cooper was of the opinion that violation of fundamental terms of the Union would be unlawful, but non-justiciable in a United Kingdom court.[48] No Scottish court has, however, held a public Act of Parliament to be void since the Union.

Substantive content of legislation: the general rule

Parliament can undoubtedly delegate its powers, setting limits to the authority of the delegate and retaining power to revoke the grant and a concurrent power to legislate. But can it effectively *deprive* itself of power to legislate on any matter or otherwise predetermine the future content of its own legislation? There is authority for the proposition that it cannot. An Act of 1919 laid down a scale of compensation for owners of compulsorily acquired slum property, and it stated that 'so far as inconsistent with that Act [other statutory] ... provisions shall not have effect'. These provisions were held to have been impliedly repealed to the extent that they were inconsistent with other provisions in an Act of 1925, even if they were intended (which was doubtful) to have permanent effect.[49]

If there is a general rule that Parliament can do anything except bind its own future action, this may be regarded either as a limitation of parliamentary sovereignty or as a necessary characteristic of that sovereignty, since sovereignty inheres in Parliament as a continuing representative institution and not in one Parliament at a given moment of time. There is another, more mundane, explanation of the rule,

---

[46] Subject to minor but significant exceptions. See the Universities (Scotland) Acts 1853 and 1932.

[47] But how is Scottish consent to be signified? Through the M.P.s for Scottish constituencies and the Scottish peers at Westminster? Through an *ad hoc* constituent body?

[48] [1963] S.C. 396 at 411–13. See also MacCormick [1972] *Public Law* 176–9; T. B. Smith [1957] *Public Law* 99. In *Gibson* v. *Lord Advocate* (1975) *Scots Law Times* 134, Lord Keith refused an application to label s. 2(1) of the European Communities Act 1972 null and void as contrary to the Act of Union of 1707. He reserved his opinion on the situation which might be created if the United Kingdom Parliament passed an Act purporting to abolish the Court of Session or the Church of Scotland.

[49] *Vauxhall Estates Ltd* v. *Liverpool Corporation* [1932] 1 K.B. 733; *Ellen Street Estates Ltd* v. *Minister of Health* [1934] 1 K.B. 590.

divorced from ideas about sovereignty: public policy requires that no legislative body be competent to frustrate its primary purpose by creating a vacuum save where expressly authorized to do so – for example, by a written constitution. Put in this form, the principle applies to non-sovereign legislatures. Local authorities are incompetent to disable themselves from making a by-law on any matter within their allotted field.[50] And if this is an important factor sustaining the rule, then there remains the possibility that parliamentary omnicompetence can be restricted where the imposition of a fetter is consonant with the proper functions of Parliament.

Territorial competence

The orthodox view is that Parliament is competent to make any law whatsoever for any part of the world whatsoever, and that United Kingdom courts are under an obligation to give effect to any such law. Courts in territories subordinate to the United Kingdom are under a like obligation, but not courts in foreign countries.[51] The obligation of courts in independent Commonwealth countries is debatable.[52]

Now, it is quite clear that Parliament can attribute legal consequences in United Kingdom law to acts done by aliens in foreign countries. It did so, for example, by the Aviation Security Act 1982.[53] And it could presumably make it an offence in United Kingdom law for a Frenchman to smoke in the streets of Paris.[54] But it is at least doubtful whether, even in terms of United Kingdom law, it has an unlimited competence to change the laws of independent countries. Since it would not, in practice, assert such authority,[55] the question is unlikely to arise before a United Kingdom court. However, untested assertions about Parliament's omnicompetence are an inadequate basis for ascribing to Parliament powers inconsistent with international comity and common sense.

---

[50] See, for example, *Cory (William) & Son Ltd* v. *City of London Corporation* [1951] 2 K.B. 475.

[51] Or, possibly, a court in a British protected state (which was not part of Her Majesty's dominions) where the Crown has only limited jurisdiction, in respect of an Act of Parliament going beyond the Crown's jurisdiction: Sir Kenneth Roberts-Wray, *Commonwealth and Colonial Law* (1966), 139–41.

[52] See pp. 76–8.

[53] See also *Joyce* v. *D.P.P.* [1946] A.C. 337; Statute of Treasons 1351 (treason can be committed by alien in foreign country).

[54] Sir Ivor Jennings, *The Law and the Constitution* (5th edn, 1959), pp. 170–71.

[55] Unless one takes the view that on or soon after UDI, Southern Rhodesia acquired the attributes of independent statehood; cf. Southern Rhodesia Act 1965; Southern Rhodesia Constitution Order 1965 (S.I. 1965, No. 1952); *Madzimbamuto* v. *Lardner-Burke* [1969] 1 A.C. 645; cf. *R.* v. *Ndhlovu* 1968 (4) S.A. 515.

Total or partial abdication by Parliament

If the United Kingdom Parliament were to proceed to liquidate itself by passing an Act transferring its functions to a new supranational European body or distributing those functions among (say) new Parliaments for England, Scotland, Wales and Northern Ireland, it would be absurd to suggest that a notional United Kingdom Parliament still existed and that it could resume its identity at any time and continue to exercise sovereign authority. Because this would be absurd, Parliament must be accepted as having the power to abdicate by extinguishing itself, thus 'committing suicide'. But what if Parliament continued to exist but purported to give away *part* of its sovereignty to another country or to new legislatures within the United Kingdom or to a supranational body?[56] Would this not be as ineffectual as an attempt by Parliament to preclude itself from repealing or amending a Licensing Act? This will be considered in three contexts: (1) Commonwealth affairs; (2) adoption of a written constitution; and (3) accession to the European Communities.

1 – Independence in the Commonwealth

The most familiar, but not the most illuminating, questions turn on the legal effect of section 4 of the Statute of Westminster 1931,[57] ostensibly precluding Parliament from legislating for a Dominion unless the Act in question recited the Dominion's request and consent. Section 4 might be interpreted as (a) laying down a rule for the construction of statutes but (b) not imposing a fetter on the omnicompetence of Parliament because (i) it merely prescribed the insertion of a particular form of words in an Act, and Parliament could not effectively bind itself in this way[58] and (ii) in any event the power of Parliament to make any law whatsoever for any place whatsoever could not be surrendered. On this last point, we have a Privy Council dictum in a Canadian appeal supporting the view stated above;[59] an equivocal

---

[56] cf. the controversy over the Irish Home Rule Bill in 1886; Marshall, op. cit., pp. 63–7; Anson (1886) 2 *L.Q.R.* 427.

[57] See pp. 46–7.

[58] cf. Maugham L.J. in *Ellen Street Estates Ltd* v. *Minister of Health* [1934] 1 K.B. at 597: Parliament 'cannot bind itself as to the form of subsequent legislation'. It is hard to know how much should be read into this dictum, since the question was whether Parliament could effectively prescribe that a statute should be repealable or alterable only by *express* words; held, it could not, even if it had purported to do so, which was doubtful.

[59] *British Coal Corporation* v. *R.* [1935] A.C. 500 at 520 ('the Imperial Parliament could, as a matter of abstract law, repeal or disregard s. 4 of the Statute').

decision of the High Court of Australia;[60] and dicta in a Privy Council appeal from Ceylon,[61] and in South African cases decided while that country was still in the Commonwealth,[62] supporting a more radical interpretation – that such a provision was a renunciation of Parliament's plenary authority to make laws for those countries otherwise than in accordance with the requirement laid down by Parliament. ('Freedom once conferred cannot be revoked.')[63] There is also an intermediate position: that United Kingdom courts would be obliged to give effect to Acts plainly intended to alter the law in Commonwealth countries despite non-compliance with the statutory conditions, but that the *local* courts, and on appeal the Privy Council (applying local law), would be entitled, or even obliged, *not* to apply such an Act.

If one looks at Independence Acts since 1960, the case for a traditionally conservative construction becomes weaker; for the United Kingdom Parliament has purported to renounce its power to legislate for those countries altogether. For example, section 1(2) of the Mauritius Independence Act 1968 provides: 'No Act of the Parliament of the United Kingdom passed on or after the appointed day [i.e., independence day] shall extend, or be deemed to extend, to Mauritius as part of its law; . . .' Is Parliament competent simply to resume its legislative sovereignty over Mauritius tomorrow?

From the point of view of the Mauritian courts, the answer is clearly not. The words of the Independence Act are unambiguous. Moreover the achievement of independence should in itself be understood as having liberated the legal order of Mauritius from its hierarchical subordination to that of the United Kingdom, so that the omnicompetence of the United Kingdom Parliament ceased to prevail in the local

---

[60] *Copyright Owners Reproduction Society* v. *E.M.I.* (*Australia*) *Pty Ltd* (1958) 100 C.L.R. 597. The decision (see p. 31, note 41) did not give a clear indication of what the attitude of Australian courts would have been had a United Kingdom statute purported unambiguously to change the law of Australia without reciting the necessary request and consent of the Commonwealth of Australia. cf. Hanks in (1968) 42 *A.L.J.* 286. (The power of the U.K. Parliament to legislate for Australia was ended by the Australia Act 1986: see below, pp. 663–4.)

[61] *Ibralebbe* v. *R.* [1964] A.C. 900 at 918 (on the irrevocable 'surrender' of Parliament's power by the Ceylon Independence Act 1947) and 924 (on the surrender of the Crown's prerogative legislative power).

[62] *Ndlwana* v. *Hofmeyr* [1937] A.D. 229 at 237; *Harris* v. *Donges* [1952] 1 T.L.R. 1245 at 1261, *sub nom. Harris* v. *Minister of the Interior* 1952 (2) S.A. 428.

[63] *Ndlwana* v. *Hofmeyr*, above. See, to like effect, Rand (1960) 38 *Can. Bar Rev.* 135 at 149; *Blackburn* v. *Att.-Gen.* [1971] 1 W.L.R. 1037 at 1040, *per* Lord Denning M.R. (though his Lordship also cited, without disapproval, the dictum in the *British Coal Corporation* case, note 59).

legal system.[64] And, looking at the matter from a common-sense point of view, one must suggest that English courts should adopt the same attitude. The United Kingdom Government and Parliament have renounced their authority over Mauritius, surrendering it to the competent authorities in Mauritius. One must also recognize that common sense does not always prevail in legal theory.[65]

2 – A written constitution

If the rule of judicial obedience to Acts of Parliament can be reformulated so that Parliament can effectively deprive itself of part of its sovereignty by surrendering it or transferring it to authorities *outside* the territorial limits of the United Kingdom, why can it not be reformulated by accepting that Parliament can do exactly the same thing *within* the territorial limits of the Upper Kingdom? Suppose, for example, that a federal constitution were enacted, retaining a United Kingdom Parliament but purporting to restrict its legislative powers. For the courts dogmatically to insist that, so long as the United Kingdom Parliament existed, there was a mysterious rule, both fundamental and unalterable, precluding them from recognizing the efficacy of a transfer of part of its absolute sovereignty to Welsh and Scottish Parliaments, would be extremely odd, if the new federal constitution restricting parliamentary competence was known to have general public support as well as a parliamentary majority behind it. One's guess is that rather than make themselves ridiculous, the courts would fall into line and vary the 'fundamental' rule. They could vary it *ad hoc* (by declaring in a concrete case that an enactment of the reconstituted United Kingdom Parliament was inoperative) or by a general pronouncement (as when the House of Lords, acting extra-judicially, announced the abandonment of the self-imposed basic rule that it was bound by its own earlier decisions).[66] Law in the courts

---

[64] See Kenneth Robinson in *Essays in Imperial Government* (ed. Robinson and A. F. Madden), p. 249. The case would be even clearer if Mauritius had become a republic.

[65] cf. p. 75.

[66] [1966] 1 W.L.R. 1234 (Practice Statement). Rupert Cross, *Precedent in English Law* (3rd edn, 1977), pp. 209–10, takes the view that a similar Practice Statement modifying the rule of absolute judicial obedience to Acts of Parliament would be strictly *ultra vires*, though if it were acquiesced in and acted upon it would effect a legal revolution. See also H. W. R. Wade, 'The basis of legal sovereignty' [1955] *Camb. L.J.* 172 (an important and influential article), arguing that this basic rule or ultimate legal principle is alterable by judicial decision but not by statute. I have difficulty in understanding why a purported statutory modification of the present customary common-law rule should be treated either as nugatory or as less 'binding' than other statutory enactments merely because

ought not to rest on assumptions that blithely ignore fundamental changes in constitutional structure.

One can carry this argument still farther. At present Parliament, as we have noted, is incapacitated from binding its own future action as to the substantive content of legislation where this would leave a legislative vacuum. But if Parliament adopted a written constitution under which no legislature in the United Kingdom was competent to violate certain rights and freedoms (for example, by enacting *ex post facto* penal legislation), it would be sensible for the judges to uphold the constitution against future legislative encroachments, provided at least there was a prescribed procedure for constitutional amendment. In other words, the fundamental rule of judicial obligation ought to be regarded as flexible, not immutable; as being susceptible to reformulation in the light of drastic innovations in legislative practice and corresponding changes in the climate of informed opinion about the limits of legislative authority.[67]

3 – Effect of accession to the European Community[68]

As was pointed out in an earlier chapter, our constitutional law must now take into account Community legislation made by organs not subordinate to Parliament. In particular, the Council of Ministers and the Commission are empowered by the treaties to make regulations having direct effect in member States and creating individual rights and duties enforceable in national courts. The concept of 'directly applicable' Community rules is recognized and implemented by section 2(1) of the European Communities Act 1972. Certain provisions of the

---

the present rule (i) is extremely important and (ii) was established neither by statute nor by judicial decision but by judicial accommodation to political facts. Nevertheless, the argument in the text above is confined to expressions of opinion as to what the judges ought to do or are likely to do if a fundamental structural change in the British constitutional system were to be adopted, and as to the present territorial scope of the rule of judicial obedience to statutes.

[67] The duty of the courts would probably be indicated expressly or by necessary implication by the text of such a constitution. The constitution itself might be adopted by a Constituent Assembly set up by parliamentary authority, and then be submitted for the approval of the electorate at a referendum.

[68] See L. Collins, *European Community Law in the United Kingdom* (3rd edn, 1984); T. C. Hartley, *The Foundations of European Community Law* (1981); A. J. Mackenzie Stuart, *The European Communities and the Rule of Law* (1977); J. A. Usher, *European Community Law and National Law: The Irreversible Transfer* (1981); de Smith (1971) 34 *Mod. L. Rev.* 597; Mitchell, Kuypers and Gall (1972) 9 *Common Market L. Rev.* 134. See also ch. 5, below.

treaties themselves are 'directly applicable' in the sense described.[69] Directives and decisions issued by the Council or the Commission normally require further implementation by the Government or other parties to whom they are addressed, but exceptionally they too may be invoked before national courts.[70]

Questions of the highest constitutional importance have arisen: they have not yet been fully answered. English courts have acknowledged that, as a general principle, Community law prevails over English law.[71] But what if a directly applicable rule of Community law (say, a regulation) conflicts with an Act of Parliament? According to section 2(4), 'any enactment passed *or to be passed* [subject to certain exceptions] shall have effect subject to' the provisions of section 2(1). Surely this is not a mere rule of construction, to be displaced if the Act and the regulation cannot be harmonized? It states that Acts of Parliament shall *have effect subject to* directly applicable rules of Community law. We can assume that legislation already in existence on 1 January 1973 or (after that date) when the Community regulation is made will be impliedly repealed by the latter to the extent that the two sets of rules are irreconcilably in conflict. But what of post-accession United Kingdom legislation that is plainly inconsistent with a *prior* Community regulation? British courts will then try to use their ingenuity to interpret the provisions such that primacy is accorded to the Community rule *and* so that no irreconcilable difference remains. That approach was approved by the House of Lords in *Garland* v. *British Rail Engineering Ltd.*[72] But, if that method does not do the trick, some courts and tribunals have applied Community law in a few

---

[69] For example, art. 16 of the EEC Treaty: see *Re Export Tax on Art Treasures (No.1)* [1969] C.M.L. Rep. 1; ibid. (No. 2) [1972] C.M.L. Rep. 699. See also pp. 26–7. The first case in which the English courts had to *apply* the EEC Treaty was *Schorsch Meier G.m.b.H* v. *Hennin* [1975] Q.B. 416 (held, any rule at common law which required the English courts to give judgment only in sterling was incompatible with art. 106 of that Treaty): confirmed by s. 4 of the Administration of Justice Act 1977. See also *Bulmer (H.P.)* v. *J. Bollinger S.A.* [1974] Ch. 401 ('Parliament has decreed that the treaty is henceforward to be part of our law. It is equal in force to any statute': *per* Lord Denning M.R. at 418), and *Application des Gaz S.A.* v. *Falks Veritas Ltd* [1974] Ch. 381.

[70] *Grad* v. *Finanzamt Traunstein* [1971] C.M.L. Rep. 41; *S.A.C.E.* v. *Italian Ministry of Finance* [1971] C.M.L. Rep. 123.

[71] See, e.g., *Shields* v. *E. Coomes (Holdings) Ltd* [1979] 1 All E.R. 456; *Macarthys Ltd* v. *Smith* [1979] 3 All E.R. 325 and [1981] 1 All E.R. 111.

[72] [1983] A.C. 751; see also *Duke* v. *GEC Reliance* [1988] 1 All E.R. 625, and below, pp. 106–8. The House also employed that technique in *Rainey* v. *Greater Glasgow Health Board* [1987] A.C. 224.

cases in preference even to a British statute passed after accession.[73] Now, according to the traditional British doctrine, primacy should be accorded to the subsequent statute;[74] but perhaps that doctrine has been undermined by the combined effect of the wording of section 2(4) and the political fact of Britain's accession to the Community. According to well-settled Community doctrine, Community law (and not merely 'directly applicable' Community law) ought to prevail over *all* inconsistent national law, antecedent and subsequent. As the European Court of Justice (the Court of the Communities) has said, 'the member States, albeit within limited spheres, have restricted their sovereign rights',[75] and 'no appeal to provisions of internal law of any kind whatever can prevail' over this cession of authority.[76] By section 3(1) of the European Communities Act 1972, questions of Community law 'shall be determined' by our courts 'in accordance with the principles laid down by and any relevant decision of the European Court'.

The European Court gives primacy to Community law even where there is no *direct* conflict with national law. If Community rules have been promulgated to 'occupy the field' in a matter within Community competence, national Parliaments cannot pass *any* law on such a matter, except possibly for the ancillary purpose of implementing those rules locally on points of detail.[77] It seems, moreover, that if a competent Community organ has made a treaty on a matter within its competence, member States cannot legislate (or even enter into executive agreements with non-member States) so as to detract from the operation of the Community policy, at least if that policy has been embodied in Community rules.[78]

If these pronouncements are to be taken at their face value, parliamentary sovereignty is dead. However, things are not always as they seem in the Communities. For instance, West German courts have

---

[73] See, e.g., *Re an Absence in Ireland* [1977] 1 C.M.L.R. 5 (1971 regulation held to prevail over Social Security Act 1975, s. 82(5)(*a*)); *MacMahon* v. *Department of Education and Science* [1982] 3 C.M.L.R. 91 (1986 regulation applied in preference to inconsistent 1979 statutory instrument, S.I. 1979, No. 889).

[74] Although in *Prince* v. *Secretary of State for Scotland* 1985 S.L.T. 74 Lord Cameron queried whether the European Parliament Elections Act 1978 was *ultra vires* the United Kingdom Parliament because of its apparent conflict with Article 138 (3) of the EEC Treaty; he did not have to decide the point as the pursuers failed on other grounds. See (1985) 101 *L.Q.R.* 149.

[75] *Costa* v. *ENEL* [1964] C.M.L. Rep. 425 at 455. See pp. 106–8.

[76] *Re Export Tax on Art Treasures (No. 2)* [1972] C.M.L. Rep. 669 at 708.

[77] See, for example, the *Hauptzollamt Hamburg* case [1972] C.M.L. Rep. 141 at 153; the *Norddeutsches Vieh* case [1971] C.M.L. Rep. 281 at 293; *Re Imported Thai Sand Flour*, ibid. 521.

[78] *Re European Road Transport Agreement* [1971] C.M.L. Rep. 335 (dicta) – a difficult case.

yet to accept the Court's ruling that Community law prevails over inconsistent provisions of national constitutions.[79] French courts are reluctant to refer questions of Community law to the European Court. And most of the pronouncements by the Court on the primacy of Community law are made on preliminary rulings under Article 177 of the EEC Treaty, under which the Court does not interpret national law but merely delivers a general interpretation of Community law in a case referred by a national court. If the national court can then apply the Community doctrine as declared by the European Court to the case before it, it should do so. If it cannot the expectation is that the national authorities will pass amending legislation as soon as possible. This has been done in the United Kingdom, and it seems safe to assume that fresh legislation will be passed at Westminster in further cases of irreconcilable conflict.[80] If this action is not taken, the national authorities can be brought before the Court by the Commission as defaulters (Articles 169–71).[81] But the most that the Court can do is to make an unenforceable declaratory judgment against the Government in question. *It cannot hold national legislation to be void* for inconsistency with Community law. The Court is not at all like the Supreme Court of the United States.

There is also a possible intermediate position – that the doctrine of parliamentary sovereignty has been changed, but that it would fully revive in its traditional form if Parliament legislated to withdraw the United Kingdom from the European Community. Such a step would be effective in English law (although the European Court would probably hold that it was ineffective in Community law).

And so this unique Act is a fascinating exercise in equivocation, a wilful manifestation of legislative schizophrenia. Or, to vary the metaphor, the United Kingdom Government has seated Parliament on two horses, one straining towards the preservation of parliamentary sovereignty, the other galloping in the general direction of Community law supremacy.

---

[79] See the *Internationale Handelsgesellschaft* case [1972] C.M.L. Rep. 258, 330; and further [1974] 2 C.M.L. Rep. 540.

[80] For example, Equal Pay (Amendment) Regulations S.I. 1983, No. 1794 (passed after *Commission* v. *United Kingdom* [1982] I.C.R. 578); Sex Discrimination Act 1986 (passed after *Commission* v. *United Kingdom* [1974] I.R.L.R. 29 and *Marshall* v. *Southampton & S.W. Hants. AHA* [1986] I.R.L.R. 140).

[81] This was the procedure adopted in the second *Export Tax* case, after the Italian Government and Parliament had failed to give effect to the Court's ruling under art. 177 implying that this long-standing tax was incompatible with the EEC Treaty.

What is an Act of Parliament?

Let the major issues just considered now be disregarded. How far, if at all, do the courts at the present time have jurisdiction to determine whether what purports to be an Act of Parliament is, as a matter of law, an authentic statute which they are bound to apply?

The rule that judges ought to apply Acts of Parliament can be classified as a common-law rule, albeit a rule of outstanding importance. The meaning of the Queen in Parliament, and of an Act of Parliament, is governed partly by customary common law and partly by statute. The jurisdiction of the courts to examine the authenticity of purported Acts of Parliament can be considered by using inferences (in which considerations of public policy are of some consequence) drawn from common-law and statutory rules.

1   At common law, Parliament as a legislative body consists of the House of Commons, the House of Lords and the Queen. Each House must record its assent to a bill separately and the Queen has at least a formal discretion whether to assent to bills passed by them. The methods of giving and communicating the royal assent are regulated or prescribed by statute.[82] When Parliament is dissolved, its sovereignty is temporarily in abeyance since it is unable to legislate; there is a House of Commons, but it has no members because their seats have become vacant; there is a House of Lords, but it is incapacitated from sitting (except as a court of law) during a dissolution.

2   The customary common-law rule that each House has to pass a bill before it can be presented for the royal assent has been modified by statute. The Parliament Acts 1911 and 1949 authorize the presentation of a bill for the royal assent if certain conditions have been complied with, although the House of Lords has not passed the bill.

3   In order to express its sovereign will, Parliament must be constituted as Parliament and must function as Parliament within the meaning of existing common law and statute law. Unless these antecedent

---

[82] Royal Assent Act 1967. An Act of Parliament is now duly enacted if the royal assent is signified (i) by Letters Patent signed by Her Majesty under the Great Seal and pronounced in the customary manner (i.e. by Royal Commissioners in the House of Lords, the Commons also being present), or (ii) as above but announced to each House separately by the Speaker of that House (so as to avoid interruptions of the proceedings of the Commons because of the arrival of Commissioners in the Lords), or (iii) by Her Majesty in person, in the presence of both Houses. For forms of the assent, see Crown Office Rules Order 1967 (S.I. 1967, No. 802).

conditions for law-making have been fulfilled, the product should not be regarded as an authentic Act of Parliament.[83]

4 Nevertheless, if an official copy of what purports to be an Act of Parliament, bearing the appropriate customary words of enactment (normally [84] 'Be it enacted by the Queen's most excellent Majesty, by and with the advice and consent of the Lords Spiritual and Temporal, and Commons, in this present Parliament assembled, and by the authority of the same, as follows';) is produced, the courts will almost certainly accept this as conclusive evidence that the measure is authentic and has been duly passed. This follows from the decision of the House of Lords in *British Railways Board* v. *Pickin*.[85] In 1969 Mr Pickin had purchased part of a disused railway line and land adjoining it. But the Board subsequently claimed that it was the owner by virtue of a private statute, the British Railways Act 1968, section 18(1). Mr Pickin, however, alleged that in obtaining the passage of that Act in its favour, the Board had fraudulently concealed certain matters from Parliament and that section 18 was therefore ineffective and did not deprive him of his proprietary rights.[86] Such an allegation, to be tested, would require the courts to look to see what had happened in Parliament during proceedings on the bill. The House of Lords unanimously decided that the courts had no jurisdiction to do so, either in relation to a private or any other Act of Parliament.[87] As Lord Reid put it:

[83] This proposition is stated dogmatically and cannot be demonstrated to be correct, but is founded on logic. It enjoys widespread support among writers (for example, R. T. E. Latham, *The Law and the Commonwealth* (1949), pp. 523–4; Sir Ivor Jennings, *The Law and the Constitution* (5th edn, 1959), ch. 4; J. D. B. Mitchell, *Constitutional Law* (2nd edn, 1968), ch. 4; R. F. V. Heuston, Geoffrey Marshall, Hamish Gray, D. V. Cowen, B. Beinart, note 109 below).

[84] Extra words are added for money bills. The usual enacting formula was evolved in the fifteenth century. By virtue of the Statute Law Revision Act 1948, s. 3(1) (*a*), it can be omitted altogether in a revised edition of the Statutes of the Realm. *Semble* omission of a recital that the House of Commons or (unless otherwise provided by statute) the House of Lords had consented to an Act would render the measure nugatory: *The Prince's Case* (1606) 8 Co. Rep. 1a at 20a. The words of enactment have been varied by statute for measures passed under the Parliament Acts without the consent of the House of Lords: Parliament Act 1911, s. 4(1).

[85] [1974] A.C. 765.

[86] On the special procedure required for the passage of a private Act, see below p. 278.

[87] Thus applying the dicta of, among others, Lord Campbell in *Edinburgh and Dalkeith Railway Co.* v. *Wauchope* (1842) 8 Cl. & F. 710 at 725 and of Wilkes, J. in *Lee* v. *Bude and Torrington Railway Co.* (1871) L.R. 6 C.P. 576 at 582. When an amendment, agreed to by both Houses, to what became the Rent (Agriculture) Act 1976 was, by an error, omitted from the text, the Government's view was that only Parliament – and certainly

For a century or more both Parliament and the courts have been careful not to act so as to cause conflict between them. Any such investigations as the respondent seeks could easily lead to such a conflict . . . The whole trend of authority for over a century is clearly against permitting any such investigation.[88]

This decision clarifies the situation which had been the subject of much academic debate. The courts will apparently now take the view that they *lack jurisdiction* to pronounce an ostensibly authentic Act of Parliament to be a nullity even though in fact Parliament has not functioned according to existing law. But the point still requries further exploration.

The enrolled bill rule

Before *Pickin's* case much had been made of the words of Lord Campbell in *Edinburgh and Dalkeith Railway Co.* v. *Wauchope*:[89]

All that a Court of Justice can do is to look to the Parliament Roll: if from that it should appear that a bill has passed both Houses and received the Royal Assent, no Court of Justice can inquire into the mode in which it was introduced into Parliament, nor into what was done previous to its introduction, or what passed in Parliament during its progress in its various stages through Parliament.

Several comments can be made on this much-quoted passage.

1 The statement was a mere *obiter dictum*, a point missed by many commentators.

2 A peculiar sacrosanctity used to be attributed to the Parliament roll, the formal record of the High Court of Parliament,[90] upon which the originals of all Acts were engrossed in manuscript. Practice changed over the years.[91] From 1497 the original text was retained in the House of Lords and a *copy*, made on a Parliament roll, was sent to the Chancery. Since the middle of the nineteenth century, two copies of a bill as assented to have been printed on vellum, and the Clerk of the Parliaments then adds his signature for the purpose of authentication; the 'original' is kept in the House of Lords, and

---

not the courts – could correct the mistake, and the Rent (Agriculture) Amendment Act 1977 was accordingly passed to put matters right. See 925 H.C. Deb. 1581–1622 (9 February 1977). A mistake in a bill by one House may be returned to it by the other House for correction before royal assent. This happened with the Prosecution of Offences Bill in 1985: see 460 H.L. Deb. 1438, 1449 (6 and 7 March 1985). Lord Campbell's dictum was also applied in *Manuel* v. *Att.-Gen.* [1983] 1 Ch. 77, and in *Martin* v. *O'Sullivan* [1984] S.T.C. 258.

[88] *Pickin's* case at 788.

[89] See note 87.

[90] See Jennings, *The Law and the Constitution* (ibid), p. 139 and Appendix 3. But cf. R. F. V. Heuston, *Essays in Constitutional Law* (2nd edn, 1964), pp. 16–20.

[91] For a historical survey, see Bond, 'Acts of Parliament' (1958) 3 *Archives* 201.

the duplicate 'Parliament roll' copy now goes to the Public Record Office.[92] There was no reason of basic principle why these two official texts should have precluded all further judicial inquiry whatsoever into the procedure followed prior to enactment.

3   Copies of the Act are also printed by the Queen's Printer at Her Majesty's Stationery Office and sold to the public. Under section 3 of the Interpretation Act 1978 (which consolidated section 9 of the Interpretation Act 1889), judicial notice must be taken of all public Acts of Parliament passed since 1850; this states a rule of evidence[93] and does not specify what is an authentic Act of Parliament.

4   The courts will not encroach upon the exclusive preserves of the two Houses. Article 9 of the Bill of Rights 1689 provides that 'proceedings in Parliament ought not to be impeached or questioned in any court or place out of Parliament'. They fall within the province of parliamentary privilege. Hence the courts will refuse to inquire into such questions as whether either House was mistaken as to the facts, whether a bill had two, three or thirty-three readings, whether a quorum was present, and so on. Perhaps they would even disclaim jurisdiction to inquire whether a bill was in fact passed in the same form by both Houses.[94] If, however, it were to be asserted that a bill had not obtained a majority at the final reading in the House of Commons, would they, even after *Pickin*'s case, be prepared to go behind the official text of the Act and examine the Journal of the House and the notes of the official shorthand writers, on the grounds that the alleged defect was peculiarly gross and that 'a court must not decline to open its eyes to the truth'?[95] Even if they

---

[92] Erskine May, op. cit., p. 605. The Clerk of the Parliaments and the Clerk of the Records in the House of Lords kindly verified the information set out above. It must be obvious that the modern 'Parliament roll' copy of a statute need not enjoy the unique status of an original engrossed on the ancient Parliament roll, irrespective of judicial dicta suggesting that it does.

[93] For the various rules of evidence relating to the proof of Acts of Parliament, see *Halsbury's Laws of England* (4th edn), vol. 17, para. 149.

[94] Doubts on this point are expressed by Maitland, *Constitutional History of England* (1908), pp. 381–2. See also *Craies on Statute Law* (7th edn, 1971), pp. 37–40; the point is unsettled. Examples of such errors, and other irregularities in the enactment of bills, being followed by validating or amending legislation, are given by Erskine May, op. cit., pp. 606–7. The question whether the discrepancy between a bill as passed by the Commons and the bill as passed by the Lords rendered the Act invalid was actually argued before a court in *Pylkington*'s case (1455; discussed by Cowen in 16 *Mod. L. Rev.* at 275–7) but no final decision was recorded.

[95] cf. *Bribery Commissioner* v. *Ranasinghe* [1965] A.C. 172 at 194 (dealing with the jurisdiction of the courts, at least in Ceylon, to inquire whether a prescribed Speaker's certificate had been given in the due form on a bill before enactment). The comment in the text above is necessarily speculative. See further Beinart, loc. cit., for a very full review of these questions.

were so prepared it is doubtful whether a court would be prepared to conduct such an inspection without leave of the House, because the House has asserted the privilege not to have its internal proceedings investigated.[96]

5   What if it is alleged that procedural or formal requirements laid down by *statute* have not been complied with during the passage of a bill? Some modern statutes[97] have laid down procedural rules to be observed *before* a particular class of bill is introduced in Parliament. These rules are probably no more than directory; that is to say, non-compliance will not vitiate the end-product. One can arrive at this conclusion by two alternative assertions. The first is that the giving of the royal assent and publication with the appropriate words of enactment cure *all* prior defects. The second is that the rules in question are not of such fundamental importance to be regarded as conditions precedent to the validity of subsequent legislation.[98] Clearly these are different approaches, the second implying that compliance with statutory procedural rules of fundamental importance might be regarded as a condition precedent. One is not obliged to assume that fundamental rules of such a character lie within the exclusive cognizance of Parliament itself.

6   It is unlikely that a court would be prepared to issue an injunction to restrain the submission of a bill for the royal assent or otherwise intervene while the bill was before Parliament.[99] The Attorney-General could probably obtain an injunction to prevent a public body from exceeding its statutory powers by promoting a private bill before the matter came before Parliament.[100]

---

[96]   Erskine May, op. cit., pp. 89–91.

[97]   For example, Consolidation of Enactments (Procedure) Act 1949.

[98]   cf. *Clayton* v. *Heffron* (1961) 105 C.L.R. 214, where part of the procedure prescribed for the resolution of a disagreement between the two Houses of Parliament in Victoria had not been observed in the passage of a bill; held, the requirements were only directory. This decision was followed in *Cormack* v. *Cope* (1974) 131 C.L.R. 432 and in *Victoria* v. *Commonwealth of Australia and Connor* (1975) 134 C.L.R. 81. Contrast *Bribery Commissioner* v. *Ranasinghe* [1965] A.C. at 200 (held, that the giving of a Speaker's certificate was a necessary part of the legislative process, and its omission was not cured by royal assent to a bill).

[99]   The main reason being that this would be a breach of parliamentary privilege – an objection that would not apply to proceedings before a colonial legislature: *Rediffusion (Hong Kong) Ltd* v. *Att.-Gen. of Hong Kong* [1970] A.C. 1136.

[100]   *Att.-Gen.* v. *London and Home Counties Joint Electricity Authority* [1929] 1 Ch. 513 (unlawful expenditure of funds for the purpose). But the jurisdiction to award an injunction will be sparingly exercised and is unlikely to be exercised at all in proceedings between parties. See *Bilston Corpn* v. *Wolverhampton Corpn* [1942] Ch. 391 (no injunction to restrain breach of undertaking, confirmed by statute, not to oppose introduction of bill); Holdsworth (1943) 59 *L.Q.R.* 2. cf. p. 399.

7   One can nevertheless imagine situations in which a measure
purporting to be an Act of Parliament might be treated as nugatory
by a court. For example, the Parliament Acts enable certain bills to
be presented for the royal assent without the consent of the Lords,
and provide that a certificate given by the Speaker of the Commons
before a bill is presented for assent, and endorsed on the bill that
the requirements of the Acts have been complied with, shall be
conclusive for all purposes and shall not be questioned in any
court.[101] But bills to prolong the duration of a Parliament beyond
five years are explicitly excluded from the Parliament Act
procedure.[102] If such a bill were to be passed by the Commons
alone, certified by the Speaker and assented by the Queen with
words of enactment stating that it had been passed in accordance
with the Parliament Acts[103] a court should surely treat that 'Act' as
a nullity, because it was 'bad on its face'; the body purporting to
enact it would not be 'Parliament' within the meaning of existing
law. The fatal defect[104] would be apparent without any judicial
intrusion into the proceedings of either House; the purported Act
would be no more efficacious than a resolution of the House of
Commons.[105] A broadly similar analysis might be applicable to a
situation in which a Regent assented to a bill to alter the succession
to the throne or the establishment of the Church in Scotland, in
disregard of the prohibitions contained in the Regency Act 1937.[106]
These are no doubt somewhat fanciful hypotheses, but by putting
extreme examples, the limitations of an apparently rigid rule can be
exposed.

Redefinition of the meaning of Parliament

Parliament is capable of redefining itself for particular purposes. It did

---

[101] Parliament Act 1911, ss 2(2), 3; Parliament Act 1949. For the Speaker's certificate that
a bill is a money bill within the meaning of the 1911 Act, see s. 1(3) of that Act.

[102] 1911 Act, s. 2(1).

[103] As has already been indicated (see p. 33), an erroneous certificate that a bill was a
money bill would be probably accepted as conclusive unless the error was so gross as to
be indicative of bad faith. This is because the practical consequences of holding a
money bill to be a nullity might be extremely grave.

[104] Or to use the colourful phrase used in *R.* v. *Arundel* (*Countess*) (1617) Hobart 109 at
111, the 'death wound'.

[105] Which has no legal effect outside the walls of Parliament (*Stockdale* v. *Hansard* (1839) 9
Ad. & E. 1; *Bowles* v. *Bank of England* [1913] 1 Ch. 57), unless given such an effect by
Act of Parliament: see Provisional Collection of Taxes Act 1968; and ch. 17.

[106] Regency Act 1937, s. 4(2). This provision might, of course, be held to be merely
directory, though such an analysis seems implausible.

so by the Parliament Acts, which provided a simpler, optional procedure for legislation on most topics.[107] It could make the procedure simpler still by abolishing the House of Lords. What if it were to lay down a more cumbersome procedure for legislating and prescribe it as the only procedure to be followed? Suppose, for example, that Parliament were to pass a Bill of Rights Act proclaiming the rights of the citizen, and which stated that no bill to vary that Act was to be presented for the royal assent unless it had first obtained the support of a majority of the voters at a referendum, or had been passed at its final reading with the support of two-thirds of the full membership of the House of Commons; and that no bill to amend or repeal that Act was to be presented for the royal assent unless that same procedure had been followed.[108] Could Parliament nevertheless amend or repeal the Act by ordinary legislative procedure?[109]

1   It is not enough to incant the phrase: 'A sovereign Parliament cannot bind its own future action.'[110] One of the questions to be

[107] Professor H. W. R. Wade regards measures passed under this procedure as a special form of delegated legislation: see [1955] *Camb. L.J.* 172 and *Constitutional Fundamentals* (1980), pp. 27–8. I respectfully prefer Dr Geoffrey Marshall's view (*Parliamentary Sovereignty and the Commonwealth* (1957), pp. 42–6) that such legislation is primary and not delegated. Professor Hood Phillips (*Constitutional and Administrative Law* (7th edn, 1987 by Hood Phillips and Paul Jackson, p. 91) goes so far as to characterize legislation passed with a Regent's assent 'as a kind of delegated legislation', and on this ground would justify a judicial decision to the effect that an 'Act' assented to by a Regent in contravention of s. 4(2) of the 1937 Act was invalid. He has also suggested (*Reform of the Constitution* (1970), pp. 18–19, 91–2) that the Parliament Act 1949 is a nullity because the 'delegate' created in 1911 enlarged its own limited powers in passing it.

[108] Unless this last entrenching provision was present – it is absent from section 1 of the Northern Ireland Constitution Act 1973, as it was from section 1(2) of the Ireland Act 1949 – it could easily be argued that the Act imposing the special requirement could itself be amended or repealed by ordinary legislative procedure.

[109] Among the main contributions are those by Cowen (1952) 15 *Mod. L. Rev.* 282, (1953) 16 *Mod. L. Rev.* 273; Beinart [1954] *Butterworth's South African Law Rev.* 135; Geoffrey Marshall, *Parliamentary Sovereignty and the Commonwealth* (1957) and *Constitutional Theory* (1971), ch. 3; R. F. V. Heuston, *Essays in Constitutional Law* (2nd edn, 1964), ch. 4; J. D. B. Mitchell, *Constitutional Law* (2nd edn, 1968), ch. 4; Gray (1953) 10 *U. of Toronto L.J.* 54; Friedmann (1950) 24 *Australian L.J.* 103; O. Hood Phillips, op. cit., ch. 4; Harry Calvert, *Constitutional Law in Northern Ireland* (1968), ch. 1.

[110] In this context the implications of *Att.-Gen. for N.S.W.* v. *Trethowan* (1931) 44 C.L.R. 394; [1934] A.C. 526 are often misunderstood by students. Under the constitution of New South Wales as amended by local legislation passed in 1929, a bill to abolish the upper House could not be presented for the royal assent unless it had first been approved by the electorate at a referendum, and a like requirement extended to any bill to amend or repeal this procedure. Following a change of government in 1931, bills were passed by both Houses of the New South Wales Parliament to remove the referendum rule and to abolish the upper House; neither bill was submitted to a referendum. Injunctions were obtained to restrain submission of the bills for the royal assent. This may have been an inappropriate remedy (see *Hughes and Vale Pty Ltd* v.

asked is: 'What is meant by "Parliament"?' Another – essentially
the same question expressed in a different way – is whether there
cannot be new mandatory legal rules as to the manner and form of
law-making which Parliament must observe if its enactments are to
be recognized as authentic. The much-quoted dictum that 'Parliament cannot bind itself as to the form of subsequent legislation'[111]
carries us nowhere, for it was uttered merely to rebut the optimistic
argument that Parliament had protected an ordinary enactment
against implied repeal.[112] Another question, as we have already
seen, is the extent to which the courts have jurisdiction to determine
whether 'Parliament' has acted in conformity with the law behind
Parliament.

2   Modern decisions in constitutional cases arising in South Africa[113]
and Ceylon[114] show that a sovereign (i.e. omnicompetent) Parliament must function in the manner prescribed by existing law in
order validly to express its legislative will. In each of the cases the

---

Gair (1954) 90 C.L.R. 203 at 204–5), but the decision on the point of substantive law
was clearly correct. Confusion has been caused by the fact that New South Wales had a
non-sovereign legislature; and section 5 of the Colonial Laws Validity Act 1865, which
applied to New South Wales, provided that a 'colonial' legislature could make laws
relating to its constitution, powers and procedure 'in such manner and form as may . . .
be required' by existing law. The applicability of section 5 furnished one reason for
holding the improper procedure to be unlawful; the decision should have been the same,
however, even if New South Wales had had a 'sovereign' legislature: see cases cited in
notes 113 and 114, below. There is a common but wholly unfounded misconception that
because New South Wales had a non-sovereign legislature and was held to be
competent to 'bind its own future action', *it therefore follows* that a sovereign legislature
like the United Kingdom Parliament is incompetent to do so.

[111] See above, note 58.

[112] cf. *R.* v. *Drybones* [1970] S.C.R. 282 (Can.) for the position of an extraordinary
enactment (the Canadian Bill of Rights 1960) which the majority of the Supreme Court
held would prevail over inconsistent legislation not expressed to be made 'notwithstanding' the Bill of Rights.

[113] *Harris* v. *Donges* [1952] 1 T.L.R. 1245, *sub nom. Harris* v. *Minister of the Interior* 1952
(2) S.A. 428 (two-thirds' majority of both Houses of the South African Parliament
required by the South Africa Act 1909 for removal of Cape coloured voters from the
common voters' roll; held, a measure passed by both Houses sitting separately by
simple majorities was not an authentic Act of Parliament, although it had been assented
to); see also *Minister of the Interior* v. *Harris* 1952 (4) S.A. 769 (an 'Act' constituting the
two Houses as the 'High Court of Parliament' with power to override the previous
decision by a simple majority, also held to be a nullity). See, however, *Colins* v. *Minister
of the Interior* 1957 (1) S.A. 552, where the desired result was achieved by a sufficiently
circuitous route. For the literature on this series of legal battles, see Geoffrey Marshall,
Parliamentary Sovereignty and the Commonwealth (1957).

[114] *Bribery Commissioner* v. *Ranasinghe* [1965] A.C. 172 (royal assent did not cure failure to
obtain a two-thirds' majority in the lower House for a measure inconsistent with the
constitution). See further *R. (O'Brien)* v. *Military Governor, N.D.U. Internment Camp*
[1924] I.R. 32 (failure to submit a bill to a referendum held fatal to the validity of an
ostensibly authentic Act; see Heuston, op. cit., pp. 11–14).

constitution had laid down a special procedure (a two-thirds' majority of the two Houses in joint session, or a two-thirds' majority in the lower House, at final reading) to be followed for the enactment of legislation on certain important matters. In each of them the courts held that where bills dealing with these 'entrenched' matters had been passed by *ordinary* legislative majorities and had been duly assented to and printed, they could not be accepted as authentic Acts of Parliament. There was to be read into the constitution a necessary implication that 'Parliament' bore different meanings for different purposes.

3 These decisions, extremely interesting though they are as illustrations of basic principle, are of doubtful persuasive authority when we try to answer our hypothetical problem set in a British constitutional context. In the first place, in each of them the wording of a Speaker's certificate on the face of the Act or bill in question (or the absence of such a certificate) indicated that the specially prescribed procedure had not in fact been followed. Although the decisions suggest that the courts can look at the original of the bill as presented for assent (and are not confined to the bare text of the published Act), they do not offer clear guidance on the proper limits of a court's scope of inquiry if there is no requirement of a Speaker's certificate, or if a Speaker's certificate or the words of enactment are notoriously false or are alleged to be false. As far as British courts are concerned, these questions remain open. In the second place, none of them deals with the legal effects of *self-imposed* procedural requirements by the Parliaments of those countries; the requirements had been imposed by the constitutional instruments from which the Parliaments derived their authority to make law.

4 None the less, there is no *logical* reason why the United Kingdom Parliament should be incompetent so to redefine itself (or redefine the procedure for enacting legislation on any given matter) as to preclude Parliament *as ordinarily constituted* from passing a law on a matter. (There are, of course, doubts as to the jurisdiction or willingness of the courts to intervene.) If Parliament can make it easier to legislate, as by passing the Parliament Acts or abolishing the House of Lords, it can also make it harder to legislate.[115]

5 Hence a two-thirds' majority rule might be analysed either as a

---

[115] The Parliament Acts analogy has been characterized as fallacious because the Acts only created an additional and permissive means of legislating, so that no question of limitation arises. See Colin Munro, *Studies in Constitutional Law* (1987), pp. 106–7.

redefinition of the meaning of 'Parliament' or a prescription of essential procedural conditions before Parliament could speak with an authentic voice; a rule imposing a duty to hold a referendum could quite persuasively be analysed as the addition of a fourth element to 'Parliament', in much the same way as the Parliament Act procedure can be analysed as involving the conditional subtraction of one of the three elements from Parliament.

6   Such an analysis can be attacked on the ground that once it is conceded that Parliament can make legislation on any topic more difficult, one must then concede that it can make legislation impossible. If it can lay down a two-thirds' majority rule it can lay down a nine-tenths' majority rule, and a similar rule for the majority to be obtained at a referendum. In this way it could, by imposing requirements as to the manner of legislating, in practice bind itself not to change the substantive content of future legislation, and this would be contrary to both established principle and public policy; a legislative vacuum must not be created; consequently the courts ought not to recognize the legal efficacy of *any* such restrictive rule. The only ways of answering this point are that there exist *political* safeguards against the adoption of such restrictive rules, just as there are political safeguards against the enactment of preposterous laws by ordinary legislative procedure; and that a court could draw a common-sense line between binding rules regulating the manner of legislating and ineffectual rules which if accepted as binding would, in substance, stop Parliament from legislating at all.[116] One must, however, recognize the distinct possibility that a court might decide not to engage in such a delicate exercise.

To devote more space to this conundrum would hardly be worthwhile. We are in the realm of speculative conjecture. To dwell there longer would be justified only if there were a substantial likelihood that our hypothetical situation would assume practical importance.

Practical limitations on the legislative power of Parliament

Some of these limitations are considered more fully in chapters 10, 13 and 15. The possible legal effect of entry to the European Communities has already been considered. Even if membership does not curb the formal legal sovereignty of Parliament, the obligations entailed by membership mean that in practice Parliament will have to abstain from legislating, or legislating in particular ways, on a number of important

[116] See Friedmann (1950) 24 *Australian L.J.* at 105–6.

topics; and has required that legislation (mainly under delegated authority conferred by section 2(2) of the European Communities Act 1972 [117]) be passed in conformity with Community requirements.

When one asks what are the practical limitations on the exercise of parliamentary supremacy, one is also asking what are the effective restraints operating on the Government; for the legislative programme is largely dominated by the Government. In the first place, a Government's freedom of action is inhibited by its international position, and in particular by international obligations which it has undertaken. Quite apart from the pervasive influence of Community law, a Government would need to have very strong reasons for introducing legislation inconsistent with its obligations under the European Convention on Human Rights, GATT, or other multilateral conventions to which this country had acceded. Again, when the Government is obliged to seek a very large loan from external sources, it may be compelled to introduce restrictive fiscal and economic measures by legislation as a condition of receiving the money.

Secondly, the Government would not sponsor legislation which flagrantly violated a constitutional convention restricting the territorial ambit or subject-matter of legislative competence. It would not initiate legislation intended to encroach on the autonomy of an independent Commonwealth country or, for example, to impose changes in the laws of the Channel Islands on purely domestic matters. It has often been stated that the Government must not 'exceed its electoral mandate' by introducing major constitutional changes which have not been foreshadowed by its election manifesto. One may accept that there exists a loose convention to this effect, but one must recognize that unforeseen contingencies always arise during the life of a Parliament, that the country cannot exist on a diet of dissolutions, that a party's election manifesto does not have to be comprehensive and that a vote cast at a General Election does not imply conscious support for every aspect of a party's programme.

Thirdly, the Government will not introduce legislation which it believes to be incapable of enforcement. Occasionally an Act proves subsequently to be unenforceable (for example, the Southern Rhodesia Act 1965, asserting Parliament's paramount authority over the breakaway colony), but that is another matter. Nor will an Act be passed which requires the cooperation of the general public but which flies in the face of strong public opposition, such as one which would make it an offence to manufacture or sell all alcoholic liquor.

[117] See ch. 18.

Fourthly, although unpopular legislation may be passed, the Government would not introduce and its normally obedient supporters in Parliament might refuse to support legislation which would court inevitable electoral disaster in the later stages of the life of a Parliament. Repeal of all restrictions on Commonwealth immigration would fall into this category.

Fifthly, a Government's freedom of legislative initiative is circumscribed to some extent in so far as it is customary or expedient (or both) to consult in advance and pay some regard to the views of powerful organized interest groups, which are also able to exert pressure through their spokesmen in Parliament.

Sixthly, if a Government is in office without an overall majority in the House of Commons, it will obviously be at risk of losing votes on (among other things) its proposed legislation. The General Election of February 1974 resulted in the formation of a minority Labour Government, the first Government to be formed without a parliamentary majority since 1929. The October 1974 General Election gave the Government a small overall majority, but this was lost quite soon through by-election defeats. Thus the parliamentary situation was such that the Labour Government had to be careful to bring forward proposals which would carry at the least its parliamentary party. It did suffer defeats on bills, particularly relating to devolution.

Two other points must be made. First, there are still those who will solemnly affirm that Parliament ought not to legislate against the weight of public opinion; and even that the purpose of constitutional conventions is to ensure that government is conducted in accordance with public opinion. Stated in these general terms, such propositions are unacceptable. The British system of parliamentary government is above all a system of *government*. It is not a system geared to a series of opinion polls or referendums in which the garbled voice of the people is equated with deity. Among the factors which the Government and members of Parliament have to take into account is the strength of public sentiment on particular issues. But this is one factor among many. Members of Parliament are representatives but not delegates of their constituents; nor is the Cabinet a committee of the House of Commons or of Parliament. A Government and its parliamentary supporters ought to act in the way they think best in the general interests of the country. It is open to the electorate to use criticism and ridicule, to exert pressure on their representatives by legitimate means, to voice their displeasure at by-elections and to turn the Government out at the next General Election. But there is no constitutional convention to the effect that a Government which loses the confidence of the *country* must resign or advise a dissolution of Parliament, so long as it commands a majority in the House of Commons.

The second point should be stated in order to balance this account, though its connection with the idea of the supremacy of sovereignty of Parliament is only marginal. Although Parliament, for political purposes, is not to be thought of as a collective entity, and although in the last resort a Government will normally be able to bring its supporters in the House of Commons (and its supporters and opponents in the House of Lords) reluctantly to heel, the last resort is seldom reached. Because Parliament exists, because the Opposition in the House of Commons is always probing for opportunities to discredit the Government, and because Governments prefer convincing their backbenchers to bullying them, and are anxious to avoid public recriminations within the party in front of the Opposition, a Government needs to explain and justify its position to Parliament, and through Parliament to the public at large, as persuasively as possible and with an outward show of unity. Moreover, parliamentary time is not unlimited; and draconian action to curtail debate when obstructive tactics are used in the House of Commons can prove counter-productive. These factors undoubtedly influence the content of legislation, as well as curbing a Government's general freedom of action. Prudence often dictates caution and compromise.

Chapter 5

The United Kingdom and the European Community [1]

The Community and constitutional law

There can be no doubt that the United Kingdom's membership of the European Communities is of high importance in our constitutional law. No book on constitutional law can be considered complete if it fails to bring this fact home to the reader, and to point him to sources for wider and deeper reading than it is possible to supply in any such textbook. This chapter will not in itself, however, offer a comprehensive guide to the impact of membership, because it is best to consider certain aspects in their contexts throughout the book. Thus, for example, the vexed question of the effect of membership on parliamentary sovereignty was considered in the preceding chapter; [2] the place of Community law as a source of our domestic law was looked at in chapter 2; [3] the ability of the European Communities to levy taxes directly, without reference to the United Kingdom Parliament, will be considered in chapter 15 as part of the United Kingdom's financial arrangements; [4] scrutiny by Parliament of European legislation will also be looked at in that chapter; [5] the consequences of membership on our immigration law will be examined in chapter 23, [6] and there will be other,

[1] Three very helpful short studies are P.S.R.F. Mathijsen, *A Guide to European Community Law* (3rd edn, 1980); D. Lasok and J. W. Bridge, *Introduction to the Law and Institutions of the European Communities* (4th edn, 1987) and Lawrence Collins, *European Community Law in the United Kingdom* (4th edn 1987). See also K. Lipstein, *The Law of the European Community* (1974); Anthony Parry and Stephen Hardy, *E.E.C. Law* (2nd edn, 1981), T. C. Hartley, *The Foundations of European Community Law* (1981). For larger reference works see Alan Campbell, *Common Market Law* (1973); B. Rudden and D. Wyatt, *Basic Community Laws* (2nd edn, 1986); D. Wyatt and A. Dashwood, *The Substantive Law of the E.E.C.* (1980).

[2] See above, pp. 79–82.
[3] See above, pp. 26–7.
[4] See below, p. 282.
[5] See below, p. 281.
[6] See below, pp. 446, 448.

shorter, references in appropriate places. This policy is deliberate. It must be emphasized that constitutional lawyers should develop the habit, if they have not yet done so, of considering Community law where it is relevant as part and parcel of English law: to put the whole treatment of Community matters into one place in this book would not be conducive to that habit.

So this chapter will concentrate on matters which are not considered elsewhere. They are (1) the political background; (2) the purposes and institutions of the Community; and (3) Community law.

Political background

The European Coal and Steel Community (ECSC) was established in 1952.[7] The political will existed in continental Europe in the 1950s to take that initiative much further, and the European Economic Community (EEC)[8] together with the European Atomic Energy Community (EURATOM)[9] were born in 1958. This was followed by the merger of the institutions of the three Communities in 1965.[10] The EEC has undoubtedly been, and remains, the most important of the Communities, but the United Kingdom was not ready to join it at its inception: memories of the Empire were still relatively fresh; a considerable number of colonies remained; the 'special relationship' with the United States of America and relationships with the independent Commonwealth countries, taken together with fears about the loss of sovereignty which it was thought would be implicit in joining, kept us out. When the Leader of the Labour Party, Mr Gaitskell, said as late as 1962 that joining would mean the 'end of a thousand years of history'[11] he probably spoke for many. Accordingly the United Kingdom did not join the original six members[12] but tried instead to sit on a three-legged stool made up of the Commonwealth and colonies (with trade preference), the United States (particularly for political purposes) and a loose-knit European Free Trade Association (broadly consisting of European countries not in the EEC).

It became increasingly clear, however, that it should at least be discovered whether the United Kingdom could become associated with

---

[7] See Cmnd 4863 (1972) (the Treaty of Paris).
[8] See Cmnd 4864 (1972) (the Treaty of Rome).
[9] See Cmnd 4865 (1972).
[10] See Cmnd 5179 (1972).
[11] At the Labour Party conference, Brighton, October 1962.
[12] Belgium, the Federal Republic of Germany, France, Italy, Luxembourg and the Netherlands.

the European Communities on acceptable terms. The EEC countries enjoyed an economic boom in the 1950s and 1960s, while the United Kingdom's economy never really recovered from the enormous costs of the Second World War. In short, the belief grew that salvation might lie in membership of the EEC. As one of the last great acts of his Administration, Mr Macmillan applied for membership in 1961. Negotiations, led for Britain by Mr Edward Heath, dragged on until 1963, when President de Gaulle vetoed the application. The Labour Party (which in the same year had elected Mr Wilson as its Leader on the death of Mr Gaitskell) underwent a change of heart and decided that when it was next in power it too would try to enter. By that time, in 1967, the President of France was quicker off the mark: the French veto came before negotiations could take place. Finally, Mr Heath's Government of 1970 made a further attempt [13] and successful negotiations led to the conclusion of the Treaty of Brussels,[14] the European Communities Act 1972 and full United Kingdom membership from 1 January 1973.[15]

But a nagging doubt remained. Were we truly 'European'? The question could not be answered by a vote in the House of Commons or at a General Election, because different answers would be given by members of the same political party and of none. The Labour Government of 1974 therefore came to office pledged to put the issue to the people.[16] The Cabinet agreed upon a unique constitutional experiment: a referendum.[17] The Referendum Act 1975 allowed all those who would be entitled to vote at a local government election to participate in the referendum.[18] Public money was granted to the protagonists.[19] Under the superintendence of a Chief Counting Officer[20] the referendum was held on 5 June 1975, the majority of the Cabinet being in favour of continued membership.[21] The question on

[13] President de Gaulle had resigned in 1969, and his successor, President Pompidou, did not share his predecessor's fears of Anglo-Saxon domination of the EEC.

[14] See Cmnd 4862 (1972), vols. 1 and 2.

[15] Norway applied for membership at the same time, but the Norwegian electorate rejected it at a referendum. Denmark and the Republic of Ireland joined at the same time as the United Kingdom.

[16] This was to be done 'through the ballot box' – a formula which left open the possibility of a referendum or another General Election.

[17] See p. 189 below for the suspension of collective Cabinet responsibility on the matter – in itself a rare, but not unique constitutional device.

[18] Section 1(3).

[19] Section 3. Two umbrella organizations were formed, one on each side.

[20] Section 2(4).

[21] The Government had 'renegotiated' the terms on which the United Kingdom had entered the Community: see Cmnd 6003 (1975).

the ballot paper was 'Do you think that the United Kingdom should stay in the European Community (the Common Market)?' Of eligible voters, 67.2 per cent answered in the affirmative.[22]

So today the European Community comprises the following twelve States: Belgium, Denmark,[23] the Federal Republic of Germany, France, Greece,[24] the Republic of Ireland,[25] Italy, Luxembourg, the Netherlands, Portugal, Spain,[26] and the United Kingdom.[27] The European Community is usually referred to nowadays in the singular, although that term embraces all the Communities which juridically remain separate.

Purposes and institutions

The basic objectives of the EEC relate to economic development and to improved living standards for the people of the Community.[28] To those ends the Community aims to establish a customs union between member States and a common commercial policy towards non-members, to achieve free movement of persons, services and capital between States within the Community, to evolve a common agricultural policy[29] and a common transport policy, and to maintain fair competition. Although these economic aims have been paramount in the Community, political cooperation and ultimately political union were also original aspirations, and 'European Union' has recently been restated as an objective to be reached by 1992. This is made clear in the preamble to an important Community treaty, the Single European Act of 1986.[30] The Single European Act is of major significance in the development of the Community, especially through those of its provisions which are designed to speed up decision-making. Under the Act

---

[22] On the referendum see D. Butler and U. Kitzinger, *The 1975 Referendum* (1975). The Labour Party later campaigned at the 1983 General Election for withdrawal of the United Kingdom, but not during the 1987 General Election.

[23] Denmark joined at the same time as the United Kingdom.

[24] Greece joined in 1981. See the European Communities (Greek Accession) Act 1979.

[25] Ireland joined at the same time as the United Kingdom.

[26] Portugal and Spain joined in 1986. See the European Communities (Spanish and Portuguese Accession) Act 1985.

[27] Norway did not ratify its membership, following a referendum; Greenland (which is part of Denmark although self-governing) left in 1982 after a referendum.

[28] Treaty of Rome, arts. 2 and 3 (hereafter 'the EEC Treaty').

[29] The common agricultural policy has been easily the most controversial of the Community's aims.

[30] See Cmnd 9758 (1986). For explanations see Cmnd 9761 (1986); 479 H.L. Deb. 1004–9 (31 July 1986); [1987] *Camb L.J.* 1. It was made effective in the United Kingdom by the European Communities (Amendment) Act 1986.

the Community's competence is extended to cover monetary cooperation, research and technology, environmental protection and social
policy. The internal market (that area without internal frontiers against
freedom of movement) is planned to be completed by 1992. A new
decision-making process, 'cooperation procedure', will increase the
influence of the European Parliament, and 'European Political Cooperation' is designed to ensure consultation about and coordination of
foreign policy between member States. Specific institutional changes
brought about by the Single European Act will be mentioned at
appropriate points in this chapter.

The institutions of the Community are the Council of Ministers, the
Commission, the Parliament, the European Court of Justice and the
European Council. It is interesting to look first at the European
Council. It was established in 1974 in a communiqué issued by the
heads of government of the member States meeting in Paris: it was,
therefore, not mentioned in the treaties and had no further formal
recognition until the Single European Act in 1986.[31] The European
Council consists of heads of government, together with their Foreign
Ministers, and usually meets two or three times a year. Politically the
European Council is as vital as any other Community institution. For
example, through three meetings of the European Council the European
Monetary System was agreed on and established by the Brussels
resolution of December 1978. It was only at head of government level
that such issues could be determined, and the European Council is a
convenient forum in which such matters can be resolved. These regular
meetings are high-powered gatherings which can give the Communities
a sense of political direction. The European Council frequently
discusses international questions without being constrained by any
narrow view of Community interests.

The Council of Ministers [32] consists of one representative from each
member State.[33] They are frequently the Foreign Ministers.[34] There is
an ancillary and very important Committee of Permanent Representatives, composed of national officials of ambassadorial status,
which advises the Council generally and in particular on Commission
proposals.[35] The Council is the principal decision-making and legislative

[31] Art. 1. The European Council must meet at least twice a year: art. 2.
[32] Not, of course, to be confused with the European Council.
[33] EEC Treaty, art. 146.
[34] But the representation varies according to the agenda. If, for example, fisheries policy is
to be discussed Fisheries Ministers will attend.
[35] Merger Treaty, art. 4.

organ of the Communities.[36] For example, it ultimately adopts Community legislation (if it agrees that it should be adopted) proposed by the Commission, adopts the budget and concludes international agreements on behalf of the EEC.[37] There are usually some eighty meetings a year. Each member State holds the Presidency of the Council for six months in rotation, and the Commission attends upon the Council at those meetings (but has no voting rights).

Under the treaties, decisions by the Council of Ministers are usually taken only following a proposal by the Commission. Depending on the subject-matter, the decision is to be taken either (*a*) by a simple majority; or (*b*) by a 'qualified majority', special weightage being given to the larger member States,[38] or (*c*) unanimously – where the Council wishes to amend a Commission proposal.[39] In practice, however, where any vital interest of any member State is at stake (what is 'vital' being determined by the Government concerned) the decision will have to be unanimous: this is to be inferred from the interpretation given to the Luxembourg Agreement of 1966.[40] Under the Single European Act qualified majority voting is extended to areas such as transport, common customs tariffs, some aspects of freedom of establishment and services, and capital movement (but not to taxation or to freedom of movement of persons).

The Commission is the executive authority which supports the Community. It has wide executive competence and a crucial role in the process of Community legislation. It consists of seventeen members, one from each of the smaller States and two from each of the larger.[41] The members are appointed by agreement between the member States. They are Community officials (though most of them have been involved in national politics)[42] and they owe their allegiance to the

---

[36] EEC Treaty, art. 145.

[37] ibid., art. 228.

[38] The qualified majority vote is 54 votes out of a possible total of 76. France, the Federal Republic of Germany, Italy and the United Kingdom have 10 votes each; Spain has 8; Belgium, Greece, the Netherlands and Portugal have 5 each; Denmark and Ireland have 3 each, and Luxembourg has 2.

[39] EEC Treaty, arts. 148, 149.

[40] The Agreement does not record an agreement to this effect, but rather an agreement between France and the other member States to differ on this crucial point. The Agreement seemed to be broken for the first time in 1982 when a decision on farm prices was taken by a majority, even though the minority had stated that the vote would affect their vital interests. Different interpretations of the affair are, however, tenable: see Evans [1982] *Public Law* 366.

[41] Merger Treaty, art. 11. The United Kingdom, France, the Federal Republic of Germany, Spain and Italy each have two, the others each having one.

[42] The United Kingdom Commissioners have been appointed in equal numbers from the Conservative and Labour Parties.

Community, not to the government of any State. Indeed, the member States undertake not to try to influence the Commissioners in their work.[43] They hold office for renewable four-year terms. A President and five Vice-Presidents are appointed by member States from the Commissioners for renewable two-year terms.[44] Commissioners have security of tenure: only the European Court can retire a Commissioner for incapacity or misconduct, and the entire Commission could only be removed by the European Parliament – a highly unlikely prospect. The Commission is pre-eminently a supranational rather than an inter-national body: initiating, supervising, coordinating, legislating within narrow limits,[45] drawing up the budget,[46] imposing penalties on enterprises which break competition rules, instigating infringement proceedings when a member State appears to be in breach of Community law (at the rate of up to 300 a year)[47] and conducting elaborate dialogues with the Council of Ministers. Its supranational character allows the Commission above all Community institutions to represent the Community's interests.

Each Commissioner has individual responsibility for defined aspects of the work of the Communities, although the Commission takes decisions together.[48] So, for example, there are Commissioners for External Affairs, Agriculture and so on. Under each Commissioner is a Directorate-General. The total staff of the Commission is now over 11,000. The Commission's role in the legislative process is primarily to initiate legislative proposals, which go to the Council of Ministers, who act on them usually after consulting the European Parliament. It would be wrong to assume that the Commission works in isolation in making these proposals because it consults the civil service of member States and the staff of the Council of Ministers.[49] Where the Commission does have considerable power, however, is the treaty provision that once the Commission has made a proposal to the Council of Ministers, the Council can only amend it by a unanimous vote.[50]

The European Parliament was originally styled the Assembly in the treaties,[51] but in 1962 it adopted the description Parliament, a change

---

[43] Merger Treaty, art. 10.
[44] ibid., art. 14. Lord Jenkins of Hillhead, a former Deputy Leader of the Labour Party and first Leader of the Social Democratic Party, was President 1977–81.
[45] See, for example, EEC Treaty, art. 48(3) (*d*).
[46] ibid., art. 209.
[47] ibid., arts. 155 and 169.
[48] These can be majority decisions: Merger Treaty, art. 17.
[49] EEC Treaty, art. 15.
[50] ibid., art. 149.
[51] ibid., art. 137.

endorsed by the Single European Act.[52] It used to consist of representatives chosen by national Parliaments from their own members. But since 1979 the electorates of each member State elect their representatives directly, a development designed to increase the influence of the Parliament beyond its largely debating and consultative work towards greater democratic control of Community institutions. The number of members allocated to each State does not depend on population, and there are currently 518 members in total.

The United Kingdom members are elected by virtue of the European Parliament Elections Act 1978.[53] Eighty-one representatives are elected from the United Kingdom[54] for a five-year term.[55] The United Kingdom members are elected by the usual 'first past the post' electoral system, as used at parliamentary elections. Under the European Parliament (Pay and Pensions) Act 1979, section 1, representatives receive the same salary as British M.P.s, charged on the Consolidated Fund. If a representative is also an M.P., he receives one salary plus one-third. Expenses and other allowances are paid by the Parliament itself. Members are elected under party labels, and sit in party, not national, groupings in the Parliament chamber.

The powers of the Parliament remain primarily consultative, not legislative, the Council of Ministers seeking its views about Commission proposals.[56] Members of the Parliament can ask questions about the work of both bodies at a question time not unlike that of the House of Commons. It works largely through standing committees which cover all the main areas of Community competence. The Parliament has the ultimate power, never yet used, to dismiss the Commission if it votes to do so by a two-thirds majority, representing a majority of the total membership.[57] But in 1979 and again in 1984 the Parliament rejected the budgets proposed by the Commission – the most drastic actions of the Parliament since its inception. The Parliament may also bring enforcement proceedings in the European Court against the Commission or Council of Ministers if either fails to take action which it is

---

[52] The word 'Parliament' is inserted retrospectively into relevant British statutes by the European Communities (Amendment) Act 1986, s. 3.

[53] See Cmnd 6399 (1976); Cmnd 6768 (1977).

[54] Sixty-six from England, eight from Scotland, four from Wales and three from Northern Ireland: 1978 Act, s. 2. The Northern Ireland members are elected by single transferable vote. See also the European Parliament Elections Act 1981.

[55] Council Decision 76/787.

[56] Failure to do so would be a ground for challenging the validity of legislation: see EEC Treaty, arts. 173 and 190. See also *S.A. Roquettes Frères* v. *Council of Ministers* [1980] E.C.R. 3333.

[57] EEC Treaty, art. 144.

obliged to take: thus in 1985 the European Court partly upheld the Parliament's complaint that the Council had failed to adopt a common transport policy.[58]

The European Court of Justice[59] sits at Luxembourg and consists of thirteen judges appointed by agreement between the member States.[60] One judge is appointed from each member State, with the thirteenth being selected from the larger States in rotation. Judges are appointed from those who are qualified for the highest judicial office in their own State, or who are 'juriconsults of recognized competence' (a provision which allows practitioners and academics to be appointed).[61] A judge may only be removed by the unanimous vote of the other judges. The President of the Court is elected by his fellow judges. Lord Mackenzie Stewart, formerly a member of the Scottish Court of Session, was elected President in 1984. The Court is fashioned according to European models; its procedures are inquisitorial, and written submissions by counsel are more important than oral argument. Provisional conclusions are prepared by an Advocate-General, an officer who has no counterpart in the United Kingdom.[62] In interpreting legal instruments the Court may consider preparatory materials and not merely the bare text. Its judgments are frequently terse, replete with statements of general legal principle and no dissenting opinion is delivered or announced.

The Court's jurisdiction is wide-ranging. Its principal function is to see that Community law is observed. It is an 'administrative court' determining the validity of acts and decisions of Community organs broadly according to French administrative law doctrine.[63] Action may be brought by a member State or by the Commission or the Council. Luxembourg brought an action against the Parliament in 1981, claiming that a parliamentary resolution about where the Parliament

---

[58] *European Parliament* v. *Council of Ministers* [1986] 1 C.M.L.R. 138. The 1986 budget was held to have been unlawfully adopted because it had not been agreed by the Council and the Parliament: *Council of Ministers* v. *European Parliament, The Times*, 4 July 1986.

[59] See L. Neville Brown and F. Jacobs, *The Court of Justice of the European Communities* (2nd edn, 1983); D. G. Valentine, *The Court of Justice of the European Communities* (1965); Gerhard Bebr, *Judicial Control of the European Communities* (1965); L. J. Brinkhorst and H. G. Schermers, *Judicial Remedies in the European Communities* (2nd edn, 1977); J. A. Usher *European Court Practice* (1983). Selected judgments are reported in English in *The Common Market Law Reports* (C.M.L.R.), together with important decisions of national courts on matters of Community law, and all the Court's judgments are published in its official reports, which appear in all the official Community languages.

[60] EEC Treaty, arts. 165, 167.

[61] ibid., art. 167.

[62] See Slynn (1984) 33 *I.C.L.Q* 409.

[63] EEC Treaty, art. 173.

should sit was invalid.[64] Actions may be brought against member States by the Commission, or by another member State, for failure to fulfil a Community obligation.[65] The Court also hears appeals against penalties imposed by the Commission, disputes between the Communities and their officials, claims in tort and contract against the Communities, and proceedings against Community organs for wrongful failure to act. In constitutional law its most important head of jurisdiction is to give preliminary rulings, under article 177 of the EEC Treaty, on the interpretation of the treaties and the validity and interpretation of acts (including regulations and directives) of Community organs.[66] A national court or tribunal ought not to refer such a question unless an interpretation or ruling on the validity of the Community measure is necessary for its decision on the matter before it. Courts and tribunals of last instance are obliged to refer such a question unless the correct interpretation is quite clear.

Where a national court has a discretion under article 177 to refer a question to the European Court, Lord Denning M.R. offered guidelines, in *Bulmer (H.P.)* v. *J. Bollinger S.A.*[67] on how it should be exercised by English courts. Broadly, (*a*) the resolution of the question must be necessary to enable the English court to give judgment; (*b*) the decision must be conclusive of the case, and (*c*) even then the court must consider such matters as the difficulty and importance of the point, the delay and expense which a reference would involve, and the burden on the European Court. Rules of court prescribe the *procedure* for making references to the European Court from superior courts[68] but do not state the *principles* governing references. References ought to be made by lower courts if possible; this will reduce the costs of the parties and minimize the delay, which will in any event be of several months' duration.

The European Court makes its preliminary ruling under article 177, avoiding as far as possible any interpretation of municipal law. The case then returns to the originating national court which, in deciding the case, must see how (if at all) the relevant provisions of municipal law can be reconciled with the European Court's ruling.[69]

[64] *Grand Duchy of Luxembourg* v. *European Parliament* [1983] 2 C.M.L.R. 726.

[65] EEC Treaty, art. 171. See, e.g., *Commission* v. *United Kingdom* [1984] 1 All E.R. 353; *France* v. *United Kingdom* [1980] 1 C.M.L.R. 6.

[66] See below, and also F. G. Jacobs and A. Durand, *References to the European Court: Practice and Procedure* (1975).

[67] [1974] Ch. 401. See also above, p. 80.

[68] S.I. 1972, Nos. 1786, 1787, 1898.

[69] See above, pp. 26–7. The European Court considered the meaning of art. 177 in *C.I.L.F.I.T.* v. *Italian Ministry of Health* [1983] 1 C.M.L.R. 472.

The Court, like the Commission, has generally sought to extend the frontiers of Community law and to emphasize the concept of Community law supremacy. But no coercive sanction is provided against a defaulter,[70] except under the ECSC Treaty.[71] This lack of a general sanction was amply illustrated when France ignored a ruling of the Court in 1979–80 that she should resume the import of English sheep-meat.[72]

Under the Single European Act, a new Court of First Instance is to be set up to take some of the less important cases.[73]

Community law

It is not the intention here to consider a number of matters concerning Community law which are dealt with elsewhere in this book. In particular the reader is referred to the discussion of the European Communities Act 1972 in chapter 4.[74] Rather, the present limited purposes are to explain what is meant by the term 'Community law', and those important effects which it has on United Kingdom law which are not explained anywhere else in these pages.

Community law comprises[75] the primary treaties;[76] ancillary agreements entered into by the member States;[77] secondary legislation by Community organs;[78] administrative acts and decisions by those organs, and decisions and other pronouncements of the European Court of Justice. Secondary legislation[79] is made by the Council of Ministers and the Commission, and is of three types. *Regulations* are binding and directly applicable in member States.[80] They are used to ensure a uniform application of Community policies. *Directives* are also

[70] EEC Treaty, arts. 169–71. A defaulting State is obliged to comply with the Court's judgment: see *Procurer de la République* v. *Waterkyn* [1983] 2 C.M.L.R. 145.

[71] Art. 88, which empowers the Commission, with the concurrence of two-thirds of the Council of Ministers, to withhold from that member State moneys due to it and to authorize other members to subject it to fiscal sanctions.

[72] *Commission* v. *France* [1980] 1 C.M.L.R. 418.

[73] Arts. 4, 5, 11, 12, 26, 27; European Communities (Amendment) Act 1986, s. 2.

[74] See above, pp. 79–82.

[75] See also above, pp. 26–7.

[76] These may be described as the Community's basic law: see Donner (1974) 11 C.M.L.R. 127.

[77] The Communities also have treaty-making competence: EEC Treaty, arts. 210, 228, 235.

[78] ibid., art. 189; see also above, pp. 79–82.

[79] Such legislation must be reasoned, i.e., indicate the authority for it, the reasons for making it and state that any necessary opinions have been obtained. If it is not reasoned the European Court may annul it. Ibid., arts. 173, 174, 190.

[80] ibid., arts. 189, 191. See *Leonesio* v. *Italian Ministry of Agriculture* [1973] C.M.L.R. 343; *Commission* v. *United Kingdom* [1979] 2 C.M.L.R. 48.

binding, but the mode of adoption is left to each member State, subject usually to a time-limit for that adoption.[81] *Decisions* are binding on those to whom they are addressed, sometimes to member States, sometimes to individuals or companies.[82]

Community law is distinct from public international law and from national (municipal) law of member States. But it is interwoven with municipal law; it is applied mainly by the courts of member States; certain rules of Community law (notably regulations made by the Council of Ministers or the Commission) are directly applicable[83] in the sense that, of their own force, they create legal rights and duties enforceable in municipal courts. It is concerned primarily with such issues as the free movement of goods, labour, services and capital; customs duties; agriculture, and trade competition.

According to Community law doctrine, as expounded by the European Court of Justice, Community law prevails over national law (even national constitutional law) to the extent that they are inconsistent with one another. Cases of inconsistency are not confined to conflicts between directly applicable Community law and municipal law; they arise whenever municipal laws are incompatible with rights specifically conferred by rules of Community law (including provisions of the treaties, directives issued by the Council of Ministers or the Commission, and decisions of the Commission), and inconsistency may exist without direct conflict if Community rules evince an intention to cover the whole field of activity in question. The European Communities Act 1972 provides that the Community treaties shall have effect in United Kingdom law,[84] that enactments 'passed or to be passed' shall be 'construed and have effect' subject to the preceding provisions,[85] and that decisions of the European Court and the principles laid down by it (including, of course, the supremacy of Community law and the consequential denial of the legal doctrine of parliamentary sovereignty) shall be applied by United Kingdom courts. Attention has already been drawn, in chapter 4, to the incompatibility of some of these provisions

---

[81] ibid., art. 189. A directive may create rights for individuals, enforceable in their national courts: see, e.g., *Van Duyn* v. *Home Office* [1975] Ch. 358; *Marshall* v. *Southampton and S.W. Hants. A.H.A.* [1986] 2 All E.R. 584 (see above, p. 80). In *Duke* v. *GEC Reliance* [1988] 1 All E.R. 625 the House of Lords held that s. 2(4) does not constrain a British court to distort the meaning of a statute in order to enforce a Community directive against an individual when the directive has no direct effect between individuals.

[82] ibid., art. 189. The Council and the Commission also make recommendations and deliver opinions. Neither is binding.

[83] See Bebr (1970) 19 *I.C.L.Q.* 257, and above, pp. 26–7.

[84] Sections 1, 2(1).

[85] Section 2(4). See *Garland* v. *British Rail Engineering Ltd* [1983] 2 A.C. 751 (above, p. 80); *Duke* v. *GEC Reliance* [1988] 1 All E.R. 625.

with basic constitutional principles.[86] Clearly, therefore, within the Communities' legal system, Community law prevails over domestic law.[87] This has, however, been specifically denied by some national courts.[88]

In the United Kingdom issues of Community law have arisen in courts and tribunals of all ranks, from the lowliest magistrates' courts to the judicial House of Lords. It was not easy for our courts to adapt to Community law – after all, the original member States have shared a similar legal tradition which is largely alien here; and those States had had the chance to shape Community law from the start, whereas the United Kingdom did not join until fifteen years later. A cautious approach by our courts was therefore foreseeable and perhaps desirable. Nevertheless, Community law has had a substantial effect in several areas of our law, particularly in relation to freedom of movement of persons[89] and of goods,[90] free competition[91] and equal pay.[92]

[86] See above, pp. 79–82. A *possible* (though not the only) position for a United Kingdom court to adopt could be that parliamentary sovereignty has been restricted by the fact of the United Kingdom's accession, but that Parliament retains an ultimate overriding power to legislate so as to exclude the United Kingdom from the Communities.

[87] See, for example, *Costa* v. *E.N.E.L.* [1964] E.C.R. 585; *Internationale Handelsgesellschaft* case [1972] C.M.L.R. 255. The Court of Appeal had held that Community law, and in particular art. 119 of the EEC Treaty, is supreme over United Kingdom law by virtue of the European Communities Act 1972 itself: *Macarthys Ltd* v. *Smith* [1981] 1 All E.R. 111 at 120; and see Ellis (1980) 96 *L.Q.R.* 511.

[88] See, for example, *Le Ski* [1972] C.M.L.R. 330 (Belgium); *Costa* v. *E.N.E.L.* [1964] C.M.L.R. 425; *Frontini* v. *Ministero delle Finanze* [1974] 2 C.M.L.R. 372 (Italy); *Directeur Général des Douanes* v. *Societé des Cafés Jacques* [1975] 2 C.M.L.R. 336 (France). These are only *examples*: there have been other instances.

[89] See, e.g., *Van Duyn* v. *Home Office* [1975] Ch. 358; *R.* v. *Bouchereau* [1978] Q.B. 732; *R.* v. *Secretary of State for the Home Department, ex p. Dannenberg* [1984] Q.B. 766.

[90] See, e.g., *Commission* v. *United Kingdom* [1979] 2 C.M.L.R. 427; *R.* v. *Henn* [1981] A.C. 580; *Conegate Ltd* v. *Customs and Excise Commissioners* [1987] 2 W.L.R. 39.

[91] See, e.g., *Application des Gaz S.A.* v. *Falks Veritas* [1974] Ch. 381.

[92] See, e.g., *Commission* v. *United Kingdom* [1982] I.C.R. 578; *Drake* v. *Chief Adjudication Officer* [1987] Q.B. 166; *Johnston* v. *Chief Constable of the RUC* [1986] 3 All E.R. 135; *Pickstone and Others* v. *Freemans plc* [1988] 2 All E.R. 803.

Part Two

The Executive

In this Part are collected the more important or interesting rules about central government. As far as is practicable they have been set against their political background. But this is not a textbook on politics or public administration, and it does not purport to give a full account of how Britain is governed.

Textbooks on constitutional law usually deal with Parliament first and the Government afterwards. Here the order is reversed (apart from the earlier treatment of parliamentary sovereignty), mainly because the Government is more important than Parliament. But Government and Parliament (Executive and Legislature) are closely interlocked, and some matters discussed in this Part of the book will reappear in Part Three.

The Chapter on the Crown and the Royal Prerogative was becoming unwieldy and has been divided into two in this edition. Chapter 6 contains the rules of law about the monarchy; residual matters on which the Queen may still be entitled by constitutional convention to act in her personal discretion, and the scope of the royal prerogative, a bundle of rights, privileges and immunities belonging to the Crown and to the Crown alone. The controversial newspaper allegations – that the Queen disapproves of a number of Mrs Thatcher's policies – which were made (and denied) in 1986 are considered. Constitutional events in Ontario in 1985 may throw more light on the question whether and if so in what circumstances a request for a dissolution might be refused, and those events are explained. The law relating to the activities of the executive branch of government and its officers in external affairs is now examined in a new chapter 7. The common thread running through both these chapters is the Queen, or the Crown. In British constitutional law we do not recognize 'the State' as a legal concept.

Chapter 8 deals with the Privy Council, now only a 'dignified' organ of government, and with its active committees, including the Judicial Committee. In chapter 9 the roles of the Prime Minister and his or her Cabinet colleagues in the scheme of government are analysed. The chapter has been retitled more accurately to reflect its content and the relative power of the Prime Minister and the Cabinet. Account has been taken of new information about the use of both Cabinet committees and of informal groups of Ministers in arriving at Government decisions. Mrs Thatcher's style of government – now widely explained by serving and former colleagues – is inevitably considered in these developments. A new section on the confidentiality of Cabinet proceedings and papers has been added. Chapter 10 goes on to outline the structure of central government, and the material on ministerial responsibility has been transferred here to emphasize that the doctrine of ministerial responsibility does not vary according to whether a Minister is or is not a member of the Cabinet. The Westland affair, and the increased use of leaks by Ministers (which was highlighted by that affair), are described. The chapter also gives an account of bodies ancillary to Departments, and some of the rules about the organization of the civil service and the legal and constitutional position of its members.

Chapter 11 deals with some aspects of the constitutional position of the armed forces of the Crown and their members. In chapter 12 the legal and constitutional status of the remaining nationalized industries are considered, but considerable space has now been devoted to the Government's massive privatization programme. This chapter, too, has been slightly retitled to reflect the changing balance between the public and private sectors.

Chapter 6

The Crown and the Royal Prerogative

Constitutional monarchy [1]

The Queen today remains a symbol of national identity, a focal point of national loyalty, transcending partisan rivalry and strengthening social cohesion. The national anthem is 'God Save the Queen'; British coins and postage stamps bear her image; the Queen personifies the State and the nation, their history and continuity. The Government is Her Majesty's Government; government is carried on in the Queen's name; sovereignty is attributed to the Queen in Parliament; wide legal powers are vested in Her Majesty or in Her Majesty in Council; the courts are the Queen's courts. Coronations, royal weddings and funerals, and an investiture of a Prince of Wales, are great national occasions, bringing the past into the present amid splendid pageantry and ancient ritual. The Queen is pre-eminently a 'dignified' [2] element in the British constitution. She is also a pillar of the Established Church, an exemplar of family virtue, a personage to whom deference is paid by all in public life in a society where habits of deference are diminishing. She embodies the hereditary principle. She has the misfortune to be required to live in a glare of publicity and to have reposed in her expectations which no ordinary mortal can hope to fulfil. The smallest

[1] By far the best modern account is in Sir Ivor Jennings's *Cabinet Government* (3rd edn, 1959), especially chs 12–14. The most recent royal biographies are also instructive: see Sir Harold Nicolson, *King George V* (1952), Kenneth Rose, *King George V* (1984), Frances Donaldson, *Edward VIII* (1974) and Sir John Wheeler-Bennett, *King George VI* (1958). There has only been one royal autobiography: *A King's Story* (1951). For more popular accounts, see Andrew Duncan, *The Reality of Monarchy* (1970), Willie Hamilton, *My Queen and I* (1975) and Christopher Hibbert, *The Court of St James's: the Monarch at Work from Victoria to Elizabeth II* (1979). Detailed factual information is in the *Report of the Select Committee on the Civil List* (H.C. 29 (1971–2)).

[2] The term used by Walter Bagehot in his classic study, *The English Constitution* (Fontana edn, 1963), p. 61.

indiscretion or verbal lapse may be the subject of adverse comment to which she will be unable to reply on her own behalf. Perhaps in recognition of this danger the Queen does not give interviews to the media, and reporters do not put questions to her during her public engagements. She must, therefore, endeavour so to comport herself as to give offence to nobody; not only must she never do or say the wrong thing, but she must always do and say the right thing, irrespective of her private inclinations. In England at least, republican sentiment is very weak, and the strength of positive enthusiasm for the monarchy has not diminished.

From the late Victorian era till the middle years of the present century, the monarchy was an important factor cementing the unity of the British Empire. Local nationalist sentiment in the colonies was subdued by the well-inculcated loyalty of simple peoples to the occupant of the throne. In those self-governing Dominions which were populated mainly by settlers of British stock, the growth of national self-assertion could be accommodated with the fundamental concept of common allegiance to a common and indivisible Crown. This concept broke down in the Irish Free State (Eire), and then in South Africa. In 1949 the Commonwealth Prime Ministers agreed to accept the continuance of India's membership of the Commonwealth as a republic on the understanding that India would recognize the King as Head of the Commonwealth. Today, when there are forty-eight full and independent members of the Commonwealth, the Queen is head of State in only eighteen of them and is represented (except in the United Kingdom) by a Governor-General;[3] twenty-five are republics and five[4] have indigenous rulers. She remains Head of the Commonwealth, but in this symbolical capacity she exercises no constitutional function.[5] For each of those Commonwealth countries of which she is still head of State she has a separate title.

It was assumed that a convention recited in the preamble to the Statute of Westminster 1931 – that the assent of the Parliaments of the Dominions was required for any change in the law touching the succession to the throne or the royal style and titles – applied to all

---

[3] Following a military coup in Fiji in 1987 Fiji was declared a republic and her Commonwealth membership automatically lapsed (see below, p. 668). Up to that moment the Queen as Queen of Fiji had publicly urged the population to remain loyal to the lawful constitution – a rare public intervention in politics by Her Majesty.

[4] Malaysia, Lesotho, Swaziland, Tonga and Brunei.

[5] And she does not take ministerial advice on the content of her Christmas Day and Commonwealth Day messages to the Commonwealth: see Blackburn [1985] *Public Law* 361.

independent Commonwealth countries of which the King or Queen was head of State. The Dominion Prime Ministers were consulted in 1936 by Baldwin, the United Kingdom Prime Minister, to ascertain whether they would approve of Edward VIII's proposed marriage to Mrs Simpson; a majority of them emphatically agreed with the British Government's opposition to the idea, and Edward VIII abdicated. Appropriate legislation was then passed by the United Kingdom Parliament to give effect to the King's decision and to exclude him and his descendants from the line of succession.[6] The conventional procedures were also followed in 1948 when George VI ceased to be Emperor of India, and 1953 when Elizabeth II adopted separate titles for her several realms.[7]

Today the personal characteristics of a monarch's proposed consort would be unlikely to arouse strong emotions outside the United Kingdom. Since, moreover, the number of independent Commonwealth countries continuing to owe allegiance to Her Majesty will diminish as a result of republican trends, the constitutional niceties relating to the law touching the succession to the throne and the royal style and titles will probably be reduced to matters of small practical consequence.[8]

The principal convention of the British constitution is that the Queen shall exercise her formal legal powers only upon and in accordance with the advice of her Ministers, save in a few exceptional situations. In independent Commonwealth countries the powers of the Governor-General, her personal representative, are similarly restricted, except in so far as they may have been enlarged or attenuated by the text of the constitution.[9]

[6] His Majesty's Declaration of Abdication Act 1936. Only the 'Dominions' (listed in s. 1 of the Statute of Westminster 1931) are covered by this convention; today only Canada and Australia remain in that list. (For New Zealand, see below, p. 663.)

[7] The Royal Titles Act 1953 recognized the authority of the Queen to adopt a new title for the United Kingdom and for the other territories for whose foreign relations the United Kingdom Government was responsible. The style and title proclaimed for the United Kingdom and its dependencies was 'Elizabeth II, by the Grace of God of the United Kingdom of Great Britain and Northern Ireland and of her other Realms and Territories Queen, Head of the Commonwealth, Defender of the Faith'. See further de Smith (1953) 2 *I.C.L.Q.* 263. The validity of this measure in relation to Scotland (she was the first Elizabeth to be Queen of Scotland) was unsuccessfully challenged in *MacCormick* v. *Lord Advocate* 1953 S.C. 396, partly on the grounds of lack of *locus standi*.

[8] The adoption of a separate royal title for a newly independent Commonwealth country of which Her Majesty remains Queen has not recently been accompanied by the assent of the Parliaments of other independent Commonwealth countries. To this extent the convention recited in 1931 has partly lapsed.

[9] See generally de Smith, *The New Commonwealth and its Constitutions* (1964), ch. 3. See also pp. 33–4, 661.

This is not to say that the monarch must be a mere cypher. As Bagehot wrote,[10] she has 'the right to be consulted, the right to encourage, the right to warn'. He could have added that she also has the right to offer, on her own initiative, suggestions and advice to her Ministers even where she is obliged in the last resort to accept the formal advice tendered to her.

To be more explicit, she has the conventional rights to receive Cabinet papers and minutes, to be kept adequately informed by the Prime Minister (with whom she has regular weekly audiences) on matters of national policy, to receive Foreign Office dispatches and telegrams and other State papers,[11] and to be notified of proposed appointments and awards to be made in her name so that she can express her views informally. She can make such private comments as she thinks fit; she can remonstrate and offer strong objections to a proposed course of action. How much attention is paid to her views will depend upon the context and her personal experience and stature. Any objection that she may raise to the introduction of politically controversial legislation to which the Cabinet is committed is unlikely to be pressed or taken seriously, particularly if the Government is not of a conservative complexion; the monarch, aware of the monarchy's conservative image, is obliged to use extreme tact. More generally, the length and range of her experience of public affairs (the Queen has been on the throne since 1952), and her personal acquaintance with a large number of overseas dignitaries, may lend weight to suggestions she chooses to offer. George VI was never a political sage; but there are some grounds for believing that his comments in 1945 may have been instrumental in persuading Attlee to reconsider and then change his original intention of placing Bevin in the Treasury and Dalton in the Foreign Office;[12] in 1940 he urged Churchill not to recommend Beaverbrook as Minister of Aircraft Production (although fortunately the Prime Minister was able to convince the King to acquiesce);[13] and we know that in 1944 he took it upon himself in effect to direct

[10] Bagehot, op. cit., p. 111.

[11] Which take her two or three hours a day to read. Memorandum of the Queen's Private Secretary to the Select Committee on the Civil List (H.C. 29 (1971–72)), Minutes of Evidence. App. 13, § 3.

[12] Wheeler-Bennett, op. cit., p. 638; Ben Pimlott, *Hugh Dalton* (1985), ch. XXIV ('. . . it is reasonable to suppose that the King's advice was an important factor' in switching Dalton and Bevin: p. 415). Earl Attlee denied this in *The Observer*, 23 August 1959, but the accuracy of his recollection of the matter is not beyond question; see Driberg (1969) 50 *The Parliamentarian* at 165; Pimlott, ibid.

[13] See Martin Gilbert, *Finest Hour* (1983), p. 328; Sir John Colville, *The Fringes of Power* (1985), p. 211.

Churchill not to accompany the invasion force to Normandy.[14] George V had a mind of his own, as well as a high place in popular esteem, and his habits of gruff and forthright expression doubtless influenced not only the manner in which advice was presented to him but also, on occasion, the substance of that advice. He appears to have exercised some influence over senior military appointments; his expostulations addressed to the Prime Minister over the forcible feeding of militant suffragettes probably conduced to a change of policy; he did his best, though with scant success, to lower the political temperature during the recurrent Irish troubles in the first half of his reign.[15]

Any *public* disclosure of disagreement between the Queen and the Prime Minister of the day could be damaging. In 1986 a senior source within Buckingham Palace confirmed in a response to a newspaper's inquiries that the Queen was 'dismayed' by 'an uncaring Mrs Thatcher' and that the Queen disapproved of several major Government policies. The Queen's Private Secretary intervened, however, in a rare letter to the press to deny the published account.[16]

In times of national crisis the role of a non-partisan head of State as a bridge-builder is potentially significant. When the possibility of civil war in Ireland over the home-rule issue became imminent in 1914, George V took the initiative in convening an inter-party conference, with the Prime Minister's agreement, and addressed its opening session. In 1931, after the collapse of Ramsay MacDonald's Labour Government, he encouraged the formation of a National Government under MacDonald's leadership, but did not exert any improper pressure. If the normal machinery of democratic government breaks down, the monarch's ill-defined residuary discretionary powers may have to be exercised in novel or highly unusual circumstances. Obviously personal interventions of this kind may imperil the status of the monarchy; they are therefore justifiable only as the least of evils. If only because one cannot readily envisage all these hypothetical situations, it is impracticable to state exhaustively the scope of the residual powers. However, the main situations in which the Queen has, or may possibly have, a conventional right to exercise her prerogative powers[17] without or against ministerial advice can be briefly listed.[18]

[14] W. S. Churchill, *The Second World War*, vol. 5 (1951), *Closing the Ring*, pp. 547–50.
[15] Nicolson and Rose, op. cit., *passim*.
[16] See the *Sunday Times*, 20 July 1986; *The Times*, 29 July 1986; Marshall [1986] *Public Law* 505.
[17] For the definition of prerogative, see pp. 127–30.
[18] See further Rodney Brazier, *Constitutional Practice* (1988), ch. 8.

Appointment of a Prime Minister

On several occasions during the past seventy years the choice of a new Prime Minister upon the resignation of the incumbent has not been predetermined by constitutional rules, and the monarch has had to exercise a judicious discretion. For reasons to be explained in a later chapter,[19] the Queen has now been relieved of this responsibility save where no party leader commands a majority in the House of Commons.

Dismissal of a Government

If a Government, having lost a vote of confidence in the House of Commons, were to insist on remaining in office instead of offering its resignation or advising a dissolution, the Queen would be justified, after the lapse of a reasonable period of time, in requesting the Prime Minister to advise her to dissolve Parliament and, if he were to refuse, in dismissing him and his Ministers. She would also, it is submitted, be justified in dismissing her Ministers if they were purporting to subvert the democratic basis of the constitution – for example, by prolonging the life of a Parliament in order to avoid defeat at a General Election, or by obtaining an electoral majority through duress or fraudulent manipulation of the poll. Expediency would be the only factor restricting her discretion. Since such an intervention on her part would tend, in Asquith's phrase,[20] to make the Crown 'the football of contending factions' at an ensuing General Election, and since no Government has been unambiguously dismissed since 1783,[21] this, the most dramatic form of royal initiative, must be a recourse of last resort, an ultimate weapon which is liable to destroy its user.

A drama in Australia is instructive. The Queen's representative, the Governor-General Sir John Kerr, was emphatically of the opinion that he had the power and indeed the duty under the prerogative to dismiss Mr Whitlam and his Government in November 1975. The majority opposition in the Senate refused to pass appropriation bills because of alleged ministerial improprieties in obtaining overseas loans; Mr Whitlam, who had a majority in the House of Representatives, would only recommend a Senate, not a General Election; Sir John was given an undertaking by the Leader of the Opposition, Mr Fraser, that, as Prime Minister, he would recommend a General Election; Sir John then dismissed Mr Whitlam. Mr Fraser formed a minority government; the

[19] See pp. 161–4.
[20] Quoted in Jennings, op. cit., p. 408.
[21] For the equivocal precedent of 1834, see Jennings, op. cit., pp. 403–5.

Senate passed the bills, and Mr Fraser's party won the promised General Election (in which Asquith's fears about footballs were amply justified). Both the Governor-General and the Chief Justice of Australia were of the view that a British Government which could not procure the passage of legislation to raise revenue and which refused to recommend a General Election or to resign could be properly dismissed by the Queen.[22]

Insistence on a dissolution

Much the same considerations apply as those applicable to the dismissal of a Government. It is true that the Queen might urge upon the Prime Minister that a dissolution would be in the best interests of the country, and he might reluctantly agree to advise her to dissolve. But if he did not agree, and the Queen were to insist on a dissolution, then she would have to remove the Prime Minister and find a new one; the procedure upon a dissolution of Parliament entails the making of an Order in Council and the issue of a royal proclamation under the Great Seal, and this requires the cooperation of Ministers. Unless, therefore, the Prime Minister's own colleagues were prepared to form a new Government, the Queen would have to send for the Leader of the Opposition and ask him to form a Government for the purpose of an immediate dissolution. She would then become a 'football of contending factions'.

To this general analysis, one qualification must be added; she may *possibly* have a right to insist on a dissolution before agreeing to exercise her prerogative to create new peers in order to swamp opposition to the Government in the House of Lords.[23]

Refusal of a dissolution

If a Prime Minister were improperly to request a dissolution, the Queen would at least be entitled, and might perhaps be obliged, to reject it. For example, if a Prime Minister whose party had been defeated by the Opposition party at a General Election were to request an immediate second dissolution on the ground that the victory of his opponents had

---

[22] On this affair, see Polyviou, 1976 *Annual Survey of Commonwealth Law* 16; Sir John Kerr, *Matters for Judgment* (1978) and Gough Whitlam, *The Truth of the Matter* (1979). An excellent collection of essays on the many events during the Whitlam years of constitutional importance to Australia and, by analogy, to the United Kingdom is in Gareth Evans, *Labour and the Constitution 1972–1975* (1977).

[23] See pp. 120–21.

been obtained by misrepresentation of the electorate, or if Neville Chamberlain in 1940 had, instead of resigning, requested a dissolution at a time when the country was threatened with military defeat, the monarch could justifiably refuse, since resignation would be the only proper course for the Prime Minister to adopt. Undoubtedly there are other situations in which a request for dissolution could be refused; cogent arguments to this effect have been advanced over the years by monarchs, their advisers, and writers of authority. Confident identification of those situations is not easy. In the first place, in the United Kingdom there has been no unequivocal instance of an absolute rejection of a request for a dissolution in modern times,[24] though on several occasions requests have been granted with reluctance. Secondly, the absence of precedents for a refusal means that the scope of the power to refuse has to be inferred from general constitutional principles; and opinions will differ both on the definition of those principles and the inferences to be drawn from them. Hence, such a refusal would now be highly controversial, unless the request itself was manifestly improper; and this fact alone must make any attempt at definition highly tentative.

Perhaps the following proposition would command a wide measure of support: the Queen may properly refuse a Prime Minister's request for a dissolution if she has substantial grounds for believing (i) that an alternative Government, enjoying the confidence of a majority of the House of Commons, can be formed without a General Election, and (ii) that a General Election held at that time would be clearly prejudicial to the national interest.

As thus formulated, her power could seldom be appropriately exercised except where no party leader in the House of Commons enjoyed an overall majority.[25] Even then it might prove impolitic for her to exercise the power. The minority Prime Minister might resign at

---

[24] In November 1910 George V was thought to have refused a request for dissolution but to have changed his mind after discussing the matter with senior Ministers: Jennings, op. cit., p. 424. See, however, the more equivocal account of this episode given by Sir Harold Nicolson in his official biography, *King George V* (1952), pp. 125–39 and 150; Rose, op. cit., pp. 115–25.

   For extensive examinations of refusals of requests for dissolution by Governors-General and Governors in self-governing Commonwealth countries, see Eugene Forsey, *The Royal Power of Dissolution of Parliament in the British Commonwealth* (1943); H. V. Evatt, *The King and his Dominion Governors* (2nd edn, 1967). See also B. S. Markesinis, *The Theory and Practice of Dissolution of Parliament* (1972).

[25] Though Neville Chamberlain (in the hypothetical case mentioned above) still enjoyed the support of his Cabinet and a majority of the House. Refusal of a request for a dissolution in these circumstances would have been justified, however, by reason of extreme national danger.

once, protesting volubly, instead of acquiescing quietly in her decision; and she might be mistaken in her belief that a stable alternative Government could be formed without an election, in which case she would be obliged to grant the new Prime Minister what she had refused to his predecessor, thus conveying in some quarters an impression of partisanship.[26] Protests notwithstanding, a refusal would probably be justified and broadly acceptable if a Prime Minister, placed in a minority within his own Cabinet and threatened with repudiation by his parliamentary party, suddenly asked for a dissolution in order to forestall the prospect of his imminent supersession.[27] Refusal might be still more readily justifiable if the rebels were known to be prepared to form a coalition Government with an opposition party, or if the country were in the throes of a serious economic crisis or widespread civil strife. *A fortiori*, a Prime Minister who has actually been repudiated by his own parliamentary party in favour of one of his colleagues can claim no constitutional right at all to demand a dissolution. It is also possible to imagine a marginal situation in which the fact that a General Election had been held only a short while previously might tip the balance against granting a request for a dissolution.

Support for the view that the Queen might properly refuse a requested dissolution in some circumstances may be extrapolated from events in Ontario in 1985.[28] A minority Conservative Government had been formed after a General Election, but two opposition parties (who together had a majority in the Legislative Assembly) published an agreed parliamentary pact, including a resolution that any Government formed by them would not recommend a dissolution for at least two years. The minority Government was then defeated on a vote of confidence. The Lieutenant-Governor had made it known informally that any request for a second dissolution would, in view of the

[26] This was the embarrassing situation in which Lord Byng, the Governor-General of Canada, found himself in 1926. It does not follow that in refusing a dissolution to Mackenzie King and then granting one to Meighen, the former Opposition leader (who lost the ensuing General Election), Lord Byng had acted unconstitutionally; but Mackenzie King insisted that he had in fact so acted. See Forsey, op. cit., and p. 116 for the Whitlam affair.

[27] This was broadly the position in South Africa in September 1939, when the Governor-General, Sir Patrick Duncan, refused a dissolution to General Hertzog, who favoured a policy of neutrality against the views of a majority of his colleagues and his party, and had been placed in a minority on this issue in the House. Hertzog resigned and Smuts, having accepted office as Prime Minister, was able to form a Government with a stable majority. cf. Markesinis, op. cit., chs 5, 7, arguing that royal discretion is narrower than is suggested in the main text above, and rejecting the still broader view adopted by Forsey.

[28] See Brazier, op. cit., pp. 42–3.

published pact, be refused. Not surprisingly, the Conservative Premier did not recommend a further dissolution, but resigned, and the two opposition parties formed a coalition Government.

Coercion of the Lords [29]

In 1712, Queen Anne created twelve new hereditary peers in order to secure the approval of the House of Lords for a peace policy. In 1832, William IV reluctantly accepted (after having initially rejected) his Government's advice to create a sufficient number of Whig peers to carry the Reform Bill (substantially enlarging the franchise and reforming the electoral constituencies) through the House of Lords, which had rejected three similar bills in rapid succession. The creation of the new peerages became unnecessary because some Tory peers, apprised of the threat, abstained from voting against the bill, which duly passed. A broadly similar situation arose in 1910–11. The Lords had rejected the Liberal Finance Bill in 1909. They agreed to pass it only after the Government had gone to the country and had been returned to power (though the Liberal Party lost its absolute majority in the House of Commons) in January 1910.[30] The Government had decided to introduce legislation to reduce to a suspensory veto the power of the Lords to reject a bill outright. Edward VII expressed the view that it would not be justifiable to ask him to exercise his prerogative to swamp the Lords with new hereditary peers in order to pass such legislation unless the electorate had shown themselves to be in favour of it. In May 1910 he died, shortly after the introduction of the Parliament Bill. Asquith, the Prime Minister, agreed to advise the new King, George V, to dissolve Parliament so that the electorate could pronounce its verdict on the bill. The King reluctantly agreed to the creation of the requisite number of peers if the Government were returned and the Lords refused to pass the bill. This contingent promise was not disclosed till after the Government had been returned to power at the second General Election of 1910 – the results were almost identical to those in the January election – and the Lords, in July 1911, had passed wrecking amendments to the bill. In August 1911 the Lords accepted the rejection of most of their amendments by the Commons, and passed the bill by a small majority.

[29] See Jennings, op. cit., pp. 428–48, for an analysis of the precedents.
[30] The balance between the Liberals and the Conservatives was held by the Irish Nationalists and the Labour Party, who generally supported the Liberal Government. See Roy Jenkins, *Mr Balfour's Poodle* (1954), and ch. 16.

Neither in 1831–2 nor in 1910–11 was it accepted that the Government had an absolute right to require the monarch to exercise his prerogative for such a purpose. Jennings, commenting on the present conventional rules, wrote that it was 'clear that the power to refuse is extant'.[31] However, an outright refusal might compromise the political neutrality of the monarchy. The imposition of a requirement that approval of the electorate for the measure for which the exercise of the prerogative[32] was so sought should first be obtained might well be justifiable.[33] In practice the situation is unlikely to arise, now that the Parliament Acts have reduced the suspensory veto of the Lords to one month for money bills and just over a year for other public bills.[34]

Refusal of the royal assent

In 1913 and 1914, George V appears to have thought that he retained a residual power to refuse his assent to the Irish Home Rule Bill,[35] though he did in fact assent to it. Refusal of the royal assent on the ground that the monarch strongly disapproved of a bill or that it was intensely controversial would nevertheless be unconstitutional. The only circumstances in which the withholding of the royal assent might be justifiable would be if the Government itself were to advise such a course – a highly improbable contingency[36] – or possibly if it was notorious that a bill had been passed in disregard of mandatory procedural requirements; but since the Government in the latter situation would be of the opinion that the deviation would not affect the validity of the measure once it had been assented to, prudence would suggest the giving of assent.

Appointments and honours[37]

The Queen personally appoints members of her own private household; by far the most important member of her staff is her Private Secretary,

---

[31] Jennings, op. cit., p. 447. Any reasoned opinion expressed by Sir Ivor Jennings is entitled to the greatest respect.
[32] On the statutory power to create life peerages, see pp. 298, 309.
[33] See p. 117, on insistence upon a dissolution.
[34] See below, pp. 304–8. Procedural rules of the House of Lords could also delay the introduction of 'swamping' peers: see Brazier, op. cit., pp. 152–3.
[35] Jennings, op. cit., pp. 395–400.
[36] It could hardly arise unless a change of Government occurred without a General Election within the brief interval between the passage of the bill and its presentation for assent.
[37] See generally Jennings, op. cit., ch. 14.

who maintains contact with the Prime Minister and overseas dignitaries on her behalf, offers her and others informal counsel on matters of constitutional propriety and ceremonial decorum, and has been known to occupy a key position, as a liaison officer, in delicate constitutional situations.

When other appointments are made in her name, and when titles, honours and dignities are bestowed, she must act on the Prime Minister's advice (or, in the case of Commonwealth countries of which she is Queen, on the advice of the relevant Prime Minister) except on the appointment of a new Prime Minister and in the award of certain honours. Membership of the Royal Victorian Order is granted for personal services to the monarchy; normally no political implication is to be read into such an award, but in November 1965, after the unlawful unilateral declaration of independence by the Ministers in Southern Rhodesia, she created Sir Humphrey Gibbs, the loyalist Governor, a K.C.V.O., acting in her personal discretion. When he retired in July 1969 she awarded him the G.C.V.O. She is also entitled to make appointments to the Order of Merit and the Orders of the Garter and the Thistle in her discretion. Suggestions may, of course, emanate from the Prime Minister, just as she may herself initiate suggestions for the bestowal of titles, honours and dignities in respect of which she must act on the Prime Minister's advice.

The Queen also has numerous social and ceremonial functions to perform in her capacity as head of State. Among them are State visits to foreign and Commonwealth countries and the reception of heads of State from overseas. In the constitutional law of the United Kingdom a great many formal acts have to be done by her in the traditional manner, and require her personal signature or approval. She also presides in person at meetings of the Privy Council, and reads the Queen's speech at the opening of a new Parliament or a parliamentary session. She receives letters of credence from newly appointed foreign ambassadors, receives homage from new bishops, and holds some two hundred formal audiences of one sort or another in the course of a year, apart from dispensing a great deal of informal entertainment.

Legal rules affecting the monarchy

Title to the Crown is hereditary; the line of succession depends partly on statute and partly on customary common-law rules. Upon the death or abdication of a monarch, the throne and the prerogatives of the

Crown pass at once – there is no interregnum:[38] 'the king never dies' – to the person next in succession. Lineal Protestant descendants of Sophia, Electress of Hanover, are alone eligible to succeed.[39] If the reigning monarch has children, sons succeed before daughters, and in accordance with primogeniture. When George VI died leaving two daughters and no son, it was assumed that the elder daughter was entitled to succeed as Elizabeth II, and did not inherit the throne jointly with her sister as a coparcener in accordance with the feudal law of succession to real property.

Roman Catholics and persons marrying Roman Catholics are excluded by statute from the throne; and the monarch must be in communion with the Church of England, declare himself to be a Protestant, swear to maintain the Established Churches in England and Scotland, and take the Coronation Oath.[40] Until the attitude of the Church of England towards divorce is changed, it can be assumed that the monarch will be advised not to take a divorced person as consort.[41]

The law relating to the succession to the throne is uniform throughout Her Majesty's dominions. The diversification of the royal titles in 1953 implied that the Crown was no longer indivisible or undivided;[42] but although the Queen of Jamaica, for example, is probably to be regarded as a different legal person from (though the same natural person as) the Queen of the United Kingdom and its dependent territories, the Queen of some of the older Commonwealth countries is perhaps still regarded as the same legal person as the Queen in the United Kingdom even though she bears a different title. However, in so far as the Crown is still undivided, it may be unwise to read

[38] The last interregnum in British history occurred in 1688–9. James II was deemed to have abdicated on 11 December 1688 (the day he first tried to flee the country and dropped the Great Seal into the Thames). 'From that day until the day when William and Mary accepted the crown, 13 February 1689, there was no king of England' (F. W. Maitland, *Constitutional History of England* (1908), p. 284).

[39] Act of Settlement 1701. Edward VIII and his issue were excluded by His Majesty's Declaration of Abdication Act 1936.

[40] Provisions to this effect are contained *inter alia* in the Bill of Rights 1689, the Act of Settlement 1701 and the Succession to the Crown Act 1707. The Coronation Oath, prescribed by statute immediately after the Revolution of 1688, and subsequently modified by statute, has since been modified without statutory authority. Elizabeth II swore to govern the peoples of her realms and territories according to their respective laws and customs, and to maintain the established Protestant religion in the United Kingdom.

[41] This is to be inferred from the circumstances surrounding Edward VIII's decision in 1936 to abdicate, the King having been advised by the Cabinet that they and the Dominion Governments could not approve of his proposed marriage to Mrs Simpson.

[42] See pp. 112–13. The correctness of this view was confirmed in *R.* v. *Secretary of State for Foreign and Commonwealth Affairs, ex p. Indian Association of Alberta* [1982] 1 Q.B. 892 (C.A.).

implications into the concept. There is no doubt that legal proceedings can be brought by one of Her Majesty's realms against another, or by one Australian state against another, or that the prerogatives of the Crown in right of Canada may be at variance with her corresponding prerogatives in right of a province of Canada.

Immediately upon a demise of the Crown, it is customary to convene an Accession Council, composed of Privy Councillors and other leading citizens – in 1952, Commonwealth High Commissioners in London were also present – by whom the Queen is formally proclaimed. The Coronation Service will take place some months later; it is attended by picturesque ceremonial, but has no significance in relation to the legal attributes or powers of the monarch. Edward VIII was never crowned.

For most legal purposes no distinction is drawn between the Crown and the monarch; the references to the Sovereign for the time being are to be construed as references to the Crown.[43] In some contexts a distinction must necessarily be drawn. Thus, a conspiracy to cause death, or an attempt on the life, of the Queen Regnant is treason, which is still punishable by death.[44] A conspiracy or attempt to depose the Queen is treason felony.[45] Ordinary civil proceedings can be brought against the Crown but not against the Queen.[46] The general concept of allegiance, however, imports duties owed to the Queen which can equally be expressed in the form of duties owed to the Crown.

The royal family

Miscellaneous rules of law and custom affect members of the royal family. Under the archaic Royal Marriages Act 1772, the marriage of a descendant of George II (other than the issue of princesses who have married into foreign families) is void unless the Queen has signified her formal consent.[47] Such a person may marry without her consent if he is over twenty-five, provided that he gives twelve months' notice to the Privy Council and the two Houses of Parliament do not register objection during that period. The monarch's consort does not in general occupy a special position in the eyes of the law, though

---

[43] Interpretation Act 1978, ss 10, 21(2). See further, p. 127.
[44] Statute of Treasons 1351. It is also treason to commit these offences in respect of the King's consort, but not in respect of the consort of a Queen Regnant.
[45] Treason Felony Act 1848, which carries a maximum penalty of life imprisonment.
[46] See further, ch. 32.
[47] For a persuasive argument to the effect that the Act of 1772 does not apply to any of Queen Victoria's descendants, see C. d'Olivier Farran (1951) 14 *Mod. L. Rev.* 53.

violation of the chastity of a female consort is treason.[48] Prince Albert was designated as Prince Consort, and he exercised a substantial and beneficent influence over Queen Victoria in constitutional matters till his death in 1861. Prince Philip has not been so designated, but has been accorded official precedence immediately after the Queen. The monarch's eldest son becomes Duke of Cornwall on birth; he will later be created Prince of Wales. His life, the life and chastity of the Princess of Wales during marriage, and the chastity of the monarch's eldest daughter being unmarried are protected by the law of treason.[49] In accordance with precedent, Princess Anne has been created Princess Royal. The title of 'Royal Highness' is conferred upon the sons and daughters of the monarch and on the sons' wives and on the children of the monarch's sons.

Regency and Counsellors of State

No general statutory provision existed until 1937 for the exercise of the royal functions if the monarch were an infant, or were incapacitated or absent from the realm. The Regency Act 1937 dealt with these matters; it was amended by Acts of 1943 and 1953. Under the present law:

(i) There is to be a regency if the Sovereign is under eighteen years of age, or if the Sovereign is incapacitated by infirmity of mind or body or is 'for some definite cause not available' (for example through being a prisoner of war[50]) for performing the royal functions. A declaration as to the Sovereign's incapacity or unavailability is to be made by the Sovereign's spouse, the Lord Chancellor, the Speaker of the House of Commons, the Lord Chief Justice and the Master of the Rolls, or any three or more of them; and a regency will continue till a declaration as to the removal of the incapacity is similarly made. The Regent is to be that person of full age who is next in the line of succession to the throne, provided that he is a British citizen resident in the United Kingdom and is not disqualified on religious grounds. He may exercise all royal functions except that he is precluded from assenting to a bill to alter the succession to the throne or to repeal the Acts securing the Scottish religion and Church.[51]

---

[48] Statute of Treasons 1351. See also note 44.
[49] Statute of Treasons 1351.
[50] Or, arguably, if the Sovereign were simply abroad on a visit, although the Act has never been invoked in such a circumstance.
[51] For the possible effect of disregard of this prohibition (Regency Act 1937, s. 4(2)), see p. 88.

(ii) If the Sovereign is suffering from a lesser degree of incapacity than would justify the establishment of a regency, or if she is or intends to be temporarily absent from the realm, she may appoint Counsellors of State (not a Council of State) by letters patent and delegate to them such royal functions as may be specified. They may not, however, dissolve Parliament except on her express instructions,[52] or grant any title or dignity of the peerage. The Counsellors of State are to be the spouse of the Sovereign, the four persons next in succession to the throne (unless disqualified for being Regent or absent from the realm), and Queen Elizabeth the Queen Mother.

Crown revenues [53]

For many centuries no distinction was drawn in financial matters between the King in his public capacity (the Crown) and the King in his private capacity. The King was expected to live from his own means, and only for special purposes was he to have recourse to Parliament in order to obtain extra money by the levying of taxation. When he did come to Parliament, the Commons (especially under the early Stuarts) were apt to demand redress of grievances before agreeing to grant taxes or to appropriate supplies. Gradually this system broke down and parliamentary grants were made to the Sovereign for the time being for his private purposes during his lifetime. In exchange the Sovereign surrendered to the Exchequer most of the time-honoured hereditary revenues of the Crown.

In 1800 the Sovereign was enabled by statute to hold land in a *private* capacity; this is alienable and is rateable. But the Queen is personally exempt from most forms of taxation.[54] Today the Queen's private estates are managed separately from the Crown lands, which are exempt from fiscal burdens and are administered by Crown Estate Commissioners.

A Civil List Act is passed at the beginning of each reign, providing for annual sums of money[55] for Her Majesty's privy purse, salaries and

[52] When the Queen was on a Caribbean tour in 1966 leaving Counsellors of State, the request and assent for a dissolution were communicated in letters exchanged between the Prime Minister and Her Majesty: Harold Wilson, *The Labour Government 1964–1970, A Personal Record* (1971), p. 215.

[53] For the substantial body of law on this matter, see *Halsbury's Laws of England,* 4th edn, vol. 8, title 'Constitutional Law', paras 1411–1636.

[54] For the complex rules and practices in these matters, see the 1971 Report, expecially Appendices 1 and 12.

[55] The Civil List is charged on the Consolidated Fund and does not, therefore, require annual authorization by Parliament.

expenses of her household, and miscellaneous matters including annuities and expenses of some other members of the royal family. The Civil List Act 1972, amending the Civil List Act 1952, now regulates the royal grant from Parliament. The main difference introduced by the 1972 Act is that the annual sums may be increased by the Treasury at any time by statutory instrument, subject only to the power of the House of Commons to annul it; the requirement for a fresh statute for each increase was thus removed. The Civil List Act 1975 enacted that the Civil List may be supplemented by the Treasury out of money provided by Parliament.[56]

Signification of the royal pleasure

Fortunately, not every act of government done in the Queen's name requires her personal participation. Nevertheless, either by custom or by statute, she has to take part in a great number of such acts. For example, when an Order in Council has to be made, or when any other transaction has to take place in Council, she must preside at a formal meeting of the Privy Council. About ten meetings are held annually. Some royal appointments (for example, ambassadors) are made under the royal sign manual (the Queen's personal signature); some (for example, appointments of most Cabinet Ministers) are made by personal delivery of the seal of office. Many classes of acts (for example, the issue of royal proclamations, writs for the holding of elections, letters patent for the conferment of peerages, the appointment of royal commissions, and charters of incorporation for boroughs and universities, and the ratification of certain treaties) involve the affixing of the Great Seal of the Realm, of which the Lord Chancellor is custodian; this can normally be brought into use only by virtue of a warrant under the royal sign manual.

The royal prerogative [57]

The royal prerogative, 'in its nature singular and eccentrical',[58] can be roughly described as those inherent legal attributes which are unique to the Crown. For 'the Crown' we can substitute 'the Queen'. Prerogative powers belong to the Queen as a person as well as to the institution

---

[56] £5,535,700 was payable in 1988. Some royal expenses are borne on departmental votes. The Queen has not drawn the sums allocated to her privy purse.

[57] For an excellent survey of history and the prerogative, see D. L. Keir and F. H. Lawson, *Cases in Constitutional Law* (6th edn, 1979), ch. II.

[58] Blackstone, *Commentaries*, vol. 1, p. 238.

called the Crown; in law the Queen is the Crown, or Her Majesty's Government,[59] or the State, except where an Act of Parliament or common sense differentiates them expressly or by necessary implication.[60] Powers and duties are often vested by statute directly in named Ministers. But prerogatives are non-statutory attributes of the Crown, not statutory attributes of its servants.

Prerogatives are *inherent* in so far as they are derived from customary common law. They are *legal* in so far as they are recognized and enforced by courts; and, as the *Case of Proclamations* (1611)[61] made abundantly plain, their ambit is determinable by the courts. When Blackstone described the prerogative as 'that special pre-eminence which the King hath, over and above all other persons, and *out of the ordinary course of the common law*, in right of his regal dignity',[62] he was not asserting that the Crown could conclusively determine the limits of its own prerogative; he was merely emphasizing the *uniqueness* of the prerogative. Prerogative attributes are not shared with subjects, though there may be close similarities; the royal prerogative in time of real or apprehended war differs in degree rather than kind from the general common-law doctrine of necessity. The courts have stopped using the term 'Crown privilege' and employ the phrase 'public interest privilege' instead to describe the power to procure the exclusion of evidence from judicial proceedings on grounds of public interest, and it must be doubted whether this is to be regarded as a prerogative at all, because it is not a power peculiar to the Crown.[63]

The prerogative consists mainly of executive governmental powers – powers to conduct foreign relations, to make war and peace, to regulate the disposition of the armed forces, to appoint and dismiss Ministers, to dissolve Parliament, to assent to bills, and so on. The exercise of these powers is controlled by constitutional convention. It also includes immunities (for example, the Queen's personal immunity from suit or prosecution, and from liability to income tax), privileges (for example, proprietary rights over royal fish, the status of the Crown as a preferred

---

[59] Or 'Her Majesty's Government in the United Kingdom'. See, for example, Jamaica Independence Act 1962, s. 1(1), and other statutes dealing with external relations.

[60] See pp. 123, 126. For a skilful critique, see Geoffrey Marshall, *Constitutional Theory* (1971), pp. 17–34.

[61] 12 Co. Rep. 74. A proclamation forbidding under penalty new building in and around London was held to be unlawful. Similar proclamations had been issued and enforced under Elizabeth I – for example, a proclamation of July 1580 made at Nonsuch.

[62] loc. cit. (italics supplied).

[63] See especially *R. v. Lewes JJ., ex p. Home Secretary* [1973] A.C. 388 (H.L.). Another reason may be that such claims, even if made by Ministers, are reviewable by the courts: see *Conway* v. *Rimmer* [1968] A.C. 910, and ch. 32.

creditor) and miscellaneous attributes, such as the prerogative of protection which is in some aspects a legal duty.

Other definitions can be considered. To Dicey,[64] the royal prerogative was 'the residue of discretionary or arbitrary authority, which at any given time is legally left in the hands of the Crown'. This definition is incomplete because it is restricted to powers. However, it includes some important features. It stresses the *residual* features of the prerogative within the realm. The prerogative is traceable to the days before Parliament ever existed, but cannot be enlarged by the Crown except in certain dependent territories. 'It is 350 years and a civil war too late for the Queen's courts to broaden the prerogative.'[65] Prerogatives can be and have been abrogated or diminished by statute; the Crown Proceedings Act 1947 deprived the Crown (but not the monarch in her private capacity) of various immunities in civil litigation. They have also been lost by other means. For certain colonies the Crown could lose its plenary legislative powers under the prerogative by granting a representative legislature.[66] Prerogative powers in the administration of justice passed into the hands of Her Majesty's judges.[67] Other prerogatives came to be shared by subjects and lost their original character and function.[68] Some appear to have quietly withered away.[69] Yet a vanishing prerogative is a strange creature, for there is no generally accepted principle of law that a prerogative may be lost merely by desuetude.[70]

It used to be said that prerogative discretionary powers are also absolute (which is what Dicey meant by 'arbitrary') in the eyes of the courts, in the sense that once the existence, scope and form of a prerogative power were established to their satisfaction, the courts would disclaim jurisdiction to review the propriety or adequacy of the

---

[64] *Introduction to the Study of the Law of the Constitution* (10th edn, 1959), p. 424. His definition has been cited in a number of judgments.

[65] *British Broadcasting Corporation* v. *Johns* [1965] Ch. 32 at 79, *per* Diplock L.J. See also *The Zamora* [1916] 2 A.C. 77 (the Crown may mitigate but not extend its own prerogative in prize law).

[66] *Campbell* v. *Hall* (1774) 1 Cowp. 204 and ch. 34.

[67] See especially *Prohibitions del Roy* (1607) 12 Co. Rep. 63 (King could not administer justice in person). For criticisms of the casuistic reasoning adopted by the judges, see Dicey, op. cit., p. 18.

[68] For example, the prerogative writ *ne exeat regno* by which the monarch could (and possibly still can) (see Bridge (1972) 88 *L.Q.R.* 83; Anderson (1987) 104 *L.Q.R.* 246) command a subject not to leave the realm, at least in time of emergency; cf. *Felton* v. *Callis* [1969] 1 Q.B. 200 showing the strict limitations of the scope of the writ in proceedings between subjects, and see *Lipkin Gorman* v. *Cass, The Times*, 29 May 1985; *Al Nahkel for Contracting and Trading Ltd* v. *Lowe* [1986] 2 W.L.R. 317.

[69] For example, the power to impress men into the navy.

[70] F. W. Maitland, *Constitutional History of England* (1908), p. 418.

grounds upon which that power had been exercised.[71] As a result, however, of the modern development of judicial review of executive action, and in particular in the light of the opinions of the majority in *Council of Civil Service Unions* v. *Minister for the Civil Service*[72] (the G.C.H.Q. case), the last part of that proposition no longer stands. In that case the Prime Minister, as Minister for the Civil Service, gave instructions under a prerogative Order in Council forbidding staff at the Government Communications Headquarters at Cheltenham from belonging to trade unions. The House of Lords held that regardless of the source (whether statutory or prerogative) of a Minister's power, its exercise was potentially reviewable, although not all prerogative acts are justiciable.[73] So today the grounds upon which executive action is carried out in pursuance of a prerogative power are, in general, open to judicial scrutiny,[74] although the propriety of the exercise of some prerogative powers is unsuitable to and remains immune from judicial review, such as, for example, certain action taken on the grounds of national security (as in the G.C.H.Q. case itself), the conclusion of treaties,[75] the dissemination of information,[76] the refusal to commute a sentence,[77] the dissolution of Parliament, the appointment of Ministers or the granting of honours. A court might conclude that a power claimed by the Crown (for example, to take property for defence purposes) existed in law but imported a duty to pay compensation to the persons whose interests were encroached upon.[78] The refusal of a passport is now reviewable.[79]

Some general problems

If one were to devote a whole book to examining the scope of the royal

[71] See, for example, *R.* v. *Allen* (1862) 1 B. & S. 850 (grounds for entering a *nolle prosequi*); *Engelke* v. *Musmann* [1928] A.C. 433 (recognition of diplomatic representative for purpose of according diplomatic immunity – a matter now regulated by statute); *Chandler* v. *D.P.P.* [1964] A.C. 763 (disposition of armed forces; though cf. the reservation entered by Lord Devlin at 809–10) and see p. 144.

[72] [1985] A.C. 374.

[73] The trade unionists' action failed in the face of the Government's assertion of national security considerations: see below, p. 564.

[74] Such as, in limited circumstances, whether a civil servant has been dismissed fairly: *R.* v. *Civil Service Appeal Board, ex p. Bruce, The Independent*, 13 December 1988.

[75] *Blackburn* v. *Att.-Gen.* [1971] 1 W.L.R. 1037; *McWhirter* v. *Att.-Gen.* [1972] C.M.L.R. 882.

[76] *Jenkins* v. *Att.-Gen., The Times*, 13 August 1971.

[77] *Hanratty* v. *Lord Butler, The Times*, 12 May 1971.

[78] For example, *Burmah Oil Co.* v. *Lord Advocate* [1965] A.C. 75.

[79] *R.* v. *Secretary of State for Foreign and Commonwealth Affairs, ex p. Everett, The Independent*, 26 October 1988; see below, p. 454.

prerogative today,[80] one would still leave a number of questions unanswered. Writing in 1888, Maitland observed that there was 'often great uncertainty as to the exact limits' of the prerogative; and he concluded his short but masterly survey with these words: 'Thus our course is set about with difficulties, with prerogatives disused, with prerogatives of doubtful existence, with prerogatives which exist by sufferance, merely because no one has thought it worthwhile to abolish them.'[81] The problem of identification, then, is very real. No comprehensive authoritative statement was offered in medieval times; and in the seventeenth century the scope of the prerogative was hotly disputed. We can identify, as a matter of historical interest, some of the disputed and undisputed prerogatives of which the Crown has been explicitly deprived by statute. But the concept of the prerogative as a bundle of inherent and residuary attributes is intrinsically vague. In 1957 a Committee of Privy Councillors thought that telephone-tapping authorized by a Minister might possibly be justified as a manifestation of an ancient prerogative power to intercept communications between subjects;[82] yet it is more than doubtful whether such a prerogative ever existed. That the Crown still has certain prerogative powers in time of grave national emergency to enter upon, take and destroy private property seems clear. The conditions under which these powers are exercisable are far from clear, partly because the powers were never precisely defined, partly because the scope of the war prerogative was not considered in general terms by the courts for nearly three hundred years, and partly because in modern times various statutory provisions have been made for these matters.[83] Again, it is not clear how far the royal prerogative in foreign affairs and the concept of an 'act of State' are coterminous.[84]

Archaic prerogatives: a suggestion

In a Scottish appeal to the House of Lords, Lord Simon of Glaisdale said that 'a rule of the English common law, once clearly established, does not become extinct merely by disuse'; it may 'go into a cataleptic

---

[80] cf. Joseph Chitty, *The Prerogatives of the Crown* (1820) (the best-known monograph); A. B. Keith, *The King and the Imperial Crown* (1936); G. S. Robertson, *Civil Proceedings by and against the Crown* (1908).

[81] *Constitutional History of England*, pp. 418, 421.

[82] Cmnd 283 (1957), pt 1. See also *Malone* v. *Metropolitan Police Commissioner* [1979] Ch. 344. cf. R. F. V. Heuston, *Essays in Constitutional Law* (2nd edn, 1964), pp. 50–52, and below, p. 477, for the Interception of Communications Act 1985.

[83] See *Att.-Gen.* v. *De Keyser's Royal Hotel Ltd* [1920] A.C. 508; *Burmah Oil Co.* v. *Lord Advocate* [1965] A.C. 75; *Nissan* v. *Att.-Gen.* [1970] A.C. 179.

[84] *Nissan*'s case (see note 83 and pp. 145–7).

trance', but, like Sleeping Beauty, it can be revived 'in propitious circumstances'. It cannot, however, revive if it is 'grossly anomalous and anachronistic'.[85] Probably this proposition offers the best available explanation of the fate of obsolescent prerogatives like the powers to forbid a subject to leave the realm, and to impress him into naval service.[86] Conceivably the former power might revive in circumstances which are, admittedly, hard to envisage; but the latter power must surely be unresponsive to any Prince Charming.

Statute and prerogative powers

The relationship between statute and prerogative remains strangely abstruse. Statutes can bind the Crown;[87] and a prerogative can be abolished by express words. Alternatively the wording of a statute may leave no room for doubt that Parliament, when conferring powers on the Crown, intended to leave the prerogative intact;[88] or to maintain the prerogative but regulate the way in which it can be exercised.[89] Puzzles arise where Parliament neither extinguishes nor saves a prerogative but simply confers powers on the Crown in an area hitherto occupied only by prerogative. In such a situation, the Crown must indeed abide by any statutory restrictions imposed on the exercise of its powers (for example, procedural requirements, or a duty to pay compensation) and cannot fall back on its original absolute prerogative. To the extent of *this* inconsistency the prerogative is abrogated.[90] But suppose a statute merely covers the same ground as prerogative without expressly restricting the Crown's competence. Do statute and prerogative then co-exist, or is the prerogative swallowed up and superseded?[91] If superseded, does it revive when the statute is repealed?[92]

---

[85] *McKendrick* v. *Sinclair* 1972 S.L.T. (H.L.) 110 at 116, 117.

[86] See p. 129, notes 68, 69.

[87] See generally, pp. 134–6.

[88] For example, Emergency Powers (Defence) Act 1939, s. 9; Crown Proceedings Act 1947, ss 11(1), 40(1).

[89] See Royal Assent Act 1967.

[90] *Att.-Gen.* v. *De Keyser's Royal Hotel Ltd* [1920] A.C. 508 (requisitioning).

[91] See the differences of opinion on this point expressed by Lord Denning M.R. and Russell L.J. in *Sabally and N'Jie* v. *Att.-Gen.* [1965] 1 Q.B. 273. See also Sir Kenneth Roberts-Wray, *Commonwealth and Colonial Law* (1966), pp. 164–6, 169–72, 190–97. The prerogative power to maintain the peace was not abridged or placed in abeyance by the Police Act 1964, s. 41; so the Home Secretary may use that power to issue plastic bullets to chief constables even if their police authorities object. See *R.* v. *Secretary of State for the Home Department, ex p. Northumbria Police Authority* [1988] 1 All E.R. 556.

[92] For an answer derived from *Att.-Gen.* v. *De Keyser's Royal Hotel Ltd* [1920] A.C. 508 at 539, see Colin Munro, *Studies in Constitutional Law* (1987), pp. 171–2.

Answers to these questions must be tentative. Because the prerogative is tenacious and the Crown is not readily held to be bound by mere implication,[93] the courts are unlikely to hold that a prerogative has been excluded by implication unless legislation evinces a very clear intention to cover the field in question exhaustively.[94]

Assuming that a prerogative is superseded by a statute and the statute is later repealed, it is submitted that the prerogative ought not to be held to revive unless it is a major governmental attribute[95] or is otherwise consonant with contemporary conditions.[96] Hence archaic Crown privileges or immunities expressly abolished by the Crown Proceedings Act 1947 should not be construed as having been restored merely by a repeal of the relevant parts of the Act.

The prerogative today: domestic affairs

Prerogative powers in an emergency will be considered in a later chapter.[97] The other surviving prerogatives in domestic affairs are a mixed bag of residual loose ends; some linger on as reminders of feudal days, some are of major importance in the conduct of public affairs. Most of the prerogatives are rights and powers, but it may be convenient to touch first on the main prerogative attributes which are in the nature of privileges, immunities and duties.

The King (or Queen Regnant) can do no wrong. Over the years the prerogative of perfection has borne a variety of meanings, ranging from the total unaccountability of the monarch to any human agency, to the simple rule that the monarch in person cannot be prosecuted or sued for a wrongful act in the courts. The latter rule still prevails, though it

[93] See p. 134.

[94] Thus the prerogative power to declare the extent of United Kingdom territorial waters has clearly been replaced by the Territorial Sea Act 1987. It declares that the territorial sea extends to 12 nautical miles (s. 1(1)(*a*)), and that the baselines are to be established by Orders in Council made under the Act: the Territorial Waters Order in Council 1964 and the Territorial Waters (Amendment) Order in Council 1979 are deemed to have been made under the Act. (s. 1(1)(*b*)). For the earlier position under the prerogative, see *R.* v. *Kent JJ., ex p. Lye* [1967] 2 Q.B. 173; *Post Office* v. *Estuary Radio Ltd* [1968] 2 Q.B. 740; *The Fagernes* [1927] P. 311; Edeson (1973) 89 *L.Q.R.* 364.

[95] As in the *De Keyser* case (see above; power to requisition for defence purposes in wartime), in which event the prerogative may reasonably be held to lie in suspense; see [1920] A.C. at 539–40. See also ibid., 554, 561.

[96] cf. *New Windsor Corporation* v. *Taylor* [1899] A.C. 41 (local customary franchise of tollage superseded by statutory right; statute later repealed; held, old franchise was not thereby revived). The terms of sections 15 and 16(1) of the Interpretation Act 1978 may not be irrelevant in this general context. See also p. 132.

[97] See ch. 27.

is possible to bring a petition of right against the monarch in the High Court for alleged breaches of contract and a few other legal wrongs, thus obtaining a judicial remedy unaccompanied by coercive relief. Before the Crown Proceedings Act 1947 it was therefore impossible (subject to a small number of exceptions) to sue the Crown as a matter of strict law for tortious acts or omissions, or to sue the Crown vicariously for the torts of its employees. Fortunately this absurd anachronism has been substantially removed from our law.[98]

Since the days of Elizabeth I it has been acknowledged that acts done by the Crown purportedly under the prerogative may be held by the courts to be *ultra vires*[99] – a proposition challenged only by the most extreme Stuart theoreticians.

Because it may be unseemly to hold the monarch personally to account for an invalid or potentially controversial act performed by her in her public capacity, custom requires the participation of Ministers in most of such acts – for example, by countersignature, or by presence at a Privy Council meeting where formal business is transacted. Thus, it is the Ministers who attract responsibility.

The King is a preferred creditor. If a debtor is insolvent, the Crown has priority as a creditor at common law. This matter is now largely regulated by statute. But in the levying of execution or distress against the property of a subject, the Crown still enjoys priority under the prerogative.

Time does not run against the King. The normal periods of limitation did not apply to the Crown in criminal proceedings and as a plaintiff in civil litigation. In most forms of civil proceedings, and to a lesser extent in criminal proceedings, this immunity has been abrogated by statute.

The Crown is not bound by statute save by express words or necessary implication. In its origin a prerogative immunity, this proposition can also be formulated as a particular rule of statutory interpretation. It covers the imposition of obligations, restraints and other burdens. General words directed to such ends will normally be construed as excluding the Crown unless the purpose of the Act would be frustrated were the Crown held to be exempt from their operation.[100] To apply

---

[98] See ch. 32, where the state of the law is considered in more detail.

[99] See, for example, *Willion* v. *Berkley* (1561) Plow. 223; *Case of Monopolies* (1602) 11 Co. Rep. 84b.

[100] *Bombay Province* v. *Bombay Municipal Council* [1947] A.C. 88, and see *The Queen in Right of Alberta* v. *Canadian Transport Commission* (1977) 75 D.L.R. (3d) 257,

this principle rigidly today would be unreasonable. Although in some contexts it would be incongruous or contrary to public policy to hold the Crown impliedly subject to the same liabilities as the public at large, in others it would be unjust to hold the Crown exempt merely because an Act would be still workable despite the exemption of the Crown from its ambit. But the principle has, on the whole, been rigidly applied; and Crown immunity has been understood to mean that Crown tenants, and tenants of a body ancillary to the regular armed forces, do not enjoy the protection of the Rent Acts,[101] that government Departments do not have to obtain planning permission in order to effect a material change in the use of land occupied by them,[102] that land occupied for Crown purposes (for example, for use as county courts)[103] is immune from local rates,[104] that a court cannot make an order for the abatement of a nuisance committed in a hospital administered under the National Health Service,[105] and even (till the Road Traffic Acts were expressed to bind the Crown) that a Crown servant on duty driving a vehicle for Crown purposes and under superior orders to deliver a load quickly, could not be convicted of exceeding a statutory speed limit.[106]

The narrower principle, also founded on the prerogative, that the Crown is immune from central government taxation in the absence of express words or necessary intendment, has a more secure and rational basis. Why should an intention be imputed to Parliament to raise money *from* the Government? Government Departments are exempt from income tax; so is the Queen in her personal capacity;[107] civil

---

Department of Transport v. *Egoroff* (1986) 278 E.G. 1361; though cf. *Madras Electric Supply Corpn Ltd* v. *Boarland* [1955] A.C. 667 (where the word 'person' in a special rule in an Income Tax Act was held to include the Crown). The prerogative immunity in Scots law is possibly less far-reaching: Mitchell [1957] *Public Law* 304.

[101] *Territorial Forces Association* v. *Nichols* [1949] 1 K.B. 35; *Tamlin* v. *Hannaford* [1950] 1 K.B. 18 (dicta). This rule has since been modified by statute.

[102] *Ministry of Agriculture* v. *Jenkins* [1963] 2 Q.B. 317.

[103] *R.* v. *Manchester Overseers* (1954) 3 E. & B. 336.

[104] See generally *Mersey Docks and Harbour Board Trustees* v. *Cameron* (1964) 11 H.L.C. at 464–5. See now General Rate Act 1967. In any event, the Crown does in practice pay contributions in lieu of rates in respect of exempt hereditaments.

[105] *Nottingham Area No. 1 Hospital Management Committee* v. *Owen* [1958] 1 Q.B. 50. For the purposes of the legislation on food hygiene, health and safety, Crown immunity in respect of hospital premises has been removed: National Health Service (Amendment) Act 1986, ss 1, 2. For another aspect of Crown immunity (in respect of patented drugs) in connection with the National Health Service, see *Pfizer Corporation Ltd* v. *Ministry of Health* [1965] A.C. 512.

[106] *Cooper* v. *Hawkins* [1904] 2 K.B. 164. See now Road Traffic Regulation Act 1984, s. 130, binding the Crown.

[107] See p. 126, above.

servants in their private capacities are not, of course, exempt. However, difficult marginal cases arise. Public bodies which are servants or agents of the Crown, or which act as instruments of the Crown, are exempt. But how and where is a court to draw the line? The general functions of local authorities, and public corporations conducting the affairs of nationalized industries, are not performed as servants or agents of the Crown; they enjoy a substantial degree of independence from the Crown, and their functions are not unambiguously within the province of central government;[108] they do not, therefore, attract the immunities and privileges of the Crown.[109] For similar reasons the BBC has been held to be subject to income tax.[110] The Custodian of Enemy Property was held to be a Crown servant, mainly because of the degree of control that Ministers were entitled to exercise over him, and tax was therefore not payable on the income from property disposed of by him while acting in that capacity.[111] Hair-splitting distinctions may still have to be drawn where it is doubtful whether a body is a Crown agent, or where a body is clearly not a Crown agent but performs functions associated with the business of central government.

The prerogative of protection. This prerogative does not fit neatly into any analytical category. In some aspects it is a duty, in others a power.[112] The Crown has a duty to 'protect' its own subjects by granting them diplomatic protection in foreign countries; but this duty is not directly enforceable in a court of law,[113] and in any event the 'duty' is now probably limited to British citizens, British Dependent Territories citizens, British Overseas citizens and British protected persons. It is under no legal duty to grant them passports. Nor is it under any legal duty to offer armed protection to such of its intrepid subjects as engage in hazardous ventures on the high seas or in foreign countries; if it decides in its discretion to offer this form of protection,

---

[108] See *Mersey Docks and Harbour Board Trustees* v. *Gibbs* (1866) L.R. 1 H.L. 93 on the separate legal status of autonomous and semi-autonomous public authorities.

[109] See *Tamlin* v. *Hannaford* (note 101), on nationalized industries; and generally J.A.G. Griffith (1952) 9 *U. of Toronto L.J.* 169. The now defunct Central Land Board was held to be a Crown servant: *Glasgow Corporation* v. *Central Land Board* 1956 S.C. (H.L.) 1. That nationalized industries do not enjoy Crown immunities is now usually made clear by statute. See, for example, Post Office Act 1969, s. 6(5); and below, p. 220.

[110] *British Broadcasting Corporation* v. *Johns* [1965] A.C. 32.

[111] *Bank voor Handel en Scheepvaart* v. *Administrator of Hungarian Property* [1954] A.C. 584.

[112] See two thought-provoking articles by H. Lauterpacht (1947) 9 *Camb. L.J.* 330, and Glanville Williams (1948) 10 *Camb. L.J.* 54. See also Clive Parry (ed.), *A British Digest of International Law*, vol. 5, s. 3; and pp. 452–4.

[113] See *Mutasa* v. *Att.-Gen.* [1980] Q.B. 114.

it can impose a condition that the subject shall pay for the protection offered.[114] The Crown does owe limited duties of protection to persons owing allegiance, including aliens owing local allegiance; the extent and implications of these duties will be considered later.[115]

The capacity of the Crown as *parens patriae* implied a prerogative to protect the welfare of infants. This power or duty has long been exercised only through the Queen's courts by judges; in other words, it has become an 'ordinary' prerogative as distinct from an 'absolute' prerogative. But an alien infant owing allegiance is within the scope of the prerogative of protection, so that the Chancery Division has jurisdiction to exercise its discretion whether to make him a ward of court.[116] In so far as the prerogative of protection encompasses the superintendence of charities and the welfare of persons of unsound mind, it appears to have been almost entirely engulfed by statute.

Miscellaneous domestic prerogatives

Power to appoint and dismiss Ministers, to dissolve and prorogue Parliament, and to assent to legislation is derived from the prerogative. As the fountain of honour the Queen creates hereditary peerages and confers other titles and dignities. As head of the Established Church, she appoints archbishops and diocesan bishops, and assents to measures of the General Synod approved by both Houses of Parliament. As head of the armed forces, she directs their disposition and commissions officers. War is declared and a state of war terminated by virtue of the prerogative.

The diffusion of government information[117] and the regulation of the civil service[118] fall partly or wholly within the scope of the prerogative. Enemy aliens can be interned or expelled. The issue and revocation of a United Kingdom passport fall within the prerogative.

The Queen is the fountain of justice, and in relation to the administration of justice, several prerogatives remain vested in the Crown. There is a prerogative power to create new courts, but only courts to administer the common law.[119] Prosecutions for indictable offences are conducted in her name. The power to enter a *nolle prosequi*, to stop or discontinue a prosecution or indictment, is

[114] *China Navigation Co.* v. *Att.-Gen.* [1932] 2 K.B. 197.
[115] See pp. 452–4.
[116] *Re P. (G.E.) (an Infant)* [1965] Ch. 568.
[117] See note 76.
[118] See ch. 10.
[119] *Re Lord Bishop of Natal* (1864) 3 Moo. P.C.C. (N.S.) 115.

exercised by the Attorney-General[120] on behalf of Her Majesty; this power is occasionally used to secure the discontinuance of a private prosecution. The prerogative of pardon (exercisable in England only on the advice of the Home Secretary) is used to grant absolute or conditional pardons to persons convicted of criminal offences,[121] or to remit part of the sentence of imprisonment or the fine imposed. A conditional pardon substitutes, by commutation, a different penalty for that imposed by the court; whether the person convicted could reject the condition is a nice question;[122] in the last resort the Crown could, if it saw fit, grant a free pardon. Statutory authority exists for the release of prisoners on parole.[123]

The Crown also has prerogative rights and powers in respect of *bona vacantia*, sturgeon and certain swans and whales,[124] coinage, the granting of charters of incorporation, the award of franchises (including the right to hold markets and fairs, and to collect tolls[125] from bridges or ferries), the construction and supervision of harbours, and the printing and publication of statutes and other legislative instruments, the authorized version of the Bible and the Book of Common Prayer.[126]

[120] See below, p. 384.

[121] It would seem that a pardon may be granted *before* conviction; but this power is not exercised. The line between pardon before conviction and the unlawful exercise of dispensing power is thin. A pardon removes all the 'pains, penalties and punishments' flowing from a conviction, but in no sense eliminates the conviction itself, according to the Court of Appeal: *R.* v. *Foster* [1985] Q.B. 115. A statutory right to compensation for those wrongly convicted and sentenced was provided for the first time in the Criminal Justice Act 1988, s. 133.

[122] See Brett (1957) 20 *Mod. L. Rev.* 131.

[123] Criminal Justice Act 1967, ss 59–62.

[124] Other archaic prerogative proprietary rights were abolished by the Wild Creatures and Forest Laws Act 1971.

[125] See *Nyali Ltd* v. *Att.-Gen.* [1956] 1 Q.B. 1.

[126] And may license their printing and publication by others, but not so as to authorize a breach of copyright: *Oxford and Cambridge Universities* v. *Eyre and Spottiswoode Ltd* [1964] Ch. 736.

Chapter 7

The Royal Prerogative in External Affairs

General

External relations are conducted pre-eminently under prerogative powers.[1] Not only the declaration of war, the dispatch of armed forces and the annexation of territory, but also the conclusion of treaties, the accrediting and reception of diplomats, the recognition of new states and revolutionary governments fall within the scope of the prerogative. Such acts are sometimes called acts of State – assertions of State sovereignty in international relations. The term 'acts of State' is also used in other specialized senses; and it does not invariably connote an act done in pursuance of the royal prerogative.[2]

As we have already indicated, prerogative powers in relation to dependent territories are not merely a residue.[3] For colonies acquired by conquest or cession they are plenary in the absence of special circumstances; and they may be lost but later resumed.[4] For colonies acquired by settlement, its prerogative legislative power is more limited and has been largely superseded by statue. In those dependent territories which are not British possessions the prerogative is again more than a residue. In colonial-type protectorates (of which no specimens survive today) the legislative powers of the Crown, though regulated by the Foreign Jurisdiction Acts, were derived from the prerogative; and the Crown could have extended its own jurisdiction even though it may have originally been limited.[5] In British protected states (of which none survives today) which had indigenous rulers and enjoyed a degree of

---

[1] On the prerogative generally, see ch. 6.
[2] See pp. 145–7.
[3] p. 129.
[4] *Campbell* v. *Hall* (1774) 1 Cowp. 204; *Sammut* v. *Strickland* [1938] A.C. 678.
[5] *Sobhuza II* v. *Miller* [1926] A.C. 518; *Nyali* v. *Att.-Gen.* [1956] 1 Q.B.1 (affd. [1957] A.C. 253); Sir Kenneth Roberts-Wray, *Commonwealth and Colonial Law* (1966), pp. 187–97.

autonomy, the Crown did not claim unlimited jurisdiction; but it acquired such jurisdiction as it possessed by virtue of the prerogative,[6] and we must assume that in terms of British constitutional law the Crown was competent to enlarge as well as diminish it by prerogative.

Treaties and treaty implementation

Treaties[7] are international agreements. Such agreements may be called treaties, conventions, covenants, pacts, charters, agreements, protocols, even statutes, declarations or exchanges of notes. They may be bilateral or multilateral; they may be concluded between heads of State, or between governments, or between governments and international organizations. They may deal with political, defence, economic, legal, social or cultural matters. Any such international instrument to which the United Kingdom is a party binds the United Kingdom in international law. Normally it becomes binding only when ratified by the Executive, though some agreements have effect upon signature, and a few have effect only when approved by Act of Parliament. The treaty itself may specify when and in what circumstances it shall come into effect. It is a constitutional usage, and possibly a binding convention, to lay the texts of international agreements before both Houses of Parliament for twenty-one days before ratification, if ratification is required.[8]

The conclusion of a treaty is an act of State and an exercise of the royal prerogative, even though the Queen has not played a formal role in the matter (for example, by granting full powers to plenipotentiaries to negotiate and sign on her behalf, and by ratifying the treaty under the Great Seal); the prerogative, or part of it, may be exercised by the Secretary of State for Foreign and Commonwealth Affairs as her delegate. It is unnecessary to go into the details of this complex branch of the law. But one point stands out. Whereas in a number of legal systems (for example, the United States of America, West Germany), a treaty is self-executing – i.e. it becomes part of the municipal law of the land, as soon as it is finally concluded[9] – this is not the rule in United Kingdom law. With few exceptions, internationally binding obligations still need to be given legislative effect if they are to be enforced as law

6 Roberts-Wray, op. cit., p. 116.
7 See Lord McNair, *Law of Treaties* (2nd edn, 1961).
8 171 H.C. Deb. 2001 (1 April 1921). This is commonly called the 'Ponsonby' rule.
9 In the United States, however, treaties require the sanction of a two-thirds' majority in the Senate; instruments known as executive agreements do not.

by the courts of this country.[10] They may be given such effect if their provisions (or some of them) are incorporated in or scheduled to an Act of Parliament, or in a statutory instrument (for example, an Order in Council) made under the authority of an Act of Parliament.[11]

There are exceptions to the rule that the Executive cannot alter the law applied in United Kingdom courts merely by incurring international obligations. European Community treaties are cases in point, for according to Community law certain provisions of such treaties may be 'directly applicable' in the laws of member States.[12] There may be another exception. In a flight of fancy, Walter Bagehot asserted that the Crown has a prerogative power to cede Cornwall.[13] It is very doubtful whether the Crown has a prerogative to cede any part of the United Kingdom. But there have been past examples of the cession of parts of Her Majesty's dominions beyond the seas by prerogative acts[14] (for example, the recognition of American independence in 1783), especially in treaties of peace. If this prerogative has disappeared, it is not clear how, though in modern practice the transfer of British territory and the implementation of a peace treaty are always effected by statute.

The general rule is that a treaty is not a source of legal rights directly enforceable against the Crown in United Kingdom courts, even though it may be intended to benefit particular individuals (for example, where the Crown receives money from a foreign government by way of compensation for injuries done to them);[15] it is an act of State, not a

[10] This rule is clearly settled; the leading authority is *The Parlement Belge* (1879) 4 P.D. 129 at 154.

[11] For example, extradition treaties, under the Extradition Acts. If a treaty needs legislative implementation, it is unlikely to be ratified by the Crown until the necessary legislation is passed. If there is ambiguity in a statute which incorporates a treaty into United Kingdom law the courts will examine the treaty itself as an aid to interpretation of the statute: *Fothergill* v. *Monarch Airlines* [1981] A.C. 251.

[12] This is a complex point. Article 95(1) of the EEC Treaty (prohibiting various discriminatory trade practices) is directly applicable, without further enactment, in the laws of member States. But the United Kingdom has incorporated this rule into municipal law by implication in enacting the European Communities Act 1972; see ss 1, 2(1), 3, Sched. 1. Under the Act, future Community treaties (which *may* contain directly applicable provisions) are to be authenticated by Order in Council (s. 1(3) – will this be *giving statutory effect* to such a treaty?), and the Order in Council will have to be approved in draft by resolutions of both Houses if the United Kingdom is itself a party to it (ibid.). For an unsuccessful challenge to a draft Order in Council made under s. 1(3), see *R.* v. *H.M. Treasury, ex p. Smedley* [1985] Q.B. 657 (and see below, p. 350).

[13] *The English Constitution*, Introduction to the 2nd edn (Fontana edn), p. 287.

[14] See generally Roberts-Wray, op. cit., ch. 4. See also *Damodhar Gordhan* v. *Deoram Kanji* (1876) 1 App. Cas. 332.

[15] *Rustomjee* v. *R.* (1876) 2 Q.B.D. 69. The position is the same where the provisions of the treaty have been implemented by statute: *Civilian War Claimants' Association Ltd.* v. *R.* [1932] A.C. 14. But see below on Community treaties.

transaction in the nature of a contract or a declaration of trust.[16] Under the Foreign Compensation Acts 1950 and 1969, the allocation of sums received from foreign governments under treaty as compensation for the confiscation or destruction of British-owned property is made on a discretionary basis by an independent statutory body, the Foreign Compensation Commission. A claimant before the Commission may impugn in the courts a determination that he did not comply with the *statutory* conditions necessary to establish a claim, or a determination reached in disregard of minimum procedural standards,[17] but he cannot obtain a judicial declaration that he is entitled to any particular sum. Community treaties stand in a special position; they are capable in Community law (adopted in this country by the European Communities Act 1972) of conferring or imposing judicially enforceable legal rights and obligations on individuals.

Conclusive Crown certificates

In the late Victorian era a Miss Mighell issued a writ for breach of promise of marriage against a Mr Albert Baker; whereupon Mr Baker revealed to the court that he was none other than the Sultan of Johore (who had been living for a time in England under a pseudonym), and pleaded sovereign immunity from the jurisdiction of the court. On behalf of the Crown, the Colonial Office obligingly certified that he was the sovereign ruler of an independent State. The court accepted this certificate as conclusive evidence of the facts stated (although the claim of Johore, a British protected state in Malaya, to be an independent international person was tenuous in the extreme), and the defendant having thus established his immunity from suit, Miss Mighell's action could proceed no further.

This somewhat bizarre case[18] illustrates the disinclination of the courts to make an independent determination of certain questions of law and fact in politically sensitive areas; they indeed abdicated in favour of the Executive. Parliament has since asserted itself by passing the State Immunity Act 1978, which considerably extended the circum-

---

[16] Though in the *Civilian War Claimants' Association* case, Lord Atkin indicated (at 26–7) that the position might be different if the Crown purported expressly to act as trustee or agent for a subject.

[17] *Anisminic Ltd.* v. *Foreign Compensation Commission* [1969] 2 A.C. 147; cf. Foreign Compensation Act 1950, s. 4(4); Tribunals and Inquiries Act 1958, s. 11. See now Foreign Compensation Act 1969, s. 3, superseding s. 4(4) of the 1950 Act, and providing for an appeal on points of law from determinations of the Commission to the Court of Appeal. See pp. 554–5, below.

[18] *Mighell* v. *Sultan of Johore* [1894] 1 Q.B. 149.

stances in which a State will not be immune from suit in the English courts. The Act was designed to bring United Kingdom law into closer harmony with the more restrictive rules of other States. Accordingly, among other things, immunity was removed in relation to commercial transactions,[19] contracts to be performed in the United Kingdom, certain torts and actions over immovable property in the United Kingdom. A head of State, his family and personal servants, continue to enjoy sovereign immunity (section 20), but a government of an independent State and its public property,[20] although in general immune from the jurisdiction of the courts (section 1), must now submit to that jurisdiction in the circumstances set out in sections 2 to 11 of that Act.[21] Persons having diplomatic or consular status enjoy immunities of various kinds, depending on their position in the diplomatic mission or consulate. Diplomatic and consular immunities have been restated by statutes giving effect to the terms of multilateral international conventions,[22] and nothing in the State Immunity Act 1978 limits any diplomatic privileges in those statutes (section 16). Whether a person is entitled to diplomatic or consular status and, if so, to what category he belongs is conclusively determined by a certificate entered by a Secretary of State;[23] these certificates are now given under statutory authority, but the conclusiveness of certificates on questions

---

[19] See, e.g., *Alcom Ltd.* v. *Republic of Columbia* [1984] A.C. 580.

[20] Difficult questions as to the immunity of vessels owned by independent States are settled by reference to s. 10 of the 1978 Act, which enacts that ships owned by a State (or in which it has an interest) and which are used for commercial purposes will enjoy no immunity.

[21] So, e.g., a landlord successfully pleaded the Act against the French Government which had leased his property as a private dwelling: *Intpro Properties (U.K.) Ltd.* v. *Sauvel* [1983] Q.B. 1019.

[22] Diplomatic Privileges Act 1964; Consular Relations Act 1968. See also the International Organizations Acts 1968 and 1981; Diplomatic and other Privileges Act 1971; Diplomatic and Consular Premises Act 1987; Arms Control and Disarmament (Privileges and Immunities) Act 1988.

[23] Broadly speaking, under the 1964 Act (i) the head of the mission and the principal members of the staff and their families are immune not only from criminal liability but also from most forms of civil liability; (ii) members of the administrative and technical staff are immune from criminal liability but not from civil liability save in respect of acts performed in the course of their official duties; (iii) members of the domestic staff are immune neither from criminal nor from civil liability for acts outside the course of their duties. Although a certificate tendered by the Secretary of State is conclusive as to the matters specified in the text above, the courts retain jurisdiction to ascertain whether, for categories (ii) and (iii), the conduct in question took place in the course of official duties: see *Empson* v. *Smith* [1966] 1 Q.B. 426. They are also entitled to decide questions of waiver and submission to the jurisdiction. See also *Agbor* v. *Metropolitan Police Commissioner* [1969] 1 W.L.R. 703 for independent judicial determination of a question (whether premises were the 'private residence of a diplomatic agent') arising under the 1964 Act.

of sovereign and state immunity entails an exercise of the prerogative. Immunities from suit may be waived in the appropriate form. Members of many diplomatic missions in London have taken full advantage of their immunity by refusing to pay penalties for car parking offences.

By virtue of the prerogative, the Crown is also entitled to determine conclusively a range of other matters. These may be summarized as follows:

1 Whether a state of war exists between Her Majesty and a foreign country. Thus, in one case, soon after the end of armed hostilities in the Second World War, the Crown was still detaining and wished to deport a German national as an enemy alien; he brought an application for a writ of habeas corpus, contending that the state of war was at an end and that in any case Germany no longer existed as a State; the court accepted as conclusive a certificate entered by a Secretary of State contradicting these contents.[24]

2 Whether a State is recognized by Her Majesty as an independent State.[25]

3 What dealings (if any) should take place between Her Majesty's Government and a regime which comes to power unconstitutionally in a State.[26]

These issues usually arise in connection with claims to jurisdictional immunity, but they may also arise in other contexts – for example, what effect, if any, is to be accorded in English law to the enactments, orders, or judgments of organs of such a political body.[27]

We must not suppose that rules such as these are eccentricities peculiar to British constitutional law. In a number of legal systems the

---

[24] *R. v. Bottrill, ex p. Kuechenmeister* [1947] K.B. 41.

[25] For an example, see *Gur Corporation* v. *Trust Bank of Africa* [1987] Q.B. 599.

[26] The former practice of recognizing a regime as the *de jure* or *de facto* government was abandoned in 1980, mainly because 'recognition' could imply an *approval* of the new regime, which does not necessarily follow: see 984 H.C. Deb. 277–9 (written answers 25 April 1980), and Symmons [1981] *Public Law* 249.

[27] See, for example, *Carl Zeiss Stiftung* v. *Rayner and Keeler Ltd* (No. 2) [1967] 1 A.C. 853 (Foreign Secretary certified that Her Majesty's Government did not recognize the German Democratic Republic (East Germany) *de facto* or *de jure*, but that the USSR was recognized as being entitled to exercise *de jure* authority there; House of Lords accepted this declaration as conclusive, but nevertheless attributed legal effect to a decree of the unrecognized government since it was to be regarded as a subordinate organ of a recognized government). *Semble*, such a certificate is not absolutely conclusive where the question is one of usurpation of sovereignty in a British dependency: *Adams* v. *Adams* [1971] P. 188 (Rhodesia). The courts will not challenge the validity of a certificate unless it (i) is not genuine, or (ii) appears on its face to have been made *ultra vires*: *R. v. Secretary of State for Foreign and Commonwealth Affairs, ex p. Trawnik*, The Times, 21 February 1986.

courts look to the Executive for authoritative guidance on matters lying especially within the domain of external affairs; and some systems have developed a coherent concept of non-justiciable 'political questions'. In this country there is no coherent concept; moreover, some questions with marked political overtones are decided by the courts on the basis of the evidence and legal submissions where there is no provision for a conclusive executive certificate or where no such certificate is tendered.[28]

It is also true that in some systems the rules of international law form part of municipal (or domestic) law, and the courts will make an independent determination of the content and applicability of those rules. In Britain the courts adopt a rebuttable presumption that Parliament has not intended to legislate inconsistently with rules of public international law, and common-law rules will, as far as practicable, be so stated as to conform with corresponding international rules[29] but if there is a plain inconsistency, the international law rules will have to give way.[30] Only the Prize Court in wartime purports to apply international law as such, and even this court must, of course, enforce statutes conflicting with international law. Rules of Community law again stand in a special position; for United Kingdom law has effect subject to any relevant Community law rules.[31]

Acts of State and legal proceedings [32]

Acts of State are primarily prerogative acts of policy in the field of external affairs – for example, the declaration of war, the conclusion of

[28] The State Immunity Act 1978, s. 21, has improved the situation somewhat: a Secretary of State's certificate, if entered, will be conclusive, among other things, as to whether any country is a State, and who must be regarded as the head or government of a State. But problems remain: see *Agbor*'s case (note 23 above; question of entitlement to occupation of diplomatic premises in London arising out of the civil war in Nigeria). Contrast *Buck* v. *Att.-Gen.* [1965] Ch. 745, where the English Court of Appeal would have disclaimed jurisdiction, as a matter of comity, to declare the constitution of a former colony (Sierra Leone) invalid following the grant of independence; and cases where ulterior motives are attributed by prisoners to governments seeking their surrender as fugitive offenders; p. 455, below.

[29] See, for example, *Salomon* v. *Customs and Excise Commissioners* [1967] 2 Q.B. 116. If the United Kingdom legislation purports to give effect to an international convention, the wording of the convention can be considered as an aid to interpretation: *Post Office* v. *Estuary Radio Ltd* [1968] 2 Q.B. 740.

[30] See, for example, *Cheney* v. *Conn* [1968] 1 W.L.R. 242.

[31] European Communities Act 1972, ss 2(4), 3(1). See further pp. 79–82.

[32] For a typically illuminating short survey, see D. L. Keir and F. H. Lawson, *Cases in Constitutional Law* (6th edn, 1979), pp. 144–73. For full studies, see E. C. S. Wade (1934) 15 *B.Y.I.L.* 98; Holdsworth (1941) 41 *Columbia L. Rev.* 1313; Collier [1968] *Camb. L.J.* 102; Cane (1980) 29 *I.C.L.Q.* 680. See further pp. 452–5.

a treaty, an annexation of territory, the recognition of a foreign sovereign, state or government. However, there can be no all-inclusive short definition, covering the different senses in which the term 'act of State' has been used. In one aspect an act of State is a manifestation of national sovereignty by the executive branch of government. When the courts say that an act of State is not cognizable by municipal courts (i.e. United Kingdom courts, and, for most purposes, the Judicial Committee of the Privy Council), they usually mean that once it is established to their satisfaction that an act performed by or with the authority of the Crown or a foreign government falls within the legal concept of an act of State, they are not concerned with the propriety of the grounds on which it has been exercised; they do not mean that the Crown can remove a matter from their jurisdiction by the bare assertion that it is an act of State.[33]

There are certain differences of substance or terminology between some acts of State and some prerogative acts.

1 Not every prerogative act is called an act of State; the latter term is reserved for executive acts having an effect in external affairs or performed in relation to persons not fully within the protection of the Crown. The granting of a new charter to an English university is a prerogative act but is not called an act of State.

2 A cause of action against the Crown can seldom be founded on a valid act of State (for example, the conclusion of a treaty).[34] On the other hand, a lawful exercise of the prerogative (for example, the taking of property for defence purposes) may give rise to a justiciable claim against the Crown for compensation.[35]

3 It is sometimes said that the term 'act of State' refers only to acts performed outside Her Majesty's dominions. This cannot be correct. Although acts of State can be performed outside her dominions, certain acts of State (for example, the making of a treaty) may also be performed inside them. The detention of an enemy alien in

---

[33] *Entick* v. *Carrington* (1765) 19 St. Tr. 1030; *Musgrave* v. *Pulido* (1879) 5 App. Cas. 102.

[34] See p. 140; or on an annexation (*Secretary of State for India* v. *Kamachee Boye Sahaba* (1859) 12 Moo P.C.C. 22); Collier, loc. cit., at 105–9.

[35] See *Nissan* v. *Att.-Gen.* [1968] 1 Q.B. 286 (C.A.); *Att.-Gen.* v. *De Keyser's Royal Hotel Ltd* [1920] A.C. 508. Note also the distinction between prerogative powers and acts of State drawn in *Commercial and Estates Co. of Egypt* v. *Board of Trade* [1925] 1 K.B. 271 (prerogative power of angary; wartime requisitioning of goods within the realm belonging to absent neutral; compensation payable). In that case Scrutton L.J. (at 290) and Bankes L.J. (at 297) said *obiter* that act of State could never be pleaded as a defence to an action in tort arising out of an act done in the realm. But the plaintiff was non-resident and apparently did not owe local allegiance. On principle, therefore, it is arguable that act of State could have been successfully pleaded, but for the fact that the situation fell within the rules governing angary.

wartime[36] or the deportation of such a person[37] can be classified either as a prerogative act or as an act of State; this is merely a matter of terminology.

4 It is also sometimes said that act of State cannot, whereas the royal prerogative can, be pleaded by way of justification in proceedings instituted by a British citizen.[38] This suggestion will be considered below.

5 In certain situations a British citizen may successfully plead that an ostensibly unlawful act is lawful because it was carried out in pursuance of an act of State of a foreign government, the validity of which will be recognized by an English court.[39] Such acts would not generally be called prerogative acts.

6 There are doubts as to the operation of the royal prerogative outside Her Majesty's dominions,[40] doubts which do not apply with equal force to acts of State. That certain prerogative powers (for example, in relation to the disposition of the armed forces, and in relation to protected states) are exercisable on foreign soil is reasonably clear; what is not clear is where the line is to be drawn.

7 The term 'act of State' is sometimes loosely used to include acts done in pursuance of statutory authority which has superseded prerogative (for example, the conclusiveness of a certificate as to diplomatic immunity).

Acts of State and individual rights

An act of State has been described as 'an act of the executive as a matter of policy',[41] and as 'an exercise of sovereign power'.[42] Those descriptions fit most of the situations in which conduct has been held in judicial proceedings to constitute an act of State. But there have been cases in which the quality of an act of State has been attributed to the individual initiative of a not very senior Crown servant ratified by the Crown.[43] On the other hand, the requisitioning and use of a hotel in

[36] *R.* v. *Vine Street Police Station Superintendent, ex p. Liebmann* [1916] 1 K.B. 268.

[37] *Netz* v. *Chuter Ede* [1946] Ch. 224; *R.* v. *Bottrill, ex p. Kuechenmeister* [1947] K.B. 41.

[38] The phrase 'British citizen' for the purposes only of the rest of this chapter should be read as also including British Dependent Territories and British Overseas citizens, and British protected persons. See further below, pp. 440–43.

[39] *Dobree* v. *Napier* (1836) 2 Bing N.C. 781; *Carr* v. *Fracis Times and Co.* [1902] A.C. 176; Zander (1959) 53 *Am. J.I.L.* 826. The act must be within the foreign government's own jurisdiction.

[40] See *Nissan* v. *Att.-Gen.* [1970] A.C. 179; note 45, below.

[41] E. C. S. Wade (1934) 15 *B.Y.I.L.* at 103.

[42] *Salaman* v. *Secretary of State for India* [1906] 1 K.B. 613 at 639.

[43] For example, *Buron* v. *Denman* (1848) 2 Ex. 167 (see below).

Cyprus by British troops engaged in a peace-keeping operation was held not to fall within the description of an act of State.[44] Since the Law Lords gave a number of different reasons for their conclusion on this point, the case is not helpful except in so far as it suggests that nowadays only acts which are part of or necessarily incidental to a high-level policy decision (and possibly other acts expressly ratified by the Crown) will be treated as acts of State.

Many of the decisions on act of State have an archaic flavour. They deal with the annexation of territory in India and Southern Africa in the heyday of imperial expansion, when judges often seemed to be as executive-minded as the Executive. It is not certain how much weight should be attached to some of these decisions; sometimes it is not even clear what were the material facts. But the principles laid down in them may still have to be taken into account in connection with claims arising from acts done by British peace-keeping forces overseas; the age of military intervention is not over, though one can optimistically assume that nowadays intervention will seldom take place except at the request or with the concurrence of the government of the territory or country concerned or as part of a United Nations force. Unfortunately the only modern case in which the Crown pleaded act of State as a defence in legal proceedings (*Nissan* v. *Att.-Gen.*) was a disaster for students of the law. The decision of the House of Lords lacks any clear *ratio decidendi* on any point now under consideration. Important questions of law were raised but left half-answered or unanswered, and points that once seemed clear were left shrouded in obscurity.[45]

The following observations about the state of the law must therefore be regarded as very tentative.

1   Act of State can successfully be pleaded by way of defence to an

---

[44] *Nissan* v. *Att.-Gen.* [1970] A.C. 179.

[45] [1970] A.C. 179. For critiques, see Gilmour [1970] *Public Law* 120; Bridge (1971) 34 *Mod. L. Rev.* 121; Collier [1969] *Camb. L.J.* 166; see also H. W. R. Wade, *Administrative Law* (6th edn, 1988), pp. 830–31; de Smith (1969) 32 *Mod. L. Rev.* 427. N, a British subject in Cyprus, was claiming that he was entitled to (i) *compensation* for the requisitioning of his hotel, and the use of the contents, under the royal prerogative; or (ii) declarations as to a breach of contract; or (iii) a declaration that he was entitled to damages in tort for trespass to his chattels. The Crown denied the allegations and also pleaded act of State; it then withdrew the defence of act of State in respect of claim (iii). The case was not fully disposed of but determined on preliminary points of law. No majority view emerged in the Lords as to the definition of an act of State; the scope of the *defence* of act of State (for instance, when, if at all, it was available against British subjects; whether it was available against claims not sounding in tort); or whether acts of State and prerogative acts were materially distinguishable; or whether the royal prerogative to take or destroy property subject to compensation applied outside Her Majesty's dominions.

action in tort brought by an alien in respect of an ostensibly wrongful act committed against him outside Her Majesty's dominions by the Crown or with the authority, antecedent or subsequent, of the Crown: *Buron* v. *Denman* (1848), an action for trespass.[46] The rationale of this rule is twofold: an alien in a foreign country or on the high seas does not ordinarily owe allegiance to the Crown[47] and is therefore not entitled to the protection of the Crown or indeed protection against the Crown; and he can look to his own government for diplomatic redress and, if any appropriate forum exists, the institution of proceedings for a breach of international law. Whether these are adequate reasons for treating a deliberate wrong perpetrated at the instance of the Crown as being a non-justiciable matter is questionable.

2 A person who is a friendly alien (even though he is engaging in unfriendly conduct) within Her Majesty's dominions owes local allegiance and is therefore entitled to protection, so that act of State cannot be pleaded in respect of a tortious act done to him with the authority of the Crown: *Johnstone* v. *Pedlar*.[48]

3 *A fortiori*, act of State is not a defence to an action arising out of such an act done to a British citizen within Her Majesty's dominions: *Walker* v. *Baird* (1892).[49]

4 Nor, so it would seem, is act of State available as a defence to a tort committed against a British citizen outside Her Majesty's dominions (for example, Cyprus).[50]

5 The term 'British citizen' in propositions 3 and 4 does not include citizens of independent Commonwealth countries, since they have the status of 'Commonwealth citizen' in United Kingdom law only

---

[46] (1848) 2 Ex. 167. A British naval officer, with general instructions to suppress the slave trade, exceeded them by landing in West Africa, destroying a barracoon (shed) and liberating slaves belonging to a Spaniard; his conduct was ratified by the Crown and he was awarded a large gratuity. The Spaniard's action for trespass failed. Today no action for trespass to land (as distinct from goods) situate abroad would be entertained by the High Court. This point was relevant to the statement of claim in *Nissan*'s case.

[47] Unless he is an alien who has left family, goods or effects here, evincing an intention to return, or possibly if he holds a British passport. See p. 452–5.

[48] [1921] 2 A.C. 262 (seizure of money belonging to American arrested for subversive activities in Dublin, then a part of Her Majesty's dominions, not defensible as act of State). Possibly the decision would now be different if the act complained of were done in an independent Commonwealth country.

[49] [1892] A.C. 491 (seizure of lobster factory in Newfoundland, in purported implementation of a treaty with France).

[50] This defence having been abandoned in *Nissan*'s case (note 44, above). Cyprus, although within the Commonwealth, is a republic and therefore not within Her Majesty's dominions.

by virtue of their citizenship of those countries,[51] owe allegiance primarily or solely to their own states or governments,[52] and are entitled to international protection by them.

6   It is doubtful how far, if at all, aliens owing local allegiance to the Crown but temporarily absent from the realm are entitled to immunity from a plea of act of State.[53]

7   All persons, including British citizens, may become the *indirect* victims of an act of State by the Crown. Act of State in this context does mean an act of high policy. Thus, a declaration of war may frustrate contracts. Upon the acquisition of territory the Crown does not succeed to the obligations of the predecessor government, but has a free discretion whether or not to accept them: *Cook* v. *Sprigg* (1899);[54] *West Rand Central Gold Mining Co.* v. *R.* (1905).[55]

8   There is also some authority for the proposition that in certain ill-defined circumstances direct injury inflicted on British citizens may be justified under the plea of act of State. For example, it has been suggested that damage done by the armed forces in the course of a military operation falling short of war to the property of citizens on foreign soil may be an act of State and therefore non-compensable.[56] (If it were attributed to an exercise of the royal prerogative, compensation might be payable by the Crown as a matter of obligation)[57] In this sense the defence of act of State would be a by-product of an 'act of policy'. Again, the seizure of British-owned property on behalf of the Crown may possibly be so connected,

---

[51] British Nationality Act 1981, s. 37(1).

[52] For example, they cannot be convicted of treason in United Kingdom law unless the conduct in question was treasonable if done by an alien in a foreign country (ibid., s. 3(1)). See further, p. 452.

[53] See pp. 452–5, below. *Semble* in any event act of State is pleadable in respect of seizure of property within the realm belonging to a non-resident alien who does *not* owe local allegiance; though cf. note 35, above.

[54] [1899] A.C. 572 (refusal to recognize railway concession granted by former government to one who was apparently a British subject).

[55] [1905] 2 K.B. 391 (refusal to accept responsibility for allegedly wrongful seizure of gold bars by former South African Republic).

[56] There are dicta to this effect in *Nissan*'s case [1970] A.C. 179 at 221 (Lord Morris), 235 (Lord Wilberforce) and 240 (Lord Pearson); Lord Pearce (at 227) left the point open and only Lord Reid (at 213) rejected this view.

[57] *Burmah Oil Co.* v. *Lord Advocate* [1965] A.C. 75; but no compensation would be claimable as of right during a state of war or apprehended war for battle damage or denial damage, even in Her Majesty's dominions: War Damage Act 1965. In *Nissan*'s case Lord Reid (at 213) and Lord Wilberforce (at 236) doubted whether the *Burmah Oil* rule about the prerogative applied to foreign soil. (The *Burmah Oil* case arose within Her Majesty's dominions.) Lord Denning M.R. in the Court of Appeal ([1968] 1 Q.B. 286 at 340) and Lord Pearce ([1970] A.C. at 229) took the broader view of the applicability of the prerogative.

causally and in point of time, with an act of State (for example, a treaty or an annexation) as to be regarded as part of it or necessarily incidental to it;[58] but it is very doubtful whether a court ought ever to accept such an argument today.

The accidents of litigation will doubtless resolve some of these problems, and throw up new ones, before the century is out.

[58] See, for example, *Secretary of State for India* v. *Kamachee Boye Sahaba* (1859) 12 Moo. P.C.C. 22; *Salaman* v. *Secretary of State for India* [1906] 1 K.B. 613 (seizures of property of former rulers upon annexation of their territory; presumably they became British subjects on annexation). In *Cook* v. *Sprigg* [1899] A.C. 572, see note 54 above – 'a case of doubtful authority' (*per* Lord Wilberforce in *Nissan*'s case [1970] A.C. at 232) – it is not clear whether the plaintiff's property was in fact seized.

Chapter 8

The Privy Council

I

The Privy Council, like the monarchy, is an ancient and dignified institution of government. Unlike the monarchy, it is not an important feature of the British constitutional system. If the monarchy were to be abolished, a new personage or institution would have to be endowed with the functions which only a head of State can exercise. The functions now performed by the Privy Council and its committees could be distributed tomorrow among other existing organs of government, and few people in the United Kingdom would notice any difference. Only the Judicial Committee of the Privy Council, which is in fact a court, almost entirely concerned with the hearing of appeals from Commonwealth countries overseas, would obviously need to be replaced by a separate new institution.

The Privy Council today[1] has over 400 members. All are entitled to be addressed as 'The Right Honourable . . .'. Members must be British citizens in United Kingdom law, or citizens of the Republic of Ireland. Appointments are made by letters patent on the Prime Minister's advice, and are for life, though a Privy Councillor (or Counsellor) may be removed on advice or at his own request.[2] By convention, all Cabinet Ministers must be sworn as Privy Councillors.[3] It is also conventional or customary to appoint the Archbishops of Canterbury

---

[1] The Scottish Privy Council was merged with the English Privy Council in 1708, after the Act of Union. There is a separate Privy Council for Northern Ireland but no new appointment to it has been possible since 1973: Northern Ireland Constitution Act 1973, s. 32(3).

[2] Sir Edgar Speyer was removed for his pro-German sympathies after the First World War, and Mr John Profumo and Mr John Stonehouse were removed respectively in 1963 and 1976 at their own requests.

[3] For an amusing account of the swearing ceremony, see R. H. S. Crossman, *Diaries of a Cabinet Minister*, vol. 1 (1975), p. 29.

and York, the Speaker of the House of Commons, the Lords of Appeal in Ordinary (the Law Lords), the Master of the Rolls, the Lords Justices of Appeal, the Lord Chief Justice and the President of the Family Division. Senior non-Cabinet Ministers, dignitaries and eminent judges from Commonwealth countries and a small number of other persons upon whom it is appropriate to confer a special honour for public or political service (for example, leadership of the small political parties) may also be appointed.[4]

Upon admission, a new Privy Councillor must swear an oath or make an affirmation not to divulge any matter disclosed to him confidentially in the Council. The general understanding used to be that the secrecy of Cabinet proceedings is preserved by the undertaking thus given; but this view cannot be sustained either by a literal interpretation of the oath (because the Cabinet is neither the Privy Council nor a committee of the Privy Council) or after the decision in *Attorney-General* v. *Jonathan Cape Ltd* (the Crossman Diaries case).[5]

Meetings of the Privy Council are held in the presence of the Queen (or Counsellors of State if she is absent from the realm or indisposed), normally at Buckingham Palace. The business transacted is purely formal, approving and recording decisions already taken elsewhere. The Lord President of the Council, a senior Minister (who need not be a peer), is responsible for the summoning of members and the preparation of the list of business; usually only three or four members are called, and they will be Ministers concerned with the matters to be transacted; meetings of the Council are very brief; indeed, the members remain standing. On rare ceremonial occasions a larger meeting, including persons other than Ministers, is convened – for example, to proclaim a new monarch, or to hear the monarch give consent to a royal marriage.

The dissolution, summoning and prorogation[6] of Parliament are effected by royal proclamations in Council; so are the declaration and termination of a state of war, and the declaration of a statutory state of emergency. *Projets de loi* (bills) passed by the States of Jersey and Guernsey are assented to by Order in Council; and it is by Order in Council that the Royal Courts of the islands are directed to register Acts of the United Kingdom Parliament having effect in the islands.

Some Orders in Council are of a judicial character, formally

---

[4] The current annual volume of *Whitaker's Almanack* gives a list of the membership.

[5] [1976] Q.B. 752, and below, p. 190.

[6] See ch. 13.

promulgating the report (or judgment) of the Judicial Committee.[7] The great majority are legislative Orders in Council. Apart from those few Orders in Council which are still made under prerogative powers (for example, for altering the constitutions of the diminishing group of colonies,[8] for altering rates of pensions for the armed services, or for dealing with recruitment to the civil service, coinage),[9] legislative Orders in Council are made in pursuance of powers delegated to Her Majesty in Council by statute. These have exactly the same status as regulations made by individual Ministers under delegated legislative powers; they fall within the definition of 'statutory instruments',[10] are numbered and published in the annual volumes of Statutory Instruments, and differ from departmental regulations only in their formal source. Unless they are of exceptional importance (in which case parliamentary draftsmen may be enlisted) they are drafted by the legal advisers to the Department with whose business they deal. The reasons for giving Her Majesty power to make Orders in Council on certain matters instead of vesting a Minister with power to make regulations are partly traditional and partly psychological. It is more dignified and impressive for an independence constitution, or an instrument giving effect to an extradition treaty or creating new parliamentary constituencies or altering electoral boundaries, to be made by Her Majesty in Council. Or so it seems to some people; and appearance is occasionally more important than reality, even if hardly anyone is misled by the ceremonial trappings. The draft Orders are not discussed at the meeting of the Council; the Lord President reads out their titles, the Queen (who has been fully informed in advance of the business to be transacted) approves them orally, and they are then authenticated by the signature of the Clerk of the Council and the affixing of the seal of the Council.

II

Various committees of the Privy Council have been formed at different times and for a range of purposes. Today the Privy Council has a miscellany of standing committees, none of recent origin, and most resting on a statutory basis – the Universities Committee, reporting on

[7] The distinction between a judicial and a legislative Order in Council was clearly emphasized in *Ibralebbe* v. *R.* [1964] A.C. 900. See p. 31.

[8] For example, colonies originally acquired by conquest or cession, such as Gibraltar.

[9] Prerogative Orders in Council of a legislative character are published as an Appendix to the annual volumes of Statutory Instruments. They are not numbered and are not, of course, *statutory* instruments.

[10] Statutory Instruments Act 1946, s. 1, and the regulations made thereunder. See ch. 18.

petitions concerning Statutes of the Universities of Oxford and Cambridge and their colleges; a somewhat similar Scottish Universities Committee; a Baronetage Committee to report on claims to baronetcies; the Political Honours Scrutiny Committee (a committee of three persons, not being members of the Government, reporting in the first instance to the Prime Minister on the suitability of persons to be recommended by him for the award of titles and dignities at CBE level and above for political or any other services);[11] and committees on the Channel Islands and the Isle of Man, to which bills passed locally are referred for report. The Honours Committee (composed of elder statesmen, one from each of the main parties) and the Universities Committees are fairly active, non-political, advisory bodies. The Committees on the Channel Islands and the Isle of Man are composed of the Lord President, the Home Secretary and other Ministers; they are political organs of the United Kingdom Government, but seldom do they meet and deliberate as committees. There are *ad hoc* committees – for example, to consider applications by other institutions for charters and Statutes; and committees of the Council, or consisting of Privy Councillors, to consider special problems appropriate for investigation by an eminent non-partisan body, for instance the use of questionable interrogation techniques by security forces or the recruitment in this country of mercenaries to fight abroad, or the lessons of the Falklands conflict of 1982. And then there is the Judicial Committee. Hence the Privy Council is not entirely superfluous. Although all its non-judicial functions could be transferred to the Cabinet or departments of State, and its committees could be detached as autonomous statutory bodies or as advisory bodies to Departments, such a redistribution would not in every instance be as convenient as the present arrangements, and in some cases the retention of ancient forms is of political value.

III

The Judicial Committee of the Privy Council[12] can be mentioned at this point. After the abolition of the conciliar courts, the Council was

---

[11] The Prime Minister widened the function of the Committee to include examination of recommendations based on *non*-political services, but, misleadingly, the Committee's title was left unchanged: see 974 H.C. Deb. 880 (26 November 1979). It has always been the case that if the Committee reports adversely and the Prime Minister proceeds with his recommendation, the Queen is to be informed of the Committee's view.

[12] Sir Kenneth Roberts-Wray, *Commonwealth and Colonial Law* (1966), pp. 433–63; Beth [1975] *Public Law* 219.

still able to entertain appeals from the overseas dominions of the Crown. With the expansion of the colonial empire, it became essential to make adequate provision for the determination of appeals, and in 1833 Parliament constituted a Judicial Committee of the Privy Council; its composition and jurisdiction have been modified many times since.

Today the Judicial Committee consists of the Lord President (who never sits), persons who hold or have held high judicial office in the United Kingdom and are Privy Councillors, and leading members of the Judiciary from certain Commonwealth countries (notably New Zealand) from which appeals still lie to the Privy Council. The quorum of the Judicial Committee is three; normally five members sit to hear an appeal;[13] more often than not, they are the Law Lords. The Judicial Committee is sometimes referred to as the Board; its reports are in the form of advice and are promulgated, as we have seen, by Order in Council. It is not strictly bound by its own decisions. Before 1966 no dissenting opinion could be delivered, because advice to the Crown should not be divided, but this anachronistic rule has been abandoned.[14]

The Judicial Committee's jurisdiction is regulated by statute, subordinate legislative instruments, and local constitutions and legislation. It hears appeals from the superior courts of the Channel Islands, the Isle of Man, colonies and such independent Commonwealth countries as have retained the appeal from their own courts. It receives about fifty appeals each year from courts overseas. Appeals may lie as of right, with leave of the court below, or by special leave of the Judicial Committee. The power to grant special leave to appeal is a prerogative power placed on a statutory basis, and cannot be abrogated by a colony.[15] Appeals in criminal matters lie only by special leave, save in matters concerning the guarantees of fundamental rights and freedoms embodied in constitutions since 1959; generally the appeal will lie as of right in the latter class of case. Petitions for special leave to appeal are granted sparingly; and the Judicial Committee declines to act as a general Court of Criminal Appeal.

[13] In the *Australian Banks Nationalisation* case (*Commonwealth of Australia* v. *Bank of N.S.W.* [1950] A.C. 235), a Board of seven members was convened. Two members died during the hearing, which was of unprecedented length.

[14] Judicial Committee (Dissenting Opinions) Order 1966 (S.I. 1966, No. 1100); Lock [1985] *Public Law* 64.

[15] Southern Rhodesia remained a colony despite the unilateral declaration of independence (UDI) by its government in November 1965, and the purported abolition of the appeal to the Privy Council by the Smith Constitution was therefore ineffective in law; see *Madzimbamuto* v. *Lardner-Burke* [1969] 1 A.C. 645. The Appellate Division of the High Court of Southern Rhodesia refused to follow this Privy Council decision and accepted the Smith Constitution as binding: *R.* v. *Ndhlovu* 1968 (4)S.A. 515.

By virtue of the Statute of Westminster 1931, and subsequent independence Acts, independent Commonwealth countries have acquired power (subject to any restriction imposed by their own constitutions) to terminate the appeal, and a number have done so. Among Commonwealth countries which achieved independence before 1950, Canada, India, Sri Lanka and Australia[16] have abolished all appeals; appeals still lie on a wide range of matters from New Zealand but are infrequent. If a Commonwealth country which becomes a republic or comes under a separate monarchy on or after the attainment of independence still wishes to retain the appeal, this may be done by one of two methods: by providing either (i) that appeals shall be referred by the local head of State to the Judicial Committee, which will submit its report to him (as in Malaysia), or (ii) that appeal shall lie not to 'Her Majesty in Council' – the form used in the constitutions of those countries of which the Queen is still head of State – but simply to the 'Judicial Committee'.[17]

Under the constitutions of some Commonwealth countries, a superior judge cannot be removed except for inability or misbehaviour established to the satisfaction of the Judicial Committee following an adverse report by a local judicial tribunal of inquiry.

The Judicial Committee of the Privy Council is essentially a Commonwealth court, but it also has a place in the legal system of the United Kingdom. Here its jurisdiction is exclusively statutory and, like the powers of the Privy Council itself, comprises a mixed assortment.

1 It hears appeals from the decisions of certain professional disciplinary bodies, medical, dental, optical and in respect of professions ancillary to medicine. It also has a limited appellate jurisdiction from higher ecclesiastical courts, and in wartime it hears appeals from the Prize Court.

2 Under section 7 of the House of Commons Disqualification Act 1975, a member of the public may apply to the Judicial Committee for a declaration that a member of the House is subject to a statutory disqualification under that Act.

3 The Crown may, under section 4 of the Judicial Committee Act 1833, refer any matter to it for an advisory opinion. Unlike its appellate determinations, which are advisory only in form, such opinions are truly advisory, though they will almost invariably be

---

[16] Australia Act 1986, s. 11: see below, p. 665.
[17] Appeals still lie from Antigua and Barbuda, Bahamas, Barbados, Belize, Dominica, Gambia, Jamaica, Kiribati, Malaysia, Mauritius, New Zealand, St Kitts-Nevis, St Lucia, St Vincent, Singapore, Trinidad and Tobago, Tuvalu.

treated as authoritative. It would be possible so to refer a matter that was not characteristically justiciable, though in practice its advice has been sought only on legal questions.[18] The last special reference was made in 1957, at the request of the House of Commons and upon the initiative of the Committee of Privileges, in order to obtain an authoritative interpretation of the effect of an obscure eighteenth-century statute on the article of the Bill of Rights, which guarantees freedom of speech and proceedings in Parliament.[19]

[18] See Roberts-Wray, op cit., p. 449, for a synopsis of the matters specially referred. In the past, mixed questions of law and policy were occasionally referred for an advisory opinion to a mixed *ad hoc* committee of the Privy Council, composed of judicial and other members of the Council: see, for example *Re States of Jersey* (1853) 9 Moo. P.C.C. 185.

[19] *Re Parliamentary Privilege Act 1770* [1958] A.C. 331. This was one stage in the controversy in the *Strauss* case; see p. 318 below.

Chapter 9

The Prime Minister and the Cabinet [1]

In general

No series of terse comments on existing practice can be free from dogmatic assertion, or be based on sufficient or reliable information on matters which are still to a large extent confidential; nor can a brief description pay proper regard to the work of constitutional and political historians or students of politics and political sociology. Recent investigations into the processes by which major policy decisions have been made, the organization and behaviour of the two main political parties in and out of Parliament, the selection of parliamentary candidates by constituency parties, the impact of the media of information on the vicissitudes of public opinion, the realities behind voting behaviour, and so on, have contributed much to an understanding of how the British constitutional and political system works in practice. This book is concerned less with evaluation than with rules and institutions.

The rules about the principal institutions of executive government are not, of course, mainly rules of strict law. The monarchy and the Privy Council are encrusted with rules of strict law in abundance; but they are not principal institutions of executive government. The Cabinet and the Prime Minister, on the other hand, are hardly recognized in the statute book and they are almost invisible in the law reports. The Prime Minister is the keystone of the Cabinet arch, a sun around which planets revolve, an elected monarch, a President, or what you will; yet he was not mentioned in an Act of Parliament till 1917, and the main statutes relating to his office are those providing for his

[1] See Rodney Brazier, *Constitutional Practice* (1988), chs 5, 6.

salary and pension.[2] His powers and duties are determined almost exclusively by convention and usage. The Cabinet has been virtually ostracized by the parliamentary draftsman. It appeared in 1937 (also in the context of ministerial salaries) but has made little further progress towards statutory recognition.[3] Its composition, mode of selection, powers and procedures have to be elicited from political announcements, inference, breaches of confidence, and optimistic speculation. The strict law of the constitution tells us as much and as little about political parties and the Leader of the Opposition.[4]

It is nevertheless possible to list a number of conventional rules about the Prime Minister and the Cabinet. The authenticity of some of the rules is dubious, since their binding force is sometimes questionable and they are apt to change with a disconcerting frequency; moreover attempts to ascertain them are bedevilled by a paucity of reliable up-to-date information. Again, it is possible to place a variety of reasonable interpretations on the relationship between the Prime Minister and his Cabinet at any given moment (although no one would dispute the dominance of Mrs Thatcher over *her* Cabinet[5]) and nearly all commentators regard any Cabinet as being in some degree subordinate to the Prime Minister. Hardly anyone today will make out a case for the proposition that the Prime Minister is merely *primus inter pares*, the

[2] The main one is the Ministerial and other Salaries Act 1975. The maximum annual salary is £64,250. There are a few other random statutory references to the Prime Minister: see, for example, the Chevening Estate Acts 1959 and 1987; Parliamentary Commissioner Act 1967, s. 8(4); House of Commons (Administration) Act 1978, s. 1(4); National Heritage Act 1980, s. 1(2); Police Negotiating Board Act 1980, s. 1(2); National Audit Act 1983, s. 1(1); Interception of Communications Act 1985, ss 7, 8.

[3] Under the First Schedule to the Ministerial and other Salaries Act 1975 the salaries of specified Ministers are fixed according as to whether they are or are not members of the Cabinet. Cabinet papers and proceedings (certified as such by the Secretary to the Cabinet with the approval of the Prime Minister) are not to be divulged to the Parliamentary Commissioner for Administration (the 'Ombudsman') in the course of his investigations: Parliamentary Commissioner Act 1967, s. 8(4). The Cabinet Office lies outside the Commissioner's field of inquiry: ibid., Sched. 2, note 6.

[4] See Ministerial and other Salaries Act 1975, s. 2(1) (definition of the meaning of Leader of the Opposition by reference to the largest opposition party); Companies Act 1985, s. 235 (directors' reports to disclose contributions by companies to political parties). See also *John* v. *Rees* [1970] Ch. 345 (natural justice to be observed by party's national executive before disaffiliating or suspending activities of a constituency party); *Conservative and Unionist Central Office* v. *Burrell* [1982] 1 W.L.R. 522 (funds and income held by Central Office for the Conservative Party not subject to corporation tax); *R.* v. *Broadcasting Complaints Commission, ex p. Owen* [1985] Q.B. 1153 (challenge to fairness of treatment on television of S.D.P./Liberal Alliance).

[5] For testimony to this of former Cabinet colleagues, see, e.g., James Prior, *A Balance of Power* (1986), especially pp. 114–19 and ch. 8; Francis Pym, *The Politics of Consent* (1984), ch. 1; Lord Hailsham, Granada Guildhall Lecture (1985).

first among equals, except in the formal sense that all are servants of the Crown. The central feature of recent controversies is the question how far it is justifiable to speak of Prime Ministerial government rather than Cabinet government.[6] For two centuries the Cabinet has been regarded as the primary executive organ of government, discussing and deciding the main issues of national policy and coordinating the work of the Departments; but since 1945 at the latest some Prime Ministers with sufficient political authority and enjoying strong personalities have been able to dominate it.

Choice of Prime Minister [7]

The general rule is that in appointing a Prime Minister, the Queen should commission that person who appears best able to command the support of a stable majority in the House of Commons.

A change of Prime Minister may be necessary because of the resignation, death or dismissal of the incumbent. The last possibility, dismissal, would arise only in highly exceptional circumstances and, one would suppose, in a near-revolutionary situation;[8] in such a context the Queen would have to find somebody to form an emergency Government, perhaps without a majority in the House but prepared to advise a dissolution of Parliament at the earliest practicable moment. All vacancies in the office since Victoria came to the throne have arisen through resignation or death. Resignation may occur because the Government has been defeated at a General Election (as in 1945, 1951, 1964, 1970, February 1974 and 1979) or has collapsed through internal dissension (as in 1931) or has been defeated on a vote of confidence in the House of Commons (as in 1895,[9] 1923[10] and

---

6 The prime ministerial thesis has been argued by R. H. S. Crossman, Introduction to Walter Bagehot's *The English Constitution* (1963 edn) – but later, having held Cabinet office, he became more ambivalent: see *The Diaries of a Cabinet Minister*, vols. 1 (1975), 2 (1976) and 3 (1977), *passim*; John Mackintosh, *The British Cabinet* (3rd edn, 1977) – although he, too, became more guarded in each edition; and Humphrey Berkeley, *The Power of the Prime Minister* (1968). The thesis has been vigorously opposed by Herbert Morrison, *Government and Parliament* (3rd edn, 1964); Patrick Gordon Walker, *The Cabinet* (revised edn, 1972) (both of whom had sat in Cabinets); and by a former Prime Minister: Harold Wilson, *The Governance of Britain* (1976), *passim*. See also Ian Gilmour, *The Body Politic* (1969), and for a particularly well argued appraisal, A. H. Brown [1968] *Public Law* 28, 96.
7 See Brazier, op. cit., chs 2, 3.
8 See pp. 116–17.
9 When Lord Rosebery's Government was defeated on the 'cordite vote'.
10 When Baldwin's Conservative Government was defeated on an amendment to the address in reply to the King's speech. See also the 1924 case (below).

1979[11]). In such cases it is the duty of the Government as a whole to resign (unless, in the event of a defeat in the House, the Prime Minister elects to request a dissolution[12]) and of the Queen to send for the Leader of the Opposition or, when a Government resigns as soon as the results of a General Election are known and Parliament still stands dissolved, the person who was Leader of the Opposition in the House of Commons before the dissolution;[13] he will normally accept office as Prime Minister, but in an exceptional situation may prefer to advise (as Baldwin advised in 1931) that a coalition Government under another person[14] be formed. The resignation of a Prime Minister may take place for other reasons – because of ill health or old age, or because he feels or is persuaded to feel that he has become a liability to his party or an obstacle to the formation of a coalition in wartime. In these situations, which have often arisen in the last sixty years – in 1923 (Bonar Law), 1935 (MacDonald), 1940 (Neville Chamberlain), 1955 (Churchill), 1957 (Eden) and 1963 (Macmillan) – the party in office still retains a majority in the House and the Prime Minister's resignation is personal, almost as if he had died in office; the Ministers place their offices at his successor's disposal, but the Government as a whole does not vacate office. His successor may decide to make few changes, and those Ministers who continue in their posts do not have to be reappointed. But how is his successor chosen? The Queen should wait until the Government party has elected its new leader, and then send for him. This happened in 1976 when Mr Wilson announced that he would resign as soon as the Parliamentary Labour Party had elected a new leader. Mr Callaghan was elected three weeks after that announcement; Mr Wilson resigned and the Queen appointed the new Leader of

[11] When Mr Callaghan's minority Labour Government was defeated on an Opposition motion of no confidence: see 965 H.C. Deb. 461–590 (28 March 1979). Mr Callaghan forthwith requested and obtained a dissolution. The Conservative Party under Mrs Thatcher won the ensuing General Election with a 43-seat majority. A defeat on a vote of confidence has been very rare. See further Norton [1978] *Public Law* 360.

[12] Ramsay MacDonald so advised in 1924, and George V accepted his advice though he was not obliged to do so.

[13] Assuming, of course, that his party has won a majority at the General Election and he has himself been re-elected in a constituency. When an Opposition party has won an overall majority in the House at the General Election, it is conventional for the Government to resign before the new Parliament meets.

[14] In this instance, MacDonald, the outgoing Prime Minister, who cut himself adrift of the majority of his Labour colleagues. In a multi-party situation, where the Government has lost its majority but the Opposition cannot command one, the Leader of the Opposition may alternatively agree to form a minority Government. This situation arose after the February 1974 General Election. See note 17.

the Labour Party as Prime Minister.[15] With a change of Conservative Prime Minister the monarch had a personal discretion till February 1965, when the Conservative and Unionist Party adopted a new procedure for electing a party leader by ballot among Conservative M.P.s.[16] It can, therefore, be assumed that the Queen will not now have to exercise personal discretion on a change of Prime Minister resigning for personal reasons, as she had to exercise a discretion in 1955, 1957 and 1963. In 1955, however, Sir Anthony Eden (later the Earl of Avon) was the obvious successor to Churchill. On the resignations of Eden in 1957 and Macmillan in 1963 the successor was not obvious. In 1957 she consulted Sir Winston Churchill and Lord Salisbury, two elder statesmen of the party; neither of them was any longer a candidate for the office; both recommended Harold Macmillan in preference to R. A. Butler, the alternative choice, and she commissioned Macmillan to form a Government. In 1963 the position was more difficult. Macmillan, having decided to resign on grounds of health, arranged for soundings to be taken among the Cabinet, the Parliamentary Party, the Conservative peers and the constituency parties; the collective weight of opinion appeared to favour Lord Home, and Macmillan advised the Queen accordingly. Although the monarch was not obliged to seek or follow the outgoing Prime Minister's advice, she could hardly have acted otherwise in those circumstances. The procedure and its outcome gave rise to some dissatisfaction within the party, which decided to alter its practice soon afterwards.

Hence the Queen is unlikely to have to exercise such a discretion again unless no party has an overall majority in the House, or the formation of a coalition is advised, or a coalition, having been formed, disintegrates. In such situations her duty will be to take such counsel as is proper and expedient to assist her in deciding who is the most appropriate person to invite to form a Government with a reasonable prospect of maintaining itself in office. That person will normally, but not invariably, be the leader of the largest party in the House of

---

[15] Mr Callaghan was elected by the Parliamentary Labour Party under the then current party election rules. See now below, p. 265, for the 1981 changes in electing a Leader of the Labour Party.

[16] In July 1965 Mr Edward Heath was elected leader by this new procedure in succession to Sir Alec Douglas-Home (formerly Lord Home) who resigned the leadership; the party was then in opposition. The Conservatives' rules have since been amended to require annual re-election: Mr Heath so offered himself in 1975 and lost to Mrs Thatcher. Leaders of the Labour Party had always been elected annually when in opposition, but see below, p. 266.

Commons.[17] In any event, the procedures now adopted by all the major political parties for electing their own leaders seem to carry a necessary implication that the Prime Minister, when appointed, shall be a member of, or shall be about to occupy his seat[18] in, the House of Commons.

The Prime Minister's powers

The following are the principal conventions concerning the Prime Minister.

1 The Prime Minister is invariably designated First Lord of the Treasury. The legislation providing for his salary and pension presupposes that he will fulfil this dual role.

2 Although his Treasury duties may be nominal – the Minister effectively in charge of the Treasury is the Chancellor of the Exchequer – it seems to follow that the Prime Minister must be (or must become immediately after his appointment) a member of the House of Commons, if only because the House of Lords no longer has any control over finance. There are other, more obvious reasons why he must be in the Commons: the unrepresentative character of the Lords, its diminished status in the constitution since 1911, the role of the House of Commons as the political cockpit and the fact that a Government has to retain a majority in the Commons to remain in office but can flout a hostile House of Lords. Apart from Lord Home, who swiftly transmuted himself into a member of the Commons,[19] no Prime Minister has been a member of the Lords since 1902.

3 Since 1968 the Prime Minister has been designated Minister for the Civil Service. In that role and as First Lord of the Treasury he has responsibility for civil service affairs and his approval is required for proposals for the appointment of permanent heads of departments.[20] Mrs Thatcher has appointed seventeen permanent heads since coming to office.

[17] As he was after the first 1974 General Election. Mr Heath (who had lost the Election and had failed to negotiate a coalition with the Liberals) was succeeded as Prime Minister by Mr Wilson, who led the largest party, there being no majority party in the new House. Hence the Queen's part may in such circumstances be largely formal.

From 1931 to 1935 MacDonald held office as Prime Minister of the 'National' Government although he was the leader of a small minority party. He was dependent on the favour of the Conservatives, the majority party and the dominant partner in the coalition; his personal position was conspicuously weak.

[18] Where a change of Prime Minister is necessary after an election while Parliament stands dissolved.

[19] See pp. 38, 44.

[20] See pp. 196–8.

4   The Prime Minister presents a list of his proposed ministerial colleagues for the Queen's approval. She may make observations, suggestions and objections, but the Prime Minister is entitled to insist on his own choice. Junior Ministers are appointed by the Prime Minister without prior reference to the Queen, although she is of course informed of the Prime Minister's proposed junior appointments.

5   The Prime Minister decides which Ministers are to be members of the Cabinet. His selection will be determined mainly by personal inclination and political expediency. By convention or custom, certain Ministers – the Chancellor of the Exchequer, the Secretary of State for Foreign and Commonwealth Affairs, the Home Secretary, the Lord Chancellor, the Secretary of State for Scotland, the Secretary of State for Defence, and that Minister whom the Prime Minister designates as Leader of the House of Commons – must always be in a peacetime Cabinet; and it would be odd if Ministers in charge of certain other main Departments (for example, education, social services, agriculture) were to be excluded. All Cabinet Ministers must be sworn as members of the Privy Council.

6   In assigning Ministers to Departments the Prime Minister must have regard to certain well-established conventions. All Ministers [21] must be or become members of one or other House of Parliament; if a Minister is not a member of either House at the time of his appointment, he must obtain a seat at the earliest opportunity or resign. Hence although it was proper to appoint Mr Patrick Gordon Walker as Foreign Secretary in 1964 in spite of his defeat in his constituency at the General Election, it was necessary for him to resign from office when he failed to win a seat at a by-election shortly afterwards. [22] Each Department must have a ministerial spokesman in the House of Commons; no corresponding rule applies to the Lords. The Chancellor of the Exchequer must be a member of the House of Commons.

7   The Prime Minister may require a Minister to resign at any time and for any reason he thinks fit. So, for example, by 1981 Mrs Thatcher had shuffled out almost all Cabinet Ministers (popularly known as 'wets') who did not share her economic philosophy. If the Minister refuses to comply, the Prime Minister may in the last

[21] Except the Lord Advocate and the Solicitor-General for Scotland, one or both of whom have not infrequently been outside Parliament.
[22] Mr Hamish Gray lost his seat at the 1983 General Election but was created a life peer and retained ministerial office.

resort advise the Queen to dismiss him.[23] Whether there are any circumstances in which the Queen could properly refuse a Prime Minister's advice to dismiss his colleagues is debatable.[24]

8   The Prime Minister may decide to advise a dissolution without prior reference to the Cabinet. In some situations, as we have already noted,[25] it would be constitutionally proper for the Queen to refuse such a request, absolutely, temporarily or conditionally, and one of those situations may be the case of a Prime Minister, placed in a minority in his own Cabinet, seeking to appeal to the electorate against his colleagues instead of following the more appropriate course of resigning. Nevertheless, the widespread assumption that it is within the Prime Minister's sole authority to fix the date of the next General Election enhances his personal power in relation to his ministerial colleagues and his party, and in the country as a whole. All recent Prime Ministers have, however, consulted senior colleagues about the timing so as (among other things) to implicate them in it if the Election is lost.[26]

9   When Parliament is dissolved the Government continues in office; it vacates office only if the election results show that it has lost its majority in the House, in which case it must resign.

10   The Prime Minister has substantial control over the organization as well as the personnel of central government. Not only does he choose, switch, promote, demote and discard his colleagues; he places them in an informal order of seniority;[27] he may nominate one to be Deputy Prime Minister; he can take the initiative in creating a new Department or ministerial office, winding up a

[23] In 1975 Mr Heffer, Minister of State for Industry, was dismissed on the Prime Minister's advice for breaking the Cabinet guidelines agreed for the suspension of collective responsibility during the EEC referendum campaign (see below, p. 189). In 1981 Mr Speed, Under-Secretary of State for Defence, was dismissed for making a speech which contradicted the Cabinet's agreed but not then announced cuts in naval spending.

[24] Sir Ivor Jennings has asserted (*Cabinet Government* (3rd edn, 1959), p. 86) that: 'The Queen must not intervene in party politics. She must not, *therefore* [my italics], support a Prime Minister against his colleagues. Accordingly, it would be unconstitutional for the Queen to agree with the Prime Minister for the dissolution of a Government in order to allow the Prime Minister to override his colleagues.' This view is sustainable if the Prime Minister is known to have been placed, or is believed to be on the point of being placed, in a minority in his own Cabinet, but not otherwise.

[25] See pp. 117–20.

[26] See Brazier, op. cit., p. 83.

[27] A 'pecking order' emerges in the list of Ministers, published regularly in *Hansard*. The order in which the names of Cabinet Ministers appear is generally attributed to the Prime Minister's personal decision. It does not follow, however, that the Prime Minister is impliedly indicating that the second name in the list is that of his most appropriate successor.

Department, and transferring functions from one Minister to another (though in some instances the change can only be effected by legislation); he can decide to create a new committee of the Cabinet, prescribe its terms of reference and give it decision-making powers; he can determine when the Cabinet shall meet; and in the last resort he can decide what shall or shall not be discussed at Cabinet meetings. He can thus control the allocation of functions between Cabinet, Cabinet committees and individual Departments. He can also decide which non-Cabinet Ministers shall be appointed to membership of Cabinet Committees. Through his control over the Cabinet Office – a Cabinet Secretariat was created by Lloyd George in 1916 – he is in a position to see that the decisions of the Cabinet and its committees are implemented.[28]

11   He is entitled to say what issues shall be referred to him personally for decision outside the Cabinet. Inter-departmental disputes or deadlocks in Cabinet committees may be resolved by his informal rulings. And he may simply, by an uninvited personal initiative or pronouncement, confront his colleagues with a *fait accompli.*

12   The Prime Minister personally presides not only in the Cabinet but also in some of the more important standing committees of the Cabinet – for example, the Defence and Overseas Policy Committee, the committee on economic strategy, and on the supervision of the Security Service (MI5) and the Secret Intelligence Service (MI6). The Prime Minister, as the country's principal spokesman on the international scene, must inevitably concern himself closely with foreign and Commonwealth affairs, matters of defence and security, and economic policy.

13   Since the Prime Minister is an international figure and a national leader, he is potentially capable of dominating his colleagues. His visits overseas to discuss matters of high policy, his speeches, answers to questions (which are occasionally broadcast live on sound radio) and interventions in the House of Commons, his performances on television and his other public addresses attract a degree of attention which no other politician in the country is likely to emulate. Moreover, he controls the Government's information services. As leader of his party he has another powerful organization behind him to project his image in its most favourable light; for if the public reputation of the Prime Minister sags, the prospects of the party remaining in office after the next General Election will dwindle; and it is not easy to remove a party

28   On the Cabinet Office, see p. 171.

leader tenacious of office and of the authority and deference that go with it.

14 At a General Election, the voters know that they are choosing a Government. To many of them, the choice is not so much between party programmes or party images as between the personal qualities of the Prime Minister and the Leader of the Opposition. If a Prime Minister and his advisers on public relations see this as the dominant factor in voting behaviour, the consequence will be the devotion of a disproportionate amount of publicity to the Prime Minister at the expense of his colleagues. This has been seen in all recent General Elections, which to an ever-increasing extent have been fought through the medium of television. The electorate's perception of Mrs Thatcher's qualities has been a major factor in her success in winning three consecutive General Elections – a record this century – and in becoming in 1988 the longest-serving Prime Minister in one continuous period since Lord Liverpool.

15 The Prime Minister enjoys, by convention, substantial powers of patronage. Some of these powers are apt to be a nuisance – 'Damn! another bishop dead', as Lord Melbourne remarked [29] – and others, such as the power to advise on appointments to the highest judicial and military offices, are of no political advantage to him because of expectations that appointments shall be non-partisan. But there are others which enhance his personal authority, if only because the hope of preferment tends to muffle the voices of carping critics. One who attracts the favourable notice of the Prime Minister or those closest to him may cherish the prospect, if not of political office, at least of a place in the honours list, even a peerage, or perhaps the chairmanship of one of the multifarious statutory corporations, advisory and consultative bodies, royal commissions or committees of inquiry by virtue of the Prime Minister's nomination. The increase in the peripheral adjuncts of government, as the reach of central government has expanded and its workings have become more complex, has undoubtedly enlarged the area of ministerial patronage.

16 The Prime Minister is the channel of communication between the Cabinet and the Queen. It is his duty to keep her adequately informed on matters of State, and she holds a private audience

---

[29] Lord Melbourne would have welcomed the setting up of the Church Commission on Crown Appointments in 1978. It gives the Prime Minister two names for any vacant archbishopric or bishopric, stating a preference for one. The Prime Minister then passes on this advice to the Queen. Dr Runcie was appointed Archbishop of Canterbury under this new procedure in 1979.

with him weekly. These contacts tend to enhance the prestige of his office.

Prime ministerial power: some correctives

A good deal has been said about the Prime Minister but precious little about the Cabinet. Because the Prime Minister's conventional powers and general authority in the scheme of the constitution are very great, and because one can point to examples of dramatic Prime Ministerial decisions (such as Eden's decision to engage in the Suez venture, or Macmillan's decision to dismiss a third of his Cabinet) taken outside the Cabinet, one can easily be led to the conclusion that the Cabinet is no more than a Prime Minister's instrument at any given time. For reasons which must already be fairly obvious, it is too early to draw such a conclusion.

Disquisitions on the sovereignty of the Prime Minister bear some resemblance to discussions of the sovereignty of Parliament. Parliament in its wisdom might pass any number of appalling Acts without stepping beyond the limits of its constitutional authority, but somehow it does not regularly perpetrate gross abuses of its formal omnipotence. If a Prime Minister were to behave in a preposterous manner he would lose credit among his senior colleagues (who would resign if he had not already dismissed them), in the country and in his party; such a combination will be fatal to anyone but the most reckless autocrat, and a reckless autocrat who will neither resign nor mend his ways may have to be dealt with by unconventional and even extra-legal means. No modern Prime Minister has been a reckless autocrat. Illustrations of high-handed behaviour indicate not so much what a Prime Minister can do as the extent to which he may place his own position at risk. The misfortunes of Suez undermined Eden's health and personal prestige, and his resignation soon followed; Macmillan's standing in the Conservative Party and among the electorate, so strong in 1960, was not restored and may have suffered irretrievable damage by the dismissals of 1962.

The personification of a Government by the Prime Minister is also an uncertain asset. In March 1966 the size of the Labour Party's electoral victory could be attributed mainly to admiration of Harold Wilson's capacity to inspire confidence in his ability. The financial and economic crisis in the autumn of 1967 impaired the Prime Minister's personal credibility as an astute leader; his Government and his party might have suffered less in popular support if they had not been so closely identified with the qualities of their leader.

And so one soon arrives at the conclusion that few conclusions except the banal and platitudinous can be drawn from recent experience. The authority of a Prime Minister will depend mainly on such variables as the confidence and popularity he commands as a leader, his intellectual grasp of the problems of government, his tactical acumen, his performances as an orator and on the floor of the House of Commons, his ability to make quick and acceptable decisions and to carry his senior colleagues and his party with him, the stature of those colleagues (particularly as potential alternative Prime Ministers), the international climate, the state of the country's economy, sheer luck,[30] and the often fickle moods of public opinion ('It's time for a change'). In wartime the personal authority of a Prime Minister may be overwhelming, as it was under Lloyd George from 1916 to 1918 and under Churchill from 1940 to 1945; it was by no means overwhelming under Asquith from 1914 to 1916 or under Chamberlain from 1939 to 1940. One is tempted to assert that all generalizations are false, including, of course, the one just offered.

The effective power of the Prime Minister in relation to that of his ministerial colleagues has been greater in the period since 1945 than during the inter-war years. But this must not be exaggerated. The office of Prime Minister is largely what an incumbent wishes and is able to make of it. While Mrs Thatcher seems the personification of prime ministerial government, her successor may want (or be forced) to revert to more traditional understandings of collegiate Cabinet government. And no matter how versatile, energetic and able a Prime Minister may be, he can never be in a position to exercise close supervision over all the increasingly complex activities of the Departments, or indeed keep fully abreast of the technological and scientific developments with which their expert officials and advisers must be familiar. Coordination, supervision and the resolution of disagreements are achieved through inter-departmental committees, Cabinet committees and the Cabinet as a whole, as well as by the Prime Minister's informal rulings and by the machinery of the Cabinet Office.

Some of the propositions set out in the preceding sections must also be amplified or qualified. The Prime Minister does indeed control the

---

[30] Thus Macmillan's luck seemed to desert him from 1962, with security lapses, by-election reverses, his dismissal of seven Cabinet colleagues in a drastic purge (which was seen as a panic measure), the Profumo scandal (see p. 183) and his illness and resignation. Mr Callaghan's sureness of touch in dealing with the trade unions left him by the time of the 'winter of discontent' in 1978–9 – which cost Labour the 1979 General Election.

Cabinet's agenda, but in practice he will often find it imprudent and will sometimes find it impracticable to exclude discussion of a question which other Ministers regard as important. He decides when the Cabinet is to meet; he presides at meetings; he is not bound to defer to the opinion of a majority of the Cabinet on any given issue, but if he persists in bypassing or attempting to override a majority of his colleagues the Government will soon disintegrate through resignations,[31] and it is therefore in his interest to attempt by persuasion to establish a consensus in favour of his own views (if he had already formed a firm view) but not to press his colleagues too hard. The fact that by the act of resignation an individual Minister may consign himself to years in the political wilderness is not enough to encourage a Prime Minister to court mass resignations or a major revolt.

Again, it is sometimes said that the power of the Prime Minister (acquired since the First World War) to advise a dissolution of Parliament without the prior concurrence of his colleagues places in his hands an enormously potent weapon to subdue restiveness or crush rebellion within the ranks. Here analogies with nuclear weapons are relevant. They can be used, but the result is likely to be suicidal; hence threats to use them may not always be taken seriously. If the threat is carried out, the electorate may well turn away from a party in disarray and put the Opposition in office; a penal dissolution is apt to prove a boomerang and everybody knows this. This is not to say that an open threat by the Prime Minister to advise a dissolution will have no positive political impact whatsoever; but it does imply that the fairest comparison is with a threat by the Prime Minister to tender his Government's resignation. Dissent is better dealt with by bold leadership, or by accommodation and compromise, or, if necessary, by the dismissal of malcontents from the Government, or withdrawal of the party whip from backbench rebels, or simply by non-endorsement of a candidate at a General Election to be held at an indeterminate date; again, everybody knows this, and facts which everybody knows tend to condition political behaviour.

When one says that the Prime Minister controls the Cabinet Office, one is not asserting that this Office is merely his pliant instrument. The main constitutional function of the Office[32] is to provide a Secretariat for the Cabinet and its committees, distributing memoranda and agenda papers, recording proceedings and compiling and circulating

---

[31] On ministerial threats of resignation as a tactical weapon to influence government policy, see R. K. Alderman and J. A. Cross, *The Tactics of Resignation* (1967), ch. 2.

[32] See generally, R. K. Mosley, *The Story of the Cabinet Office* (1969).

minutes. Documents issued by the Secretariat go to departmental Ministers who are not members of the Cabinet. The work of the Secretariat therefore enables all Ministers to become better informed about major decisions and their factual background. This makes a Government more efficient, and incidentally justifies a reduction in the size of a Cabinet; it does not necessarily elevate the Prime Minister still higher above his colleagues, though it provides special briefs for the Prime Minister and helps him to follow up action taken in pursuance of decisions. The Cabinet Office, moreover, is not the Prime Minister's private office. It is staffed mainly by permanent civil servants, of whom a substantial proportion are officers of high seniority and standing; and the Secretary to the Cabinet, the head of this Office and just as independent as his colleagues, is possibly the most important member of the public service. Nevertheless, a Prime Minister's close personal relations with the Secretary to the Cabinet [33] will place him at an advantage in controlling the machinery of central government, and successive Prime Ministers have felt so well served by the Cabinet Office that they have seen no need to set up a Prime Minister's Department. [34] He will also have close relations with the head of the Policy Unit, which concentrates on economic, industrial and employment policy. [35]

The Prime Minister also has a small separate Private Office: this is also composed mainly of established civil servants, but it will naturally include persons whom the Prime Minister finds particularly congenial. There is also a separate Political Office, designed to keep him abreast of party feeling in the country as a whole; it is staffed by party workers. [36]

Cabinet committees and ministerial meetings

The Cabinet committee system is clearly of first-class importance in the

[33] Patrick Gordon Walker (*The Cabinet*, p. 55) comments that 'the Cabinet Secretary has become something like a Permanent Secretary to the Prime Minister'. Since 1981 he has also been Head of the Home Civil Service. Sir Robert Armstrong (1979–87) brought unprecedented publicity to the office during his evidence to the Defence Select Committee on the Westland affair in 1986 (on which see below, p. 295), and during his evidence before the Australian courts during the British Government's unsuccessful attempt to prevent the publication there of Peter Wright's *Spycatcher*.

[34] See, e.g., James Callaghan, *Time and Chance* (1987), p. 408.

[35] See Bernard Donoghue, *Prime Minister* (1987), pp. 19–25.

[36] For the roles of the Cabinet Office, Policy Unit, Private Office and Political Office in the 1974–9 Labour Government, see Bernard Donoghue, op. cit., pp. 16–37, James Callaghan, op. cit., pp. 403–8. On 1 March 1981 the Prime Minister's staff at 10 Downing Street numbered ninety-three, some of whom were part-time.

machinery of central government. But the secrecy enveloping this system is even harder to penetrate than the working of the Cabinet itself. In no official publication is there so much as a full list of these committees, let alone the names of their chairmen and members, a statement of their functions, or their relationships with the Cabinet as a whole.[37] When a Government has departed from the political scene, a fuller account of its committee system may become available;[38] contemporary details are rarely divulged. There have been two modern exceptions. It was made known at the time of the Falklands conflict in 1982 that military operations were being overseen by a Cabinet committee chaired by Mrs Thatcher and made up of four other Cabinet Ministers; it was popularly known as the War Cabinet. And in 1983 Mrs Thatcher confirmed the existence of four standing committees: the Defence and Overseas Policy Committee; the Economic Strategy Committee; the Home and Social Affairs Committee, and the Legislation Committee.[39]

A Cabinet committee properly so called is a committee of Ministers (and may include non-Cabinet Ministers), established by the Prime Minister and which has formal procedures and is serviced by the Cabinet Secretariat (but not having civil service members). Cabinet committees may be standing or *ad hoc*: the latter are set up to consider specific problems and are then dissolved. Mrs Thatcher, it has been estimated, has between thirty and thirty-five standing committees and, at any one time, some 120 *ad hoc* committees.[40] Many Cabinet committees are supported by a parallel official committee of senior civil servants belonging to the Departments most closely concerned. Some Prime Ministers (such as Mr Heath and Mr Callaghan) have also used on occasion mixed committees of Ministers and civil servants, in Mr Callaghan's case the main one being dubbed 'the seminar' on central economic questions.[41]

---

[37] The need for complete secrecy was justified by Sir Burke Trend, the Secretary to the Cabinet, giving evidence before the Franks Committee on Section 2 of the Official Secrets Act 1911 (Cmnd 5104 (1972), Minutes of Evidence, vol. 3, pp. 324–6) as being essential for the maintenance of collective responsibility for Cabinet decisions – a most unconvincing reason – and the prevention of leakages. cf. 'Whitehall's Needless Secrecy', *The Times*, 3 May 1973, naming sixteen committees.

[38] See Harold Wilson, *The Governance of Britain* (1976), pp. 62–8.

[39] See 45 H.C. Deb. *7–8* (written answers 4 July 1983). On Mrs Thatcher's Cabinet committees see Peter Hennessy, *Cabinet* (1986), pp. 100 3. For the Cabinet committee structure under Mr Callaghan see Bruce Page, *New Statesman*, 21 July 1978.

[40] Hennessy, ibid.

[41] See Donoghue, op. cit., pp. 101–2. A standing mixed committee is the Civil Contingencies Unit: see David Bonner, *Emergency Powers in Peacetime* (1985), pp. 28–32.

The use of Cabinet committees undoubtedly increases a Prime Minister's power over his colleagues. He chooses whether to establish a particular committee, what its terms of reference and membership are to be, who will be its chairman, whether any 'appeal' may be taken to the Cabinet against its decisions[42] and when to disband it. Moreover, the increased use of such committees has allowed the Prime Minister to summon the Cabinet to meet usually only once a week (compared with regular twice-weekly meetings up to the 1960s): there are thus fewer opportunities for Cabinet Ministers as a whole to raise and debate issues which the Prime Minister might prefer not to be raised. Mrs Thatcher has gone further and sometimes establishes decisions through informal meetings of Ministers, outside the formal Cabinet committee structure, made up of selected colleagues who are likely to further her preferred solutions.[43]

Confidentiality of proceedings and papers

The Cabinet and its committees must be able to deliberate in private and with some certainty that neither their proceedings nor their papers will subsequently be made public without their consent. The conventional reasons which ensure that Ministers themselves do not make unauthorized disclosures[44] stem from the tradition of secrecy in Westminster and Whitehall, loyalty to colleagues, a desire not to inhibit future discussion and the ultimate political threat – dismissal. There are also guidelines recommended by the Radcliffe Committee on Ministerial Memoirs[45] which require fifteen years to elapse before certain types of Cabinet material may be disclosed by former Ministers; not all ex-Ministers have, however, abided by them.[46] Now, Ministers still in office do not maintain a stony silence when they are not making official utterances: they leak information to journalists when it is in their interests to do so – for example, to distance themselves from an unpopular Government decision and to let their

[42] Mr Wilson gave Cabinet committees executive authority and only allowed 'appeals' with the consent of their chairmen: see Harold Wilson, op. cit., pp. 65–6.

[43] See Lord Hailsham (1987) 1 *Contemporary Record* 58; James Prior, op. cit., pp. 133–4.

[44] For the power of the courts to ensure confidentiality see *Att.-Gen.* v. *Jonathan Cape Ltd* [1976] Q.B. 752: see below, p. 190. Ministers cannot, it seems, be prosecuted under the Official Secrets Act 1911, s. 2 (on which see below, p. 493) because they may authorize themselves to disclose information: see Report of the Franks Committee on Section 2 of the Official Secrets Act 1911, Cmnd 5104 (1972), pp. 14–15.

[45] Cmnd 6386 (1976).

[46] Notably by Richard Crossman's literary executors in publishing his three-volume *Diaries of a Cabinet Minister*; by Barbara Castle, *The Castle Diaries 1974–1976* (1980), and Hugh Jenkins, *The Culture Gap* (1979).

supporters know their views.[47] Leaks by or on behalf of Ministers can make a nonsense of the confidentiality of Cabinet discussions, but at least the public is better informed than it would otherwise be.

Cabinet papers are Crown property, and so improper publication of them could be actionable as in breach of the Crown's copyright. Former Ministers who wish to refresh their memories from papers which they saw while in office may see them in the Cabinet Office where, on resignation, their papers are deposited. Access to one Government's papers by a successor Administration is governed by a number of understandings.[48] So, Ministers may not see the papers of a previous Government of a different party (because they might want to make party political capital out of them) unless the former Prime Minister of that Government agrees (or, if he is not available, the current Leader of the relevant party); they may see the papers of previous Administrations of their own party. Some papers deemed to be in the public domain, such as Ministers' letters to M.P.s, are freely available to former Ministers. These are sensible, workmanlike arrangements.

[47] See below, p. 189.
[48] See Lord Hunt of Tamworth [1982] *Public Law* 514.

Chapter 10

Ministers, Departments and Civil Servants

Central government

Ministers and Departments [1]

In 1989 there were twenty-two Cabinet Ministers and thirty full Ministers, as well as the four Law Officers of the Crown, who were not members of the Cabinet. In addition, there were over fifty junior Ministers – parliamentary under-secretaries of state,[2] parliamentary secretaries, financial secretaries, Government whips,[3] and the like. In short, the Ministry numbered over one hundred. A large majority of those full Ministers who sat in the Commons had unpaid back-bench M.P.s as their parliamentary private secretaries. All but thirteen of the senior Ministers were members of the Commons. About a fifth of the membership of the House of Commons consisted of members of the Government or M.P.s closely associated with the work of Ministers, though the maximum number of holders of paid ministerial offices, who may sit and vote in the House, is fixed by statute at ninety-five.[4] Yet in 1914 when the Government had already begun to assume responsibility for providing minimum standards of social welfare, the number of senior ministerial offices, excluding the Law Officers, was

[1] See Rodney Brazier, *Constitutional Practice* (1988), ch. 7.

[2] If the Minister in charge of a Department is a Secretary of State.

[3] Government whips have various designations. The Government Chief Whip in the House of Commons is the Parliamentary Secretary to the Treasury. Other Government whips in the Commons hold nominal offices in the Royal Household or are styled Junior Lords of the Treasury or merely Assistant Whips. In the Lords all Government whips hold nominal offices connected with the Royal Household.

[4] House of Commons Disqualification Act 1975, s. 2(1). The maximum numbers of holders of various classes of political offices to whom salaries may be paid are also fixed by statute: Ministerial and other Salaries Act 1975, s. 1 and sched. 1.

only twenty-one. The big increase since that time is attributable to a large expansion in the function and activity of central government.

It cannot be said that there have been changes of high constitutional importance in the machinery of central government during the last few years. The most interesting development has probably been the evolution of five very large Departments – the Ministry of Defence; the Foreign and Commonwealth Office; the Department of Health and Social Security; the Department of the Environment; the Department of Trade and Industry. In 1970 the powers formerly exercised by three separate Ministers (Housing and Local Government; Transport; Public Building and Works) were vested in a Secretary of State for the Environment. The Ministry of Technology and the Board of Trade were absorbed by a Department of Trade and Industry. In 1976 Mr Callaghan decided that the Department of the Environment was too cumbersome and created a Secretary of State for Transport, removing transport responsibilities from Environment. Similarly, Mrs Thatcher split the DHSS into a Department of Health and a Department of Social Security in 1988.

A second feature, of longer standing, is the large number of full Ministers not in charge of Departments. This is attributable partly to the extensive involvement of central government in economic and social affairs, and partly to the need for having full Ministers available for the conduct of discussions and negotiations outside England or with national interest groups. In 1989, twenty-five of these 'deputy' ministers were styled Ministers of State.

Departments and other agencies

Under the British system of government it is expected that there shall be a Minister politically accountable for the more controversial acts of central government agencies. Political accountability cannot readily be achieved unless the activity is carried on by a Department or Office directly headed by a Minister.

This general proposition needs to be qualified. Although the prospects for taking major government activities 'out of politics' are limited, the allocation of government functions to largely autonomous bodies has become an important feature of public administration in Britain today. None of the remaining nationalized industries is run by a government Department, though Ministers retain a restricted range of powers and duties in relation to them.[5] Then there are miscellaneous other bodies

[5] See ch. 12.

performing what can broadly be described as functions of central government but lying outside the reach of detailed ministerial control. Most of them are statutory creations, but a few are non-statutory; some are incorporated, some are not; their sources of revenue are various; none is headed by civil servants, but some are staffed by them; some have executive powers, some are merely advisory, some are both; there is no common pattern. Their powers may involve the provision of a public service (for example, the British Broadcasting Corporation, the Commonwealth War Graves Commission, the Forestry Commission, the National Museums and Art Galleries), the regulation or management of a public service (for example, the Independent Broadcasting Authority, the Countryside Commission), or the regulation or promotion of private and public activity (for example, the Civil Aviation Authority, the Commission for Racial Equality, the Development Commission, the Arts Council, the various agricultural and horticultural marketing boards, the Advisory, Conciliation and Arbitration Service, the National Research Development Corporation, the British Tourist Authority). The functions of the British Council, which is not a government Department – its officers and servants are not civil servants – range over all these fields and are also advisory.

Then there is an assortment of bodies staffed mainly or entirely by civil servants but without any ministerial head, though a Minister is answerable in Parliament for some or all of their activities.[6] They have been kept at arm's length from the principal Departments for a variety of reasons: because they perform specialized functions which are not likely to be politically controversial; because some of these functions ought not to be the subject of political controversy (for example, because they are judicial or analogous to the judicial); or because the organ was originally created outside the framework of a political Department and there has never been a sufficiently strong reason for bringing it within one. Some are so closely associated with a political Department that they are in effect sub-departments, for example, the Board of Inland Revenue, the Board of Customs and Excise, the Export Credits Guarantee Department, and the Intervention Board for Agricultural Produce, the Government Actuary's Department, the Royal Mint, the

---

[6] Thus, the Chancellor of the Exchequer answers a question in the House of Commons in connection with Her Majesty's Stationery Office, the Central Office of Information, the Treasury Solicitor, the Department of the Government Actuary, the Royal Mint and the National Debt Office; the Meteorological Office is answered for by the Secretary of State for Defence, the General Register Office by the Secretary of State for Social Services; the Secretary of State for the Environment answers for the Ordnance Survey. The Lord Chancellor answers in the Lords for the Land Registry and the Public Record Office.

National Debt Office, and the Treasury Solicitor's Office. Others, to which a separate Supply vote may be allocated in the Civil Estimates,[7] are more loosely associated with political Departments – for example, the Central Office of Information, Her Majesty's Stationery Office, the Charity Commission, the Crown Estate Office, the Registry of Friendly Societies, the Public Works Loan Board, the Land Registry, the Ordnance Survey, the Meteorological Office, the Public Record Office, the Registrar General's Office.

Whether every one of the bodies listed in the latter group is properly to be described as a government Department is questionable. There is no recognized definition of a government Department; normally it is understood to mean a central government body staffed by civil servants and receiving its funds directly out of moneys provided by Parliament,[8] but anomalies abound; the 'rich Byzantine structure'[9] of British central government is nowhere more apparent than in these twilight zones.

The National Economic Development Council and the Development Commission are undoubtedly instruments of central government policy, but their functions are advisory, their membership is partly or wholly non-official and they would not ordinarily be thought of as government Departments. The Law Commissions also owe their existence to an act of policy; but their chairmen are superior judges and their members, though salaried, are entirely independent of the Government, and their functions are also advisory; probably they should no more be regarded as government Departments than the Council on Tribunals.

Government Departments dealing with domestic affairs make use of a great number of standing advisory committees and councils composed of outside experts or representatives of interest groups. Occasionally, the functions of such a committee (for example, the Social Security Advisory Committee) are prescribed by statute; usually the committee rests on a less formal basis. At a more exalted level, there are the advisory councils concerned with government-sponsored research:[10] the Medical, Agricultural, Science, Economic and Social Science and Natural Environment Research Councils. A full description of the machinery of central government would require an account of the functions exercised by these multifarious ancillary bodies.

[7] This feature is, however, inconclusive of status. For example, there is a separate vote for the British Council.

[8] W. J. M. Mackenzie and J. W. Grove, *Central Administration in Britain* (1957), pp. 183–4; see also Sir Ivor Jennings, *Cabinet Government* (3rd edn, 1959), ch. 4. Schedule 2 to the Parliamentary Commissioner Act 1967 lists government Departments and other authorities subject to investigation, without distinguishing the one group from the other.

[9] Brian Chapman, *British Government Observed* (1963), p. 18.

[10] cf. Science and Technology Act 1965.

Matters historical and legal[11]

Of the modern ministerial offices, a few, such as those of Lord Chancellor, Lord President of the Council, Chancellor of the Duchy of Lancaster and Lord Privy Seal, are traceable to the Tudor period and even earlier. The office of Secretary of State developed from a secretarial office in the royal household and became, in the seventeenth century, an important ministerial post. In Charles II's time there were two Secretaries of State; by 1784 there were three; the numbers increased as the functions of government extended and became more complex, and today there are fourteen.[12] Their individual responsibilities are seldom prescribed by statute, and indeed where powers and duties are conferred by legislation on 'a' or 'the' Secretary of State, the function could, as a matter of strict law, be exercised by any of the Secretaries of State unless one is specifically designated by the Act or Order.

The office of Chancellor of the Exchequer is less ancient; the Lord High Treasurer[13] was a high officer of State in Tudor times and before, but the office was put into commission and discharged by a board composed of Lords Commissioners of the Treasury in 1714. The Board never meets, but the First Lord of the Treasury is now invariably the Prime Minister, and the second Lord, in charge of the Treasury, the principal Department of State, is the Chancellor of the Exchequer; the Junior Lords sign formal Treasury warrants, but their main function is to act as Government whips in the Commons. Several of the surviving medieval offices of the Royal Household are occupied by Government whips in the Lords.

The existence of some ministerial offices (for example, Lord Chancellor, Secretary of State) is derived from the prerogative, but statutory functions can be assigned to a prerogative office-holder. The majority of ministerial offices have been established by legislation. The Minister is created a corporation sole, given a seal of office and entrusted with a loosely defined range of functions which can be supplemented by other statutes and statutory instruments. In general, legislation recognizes the Minister, not his Department; and acts done by departmental officials will be performed in the Minister's name. Under the Ministers of the Crown Act 1975, functions may be transferred by Order in Council from one Minister to another, the designations of Ministers may be

[11] See Brazier, ibid.
[12] The maximum number cannot, in practice, exceed twenty-one: Ministerial and other Salaries Act 1975, Sched. 1, Part V.
[13] Mackenzie and Grove, op. cit., pp. 167–70.

altered, and Ministers and their Departments may be similarly wound up. In order to create a ministerial office with entirely new executive functions, an Act of Parliament is required unless the office is that of a Secretary of State. All Ministers hold office during Her Majesty's pleasure and are removable, by convention, on the advice of the Prime Minister.

Within the general framework of the principle that a Minister must not allow a conflict to develop between his public responsibilities and his private interests, detailed rules and criteria had been laid down by Prime Ministers limiting the permissible range of private activities of members of a Government.[14] For example, Ministers must not hold directorships in public companies or engage in speculative investments in respect of which information acquired in their official capacities might be beneficial; though they are not required to dispose of all private shareholdings. Association with non-profit-making organizations may also be incompatible with the discharge of ministerial duties. The principles are flexible enough to accommodate special cases when it appears to the Prime Minister expedient to do so. When Mr Frank Cousins became Minister of Technology in 1964 he was allowed to retain the office of General Secretary of the Transport and General Workers' Union on indefinite leave; on his resignation from ministerial office in 1966 he resumed his activities as union secretary.

Ministerial responsibility [15]

That Ministers are 'collectively responsible' is an undoubted constitutional convention. But what does collective responsibility signify? In many of the newly independent Commonwealth countries British conventions have been spelt out in some detail, often with modifications, in the texts of the constitutions. On Cabinet responsibility, Barbados is nevertheless laconic. 'The Cabinet shall be the principal instrument of policy and shall be charged with the general direction and control of the government of Barbados and shall be collectively responsible therefor to Parliament.'[16] It is wise not to attempt to define in a constitutional document what exactly collective responsibility means, because the outlines of the concept are so vague and blurred. It can be described at a high level of generality; it can be illustrated by specific examples; a

---

[14] The rules are set out in *Questions of Procedure for Ministers*, a copy of which is given to each new Minister.
[15] See Brazier, ibid.
[16] Barbados Independence Order 1966 (S.I. 1966, No. 1455), Schedule, s. 64(2).

182   *The Executive*

neat but comprehensive set of propositions cannot be devised, if only because the gulf between traditional constitutional theory (to which lip-service may still be paid) and political practice yawns so widely.

Responsible for what and to whom? And what exactly do we mean by 'responsible'? Does the substitution of words like 'accountable' or 'answerable' clarify the issues at all?[17] Perhaps it is more helpful to begin with the concept of the *individual responsibility* of Ministers, which raises some of the questions in a still more difficult way. Historically, moreover, the principle of individual ministerial responsibility preceded the doctrine of collective responsibility.

All Ministers, whether they be in or outside the Cabinet, are responsible for their personal acts, the general conduct of their Departments and acts done (or left undone) in their name by their departmental officials. Responsibility may be political, legal, or both political and legal; and the meaning of responsibility, and the persons or bodies to whom it is owed, will vary according to the context.

Ministers are legally responsible in their private capacities for acts which they order or authorize to be done, or in which they actively participate. If, for example, such an act proves to be a trespass, the Minister can be sued personally for damages as a tortfeasor. To Dicey, the personal liability of Ministers and officials for civil wrongs before the ordinary courts applying the ordinary law of the land, subject to any special statutory powers that might be vested in them to encroach on private rights, was a cardinal feature of the rule of law in Britain. Today this aspect of ministerial responsibility is of little practical importance, for since 1947 it has been possible to sue the Crown as the Minister's employer for torts committed in the purported exercise of legal powers and duties.

Ministers are legally and politically responsible for formal acts done by the monarch, under prerogative or statutory powers, in which they have participated by virtue of their attendance at a meeting of the Privy Council, or their countersignature of the royal sign manual or their custody of a royal seal. The strictly legal rationale of these customary procedures has now disappeared.

Ministers are politically answerable in respect of matters lying within their statutory or conventional fields of responsibility. They are responsible not only for their personal acts but for the conduct of their

[17] cf. Geoffrey Marshall and G. C. Moodie, *Some Problems of the Constitution* (5th edn, 1971); John P. Mackintosh, *The British Cabinet* (3rd edn, 1977); D. N. Chester and Nona Bowring, *Questions in Parliament* (1962), Appendix 2; Henry Parris, *Constitutional Bureaucracy* (1969), chs 3, 4, 10.

Departments. The area of statutory responsibility is determined by the legislation (if any) establishing their offices and particular Acts and subordinate legislative instruments endowing them with powers and duties. If a Minister has no power or duty to take any action with regard to a matter, he cannot properly be left accountable to Parliament for what is done or left undone; hence, a Minister is not expected to answer parliamentary questions about the day-to-day administration of nationalized industries[18] and many other public corporations, or most of the activities of local government authorities or the police.[19] To some Ministers powers and duties are assigned by convention – for example, to the Secretary of State for Foreign and Commonwealth Affairs, most of whose functions are non-statutory; to the Home Secretary in respect of advice on the exercise of the prerogative of pardon; to the Attorney-General in respect of decisions whether to enter a *nolle prosequi* to stop a trial on indictment. The conventions may, like those just referred to, be well established, surviving changes of government; or they may be the product of an informal re-allocation by the Prime Minister of responsibilities among his Ministers, especially Ministers such as the Lord President of the Council, the Lord Privy Seal, the Chancellor of the Duchy of Lancaster and the Paymaster-General, whose formal departmental functions are small or nominal.

The meaning of political responsibility cannot be precisely defined. If a Minister is personally blameworthy, he ought to make a public admission of his responsibility. Personal culpability may be attributable to private or public conduct unbecoming to a Minister of the Crown, in which case there will be an expectation that he will resign;[20] or to bad judgement or departmental maladministration, in which case there cannot be said to be any clear-cut convention about a duty to offer resignation.[21] Unless the Prime Minister is unwilling to stand by the

[18] But see p. 222.
[19] See ch. 20.
[20] Mr Parkinson resigned in 1983 when it became known that a woman who was not his wife was expecting his child. He was reappointed to the Cabinet in 1987. Earl Jellicoe and Mr Lambton resigned in 1973 following revelations that they had been associating with prostitutes. Mr John Profumo resigned in 1963 after it was revealed that he had made a false statement to the House of Commons in rebuttal of allegations about his private life. For a list of resignations this century and notes on the reasons, see David Butler and Gareth Butler, *British Political Facts 1900–1985* (6th edn, 1986), pp. 85–7.
[21] The Foreign Secretary, Lord Carrington, and two other Foreign and Commonwealth Office Ministers felt compelled to leave office in 1982 after the Argentinian invasion of the Falkland Islands because they believed that their department had not adequately assessed Argentina's intentions. See also Finer (1956) 34 *Public Administration* 377; Madgwick (1966–7) 20 *Parliamentary Affairs* 59; R. K. Alderman and J. A. Cross, *The Tactics of Resignation* (1967).

Minister under attack – and in this context the personal authority of a Prime Minister is of great importance – a Minister may choose, and has not infrequently chosen in recent years, to brazen out appalling indiscretions, gross errors and omissions, plans gone awry and revelations of disastrous mismanagement within his Department. If the Opposition is allowed time to move a vote of censure, or if an Opposition Day is selected for the purpose of moving a motion to reduce the Minister's salary, the Minister can confidently expect to emerge triumphant in the division lobbies, with members voting strictly along party lines. Yet his victory may prove to be Pyrrhic and ephemeral. The Prime Minister may shift him to another office carrying less prestige in the next ministerial reshuffle; he may 'kick him upstairs' to the Lords; he may quietly call for the Minister's resignation at a moment less embarrassing for the Government, or gratefully accept a half-hearted offer of resignation if it comes. A Minister who is incapable of explaining and justifying his conduct of affairs persuasively in the face of a hostile Opposition, or to the satisfaction of his own backbenchers, is a liability to the Government and the party. So Mr Leon Brittan had to resign in 1986 following the improper leaking of a Law Officer's letter with Mr Brittan's approval by a civil servant in his Department during the Westland affair.[22]

Given that the idea of ministerial culpability for personal failings is so shapeless, a detailed analysis of *degrees* of ministerial responsibility for the conduct of departmental affairs and officials would not be very helpful. A Minister is expected to answer questions about these matters in Parliament unless the question must be disallowed by parliamentary practice (for example, because it deals with an issue *sub judice*) or unless the Minister feels bound to refuse an answer or a full answer on grounds of national security, in which case he will have to face the prospect of personal criticism.[23] In answering questions or in replying to a debate, he cannot be expected to accept that he is himself culpable whenever a departmental official has committed a dishonest act or has disobeyed instructions or exceeded his authority. He is entitled to explain in public what has occurred; but he cannot totally absolve himself of responsibility. To use a colloquialism which, eluding exact definition, is still well understood, he must, in the last resort, 'carry the

---

[22] On Westland, see below, p. 188.
[23] For a list of matters on which successive Ministers have refused to answer questions, either for reasons of public interest or because they lie outside the field of ministerial responsibility, see *Report of the Select Committee on Parliamentary Questions* (H.C. 393 (1971–2), pp. 114–17).

can'.[24] If maladministration within his Department is attributable to bad organization or procedures or defective supervision, or exists on such a large scale or at so high a level that he ought to have been able to prevent it, then he is in some degree blameworthy.[25] But Sir Thomas Dugdale's personal decision to resign as Minister of Agriculture in 1954 because of the exposure of maladministration by senior officials in the over-celebrated Crichel Down affair[26] was not demanded by convention; certainly other Ministers have not sought to emulate him by exacting the supreme political penalty on themselves, and it would be unrealistic to expect them to do so, particularly if wide decision-making powers have been delegated to the official concerned.[27] The further the Minister was, geographically or hierarchically, from the events complained of, the less he will generally be expected to take the blame for them and resign. So Mr Lennox-Boyd did not resign as Colonial Secretary in 1959 after fifty-two people had been killed by the security forces in Nyasaland,[28] nor did Mr Whitelaw as Home Secretary in 1982 after an intruder had confronted the Queen in her bedroom, nor did Mr Prior as Northern Ireland Secretary after a mass prison escape in Northern Ireland.[29]

The political answerability of Ministers has helped to preserve the impartiality and anonymity of civil servants; they have been reasonably secure from public censure and, therefore, find it easier to give unstinted loyalty to a succession of political masters. But official anonymity has not been an unmixed blessing; and, as the Fulton Committee on the civil service pointed out,[30] it is gradually being eroded. It is being eroded, in particular, by the activities of departmental select committees of the House of Commons[31] and the Parliamentary

---

[24] cf. the Report of the Parker Committee on the Use of Authorized Procedures for Interrogation of Persons Suspected of Terrorism in Northern Ireland (Cmnd 4901 (1972)), indicating that the unlawful practices adopted had never in fact been authorized by a Minister and may not have even been known to Ministers. They were nevertheless politically answerable for the conduct of the security forces.

[25] cf. the slightly different formulation by the then Home Secretary, Sir David Maxwell Fyfe, in 530 H.C. Deb. 1285–8 (20 July 1954), quoted in Geoffrey Wilson, *Cases and Materials on Constitutional and Administrative Law* (2nd edn, 1976), pp. 162–4.

[26] Cmnd 9176 (1953); Cmnd 9220 (1957); Geoffrey Marshall, *Constitutional Conventions* (1984), p. 66; J. A. G. Griffith (1955) 18 *Mod. L. Rev.* 557, (1987) 1 *Contemporary Record* 35. Dugdale was later elevated to the peerage as Lord Crathorne.

[27] As in the Vehicle and General affair; note 34.

[28] See Harold Macmillan, *Riding the Storm* (1971), pp. 733–8.

[29] Mr Prior's offered resignation was refused by Mrs Thatcher: see James Prior, *A Balance of Power* (1986), p. 232.

[30] Cmnd 3638 (1968), vol. 1, p. 33.

[31] See ch. 15.

Commissioner for Administration[32] (the Ombudsman). The Parliamentary Commissioner not only scrutinizes departmental procedures but has, on rare occasions, singled out identifiable civil servants for criticism.[33] He has yet to go as far as the judicial tribunal of inquiry on the collapse of the Vehicle and General Insurance Co. (1972), which affixed blame on a named senior civil servant in the Department of Trade and Industry for failing to set in motion an investigation of the Company's affairs, but exonerated the responsible Ministers.[34] If this type of inquisition were to become frequent, it would be impossible to expect civil servants not to answer back. Nevertheless, ministerial responsibility remains as a protective, if slightly tattered, cloak for the civil service, and at least no serious complaint of political partisanship against senior civil servants has yet been substantiated.

The *collective responsibility* of Ministers to the House of Commons is still sometimes spoken of as a democratic bulwark of the British constitution. After all, did not five Governments resign between the years 1852 and 1859 as a result of being defeated on votes of confidence in the House?[35] (True, democracy was then a pejorative term, but who cares?) Rather more to the point is that only two Governments, both in a minority in the Commons, have lost the confidence of that House since 1924. In that year Ramsay MacDonald's first Labour Government found itself deserted by its Liberal allies. Mr Callaghan, who took over a tiny Labour majority on Mr Wilson's retirement in 1976, lost his majority through by-election defeats and defections; and his Government was defeated on a Conservative motion of no confidence in 1979.[36] But the very unusual parliamentary background to these defeats must be stressed: both were *minority* Governments – an extremely rare phenomenon in modern British constitutional history. On several occasions since 1945, Governments have been defeated in the House on particular issues because their whips have been out-manoeuvred by the Opposition or because of absenteeism. The Government has then usually mustered in its full resources and procured a reversal of the vote. There has been no other defeat on an unequivocal

---

[32] See ch. 33.

[33] See, for example, H.C. 316 (1968–9) (*Third Report of the Parliamentary Commissioner for the Session 1968–9*).

[34] H.C. 133 (1971–2); the report was debated in 835 H.C. Deb. 33–161 (1 May 1972). There was much criticism that the civil servant concerned had not been granted adequate facilities to defend himself before the tribunal of inquiry.

[35] Particulars are supplied by Jennings, *Cabinet Government* (3rd edn, 1959), pp. 512–15.

[36] See above, pp. 62–3.

issue of confidence,[37] such as the budget resolutions or the address in reply to the Queen's speech at the opening of a session. Mr Harold Wilson was able to sustain himself in office from 1964 to 1966 with a majority of less than six; and he then won a handsome victory at a General Election held at the most advantageous moment for his party. And again the Labour Government of March to October 1974 survived without a majority, and, after the October 1974 Election, continued at first with a tiny, then without, a majority – although a number of defeats were sustained. That Government's success in the Commons until it was driven to the country in 1979 was partly the result of the pact which it concluded with the Liberals in March 1977 and which continued until the end of the 1977–8 parliamentary session. In return for Liberal votes 'in the pursuit of economic recovery' the Government gave various undertakings about Government policy to Liberal M.P.s.[38] To go further back, Neville Chamberlain, on the other hand, decided to resign after a vote in the House on a motion of censure in May 1940; but the motion was defeated by eighty-one votes. It is a nice question which was the more significant fact – that he retained a substantial parliamentary majority after having forfeited the confidence of the general public, or that thirty-three Conservatives voted against their own leader and eighty others abstained.

Because a Government must maintain a majority in the House of Commons as a condition of survival – it can ignore defeats in the Lords – it has to ensure party solidarity. Doubtless this reduces the results of most of the contentious debates in the House to foregone conclusions; but a Government which is driven to rely on disciplinary sanctions and threats of sanctions, and an autocratic disregard of the interests of the Opposition and private members generally in the allocation of parliamentary time, is not going to endear itself to the electorate. The fact that the executive branch is parliamentary has an influence, which cannot be quantified, on the style of British politics.

Collective responsibility also implies that all Cabinet Ministers assume responsibility for Cabinet decisions and action taken to implement those decisions. A Minister may disagree with a decision[39] or with the manner of its implementation, but if he wishes to express

[37] There is no formal definition of a matter of confidence. If a Government explicitly states that it regards a vote as one of confidence, or if the Opposition has moved a motion of no confidence, the Government must, of course, stand or fall by the result.

[38] See Alistair Michie and Simon Hoggart, *The Pact* (1978), and David Steel, *A House Divided* (1980).

[39] But the practice of having his dissent recorded in the minutes was ended in 1964: see Harold Wilson, *The Governance of Britain* (1976), pp. 58–9.

dissent in public he should first resign. The Westland affair[40] is instructive. The Westland company supplied helicopters to the Ministry of Defence; and by 1985 urgently needed financial reconstruction. Two rival packages were on offer, one emanating from the United States, the other from a European consortium. Mr Michael Heseltine (the Defence Secretary) preferred the European option, while Mr Leon Brittan (the Trade and Industry Secretary) and perhaps the Prime Minister as well favoured the other. The Cabinet as a whole was supposed to be neutral as between the competing offers. At a Cabinet meeting in January 1986 it was agreed that, to prevent Ministers from speaking with different voices on the issue, all further ministerial statements on Westland would be cleared by the Cabinet Office. Mr Heseltine considered this to be an attempt at censorship by the Prime Minister which he could not accept; he also thought that Mrs Thatcher had unilaterally cancelled an arranged Cabinet committee meeting on Westland, and that both these events showed that the Cabinet government system was breaking down.[41] He therefore resigned.

A number of points need to be added to explain and qualify the obligation of public unanimity which flows from the doctrine of collective responsibility.

1   The convention of public unanimity is settled, at least to the extent that it will be regarded as constitutionally improper for a Minister to remain in office if he has overtly dissociated himself from Cabinet policy. It is open to the Prime Minister to condone a verbal indiscretion by a colleague, and even to overlook a studied refusal by a colleague to offer positive commendation of a policy which he dislikes, though the line between half-hearted formal acquiescence and hints of real disagreement may wear thin. Mr Peter Walker has been said to make some extra-parliamentary speeches in such a way as to make clear his lukewarm approval of Mrs Thatcher's economic policies, despite being a Cabinet Minister since 1979. During the 1974–9 Labour Governments some Cabinet Ministers, notably but not only Mr Tony Benn, came very close to public dissociation from Government policy. Mr Wilson had to issue a not wholly successful minute to Ministers reminding them of the doctrine of collective Cabinet responsibility. In this century the

---

[40] On which see Marshall [1986] *Public Law* 184; M. Linklater and D. Leigh, *Not With Honour* (1986); Defence Select Committee, H.C. 519 (1985–6); Cmnd 9916 (1986); H.C. 92 (1985–6); Cmnd 9841 (1986).

[41] See his account in *The Observer*, 12 January 1986.

convention has been expressly waived three times. In 1975 that convention, in so far as it required Ministers not to disagree with Cabinet decisions in public, was waived by the Cabinet to allow those Ministers who disagreed to say in public, but outside Parliament, that they dissented from the Cabinet's recommendation that the electorate should vote to remain in the EEC in the referendum held under the Referendum Act of that year. Once the referendum result was announced, full collective responsibility was restored. Secondly, the doctrine was waived on an *ad hoc* basis, for the purposes of what became the European Parliament Elections Act 1978, because of the deep divisions in the Labour Cabinet and parliamentary party over direct elections to the European Parliament. Indeed, the Prime Minister, Mr Callaghan, was moved to remark that '. . . I certainly think that the doctrine should apply, except in cases where I announce that it does not.'[42] Both of those suspensions were a success for the Prime Ministers concerned. But the third, and earlier, experiment adopted by the 'National' Government in 1932 over its protectionist policies, and which was intended to allow the coalition parties to 'agree to differ' indefinitely, failed after only a few months.[43] Such experiments are obviously rare and, despite occasional deviations from the norm, the general principle stated above is clear.

2 Public unanimity conforms to expectations of the electorate (which frowns upon a Government in disarray) and strengthens the hands of a Government in relation to its own backbench dissenters, the Opposition and political commentators, all of whom are alert to any suspicion of discord within the Cabinet. But from time to time, when a Minister finds the strains of maintaining a tight-lipped silence insupportable, he will deliberately 'leak' his 'unattributable' private views to a journalist. Leaking is resorted to by Ministers – and the Prime Minister – to fortify or explain their positions. Unprecedented leaking took place during the Westland affair. Political correspondents at Westminster receive daily 'briefings on Lobby terms' from the Prime Minister's Press Secretary; in return for the information divulged those terms require that the exact source not be identified.[44] Such 'briefing' is said to involve the

---

[42] 933 II.C. Deb. *552* (16 June 1977).
[43] See David Marquand, *Ramsay MacDonald* (1977), ch. 28.
[44] Now well documented. See Jeremy Tunstall, *The Westminster Lobby Correspondents* (1970); Patrick Gordon Walker, *The Cabinet* (1972 edn), pp. 26–33; Michael Cockerell *et al.*, *Sources Close to the Prime Minister* (1984).

authorized disclosure of information, but the distinction between such 'briefing' and 'leaking' may be too subtle for most of us.[45] Leaking and briefing remain essential to the maintenance of collective responsibility, and are underpinned by the symbiotic relationship between leaker and journalist.

3   The obligation to preserve an outward show of unanimity about past decisions is supposed to continue after the Government, or the Minister who had been placed in a minority, has left office. But the force of this obligation is very weak.

(*a*) If a Minister has decided to resign because of disagreement on a policy issue[46] he is customarily allowed to publish the nature of the disagreement in his letter of resignation and to make a resignation speech in Parliament if he so wishes.

The general principle is that disclosures of Cabinet discussions or decisions by former Ministers are permissible only with the Sovereign's consent, communicated by the Prime Minister of the day through the medium of the Cabinet Office.[47] The national interest, and the interest in encouraging the utmost frankness in Cabinet discussions leading up to a policy decision, will sometimes be prejudiced if it is thought that Ministers will be at liberty to rush into print or be propelled on to the television screen with their memoirs and reminiscences as soon as they leave office. Yet over the years, and particularly since 1970, ex-Ministers have disclosed with impunity Cabinet discussions and disagreements; the general principle has now been tested in the courts and found wanting. Mr Richard Crossman held various Cabinet posts in the Labour Governments of 1964–70. He kept detailed diaries of his life and work as a Minister. After he left office the *Sunday Times* wanted to serialize them, and after his death in 1974 his literary executors wished to publish them in book form. The Secretary to the Cabinet was not satisfied by the cuts which they were prepared to make, so the Attorney-General brought an action against the newspaper, the executors and the book publishers seeking a permanent injunction to prevent such publication. He relied on both the confidential nature of the materials, which flowed from the convention of

---

[45] cf. Mr James Callaghan, giving evidence to the Franks Committee on Official Secrecy: 'You know the difference between leaking and briefing. Briefing is what I do and leaking is what you do' (Cmnd 5104 (1972), vol. 4, p. 187).

[46] See Alderman and Cross, op. cit., Appendix. For examples, see Butler and Butler, ibid.

[47] It may be doubted whether ex-Ministers invariably still obtain such clearance for their resignation statements: see Brazier, op. cit., p. 74.

collective Cabinet responsibility, and also on the argument that free discussion in future Cabinets would be inhibited if the materials were published in a way which disclosed the attitudes and views of individual Ministers – and civil servants. The Attorney-General did *not* rely on Mr Crossman's oath as a Privy Councillor or on the Official Secrets Acts (both of which had previously been assumed to buttress the secrecy of Cabinet discussions and to form the bases of the vetting procedure). The injunctions were refused.[48]

The Lord Chief Justice held that the courts indeed have the power to prevent publication of Cabinet material if such publication (i) would be a breach of confidence and (ii) would be against the public interest in prejudicing the maintenance of the doctrine of collective responsibility. However, there would, in his Lordship's view, come a time when the confidential nature of the material ceased to exist, such time depending on the circumstances of each case; as nearly ten years had elapsed since the events contained in the first volume of the diaries, publication could not prejudice the doctrine of collective responsibility in the 1975 Cabinet – despite the fact that many of its members had sat in the Cabinet with Mr Crossman. Only time and the literary efforts of ex-Ministers (and ex-Prime Ministers?) will show where this case leaves the 'convention' of collective responsibility.[49]

(*b*) The convention (such as it is) extends to decisions of which a Minister was not aware at the time but to which he subsequently gave his tacit approval by continuing in office with full knowledge of the facts. But here the force of the convention is even weaker. One can hardly expect a Minister to accept the same degree of responsibility for a decision in which he had no opportunity to participate as for a decision where he had such an opportunity.

(*c*) For this reason the *ex post facto* responsibility of non-Cabinet Ministers for Cabinet decisions is not at all clear-cut, unless the Minister concerned was a member of a Cabinet committee which took or recommended the actual decision. Criticism of a Cabinet decision by the Minister after his departure from office may be

---

[48] *Att.-Gen.* v. *Jonathan Cape Ltd and others, Att.-General* v. *Times Newspapers Ltd* [1976] Q.B. 752. The report of the case also provides fascinating details about the vetting procedure and the role of the Secretary to the Cabinet in it, on which also see Cmnd 5104 (1972), vol. 3, pp. 330–32.

[49] For the sequel see the Radcliffe Report on Ministerial Memoirs, Cmnd 6386 (1976), which, among other things, recommended that fifteen years should elapse before certain types of material should be published by former Ministers. The Report was accepted by the Prime Minister. See further, Wright (1977) 30 *Parliamentary Affairs* 293; Hugo Young, *The Crossman Affair* (1976); Barbara Castle, *The Castle Diaries 1974–1976* (1980).

condoned, if he learned of it only when Cabinet minutes were circulated to him; it ought to be excused if the decision was never brought to his notice at all.

4   Nevertheless, a non-Cabinet Minister will not be allowed to express public disagreement with government policy and remain in office, unless it is expedient for the Prime Minister to overlook the transgression; for a transgression it is. The practice followed in Attlee's government after 1945 was instructive. The Government Chief Whip in the House of Lords described the Government handling of a dock labour dispute as 'absolutely crazy'; out he went. The Parliamentary Secretary to the Ministry of Agriculture did not survive his public criticism of the Government's 'feather-bedding' of farmers. And out went a group of parliamentary private secretaries (not even Ministers, but unpaid aides to individual Ministers) who failed to support the Government in an important division on the Ireland Bill which recognized (*inter alia*) the continued partition of Ireland. Such an involvement of non-Cabinet Ministers in the consequences of the doctrine of collective responsibility has been followed by all Prime Ministers since Attlee.

5   Just as Ministers are expected to be loyal to their colleagues, so they can reasonably claim to be entitled to the loyalty of their colleagues if they run into public criticism in implementing agreed Cabinet policies. If they implement them badly, or if they incur criticism as a result of purely departmental failings or indications of personal ineptitude, they will not have any corresponding claim to corporate solidarity. In 1935, the Foreign Secretary, Sir Samuel Hoare, exceeded his mandate by concurring in an agreement that would have given the Italian invaders of Abyssinia a slice of that country. The Cabinet would have repudiated Hoare but decided to stand by him. When the terms of the agreement were published, a national outcry arose. In an attempt to retrieve its reputation, the Cabinet then insisted on Hoare's resignation. In the circumstances this was a clear breach of convention. Hoare was duly rewarded for allowing himself to be sacrificed for the national good; he was given another, not quite so exalted, Cabinet post a few months later.

The civil service

A civil servant is a Crown servant (other than the holder of a political or judicial office or a member of the armed forces) appointed directly or indirectly by the Crown, and paid wholly out of funds provided by

Parliament and employed in a Department of government. The definition of a civil servant has not yet given rise to serious legal problems; the meaning of the term 'Crown Servant' (which may include bodies corporate) has posed bigger difficulties.[50]

It is not, of course, realistic to think of the civil service only as a body of advisers to Ministers. First, a great number of decisions, the responsibility for taking which is committed by law to Ministers, are in fact taken by civil servants in the Minister's name without reference to the Minister personally.[51] Unless the class of decision is so important that nothing less than the Minister's personal attention is appropriate, the courts will accept the propriety of such a procedure even though the Minister has not explicitly authorized the civil servant to make the decisions.[52] However, in immigration law special legal consequences are attached to decisions taken by the Secretary of State in person.[53] Secondly, some statutes vest powers of decision directly in named classes of civil servants (for example, customs and excise officers, inspectors at town planning inquiries). Thirdly, in some Departments large questions of policy will in practice be decided by civil servants with the Minister's formal concurrence. A combination of thrustful and strong-minded senior civil servants, complex issues demanding both a substantial body of factual knowledge and an appreciation of the personal qualities of persons with whom the Department has to deal, and an inexperienced, indolent, ill-endowed or indecisive Minister, will sometimes lead to a situation in which a Minister dwindles to a political mouthpiece of his civil servants. Civil servants may seek to influence a ministerial decision in a particular direction by their methods of selecting and summarizing facts, stating the problems and presenting alternative courses of action to the Minister, and they are usually expert in putting to a Minister the objections against a decision that he may wish to take; but they are aware of the need for preserving political neutrality by conscious self-restraint, and the constitutional importance of having an effective political head of their Department.[54] Ministers, if only for reasons of self-respect and personal ambition, know that they must be able to present departmental decisions

---

[50] See pp. 135–6, 220–21, 629–30.
[51] A point made spectacularly but perhaps over-emphatically by the judicial tribunal of inquiry into the *Vehicle & General Insurance Co.* affair: H.C. 133 (1971–2); see p. 186.
[52] *Carltona Ltd.* v. *Commissioners of Works* [1943] 2 All E.R. 560; *Lewisham Borough* v. *Roberts* [1949] 2 K.B. 608 at 629; *R.* v. *Skinner* [1968] 2 Q.B. 700.
[53] Immigration Act 1971, ss 13(5), 14(3), 15(4); see ch. 23.
[54] See R. H. S. Crossman, *Diaries of a Cabinet Minister*, vols 1–3 (1975–7), *passim*.

persuasively to their colleagues, to Parliament, to the public at large and to any groups with whom they have been negotiating.

Following the Westland affair[55] the Treasury and Civil Service Select Committee made many recommendations for the reform of the duties and responsibilities of civil servants in relation to Ministers.[56] The Government in effect rejected all of them, including a proposal that civil servants should be free to give evidence to select committees about alleged misconduct in Government Departments (rather than passing it to more senior members of the service).[57]

Political activities of civil servants

Overt political partisanship cannot be reconciled with the principle of official impartiality. Civil servants are disqualified by statute for membership of the House of Commons; and a civil servant who wishes to stand at a parliamentary election is obliged by regulations of the service to resign his post before announcing himself as a candidate or prospective candidate, though in certain cases[58] he will be entitled to reinstatement if he is not elected or after he has ceased to be a member of the House. By pursuing logic to a facile conclusion, one will rapidly decide that all civil servants ought to be denied every form of political activity except that of casting a vote at an election. But the reasons of public policy that impose the utmost discretion on civil servants closely associated with the work of their Minister are largely irrelevant to the van driver, the worker in the Royal Mint, the porter and the junior clerk. In order to allow civil servants a reasonable measure of freedom of political expression, they are divided into three main groups.[59] The 'politically restricted' are senior members of the service; they are debarred from national political activities (including the public expression of views on matters of national political policy), but are entitled to take part, with the permission of their Department, in local political activities, provided that they act 'with moderation and discretion, particularly in matters affecting their own Department'. Secondly, there is a large

---

[55] See above, p. 188.

[56] See H.C. 92 (1985–6).

[57] See Cmnd 9841 (1986). The civil service continues to be guided in these matters by a Note of Guidance issued by the Head of the Home Civil Service. For the latest text see 123 H.C. Deb. *572–5* (written answers 2 December 1987).

[58] Those civil servants who are not in the 'restricted' or 'intermediate' groups: see below.

[59] The rules are stated in the Civil Service Pay and Conditions of Service Code, which also contains the recommendations of the Masterman Committee (Cmd 7718 (1944)) and of the Armitage Committee (Cmnd 7057 (1978)).

'intermediate' group, consisting of clerical officers, typists and persons charged with technical and specialized responsibilities not involving questions of political policy. Members of this group may be given permission by their Department to take part in both national and local political activities; permission is likely to be refused, however, to officers who come into direct contact with members of the public in the course of participating in discretionary decisions (for example, at jobcentres or tax offices) or who are closely associated, though in a subordinate capacity, with Ministers and senior policymakers. Following the Armitage Committee Report,[60] the 'intermediate group' was increased by some 175,000 civil servants in the executive officer grade who were transferred to that group from the 'restricted category'. The remainder of the civil service, and much the largest group, is politically unrestricted,[61] except in so far as they have to observe the Official Secrets Acts, may not engage in political activity while on duty or in uniform or on official premises, and have to observe a due measure of restraint so as to avoid embarrassing their Ministers and Departments.

Private interests of civil servants[62]

There is no precisely formulated code of conduct governing the private economic activities of civil servants, but they must not allow a conflict to develop between their public responsibilities and their private interests as shareholders and investors. Fortunately, cases of corruption among senior civil servants are exceedingly rare.[63] A certain amount of disquiet has been caused by the frequency with which senior officers, upon their retirement, are appointed to executive or advisory posts in commercial and industrial firms with which they have conducted direct negotiations while they were officials; but under rules of the service such offers of appointment cannot be accepted within two years of retirement except with the consent of the Government.[64]

---

[60] Cmnd 7057 (1978).

[61] Subject to the rules about parliamentary candidature.

[62] See Chester and Wilson, *Organization of British Central Government*, pp. 117–19.

[63] But not unknown. In the wake of the 'Poulson affair' a Royal Commission on Standards of Conduct in Public Life was set up in 1974. In its report, Cmnd 6524 (1976), sweeping changes in the law were recommended, including new statutory rules which would affect civil servants. The Commission recorded that from 1966 to 1976 seventeen civil servants had been convicted on corruption charges. See further, below p. 401.

[64] *The Civil Service*, vol. 4, pp. 393–6.

Anonymity and secrecy

Government Departments have often been criticized for their disinclination to divulge interesting and useful information to members of the public.[65] The fiction that all departmental decisions were taken by the Minister (who is alone politically answerable for them), coupled with a deep-seated belief that any exposure of the processes of departmental decision-making would tend to cause trouble and reduce administrative efficiency, brought about a state of affairs in which secretiveness was sometimes carried to absurd lengths. Inspectors' reports to Ministers on housing and town planning inquiries were not disclosed – and the courts upheld the departmental view that natural justice did not require their disclosure[66] – till 1958.[67] The Franks Committee's emphasis on the need for openness in the procedures for taking decisions on matters directly impinging on individual rights led to a healthy ventilation of the corridors of Whitehall which has enhanced public confidence in the processes followed. The prevailing image of central administration is less monolithic. And it is fair to say that, for many years past, senior civil servants have been more accessible for informal interviews than their bureaucratic counterparts in a number of other countries (provided, at least, that the interviewer was not proposing to publish 'confidential' information); and that formal and informal consultations between officials and representatives of organized interest groups has long been a feature of central administration in Britain.

In 1977 the then Government agreed to make publicly available as far as possible the information used as the background to major policy studies, and heads of departments were actually encouraged in a letter to them from the then Head of the Home Civil Service, Sir Douglas Allen, to cooperate fully in this sortie into 'open government'.[68]

Regulation, organization and structure[69]

The civil service is regulated primarily under the royal prerogative. Formal prerogative Orders in Council relating to the civil service are, however, few: the main one was promulgated in 1982. Regulations,

---

[65] For measured criticisms, see D. G. T. Williams, *Not in the Public Interest* (1965); Report of the Fulton Committee on the Civil Service, Cmnd 3638 (1968), ch. 8.

[66] *Local Government Board* v. *Arlidge* [1915] A.C. 120.

[67] See further, ch. 31.

[68] Sir Douglas was raised to the peerage as Lord Croham on his retirement: his epistle is immortalized under the name of the 'Croham Directive'. For the text, see 942 H.C. Deb *691–4* (written answers 26 January 1978).

[69] See Peter Kellner and Lord Crowther-Hunt, *The Civil Servants* (1980).

minutes and circulars issued formerly by the Treasury, and between 1968 and 1981 by the Civil Service Department, have been the main substance of the law and custom of the civil service; they are supplemented by a few statutes (for example, the Superannuation Acts) and judicial decisions (for example, on civil liability, tenure of office). The Secretary to the Cabinet is also Head of the Home Civil Service. There is a separate Head of the Diplomatic Service (the Permanent Under-Secretary of State to the Foreign and Commonwealth Office). The Civil Service Commissioners are mainly responsible for the recruitment and selection of civil servants by competitive examination and interview. Departments also recruit their own specialist and temporary staff by other methods; promotions within the service, except at the very highest levels, are matters reserved for individual Departments. Top appointments to Permanent Under-Secretary and Deputy Under-Secretary are made by the Prime Minister on the recommendation of the Head of the Home Civil Service, who is assisted by the Senior Appointments Selection Committee, composed of senior Permanent Under-Secretaries and a few senior professional officers.[70]

The elaborate procedural and substantive rules relating to conditions of service, promotions and tenure have been evolved to a large extent by means of collective agreements reached by the system of National and Departmental Whitley Councils, at which representatives of the 'official' side of the civil service (senior officials) negotiate and consult with representatives of the trade union side. If agreement cannot be reached, the matter may be committed to an arbitral body or the Government may take a unilateral decision. In any event, the Whitley system is technically only advisory.[71] The rules governing 'established' (or permanent) civil servants are published in the Civil Service Pay and Conditions Code.

The recommendations of the Fulton Committee on the Civil Service[72] gave impetus to change. The Civil Service Department was created soon afterwards. It was abolished in 1981, responsibility for civil service manpower, pay and superannuation returning to the Treasury, while responsibility for organization, management, recruitment policy, training, personnel matters and for overall efficiency was transferred to a

---

[70] *Top Jobs in Whitehall* (1986), Royal Institute of Public Affairs. By 1985 Mrs Thatcher had appointed 43 Permanent Secretaries and 138 Deputy Secretaries.

[71] See evidence submitted to the Fulton Committee, vol. 4, pp. 500–510. Some matters are dealt with by direct negotiation with the various staff associations. See further, B. A. Hepple and Paul O'Higgins, *Public Employee Trade Unionism in the United Kingdom. The Legal Framework* (1971).

[72] Cmnd 3638 (1968).

new Management and Personnel Office within the Cabinet Office. In 1987 the functions of the Management and Personnel Office were divided between the Treasury and a new Office of the Minister for the Civil Service, the Management and Personnel Office being abolished.[73] In 1970 a Civil Service College for advanced training was opened. Within the service, separate grades have been merged or grouped together; stratification has diminished, promotions and transfers have been facilitated. Special arrangements have been made for the compulsory retirement of the inefficient. Modern methods of job analysis, personnel management, planning and budgetary accounting, bandied around by their abstruse initials, are all the rage.

The Heath Government also introduced a small top-level Central Policy Review Staff, headed by a Labour peer and industrialist, to advise Ministers on forward planning, the allocation of priorities and issues cutting across departmental boundaries, such as the Concorde project, sponsored research, the role of the City of London, and policy on energy, population and the regions.[74] Mrs Thatcher abolished the C.P.R.S. in 1983.

Mrs Thatcher has begun to implement important recommendations of the Number Ten Efficiency Unit on management in the civil service.[75] The main aim is to ensure that to the greatest practicable extent executive functions of government (as distinct from policy formulation) are carried out by new 'agencies' within government Departments. Responsibility for day to day operations of each of these agencies is to be delegated to a chief executive, who would be responsible for management within a framework of policy objectives and resources set by the relevant Minister, in consultation with the Treasury. Each agency will be accountable to Parliament through its Minister, who would, however, be expected to let the chief executive manage. The agencies' staff will remain civil servants. The Government plans to increase the number of agencies: the first ones include unemployment offices and jobcentres, the Driver and Vehicle Licensing Centre at Swansea, the Passport Office, Her Majesty's Stationery Office, and the Meteorological Office. Up to 70,000 civil servants will be managed in this new way by 1989; the Efficiency Unit report envisaged that eventually the number of policy-makers in the civil service could be as few as 20,000.

---

[73] S.I. 1987, No. 2039. The Office of the Minister for the Civil Service is a sub-department of the Cabinet Office.
[74] See James (1986) XXXIV *Political Studies* 423.
[75] See the Prime Minister's statement at 127 H.C. Deb. 1149 (18 February 1988).

The remarkably high degree of security enjoyed by established civil servants, surpassed only by the Judiciary, was not recognized by rules applied in the courts. In the eyes of the common law, civil servants held their offices at the pleasure of the Crown. Their offices would be vacated summarily at any time for any reason that Her Majesty thought fit.

The common-law rule that a civil servant has no right of recourse to the courts for wrongful dismissal is reasonably clear.[76] But what is the basis of the rule; and are there any exceptions to it? It has sometimes been said that a civil servant enjoys a legal status but is not employed under a contract.[77] Even if this is so, it would not preclude the officer from recovering damages for wrongful dismissal, or, indeed, a declaration that he was entitled to reinstatement.[78] And at least one decision of the House of Lords has rested ambiguously on the presupposition that the relationship between civil servants and the Crown is contractual.[79]

Again, the fact that the power to appoint and regulate the conduct of civil servants is derived from the royal prerogative is not inconsistent with the existence of a contract of employment. The Crown can enter into binding contracts (for example, for the supply of food) in the exercise of its prerogative functions.

Yet, assuming that the relationship is contractual, it appears that the right to dismiss at pleasure cannot be displaced by engagement for a fixed period,[80] or by official circulars[81] or non-statutory regulations[82] laying down a regular procedure to be followed before dismissal. It is indeed doubtful whether any ostensibly contractual term inconsistent with the power of the Crown to dismiss at pleasure (for example, a statement that a Crown servant would be dismissible only 'for cause',[83] or for inability or misbehaviour) would be endorsed by a court, unless, of course, the restriction on the Crown's freedom to dispense with a

---

[76] See, for example, *Shenton* v. *Smith* [1895] A.C. 229 (P.C.); *Terrell* v. *Secretary of State for the Colonies* [1953] 2 Q.B. 482. But see below on the statutory position.

[77] See Blair (1958) 21 *Mod. L. Rev.* 265, [1958] *Public Law* 32.

[78] cf. *Vine* v. *National Dock Labour Board* [1957] A.C. 488 (dock labourers); *Ridge* v. *Baldwin* [1964] A.C. 40 (chief constables).

[79] *Sutton* v. *Att.-Gen.* (1923) 39 T.L.R. 294. The point was not argued and the precedent is therefore *sub silentio*; but all the Law Lords assumed that the engagement in question was contractual. See now *Kodeeswaran* v. *Att.-Gen. of Ceylon* [1970] A.C. 1111 (P.C.) supporting this view.

[80] *Dunn* v. *R.* [1896] 1 Q.B. 116.

[81] *Rodwell* v. *Thomas* [1944] K.B. 596. But see *Sutton* v. *Att.-Gen.* (note 79); and Blair [1958] *Public Law* at 43-6.

[82] *Riordan* v. *War Office* [1959] 1 W.L.R. 1046.

[83] Though cf. *Reilly* v. *R.* [1934] A.C. 176 at 179-80 (dicta); *Robertson* v. *Minister of Pensions* [1949] 1 K.B. 227 at 231 (dictum).

servant at will had been imposed by statute.[84] Now, if the power to dismiss at pleasure were to be construed as an ordinary implied term of a contract, it could be displaced by an express term of a contractual engagement incompatible with it.[85] If it cannot be so displaced, this must be either because the Crown is incapacitated from fettering its future executive discretion in this way[86] (so that an incompatible undertaking would simply be *ultra vires* and void[87]) or because it is a special kind of implied term, imported by precedent and for reasons of public policy into all engagements with the Crown irrespective of their wording. These rationalizations of the rule are unconvincing and cast doubt on the content of the rule. Public policy may indeed suggest that an unsuitable or redundant civil servant should be dispensable at any time when the interests of the State so demand; but this merely means that a court of law ought not to award a declaration that a dismissed civil servant is entitled to reinstatement; it does not imply that he should be denied monetary compensation for wrongful dismissal.

The Industrial Relations Act 1971 made an important addition to the law, which was subsequently strengthened and is now contained in the Employment Protection (Consolidation) Act 1978. If a civil servant is unfairly dismissed an industrial tribunal may order that he be re-instated or re-engaged, and that he receive compensation.[88]

The Court of Appeal has held[89] that a decision of the Civil Service Appeal Board (which had confirmed that a former civil servant in the Inland Revenue had been fairly dismissed) was susceptible to judicial review by the courts. The court accepted that the applicant held his post at the Crown's pleasure, having no contract of employment with it, and decided that the usual remedy for a civil servant who believed that he had been unfairly dismissed was to go to an industrial tribunal.

The salaries of civil servants are determined by standing references to arbitral bodies. There have been judicial dicta to the effect that a civil

---

[84] As in *Gould* v. *Stuart* [1896] A.C. 575 (P.C.). See also below.

[85] See dicta cited in note 83, above; and see *Sutton* v. *Att.-Gen.* (1923) 39 T.L.R. 294.

[86] cf. *Rederiaktiebolaget Amphitrite* v. *R.* [1921] 3 K.B. 500; pp. 629–30, below.

[87] See *Riordan*'s case [1959] 1 W.L.R. at 1053; *Rodwell* v. *Thomas* [1944] K.B. at 602.

[88] Sections 67–79, 138. The concept of 'unfair' dismissal is related to non-observance of the principles laid down in the Code of Practice prepared by the Advisory, Conciliation and Arbitration Service. A Minister may exclude a Crown employee from the protection of the Act on grounds of national security: s. 138(4). The Foreign and Commonwealth Secretary did so in relation to employees at the Government Communication Headquarters at Cheltenham in 1984; see *Council of Civil Service Unions* v. *Minister for the Civil Service* [1985] A.C. 374 and above p. 130.

[89] *R.* v. *Civil Service Appeal Board, ex p. Bruce,* the *Independent,* 13 December 1988.

servant has no legally enforceable right to his pay.[90] Even if this is a correct statement of the common-law rule regarding future payments, it is now clear that at common law a civil servant is entitled to recover any part of his salary withheld from him in respect of the work he has already done.[91]

The superannuation of civil servants is regulated by statute, but before 1972 the wording of the legislation presupposed a lack of judicially enforceable entitlement to the rates of superannuation prescribed or indeed to any pension at all.[92] Questions of law arising out of civil service superannuation schemes are now potentially justiciable.[93]

Security procedures[94]

The growth of peacetime espionage, particularly in connection with nuclear research and technology, led to the adoption of special security measures within the civil service in 1948. Following the defection of two senior Foreign Service officials, Burgess and Maclean, to the Soviet Union, and the conviction of some Crown servants, including George Blake, an important controller of British agents,[95] for espionage, committees were appointed to investigate and report on security procedures. Their recommendations[96] resulted in the introduction of new procedures. Typically, all the new rules rest on a non-statutory basis.

The procedures have been applied to only a small proportion of civil servants, holding positions where personal unreliability might give rise to serious risks to national security. They have been more selective (though not necessarily more efficacious) than those adopted in the United States; and British civil servants have not had to endure the solemn silliness of indiscriminate loyalty oaths.

[90] *Mulvenna* v. *Admiralty* 1926 S.C. 842 at 859; *Lucas* v. *Lucas* [1943] P. 68 at 78 (criticized by Logan (1945) *L.Q.R.* 240).

[91] *Kodeeswaran* v. *Att.-Gen. of Ceylon* [1970] A.C. 1111, disapproving dicta to the contrary effect and applying general principles.

[92] Superannuation Act 1965, s. 79. See *Nixon* v. *Att.-Gen.* [1931] A.C. 184.

[93] Superannuation Act 1972, s. 2(6).

[94] See Harry Street, *Freedom, the Individual and the Law* (5th edn, 1982), pp. 236–47; D. G. T. Williams, *Not in the Public Interest* (1965), chs 3, 7, 9; Geoffrey Wilson, *Cases and Materials on Constitutional and Administrative Law* (2nd edn, 1976), pp. 89–98.

[95] *R.* v. *Blake* [1962] 2 Q.B. 377. For his activities he was sentenced to three consecutive terms of imprisonment of fourteen years each. He escaped from prison to Eastern Europe in 1967, and was subsequently awarded the Order of Lenin.

[96] Cmd 9715 (1955) (the Privy Councillors' Report); Cmnd 1681 (1962) (the Radcliffe Report).

In 1948 it was decided that civil servants with Communist or Fascist affiliations should not be employed in work vital to the security of the State. Where practicable they would be transferred to non-secret work. From a provisional decision by a Minister that an official ought to be transferred or removed on security grounds, an appeal would lie to an advisory tribunal, the 'Three Advisers', who would meet in private. In 1952 civil servants employed on top secret work became subject to a more rigorous form of scrutiny, known as 'positive vetting', extending to general character defects; no reference to the Three Advisers would lie from an executive decision in this context. High-level reports on security measures, published in 1955 and 1962,[97] emphasized that personality or behavioural defects or disorders, such as homosexual conduct, alcoholism and drug addiction (which might render an official vulnerable to blackmail or subject to financial temptation), as well as known political affiliations or sympathies, were indicators of security risks; but precautionary measures in such cases were left to departmental action. Security procedures were modified in 1957; and in 1964 a new, and almost inevitably non-statutory, organ, the Security Commission, under the chairmanship of a superior judge, was set up to investigate, at the Prime Minister's request, breaches of security in the public service, and to report and advise generally on security arrangements.[98]

Mrs Thatcher announced a further extension of security measures in 1985.[99] They apply to all those employed on work the nature of which is vital to the security of the State, whether they be civil servants or employees of private companies. Communist or Fascist affiliations would continue to be inconsistent with security-sensitive work; so now would membership of or association with a subversive group (acknowledged as such by a Minister) whose aims were to undermine or overthrow parliamentary democracy in the United Kingdom by political, industrial or violent means. Moreover, Ministers could use this extended definition to bar trade union officials from any Government establishment or to refuse to negotiate with them because they might need access to classified information during the course of those negotiations.

Proceedings before the Three Advisers (two of whom are normally retired civil servants with a High Court judge as chairman, and whose findings are not binding on the Minister) do not conform to the standards of natural justice imposed on a judicial tribunal. After the

---

[97] See above, note 96.
[98] The other members of this standing commission are judges and very senior ex-members of the civil service and the armed forces.
[99] 76 H.C. Deb. *621* (written answers 3 April 1985); 78 H.C. Deb. *895–902* (9 May 1985).

Minister has decided that a *prima facie* case has been made out – there is no preliminary hearing[100] – particulars of the allegations are disclosed to the Advisers, but the civil servant will not be supplied with details which would reveal the sources of the information against him. The civil servant may appear in person, but he cannot be represented by a lawyer or anybody else; he is merely entitled to be accompanied by a friend when he is presenting his opening statement. He may call witnesses to testify to his character and record, but he is unable to cross-examine the anonymous and invisible informants. The advice tendered by the tribunal to the Minister is not revealed.

This procedure may well be 'a travesty of justice as Englishmen are accustomed to it'.[101] The Franks Committee had insisted[102] that the proceedings of statutory administrative tribunals should be character- ized by 'openness, fairness and impartiality'; it is questionable whether any of these criteria is met by the machinery outlined above, though it can be assumed that Ministers and the Advisers do their best to act fairly. But to speak of a travesty belittles the fact that even the most lenient security programme must rest on a harsh assumption: that measures injurious to possibly innocent persons will have to be taken on the basis of reasonable suspicions, suspicions insufficient to justify a prosecution. The balance will inevitably be delicate. We have no means of evaluating the soundness of the decisions that have in fact been taken, or how much harm might be done if the 'defendant' or the representative he would prefer to choose were to be supplied with full particulars of the case against him and were to be given the right to confront informants. It is worth mentioning that in the first thirteen years of the special security programme, only twenty-four civil servants were dismissed and twenty-four others were induced to resign on security grounds, and eighty-three were transferred to non-secret work.[103] During the two world wars, thousands of innocent and innocuous persons were placed in preventive detention as a result of policy decisions and excesses of executive zeal.

Security precautions extend beyond the civil service and the Atomic Energy Authority.[104] Government contracts placed with private firms for secret work include terms which have the effect of barring any

[100] Though the civil servant may make written representations to the Minister.
[101] Street, op. cit., p. 244.
[102] Cmnd 218 (1957), p. 5.
[103] Joelson [1963] *Public Law* 51, at 56–7.
[104] Under the First Schedule to the Atomic Energy Authority Act 1954, the Authority may not terminate the employment of any of its employees on security grounds without the consent of the Minister (now the Secretary of State for Energy).

employee of the firm who is designated by the Minister as a security risk from having access to secret matters. In 1955 ICI dismissed their assistant solicitor because the Government, on ostensibly flimsy grounds, refused to place with them any further secret contract to which he would have access. Such an employee is now able to have his case referred to the Three Advisers.[105]

Special advisers

In the 1970s individual Ministers started the practice of appointing one or two personal advisers.[106] They are now in two groups.[107] 'Political advisers' are not civil servants and are paid from party, not public, funds. Their functions are to give Ministers advice on implementing their party manifesto, and information about party opinion. 'Special advisers' are civil servants with terms of appointment similar to those of other civil servants, who give independent, non-party political advice. All advisers leave office with the Minister. The aim is to provide a Minister with mainly political advice about his responsibilities, especially in the carrying out of his party's manifesto programme. The Treasury and Civil Service Select Committee has recommended an extension of this idea, so that all Ministers would have policy units staffed by non-civil servants.[108]

[105] For non-statutory references of politically sensitive immigration 'appeals' to the Three Advisers, see ch. 23.
[106] See Mitchell (1978) 56 *Public Administration* 87; Hoskyns (1983) 36 *Parliamentary Affairs* 137 at 146; Harold Wilson, *The Governance of Britain* (1976), Appendix V.
[107] See Mrs Thatcher's explanation in 58 H.C. Deb. *155–6* (written answers 10 April 1984).
[108] See H.C. *92* (1985–6), para. 5.

Chapter 11

Constitutional Position of the Armed Forces

Structure and status[1]

The armed forces are instruments of the central government, equipped, disciplined and trained for the exercise of physical force in the interests of the State. In a large number of new states, and in a few that are not so new, the military servants of the State have recently become masters. No constitutional or legal device can afford a guarantee against a military take-over when the political structure is in a condition of decadence or collapse. The British rules relating to the status of the armed forces presuppose a set of public attitudes and assumptions towards the roles of the civil and military powers within the State. The primacy of the civil power is a sociological as well as a constitutional fact. No British Government has been overthrown by military force since 1688. No senior officer of the regular armed forces has ever been Prime Minister except the Duke of Wellington (1828–30, 1834), and he had long since retired from active service.

The feudal levy, supplied by military tenants of the Crown, was abolished in 1660. The pre-Norman *fyrd*, a national levy, had been transformed into the militia, and it was regulated by statute in 1661. But such was the rancour aroused by James II's use of troops that the Bill of Rights 1689 prohibited the raising or maintenance of a standing army within the realm in time of peace without the consent of Parliament. Since a regular armed force was necessary at that time, a Mutiny Act, giving a requisite parliamentary authority, was passed but was limited to a year's duration. Annual Mutiny Acts were passed for nearly two hundred years. In 1881 an Army Act was passed, embodying rules of military law which had previously been embodied in the

[1] This chapter will not deal with the reserve forces (see Reserve Forces Acts 1980 and 1982) or the auxiliary, territorial or women's services.

Mutiny Acts and articles of war.[2] When a separate air force was created in 1917, a similar Act was passed. These were kept alive for periods of twelve months by Army and Air Force (Annual) Acts. In 1955 the Army and Air Force Acts were revised and consolidated, and the system of annual renewal was modified; instead of an annual Act of Parliament (the debates on which provided the Opposition with a useful opportunity for consuming legislative time) they would be renewed from year to year by Orders in Council, which would be subject to approval in draft by both Houses of Parliament. After five years of renewal, however, a fresh Act of Parliament is required. The current enabling statute is the Armed Forces Act 1986; it will expire in 1991 before which a new Act will, no doubt, be passed.

The maintenance of a navy, which was seldom, if ever, regarded as an instrument of royal oppression, has never needed parliamentary approval. The navy exists by virtue of the royal prerogative; indeed, the prerogative power to impress seafaring men into the navy has never been expressly abrogated. But naval discipline is dependent on an Act of Parliament (the Navy Discipline Act 1957, as amended), and the money needed for the navy, as for the other armed services, has to be determined by the Government and authorized by Parliament. Parliamentary debate on any of the armed services may take place on the presentation of the annual estimates, the introduction of supply legislation, and any other legislative measures relating to them. Since 1971 the Naval Discipline Act has been renewable in the same way as the Armed Forces Act.

How far the army and the air force are regulated by prerogative is an interesting but obscure question. The disposition of the forces[3] and the commissioning of officers certainly fall within the scope of the prerogative. The enforcement of military discipline and the trial of offences under military law are regulated by statute; and statutory regulations made by the Defence Council may prescribe terms and conditions of service.[4] Pay and pensions are determined by royal warrants under the prerogative. Although the relationship between a member of the forces and his employer, the Crown, has a distinct statutory flavour, there is ample judicial authority for the proposition that, save where a sentence has been imposed by a court-martial or

[2] Till the eighteenth century, articles of war for the governance of soldiers had been issued only in time of war.

[3] *Chandler* v. *D.P.P.* [1964] A.C. 763. It is most unlikely to be justiciable even after *Council of Civil Service Unions* v. *Minister for the Civil Service* [1985] A.C. 374 (see above, p. 130).

[4] Armed Forces Act 1966, s. 2.

other statutory disciplinary authority, the relations between the soldier and the Crown are not cognizable by the courts. Not only is he disabled from suing for wrongful reduction of pay[5] or arrears of pay,[6] but he cannot sue for wrongful dismissal[7] even, it seems, in the face of inconsistent statutory or contractual provisions; nor can an officer resign his commission without leave.[8] An ex-member of the forces cannot sue for his pension. The rules are based partly on the prerogative and partly on an overriding judge-made concept of public policy which frowns upon litigation between the soldier and his employer. On the other hand, the Crown can hold the soldier to the terms of his enlistment to serve for a term of years unless he purchases his discharge, and it exercises this power.

Central government organization for defence is now based partly on prerogative but mainly on statute.[9] There are a Secretary of State and two Ministers of State, one for the Armed Forces, the other for Defence Procurement, each having a parliamentary under-secretary of state. Within the Ministry of Defence there is located a Procurement Executive, using up-to-date managerial and accounting techniques.[10]

There is a chiefs of staff committee, composed of the Chief of Defence Staff and the chiefs of staff of the three services; they have a right of direct access to the Prime Minister and are occasionally asked to attend Cabinet meetings. The detailed regulation of the services is entrusted to a statutory Defence Council consisting of the Secretary of State and the Ministers of State, the chiefs of staff, the Permanent Under-Secretary of State to the Ministry of Defence and the Chief Executive for Procurement. For each of the three services there is a separate Defence Board. At Cabinet level there is a Defence and Oversea Policy Committee, presided over by the Prime Minister; the Secretary of State for Foreign and Commonwealth Affairs, the Chancellor of the Exchequer and the Home Secretary are among its members; the service chiefs of staff are frequently invited to attend. The Security Service (MI5, which is responsible for internal security) and

---

[5] *Worthington* v. *Robinson* (1897) 75 L.T. (N.S.) 446 (an action against a superior officer); *Leaman* v. *R.* [1920] 3 K.B. 663; cf. Logan (1945) 61 *L.Q.R.* at 260.

[6] *Ex p. Napier* (1852) 21 L.J.Q.B. 332; cf. Glanville Williams, *Crown Proceedings*, 69.

[7] *Re Poe* (1833) 5 B. & Ad. 681; *Grant* v. *Secretary of State for India* (1877) 2 C.P.D. 445; *De Dohse* v. *R.* (1886) 3 T.L.R. 114. The Employment Protection (Consolidation) Act 1978 does not affect the position; it does not apply to military servants of the Crown: s. 138(3).

[8] *Marks* v. *Commonwealth of Australia* (1964) 111 C.L.R. 549; *O'Day* v. *Commonwealth*, ibid., 599.

[9] See Cmnd 2097 (1963) and Cmnd (1984); Defence (Transfer of Functions) Act 1964 and statutory Orders in Council made thereunder.

[10] Cmnd 4641 (1971); Colin Turpin, *Government Contracts* (1965), pp. 122–3.

the Secret Intelligence Service (MI6, which gathers intelligence from outside the country) have intimate links with the Prime Minister, the Secretary to the Cabinet, the Ministry of Defence, the Foreign Office, the Home Office and the Special Branch of the Metropolitan Police.[11]

In Britain, as in a large number of other countries, there is a tendency for regular officers in the armed services to show a profound distaste for party politics or to hold views sympathetic to the far right wing in politics; or to entertain both attitudes simultaneously, if sometimes unwittingly. But it is part of the service tradition to accept a position of subordination to the civil power – a tradition rudely interrupted by the Curragh incident in Ireland early in 1914,[12] but unbroken since then[13] – and although the British public has often been disenchanted with its political leaders, it is averse from turning to the regular armed forces for salvation. Even in times of civil disorder within the realm, the forces must normally (as we shall see in a later chapter)[14] act only under the direction of the civil authorities.

Military law and the civil law

As Dicey emphasized, a soldier[15] is, for most purposes, a civilian in uniform. Although he is subject to certain special rules of law, he is not exempt from the general law of the land.[16]

Those rules which differentiate soldiers from other sections of the community are a consequence of their special responsibilities. Regular soldiers, like civil servants, are disqualified for membership of the House of Commons.[17] The regulations of the service restricting the political activities of members of the forces are stricter than the

[11] cf. D. G. T. Williams, *Not in the Public Interest* (1972), chs 7, 8; Cmnd 2152 (1963) (the Denning Report). The Director-General of MI5 is directly answerable to the Home Secretary. For rare parliamentary debates on MI5 and MI6 see 106 H.C. Deb. *932–86* (3 December 1986) – an unsuccessful attempt to establish a parliamentary scrutiny committee over the two Services – and 483 H.L. Deb. *174–209* (17 December 1986).

[12] cf. Kenneth Rose, *King George V* (1984), pp. 153–7 (when fifty-eight officers in Dublin, including a General, purported to resign their commissions rather than take part in coercing Ulster into an undivided self-governing Ireland).

[13] It is possible, however, that the Wilson Government's decision not to attempt to crush by force the rebellion in Southern Rhodesia in or after November 1965 was partly influenced by doubts as to the morale of the troops.

[14] See ch. 27.

[15] 'Soldier' is here used to include members of the navy, the air force and the marines, as well as the army, subject to verbal modifications.

[16] *Introduction to the Study of the Law of the Constitution* (10th edn), ch. 9. See also *Lynch v. Fitzgerald* [1938] I.R. 382; Keir and Lawson, *Cases in Constitutional Law* (6th edn, 1979), p. 206.

[17] House of Commons Disqualification Act 1975, s. 1(1).

corresponding rules for civil servants. A regular soldier is absolutely prohibited from standing as a parliamentary candidate. In practice a serviceman who applied for nomination papers as a parliamentary candidate would be given his discharge by the service authorities: he must, however, first satisfy a special advisory committee as to his *bona fides*.[18]

Scrving members of the forces are entitled to vote by post or proxy at elections; they are exempt from jury service; they may make informal wills while on actual military service.

Serving members of the armed forces are subject to military law as well as the ordinary law of the land. Military law is a readily ascertainable body of rules, collected in the official *Manual of Military Law*.[19] It is primarily a body of criminal law, contained in statutes and subordinate legislative instruments. It must be sharply distinguished from martial law, which is not a crystallized code of rules at all but a state of affairs in which there has been a complete breakdown of civil authority and the governance of the populace is handed over to or assumed by a military commander.[20]

In the United Kingdom, certain very serious criminal offences committed by members of the forces are triable only by the civil (i.e. ordinary criminal) courts. Other offences are triable by court-martial. A court-martial is composed of military officers sitting without a jury; they are assisted by a judge advocate, a barrister who sums up the evidence and advises the court on questions of law. Minor offences are triable summarily by commanding officers. A number of offences under military law have no equivalent in the ordinary criminal law – for example, conduct to the prejudice of good order and military discipline.

Till 1951 the enforcement of military discipline and the criminal law by courts-martial was largely a self-contained system; only superior officers and, in the last resort, the Army Council (as it then was) could review a conviction of a person subject to military law or the sentence imposed on him, with an ultimate right of recourse to the royal prerogative of mercy. True, the High Court would issue habeas corpus to direct the release of a person detained by the military authorities if he was not subject to military law, or certiorari to quash a decision if jurisdiction had been manifestly exceeded.[21] But although the High Court was capable of exercising the same supervisory jurisdiction (by

[18] R. L. Leonard, *Elections in Britain* (1968), pp. 64–5.
[19] See also Stuart-Smith (1969) 85 *L.Q.R.* 478.
[20] See ch. 27.
[21] As in *R* v. *Wormwood Scrubs Prison Governor; ex p. Boydell* [1948] 2 K.B. 193.

orders of certiorari, prohibition and mandamus) over courts-martial as over other inferior statutory tribunals, in practice it was extremely reluctant to intervene even when grave procedural irregularities had been established;[22] the judges affirmed that they would interfere if the 'civil rights' of an individual had been infringed, but were conspicuously vague in explaining what they meant by the civil rights of a soldier.[23] A similar reluctance to appear to prejudice the administration of military discipline in any way whatsoever was exhibited by the courts in other contexts: in the decisions on dismissal and pay; in decisions that no action would lie against members of a court-martial or a commanding officer for false imprisonment or malicious prosecution while acting within their jurisdiction even if actuated by improper motives and lacking reasonable cause,[24] and that reports written by a superior officer upon another officer in the course of duty[25] and the proceedings of a military court of inquiry enjoyed absolute privilege in the law of defamation.[26] Military discipline and justice in the courts seemed to be uneasy bedfellows.

Some of the older decisions on immunity from civil liability may still be good law. But the administration of military discipline is no longer a self-contained system. In 1951 a Courts-Martial Appeal Court, composed of High Court judges and Scottish and Northern Ireland judges of like status, was constituted and given jurisdiction to hear appeals from courts-martial after internal review procedures had been exhausted. Thus was reasserted the primacy of the civil power. Recourse to the common-law supervisory remedies (other than habeas corpus) became largely superfluous; in any event these remedies have territorial limitations, whereas the jurisdiction of the new court extends to courts-martial held in any part of the world.

Under the present law[27] appeal will lie to the court, after military remedies have been exhausted, against a conviction by a court-martial. Leave of the Appeal Court must be obtained, and the court has no jurisdiction to entertain an appeal against sentence alone. A further appeal will lie to the House of Lords at the instance of the accused or the Defence Council (the respondent) if the Appeal Court or the Lords give

---

[22] As in *R* v. *Army Council, ex p. Ravenscroft* [1917] 2 K.B. 504; *R* v. *Secretary of State for War, ex p. Martyn* [1949] 2 All E.R. 242; *R.* v. *O.C. Depot Battalion, R.A.S.C. Colchester, ex p. Elliott*, ibid. 373.

[23] See *Re Mansergh* (1861) 1 B. & S. 400, and *Martyn*'s and *Elliott*'s cases, above.

[24] *Heddon* v. *Evans* (1919) 35 T.L.R. 642. See also *Johnstone* v. *Sutton* (1786) 1 T.R. 493, 510, 784; *Fraser* v. *Balfour* (1918) 34 T.L.R. 502.

[25] *Dawkins* v. *Paulet* (1869) L.R. 5 Q.B. 94.

[26] *Dawkins* v. *Rokeby* (1875) L.R. 7 H.L. 744.

[27] Consolidated in the Courts-Martial (Appeals) Act 1968.

leave and the Appeal Court certifies that a point of law of general public importance is involved. The royal prerogative of mercy is preserved.

Superior orders

Before 1966 a member of the forces might incur double jeopardy. If he were convicted of an offence under military law, he could still be charged with and convicted of the same offence in a civil court, though the latter was to take into account any sentence imposed by the military authorities. (Conviction by a civil court precluded trial for the same offence by court-martial, though the facts constituting the civil offence might give rise to a separate *disciplinary* charge under military law.) Since 1966 the anomaly has been largely removed. Conviction by a court-martial precludes trial by a civil court for any offence that is substantially the same.[28]

A member of the forces may nevertheless stand in double jeopardy in a different context. If, in obedience to superior orders, he commits a criminal offence or a civil wrong (for example, wounding a rioter in circumstances where this is not reasonably justifiable) he may incur legal liability before the ordinary courts. If, on the other hand, he refuses to obey an order because he believes it to be unlawful, he may be court-martialled. It may be said that the dilemma is unreal because it is not an offence under military law to disobey an unlawful command; a soldier cannot be convicted for disobedience unless the command was lawful. But since a soldier is a member of a disciplined force conditioned to the habit of obedience, and since, moreover, a court-martial may well hold the command to be lawful, the dilemma and the risk can be very real. Is it reasonable, then, to assert that obedience to superior orders can never be a defence to an unlawful act in proceedings before the courts? The Nuremberg War Crimes trials proceeded on the footing that superior orders were no defence, though they might be pleaded in mitigation of punishment. This general proposition is adopted in modern editions of the *Manual of Military Law*, though it is conceded that obedience to superior orders may afford a defence to particular offences, for instance, negativing the existence of criminal intent where this is relevant. Doubts as to the content of the rule still persist. In a much-quoted South African case, decided during the Boer War,[29] it was held that an honest belief in the

---

[28] See Armed Forces Act 1966, ss 25, 26, 35.
[29] *R* v. *Smith* (1900) Cape of Good Hope S.C. 561. See also *Keighley* v. *Bell* (1886) 4 F. & F. 763 at 790, *per* Willes J.

lawfulness of an order to shoot an African civilian was a good defence to a charge of murder, the order not being manifestly illegal. The dangers of such a principle are illustrated by the facts of the case; and there is no general rule of criminal law that a reasonable mistake of law is a defence.[30] Yet a reasonable mistake induced by an order given by a military superior to do an act which, in the circumstances, is not manifestly illegal may in some situations be akin to the operation of duress on a soldier, and can fairly be analysed in that fashion. The civil liability of the soldier will not necessarily be governed by the same considerations, particularly where vicarious liability can be affixed to the Crown.

Civilians and courts-martial

Courts-martial outside the United Kingdom have jurisdiction over a wide range of civilian dependants and employees of the forces. Their jurisdiction extends not only to all criminal offences under English law but also to certain offences of a disciplinary nature (for example, breach of a local curfew). The jurisdiction embraces criminal offences in respect of which United Kingdom courts have no extraterritorial jurisdiction, and others which, if committed in the United Kingdom, would be triable only in a civil court.

This is not an entirely satisfactory state of affairs: pre-trial safeguards are not as efficacious as in a civil court; guilt and sentence are determined by a simple majority of a panel of military officers who will hardly ever have legal qualifications; the accused will often lack the services of a lawyer to defend him.[31] The existence of the Courts-Martial Appeal Court is an ameliorating factor but cannot cure every defect.[32] The Armed Forces Act 1976, sections 6 to 9 and schedules 3 and 4, meet these objections to some extent. Standing Civilian Courts have been established, consisting of a 'magistrate' – an assistant to the Judge Advocate General who will have knowledge of the law – and not more than two assessors drawn from a panel of civilians and military officers. An accused has the right of appeal to a court-martial, or to elect to be tried by court-martial instead of by the Standing Civilian

---

[30] See J. C. Smith and Brian Hogan, *Criminal Law* (6th edn, 1988), p. 207. cf. Ashworth [1974] *Crim. L.R.* 562.

[31] The accused is, however, entitled to be represented by a defending officer. On the quality of judge advocates, see Borrie (1969) 32 *Mod. L. Rev.* 35 at 47–8.

[32] cf. the position under American constitutional law as interpreted by the Supreme Court of the United States: *Reid* v. *Covert* 354 U.S. 1 (1957), and subsequent cases holding that trial of civilian dependants and employees by court-martial was unconstitutional.

Court. Regulations have been made by the Secretary of State which deal with the procedure of the Court, including the question of the representation of an accused person before it.[33]

Under the Visiting Forces Act 1952, members of visiting Commonwealth forces, and of such other countries as may be designated by Order in Council (in pursuance of an international agreement for common defence), stationed in the United Kingdom, and their civilian components, are exempt from the jurisdiction of the ordinary criminal courts in respect of offences[34] committed on duty or against the persons of forces personnel or the property of the forces and their personnel; the operation of the Act has been extended to certain British dependencies. In addition, tort claims are settled by special arrangements and are not determinable by the ordinary courts unless the claimant is denied satisfaction through administrative channels.

[33] See generally Rowe and Jetha (1977) 40 *Mod. L. Rev.* 444.

[34] See note 32 on constitutional limitation of the jurisdiction of American courts-martial over civilians – a point not yet established in 1952, when the agreement was made and the Act was passed. American courts-martial try American servicemen for those criminal offences excluded from the jurisdiction of the local courts.

Chapter 12

Public Boards and the Economy

Government and quasi-government bodies[1]

Britain is governed primarily by central government Departments and elected local authorities. We have seen that, apart from Departments directly headed by Ministers, there are also subordinate central Departments or sub-departments which are not Ministries; they are not directly headed by a Minister, but they consist of civil servants and a Minister usually has substantial or full control over them.[2] Subordinate Departments shade off into bodies auxiliary to but not integral parts of the executive branch of government, bodies managerial, regulatory, promotional, investigatory and advisory, bodies that defy orderly classification by reference to any meaningful criteria, if only because they have been set up by Government and Parliament *ad hoc* to discharge a variety of specialized tasks best performed by institutions partly autonomous and free from comprehensive political control. The least incoherent group of these 'quasi-governmental' bodies are the corporations administering nationalized industries.

Central government in the narrower sense is not conducted exclusively in Whitehall and its environs. Quite apart from the substantial devolution of responsibility for Scottish affairs to sub-departments of the Scottish Office located in Edinburgh, and the lesser measure of devolution for Welsh affairs to the Welsh Office,[3] several of the United Kingdom Departments maintain regional and local organizations and offices.[4] Among the Departments with regional offices are the Department of the Environment, the Ministry of Agriculture, Fisheries and

[1] cf. Sir Arthur Street, 'Quasi-Government Bodies since 1918', in *British Government since 1918* (Institute of Public Administration, 1950).
[2] pp. 177–9.
[3] See ch. 3.
[4] See A. H. Hanson and Malcolm Walles, *Governing Britain* (4th edn, 1984), ch. 10.

Food, the Department of Trade and Industry and the Department of Social Security. Still better known are the local jobcentres of the Department of Employment, social security offices and inland revenue offices. Immigration officers of the Home Office, and customs officers of the Board of Customs and Exercise, are stationed at seaports and airports. And various public corporations, particularly those managing nationalized industries, are organized partly on a regional basis.

There is no pattern of regional government in the United Kingdom. There is a patchwork quilt of overlapping *ad hoc* regions for the provision, regulation or coordination of particular services. Functional regionalism moved a stage further in 1973 with the reorganization of the National Health Service and water authorities on a regional basis. The Government did not, however, accept the Redcliffe-Maud Commission's recommendations for establishing provincial councils in England as indirectly elected regional planning authorities.[5]

The role of government in the mixed economy and the welfare State: a brief sketch

1. A number of public services are provided by elected local authorities.[6] These services include schools, sanitation, street lighting, traffic control, housing, environmental planning and certain welfare services (for example, child care).

2. A few local public services are provided or regulated by *ad hoc* authorities composed wholly or mainly of members of the local authorities in the area.[7]

3. A large proportion of social services are provided directly or indirectly by the central government. Social security benefits are dispensed by the Department of Social Security through local offices. The Department of Health organizes and controls the National Health Service; hospitals are managed out of central government funds by appointed Regional Health Authorities and District Health Authorities.

4. Land use is closely regulated by the Department of the Environment and local planning authorities. Government action to create new towns

[5] Report of the Royal Commission on Local Government in England (Cmnd 4040 (1969)), ch. 10.
[6] See ch. 21.
[7] J. F. Garner, *Administrative Law* (6th edn, 1986 by Garner and B. L. Jones), pp. 333–5.

administered by development corporations has checked the concentration of industry and population in big conurbations.

5. A public service may be operated directly by a government Department. The one conspicuous example was the Post Office, which became a semi-autonomous public corporation in 1969 after more than a century of departmental operation.

6. Governments may participate in or regulate the economy in a variety of ways.[8] They may take over the assets of a privately owned company and appoint its directors without destroying its legal capacity as a company; thus Cable and Wireless Ltd, a company responsible for international telecommunications, became government-owned in 1947: it was returned to the private sector in 1981.[9] They may acquire a majority or minority shareholding in a privately owned company in return for the right to appoint directors;[10] the British Aerospace Act 1980 and the Civil Aviation Act 1980 are examples. They may and do grant subsidies and loans, and offer tax incentives, to commercial and industrial firms for research and development or to prevent large-scale unemployment by salvaging an ailing firm or industry or to promote development in a needy region, although such intervention has been much reduced under the present Government.[11] They may influence the location of industry by systems of licensing. They may set up a semi-autonomous public corporation like the Highlands and Islands Development Board and supply it with public funds. They may constitute a semi-autonomous body like the Monopolies and Mergers Commission, the Office of Fair Trading and the Restrictive Practices Court to regulate aspects of private enterprise. If fiscal controls and tax policies are incapable of restraining inflation or maintaining a satisfactory balance of payments or keeping unemployment down to an acceptable level or encouraging economic development, growth or productivity, then a compulsory restriction of prices, charges and incomes may have to be imposed, monitored by semi-autonomous boards, although not under Mrs Thatcher's Administration.

Nationalization of industry through the vesting of privately or locally owned assets in a (usually monopolistic) public corporation, subject to the payment of compensation, became the most characteristic

---

[8] See G. Ganz, *Government and Industry*.
[9] See Telecommunications Act 1981.
[10] See T. C. Daintith in W. Friedmann and J. F. Garner (eds), *Government Enterprise* (1970), ch. 3.
[11] The principal legislative instrument for achieving these purposes is the Industry Act 1982. Regional development is promoted by EEC policies, through a Regional Development Fund which helps employment in the poorer areas of the Community.

feature of public enterprise after 1945 and down to the 1980s. There has been a broad general pattern: a new body corporate is constituted; its governing body is appointed by a Minister and is then given a substantial degree of freedom to conduct the enterprise in day-to-day matters in its own discretion; the Minister retains powers to give it directions of a general character and certain specific powers; Treasury sanction is required for ventures with large financial implications; the corporation has its own assets and is expected broadly to pay its own way; its employees are not civil servants. The form of nationalization was suggested partly by the British Broadcasting Corporation, partly by the experience of the London Passenger Transport Board. Nationalization as an instrument of political and economic policy was conceived by the Labour Party and implemented when the first Labour Government with an overall majority in the House of Commons came to power in 1945.[12] Private ownership of the principal means of production and distribution was regarded as morally wrong and detrimental to the public interest; it was necessary to supplant the profit motive with a zeal for public service, to revivify declining industries, to achieve levels of efficiency which private enterprise was incapable of reaching, and to install the Government on the commanding heights of the economy. Coal, electricity, gas, inland transport, airways, and the iron and steel industry were nationalized between 1946 and 1951. Iron and steel were denationalized under a Conservative Government in 1953, and renationalized under a Labour Government in 1967.[13]

Nationalized industries: legal and constitutional issues

Detailed examination of the structure, organization and functions of individual nationalized industries falls outside the scope of this book.[14] The main bodies conducting the affairs of the industries are British Coal[15] (which has divisional executives); the Central Electricity Generating Board and area electricity boards (responsible for generation,

---

[12] See generally W. A. Robson, *Nationalized Industry and Public Ownership* (2nd edn, 1962): A. H. Hanson, *Parliament and Public Ownership* (1961); W. Friedmann and J. F. Garner (eds), *Government Enterprise* (1970); David Coombes, *State Enterprise: Business or Politics?* (1971); C. D. Foster, *Politics, Finance and the Role of Economics* (1971); Richard Pryke, *Public Enterprise in Practice* (1971).

[13] The current statute is the Iron and Steel Act 1982.

[14] See further Tony Prosser, *Nationalized Industries and Public Control* (1986); Robson, op. cit.; J. A. G. Griffith and H. Street, *Principles of Administrative Law* (5th edn), ch. 7; J. F. Garner, op. cit., ch. 12; J. D. B. Mitchell, *Constitutional Law* (2nd edn), ch. 12; Friedmann and Garner, op. cit., chs 1, 2.

[15] The National Coal Board became the British Coal Corporation by the Coal Industry Act 1987, s. 1.

transmission and distribution) and the Electricity Council (a coordinating body which advises the Secretary of State);[16] the South of Scotland Electricity Board and the North of Scotland Hydro-electricity Board; British Shipbuilders;[17] the United Kingdom Atomic Energy Authority;[18] the British Steel Corporation;[19] the Post Office;[20] a complex network of inland transport authorities,[21] including the British Railways Board, the British Transport Docks Board, the British Waterways Board, the Scottish Transport Group, the London Regional Transport[22] and other regional transport authorities designated by the Secretary of State, and the British Broadcasting Corporation, which operates under a royal charter and a quinquennial licence.[23]

The responsible Minister (the Secretary of State for Trade and Industry,[24] or for the Environment, or for Scotland) appoints[25] (or advises the appointment of) members of the governing boards; the members will hold office for fixed periods; the Minister has powers of dismissal (which have seldom been exercised[26]) and a power not to re-appoint them.[27] Broad policy control rests in the hands of the Minister; day-to-day administrative control lies in the hands of the governing bodies; an indeterminate zone where policy merges with day-to-day administration lies between. A typical statutory provision is that the

[16] The electricity and water industries are due to be privatized (see below, p. 225): see Public Utility Transfers and Water Charges Act 1988; Electricity and Water Bills 1988–9.

[17] British Shipbuilders Act 1977.

[18] Atomic Energy Authority Acts 1954 and 1986.

[19] Iron and Steel Act 1982. The industry is to be privatized under the British Steel Act 1988.

[20] Post Office Act 1969.

[21] See Transport Act 1968, amending the Transport Act 1962. The original nationalization Act was the Transport Act 1947; none of the nationalized industries has undergone so much structural change as the transport services.

[22] Replacing the London Transport Executive under the London Regional Transport Act 1984.

[23] The BBC is operating under a Licence and Agreement which run to 1996 and are published in Cmnd 8233 (1981). The Independent Broadcasting Authority (the Broadcasting Act 1981) is a regulatory rather than an operational body; commercial television and radio programmes are provided through regional programme companies to which it allocates contracts. The life of the IBA was extended to 31 December 1996 by the Broadcasting Act 1980 (now consolidated in the Broadcasting Act 1981).

[24] Who is generally responsible for the Post Office. The Home Secretary has in practice a lesser responsibility for broadcasting; the Governors of the BBC are formally appointed by Her Majesty in Council. The BBC is *sui generis*; Ministers' powers are very wide, but politicians have observed a self-denying ordinance.

[25] In 1978 worker-directors were appointed to British Steel and the Post Office.

[26] But in 1970 the Minister terminated the appointment of the then chairman of the Post Office.

[27] The Minister did not renew contracts of the Chairman of British Steel in 1980 or of the Chairman of the Central Electricity Generating Board in 1977.

Minister shall have power to give the board directions of a general character as to the exercise of its functions on matters appearing to him to affect the national interest.[28] In some instances – for example the Atomic Energy Authority[29] and the British Steel Corporation[30] – he will have a general power to give specific directions, subject to qualifications. The nationalization Acts also confer upon the Minister particular powers. Thus, the Minister is empowered to prescribe the form of the corporation's accounts and appoint auditors, except where (as with the Atomic Energy Authority) the accounts are audited by the Comptroller and Auditor-General; his sanction is required for large schemes of capital investment or reconstruction or public borrowing; in some instances he may advance sums (for example, for maintaining uneconomic railway services).[31] Ministerial and Treasury approval is also needed for money advanced out of the National Loans Fund for any large-scale scheme of public investment or borrowing. The Minister will be entitled to call for information from the board regarding its activities. The board must present its accounts and an annual report to the Minister. He is usually empowered to prescribe schemes for training and research; or his approval of such schemes will be necessary. There is no set pattern of ministerial authority.

In most cases the corporations have been expected and required to conduct their affairs as commercial undertakings operating in the public interest and to be financially self-supporting over a period of years; the BBC and the Atomic Energy Authority, which are financed primarily out of licence fees prescribed by the Government and direct government grants respectively, have always been exceptions. Solvency has not, however, always proved to be an attainable objective and financial obligations have had to be modified. The maintenance of an arm's length relationship between Ministers and boards has also been impracticable in some instances, because of (1) the political repercussions of many day-to-day decisions, or errors or misfortunes in management – for example, public reaction to power cuts, or increases in fares or charges, or closure of uneconomic pits or transport services, or the dislocation caused by strikes in major industries providing public services; (2) pressure by individual M.P.s to secure ministerial intervention in various matters of detailed management, and party political criticism of the performance of industries that were nationalized as an

---

[28] For example, Coal Industry Nationalization Act 1946, s. 3(1).
[29] Atomic Energy Authority Act 1954, s. 3; Atomic Energy Authority Act 1986, s. 6.
[30] Iron and Steel Act 1982, s. 3.
[31] Transport Act 1968, s. 39.

act of political conviction; (3) the unforeseen dependence of some nationalized industries on government financial aid and therefore more detailed government control. Frequently the Government has been impelled to intervene in serious labour disputes involving the industries; to supplement the boards' resources in order to enable them to arrive at wage settlements; to write off massive deficits; and to finance programmes for expansion or rationalization. As will be seen below, the present Government has sought to avoid having to act in these ways by privatizing (the vogue word for denationalizing) many industries.

In some industries the Minister has offered little policy guidance; in others he has frequently intervened in matters of detail but without giving formal directions. Very few *general* statutory directions on matters of national policy have been given by Ministers to boards. Ministers prefer to exert informal pressure on boards; this has been facilitated by regular personal contacts with their chairmen. Constitutionally this may be an unsatisfactory anomaly. More clearly demarcated powers and prohibitions can be enshrined in legislation; the outcome will not necessarily be conducive to efficiency or harmony.

Legal status

The corporations can sue and be sued in their own names. Their employees are their own officers and servants. It is doubtful whether any of the corporations is an agent or servant of the Crown enjoying Crown immunities and privileges;[32] some statutes have placed these questions beyond doubt.[33] The National Health Service authorities on the other hand exercise their functions on behalf of the Crown.[34] The Atomic Energy Authority was a marginal case until 1986, for until then it was closely controlled by the Secretary of State and derived its revenue mainly from the central government; for most legal purposes other than liability to rates and taxes it was treated as an autonomous body corporate, not as a Crown servant.[35] The Atomic Energy Authority Act 1986 retained the Secretary of State's control (and

---

[32] *Tamlin* v. *Hannaford* [1950] 1 K.B. 18 (former British Transport Commission); *BBC* v. *Johns* [1965] Ch. 32, p. 135.

[33] For example, Transport Act 1968, ss 52(5), 160–162; Post Office Act 1969, s. 6(5).

[34] *Nottingham No. 1 Area Hospital Management Committee* v. *Owen* [1958] 1 Q.B. 50. See also *Pfizer Ltd* v. *Ministry of Health* [1965] A.C. 512. The situation was unaltered by the National Health Service Reorganization Act 1973: *Wood* v. *Leeds Area Health Authority* [1974] I.C.R. 535. The governing Act is now the National Health Service Act 1977. But the regional health authorities can sue and be sued in their own names.

[35] Atomic Energy Authority Act 1954, s. 6.

indeed added to it)[36] but placed the Authority on a commercial basis.[37]

The legal powers vested in the corporations are extensive, and although a person having a sufficient legal interest can impugn the validity of their acts and decisions, successful challenges will be rare, first because of the breadth of their powers[38] and, secondly, because of the disinclination of the courts to afford *locus standi* to members of the general public,[39] though it is open to the Attorney-General to sue for an injunction or a declaration.[40]

The primary legal duties of the corporations are so broadly drawn (for example, 'to provide an efficient service . . .') that they must be regarded as non-justiciable; indeed, the general duties of the British Railways Board are expressly declared to be unenforceable in a court,[41] though section 106(1) of the Transport Act 1968 goes to the other extreme by providing that the maintenance duties of the British Waterways Board may be enforced in judicial proceedings by any person. Whether a duty is potentially susceptible of judicial enforcement must depend mainly on the degree of precision with which it is formulated.[42] If a board were to refuse to comply with its duty to act in conformity with a direction properly issued to it by a Minister, the latter could presumably compel performance of the duty by obtaining an order of mandamus, or alternatively be awarded a judicial declaration that the board was in breach of its duty; but matters have yet to be brought to this pass, and in such a situation a Minister might prefer to exercise his powers of dismissal.[43]

Public accountability and extra-judicial safeguards

The main reason for vesting the ownership of nationalized industries in semi-autonomous public corporations, instead of bringing them within

[36] 1986 Act, s. 6 (duty to act on lines approved by Secretary of State).

[37] See ss 1–5.

[38] See, for example, *Roberts (Charles) & Co.* v. *British Railways Board* [1965] 1 W.L.R. 396; though cf. *South of Scotland Electricity Board* v. *British Oxygen Co.* [1956] 1 W.L.R. 1069; [1959] 1 W.L.R. 587.

[39] *See, for example, McWhirter*'s case (note 42), and p. 486.

[40] See pp. 384, 594–6.

[41] Transport Act 1968, s. 1(3). See also Iron and Steel Act 1982, s. 14; Post Office Act 1969, s. 9(4).

[42] Hence it appears that the duty of the IBA to satisfy themselves that as far as possible programmes do not include matter offensive to public feeling (Broadcasting Act 1981, s. 4(1)(*a*)) falls narrowly within the area of duties enforceable at the suit of the Attorney-General; *Att.-Gen., ex rel. McWhirter* v. *IBA* [1973] Q.B. 629.

[43] All the members of the governing body of RTE (the Irish equivalent of the BBC) were dismissed in November 1972. As a matter of strict law, it would be possible for the BBC's licence to be revoked.

the framework of normal departmental administration, was to encourage a competitive spirit of initiative and enterprise. The civil service ethos would, it was thought, inhibit the managerial staff of the industries from making untried experiments in new fields; it would induce an excess of caution and addiction to precedent; officials would always be looking over their shoulders, apprehensive of the parliamentary inquisitor. Hence an attempt was made to insulate the industries from the rigours of question time by restricting ministerial responsibility for the conduct of their affairs.[44] Against this background, the scope of parliamentary scrutiny is inevitably more limited than it was in relation to the Post Office before it ceased to be a government Department.

Parliamentary questions. Since 1948 the Speaker has allowed questions to be put to Ministers about day-to-day administration of the nationalized industries provided it appears to him that such a question raises a matter of urgent public importance: it is up to Ministers whether to answer them. When in doubt, the clerks at the table (who in the first instance receive notice of questions to be put in the House) have generally taken a broad view of the latitude thus granted in accepting questions;[45] and Ministers have not often refused to answer a question on the ground that it related to day-to-day management or administration, though some of the questions tabled and answered might well have been rejected on that ground.[46]

Clearly a Minister can properly be asked to answer a question within the field of his statutory responsibility – for example, a question about appointments he has made and has power to terminate or has terminated or why he has or has not given an approval or a specific direction which he is required or empowered by statute to give. A Minister can also be asked questions about his extra-statutory official activities (for example, informal consultations with board chairmen) if they come to the notice of M.P.s. The more difficult cases – and the pegs on which the majority of questions about nationalized industries are hung – are questions about whether the Minister proposes to give (or why the Minister has not given) certain directions of a general character to a board in the national interest, and questions asking the Minister to obtain statistical information from a board. The former type of question often relates to a matter of marginal generality; the latter may

---

[44] See the White Paper on the Nationalized Industries, Cmnd 7131 (1978).
[45] See generally D. N. Chester and Nona Bowring, *Questions in Parliament*, pp. 301–5.
[46] First Report of the Select Committee on Nationalized Industries for 1967–8 (H.C. *371–I* of 1967–8), paras 852–3.

be strictly admissible but tends to involve the staff of the boards in a large amount of work. (Members can and do address still more questions direct to the chairmen of the boards.)[47] The insulation of the boards from political accountability through questions to Ministers is therefore far from complete. And question time in the House of Commons is the cockpit of party conflict.

Parliamentary debate. Debate on the conduct of a nationalized industry may take place on public bills (especially bills increasing a corporation's borrowing powers or reconstructing the organization of the industry), on private bills promoted by one of the corporations and on subordinate legislation concerning the industries; on substantive motions to discuss a particular matter, or on one of those twenty days where the topics for debate are chosen by the Opposition[48] or on the annual reports and accounts of the corporations after they have been laid before Parliament; or a private member may lead a brief debate on the affairs of a public corporation on the daily motion for the adjournment of the House of Commons. The rules of procedure governing debate are generally less restrictive than those governing the scope of parliamentary questions, and the issues raised may range beyond the area of ministerial responsibility.

Select committees of the House of Commons. Until 1979 the Select Committee on Nationalized Industries examined the activities of public corporations and reported to the House of Commons. It produced many valuable reports. That committee was abolished when the fourteen new select committees were set up in 1979.[49] Departmental select committees scrutinize relevant nationalized industries – the Transport Committee British Rail, the Energy Committee British Coal, and so on. The new arrangements authorized the setting up of a subcommittee drawn from the membership of two or more of a number of committees to consider any matter affecting two or more nationalized industries, but the power has not been used.[50]

Other controls. The Government has appointed, over the years, *ad hoc*

[47] In 1966, 550 questions were tabled on British Railways alone in the two Houses; the Board had no reply to 246 of them. M.P.s also sent over 1100 letters to the chairman of the Board: loc. cit., para. 856.
[48] See below, p. 303.
[49] See pp. 292–6.
[50] See S.O. No. 130(4). The Liaison Committee (see below, p. 294) recommended in 1982 that it be repealed: H.C. *92* (1982–3), para. 42.

inquiries, headed by independent experts, to examine and report on aspects of certain nationalized industries. Some of these reports have been followed by statutory reorganization.

The Monopolies and Mergers Commission, too, has been an important agency for reviewing nationalized industries. The Competition Act 1980 enables the Secretary of State to refer to it questions about the efficiency and costs of the service provided, and the possible abuse of monopoly power, by nationalized industries. It has produced a number of reports.[51]

The accounts of the nationalized industries (apart from atomic energy) are not audited by the Comptroller and Auditor-General.[52] The expenditure and administration of those public corporations (such as the BBC) which are subsidized out of moneys provided by Parliament are subject to scrutiny by the Treasury and Civil Service Committee of the House.[53]

The nationalized electricity and inland transport bodies have national and area consultative committees or councils; civil aviation has an Air Transport Users' committee. The Post Office has a Post Office Users' National Council. These associated bodies, mainly appointed by the superintending Minister, have no executive powers; in general – there is no fixed pattern – their functions are to represent the consumer interest, to receive and consider complaints by members of the public, and to advise the Minister or the relevant board on matters referred to them or in some cases on their own initiative. The general consensus of opinion is that as guardians of the interests of consumers these bodies have not fulfilled a conspicuously significant function;[54] nevertheless, in September 1970 objections by the Post Office Users' National Council to certain proposed increases in postal charges were followed by a formal ministerial directive to the Post Office not to impose them. In 1978 two consumer representatives were appointed to the Post Office board.

Public corporations are not within the jurisdiction of the Parlia-

---

[51] See, e.g., Inner London letter post (1980); London and S.E. commuter services (1980); Central Electricity Generating Board (1981); Severn Trent Water Authority (1981); a report on five bus companies (1982); a report on the sewage functions of two water authorities (1982); National Coal Board – development and supply of coal (1983); Caledonian MacBrayne shipping societies (1983).

[52] The Government successfully resisted an attempt to include this auditing in the National Audit Act 1983.

[53] For these committees, see pp. 292–6.

[54] J. A. G. Griffith and H. Street, *Principles of Administrative Law* (5th edn), pp. 316–21; J. F. Garner, op. cit., pp. 313–17; a Justice Report, *The Citizen and the Public Agencies* (1976).

mentary Commissioner for Administration. However, Regional and District Health Authorities are supervised by separate Health Commissioners for England and Wales.[55]

Yet there is a real dilemma: watchdogs whose bark is feeble and whose bite is imperceptible are hardly worth keeping; but the nationalized industries, already subjected to a depth and range of public scrutiny to which no privately owned industrial undertaking has to submit, are understandably reluctant to encourage the development of more effective oversight of their operations.[56] They complain that the controls are already restrictive. Their budgets and investment proposals are subject to close scrutiny by economists within the relevant Department and by Treasury experts; then by a Cabinet committee; then come management audit and external audit by Government appointees; the possibility of reference to the Monopolies and Mergers Commission; the Treasury and Civil Service Committee; debate in the House of Commons; and finally Consumer Councils.[57]

The position of the broadcasting authorities is different. The BBC has an appointed but independent General Advisory Council; the IBA also has a number of specialized advisory committees on such matters as religious and educational broadcasting, the maintenance of advertising standards and local commercial radio broadcasting. Complaints are dealt with primarily by internal procedures. A Broadcasting Complaints Commission for all channels exists by virtue of the Broadcasting Act 1981, Part III.[58]

Privatization

All the above needs to be read in the context of the privatization policy of Mrs Thatcher's Government. It believes that some nationalized industries could be more efficiently run from the private sector, that privatization (which allows the public to increase its share-owning) is popular and that revenue can be raised from sales of nationalized undertakings. Its privatization programme[59] has been massive

---

[55] National Health Service Act 1977. In 1976 the Justice Report, *The Citizen and the Public Agencies*, recommended the institution of an Ombudsman for the public agencies.
[56] Representative expert bodies may, however, perform valuable advisory functions. See, for example, *Consumer Consultative Machinery in the Nationalized Industries* (HMSO, 1968).
[57] And see Sir Arthur Knight (1983) *Political Quarterly* 24.
[58] See *R. v. Broadcasting Complaints Commission, ex p. Owen* [1985] Q.B. 1153 for the functions of the Commission.
[59] On which see Graham and Prosser (1987) 50 *Mod. L. Rev.* 16.

compared with other post-war Conservative Governments:[60] since 1979, forty per cent of nationalized industries have been returned to private hands, and some £18 billion in revenue has been raised thereby.

Three methods have been used to achieve privatization. First, legislation may be passed to create a public company in which the public may buy shares. This was done, for example, in relation to British Telecom,[61] British Airways,[62] British Aerospace,[63] British Gas[64] and the British Airports Authority.[65] Secondly, the Government may sell shares which it owns in certain undertakings, as it did with, for instance, its holdings in the National Bus Company[66] and British Leyland.[67] Thirdly, the Government may authorize a nationalized industry to dispose of part of its assets, as with, for example, British Rail Hotels and Sealink.[68] More privatization is planned: British Steel, British Rail Engineering Ltd water and electricity have been designated for return to the private sector.

Fresh regulatory systems are enacted for some privatized companies: so a Director-General of the Office of Telecommunications ('Oftel') operates under the Telecommunications Act 1984 to supervise the licensing of telecommunications operators and, through conditions in their licences, can affect the prices which they charge to telephone users; and the Director-General of Gas Supply has regulatory functions under the Gas Act 1986.

The popularity of privatization with the public (as witnessed by the number who have bought shares under the programme) and the vast revenues which it has generated mean that renationalization under a Labour Government would be impossible. The Labour Party therefore committed itself at the 1987 General Election to legislate to take back certain industries (notably British Telecom) in return for Government stock.

[60] The 1951–64 Conservative Government only denationalized steel; the 1970–74 Government denationalized Thomas Cook and the Carlisle state-run breweries – but it nationalized Rolls-Royce in 1971.
[61] Telecommunications Act 1981 and 1984.
[62] Civil Aviation Act 1980.
[63] British Aerospace Act 1980.
[64] Gas Act 1986.
[65] Airports Act 1986. Other enterprises privatized in this way include B.P. (in 1979 and 1987), Cable and Wireless Ltd, Amersham International, Britoil, Associated British Ports, Enterprize Oil, Jaguar, and Rolls-Royce Ltd.
[66] Transport Act 1985.
[67] Others have included Government holdings in the National Freight Corporation, Scott Lithgow, Yarrow Shipbuilders, Vosper Thorneycroft, Swan Hunter, Vickers, and Unipart.
[68] Transport Act 1981.

Part Three

Parliament and Legislation

Chapter 13 deals first with some of the basic rules about the working of Parliament (for example, adjournment, prorogation and dissolution), and then with the general functions of parliamentary institutions within the scheme of the British constitution. Once again we observe the close interrelationship of the Executive and the Legislature. But although the Government is the dominant force in Parliament and although legislation is primarily a function of the Government in office, it is an oversimplification to speak of Cabinet or Prime Ministerial dictatorship.

The next two chapters are about the House of Commons. First, in chapter 14, there are the rules relating to the right to vote, the delimitation of constituencies (a controversial topic), the conduct of electoral campaigns and the system of voting (*another* controversial topic: a comment is offered on some alternative systems), legal disqualifications for membership, the selection of candidates, and ways of disputing the validity of elections. Chapter 14 has been expanded somewhat to give more detail on electoral law. The Representation of the People Act 1985 is fully incorporated in it so as to explain, for example, the more liberal rules about absent voting and the right of overseas electors to vote. Mention is also made of Labour's plan to have constituency electoral colleges to select parliamentary candidates. Chapter 15 considers the functions and procedure of the House of Commons, including the process of legislation, discussion of financial matters, scrutiny of policy and administration, and the roles of backbenchers. The new machinery for determining the levels of M.P.s' pay and allowances is noted, as are further reports from the Select Committee on Procedure (which largely remain unimplemented). The treatment of the departmental select committees has been considerably extended, and the light thrown by the Westland affair on the law and practice relating to the powers of those committees is examined. In these two chapters the roles of national political parties are far from ignored. Chapter 15 includes comments on Community legislation, and the effects of Community membership on financial legislation.

There follows a chapter on the House of Lords and the means of resolving conflicts between the two Houses; this includes a review of the changes which have been made in the membership and functions of the upper House, and comments on possible reforms of it.

In chapter 17 we are on well-trodden ground – the privileges and immunities of the Houses of Parliament and of their members acting in their capacity as members. Select committees of the House of Commons have recommended some reforms in the law of parliamentary privilege, and the House has implemented some of them.

Part Three concludes with a chapter on subordinate legislation (mainly legislation by Ministers under powers delegated by Act of Parliament). Delegated legislation could alternatively have been discussed in Part Six of the book ('Administrative Law'), but it has been placed here because it *is* legislation and, like most of Parliament's own general legislative output, it is initiated by Ministers. Particular attention is paid to the special safeguards against the abuse of delegated powers. Attitudes towards the dangers inherent in delegated legislation have often been excessively alarmist – a point underlined in the course of this chapter. But some recent developments, and in particular accession to the European Community, have brought the need for adequate safeguards into the foreground once again.

Chapter 13

Parliament: Background and Framework

Some basic rules

Frequency of Parliaments

The Bill of Rights 1689 provided that Parliament 'ought to be held frequently'. By virtue of the Meeting of Parliament Act 1694 (which is still in force) not more than three years must elapse between the dissolution of one Parliament and the meeting of its successor. In practice, and by convention, Parliament must be summoned to meet each year. The most remunerative taxes and grants of supply to the Crown are provided by Act of Parliament annually; and authority for the maintenance of the army and its discipline requires annual renewal by the authority of both Houses.[1]

The two Houses. The House of Commons is a wholly elected body; the House of Lords is wholly non-elected. Since the late Middle Ages it has been an accepted rule that the two Houses meet, deliberate and vote separately. There is no statutory or other provision for joint sessions, though for certain purposes there can be joint select committees. A bill may be introduced in either House unless it is a Finance Bill (authorizing taxation) or a Consolidated Fund or Appropriation Bill (authorizing national expenditure), in which case convention and the privileges of the Commons require that it be introduced in that House and by a Minister. Other money bills may be introduced in the Lords (H.C.S.O. No. 78). But it is a constitutional convention, and one of fundamental importance, that every amendment or motion to authorize central government expenditure, or to increase or impose a tax,

[1] See above, pp. 205–6.

must have the Queen's recommendation [2] – that is to say, it must be introduced or moved by a Minister. This necessarily implies that the power of the purse belongs to the Government and not to private members. Hence, if a bill introduced by a private member requires the expenditure of public money for the fulfilment of its purposes – and it does so require more often than not – the member must be able to persuade a Minister to move a financial resolution in the House; otherwise the bill cannot be passed. No such restriction applies in the United States Congress or in a number of other foreign legislatures.

The customary common-law rule is that a bill cannot become law unless it has been passed by both Houses and assented to by the Queen. Under the Parliament Acts 1911 and 1949 most classes of bills may, after a period of delay, be presented for the royal assent, although they have not been passed by the Lords. [3]

Duration of a Parliament

In 1694 it was enacted that no Parliament was to last more than three years. This provision was repealed by the Septennial Act 1715 (passed in the state of alarm engendered by the first Jacobite revolt) which extended the maximum duration of a Parliament to seven years. The Parliament Act 1911 reduced this period to five years (s. 7), and laid it down that the new procedure whereby a bill could be presented for assent without the Lords' consent was not to apply to bills to prolong the life of Parliament (s. 2(1)); these rules are still in force. Parliament may, however, prolong its own life by an Act passed in the normal manner. Thus, the Parliament elected in 1910 was prolonged by Annual Acts during the First World War, and was not dissolved till November 1918; the Parliament elected in 1935 was similarly prolonged during the Second World War and was dissolved in June 1945. An attempt by a Government to procure the deferment of a General Election in any situation other than one of armed conflict would provoke a serious constitutional crisis.

Parliament may be, and nearly always is, dissolved by the exercise of the royal prerogative before its five-year term comes to an end. We have already considered the constitutional conventions regulating the exercise of this prerogative. [4] The main practical effect of these conventions (save in those circumstances in which the Queen is entitled

---

[2] These rules are partly embodied in standing orders of the House (S.O. Nos 46–8, 77–8).
[3] See pp. 304–8.
[4] See pp. 117–20.

to refuse a request for dissolution) is to enable the Prime Minister to choose the most advantageous, or least disadvantageous, date for a General Election. The fact that this power lies in his hands tends both to enhance his stature within the Government and to rally the ranks of party waverers once it is suspected that a dissolution may be imminent. If the power to dissolve were to be eliminated (so that we had Parliaments of fixed duration) or narrowly restricted, one could expect party discipline within the House of Commons to be more difficult to enforce.

The modern practice is for the Prime Minister to announce the date of the dissolution and election (after he has tendered the necessary request to Her Majesty) about ten days before the actual dissolution. Dissolution is effected by a royal proclamation in Council, which also names the date for the summoning of the new Parliament. In practice polling day will be about a month after the announcement of the intended dissolution,[5] and a couple of weeks will elapse thereafter before the new Parliament meets.

The proclamation is followed immediately by an Order in Council, directing the Lord Chancellor to issue writs to the returning officer (who will be the mayor or chairman of a local authority or the sheriff of a county) in each constituency to cause an election to be held on the day named, and writs of summons to individual peers and bishops to attend the meeting of the new Parliament.

The commencement of a Parliament is accompanied by picturesque ceremonial. Parliament is formally opened by Lords Commissioners in the House of Lords. The Commons repair to their own chamber to elect a Speaker and swear in members. The following day or shortly afterwards, Her Majesty attends in person to read the Queen's speech in the House of Lords;[6] this speech is prepared for her under the direction of the Prime Minister, and outlines the Government's legislative programme for the session and its broad policies. The Commons are present at the bar of the House of Lords. The main substantive business of the new Parliament begins with a general debate in each House on the address in reply to the Queen's speech.

At common law, Parliament was dissolved automatically by a demise of the Crown (the death or abdication of the monarch). This rule was abrogated by statute in 1707. Under the present law[7] the effects of a demise of the Crown are: (i) the two Houses are to meet immediately if

---

[5] See R. L. Leonard, *Elections in Britain* (1968), pp. 7–8.
[6] If she is unable to attend personally, the Lord Chancellor reads it on her behalf.
[7] Succession to the Crown Act 1707; Representation of the People Act 1867; Representation of the People Act 1985, s. 20.

prorogued or adjourned; and (ii) if the demise of the Crown occurs while Parliament is dissolved and before polling day, the meeting of Parliament after the election is to be delayed for fourteen days.

Sessions: prorogation and adjournment. It is the invariable custom for the life of a Parliament to be divided up into a number of sessions. These are usually of about one year's duration, though there is no fixed practice. If Parliament were not to sit at all for a full year, some vital Acts which have to be renewed or passed annually would lapse. A speech from the throne is read by the Queen in the Lords, with the Commons in attendance, at the opening of each session. Typically, a session will begin and end in October and will be interspersed with adjournments each night, at weekends, at Christmas, Easter and Whitsun, and during the long summer recess beginning late in July. It is possible for the Commons to be sitting while the Lords are adjourned. Nowadays the Commons sit for about 180 days altogether during a calendar year. Each House determines, on the Government's initiative, on which dates it will adjourn and reassemble.

A session of Parliament is terminated by prorogation, a prerogative act; a short formal speech is made on behalf of the Queen, summarizing the work done during the session, and the Parliament stands prorogued till a named date, which (unless prorogation precedes a dissolution) will be only a few days later, when a new session will be opened by the reading of the Queen's speech. These dates are decided on the Government's advice. Prorogation has the effect of causing all public bills that have not yet passed into law to lapse; if they are to be reintroduced in the new session they must go through all their stages again. Private bills (i.e. bills of a local or personal character) are carried forward into the new session by resolution of each House, so that they can be continued at the stage they have already reached. The main casualties of a prorogation will be public bills introduced by private members (private members' bills) but occasionally bills introduced by Ministers (government bills) will lapse too. Prorogation therefore serves two purposes: to induce the Government to manage its legislative programme efficiently, and to discourage backbenchers from getting above themselves.

The reason why Parliament is adjourned, instead of standing prorogued, in midsummer is strictly practical. In the first place, if it becomes necessary to recall a prorogued Parliament to deal with a matter of unexpected urgency, a royal proclamation has to be issued. It is simpler and may be more expeditious to reassemble an adjourned

Parliament; this can be done by the Speaker and the Lord Chancellor acting on the Prime Minister's request.[8] Secondly, at the end of a summer recess it is often desirable to spend a few days dealing with unfinished legislative business (for example, considering late Lords' amendments to Government bills), debating an important issue that has arisen during the recess or making policy announcements before the session terminates.

The role of Parliament

It has often been said that Parliament has three main constitutional functions: making laws; controlling national expenditure and taxation; and a third class of function, comprising criticism of national policy, scrutiny of central administration, and procuring the redress of individual grievances.

A preliminary difficulty with this classification is that the word 'Parliament' is being used in different senses. There are more serious difficulties inherent in any classification by reference to function when expressed in legal or institutional terms. The familiar classification is too much at variance with the facts. Legislation is primarily a function of Government. Even if one ignores the mass of non-parliamentary or subordinate legislation made by the Queen in Council or Ministers, a very large majority of Government bills, introduced into Parliament by Ministers, are passed into law substantially in their original form. In 1985–6, fifty Government bills were introduced and all but two (which were able to be carried over to the following session) were passed. In the 1985–6 session seventeen out of 107 private members' bills actually introduced became law. Again Parliament 'controls' national finance in the formal sense that its sanction is needed for the imposition of taxation and the authorization of expenditure; but bills authorizing public expenditure are dominated even more than the content of ordinary legislation by the will of the Government, and in particular the views of the Treasury. A lot of time in the House of Commons is spent on debating what are in form financial matters; but the House has largely given up the pretence that it has real authority over these

---

[8] This practice is provided for in standing orders of the House of Commons (S.O. No. 12) and sessional orders of the House of Lords. The Speaker and the Lord Chancellor are not obliged to comply with the Prime Minister's request, but it would be remarkable if they were to refuse unless no substantial reason for the request was supplied.

Parliament must also be summoned to meet within five days if a royal proclamation of a state of emergency is made under the Emergency Powers Acts 1920 and 1964. See ch. 27.

measures, and most debates on public expenditure concentrate on aspects of policy and administration to which questions of expenditure may be only peripheral.

The deeper one digs, the bigger yawns the gulf between appearance and reality. Neither Parliament nor the House of Commons acts as a collective entity save on special and rare occasions. In recent years political scientists, though prone to disparage or be ignorant of legal rules, have rightly concentrated their attention on party organization and activity in and out of Parliament;[9] the role of pressure groups operating on Ministers, civil servants, parties and M.P.s; the potential expansion of select scrutinizing committees; the meaning of public opinion;[10] and the nature of General Elections to the House of Commons. In other words, parliamentary institutions cannot meaning-fully be considered in isolation from the forces which influence decisions; and some of those decisions may not even require to be formally registered by Parliament. Having made this point, we must reiterate that this is a book about constitutional law and not a general work on British government. Our main emphasis must, therefore, be placed on aspects of parliamentary institutions which are not necessarily the most important.

Against this complex background, the question: What is the constitu-tional role (or what are the functions) of Parliament? becomes altogether too ambiguous. Answers will depend on whether one is thinking of the Queen in Parliament, the two Houses, or the House of Commons alone; on whether one is thinking of all the members on the Government side, or of those members on the Government side who are not Ministers, or of members on the Opposition side; on whether one is thinking of the political activities of members outside as well as inside Parliament. One can set out the following general proposi-tions.

1   The House of Commons gives the Government a legitimate foundation. The Prime Minister must be that person who is best able to command the support of a majority of members of the House; he is normally the leader of the majority party; the majority party in the House is identified by the party affiliations of the successful candidates in individual constituencies at a General

---

[9] The last major work written by Sir Ivor Jennings, the most eminent of modern British constitutional lawyers, was a three-volume treatise on *Party Politics* (1960–62).

[10] See especially David Butler and Donald Stokes, *Political Change in Britain* (2nd edn, 1974).

Election. The Prime Minister forms a Government;[11] the members of the Government must be or become members of one or other House. Thereafter supporters of the Government in the House of Commons sustain it in office by thwarting the Opposition's motions of censure and enabling the Government to enact its legislative programme.

2   The role of the Opposition in the House of Commons must be conditioned by the constant need to present itself to the electorate as the alternative Government. This objective can be frustrating when the next General Election may be four years distant. But it will not be thought of as unattainable, for the main political parties are broadly based; they are not reflections of a permanent majority or minority group (the situation in Northern Ireland was essentially different); there is a sizeable floating vote; we have free elections; only three times this century has the same party won three consecutive General Elections.[12] (Mrs Thatcher's winning hat trick of General Elections of course dismayed the Opposition; but they will no doubt fortify themselves with the thought that the Conservatives' luck cannot hold indefinitely.) To say that the function of the Opposition is to oppose would be an over-simplification; a substantial majority of Government bills are passed without any move to reject them, and there is a large area of common ground between the two main parties on matters of national policy. The Prime Minister often gives the Leader of the Opposition confidential information and consults with him privately on non-party matters of national concern. But in fulfilling its role the Opposition will frequently attack the Government in debate and at question time on issues of principle and detail. Parliament is the only public forum in which Ministers are obliged to present reasoned (and sometimes unprepared) answers to these criticisms.

3   Irrespective of the political complexion of the Government in office, the Conservative Party remains the largest single group in the House of Lords. But because of the peculiar composition and limited powers of the upper House, the roles of Government and Opposition in the Lords cannot be considered in the same terms as in the Commons. Perhaps incongruously, it is possible to review the

---

[11] The Government, when formed, does not (as in some countries) have to obtain a formal parliamentary vote of confidence.

[12] The Liberals in 1906 and 1910 (twice), though in the 1910 elections they failed to obtain an overall majority of seats in the Commons and retained office only with the support of minority parties; and the Conservatives in 1951, 1955 and 1959; and again in 1979, 1983 and 1987.

constitutional functions of the House of Lords more coherently than those of the House of Commons.[13]

4   In both Houses, and particularly in the Commons, the Government's policies and its conduct of administration are subjected to open scrutiny; and adverse criticism does not come only from members on the Opposition side. To this extent Parliament is a 'grand inquest of the nation'. Voting figures in the division lobbies tell only part of the story. Criticism often takes the form of putting down detailed amendments to Government bills; these amendments are not necessarily, or indeed usually, prompted by considerations of party politics and Ministers will seldom be able to afford merely to brush them aside. Fuller investigation of aspects of policy and administration will be a matter for select scrutinizing committees.

5   The House of Commons provides a forum for ventilating the grievances of individuals, localities and organized groups. An M.P. may raise such an issue by asking a parliamentary question, putting down an 'early-day' motion, raising the matter in debate (especially the debate on the daily adjournment of the House), putting down amendments to bills, or seeking to introduce a private member's bill himself. However, effective *redress* for injustices suffered by individuals at the hands of the Administration is more likely to be achieved outside Parliament, by members' letters and other representations to Ministers, or through an inquiry by the Parliamentary Commissioner for Administration into a complaint of maladministration referred to him by an M.P., through a more formal committee or tribunal of inquiry or by statutory machinery for appeal or by judicial review.

6   The publicity given to its proceedings, moreover, tends to enhance public interest in public affairs, and to educate and inform by the wider diffusion of facts, arguments and statements of policy. This tendency must not be exaggerated. Few people read *Hansard*; in England only four daily newspapers, with a total circulation of barely three millions, offer even a moderately adequate coverage of parliamentary proceedings; most of the electorate now obtains its information about current affairs mainly from television programmes, and party political broadcasts are not popular with viewers except during an election campaign; only important set-piece debates are broadcast live on the radio; professions of intent by politicians are regarded with widespread scepticism; because the outcome of divisions in the House of Commons is normally a

[13] See ch. 16.

foregone conclusion, parliamentary debates fail to attract the attention given to contests where the result is in doubt. Perhaps the televising of proceedings (a six-month experiment has been approved by the House) might arouse greater public interest.

Chapter 14

The House of Commons: Elections and Members

The electoral system

The franchise

In order to exercise the franchise in a parliamentary constituency, a person must be included in the electoral register for that constituency. The register is compiled annually, on the basis of information provided by householders, by the registration officer, who will be the chief executive of a local authority. A person, though legally qualified to vote in every other respect, will not be permitted to vote if his name is not on the register.

To be included in the register, a person must[1] 1. be eighteen years of age, or be due to attain his eighteenth birthday within twelve months of the publication of the register, thus becoming eligible to vote in an election held after his birthday; 2. be a Commonwealth citizen or a citizen of the Republic of Ireland; 3. not be subject to any legal incapacity;[2] and 4. be resident in the constituency on the qualifying date (10 October in Great Britain)[3] for compiling the register.

The following points should be noted.

(a) It is a criminal offence for a person to vote in more than one constituency even though his name appears on the electoral register for each constituency. Again, it is an offence to vote if one knows or has reasonable grounds for believing that, notwithstanding one's appearance on the electoral register, one is subject to a legal disqualification. Hence although absence from the register is conclusive of inability to vote, presence on the register is not conclusive of entitlement to vote.

---

[1] Representation of the People Act 1983, s. 1; hereafter 'the 1983 Act'. On electoral law generally, see Erskine May, *Parliamentary Practice* (20th edn, 1983) chs. 2, 3; H. F. Rawlings, *Law and the Electoral Process* (1988).

[2] See p. 240.

[3] 1983 Act, s. 4(1).

(*b*) The term 'Commonwealth citizen' includes, as well as British citizens, British Dependent Territories citizens and British Overseas citizens,[4] together with citizens of independent Commonwealth countries.[5] Citizens of the Republic of Ireland (which is not a Commonwealth country) are not British citizens in United Kingdom law, but they are excluded from the definition of aliens[6] and are accorded much the same rights and privileges in the United Kingdom as citizens of Commonwealth countries.[7]

(*c*) To be included in the register, a person who is otherwise qualified needs to be 'resident' at an address in the constituency only on the qualifying date.[8] No *period* of residence is necessary, except in Northern Ireland where three months' continuous residence is required. A person ought not to be put on the register unless his *ordinary* place of residence[9] is in the constituency. However, it is irrelevant that his place of residence is, for example, merely a tent: if, as a matter of fact, that is the person's residence, he or she is entitled to be registered there.[10] And university students pursuing their courses of study are entitled to be registered in the constituency where they are residing for that purpose.[11]

(*d*) Persons with service qualifications (members of the armed forces, Crown servants and British Council officials overseas, and their spouses living overseas with them), and merchant seamen, are entitled to be treated as if they were resident in a constituency on the qualifying date, provided that they would have been so resident but for their assignment elsewhere.[12]

(*e*) A British citizen resident outside the United Kingdom may vote as an overseas elector.[13] To do so he must be qualified but for that absence, and have been included on a register in a constituency not

[4] British Nationality Act 1981, s. 37(1)(*a*). See pp. 441–3.
[5] ibid., s. 37(1)(*b*).
[6] ibid., s. 50(1).
[7] See generally the Ireland Act 1949, s. 2 and the Representation of the People Act 1983, s. 1.
[8] 1983 Act, s. 5.
[9] A prison will not be accepted as an address for the registration of a person incarcerated there: 1983 Act, s. 5(3). A mentally disordered person is not resident at the place where he is *detained:* ibid., s. 7(1). A *voluntary* mental patient may register at a place outside his psychiatric hospital and obtain a postal vote: ibid., ss 7, 19.
[10] *Hipperson* v. *Electoral Registration Officer for Newbury* [1985] Q.B. 1060 (women protesting at Greenham Common).
[11] *Fox* v. *Stirk* [1970] 2 Q.B. 463. If they have a home in another constituency, they can be registered there as well.
[12] See 1983 Act, ss 14–17, and pp. 238, 245.
[13] Representation of the People Act 1985, ss 1–4. He may also vote in elections to the European Parliament.

more than five years before the date on which he wishes to qualify as an overseas elector. He must make an overseas elector's declaration, and may vote by post or proxy.[14] Some 12,000 people were qualified to vote in the 1987 General Election in this way.[15]

Disqualification. The following classes of persons are not entitled to exercise the franchise, even if their names appear on the electoral register.

(i) Aliens.[16]
(ii) Minors (persons under eighteen years of age).
(iii) Peers, other than peers of Ireland.[17]
(iv) Persons serving sentences of imprisonment, or who are unlawfully at large having escaped.[18]
(v) Persons convicted of corrupt practices at elections (who are disfranchised for five years); and persons convicted of illegal practices at elections (election offences of a lesser order), who are also disfranchised for five years but only in respect of the constituency in question. The line drawn between corrupt and illegal practices is not altogether logical. To incur unauthorized expenditure to promote the election of a candidate is a corrupt practice; to publish a false statement that a candidate has withdrawn from the contest is an illegal practice.

The register[19]

The registration officer[20] must issue a provisional electoral register for the constituency on 28 November; this is to be exhibited in public libraries and other public buildings. He must also keep lists of voters entitled to vote by post or proxy.[21] If he realizes that he has made a

---

[14] See below, p. 246.
[15] See 114 H.C. Deb. *531–4* (written answers 22 April 1987).
[16] This term excludes citizens of the Republic of Ireland (see above).
[17] By custom the Lords Spiritual (see p. 297) do not vote, although the courts have never ruled on the matter. The Archbishop of Canterbury voted in the 1983 General Election, but the Anglican bishops subsequently declared that they would in future abide by the custom. See 443 H.L. Deb. *242–5* (29 June 1983).
[18] Representation of the People Act 1983, s. 3, as amended by the Representation of the People Act 1985, Sched. 4. Such a person may, of course, have been correctly included in the electoral register before his term of detention began.
[19] 1983 Act, ss 9–13.
[20] The sheriffs of counties, chairmen of district councils and mayors of London boroughs are returning officers, but their duties are delegated to registration officers: Local Government Act 1972, ss 39, 40.
[21] 1985 Act, ss 6–7. On postal and proxy voting, see below, p. 246.

mistake in compiling the register, then (subject to any appeal from a decision on a claim or objection) he must correct it.[22] Any person may object to the inclusion or exclusion of any name by 16 December; the registration officer must hear and determine any objection and may rectify the register accordingly. An appeal lies from his determinations to the county court and thence, on a point of law, to the Court of Appeal; alternatively his determination, or that of the Circuit judge, may be impeached before a Divisional Court of the Queen's Bench Division.[23] The register for the constituency comes into force on 16 February and is operative for any election held there during the following twelve months.

Delimitation of constituencies

In the American Constitution it is laid down[24] that no state shall deny any person within its jurisdiction 'the equal protection of the laws'. In *Baker* v. *Carr* (1962),[25] one of the most remarkable and influential decisions ever given by the United States Supreme Court, it was held that the equal protection clause implied the doctrine of 'one man, one vote, one value', so that electoral districts (constituencies) established under state law for the federal House of Representatives had to have approximately equal numbers of electors. This decision, and others that followed,[26] led to a massive legislative reapportionment of electoral districts not only for congressional elections but also at the state and local levels so as to modify the prevailing over-representation of sparsely populated rural areas.

No decision of a United Kingdom court could propel Parliament willy-nilly into radical reform. The present machinery for constituency delimitation, based on a scheme introduced in 1944,[27] is designed to

---

[22] 1983 Act, s. 11.

[23] By an application, made by a party aggrieved, for an order of certiorari to quash the determination (for example, for excess of jurisdiction) or for an order of mandamus to compel him to perform his public duty.

[24] Fourteenth Amendment, s. 1.

[25] 369 U.S. 186 (1962).

[26] See, for example, *Reynolds* v. *Sims* 377 U.S. 533 (1964) (principle of broadly equal electoral districts held to govern representation in *both* houses of a state legislature; contrast the position in the United States Senate).

[27] See generally David Butler, *The British Electoral System since 1918* (2nd edn, 1963). The original Act was the House of Commons (Redistribution of Seats) Act 1944. There had been no general redistribution since 1918 despite the movement of population from city centres to suburbs. The movement was accelerated during and after the Second World War; and new towns to siphon off population from the big cities were deliberately created and expanded as an act of policy.

work impartially and to promote approximately equal electorates; but the last word rests with Parliament, and politics tends to keep creeping in.

Under the Parliamentary Constituencies Act 1986 (which consolidated the House of Commons (Redistribution of Seats) Acts 1949 to 1979), four Boundary Commissions, one each for England, Scotland, Wales and Northern Ireland, are charged with the duties of reviewing representation in the House of Commons, and submitting to the Secretary of State reports recommending such redistribution of seats as may be necessary at intervals of not less than ten or more than fifteen years. As soon as may be after they have reported, the Home Secretary must lay their reports before Parliament, *together with* drafts of Orders in Council giving effect, with or without modifications, to their recommendations for boundary changes. The Act thus permits the Home Secretary to vary but not to ignore or reject the recommendations. If the draft Orders are approved by resolutions of each House, Orders in Council will then be made, and will have effect at the next General Election.

The chairman of each Commission is the Speaker of the House of Commons; the deputy chairman must be a superior judge; each Commission has two other members who are not to be M.P.s, and is advised by senior public officials – in England, the Registrar-General and the Director-General of Ordnance Survey. The Commissions are guided by a number of rules laid down in the Act. When a Commission has provisionally decided to recommend changes, it must give public notice of its proposals in the constituencies concerned and invite representations to be made to it; it may conduct local inquiries. The total number of constituencies (all of which are to be represented by a single member) for Great Britain is not to be substantially greater or less than 613; this number is to include at least seventy-one Scottish and thirty-five Welsh constituencies; there are also to be seventeen constituencies in Northern Ireland.[28] The electorate of a constituency is to be as near as practicable to a quota ascertained by dividing the total electorate within the region covered by a Commission by the number of constituencies in that region; deviations from the quota are permissible in order to respect local government boundaries or for reasons of geographical dispersal. The total number of United Kingdom constituencies is not fixed by Act of Parliament; it is currently 650.

Each set of proposals by the Commissions has proved controversial.

---

[28] An increase from 12 made by virtue of the House of Commons (Redistribution of Seats) Act 1979.

The first reports of the Commissioners, in 1948, recommended very extensive boundary changes in the light of shifts in the distribution of population since 1918; the Commission for England also deviated from the rules to give an advantageous weightage to rural areas, which happened to be mainly Conservative; the Labour Government redressed the balance by introducing amending legislation to add seventeen urban seats, eight of which were in fact won in 1950 by Conservative candidates. The 1954 reports of the Commissions were implemented in full but aroused a good deal of local resentment. Two unsuccessful attempts were made to impugn the validity of recommendations or draft Orders in Council in the courts.[29] For technical reasons it was not easy to see how in practice the courts could be persuaded to go into the question of *vires*.[30] The 1969 recommendations[31] precipitated a crisis. If they had been fully implemented, the Labour Party might possibly have lost about ten seats at the next election, mainly through the disappearance of depopulated urban constituencies. Some weeks after they had been received, the Home Secretary presented them to Parliament[32] but did not produce draft Orders in Council to give effect

[29] *Hammersmith B.C.* v. *Boundary Commission of England. The Times*, 15 December 1954 (attempt to obtain mandatory injunction to direct the Commission to withdraw its recommendations *after* it had reported; held, the Commission had no power to do this); *Harper* v. *Home Secretary* [1955] Ch. 238 (attempt to prevent draft Order in Council, already approved by both Houses, from being presented to Her Majesty in Council). See generally Craig [1959] *Public Law* 23.

[30] Among the difficulties are the unavailability of injunctions against Crown servants acting as such (Crown Proceedings Act 1947, s. 21), the fact that the courts are fearful of encroaching on parliamentary privilege by interfering with a 'proceeding in Parliament' (though this objection would not arise if there were a reasonable interval between publication of the report and laying before Parliament) and the provision of the 1949 Act (unaffected by the 1958 Act or by the Parliamentary Constituencies Act 1986) that the validity of an Order in Council thus made cannot be called in question in any legal proceedings whatsoever (1986 Act, s. 4(7)). In an extreme case a court might nevertheless be persuaded to intervene; and in any event it might be possible to obtain an order of mandamus to compel the Home Secretary to comply with his express statutory duties (see p. 244).

[31] The period between reviews had been extended to a maximum of fifteen years by the 1958 Act.

[32] The reports were published as Command Papers, and presented to the House of Commons (see S.O. No. 137) by being placed in the Votes and Proceedings Office. It was at first claimed on behalf of the Home Secretary that they had not been 'laid' before Parliament within the meaning of the parent Act; hence the duty to lay draft Orders in Council at the same time did not arise. When the reports were presented to the House a second time, accompanied by draft Orders (see below), they were expressed to have been laid in pursuance of the Act; again they were deposited in the Votes and Proceedings Office. It seems artificial in the extreme to contend that the first laying was not a performance of a statutory duty but an act of obedience to Her Majesty's command. cf. *Att.-Gen.* v. *De Keyser's Royal Hotel Ltd* [1920] A.C. 508; p. 132 above. And see *R.* v. *Immigration Appeal Tribunal, ex p. Joyles* [1972] 1 W.L.R. 1390, showing that presenting a Command Paper to the House *is* laying within the meaning of the Act.

to them, either with or without amendment. Instead, the Government decided to implement them only in part, explaining that local government areas were being subjected to a comprehensive review, that there ought not to be too big a discrepancy between local government and parliamentary constituency boundaries, and that it would be undesirable to have two major delimitations within the course of a few years. The Home Secretary introduced a new House of Commons (Redistribution of Seats) Bill, implementing the recommendations for Greater London and a few very large constituencies but absolving him from performance of his existing statutory duty to give effect to the Commissions' recommendations. The Opposition and some independent critics maintained that the bill involved gerrymandering. The Conservative majority in the Lords passed the bill but only subject to wrecking amendments. The two Houses adjourned for the summer recess in a state of deadlock, with the Home Secretary facing the prospect of an application to the High Court for an order of mandamus to compel him to carry out his legal duties. When Parliament reassembled, the Home Secretary moved compromise amendments, and warned that if the Lords rejected them, he would lay all the recommendations for constituency changes together with draft Orders giving effect to them, but would ask Government supporters not to approve any of them. The Lords rejected the Commons' amendments to the bill. The application for mandamus was withdrawn,[33] the Home Secretary having declared that he would comply with his statutory duty. The bill lapsed on prorogation, and no attempt was made the following session to override the Lords under the Parliament Acts procedure. Instead, the reports and draft Orders giving effect to them were laid before the Commons by the Home Secretary; and the draft Orders were duly voted down by the House.[34] The subsequent General Election in 1970 was therefore conducted on the basis of the 1954 delimitation. In November 1970 the new Conservative Home Secretary reintroduced the draft Orders and they were given parliamentary approval.[35]

[33] *R.* v. *Home Secretary, ex p. McWhirter, The Times,* 21 October 1969. No order was made as to costs and the Home Secretary agreed to make an *ex gratia* payment to the costs of the applicant, a voter in one of the constituencies affected by the English Commission's recommendations. The several interesting issues raised by the application (for example, whether it constituted an impeachment of 'proceedings in Parliament'; see ch. 17) were not determined.

[34] 791 H.C. Deb. *428–571* (12 November 1969). The Attorney-General, winding up the debate for the Government, declared (col. 550) that the Home Secretary's actions had been 'lawful . . . sensible and wise', and that only 'the malicious and the misinformed could be capable of taking any other view'.

[35] S.I. 1970, Nos. 1674, 1675, 1678, 1680.

In 1983 the Labour Party again objected to the effects of the recommendations of the Boundary Commission for England, as it believed that once more they would cost the Party seats at the General Election. The Leader and other senior members of the Labour Party sought orders of prohibition and injunctions to restrain the Commission from submitting its proposals to the Home Secretary on the ground that the Commission had misdirected itself in law. The Court of Appeal rejected the challenge, broadly because the Commission had in its view properly interpreted the rules in and under the House of Commons (Redistribution of Seats) Acts of 1949 and 1958 and had exercised its discretion on all points reasonably.[36] The changes were implemented in the ordinary way.

Method of voting[37]

The general rule is that on election day voters must go in person to the appropriate polling station in their constituency, where they will be handed a ballot paper listing the names of the candidates. The voter enters a polling booth and makes a cross in a space alongside the name of one candidate; the voter folds the ballot paper and drops it into a sealed ballot box. The fiction that a voter chooses the most suitable candidate irrespective of his party affiliations was maintained by a rule precluding the incorporation in the ballot paper of words indicating the political attitudes of candidates – a rule which caused some difficulty not so long ago in a Welsh constituency where there were three candidates named Jones – till 1969 when a statute permitted the insertion of up to six words descriptive of the candidate's political associations.[38]

In the celebrated case of *Ashby* v. *White* (1703)[39] it was held that the right to vote was in the nature of a proprietary right, and that a returning officer refusing for improper motives to allow a qualified elector to cast his vote was liable in damages. Under section 63 of the Representation of the People Act 1983,[40] no civil liability is incurred by an election officer in respect of a breach of his official duties, though he may be criminally liable. No election officer may refuse to give a ballot

---

[36] *R.* v. *Boundary Commission for England, ex p. Foot and others* [1983] Q.B. 600. In appropriate cases relief would be granted by a declaration, not prohibition, as the latter would wholly preclude Parliament from considering the Commission's proposals: ibid. pp. 645–6.

[37] See Representation of the People Act 1985, s. 5.

[38] See now 1983 Act, s. 23 and sched. 1, rule 6(2), (3).

[39] 2 Ld. Raym. 938.

[40] As amended by the Representation of the People Act 1985, sched. 4.

paper to a person whose name appears on the register – save in Northern Ireland:[41] there, voters must first furnish a specified identity document,[42] and if there is reasonable doubt whether the voter is who he claims to be he may be refused a ballot paper.[43] In England, Wales and Scotland, if the election officer has grounds for believing that any such person is legally disqualified (for example, by reason of minority, or because he has already voted) it is his duty so to warn him; if that person nevertheless proceeds to vote though disqualified, he may be prosecuted for an election offence.

Special arrangements are made for casting of votes by persons with service qualifications and by persons who have applied to be registered as absent voters.[44] As a general rule, service and absent voters may vote by post or by proxy. To qualify as an absent voter an elector may either be registered as such for an indefinite period (because, for example, of the nature of his employment, or his infirmity), or for a particular election (because, for instance, he will be away on holiday on the day of the poll).

At the close of the polls (10 p.m.) the ballot boxes are transported to a central counting station in the constituency and emptied, and the ballot papers are counted together with postal and proxy votes. The candidate with the largest number of votes is declared by the returning officer to be elected. There is no requirement that a candidate obtain a minimum percentage of the total vote to be elected.

By-elections to fill vacancies caused by death, resignation or other cause are conducted in essentially the same manner.

The British system of election is often called 'first past the post'. It has been criticized as unfair to parties other than Conservative or Labour. For example, at the General Election of 1987, Social Democratic and Liberal Alliance candidates obtained 22.6 per cent of the national vote, but only 3 per cent of the seats in the House: Labour achieved only rather more of the popular votes (30.8 per cent), but the system awarded it 36 per cent of the seats. The figures above speak of injustice.[45] But the first past the post system is traditionally defended

---

[41] Elections (Northern Ireland) Act 1985, s. 1(2).

[42] i.e. a driving licence, DHSS payment or order book, NHS card or marriage certificate: ibid.

[43] A refusal is subject to any election petition (see below, p. 258), but is otherwise final: ibid., s. 2.

[44] See 1985 Act, ss 6–9.

[45] For a powerful criticism, see H.W.R. Wade, *Constitutional Fundamentals* (1980), ch. 2, in which the author calls for a redistribution of seats on a more representative basis, election to the Commons by proportional representation and a fair system for the selection of candidates.

by arguing that a General Election is, in effect, the choice of a Government. A party winning 48 per cent of the national vote is almost certain to have an overall majority of seats in the House.[46] Many people who might otherwise be inclined to vote for non-Conservative and non-Labour candidates traditionally have either abstained from voting or have voted for a candidate of one of the two major parties in order not to 'waste' their vote; they have believed that the election of a few more members from the smaller parties will not affect the formation of the next Government.

There is obviously a case for reforming the electoral system with a view to reducing the discrepancy between votes cast for and seats won by a party campaigning on a national scale. That case has been argued for years by the Liberal Party and subsequently by the Democrats;[47] and proportional representation has been introduced in part of the United Kingdom – Northern Ireland (for the Northern Ireland Assembly in 1973, and for Northern Ireland elections to the European Parliament in 1978). The most favoured systems[48] are the alternative vote and proportional representation. The *alternative vote* is used in single-member constituencies at elections to the Australian House of Representatives when there are more than two candidates. The voter must place the candidates in order of preference by marking his ballot-paper 1,2,3 ... If no candidate obtains an absolute majority by counting first preferences, the candidate at the bottom of the poll is eliminated, and his second preference votes are distributed among the other candidates, and so on (if necessary) till one candidate has more than 50 per cent of the vote. The result may be that the candidate placed second on the first count wins the seat. A closer correspondence between votes cast and seats won can be achieved by a system of *proportional representation*. The best-known proportional systems are

---

[46] Only in 1931 and in 1935 has a party achieved over 50 per cent of the vote. Even Mrs Thatcher's landslide majority of 144 seats in 1983 was obtained with only 42·4 per cent of the votes cast; her 101-seat majority in 1987 resulted from a slightly smaller percentage.

[47] S.D.P./Liberal Alliance, *Electoral Reform: Fairer Voting in Natural Constituencies* (1982); such reform was advocated in the Alliance manifestos at the 1983 and 1987 General Elections. But the Liberal Party claim that the present electoral system is in breach of a provision of the European Convention on Human Rights which guarantees the free expression of the people's will was rejected by the European Commission on Human Rights in *Liberal Party* v. *United Kingdom* (1980) 4 E.H.R.R. 106.

[48] For fuller details see, for example, Enid Lakeman, *How Democracies Vote* (3rd edn, 1970) and *Power to Elect* (1982); S. E. Finer, *Adversary Politics and Electoral Reform* (1975); V. Bogdanor and D. Butler, *Democracy and Elections* (1983); Blake Report of the Hansard Commission (1976); Oliver [1983] *Public Law* 108.

the single transferable vote (STV) and the party list system; there are numerous variants, including mixed systems. Proportional systems require multi-member constituencies. Under STV (which is used in elections in the republics of Ireland and Malta and for the Australian Senate) the voter marks his preferences numerically against the names of candidates; where a candidate has obtained a large enough percentage of the total poll to ensure that he must be elected,[49] his second preferences are redistributed among the other candidates, and so on till all the seats are filled. The larger the number of seats to be filled in a constituency, the more closely will their allocation reflect the electoral support enjoyed by the various candidates. Under the party list system in its simplest form, each party puts up a national list of candidates in ranking order; each voter casts a single vote for one party list; a party obtaining 40 per cent of the national vote will fill 40 per cent of the seats with the candidates ranked highest in its list.

Various Western European countries use proportional electoral systems. More often than not they bring about coalition or minority governments because no party wins an overall majority. But plans for basic changes in the electoral system in the United Kingdom founder on the combined hostility of the two main parties. Each party believes that under the first-past-the-post system it has a good chance of winning the next (or next but one) General Election with an outright majority; and to win an election is to win power for four or five years. Why, then, meddle with our ancient institutions which have served us so well for so long? At least in this context, 'consensus politics' is not a figment of the imagination.

Members

Before touching upon the conduct of an election campaign, we need to say something of the qualifications for membership of the House of Commons and the ways in which a candidate may be selected.

Disqualification for membership of the House

There are three preliminary points. First, there is no list of basic qualifications; there is simply a list of disqualifications. The former property and residential qualifications for candidates were abolished

---

[49] If, for example, four seats are to be filled in a constituency where 100,000 persons vote, a candidate obtaining $[100,000/(4 + 1)] + 1$ (i.e. 20,001) votes from first preferences will be declared elected, because it is impossible for any four other candidates to beat him.

long ago; it is indeed fairly unusual for a candidate from one of the two main national parties to be a local man, though he is often expected by his constituency party to take up local residence when he becomes their prospective candidate. Secondly, some disqualifications, significant in their day, have been removed by statute as being obnoxious or unnecessary. All religious disqualifications had been removed by 1888; the disqualification (or lack of qualification) of women was removed in 1918; the remaining disqualifications attached to Government contractors and Crown pensioners were abolished in 1957. Thirdly, if a candidate is subject to a legal disqualification, the returning officer is not allowed to reject his nomination papers if they are otherwise in order; his rights to be elected and to sit in the Commons are determinable (as we shall see) by other means if he is elected to the seat.

The following are disqualified.[50]

1   Aliens. These are persons who are neither British citizens nor Commonwealth citizens nor citizens of the Republic of Ireland.[51]
2   Persons under twenty-one years of age.[52]
3   Persons suffering from severe mental illness. They were disqualified at common law; the non-statutory disqualification has been supplemented by section 141 of the Mental Health Act 1983 under which the Speaker must be notified if a member is detained as a mental patient; if the member is still detained as a mental patient six months later, his seat will be vacated.
4   Peers and peeresses in their own right,[53] other than peers of Ireland (who are not qualified to sit in the House of Lords[54]).
5   Persons who receive a prison sentence of more than one year, or an indefinite sentence, are disqualified from membership of the House while detained.[55] If a person so disqualified is elected to the

---

[50] See Sir Thomas Erskine May, *Parliamentary Practice* (20th edn, 1983), ch. 3; *Halsbury's Laws of England* (4th edn), vol. 34, *Parliament*, with Cumulative Supplement. Some disqualifications do not automatically cause vacation of the seat but debar a member from sitting and voting while subject to the disability. In practice it is impossible to *sit* without participating in a vote; the recurrent formal resolutions passed every day without a division will entail a unanimous vote.

[51] For definitions of these terms see above, p. 239.

[52] This provision was preserved by the Family Law Reform Act 1969 which for most legal purposes reduced the age of majority to eighteen; see s. 1(4) of that Act and para. 2 of schedule 2. Before 1832 several infants (including Charles James Fox) nevertheless sat as members.

[53] For the meaning of this concept, see pp. 297-8.

[54] See *Re Earl of Antrim's Petition* [1967] 1 A.C. 691.

[55] Representation of the People Act 1981, s. 1. The Act is also retrospective to include such sentences passed before 1981, a provision which has rightly been criticized: see Walker [1982] *Public Law* 389.

House, then that election is void, and if a sitting member is so disqualified his seat is vacated.[56] A member who is imprisoned for any other lesser period for an offence other than treason is merely prevented from sitting and voting while serving his sentence,[57] but the House could vote to expel him. A person serving a definite prison sentence of less than one year for a non-treasonable crime is not disqualified from election. Persons serving sentences for treason are disqualified.[58]

6   Bankrupts. Persons adjudged bankrupt by a court are disqualified from being elected to, or sitting or voting in, the House. The disqualification ceases on discharge from bankruptcy. The court must inform the Speaker forthwith of a member's declaration of bankruptcy and, if that bankruptcy lasts for six months or more, his seat is vacated.[59]

7   Persons convicted of corrupt and illegal practices at elections. These disqualifications are rather more extensive than those affecting the exercise of the franchise by persons so convicted.[60]

8   Clergy. A motley collection of statutory provisions, enacted at different times to meet particular problems, disqualify some ministers of religion but not others. Ministers of the Church of England, the Episcopalian Church of Scotland and all other Protestant clergymen (including ministers of the Church of Ireland)[61] ordained by bishops, except ministers of the disestablished Church of Wales, are disqualified; so are Roman Catholic priests, and ministers of the Established (Presbyterian) Church of Scotland; but nonconformist ministers, and ministers of non-Christian denominations, are not disqualified. To say that the law is a mass of archaic anomalies is one thing; to rationalize it, given the discordant sentiments expressed by the religious bodies themselves, is another. A select committee of the House which investigated the whole matter in the early 1950s recommended[62] that no change be then made, and the same view was taken by

---

[56] ibid., s. 2.
[57] This appears to be the result of the amendment of s. 2 of the Forfeiture Act 1870 by s. 10 of and Part III of the Third Schedule to the Criminal Law Act 1967.
[58] Forfeiture Act 1870 (as amended by the Criminal Law Act 1967, Sched. 3).
[59] Insolvency Act 1986, s. 427. The old rule which continued a member's disqualification for five years after discharge was repealed by the 1986 Act.
[60] Representation of the People Act 1983, ss 159, 160, 173, 174; see also p. 240.
[61] *Re MacManaway* [1951] A.C. 161.
[62] H.C. 200 (1952–3).

another select committee a few years later.[63] This strange tangle is likely to be with us for some time.[64]

9   Ministers of the Crown. Not more than ninety-five holders of specified ministerial offices may sit and vote at any one time in the House of Commons (House of Commons Disqualification Act 1975, s. 2(1) and Schedule 2). Since by convention a Minister must have or obtain a seat in one or other House, the appointment of a person to ministerial office when the maximum number has already been reached implies that he must be a peer or be granted a peerage; or that a sitting member be granted a peerage to make room for him; or that legislation be passed rapidly to regularize the position; or (possibly) that the new Minister be given an office not hitherto recognized by statute; though amending legislation would again be needed to provide him with a salary and legal powers.[65] The maximum number of persons to whom salaries may be paid as holders of certain ministerial offices is prescribed by statute.[66] In 1937 the Ministers of the Crown Act rationalized the law by grouping ministerial offices and specifying how many holders of offices in each group could sit and vote in (i.e. be members of) the House of Commons at any one time. The permissible number was enlarged by individual Acts creating new Ministers, and again, in more general terms, by statutes passed in 1957 and in 1964. The governing statute is now the House of Commons Disqualification Act 1975.[67] The modern policy is to strike a balance between the principle that every major Department ought to have a ministerial spokesman in the Commons and the undesirability of having the Government side of the House overweighted by Ministers at the expense of backbenchers.

10   Holders of public offices. The meaning of an office or place of profit which disqualified or rendered its holder liable to vacate his seat and stand for re-election remained obscure, and also highly inconvenient, for till 1951 a common informer could sue a disqualified member for a penalty of £500 for each day on which he had sat and voted; frequently Parliament would be asked to

[63] Select Committee on the House of Commons Disqualification Bill (H.C. *349* (1955–6)).
[64] Though informed opinion in the Church of England now seems to favour repeal of the disqualifications: see *Church and State* (1970), pp. 57–8 (The Report of the Archbishops' Commission).
[65] The last two expedients were resorted to in 1964 when Mr Wilson appointed a number of Ministers in excess of the maximum then authorized: see Park (1965) 28 *Mod. L. Rev.* 338.
[66] Ministerial and other Salaries Act 1975.
[67] Section 2(1) and sched. 2.

pass an Act indemnifying an individual member against the legal consequences of having accepted in good faith a position (for example, unpaid membership of a special tribunal) which might still be construed as an office or place of 'profit' in the gift of the Crown. The only remedy was to replace the general phrase by an explicit list of offices, tenure of which ought to disqualify because they required a degree of political impartiality or a burden of continuing responsibility incompatible with membership of the House of Commons. A bill to this effect was introduced in 1955, amended after detailed examination by a select committee of the House,[68] and passed into law as the House of Commons Disqualification Act 1957 (now the House of Commons Disqualification Act 1975).

The main classes of persons thus disqualified for membership are as follows.

(*a*) Professional full-time judges.
(*b*) Civil servants.
(*c*) Members of the regular armed forces.
(*d*) Full-time members of a police force.
(*e*) Members of the legislatures of non-Commonwealth countries.[69]
(*f*) Members of independent public boards and commissions, the chairman and sometimes the members of 'administrative' tribunals, and other persons occupying offices requiring political neutrality, judicial detachment or other characteristics inconsistent with membership of the House. These disqualifying posts are listed in full in the First Schedule to the 1975 Act; the list may be varied by statute, or by Order in Council made in pursuance of a resolution of the House. The 1975 Act may be reprinted in an amended and up-to-date form so that candidates and members may know how they stand.

11   Acceptance of the offices of bailiff or steward of the Chiltern Hundreds or the Manor of Northstead. This is the traditional manner of resigning membership; these offices are sinecures and nominal offices of profit under the Crown, and acceptance of any of them is expressly preserved as a ground of disqualification by section 4 of the 1975 Act.

12   Expulsion by resolution of the House. The House may declare a member's seat vacant, either because he has incurred a legal

---

[68] For the report of the Select Committee, see H.C. *349* (1955–6). For the report of an earlier committee, reviewing more fully the history of the problem, see H.C. *120* (1940–41).

[69] This excludes members of the Parliament of the Republic of Ireland.

disqualification or for any other reason whatsoever; this is one of its privileges. It cannot, however, prevent that person from standing as a candidate at a by-election.[70]

Effect of disqualification. (1) If a person already subject to a legal incapacity (for example, peerage) is elected to membership then (*a*) the House may declare his seat vacant, or (*b*) a petition may be lodged to have him unseated in pursuance of the finding by an election court that his election was void.[71] (2) If a sitting member incurs a disqualification, then (*a*) the House may declare his seat vacant, if it is not automatically vacated by the nature of the disqualification; or (*b*) any member of the public may apply to the Privy Council for a declaration that a member is disqualified under the 1975 Act; the matter is to be referred to the Judicial Committee;[72] or (*c*) the House itself may petition the Crown to have the matter referred to the Judicial Committee for an advisory opinion;[73] or (*d*) the House may, if it thinks fit, waive the effect of a disqualification under the 1975 Act if it has already been removed;[74] or (*e*) a common informer may still pursue his action for penalties against an episcopally ordained clergyman who sits and votes while subject to the disqualification.[75]

Selection of candidates

Under our present system of two alternately dominant parties, a large majority of seats will be 'safe' for either the Conservative or the Labour candidate at a General Election,[76] unless there is a substantial swing in

---

[70] See p. 324.

[71] For election petitions, see pp. 258–9. When Mr Tony Benn succeeded to his father's peerage as Viscount Stansgate, he argued that he was entitled to retain his seat in the Commons because he had not applied for a writ of summons to the Lords. The House referred the matter to the Committee of Privileges; the Committee found against Mr Benn and the House adopted its report and declared his seat vacant. He stood as a candidate at the ensuing by-election, which he won, but was unseated on an election petition by his defeated opponent: *Re Parliamentary Election for Bristol South-East* (1961), reported [1964] 2 Q.B. 257. When the Peerage Act 1963 was passed he immediately disclaimed his peerage and was able to regain his seat.

[72] House of Commons Disqualification Act 1975, s. 7. The applicant must furnish security for costs. No such proceeding has been brought; this is hardly surprising.

[73] Under section 4 of the Judicial Committee Act 1833. This procedure was adopted in *Re MacManaway* [1951] A.C. 161.

[74] As by resignation from the disqualifying office: 1975 Act, s. 6.

[75] Under the House of Commons (Clergy Disqualification) Act 1801.

[76] The position may be more fluid at a by-election, where candidates from smaller national or regional parties, or even independents, may benefit from a big 'protest' vote or large-scale abstentions. At by-elections the voters know that they are not participating in the choice of a Government.

public support away from one of the parties, in which case safe seats may become marginal. Hence the selection of the official candidate for the Conservative or Labour Party, as the case may be, will as a rule effectively determine who will win the seat. For most of those who vote, a General Election is a ritualistic affirmation of support for (or hostility to) one of the two main national parties and a means of choosing a Government; and an unattractive candidate will seldom cause his party to lose the seat. In England, it is rare, but not impossible,[77] for an Independent M.P. to be elected even at a by-election.[78] In both Scotland and Wales the pattern is nowadays far from the same as in England. Nationalists and Democrats may win a fair proportion of the seats, and the personal attributes of candidates will sometimes count for more than the blessing of a mass party organization. Northern Ireland, too, may provide a number of Independent M.P.s in the Commons.

The role of political parties in the British system of government is too big a topic to be considered adequately in a primarily legal work.[79] The part played by the parties in the House of Commons will be briefly touched on in the next chapter. In the selection of candidates, party choice is wholly unregulated by rules of strict law, and depends on extra-legal[80] party rules and practices. In many states in the United States of America, and in a few other countries, statutory provision is made for primary elections to select official party candidates. This democratic safeguard is absent in Britain (though recently some Conservative constituency associations have conducted informal polls to select prospective party candidates), and party choice is sometimes still determined by an inner group of party activists and national office-holders.

Selection[81] is mainly a matter for local constituency parties. In the Labour Party, nominations of prospective candidates come from ward branches and affiliated organizations (normally trade unions). Labour Party headquarters has lists of officially approved candidates. The executive committee of the constituency party draws up a short list, and the candidate is then chosen, subject to the approval of the National Executive Committee of the party, by a selection conference of the constituency party's general management committee. At the 1987 Labour Party conference it was decided to establish an electoral college

---

[77] See p. 255.

[78] For the figures from 1900 to 1979, see David Butler and Gareth Butler, *British Political Facts 1900–1985* (6th edn, 1986), pp. 172–3.

[79] The leading modern work is R. T. McKenzie, *British Political Parties* (2nd edn, 1970).

[80] Though cf. *John* v. *Rees* [1970] Ch. 345 (natural justice to be observed in disaffiliation or suspension of local party organization).

[81] See R. L. Leonard, *Elections in Britain* (1968), pp. 65–81 for a good short account, and Michael Rush, *The Selection of Parliamentary Candidates* (1969) for a very full study.

in every constituency to select parliamentary candidates; trade union representatives would have 40 per cent of each college's votes and ordinary members 60 per cent. Occasionally a prospective candidate, or a sitting member, is vetoed as an official candidate by the National Executive Committee; this will lead to the nomination of another candidate with official backing at the national level, and may entail disaffiliation of the constituency party. A Labour candidate lacking official backing will normally have no chance at all of being elected. Many Labour M.P.s are sponsored by trade unions.[82]

Selection procedure among the Conservatives is broadly similar to that of the Labour Party, though ratification of the final choice is made by a general meeting of the whole constituency association[83] (and occasionally by postal ballot of members). The Conservative Central Office also has its approved list, but it hardly ever refuses to endorse a local choice. Conservative candidates and M.P.s are not allowed to make more than a nominal contribution to their constituency association's funds. In practice Conservative M.P.s come from a smaller range of social groups than Labour M.P.s, more having been to public schools and Oxbridge, and very few manual workers occupy Conservative seats. Nevertheless, the differences between the social complexions of the front benches of the two parliamentary parties are now less striking than their similarities.

There is no constitutional procedure whereby an M.P. can be compelled by his constituents to vacate his seat, but it is open to the constituency party or association to adopt a different candidate at the next General Election if they are dissatisfied with their member's conduct or political stance. This can be a very real threat to a member's independence. Since 1980 the Labour Party has had an automatic reselection process: each M.P. must undergo reselection (or, if he is unlucky, deselection) once in every Parliament. Several Labour M.P.s have thereby indirectly lost their seats. A member may, of course, be refused official backing by party headquarters at an election. It is also open to the national party headquarters to seek to protect the member; but their practical freedom of action is restricted, especially in the Conservative Party.[84]

---

[82] See K. Ewing, *The Funding of Political Parties in Britain* (1987). Companies contributing to national party funds must now disclose the fact in their accounts: Companies Act 1985, s. 235. As was to be expected, the contributions go overwhelmingly to the Conservative Party. A large part of the Labour Party's income is derived from trade unions and the political levy imposed on their members.

[83] Democrat candidates are chosen by secret ballot at constituency party meetings (although postal votes may be cast by absentees), and S.D.P. candidates by postal vote in the constituencies.

[84] Peter G. J. Pulzer, *Political Representation and Elections in Britain* (2nd edn, 1972), pp. 77–81.

Electoral campaigns

Following a dissolution, candidates wishing to stand for election must submit nomination papers (signed by a proposer, a seconder and eight other voters) to the returning officer within eight clear days; polling day will be nine clear days afterwards – in practice on a Thursday. The rules governing by-elections are basically the same except that the issue of the writ for holding an election will be made by the Speaker on the resolution of the House of Commons. By custom the necessary motion is moved by a whip from the party which held the seat before the vacancy arose.[85] A party fearing loss of such a seat sometimes refrains from moving the motion for months, leaving the constituency unrepresented.[86] The Recess Elections Act 1975, which replaced earlier statutory provisions, puts the Speaker under a duty to issue writs for by-elections at the request of any two members during a parliamentary recess; it would be interesting to see this procedure invoked against the wishes of the party that held the seat.

Before party candidates are nominated, it is usual for them to be formally adopted at a special constituency members' meeting, though that is not required by law. But every candidate must appoint an election agent (who may be himself), and the agent will be accountable to the returning officer after the polls for election expenditure. Some frivolous candidatures may still be discouraged by the rule that upon nomination a candidate must deposit the sum of £500 which will be forfeited if he fails to obtain more than one-twentieth of the votes cast.[87]

Attempts have been made by legal regulation to ensure as far as possible that election campaigns are fairly conducted.[88] Bribery, treating and undue influence in the nature of duress are corrupt practices. Candidates are allowed to send an election address to each voter free of postage, and are not to be refused permission to hire schools maintained by the local education authority for election meetings. Under non-statutory agreements between the main parties,

---

[85] A custom confirmed by the House in 1983 when an Opposition party sought to move for a by-election writ against the wishes of the Government which had held the seat in question: 11 H.C. Deb. *164–71* (19 April 1983).

[86] Swindon was without a member for seven months in 1969. A Speaker's Conference on Electoral Law has recommended that normally a writ should be sought within 3 months of a vacancy: see Cmnd 5000 (1973).

[87] Representation of the People Act 1985, s. 13. Before that Act the deposit had been £150 and a poll of one-eighth of the votes cast saved it.

[88] Probably the best account of the details of electoral law is in Halsbury's *Laws of England* (4th edn), vol. 15, *Elections*, with Cumulative Supplement.

the broadcasting authorities allocate time for party election programmes in a reasonably equitable manner on a national basis. At the 1987 General Election the Conservative, Labour and Alliance parties were given the same number of election programmes, an allocation of time reflected in news and current affairs programmes.[89] And expenditure on elections is limited by law so that not too much weight shall be given to the power of the purse. The law relating to election expenses is in some respects intricate, obscure and unsatisfactory — characteristics reflecting not merely the intrinsic difficulty of detailed regulation but also the influence of vested interests in the main parties which would prefer the law to be vague on certain points. The main general rules are as follows.

1 That no expenditure may be incurred with a view to promoting or procuring the election of a candidate at an election by any person other than the candidate himself or his agent or a person authorized by the agent.[90]
2 That the maximum expenditure to be incurred at an election shall be restricted to £3,370 for a constituency, plus 3.8p for each registered voter in a county constituency, and 2.9p for each registered voter in a borough constituency.[91]
3 That certain kinds of expenditure (notably on broadcasting from outside the United Kingdom except by arrangement with the BBC and the IBA)[92] which might give a wealthy party an unfair advantage shall be absolutely prohibited. The cost of national party election broadcasts and of postage for candidates' election addresses is, however, met by the State.

The difficulties are mostly concerned with the first of these rules, taken in conjunction with the second. What is the relevant period for the purpose of election expenditure? Does it begin with the announcement of a forthcoming dissolution, the proclamation of dissolution, the

---

[89] See Boyle [1986] *Public Law* 562.
[90] Representation of the People Act 1983, s. 75. Criticism of an opponent is capable of promoting the election of a candidate who might incur an unauthorized expense in so doing: *D.P.P.* v. *Luft* [1977] A.C. 962.
[91] 1983 Act, s. 76(1), (2), (3) and 76A (added by the Representation of the People Act 1985, s. 14) allows the Secretary of State to raise these amounts by statutory instrument 'where in his opinion there has been a change in the value of money' since the previous increase – the phenomenon of inflation thus being recognized in the statute book. The latest provision is in S.I. 1987, No. 903.
[92] 1983 Act, s. 92. Broadcasts within this country about a constituency during an election period cannot include a candidate without that candidate's consent: a veto is given to a candidate who would actively participate in a broadcast (as in an interview), but not to a candidate who would merely be shown in it (for example, on film canvassing: *Marshall* v. *BBC* [1979] 1 W.L.R. 1071).

adoption of candidates, the presentation of nomination papers?[93] Probably the earliest of these dates is the relevant one,[94] though in a sense the party organizations are waging a continuous electoral campaign throughout the life of a Parliament. Again, does expenditure at the national level during the election period have to be apportioned between all constituencies in which the party's candidates are standing, or is it only relevant to consider propaganda distributed or otherwise used in the particular constituency? British electoral law places its emphasis, with a disarming lack of conviction, on the individual constituency and the individual candidate; and the general interpretation, supported directly or indirectly by two modern judicial decisions, is that only expenditure for the purpose of promoting the election of an individual candidate in his constituency (as distinct from expenditure directed to procuring the election or defeat of candidates of a particular party in general) has to be counted as an election expense.[95] Neither of the main parties is likely to challenge this benevolent interpretation. In any event, newspaper articles and comments and political broadcasting programmes (as distinct from advertisements) are expressly excluded from the definition of election expenses, even if the money is spent with a view to promoting the election of a particular candidate.[96]

References in this chapter to the role of the returning officer must not obscure the fact that the burden of organizing the machinery of an election, and particularly the poll and the count, rest mainly on the registration officer.

Election petitions

A voter or a defeated candidate may lodge a petition against the validity of an election.[97] Since 1868 petitions have been heard by an election court, now consisting in England of two judges of the Queen's Bench Division, who may sit in the constituency in question.

[93] Authorities are considered in *Halsbury's Laws of England* (4th edn), vol. 15, paras 707–12.

[94] See s.93 of the 1983 Act, adopting the announcement of dissolution for the purpose of rules concerning broadcasts 'during' elections.

[95] See *R.* v. *Tronoh Mines Ltd* [1952] 1 All E.R. 697 (newspaper advertisement by company advocating defeat of the Labour Government at the impending General Election of 1951, held not an election expense within the meaning of s. 63 of the 1949 Act: now s. 75 of the 1983 Act); see also *Grieve* v. *Douglas-Home* [1965] S.C. 313 (party political broadcast featuring the then Prime Minister held not to be expenditure 'with a view to' procuring his election in his constituency).

[96] 1983 Act, s. 75(1); this amendment resolved any doubt that survived the decision in *Grieve* v. *Douglas-Home* (see above) on party political broadcasts.

[97] The law is now governed by Part III of the Representation of the People Act 1983.

Petitions based on illegal or corrupt practices or other irregularities at parliamentary elections are now extremely rare; this is partly because very close contests are uncommon and even if the court finds that irregularities were present it may determine that the result ought to stand since they were unlikely to have affected the result.[98] A petition may also be lodged on the ground that the successful candidate was subject to a legal incapacity – for example, peerage.[99] In such a case the court may, if satisfied that the incapacity existed, either declare the election void (so that a by-election has to be held) or, if satisfied that the voters for the successful candidate had had his incapacity sufficiently brought to their notice so that they must be deemed deliberately to have thrown their votes away, award the seat to the runner-up.[100] Normally the petition has to be lodged within three weeks of the date of the election.

In form the judgment of an election court is a report to the Speaker, which the House is directed by statute to accept. By the act of resolving that the report be recorded in the Journals of the House, the empty shell of the ancient privilege of the House is preserved.

The other methods by which the qualification of an elected member to sit in the House may be challenged and determined have already been noted.[101]

[98] There are other reasons, including the maxim that dog does not bite dog: see Geoffrey Wilson, *Cases and Materials* (2nd edn, 1976), pp. 131–2.

[99] See *Re Parliamentary Election for Bristol South-East* [1964] 2 Q.B. 257 (the Stansgate Peerage case). See also the Northern Ireland cases of *Mitchell* and *Clarke* [1958] N.I. 143, 151 (successful candidates serving long sentences for felony, then a disqualification for election).

[100] Thus, the Bristol South-East seat was awarded to Viscount Stansgate's (Mr Tony Benn's) defeated opponent after the by-election caused by the resolution of the House declaring the seat to be vacant.

[101] See p. 253.

Chapter 15

The House of Commons: Functions and Procedure [1]

Introduction

Officers

The House of Commons has 650 members, including the Speaker. The first business of the House at the opening of a new Parliament is to elect a Speaker from among its members; the Queen formally signifies her approval of the Commons' choice. The Speaker is expected to be an absolutely impartial chairman of debate; in no sense is he a spokesman for the Government. In early days he was the spokesman for the Commons in relation to the Crown and the Lords. His function of presenting the views of the Commons to the monarch made his position fraught with hazard, and the show of reluctance that he puts up today as he is propelled gently to the Speaker's chair after his election is a reminder of things past.

His election is normally unopposed in the House, and he is not always a member on the Government side. He can be removed by a simple resolution of the House, but this state of affairs will arise only if he has comported himself with serious impropriety. The usual practice is to re-elect the Speaker of the preceding Parliament if he has been returned at the General Election and is willing to stand for office again. As Speaker he detaches himself from his former party affiliations, although his seat will often be contested by other parties at a General Election. [2]

---

[1] See generally Rodney Brazier, *Constitutional Practice* (1988), ch. 9.
[2] Suggestions that the Speaker's constituents are in effect unrepresented in the House because of his non-political role overlook the fact that he will take up their problems with Ministers and in that capacity may carry greater weight than an ordinary backbencher. On the Speakership, see Lord Selwyn-Lloyd, *Mr Speaker, Sir* (1976); Philip Laundy, *The Office of Speaker* (1984).

The Speaker does not participate in debate, even when the House is sitting in committee. Nor does he vote on a motion, unless a casting vote from the chair is required; the manner in which he is to cast such a vote is circumscribed by precedent. His main functions in the House are to maintain decorum in debate, to call upon members to speak, to give rulings on points of order and on a question whether a *prima facie* case of breach of privilege has been established, and to act as the servant of the House (for example, in directing the issue of writs for filling vacancies) or as its spokesman (for example, in delivering a reprimand or admonition to one found guilty of contempt of the House; or in communications with legislatures overseas or on ceremonial occasions). As the incarnation of the ancient dignity of the House, he is habitually treated with great respect, indeed deference. Important discretionary functions fall to be discharged by him from time to time – for example, certifying whether a bill is a money bill within the meaning of the Parliament Act 1911; suspending a member for a day for disorderly conduct, or naming a member (who may then incur a period of suspension) for persistent disregard of the authority of the chair;[3] appointing members of the panel of chairmen of committees at the beginning of each session;[4] deciding whether to accept a motion for the closure of debate, and whether to put to the House for debate a question raised as an urgent matter of public importance. He has the same rate of salary as a Cabinet Minister, charged on the Consolidated Fund so that it does not require annual renewal, and a house within the Palace of Westminster. When he retires he will be offered a peerage; the former custom of making a retiring Speaker a viscount was revived in 1983 for Mr George Thomas.

The office of Deputy Speaker is filled by three members elected by the House – the Chairman and Deputy Chairmen of Ways and Means. At least two belong to the party in office, but when in the chair, they are expected to observe the same impartiality as the Speaker. Most of the Speaker's powers are exercisable by them.

The Speaker is assisted by the Clerk of the House of Commons, the other clerks at the table (whose functions are by no means merely clerical), a personal legal adviser, Speaker's Counsel, and an administrative officer, Speaker's Secretary. The Serjeant at Arms attends upon the Speaker; he executes orders of the House (for example, to clear the public galleries; to take a person into custody), and is generally responsible for the domestic staff arrangements of the House.

---

[3] See p. 327, note 55.
[4] For the functions of the Business Committee of the House (consisting of the chairmen, and other members nominated by the Speaker), see pp. 269–70.

Records

The formal record of the transactions of the House is the Journal of the House, published annually. The Journals do not purport to summarize all that has occurred in debate. They are admissible in evidence in court. Each day the votes and proceedings of the House are recorded and circulated to members; they will record the decisions of the House and its committees, and in due course their substance will be entered in the Journals. The official report (*Hansard*) is a daily verbatim transcript of all that was said and done in the House in the course of parliamentary business; it includes, in what is in effect an appendix, written answers to questions. This is published by Her Majesty's Stationery Office with the authority of the House. It does not include reports of the proceedings of standing committees or select committees, which are published separately. Reports ordered to be laid before the House of Commons and published otherwise than in pursuance of royal or ministerial authority are called House of Commons papers, as distinct from Command papers. The Lords have their own Journals, minutes of proceedings, official reports, and series of papers.

The law and custom of Parliament

The main essentials of parliamentary procedure are contained in the standing orders[5] of the House, which are published by the Stationery Office from time to time and may be varied by a simple majority of the House, and in sessional orders which, for example, authorize the appointment of select committees which the House has not yet decided to establish on a permanent basis. Changes in these orders frequently emanate from recommendations of the Select Committee on Procedure. Separate standing orders for private bills are issued.

In addition, the conduct of parliamentary proceedings is regulated to a small extent by statute (for example, the procedure on consolidation bills) and common law; and to a large extent by resolutions of the House, Speakers' rulings and unwritten customs or conventions. Some of the most important practices governing the allocation of parliamentary time are not enshrined in any formal authoritative document.

Parliamentary privilege[6] stands in a slightly different category, though it is clearly part of the law and custom of Parliament. It is to be found partly in legislation and case-law, mainly in resolutions of each

[5] The standing orders referred to are the 1986 version: see H.C. 1 (1986–7).
[6] See ch. 17.

House, and hardly at all in standing or sessional orders or in unwritten conventions.

The debating chamber

In many legislatures the chamber is in the shape of a horseshoe, and members are able to signify their ideological position by placing themselves on the far left, the far right, or at a suitable intermediate point; speeches are normally delivered from a rostrum. The chamber of the House of Commons is rectangular; the Government benches are on the right of the elevated Speaker's chair, the Opposition are to his left. Today this division symbolizes the character of parliamentary government. Ministers sit on the Government front bench and their supporters behind them; the Opposition front bench faces them. On each side of the House the undemarcated line between frontbenchers and backbenchers will be significant. Members speak from their places and do not declaim from a rostrum; this conduces to an informal style of debate, discouraging the rhetorical flourish.[7] However, informality has its limits. Members must address themselves to the chair; when referring to other members they are to mention them not by name but by description ('the honourable member for Stretchford East'); pejorative epithets are out of order; smoking and reading newspapers are not permitted.

Facilities for members

The number of seats in the House is insufficient to accommodate all members at any one time. This dearth of space (which seldom gives rise to problems except immediately before an important division on a motion) is deliberately designed to foster the atmosphere of an intimate club; it also harks back to the days when for most members politics were far from being a full-time occupation. (Salaries were not paid to members till shortly before the First World War.) Up to 1988 M.P.s were embarrassed by having periodically to vote themselves pay rises. Now their pay is linked to a percentage of the salary earned by a senior principal in the civil service, so that as civil service salaries rise, so automatically will those of M.P.s.[8] Currently M.P.s are paid £24,017 a

[7] One of the arguments adduced against permitting television broadcasting of debates is that this would encourage members to 'play to the gallery'. But, following experiments, the Commons (as with the Lords) has allowed *sound* broadcasting of proceedings since 1978, and experimental televising of the Commons has been approved.

[8] That linkage must be approved within the first 3 months of each Parliament: see 46 H.C. Deb. 329–52 (19 July 1983); 120 H.C. Deb. 295–341 (21 July 1987).

year. They may also claim an office costs allowance for out of pocket office, secretarial and research expenses, up to a current maximum of £20,140 a year.[9] M.P.s whose homes are outside London receive a London allowance of some £8,000 a year.[10] All travel within the United Kingdom on parliamentary business is either free or qualifies for a car mileage allowance, and telephone calls and postage from the House are free. The facilities provided for members outside the chamber are on the whole unimpressive: for example, less than half of all M.P.s have private offices, the rest having to share. There is, however, an excellent library with a useful reference service.[11] The House frequently sits late into the night. Since members normally have a multiplicity of responsibilities besides attendance in the House, it is perhaps surprising that the quality of backbenchers is good and has almost certainly improved since the 1950s; this is hardly attributable to financial rewards,[12] a sense of security[13] or leisured ease, or a feeling that a backbencher is likely to set the course of the ship of state, but rather to such factors as the hope of ministerial office one fine day, a sense of excitement at being 'in the know' and close to the hub of political activity, or a desire to attract public attention to one's causes, opinions or oneself. M.P.s are on the whole a good deal more articulate than the average member of the community, and it is unkind to criticize them for having sought a place in that forum which offers the most dignified platform for eloquence and enshrines their public utterances in imperishable prose.

Parties in the House [14]

In 1937 the Ministers of the Crown Act formally recognized the status of the Leader of the Opposition, providing for a salary, charged on the

---

[9] This, too, is indexed and so rises automatically.

[10] Those living in inner London receive only £1,000.

[11] See M. Rush and M. Shaw (eds), *The House of Commons: Services and Facilities* (1974); M. Rush (ed.), *Services and Facilities of the House of Commons* (1983).

[12] Bribery of members is almost unknown. On sponsorship and retainers by pressure groups, see pp. 255, 271, 320. Fringe benefits, such as invitations to appear on television and write articles for the press are, of, course, a not unattractive by-product of political fame and acumen for some members.

[13] M.P.s do, however, qualify for a pension: see Parliamentary and other Pensions Act 1972; Parliamentary and other Pensions and Salaries Act 1976; Parliamentary Pensions etc. Act 1984; Parliamentary and other Pensions Act 1987. If an M.P. loses his seat at an election he may also receive a resettlement grant.

[14] See especially Peter G. Richards, *The Backbenchers* (1972), chs 3, 11. This book is a valuable and concise work of reference. See also Dick Leonard and Valentine Herman (eds), *The Backbencher and Parliament* (1972).

Consolidated Fund, to be paid to him. This was right and proper, for he or she is the alternative Prime Minister, and a fundamental feature of the British parliamentary system is that the leadership of the largest opposition party really is an alternative Government and should therefore be encouraged to behave like one; in short, being Leader of the Opposition[15] is a full-time job. Under the Ministerial and other Salaries Act 1975, his salary is currently £49,707, and that of the Opposition Chief Whip in the Commons is £46,737. Salaries are also paid to two Assistant Opposition Whips, and to the Leader of the Opposition and the Chief Opposition Whip in the Lords.[16]

At a special Labour Party Conference in January 1981 it was decided that in future the Leader and Deputy Leader of the Labour Party would be elected by an 'electoral college', in which 40 per cent of the votes would be cast by trade unions, 30 per cent by the constituency parties and 30 per cent by the Parliamentary Labour Party. The Leader would, moreover, be subject to re-election every year, regardless of whether the Party was in or out of office.[17] Mr Kinnock was elected under this system in 1983 on the resignation of Mr Foot and was re-elected in 1988. The Chief Whip, the Chairman of the Parliamentary Party (a backbencher), fifteen M.P.s and three peers are elected annually by the Parliamentary Party; collectively they form the Parliamentary Committee or Shadow Cabinet. Decisions of the Shadow Cabinet – the allocation of subject responsibilities to its members is a matter for the Party Leader – are reported weekly to the Parliamentary Party. Lurking in the background lie the National Executive Committee of the Party (elected by the party's annual

---

[15] Defined (Ministerial and other Salaries Act 1975, s. 2(1)) as that member 'who is for the time being the Leader of the party in that House in opposition to Her Majesty's Government having the greatest numerical strength in the House . . .' Any dispute as to who is the occupant of this post is to be determined conclusively by the Speaker.

[16] The House of Commons resolved in 1975 that money from public funds should be paid to Opposition parties to help their parliamentary work, calculated on the number of seats and votes won at the previous General Election: 888 H.C. Deb. *1869–1934* (20 March 1975). It is known as 'Short money' after the Leader of the House who introduced the concept. The present formula for fixing the allowance was approved in 1988: see 135 H.C. Deb. *1084–6* (21 June 1988). A party can receive an annual maximum of £840,000. The Report of the Committee on Financial Aid to Political Parties, Cmnd 6601 (1976), recommended a different system of state funding, but it has not been implemented. See further Michael Pinto-Duschinsky, *British Political Finance 1830–1980* (1982); Hansard Society, *Paying for Politics* (1981); K. Ewing, *The Funding of Political Parties in Britain* (1987).

[17] One consequence of this change was the creation in 1981 of the Social Democratic Party, of which the nucleus was a dozen or so M.P.s who left Labour's ranks. This number increased in subsequent defections, but only 6 S.D.P. M.P.s were returned at the 1983 General Election, and 5 at that of 1987.

national conference and including prominent trade unionists and other non-parliamentary figures) and the resolutions passed by the annual conference itself.

In the Conservative Party, the Party Leader is elected by the Parliamentary Party, and is then presented to a meeting of Conservatives drawn widely from the Party and which acts as a nominal electoral college: in effect its function is to acclaim the Leader. In 1975 Mr Heath accepted changes in the election rules, and offered himself for re-election: he lost to Mrs Thatcher. The new rules require annual re-election. The Leader appoints the Deputy Leader, the Chief Whip, the Party Chairman and the Shadow Cabinet; he or she also has ultimate control of the party bureaucracy, a function vested, within the Labour Party, in the National Executive Committee. The Party's annual conference[18] has tended to be more deferential than the corresponding Labour Party conference, and indeed of late has been contrived to appear as a telegenic party rally. Within the Parliamentary Party there are elected specialized and regional committees. All backbench members belong to the 1922 committee, a body to which the leadership must pay careful attention despite the fact that in form this committee is only a discussion group.[19]

Party organization within the House is therefore far from being a haphazard affair. Whether a party is in office or in opposition, the role of the whips is of crucial importance in conveying the views of the rank and file to the leadership and vice versa; in keeping members informed by circular of forthcoming parliamentary business; in giving the expected times of divisions in order to secure a high attendance – by underlining the matter once, twice, or thrice; failure to comply with a three-line whip without a very good excuse is often to be construed as an act of rebellion against the leadership – in arranging, in consultation with whips on the other side, for an indisposed member, or one with an urgent outside commitment, to absent himself by 'pairing' him with another member who also wishes to be absent from the division, so that neither party will obtain an advantage; in making informal recommendations to the leadership about the suitability of backbenchers for preferment; in supplying names of members to serve on committees of the House and in helping to impose party discipline by suasion, admonition and, if necessary, threats that the party whip may be

[18] The conference is called the Annual Conference of the National Union of Conservative and Unionist Associations.
[19] John P. Mackintosh, *The British Cabinet* (3rd edn, 1977), pp. 594–5, mentions some of the decisions influenced by the committee.

withdrawn or that the ultimate sanction of expulsion from the Parliamentary Party may be imposed.[20] However, disciplinary penalties on Labour members may be imposed only by the Parliamentary Party itself and the Conservative whip is hardly ever withdrawn. Those Labour M.P.s who, by defying a three-line whip, enabled the European Communities Bill to pass, were not disciplined. All Government whips are now salaried and the Chief Whip attends Cabinet meetings. The senior whips also have an important part to play in organizing the distribution of parliamentary time 'through the usual channels'.

Business of the House [21]

The House normally sits from 2.30 p.m. till at least 10.30 p.m. from Monday to Thursday and from 9.30 a.m. to 3 p.m. on Friday.[22] Standing orders recognize that priority shall be given to Government business,[23] but allocate twenty Fridays during a session to private members' bills and motions.[24] In practice private members are allowed to determine the course of business on other occasions – for example, in debates on the daily adjournment or the recess, and at question time. An approximately equal amount of time to that allocated to private members is placed at the disposal of the official Opposition, which chooses the topics for debates on Opposition Days. Twenty such days are so allotted, seventeen being at the disposal of the Leader of the Opposition, three being reserved for the second largest opposition party.[25] If, moreover, the Opposition wishes to put down a motion of censure on the Government it is incumbent on the Government to give up a day for such a debate unless the request is part of a campaign of obstruction.

Government business includes not only bills but also motions to debate reports of committees and royal commissions (on which the Government will express its views and submit to comment and criticism), motions to approve certain subordinate legislative instruments, formal Government statements, procedural motions (for example, to curtail debate on a bill), and more general motions which serve as a peg on which a debate may hang.

---

[20] See Donald Wade, *Behind the Speaker's Chair* (1978).
[21] On this topic and many other aspects of parliamentary institutions, Sir Ivor Jennings's *Parliament* (2nd edn, 1957) is still of great value, though it needs to be supplemented by more recent studies.
[22] S.O. No. 11.
[23] S.O. Nos 13(1), 24.
[24] S.O. No. 13(4), (7).
[25] S.O. No. 13(2) and see 28 H.C. Deb. *118–84* (19 July 1982).

This picture hardly corresponds with the image of a legislative body dominated by the Executive, particularly when one recalls that the Executive has to pay regard to the views of powerful pressure groups, to stirrings among its backbenchers and party loyalists outside Parliament, and in some contexts to the voice of public opinion – not to speak of international pressures, and political popularity polls and by-election results in so far as they may influence political morale. Furthermore, a good deal of the time spent on Government bills is absorbed by critical speeches and debates on amendments. On the other hand, not all parliamentary business is transacted on the floor of the House. And a Government with an overall majority in the House is almost certain to succeed, by marshalling support in the division lobbies and if necessary using its majority to alter the parliamentary timetable, in securing the enactment of the great bulk of its legislative programme.

Form and substance are therefore intertwined but in convoluted shapes. The main responsibility for the business of the House is vested in the Leader of the House of Commons (usually the Lord President of the Council but occasionally the Lord Privy Seal), assisted by the Government Chief Whip. They are expected to consult their opposite numbers 'behind the Speaker's chair'; parliamentary time is allocated 'through the usual channels' on a basis of bargain and compromise, on the understanding that, subject to standing orders and convention, the Government has the biggest claim and may be able to impose its own priorities by resolutions suspending standing orders or otherwise adjusting the normal timetable. Each Thursday in the House the Leader of the Opposition asks the Leader of the House to announce the business of the House for the forthcoming week. This is a question to which he may know the answer already; if he or any other member is dissatisfied (as is invariably the case), there is then an opportunity for public protest, and the Government, anxious not to leave itself open to justifiable criticism, will have already taken this possibility into account.

The following devices are available to enlarge the amount of time available to the Government – and, indeed, the House generally – for debate on the floor of the House.

1 Bills may be debated in standing committee (and second reading committee), so that other proceedings can take place on the floor of the House. The use of these small committees, sitting 'upstairs', has become a very important feature of contemporary parliamentary procedure.

2 Standing orders relating to times may be suspended to postpone the time of the daily adjournment (a device frequently resorted to) or provide for special sittings on Friday evenings or weekends (a device unpopular in nearly all quarters). Again, the provisional date of adjournment for a recess may be postponed if urgent business is incomplete; a motion for this purpose may be resisted by the Opposition.

3 Standing orders may be suspended so as to enable the Government to annex private members' time. Any proposal to this effect would be deeply resented today.

4 Procedural devices are available for shortening debate, and are sometimes used to prevent protraction of the proceedings by the official Opposition or backbenchers. The first is the *closure*.[26] In its simplest form, this involves a member (usually a Government whip, rising at a prearranged time) purporting to move, in the course of debate, that 'the question be now put'. Unless the Speaker (or Deputy Speaker) regards such a motion as an abuse of the rules of the House or an infringement of the rights of the minority, he must put this question forthwith without further discussion; if the motion is passed, with at least 100 members voting in favour, then the question then under debate (for example, that the bill be read a second time, or that the House do now adjourn) is put to the House and voted on immediately. The closure was first introduced into the House on the Speaker's responsibility in 1881 after a continuous filibuster of forty-one hours by Irish home rulers who had decided that if Britain would not let Ireland govern herself, the Irish would do their best to prevent Britain governing herself; standing orders were adopted in 1882 to regularize the situation. The *guillotine* is a form of closure by compartments. If debate on a bill, particularly in committee, is likely to be, or is being, unduly protracted, the Leader of the House introduces a resolution under which a prescribed maximum number of days will be allocated to each stage of the bill. Prior agreement between the two sides is rarely sought, debate on such a motion is likely to be acrimonious, and a tedious three-hour debate will follow usually ending in a Government victory in the division.[27] When the resolution has been passed, detailed compart-

---

[26] See S.O. Nos 35, 36. See also S.O. No. 10, which enables a Minister to move suspension of a late sitting till the following day.

[27] A sensible proposal from the Select Committee on Procedure that an automatic timetable be adopted for bills likely to take more than twenty-five hours in committee was rejected by the House in 1986: see H.C. 324 (1985–6); 92 H.C. Deb. 1083–136 (27 February 1986).

mentalization of the bill will be effected by the Business Committee of the House, and in standing committee by a sub-committee.[28] The Business Committee is established *ad hoc* in relation to particular bills to deal with such allocation of time. When the appointed hour is reached the guillotine falls; the chairman must interrupt debate and the committee (or the House) must pass on to the next phase even though many amendments have not yet been reached. One should also mention in this context a separate matter – the power (formerly called the *kangaroo*) vested in the Speaker at report stage and the chairman in committee to select for discussion some amendments to a bill and not to call (thus jumping over) others covering substantially the same ground. This power, unlike the closure and guillotine, is conferred not by resolution of the House but by standing orders,[29] is frequently exercised, and rarely evokes serious controversy.

Legislation[30]

Most of us want to see some parts of English law changed, so as to rectify an injustice or an anomaly, or to prohibit conduct of which we strongly disapprove, or to enable something to be done in the interests of the general public or a section of it or merely ourselves. But if we are to transform our prescriptions into remedial medicine, we need power, influence or persistence, or a combination of all three. If the general law of the land is to be altered, Parliament must pass an Act, or Ministers must be persuaded to make new regulations under powers already vested in them by statute. Most of the public bills introduced into Parliament emanate from government Departments; nearly all of them will be passed.[31] A fair number of bills are introduced by private members; not many of them will reach the statute book. The vast bulk of rules and regulations made under statutory authority are departmental, apart from local by-laws. If, then, one cannot be a Minister or a senior civil servant, one ought to start a campaign, or better still, form or join an organization likely to influence the lawmakers. One can hope to exercise some influence within a major political party, particularly if

---

[28] S.O. Nos 80, 81, 103.
[29] S.O. Nos 31, 89(3).
[30] See I. Burton and G. Drewry, *Legislation and Public Policy* (1981); D. R. Miers and A. C. Page, *Legislation* (1982).
[31] A spectacular exception was the loss of the Shops Bill (which would have reformed the law on Sunday trading) at second reading by 296 votes to 282, despite a Government three-line whip: see 95 H.C. Deb. *584–702* (14 April 1986).

one is elected to the House of Commons; though party discipline will impose its constraints. Or one can join what is usually called a pressure group. And perhaps one will be moved to form or join such a group in order to prevent the law being changed for the worse.

Pressure groups fall into two main classes, the sectional or interest groups and the promotional or 'cause' groups. To the former class belong such powerful groups as the Trades Union Congress, the Confederation of British Industry, the National Farmers' Union, the British Medical Association, and associations representing different categories of local authorities. The degree of influence wielded by some of these bodies may vary according as the Government is Labour or Conservative. In 1971 and 1972 individual unions demonstrated their power in resisting implementation of the Conservative Government's industrial relations and wages policies, and their part in the incomes policies of the Labour Governments from 1974 to 1979 was crucial. The withdrawal of union support for Government economic policies and the 1978–9 'winter of discontent' cost the Labour Government the 1979 Election. The influence of the Confederation of British Industry, less obtrusive but more pervasive, resting on technical expertise, ample funds, representation on numerous official, advisory and consultative bodies, familiarity with the corridors of power and contacts with Ministers, civil servants, M.P.s and peers, must obviously be greater under a Conservative Government. The major sectional pressure groups are always significant, because a Government needs their cooperation and sometimes cannot withstand their opposition; because they represent large organized elements of the community; because they are wealthy, and can use their funds to employ research staff and to mount extensive publicity campaigns if necessary; because they have, or may be able to obtain, active members and sympathizers in Parliament; because they are represented on advisory bodies connected with Departments; because their office-holders will have direct access to Ministers and senior civil servants. In order to avoid any conflict of interest, the House maintains a Register of M.P.s' Interests.[32] For a Department to introduce a bill directly affecting the interests of such an organization without prior consultation with its representatives is

[32] See Report of the Select Committee on Members' Interests (Declaration), H.C. *102* (1974–5). For the current Register see H.C. 155 (1986–7). M.P.s must register specified classes of pecuniary interest or benefit, now also including lobbying activities (namely, paid activity in public relations and political and parliamentary advice and consultancy): see 89 H.C. Deb. *216–54* (17 December 1985). See generally Erskine May, *Parliamentary Practice* (20th edn, 1983), pp. 435–9. For issues of parliamentary privilege, see below, pp. 320–21.

exceptional; it is still more exceptional for regulations to be made without such consultation. Consultation does not presuppose concurrence, but the content of the bill or the regulations will frequently be influenced by these discussions. In the case of bills, moreover, detailed amendments put down in Parliament often originate from a pressure group. And a few bills passed, and a larger number of regulations made, during the course of a year will be traceable to the initiative of pressure groups, operating on Departments and private members.

The pressure group which exists to promote a cause (for example, the RSPCA, the Howard League for Penal Reform, Justice, the Lord's Day Observance Society) rather than a sectional interest is far less likely to be consulted at the formative stage of legislation, but it may help to procure the enactment of legislation (usually introduced as a private member's bill) or the amendment of bills. Relatively small but energetic and well-organized pressure groups, using special reports or adept propaganda directed towards influential persons rather than the general public, have been largely instrumental in converting parliamentary majorities to such causes as the abolition of capital punishment for murder, reform of the criminal law relating to abortion and homosexual acts, the abolition of theatre censorship, and the importation of the Ombudsman under the name of the Parliamentary Commissioner for Administration. The European Movement played a part in converting sceptics into supporters of British accession to the EEC.

The end-product of legislation is an interplay of departmental initiative, party political policies, pressure group activities and initiative of individual M.P.s or groups of M.P.s. A glance through the Public General Acts for almost any year bears out this proposition.

This evidence suggests that the picture of parliamentary legislation as a function of government is slightly over-coloured but by no means a caricature; and that it is easy to over-emphasize the parts played by party political programmes (except during the first year of a new Parliament) and pressure group activities in determining the content of the statute book.

Legislative procedure[33]

There is a Legislation Committee of the Cabinet, which considers departmental and inter-departmental proposals for new Government

[33] The principal source of information is *The Process of Legislation*, Second Report of the Select Committee on Procedure, July 1971 (H.C. 538 (1970–71)). See also J. A. G. Griffith, *Parliamentary Scrutiny of Government Bills* (1974).

bills in principle and arranges provisional priorities; it considers later approved bills in detail, allocates firm priorities and keeps the parliamentary timetable under close review. A senior member of the Cabinet is designated by the Prime Minister to be chairman of the Committee.

Consultation with interest groups is likely to be most active when a bill has been approved in principle, though it may take place before any firm decision has been made (for example, after publication of the report of an independent committee or royal commission) to which the group will almost certainly have submitted evidence. Governments issue a large number of Green Papers and consultation documents, setting out tentative legislative proposals for public discussion. White Papers, setting out firm decisions prior to publication of bills, may follow.

A memorandum of instructions will be prepared by the sponsoring Department, or possibly an inter-departmental committee, for submission to Parliamentary Counsel, who will prepare a first draft of the bill. The bill may undergo several drafts before it is introduced into Parliament. The final draft will be scrutinized by a Law Officer of the Crown as well as the Legislation Committee. Responsibility for the European Communities Bill was generally ascribed to the then Solicitor-General, Sir Geoffrey Howe.

Introduction and first reading

Bills may be introduced in the Commons or the Lords. In the interests of good tactical management, a number of Government bills which are not likely to arouse party political opposition begin their career in the Lords. The existence of the upper House makes it possible to have more adequate parliamentary debates on legislation than would be the case if we had a unicameral Legislature. Money bills, however, must normally be introduced in the Commons[34] and a tax bill must be preceded by a resolution of the Commons approving its introduction.

The normal method of introducing a public bill into the Commons is by its ministerial sponsors presenting a dummy print of the bill at the table; one of the clerks then reads out the title of the bill, which is thus deemed to have been read a first time; the bill is ordered to be printed and published, and a date fixed for the second reading.

Public bills introduced by private members can obtain a first reading in one of three ways. The first is by obtaining a high place in the ballot for the right to introduce private members' bills.[35] In practice a

---

[34] But cf. p. 229.
[35] See S.O. No. 13(6), and see D. Marsh and M. Read, *Private Members' Bills* (1988).

member needs a high place to have any real prospect of seeing his bill pass through all its stages into law. The ten M.P.s placed highest in the ballot may each claim up to £200 as drafting expenses. Promotional pressure groups and sometimes the Government whips will seek to induce a well-placed private member to introduce a bill of their own devising. Several Law Commission bills have been enacted in this way. If the Government is particularly well disposed to a bill, a Minister will move any necessary money resolution, and the assistance of Parliamentary Counsel may be made available to its sponsor. Sometimes a Government may give up part of its own time to enable the bill to pass its final stages in the House.[36] Secondly, a private member's bill may be introduced without leave of the House under S.O. No. 58. If such a bill is unopposed and skilfully managed, it has a chance of becoming law. Thirdly, any member may get up in his place at the beginning of public business on Tuesdays or Wednesdays and ask leave of the House to introduce a bill.[37] The Speaker may allow him a few minutes to explain the nature and objects of the bill and also another member a similar opportunity to speak in opposition; the House then divides on the question whether to give leave. Even if this preliminary hurdle is cleared, bills introduced under the 'ten-minute rule' seldom pass into law because they cannot even be debated unless the Government is prepared to surrender some of its own time.[38]

Before a private bill – a bill of a local or personal character – can be introduced and read a first time, elaborate statutory provisions and special standing orders have to be complied with. Private bills of a personal character are now almost obsolete.[39] The bills were used extensively in the nineteenth century to provide for the naturalization of aliens and for divorces entitling the parties to remarry, until these changes in status could be effected by administrative action or judicial decrees under general enabling legislation. The nineteenth-century flurry of railway private bills is now part of economic history. Yet private legislation is not dying out. In the 1985–6 session sixty-nine

---

[36] For a list of such bills see 62 H.C. Deb. *495–6* (written answers 28 June 1984). Occasionally the Government may be forced into legislative action by the popularity of such a bill, as happened with a bill to end solicitors' conveyancing monopoly in 1985.

[37] See S.O. No. 19.

[38] On average eighty private members' bills were introduced, of which ten were enacted, each session from 1960 to 1986: see 109 H.C. Deb. *117–23* (written answers 26 January 1987).

[39] Especially following the enactment of the Marriage (Prohibited Degrees of Relationship) Act 1986, s. 1, which removes some of the previous need for a private bill to sanction marriage between related people.

Public General Acts were passed, but there were also twenty-six 'Local and Personal' Acts. Private bills are promoted mainly by local authorities seeking to acquire special powers; some are promoted by other public corporations, and a few by large public companies.

A local authority cannot promote a private bill to alter a local government area or to alter its status or electoral arrangements.[40] If a county or district authority wishes to promote a bill, it must give public notice, pass the necessary resolutions by an absolute majority, and confirm the resolution after the bill has been deposited in Parliament.[41] Within the House, the bill must pass the close scrutiny of the Examiners of private bills, who have to be satisfied that all the preliminary formalities, including the giving of notice to persons directly affected,[42] have been complied with. If these obstacles are successfully overcome, the bill is given a first reading.

Second reading

The occasion provided for parliamentary debate on the principles of a bill is the second reading stage.[43] No amendment to individual clauses is permissible. Rejection of a bill at second reading may be moved either by a reasoned amendment explaining why the bill should not be read a second time or by an amendment to postpone second reading. A private member's bill may be simply 'talked out' because the allotted time has expired. Private bills are normally unopposed at second reading.

Historically the second reading stage has always taken place in the House itself. The second reading debate on a bill may be conducted in committee in two sets of circumstances.

1 On the motion of a Minister, a bill certified by the Speaker as relating exclusively to Scotland may be referred to the Scottish Grand Committee (consisting of all members for Scottish seats) for this purpose (S.O. Nos 93, 94), provided that fewer than ten members object.

2 Any other public bill may now similarly be referred to a special second reading committee, consisting of between sixteen and fifty

---

[40] Local Government Act 1972, s. 70.

[41] ibid., s. 239.

[42] cf. *British Railways Board* v. *Pickin* [1974] A.C. 765, above, p. 84.

[43] The Speaker may announce that, because of the large number of M.P.s wishing to speak, he will limit backbench contributions to ten minutes. The debates in which he may do so are specified in the Standing Order: see 136 H.C. Deb. *503–4* (13 July 1988).

members provided that ten days' notice of the motion is given and fewer than twenty members object (S.O. No. 90). Few bills were at first so referred (and none at all in 1968 or 1969), but the use of the committees has increased markedly of late.[44]

The Committee reports to the House, which formally resolves that the bill be read a second time.

Money resolution

Till 1967 financial clauses in a bill had to be considered in Committee of the Whole House, with the Speaker out of the chair;[45] the Speaker then reoccupied the chair and the financial resolution was formally reported to the House. To save time, the financial resolution has now been telescoped into a single stage, the Speaker remaining in the chair. The necessary motion must still be moved by a Minister, a requirement which means that a backbench M.P. cannot introduce a bill designed to impose or increase a tax or to authorize expenditure.

Committee stage

The committee stage of a bill follows second reading. It is the stage most likely to be guillotined if the two sides of the House are unable to agree on a timetable. There has been a big increase in the use of standing committees since the Second World War. Now all public bills other than the annual bills providing for public expenditure and bills for the confirmation of provisional orders[46] go to standing committees unless the House otherwise resolves; since 1968 the annual Finance Bill (providing for taxation) has been taken partly in standing committee. The alternative is for a bill to be taken in Committee of the Whole House, which means that the House cannot proceed with any other

[44] S.O. 90(2) allows private members' bills to be referred to a second reading committee with the leave of the House. This could increase the work load of such committees, especially for uncontroversial private members bills, but few have been so referred.

[45] The need for the Speaker to leave the chair on such occasions was explicable on the grounds that the power of the Commons to withhold taxes and supplies from the Crown was historically of paramount importance, and the Speaker had at times been under the monarch's influence.

[46] Certain public general Acts empower Ministers to make provisional orders conferring special powers on public authorities. These orders are provisional in that they do not have effect till confirmed by a Provisional Order Confirmation Act. A provisional order usually entails a local inquiry at which objectors may be heard; the provisional order confirmation bill is technically a public bill, but its committee stage is similar to the committee stage of a private bill (see below).

business while the committee is sitting. Bills that are thought by the Government to be straightforward and not seriously controversial, and bills of major constitutional importance (such as the European Communities Bill or a bill to reform the Lords or to provide for devolution of power to Scotland or Wales) will be debated in Committee of the Whole House. The prospect of massive expenditure of time on the Parliament (No. 2) Bill in Committee of the Whole House induced the Government to withdraw it in April 1969; if the bill had been sent upstairs to a standing committee in the first place, the Government might perhaps have maintained patience.[47]

Standing committees consist of between sixteen and fifty members, chosen by the Committee of Selection in accordance with party strengths,[48] and having regard to their special qualifications. They usually sit in the morning. Scottish bills may be committed to a Scotish standing committee unless the second reading has been opposed by more than six members,[49] and bills dealing purely with Wales and Monmouthshire to the Welsh Grand Committee including all M.P.s from that area.[50]

In committee amendments to individual clauses of the bill are debated;[51] if no amendment to a clause is put down, that clause cannot be discussed except on the motion that the clause stand part of the bill. Proceedings are rather less formal than in the House; members may speak more than once to the same question. The Law Officers of the Crown[52] have the right to attend standing committees and take part in their deliberations, but they are not entitled to vote unless they are members of the committee; their presence is often important, for obscurities in drafting need to be clarified and the implications of proposed amendments made clear. The Minister in charge of a bill (who can speak on a Finance Bill even if he is not a member of the

---

[47] See pp. 311–13. But if a guillotine motion had become necessary at any stage, the Government would have been apprehensive about the outcome, given the opposition of many of their backbenchers to the bill.

[48] If the Government does not have a majority in the House, the best it can hope for is parity with combined opposition parties on standing committees. This was the solution arrived at in 1976 when the Government, following the loss of a by-election and the defection of an M.P. to the Opposition benches, was put into a minority in the House of Commons.

[49] S.O. Nos 93, 94, 95.

[50] S.O. No. 98. Up to five other M.P.s may be added. Not much use is made of this Committee for legislative purposes: see above, p. 48. There is also a Northern Ireland Committee, consisting of all Northern Irish M.P.s and not more than twenty others, which considers such matters affecting the province as may be referred to it (S.O. No. 99).

[51] Subject to the chairman's power to select amendments: see p. 270.

[52] See pp. 384–6.

committee) will frequently put down amendments to his own bill in committee in the light of afterthoughts by members of the Government or officials or parliamentary draftsmen, or other representations made from inside or outside the House following second reading. Amendments put down by backbenchers or the Opposition front bench will sometimes be accepted, or withdrawn on the understanding that the Minister will reconsider the matter in an attempt to meet the point in an alternative formulation. Hundreds of amendments were made to the Local Government Bill 1972 during its passage through Parliament. The European Communities Bill, on the other hand, though intensely controversial and a prodigious consumer of parliamentary time, was not amended at all.

To anyone at all familiar with American legislative bodies, it will be apparent that proceedings in committee on a bill are fundamentally different in the two countries.[53] In 1980, however, the House took a small step in the direction of the United States. A special standing committee was appointed to which a small number of bills (about three each session) could be committed. For up to twenty-eight days it can send for persons, papers and records, and hold up to four morning sittings. The first such sitting is in private, but the others are *in public*, to receive oral evidence from interested groups.[54] Although provision for special standing committees is now in standing orders,[55] only five bills have been considered in them. The only other British analogy with the congressional legislative committee is the select committee. But only in exceptional circumstances will a bill be committed to a select committee; in Britain such a committee is used predominantly as a device for parliamentary scrutiny of administration. However, statute law repeal bills (to clear away dead wood from the statute book)[56] and consolidation bills (to bring together all the existing statute law on a matter in one Act, subject to minor modifications)[57] go to a joint select committee of the two Houses. Such bills now emanate from the Law Commissions.

Proceedings in committee on an unopposed private bill and also on a

---

[53] See Caspar (1978) 26 *American Journal of Comparative Law* 359.

[54] See 991 Deb. 835–6 (30 October 1980).

[55] See S.O. No. 91. The Select Committee on Procedure has urged that more use be made of such committees: see H.C. *49* (1984–5), paras 11–13.

[56] Statute Law (Repeals) Acts are now regularly drafted by the Law Commissions.

[57] Some interesting variations from ordinary legislative procedure are prescribed by the Consolidation of Enactments (Procedure) Act 1949. *Quaere* whether observance of the special procedure laid down is mandatory. See Erskine May, op. cit., pp. 558–9.

hybrid bill,[58] and to a large extent on a provisional order confirmation bill,[59] are quite different from those on public bills. A private bill will be considered by a small committee, of four in the Commons or five in the Lords. The bill will have been drafted by parliamentary agents. The promoters must prove the preamble, stating the facts accounting for the bill and its objects, to the satisfaction of the committee; petitioners against the bill, having established their *locus standi*, may argue against the preamble and put down amendments to clauses; the parties may be represented by counsel, call evidence and make submissions. The proceedings of the committee have the outward trappings of a quasi-judicial contest between parties, though the committees may give paramountcy to extraneous factors directed to the furtherance of the public interest.[60]

Report stage

The bill, as amended, is reported to the House. The Speaker takes the chair. If it is a private bill, the report stage may be a formality. If a public bill considered in Committee of the Whole House emerges unamended, there is no report stage. If a bill has been considered in standing committee, other members may wish to put down their amendments on report, subject again to the Speaker's power of selection. Again, if the Government has afterthoughts it may decide to put down amendments or new clauses or schedules on report. It is possible for a bill to be sent back to committee at report stage. Bills considered at second reading in standing committee or by the Scottish Grand Committee may have their report stage taken before such a committee if a Minister so moves and fewer than twenty members object.[61]

Third reading

More often than not, a bill is read a third time immediately the report stage is concluded. The third reading will not be debated at all unless six or more members give notice that they wish for a debate or a

---

[58] A recent example was the Channel Tunnel Act 1987. As to hybridity, see S.O. No. 59. The furious parliamentary debates in 1976–7 over whether the Aircraft and Shipbuilding Industries Bill ought to have been passed by the special hybrid procedure cast light as well as heat on the subject of hybridity.

[59] See below, pp. 342–3. Such bills are almost obsolete.

[60] A joint select committee was appointed in 1987 to consider possible changes to private bill procedure.

[61] S.O. No. 92. A standing committee (other than the Scottish Grand Committee) so constituted must have between twenty and eighty members.

postponement.[62] If there is a debate, it will be brief and general in its terms. Only minor verbal amendments may be made; the bill may, theoretically at least, nevertheless be rejected at the end of the debate

Lords' bills and amendments

The procedure on bills in the Lords is similar to that in the Commons, but there is no money resolution stage and the committee stage is taken in the whole House, with the Lord Chairman of Committees in the chair, and there is no provision in standing orders for the closure or guillotining of debate. A public bill passed by the Lords cannot become law unless the Commons also pass it. A public bill passed by the Commons can become law under the Parliament Acts procedure although the Lords fail to pass it without amendment or reject it. Disagreements between the two Houses on clauses of a bill may be resolved in this manner, but it is more usual for one House (normally the Lords) to give way or for a compromise to be reached; a small committee is appointed by one House to give reasons why it disagrees with the other's amendments.

Quorum in the Commons

The general rule (subject to exceptions for certain hours and days and certain types of business) is that the quorum of the House and in Committee of the Whole House is forty.[63] This means not that forty members have in fact to be present in the chamber at all relevant times, but that if the House divides on a motion, the business under discussion stands over till the next sitting unless forty or more members have taken part in the division. It is the responsibility of the Government whips to ensure that a sufficient number of their back-benchers are in the vicinity of the chamber to scurry in when a vote is called for. In standing committee the quorum is one-third of its members or seventeen, whichever is the less.[64]

Royal assent

Under the procedure introduced by the Royal Assent Act 1967, the House can simply be notified that the royal assent to a bill has been

[62] S.O. No. 75.
[63] S.O. No. 40.
[64] S.O. No. 89(1). Private members' bills are no longer 'counted out'.

granted, and it does not have to interrupt its proceedings and adjourn to the Lords' chamber to hear the royal assent signified orally.

Community legislation

Community legislation directly applicable without further enactment in this country[65] does not pass through any of these stages. Such legislation consists of regulations made by the Council of Ministers or the Commission. In Community law, regulations are secondary legislation. In United Kingdom law they must rank as primary and not delegated legislation. Existing and new machinery has been used to scrutinize Community matters. Thus it has become customary for part of question time to be given over to Community matters; Ministers make statements to the House on their part in the Council of Ministers; and there are periodic debates. The new machinery centres in the House of Commons (similar provision is made in the Lords) on the Select Committee on European Legislation, which considers draft Community legislation and other documents published by the Commission for submission to the Council. The Government prepares explanatory memoranda, and the Committee can seek information from Government departments. The Committee is charged with drawing the attention of the House to documents which raise questions of legal or political importance, to report what matters of principle or policy may be affected thereby, and to make recommendations to the House. The Government finds time to debate those materials which the Committee recommends for debate. But difficulties remain, primarily as a result of the mass of paper which the Committee and M.P.s must try to examine.

Financial procedure

The main departmental responsibility for the management of the national economy rests with the Treasury, under the Chancellor of the Exchequer.[66] A department bearing the main brunt of decisions affecting national income and expenditure, the value of the pound, the country's international balance of payments and the cost of living is necessarily of crucial importance.

[65] European Communities Act 1972, s. 2(1).
[66] See generally Samuel Brittan, *Steering the Economy: The Role of the Treasury* (1971); Lord Bridges, *The Treasury* (2nd edn, 1966); Henry Roseveare, *The Treasury* (1973); Joel Barnett, *The Treasury* (1982).

The initiative in tax policy is vested in the Treasury alone.[67] The details of the Chancellor of the Exchequer's budget speech are revealed to all his Cabinet colleagues only the day before it is delivered in the House. In matters of public expenditure, Treasury approval is required for all large-scale items, not only at the central departmental level but also by public corporations and, directly or indirectly, by local authorities. The hand of the Treasury extends to approval of the standard terms of Government contracts and pricing policies. The influence of the Treasury at any given time is, of course, partly dependent on the personal stature of the Chancellor, and his ability to carry the Prime Minister and the Cabinet along with him. That influence has traditionally been exercised in the interests of economy and caution. In 1958 Mr Peter Thorneycroft, unable to convince the Cabinet of the need for scaling down the annual estimates, resigned with his two junior Ministers; the Macmillan Government survived his departure.

Taxation

Taxes are collected by or under the Board of Inland Revenue, and the Board of Customs and Excise. Some taxes – for example, stamp duties, capital transfer tax – imposed by statute have effect till the statute is amended. Others – notably income tax – have effect only till the end of the tax year and require renewal by Parliament in the annual Finance Act. No charge may lawfully be levied on the subject by the Crown except under authority conferred by express statutory language; the fact that an Act may be unworkable unless charges are imposed in the course of its administration is irrelevant.[68]

Membership of the Communities has had major constitutional effects. First, the United Kingdom has agreed to adopt the Communities' common external tariff and its agricultural policy (involving the imposition of import levies).[69] Secondly, the rates of customs duties

---

[67] Subject to Community rules: see below.

[68] The leading cases are *Att.-Gen.* v. *Wilts United Dairies Ltd* (1921) 37 T.L.R. 884, and *Cape Brandy Syndicate* v. *I.R.C.* [1921] 1 K.B. 64. See also *Liverpool Corporation* v. *Maiden (Arthur) Ltd* [1938] 4 All E.R. 200 (local authorities). The Bill of Rights provides that no charge on the subject should be levied by pretence of prerogative without the consent of Parliament, but the principle stated in the text above ranges beyond prerogative exactions and, indeed, beyond central government. However, charges may be imposed by the Crown on the subject without express statutory authority for providing services (*China Navigation Co.* v. *Att.-Gen.* [1932] 2 K.B. 197) which it is under no prior obligation to furnish.

[69] An Intervention Board for Agricultural Produce implements the agricultural policy (European Communities Act 1972, s. 6).

and agricultural levies can be varied by directly applicable Community regulations.[70] Thirdly, the Communities are to be progressively financed out of their 'own resources', which comprise the proceeds of customs duties (less 10 per cent for the cost of administration), agricultural levies, and eventually up to 1 per cent of a harmonized value added tax, all collected by member States for Community purposes.[71] United Kingdom authorities levy and collect money under Community law as agents for the Communities. Moreover, payments required to meet Britain's Community obligations are charged on the Consolidated Fund.[72]

Before 1968 the budget was introduced in the Committee of Ways and Means, a Committee of the Whole House, with the Speaker out of the chair. This committee has now been abolished and the budget speech is made by the Chancellor in the House itself. At the same time, a White Paper is published containing a Financial Statement and Budget Report ('the Red Book'); this now includes economic data for the recent past and predictions for the immediate future, some of which have been transferred from the Budget speech, and other parts of which have been added as a result of parliamentary pressure.

The budget will normally be introduced in late March or early April. For tax purposes the financial year runs from 6 April to 5 April in the following year. The Finance Bill, incorporating tax legislation, is unlikely to receive the royal assent till late July. But authority to collect the most remunerative taxes will have expired on 5 April. In order to bridge this gap, statutory authority exists[73] to enable essential taxes to be levied immediately after the budget. As soon as the Chancellor sits down, resolutions approving these tax proposals are passed and have statutory effect forthwith by virtue of the Provisional Collection of Taxes Act 1968. Under section 5 of this Act (as amended), resolutions can be (and are) passed, giving provisional statutory effect, for ten

---

[70] European Communities Act 1972, ss 2(1), 5,6.

[71] This was agreed by the Communities in 1970 (Cmnd 4867 (1972)), and promulgated by a Community regulation in 1971, subject to modifications agreed in the instruments of accession (Cmnd 4862 – 1 (1972), pp. 51–3). See also European Communities Act, s. 1; sched. 1, para. 6; European Communities (Finance) Acts 1985 and 1988.

[72] European Communities Act 1972, s. 2(3). See for Consolidated Fund Services, p. 286. The purpose of charging these monies on the Consolidated Fund is to reduce parliamentary scrutiny over them. See further 831 H.C. Deb. *1137–242* (22 February 1972).

[73] It was needed because such taxes could not lawfully be imposed merely on the strength of budget resolutions: *Bowles* v. *Bank of England* [1913] 1 Ch. 57. The position was regulated for the future by the Provisional Collection of Taxes Act 1913.

days,[74] to the proposed new rates of income tax, value added tax, corporation tax and customs and excise duties for the financial year; they must be confirmed by the House within ten days; the Finance Bill must be read a second time within twenty-five days and passed into law by 5 August, if the resolutions were passed in March or April, or within four months in other circumstances, otherwise the collection of taxes on the basis of the resolutions becomes retroactively invalid. This tends, of course, to restrict the period in which it is practicable to dissolve Parliament.

Debate on the budget will continue for several days on a general resolution which does not have to be passed forthwith. The Finance Bill is then published and read a second time. At the committee stage – if taken in standing committee, many additional days become available for the business of the House – a very large number of amendments will be put down and some will be accepted or compromise amendments put down by the Government. The Government cannot be too amenable, because the sum to be raised by taxation is geared both to its general economic policy and its commitments as to the quantum of expenditure, but minor concessions are possible. Since there will not have been a full range of prior consultations with interest groups or expert committees before the budget is introduced, the practical implications of the proposed changes in tax law will not always have been appreciated by the Treasury, and it may welcome suggestions – for example, that a particular tax will cause undue hardship or be too difficult or costly to enforce. The bill will usually also modify aspects of tax law which do not need annual enactment.

Amendments will again be put down when the bill is reported to the House. After third reading, proceedings in the Lords will be a formality.

Supplementary budgets and other legislation to levy money (for example, to introduce higher National Health Service charges) may be introduced during a parliamentary session.

National expenditure

Public expenditure also requires statutory authority. About two-thirds of central government expenditure is customarily authorized on an annual basis.

---

[74] See also s. 1 of the 1968 Act, under which the resolutions can be given firm statutory effect (subject to the provisos mentioned in the text above) without a confirming resolution. Even if the budget resolutions are not moved until after 5 April, s. 2 of the 1968 Act gives provisional effect to them.

As expenditure in the public sector of the national economy has grown, new machinery for coordinating departmental programmes has had to be constructed.[75] Under this new system all forms of public expenditure, including those of nationalized industries and local government, are surveyed. At the heart of these arrangements is the Public Expenditure Survey Committee (PESC), a committee of civil servants chaired by a Treasury official, and including the department financial officers. From November to May Treasury and Departments seek to agree on the projected cost over the next four years of existing departmental policies. The Minister responsible is the Chief Secretary to the Treasury (often in the Cabinet), not the Chancellor of the Exchequer. PESC writes a report on the basis of these discussions projecting the cost of present policies and outlining remaining areas of disagreement. This report (highly confidential and not published) goes to the Chancellor in June. By November the Cabinet decides on expenditure for the whole of the public sector and publishes its conclusions in a Public Expenditure White Paper between November and February. This White Paper sets out the Government's expenditure plans in fifteen main programmes over a period of four years, year one being the year in which it is published. Parliament debates this White Paper. From 1989, however, the Public Expenditure White Paper will be replaced by an annual report from each department which will be published at budget time and will set out the department's performance, objectives and spending. The general economic background to public spending will be explained in the Chancellor's Autumn Statement. These changes follow recommendations from Commons' select committees, and are designed to make comparison easier with the annual estimates and thus to improve parliamentary scrutiny.

Bulky volumes of the estimates are published in February and March. They are divided into classes, 'votes' (for individual Departments, sub-Departments, and certain other bodies financed out of central funds), sub-heads and further details; the corresponding figures for the current year are set out. For the purpose of national expenditure, the financial year extends from 1 April to 31 March. Parliament has to debate the estimates – redress of grievances precedes supply – and the result of its deliberations (or rather, the deliberations of the House of Commons) will be embodied in the Appropriation Act, which is usually passed in July. The Act authorizes the withdrawal from the Bank of England, and the expenditure, of the sum total of the

---

[75] The best account of these new arrangements is still H. Heclo and A. Wildavsky, *The Private Government of Public Money* (2nd edn, 1983).

estimates, and appropriates in its schedules money for prescribed votes. But the Government needs drawing and borrowing powers before this. To bridge the gap, a sum (called the vote on account) authorizing the prospective expenditure of 35 to 40 per cent of the total sought will be granted by one or more Consolidated Fund Acts passed before the beginning of the financial year. These Acts will also authorize expenditure on supplementary estimates for the year just ending, and may ratify an excess vote to a Department which overspent its alloted sum in the previous year.[76]

Those items of expenditure for which annual authority is needed are called Supply Services; the others (comprising interest on the national debt, the Civil List, and the salaries of judges, the Speaker, the Leader of the Opposition and other persons whose conduct in office ought not to be the subject of annual debate, and now sums required for the discharge of Community obligations) are Consolidated Fund Services. The Consolidated Fund is a notional account kept at the Bank of England. In 1968 many of its functions and revenues were allotted to a new account, the National Transactions Capital Account.[77]

The estimates are prepared in Government Departments and are then vetted by the Treasury, which usually demands cuts in them. Recently a Cabinet committee known colloquially as the Star Chamber has achieved final agreement each year between individual Ministers and the Treasury over the estimates. Three Estimates Days are then devoted in the House before 5 August each year to debate selected estimates.

Public Expenditure White Paper figures used to be at constant prices and therefore unaffected by inflation; they are now in terms of cash (as are the Supply Estimates), and include a built-in allowance for inflation between the date at which they were first drawn up and the date on which the money is spent. Cash limits are included in the Supply Estimates, and the Estimates are subject to parliamentary approval. Increases in cash limits on voted expenditure are subject to parliamentary approval of the necessary Supplementary Estimates.[78]

Another mechanism is the Treasury and Civil Service Committee, one of the fourteen new select committees set up in 1979.[79] This committee replaces the Expenditure Committee which has been abolished. It consists of eleven members under the chairmanship of a senior

---

[76] Unappropriated sums can be made available in an emergency out of the Civil Contingencies Fund. Such grants are scrutinized by the Comptroller and Auditor-General and the Public Accounts Committee (see below) and are often the subject of a critical report.

[77] See National Loans Act 1968, and Leo Pliatzky, *Getting and Spending* (1982).

[78] Memorandum on the Supply Estimates 1983–4, Cmnd 8817, para. 50.

[79] See below, pp. 292–6.

M.P., usually a former Treasury Minister. Its terms of reference authorize it to examine the expenditure, administration and policy of (*inter alia*) the Treasury, Board of Inland Revenue and Board of Customs and Excise. It is authorized to appoint one sub-committee. The committee makes full use of its powers to require the presence of senior Ministers, including the Chancellor of the Exchequer, and officials, and actively seeks the production of departmental papers. Among the subjects of inquiry on which it has embarked are the general management of the economy, covering control of public expenditure, responsibilities of the Comptroller and Auditor-General, taxation and monetary policies. Its declared aims are to monitor the Treasury and economic policy, and to keep Parliament and public better informed so as to broaden discussion of economic policies.

The Public Accounts Committee[80] was established in 1861 and is composed of fifteen members. Although, as in all select and standing committees, they are selected according to party strengths, the committee is scrupulously non-partisan – so much so that there is a well-settled convention that its chairman shall be a member of the Opposition; he is usually a former junior Minister at the Treasury. Its task is to ensure that parliamentary grants have been applied to the objects which Parliament prescribed. It bases its examination of government spending and of departmental administration on the reports of the Comptroller and Auditor-General. Accordingly its reports are not confined to financial irregularities but also cover wasteful and extravagant expenditure and imprudent contractual transactions.[81] The fact that the Comptroller and Auditor-General sits with the Committee strengthens its position greatly when it interrogates departmental accounting and finance officers. Its reports are treated with the greatest respect in Whitehall and are debated annually by the Commons.

The Comptroller and Auditor-General is a key figure in the system of parliamentary control of finance. He is an officer of the House of Commons, not a civil servant. He is appointed by the Crown on an address presented to the Crown by the Commons and moved by the Prime Minister acting with the agreement of the Chairman of the Public Accounts Committee.[82] He is removable only for misbehaviour

---

[80] See Basil Chubb, *The Control of Public Expenditure* (1952); E. L. Normanton, *The Accountability and Audit of Governments* (1966).

[81] For example, the Ministry of Defence was criticized in 1986 over the £880m wasted on the Nimrod early-warning system, which was then cancelled – 'a major example of how not to approach' the making of contracts: see H.C. *104* (1986–7).

[82] National Audit Act 1983, section 1. For the first appointment under the 1983 Act see 124 H.C. Deb. *1185–94* (16 December 1987).

in pursuance of an address from both Houses of Parliament, and his salary is charged on the Consolidated Fund. His department, the National Audit Office,[83] has a staff of several hundreds appointed by him.

The Comptroller and Auditor-General is empowered to carry out examinations into the economy, efficiency and effectiveness with which various authorities or bodies have used their resources in discharging their functions, but not to question the merits of their policy objectives.[84] His powers do not extend to the nationalized industries.[85] The private member's bill which became the National Audit Act originally included nationalized industries, but its sponsor, Mr Norman St John-Stevas, had to delete these as the price of ensuring that the Government did not obstruct the passage of the Bill. The Government has, however, used its powers under the Competition Act 1980, s. 11, to refer the accounts of several nationalized industries for audit by the Monopolies and Mergers Commission. The estimates for the Office are laid before Parliament after being approved by the Public Accounts Commission which includes the Chairman of the Committee of Public Accounts[86] and the Leader of the House of Commons.[87] It works closely with the departmental accounting officers, who are normally the permanent secretaries, and the departmental financial officers who head departmental financial branches.

The Comptroller and Auditor-General is responsible as designated auditor for the annual examination and certification of some 450 accounts involving net annual expenditure in excess of £50,000 million. In addition to the Appropriation Accounts, store accounts and trading funds and accounts of all Government Departments, these include the accounts of a wide range of statutory boards and authorities as well as of certain international bodies and UN agencies. The C & AG examines and reports to Parliament on Inland Revenue, Customs and Excise and other revenue accounts. Without being designated auditor he has been granted access to inspect the books of more than 500 bodies of widely varying types which depend to a greater or lesser extent on finance from public funds. This enables him to report to Parliament in such cases where it might not be appropriate or necessary for him to be appointed auditor. The C & AG's responsibilities do not, however, extend, within the public sector, to local authorities and

---

[83] Section 3 and sched. 2 of the 1983 Act.
[84] Sections 6 and 7.
[85] Section 7(4) and sched. 4.
[86] Section 2 and sched. 1.
[87] Section 4(2).

nationalized industries, or, within the private sector, to numerous companies and other businesses and organizations in receipt of voted moneys. His reports draw attention not only to financial irregularities but also to wasteful and extravagant expenditure and imprudent contractual transactions. Their weakness is that the malpractices or blunders to which they refer will have occurred not less than a year beforehand and sometimes a good deal farther back, and the money may have been squandered beyond recall. But the report of an inquest may not be unproductive as a spur to remedial action; for instance, the adverse report of the Public Accounts Committee on excess profits made by an armaments firm under a contract for the supply of a guided missile led to a repayment by the firm and tighter contracting procedures.

One of the Committee's 1979–80 reports shows what an indispensable watchdog it is. It uncovered overpayments of offshore suppliers' interest relief grants of £16 m. with further contemplated overpayments of £44 m. in breach of Treasury guidelines and complained with 'great concern and amazement' that it was given 'grossly inaccurate and misleading evidence' by the Permanent Under Secretary of the Department of Energy. On the other hand, the Committee was only able to act as coroner in 1984 over the ill-fated De Lorean car factory project in Northern Ireland, because the £77 m. of public money had been spent and lost. The Committee thought that this was 'one of the gravest cases of the misuse of public resources for many years'. And in 1987 the Committee reported that, despite the fresh provision in the National Audit Act 1983, 'Parliament's consideration of the annual estimates – the key constitutional control – remains largely a formality.'[88]

Scrutiny of policy and administration

Under Standing Order No. 41, the Speaker or chairman may direct a member who persists in tedious repetition to discontinue his speech. This is a useful working rule; and this important section will therefore be abbreviated.

The general role of the official Opposition has already been considered. Its main procedural opportunities for criticizing the Government or individual members arise in the debate on the address in reply to the Queen's speech at the beginning of a session, debates on the budget and on Opposition Days, debates on motions of censure or

---

[88] See H.C. *98* (1986–7). And see M. Elliott in J. Jowell and D. Oliver (ed.), *The Changing Constitution* (1986), ch. 7.

other substantive motions (for example, on a formal motion for the adjournment) for which the Government gives up part of its own time, second reading debates, and at question time. But the time saved by procedural changes enabling more legislation to be considered in standing committees has been filled by Government legislation rather than general debate.[89] Backbenchers have their opportunities on the occasions set aside for private members' motions, on the motion for the adjournment each day and before a recess, at question time and, if any succeed in catching the Speaker's eye, in the course of general debate. They can also put their names to 'early day motions', which are in the nature of demonstrations of protest, concern or occasionally loyalty; these motions are tabled but are hardly ever debated in the House.

Ordinary business may be interrupted to debate a matter of urgency under Standing Order No. 20. A motion to adjourn to discuss 'a specific and important matter that should have urgent consideration' can be moved by any member, at short notice, immediately after question time. It lies within the Speaker's discretion whether to allow the motion to be put; leave is not readily granted. If this obstacle is overcome, and if the motion is approved by the House or supported by forty members rising in their places, the motion will be debated either that evening or the following day.

Members and question time[90]

Members of Parliament receive hundreds of thousands of letters from members of the public each year, making complaints which usually call for some kind of remedial action or request for information. In addition, most members hold local 'surgeries' to deal with the personal problems of their constituents. If a matter calling for further action falls within the area of ministerial responsibility, the member will usually write to the Minister about it and perhaps talk to him personally; if no satisfactory answer is received, the member may well decide to raise the issue at question time, or pass a complaint alleging injustice caused by maladministration to the Parliamentary Commissioner for Administration to investigate. If a grave public scandal is suspected, and pressure is exerted on the Government, a special independent inquiry or a formal tribunal of inquiry may be set up.[91]

[89] H.C. *538* (1970), para. 4.
[90] See D. N. Chester and Nona Bowring, *Questions in Parliament* (1962); D. N. Chester in S. A. Walkland and M. Ryle (eds), *The Commons Today* (revised edn, 1981).
[91] See chs 31 and 33 for the investigation of alleged abuses under the Parliamentary Commissioner Act 1967 and the Tribunals of Inquiry (Evidence) Act 1921.

Tabling questions in the House is one form of obtaining publicity for individual grievances; redress may be forthcoming because a parliamentary question is threatened, or because it has been put down, or because the answer given to the question is manifestly unsatisfactory and the Minister feels that he is appearing in a bad light, or because the member presses home his point by giving notice that he will raise the issue again on a half-hourly debate on the daily adjournment; but if no redress has been granted by question time, the likelihood is that no redress will be offered at all. A question to a Minister is rather a method of ventilating a grievance than of securing a remedy.

Questions to Ministers may serve other purposes. They may even be put for the purpose of eliciting factual information, in which case an oral answer will seldom be requested; the answer will then be given in writing, and circulated together with answers to oral questions which there was no time to reach. (Question time lasts for some forty-five minutes, on Mondays to Thursdays.) They may be inspired questions; a member is asked to put down a question so that the responsible Minister can make a public statement.[92] They may be, and often are, carefully designed to cause a Minister the maximum amount of embarrassment. Although a question for which an oral answer is requested must normally be tabled two days in advance, the question may be an opening gambit, to be followed by a supplementary question of which no prior notice is given. (It does not, however, overtax a Minister's Private Office to work out in good time what the supplementary questions are likely to be.)[93] Parliamentary reputations have been made and ruined in the rapid cut and thrust of question time. For a few minutes the House comes to life audibly and visibly: wit,[94] feigned or genuine outrage, cheers and jeers intrude upon the solemnity of the proceedings; Government and Opposition are briefly locked in fascinating verbal combat; the Prime Minister and the Leader of the Opposition may gain or lose a point or two in the public opinion

---

[92] But a Minister should not carry this practice to a point where opposition questions cannot be put; nor should departmental civil servants be induced to take part in such a game. See Report of the Select Committee on Parliamentary Questions (H.C. *393* (1971–2)).

[93] Ministers do not, therefore, go like lambs to the slaughter: they are (or should be) ready with supplementary *answers.* 'One evening I found Churchill at the Cabinet table . . . "What are you doing, Prime Minister?" I asked. "Oh, Parliamentary questions. Preparing improvisations! Very hard work!"': Harold Macmillan, *Tides of Fortune* (1969), p. 496.

[94] Winston Churchill, still Prime Minister at seventy-nine, was asked to constitute a Ministry of Fisheries separate from the Ministry of Agriculture. Explaining his refusal, he observed that 'there are many ancient links between fish and chips' (528 H.C. Deb. *2274*), 17 June 1954.

polls; a backbencher shows his ministerial potential, and the House wonders how much longer the Minister of Cosmology can last.

Whatever may be the intrinsic value of parliamentary questions, their popularity with M.P.s is beyond doubt. In the 1985–6 session 31,800 questions were put down for written, and 18,100 for oral, answer. The average cost of answering a question orally is £75, and in writing £45. If the cost of answering a given question is likely to exceed £250 a Minister may refuse to answer it.[95]

As has already been pointed out,[96] questions may and normally will be refused if they relate to matters lying outside the field of ministerial responsibility. Among inadmissible questions[97] are those on matters *sub judice*, but the scope of this exclusionary rule has now been narrowed so as to enable the Speaker to admit questions in his discretion though they relate to matters pending adjudication in a civil court, if the issue raised concerns a matter of national importance or the exercise of a Minister's discretion challengeable only on narrow grounds before the court.[98] A Minister may also decline to answer a question on the ground of disproportionate cost, currently set at £250.

Departmental select committees of the House [99]

A serious weakness of the House of Commons is the ineffectual role of so many backbenchers – no less ineffectual because it cannot be quantified. Able men and women discover that their opportunities to contribute significantly to debate are few, that their influence on Government policy from the backbenches or in opposition seems negligible, that even in the privacy of parliamentary party meetings the leadership is rarely moved by their arguments and that the conduct of public administration cannot be effectively scrutinized by the House. If Parliament is the grand inquest of the nation, the roles of coroner and corpse are apt to be confused.

---

[95] See 129 H.C. Deb. *429* (written answers 14 March 1988).

[96] See pp. 184–5, 219–20.

[97] See Erskine May, op. cit., pp. 337–44. The lists of inadmissible areas covers three pages of small print.

[98] 839 H.C. Deb. *1589–1627* (28 June 1972), a relaxation directly related to controversial proceedings before the (since abolished) National Industrial Relations Court; see H.C. *298* (1971–2). But the relaxation in 1972 was intended to be a deliberate one by the House of the *sub judice* rule in the area of public policy, which was not confined to that Court or to the Act which established it, and the Speaker exercises his discretion in favour of freer debate in every case where he properly can: 916 H.C. Deb. *882–4* (29 July 1976).

[99] See D. Englefield, *Commons Select Committees: Catalysts for Change?* (1984); D. Hill, *Parliamentary Select Committees in Action* (1984); G. Drewry, *The New Select Committees* (1985), and ch. 6 in Jowell and Oliver, op. cit.

Any effective participation of backbench M.P.s in decision-making will continue to present very great difficulties as long as Governments maintain majorities in the House with the aid of an electoral system under which the winner can expect to take almost all, and as long as constitutional rules leave the spending power entirely in the hands of the Executive. But, as the experience of the Public Accounts Committee has shown, it is possible, within the existing British parliamentary system, for members to *influence* the conduct of administration and to modify aspects of policy by their scrutiny of administrative activity as members of select committees.

Very modest moves in favour of backbenchers were made in 1967 when Select Committees on Agriculture and on Science and Technology were established. The experiment was not an unqualified success. The Select Committee on Agriculture was discontinued in 1969 by a decision of the Government which the House ratified. A few other specialized select committees were formed subsequently, including one on race relations and immigration and another on the Parliamentary Commissioner for Administration (which rapidly justified its existence).[100] These committees offered some detailed and imaginative suggestions for administrative reorganization, and made themselves, the House in general and interested members of the public better informed about central administration and the views of the administered.

It was not until 1979 that a bold experiment to extend the opportunity for M.P.s to scrutinize the Executive through specialized select committees was started. In its breadth and concept it was far more radical than anything which had gone before. Following a report of the Select Committee on Procedure[101] the incoming Conservative Government, committed to offering the House the chance to reform its methods, afforded the House the opportunity to set up twelve new committees to examine the expenditure, administration and policy of designated government departments, with the power to send for papers and witnesses and to appoint sub-committees. The House took that opportunity.[102] The new departmental select committees, each with a fixed membership of between nine and eleven (most have eleven) M.P.s, are on Agriculture; Defence; Education, Science and the Arts; Employment; Energy; Environment; Foreign Affairs; Home Affairs; Trade and Industry; Social Services (overseeing the Departments of Health and of

[100] See further ch. 33.
[101] See H.C. *588–I* (1977–8).
[102] 969 H.C. Deb. *33–252* (25 June 1979).

Social Security); Transport; and Treasury and the Civil Service (overseeing the Treasury, the civil service and the Boards of Inland Revenue and of Customs and Excise).[103] Two other departmental select committees, on Scottish and Welsh Affairs respectively, were set up a little later in the year.[104] There is no committee to oversee the Lord Chancellor's Department, as a result of dubious Government claims that such a committee might prejudice judicial independence. Members of the new committees are chosen by the Committee of Selection. This device has been criticized because that Committee is itself nominated by the Whips: the uncharitable take the view not only that it would keep the most outspoken of the Government's critics away from such delicate work but also that frontbench patronage would be enhanced. In recommending M.P.s for membership the Committee of Selection reflects the party balance in the House as a whole. The Select Committee on the Parliamentary Commissioner for Administration remains, as do those on Public Accounts, European Legislation, Members' Interests and Sound Broadcasting (of Commons proceedings), together with the Joint Select Committee on Statutory Instruments, the Committee of Privileges and the Select Committee on Procedure.

But under the new system two notable casualties were the Select Committee on Nationalized Industries and the Expenditure Committee. The Government's justification was that a sub-committee may be formed from a number of the new committees to consider any matter affecting two or more nationalized industries (it has not been), and that the Select Committee on the Treasury and the Civil Service would take over the work of the general sub-committee of the Expenditure Committee (which it successfully has).

A new select committee, known as the Liaison Committee and consisting of the chairmen of the departmental select committees, was set up in 1980 to consider general matters relating to the work of the new scheme.[105]

The committees decide for themselves which topics to investigate, in consultation with the Liaison Committee so as to avoid duplication of effort. The Foreign Affairs, Home Affairs and Treasury and Civil Service Committees may nominate sub-committees so that simultaneous

[103] See S.O. No. 130.

[104] They are not to be confused with the Scottish and Welsh Grand Committees, which remain, and on which see above, pp. 48–9. The Northern Ireland Committee (see above, p. 277) also stays.

[105] 977 H.C. Deb. *1687–1718* (31 January 1980). For its general reports on the progress of the departmental committees, see H.C. *92* (1982–3), H.C. *363* (1984–5).

investigations may be conducted by each of those Committees. The formal powers of the committees to send for persons, papers and records have only had to be exercised once:[106] an informal invitation to give or supply evidence usually does the trick. Those formal powers embrace Ministers (even Prime Ministers) and civil servants (even the Head of the Home Civil Service and Secretary to the Cabinet).[107] But in the aftermath of the Westland affair [108] the Defence Select Committee wanted to examine named civil servants who had been involved in the improper leaking to the press of the Solicitor-General's letter: the Government opposed this, and the Committee (which at one stage threatened to invoke its formal powers) agreed to a compromise in which the Cabinet Secretary and the Permanent Under-Secretary at the Department of Trade and Industry attended instead.[109] At no stage during this episode, however, did any select committee concede that its ultimate legal powers (which had been conferred on the committees by the House and which were underpinned by the ability of the House to punish for contempt) were restricted in any way claimed by the Government.

The extraction of evidence from witnesses has, on the whole, been an easy process. But the Government continues to insist that civil servants remain subject to ministerial direction, and in any case may not give evidence at all on certain matters.[110] And, just occasionally, a Minister himself may refuse to answer questions – a refusal which amounted to stonewalling by Mr Leon Brittan during his evidence on Westland to the Defence Committee.[111]

The departmental select committees provide a forum in which Ministers, civil servants and others can be cross-examined at a length and more thoroughly than in any other way at present open to the House of Commons. Their members have acquired knowledge and have developed expertise about departments; the committees usually

[106] In 1982, when the Energy Select Committee made a formal order against Mr Arthur Scargill, with which he fully complied. Any refusal to comply would be referred to the House to deal with as a contempt of the House: see Erskine May, op. cit., ch. 10.

[107] The Government promised in 1979 that Ministers would attend if asked: see 969 H.C. Deb. *45* (25 June 1979). Occasionally the Prime Minister has directed that a Minister other than the one sought should attend.

[108] See above, p. 188.

[109] See H.C. *519* (1985–6), paras 225–33.

[110] In particular, they must follow the Memorandum of Guidance issued by the Cabinet Secretary (see above, p. 194 and note 57). This restriction has been heavily criticized by the Treasury and Civil Service Committee (see H.C. *62* (1986–7)) and by the Liaison Committee (see H.C. *100* (1986–7)). For the Government's defence of its attitude, see Cm 78 (1987), paras 9–12.

[111] See H.C. *519* (1985–6), paras 203–4.

publish unanimous reports which can cross party lines so as to present powerful all-party criticism of the Government;[112] and, according to the Liaison Committee, they have markedly improved the flow of information to the House as a whole. A continuing weakness of the system is, however, that only a small number of the reports issued are debated substantively in the House: by 1985, only five had been so debated from a total of 275 reports issued.[113]

[112] See, e.g., H.C. *533* (1979–80) – the Foreign Affairs Committee's critical reaction to a Government plan to increase university fees for overseas students; there are several other examples. An unusual example of a report in which Government and Opposition members divided on party lines was the Foreign Affairs Committee's report on the sinking of the *General Belgrano* during the Falklands conflict: see H.C. *11* (1984–5).

[113] 83 H.C. Deb. *371–2* (written answers 22 July 1985). But the Government does routinely publish a response to each committee report, usually as a White Paper.

Chapter 16

The House of Lords [1]

Composition

The superior judges and the Law Officers of the Crown still receive writs of summons to attend with the Lords at the opening of a new Parliament, but they never take part in the proceedings of the House unless they are peers. The following are entitled to membership.

1 The Lords Spiritual. These are the Archbishops of Canterbury and York, the Bishops of London, Durham and Winchester, and the next twenty-one senior diocesan bishops of the Church of England, seniority being determined by the date of appointment to a see;[2] they cease to be eligible to sit as Lords Spiritual after retirement at seventy. Other ecclesiastics may sit only if granted peerages. In early Tudor times the Lords Spiritual had constituted half the membership of the House.

2 Hereditary peers of England (before 1707), Great Britain (1707–1800) and the United Kingdom (1801–): they are dukes, marquesses, earls, viscounts or barons.[3] In 1989 they were just over nine hundred in number; more than half of the hereditary peerages of the United Kingdom had been created (on the advice of the Prime Minister) since 1900, though none was conferred from 1965 to 1983.[4] Some of the surviving ancient hereditary peerages were

---

[1] See Rodney Brazier, *Constitutional Practice* (1988), ch. 10.

[2] The Bishop of Sodor and Man is excluded because the Isle of Man is not part of the United Kingdom: see Erskine May, *Parliamentary Practice* (20th edn, 1983), p.5.

[3] The holder of a peerage other than a dukedom may simply be known as 'Lord' X. A baron is almost invariably so styled. Some confusion can be caused by 'courtesy titles'; thus, the eldest son of the Duke of Marlborough has the courtesy title of the Marquess of (or Lord) Blandford, but he is not a peer.

[4] When viscountcies were recommended for Mr George Thomas and Mr William Whitelaw. Mr Harold Macmillan was created Earl of Stockton in 1984.

created by the issue of a royal writ of summons followed by the actual taking of a seat; such peerages descended to heirs general, including women. All modern hereditary peerages have been created by letters patent; they do not descend to women unless there is an express provision in the letters patent for inheritance by heirs female. But although a woman might be a peeress in her own right, she had no right at common law to take a seat in the Lords; and this disability was not removed by the general words of the Sex Disqualification (Removal) Act 1919: see *Viscountess Rhondda's* case (1922).[5] Under the Life Peerages Act 1958 a life peerage conferring the right to sit can be bestowed upon a woman; and the Peerage Act 1963 enabled all peeresses in their own right to sit in the Lords.[6]

3   Peers of Scotland, who have inherited peerages created before the Act of Union.[7] Till the Peerage Act 1963 they elected sixteen of their own number to represent them for the duration of a Parliament; now they have an unrestricted right to take their seats. Peers of Ireland no longer have any right to sit in the Lords[8] but may be elected to the Commons.

4   Life peers, created under the 1958 Act; they number over three hundred and fifty. Non-hereditary peerages had been created under the prerogative, but it was held in the nineteenth century that conferment of such a peerage bestowed no right to sit in the Lords; such a right could only be given by statute.[9] It was thought that a number of persons with radical sympathies who were prominent in public life would be willing to accept life peerages but not hereditary peerages; the Life Peerages Act was passed mainly in the hope of strengthening and broadening the composition of the House of Lords. Once a year a list of new 'working' life peers is drawn up by the Prime Minister after consultation with the Leader of the Opposition (and occasionally with other party Leaders).

5   Lords of Appeal in Ordinary, appointed for life under the Appellate Jurisdiction Acts. They are appointed as judges, usually from the

---

[5] [1922] 2 A.C. 339 – an unconvincing report by a majority of the Committee of Privileges of the House of Lords, praying in aid the presumption of statutory intent against the indirect introduction of major constitutional change.

[6] The wife of a peer is not, as such, a peeress in her own right. She may be elected to a seat in the Commons.

[7] Any Scotsman on whom a peerage has been bestowed since the Act of Union has been a peer of the United Kingdom.

[8] *Re Earl of Antrim's Petition* [1967] 1 A.C. 691. Before 1922, when the Irish Free State was constituted, peers of Ireland elected twenty-eight representative peers for life. The machinery for filling vacancies caused by death then lapsed.

[9] *Wensleydale Peerage Case* (1856) 5 H.L.C. 958; see p. 309, below.

Court of Appeal, but are not precluded from taking part in general debate,[10] and they are indeed still entitled to sit in the House after they have retired from judicial office. The maximum number entitled to be paid as Lords of Appeal at any one time is now eleven.

It will be seen that some members of the House of Lords (the Lords Spiritual) are not peers, and that not all peers (for example, peers of Ireland) are entitled to sit. Alienage, infancy, bankruptcy and imprisonment for treason are also disqualifications for sitting.[11] There is no provision for expulsion of a peer by resolution of the House in its legislative capacity.

The potential membership of the House is over one thousand. Some peers who have succeeded to hereditary peerages have never applied for writs of summons;[12] other peers have been granted, or have been deemed to obtain, leave of absence[13] under a standing order designed to discourage habitual absentees ('backwoodsmen') from descending on Westminster in strength to vote down a controversial reform measure emanating from the Commons. The average daily attendance is about three hundred,[14] but the number can still rise sharply on an important occasion. On 28 October 1971 the House voted 451 to 58 in favour of the principle of entry into the Common Market.

A peerage may fall into abeyance or become extinct, but cannot be alienated; nor could it be renounced at common law. Mr Tony Benn's persistent campaign to disclaim the Stansgate peerage to which he had succeeded came to fruition in the Peerage Act 1963.[15] Under this Act a peer may disclaim for his own lifetime a hereditary peerage to which he has succeeded, provided that he makes the disclaimer within twelve

[10] See generally Drewry and Morgan (1969) 22 *Parliamentary Affairs* 226; Louis Blom-Cooper and Gavin Drewry, *Final Appeal* (1972), ch. 10.
[11] Mental disorder does not disqualify: see H.L. 254 (1983–4), pp. 5–6, and Leopold [1985] *Public Law* 9.
[12] The number in 1988 was 86.
[13] Erskine May, op. cit., p. 222. In 1985–6, 135 members of the Lords had leave of absence. At the beginning of each Parliament the Lord Chancellor sends a letter to each member asking if he wishes to apply for leave of absence; and at the beginning of each session he puts the same question to members who have neither applied for leave of absence nor attended, or who have been granted leave of absence for the previous session. One who has obtained leave of absence for that Parliament or that session, or who has not replied to the letter, is expected not to attend the House during the relevant period unless he gives a month's notice of his desire to attend, though he cannot apparently be prevented from speaking or voting if he nevertheless presents himself.
[14] In the 1985–6 session it was 317. In 1955 (before the Life Peerages Act 1958) it was only ninety-two. The attendance record of peers of first creation was, not surprisingly, better than that of peers by inheritance.
[15] See Tony Benn, *Out of the Wilderness: Diaries 1963–7* (1987), ch. 2.

months of succession or coming of age. If he is an M.P., or a parliamentary candidate who is then elected to the Commons, he has only a month in which to make up his mind. After disclaimer, he becomes a commoner; he may subsequently be granted a life peerage but not a hereditary peerage. One upon whom a peerage has been personally conferred cannot disclaim it. Seventeen peers by inheritance had in fact disclaimed their peerages by 1989; not surprisingly, Mr Benn was the first of the few. The Earl of Home soon disclaimed his peerages in 1963 and became an M.P. after having been appointed Prime Minister;[16] Viscount Hailsham (Mr Quintin Hogg) also rejoined Mr Benn in the Commons but returned to the Lords as a life peer on being appointed Lord Chancellor in 1970. The effect of the Act has not seriously affected the balance between the two Houses, but it has belatedly removed a source of injustice to reluctant peers.

Peers are not paid a salary for attendance, but they may claim reimbursement for all travel on parliamentary business, and for daily subsistence up to £20 a day, for overnight subsistence up to £52 a day and a general office, secretarial and research allowance of up to £22 a day.

The House of Lords allows its proceedings to be televised, an arrangement made permanent in 1986.[17] The other House, by contrast, has dragged its feet over this highly desirable move.

Functions and work of the House [18]

The Lord Chancellor, sitting on the woolsack, presides in the House,[19] but he lacks, and does not need, the coercive disciplinary powers of the Speaker of the Commons. Proceedings in the Lords sometimes resemble a game of cricket without an umpire; probably no other legislative body maintains so high a degree of gentle decorum. Another engaging eccentricity is that the Lord Chancellor often leaves the impartial (and extremely comfortable) cushion of the woolsack to speak for the Government.[20] When the House is in committee the chair is taken by the Lord Chairman of Committees. The House has a Gentleman Usher of the Black Rod to attend on the Lord Chancellor and execute the

[16] He received a life peerage as Lord Home of the Hirsel on his retirement from the Commons in 1974.

[17] See 474 H.L. Deb. 963–1005; 1278–9 (12 and 15 May 1986).

[18] See D. Shell, *The House of Lords* (1988).

[19] That part of his salary which he receives as Speaker of the House of Lords is not charged on the Consolidated Fund, though the salary of the Speaker of the House of Commons is so charged. See Ministerial and other Salaries Act 1975, s. 1.

[20] Another Minister is Leader of the House of Lords.

orders of the House. The clerk of the House is styled Clerk of the Parliaments; he prepares and presents bills for the royal assent; he is removable only on an address by the Lords. The House sits for about 150 days in an average session.

The White Paper of 1968 referred [21] to seven functions of the House: (i) its appellate role; (ii) the provision of a forum for debate on matters of public interest; (iii) the revision of Commons' bills; (iv) the initiation of less controversial public bills; (v) the consideration of subordinate legislation; (vi) scrutiny of the activities of the Executive; and (vii) scrutiny of private legislation. [22]

The judicial functions of the House (i) will be considered separately; [23] so will function (v). [24] Function (vi) is not performed adequately; a stronger, reformed second chamber could do better. Reference has already been made to function (vii). The second, third and fourth functions are of some consequence.

Several factors impair the efficiency of the Lords. The House is aristocratic and non-elective; its members do not represent any body of constituents and are thought of as speaking for a small section of the community. Moreover, as is well known, a peerage is often granted as a reward to party loyalists or as a consolation for Ministers who, no longer measuring up to their jobs, are 'kicked upstairs'. The Conservatives always form the largest group. Governments do not depend on the favour of the Lords for their continuance in office. The House has no power over money matters; it cannot impose its will on the Commons in legislation but can be overridden by the Commons; it is vulnerable to a hostile Labour Government because of lack of a firm basis of public support, and, conscious of this fact, is very reluctant to exercise the suspensory powers over legislation which it retains; [25] the Government can brush aside opposition in the Lords more readily than in the Commons, mainly because a high-handed attitude on its part is less likely to have adverse electoral repercussions; the Government front bench in the Lords is seldom strong and much of the excitement aroused by questions and debates in the Commons is therefore lacking in the Lords.

[21] House of Lords Reform, Cmnd 3799, pp. 2–3.
[22] In the 1985–6 session the House divided its time as follows, in percentages: consideration of Commons bills: 58; general debates: 16; questions: 11; ministerial statements, subordinate legislation: each 4; debates on European Community Committee reports: 2·5; private bills: 0·5; other: 4.
[23] See pp. 308–10.
[24] See p. 348.
[25] But see below, pp. 306–7.

On the other hand, the quality of members and speeches is often high. Those upon whom peerages are conferred are usually persons of considerable experience of politics,[26] the public service or industry or who have otherwise made their mark in public or intellectual life. They bring to the House a wide range of expertise. They tend to be elderly, but there is a leavening of young peers by succession. In recent years the House has become markedly more liberal in its outlook towards matters of social and penal reform; the effect of the Life Peerages Act has been conspicuously beneficial. For example, the original initiative in relaxing the law relating to homosexual conduct (the Sexual Offences Act 1967) came from the Lords, not the Commons; a big majority in the Lords against the abolition of capital punishment for murder in the early postwar period was converted to an abolitionist majority in the mid-1960s.[27] The leisurely timetable of the Lords gives the backbencher more opportunities to speak than in the Commons; and debates on matters which cut across party lines, raising controversial moral issues out of which the Government is more likely to incur odium than attract credit by adopting a positive position, can easily be arranged in the Lords. Again, the political balance has become more evenly weighted save on highly contentious party occasions. Making allowance for those peers on leave of absence, the Conservatives are in a minority in the total membership of the House: in 1989 there were 425 Conservative peers, 288 crossbenchers, 113 Labour, 57 Democrats and 23 Social Democrats. It is however, the case that the Conservative Party forms the largest single group in an average day's attendance.

The House of Lords as at present constituted is a useful legislative chamber. As has been mentioned, many of the less controversial Government bills are introduced there; the debates will often be well informed; helpful amendments to law reform bills may be moved by Law Lords at committee stage. An example of a major piece of legislation thus introduced was the Courts Act 1971. The Government's legislative output is thereby enlarged and its efficiency improved. (It should, however, be noted that a majority of Commons' bills are passed wholly unamended every session.) The utility of the Lords as a forum

---

[26] For example, by 1988 only eleven former Cabinet Ministers who had left the Commons since 1964 remained outside the House of Lords.

[27] This can be partly explained by reference to a change of attitude among the bishops and to some extent among the Law Lords. See the debates on the bill which became the Murder (Abolition of Death Penalty) Act 1965. In December 1969 a Government motion to give the measure permanent effect was passed on a free vote by the Lords as well as the Commons. See also Janet Morgan, *The House of Lords and the Labour Government 1964–1970* (1975).

for the consideration of private bills is well recognized. Not so generally appreciated is its value as a chamber for the introduction of private members' bills which may be crowded out in the Commons; in every session two or three such bills, not usually of a controversial character, become law. A controversial backbench bill originating in the Lords is unlikely to pass into law that session, but by attracting publicity it can lead to the implementation of a reform soon afterwards; the Sexual Offences Act 1967 is an illustration. The function of the Lords in revising Commons' bills is potentially more important, but is not very satisfactory in practice, mainly because the Lords are apprehensive about the consequences of using their delaying powers by insisting on amendments to a Labour Government's bills, and partly because of the amateurish lack of organization within the House. The latter failure, coupled with large-scale absenteeism, is also responsible for the failure of the House to perform properly what could be its most important function, scrutiny of central administration.

Occasionally the revising powers of the Lords are used with significant effect. The House, for example, successfully insisted that the bill which became the Foreign Compensation Act 1969 should (contrary to the Government's original wishes) make provision for a limited right of appeal to the Court of Appeal from the Commission's determinations about its jurisdiction. That episode showed the potential value of a well-informed second chamber. It also illustrates, incidentally, how a second chamber may be used by the Government to interpolate into a bill its afterthoughts instead of having to introduce an amending bill later.

This last point was illustrated still more aptly in 1972, when 610 Lords' amendments were made to the controversial and complex Local Government Bill after it had been passed by the Commons. The vast majority of those amendments were introduced by the Government.

The House of Lords regularly appoints select committees to investigate matters of concern to it. Some of the reports of those committees are critical of the policies of the Government of the day, regardless of its political colour: so, for example, the Report of the Select Committee on Unemployment urged major changes in the Conservative Government's employment policies.[28] The reports are always a useful source of information, and the House routinely debates all select committee reports – an attribute which the other House does not enjoy in relation to the reports of its departmental select committees.[29]

---

[28] See H.L. 142 (1981–2).
[29] See above, p. 296.

Disagreements between the two Houses

Till 1911 the Lords and the Commons had coordinate legislative authority except in money matters.[30] By convention, and according to the privileges claimed by the Commons, bills dealing wholly or mainly with taxation or public expenditure had to be introduced in the Commons, and their money clauses could not be amended by the Lords, though the Lords retained at least a formal right to reject them. Nor could the Lords amend the financial clauses of non-money bills, save where the Commons decided not to insist on but instead to waive their privilege of having exclusive cognizance of such matters. This is broadly the constitutional position in relation to financial matters today (though see p. 229), but superimposed is the drastic rule introduced by the Parliament Act 1911.

In 1909 the House of Lords rejected the Finance Bill; they passed it in 1910 after the Liberal Government had been returned to office at a General Election. Following the second General Election of 1910, at which the Liberals retained power, the Lords were induced to pass the Parliament Bill under the threat of being swamped by a massive influx of new Liberal peers.[31] The Parliament Act 1911 was amended by the Parliament Act 1949, but not so as to affect its provisions relating to money bills.

Money bills. For the purpose of s. 1 of the Parliament Act 1911, a money bill is one which in the opinion of the Speaker contains provisions *exclusively* relating to central government taxation, expenditure or loans. If before a bill leaves the Commons the Speaker certifies it as a money bill, then it may be presented for the royal assent notwithstanding that the Lords have failed to pass it without amendment after it has been before them for one month. The Speaker's certificate is to be endorsed on the bill; once given, it is conclusive for all purposes;[32] before giving it, he must, if practicable, consult two members of the chairmen's panel. It will be noted that the statutory definition of a money bill is narrow; not every Finance Bill has been so certified. But the combination of strict law and convention has deprived the Lords of all effective authority over raising and spending money.

Other bills. Other public bills (including private members' bills) passed

---

[30] See Erskine May, op. cit., ch. 31.
[31] For a readable account of the crisis, see Roy Jenkins, *Mr Balfour's Poodle* (1954).
[32] Though cf. pp. 33, 88.

by the Commons may also be passed into law against the opposition of the Lords. (The Commons may kill a Lords' bill simply by not passing it.) Under section 2 of the Parliament Act 1911, a bill could be presented for the royal assent if (1) it had been passed by the Commons in three consecutive sessions (whether of the same Parliament or not) in the same form or subject only to such amendments as were certified by the Speaker as being necessary through the effluxion of time or to Lords' amendments agreed to in the preceding session by the Commons; (2) the Lords had failed to pass it in each of the three sessions; (3) two years had elapsed between the second reading of the bill in the Commons in the first session and its third reading in the Commons in the third session; (4) the bill had been sent up to the Lords at least one month before the end of each session; and (5) the Speaker had certified that the requirements of the Parliament Act had been complied with. By the Parliament Act 1949 the number of sessions was reduced from three to two and the interval of time from two years to one. Hence the suspensory veto of the Lords has been reduced to one year and one month.[33]

These provisions do not, however, apply to bills to prolong the maximum duration of a Parliament beyond five years, or to provisional order confirmation bills;[34] nor do they apply to private bills or to subordinate legislation. Only by resorting to the unlikely, and probably self-defeating, expedient of requesting the monarch to create a sufficient number of new peers for the purpose,[35] could a Government secure the passage of such a bill against the adamant opposition of the Lords.

Only three Acts have been passed over the heads of the Lords under the Parliament Act procedure: the Welsh Church Act 1914 (disestablishing the Church of Wales); the Government of Ireland Act 1914 (providing for home rule for Ireland; the outbreak of the First World War followed at once, and this Act was never brought into operation; self-government was introduced after the war, along with partition); and the Parliament Act 1949. The 1949 Act was ostensibly designed to forestall prospective Conservative opposition to a measure for the

---

[33] If the Lords neither reject the bill nor amend it in a manner unacceptable to the Commons but merely adjourn proceedings on the bill, the Speaker is likely to certify that the requirements of the Parliament Acts have been complied with immediately before the end of the session so that the bill can be presented for the royal assent. See Eric Taylor, *The House of Commons at Work* (9th edn, 1979), pp. 112–13. In practice the suspensory veto is unlikely to exceed a year.

[34] cf. p. 276.

[35] See pp. 120–21.

nationalization of the iron and steel industry. A Parliament Bill was introduced late in 1947 and was passed by the Commons; the second reading in the Lords was adjourned while a conference of party leaders discussed schemes for the future composition and powers of the Lords; the conference broke down on the question of the period of delaying power over legislation; the Lords then rejected the bill on second reading by a large majority, and after the bill had again been passed and rejected in the next two sessions it was submitted for the royal assent.[36] The Government nevertheless found it expedient to accept a Lords' amendment to the Iron and Steel Bill, postponing its operation; the Government lost office soon afterwards and that measure did not come fully into effect.

The House of Lords used its suspensory veto to the full over the Labour Government's Trade Union and Labour Relations (Amendment) Bill. Only when it became clear that the Government would cause the Bill to be passed under the Parliament Acts did the House of Lords withdraw its strong objections and allow the measure to go for royal assent in 1976, having forced a delay of slightly under one year.[37] The opposition peers could claim that they had ensured the maximum time for the Commons to reconsider the measure in a proper exercise of the constitutional function enshrined in the Parliament Acts.

Under the Government's 1968 proposals for Lords' reform, the period of delay would have been reduced to sixty parliamentary days from the date of disagreement between the two Houses. Provision would also have been made for enabling the Commons to override by a simple resolution the Lords' disapproval of such delegated legislation as was subject to parliamentary proceedings.[38]

In practice full-scale collisions between the two Houses have been infrequent. The Lords have not rejected any of the nationalization bills passed by the Commons under Labour Governments; they have inserted many amendments, but most have been withdrawn after the Commons have insisted on their unacceptability, or a compromise has been reached after discussions between party leaders in the two Houses; some Lords' amendments to Government bills have been accepted on

---

[36] Professor Hood Phillips has argued (*Reform of the Constitution* (1970), pp. 18–19, 91–2) that the Parliament Act of 1949 may be a nullity, because it was enacted by a 'delegate' with limited powers (i.e. the King and Commons under the Parliament Act 1911 procedure) and a delegate cannot enlarge its own powers. But even if one accepts the view (rejected above at p. 89) that legislation passed under the 1911 Act procedure is 'delegated' and subordinate, it is questionable whether the 1949 Act was *ultra vires* according to the canons of statutory interpretation.

[37] The Bill became the Trade Union and Labour Relations (Amendment) Act 1976.

[38] Cmnd 3799 (1968), pp. 21–3. See ch. 18.

their merits or for reasons of prudence.[39] There have, however, been two recent exceptions to this accommodation which provide the boldest instances of the House of Lords holding up and amending major pieces of Government legislation. First, the Aircraft and Shipbuilding Industries Bill was introduced in the 1975–6 session and passed the House of Commons. The Lords, however, attached amendments which would have withdrawn the ship-repairing industry from the Bill, and insisted on those amendments. That session of Parliament ended and the Bill was lost. It was reintroduced in the 1976–7 session and passed when the Government gave way over the ship-repairing clauses.[40] It received the royal assent on 17 March 1977. Secondly, the House of Lords passed by a majority of 48 a wrecking amendment to the Local Government (Interim Provisions) Bill in 1984, so that the Conservative Government was forced to reconsider its plan to abolish the 1984 elections to the Greater London Council and to the metropolitan county councils and to put in nominated boards pending the abolition of those authorities. In view of the general unpopularity of the proposed abolition of elections and the number of Conservative defections and abstentions which contributed to the majority of 48, the Government had to cause the Bill to be amended so as to extend the life of the authorities to 1986 without elections in 1984 and to dispense with the expedient of nominated boards; the episode caused some regular critics of the existence of the House of Lords (such as Mr Ken Livingstone, Leader of the GLC) for a while to become its most ardent champions.

The House of Lords is, indeed, tending to behave in an even-handed manner towards the legislation of Governments of both parties. Mrs Thatcher's Government sustained its one hundredth legislative defeat in the Lords in October 1986 – roughly at the same rate of setback as that inflicted on the 1964 Labour Government. This attitude has enhanced the House in the eyes of the general public, who also seem pleased with what they have seen of the working House on television.

In the last analysis the most important reason why a non-Conservative Government has seldom run into serious trouble with the

[39] In 1947–8 the Commons, on a free vote, inserted in the Criminal Justice Bill a clause moved by a backbencher which would have abolished the death penalty; the backwoodsmen emerged, and the Lords passed an amendment by a large majority to delete the clause; the Government dropped the clause from the bill. It is unlikely that the Parliament Act procedure would be invoked to secure the passage of any private member's bill.

[40] The House of Lords had also effectively killed the House of Commons (Redistribution of Seats) Bill in 1969. The Government, unwilling either to accept the Lords' amendments or to resort to the Parliament Acts, decided to withdraw the Bill: see further pp. 243–4 and 348.

Lords as at present constituted is a fear of the consequences of self-assertion which the Conservative leadership in the Lords rightly entertains. The Prime Minister might, for example, obtain a dissolution of Parliament in an endeavour to distract public attention from more embarrassing and relevant problems, and the Government might then contrive to win a sufficient measure of support to be returned to power, pledged to end the Lords (under the Parliament Acts procedure, if necessary[41]) and perhaps even the hereditary peerage itself.

Judicial duties of the Lords[42]

The Lords have functions of a judicial nature incidental to their capacity as a legislative body, though inasmuch as the House is a superior court of record, their determination may be reported in the law reports. Claims to peerages[43] and to a right to sit in the House by virtue of the grant of a peerage are referred to the Committee of Privileges of the House; the House traditionally adopts the Committee's report.[44] This procedure is also adopted when allegations of breach of the privileges of the House are made.

Magna Carta had laid it down that a free man was entitled to trial by his peers. This principle survived in the House of Lords till 1948; a peer (or his wife) charged with treason or felony was tried by the whole House of Lords; this expensive anachronism was abolished by the Criminal Justice Act 1948 and peers are now tried in the ordinary courts.

The process of impeachment is obsolete but has never been abolished. If a person were to be impeached today he would be tried by the whole House of Lords, with the House of Commons as his accusers.

Another function of a judicial nature, harking back to the days when the High Court of Parliament was a judicial as well as a legislative body, was the enactment of a bill of attainder, not by the Lords alone but by the Queen in Parliament. An act of attainder is a legislative judgment declaring a person to have been guilty of treason or other

[41] On whether the House of Lords could lawfully be abolished, see Mirfield (1979) 95 *L.Q.R.* 37 and Winterton, ibid., 386.

[42] See Robert Stevens, *Law and Politics: The House of Lords as a Judicial Body 1800–1976* (1979); Alan Paterson, *The Law Lords* (1982).

[43] Disputes as to the validity of the creation of a new peerage are decided by the House of its own motion. Disputes as to who (if anyone) is entitled to an old peerage are determinable by the Attorney-General on behalf of the Crown but are normally referred, in practice, to the House.

[44] See, e.g., *Ampthill Peerage Case* [1977] A.C. 547; *Annandale and Hartfell Peerage Claim* [1986] A.C. 319 (earldom revived after almost 200 years in abeyance).

high crimes. Over 270 years have passed since this ugly manifestation of 'parliamentary judicature' was last expressed. The offences of which a man was attainted were not necessarily crimes at the time when the acts complained of were committed. Modern constitutional bills of rights will usually debar the Legislature from enacting *ex post facto* penal laws,[45] and the constitution may also, either expressly[46] or by implication,[47] invalidate bills of attainder.[48]

The House of Lords is also a court of appeal, at the apex of the ordinary hierarchy of courts in the United Kingdom.[49] In this capacity it exercises the ancient jurisdiction of the High Court of Parliament. It ceased to exercise original jurisdiction in the seventeenth century. The exercise of its appellate jurisdiction gave rise to some awkward problems; the quorum of the House in its judicial as in its legislative capacity is three, and there were not always three hereditary peers with judicial experience available to sit; the judges of the common law courts could, however, be called in to offer advice.[50]

An attempt was made to strengthen the judicial element in the Lords in the mid-nineteenth century by conferring a life peerage on a judge of the Court of Exchequer, Sir James Parke; the Committee of Privileges reported that a life peer was unable to take his seat,[51] and Parke had to be given a hereditary peerage. The idea of diluting the hereditary peerage with lawyers and their progeny was unattractive to the Lords; and the need for a second and not very distinguished appellate court was not readily apparent to laymen or indeed the bar. Under the Judicature Act of 1873 the appellate jurisdiction of the Lords was to be abolished; but after the Conservatives had ousted the Liberals at the General Election of 1874 a determined and successful campaign to restore that jurisdiction was mounted.[52] The Appellate Jurisdiction Act

[45] For example, Constitution of India, art. 20(1).
[46] For example, Constitution of the United States, art. 1, s. 9.
[47] For example, where the constitution vests the judicial power exclusively in the Judiciary. And before Ceylon became the Republic of Sri Lanka under a new constitution in 1972, the power of the Ceylon Parliament to make laws for the peace, order, and good government of Ceylon did not import a power to pass an Act for the condemnation of a particular individual: *Liyanage* v. *R.* [1967] 1 A.C. 259; though cf. *Kariapper* v. *Wijesinha* [1968] A.C. 717.
[48] Express references to 'bills of attainder' in modern constitutions are uncommon because of the ambiguity of the phrase – an ambiguity emphasized by trends of interpretation in the United States Supreme Court.
[49] For a full study, see Louis Blom-Cooper and Gavin Drewry, *Final Appeal* (1972).
[50] The last case in which such advice was sought was *Allen* v. *Flood* [1898] A.C. 1. The advice given by the judges in that case was not accepted.
[51] *Wensleydale Peerage Case* (1856); above, note 9. Sir James Parke was a Baron of the Exchequer, but not the holder of a title of baronage.
[52] See Stevens (1964) 80 *L.Q.R.* 343.

1876 provided for the appointment of two (there may now be eleven) Lords of Appeal in Ordinary, life peers who had held high judicial office for two years or were barristers of fifteen years' standing; they were given a *statutory* right to sit in the Lords. They retire at seventy-five but may still be asked by the Lord Chancellor to sit. By convention, at least two must be Scots lawyers. The Lord Chancellor, ex-Lords Chancellor and other peers who hold or have held high judicial office may also make up the necessary judicial quorum; in practice five Law Lords normally sit to hear an appeal. Lay peers are not precluded by statute from sitting uninvited with the Law Lords to hear an appeal, but by convention they abstain from doing so; the last time when such a peer sat was in 1883 and his participation in the proceedings (including his vote on the appeal) was simply ignored.

In its capacity as a court of appeal the House sits as an appellate committee; it adjourns to the chamber of the House for the formal delivery of opinions, which have been handed out in writing shortly beforehand and are not now read out by their Lordships. It may sit during a prorogation or dissolution of Parliament.

The House entertains civil and criminal appeals, with leave of itself or the court below, from the Court of Appeal. It also hears appeals from the Courts-Martial Appeal Court and in certain cases direct from the Divisional Court of the Queen's Bench Division, and individual High Court judges, under restrictive conditions. It exercises civil but not criminal appellate jurisdiction in respect of the Scottish courts, and hears both civil and criminal appeals from Northern Ireland.

Approaches to reform

The preamble to the Parliament Act 1911 recited the intention 'to substitute for the House of Lords as it at present exists a second chamber constituted on a popular instead of a hereditary basis . . .' In 1917 the Bryce conference proposed[53] that three-quarters of the members of the second chamber should be indirectly elected on a regional basis by the House of Commons; this scheme, unpropitious in its timing and, like all other schemes for reform of the Lords, inconveniently controversial, was placed in a pigeon-hole, and there it remains. The inter-party conference convened after the second Parliament Bill had been passed by the Commons reached a substantial measure of agreement on an outline plan for a reconstituted upper House; the principle of indirect election, and inheritance as an

[53] Cd 9038 (1917).

automatic qualification for membership, were alike rejected; it was accepted that the House ought to be complementary to rather than a rival of the Commons, and that as far as possible matters should be so contrived that no party had a permanent majority in it.[54] Nothing was done to implement these proposals. Subsequent reforms have not undermined the hereditary principle, but the Life Peerages Act 1958 has led to an improvement in the quality of debate, an increase in the number of regular attenders and a modification in the political complexion of the more conscientious body of participants;[55] and standing orders providing for leave of absence have also helped. But a vote strictly along party lines on a matter attracting a large attendance will almost invariably give the Conservatives a majority.[56]

Discussions about the reform of the Lords have cut across party divisions without bringing about the impetus or sense of urgency needed to carry a scheme through the Commons. Agreement in principle amongst the sophisticated tends to be less than whole-hearted and to beget new disagreements when principle is translated into detail. Real enthusiasm for Lords' reform is too often to be found among the eccentric and the naïve, who may have little idea of the mediocre performance of second chambers in so many other countries or of the limited expectations that can reasonably be reposed in a reconstituted British second chamber. Party political considerations also inhibit a determined approach to reform. Conservatives would, on the whole, like to see a less unrepresentative upper House brought into existence, but preferably by agreement and under a Labour Government; for a stronger upper House would be readier to exercise its authority, and if this were used to the detriment of a Labour Government (for example, by delaying bills) the Conservatives would not have to incur the unpopularity that would be attached to the reformed House's progenitor. Radicals have tended either to favour abolition of the Lords or to let sleeping dogs lie; an unrepresentative second chamber is now unlikely to do more than growl, and occasionally bark, at a Government of the Left, whereas a renovated and more self-assured body might bite hard.

In this context the Government's abortive scheme of 1968[57] was an imaginative effort to grapple with an elusive set of problems. Briefly, it envisaged a House stronger in its composition (though with reduced

[54] Cmd 7380 (1948).
[55] This was also influenced, of course, by life peerages granted on the advice of Mr Wilson and Mr Callaghan during 1964–70 and 1974–9.
[56] See above, p. 302, for party allegiances in the House of Lords.
[57] House of Lords Reform, Cmnd 3799 (1968).

delaying powers), so constituted that no party would have a permanent overall majority; but the Government of the day would have a 10 per cent majority over the combined opposition parties, with crossbench peers (including the Law Lords) and bishops holding the balance. The House would, in effect, have two tiers – those members with voting rights and those who would be entitled to sit and speak but not vote. The voting House would have 200 to 250 members apart from bishops and serving Law Lords; the members would be those hereditary peers of first creation and life peers who were prepared to attend regularly; about eighty new Labour life peers would have had to be created if the bill had become law in 1969, in order to bring the Government side up to strength. There would be a retiring age for voting members and they would be paid a salary. Non-voting members would be those peers of first creation who were unable or unwilling to meet the attendance requirements, and all existing peers by inheritance; subsequently, however, inheritance of a peerage would no longer of itself qualify for membership of the House at all.

By June 1968 a large measure of agreement had been reached. Then the Government, irritated by the refusal of the Lords to approve (at the first time of asking) an Order in Council imposing mandatory UN sanctions against Rhodesia, broke off the talks and produced its own scheme, closely based on what had already been agreed. A White Paper embodying the Government's proposals was debated in November 1968. It was approved in principle by the Commons by 270 votes to 159. The breakdown of the voting figures is remarkable; although the Government had put on a three-line whip, and although the Opposition front benches were in general sympathy with the proposals, 45 Labour backbenchers, 104 Conservatives, 8 Liberals and 2 other members voted in the Noes lobby. The Lords agreed to the proposals by 251 votes to 56.

Nevertheless (or perhaps consequently) trouble lay ahead for the Government. A bill to implement the proposals, the Parliament (No. 2) Bill, was read a second time in the Commons. But when it went to Committee of the Whole House, a multitude of amendments were put down by backbenchers. Many members objected to the excessive patronage that the scheme would have placed in the Prime Minister's hands; some Conservatives objected to the erosion of the hereditary principle or the weakening of the party's strength in the upper House; some Labour members saw the proposals as a means of shoring up a crumbling citadel of aristocratic privilege and wealth which ought to be demolished altogether or left alone to crumble away. In the end the

Government gave up. In April it withdrew the bill, to make room for a still more controversial Industrial Relations Bill which was never introduced at all during that Parliament.

There have been no Government-sponsored measures to seek reform of the House of Lords since 1968. The Labour Party conference in 1977 adopted a policy of abolition of the House in favour of a unicameral Parliament consisting of the Commons alone.[58] The S.D.P./Liberal Alliance has favoured a reformed House of Lords based on a mixture of half its members being directly elected by proportional representation, half being nominated for life by the Queen on the advice of the Prime Minister and a committee of senior Privy Councillors from all the parties.[59] The present Government has no plans for change.[60]

[58] That policy appeared in its 1983 General Election manifesto, but not in that for the 1987 Election.

[59] See *Towards a New Constitutional Settlement* (1983).

[60] A Conservative Party committee under Lord Home in 1978 recommended reform based on 268 members directly elected by proportional representation and 134 members nominated for life by the Queen on the Prime Minister's advice. See The House of Lords: Report of the Conservative Review Committee (1978).

Chapter 17

Parliamentary Privilege

General

Parliamentary privilege[1] is part of the law and custom of Parliament. It consists of special rules evolved by the two Houses in order to protect themselves collectively, and their members acting in their public capacities, against outside interference, so as to enable them to carry out their constitutional functions effectively. Most of these special rules are non-statutory; they have been laid down by resolutions of the two Houses or by Speakers' rulings. Some are statutory. They are part of the common law in so far as their existence and validity are recognized by the courts, but they are, in general, enforced not by the courts but by each House. The two Houses justify the special rights, powers and immunities conferred by parliamentary privilege as being necessary for the welfare of the nation. Citizens denied legal redress against M.P.s, or adjudged by the House of Commons to have committed a high contempt and a breach of its privileges, tend to be less impressed by these claims. The connotation of the word 'privilege', is, moreover, unattractive. A select committee of the House of Commons, appointed to review the law of parliamentary privilege, recommended in 1967 that the expression 'parliamentary privilege' should be sent to the lumber room, and that the House should instead speak of its 'rights and immunities',[2] but the committee's recommendations for the relinquishment of particular rights and immunities were extremely cautious. As

---

[1] For an authoritative study, see Erskine May's *Parliamentary Practice* (20th edn, 1983), chs 5–11. For valuable critiques, see *Report from the Select Committee on Parliamentary Privilege*, H.C. *34* (1967–8), and *Third Report from the Committee of Privileges: Recommendations of the Select Committee on Parliamentary Privilege* (H.C. *417* (1976–7)). See also Colin Munro, *Studies in Constitutional Law* (1987), ch. 7.

[2] H.C. *34* (1967–8), vi, viii, xlix.

will be seen at appropriate points in this chapter, the House took some action in 1978 on the committee's report.

The privileges of the Lords closely resemble those of the Commons, and will not be considered separately.

Privileges of the Commons

At the commencement of a Parliament the newly elected Speaker claims from the Crown 'all the ancient and undoubted privileges' of the House, and in particular freedom of speech in debate, freedom from arrest and freedom of access to the monarch through the Speaker; and he requests that a favourable construction be placed on the Commons' proceedings.[3] The most important privileges not specifically claimed are the right of the House to regulate its own composition, its right to have exclusive cognizance of matters arising within its precincts, the right to punish for contempt and breach of privilege, its privileges in relation to the Lords in financial matters,[4] and its claim to be the sole judge of the extent of its own privileges.[5] The difference between the privileges expressly claimed and those not expressly claimed is one of form, not of substance.

Freedom of speech

This is the most crucial and controversial parliamentary privilege. Article 9 of the Bill of Rights provided

that the freedom of speech, and debates or proceedings in Parliament ought not to be impeached or questioned in any court or place out of Parliament.

This is the basis of the modern law. Its interpretation and implications are of primary importance.

1 No action or prosecution can be brought against a member for any words used in the course of parliamentary proceedings. This rule is absolute. Thus, a member cannot be prosecuted or threatened with

---

[3] These last two privileges (or claims) relate back to the days when the attitude of the monarch towards petitions by the Commons and its spokesman was apt to be tempestuous.

[4] See ch. 16.

[5] Among the less important privileges are immunity from attendance in court as jurors or (with certain exceptions) as witnesses; and the right of impeachment. The Select Committee (note 1 above) recommended that the right of impeachment be abolished by statute.

prosecution for sedition[6] or a breach of the Official Secrets Acts[7] for such words; a prosecution or threat to prosecute would probably be treated by the House as a breach of its own privileges.[8] If a member were to be sued for libel or slander in respect of words used in Parliament (other than in casual conversation not connected with parliamentary business) the writ should be struck out as disclosing no cause of action; if the case were to come to trial the court would hold that the member was protected by absolute privilege in the law of defamation[9] – i.e. that no action would lie against him even if his remarks were shown to be defamatory, untrue and unfair. The defence of absolute privilege (which has no necessary connection with parliamentary privilege) also extends to judges acting in their official capacities; the risk that the immunity from suit may be abused is considered less than the risk that the absence of absolute privilege might deter M.P.s and judges from speaking bluntly, even harshly, when it is their duty to do so.

2 Parliamentary privilege (and absolute privilege in the law of defamation) also attaches to statements in official reports of the proceedings of the two Houses and their committees, and to other papers published by order of the House. This rule was laid down by the Parliamentary Papers Act 1840, passed in consequence of a judicial decision (*Stockdale* v. *Hansard*[10]) that parliamentary papers were protected not by parliamentary privilege but only by qualified privilege in the law of defamation – i.e. that untrue and libellous statements made in such documents were actionable if shown to have been actuated by malice.

3 What is the meaning of 'proceedings in Parliament'? A partial answer has been accepted by the House on the recommendation of the Committee of Privileges,[11] namely, that any communication between an M.P. and a Minister or an officer of the House concerning the business of the House should be absolutely privileged – but the House realizes that the crucial phrase 'business of the

---

[6] *Elliot*'s case (1629) 3 St. Tr. 294.

[7] *Case of Duncan Sandys* (1938). See Geoffrey Wilson, *Cases and Materials* (2nd edn, 1976), pp. 450–55; H.C. *101* (1938–9). Sandys had complained that he had been threatened with prosecution for refusing to divulge his sources of information in connection with a parliamentary question he had put down about a shortage of anti-aircraft equipment.

[8] This is to be inferred from the report of the Select Committee on the *Sandys* case and its adoption by the House. Members can be prosecuted for these offences in respect of disclosures or utterances which are not part of proceedings in Parliament.

[9] *Dillon* v. *Balfour* (1887) 20 Ir.L.R. 600; *Goffin* v. *Donnelly* (1881) 6 Q.B.D. 307.

[10] (1839) 9 A. & E. 1; see p. 330.

[11] H.C. *417* (1976–7), iii; 943 H.C. Deb. *1155–98* (6 February 1978).

House' needs to be defined by legislation. That legislation has not been forthcoming. Contributions to debate and committee discussions, oral questions, answers to parliamentary questions and voting are clearly within the definition; so are the execution of the orders of the House and the tabling of parliamentary questions. Acts done and words spoken within the precincts of Parliament which have nothing whatsoever to do with parliamentary proceedings[12] are clearly not protected. In between lie many transactions and situations that do not lend themselves easily to classification.[13] If a member tables a question and a Minister invites him to discuss it with him, the correspondence or conversations appear to be covered by parliamentary privilege.[14] It is arguable that unsolicited communications with a Minister are also covered if they are immediately related to a question or motion already tabled or a matter currently being debated in the House. If the issue has ceased to be before the House, such communications are probably no longer to be regarded as part of a proceeding *in* Parliament.

Communications with Ministers in respect of matters which may never arise in the House will not normally be covered by parliamentary privilege. Not every act done by a member in his capacity as a member is so protected.[15] So, for example, it is not a proceeding in Parliament when a member arranges for a film to be shown in a private room at the House, that film being the subject of an injunction which prevented it from being shown publicly.[16] A member's letter to or interview with a Minister, raising an issue of concern to an individual member of the public or a group of his constituents or any other section of the community, *may* lead to the putting down of a parliamentary question if no satisfactory informal answer is forthcoming; the issue thus raised may be a substitute for a *formal* parliamentary question (which would be privileged); but where is the line to be drawn between proceedings *in* Parliament

---

[12] See, for example, *Rivlin* v. *Bilainkin* [1953] 1 Q.B. 485 (member of the public posting a defamatory letter within the House, not protected). But see Lock (1983) *Industrial Law Journal* 28.

[13] See, for example, *Ex p. Wason* (1869) L.R. 4 Q.B. 573 (no private prosecution for alleged conspiracy to deceive the House of Lords by false statements in the House; the matter lay within scope of parliamentary privilege). See also *Att.-Gen. of Ceylon* v. *Livera* [1963] A.C. 103 at 120–22 for judicial comment on marginal situations.

[14] Speaker's Ruling, 591 H.C. Deb. 809–13 (14 July 1958).

[15] See generally de Smith (1958) 21 *Mod. L. Rev.* at 477–82.

[16] The Committee of Privileges so decided after the Speaker had directed that the film (about a secret spy satellite, 'Project Zircon') be not shown at the House of Commons pending a decision on the matter by the House as a whole: see H.C. 365 (1986–7); Bradley [1987] *Public Law* 1 and 488.

and matters merely antecedent to possible proceedings in Parliament?

The leading modern case is that of *G. R. Strauss* (1957–8). Mr Strauss, Labour M.P. and formerly Minister of Supply, wrote to a Minister complaining about certain activities of an area board of a nationalized industry. The Minister disclaimed responsibility on the ground that the matter was one of day-to-day administration, and passed the letter on to the board. The board threatened to sue Mr Strauss for libel. Mr Strauss then raised this threat in the House as a question of privilege. The question was referred to the Committee of Privileges, which reported[17] that in writing his letter Mr Strauss was engaged in a proceeding in Parliament, and that the members of the board and their solicitors, by threatening legal proceedings against him in respect of his allegations, were in breach of parliamentary privilege. They recommended (somewhat inconsistently) that the question whether Article 9 of the Bill of Rights, restating the privilege of freedom of speech, had been impliedly repealed by an obscure eighteenth-century statute should be referred to the Judicial Committee of the Privy Council for an advisory opinion. The question was so referred; the Judicial Committee advised that the Bill of Rights (whatever it might mean) stood intact.[18] The House accepted this advice and then debated the Report of the Committee of Privileges. On a free vote it rejected by 218 to 213 the Committee's finding that in writing his letter Mr Strauss had been engaged in a proceeding in Parliament.[19]

The decision is not binding on the House when future cases arise. And the Select Committee on Parliamentary Privilege in 1967 was 'strongly of the opinion' that the decision of the House in the *Strauss* case should be reversed by legislation.[20] At present the probability is that a court would hold a letter written by an M.P. to a Minister on a matter lying within the Minister's general area of responsibility[21] to be protected only by qualified privilege in the law

---

[17] H.C. *305* (1956–7).

[18] *Re Parliamentary Privilege Act 1770* [1958] A.C. 331.

[19] 591 H.C. Deb. *207–346* (8 July 1958). See also Lock [1985] *Public Law* 64.

[20] H.C. *34* (1967–8), xxvii. The Report had been published *nineteen months* before it was debated in the House. Some of its main recommendations have been implemented by the House by resolution – but then only after a delay of 10 years, and necessary legislation is still awaited: see 943 H.C. Deb. *1155–98* (6 February 1978), and D. G. T. Williams [1978] *Camb. L.J.* 1.

[21] e.g. a letter by an M.P. to the Lord Chancellor complaining of solicitors' conduct, even though the Lord Chancellor has no direct disciplinary authority over them: *Beech* v. *Freeson* [1972] 1 Q.B. 14.

of defamation, unless the letter was ancillary, or an immediate preliminary, to proceedings within Parliament itself. Public policy considerations can be canvassed on either side. Letters from members of the public to M.P.s (and presumably from M.P.s to members of the public) on matters of public concern[22] enjoy only qualified privilege.[23] So do fair and accurate newspaper reports of parliamentary proceedings.[24] A statutory extension of the scope of parliamentary privilege to ease the minds of M.P.s potentially threatened with libel actions (and heavy bills of costs) would be widely interpreted as a self-endowed licence to make maliciously defamatory comments with impunity.[25] On the other hand, in 1967 communications between M.P.s and the Parliamentary Commissioner for Administration were accorded absolute privilege by statute.[26]

4 Matters arising in the course of parliamentary proceedings cannot be challenged or relied on for the purpose of supporting legal proceedings based on events that occurred outside Parliament; for example, if an M.P. is sued for libel in connection with his remarks in a television interview, and he pleads qualified privilege or fair comment, the plaintiff is not allowed to use the defendant's comments in the House to show that the latter was actuated by malice.[27]

5 A member of the Commons who abuses his privilege of freedom of speech may be subjected to disciplinary sanctions by the House;[28] it is only outside Parliament that his parliamentary freedom of speech cannot be impeached.

6 The House still reserves to itself the right to treat the institution of legal proceedings against a member in respect of a matter covered,

---

[22] Unless the M.P. is communicating to a complainant a report from the Parliamentary Commissioner for Administration (Parliamentary Commissioner Act 1967 s. 10(5)); in which case he will enjoy absolute privilege.

[23] *R.* v. *Rule* [1937] 2 K.B. 375 (complaint by constituent to M.P. about public officers); see also *Beach* v. *Freeson* (above; complaint by M.P. to Lord Chancellor and Law Society).

[24] *Wason* v. *Walter* (1868) L.R. 4 Q.B. 73.

[25] It would seem that in an action for defamation, an M.P. who passes on a letter from a member of the public will not lose his qualified privilege by becoming automatically infected with the malice of his informant: *Meekins* v. *Henson* [1964] 1 Q.B. 472; *Egger* v. *Chelmsford* [1965] 1 Q.B. 248.

[26] Parliamentary Commissioner Act 1967, s. 10(5).

[27] *Church of Scientology of California* v. *Johnson-Smith* [1972] 1 Q.B. 522; *R.* v. *Secretary of State for Trade, ex p. Anderson Strathclyde plc* [1983] 2 All E.R. 233. See also *Dingle* v. *Associated Newspapers Ltd* [1960] 2 Q.B. 405 (action for libel against newspaper; plaintiff not entitled to contend that proceedings of select committee of House, on which offending comments were based, were void for procedural irregularity).

[28] H.C. *34* (1967–8), xxii, xxiii.

in its opinion, by parliamentary privilege, as a breach of its own privileges; but the Select Committee on Parliamentary Privilege recommended in 1967 that save in exceptional circumstances (for example, where a member is being improperly obstructed in the performance of his parliamentary functions) such matters should be left to the ordinary processes of the courts.[29] No action has been taken on that recommendation.

7   Substantial interference with the exercise of a member's freedom of speech and action in his parliamentary capacity, by threats, molestation, bribes or other improper inducements may be treated by the House as a contempt or breach of privilege. What if a member agrees to act as the parliamentary spokesman for an outside pressure group? The inconclusive case of *W. J. Brown* (1947)[30] neatly stated the problems. Brown, who had been general secretary of the Civil Service Clerical Association, was elected as an Independent M.P. He entered into an agreement with the Association whereby he became their salaried 'parliamentary general secretary' but would retain full freedom to engage in his own political activities. The executive committee of the Association later became dissatisfied with his political attitudes and proposed to recommend the termination of the agreement. Brown claimed that this proposal was a breach of parliamentary privilege in that it was calculated to influence him in his conduct as an M.P. by threatening him with a financial penalty. The Committee of Privileges, dividing (unusually) along party lines, reported[31] that on the facts no breach of privilege had been committed, but it recognized that the exertion of outside financial pressure on a member for the purpose of influencing his conduct as a member could well be a breach of privilege. The House, adopting the report, resolved that it was inconsistent with the maintenance of the privilege of freedom of speech for a member to *enter into* a contractual agreement with an outside body fettering his freedom of action or stipulating that he was to act as that body's parliamentary representative.[32] In any event a court would almost certainly refuse to enforce such a contract on grounds of public policy.[33]

---

[29] H.C. *34* (1967–8), xvi–xvii. See generally de Smith (1958) 21 *Mod. L. Rev.* 465.

[30] H.C. *118* (1946–7).

[31] H.C. *118* (1946–7).

[32] The duty of a member being to his constituents and to the country as a whole, rather than to any particular section thereof (440 H.C. Deb. *365* (15 July 1947)).

[33] See *Amalgamated Society of Railway Servants* v. *Osborne* [1910] A.C. 87 at 110–15 for the rationale of such a judicial attitude.

A clearer case arose in June 1975. The Yorkshire Area Council of the National Union of Mineworkers resolved to restrict the parliamentary conduct of M.P.s sponsored by the Area branch, in particular by requiring that such M.P.s *should not vote* on any issue contrary to union policy on the industry. The threat of withdrawal of sponsorship for recalcitrant M.P.s was suggested. The Committee of Privileges found that there had been a serious breach of privilege – but the National Executive of the N U M passed a motion to nullify the Yorkshire Area Council's resolution, so no further action was needed.[34] It is impossible to believe that financial aid tendered to members by sectional interest groups has always been granted on the understanding that a member is under no kind of obligation whatsoever to promote the interests of that group. The Select Committee on Parliamentary Privilege accepted as a fact the existence of such relationships and pointed out that a member speaking on a topic in which he had a financial interest might be guilty of a contempt of the House if he failed to disclose his interest. The Select Committee on Members' Interests, reporting in 1969,[35] expressed itself still more guardedly, emphasizing the distinction between improper inducements held out to or accepted by members for the promotion of *specific* matters in their parliamentary capacities, and *regular* financial assistance offered to members by outside organizations; the latter type of relationship was regarded (subject to the formal qualification interposed by the resolution of the House in *Brown*'s case) as being quite proper.

Threats of disciplinary action against members by party whips have been ruled not to constitute infringements of the privilege of freedom of speech because they are part of the conventionally established machinery of political organization within the House. Nevertheless, pressure exerted on a member by whips may influence his conduct far more significantly than any connection he may have with an outside interest group.

8   In order to protect its freedom of speech, the House asserts ancillary privileges. It may resolve to clear the visitors' gallery by excluding strangers; in wartime it has often gone into secret session. Leave of the House had to be obtained for evidence to be given in court of anything that occurred in the course of parliamentary proceedings, until the rule was discontinued in 1980. The House

[34] H.C. *634* (1974–5).
[35] H.C. *57* (1969–70), viii–x. See also above, p. 271 on the Register of Members' Interests.

used to treat publication of its debates as a breach of privilege; assertion of this privilege has been discontinued. The publication of leaks from the private deliberations of select committees, or of their draft reports, remains a breach of privilege, based on a resolution of the House passed in 1832. So in the case of *Richard Evans* (1985–6) a draft report of the Environment Select Committee about nuclear waste disposal was prematurely leaked to Mr Evans, a newspaper journalist. His newspaper published an article based on the leak. This was an admitted breach of privilege, but publication was defended on the ground that it was in the public interest. The leaker's identity was never established. The Committee of Privileges recommended that Mr Evans be suspended from Westminster for six months,[36] but the House, while acknowledging that it would be proper to punish an M.P. who leaked in such circumstances, sensibly refused to punish Mr Evans who was 'merely doing his job'.[37]

Freedom from arrest

This immunity has lost most of its early importance, and in 1967 the Committee on Parliamentary Privilege recommended its abolition.[38] It does not protect members from arrest on criminal charges,[39] or from preventive detention as security suspects in wartime;[40] though their arrest or detention must not be based on anything they have said in the course of parliamentary proceedings. The privilege protects members from arrest in civil matters for wilful disobedience to a court order – for example, refusal to comply with the terms of a maintenance order.[41] It extends for the period of a session and forty days before and after.

---

[36] H.C. *376* (1985–6).

[37] 98 H.C. Deb. *293–332* (20 May 1986).

[38] H.C. *34* (1967–8), xxix.

[39] The court which sentences an M.P. to imprisonment informs the Speaker, who informs the House. See, e.g., 125 H.C. Deb. *3* (11 January 1988). A warrant for the arrest of Mr Ron Brown M.P. was issued in 1988 after he had failed to appear to face a private prosecution alleging criminal damage to the Commons' mace. The D.P.P., however, took over the proceedings and discontinued them.

[40] *Ramsay's* case (1940).

[41] *Stourton* v. *Stourton* [1963] P. 302 (where privilege from arrest was successfully claimed by a peer). Members are privileged from arrest for civil but not criminal contempt of court: Erskine May, *Parliamentary Practice*, op. cit., pp. 99–105; *Wellesley* v. *Earl of Beaufort* (1831) 2 Russ. & M. 639. There are difficult marginal cases (see Enid Campbell, *Parliamentary Privilege in Australia* (1966), 59–63; Sawer (1971) 7 *U. of Queensland L.J.* 226), but broadly it seems that members are immune from detention imposed by a court if the purpose of the detention is coercive as distinct from punitive.

Imprisonment of defendants in civil proceedings, and in particular of debtors who were unavoidably prevented from discharging their obligations, was a commonplace matter till the latter part of the nineteenth century; nowadays arrest in civil cases is confined to a narrow range of situations where the defendant is as a rule seriously at fault.

Right of the House of Commons to provide for its own composition

This privilege is now partly regulated by statute. For example, the trial of disputed election returns has been committed to an election court; the question whether a member is subject to a legal disqualification may be determinable by an election court or the Judicial Committee of the Privy Council. Within its narrowed field, the privilege is nevertheless important. The House has the exclusive right, while it is sitting, to determine by resolution when a writ for the holding of a by-election shall be issued. It can declare a member's seat vacant on the ground that he has incurred a legal disqualification or for any other reason it thinks fit and the courts cannot interfere; this is why it would be lawful for the Government to use its majority in the House to expel all Opposition members.[42] Self-restraint, influenced by fair-mindedness and expediency, alone prevents abuse of its privilege. The inexpediency of abuse was illustrated by the case of *John Wilkes*, the rake, wit and radical demagogue, who was elected to the House of Commons; the corrupt House decided that he was unfit to share their company, and expelled him. But the House has no privilege to prevent any person from standing as a candidate at a by-election. Wilkes was duly re-elected, and his seat was again declared vacant by the House; after this absurd process had been repeated, the House resolved in 1770 that his election was void and that the seat be awarded to the runner-up. Wilkes was again elected in 1774; the House took no step to unseat him, and in 1782 the House resolved to expunge the resolution of 1770 from its Journals.

The only modern examples of expulsion for reasons other than legal disqualification are of members who had been convicted of criminal

---

[42] Under a written constitution, the grounds for expulsion could be judicially reviewable. cf. *Powell* v. *McCormack* 395 U.S. 486 (1970) (the case of Adam Clayton Powell, the former Congressman for Harlem).

offences involving moral turpitude or who have committed gross contempts of the House.[43]

Right to have exclusive cognizance of matters arising within the House

This right is closely linked with the rule that proceedings in Parliament cannot be called in question in any court. The leading case is *Bradlaugh* v. *Gossett* (1884).[44] Bradlaugh, a militant atheist, was elected to the House. After some vacillation, the House decided to allow him to make an affirmation of allegiance in lieu of taking an oath. A common informer then sued Bradlaugh for penalties on the ground that he was not qualified to sit and vote because he did not come within the classes of persons permitted by statute to affirm instead of taking an oath; and the courts held that Bradlaugh was not entitled to affirm.[45] Bradlaugh's seat became vacant; he was re-elected, and then sought to take the oath rather than be excluded from sitting. The House refused to allow him to do so, although on a proper construction of the Parliamentary Oaths Act 1866 he appeared entitled to take the oath if he chose, despite his position as a non-believer. Subsequently it resolved to exclude him from the House until he undertook not to disturb its proceedings. Bradlaugh brought an action, claiming a declaration that the resolution was void, and an injunction to restrain the Serjeant at Arms (Gossett) from excluding him. The court held that it had no jurisdiction to interfere. Assuming that the House had misinterpreted the Act, the matter would still fall within the exclusive privilege of the House to regulate its own proceedings. Similarly, if the House had resolved to allow Bradlaugh to take the oath, the courts would have had no power to pronounce upon that decision. But if proceedings were brought to recover a penalty from him as a disqualified person, it would be incumbent on the court to interpret the Act. In such a case the jurisdiction of the courts could not be excluded even by a resolution of the House purporting to protect Bradlaugh against an action for

---

[43] In 1947 Garry Allighan M.P. was expelled for contempt. He had made unsubstantiated allegations that M.P.s had given particulars of parliamentary party meetings, held within the precincts of the Palace of Westminster, to journalists for money or while under the influence of drink. He was himself receiving payments from a newspaper for disclosing such information and had given false answers to questions put to him in the Committee of Privileges.

[44] 12 Q.B.D. 271.

[45] *Clarke* v. *Bradlaugh* (1881) 7 Q.B.D. 38. It was later held, however, that only the Crown could recover the penalties prescribed by statute: *Bradlaugh* v. *Clarke* (1883) 8 App. Cas. 354.

penalties, for the privileges of Parliament did not extend to such a matter arising outside the House.[46]

The House has not asserted a general jurisdiction over matters arising within the walls of the House if they have no direct connection with its proceedings. Theft, rape or murder are issues to be left to the criminal courts; in any event, the penal powers of the House are inadequate to deal with ordinary crimes.[47] If two members came to blows in the House, the courts and the House would have a *concurrent* jurisdiction; a magistrate could properly issue a summons for assault and try the case,[48] and the House might also decide that the fracas amounted to a contempt of the House. But when in doubt, a court may elect to tread warily for fear of encroaching on what the House may deem to be its own exclusive preserves. When A. P. Herbert, who was campaigning to liberalize the liquor licensing laws and who was soon to become an Independent M.P., decided to embarrass the members of the Kitchen Committee of the House by applying for summonses against them for selling drinks in the members' bar without a justices' licence, the chief metropolitan magistrate refused to issue summonses; and the Divisional Court of the King's Bench Division, taking a remarkably generous view of the scope of the internal affairs of the House of Commons, held that he had been right to decline jurisdiction because of parliamentary privilege.[49]

Right to punish for breach of privilege and contempt

The House can vindicate its own privileges by taking disciplinary action against members and others whom it adjudges to have broken them. All breaches of privilege are contempts of the House. But there is also a wide range of contempts that do not fall within the scope of any nominate privilege. The following are examples of contempts:[50] offering bribes to members; molesting or otherwise obstructing members or officers of the House in the performance of their duties; casting

---

[46] (1884) 12 Q.B.D. at 281–2, *per* Stephen J. See also *Papworth* v. *Coventry* [1967] 1 W.L.R. 663 at 669–70.

[47] See p. 327. In 1970, CS gas was projected into the chamber by a member of the public as a gesture of protest. The House left the matter to be dealt with by the police and the courts.

[48] In *Eliot*'s case (note 6 above) where the conviction for *sedition* was ultimately quashed on a writ of error, the defendants' conviction for assaulting the Speaker in the House still stood. See also *Bradlaugh* v. *Gossett* (above) at 283–4.

[49] *R* v. *Graham-Campbell, ex p. Herbert* [1935] 1 K.B. 594.

[50] See Erskine May, *Parliamentary Practice*, op. cit., ch. 10.

imputations reflecting on the dignity of the House by, for example, insulting the House or its members; attempting to disrupt the proceedings of the House; tampering with witnesses before select committees of the House; refusing to give evidence, or giving false evidence, before a committee of the House. These contempts are often called breaches of privilege; this usage is misleading, for the House has accepted that it cannot by resolution enlarge the scope of its own privileges, but has not closed the categories of contempt; and – to take but one example – if revolutionary students shouted down witnesses giving evidence at a university before an itinerant select committee, they would be guilty of a contempt of the House. No matter whether the offence is styled a breach of privilege or a contempt or both, the penal powers of the House are the same.

A complaint of 'breach of privilege' must be raised by a member as soon as is reasonably practicable.[51] If the Speaker rules that a *prima facie* case has been made out, the matter is referred to the Committee of Privileges, a select committee which since the 1974–5 session has been appointed for the duration of a Parliament and which has always been nominated in proportion to party strengths. In investigating the complaint, the Committee can require the attendance of witnesses and the production of documents; refusal to comply with its commands or to answer questions is a contempt. It does not, in practice, afford the persons against whom the complaints have been made any opportunity of being legally represented, and has sometimes reported that a complaint has been established although the 'defendant' has not been given any hearing at all. In the *Strauss* case[52] the Committee condemned the members of the area board without hearing them. Since, moreover, the members of the Committee are in a sense judges in their own cause, this disregard of the elements of natural justice is open to severe criticism. In 1967 the Select Committee on Parliamentary Privilege recommended a number of procedural reforms, which would give all persons directly concerned a right to attend its hearings, make submissions, and call, examine and cross-examine witnesses; and rights to seek the Committee's leave to be legally represented and to ask for legal aid.[53] These necessary reforms had yet to be brought into effect at

[51] The earlier rule – that the complaint had to be raised 'at the earliest opportunity' – was thought to be too restrictive, and was altered to the formulation given in the text: see 943 H.C. Deb. *1155–98* (6 February 1978). The Speaker may decide not to pursue it if an immediate, unqualified apology is made to him: see, for example, 902 H.C. Deb. *1392–3* (17 December 1975).

[52] See p. 318.

[53] H.C. *34* (1967–8), xiv–xlvii.

the time of writing. There is also a case (which the Select Committee did not accept) for codifying contempts so as to introduce certainty at the expense of flexibility.[54] In some Commonwealth countries, not only are breaches of privilege and contempts codified by statute but allegations of breach of privilege and contempt are triable by the courts.

The Committee of Privileges may find that a complaint has been established but recommend that no further action be taken. It may recommend that the House resolve that the person guilty of contempt be admonished or reprimanded by the Speaker at the bar of the House; or that a member found guilty of contempt be suspended[55] or expelled from the House; or that a member, or a member of the public, be committed to prison for contempt. The recommendations of the Committee are nearly always, but not invariably, adopted by the House. The power of the House to impose fines for contempt was last exercised three hundred years ago and is now obsolete; the Select Committee in 1967 recommended that this power be revived by statute.[56] No person has been committed to prison for contempt since 1800 (and then only for one night). Imprisonment terminates on prorogation though it can be renewed in the next session. The House of Lords, as a court of record, may impose fines and may commit for a fixed term extending beyond prorogation. Offenders may be taken into the custody of the Serjeant at Arms (or Black Rod) and thence committed to prison if the House has so directed. Provided that the order of the House or Speaker's warrant is duly made out, the Serjeant at Arms may forcibly enter private property to carry out an arrest,[57] and is entitled to call upon the police or even the armed forces for any necessary assistance in executing the orders of the House.[58]

---

[54] The House has, however, accepted guidelines on when its power to punish should be used. These are (a) that the power should be resorted to as sparingly as possible, and (b) then only when the House is satisfied that to exercise the power is essential to provide reasonable protection for the House, its members or its officers, from such improper obstruction or attempt at or threat of obstruction as causes, or is likely to cause, substantial interference with the performance of their respective functions: see 943 H.C. Deb. *1155–98* (6 February 1978). This change was designed to ward off petty complaints.

[55] The Speaker may also order a member to withdraw from a day's sitting for grossly disorderly conduct (S.O. No. 42); and if he names a member for persistent disregard of the authority of the chair or other serious misconduct in the House, that member may be suspended forthwith upon a resolution of the House, the period of suspension for a first offender being five days (S.O. No. 43). These provisions do not affect the general inherent power of the House to suspend a member for contempt.

[56] The House accepted this recommendation in 1978, but no bill has been introduced.

[57] *Burdett* v. *Abbot* (1811) 14 East I.

[58] ibid. See further H.C. (1967–8), pp. 115–65, 206–9 for details of the procedure adopted.

The Select Committee of 1967 confirmed what was already apparent – that some members had been too ready to invoke the jurisdiction of the House to deal with personal affronts as questions of privilege. It recommended that recourse to this jurisdiction should be confined to those cases where the exercise of the functions of the House was liable to be seriously impeded and, as has been seen above, the House has accepted this recommendation;[59] that where members considered themselves to have been defamed by newspaper comments or statements by individuals, they should normally be content to pursue their remedies in the ordinary courts – but the House has expressly retained the right of a member to bring an alleged breach of privilege to the Commons even if he has a civil remedy;[60] and that where proceedings were brought in the House for contempt, justification or reasonable belief in the allegations complained of should be admissible as defences.

Since 1967 the number of trivial complaints of breach of privilege has diminished. But it is incongruous, to say the least, that members of the House of Commons should be more sensitive than judges to hostile criticism.[61] It is also noteworthy that, whereas an appeal lies from a conviction for contempt of court, no such appeal lies from a finding of contempt of the House; this rule would be left unchanged by the Select Committee's proposals. Fortunately the House has on the whole dealt sensibly with contemnors; where the Committee of Privileges has found a complaint proved, it has usually recommended that no disciplinary action be taken and the House has regularly accepted such a recommendation.

Parliamentary privilege and the courts

There are points of similarity between the royal prerogative and parliamentary privilege. Both are recognized as part of the law of the land; both embody special rules evolved for public purposes. The Crown cannot enlarge its own prerogatives within the realm; the two Houses have recognized that they cannot extend their privileges, though their attitude towards 'contempts' not falling within the scope of a nominate privilege is ambiguous. But there are material differences between prerogative and privilege. The prerogative is essentially a residuum of ancient common-law attributes, attenuated by judicial

---

[59] See above, note 54.
[60] 943 H.C. Deb. *1155–98* (6 February 1978).
[61] For a modern (and tolerant) judicial attitude towards the concept of contempt of court, see *R.* v. *Metropolitan Police Commissioner, ex p. Blackburn (No. 2)* [1968] 2 Q.B. 150.

decisions and legislation. The growth of parliamentary privilege can be traced in resolutions and rulings recorded in the Journals of the two Houses; and privilege has been and can still be expanded, as well as abrogated by statute. Acts done within the recognized area of pre-rogative may be reviewed by the courts: acts done by either House within its acknowledged field of privilege are unreviewable.[62] The Crown cannot commit persons to prison for infringing its prerogatives; the two Houses can commit for breach of privilege, or enforce obedience to privilege by milder forms of direct action. The most interesting difference between the two bodies of law is that, whereas the Crown has long since ceased to claim to be the sole judge of the limits of its prerogative, the two Houses (and the House of Commons in particular) still assert that they are the sole judges of the *extent* of their own privileges – a claim to which the courts do not accede. For example, a decision by the House of Commons that Mr Strauss's letter to the Minister *was* a 'proceeding in Parliament' would not have been treated as binding by the courts if the board had sued Mr Strauss;[63] the House, on the other hand, might have not only rejected the courts' interpretation but also treated it as an encroachment on its own privileges, and therefore a contempt, on the part of the plaintiffs, their legal advisers and the judges.

The claim of the House to be the sole interpreter of its own privileges has given rise to two major constitutional conflicts. In the first of them, the House of Lords (as an appellate court) held (*Ashby* v. *White*)[64] that a voter at Aylesbury, whose vote the returning officer had maliciously refused to accept, was entitled to damages. The House of Commons protested that this decision violated their exclusive privileges relating to parliamentary elections. Other Aylesbury voters brought similar actions against the returning officer; the House ordered them to be committed to prison. An application was made for writs of habeas corpus to secure their release from unlawful detention. In *Paty*'s case (1704) the court refused the writ;[65] counsel for the applicants, who intended to bring the case before the House of Lords, was promptly committed by

---

[62] See *Bradlaugh* v. *Gossett* (1884) 12 Q.B.D. 271.

[63] The situation in *Bradlaugh* v. *Gossett* was different in as much as the resolution of the House in that case, ill-founded or well-founded, undoubtedly fell within the scope of the privilege of the House to regulate its own internal affairs.

[64] See 2 Ld. Raym. 938, 3 Ld. Raym. 320; 14 St. Tr. 695.

[65] Ld. Raym. 1105, Holt C.J. (rightly) dissenting on the ground that the cause of commitment stated in the return of the writ was insufficient in law; the facts alleged to constitute the contempt of the House had been explicitly averred.

the Commons to join his clients. The deadlock was broken only by a prorogation of Parliament.

The central issue revived, in a more spectacular form, at the beginning of Victoria's reign. One Stockdale published an illustrated treatise on the reproductive system. The book was found circulating among prison inmates. Stockdale considered himself to have been defamed by comments on his work made in a report by prison inspectors, published by order of the House of Commons, and sued Hansard, the parliamentary printers (then a commercial firm) for libel. The defendants were ordered by the Commons to plead that the publication was covered by parliamentary privilege. The Court of Queen's Bench rejected this plea, holding that as a matter of law such a publication was not comprised within the area of parliamentary privilege and awarded damages to Stockdale (*Stockdale* v. *Hansard*);[66] no resolution of the House could deprive the courts of their authority to interpret and apply the law of the land in a matter affecting the rights of subjects. Stockdale brought another action against Hansard; the defendants, on the instructions of the House, entered no plea, and the plaintiff was again awarded damages. There were two sequels.[67]

(i) Execution had been levied by the Sheriff of Middlesex on Hansard's property to recover the damages. The House resolved to commit the Sheriff for breach of privilege and contempt. He applied for habeas corpus on the ground that he was being unlawfully detained (*Sheriff of Middlesex*'s case (1840)).[68] The Speaker's warrant was 'general', in that it had not recited the facts allegedly constituting the contempt. The court dismissed the application, on the ground that it would be unseemly to inquire further. Even if the House of Commons were not a superior court of record, it was entitled to as much respect as if it were; and on a habeas corpus application one superior court would not investigate the truth of the facts stated by another as a cause of commitment for contempt.[69] If, however, the facts constituting the

---

[66] (1839) 9 A. & E. I.

[67] Four, if one includes the commitments of Stockdale and his solicitor for contempt of the House (cf. *Howard* v. *Gossett* (1845) 10 Q.B. 359, 411).

[68] 11 A. & E. 273. In fact the two Sheriffs of Middlesex were committed by the House.

[69] The precedents were the *Earl of Shaftesbury*'s case (1677) 1 Mod. 144; *Murray*'s case (1751) 1 Wils. 299; and a considered dictum in *Burdett* v. *Abbot* (1811) 14 East at 150. In *Paty*'s case (above) a majority of the court had held their jurisdiction to be excluded even though the facts constituting the alleged contempt were specified in the return to the writ. The *Sheriff of Middlesex*'s case was followed by the High Court of Australia in *R.* v. *Richards. ex p. Fitzpatrick and Browne* (1955) 92 C.L.R. 157 (held, also, that a House of Parliament in the Commonwealth of Australia could commit for a fixed term). See Enid Campbell, *Parliamentary Privilege in Australia* (1966), ch. 7.

alleged contempt had been set out by the respondent to the application, and they could not reasonably be construed as amounting to a contempt of the House, the court would be at liberty to intervene.[70]

(ii) Parliament passed the Parliamentary Papers Act 1840, conferring absolute privilege on statements in parliamentary papers, and thus achieving what could not be attained by a mere resolution.

The refusal on the part of the courts to award habeas corpus to release the Sheriff from arbitrary detention is obviously open to criticism.[71] It was supported by precedent and was defended on grounds of principle; but the court had chosen to blind itself to notorious reality, and to countenance injustice. Although 'the old dualism remains unresolved',[72] in the sense that the courts still do not accept the conclusiveness of the House's pronouncements as to the scope of its own privileges and the House denies that the courts have jurisdiction to determine such a matter at all, it is not unfair to say that the courts have 'yielded the key of the fortress'[73] by accepting that the House can enforce its own view by first committing an innocent offender to prison and then refusing to give particulars of his alleged breach of privilege. Fortunately the House of Commons has not acted in such an overbearing manner since Stockdale's time; it has, moreover, acquiesced in the assumption of jurisdiction by the courts in several marginal cases, and the courts have shown circumspection when called upon to exercise jurisdiction.

Nevertheless, the House has, more than once, reiterated its own position in recent years, and only by a narrow margin was the prospect of a similar conflict averted in 1958.[74] Judges are not always better equipped than other persons to decide questions of law set in political contexts. But the unhappy combination of uncodified contempts, an unsatisfactory procedure for investigating allegations of contempt, and

[70] Adopting Holt C.J.'s view in *Paty*'s case (above) and Lord Ellenborough's dictum in *Burdett* v. *Abbot* (1811) 14 East at 150.

[71] Contrast the decisions of the Supreme Court of India in *Special Reference No. 1 of 1964* A.I.R. 1965 S.C. 746, where a general warrant of commitment for breach of privilege was held not to exclude the court's jurisdiction to inquire into the legality of the commitment. See *Annual Survey of Commonwealth Law for 1965*, pp. 41–4.

[72] *Re Parliamentary Privilege Act 1770* [1958] A.C. 331 at 354 (quoting Erskine May).

[73] Keir and Lawson, *Cases in Constitutional Law* (6th edn, 1979), p. 225.

[74] If the House had endorsed the report of the Committee of Privileges in the *Strauss* case, it is not at all certain that this would have deterred the board from proceeding with an action against Mr Strauss. In the 'Project Zircon' affair (see above, p. 317) in 1987 the Attorney-General's application for an injunction to prevent a named M.P. from showing the film complained of at the House of Commons was rejected by the court on the ground that it is for the House to regulate its own proceedings. It was astonishing that the Attorney-General made that particular application at all.

the insistence of the House that it must have the first and last word in matters touching the interests of its members as members, irrespective of the impact of its decisions on the interests of members of the public, suggests that the House ought to relinquish its jurisdiction over breaches of privilege and contempts to the courts, as it has in effect relinquished its privilege to determine disputed election returns.

Chapter 18

Subordinate Legislation

General

Parliament is not the sole source of new law. The superior courts make new law by laying down rules in decided cases which form binding precedents – binding till they are overruled (by statute or in a later case), or distinguished, or otherwise explained away. Judicial law-making is almost surreptitious; a new departure is usually rationalized as a rediscovery of a long-lost principle, or as an application of an established rule to a novel set of material facts, or as the ascertainment of an unexpressed parliamentary intent. Although the idea that the courts merely declare and apply pre-existing norms may be a polite fiction, the supposed need for this verbal camouflage rests on a widely held assumption that it is for Parliament, not for the Judiciary, to bring the law up to date. The room for judicial manoeuvre is restricted by the framework of constitutional thought within which the courts operate.

As we have already noted,[1] such Community legislation as has direct effect in Britain is really *primary*, not *subordinate*, legislation, because the Community organs are not subordinate to Parliament in the eyes of Community law and their legislative output does not derive its legal force from any delegation of authority by Parliament. Community legislation is indeed normally 'secondary' in the sense that it consists of regulations made by the Council or the Commission in pursuance of powers conferred by the Community treaties, and it is therefore subordinate *within the Community legal order*, but not within our legal order.

There are other legislative institutions, forming part of the executive branch of government. The Crown, Ministers, some Departments of State, public corporations and local authorities have law-making

[1] See pp. 26–7, 79–82, 106–8.

powers. When we speak of subordinate legislation, we mean primarily the rules and regulations made by these executive bodies. We also include rules of court made by independent statutory committees composed mainly of judges. Such legislation is *subordinate* in that it is made by bodies endowed with limited powers (usually conferred by Parliament), and is always subject to abrogation or alteration by Act of Parliament. Unlike legislation by the Queen in Parliament, it may, moreover, be held by a court to be *ultra vires.*

The only significant source of subordinate legislation made otherwise than in pursuance of powers delegated by Parliament is the royal prerogative. But the Crown has no general inherent power to alter the law of the land.[2] It has limited prerogative powers to make new constitutions and to legislate for a dwindling number of colonies acquired by conquest or cession, and to regulate the affairs of the civil service and the armed services.

The great bulk of subordinate legislation is made by virtue of parliamentary authority. Parliament delegates powers to legislate; the end-product is *delegated legislation.* The average annual output of delegated legislation easily exceeds the amount of parliamentary legislation. The Public General Acts cover, on average, over 2,000 pages each year, and published *Statutory Instruments* almost 6,000 pages. (*Statutory Instruments*[3] do not include by-laws made by local authorities or public corporations.) Roughly 2,000 sets of rules and regulations are made by Ministers or the Crown in Council or other central rule-making authorities in the course of a year; the total number of public and private Acts of Parliament will be about 100.

Some have depicted this state of affairs as an abdication by Parliament from its principal constitutional role in favour of the Executive.[4] Acts of Parliament, sponsored by government Departments and passed into law with the acquiescence of a docile parliamentary majority, give the Executive sweeping legislative powers; and safeguards against the abuse of those powers are inadequate. The most celebrated denunciation of delegation to the Executive came in 1929 from Lord Hewart, the then Lord Chief Justice of England. In his book, *The New*

---

[2] *Case of Proclamations* (1611) 12 Co. Rep. 74.

[3] For the meaning of this term, see p. 342. There are also half a dozen pages of prerogative instruments each year.

[4] See especially Lord Hewart of Bury, *The New Despotism* (1929); C. K. Allen, *Bureaucracy Triumphant* (1931); *Law and Orders* (though the 3rd edn (1965) of this work was more restrained than the first); G. W. Keeton, *The Passing of Parliament* (1952). For more detached appraisals, see C. T. Carr, *Delegated Legislation* (1921); *Concerning English Administrative Law* (1941); John Willis, *The Parliamentary Powers of English Government Departments* (1933).

Despotism, he attributed over-generous delegations of legislative power to a deep-laid bureaucratic conspiracy. The Committee on Ministers Powers, hastily appointed in anticipation of the furore that Hewart's book would arouse, reported in 1932 that the conspiratorial allegations were unsupported by 'the smallest shred of evidence'.[5] Nevertheless, the idea still persists in some quarters that delegation of legislative power to the Executive is at best a necessary evil, a constitutional impropriety to be half-heartedly condoned on grounds of expediency, but a potentially serious threat to the liberties of the subject. Doubtless this bogey will stubbornly refuse to be laid to rest, but a few elementary points can be made.

1 Executive initiative is the dominant feature of parliamentary legislation. It is a still more dominant feature of delegated legislation. The difference is one of degree. Differences of degree can indeed be extremely important. Delegated legislation, unlike parliamentary legislation, has no committee stage at which amendments can be put down;[6] seldom is it debated in Parliament at all. None the less, prior consultation with advisory bodies and organized interest groups is a more conspicuous characteristic of delegated legislation than of parliamentary legislation.[7]

2 Most of the doom-laden prophecies were based on the experience of war and its immediate aftermath. In both the world wars of this century, vast law-making powers were delegated to the Executive. The Defence of the Realm Acts 1914–15 conferred a general power to make Orders in Council for securing the public safety and the defence of the realm. The Emergency Powers (Defence) Acts 1939–40 were more explicit but equally permissive, and the 1940 Act specified that Defence Regulations could make provisions 'requiring persons to place themselves, their services, and their property at the disposal of His Majesty'. These enormous powers were not always exercised reasonably. Some Defence Regulations remained in force too long after the war was over; and new regulations and orders, sometimes unpopular or ill-conceived, were made under post-war emergency legislation.[8] However, most of them were revoked or

---

[5] Cmd 4060 (1932), p. 59.
[6] With the exception of special procedure orders; see p. 343.
[7] See generally S. A. Walkland, *The Legislative Process in Great Britain* (1968), ch. 5.
[8] Food rationing regulations were naturally among the least popular. According to a well-authenticated story, Churchill, on his return to office as Prime Minister in 1951, gave instructions that the food ration be constructed in the form of a model so that he could assess the quantity better. When the model was laid before him, he remarked 'Not a bad meal!' On being told that the model represented a week's rations he exploded: '. . . the people are starving . . .' (Harold Macmillan, *Tides of Fortune* (1969), pp. 490 91).

lapsed long ago. This fact does not, of course, imply that contemporary criticism was groundless or had no effect.

3 Open a recent volume of *Statutory Instruments* and read the first hundred pages. The tedium of wading through a mass of abstruse technicalities, barely comprehensible to anyone lacking expert knowledge of the subject-matter, is at least an instructive experience; and if one has the moral stamina, one can plough on through another five thousand pages. With such dull subject-matter, delegated legislation is in fact a dull subject for many of us.

4 Parliamentary scrutiny of delegated legislation admittedly tends to be perfunctory. But a select committee of the House of Commons examines statutory instruments which may be open to objection on constitutional grounds.[9] This committee, however, reports adversely on only a tiny number of instruments scrutinized. Before launching into a general denunciation of the content of delegated legislation, it is best to equip oneself with a sense of proportion.

5 Root and branch attacks on delegated legislation have often been prompted by a hearty dislike of public encroachments on freedom of property and contract. The assailants would have found the regulatory provisions no less objectionable if they had been embodied in Acts of Parliament rather than in rules and regulations.

There is one further preliminary point. Delegated legislation is sometimes confused with the establishment and work of administrative tribunals. Their only common feature is that both are substitutes: delegated legislation may be resorted to instead of Acts of Parliament, and administrative tribunals instead of courts. If substitutes are always a poor second best, if Parliament and the ordinary courts are the only acceptable media for legislation and adjudication, and if administrative law means delegated legislation plus administrative adjudication and is a negation of the rule of law, then it is right to place the two phenomena side by side in the same rogues' gallery. If one disagrees with these propositions, there is little point in discussing delegated legislation in conjunction with special tribunals. Such a discussion also generates confusion. The line between legislation and adjudication may often be thin, but legislation is basically the making of new rules of general application [10] for the future, and adjudication is the determination of individual claims and controversies. If new general rules emerge

[9] See p. 348–50.
[10] The difference between 'general' legislation and 'particular' executive action or judicial decisions is one of degree and sometimes imperceptible. See Walkland, op. cit., pp. 9–10; de Smith, *Judicial Review of Administrative Action* (4th edn, 1980), ch. 2.

from adjudication, this is incidental to the main purpose of the process. Obviously, statutory regulations laying down a new procedure for determining claims to social security benefits are different in kind from a decision by a social security appeal tribunal that X is or is not entitled to a benefit he has claimed in reliance on the existing rules.[11] Moreover, new tribunals are almost invariably constituted by Acts of Parliament; the normal role of delegated legislation in relation to tribunals will be to lay down detailed rules of procedure and to express in more precise terms the general functions confided in the tribunals by the enabling Act.

Delegated legislation: functions and fears

Historical note[12]

Before 1832 Parliament delegated rule-making powers to the Executive spasmodically and, on the whole, sparingly. The plenitude of legislative authority devolved on Henry VIII by the Statute of Proclamations 1539 was not to be rivalled till 1914; the functions of central government were not wide enough to justify delegation on the grand scale. The Poor Law Amendment Act 1834, empowering the Poor Law Commissioners generally to make regulations for the management of the poor, marked the beginning of a new epoch. As the trend towards collectivism gathered momentum after 1870, so did delegations of legislative authority to the central government rapidly increase. But if this development threatened to undermine the fabric of the constitution, the dangers were hardly perceived. Dicey, among constitutional lawyers the most articulate exponent of Whiggish individualism, thought that Parliament was far too conservative in its attempts to unburden itself of detail; and, uncharacteristically, he commended the example of France, where executive decrees amplifying the general principles of legislation ranged over large areas of the law.[13] The phase of vehement denunciation began in the 1920s. Temperatures were lowered by the Report of the Committee on Ministers' Powers in 1932[14] and have never reached the same height again. The Report provided an entirely convincing

---

[11] Some special tribunals have the duty of deciding in their discretion whether to *vary* existing rights (for example, by fixing fair rents) or to grant new rights and privileges (for example, licences).

[12] See also Cmd 4060 (1932), pp. 10–15.

[13] *Introduction to the Study of the Law of the Constitution* (10th edn, 1959), pp. 52–3.

[14] Cmd 4060. The Committee is often called the Donoughmore Committee, after the name of its first chairman.

account of the reasons why the delegation of legislative powers to Ministers was indispensable, as well as indicating some real or potential dangers in the practice and suggesting safeguards against abuses. Amid the torrent of regulations descending from Whitehall between 1939 and 1950, few voices were raised to question the constitutional propriety of delegation. The main constitutional issues were: Where should the lines be drawn between parliamentary and delegated legislation? And how could safeguards against the misuse of delegated powers be improved? These issues became less important as other horses emerged to be flogged.

Purposes of delegation

The reasons for delegating legislative powers to the Executive can be summed up in one phrase: the promotion of efficiency.

1   It is inefficient and unnecessary to incorporate a mass of complex detail in a parliamentary bill, or indeed in the schedules to such a bill, unless such provisions are designed to make really important changes in the law (for example, imposing substantial criminal liabilities or altering taxes), in which case they ought to be exposed to full parliamentary scrutiny. Few members of any Parliament will have the expert knowledge required to table and debate amendments to highly technical legislation; but a dogged group of the initiated can consume parliamentary time in this way, often for the ulterior purpose of impeding a Government's general legislative programme. Delegation saves parliamentary time.

2   The enactment of tortuous and cumbersome legislation, bulging with minutiae, disfigures the statute book and tends to detract from the prestige of Parliament. One can admire the diligence of the draftsmen of the Land Commission Act 1967[15] without being entranced by their product; some of the provisions of this convoluted statute should have been left to subordinate legislation.

3   It may be impossible to bring a major Act (for example, on town planning, social security, nationalization of an industry, or reform of local government structure) into operation the day it receives the royal assent. Postponement may be necessary in order to undertake administrative reorganization or to conduct detailed consultations with various bodies with a view to modifying the general principles of the Act in their application to particular areas or sections of the

[15] Now repealed: Land Commission (Dissolution) Act 1971.

community. Sometimes this can be effected by fixing the operative date when the bill is passed.[16] Sometimes this is impracticable, and the Act will therefore provide that it will come into force on such day as Her Majesty by Order in Council (or a Minister by statutory instrument) shall appoint. In any event, powers to make supplementary regulations on aspects of the new design will almost certainly be needed in the interest of flexibility, fairness and efficiency.

4 When an Act is passed, it is often reasonable to suppose that new contingencies (such as cases of special hardship, or technological developments) will arise although their exact form cannot be predicted at the date of enactment. It will be more sensible to give the responsible Minister powers to make regulations to amplify the Act should such contingencies arise than to compel him to rely on the chance of finding a place for amending legislation in an already long legislative queue.

5 Swift emergency action may have to be taken during a parliamentary recess or at a time when serious damage may be done if the normal processes of parliamentary legislation have to be followed. Sudden outbreaks of epidemics, natural disasters, the discovery and introduction of new dangerous drugs or poisons, paralysis of the economy by industrial stoppages or a threat to the stability of the pound resulting from an international financial crisis, may call for the immediate exercise of rule-making powers. Sometimes, of course, it is feasible to rush a bill through all its stages in both Houses within a few hours; the Emergency Powers (Defence) Act 1939 and the Southern Rhodesia Act 1965 (consequential on UDI) fell into this exceptional category. Sometimes a possible need for urgent action can be provided for by the enabling Act in the form of a grant of *executive* powers if *general* emergency regulations are unlikely to be required. However, when in March 1972 the United Kingdom Government decided that it was imperative to impose direct rule on Northern Ireland and suspend the institutions of Stormont, the Northern Ireland (Temporary Provisions) Act 1972 not only vested *executive* authority in respect of Northern Ireland in the Secretary of State, but also provided that Orders in Council could be made on any matter within the competence of the Northern Ireland Parliament. A series of important legislative changes have been made under this wide-ranging delegated power.[17]

[16] Different dates may be fixed for bringing into operation different parts of an Act.
[17] See further above, ch. 3.

6   Changes in the constitutions of dependent territories, and constitutions adopted immediately before independence, are better embodied
in Orders in Council than in Acts of Parliament. This is not because
they are unimportant but because they are almost invariably the
outcome of an intergovernmental negotiation, and if it were open to
Parliament to delete or modify individual provisions of the constitution a delicate balance might be upset and the political consequences
could then be very serious.

Where delegation is open to criticism

1   It is a primary function of Parliament to determine the guidelines of
legislative policy.[18] Parliament should not, therefore, delegate to
Ministers power to make regulations on matters of general principle
unless it lays down in the enabling Act standards delimiting the
boundaries of the delegate's discretion. Skeleton legislation is
justifiable only in order to deal with a state of dire emergency (such
as the Northern Ireland situation since 1972) or a quite exceptional
situation, such as has been created by Britain's accession to the
European Communities. In countries with written constitutions, a
blanket delegation of legislative power to the Executive may be held
to be unconstitutional.[19]

2   Grants of delegated power ought not to be so expressed that it
becomes impossible in practice for the courts to review the limits of
the powers exercised. Statutory formulae purporting to oust the
jurisdiction of the courts by express language [20] are now uncommon.
Less uncommon are statutory provisions endowing Ministers with
powers which in their opinion are requisite or expedient for a
broadly framed statutory purpose. When the validity of regulations
made in pursuance of such powers is challenged, very strong
grounds will have to be adduced before a court will be persuaded to
intervene.[21] Moreover, Ministers, and their advisers endowed with
so large a discretion may be unable to resist temptations to stretch

---

[18] See generally Griffith (1951) 14 *Mod. L. Rev.* 279, 425.
[19] See, for example, *Kent* v. *Dulles* 357 U.S. 116 (1958) (United States); *Re Delhi Laws Act*
(1951) S.C.R. 747 (India), though see H. M. Seervai, *Constitutional Law of India* (2nd
edn, 1975), pp. 874–86.
[20] See pp. 354–5.
[21] The point is well made by Lord Diplock *obiter* in *McEldowney* v. *Forde* [1971] A.C. 632
at 659–61, though see *Utah Construction and Engineering Co.* v. *Pataky* [1966] A.C. 629;
Customs and Excise Commissioners v. *Cure and Deeley Ltd* [1962] 1 Q.B. 340. See also
pp. 353–4.

their powers beyond reasonable limits. Such delegations may thus offend against proposition (1).

3   Criticism has been levelled against the so-called 'Henry VIII clause', under which Parliament delegates authority to make regulations amending Acts of Parliament.[22] This formulation is not widely used, and it is normally innocuous if the grant of power is confined to a limited period for the purpose of enabling draftsmen to make consequential adaptations to miscellaneous enactments that may have been overlooked when the principal Act was passed.[23]

4   Seldom if ever will a grant of power to make regulations imposing liabilities with retroactive effect be justified.[24]

5   The power to impose or vary taxation is, in general, too important to be delegated by Parliament. But a flexible power to make regulations modifying, for example, rates of indirect taxation or customs duties may be a valuable ancillary instrument for the management of the economy.[25]

6   In the interests of certainty, Parliament ought to identify the recipient of its delegated powers, and when delegating legislative authority it should not authorize sub-delegation of those powers to unnamed persons. In and immediately after the Second World War, when sub-delegation was expressly authorized by the Emergency Powers (Defence) Acts and their successors, instances of five-tier delegation arose.[26]

The European Communities Act 1972

Quite apart from Community regulations which are directly applicable of their own force (section 2(1)), further regulations have been and will have to be made in this country under powers delegated by the Act (section 2(2)) to give effect to Community directives and decisions and also to implement in fuller detail some Community regulations. Orders

---

[22] cf. Cmd 4060 (1932), pp. 36–8, 59–61, 65.

[23] See, for example, Kenya Independence Act 1963, s. 5(4). An unusual power to amend the parent Act itself was conferred by section 16(2) of the Race Relations Act 1968 (see now the Race Relations Act 1976, s. 71). And see the extraordinary device in the Remuneration, Charges and Grants Act 1975, s. 1 (which lapsed in 1978).

[24] Such legislation is likely to be held to be *ultra vires* unless retroactive operation has been expressly authorized by the enabling Act. cf. authorities cited in *The Abadesa* [1968] P. 656 at 659. See also *Master Ladies Tailors Organisation* v. *Minister of Labour and National Service* [1950] 2 All E.R. 525 at 528. See, however, *Sabally & N'Jie* v. *Att.-Gen.* [1965] 1 Q.B. 273.

[25] cf. Excise Duties (Surcharges or Rebates) Act 1979, s. 1.

[26] J. A. G. Griffith and H. Street, *Principles of Administrative Law* (5th edn, 1973), pp. 59–66.

in Council and departmental regulations made under these delegated powers *have the effect of Acts of Parliament* and can include any provision that might be made in an Act of Parliament (section 2(4))[27] except that they are not to impose or increase taxation[28] or have retroactive effect or sub-delegate legislative powers (other than power to make procedural rules for courts and tribunals) or create a new criminal offence punishable with more than two years' imprisonment or a fine more than £2,000. This is probably the most sweeping grant of delegated legislative powers to the Executive in modern times except under emergency conditions.

Statutory instruments

Subordinate legislation may be designated as rules, regulations, orders, by-laws, schemes, measures, or by a variety of other appellations. The most important generic description is 'statutory instrument'. The definition of this term is complex and raises difficult points of interpretation.[29] Broadly, the term covers delegated legislation made under (1) powers conferred by statutes after 1947 on Her Majesty in Council, or on Ministers or Departments, to make, confirm or approve subordinate legislation where the enabling Act says that the power shall be exercisable by statutory instrument, and (2) powers conferred by statutes before 1948 on these authorities or other rule-making authorities (such as the Rule Committee of the Supreme Court) to make subordinate legislation, and on Ministers to confirm or approve instruments of a legislative (but not of an executive) character which also have to be laid before Parliament. A statutory instrument comes into effect when made unless (as is nearly always the case) the instrument specifies a later date on which it is to come into operation.

By-laws of local authorities and public corporations are not statutory instruments. Nor are measures of the General Synod of the Church of England.[30] Nor are provisional orders, which do not have legal effect till confirmed by Act of Parliament and are therefore not a form of

[27] For section 2(4), see pp. 79–81. Clearly such regulations can repeal or amend Acts of Parliament in force at the time when they are made. But it is arguable that the regulations will be *ultra vires* unless related to Community affairs.

[28] But taxation can be imposed by directly applicable Community instruments (s. 2(1)).

[29] For a full analysis, see Griffith and Street, op. cit., pp. 42–56, considering the meaning of the Statutory Instruments Act 1946 and regulations and an Order in Council made thereunder in 1947.

[30] Made in pursuance of the Synodical Government Measure 1969; these measures are submitted for the royal assent if approved by both Houses of Parliament.

delegated legislation at all. For most legal purposes, 'special procedure orders', which have replaced provisional orders under a number of Acts of Parliament, are statutory instruments; they will normally have legal effect without a confirmation Act.[31] Compulsory purchase orders, being of an executive rather than a legislative character, are not usually classified as statutory instruments. Nor, in general, are instruments made in pursuance of sub-delegated powers, but it is possible for them to fall within the definition of statutory instruments.[32] Nor, of course, are resolutions of the House of Commons statutory instruments; normally their legal effect is confined to matters arising within the House; but under some modern Acts of constitutional importance such resolutions have been accorded legislative effect.[33]

Statutory instruments must be printed, numbered, published and sold. They are also published in annual volumes in chronological sequence. However, local or temporary instruments, instruments made available in a separate series to persons directly concerned, and very bulky schedules, may be exempted from the requirement of publication. The annual volumes were called *Statutory Rules and Orders* before 1948;[34] since 1948 they have been entitled *Statutory Instruments*. Prerogative legislative instruments are unnumbered but are published and appear in an appendix to each volume.

Government statements of policy and intent, departmental circulars giving instructions to local authorities, and procedural rules issued by certain other public bodies, may be legislative in effect and will usually be published; but they will not be published as statutory instruments even if made in pursuance of statutory powers.[35] The extra-statutory concessions offered by the Inland Revenue in favour of taxpayers are

---

[31] See Statutory Orders (Special Procedure) Acts 1945 and 1965; the procedure on such orders (which is attracted where an Act prescribes that an order authorized to be made shall be 'subject to a special parliamentary procedure') involves opportunities to object to the order at a local inquiry and also by petition to Parliament; the order may be amended in pursuance of a report by a joint committee of the two Houses.

[32] Regulations made by designated Ministers under the European Communities Act 1972 (see European Communities (Designation) Order 1972 (S.I. 1972, No. 1811)) are statutory instruments (s. 2(2); Sched. 2, para. 2(1)).

[33] See Provisional Collection of Taxes Acts 1913 and 1968 (temporary authority to collect income tax and other annual taxes); Exchequer and Audit Department Act 1957, s. 1(3) (increase in salary of Comptroller and Auditor-General); Parliamentary Commissioner Act 1967, s. 2(2) (increase in salary of Parliamentary Commissioner for Administration). See also House of Commons Disqualification Act 1975, s. 6(2), (3) (relieving M.P.s from effect of disqualification); Murder (Abolition of Death Penalty) Act 1965, s. 1.

[34] There is also a consolidation entitled *Statutory Rules and Orders and Statutory Instruments Revised*, comprising subordinate legislation in force at the end of 1948.

[35] cf. *Blackpool Corporation* v. *Locker* [1948] 1 K.B. 349.

clearly legislative in substance [36] but, just as clearly, are not within the definition of statutory instruments. The Immigration Rules are not classified as statutory instruments, perhaps because it is not clear that the power to make them is directly conferred by statute. Nor are the Codes of Practice made under the Police and Criminal Evidence Act 1984, and the Highway Code, which do not have quite the same legal force.

Safeguards

Contraceptive and ante-natal

The most effective safeguard against the abuse of delegated powers is not to delegate them in such terms as to invite abuse. When a bill is first drafted by parliamentary counsel on instructions given by the sponsoring Department, it will go to that Department, to the Legislation Committee of the Cabinet (of which the Lord Chancellor and the Law Officers of the Crown are members) and may go to a specialized Cabinet committee or an inter-departmental committee.

A number of policy and technical decisions have to be taken: where the lines should be drawn between matters explicitly to be set out in the bill and matters to be left for amplification by the exercise of delegated powers; how precisely the limits of delegated power are to be worded; whether the Act should require subordinate legislation to be laid before Parliament at all, and if so, whether it should also be subject to annulment by resolution of either House, or should require approval by affirmative resolution of one or both Houses; and so on. To what extent general criteria have been formulated as guides to making these decisions is far from clear, though it can be assumed that the parliamentary draftsmen have regard to precedents and do not accede automatically to every eccentric departmental request. If the draftsmen consider an aspect of a draft bill to be objectionable on grounds of constitutional principle, they may succeed in carrying the sponsoring Department's legal advisers with them. If this is not enough and they wish to press their point, they will have a further opportunity when the final draft of the bill is examined by the Law Officers.

The Legislation Committee of the Cabinet also reviews departmental drafts of statutory instruments which are of exceptional importance or special interest to other Departments or may give rise to criticism on

---

[36] cf. *R.* v. *Customs and Excise Commissioners, ex p. Cook* [1970] 1 W.L.R. 450 at 454–5 (where attention was drawn to the lack of any legal basis for concessions made by the Customs and Excise).

the grounds that they are unusual in their content or of doubtful constitutional propriety. The departmental legal advisers may obtain the aid of parliamentary counsel in preparing the draft of a particularly important instrument.[37]

Before regulations are made by a Department, prior consultation with advisory bodies and organized interest groups is the general practice.[38] Statutes often require that named bodies, or organizations identified by description (for example, representative of local authorities) be consulted in advance. Procedural regulations for tribunals and inquiries have to be submitted in draft to the Council on Tribunals.[39] Drafts of social security regulations have to be submitted to the Social Security Advisory Committee, a statutory body; the Committee must notify persons and bodies likely to be affected and give an opportunity for objections to be lodged; the Committee submits its report to the Secretary of State who, when he makes the regulations, must also lay the report before Parliament and state how far he has given effect to the Committee's recommendations and why he has not accepted them. In practice he has almost invariably accepted them.[40]

Under a few statutes, the initiative in preparing draft rules and regulations (for example, for agricultural marketing schemes) is given to bodies representing persons engaged in the occupation, and occasionally to individuals so engaged; such schemes cannot normally be given legislative effect without the responsible Minister's approval.

By-laws made by local authorities are subject to confirmation by the appropriate Minister, who is in most cases the Secretary of State for the Environment. Sets of model by-laws are available, and local by-laws deviating widely from these without special reasons are unlikely to be confirmed.

Publicity

'Does any human being read through this mass of departmental legislation?' asked Lord Hewart.[41] Perhaps not; but since ignorance of the law is, in general, no excuse for breaking it, regulations ought to be readily available to members of the public and their legal advisers as soon as they come into force. The principles governing publication

---

[37] S. A. Walkland, *The Legislative Process in Great Britain* (1968), pp. 63–5.
[38] Griffith and Street, op. cit., pp. 123–39; Garner [1964] *Public Law* 105.
[39] Tribunals and Inquiries Act 1971, ss 10, 11.
[40] Griffith and Street, op. cit., pp. 130–36; Social Security Act 1980, ss 9(1), 10, sched. 3.
[41] *The New Despotism* (1929), pp. 96–7.

have already been noted.[42] An instrument may nevertheless have legal effect before it is published and available for sale at a government bookshop.[43] This is unusual; indeed, Departments now try to follow a general rule that an instrument shall not come into operation for twenty-one days after being laid before Parliament.[44] But to mitigate the hardship that may still arise, section 3(2) of the Statutory Instruments Act 1946 provides that it shall be a defence to criminal proceedings for contravening an instrument to prove that the instrument has not been issued at the date of the contravention unless the prosecution proves that reasonable steps have previously been taken to bring its purport to the notice of the public or persons likely to be affected or the person charged.

In the best of all possible worlds, statutory instruments would be not only available but also intelligible. This desideratum may be unattainable, but the opaque has become translucent by the modern practice of appending brief explanatory notes at the end of statutory instruments, indicating their general purport and effect.

Parliamentary proceedings[45]

The parent Act may or may not require the instrument to be laid before Parliament. If there is no requirement as to laying,[46] a member of Parliament who gets to know of the instrument may still put down a question about it to the responsible Minister or seek to raise the matter in debate. If the instrument has merely to be laid, or laid in draft, before Parliament, it will be delivered to the Votes and Proceedings Office of the House of Commons.[47] No opportunity is provided by parliamentary procedure for the instrument to be discussed, but its existence will at least be brought to the notice of members and the Minister is more likely to be questioned about it than if it is not laid before Parliament at all. Moreover, any instrument required to be laid

[42] p. 343.
[43] See *R.* v. *Sheer Metalcraft Ltd* [1954] 1 Q.B. 586. Contrast *Johnson* v. *Sargant & Sons* [1918] 1 K.B. 101 (statutory order held not to have effect till it became known; the authority of this decision is now doubtful). See further Lanham (1974) 37 *Mod. L.R.* 510.
[44] H.C. *475* (1971–2), para. 62. But not all instruments have to be laid before Parliament: see below.
[45] See John E. Kersell, *Parliamentary Supervision of Delegated Legislation* (1960); *Report of the Joint Select Committee on Delegated Legislation* (H.C. *169* (1977–8)).
[46] The large majority of statutory instruments in this category are instruments of a local nature.
[47] S.O. No. 138; Laying of Documents before Parliament (Interpretation) Act 1948, s. 1.

before Parliament does not become operative until so laid, unless it is essential for it to become operative at once, in which case the reason must be notified to the Lord Chancellor and the Speaker forthwith.[48]

It is more common for the enabling Act to provide that an instrument shall be laid, or laid in draft, subject to the negative resolution procedure. This means that it is open to any member to move a prayer to annul the instrument (or, if it has been laid in draft, to move that it not be made) within forty days of being laid.[49] Such motions are put at the end of the day's business; debate on such a motion must be terminated or adjourned not later than 11.30 p.m. in the Commons.[50] In 1973 provision was made[51] for statutory instruments against which a negative resolution has been moved, or which are subject to the affirmative resolution procedure (see below), to be considered on their merits by new standing committees of the House of Commons – but this procedure can only be invoked *at the instance of a Minister*.

A minority of instruments are required to be laid, or laid in draft, subject to an affirmative resolution of one or both Houses; unless a resolution approving the instrument is passed within the period (if any) prescribed by the enabling Act, the instrument ceases to have effect or cannot be made.[52] Instruments made subject to that procedure are normally those regarded as being of special constitutional importance (for example, varying constituency boundaries) or imposing taxation (in which case an affirmative resolution of the Commons alone will be needed). A statutory instrument made under the European Communities Act *may* be laid in draft subject to the affirmative resolution procedure; if not so laid in draft, it shall be subject to the negative resolution procedure.[53]

The value of the negative resolution procedure is not easily assessed. Motions to annual statutory instruments are infrequent; rarely are they successful,[54] and it is open to the Minister to present the instrument

---

[48] Statutory Instruments Act 1946, s. 4(1). See also above, and S.O. No. 139.

[49] ibid., s. 5(1).

[50] S.O. No. 15.

[51] S.O. No. 101; 853 H.C. Deb. *680–95* (22 March 1973).

[52] Passing a negative resolution or failing to pass an affirmative resolution does not have the effect of invalidating anything already done in pursuance of the instrument.

[53] 1972 Act, sched. 2, para. 2(2).

[54] A spectacular exception to the general rule was the rejection of the revised Immigration Rules (not technically a statutory instrument, but the distinction is immaterial) made under section 3(2) of the Immigration Act 1971: see 34 H.C. Deb. *355–440* (15 December 1982). Revised Immigration Rules had to be introduced. The House of Lords has *never* carried a negative resolution (H.C. *475* (1971–2), para. 13), although (or because) their opposition cannot be overriden under the Parliament Acts procedure.

afresh; but from time to time a Minister withdraws an instrument in the face of hostile criticism and may perhaps submit it in a revised form. One substantial criticism of this procedure is that because of pressure on parliamentary time it is not always possible to debate a prayer to annul an instrument.[55] Hardly ever does an Act make provision for the amendment of a statutory instrument. But the possibility that damaging parliamentary publicity may result from a debate on an ill-drafted or otherwise objectionable instrument is of some utility as a safeguard against the misuse of delegated power.

The affirmative resolution procedure is more important, in that the Government must find time to explain why the instrument should be approved and thus lays itself open to critical comment. In November 1969 the Home Secretary laid himself open to acrimonious criticism by moving (successfully) that four draft Orders in Council purporting to give effect to Boundary Commission recommendations be not approved by the Commons.[56] But if all statutory instruments were made subject to this procedure, a primary object of delegating legislative powers to the Executive – to make for economical use of parliamentary time – would be frustrated.

Parliamentary scrutinizing committees

In 1944 a Select Committee of the House of Commons on Statutory Rules and Orders was appointed to examine and report on certain aspects of regulations laid before the House. That the Executive should commend the subjection of its legislative output to a new form of detailed parliamentary scrutiny in time of war is remarkably interesting. The Committee is appointed for the whole of each Parliament. The name was changed to the Select Committee on Statutory Instruments, and in 1973 it became the Joint Select Committee on Statutory Instruments. This Committee replaced both the House of Commons Committee and the House of Lords Special Orders Committee.[57] The terms of reference of the Joint Select Committee today are to consider every statutory instrument of a general character and various other instruments which, under the parent Act, were laid or laid in draft before the House subject to the negative or affirmative resolution

---

[55] H.C. *538* (1970–1), paras 41–6; H.C. *475* (1971–2), paras 95–128, for proposals for enlargement of the opportunities.

[56] See pp. 243–4, 307.

[57] Although the function of the latter of examining instruments against which persons whose interests are directly affected may petition is now vested in the Lords' Hybrid Instruments Committee, set up in 1975.

procedure, with a view to deciding whether the special attention of the House should be drawn to the instrument on any of these grounds: that (i) it imposes charges on the subject or the public revenue; (ii) it is ostensibly immunized by the parent Act against challenge in the courts; (iii) it purports to have retrospective effect in the absence of express authority given by the parent Act; (iv) there appears to have been unjustifiable delay in publication or laying before Parliament; (v) where it is essential for an instrument to come into effect before being laid, there has been unjustifiable delay in notifying the Speaker of this fact and the reasons; (vi) where the instrument gives rise to doubts whether it is *intra vires*, or where it appears to make an unusual or unexpected use of the powers conferred by the parent statute; (vii) where it requires elucidation; or (viii) where the draftsmanship appears to be defective; or any ground 'which does not impinge on its merits or on the policy behind it; and to report their decision with the reason thereof in any particular case'.[58]

Before deciding to draw the attention of the House to an instrument on any of these grounds, the Committee must give the Department concerned an opportunity of putting its case.

The Committee consists of seven members of each House, of whom two are a quorum. It is assisted by Counsel to the Speaker and by Counsel to the Lord Chairman of Committees. That its function is strictly technical and non-partisan is emphasized by the convention that the chairman shall be a member of the Opposition. Its concern is with efficiency and constitutional propriety, extending beyond (but including) consideration of the strict legality of the powers exercised by the prescribed authority. It can comment, and has commented, on inconsistencies in legislative practice (for example, in providing for parliamentary proceedings on some instruments but not on others of a similar character) and on unsatisfactory features of sub-delegation of powers. In its early years many of its adverse reports were based on undue delay in publication or laying before Parliament; departmental procrastination suddenly became very rare. The fact that regulations are on the whole less obscurely drafted than they were forty-five years ago can be partly attributed to its influence. Perhaps the patient drudgery of the Committee has had a highly salutary effect on overweening bureaucrats; perhaps the dangers of abuse of delegated legislative powers were greatly exaggerated by some critics. That a few

---

[58] The words in quotation marks had been added in 1971. M.P.s consider without peers those instruments which the parent Act directs to be laid before and to be subject to proceedings in the House of Commons only.

instruments made an unusual use of the powers granted, and that others were obscurely worded – these had become the main grounds for adverse reports by the 1960s – was hardly surprising. What was surprising was the small size of this problem viewed by an experienced scrutinizing committee.[59]

No special opportunity has been provided by parliamentary procedure for debating the Committee's reports; this must have detracted from its efficiency. But an adverse report delivered swiftly enough may lead to a prayer for annulment, or opposition to an affirmative resolution; or such a report may persuade a Department to amend or revoke an instrument.

Judicial review

The courts may hold a subordinate legislative instrument to be invalid if it is *ultra vires*, i.e. in excess of powers. This jurisdiction extends to prerogative instruments as well as statutory rules, regulations and by-laws. The validity of such instruments may be impugned directly or indirectly. Direct frontal challenges are unusual and are seldom successful; a plaintiff may find it impossible to establish that his personal interests are sufficiently affected by a general legislative instrument to give him title to sue.[60] Collateral, or indirect, attack is more common; a person is prosecuted for breach of a regulation or by-law, or is sued for breach of a contract the binding force of which is dependent on the validity of a regulation or by-law, and his defence is that the regulation or by-law is invalid. Under Community law this appears to be the only method by which *Community* instruments can be impeached before national courts as being *ultra vires* the treaties.[61]

An instrument may be invalid because of a formal or procedural defect, or because it goes beyond the limited scope of delegated authority on a matter of substance. Challenges based on defects of form or procedure present difficulties in that not every such defect is a source of invalidity. Formal or procedural requirements are classifiable

---

[59] That said, however, the Committee (in H.L. 51 and H.C. 169 (1977–8)) criticized the Government for giving Ministers wide discretionary powers in certain statutory instruments to amend statutory instruments, for omitting essential detail from statutory instruments, and for allowing inadequate time to elapse between the laying, publication and coming into force of some instruments.

[60] But see *R. v. H. M. Treasury, ex. p. Smedley* [1985] Q.B. 657 (taxpayer had standing to challenge draft Order in Council which would authorize spending from Consolidated Fund); *Hotel and Catering Industry Training Board* v. *Automobile Proprietary Co.* [1969] 1 W.L.R. 697 (declaration that a statutory instrument was *ultra vires* granted).

[61] Hartley [1981] *Crim. L. Rev.* 85.

as either mandatory or directory. Non-compliance with a mandatory requirement is a potentially vitiating defect; if, however, the requirement is construed as being merely directory, the courts may take the view that substantial compliance is enough or even that total non-compliance is a mere error that does not affect the validity of what has been done. Prediction of how a court will regard non-compliance is difficult; precedents afford little guidance, and although the practical importance of non-compliance with the duty is the main criterion, a court will sometimes take a stringent view of failure to observe a minor formality.[62] Non-observance of duties to consult with a specified body[63] or consider objections or give an opportunity to be heard[64] are likely to be held to render regulations invalid. Rather surprisingly, it appears that mere failure to publish an instrument does not render it invalid if other prescribed preliminaries have been observed;[65] the effect of breach of a duty to lay a statutory instrument before Parliament is doubtful, but this may well be held to render the instrument inoperative.[66]

If power is delegated only to do X, the delegate cannot do Y, unless Y is necessarily implicit in or incidental to the power to do X. Power granted for purpose A cannot be used instead for purpose B. These ostensibly straightforward questions of statutory interpretation may give rise to considerable problems in practice – for example, where the statutory purpose is not clearly defined,[67] or where the existence of a link between the subject-matter of the delegated power and the statutory purpose is expressed by the parent Act to be determinable by the delegate himself.[68] Again, a strictly literal interpretation of the enabling section may frustrate the general object of the Act or wreak injustice; a court will not necessarily shut its eyes to this possibility. Nor will a court disregard the context in which regulations have been made; regulations made in a state of grave emergency may be construed more benevolently in favour of the Executive than regulations made under the same powers when the seriousness of the emergency has diminished.

---

[62] See, for example, *Patchett* v. *Leathem* (1949) 65 T.L.R. 69.

[63] *Agricultural etc. Training Board* v. *Aylesbury Mushrooms Ltd* [1972] 1 W.L.R. 190.

[64] *R.* v. *Housing Appeal Tribunal* [1920] 3 K.B. 334 at 342, 343, 346.

[65] See pp. 345–6; but note the mitigating effect of s. 3(2) of the Statutory Instruments Act 1946.

[66] *R.* v. *Sheer Metalcraft Ltd* [1954] 1 Q.B. 586 at 590. It is still open to the courts to resolve these difficult issues.

[67] cf. the 3:2 division of opinion in the House of Lords in *McEldowney* v. *Forde* [1971] A.C. 632, a case arising under the Northern Ireland Civil Authorities (Special Powers) Act 1922 (now repd).

[68] See pp. 340–41, 353–4.

Forecasts of how a court may construe the validity of regulations are further complicated by other factors. Thus, ordinary literal interpretation may be modified in the light of common-law presumptions of legislative intent. For instance, there is a presumption that express statutory authority is needed to validate the exercise of delegated powers interfering with the liberty of the person, or excluding the citizen from access to the ordinary courts for the determination of his legal rights and liabilities,[69] or imposing taxation,[70] or taking away property rights without compensation.[71] The circumstances in which these presumptions will carry decisive weight are not easy to predict.[72] In the First World War, power to make regulations for securing the public safety and the defence of the realm was held to justify the making of a regulation for the preventive detention of British subjects on security grounds without trial,[73] notwithstanding the strong common-law presumption in favour of individual liberty. Three years later a court held that the same statutory power was not wide enough to validate a wartime regulation prohibiting landlords from taking legal proceedings for possession orders, against tenants who were munition workers, without the prior consent of a Minister.[74] In the Second World War, an undoubtedly valid defence regulation, providing that a Secretary of State could make orders for the detention of persons whom he had 'reasonable cause' to believe to be of hostile origin or associations and in need of subjection to preventive control, was not construed by the courts as importing an objectively determinable test of reasonableness. To establish the invalidity of a detention order, a detainee would have to discharge the impossible burden of proving that the Secretary of State did not genuinely believe he had 'reasonable cause'.[75] In a number of cases in which the validity of subordinate legislation and executive acts affecting property rights was challenged during and immediately after

---

[69] *Chester* v. *Bateson* [1920] 1 K.B. 829; *Customs and Excise Commissioners* v. *Cure & Deeley Ltd* [1962] 1 Q.B. 340.

[70] *Cure & Deeley*'s case (above); see also *Att.-Gen.* v. *Wilts United Dairies Ltd* (1921) 37 T.L.R. 884 (C.A.), but see p. 282, above.

[71] For example, *Newcastle Breweries Ltd* v. *R.* [1920] 1 K.B. 854.

[72] Contrast, for example, in the field of town planning decisions (executive acts), the case of *Hall & Co.* v. *Shoreham-by-Sea U.D.C.* [1964] 1 W.L.R. 240 (presumption against deprivation of property rights without compensation applied) with *Westminster Bank Ltd.* v. *Beverley B.C.* [1971] A.C. 508 (presumption not applied).

[73] *R.* v. *Halliday, ex p. Zadig* [1917] A.C. 260.

[74] *Chester* v. *Bateson* [1920] 1 K.B. 829.

[75] *Liversidge* v. *Anderson* [1942] A.C. 206. Contrast, on the meaning of 'reasonable cause' or 'reasonable grounds', *Nakkuda Ali* v. *Jayaratne* [1951] A.C. 66 at 76–7. The only other ground on which a detention order could be challenged was that it had been improperly made out: *R.* v. *Secretary of State for Home Affairs, ex p. Budd* [1942] 2 K.B. 14 at 22. See ch. 27.

the Second World War, the courts adopted a strictly literal interpretation of the enabling legislation in favour of the Executive. The enabling Act was typically expressed in the form: 'If it appears to' or 'if in the opinion of' the Minister, or 'if the Minister is satisfied that' a given state of affairs existed, he could make such orders as appeared to him necessary or expedient for a generally worded purpose.[76] By the early 1950s this self-denying ordinance had been slightly modified. The Judicial Committee of the Privy Council could state that a power so exercised had to be 'capable of being related to one of the prescribed purposes'.[77]

In 1961 the pendulum had swung far enough for a High Court judge (invoking common-law presumptions of legislative intent) to hold that a statutory power authorizing the Commissioners of Customs and Excise to make regulations 'for any matter for which provision appears to them necessary for the purpose of giving effect to the Act' was too narrow to validate a regulation by which they gave themselves power to determine conclusively what amount of purchase tax was payable in individual cases.[78] This is perhaps an extreme case of judicial activism. Nowadays the courts are unlikely to review the matter *de novo* but to ask whether the competent authority had misdirected itself and whether the regulations were reasonably capable of being related to the grant of power.[79]

Judicial tests for the validity of by-laws have generally been understood to be stricter than the tests for the validity of regulations made by Ministers or Her Majesty in Council. Although by-laws made by elected local authorities for the general welfare are to be benevolently construed,[80] they may be still held *ultra vires* and invalid if they are excessively uncertain in their terms or repugnant to the general law of the land or manifestly unreasonable. The English courts have yet to

---

[76] For example, *R.* v. *Comptroller General of Patents, ex p. Bayer Products Ltd* [1941] 2 K.B. 306; *Point of Ayr Collieries Ltd.* v. *Lloyd-George* [1943] 2 All E.R. 547. In *Carltona Ltd* v. *Commissioners of Works* [1943] 2 All E.R. 560 at 564, Lord Greene M.R. said, 'All that the court can do is to see that the power . . . falls within the four corners of the power given by the legislature and [is] exercised in good faith. Apart from that, the courts have no power at all to inquire into the reasonableness, the policy, the sense, or any other aspect of the transaction.'

[77] *Att.-Gen. for Canada* v. *Hallet & Carey Ltd* [1952] A.C. 427 at 450.

[78] *Customs and Excise Commissioners* v. *Cure & Deeley Ltd* [1962] 1 Q.B. 340 (*per* Sachs J.). See to like effect, *Reade* v. *Smith* [1959] N.Z.L.R. 996 (applied in *Labour Department* v. *Merritt Beazley Homes Ltd* [1976] 1 N.Z.L.R. 505). cf., however, *Marsh (Wholesale) Ltd* v. *Customs and Excise Commissioners* (1970) 2 Q.B. 206.

[79] See note 21 above; *Hallet and Cary*'s case (note 77); *Secretary of State for Employment* v. *ASLEF (No. 2)* [1972] 2 Q.B. 455.

[80] *Kruse* v. *Johnson* [1898] 2 Q.B. 91 at 99–100; applied in *Burnley Borough Council* v. *England* (1978) 77 L.G.R. 227 (by-law made by local council banning dogs from parks and children's playgrounds not unreasonable).

hold a statutory instrument to be *ultra vires* explicitly on these grounds alone. But a court might hold an instrument to be too vague to be capable of being related to a permitted purpose;[81] so offensive to the general principles of the law as to be beyond the contemplation of the enabling Act;[82] or so unreasonable that it could not be ascribed to the enabling provisions.[83] Perhaps, then, the differences in the scope of judicial review of by-laws, on the one hand, and statutory instruments, on the other, are only matters of degree or even verbal distinctions.

Although no English authority directly covers the point, it is highly probable that the courts, applying the maxim *delegatus non potest delegare*, will hold that the recipient of delegated legislative power cannot validly sub-delegate any part of its rule-making power to another in the absence of express statutory authorization.[84] But a power vested in a Minister or a Department to make regulations can validly be exercised by an official authorized by his superiors to act in that behalf; this is not an example of sub-delegation, for the official is the Minister's other self, his *alter ego*.[85]

In the past a great deal of heat was generated by statutory provisions purporting to oust judicial review of the validity of regulations, orders and administrative decisions and determinations.[86] The formula providing that a regulation or order, when made, was to have effect 'as if enacted in the Act', has fallen into desuetude. Whether the courts regarded it as excluding them from determining the *vires* of a subordinate instrument was never entirely clear.[87] A provision that the making or confirmation of an order was to be 'conclusive evidence' that the requirements of the Act had been complied with was probably effective to exclude judicial review,[88] despite the traditional disfavour shown by the courts to language ostensibly depriving them of their inherent supervisory jurisdiction. Exclusionary formulae create a bad impression and are seldom used today unless finality is all-important.

---

[81] *McEldowney* v. *Forde* [1971] A.C. 632 at 643, 645, 653, 665.

[82] For example, by authorizing the condemnation of a person without allowing him an opportunity of being heard on his own behalf (*R.* v. *Housing Appeal Tribunal* [1920] 3 K.B. 334) or by taking away his common-law right of access to the courts: *Chester* v. *Bateson*; *Cure & Deeley*'s case (above).

[83] See note 81, above.

[84] See *Jackson, Stansfield & Sons* v. *Butterworth* [1948] 2 All E.R. 558 at 564–6, and below, pp. 572–3.

[85] *R.* v. *Skinner* [1968] 2 Q.B. 700.

[86] See generally de Smith, *Judicial Review of Administrative Action* (4th edn, 1980), ch. 7.

[87] *Institute of Patent Agents* v. *Lockwood* [1894] A.C. 347 supported the view that such a provision barred judicial review; *Minister of Health* v. *R., ex p. Yaffe* [1931] A.C. 494 indicated that it did not. Various intermediate positions are possible.

[88] *Ex p. Ringer* (1909) 73 J.P. 436.

The Extradition Act 1870 and the Parliamentary Constituencies Act 1986 still have provisions to the effect that Orders in Council made thereunder shall not be questioned in any legal proceedings; the subject-matter of such Orders (application of an extradition treaty to a foreign State, and the determination of constituency boundaries) may justify the exclusion of judicial review.[89] Similar formulae purporting to protect judicial-type administrative determinations against judicial review are made nugatory (with certain exceptions) by section 14 of the Tribunals and Inquiries Act 1971, if contained in Acts passed before August 1958.[90] In the present climate of opinion, one would not expect to see delegated legislation afforded special statutory protection save in highly exceptional circumstances. As we have seen, Orders in Council and regulations made in this country under the European Communities Act 1972 for the fulfilment of Community obligations enjoy extraordinary protection inasmuch as they are assimilated for most purposes to Acts of Parliament.[91]

[89] Extradition Act 1870, s.5; Parliamentary Constituencies Act 1986, s. 4(7). See also Parliament Act 1911, s. 3; Parliament Act 1949, s. 2(2) (Speaker's certificates); West Indies Act 1967, s. 18. Judicial review of subordinate legislation is not excluded merely because provision has been made by the parent Act for the affirmative or negative resolution procedure (*R. v. Electricity Commissioners* [1924] 1 K.B. 171), but judicial intervention while an instrument was still before either House might be regarded as an encroachment on parliamentary privilege.

[90] See further pp. 552, 555–7.

[91] See p. 341. But, as was indicated, jurisdiction to determine the *vires* of such instruments is not entirely excluded.

Part Four

Justice, Police and Local Government

In this part, three important subjects will be examined which shade off into one another.

First, in chapter 19 some features of the administration of justice in England are considered. For detailed accounts of the structure and working of the English legal system, readers should consult textbooks devoted to the subject; here only an outline sketch is presented. The working of the Crown Prosecution Service is explained, and the roles of the amateur in the legal system – as magistrates and jurors – are touched on. The final abolition of the peremptory challenge to jurors is noted. More detail is devoted to the rules of law and convention, professional traditions and political practices, that help to sustain the independence of the Judiciary. The Lord Chancellor's policies and practices in relation to the appointment and promotion of the Judiciary have become clearer and are explained. This is a convenient place for considering the law of contempt of court, both in the Contempt of Court Act 1981 and in the case law upon it. The roles of Ministers (including the Attorney-General) and the Director of Public Prosecutions in the administration of justice are also considered. Every one of these topics is of constitutional interest and distinguishes the English system from a great many other legal systems.

Secondly, in chapter 20, some features of the constitutional status of the police, the officers directly responsible for enforcement of the criminal law and the maintenance of the Queen's peace, are examined; some of their powers and duties are more fully explained in chapters 22–6.

The status of a police officer is anomalous: in some respects he is an instrument of the executive branch of government, in others a local officer, and in others an independent public officer, but he cannot be fitted neatly into any category. Control over the police is partly a matter for the Home Office, partly for local police authorities, but a chief constable of a local force enjoys a very substantial measure of personal autonomy and authority. Public duties are cast on him by law to secure the due enforcement of law and order within his area of command; but the means of compelling him to perform those duties are still unclear. The chapter ends with a comment on the thorny problem of investigating complaints against police officers and of the provision made for this by the Police and Criminal Evidence Act 1984.

'Police' is often listed among local government services, though local control over the conduct of a force may be tenuous. Chapter 21 is in the nature of an essay on local government law. Books on this specialized subject are available for consultation, and this chapter does not attempt to offer a detailed synopsis of the whole field. Much rewriting has had to be undertaken to keep up with the Conservative Government's policies and legislation on local government. The Greater London Council and the metropolitan county councils have been abolished; domestic rates in Scotland are being replaced by a community charge, or poll tax, and England and Wales follow suit in 1990; earlier controls on rate-capping will continue in relation to the community charge; the use of local revenues for political publicity has been banned; and the Education Reform Act 1988, the Housing Act 1988 and the Local Government Act 1988 all further weaken local authority powers. This redefinition of relative central and local government power remains a controversial constitutional issue.

Chapter 19

The Administration of Justice

Courts [1]

Criminal jurisdiction

The most striking feature of the English legal system is the part played by the layman, as justice of the peace, as juror or as the initiator of criminal proceedings. It is open to an aggrieved member of the public to lay an information before a magistrate asking him to issue a summons, or in some cases an arrest warrant, against another person for a criminal offence (for example, assault). In practice most of these members of the public are police officers and prosecutions are largely conducted by the Crown Prosecution Service, but purely private prosecutions are not uncommon. For some serious offences (for example, against the Official Secrets Acts) the Attorney-General's leave must be obtained before a prosecution can be instituted. There are other offences for which only the Director of Public Prosecutions, or only a local authority, may prosecute.

Before 1986 criminal prosecutions were mainly conducted by or on behalf of the police. This unsatisfactory state of affairs, involving the police in both the detection and the prosecution of crime, was widely recognized and was ultimately condemned by the Royal Commission on Criminal Procedure. [2] The Government accepted the case for transferring the main prosecution role to an independent body, [3] and it

---

[1] The leading work is R. M. Jackson's *Machinery of Justice in England* (7th edn, 1977). See also Geoffrey Wilson, *Cases and Materials on the English Legal System* (1973) and, for a lively critique of the system, *The Judiciary* (*A Report by a Subcommittee of Justice*, 1972). Only a brief outline of the system in England and Wales is offered in this chapter. Some important questions, like the cost of litigation and the award of costs, are omitted.

[2] Cmnd 8092 (1981).

[3] See Cmnd 9074 (1983).

secured the passage of the Prosecution of Offences Act 1985. The right to bring a private prosecution is expressly retained under the Act[4] so that, as well as the individual citizen keeping that right, the power of local authorities, Government Departments and others to prosecute under existing legislation is retained. It is still for the police to decide whether to initiate a public prosecution and, if they decide to do so, to lay an information. But the Crown Prosecution Service (CPS) actually conducts criminal prosecutions on behalf of the Crown, and may also decide which prosecutions should be discontinued.[5]

The Director of Public Prosecutions (the DPP)[6] is at the head of the CPS.[7] It is his duty to take over and to conduct all criminal proceedings which have been instituted by the police, to take over all criminal proceedings which appear to him to be important or difficult, and also to appear for the prosecution when directed to do so by a court in certain criminal appeals. He may also advise police forces on all matters relating to offences. The actual daily conduct of proceedings is in the hands of Crown Prosecutors[8] under a Chief Crown Prosecutor in each prosecution area. They operate under a Code for Crown Prosecutors issued by the DPP[9] and which is annexed to his annual report to Parliament.[10] The Crown Prosecutors have all the DPP's powers in relation to the institution and conduct of criminal proceedings, including the important power to discontinue cases in the magistrates' court.[11]

Apart from the issue of summonses and warrants, the chief functions of magistrates are the trial of summary offences, and the conduct of preliminary inquiries into indictable offences which are triable by a higher court.[12] Magistrates may be either lay justices of the peace – the office originated over six hundred years ago – or professional stipendiary magistrates. There are some 27,500 active justices of the peace in

---

[4] 1985 Act, s. 6.

[5] This power to discontinue, when exercised, could affect police decisions whether to initiate proceedings in similar cases in the future.

[6] See further below, p. 385.

[7] 1985 Act, ss 1–3.

[8] ibid., ss 4, 5.

[9] ibid., s. 10.

[10] See H.C. *14* (1987–8), Annex B. According to that report the number of cases referred to the DPP for guidance has fallen to half the number referred in 1985, so that fears of overcentralization seem to be unfounded.

[11] 1985 Act, s. 23.

[12] This is an oversimplification especially since the enactment of the Criminal Law Act 1977 and later legislation which provides for specified offences to be tried either only summarily (before magistrates), or only on indictment (in the Crown Court), or 'either way'.

England and Wales, sitting in over a thousand magistrates' courts, but just sixty-three stipendiaries, of whom all but fourteen are metropolitan magistrates sitting in the London area. There are no juries in magistrates' courts; in trying offences, magistrates are judges of law and fact and impose sentence. Metropolitan stipendiary magistrates always sit alone to hear summary cases; other stipendiaries usually sit unaccompanied by lay justices; the size of a lay bench will be between two and seven (and will usually be two or three), under a chairman elected by the magistrates. Magistrates must normally sit in open court, but when they sit as examining justices conducting a preliminary inquiry to determine whether there is sufficient evidence to commit a defendant for trial before a higher court, the evidence given at these proceedings cannot be reported contemporaneously except at the defendant's request, unless the magistrates discharge him.[13]

On conviction, magistrates cannot, in general, impose a sentence of more than six months' imprisonment or a fine of more than £2,000; they may, however, commit an offender for sentence at the Crown Court if the offence is one punishable by a heavier sentence and their own powers are inadequate to meet the case. They may also remand defendants in custody; in certain circumstances they may make recommendations for deportation upon conviction; they may bind over a defendant by requiring him to enter into recognizances, with or without sureties, to be of good behaviour or to keep the peace, and send him to prison if he refuses.[14] These are formidable powers to vest in amateurs[15] whose knowledge of legal technicalities and techniques may be rudimentary. The picture is not in fact quite as alarming as it may appear. Magistrates are advised on points of law and procedure by a clerk of the court, who is normally a full-time officer and who is usually legally qualified. All newly appointed justices are obliged to

---

[13] Magistrates' Courts Act 1980, ss 4(2), 8. If there are two or more accused and one objects to contemporaneous reporting, the court will only order that reporting restrictions be lifted if it is satisfied that it is in the interests of justice to do so: Magistrates' Courts Act 1980, s. 8(2A). In certain circumstances committal proceedings may be (and frequently are) based on written depositions: 1980 Act, s. 102.

[14] This is really a form of preventive justice. Other alternatives after a case has been proved include absolute discharge, conditional discharge, community service orders and putting on probation: Powers of Criminal Courts Act 1973. For young offenders, a different set of sanctions or welfare orders is prescribed; see Children and Young Persons Act 1969, Criminal Justice Act 1982, ss 1–28, Criminal Justice Act 1988, Part IX, and *The Sentence of the Court* (4th edn, 1986), chs 10–11.

[15] The 'great unpaid' have received travelling and subsistence allowances for loss of earnings since 1949. The governing provision is now the Justices of the Peace Act 1979, s. 12 (itself a major consolidating measure).

undergo a course of preliminary training; they are also obliged to attend refresher courses and conferences; they are kept informed by advisory Home Office circulars about sentencing policies and problems and other developments on the treatment of offenders. The infirm and incompetent can be placed on a supplemental list where they will be ineligible to perform judicial functions. In any event, magistrates are now retired or placed on the supplemental list at seventy. There are about 10,000 magistrates on the supplemental list. Except in the City of London, the *ex officio* magistrate has almost disappeared.[16] There is no adequate means of assessing the quality of criminal justice dispensed by lay magistrates, but the asperity of criticism formerly levelled against them has been softened in the last forty years and there is a dearth of enthusiasm for the professional magistrate sitting alone.

Young offenders, and young persons in need of care and protection, are normally brought before juvenile courts, differently constituted from ordinary magistrates' courts and following a less formal procedure. They are composed predominantly of lay magistrates.[17]

Fundamental changes in the system of criminal courts were introduced by the Courts Act 1971, which came into force on 1 January 1972. The reforms were based on the Report of the Beeching Commission on Assizes and Quarter Sessions.[18]

The Crown Court, which replaced other criminal courts, the most important of which were Assizes and Quarter Sessions, is part of the Supreme Court of Judicature.[19] It consists of High Court judges, Circuit judges, part-time Recorders and Assistant Recorders and, in certain circumstances, justices of the peace. There are 394 Circuit judges who are now appointed exclusively from the ranks of Recorders, and who sit in the Crown Court and the county court. Recorders are required to sit for twenty days a year in the Crown Court. They must be barristers or solicitors of at least ten years' standing; a large majority are in fact barristers. Recorders are now appointed by the Lord Chancellor from the pool of Assistant Recorders (of whom there are about 450), who are barristers or solicitors of at least ten years' standing and who sit part-time mainly in the Crown Court. After about

---

[16] See Justices of the Peace Act 1979, s. 39.
[17] See *The Sentence of the Court* (above, note 14), paras 11.3–11.18. The emphasis has shifted from criminal responsibility and sanctions towards civil responsibility and remedial orders.
[18] Cmnd 4153 (1969).
[19] See generally the Supreme Court Act 1981.

three to five years of such work an Assistant Recorder is considered for promotion to Recorder; if he is not promoted, his judicial assistance is dispensed with.[20] The qualification for appointment as a Circuit judge is to be a barrister of ten years' standing or to have been a Recorder for three years;[21] it is therefore possible for a solicitor of at least thirteen years' standing to become a Circuit judge. There are over thirty solicitor-Circuit judges in office at the moment.

The Crown Court sits in twenty-four main provincial centres, staffed by High Court and Circuit judges, and by Recorders and Assistant Recorders. Here the High Court judge will wear two hats. Sitting in the *High Court*, he will hear civil cases; sitting in the *Crown Court*, he will hear the most serious criminal cases. But there is flexibility: the very serious criminal cases can be assigned to a Circuit judge, and a Circuit judge can also hear certain *High Court* civil cases. There is a second tier of centres, served by High Court and Circuit judges, where only criminal cases are heard. Then there is a third tier, staffed by Circuit judges only. There are 113 major centres for the administration of criminal justice outside London.

Offences are divided into four classes. Indictable offences in the first class must be tried by a High Court judge; in the second class they must be tried by a High Court judge unless the judge presiding over a circuit releases a case to another judge; in the third class they may be tried by a High Court judge or Circuit judge or Recorder. The fourth class of offence (cases triable 'either way' under the Criminal Law Act 1977, together with a few other specified offences) will normally be tried by a Circuit judge or Recorder.[22] There are detailed rules directing or guiding magistrates as to the class of centre to which a particular case should be committed. All trials on indictment are by jury.

Juries are now selected more or less at random[23] from among registered electors between the ages of eighteen and sixty-five who have

---

[20] Information about the Lord Chancellor's appointments policy has been published in *Judicial Appointments* (Lord Chancellor's Department, 1986).

[21] Administration of Justice Act 1977, s. 12.

[22] Criminal Law Act 1977, ss 14–17; Practice Direction (Crime: Crown Court Business) [1987] 3 All E.R. 1064.

[23] But the controversial issue of 'jury vetting' has made the choice less random and has produced conflicting judicial attitudes towards its constitutionality: see, for example, *R. v. Sheffield C.C., ex p. Brownlow* [1980] Q.B. 530, C.A.; cf. *R. v. Mason* [1980] 3 W.L.R. 617, C.A.; 979 H.C. Deb. *948* (25 February 1980), and the Attorney-General's statement and new guidelines 989 H.C. Deb. *1929–40* (1 August 1980) and (1988) 138 *N.L.J.* 358–60. The Attorney-General authorized jury vetting in relation to 18 defendants between 1980–85: see 72 H.C. Deb. *383–5* (4 February 1985). Since 1988 he has only approved Crown objections to potential jurors in cases involving terrorism or national security.

resided for five years or more in the British Islands since childhood.[24] The right of a defendant to object to a potential juror without cause ('the peremptory challenge') was finally abolished in 1988.[25] The jury is perhaps the most venerated English institution, lauded as a bulwark against oppression and the common-sense voice of twelve ordinary citizens. But uneasiness about the merits of jury trial has grown of late,[26] though some of the doubts cannot be reliably substantiated. In civil cases trial by jury is now rare – hardly 30 cases a year. In criminal cases the accuracy of findings by juries and the processes by which they are reached are not infrequently questioned. Bribery and intimidation of jurors are thought to be extremely uncommon; nevertheless, because this problem arose in trials involving members of London gangs, the rule that a jury's verdict in criminal proceedings had to be unanimous was varied in 1967; a majority verdict may be accepted by the court if ten jurors agree that the accused is guilty.[27] In civil cases majority verdicts are acceptable with the consent of the parties, and without their consent subject to safeguards similar to those laid down in criminal proceedings.[28]

The system of appeals in criminal cases is complicated:[29]

1   A person convicted by a magistrates' court can appeal to the Crown Court on a question of law, fact or sentence; the appeal is by way of rehearing without a jury; a sentence may be increased.

2   Alternatively, either the prosecutor or the defendant may appeal on a point of law by case stated[30] from a conviction by a magistrates' court, or a determination by the Crown Court *on appeal or a committal for sentence*, to a Divisional Court of the Queen's Bench

---

[24] See generally Juries Act 1974. Electors aged between 65 and 70 may now serve as jurors, but they have the right to decline: Criminal Justice Act 1988, s. 119. Jurors are paid travelling and subsistence allowances and compensation for loss of earnings. Subject to certain exceptions, service is compulsory. Juries are still used in coroners' courts: see Coroners' Act 1988, ss 9–12.

[25] Criminal Justice Act 1988, s. 118.

[26] See, for example, Criminal Law Revision Committee, 11th Report, *Evidence (General)*, Cmnd 4991 (1972) and John Baldwin and M. McConville, *Jury Trials* (1979).

[27] See now Juries Act 1974, s. 17. If there are only ten jurors – the normal size of a jury is eleven or twelve – nine must concur in the finding of guilt. The court must not accept a majority verdict unless the jury has deliberated for at least two hours. Moreover, people who have been sentenced to or served prison and other penalties are disqualified from service for specified periods: Juries Act 1974, Sched. 1, Part III, as substituted by the Juries (Disqualification) Act 1984.

[28] Juries Act 1974, s. 17.

[29] Part of this branch of the law was consolidated in the Criminal Appeal Act 1968. It was modified by the Courts Act 1971.

[30] The clerk of the court draws up a statement of the facts found and the basis of the decision, and this is signed by the magistrates.

Division, consisting of two or more (usually three and occasionally five) judges of that Division of the High Court. This course is followed where an authoritative legal ruling is sought.

3   From the Divisional Court, a further appeal on a point of law will lie direct to the House of Lords, but only with leave, which is not to be granted unless the Divisional Court certifies that a point of law of general public importance is involved, and that court or the House of Lords is of the opinion that it should be considered by the House.

4   From convictions in the Crown Court appeals lie against conviction or sentence to the Criminal Division of the Court of Appeal, subject to various restrictive conditions.[31] The Criminal Division sits in at least two courts, composed partly of Lords Justices of Appeal and partly of Queen's Bench judges. If new relevant evidence is received by the court, it has discretion to order the appellant to be retried.[32]

5   A further appeal on a point of law will lie from the Court of Appeal to the House of Lords, subject to similar conditions to those in paragraph 3 above.

Ancillary points, not directly linked with appeals, need to be mentioned. First, the Home Secretary may refer the whole of a case after a conviction on indictment to the Court of Appeal; the effect is much as if the person convicted had lodged an appeal. Secondly, he may refer any aspect of such a case to the Court of Appeal for their opinion.[33] Thirdly, he may advise the Queen to exercise the prerogative of pardon. Fourthly, a prisoner may be released on licence on the recommendation of the Parole Board (and in certain cases merely on the recommendation of a local review committee) after serving a third of his sentence.[34] Fifthly, the Attorney-General may refer to the Court of Appeal a point of law arising out of an acquittal in a trial on indictment.[35] Sixthly, sentences passed for certain serious offences may be referred to the Court of Appeal by the Attorney-General if he thinks that the trial judge had been unduly lenient; the Court of Appeal may

[31] For example, leave of the court below is required for an appeal on a question of fact, and leave of the Court of Appeal if an appeal is to be lodged against sentence. The Court of Appeal cannot increase the total period of sentence already imposed, except on an Attorney-General's reference against an 'unduly lenient' sentence: see below and p. 366, note 36.

[32] Criminal Appeal Act 1968, ss 7, 8, 23; Criminal Justice Act 1988, s. 43.

[33] ibid., s. 17.

[34] Criminal Justice Act 1967, ss 59–64; Sched. 2; Criminal Law Act 1977, s. 65 and Sched. 12; Criminal Justice Act 1972, s. 35; Criminal Justice Act 1982, s. 33.

[35] Criminal Justice Act 1972, s. 36. Whatever be the opinion of the court, the acquittal will still stand.

then substitute any sentence which it thinks appropriate.[36] Seventhly, determinations by magistrates' courts and the Crown Court are subject to review by the Divisional Court of the Queen's Bench Division exercising its supervisory jurisdiction – for example, an order of certiorari to quash a conviction (other than a conviction by the Crown Court in a trial on indictment) can be obtained if the court has exceeded its jurisdiction or broken the rules of natural justice.[37] Eighthly, a person deprived of his liberty without lawful authority may procure his release by the award of a writ of habeas corpus.[38]

Civil jurisdiction [39]

Many justiciable claims and controversies in non-criminal matters are determined by bodies other than the ordinary courts – by special statutory tribunals, or local authorities, or Ministers (through departmental officials), or named classes of officials, or domestic tribunals (committees of clubs, trades unions and so on). Businessmen often provide in their commercial contracts that disputes shall be submitted to arbitration. Of late there have been experiments in establishing informal small claims courts. There are also specialized courts such as the Restrictive Practices Court and the Patents Court, outside the mainstream of the ordinary judicial system. But in almost all cases the general superior courts preserve an appellate or a supervisory jurisdiction.

Magistrates' courts have a limited civil jurisdiction. They have power to make affiliation orders, and maintenance and separation orders and decisions as to custody of children in matrimonial cases; appeal on points of law lies to a Divisional Court of the Family Division of the High Court. They also have various functions in the general field of administrative law, particularly in respect of licensing and the hearing of appeals against local authority licensing decisions; appeal usually lies to the Crown Court, with a further (or alternative) appeal by case stated on points of law to the Divisional Court of the Queen's Bench Division.

The county courts are the main courts of civil jurisdiction.[40] There

---

[36] Criminal Justice Act 1988, ss 35, 36. The offences are those which are triable only on indictment or as are specified by statutory instrument.

[37] See ch. 30.

[38] See pp. 471–6.

[39] A Report recommending radical reforms in the civil justice system has been published by the Lord Chancellor's Review Body on Civil Justice: see Cm 394 (1988).

[40] See County Courts Act 1984.

never has been any necessary connection between a county court area and an administrative or geographical county. In the county courts undefended divorce petitions are heard, but their main function is to determine small monetary claims. To an increasing extent judicial functions in minor county court cases have been devolved upon registrars, who are solicitors. In practice most of the nearly two million cases that come before county courts each year are undefended; these are mainly plaints issued in respect of debts.

Their monetary jurisdiction in contract and tort has been progressively raised; in 1989 the maximum claim they could entertain was for £5,000. They also exercise a miscellany of functions in the fields of equity, bankruptcy, and landlord and tenant (notably applications for possession orders), and a wide range of jurisdiction, mainly original but sometimes appellate, arising under modern collectivist legislation. Appeals lie, normally on points of law only, to the Court of Appeal (Civil Division).

The Supreme Court of Judicature consists of the Court of Appeal, the High Court and the Crown Court. The Court of Appeal has two divisions, civil and criminal: it is presided over by the Master of the Rolls, and has up to twenty-eight Lords Justices of Appeal. It normally sits with a bench of two or three; the Lord Chief Justice presides in one court of the Criminal Division; other High Court judges are often called upon to sit to hear criminal appeals, but less frequently to hear civil appeals. Appeals on the civil side lie mainly from county courts and the High Court; the court may be leapfrogged and an appeal raising a point of law of exceptional difficulty or importance calling for a reconsideration of a binding precedent may, with leave of the House of Lords, lie direct from the High Court to the Lords.[41]

The High Court sits in three divisions: the Queen's Bench, the Chancery, and the Family Divisions. The Family Division replaced the Probate, Divorce and Admiralty Division ('the court of wrecks') in October 1971. On appointment, a judge is assigned to one of the three divisions. The Lord Chief Justice presides in the Queen's Bench Division; the Lord Chancellor, who never sits, is nominally president of the Chancery Division and there is a Vice-Chancellor who is a Chancery judge; there is a President of the Family Division. The maximum number of other High Court judges (called puisne judges) is

---

[41] Administration of Justice Act 1969, ss 12–16. A certificate must first be given by the trial judge, and the parties must consent to the leapfrogging appeal.

eighty-five.[42] The original civil jurisdiction of the High Court is unlimited as to amount and persons but subject to territorial limitations. Distribution of work between the three divisions is governed partly by statute, partly by rules of court, partly by custom, and there is a substantial area of concurrent jurisdiction; for example, actions claiming injunctions or declarations are usually brought in the Chancery Division but can be instituted in the Queen's Bench Division or even the Family Division. The High Court also has appellate and supervisory jurisdiction in relation to inferior tribunals, a jurisdiction normally exercised by a Divisional Court of the Queen's Bench Division, and power to issue writs of habeas corpus.[43] The High Court, like the Court of Appeal, sits in the Royal Courts of Justice (the Law Courts) in London, and also (as has been seen) juxtaposed with the Crown Court at the top-tier provincial centres. There Queen's Bench judges sit as Crown Court judges for criminal cases too.[44]

The House of Lords as a 'final' appellate court has already been mentioned.[45] In 1966 it reasserted power to overrule its own decisions.[46]

Independence of the Judiciary [47]

It is clearly of great importance that justice be dispensed even-handedly in the courts and that the general public feel confident in the integrity and the impartiality of the Judiciary. Where the Government of the day has an interest in the outcome of judicial proceedings, the court should not act merely as a mouthpiece of the Executive. The Judiciary must therefore be secure from undue influence and autonomous within its own field.

These propositions may seem platitudinous. But in many countries some of them would be rejected. Whereas all governments would agree that there should be public confidence in the administration of justice, and that judges ought not to accept bribes or decide cases on the basis of personal friendship or animosity, many would not agree that the Judiciary ought to be independent of the Executive. On the contrary, they would say that the judges have not to be impartial between the

---

[42] Supreme Court Act 1981, s. 4; Maximum Number of Judges Order 1987, S.I. 1987, No. 2059.
[43] See pp. 584–5.
[44] See p. 363.
[45] pp. 308–10 and above. But see pp. 104–6 on the European Court of Justice.
[46] Practice Statement [1966] 1 W.L.R. 1234.
[47] See Rodney Brazier, *Constitutional Practice* (1988), ch. 11.

people and the enemies of the people; that since the Government (or the Party) is the voice of the people, critics of the régime or bourgeois elements or other classes of persons stigmatized as anti-social must be dealt with severely by the courts, which are instruments of State policy. And judges who talk out of turn or acquit persons charged with sedition or refuse to join the Party or (as the case may be) fail to uphold and apply the edicts of the military régime may be dismissed.

In many other countries, the principles of judicial independence are acknowledged but are substantially qualified in practice. This is hardly surprising when one considers the implications that can be and have been read into the concept. Does judicial independence imply that the Executive must have no voice, or a muted voice, in the appointment or promotion of judges? Does it imply that neither the Executive nor the Legislature shall be competent to remove judges? If the principle carries these implications – and it is arguable that it should import them – it is imperfectly realized in Britain. Does it imply that judges should be entirely aloof from public sentiment and always disregard the strength of local feeling on an issue before them? If not, to what extent should judges take into account considerations of public policy, and how far can the Government or its unruly supporters or opponents be permitted to determine what is the public interest? In Britain these questions seldom arise in an acutely controversial form,[48] but judges not infrequently have to determine what is in the public interest, or whether a transaction is contrary to public policy, or whether it is necesssary to impose a deterrent sentence because of the prevalence of a social evil; and in coming to such decisions they are expected to have some regard to the general sense of the community and not to rely merely on idiosyncratic opinions.[49] Moreover, in some political contexts the

[48] Though cf. the controversies which arose in 1972 out of the application of the Industrial Relations Act 1971 (since repd). See, for example, John Griffith, 'Reflections on the Rule of the Law', *New Statesman*, 24 November 1972, for sharp criticism, and his *The Politics of the Judiciary* (3rd edn, 1985); *Churchman* v. *Joint Shop Stewards' Committee* [1972] 1 W.L.R. 1094; and see p. 383, on the Official Solicitor. When in 1975 a High Court judge ordered the fees of counsel and solicitors in a case before him to be reduced because of their conduct of the case, his decision was reversed by the Court of Appeal: *R.* v. *McFadden*, *The Times*, 11 December 1975. But, undeterred, the judge called an unprecedented press conference and wrote to *The Times*. A motion was tabled in the Commons to remove him, but no debate ensued and the matter lapsed.

[49] There have been a number of instances since the late 1970s in which individual judges have been publicly criticized because of remarks made or attitudes displayed in court to which exception was taken either by M.P.s or by their superiors. See, for example, the 'early day' motion referred to at 933 H.C. Deb. 1747–8 and 1751 (23 June 1977) and the controversies caused by Judge McKinnon (*The Times*, 13 January 1978) and Melford Stevenson J. (*The Times*, 6 July 1978); see further Brazier, op. cit., pp. 240 54.

courts allow the Executive [50] or the House of Commons [51] the first and last word. Here we are enmeshed in the thicket of questions of degree, where generalizations are not very helpful.

Can we not at least agree that the protection of judicial independence in a liberal democracy demands that it should be unconstitutional for the Legislature to invade the domain of the Judiciary by pronouncing judgment (as in a bill of attainder) [52] or reversing a judicial decision with retroactive effect, [53] or enabling the Executive to designate which judges shall sit to hear a particular case, [54] or abolishing a judicial office while it has a substantive holder, [55] or reducing judicial salaries? [56] In Britain such measures would generally be regarded, in the absence of extraordinary circumstances, as unconstitutional in the sense of being contrary to constitutional convention. But in a number of Commonwealth countries they would be not only 'unconstitutional' but also invalid. And in some Commonwealth countries it would also be unconstitutional to impair the independence of the Judiciary by endowing them with functions extraneous to the judicial, [57] or to purport to oust the jurisdiction of the courts to decide the constitutionality of legislative or executive action. [58]

Appointment [59]

Appointments of High Court and Circuit judges, Recorders, Assistant Recorders and stipendiary and lay magistrates are made either by or on the advice of the Lord Chancellor. He also decides whether to renew part-time judicial appointments. Since the Lord Chancellor is himself a political appointee and a member of the Cabinet, there appears to be

---

[50] See, for example, *Chandler* v. *D.P.P.* [1964] A.C. 763; and other cases cited above, pp. 142–5.

[51] See, for example, the *Sheriff of Middlesex*'s case (1840) 11 A. & E. 273; *Bradlaugh* v. *Gossett* (1884) 12 Q.B.D. 271.

[52] See *Liyanage* v. *R.* [1967] 1 A.C. 259 (Ceylon); though cf. *Kariapper* v. *Wijesinha* [1968] A.C. 717; *Australian Communist Party* v. *Commonwealth of Australia* (1951) 83 C.L.R. 1.

[53] cf. *Burmah Oil Co.* v. *Lord Advocate* [1965] A.C. 75; War Damage Act 1965.

[54] *R.* v. *Liyanage* (1963) 64 New L.R. 313 (Ceylon); see Thomas M. Franck, *Comparative Constitutional Process* (1968), pp. 384–98. The court held that this power was one properly reposed only in members of the Judicature.

[55] See, for example, Constitution of Jamaica (S.I. 1952, No. 1550, Sched. 2), s. 97(3).

[56] For example, Constitution of India, art. 124(2), proviso.

[57] *Att.-Gen. for Australia* v. *R. and the Boilermakers' Society of Australasia* [1957] A.C. 288. See also *Hinds* v. *R.* [1977] A.C. 195.

[58] For example, *Balewa* v. *Doherty* [1963] 1 W.L.R. 949 (P.C., Nigeria).

[59] See *Judicial Appointments* (1986), which describes the Lord Chancellor's principles and practices in some detail in relation to the lower judiciary, but much less fully in relation to the senior judiciary.

ample scope for political patronage. Appointments to the Court of Appeal and to the House of Lords, and to the offices of Lord Chief Justice, Master of the Rolls and President of the Family Division, are made on the advice of the Prime Minister after consultation with the Lord Chancellor.[60] In a number of new Commonwealth countries judicial appointments other than Chief Justice are made on the advice of a Judicial Service Commission, presided over by the Chief Justice and composed mainly of judicial members. In practice appointments in England and Wales are no longer made on political grounds, except to the lay magistracy. Justices of the Peace are appointed by the Lord Chancellor on the recommendation of local advisory committees whose membership has not, in general, been disclosed; but the Lord Chancellor has recommended all committees to publish their membership by 1992 at the latest. In a circular to advisory committees in 1966, the then Lord Chancellor made it clear that political affiliations ought not to be disregarded because it was important that 'justices should be drawn from all sections of the community and should represent all shades of opinion'.[61]

Before 1914 it was quite common for M.P.s belonging to the party in office to be appointed to the High Court.[62] Since 1945 hardly any judicial appointment in England appears to have been influenced by political considerations.[63] Professional standing at the bar and personal suitability are ostensibly the sole criteria. The Lord Chancellor is likely to consult the Lord Chief Justice, the Master of the Rolls, the Vice-Chancellor and the President of the Family Division before submitting a recommendation. Not long ago the Attorney-General was understood to have the first refusal of a vacancy in the office of Lord Chief Justice. In 1922 Lord Hewart, then Attorney-General, was appointed; in 1940 he was succeeded by Lord Caldecote, formerly Attorney-General and at the time Lord Chancellor. But in 1946 Caldecote was succeeded by Lord Goddard, a Law Lord who was far from being a Labour sympathizer[64] and in 1958 Lord Parker, a Lord Justice of Appeal, assumed the office. In 1971 Lord Parker was succeeded by Lord

---

[60] See Lord Hailsham, *The Door Wherein I Went* (1975), p. 254.

[61] In the counties the chairman of the advisory committee is the Lord Lieutenant; in districts the chairman is appointed by the Lord Chancellor. The main political parties will be represented on the Committee. See Richards [1961] *Public Law* 134.

[62] See generally, H. J. Laski, *Studies in Law and Politics* (1932), pp. 168–80.

[63] This comment does not apply to Scottish judicial appointments. See Willock (1969) 14 *Juridical Review* (N.S.) 193.

[64] Viscount Jowitt, Lord Chancellor under the Attlee Governments (1945–51), went to great pains not to afford any ground for suspicion that appointments to high judicial office were politically influenced.

Widgery, also a Lord Justice of Appeal. His successor in 1980, Lord
Lane, had briefly been a Lord of Appeal in Ordinary. There is no
reason, however, why the Law Officers of the Crown, and other
barristers in politics, should not be eligible for appointment to high
judicial office, provided that they possess the appropriate qualities of
character, temperament and intellect. Political affiliations may nevertheless operate as a disqualification inasmuch as an active proponent of
revolution may be regarded as unsuitable to occupy what is in one
aspect a high office of State.

A lawyer seeking appointment as a Recorder or professional magistrate should make the fact known to the Lord Chancellor's Department;
candidates for such appointments are not easily identified.[65] As we
have seen, solicitors as well as barristers are eligible for these appointments, and a solicitor may become a Circuit judge after three
years' service as a Recorder. Solicitors also exercise judicial functions
as Masters of the Supreme Court, county court registrars and chairmen
of special tribunals. But at present full-time judgeships are reserved for
members of the bar.[66] This exclusiveness has had certain advantages.
Members of the bar alone have had the right of audience in the
superior courts;[67] they rub shoulders out of court with the judges, who
remain members of their Inns; the bar is an autonomous, individualistic
but tightly knit profession, maintaining extraordinarily high standards
of professional conduct, partly, perhaps, because the number of
barristers in private practice in England and Wales is still only some
five thousand. Recent developments, and in particular the growth of
the size of the Judiciary, portend an erosion of exclusiveness. One
class of lawyer, the full-time academic lawyer, is still in practice
excluded from serious consideration for appointment to a superior
judgeship. On this matter there are real difficulties to overcome. It
would be a risk to appoint a person with little experience of
advocacy to be a judge of first instance. To appoint him to the
Court of Appeal or the House of Lords might evoke serious resentment among the puisne judges.

---

[65] The Lord Chancellor's Department, however, each year reviews the careers of all
practising barristers under fifty to see who might receive judicial appointments: *Judicial
Appointments* (1986), p. 11.

[66] High Court puisne judges must be barristers of at least ten years' standing and other
superior judges must be barristers of at least fifteen years' standing (except that the Law
Lords may alternatively have held high judicial office for two years).

[67] Solicitors have a right of audience in county courts, limited rights of audience in the
Crown Court (Practice Directions [1972] 1 W.L.R. 5 and 307), and in the Supreme Court
in formal and unopposed proceedings (Practice Direction [1986] 1 W.L.R. 545, adopted
after *Abse* v. *Smith* [1986] Q.B. 536).

Promotion

In Britain the Judiciary is not a career service. In many countries a young man will join the judicial service, starting at the bottom and working his way upwards through the hierarchy. Such a system may tend to inhibit forthright independent-mindedness, particularly if promotion is determined by a Minister of Justice.[68] But in Britain appointments to the High Court are made from the ranks of successful practitioners;[69] professional magistrates are not promoted to the High Court, and promotions of Circuit judges have been rare;[70] advancement from the High Court to the Court of Appeal may be gratifying, but it carries little increase in salary;[71] appointment to the House of Lords means a relatively small increment in salary though by some a peerage is highly valued. There is no great material inducement to encourage a member of the Judiciary to curry favour with the politicians or his judicial superiors; any attempt to procure advancement by such means would bring a judge into disfavour. Moreover, a Prime Minister or Lord Chancellor has little incentive to take political considerations into account when recommending promotion or, indeed, the initial appointment of a judge. Matters might be different if we had a written constitution with entrenched guarantees and prohibitions subject to judicial interpretation, especially if it were difficult to procure constitutional amendments overturning the effect of inconvenient decisions.

Since the early 1980s the Lord Chancellor's policy has been to appoint and to promote to full-time judicial offices only those who have satisfactorily served in relevant part-time appointments. So a career progression has developed, from Assistant Recorder to Recorder to Circuit judge, and it will gradually be extended to take in High Court appointments as well.[72] A similar progression is discernible in the senior judiciary, appointments being made to the Court of Appeal exclusively from the High Court, and to the House of Lords from the Court of Appeal.

---

[68] In Commonwealth countries where there is a Judicial Service Commission, promotion is a matter for the Commission. This system may induce a different kind of deference.

[69] For their social background, see Henry Cecil, *The English Judge* (1972 edn), ch. 1.

[70] Promotions of Circuit judges to be High Court judges may well, however, become more common in future. At the present time there are indications of hierarchical tendencies at the lower end of the scale – for example, a magistrates' clerk may become a professional magistrate and then a deputy Circuit judge or Circuit judge.

[71] Every new Lord Justice is, however, made a Privy Councillor.

[72] See *Judicial Appointments* (1986), p. 13.

Salaries

Judicial salaries and pensions are substantial by international standards. A puisne judge of the High Court is paid £68,500 a year, and is a charge on Consolidated Fund Standing Services.[73] Salaries may be increased, but not reduced, by the Lord Chancellor with the consent of the Minister for the Civil Service.[74] After fifteen years' service a judge can retire on a pension equal to half his salary.[75] Practitioners are often earning more in fees than a judicial salary when appointed to the bench, but a judgeship affords not only great dignity but financial security.[76]

The Act of Settlement 1701 had provided that judges' salaries were to be 'ascertained and established'. Till well into the eighteenth century judicial salaries were nevertheless low. Judicial incomes were supplemented by fees from suitors and other sources, sundry perquisites of office and the exercise of patronage.[77] These standing temptations to corruption – which had been all the greater so long as judicial salaries had to be met out of the King's privy purse[78] – under the Stuarts they were often in arrears – were finally removed by an Act of 1826 which raised the salaries of superior judges to £5,000 and abolished their income from fees.

Rules tending to protect judicial independence

Insulation from politics. First, full-time judges are disqualified from membership of the House of Commons.[79] Secondly, by convention judges must refrain from politically partisan activities; and although

[73] See above, p. 286.
[74] Administration of Justice Act, 1973 s. 9(1); Supreme Court Act 1981, s. 12. Lords of Appeal in Ordinary, the Lord Chief Justice and the Master of the Rolls each receive £78,750 a year; Lords Justices of Appeal, the President of the Family Division and the Vice-Chancellor, £75,000. Circuit judges each receive £45,800 and stipendiary magistrates £37,500.
[75] Judicial Pensions Act 1981, s. 2.
[76] In 1970 a High Court judge resigned and became a member of a firm of merchant bankers; his decision aroused some professional criticism.
[77] See generally W. S. Holdsworth, *History of English Law*, vol. 1, pp. 252–5.
[78] For this reason William III had refused his assent in 1692 to a bill to increase judicial salaries to £1,000: Sir Kenneth Roberts-Wray, *Commonwealth and Colonial Law* (1966), pp. 485–6.
[79] House of Commons Disqualification Act 1975, ss 1(1) (*a*), 1(2); First schedule. The disqualification of part-time Recorders for election in those constituencies where they exercised jurisdiction was repealed by the Courts Act 1971, sched. 11, and, it would seem (despite the general words of sched. 8 to that Act), not replaced. For Law Lords in the upper House, see ch. 16. The last judge (other than the Lord Chancellor) to hold Cabinet office was Lord Ellenborough, Chief Justice of the King's Bench, in 1806.

they can criticize the wording and content of legislation and the conduct of members of the Executive, they should be careful not to take sides in matters of political controversy – a precept more easily formulated than followed,[80] for ostensibly non-political matters of public concern are apt to become party issues unexpectedly. Thirdly, by convention members of the Executive are expected to preserve a reciprocal restraint when commenting on the words and deeds of judges, though if criticized by a judge they are not obliged to remain mute, and if a judge makes politically controversial remarks a robust answer can be offered. Fourthly, in parliamentary practice members of the House of Commons are not permitted to cast aspersions on the conduct of a judge at question time, or in the course of debate except on a motion specifically criticizing the judge or supporting an address for his removal;[81] and in general a matter cannot be raised in Parliament if it is *sub judice*.[82] Fifthly, the courts disclaim jurisdiction to inquire into proceedings in Parliament.[83] Sixthly, the charging of judicial salaries on the Consolidated Fund means that since Parliament does not authorize them annually, there is no adequate opportunity to censure judges in the debates on the estimates.

Some hold the view that the independence of the Judiciary may be prejudiced if judges are entrusted with functions alien to the judicial; or if provision is made for courts to give advisory opinions to the Executive on questions of law. The former view does not seem to be generally accepted by the present generation of English judges; they sit in the Restrictive Practices Court and sat in the National Industrial Relations Court during its brief life from 1971 to 1974, and they accept appointments as chairmen of inquiries into alleged public scandals, major industrial disputes, police pay and conditions in the prisons and other politically contentious matters; they conceive these functions to be aspects of their duty towards the State.[84] There are various objections to the advisory judicial opinion, but they have only a tenous connection with judicial involvement in executive policy. The fact that

---

[80] It tends to be followed more rigorously in England than in Scotland.

[81] For a slight relaxation of this rule, see the Speaker's Ruling 935 H.C. Deb. *1381–4* (19 July 1977). If a judge writes a letter to an M.P., its contents may be criticized by M.P.s: see 128 H.C. Deb. *166* (23 February 1988). (An M.P. had written to the Master of the Rolls about one of his judgments; Lord Donaldson M.R. replied; the Speaker ruled that M.P.s could comment on that reply.)

[82] For an exception introduced in 1972, see p. 292.

[83] See pp. 315–16, 319–320, 328–32.

[84] For a helpful catalogue and critique, see Zellick [1972] *Public Law* 1 and, for an exhaustive list of extra-judicial inquiries carried out by judges, see David Butler and Gareth Butler, *British Political Facts 1900–1985* (6th edn, 1986), pp. 299–303.

the Stuarts used judges as advisers and brought undue pressure to bear on them in private consultation does not imply that a publicly delivered advisory opinion on a specific question of law would prejudice judicial impartiality today.[85]

Judicial immunities in legal proceedings.[86] The majority in a Court of Appeal case[87] decided that every judge of the superior and inferior courts – including magistrates – was entitled to protection from liability in damages for anything done while acting judicially. As long as he acted under the honest belief that his conduct was within his jurisdiction, he was protected even though a mistake of law or fact led him outside his jurisdiction. The House of Lords has now reluctantly held that that decision must be overruled at least to the extent that magistrates will be held liable if they exceed their jurisdiction.[88] While acting *within their jurisdiction*, members of other tribunals closely resembling courts[89] enjoy a similar immunity in respect of defamatory words, but a right of action may possibly lie against such officers for malicious *acts*,[90] and will lie for tortious acts done outside their jurisdiction where jurisdiction has been exceeded because of an error of law or an unreasonable mistake of fact.[91]

Judicial immunities from suit are conferred not for the benefit of judges but for the benefit of the administration of justice. The risk that a judge may abuse his privilege by making gratuitously defamatory

[85] Advisory opinions may be obtained from the Judicial Committee of the Privy Council under section 4 of the Judicial Committee Act 1833; see pp. 157–8; see also Criminal Justice Act 1972, s. 36 (p. 365). In Canada advisory opinions on the constitutionality of legislation have frequently been delivered by the courts. The International Court of Justice has also given several advisory opinions.

[86] See Margaret Brazier [1976] *Public Law* 397.

[87] *Sirros* v. *Moore and others* [1975] Q.B. 118.

[88] *McC.* v. *Mullan* [1985] A.C. 528. See also *R.* v. *Waltham Forest JJ., ex p. Solanke* [1986] Q.B. 479 (held, justices acted in execution of their office by committing man to prison for non-payment of money due to his wife under a High Court order, even though the order had not been registered).

[89] See, for example, *Addis* v. *Crocker* [1961] 1 Q.B. 11 (Disciplinary Committee of the Law Society). The courts have, in general, refused to hold members of administrative tribunals to be protected by absolute privilege; they enjoy qualified privilege which is destroyed by proof of malice.

[90] See, on this difficult topic, *Everett* v. *Griffiths* [1921] 1 A.C. 631; *O'Connor* v. *Isaacs* [1956] 2 Q.B. 288; Justices of the Peace Act 1979, ss 44–5; Amnon Rubinstein, *Jurisdiction and Illegality* (1965), pp. 128–33; Sheridan (1951) 14 *Mod. L. Rev.* 267; Thompson (1958) 21 *Mod. L. Rev.* 517; Margaret Brazier [1976] *Public Law* 397.

[91] *Houlden* v. *Smith* (1850) 15 Q.B. 841; *Palmer* v. *Crone* [1927] 1 K.B. 804. Even before *Sirros* v. *Moore and others* (above, note 87), a magistrate who had had to pay damages or costs in respect of proceedings instituted against him in the purported exercise of his duties has since 1964 been entitled to be indemnified out of public funds provided that he had acted reasonably and in good faith: see now Justices of the Peace Act 1979, s. 53.

remarks for reasons of personal rancour is considered to be less than the risk of his abstaining for reasons of prudence from condemning iniquity in appropriate language. In the public interest, absolute privilege also attaches to words used by the parties, counsel and witnesses in the course of judicial proceedings.[92] Nor can jurors be punished for their verdict.[93]

There may be circumstances in which a judge wrongfully declining to hear a case within his jurisdiction will incur civil liability to a person aggrieved.[94] Under the Habeas Corpus Act 1679 a judge wrongfully (and presumably wilfully) refusing to issue a writ of habeas corpus is liable to a penalty of £500 recoverable by the prisoner.

The general rules of judicial immunity do not extend to giving a judge or magistrate an open licence to be corrupt or oppressive. Corruption would be a ground for prosecution. Oppressive conduct would result in the removal of a magistrate, and the same fate might befall an oppressive judge.[95]

Contempt of court.[96] Disobedience to a court order is a civil contempt, punishable in the discretion of the court by imprisonment. This rule has nothing to do with judicial independence. Criminal contempts fall into three main categories. First, there are contempts in the face of the court – for example, the interruption of a High Court libel action by a group of Welsh nationalist student demonstrators,[97] or a wilful refusal by a witness to answer questions put to him.[98] Secondly, there is conduct

---

[92] Neither a barrister nor (it seems) a solicitor can be sued for negligence in respect of his conduct of a client's case as an advocate: *Rondel* v. *Worsley* [1969] 1 A.C. 191. Solicitors are liable for professional negligence in other contexts, and in *Saif Ali and another* v. *Sydney Mitchell & Co.* [1980] A.C. 198 the House of Lords held that the immunity of barristers in respect of pre-trial acts or omissions was not to be given any wider application than was absolutely necessary in the interests of the administration of justice, although on the facts the barrister could not be said to have been negligent.

[93] *Bushell's* case (1670) Vaugh. 135.

[94] See *Ferguson* v. *Earl Kinnoull* (1842) 2 Cl. & F. 251.

[95] See pp. 380–81.

[96] See G. J. Borrie and N. V. Lowe, *The Law of Contempt* (2nd edn, 1983); A. Arlidge and D. Eady, *The Law of Contempt* (1982); C. J. Miller, *Contempt of Court* (1975). See further the Phillimore Report on Contempt of Court, Cmnd 5794 (1974), and Contempt of Court: a discussion paper, Cmnd 7145 (1978).

[97] *Morris* v. *Crown Office* [1970] 2 Q.B. 114 (power of judges to sentence summarily), *Balogh* v. *St Albans Crown Court* [1975] Q.B. 73 (a gross interference with the course of justice in a case tried or about to be tried can be punished either by the judge who had seen the contempt or by a judge in another court to whom it had been reported: the jurisdiction is not limited only to contempt committed 'in the face of the court').

[98] It is not contempt for a person to refuse to disclose a source of information contained in a publication for which he is responsible, unless the court decides that disclosure is necessary in the interests of justice or national security or for the prevention of disorder

which creates a substantial risk that the course of justice in a case will be seriously impeded or prejudiced[99] – for example, publishing newspaper comment or broadcasting a television programme tending to show (in criminal proceedings) that a person not yet convicted, but who is either wanted under an arrest warrant, or who has been arrested or charged, is guilty, or (in civil proceedings) ascribing liability after arrangements for a hearing have been made, or after a hearing has begun – at the earliest of which events the proceedings become 'active';[100] or disclosing a party's past convictions; or putting pressure on witnesses to alter their evidence or not to give evidence; or publishing a report of legal proceedings in which the court has, in order to avoid a substantial risk to the administration of justice in them, ordered the publication of any report to be postponed for as long as it thinks fit;[101] or obtaining, disclosing or soliciting opinions expressed, arguments advanced or votes cast by members of a jury in the course of its deliberations.[102] Thirdly, there is conduct scandalizing the court by scurrilous criticism or imputations of partiality.[103] The limits of permissible criticism have been extended by the courts themselves in recent years. In a case report in 1936, the Judicial Committee, allowing an appeal against a conviction and fine imposed on the author of a newpaper article criticizing sentences imposed by local judges, held that members of the public were immune provided that they refrained from imputing improper motives to the judges and were not actuated by malice. 'Justice must not be a cloistered virtue; she must be allowed to suffer the scrutiny and respectful, even the outspoken, comments of ordinary men.'[104] Today, even disrespectful comments will not necessar-

---

or crime: Contempt of Court Act 1981, s. 10 and *Secretary of State for Defence* v. *Guardian Newspapers Ltd* [1985] A.C. 339: held 'necessary' was to be construed strictly, not as a synonym for 'convenient'; followed in *Maxwell* v. *Pressdram Ltd* [1987] 1 All E. R. 656. 'Prevention of crime' means crime generally, rather than any particular crime: *Re an Inquiry under the Company Securities (Insider Dealing) Act 1985* [1988] 1 All E. R. 203.

[99] 1981 Act, ss 1, 2(2). In *Att.-Gen.* v. *News Group Newspapers Ltd* [1987] Q.B. 1 an injunction to restrain further publication of allegedly defamatory material was refused because the trial would not begin for at least 10 months and a *substantial* risk of serious prejudice would not be caused by such publication.

[100] ibid., s. 2 and sched. 1. Even if proceedings are not 'active', where the conduct complained of is specifically *intended* to impede or prejudice the administration of justice the courts have a common-law power to commit for contempt which is saved by the 1981 Act, s. 6(c): see *Att.-Gen.* v. *Newspaper Publishing plc* [1987] 3 All E.R. 276.

[101] ibid., s. 4(2). See Practice Direction [1982] 1 W.L.R. 1475; *R.* v. *Horsham Justices, ex p. Farquharson* [1982] Q.B. 762.

[102] ibid., s. 8.

[103] *McLeod* v. *St Aubyn* [1899] A.C. 549; *R.* v. *Gray* [1900] 2 Q.B. 36; *R.* v. *Editor of the New Statesman* (1928) 44 T.L.R. 301. See Walker (1985) 101 *L.Q.R.* 359.

[104] *Ambard* v. *Att.-Gen. for Trinidad and Tobago* [1936] A.C. 322 at 335.

ily be construed as contempts of court. In a case decided in 1968,[105] the Court of Appeal declined to hold that an article by a Q.C. (soon to be Lord Chancellor) in *Punch*, embodying robust, jocular and inaccurate denunciations of judgments by the court, was a contempt. Lord Denning M.R. said that the court would 'never use this jurisdiction as a means to uphold our dignity. We do not fear criticism, nor do we resent it.' Salmon L.J. said that 'no criticism of a judge, however vigorous, can amount to contempt of court, providing it keeps within the limits of courtesy and good faith'. Judges may adopt differing standards, but the tendency is to show more indulgence towards outspoken criticism alleging ignorance of the law or excessive harshness or leniency in sentencing. The Law Commission has recommended that this aspect of contempt be narrowed by the creation of a new offence of making false statements alleging corruption in the performance of judicial duties.[106]

Magistrates' courts can punish for contempt in connection with their proceedings. Any person who wilfully insults the justices or any witness before them or an officer of the court or any solicitor or barrister having business in the court during their sitting, or attendance, or in going to or returning from the court, or who wilfully interrupts the proceedings or misbehaves in court, is liable to a maximum penalty of one month in prison or a £2,000 fine or both.[107]

The maximum penalty for contempt of other courts[108] is two years' imprisonment.[109] An appeal against conviction lies to a higher court. It is a defence that a publisher or a disseminator of a contempt, having taken all reasonable care, did not know and had no reason to suspect that relevant proceedings were 'active', or that the publication contained a contempt.[110] A publication made of a discussion in good faith of public affairs or other matters of general public interest is not a contempt if the risk of impediment or prejudice to particular legal proceedings is merely incidental to the discussion.[111]

---

[105] *R.* v. *Metropolitan Police Commissioner, ex p. Blackburn (No. 2)* [1968] 2 Q.B. 150.
[106] Law Com. No. 96 (1979).
[107] Contempt of Court Act 1981, s. 12.
[108] Defined as any tribunal or body exercising the judicial power of the State: ibid., s. 19 (e.g. a coroner's court: see *R.* v. *West Yorkshire Coroner, ex p. Smith (No. 2)* [1985] 1 All E.R. 100).
[109] ibid., s. 14(1). Consecutive sentences are appropriate for each of a number of acts of contempt: *Lee* v. *Walker* [1985] 1 All E.R. 781.
[110] ibid., s. 3(1), (2).
[111] ibid., s. 5. See *Att.-Gen.* v. *English* [1983] 1 A.C. 116.

Security of judicial tenure

Before 1688 judges generally held office during the King's pleasure. When they incurred his displeasure they were apt to be summarily dismissed.

After the 'Glorious Revolution' of 1688 all superior judges were appointed during good behaviour. The Act of Settlement 1701 placed the terms of appointment on a statutory basis: judges' commissions were to be made *quamdiu se bene gesserint* [as long as they behave themselves], 'but upon the address of both Houses of Parliament it shall be lawful to remove them'. This has often been understood to mean that a judge is irremovable except for misbehaviour, in pursuance of an address submitted to the Crown by both Houses praying for his removal on that ground. However, the better interpretation of the Act, and of modern Acts replacing it with slightly different wording,[112] is that a judge is in strict law removable by the Crown *either* for misbehaviour *or* on any other ground in pursuance of a parliamentary address.[113] Misbehaviour would include conviction for an offence involving moral turpitude, and persistent neglect of duties; it does not appear to cover mental infirmity. Removal from an office held during good behaviour has traditionally been effected by proceedings commenced by a writ of *scire facias*. Probably this procedure still survives;[114] it would seem that alternatively the Attorney-General could move for an injunction in the High Court to restrain the judge from continuing to act in an office to which he was no longer entitled, but the judge would have to be given prior notice and a fair opportunity to be heard before being removed.[115]

In practice no judge is likely to be removed except upon a parliamentary address based on the judge's misbehaviour. Only one judge has in fact been so removed since the Act of Settlement – Sir Jonah Barrington, an Irish judge, in 1830.[116] A few other addresses were moved unsuccessfully in the nineteenth century; the judges were

---

[112] Supreme Court Act 1981, s. 11(3) (tenure 'during good behaviour, subject to' a power of removal by the Crown upon an address by both Houses); Appellate Jurisdiction Act 1876, s. 6 (Lords of Appeal in Ordinary).

[113] See the discussion in Sir Kenneth Roberts-Wray, *Commonwealth and Colonial Law* (1966), pp. 486–90.

[114] Despite the wording of the First Schedule to the Crown Proceedings Act 1947 the repeal of the writ may refer only to its use for the recovery of Crown debts.

[115] In accordance with the rules of natural justice: see authorities quoted in *Ridge* v. *Baldwin* [1964] A.C. 40.

[116] Half-hearted attempts to remove the President of the National Industrial Relations Court never reached the stage of putting down a motion, cf. notes 48 and 49.

permitted to defend themselves and be represented by counsel.[117] But the strictly legal safeguards of security of tenure are weak. The death of parliamentary addresses is attributable to the self-restraint of politicians and the circumspection maintained by the Judiciary.[118] It would be more satisfactory to introduce a new procedure whereby a judge would be removable either for mental or physical incapacity or misbehaviour in pursuance of the report of a judicial tribunal of inquiry, and on no other ground. Such a procedure has been incorporated in a number of Commonwealth constitutions since 1957.[119] The Lord Chancellor may, with the concurrence of senior judges, declare vacant the office of a superior judge who is subject to permanent medical incapacity and who is, through illness, unable to tender his resignation.[120]

Till December 1959 tenure during good behaviour was tantamount to life tenure. Superior judges appointed since then must retire at seventy-five.[121]

Circuit judges and Recorders are removable by the Lord Chancellor for incapacity or misbehaviour;[122] they have an implied right to be heard on their own behalf.[123] The normal age for compulsory retirement of a Circuit judge is seventy-two.

Magistrates have no legal security of tenure, but they may be placed on the supplemental list for infirmity or non-judicial behaviour or removed altogether from the commission of the peace. About a dozen lay magistrates are dismissed each year.[124] Both lay and stipendiary magistrates are placed on the supplemental list or retired at seventy.[125]

The Executive and the administration of justice

There is no Minister of Justice in England. Executive responsibilities in

[117] See Alpheus Todd, *Parliamentary Government in England*, vol. 2, pp. 726–44, for particulars of the nineteenth-century cases.

[118] From time to time senior judges have doubtless persuaded their aberrant or infirm brethren to resign.

[119] Roberts-Wray, op. cit., pp. 490–501.

[120] Supreme Court Act 1981, s. 11(8), (9).

[121] ibid., s. 11(2).

[122] Courts Act 1971, ss 17(4), 21(6). A Circuit judge was removed in 1983 following his conviction for smuggling and a £2,000 fine. The Lord Chancellor is directed to satisfy himself before recommending a person for appointment as a Circuit judge that that person's health is satisfactory (s. 16(4)).

A Recorder may also be removed for failure to comply with the conditions of his appointment as to requirements to officiate (s. 21(3), (6)). He will be appointed for a fixed term, which may be renewed but not beyond the age of seventy-two.

[123] *Ex p. Ramshay* (1852) 18 Q.B. 173.

[124] Lord Hailsham L.C., *The Times*, 1 October 1985.

[125] Justices of the Peace Act 1979, ss 8, 14.

relation to the administration of justice are distributed among several Ministers – the Lord Chancellor, the Home Secretary, and the Law Officers of the Crown (the Attorney-General and the Solicitor-General for England and Wales). The Scottish Law Officers are the Lord Advocate and the Solicitor-General for Scotland; the Secretary of State for Scotland also has responsibility for aspects of the Scottish legal system, which differs in many ways from the English.

The Lord Chancellor's duties[126] are multifarious, demanding the utmost delicacy and an extensive familiarity with lawyers and the law. As we have seen, he is head of the Judiciary, a Cabinet Minister and Speaker of the House of Lords. He seldom sits as a judge, but is responsible for arranging who shall sit to hear cases in the House of Lords and the Judicial Committee of the Privy Council. Many of his functions in relation to judicial appointments have been mentioned, but there are others; thus he appoints Chancery Masters, the senior Master of the Queen's Bench Division, judges' clerks, county court registrars and the legally qualified chairmen of certain statutory tribunals. He is chairman of the committees that make rules of procedure for the Supreme Court[127] and the Crown Court and appoints the members of the corresponding body for county courts. To an increasing extent he has assumed responsibilities for matters connected with the administration of criminal justice. It was he, not the Home Secretary, who was the progenitor of the Courts Act 1971, and it is he who appoints the officials of the Crown Court. He is also the Minister responsible for law reform on the civil side. In this context by far the most important advisory body is the Law Commission,[128] composed of a High Court judge as chairman and full-time Commissioners appointed by the Lord Chancellor. The Commission has a small but highly qualified research staff, and parliamentary counsel are attached to it as draftsmen. Before the Commission issues a formal report with firm proposals, it will hold extensive consultations, usually produce a preliminary working paper, meet with a specialist advisory committee and invite comments from representative bodies of lawyers and individuals. The Commission has produced detailed schemes ranging from divorce law reform to codification of the criminal law and statute law revision, and its reports have

---

[126] They are summarized in R. F. V. Heuston, *Lives of the Lord Chancellors 1885–1940* (1964), Introduction. Doubts as to whether a Roman Catholic may hold the office have been removed in favour of adherents of that faith: Lord Chancellor (Tenure of Office and Discharge of Ecclesiastical Functions) Act 1974.

[127] cf. *Bates* v. *Lord Hailsham of St Marylebone* [1972] 1 W.L.R. 1373.

[128] See Law Commissions Act 1965. There is a separate Law Commission for Scotland. The Commissions have also made numerous reports on criminal law reforms.

strengthened the position of the Lord Chancellor, jostling with his ministerial colleagues for places in the legislative queue. Several bills emanating from the Law Commission have been passed as private members' bills. The Law Reform Committee is one of the part-time bodies which advises the Lord Chancellor. Again, he appoints the members of the Council on Tribunals [129] which has various supervisory, consultative and advisory functions with regard to statutory tribunals and inquiries; the Council makes reports to him. He exercises a general superintendence over the legal aid and advice scheme in civil matters for persons of modest means; the scheme is administered by the Legal Aid Board, which is appointed by him.[130] Administrative responsibility for the legal aid scheme in criminal matters has been transferred to the Lord Chancellor from the Home Secretary; decisions to grant legal aid orders are made by the criminal courts themselves.[131] If the Lord Chancellor has not enough to occupy his time, he can make speeches for the Government in the House of Lords or address his mind to his extensive ecclesiastical patronage or his responsibilities for the Land Registry and the Public Record Office.

Another function of the Lord Chancellor is to appoint the Official Solicitor to the Supreme Court and to give him general directions as to the performance of his duties. Among the multifarious duties performed by the Official Solicitor as a 'general sweeper-up · of messes'[132] is representation of infants, mental patients and persons committed for contempt of court, particularly if they are unrepresented in forthcoming judicial proceedings.

The Home Secretary is in effect the Minister of the Interior, though he also has responsibilities for Westminster's relations with the Channel Islands and the Isle of Man. Some of his responsibilities with regard to law and order have only a tenuous connection with the administration of justice – for example, implementing (or not implementing) the reports of constituency boundary commissions; superintending the machinery for the conduct of elections; immigration, deportation, extradition, naturalization and the general regulation of aliens and Commonwealth immigrants; control of firearms, poisons and dangerous drugs. The Director General of the Security Service (M I5) is personally answerable to him. Other functions impinge on the administration of justice; he is the

---

[129] See ch. 31.
[130] See Legal Aid Act 1988, Part II; and Parts IV (advice and assistance), IV (civil legal aid) and V (criminal legal aid).
[131] Legal Aid Act 1974, Part II. See further *R.* v. *Derby JJ., ex p. Kooner* [1971] 1 Q.B. 147 (implied duty of magistrates to provide counsel in committal proceedings for murder).
[132] The then Official Solicitor's own description (1966) 63 *Law Society's Gazette* at 338.

police authority for the Metropolitan Police and supervises local police forces;[133] he is generally responsible for the penal system and the treatment of offenders, and looks after prisons, other custodial establishments and the probation service; he has administrative responsibilities for magistrates' courts and the general working of the system of lay magistrates (though the Lord Chancellor and local magistrates' courts committees discharge important functions in this field). It is he who advises the Queen on the exercise of the prerogative of mercy. He is broadly responsible for not only the administration but also the reform of the criminal law, and is advised by a Criminal Law Revision Committee.

The Attorney-General[134] is the principal legal adviser to government Departments. He appears in court on their behalf in important cases, and gives them formal and informal opinions on difficult questions of law out of court. Reference has already been made to his important role in scrutinizing drafts of bills; he is also a valuable member of committees on bills. These functions, and some of his other responsibilities,[135] are dischargeable by the Solicitor-General (who is not a solicitor). The Law Officers, though members of the Government, do not now have seats in the Cabinet.

The Attorney-General has a number of non-political functions. As guardian of the public interest, he may institute civil proceedings in the High Court for the vindication of public rights – for example, to restrain a local authority from exceeding its powers, or a private individual from perpetrating repeated breaches of by-laws or other minor criminal offences. He may take such proceedings on his own initiative or at the request of other persons or bodies lacking a sufficient personal interest to sue on their behalf; he has an absolute discretion whether to proceed.[136] Again, he appears as an independent officer of State before judicial tribunals of inquiry. His role in criminal proceedings is of special constitutional importance. He can select the place of trial on indictment.[137] He can enter a *nolle prosequi* to stop any trial of an indictable offence: this incidentally allows him to grant immunity from prosecution, frequently in return for information. His leave is required before certain classes of criminal proceedings (for example, for breaches of the Official Secrets Acts) can be instituted. He

---

[133] See ch. 20.
[134] For the fullest accounts, see J. Ll. J. Edwards, *The Law Officers of the Crown* (1964) and *The Attorney-General: Politics and the Public Interest* (1984).
[135] See Law Officers Act 1944.
[136] See generally de Smith, *Judicial Review of Administrative Action* (4th edn, 1980), ch. 9 and *Gouriet* v. *Union of Post Office Workers* [1978] A.C. 435.
[137] He can also determine the venue in civil cases involving the Crown.

can institute criminal proceedings, or instruct the Director of Public Prosecutions to take over a private prosecution and offer no evidence if a *nolle prosequi* cannot be entered or if it is preferable not to go through the formality of entering a *nolle prosequi*. These discretionary powers are probably unchallengeable in any court,[138] and they could be abused to serve party political purposes. But in performing these functions he is obliged by convention to exercise an independent discretion, not dictated by his colleagues in the Government, though he is at liberty to (and sometimes should) consult them and obtain their views in a case with political implications. In 1985 the Attorney-General's decision (taken after he had consulted the Solicitor-General and the Director of Public Prosecutions) to prosecute Clive Ponting under section 2 of the Official Secrets Act 1911 for leaking confidential information to Tam Dalyell M.P. about the sinking of the *General Belgrano* in the Falklands conflict aroused much controversy. Mr Ponting was acquitted.[139] Similarly, his role in the decision in 1987 to investigate possible breaches of that section arising out of an article in the *New Statesman* on the parliamentary funding of a spy satellite, 'Project Zircon', caused considerable parliamentary debate.[140] In 1924 the circumstances in which the Attorney-General was suspected of having yielded to Cabinet pressure in withdrawing a prosecution for sedition led to a successful vote of censure on the Government and its downfall.[141] He appoints, is politically answerable for, and 'superintends' the Director of Public Prosecutions,[142] an official appointed by the Home Secretary but with his own Department. The Director of Public Prosecutions himself instructs counsel and solicitors to conduct prosecutions in cases referred to him by Departments and in other serious or important cases (in some of which he alone is entitled to prosecute, or proceedings cannot be undertaken except with his leave), and can take over prosecutions from private persons. He undertakes about three thousand such prosecutions a year. He also advises the police at their request whether there is sufficient evidence to justify a prosecution. His advice, though not binding, carries great weight.

[138] See *R.* v. *Allen* (1862) 1 B. & S. 850 on the prerogative power to enter a *nolle prosequi*. cf. Dickens (1972) 35 *Mod L. Rev.* 347, suggesting that in some contexts his discretion may not be unlimited. And see p. 595, below.

[139] See 73 H.C. Deb. *737–830* (18 February 1985); Clive Ponting, *The Right to Know* (1985). *R.* v. *Ponting* [1985] *Crim. L. Rev.* 318.

[140] See 109 H.C. Deb. *330* (written answers 29 January 1987); 109 H.C. Deb. *815–62* (3 February 1987). No prosecutions followed.

[141] Edwards, op. cit., chs 10 and 11; Geoffrey Wilson, *Cases and Materials* (2nd edn, 1976), pp. 514–19.

[142] Prosecution of Offences Act 1985, s. 2. See above, p. 360.

In a number of newly self-governing Commonwealth countries with politically appointed Attorney-Generals, the Director of Public Prosecutions is given judicial security of tenure by the constitution and is vested with an exclusive independent responsibility for decisions to take over, continue or discontinue prosecutions. Where he decides to institute criminal proceedings himself, the constitution will provide that he shall not act under the direction of any other person. This constitutional device – and there are others designed to produce a similar effect [143] – emphasizes both the importance attached to the maintenance of public confidence in the process of prosecution and the precarious delicacy of the balance achieved by habits of political self-restraint in Britain. It is not too much to say that in Britain the independence of the Judiciary and the impartiality of the administration of criminal justice are maintained *in spite of* the strictly legal powers vested in Parliament and the Executive.

[143] cf. Roberts-Wray, op. cit., pp. 354–5.

Chapter 20

Police[1]

Status[2] and functions

A police officer has often been likened to a citizen in uniform. In the first place, every citizen has powers to arrest without warrant and to use reasonable force in the prevention of crime;[3] the police are the specialists. Secondly, for most offences it is open to any person to institute a prosecution; it so happens that the initiators are usually policemen.[4] Thirdly, a person unlawfully arrested by a police officer is not obliged to submit tamely to restraint; he can use reasonable force to free himself. Fourthly, police officers are not above the law, and if they exceed their powers and duties they can be sued or prosecuted in the ordinary courts according to the general principles of civil and criminal liability.

For a number of reasons this kind of analogy is not very helpful. Police officers have powers of arrest, entry, search and seizure going far beyond those of the ordinary citizen.[5] If a police officer arrests the wrong man, even if no criminal offence has been committed at all, the arrest is not necessarily wrongful in the sense of being unlawful; special defences are available to the police.[6] Since police powers of arrest are extensive, discreet non-resistance may be the better part of valour; the

[1] See L. Lustgarten, *The Governance of Police* (1986).
[2] For a searching and unorthodox analysis, see Geoffrey Marshall, *Police and Government* (1965). See, however, the judgments in the Court of Appeal in *R. v. Metropolitan Police Commissioner, ex p. Blackburn* [1968] 2 Q.B. 118.
[3] Police and Criminal Evidence Act 1984, s. 24; Criminal Law Act 1967, s. 3. See further ch. 24.
[4] See above, p. 360. In Scotland most prosecutions are launched by Procurators-Fiscal, who are appointed by and responsible to the Lord Advocate; the police cannot initiate a prosecution, or indeed decide whether to prosecute.
[5] See L. H. Leigh, *Police Powers in England and Wales* (2nd edn, 1985); St J. Robilliard and J. McEwan, *Police Powers and the Individual* (1986).
[6] See generally ch. 24.

citizen can vindicate his rights (if any) after the event. Police powers to prosecute for criminal offences may not differ significantly from those of other persons; in practice, however, the exercise of police discretion whether or not to start criminal proceedings can be of great importance. Again, the police have special common-law duties in connection with the maintenance of law and order,[7] and it is a statutory offence for anyone wilfully to obstruct a constable in the execution of his duties.[8] It is also a statutory offence to waste the time of the police by knowingly making false reports that require investigation.[9] It is no part of a citizen's duties to investigate alleged crimes, take statements and interrogate suspects; but these are duties of the police, which are now largely governed by the Police and Criminal Evidence Act 1984.[10] Police officers have, but the ordinary citizen has not, coercive powers to regulate traffic, processions and the conduct of public meetings. Members of a police force cannot become M.P.s[11] or indeed 'take any active part in politics'.[12] It is an offence to incite them to 'disaffection';[13] officers below the rank of superintendent cannot join a trade union[14] (though they belong to a statutory negotiating body, the Police Federation);[15] they are subject to a detailed disciplinary code.

---

[7] cf. *Blackburn*'s case (above) where the court conceded that a chief constable had discretionary powers in this field but emphasized that they were not absolute. In this case the Commissioner had decided for the time being not to prosecute gaming clubs for breaches of the Gaming Acts in the absence of special circumstances; held, that this was a breach of legal duty owed to the general public, and potentially enforceable in an appropriate form of proceedings against the Commissioner. See further *Buckoke* v. *G.L.C.* [1971] Ch. 655 (wide discretion of police not to prosecute fire engine drivers ignoring red traffic signals); *R.* v. *Metropolitan Police Commissioner, ex p. Blackburn (No. 3)* [1973] Q.B. 241 (reasonable discretion conceded to police in enforcing obscenity laws).

The police have a duty to protect persons and their property against reasonably apprehended violence. In principle, therefore, a police authority cannot impose a charge for supplying extra protection to persons in need of it. However, if 'special' protection is requested going beyond what is reasonably necessary in the circumstances, a charge can be made by the police as a condition of supplying it: Police Act 1964, s. 15 (giving statutory effect to the rule laid down in *Glasbrook Bros. Ltd* v. *Glamorgan C.C.* [1925] A.C. 270). Chief constables have a discretion in determining the ambit of their duty in any given situation, but their opinion is not conclusive and the issue of financial liability for 'special' protection is potentially justiciable. See generally Weatherill [1988] *Public Law* 106.

[8] Police Act 1964, s. 51(3); pp. 468–70.

[9] Criminal Law Act 1967, s. 5(2).

[10] See Part V; pp. 470–71.

[11] House of Commons Disqualification Act 1975, s. 1.

[12] Police (Discipline) Regulations 1985, S.I. 1985, No. 518.

[13] Police Act 1964, s. 53.

[14] Officers of that rank, and above, are represented, respectively, by non-statutory bodies, the Superintendents' Association and the Association of Chief Police Officers: ibid., s. 44(6).

[15] ibid., ss 44, 47. But the Home Secretary may authorize the Police Federation to become

Constables are public officers. It is arguable that they are Crown servants. On appointment, a constable must declare that he will well and truly serve the Queen. For certain purposes he is undoubtedly an officer of the Crown;[16] and the maintenance of law and order, the preservation of the 'Queen's peace', is pre-eminently a function of executive government; and books on local government law list 'police' among the local government services. A police officer is not paid directly out of central government funds, and except in the Metropolitan area he is neither appointed nor dismissible even indirectly by the Crown. He is appointed and dismissible by the chief constable of a local police force (if he is below the rank of assistant chief constable) and paid by the local police authority. He is under the command of the chief constable, who is appointed by the local authority and can be removed by that authority on prescribed grounds. If a police officer commits a tort, such as assault or negligence, in the purported exercise of his duties, vicarious liability attaches not to the Crown[17] or the local authority[18] but to the chief constable, who is entitled to be indemnified out of local police funds.[19]

A chief constable is nobody's servant but an independent officer upon whom powers and duties are directly conferred by law for the benefit of the populace.[20] His constitutional status remains anomalous and puzzling, even after the re-organization of the police system implemented by the Police Act 1964. It is still not clear whether anyone is entitled to give him instructions as to the performance of any of his duties, or to what extent the Home Secretary is politically answerable for decisions taken by chief constables outside the Metropolis. The rank and file of a police force obviously do not enjoy a comparable degree of autonomy, but one cannot identify any single person or body as their employer and for this reason they can still be regarded as 'independent' public officers rather than employees.

---

associated with a body outside the police service: Police Act 1972, s. 1, and under the Police Negotiating Board Act 1980, s. 1, the Board may consider matters such as pay, hours of duty, leave and pensions.

[16] See the review of authority and principle in *Att.-Gen. for New South Wales* v. *Perpetual Trustee Co.* [1955] A.C. 457; and see also *Fisher* v. *Oldham Corporation* [1930] 2 K.B. 364. For the purpose of the Official Secrets Acts a police officer is a person holding office under the Crown: *Lewis* v. *Cattle* [1938] 2 K.B. 454. And see *Coomber* v. *Berks JJ.* (1883) 9 App. Cas. 61.

[17] See Crown Proceedings Act 1947, s. 2(6).

[18] *Fisher* v. *Oldham Corporation* (above; wrongful arrest).

[19] Police Act 1964, s. 48. There is a *discretion* to indemnify police officers in other circumstances.

[20] See *R.* v. *Metropolitan Police Commissioner, ex p. Blackburn* [1968] 2 Q.B. 118 at 135–6, 138, 148–9.

Organization and control

The absence of a national police force is explained partly by apprehensions of central political control but mainly by the course of
historical development.[21] The organization of professional disciplined
police forces only began at the end of the eighteenth century. In 1829
the Metropolitan Police Force was created under the direction of the
Home Secretary, Sir Robert Peel.[22] The establishment of borough
police forces was made compulsory in 1835 and county forces in 1856.
If the broad pattern of local organization were to be disrupted, this
would be construed as yet another blow at the principle of local
government. In 1962 a majority of members of the Royal Commission
on the Police opposed the idea of centralization, but recommended
rationalization and closer Home Office involvement in promoting
coordination and efficiency.[23] Most of its recommendations were
accepted.

The police authority for the Metropolitan Police District (which
excludes the City of London with its unique system) is the Home
Secretary. He recommends the appointment of the Commissioner who
commands the force, and Assistant Commissioners. He appears to have
a general power, exercised in practice with great restraint, to give
directions to the Commissioner as to the operational control of the
Metropolitan Police, and can be asked detailed questions in Parliament
about the conduct of the force; but according to views expressed by the
Court of Appeal he cannot give directions to the Commissioner as to
the institution of prosecutions.[24] However, the special position of a
police authority was illustrated in 1972 where Mr Reginald Maudling
was impelled to resign from the office of Home Secretary because the
Special Branch of the Metropolitan Police would be inquiring into the
activities of one of his former business associates. Over local forces the
Home Secretary's power is indirect, though it was extended by the

---

[21] The leading single-volume work is T. A. Critchley, *A History of the Police in England and
Wales, 900–1966* (2nd edn, 1978). See also F. W. Maitland, *Justice and Police* (1885); C.
K. Allen, *The Queen's Peace* (1953). For a monumental and highly readable survey, see
L. Radzinowicz, *A History of English Criminal Law and its Administration from 1750* (4
vols).

[22] Hence the term 'bobbies'.

[23] Cmnd 1728 (1962). For comments on this Report see Hart [1963] *Public Law* 283; and
on the Police Act 1964, Regan [1966] *Public Law* 13; Pollard [1966] *Public Law* 35.

[24] Or according to the views expressed in the judgments in that case (*R.* v. *Metropolitan
Police Commissioner, ex p. Blackburn* [1968] 2 Q.B. 118), other aspects of law
enforcement; *sed quare*. The Director General of the Security Service is directly
answerable to the Home Secretary, and he also works in collaboration with the Special
Branch of the Metropolitan Police.

Police Act 1964.[25] Each local police authority outside London is composed in the same way; two-thirds of its members are local councillors and one-third lay magistrates. Combined authorities constituted by amalgamations have the same proportions of councillors and magistrates. Police are a county responsibility. Following the abolition of the metropolitan county councils,[26] metropolitan county police authorities were established for those areas.[27] The police authority appoints a chief constable, a deputy chief constable and assistant chief constables, subject to the concurrence of the Home Secretary. A chief constable must have had two years' experience in another police force in the rank of inspector or above. The authority may, with the Home Secretary's approval, retire a chief, deputy or assistant chief constable compulsorily in the interests of efficiency.[28] The Home Secretary may also require an authority to retire a chief constable on this ground,[29] in which case he must appoint an independent person to conduct an inquiry into any representations made by the officer concerned; where compulsory retirement is imposed by a police authority he *may* cause such an inquiry to be held; in any event the officer must be given adequate notice coupled with a fair opportunity to be heard, according to natural justice. Senior officers are also dismissible for a breach of disciplinary regulations, after a hearing before an independent person; an appeal lies to the Home Secretary. The chief constable himself appoints and promotes other ranks and is the disciplinary authority;[30] disciplinary procedure is judicialized, and the chief constable must not sit if he is in effect a party to the proceedings or a witness; appeal again lies to the Home Secretary.[31]

Operational control is vested in the chief constable. The police authority is charged with the duty of securing the maintenance of an adequate and efficient local police force.[32] Subject to Home Office

---

[25] The Act was amended by the Local Government Act 1972, ss 107, 196, 272, Sched. 30.

[26] See below, pp. 397–8.

[27] Local Government Act 1985, s. 24.

[28] Police Act 1964, ss 5(4), 6(5). The officer must first be given an opportunity to make representations on his own behalf; cf. *Ridge* v. *Baldwin* [1964] A.C. 40, where this right was inferred from his status as the holder of a public office.

[29] Police Act 1964, s. 29. In 1985 the Home Secretary required the Derbyshire police authority to retire its chief constable in the interests of efficiency – the first use of this power.

[30] He is also responsible for the appointment and dismissal of special constables and police cadets.

[31] See S.I. 1985, No. 518, Reg. 12; Police Act 1964, s. 33(3); Police and Criminal Evidence Act 1984, s. 101. Officers of all ranks have the right to legal representation at disciplinary proceedings: S.I. 1985, No. 518 (reversing the effect of *Maynard* v. *Osmond* [1977] Q.B. 240).

[32] Police Act 1964, s. 4(1).

regulations or approval, it is responsible for determining the size and establishment of the force and providing and maintaining buildings, vehicles and equipment.[33] It is entitled to receive an annual report from the chief constable on the policing of the area, and to request him to give other reports from time to time, but with the Home Secretary's concurrence he may decline to supply information if its disclosure would be contrary to the public interest or unnecessary for the discharge of the authority's functions.[34] The scope of these exceptions is as obscure as the scope of those functions. It can be inferred that the authority may properly give the chief constable advice; it is doubtful whether it is competent to give him any instructions outside the administrative sphere,[35] and it cannot instruct him whether or how to comply with his duty to enforce the criminal law.[36]

The powers of the Home Office now dwarf those of local police authorities.[37] The Home Secretary's powers in relation to senior appointments and appeals have already been mentioned. In addition, he has and exercises powers to make regulations[38] on establishment, discipline, pay, pensions, allowances, training, duties, leave, housing, uniforms and equipment. He too is required to exercise his functions so as to promote policy efficiency.[39] He has powers of inspection, withholding grants, inquiry and compulsory amalgamation of forces; and he may call upon chief constables to furnish him with reports on the policing of their areas.[40] There is a central inspectorate of police, with a Chief Inspector of Constabulary who makes an annual report to him; the report is published and laid before Parliament. The Home Office grant to local police forces is 50 per cent of the net expenditure of the force, the other half being raised by precepts on the local authorities within the police district. The Home Secretary has a discretion to withhold a grant if dissatisfied with the efficiency of a local force or with a proposed appointment to a senior post; this power

---

[33] ibid., s. 4(4). This statutory responsibility does not affect the Home Secretary's power under the royal prerogative to supply chief constables directly with, e.g., CS gas: see *R.* v. *Secretary of State for the Home Department, ex p. Northumbria Police Authority*, [1988] 1 All E.R. 556 (C.A.).

[34] ibid., s. 12.

[35] Councillors may put questions to a designated member of a police authority as to the exercise of the authority's functions (s. 11).

[36] *R.* v. *Metropolitan Police Commissioner, ex p. Blackburn* [1968] 2 Q.B. 118 (duty owed to members of the public).

[37] See especially Regan [1966] *Public Law* 13.

[38] See Police (Discipline) Regulations 1985 (S.I. 1985, No. 518) for the wide range of topics covered.

[39] Police Act 1964, s. 28.

[40] ibid., s. 30. An annual report must be submitted. See generally Part II of the Act.

is no formality, and has been threatened or exercised several times since 1945. He can impose a compulsory scheme for amalgamation of forces by statutory instrument after holding a local inquiry, if the local police authorities concerned fail to produce an acceptable voluntary scheme; the number of separate forces was in fact substantially reduced after the Police Act 1964. He can conduct an *ad hoc* independent inquiry into the conduct of a force. The only important power not explicitly confided in him is to direct chief constables as to the conduct of their forces, but the power of suasion is reinforced by the other sanctions available to him.

Both in strict law and in their practical operation, these go far beyond the normal range of powers exercised by central government Departments over local authorities and their officers. Moreover, the general power to call for reports from chief constables means that parliamentary accountability of the Home Secretary for local police matters is potentially wide. And it must be stressed that under section 28 of the Police Act 1964 the Secretary of State is placed under a duty to use his enumerated powers 'in such manner and to such extent as appears to him to be best calculated to promote the efficiency of the police'. However, Home Secretaries still take a restrictive view of their obligations to answer parliamentary questions about law enforcement outside the Metropolis.

The inner city riots in 1981, and particularly the violent disorder associated with some industrial disputes during the 1980s (such as the miners' strike of 1984–5[41]) produced tension between chief constables and certain local councils and police authorities, and between the latter bodies and the Government. The creation in 1982 of an *ad hoc* national reporting centre at Scotland Yard to coordinate reinforcements for hard-pressed local forces exacerbated this tension, because some people believed that it was the beginning of a national police force designed, broadly, to do the Government's bidding. That fear was unfounded: but certainly the Government gave moral and political support to chief constables who used their resources to the full to contain disorder.

The Police and Criminal Evidence Act 1984[42] requires each chief constable to arrange in his area to obtain the views of local inhabitants about policing and to seek their cooperation in preventing crime.

A number of police forces exist outside the scheme of the Police Act 1964. The main ones are the Ministry of Defence Police[43] and the British Transport Police.[44]

---

[41] See S. Spencer, *Called to Account* (1985).
[42] Section 106.
[43] Ministry of Defence Police Act 1987.
[44] Transport Act 1962, ss 69–71.

Complaints

The police in Britain have attached very great importance to the maintenance of friendly relations with the general public. For this purpose they need the backing of the Home Secretary and local police authorities. They will, moreover, go to considerable lengths to avoid the appearance of partisan bias, to be approachable and generally to be at one with the people, offering helpful advice, answering silly questions, directing passers-by to their destinations, looking after lost children and generally taking on a number of responsibilities cast on them neither by statute nor by common law. Except in parts of Northern Ireland, the police have contrived on the whole to retain the confidence of the bulk of the local community. They have been least successful in their relations with younger coloured immigrants.[45]

Complaints of unnecessary harshness and of malpractices in conducting investigations and interrogations are not uncommon and are sometimes substantiated. On the other hand, complaints are often instigated by miscreants or persons with political axes to grind, and it is understandable that the police would wish complaints to be investigated by those who are sympathetically aware of their own problems. It is especially important that the complaints procedure be fair, because the aggrieved citizen in reality has no other form of redress – for how is he expected to obtain evidence against the police? An action in the courts would be doomed without it, and could be very expensive as a result. The Parliamentary Commissioner for Administration has never had power to investigate complaints against the individual members of police forces or against local policy authorities, and his jurisdiction to consider complaints against the Home Secretary in respect of police affairs (for example, in the Metropolitan Police District) has been construed as covering administrative matters only.[46] The Police Act 1976 went part of the way towards introducing an independent element in police complaints procedures while keeping a police presence. The result was not, however, entirely satisfactory,[47] and the Government

---

[45] See, for example, *Police–Immigrant Relations*, a Report of the House of Commons Select Committee on Race Relations and Immigration (H.C. *471–1* (1971–72)); Lord Scarman, The Brixton Disorders, Cmnd 8427 (1981).

[46] Under Schedule 2 to the Parliamentary Commissioner Act 1967 complaints against the Home Office can be entertained. Under paragraph 5 of Schedule 3 action taken by or with the authority of the Secretary of State for the purpose of investigating crime cannot be inquired into. See also section 5(2) of the Act, conditionally barring investigation of complaints about maladministration in connection with disciplinary matters. *Semble* Home Office refusal to consent to a senior local appointment could be investigated on a complaint initiated by the person aggrieved.

[47] For a statement of the criticisms of the 1976 procedures see Police Complaints Board:

decided to develop it further. The Police and Criminal Evidence Act 1984, Part IX, is the result.[48]

When a member of the public makes a complaint against the police it must be forwarded to the chief constable who has to decide whether it should be formally investigated.[49] In order to do so he may request the help of an officer from another police area.[50] The chief constable must refer certain serious (and may refer other) complaints to the Police Complaints Authority, which consists of a chairman and not less than eight members, none of whom shall be or have been police officers.[51] It is then the duty of the Authority to supervise the complaint, and it may ask an officer from another force to investigate such a complaint. At the end of the investigation the Authority reports to the chief constable.[52] If as a result the chief constable thinks that a criminal prosecution (rather than internal police disciplinary action) could be started against one of his officers, he must refer the matter to the Director of Public Prosecutions. Should the chief constable decide not to do so, the Authority can direct him to do so, or it may in the alternative direct him to begin police disciplinary measures if he decides not even to do that.[53] There is therefore a substantial independent element involved in these procedures.

The chief constable, or the Authority, may direct that disciplinary charges be brought against a police officer following a complaint. A disciplinary tribunal consisting of the chief constable and two members of the Authority decides whether the charge is proved or not, by a majority if necessary; if there is a finding of guilt, the chief constable decides on the punishment, after considering any recommendation from the chairman (who must have consulted the other members on the

---

Triennial Review Report, Cmnd 7966 (1980); the Board thought that the criticisms were unfounded. See also House of Commons Home Affairs Committee, H.C. *98* (1981–2).

[48] The scheme is explained in Cmnd 9072 (1983). See also V. Bevan and K. Lidstone, *A Guide to the Police and Criminal Evidence Act 1984* (1985), ch. 9; Robilliard and McEwan, op. cit., ch. 7; S.I. 1985, Nos 520, 671, 673.

[49] Provision is made in the Police and Criminal Evidence Act 1984, s. 85 for informal resolution of complaints. Complaints against an officer of chief superintendent rank and above must be referred to the local police authority: the chief constable has no jurisdiction. So in the case of Mr John Stalker, Deputy Chief Constable of Greater Manchester, the police authority appointed the Chief Constable of West Yorkshire to investigate complaints which had been made against him. The chief constable investigated and reported to the police authority, which exonerated Mr Stalker.

[50] ibid.

[51] 1984 Act, s. 83 and sched. 4.

[52] ibid., s. 89.

[53] ibid., ss 92, 93.

matter).[54] If the policeman is charged with a criminal offence and is acquitted or convicted of it, he may not be charged with a disciplinary offence which is in substance the same as that criminal offence; but if the disciplinary charge itself consists in having been found guilty of a crime, that provision does not apply.[55]

It remains to be seen whether the 1984 Act has established a system which will enjoy the equal confidence of police and public, but it seems to be a major improvement on what went before. The Authority, at any rate, believes that Part IX of the 1984 Act is working well.[56] It may be that the Act is yet another step in the desirable evolution of police complaints procedures into a fully independent process.

[54] ibid., s. 94.
[55] ibid., s. 104.
[56] See Police Complaints Authority, Triennial Review 1985–1988, H.C. *466* (1987–8).

Chapter 21

Local Government:
A Sketch

This chapter is concerned with local government in England and Wales, the structure of which was radically changed by the Local Government Act 1972[1] and further revised by the Local Government Act 1985. Scottish local government was reconstructed by the Local Government (Scotland) Act 1973.[2] In Northern Ireland, where the position is fundamentally different, the complex and controversial local government system has been simplified under Northern Ireland legislation, and major local authority functions have been or are being transferred to the central government or *ad hoc* bodies.

Structure and functions

Under the Local Government Act 1972 England was divided into six metropolitan counties outside London (Greater Manchester, Merseyside, South Yorkshire, Tyne and Wear, West Midlands, and West Yorkshire), and thirty-nine non-metropolitan counties. The Conservative Government made a surprise commitment in its 1983 General Election manifesto to abolish the Greater London Council and the metropolitan county councils. On its confirmation in power at that Election it introduced what became the Local Government (Interim Provisions) Act 1984 and the Local Government Act 1985 which

[1] For the background, see Report of the Royal Commission on Local Government in England, Cmnd 4040 (1969); and also Cmnd 4276 (1970), Cmnd 4584 (1971). The changes in Wales were foreshadowed in Cmnd 3340 (1967). The main works are C. A. Cross, *Principles of Local Government Law* (7th edn, 1986 by Cross and S. Bailey); Keith Davies, *Local Government Law* (1983); A. Alexander, *The Politics of Local Government in the United Kingdom* (1982); M. Loughlin, *Local Government in the Modern State* (1986). See also J. F. Garner, *Administrative Law* (6th edn, 1986 by Garner and B. L. Jones), chs 13–19.

[2] See Cmnd 4150 (1969), Cmnd 9583 (1971). See also the Civic Government (Scotland) Act 1982.

secured that abolition.[3] The 1985 Act makes provision for joint authorities in each former metropolitan county area (made up of representatives from the district councils) and which have responsibility for county police, fire service, civil defence, and transport authorities.[4] The Local Government Act 1972 had divided the metropolitan counties into metropolitan districts, thirty-six in all. These remain, as do the names of the metropolitan counties as geographical units. For instance, the county borough of Manchester together with the parish of Ringway is one of twelve districts in the metropolitan county of Greater Manchester. The non-metropolitan counties are divided into districts; there are 296. Each county and district has its own council with executive powers and duties.

The most striking feature of the structural changes made by the 1972 Act was the abolition of the county borough. Like Bristol, these powerful unitary authorities became county districts, or like Liverpool, metropolitan districts; or they were merged with other authorities to form a district. However, a district council may petition for the district to be given the title of a borough, and existing cities and boroughs retain their formal dignities. Rural districts in almost every instance were merged with other local government areas to form county districts. Parish councils remain intact; there is also provision for urban parishes to be constituted and for parishes to be designated as towns.

In Wales the number of counties was reduced under the 1972 Act to eight; there are thirty-seven county districts. There are community councils, exercising functions broadly similar to those of parish councils and meetings in England.

Non-metropolitan county councils are responsible for education, personal social services, libraries, museums and art galleries, most aspects of transport (including highways, parking and lighting), structure plans and national parks in town and country planning (with concurrent powers in most other aspects), refuse disposal, consumer protection services (for example, weights and measures, foods and drugs), police and fire services, residual housing powers, and certain other functions exercisable concurrently with districts. Among the more important matters for which districts have primary or sole responsibility are housing, public health, markets, refuse collection, and local plans and development control in the field of town and country planning. In the metropolitan county areas, the district councils are the authorities responsible for education, personal social services and libraries; as

---

[3] See Cmnd 9063 (1983).
[4] Local Government Act 1985, ss 23–42.

already explained, joint county authorities have charge of police, fire, civil defence and transport, while most other services have been devolved to the district authorities (in Greater London, to the London boroughs).

The demarcation of functions is in some respects complex and awkward, but one class of authority may agree that its functions shall be discharged by another as its agent (s. 101), and authorities may appoint joint committees (s. 102). Parish councils have limited functions – for instance, responsibilities for footpaths, cemeteries, swimming baths, parks, open spaces and allotments, with some new ones – for instance, car parks and entertainments.

Local Government Boundary Commissions for England and Wales may make recommendations to the Secretary of State about alterations in the status of counties and districts, the alteration of local government areas and the construction of new areas, and changes in electoral arrangements (Part 4); the Commission for England has a limited jurisdiction in relation to London boroughs. No local authority can promote a private bill for altering the status, area or electoral arrangements for any local government unit or for forming or abolishing such a unit (s. 70).[5]

The 1972 Act (in section 262) also sought to clear up the mass of frequently inaccessible local legislation. Save where any specified Act is continued in force by statutory instrument, all existing local Acts ceased to have effect in metropolitan counties in 1979, and in non-metropolitan counties in 1986. The staging was designed to allow the new authorities to seek the re-enactment of essential local legislation, and the process has been helped by the Local Government (Miscellaneous Provisions) Act 1976 which conferred powers generally on local authorities which, before that Act, were usually obtained only by virtue of local Acts of Parliament.

Members, meetings, committees and officials

In English local government authorities there is no clearly identifiable executive branch of government. Detailed administrative decisions are made by resolutions of the council itself or its committees and subcommittees, or by officials acting under specially delegated powers.[6] The council chairman is elected to hold office for one year, and he will seldom be re-elected; in any event, he is far from being a first Minister.

[5] It is thought that the Attorney-General could obtain an injunction to restrain the introduction of such a bill before it was submitted to Parliament. See p. 87.
[6] On delegation, see pp. 404–5, 407–8.

There is no Ministry though there may be a committee with primary responsibilities for the coordination of policy; nor does a doctrine of collective responsibility (in the sense of an obligation to show or maintain unanimity) apply to committee decisions except in so far as this is required by party decisions. The council's permanent officials, unlike senior civil servants, serve the council and its committees as a whole, not merely the dominant group in those bodies.

Members

County councillors are elected for a period of four years to represent electoral divisions; all retire together. District councillors represent wards; in metropolitan districts, one third retire in each year other than an election year for the county council; in others, councillors may either retire together every fourth year or follow the metropolitan district pattern. There is no provision for a dissolution between fixed dates of elections.

The basic rules governing the conduct of local elections are similar to those for parliamentary elections. The qualifications of voters are almost identical;[7] qualification to vote can no longer be founded exclusively on the occupation of property. To be qualified for election as a councillor, however, a person must either be on the local register of electors or have been resident or have occupied property or have had his principal place of work within the area of the local authority for the twelve months preceding nomination day and the date of the election.[8] There are also differences in the list of disqualifications.[9] The main disqualification is tenure of an office of profit at the disposal of the local authority or any of its committees; this disqualifies not only council officials but also local schoolteachers.[10] Bankruptcy, surcharge by a local government auditor,[11] conviction for corrupt or illegal practices, and incurring a sentence of three months' imprisonment within five years of an election, also disqualify. Qualification to sit may be challenged either by an election petition or by moving for an injunction and a declaration that the seat is vacant. A council cannot expel one of its members, but a member's seat becomes vacant if he absents himself from meetings for six consecutive months without leave.

[7] For parliamentary elections, see pp. 238–40. Peers may, however, vote in local government elections.
[8] Local Government Act 1972, s. 79.
[9] ss 80, 81.
[10] Subject to certain exceptions (ss 80(2), (3), 81(4)).
[11] See p. 413.

The chairmen and vice-chairmen of county and district councils may be paid such expense allowances as the council thinks reasonable. Other members of the council receive travelling and subsistence allowances, and a flat-rate taxable attendance allowance or (for non-elected committee members) a small reimbursement for loss of earnings while on council business.[12] The burden of committee work can be substantial,[13] and the services of council members are almost gratuitous.

We have noted that M.P.s are now bound by resolutions of the House of Commons which seek to regulate conflicts of private and public interest.[14] For members of local authorities there are statutory rules.[15] Their general effect is as follows. A member who has a direct or indirect financial interest in a matter arising before the council or any of its committees must disclose that interest as soon as practicable, and he is disqualified from speaking or voting on that matter save where his interest is so remote or insignificant that it cannot reasonably be regarded as likely to influence him. Non-compliance with these requirements is a criminal offence, and if a disqualified member takes part in a proceeding analogous to that of a judicial tribunal (for example, where the council is exercising licensing functions), the decision can be quashed at the instance of a person aggrieved.[16] But on grounds of necessity or in the interests of the inhabitants of the area the Secretary of State for the Environment may remove a statutory disability imposed on a member. This dispensing power has been liberally exercised where exemption is requested from disqualification for speaking on a matter, less liberally where exemption from disqualification for voting is sought.

It used to be thought that the incidence of corrupt practices in local government was low. But following especially the revelations in the 'Poulson affair'[17] the Royal Commission on Standards of Conduct in Public Life was set up in 1974. It reported in 1976.[18] The Commission found that over the previous decade fourteen councillors and seventy

---

[12] ss 3(5), 5(4), 173, 174. A councillor may in the alternative choose to receive a 'financial loss allowance' under s. 24 of the Local Government, Planning and Land Act 1980.

[13] County borough councillors spent an average of two and a half hours a day on council business (Cmnd 4040 (1969), § 506). 'Special responsibility allowances' are now payable, however, under s. 26 of the 1980 Act.

[14] See p. 271.

[15] See 1972 Act, ss 94–8 for details.

[16] *R.* v. *Hendon R.D.C., ex p. Chorley* [1933] 2 K.B. 696 (grant of opposed planning permission). cf. *Murray* v. *Epsom Local Board* [1897] 1 Ch. 35 (decision to remove obstructions to passage of vehicles; interest of member had no effect on validity of decision).

[17] See above p, 195.

[18] Cmnd 6524 (1976).

local authority employees had been convicted on corruption charges, and ten councillors had been convicted on charges of failing to disclose an interest. Such figures, the Commission felt, were not alarming when it is remembered that 26,000 councillors held office in the United Kingdom – but corrupt dealings are secretive; crimes are hard to prove; there was no room for complacency. The creation of new offences and greater powers for the police, especially to inspect financial records, were recommended. Further, the Commission was of the view that there should be a statutory obligation on councillors to enter prescribed information at annual intervals in a register maintained for the purpose.[19] Legislation to give effect to these proposals is still awaited. The Widdicombe Report on the Conduct of Local Authority Business[20] advocated even more radical changes, including the taking by councillors of an oath of acceptance of a national code of conduct on local government, and a strengthening of the statutory requirements on the disclosure of financial interests.

There are Commissions for Local Administration, one for England and one for Wales, established under the Local Government Act 1974, Part III. The English Commission consists of three Local Commissioners, each of whom is responsible for a geographical area; the Parliamentary Commissioner for Administration is a member *ex officio*. They have jurisdiction to investigate alleged maladministration (which is not defined in the Act)[21] by a local authority, a police authority (*not* the police) or a water authority, provided that the action or want of action occurred after 1 April 1974. If a complaint is investigated a report is normally issued, and the authority investigated must tell the Commissioner of the steps it intends to take in the light of the report. An authority may incur expenditure in compensating a person who has suffered injustice in consequence of maladministration: Local Government Act 1978, section 1. Under section 184 of the Local Government, Planning and Land Act 1980 a local authority can no longer refuse to disclose documents to a Local Commissioner for Administration.[22] In 1977 the Government had promised legislation to give the Commissioners an unrestricted right of access.[23] In their

---

[19] This would supersede the agreement reached by the Government and local authority associations to maintain a voluntary register following the Report of the Committee on Local Government Rules of Conduct, Cmnd 5636 (1974), which had recommended a statutory register.

[20] Cmnd 9797 (1986); see McAuslan [1987] *Public Law* 154.

[21] But see *R v Local Commissioner for Administration ex p. Bradford City Council* [1979] 2 All E.R. 881, especially the judgment of Lord Denning M.R.

[22] Reversing *Re a complaint against Liverpool City Council* [1977] 1 W.L.R. 995.

[23] 932 H.C. Deb. *478* (written answers 25 May 1977).

annual report for the year ending March 1988[24] the Commissioners recorded that 4,229 complaints had been received. Of those complaints, 332 led to the issue of formal reports: 222 of them spoke of maladministration leading to injustice. Many complaints were, however, as usual settled before that stage. Most complaints were about housing and planning procedures. The average time taken to deal with complaints is between three and six months. If a Commissioner exceeds his jurisdiction when reporting on a complaint, a local authority is entitled to relief from the courts by way of judicial review.[25] No system of independent investigation, however, can be expected to reveal the extent to which local businessmen benefit from the inside information they obtain about council policies in their public capacity. In fairness, one must also emphasize the accessibility of councillors to their constituents, and the zeal with which many of them seek to obtain redress for legitimate grievances. In a sense they are themselves local Ombudsmen.

Meetings

Meetings of councils are largely concerned with consideration and ratification of reports and recommendations by committees and officers. Discussions tend to become more animated when politically contentious issues arise. The growth of party politics in local government is a modern phenomenon; Labour groups in particular will cleave to a party line and may enforce discipline by the sanction of expulsion from the party group, a development which has been seen particularly in certain London boroughs and northern cities. There has been a concomitant growth in Conservative, Social and Liberal Democratic, and Scottish and Welsh Nationalist councillors. A dwindling proportion of local councillors, particularly in rural areas, stand as Independents or as members of Ratepayers' Associations; often they are crypto-Conservatives. Nowadays local elections give a rough indication of trends of national political opinion, but turn-outs at the polls are low; moreover, the personal standing of candidates at local elections matters far more than the qualities of individual candidates at parliamentary elections.

Council meetings are presided over by the chairman. Procedure is regulated by standing orders, which may give the council power to

[24] Your Local Ombudsman: Report of the Commission for Local Administration in England for the year ended 31 March 1988.
[25] See *R. v. Commissioner for Local Administration, ex p. Eastleigh Borough Council*, [1988] 3 All E.R. 151.

exclude a member for disorderly conduct. Under the Public Bodies (Admission to Meetings) Act 1960, members of the public and the press are entitled to be present at meetings of the council, committees of the whole council and local education committees, unless the authority resolves that publicity would be contrary to the public interest by reason of the confidential nature of the business to be transacted or for any other special reason. This principle of publicity did not extend to meetings of other council committees, even committees to which executive decision-making powers had been delegated by the council; but the principle was thus extended by section 100 of the 1972 Act.

Local authority openness has been enhanced by the Local Government (Access to Information) Act 1985 – the first legislative success of the freedom of information campaign. That Act adds new sections 100A to 100K to the Local Government Act 1972.[26] All councils (other than parish and community councils[27]) must give public notice of council, council committee and sub-committee meetings, and copies of relevant documents must be made available. Such meetings must normally be open to the public, unless there is a risk that confidential information of a certain type might be disclosed,[28] in which case the public may be excluded.[29] The agenda, minutes and any relevant reports for such meetings must also be made available for public inspection for a period of six years. Meetings and documents of Community Health Councils were also brought within these provisions by the Community Health Councils (Access to Information) Act 1988.

Committees

Committee structure depends partly on the functions vested in a local authority. Under the 1972 Act the number of committees that a local authority is *required* to appoint was reduced, but the relevant authority must appoint an education committee, a police committee and a social services committee. There are also likely to be a policy and resources committee (with sub-committees on management services, finance and

---

[26] And new ss 50A–K to the Local Government (Scotland) Act 1973.

[27] And certain other authorities, including the joint county authorities in metropolitan counties, and the Inner London Education Authority.

[28] i.e. information furnished by a Government Department on terms which forbid disclosure, or information the disclosure of which is forbidden by any enactment or by a court order.

[29] The right of admission remains subject to the power to exclude the public in order to suppress or prevent disorder: 1972 Act, s. 100A(8). See also *R.* v. *Brent Health Authority, ex p. Francis* [1985] Q.B. 869.

estates), committees dealing with the various services administered by the authority (for example, housing, planning, parks), and *ad hoc* committees constituted for special purposes. There may be joint committees of two or more authorities. All committees of the council other than the finance committee and statutory committees whose composition is prescribed by law may co-opt outside members provided that two-thirds of the committee consists of members of the council. This numerical limitation does not apply to sub-committees.[30]

The powers vested in a committee may be to make recommendations to the council, or to make decisions which are merely reported to the council, or a combination of both types. A council is entitled to delegate to a committee or sub-committee (except in the case of statutory committees) any power to make decisions on behalf of the council other than power to raise money. Such a committee may also delegate powers to sub-committees.[31] These express grants of power overcome the common-law rule against sub-delegation (*delegatus non potest delegare*).[32] The council retains a concurrent power to make decisions within the scope of the delegated area,[33] but if the committee has already made a decision directly affecting individual interests the council cannot lawfully rescind or vary it,[34] though it may proceed to revoke the authority of the committee or any of its members.[35] Delegation relationships have brought forth a crop of technical legal problems, some of which remain unsolved.[36]

There is, of course, no legal reason why a committee or sub-committee endowed with executive powers should not empower a group of members or its chairman to recommend decisions (in consultation with senior officials) in individual cases, subject to the committee's or sub-committee's subsequent approval. This is in fact how a great number of detailed decisions are taken by local authorities.

Officials

The principal officer of a local authority is the chief executive or clerk to the council. His status has not been quite the same as that of a

[30] 1972 Act, ss 101, 102.
[31] ibid.
[32] *Cook* v. *Ward* (1877) 2 C.P.D. 255. Delegation of decision-making power to a sub-committee was generally unlawful before the 1972 Act.
[33] *Huth* v. *Clarke* (1890) 25 Q.B.D. 391; 1972 Act, s. 101(4).
[34] *Battelley* v. *Finsbury B.C.* (1958) 56 L.G.R. 165 (appointment of a council official by a committee).
[35] *Manton* v. *Brighton B.C.* [1951] 2 K.B. 393.
[36] See de Smith, *Judicial Review of Administrative Action* (4th edn, 1980), ch. 6.

permanent secretary to a government Department. He has had no general authority to act in the council's name, and his hierarchical authority over other 'departmental' heads (for example, the surveyor, or the chief education officer) has been nebulous and incomplete. Clerks to the larger local authorities used to be almost invariably solicitors; the lawyer plays a more prominent role in local administration than in the civil service. But under the current system a more varied set of patterns of authority has been introduced, and the chief executive is frequently not a lawyer.

Statutory obligations are cast on various classes of local authorities to appoint specific officers (for example, chief education officer, trading standards officers); the list was shortened by the 1972 Act,[37] and there is no express obligation to appoint a clerk to the council or a treasurer, though clearly councils will have to appoint officers of comparable status. Of the senior officers, some are appointable or dismissible only with the consent of a Minister; but no Minister enjoys a power in respect of local government officers corresponding to the Home Secretary's power to retire a chief constable.

Superannuation is determined by statute; the Secretary of State for the Environment has appellate functions in individual cases. Pay and conditions of service are negotiated by national and provincial councils composed of representatives of the local authorities and their employees. National staff commissions to advise the Secretary of State on such matters as recruitment and transfer have been appointed under the 1972 Act. Unlike civil servants, local government officers do not hold office subject to an overriding common-law rule of dismissibility at pleasure. Many local officers have binding contracts of employment. By statute, they are to hold office on 'such reasonable terms and conditions, including conditions as to remuneration' as the appointing authority thinks fit.[38] In some instances a Secretary of State's concurrence is required before they can be removed. An officer who is unfairly dismissed may be awarded compensation by an industrial tribunal, which may also order that he be reinstated.

On the whole, the legal powers and duties of local government officers in relation to the public have been very limited. This generalization must be qualified. In the first place, special fiduciary duties have been cast on a borough or county treasurer in the interests of the ratepayers, and if he complies with an order to pay out money for a purpose unauthorized by law he may be sued for recovery of the money

[37] s. 112(1), (3), (4).
[38] s. 112(2).

or restrained by injunction[39] or surcharged following adverse findings by the auditor.[40] Under the 1972 Act it may be that his position in these matters is no different from that of any other local government officer. Secondly, an officer having ostensible authority to bind his employers by contract may bind the local authority according to the general principles of agency although he is not in fact acting within the scope of his authorization.[41] Thirdly, the 1972 Act gives local authorities and their committees and sub-committees the general power (subject only to limited exceptions) to 'arrange' for the discharge of their functions by an official, whose acts will bind the authorities.[42] This provision extended the power that had existed since 1968 and which allowed a local planning authority to delegate to one of its officers power to determine in writing various classes of planning application, the authority being bound by his decisions.

Suppose that, under the new system, an official to whom no authorization has in fact been given purports to give a prospective builder an assurance that planning permission is not required for certain constructional work. The builder goes ahead on the faith of this assurance. The local authority then issues an enforcement notice, requiring him to discontinue the work and to demolish the buildings already put up, because he needed planning permission and did not obtain it. The builder contends that the local authority is 'estopped' (debarred) from repudiating the unauthorized assurance given by its officer, on which he has relied to his detriment. What then?

The general principle is that if public bodies or their officers give assurances that lie outside their powers, such assurances are void.[43] They can go back on such assurances, for they cannot by their own conduct extend their powers.[44] It may be that it is open to a court to treat minor deviations from the prescribed form or procedure for exercising a power as being merely non-compliance with a discretionary

---

[39] See *Att.-Gen.* v. *Wilson* (1840) Cr. & Phil. 1; *Att.-Gen.* v. *De Winton* [1906] 2 Ch. 106. For financial duties of officers and disclosure of pecuniary interest in contracts, see 1972 Act, ss 114, 115, 117.

[40] See p. 413.

[41] On agency in public law, see pp. 415, 629. The agent cannot bind the local authority to act *ultra vires*.

[42] Local Government Act 1972, s. 101. Delegation to a *member* of the authority, such as a committee chairman, is *ultra vires* the section: *R.* v. *Secretary of State for the Environment, ex p. Hillingdon L.B.C.* [1986] 1 W.L.R. 807. A local authority can even arrange for its functions in relation to a statutory committee to be discharged by an official. Power to raise money cannot be delegated.

[43] *Howell* v. *Falmouth Boat Construction Co.* [1951] A.C. 837.

[44] *Rhyl U.D.C.* v. *Rhyl Amusements Ltd*]1959] 1 W.L.R. 465; *Laker Airways Ltd* v. *Department of Trade* [1977] Q.B. 643.

requirement, not affecting the validity of what has been done.[45] And it may also be that, where an officer who has either real or ostensible authority to take a decision or give an assurance on behalf of his authority misleads a member of the public who suffers actual detriment as a result of acting on the misleading assurance,[46] his employing authority is estopped from going back on the assurance, provided that the authority itself would have had the power to make the decision or give the assurance emanating from its officer.[47] But the courts have lately shown reluctance to extend the doctrine of estoppel in administrative law.[48] The effect on local government officers of the threat of estoppel hanging over them, and the undesirability of permitting a careless statement from an officer to undermine local policy, are powerful incentives to the courts to call a halt to any further encroachment of estoppel in this area.[49] In an attempt to balance the conflicting interests, the courts have held that while an authority cannot be fettered from exercising its lawful powers it must hear representations before departing from a policy on which many affected parties have relied and acted.[50]

A local authority may also be vicariously liable in tort for damage caused by negligent mis-statements by its employees in circumstances where there is a duty to exercise reasonable care.[51]

Local government employees remain personally liable for torts committed by them, whether or not they were purporting to act in the course of their duties and whether or not the local authority is vicariously liable for the tort. But some of them have statutory powers to enter property, carry out inspections, surveys and tests, seize and destroy contaminated food and so on, which might be actionable trespasses or nuisances if done by private persons; and in some instances officers committing torts in the purported exercise of public

[45]   *Wells* v. *Minister of Housing and Local Government* [1967] 1 W.L.R. 1000.
[46]   *Norfolk C.C.* v. *Secretary of State for the Environment* [1973] 1 W.L.R. 1400.
[47]   *Lever Finance Ltd* v. *Westminster (City) L.B.C.* [1971] 1 Q.B. 222; *Robertson* v. *Minister of Pensions* [1949] 1 K.B. 227.
[48]   So, e.g., *Lever Finance* was criticized in *Western Fish Products* v. *Penrith District Council* [1981] 2 All E.R. 204; the C.A. asserted that no estoppel could prevent a statutory body from exercising its discretion.
[49]   See *Brooks and Barton* v. *Secretary of State for the Environment* (1976) 75 L.G.R. 285; *Western Fish Products* v. *Penrith D.C.* (1978) 77 L.G.R. 185.
[50]   *R.* v. *Liverpool Corporation, ex p. Liverpool Taxi Fleet Operators' Association* [1972] 2 Q.B. 299; *H.T.V.* v. *Price Commission* [1976] I.C.R. 170.
[51]   cf. *Hedley, Byrne & Co.* v. *Heller & Partners Ltd* [1964] A.C. 465; *Ministry of Housing and Local Government* v. *Sharp* [1970] 2 Q.B. 223.

functions have been exempted from liability provided that they have acted in good faith.[52]

Finance [53]

Income

Local authorities derive their income from three main sources: rates (until 1990); rentals, transport undertakings, entertainments and other facilities and services; and central government grants. Rates account for a third of their income and general grants for a slightly higher percentage. Heavy dependence on central grants has been a long-standing source of weakness in English local government.

Rates [54] are local taxes, imposed not on income or wealth but upon the occupation of land and buildings. For each rating area a valuation officer of the Inland Revenue compiles a valuation list, incorporating his assessment of the net annual value of each hereditament. The rating authority (a London borough or county district) decides annually how much it needs to raise by way of rates, and fixes the general rate at x or y pence in the pound accordingly.[55] Thus, if the rateable value of its area is £1 million, and it has to raise £600,000, it will decide to levy a rate of 60p in the pound, and a householder whose property is valued at £200 per annum will have to pay £120 in rates in two instalments. County councils and *ad hoc* local statutory authorities obtain income from rates by issuing an annual precept to the rating authorities within their area; the rating authorities must have regard to the amount precepted when determining their own rates.

Appeals against individual assessments in the valuation list lie to local valuation courts and thence to the Lands Tribunal. Farm land is

[52] See, for example, Public Health (Control of Diseases) Act 1985, s. 69. In general the courts will construe this immunity as extending only to situations where the officer has also exercised reasonable care.

[53] See the Local Government Act 1974, Parts I and II; the Local Government Finance Act 1982; the Local Government (Miscellaneous Provisions) (Scotland) Act 1981, and the Report of the Layfield Committee of Inquiry into Local Government Finance, Cmnd 6453 (1976), which recommended a local income tax and reform of the rating system; Paying for Local Government (1986) – a Green Paper on the community charge; Local Government Finance Act 1988.

[54] See the General Rate Act 1967; Local Government Act 1972, ss 147–9, Local Government Act 1974, Part II; Local Government, Planning and Land Act 1980, ss 28–47; Local Government Finance Act 1982, Part II; Rates Act 1984 (the 'rate-capping' Act); Rate Support Grants Act 1986; Rate Support Grants Act 1988.

[55] The rate must be fixed by 1 April each year: Local Government Act 1986, s. 1(1). In 1985 13 councils had failed to set a rate in order to put pressure on the Government for more grant aid: see below, p. 414.

not liable to rates, and certain other classes of hereditaments are partly or wholly exempt. Ratepayers whose income is low may be entitled to claim a rebate from the local authority.

Although hallowed by antiquity and deficient in the excruciating complexities obfuscating some forms of central taxation, rates are not a satisfactory source of revenue. They bear most heavily on the occupier with a large family and a large house. Moreover, the product of the same percentage rate will vary enormously from one rating area to another. And very big disparities between the services offered by authorities equal in status are not politically acceptable. For these reasons the Government has caused Parliament to enact legislation to abolish domestic rates in Scotland [56] and in England and Wales. In relation to England and Wales the Local Government Finance Act 1988 envisages the abolition of domestic rates and the substitution of a community charge (commonly known as a poll tax) in April 1990.[57] The community charge would be paid by all people aged eighteen and over residing in each local authority area.[58] Community charges officers have the major task of compiling and maintaining community charges registers in their areas, the first of which must be completed by December 1989. The rate of charge must be set by each local authority so that every resident in that area pays the same amount, although rebates for those on low incomes will be provided for by statutory instrument, probably up to 80 per cent of the charge. The Government believes that, as all electors in each local council area must pay the same charge, high-spending authorities who set a high level of charge will be vulnerable to rejection at the polls. Non-domestic rating will continue, but at a uniform business rate;[59] the Government estimates that the community charge will raise about 25 per cent of local revenue, business rates a further 25 per cent, and 50 per cent would be represented by Government grant.

The chequered history of central grants need not be traced. At one time the percentage grant was favoured, but this tended to direct local authorities from the path of economy unless their conduct of the service in question was subject to detailed regulation and scrutiny. A 50 per cent grant is still paid to local police authorities. Miscellaneous grants and subsidies are paid for specific purposes – for example, for housing construction and improvements, for aspects of the acquisition

[56] Abolition of Domestic Rates, Etc. (Scotland) Act 1987; see Himsworth and Walker [1987] *Public Law* 586.

[57] 1988 Act, Part I.

[58] Save prisoners, diplomats, members of visiting forces, the severely mentally handicapped, hospital patients and residents of residential homes.

[59] 1988 Act, Part III.

and development of land for planning purposes, for the construction and improvement of major roads, and for the benefit of local authorities having special responsibilities because of a high concentration of Commonwealth immigrants.[60] Grants are also made to meet the cost of rate rebates. The other form of grant is the block grant, not appropriated to specific services; its nomenclature has varied, but together with the 'domestic rate relief grant' it is now the 'rate support grant'. The sum to be allocated is determined by the Secretary of State in the light of the general economic situation and after consultation with local authority associations; he lays a rate support grant order, which is subject to the affirmative procedure, before the House of Commons each year.[61] The sums received by individual authorities vary considerably: they are dependent on local financial resources compared with the national average, and an assortment of factors such as population density, road mileage, and the proportions of school-children and old people. Rises in the costs of local authority services are borne partly out of central government funds, and the amount of the central grant has increased. But although block grants offer local authorities greater freedom of manoeuvre than ear-marked grants, the Secretary of State is enabled to control expenditure by local authorities in general and thereby to influence expenditure on particular services, and if he is dissatisfied with the standards maintained by an authority, he may reduce the grant to that authority after he has given it an opportunity to make representations to him and then obtained the approval of the House of Commons for his decision.[62] Under the Local Government Finance Act 1988, the Secretary of State will make one 'revenue support grant', arrived at in a similar way to the rate support grant.

The present Government has been determined to control the ability of certain 'high-spending' local authorities to increase their rates so as to finance such expenditure. The Rates Act 1984 was enacted for the purpose. Under Part I of that Act the Secretary of State for the Environment may report to the House of Commons those local authorities which, in his opinion, have excessive levels of expenditure in relation to general economic conditions, and he may determine for them the permissible maximum rate which they may lawfully set, thus

[60] On the last point, see Local Government Act 1966, s. 11. And see, for a more general power to make grants to especially needy authorities, Local Government Grants (Social Need) Act 1969.

[61] Local Government, Planning and Land Act 1980, ss 48–68; Local Government Finance Act 1982, ss 8–10.

[62] 1980 Act, ss 48–52. The courts will not interfere in decisions on the level of rate support grant: see *R.* v. *Secretary of State for the Environment, ex p. Nottinghamshire County Council* [1986] A.C. 240.

'rate-capping' them. The Secretary of State has rate-capped a number of authorities – not all of them Labour controlled. A similar system to limit the levels of community charge will operate under the Local Government Finance Act 1988.

Borrowing

Local authorities have general statutory borrowing powers for acquiring land and constructing buildings and public works: indeed nearly all major capital expenditure is financed out of loans. The exercise of borrowing powers has been subjected to detailed and strict central control, which was relaxed in 1971. A loan sanction must be obtained from the Secretary of State for the Environment and may be refused for a number of reasons, including the need for restricting the general level of public investment and spending.

Expenditure

Spending by local authorities is subject to more direct legal restraints. The general rule is that the local authorities can spend money only for purposes authorized by statute. Any other expenditure will be *ultra vires* and can be restrained in proceedings instituted in the High Court by the Attorney-General (on his own initiative or at the relation of a ratepayer)[63] claiming an injunction or a declaration or both. Acts reasonably incidental to powers expressly granted will be valid. To take two familiar examples, one on each side of the line, a local authority could lawfully set up a stationery, printing and binding works to deal with council documents though not explicitly empowered to do so,[64] but an authority empowered to establish washhouses where people could come to do their own washing could not embark upon a venture in municipal enterprise by setting up a laundry where most of the work was done by council employees.[65] The 1972 Act stretches the concept of incidental powers by providing that local authorities have power to do anything calculated to facilitate, or conducive to, the discharge of any of their functions.[66]

The courts have held that local authority funds are impressed with some characteristics of a public trust, and that councils owe a fiduciary duty to their ratepayers to spend money only for purposes authorized

[63] Or even possibly a ratepayer suing on his own behalf: *Prescott* v. *Birmingham Corporation* [1955] Ch. 210 (an action for a declaration).
[64] *Att.-Gen.* v. *Smethwick Corporation* [1932] 1 Ch. 562.
[65] *Att.-Gen.* v. *Fulham Corporation* [1921] 1 Ch. 440.
[66] Local Government Act 1972, s. 111(1).

by law and in accordance with proper legal principles. For example, local authorities cannot, in the absence of express statutory authority, subsidize the rents of private tenants, irrespective of the tenants' means,[67] or make free gifts to the aged,[68] or set themselves up as model employers and pay wages far in excess of those paid by private commercial or industrial undertakings. In the offensive words of Lord Atkinson (*Roberts* v. *Hopwood* (1925)), the council must have regard to businesslike considerations and the interests of their ratepayers, and not allow itself to be guided by 'eccentric principles of socialistic philanthropy, or by a feminist ambition to secure the equality of the sexes in the matter of wages . . .'.[69]

Since 1963 local authorities have been empowered by statute to incur a small amount of expenditure for any purpose not otherwise authorized which in their opinion is in the interests of their area or its inhabitants.[70] To this extent they have been relieved of the inhibitions imposed by the *ultra vires* doctrine – but to no more than that extent, for the new local authorities constituted under the London Government Act 1963 and the Local Government Act 1972 are statutory corporations even though some may still be styled boroughs.[71] They are thus limited to statutory functions.

The spending of the Greater London Council and other metropolitan county councils on publicity to oppose their abolition led to the passing of legislation[72] which prohibits local authorities from publishing any material which appears to be designed to affect support for a political party.

Audit[73]

The accounts of all local authorities are subject to audit. Under the

[67] *Taylor* v. *Munrow* [1960] 1 W.L.R. 151.
[68] *Prescott* v. *Birmingham Corporation* (see above; free travel concessions on corporation's transport undertaking). What was there held unlawful is now authorized by statute: Travel Concessions Act 1964.
[69] [1925] A.C. 578 at 594. See, for the background and aftermath, Keith-Lucas [1962] *Public Law* 52. Under the law as it then stood, the authority had an ostensibly unrestricted discretion to pay such wages as it thought fit to its employees; the district auditor and the courts imposed limitations on the exercise of this discretion. The present law empowers local authorities to pay 'reasonable remuneration'.
[70] Local Government (Financial Provisions) Act 1963, s. 6, replaced by Local Government Act 1972, s. 137. The sum to be thus used must not exceed the product of a 2p rate in any given year (1972 Act).
[71] The City of London Corporation is still a common-law corporation.
[72] Local Government Act 1986, s. 2.
[73] See R. Jones, *Local Government Audit Law* (2nd edn, 1985).

Local Government Finance Act 1982 the Audit Commission[74] undertakes the audit of local authority accounts and for the purpose
appoints auditors – either officers of the Commission or private
accountants.[75] A local authority must be consulted before an appointment is made,[76] but it may no longer choose whom to appoint.

Public notice is given of the annual audit and the accounts must be
open to public inspection. Any local government elector may appear
before the auditor and object to an item in the accounts. The auditor
may apply to the High Court or to the county court for a declaration
that any item of account is contrary to law, and the court may order any
person responsible for incurring or authorizing it to repay it and, if such
expenditure exceeds £2,000 and he was a member of a local authority at
the time of that expenditure, may order his disqualification from
membership for a specified period. An aggrieved elector may appeal to
the court against an auditor's decision not to apply for a declaration of
unlawfulness.[77] If the ground for complaint is alleged to be wilful
misconduct[78] – for example, deliberately refusing to set a rate as a
protest against Government policy towards local government – the
Audit Commission may demand that any revenue lost as a result be paid
directly by the responsible councillors.[79]

Local authorities and the courts: in brief

Like other public corporations, local authorities can sue and be sued,
prosecute and be prosecuted, in the courts. They are not Crown
servants and have never enjoyed the legal immunities and privileges of
the Crown;[80] thus, courts can award coercive orders, such as injunctions
and orders of mandamus, against them.[81] Their civil liability is

[74] 1982 Act, s. 11.
[75] s. 13(1).
[76] s. 13(3).
[77] s. 19. Acting reasonably or in the belief that the expenditure was lawful are defences.
[78] See s. 20.
[79] As happened in 1985 when a total of 13 councils acted in that way. The Audit
Commission claimed £233,000 from 80 councillors, an assessment upheld in *Lloyd and
Others* v. *McMahon* [1987] A.C. 625. The Government's reaction to the councillors'
conduct was the Local Government Act 1986, s. 1 (see above, p. 409).
[80] The leading case, dealing with the liability of an *ad hoc* statutory authority for tort (but
also governing the liability of local authorities) at a time when the Crown was exempt
from tortious liability, is *Mersey Docks and Harbour Board Trustees* v. *Gibbs* (1866)
L.R.1. H.L.93.
[81] On Crown privilege and local authorities, see *Blackpool Corporation* v. *Locker* [1948] 1
K.B. 349; but see p. 642, note 70.

determined by rules essentially the same as those applicable to non-public bodies, subject to a number of particular exceptions.

1　The power of a local authority to institute civil proceedings in its own name for the protection of the interests of local inhabitants has, on the whole, been narrowly interpreted;[82] but it is wider under the 1972 Act.[83] Yet in a case under the 1933 Act a local authority was held entitled to bring an action for libel against a hostile critic for the protection of its 'governing reputation'.[84]

2　Aspects of the *ultra vires* doctrine have already been noted. If a local authority steps outside the limits of its public powers, the defect cannot be cured merely by the acquiescence of persons adversely affected;[85] nor, *in general*, is the local authority itself precluded from asserting the invalidity of its own acts if another person seeks to rely on their legality.[86] Nor is it estopped by its acquiescence in acts by other persons from exercising its powers or duties to assert its rights against them;[87] and in the absence of statutory authority to that effect it cannot grant a valid dispensation from compliance with a statute or by-law.[88]

3　By-laws, as we have already seen, can be impugned on various grounds, each of which can be classified under the general rubric of *vires*.[89]

4　Contracts of local authorities are governed basically by private law rules, though they may contain standard terms and the disparity of bargaining power between the parties (for example, in a contract for letting a council house or flat) may be such that a contract will be analogous to a by-law. Since 1960 local authority contracts have not had to be made under seal. The general rules of agency apply, but a local authority can neither make nor become bound by a contract which is *ultra vires*. Apart from the effects of the *ultra vires* doctrine, freedom of contract is not absolute. The appointment and

[82] Local Government Act 1933, s. 276.

[83] s. 222; see *Solihull M.B.C.* v. *Maxfern Ltd* [1977] 1 W.L.R. 127; *Stoke-on-Trent City Council* v. *B. & Q. (Retail) Ltd* [1984] 2 All E.R. 332 (H.L.).

[84] *Bognor Regis U.D.C.* v. *Campion* [1972] 2 Q.B. 169 (criticized by Weir [1972A] *Camb. L.J.* 238).

[85] *Swallow and Pearson* v. *Middlesex C.C.* [1953] 1 W.L.R. 422.

[86] *Rhyl U.D.C.* v. *Rhyl Amusements Ltd* [1959] 1 W.L.R. 465; but see p. 407.

[87] *Islington Vestry* v. *Hornsey U.D.C.* [1900] 1 Ch. 695 (informal agreement to receive sewage could be repudiated; local authority could not lawfully bind itself thus).

[88] *Yabbicom* v. *R.* [1899] 1 Q.B. 444; *Redbridge L.B.C.* v. *Jaques* [1970] 1 W.L.R. 1604; *Cambridgeshire & Isle of Ely C.C.* v. *Rust* [1972] 2 Q.B. 426. For an example of an express dispensing power, see Greater London Council (General Powers) Act 1971, s. 4.

[89] See generally *Kruse* v. *Johnson* [1898] 2 Q.B. 91; and p. 353, above.

tenure of certain senior local government officers are regulated by statute. And there is a general principle of law that public authorities cannot preclude themselves from exercising their more important discretionary powers or performing their public duties by incompatible contractual or other undertakings.[90] For example, a local authority cannot bind itself to grant or not to revoke a grant of planning permission[91] or not to make a particular kind of by-law.[92] If it makes a by-law rendering performance of a contractor's obligations more burdensome, the contractor cannot thereupon repudiate the contract, though the actual operation of the burden may subsequently entitle him to treat the contract as having been frustrated.[93]

5   Local authorities are not liable in tort for doing what Parliament has authorized them to do, but the general rule[94] is that they must exercise their powers reasonably so as to avoid unnecessary encroachments on private rights; otherwise they may be liable for negligence, nuisance or trespass. There is no sound reason of principle why a local authority should be immune from liability because it is acting *ultra vires* when it commits a tort,[95] though if the tort has been committed by one of its servants[96] there may be difficulty in establishing for the purpose of vicarious liability that he was acting in the general course of his employment. In some contexts local authorities are subject to liability without fault and liability for breach of statutory duty on much the same basis as private persons.[97] Highway authorities used to be exempt from civil liability for injury attributable to negligent failure to repair, but this immunity was abolished by statute.[98] There is no general principle of law that public authorities are free from liability in respect of damage caused by non-feasance (inaction).[99] The difficulty faced by

[90] See, for example, *Ayr Harbour Trustees* v. *Oswald* (1833) 8 App. Cas. 623; and generally, J. D. B. Mitchell, *The Contracts of Public Authorities* (1954).

[91] *Ransom & Luck Ltd* v. *Surbiton B.C.* [1949] Ch. 180.

[92] *Cory (William) & Son Ltd* v. *City of London Corporation* [1951] 2 K.B. 475 (dicta).

[93] *Cory*'s case (above).

[94] Subject to various exceptions: see, for example, *Marriage* v. *East Norfolk Rivers Catchment Board* [1950] 1 K.B. 284; *Dormer* v. *Newcastle-upon-Tyne Corporation* [1940] 2 K.B. 204 at 217–19 (applying a narrow test of the duty to act reasonably).

[95] See *Campbell* v. *Paddington Corporation* [1911] 1 K.B. 869 (held liable).

[96] On the question who is a servant of a local authority in attributing vicarious liability for his torts, see *Stanbury* v. *Exeter Corporation* [1905] 2 K.B. 838; *Fisher* v. *Oldham Corporation* [1930] 2 K.B. 364.

[97] *Thornton* v. *Kirklees M.B.C.* [1979] Q.B. 626; *Meade* v. *Haringey L.B.C.* [1979] 1 W.L.R. 637.

[98] Highways Act 1980, Part IV, replacing a 1961 Act.

[99] But in some contexts the distinction between misfeasance and non-feasance is still material: see *Bradbury* v. *Enfield L.B.C.* [1967] 1 W.L.R. 1311.

a plaintiff claiming in respect of damage caused by inaction on the part of the authority will be to prove that the damage suffered did result from the authority's failure to act, and not from a precedent and still operative cause.[100] The wilful misuse of statutory powers, causing economic loss, may possibly be an independent tort,[101] and some forms of misconduct in public office are common-law offences.[102] Torts committed by public officers (and presumably public bodies) acting arbitrarily and oppressively may lead to an award of exemplary damages.[103]

6 The exercise of discretionary powers by local authorities is governed by the general standards applied by the courts to other public bodies. These will be considered in a later chapter.[104] The performance of certain public duties cast upon a local authority may be enforced by an order of mandamus. When a person claims damages for negligence against a local authority and the substance of the alleged negligence is the careless exercise or failure to exercise a discretionary power, it is not enough for the plaintiff to prove that the authority is in breach of a duty of care owed to him under the normal principles of negligence. He must also establish that the alleged negligence is not simply a failure to take reasonable care in relation to the plaintiff's interest, but is a misuse of the discretionary power itself. He must prove that the authority acted *ultra vires*, either in its negligent operation of the power or in its failure to exercise that power at all.[105] To take a hypothetical example, if a student contracted food poisoning after eating in a restaurant which he later discovered had filthy kitchens which were crawling with vermin, would he be able to sue the local authority for their failure to exercise their powers to inspect and close public eating places? He could succeed only if he satisfied the court that if the restaurant had been inspected the inspection was so cursory or careless that it was in no sense a proper exercise of the power used by the inspector on the authority's behalf. Had no inspection been made the student would have to show that not inspecting that particular restaurant was a misuse of discretion by the authority bearing in mind all the

---

[100] *East Suffolk Rivers Catchment Board* v. *Kent* [1941] A.C. 74 and *Dutton* v. *Bognor Regis U.D.C.* [1972] 1 Q.B. 373 *per* Stamp L.J. at 412.
[101] See *David* v. *Abdul Cader* [1963] 1 W.L.R. 834.
[102] See, for example, *R.* v. *Llewellyn-Jones* [1968] 1 Q.B. 429.
[103] *Broome* v. *Cassell & Co.* [1972] A.C. 1927 (dicta).
[104] ch. 29. See further D. G. T. Williams in J. A. Andrews (ed.), *Welsh Studies in Public Law* (1970), ch. 8.
[105] *Anns* v. *Merton L.B.C.* [1978] A.C. 882.

other calls on the available inspectors' time and the general policy adopted by the authority.[106]

7 Legal disputes (for example, about entitlement to money or property) between two local authorities, or between a local authority and another public corporation or a government Department, may be resolved by the award of a binding declaration by the High Court. Again, a local authority may obtain a declaration as to the scope of its rights, duties or powers, provided that a genuine disputed question of law is directly in issue.[107]

8 Special statutory remedies are available to persons aggrieved by certain local authority decisions. From decisions to refuse or revoke a licence to carry on an occupation, an appeal may lie to a magistrates' court and thence to a Crown Court; appeals against demolition and closing orders in respect of houses unfit for human habitation lie to a county court. In such cases appeals are not usually confined to questions of law or fact; the court can review the merits of the decision and change it, paying due regard to the special knowledge of the local authority making the decision.[108] Review of local authority decisions by the superior courts is normally limited to questions of legality.

Central control reviewed[109]

Central–local government relationships are sometimes described in the language of partnership. The foregoing account has implied that if this is partnership, it is a partnership (to use an analogy taken from a different context) between the rider and the horse; and the present Government has ridden that horse on a much shorter rein. In providing some services the local authorities still enjoy a large measure of autonomy. Moreover, the local authority associations influence the content of parliamentary and subordinate legislation. Government Departments regularly consult them on matters affecting local interests and great weight may be given to their representations. And from time to time the associations are instrumental in the initiation of legislation, including private members' bills. Again, everyday communications between the central Departments and individual local authorities are

[106] See *Haydon* v. *Kent C.C.* [1970] Q.B. 343.
[107] ch. 30. See *Ealing L.B.C.* v. *Race Relations Board* [1972] A.C. 342.
[108] *Sagnata Investments Ltd* v. *Norwich Corporation* [1971] 2 Q.B. 614.
[109] The most illuminating survey is J. A. G. Griffith, *Central Departments and Local Authorities* (1966), ch. 1. See also M. Elliott, *Central–Local Government Relations* (1982).

not a one-way process, and departmental officials are made aware of local experience and problems; this awareness affects the content of policy and the manner of exerting ultimate control.

Nevertheless, the array of controls is formidable. Where Ministers have statutory responsibilities for promoting the efficiency of services provided locally, or for coordinating or managing such services on a national scale, detailed central regulation of the administration of the services tends to follow. At the very least, the Department will be concerned to ensure a national minimum standard. We have noted the extensive control exercised by the Home Secretary over police matters by means of regulations, control of senior appointments, entertaining disciplinary appeals, inspection, financial grants, compulsory amalgamation and special inquiry. The control over local educational matters – and education is the most costly local service – exercised by the Secretary of State for Education and Science is also substantial. Control of town and country planning and housing matters by the Secretary of State for the Environment, and of public health by the Secretary of State for Health, is somewhat less detailed; but no one reading through two years' output of town and country planning regulations will doubt the reality of central control over matters of procedure and substance. And lurking not far behind the scenes lies the Treasury, with its general responsibilities for national expenditure and economic planning.

In brief, the apparatus of departmental controls [110] includes power to make or withhold grants; to control borrowing for capital projects; [111] to set a maximum rate in the pound which may be levied in any year by any local authority designated by the Secretary of State ('rate-capping'); [112] to prescribe rules for the conduct of a local service, directly by regulations (and in some cases administrative instructions), or indirectly through the introduction of parliamentary legislation; to inspect certain services (for example, police, education); to confirm or refuse to confirm by-laws, compulsory purchase orders, educational schemes, senior appointments, and so on; to entertain appeals in respect of certain local authority decisions (for example, refusals of

[110] Audit is a form of central control, but the auditors are substantially autonomous quasi-judicial officers, subject to judicial rather than administrative surveillance. Similarly the Attorney General's power to take proceedings to restrain unlawful expenditure and *ultra vires* acts generally stands on a different footing from central political and administrative controls.

[111] Including the very important power to attach detailed conditions when issuing loan sanctions.

[112] Rates Act 1984, Part I: see above, p. 411.

planning permission); to conduct local inquiries under particular statutory powers (for example, where objections have been lodged to compulsory purchase orders, or into complaints about the conduct of a police force); and to exercise default powers, by removing responsibility for the conduct of a service from one authority to another or taking over responsibility at the centre or by issuing a mandatory order or obtaining from courts an order of mandamus to compel the authority to carry out its statutory duties. Against that legal background, the extra-statutory powers of central Departments to issue advisory and hortatory circulars to local authorities bear no comparison with the functions of an information bureau.

Mrs Thatcher's Government has weakened local council control in several areas, and has plans to weaken it further. The power to rate-cap has already been noted.[113] Under the Education Reform Act 1988 the Secretary of State for Education and Science may prescribe a national curriculum which must be taught and examined in all local authority schools;[114] schools would be allowed to opt out of local authority control following a vote to do so by the parents (and become dependent on Department of Education and Science grants);[115] the Inner London Education Authority will be abolished in 1990,[116] and city technology colleges will be established under the direct authority of the Department.[117] Under the Local Government Act 1988 local authorities are required to seek competitive tenders for such things as refuse collection, cleaning and school meals;[118] and they must exclude specified non-commercial considerations when placing public supply or works contracts.[119] Under the Housing Act 1988[120] local authority tenants will be able to end local council ownership of their houses. This all represents the most radical switch of power away from local government in modern times.

[113] See above, p. 411.
[114] Sections 1 to 18.
[115] Sections 50–61.
[116] Section 141.
[117] Section 94.
[118] Part I and Schedule 1.
[119] Part II and Schedule 2.
[120] Part IV.

Part Five

Civil Rights and Freedoms

This Part of the book covers topics which are both controversial and of immediate contemporary interest.

A new chapter 22, The Protection of Human Rights, has been included to set the chapters which follow in this Part into context, to consider fully the European Convention on Human Rights (especially as it has affected United Kingdom law and practice), to evaluate the arguments in favour of and against a new bill of rights for the United Kingdom, and to take in the law relating to racial and sexual discrimination which was formerly contained elsewhere in the book.

Chapter 23 begins with a discussion of the concept of British citizenship and the implications of that status. The complex rules governing the immigration and deportation of Commonwealth citizens and aliens, and the distinction drawn between those with and without the right of abode, are also outlined. Among the statutes considered are the British Nationality Act 1981 and the Immigration Act 1971, and the rules made under the latter Act (which give special rights to nationals of Community members). Further restrictions enacted against immigration in recent years are noted. Some aspects of the concepts of allegiance and protection (already touched on in the latter part of chapter 7) and the rules about British passports are then discussed. The law on the extradition of fugitive offenders is also brought into chapter 23, because it tends to raise the same *kinds* of issues covered in the early part of the chapter.

In chapter 24 we deal with liberty of the person. It examines the main features of English law on liberty of the person, and the major – and controversial – Police and Criminal Evidence Act 1984 is incorporated. Special reference is made to police powers of arrest, interrogation, search and seizure; the offence of wilfully obstructing a police officer in the execution of his duty; and remedies against unlawful physical restraint, including the writ of habeas corpus. The chapter includes a brief note on the law of privacy, and of confidentiality, the latter having been propelled to prominence during the Government's extensive litigation over Mr Peter Wright's memoirs, *Spycatcher*.

Chapter 25 is concerned with another basic freedom – freedom of expression. In order to ascertain the scope of this freedom, the circumstances in which a person may be prevented from expressing himself at all (such as the operation of the Official Secrets Act) or through particular media – for example, the cinema, the press, the broadcasting services – have to be considered first. Then there is the miscellany of criminal or civil wrongs that may be committed by speech or written words or pictorial representations – for instance, treason, sedition, breaches of the Official Secrets Act, blasphemy, defamation, contempt of court or of a House of Parliament, the offences under the Public Order Act 1986, sections 4 and 5, incitement to racial hatred, and, of course, offences in connection with 'obscene' publications. The failure of a private Member's bill to reform section 2 of the Official Secrets Act 1911, and the Government's White Paper and Bill in response, are noted.

In chapter 26 freedom of assembly and association are examined, substantially omitting the big subject of trade union law. Here again, what one is allowed to do depends on whether any other person is entitled to prevent one, and what specific wrongs one is liable to commit in attempts at self-expression. The law is closely related to that stated in Chapter 25 but has a number of special features. There is no general right to conduct a public meeting in a street or an open space. Much rewriting has been done to incorporate the new police powers over processions and public assemblies provided for in Part II of the Public Order Act 1986, together with the new statutory offences of riot, violent disorder and affray contained in Part I of that Act.

Part Five concludes with a chapter on states of emergency (which are clearly regulated by statute), the powers of the Crown in wartime, and the nature of a state of martial law.

Chapter 22

The Protection of Human Rights

Fundamental rights

'Now, most foreign constitution-makers have begun with declarations of rights. For this they have often been in no wise to blame.'[1] Here Dicey seems almost as patronizing as Mr. Podsnap of *Our Mutual Friend*: other countries 'do – I am sorry to be obliged to say it – *as* they do'. But he was at least more restrained than his mentor, Jeremy Bentham, to whom the French revolutionary Declaration of the Rights of Man was 'rhetorical nonsense – nonsense upon stilts'. There is indeed something peculiarly exasperating about a broad affirmation of fundamental human rights unaccompanied by any machinery for giving them effective legal protection. This is what Dicey had in mind: 'The Habeas Corpus Acts declare no principle and define no rights, but they are for practical purposes worth a hundred constitutional articles guaranteeing individual liberty.'[2] Had he been alive in 1948, he might have added 'or a thousand Universal Declarations of Human Rights'.

The traditional legal approach to civil liberties in Britain can be summed up in three propositions. First, freedoms are not to be guaranteed by statements of general principle. Secondly, they are residual. Freedom of public assembly, for example, means the liberty to gather wherever one chooses except in so far as others are legally entitled to prevent the assembly from being held or in so far as the holding or conduct of the assembly is a civil wrong or a criminal offence. To define the content of liberty one has merely to subtract from its totality the sum of the legal restraints to which it is subject. Thirdly, for every wrongful encroachment upon one's liberty there is a

---

[1] *Introduction to the Study of the Law of the Constitution* (10th edn), p. 198.
[2] ibid., p. 199. See also Jennings, *The Approach to Self-Government*, p. 20. See generally de Smith, *The New Commonwealth and its Constitutions* (1964), pp. 161–77.

legal remedy awarded by an independent court of justice. *Ubi jus, ibi remedium.*

These are still the formal legal foundations of most of our civil liberties. Those foundations do not necessarily make for the best of all possible worlds, even in the United Kingdom. If the constitution of Northern Ireland had been equipped from the outset with more detailed guarantees against religious discrimination, coupled with efficacious machinery for their enforcement, it is just conceivable – one cannot put it more highly – that the worst of the current troubles might have been averted.[3] If the American constitutional Bill of Rights had been transported to Britain along with Marshall Aid in the late 1940s, our laws relating to police powers of interrogation, search and seizure, legal aid for persons suspected or accused of crime, obscene publications, passports and the delimitation of electoral constituencies might have been more satisfactory though more uncertain. For the American Bill of Rights has reasonably effective machinery for judicial interpretation and enforcement of its provisions. Its terms would also have made it more difficult for Parliament and the Government to nationalize industries and implement town and country planning policies; it might have led to more criminals escaping justice; it would surely have struck down some of our immigration legislation.

Objections to effective constitutional guarantees of human rights may be still more vehement than objections to pious platitudes. Effective guarantees obstruct governments from doing what they want to do and are expected to do. They are therefore said to be undemocratic because they obstruct fulfilment of the will of the people as expressed by their elected representatives. They lead to 'government by judges', if the constitution is hard to amend. There will be political appointments to the bench, and public confidence in the impartial administration of justice may dwindle. Justiciable guarantees and prohibitions induce delay and uncertainty, because politicians will not be sure what they are entitled to do until the judges have told them; they engender a litigious spirit; they are irreconcilable with our ancient traditions; they are, moreover, unnecessary.

These objections cannot be disregarded. However, a number of comments must be made to put those points into a United Kingdom context and to show that the protection of human rights through a special constitutional document is neither unknown to the United Kingdom nor entirely alien to British experience.

[3] For constitutional guarantees in Northern Ireland, see ch. 3.

1   It is possible to have a bill of rights enacted as an ordinary statute without constitutional entrenchment. Canada adopted this course from 1960 to 1982. Federal legislation was to be so construed and applied as to conform to the Canadian Bill of Rights except in an emergency or unless an Act expressly stated that it was to have effect notwithstanding the Bill of Rights. Its overt impact was not at first impressive. The courts held that it did not prevail over subsequent inconsistent Acts of the Federal Parliament. But it served as a guide to interpretation; and legislative draftsmen were at pains to conform to the standards it laid down. Its indirect effect on the content of legislation may have been considerable. Thus discussion about possible new constitutional guarantees for the United Kingdom need not run into the sands of unnecessary argument about whether, in English law, they could be entrenched.

2   The constitutions of a large majority of newly independent and partly self-governing Commonwealth countries have been equipped with full-scale entrenched bills of rights, based on the general pattern of the European Convention on Human Rights.[4] During its declining years, the Colonial Office moved from apathy or hostility towards this idea and began actively to press it on colonial politicians. The unmentionable became indispensable. What was obnoxious to the Westminster model has been the glory of Westminster's export models. Perhaps, after all, time-honoured Anglo-Saxon attitudes towards constitutional guarantees of fundamental rights have been slightly exaggerated. True, in many developing Commonwealth countries the guarantees exist – if they survive at all – only on paper. Yet nobody reading the judgments of the Judicial Committee of the Privy Council in two appeals (holding invalid a Maltese ministerial circular restricting freedom of the press,[5] and the discriminatory citizenship legislation in Sierra Leone[6] can doubt that (to put it at its lowest) there is something to be said in favour of restricting legislative and administrative competence by constitutional guarantees.

3   As was seen in chapter 5, United Kingdom membership of the European Community has allowed individual British citizens to take advantage of certain rights under Community law. Such law is, therefore, an additional source of human rights.

[4] The beginnings of the trend are explained and analysed in de Smith, op. cit., ch. 5.
[5] See *Olivier* v. *Buttigieg* [1967] 1 A.C. 115.
[6] *Akar* v. *Att. Gen. of Sierra Leone* [1970] A.C. 853. With these two decisions there should be studied the remarkable judgment in *Liyanage* v. *R.* [1967] 1 A.C. 259 (Ceylon; implied prohibition read into a constitution not containing a wide range of guarantees).

4   The United Kingdom has, since 1953 in fact, been subject to a modern bill of rights with its own machinery for interpretation, and during that time United Kingdom law and practice has on occasion been altered so as to conform to it. That bill is the European Convention on Human Rights. It will now be looked at in some detail.

The European Convention on Human Rights [7]

The European Convention on Human Rights came into force in 1953 in the States (including the United Kingdom) that had ratified it. Those States form the Council of Europe, which had itself been established in 1949 and which today has twenty-one members. [8] The United Kingdom is bound by the Convention as a treaty in international law: [9] it has not been enacted as part of United Kingdom law, but because of the international law obligation to observe its terms the Convention provides a restraint on the legislative authority of the United Kingdom Parliament [10] and a fruitful source of rights for the individual.

The Convention specifies certain basic rights which the West European liberal democracies were able to agree on in the early 1950s. [11] Those rights and freedoms, in summary, include the right to life (art. 2); freedom from torture or inhuman or degrading treatment or punishment (art. 3); freedom from slavery or forced labour (art. 4); the right to liberty and security of the person (art. 5); the right to a fair trial by an impartial tribunal (art. 6); the prohibition of retrospective criminal laws (art. 7); the right to respect for a person's private and family life, his home and correspondence (art. 8); freedom of thought, conscience and religion (art. 9); freedom of expression (art. 10); freedom of peaceful assembly and association, including the right to join a trade union (art. 11), and the right to marry and found a family (art. 12). Those rights are to be enjoyed without discrimination on any ground such as sex, race, colour, language, religion, political or other opinion, national or social origin, association with a national minority,

---

[7] See Cmnd. 8969 (1953); Cmnd. 9221 (1954); Ian Brownlie, *Basic Documents on Human Rights* (1971); R. Beddard, *Human Rights and Europe* (2nd edn, 1980); A. H. Robertson, *Human Rights in Europe* (2nd edn, 1977); J. E. S. Fawcett, *The Application of the European Convention on Human Rights* (2nd edn, 1987); F. G. Jacobs, *The European Convention on Human Rights* (1975).

[8] Austria, Belgium, Cyprus, Denmark, France, Federal Republic of Germany, Greece, Iceland, Ireland, Italy, Liechtenstein, Luxembourg, Malta, Netherlands, Norway, Portugal, Spain, Sweden, Switzerland, Turkey, United Kingdom.

[9] See above, p. 140.

[10] See above, ch. 4.

[11] Thus some rights which might appear in a comprehensive modern document, such as rights of property, are omitted.

property, birth or other status. Further rights were added by the First Protocol to the Convention. Thus every person is entitled, under that Protocol, to the peaceful enjoyment of his possessions (art. 1), to education (and States must respect parents' rights to the education of their children in conformity with their religious and philosophical convictions) (art. 2),[12] and to take part in free elections by secret ballot (art. 3).

The Convention also explains (lest this all seems too good to be true) the circumstances in which a protected right can be abridged or removed. Thus there is, for example, no blanket guarantee of freedom of speech, which can never mean what it appears to say; nor is there any guarantee of 'due process of law' which can mean anything a judge thinks fit. Freedom of expression is qualified by a number of provisos: the State may license broadcasting and cinemas; such restrictions on freedom of expression may be imposed 'as are necessary in a democratic society, in the interests of national security, territorial integrity or public safety, for the prevention of disorder or crime, for the protection of health or morals, for the protection of the reputation or rights of others, for preventing the disclosure of information received in confidence, or for maintaining the authority and impartiality of the judiciary' (art. 10). Derogation from some rights and freedoms is permissible in time of grave emergency, but only 'to the extent strictly required by the exigencies of the situation' (art. 15) – a derogation which has taken place in relation to Northern Ireland. Any derogation must be reported to the Secretary General of the Council of Europe. No derogation from certain rights (for example, freedom from torture or inhuman or degrading punishment or treatment) is permissible at all. Because the terms of the European Convention have not been incorporated as part of United Kingdom law, the courts in the United Kingdom cannot apply them directly.[13] If there is no British legislation on the subject-matter of a dispute, it seems that the courts *need not* take the Convention into account;[14] and, plainly, the terms of the Convention cannot prevail over inconsistent statutory provisions. On the other hand the courts, in construing legislation passed since 1953, may take note of the Convention and presume that Parliament did not intend to

---

[12] The United Kingdom limited its acceptance of that article.
[13] See, e.g., *Malone* v. *United Kingdom* [1984] Ch. 344; *Kaur* v. *Lord Advocate* [1981] S.L.T. 322; *R.* v. *Secretary of State for the Home Department, ex. p. Weeks*, The *Guardian*, 17 February 1988.
[14] *Malone* v. *United Kingdom* (above).
[15] See, e.g., *Garland* v. *British Rail Engineering Ltd* [1983] 2 A.C. 751; *R.* v. *Secretary of State for the Home Department, ex. p. Bhajan Singh* [1976] Q.B. 198; *R.* v. *Secretary of State for the Home Department, ex. p. Phansopkar* [1976] Q.B. 606.

legislate inconsistently with it.[15] An aggrieved British citizen must, therefore, go to the European machinery which is provided for the vindication of his rights under the Convention.

The *European Commission of Human Rights* is elected by the Committee of Ministers of the Council of Europe (although, once elected, Commissioners serve as independent officers, not as representatives from the State parties to the Convention). The Commission receives and investigates alleged breaches of the Convention, either at the request of one State party against another (art. 24), or at the petition of an individual against his own State (art. 25) – provided in the latter case that his State has recognized the right of individual petition (as the United Kingdom has done since 1966[16]). Individual petitions are numerically much the more important: only some dozen inter-State cases have been considered so far by the Commission, as against some 10,000 individual petitions. If the Commission decides that a petition is admissible[17] – and less than 300 to date have been – the Commission inquires into it, attempting in the first instance to achieve a friendly settlement (art. 28). If that does not succeed the Commission reports to the State concerned and to the Committee of Ministers (art. 31); the Committee, by a two-thirds majority vote, may then decide whether there has been a breach and, if so, may refer the case to the European Court of Human Rights.

The *European Court of Human Rights* is composed of twenty-one judges sitting in Strasbourg. It can consider, in a bench of seven judges, a case only if (*a*) the State involved has accepted the compulsory jurisdiction of the Court (art. 46)[18] or has consented to the court hearing the particular case (art. 47), and (*b*) the Commission or a State has referred it. An individual cannot, therefore, take his petition straight to the Court. The Court's decision is final, and it can award compensation to a successful petitioner (art. 50); although the Court has no coercive powers, the State parties undertake to abide by its rulings, the implementation of which is overseen by the Committee of Ministers.

The Commission has dealt with a number of individual petitions alleging that United Kingdom immigration law was in breach of the Convention. So, for instance, a number of East Africans who were

---

[16] It has been renewed for five-year periods, the latest from 1986.
[17] The petitioner must first have exhausted local remedies, and his petition must be brought within six months of the final local decision (art. 26); manifestly ill-founded petitions and any which abuse the right of petition will be rejected (art. 27).
[18] The United Kingdom accepted it in 1966.

refused permission to enter the United Kingdom petitioned on the ground that the law was degrading, interfered with family life and was discriminatory (thus violating arts 3, 8 and 14). The Commission agreed.[19] Many petitions against the United Kingdom have been withdrawn when the British Government has agreed to take action in particular cases, or to change the general law. The European Court of Human Rights has ruled against the United Kingdom some dozen times.[20] The first of those cases to be considered by the Court on an individual petition was *Golder* v. *United Kingdom*,[21] in which it was held that the refusal of legal advice to a prisoner who was contemplating a defamation action against a prison officer infringed the right of respect for private life and correspondence (art. 8), and the guarantee of a fair hearing (art. 6).[22] In *Campbell and Fell* v. *United Kingdom*[23] the procedure of a prison board of visitors was also held to violate that latter right. In *Tyrer* v. *United Kingdom*[24] and in *Campbell and Cozans* v. *United Kingdom*[25] the Court held respectively that birching in the Isle of Man was a degrading punishment (contrary to art. 3), and that corporal punishment in Scottish schools infringed the right of parents to have their children educated according to their philosophical convictions (under art. 2 of the First Protocol). Legislation in Northern Ireland which penalized consenting adult homosexual conduct was held in *Dudgeon* v. *United Kingdom*[26] to infringe the individual's right to respect for his private life (art. 8). The law of contempt of court[27] was declared to be in breach of the guarantee of freedom of expression (contrary to art. 10) in *Sunday Times Ltd* v. *United Kingdom*.[28] The procedure for the recall of mentally ill patients who had been conditionally released was declared to contravene the right to liberty of the person (art. 5) in *X.* v. *United Kingdom*[29] and in *Young, James and*

[19] The Commission so reported to the Commission of Ministers. The U.K. allowed the petitioners to enter, thus ending the particular complaint.

[20] See 136 H.C. Deb. *215–16* (written answers 13 July 1988). The first inter-State case was *Republic of Ireland* v. *United Kingdom* (1978) 2 E.H.R.R. 25, in which the U.K. admitted that certain interrogation techniques which had been used in Northern Ireland violated art. 3 – but they had been abandoned.

[21] (1975) 1 E.H.R.R. 524.

[22] A similar breach was found in *Silver* v. *United Kingdom* (1983) 5 E.H.R.R. 347.

[23] (1985) 7 E.H.R.R. 165.

[24] (1978) 2 E.H.R.R. 1.

[25] (1982) 4 E.H.R.R. 293.

[26] (1981) 4 E.H.R.R. 149.

[27] As it had been declared in *Att.-Gen.* v. *Times Newspapers Ltd* [1974] A.C. 273.

[28] (1979) 2 E.H.R.R. 245. But the Obscene Publications Act 1959 was held to conform to the right of freedom of expression in *Handyside* v. *United Kingdom* (1976) 1 E.H.R.R. 737.

[29] (1981) 4 E.H.R.R. 188.

Webster v. *United Kingdom*[30] provisions of the Trade Union and Labour Relations Act 1974 were held to violate the worker's right not to join a trade union (contrary to art. 11). And in *Abdulaziz and Others* v. *United Kingdom*[31] a provision of United Kingdom immigration law was declared discriminatory as between the rights of wives and of husbands to join spouses lawfully settled in the United Kingdom.

As a consequence of all these cases the British Government was either able to inform the Court that the law complained of had already been changed, or that appropriate legislative or administrative action would be taken to comply with the Court's judgments. The effect of the European Convention must obviously be considered when legislation is being drafted, and in that way as well as through the work of the Commission and the Court the European Convention is a worthwhile guarantor of rights.

A new bill of rights?

The lack of a comprehensive and easily accessible statement of fundamental rights and freedoms enforceable in the United Kingdom, the delay and inconvenience of going to Strasbourg, reliance on the accidents of litigation to disclose enforceable Community rights, among other factors, has led to discussion since the 1970s of whether the United Kingdom should adopt a new bill of rights of her own.[32] In 1977 the Standing Advisory Commission on Human Rights in Northern Ireland recommended that a bill of rights for the whole United Kingdom would be the best way to protect rights in the province.[33] The Home Office had published a Green Paper in 1976.[34] A select committee of the House of Lords in 1978 considered the desirability and possible form of a bill of rights,[35] and recommended that (if one were to be adopted) the way forward would be to incorporate the European Convention into domestic law.[36] There have been a number of attempts by backbench peers and M.P.s to do just that,[37] the last being

[30] (1981) 4 E.H.R.R. 188.
[31] (1981) 4 E.H.R.R. 38.
[32] See Lord Scarman, *English Law – the New Dimension* (1974); M. Zander, *A Bill of Rights?* (3rd edn, 1985); P. T. Wallington and J. McBride, *Civil Liberties and a Bill of Rights* (1976); H. W. R. Wade, *Constitutional Fundamentals* (1980).
[33] Cmnd. 7009 (1977).
[34] Legislation on Human Rights (1976).
[35] H.L. 176 (1977–8).
[36] On this, see J. Jaconelli, *Enacting a Bill of Rights: The Legal Problems* (1980), ch. 9.
[37] The House of Lords approved bills sponsored by Lord Wade in 1981 and by Lord Scarman in 1985.

the Human Rights Bill which narrowly failed to obtain a second reading in the House of Commons in 1987.[38] The present Government does not believe that a new bill of rights is necessary or desirable.

There are various models to hand for a new bill of rights, ranging from (for example) an Act incorporating the European Convention into United Kingdom law, to a statute which declared certain rights and provided that they would prevail over *prior* inconsistent legislation, to one which would go further and entrench those against *subsequent* inconsistent attempts at legislation.[39] What is lacking is not a serviceable scheme, but any political consensus for its adoption. Some lawyers and others object to the greater power which a new bill could give to unaccountable judges to the detriment of Parliament.[40] Others believe that only a fully entrenched and comprehensive new bill would be worth the effort.[41] Some politicians are nervous that a bill of rights might hamper the implementation of their manifesto promises. And there would be general dissent, if a new bill were drafted from scratch, over some issues which are likely to remain of party political controversy – the electoral system, private medicine, trade union rights and so on. On purely pragmatic grounds there is a sound argument that, as the United Kingdom is a party to the European Convention, it would be better for the parties to disputes under it to have them resolved in the United Kingdom, saving delay, inconvenience, expense and the occasional condemnation of the Government of the day by a 'foreign' court. There would be drawbacks in such a course, for the Convention is over thirty years old, is not comprehensive,[42] and because account might still have to be taken of the European Court's interpretation of it.[43]

For the time being, the English method of reforming proved abuses by specific legislation as they are disclosed will continue. Two examples concern discrimination on grounds of race or sex.

Racial discrimination[44]

Britain has no laws which discriminate against persons on account of their race and colour. A Jew, a Chinese, a Negro, for example, all enjoy

[38] 109 H.C. Deb. *1123-89* (6 February 1987).
[39] The latter is the least likely to be taken up because of doubts about its efficacy in the face of the orthodox doctrine of parliamentary sovereignty: see above, ch. 4
[40] See, e.g., J. A. G. Griffith (1979) 42 *Mod. L. Rev.* 1.
[41] See, e.g., Lord Scarman, op. cit.
[42] See note 11, above.
[43] See, however, Arnhill [1985] *Public Law* 378.
[44] See I. A. MacDonald, *Race Relations: the New Law* (1977); L. Lustgarten, *The Legal Control of Racial Discrimination* (1980).

the same voting rights: they must merely comply with the same rules about nationality and residence as everybody else. They are equally entitled to the facilities for education and to the benefit of social services. The law does not order segregation in public transport or anywhere else. In these respects Britain is free from the legal restraints which have agitated the United States so much. In this sense, there is equality before the law.

An equally important practical question is the effectiveness with which the law takes positive steps to ensure that persons are not discriminated against on account of race or colour. To say that the law does not discriminate is one thing, but does the law compel persons not to discriminate, or otherwise protect those who are liable to be discriminated against?

It was to deal with this question that Parliament for the first time introduced legislative controls in the Race Relations Act 1965. That Act had limited application and was based on inadequate research, but experience of its operation was helpful in preparing the much more comprehensive Race Relations Act 1968 which replaced it.

The main emphasis of the 1965 Act was placed not on punishment but on rendering certain discriminatory practices unlawful and devising machinery to reduce friction and promote conciliation. The Act made it unlawful for the proprietors, managers or other employees of certain places of public resort – hotels, restaurants, cafés, public houses, theatres, cinemas, dance halls, sports grounds, swimming pools and other places of public entertainment or recreation – and public transport undertakings to practise discrimination on the ground of colour, race or ethnic or national origins against persons seeking to use these facilities. Complaints of discrimination were to be made to local conciliation committees of the Race Relations Board, a body of three members appointed by the Home Secretary; the Board was to make annual reports to be laid before Parliament. A committee would investigate the complaint and try to reach a settlement and obtain an assurance that discrimination would cease. If it was unsuccessful it would report to the Board; the Board was to report to the Attorney-General if it considered that a course of discriminatory conduct in contravention of the Act was likely to continue, and the Attorney-General could then apply to the High Court or a county court for an injunction to restrain its continuance. Neither the committees nor the Board had any power to obtain information or subpoena witnesses, and no new civil remedy was given to a person aggrieved by discriminatory acts. Section 5 of the Act invalidated discriminatory restrictions on the disposal of tenancies other than in premises occupied by the owner or head tenant.

In 1967 there was published a penetrating critique of the Act with suggestions for legislative reform drawing on the experience of civil rights legislation in the United States and Canada.[45] The Race Relations Act 1968 (the enactment of which was doubtless accelerated by the bad impression created by the Commonwealth Immigrants Act 1968) gave effect to a number of these suggestions. The Act defined discrimination so as to include segregation and a single act of discrimination could be unlawful. The ambit of unlawful discrimination was extended to cover the provision to the public, or to a section of the public, of goods and facilities (including trading, banking, insurance, credit, education and professional services); employment, and trade unions and business associations; the provision of housing accommodation and business premises; and advertisements and other notices. A number of exceptions to the general rule were introduced for particular employment and housing situations.[46] The provisions of the Act were made generally applicable to the Crown and the police.[47]

The Act posed some difficult problems of interpretation. Discrimination on the grounds of a person's present nationality (as distinct from his 'national origins') was not contrary to the Act.[48] The House of Lords held that private social or political clubs with a genuinely selective membership did not discriminate unlawfully within the meaning of the Act by operating a colour or racial bar inasmuch as they were not providing facilities to 'the public or a section of the public'.[49]

The Act altered the procedure for investigation of complaints, strengthening the powers and enlarging the size of the Race Relations Board. Complaints might be made direct to the Board; the Board could also decide to undertake an inquiry into suspected discrimination of its own motion, and it could appoint assessors to assist it. Conciliation and investigation procedures were spelt out, but were essentially informal, and the Board and area committees had no power to compel

[45] Harry Street, Geoffrey Howe and Geoffrey Bindman, *Report on Discrimination Legislation* (1967).
[46] ss 1–9.
[47] s. 27; subject to various exceptions – for example, the Crown was not placed under a duty to employ aliens on the same basis as British citizens (s. 27(9)(a)).
[48] *Ealing L.B.C.* v. *Race Relations Board* [1972] A.C. 342.
[49] *Race Relations Board* v. *Charter* [1973] A.C. 868 (Indian excluded on racial grounds from local Conservative club).

attendance or the production of information. Complaints about employment, unions and employers' associations were referred in the first instance to the Secretary of State for Employment; in certain circumstances the Board would carry out the investigation. The Act also provided for the establishment of a Community Relations Commission, an advisory, research, coordinating and promotional body.

Under the 1968 Act, the power to bring civil proceedings for an injunction to restrain a course of discriminatory conduct was transferred from the Attorney-General to the Race Relations Board. The Board might also be awarded a declaration that a discriminatory act was unlawful and special damages and damages for loss of opportunity (but not damages for humiliation and distress) on behalf of a person damnified by such an act (ss 19–22). Courts, moreover, were expressly empowered (s. 23) to revise the terms of contracts in such proceedings so as to bring them into conformity with the Act. The county courts in which these proceedings were brought were specially designated by the Lord Chancellor, and the judge had to be assisted by two expert assessors.

The 1968 Act has been replaced by the Race Relations Act 1976. This Act has two aims, to harmonize with the machinery for sex discrimination put into operation in 1976 (and examined below) and to make good some of the defects revealed in the 1968 Act. The Act abolished both the Race Relations Board and the Community Relations Commission, and one body alone, the Commission for Racial Equality, administers it. The Commission consists of a chairman and not more than fourteen members appointed by the Home Secretary; the various racial minorities are substantially represented in its composition.

A person discriminates if on racial grounds he treats another less favourably than he treats or would treat other persons. The 'racial grounds' are extended so as to include nationality and citizenship.[50] A new provision makes it unlawful to apply a requirement on condition which (irrespective of motive) is such that the proportion of persons of a particular colour, race, nationality or ethnic or natural origins able to comply with it is considerably smaller than the proportion of other persons able to do so, and which is not justifiable on racial grounds. The ambit of the Act is substantially the same as before, but certain anomalies are removed. Where principals engage somebody personally

[50] Reversing *Ealing L.B.C.* v. *Race Relations Board*, above. In *Mandla* v. *Dowell Lee* [1983] 2 A.C. 584, the House of Lords held that Sikhs were a 'racial group' within s. 3(1) of the 1976 Act.

to execute labour or work, or where a firm of six or more partners offers new partnerships, the Act applies. Bodies which confer authorization to engage in a particular trade or profession are covered. Clubs with twenty-five or more members are affected.[51] Advertisements for jobs outside the U.K. are brought within its scope.

It is the aggrieved individual, not the Commission, who instigates a complaint of discrimination. The Commission will, on application, be able to give assistance to a claimant or potential claimant where the case raises an issue of principle or it is unreasonable, for instance, by reason of the case's complexity, or the respective positions of the parties to the dispute, to expect the claimant to proceed on his own behalf. 'Assistance' includes advice, conciliation, arranging for legal advice and assistance, and representation. The 1976 Act scraps the previous arrangements under which local race relations committees used to seek conciliation of all complaints under the legislation.

If the alleged discrimination is in the field of employment, he complains to an industrial tribunal. It is hoped that conciliation officers of the Advisory, Conciliation and Arbitration Service of the Department of Employment will, by their advice, cause most cases to be settled without a hearing before the tribunal. The complainant has the burden of proving discrimination before the tribunal. If he wins, the tribunal may declare his right, or award compensation, or recommend that the employer take action to obviate or reduce the adverse effect on the complainant of the act of discrimination.

Complaints regarding bodies over which the Secretary of State for Education and Science exercises powers are first made to him, and he has two months in which to act. Subject to that, all complaints regarding education, housing and the provision of goods, facilities and services are made to county courts. The complainant has the burden of proving discrimination. If he succeeds the court has power to award damages (including damages for injured feelings) and to grant an injunction restraining the defendant from discriminating unlawfully against the plaintiff.

Complaints about discriminatory advertisements are handled by the Commission, which can if necessary institute proceedings in the county court, seeking an injunction. One of its main functions is to conduct investigations into discriminatory practices. It has powers to require the furnishing of information and the production of documents; it can seek an order in the county court ordering anyone who refuses to produce

[51] Reversing *Race Relations Board* v. *Dockers' Labour Club and Institute Ltd* [1976] A.C. 285.

the information. If its investigation (after hearing the person investigated) reveals discrimination it may issue a non-discrimination notice requiring him to cease, but an appeal lies to the county court or industrial tribunal, as the case may be. It is empowered to ensure that in the subsequent five years the notice is complied with, and if necessary, to apply to the county court (in the field of employment) for an injunction. It collects information about all individual complaints and monitors the legislation generally.

Much in the 1976 Act is an improvement on the earlier Acts. Particularly welcome is the power of the Commission to enforce production of documents. For the first time the Commission should be able to uncover any widespread discriminatory practices and secure their cessation. The power of the courts to grant injunctions restraining discriminatory activities is also important. What causes most disquiet in this Act is the imposition on the aggrieved of the task of pursuing his complaint, without legal aid, before an industrial tribunal. There has always been difficulty about overcoming the fear of an aggrieved person to report discrimination. In the past he has known that the case would be handled for him at every stage by the central body; all he had to do was to report his complaint. It remains to be seen how much unlawful discrimination will now go unchecked because timid, harassed, ignorant or poor victims will not take cases themselves. It also remains to be seen whether the Government will be more effective than in the past in weeding out discriminatory practices by those with whom it makes contracts.

Nobody should believe that law alone can create racial harmony; yet without legal sanctions, the prospects are much worse. This Act creates the legislative framework for better race relations in all those areas of potential conflict.

The 1976 Act also extends the scope of the criminal law. Succumbing to pressure consequent on incidents at Fascist meetings, the Government in the Race Relations Act 1965 made it a crime for a person to publish or distribute threatening, abusive or insulting words, if the matter or words were likely to stir up hatred against any section of the public in Great Britain on grounds of colour, race or ethnic or national origins, or citizenship. There was disquiet when this new crime was introduced in 1965 especially because the content made the publication criminal even though no public disorder resulted. The offence under section 70 of the 1976 Act is wider in that it is no longer necessary to prove an intention to stir up hatred. The Public Order Act 1986, Part III, now provides for these offences (see p. 502).

Sex discrimination

Not until 1976 had Britain any laws in force designed to counter sex discrimination. Now there are two inter-related Acts, the Equal Pay Act 1970 and the Sex Discrimination Act 1975, which became operative simultaneously.

The Equal Pay Act provides that women are to have equal pay in three circumstances. The first is when they are doing 'like' work. If the jobs are not identical, but the differences in job content are not significant or, though significant, do not recur frequently (for example, a man would lift heavy weights once a month), then it is 'like work'. The second is where an official job evaluation study has been made and this rates the work as equivalent to men's work. The third case is where a collective bargaining agreement has been made between employer and trade union which provides different rates for men and women; any such agreement can be referred to the Industrial Arbitration Board so that any offending clauses are removed.

A woman who believes that she is not getting equal pay has to make a claim to an industrial tribunal. She will have to satisfy the tribunal that her work is the same as or similar to a man's. Once she proves that, the onus is then on the employer to prove that there are material differences between the man's situation and the woman's other than sex, which constitute a genuine reason for the difference in the treatment awarded them: an obvious example of a material difference would be where the woman worked day shifts, but the man worked regular night shifts. If the woman wins she is awarded compensation which may include up to two years' arrears of pay. In 1982 the European Court of Justice held that the United Kingdom had failed to apply the principle of equal pay for work of equal value for which no system of job classification exists.[52] Changes were then made in English law.[53]

The Act applies not only to basic pay but to other matters in a woman's contract of employment. It therefore may extend also to overtime pay, bonus payments, sick pay schemes, health insurance, holiday pay, and length of holidays, luncheon vouchers, other fringe benefits and rest periods provided for in her contract. A successful claimant will be also awarded the appropriate cash damages to compensate her for having been deprived of any such benefit. The House of Lords has held that a woman cook at Cammell Laird Shipbuilders was entitled to the same pay as a carpenter, or a joiner, or a thermal insulation engineer, employed

[52] *European Commission* v. *U.K.* (1982) 3 C.M.L.R. 284.
[53] Equal Pay (Amendment) Regulations 1983. And see Townshend-Smith (1984) 47 *Mod. L. Rev.* 201. See generally D. Pannick, *Sex Discrimination Law* (1985).

by the company, because she did work of equal value to them.[54]

The Sex Discrimination Act 1975 covers much more ground than the Equal Pay Act. Like the Equal Pay Act it applies to employment, but if the complaint is about money under a contract of employment, the Equal Pay Act governs the matter. Its concern on employment is with every aspect of an employer's relations with his workers. It may be his recruiting policy (say advertising only for boy school-leavers), his advertisements for vacancies, arrangements for interviewing, training methods, selection for promotion or transfer, lay-offs, redundancy or dismissal. Complaints about matters other than money, such as company cars or cheap loans, fall within either Act. Trade unions and employment agencies are also within the net of the 1975 Act. A printing union operating where there is a closed shop cannot keep a male preserve by barring women from the union. The Sex Discrimination Act 1975, s. 6(3), exempted from its provisions private households and businesses employing not more than five workers. That exemption was held to be contrary to European Community law,[55] and the Sex Discrimination Act 1986 was passed to repeal it and to exempt employment where work is done in a private house involving a degree of contact which might reasonably involve an objection by a worker of a particular sex.[56]

As the title of the Act indicates, its business is discrimination. This it defines under four heads: treating a woman less favourably than a man on account of sex; conversely treating a man less favourably than a woman (maternity excepted!); treating a married person less favourably, on grounds of marriage, than a single person; and fourthly, victimization because someone has invoked either of the Acts. Indirect discrimination is also outlawed when tests are applied which appear neutral but place one sex (or married people) at a disadvantage; for example, all clerks must be at least 5 ft 8 in. tall. Complaints about discrimination in employment and training are made to an industrial tribunal which may award compensation.

The 1975 Act also affects education. It is unlawful for those responsible for an educational establishment – other than single sex institutions (including school governors and university governing bodies) – to discriminate on grounds of sex in admissions policy – no medical school can lawfully operate a quota system for girls – or require higher A-levels from them, or in the benefits and facilities

---

[54] *Hayward* v. *Cammell Laird Shipbuilders Ltd* [1988] 2 All E.R. 257.
[55] *Commission* v. *United Kingdom* [1984] 1 All E.R. 353.
[56] See 1986 Act, s. 1.

offered. A local education authority may not provide worse science laboratories in its girls' schools than in its boys' schools. Other matters where sex discrimination is outlawed include: the provision to the public of goods, facilities or services, including facilities offered by building societies, insurance companies, banks, credit institutions and H.P. companies; restaurants, public houses and places of entertainment; local authorities and transport authorities. The disposal of residential or business premises is affected. These changes in the law affect many common business practices, such as making the husband sign the H.P. contract when the wife, who has a good job of her own, is buying the article, or the building society that looks askance at spinster borrowers. Pubs are not allowed all-male bars; hotel cocktail bars cannot deny admission to unaccompanied women. Local authorities cannot throw out of her council flat the separated wife who can pay the rent. Complaints under the headings in this paragraph lie to the county court.

Another innovation of this Act is the establishment of the Equal Opportunities Commission. This has power to conduct formal investigations into any person it believes to be discriminating unlawfully. It may compel him to give evidence or to produce documents. It may apply to court for an injunction, disobedience to which would be a contempt of court in various circumstances. It may have served a non-discrimination notice against someone it is satisfied is discriminating, and who has not successfully appealed against it; within five years it may seek an injunction to prevent his continuing to discriminate. It may also do so against someone whom an individual has successfully sued for discrimination.

It may itself sue an individual and seek an injunction if his unlawful discrimination is proved. If someone publishes an advertisement which indicates an intention to discriminate unlawfully, it may seek to prevent him by obtaining an injunction. In effect the Commission is expected to see that the law is complied with, even though individual victims do not themselves choose to seek its protection. Had the Act merely left it to aggrieved individuals to sue, its impact might have been negligible. The Commission has the chance to unearth sex discrimination in all the areas covered by the Act, not only employment, to investigate where it has suspicions and to confront offenders with the prospect of imprisonment for defying a court order to desist from discriminatory practices.

Chapter 23

Citizens, Aliens and Others

Background

The concept of a British subject at common law was rooted in the idea of allegiance, the bond which linked a man with his feudal lord. In return for allegiance a man was entitled to his lord's protection. Persons born within His Majesty's dominions owed the King natural allegiance and were his subjects.[1] Aliens within those dominions owed a temporary local allegiance. No one could divest himself of his natural allegiance; and violation of the duty of allegiance might constitute treason.

The common law has been greatly altered by a series of statutes. Until 1983 the principal statute was the British Nationality Act 1948. That Act was part of a complex arrangement between the independent Commonwealth countries whereby each was to have its own nationality laws but would recognize as British subjects nationals of other member States. The British Government chose the United Kingdom and Colonies as the composite unit of citizenship whose members became British subjects.

A rapid rise in the influx of British subjects from the West Indies, Pakistan and India led to the passing of the Commonwealth Immigrants Act 1962 which imposed for the first time restrictions on the freedom of Commonwealth citizens to migrate to the United Kingdom. Other statutory restrictions followed, until in 1971 the Immigration Act superseded these Acts by a detailed control of immigration and deportation of aliens as well as of Commonwealth citizens. The consequence was that citizenship under the 1948 Act no longer clearly indicated who was free to settle in the United Kingdom. The British Nationality Act 1981 (which came into force in 1983) was intended to

---

[1] *Calvin's* case (1607) 7 Co. Rep. 1a (Scotsman born after the union of the Crowns was not an alien in England).

create a closer relationship between citizenship and the right to enter the United Kingdom.[2] It created three main forms of status: British citizenship, British Dependent Territories citizenship and British Overseas citizenship.

Anyone who at the end of 1982 was a citizen of the United Kingdom and Colonies and had the right of abode in the United Kingdom under the Immigration Act 1971 became a British citizen. A person had the right of abode if (a) he were born, adopted, naturalized or registered in the United Kingdom or the Islands (the Channel Islands and the Isle of Man); or (b) his parent had that citizenship at the time of birth or adoption, provided that the parent had either acquired citizenship in the United Kingdom or the Islands or been born to or adopted by a citizen parent (that is, our citizen's grandparent) who at that time had citizenship acquired in the United Kingdom or the Islands; or (c) settled at any time in the United Kingdom and Islands and had been ordinarily resident there as a citizen for the last five years or more; or if (d) though not a citizen of the United Kingdom and Colonies, was a Commonwealth citizen born to or adopted by a parent who had that citizenship of the United Kingdom and Colonies by birth in the United Kingdom or Islands; or if (e) being married to someone having the above right of abode, had obtained registration as a citizen.

From 1983 birth in the United Kingdom ceased to be a sufficient qualification. If either parent at the time of the birth is either a British citizen or ordinarily resident in the United Kingdom, British citizenship is acquired. Others born in the United Kingdom are entitled to be registered if they have spent the first 10 years of their life here, or if a parent subsequently becomes a citizen or ordinarily resident here while the child is still a minor. A child adopted through a United Kingdom court order becomes a British citizen if an adopter is a British citizen.

A child born abroad to parents either of whom is a British citizen other than by descent will be a British citizen by descent. If a parent is a British citizen (even by descent) serving overseas in Crown or European Community service, the child born abroad is also a British citizen.

There are complex rules about obtaining British citizenship by registration. Certain classes of minor may seek registration.[3] At his discretion the Home Secretary may naturalize certain categories of applicant intending to make their principal home here and whom he is

---

[2] What follows is a general summary of the law regarding nationality and immigration. The rules are hedged about with exceptions and qualifications. It is impossible to include these in this brief account. For a more detailed review see Blake (1982) 45 *Mod. L. Rev.* 179; White and Hampson [1982] *Public Law* 6.

[3] See British Nationality Act 1981, ss 3, 4, 5 and 7.

satisfied to be of good character and to have a good knowledge of the English language. They include those with five years' residence in the United Kingdom or those married to British citizens.[4] There is no appeal against his refusal. The Home Secretary can deprive a naturalized or registered citizen of his citizenship if he is satisfied that the registration or certificate of naturalization was obtained by means of fraud, false representation or the concealment of any material facts.[5] He also has power to deprive on grounds of disaffection, assisting the enemy in war time, and of certain terms of imprisonment.[6] He must be satisfied that it is not conducive to the public good that he remain a British citizen.[7]

The second category of citizenship is that of British Dependent Territories citizenship. It is, in essence, a colonial citizenship and carries no right of entry into the United Kingdom. If a citizen of the United Kingdom and Colonies acquired that citizenship through his own connection with the dependent territory (by birth, naturalization or registration) he qualifies. This applies at the moment to people in Hong Kong in particular, of whom some 3·25 million were British Dependent Territories citizens in 1988. Following the agreement to retrocede Hong Kong to China in 1997,[8] provision has been made[9] to allow such citizens in Hong Kong to acquire a new status of British National (Overseas), and for their current status to end in 1997. Many Falkland Islanders were also British Dependent Territories citizens, but in the wake of the Argentinian invasion the British Nationality (Falkland Islands) Act 1983 was passed: it conferred British citizenship on Falkland Islanders born before 1 January 1983. People born in the Islands after that date acquire their citizenship status through the provisions of the British Nationality Act 1981. And Gibraltarians who have British Dependent Territories citizenship and who are nationals of the United Kingdom for the purpose of European Community treaties may register as British citizens.[10]

British Overseas citizenship is a residual and transitional status acquired from 1983 by all citizens of the United Kingdom and Colonies who have not become British or British Dependent Territories citizens.

[4] ibid., ss 4, 44, and sched. 1.
[5] ibid., s. 40(1).
[6] ibid., s. 40(3).
[7] ibid., s. 40(5). For the right to have the matter referred to a committee of inquiry, see s. 40(7). See *R.* v. *Secretary of State for the Home Department, ex P. Akhtar* [1981] Q.B. 46.
[8] See below, p. 657.
[9] S.I. 1986, No. 948, made under the Hong Kong Act 1985: see Cmnd 9637 (1985); 89 H.C. Deb. *1270–1306* (16 January 1986); 97 H.C. Deb. *655–78* (13 May 1986).
[10] British Nationality Act 1981, s. 5.

The largest groups are living in Malaysia, India and East Africa and may number about 1·5 million. Every person who under the 1981 Act is a British citizen, a British Dependent Territories citizen or a British Overseas citizen has the status of a Commonwealth citizen.[11]

The Immigration Act 1971 [12]

The Immigration Act 1971 (as amended by the British Nationality Act 1981[13]), together with statutory instruments made in pursuance of it, and supplemented by detailed Immigration Rules,[14] now regulates immigration and deportation.

The critical issue now is whether a person has a right of abode for the purpose of the 1971 Act. All British citizens have that right.[15] In addition Commonwealth citizens who before the 1981 Act had a right of abode retain a right of abode for their lifetime.[16] The latter group, when seeking to enter, have to prove their right of abode by a certificate of entitlement.[17] Little special significance is attributed to the holding of a United Kingdom passport.[18] British citizens are free from immigration control. Citizens of the Republic of Ireland and other Community nationals also have rights to enter and settle in the United Kingdom which Commonwealth citizens without a right of abode lack.[19]

---

[11] Section 37(1).

[12] See J. M. Evans, *Immigration Law* (2nd edn, 1983); I. A. MacDonald, *Immigration Law and Practice in the United Kingdom* (1983); L. Grant and I. Martin, *Immigration Law and Practice* (1982, *Supplement* 1985).

[13] Section 39 and sched. 4.

[14] Statement of Changes in Immigration Rules, H.C. *169* (1982–3); H.C. *503* (1984–5).

[15] Immigration Act 1971, s. 2(1) as amended by s. 39(2) of the 1981 Act.

[16] ibid.

[17] Section 2(3) and s. 3(9) of the 1971 Act as amended by s. 39(2) of the 1981 Act.

[18] Except that citizens holding U.K. passports not endorsed to the effect that the holder is subject to immigration control are admitted without proof of patriality, and should be admitted (even though their passports are so endorsed) if they hold a special voucher or entry certificate. See also S.I. 1972, No. 1613, r. 5.

However, the United Kingdom Government's responsibility under the European Convention on Human Rights for indignities caused to United Kingdom passport holders who are refused entry is not excluded merely by designating them as 'non-patrial'. Under the European Convention the European Commission on Human Rights in 1974 reported to the Committee of Ministers that, in relation to twenty-five East African Asian citizens of the U.K. and Colonies whom the U.K. had refused to admit for settlement in the U.K., the U.K. government had violated art. 3 of the Convention relating to degrading treatment. A lengthy extract from the report is set out in H.C. *434* (1979–80), First Report from the Home Affairs Committee, Appendix 2. The Committee of Ministers took no action on the report; Appendix 3.

[19] It is a criminal offence for the owner of a ship or aircraft, or a carrier, to allow any person who requires leave to enter the U.K. to arrive in the U.K. without any necessary passport and visa: Immigration (Carriers' Liability) Act 1987.

Three special comments ought to be made at this point about those other than Community nationals who have no right of abode. First, those who were already settled here in this country on 1 January 1973 (that is, being ordinarily resident here without any time limit imposed by immigration legislation: see Immigration Act 1971, sections 2(3)(*d*), 8(5), 33) are regarded as having been given indefinite leave to enter and remain here (section 1(2)); and although this does not in itself exempt them from liability to deportation, they may become exempt after five years' residence here, provided that they are Commonwealth or Irish citizens (section 7). Secondly, the immigration rules must not render a Commonwealth citizen or his wife or children any less free to come and go than before the Act (section 1(5)). Thirdly, Commonwealth citizens with a *grandparent* born here (but not qualifying for the right of abode) are allowed under the immigration rules to enter without a work permit to seek work here, provided that they have an entry clearance,[20] though they remain liable to deportation. This concession, which benefits several million Commonwealth citizens, placated Conservative critics who objected to the preference given by the former draft rules to Community nationals over citizens of the old Commonwealth countries.

A prospective immigrant who is not a British citizen, whether he be a Commonwealth citizen or an alien, is refused entry to take up employment unless he can produce a work permit[21] and permits are issued by the Department of Employment for a specific post for a limited period (normally not more than twelve months[22] in the first instance) with a particular employer. The period for which a work permit will be extended is normally three years.[23] Work permits are not needed for certain specialized forms of employment. There are rules[24] for sea and air crews, visitors, returning residents, students, *au pair* girls, businessmen and self-employed persons, writers and artists, young Commonwealth citizens coming for working holidays, fiancés, fiancées and family dependants.[25] A very wide range of entry conditions may be imposed. Visitors from Ghana, Nigeria, Bangladesh, India and Pakistan

---

[20] H.C. 169 (1982–3), § 29. Entry clearances are obtainable through the appropriate U.K. representative in the country concerned (§ 11).

[21] H.C. 169 § 115.

[22] H.C. 169 § 116.

[23] H.C. 169 § 116.

[24] See generally H.C. 169 (1982–3). Under H.C. 208 (1987–8), visitors may stay for a maximum of six months, and businessmen and the self-employed for up to one year (and they may then apply for an extension of a further three years).

[25] The wives (and children) of male Commonwealth citizens who were settled in the U.K. before 1973 no longer have an unqualified right to join their husbands (and fathers): Immigration Act 1988, s. 1.

must have a visa issued by the British High Commission in those countries before they will be allowed to enter the United Kingdom.[26] Since 1988 people of independent means, writers and artists, businessmen and the self-employed may obtain leave to enter and remain for one year, and *au pairs* for up to two years; the maximum period for a visit has been reduced to six months.[27] Persons with diplomatic or similar status are exempt from control.[28]

Political asylum should be granted, under the immigration rules, to a person seeking entry if the only country to which he could be removed is one to which he is unwilling to go owing to a well-founded fear of persecution for reasons of race, religion, nationality, membership of a particular social group or political opinion.[29] The decision is made by the Home Office but leave to enter will not be refused if removal would be contrary to the provisions of the Convention and Protocol relating to the Status of Refugees.[30]

In respect of persons seeking to come here for *settlement*, the rules contain very complicated and detailed provisions.[31] Two sets of exceptions to these immigration controls are of major importance:

(*a*) *Citizens of the Republic of Ireland.* Citizens of the Republic of Ireland are not aliens in United Kingdom law.[32] Immigration controls have not been applied to them except under emergency conditions in Northern Ireland. The British Islands and the Republic of Ireland now form a Common Travel Area, and bona fide local journeys within that area by persons already resident there are not restricted by immigration requirements.[33] However, it is open to the Home Secretary to refuse entry to an Irish citizen if he deems it conducive to the public good in the interests of national security, or if that citizen has already been refused leave to enter, and it is possible under the 1971 Act for him to exclude the Republic from the Common Travel Area.[34] Under the

---

[26] Statement of Changes to Immigration Rules, Cmnd 9914 (1986).
[27] Statement of Changes to Immigration Rules, H.C. 208 (1987–8).
[28] 1971 Act, s. 8 (2), (3); S.I. 1972, No. 1613, and S.I. 1977, No. 693.
[29] H.C. 169 §§ 65 and 73. See *R.* v. *Secretary of State for the Home Department, ex. p. Bugdaycay* [1987] 2 A.C. 514.
[30] Cmnd 3906.
[31] H.C. 169. A British Overseas citizen coming here for this purpose needs a special voucher or corresponding entry certificate issued to him by a British Government representative overseas (H.C. 169, § 45); there is no express corresponding provision for aliens. The issue of vouchers is rigorously controlled.
[32] British Nationality Act 1981, s. 50(1).
[33] Immigration Act 1971, ss 1(3), 9; sched. 4; S.I. 1972, No. 1610.
[34] 1971 Act, s. 9(4), (6).

Prevention of Terrorism (Temporary Provisions) Act 1984 the Home Secretary may exclude from the U.K. anyone (including Irish citizens but excepting one who has been ordinarily resident throughout the last three years) if it appears to him expedient in order to prevent acts of terrorism designed to influence public opinion or Government policy with respect to affairs in Northern Ireland,[35] and many Irish citizens have been so excluded.

(*b*) *EEC Nationals.* The immigration rules, purporting to implement Community obligations,[36] provide that when an EEC national (other than an Irish citizen) is given leave to enter, no condition may be imposed restricting his employment or occupation in the United Kingdom.[37] Prospective workers, businessmen and self-employed persons are admitted without a work permit or other prior consent,[38] and the rights of their dependants to accompany or join them are appreciably wider than those with respect to others who are not British citizens.[39] In Community law, restrictions of freedom of migration of Community nationals can be imposed by member states only for reasons of public security, public health and certain facets of the public interest.[40]

Status within the United Kingdom of those having no right of abode

(*a*) *Commonwealth citizens.* They are liable to deportation for breach of entry conditions (for example, overstaying their period of entry or taking up a different job without leave) and on other grounds, though there is no formal restriction of movement within the country and they are not required to register with the police. Nevertheless, given the type of condition that is imposed on them, they suffer a substantial curtailment of their civil liberties.

(*b*) *Citizens of the Republic of Ireland.* Although not British citizens, they are entitled to exercise the franchise and be elected to public office; and rules of law applicable to British subjects before the British

---

[35] 1984 Act, s. 3.
[36] For which see EEC Treaty, arts 3(c), 48–58 and regulations and directives issued thereunder.
[37] H.C. 169 § 67.
[38] Admission of Community nationals for employment will normally be for six months. If they establish themselves they will normally be given a residence permit for five years. See generally H.C. 169 § 70, 140–46.
[39] H.C. 169 (1982–3) § 68.
[40] And see H.C. 169 § 69.

Nationality Act 1948 still apply to them unless subsequently excluded.[41] They are, however, liable to deportation, and it is an offence to re-enter the United Kingdom while subject to a deportation order; though given the absence of effective immigration controls this is not exactly a rigorous sanction.

(c) *Aliens* (*other than EEC nationals*). In order to enter the country at all, an alien must normally have an acceptable national passport or travel document, and in some cases he needs a visa or other entry clearance.[42] If he is given limited leave to enter, he may be subject to a condition requiring him to register with the police, and if he is granted an extension enabling him to remain longer than six months such a condition will then normally be imposed.[43]

Aliens cannot exercise the franchise, sit in either House of Parliament or hold any office under the Crown within the United Kingdom unless the responsible Minister certifies either that suitably qualified British citizens are not available for such a post or that the alien has exceptional qualifications.[44] Nor, in general, may they hold other public office.[45] Aliens are subject to a limited range of other occupational, professional and proprietary disabilities. Certain classes of aliens (members of visiting forces[46] and persons enjoying diplomatic and other privileges[47]) enjoy immunities from the operation of various rules of United Kingdom law and in some instances are exempt from amenability to the jurisdiction of the courts.

An 'enemy alien', in the sense of a citizen of a country with which Her Majesty is in a state of war, is liable to internment or expulsion under the prerogative;[48] but if he is registered and allowed to remain within this country[49] he has an implied licence from the Crown to take legal proceedings for the protection of his interests. The term 'enemy alien' may alternatively refer to a person or company carrying on business in an enemy country.[50] Such a person or corporation need not

---

[41] On the last point, see British Nationality Act 1948, s. 3(2); Ireland Act 1949, s. 3(1). See also note 32, above.
[42] H.C. 169 (1982–3).
[43] H.C. 169 § 74.
[44] Aliens Employment Act 1955, s. 1.
[45] Act of Settlement 1701, s. 3.
[46] Visiting Forces Act 1952; p. 213.
[47] See p. 143.
[48] See p. 144. A state of war for this purpose does not appear to cover a mere state of armed conflict in the absence of a prerogative declaration.
[49] At large or as an internee, but not as a combatant.
[50] See generally McNair and Watts, *Legal Effects of War* (4th edn, 1966).

be an enemy alien in the first sense of the term, or indeed an alien at all. But an alien in this second sense cannot sue in British courts, though if sued he can defend an action and lodge an appeal.[51] His property within the realm can be confiscated and handed over to a Custodian of Enemy Property.

(*d*) *EEC nationals.* Their rights to enter and remain in this country, surpassing those citizens without right of abode, have already been noted. Within this country the general rule is that they cannot be discriminated against by reason of their non-citizen status except in relation to employment in the public service.

Deportation

Not until the passing of the Commonwealth Immigrants Act 1962 were Commonwealth citizens subject to deportation, although the Home Secretary already had that power in respect of aliens by virtue of the Aliens Order 1953. The Immigration Act 1971, as amended by the British Nationality Act 1981, now regulates the deportation of all who are not British citizens.

Apart from those Commonwealth citizens (and Irish citizens) who were ordinarily resident in the United Kingdom on 1 January 1973,[52] and special groups like diplomats and their households and consuls, anyone who is not a British citizen is now subject to deportation if (i) the Home Secretary deems it to be 'conducive to the public good', or (ii) the person is over seventeen and recommended for deportation by a court on conviction for an offence punishable with imprisonment, and the recommendation is accepted by the Home Secretary,[53] or (iii) he breaks entry conditions or overstays his permitted period of entry or (iv) he or she is the infant child or wife of a person against whom a deportation order is made.[54] Grounds (i) and (iv) are new for

[51] *Porter* v. *Freudenberg* [1915] 1 K.B. 857.

[52] Who, if at all times ordinarily resident here since then, cannot be deported on grounds of 'public good', and if ordinarily resident here for the last five years, cannot be deported at all (Immigration Act 1971, s. 7), unless they are in U.K. unlawfully: see *R.* v. *Pentonville Prison Governor ex p. Azam* [1974] A.C. 18.

[53] For the factors which the Home Secretary considers, see Immigration Rules H.C. 169 (1982–3) § 156. In *R.* v. *Nazari* [1980] 1 W.L.R. 1366 the Court of Appeal laid down the guidelines for courts when making recommendations for deportation. The court should give reasons for its recommendation: *R.* v. *Home Secretary ex p. Santillo* [1981] Q.B. 778. In *R.* v. *Home Secretary ex p. Dannenberg* [1984] Q.B. 766, the Court of Appeal quashed a deportation order for an EEC citizen on the ground that the court gave no reason for its recommendation.

[54] 1971 Act, ss 3(5), (6), 5, 6; sched. 3. See *R.* v. *Secretary of State for the Home*

Commonwealth and Irish citizens. Deportation of the family with their head is not automatic; they may be allowed to stay on compassionate grounds.[55] A person liable to deportation as a 'family deportee', or as a result of a recommendation of a court, may be given financial assistance to leave instead of being deported.[56]

The deportation provisions of the 1971 Act do not exclude Community nationals from their application. On reference from the U.K. the European Court has held that deportation on the ground of a criminal conviction is justified only if there is a genuine and serious threat to a fundamental interest of society going beyond the disturbance of the social order which every crime inevitably involves.[57] An EEC directive provides that deportation must be exclusively on the ground of the individual's personal conduct whereas the Act allows for deportation because another member of his family has been ordered to be deported.[58]

Appeals

The appelate system laid down by the Immigration Act 1971 is too complex to describe in detail, but some features are of constitutional interest.

The normal channel of appeal from the decision of an immigration officer is to an adjudicator, and thence with leave to the independent Immigration Appeal Tribunal.[59] An appeal against a decision given in conformity with the immigration rules must be dismissed, except in so far as there is a disputed question of fact; but except where otherwise stated, the adjudicating body may review the exercise of a discretion by an immigration officer or the Secretary of State himself.[60]

In brief, appeals lie[61] to an adjudicator against (*a*) exclusion from

---

Department, ex p. *Khawaja* [1984] A.C. 74; *R.* v. *Immigration Appeal Tribunal, ex p. Patel, The Independent*, 5 May 1988 (deportation is conducive to the public good both where a person has obtained entry by deception, and where, having entered lawfully, a person obtains leave to stay by deception).

[55] H.C. 169 §§ 160–64.

[56] 1971 Act, s. 5(6). Financial contributions may also be made to assist non-British citizens wishing to leave this country to live permanently elsewhere (s. 29).

[57] *R.* v. *Bouchereau* [1978] Q.B. 732, where the magistrate decided that possessing a small quantity of drugs did not justify deportation.

[58] Directive 64/221 and *R* v. *Bouchereau*, above. Section 3(5) of the Immigration Act 1971.

[59] For the procedural rules, see S.I. 1972, No. 1684. Members of the tribunal are appointed by the Lord Chancellor and adjudicators by the Secretary of State.

[60] Immigration Act 1971, ss 19, 20.

[61] ibid., ss 13–17.

the United Kingdom (by refusal of entry or an entry clearance), but not while the appellant is in the U.K. unless (in certain circumstances) he is refused leave at the port of entry; (*b*) variation of or refusal to vary the conditions of entry (for example, duration of stay or location or type of employment); (*c*) deportation orders (other than orders made in pursuance of a recommendation by a court after a conviction), and refusals to revoke a deportation order already in force (provided that the appellant is out of the country), but the appeal lies to the Appeal Tribunal and not to an adjudicator if the deportation order was made on grounds of 'public good' or if the appellants are 'family deportees'; (*d*) directions for removal, including objections to being removed to a particular country or territory. Small disbursements have been made out of public funds (section 23) to enable the Immigrants Advisory Service, a voluntary body, to assist immigrant appellants. If on an appeal it is alleged that an entry document is a forgery, and that disclosure of the method of its detection would be contrary to the public interest, the investigation of that allegation takes places in the absence of the appellant and his representative (section 22(4)). A person who appeals against refusal of leave to enter and does not hold entry clearance or a work permit may exercise his right of appeal only whilst he is outside the United Kingdom.[62]

There is no right of appeal at all against:

1   Refusal of entry if the Secretary of State certifies that he personally directed that the applicant be excluded because exclusion would be conducive to the public good, or if entry was refused in obedience to such a direction (section 13(5)).
2   Reduction of or refusal to increase the permitted period of entry, if (*a*) the Secretary of State certifies that the appellant's deportation would be conducive to the public good in the interests of national security or good international relations or for other political reasons, or (*b*) the Secretary of State took the decision in person (section 14(3)).
3   A decision to make a deportation order against him on 'conducive' grounds as in 2(*a*) above (section 15(3)), except that appeal lies as to the destination.
4   Refusal to revoke an existing deportation order if revocation has been refused by the Secretary of State in person or if he certifies that exclusion was conducive to the public good (section 15(4)).

[62]   ibid., s. 13(3).

It is most unusual – it may indeed be an innovation – for legislation to attribute special effects to the fact that a Minister has taken a decision in person. No less interesting is the method of dealing with the delicate situations mentioned in (2) and (3) above where the 'public good' is allegedly bound up with security or political factors. But although there is no provision for *appeal* in such cases, there is an extra-statutory reference, at the request of the person aggrieved, to the Three Advisers who deal with civil servants' appeals against security dismissals and transfers.[63] The immigrant may state his case before them. Their advice to the Home Secretary is neither disclosed nor binding on him.[64]

A person would normally be expected to exhaust his rights of appeal under the Immigration Act before seeking judicial review.[65] Where appropriate an aggrieved person might make an application for judicial review under the Supreme Court Act 1981, section 31, and Order 53[66] or seek a writ of habeas corpus.[67] He might, for example, establish an excess of power by the Home Office[68] or by an immigration officer. Where an immigration officer has exercised his power to detain and remove an illegal immigrant, the court has to be satisfied, on the civil standard of proof to a high degree of probability, that in fact the applicant was an illegal immigrant when removed.[69] If he could discharge the heavy onus of proving that the Home Secretary abused his discretionary powers he could challenge a decision.[70] He could challenge as a question of law the official interpretation of the Act[71] or presumably of the Immigration Rules. Proof that an immigration

[63] 819 H.C. Deb 375–7 (15 June 1971); see also p. 202, above.
[64] In *R.* v. *Home Secretary, ex p. Hosenball* [1971] 1 W.L.R. 766 two journalists were deported for publishing information harmful to the security services. They challenged the validity of the deportation order; the Court of Appeal held the normal rules of natural justice did not apply so that the order was valid even though they were not given the evidence against them or the panel's report to the Home Secretary. The European Commission of Human Rights subsequently held that their application regarding that decision was inadmissible. This is the only case where this provision has been used.
[65] *R.* v. *Chief Immigration Officer, Heathrow, ex p. Salamat Bibi* [1976] 1 W.L.R. 979.
[66] See p. 585.
[67] See p. 471. The House of Lords discussed this remedy in relation to immigration law in *R.* v. *Secretary of State for the Home Department, ex p. Khawaja* [1984] A.C. 74.
[68] *R.* v. *Governor of Richmond Remand Centre, ex p. Asghar* [1971] 1 W.L.R. 129. And see *R.* v. *Home Secretary, ex p. Phansopkar* [1976] Q.B. 606.
[69] *R.* v. *Secretary of State for the Home Department, ex p. Khawaja* [1984] A.C. 74.
[70] *R.* v. *Brixton Prison Governor, ex p. Soblen* [1963] 2 Q.B. 243 shows how difficult it is to satisfy the courts of that. The applicant unsuccessfully maintained that the Home Secretary's dominant purpose in deporting him was to effect extradition to the United States for a non-extraditable offence. And see *R.* v. *Home Secretary, ex p. Hosenball* [1977] 1 W.L.R. 766, above.
[71] *In re Abdul Manan* [1971] 2 All E.R. 1016.; *R.* v. *Immigration Appeal Tribunal, ex p. Singh* [1986] 1 W.L.R. 910.

officer conducted his investigation unfairly would make the decision reviewable as a breach of the rules of natural justice.[72] On the other hand, when interpreting the now repealed Aliens Order, the courts held that the Home Secretary need not give a hearing before deporting an alien.[73] The Court of Appeal has, however, decided that judicial review is not to be used so as to avoid the appeal procedures in the Immigration Act 1971.[74] If, on the other hand, the Home Secretary acts unreasonably according to *Wednesbury* principles[75] in deciding a question of status (such as that of refugee), then judicial review may be successfully sought.[76]

The power of the Home Secretary to make exclusion orders under the Prevention of Terrorism (Temporary Provisions) Act 1984[77] preventing those concerned with acts of terrorism from entering or remaining in Great Britain, Northern Ireland or the U.K. has been previously mentioned. A person served with an exclusion order may object to the Home Secretary within seven days and, if he requests, may be interviewed by an adviser nominated by the Home Secretary. The Home Secretary then reconsiders the case after receiving a report from his adviser.[78] This procedure is executive only and so is not subject to any effective judicial review.

Allegiance and protection[79]

At common law, one who owes allegiance to the Crown is entitled to the Crown's protection; allegiance and protection are said to be correlative duties. The basic legal consequences of these principles at common law are as follows.

1   Violation of allegiance by levying war against the Queen within the realm or adhering to the Queen's enemies[80] is high treason, an offence still attracting the death penalty.

2   One who enjoys the protection of the Crown (*a*) is entitled to be

[72] *Re H.K.* [1967] 2 Q.B. 617.
[73] *Soblen's case*, above, and *Schmidt* v. *Home Secretary* [1969] 2 Ch. 149.
[74] *R.* v. *Secretary of State for the Home Department, ex p. Swati* [1986] 1 W.L.R. 477.
[75] See below, p. 578.
[76] See *R.* v. *Secretary of State for the Home Department, ex p. Bugdaycay* [1987] 2 A.C. 514, H.L.
[77] And see Prevention of Terrorism (Supplemental Temporary Provisions) Order 1984, S.I. 1984, No. 418.
[78] 1984 Act, s. 7.
[79] See H. Lauterpacht (1947) 19 *Camb. L.J.* 330; Glanville Williams (1948) 10 *Camb. L.J.* 54; J. C. Smith and Brian Hogan, *Criminal Law* (6th edn, 1988), pp. 829–31.
[80] Acquisition of enemy nationality by a British citizen in wartime is treasonable: *R.* v. *Lynch* [1903] 1 K.B. 444.

physically protected by the Crown against armed attack within Her Majesty's dominions;[81] (*b*) is entitled to be afforded diplomatic protection by the Crown;[82] (*c*) may be made a ward of court, if a minor,[83] and (*d*) can sue the Crown or its officers if the Crown commits or orders, authorizes or ratifies unlawful acts in relation to him, inasmuch as act of State is not generally available as a justification for *prima facie* wrongful interference with the legal rights of a person owing allegiance.[84]

Allegiance is owed by:

1 British citizens wherever they may be;
2 friendly aliens within Her Majesty's dominions;
3 friendly aliens outside Her Majesty's dominions if they are (*a*) ordinarily resident within them but are temporarily absent and evince an intention to return by leaving family or property there; or (*b*) are in possession of a current British passport or a travel document entitling them to return;[85] and
4 enemy aliens within Her Majesty's dominions with the express or implied licence of the Crown; this appears to cover all enemy aliens except combatants[86] other than prisoners of war.

The local allegiance of an alien does not cease to be owed merely because the part of Her Majesty's dominions in which he is resident is occupied by hostile forces.[87] It is not clear what is the legal foundation for the suggestion[88] that the Crown may expressly withdraw its protection from a friendly alien within Her Majesty's dominions.

This pattern of rules, founded on conceptual reasoning, is nevertheless irregular. For example, it is impossible to believe that the Crown has any kind of legal *duty* to afford diplomatic protection to an alien outside Her Majesty's dominions, even if he has obtained a United Kingdom passport by misrepresenting his citizenship.[89] Nor, it is

---

[81] See generally *China Navigation Co.* v. *Att.-Gen.* [1932] 2 K.B. 197, and *Mutasa* v. *Att.-Gen.* [1980] Q.B. 114. Hence the Crown cannot demand payment as a condition of granting such protection; *aliter* if such protection is granted outside Her Majesty's dominions to a person voluntarily exposing himself to a special hazard.

[82] *Joyce* v. *D.P.P.* [1946] A.C. 347 (treason); but see below.

[83] *Re P.* (*G.E.*) (*an Infant*) [1965] Ch. 568.

[84] *Johnstone* v. *Pedlar* [1921] 2 A.C. 262; see also *Nissan* v. *Att.-Gen.* [1970] A.C. 179 and pp. 149–50 above, indicating possible exceptions to the general rule.

[85] *Joyce*'s case; *Re P.* (*G.E.*) (see above).

[86] *Joyce*'s case [1946] A.C. at 368.

[87] *De Jager* v. *Att.-Gen. of Natal* [1907] A.C. 326 (treason).

[88] Made *obiter* in *Johnstone* v. *Pedlar* (above).

[89] Williams (1948) 10 *Camb. L.J.* 54, pointing out the flaw in the *ratio decidendi* of *Joyce*'s

thought, would the Crown be incapacitated from pleading act of State in defence to an action in tort brought by him for ostensibly wrongful acts outside Her Majesty's dominions. Resident enemy aliens can commit treason, but they do not enjoy that modest degree of protection against the Crown which would render them immune from being interned or expelled under the prerogative. Allegiance and protection are not fully correlative duties for every purpose and the implications of protection may vary according to the content.

A Commonwealth citizen who is not a British citizen is not guilty of any offence in United Kingdom law in respect of any act or omission committed either in his own country or in a foreign country unless it would be an offence if committed by an alien in a foreign country (section 3(1) of the 1948 Act). This means that a citizen of Canada or India, for instance, cannot be convicted of treason in the United Kingdom for anything done in Canada or India unless his conduct would have been equally treasonable if perpetrated by a Frenchman in France (for example, because he was ordinarily resident in the United Kingdom or perhaps held a current United Kingdom passport).

Passports: a note

United Kingdom passports are issued under the royal prerogative by the Passport Office, a sub-department of the Home Office. They may be refused, revoked and impounded in the absolute discretion of the Crown, and there is no formal machinery for appeal, but a person aggrieved can obtain judicial review of a decision adverse to his interests.[90] In form a passport is a request in the Queen's name to afford the holder free passage and any necessary assistance; it is also a certificate of identity and citizenship. A holder (provided, at least, that he is in fact a citizen) is entitled to the diplomatic protection of the

---

case. Joyce, an American citizen, had obtained a British passport in 1939; he went to Germany and, as 'Lord Haw-Haw', broadcast Nazi propaganda; held, he owed allegiance by virtue of the passport and was guilty of treason. Clearly, however, the Crown owed no *duty* to protect him by the *fact* of his having the passport. Why, then, did Joyce owe allegiance while in Germany?

[90] *R.* v. *Secretary of State for Foreign and Commonwealth Affairs, ex p. Everett, The Independent*, 26 October 1988. This moves English law nearer the position in the U.S.A. and India, where the highest courts have held that the Executive has not an arbitrary discretion to refuse or revoke a passport and thus derogate from a citizen's freedom of movement. See, for example, *Kent* v. *Dulles* 357 U.S. 116 (1958). Justice, *Going Abroad: A Report on Passports* (1975), is a good summary of the present practice, which recommends the enactment of a statute conferring upon all citizens the legal right to a passport. And see Jaconelli (1975) 38 *Mod. L. Rev.* 314.

United Kingdom Government in a foreign country, though any such duty cast upon the Crown does not appear to be directly enforceable in judicial proceedings. The Government has stated that in practice passports are withheld in four classes of case: (i) a minor whose journey is known to be contrary to a court order, to the wishes of a parent or other person or authority to whom a court has awarded custody, care and control, or to the provisions of section 25(1) of the Children and Young Persons Act 1933, as amended, or section 52 of the Adoption Act 1958, as amended; (ii) a person for whose arrest a warrant has been issued in the United Kingdom, or who is wanted by the United Kingdom police on suspicion of a serious crime; (iii) in very rare cases, a person whose past or proposed activities are so demonstrably undesirable that the grant or continued enjoyment of passport facilities would be contrary to the public interest; (iv) a person repatriated at public expense, until the debt has been repaid. Under successive Administrations it has been extremely rare to refuse a person under category (iii). Decisions in these cases are always taken personally by the Secretary of State.[91]

In practice it is extremely difficult to travel outside the country without a valid passport or national identity card, because carriers will demand production of passports by passengers, and immigration authorities elsewhere will not normally accept the entry of non-holders. Since any decision not to grant, or to revoke or withhold, a passport may seriously restrict freedom of movement, there should be a statutory procedure for appeal or review, with special arrangements for politically sensitive cases.

Fugitive offenders

Special statutory rules govern the surrender from the United Kingdom of fugitives from criminal justice in other countries. The ease of modern travel, especially by air, and the continuing scourge of international terrorism mean that effective arrangements for the extradition of alleged criminals must be maintained, and from time to time updated and improved. To those ends the Government made proposals for reform in 1985,[92] which are contained in the Criminal Justice Act 1988, sections 1 to 22 and Schedule 1. These rules apply, in general, to all persons, irrespective of their citizenship. The relevant body of rules depends on

[91] 416 H.L. Deb. 558 (22 January 1981).
[92] Green Paper on Extradition, Cmnd 9421 (1985); Criminal Justice: Plans for Legislation, Cmnd 9658 (1986).

the country seeking extradition. Rendition to the Republic of Ireland is effected by a single procedure under the Backing of Warrants (Republic of Ireland) Act 1965; to Commonwealth countries under the Fugitive Offenders Act 1967; and to foreign countries under the Extradition Act 1870 (as amended), in each case as amended by the Criminal Justice Act 1988. As has been noted,[93] a deportation order may, in certain circumstances, have the same practical effect as an extradition order.

Extradition to foreign countries is regulated by statute and treaty. There can be no extradition (as distinct from deportation) to a foreign State in the absence of a bilateral treaty to which effect is given in United Kingdom law by an Order in Council made in pursuance of the Extradition Acts. The terms of such an Order in Council must be compatible with the Acts – for example, it cannot provide for surrender of a person charged with an offence that is not an extradition crime scheduled to the Act – but there is scope for variation; thus, some extradition treaties exclude the rendition of nationals of one or both of the contracting states.

Extradition proceedings are started by a foreign government[94] issuing a request for extradition to the Home Secretary.[95] He may, if satisfied that the request is lawfully made, issue a warrant to proceed to a metropolitan stipendiary magistrate (or, in Scotland, to the sheriff of Lothian and Borders), who in turn may issue an arrest warrant.[96] On arrest the wanted person is brought before the metropolitan magistrate and, if he is satisfied that the authority to proceed relates to an extradition crime and that the person is the one named, he must issue a certificate to commit him to the Home Secretary's custody.[97] (Before the passage of the Criminal Justice Act 1988 the magistrate had to consider the evidence against the accused and satisfy himself that there would, in English law, be a *prima facie* case to answer. That judicial process was removed by the 1988 Act, except in relation to extradition requests from Commonwealth countries.) An extradition crime is one which, if committed in the United Kingdom, would be an offence punishable with twelve months' imprisonment or more and which is so punishable in the requesting State (or which is an extraterritorial offence against the law of that State) – all subject to certain

---

[93] *Soblen*'s case above, p. 451.

[94] Commonwealth countries, British colonies and the Republic of Ireland are outside these general provisions: see s. 1(4). The 1988 Act contains amendments to the relevant legislation in relation to those which are considered below.

[95] 1988 Act, s. 4.

[96] ibid., s. 7.

[97] ibid., s. 6.

conditions.[98] In no case may a person be returned to a foreign State under the 1988 Act if it appears that the offence alleged is of a political character, or is an offence only under military and not under civil law, or that the request is in fact made in order to punish the accused on account of his race, religion, nationality or political opinions.[99] If the magistrate refuses to commit the accused to the Home Secretary's custody the foreign State may 'question' the proceedings in the High Court;[100] if the accused is committed, he may apply for habeas corpus.[101] The Home Secretary must give the accused a written notice explaining that he may make representations to him why he should not be returned; the accused may seek judicial review of the Home Secretary's decision (but not on the ground that he did not have evidence before him to justify return).[102] If at least fifteen days elapse after committal, and any judicial proceedings are completed, the accused may be returned under the Home Secretary's warrant.[103]

It is too early to know what the courts will make of these provisions, but no doubt some of the cases on the former law will continue to be relevant. So, the metropolitan magistrate (and the High Court on a habeas corpus application) may consider whether the offence was one within the Act, the Order of Council and the treaty; whether the surrender of the accused is being sought for the purpose of detaining or trying him for a different offence; and whether it is being sought for an offence of a political character or in order to try or punish him for an offence[104] of a political character.[105] The House of Lords has, however, held that the courts have no jurisdiction to refuse extradition on the ground that surrender would be oppressive,[106] or even on the

[98] ibid., s. 1(7). The conditions are that (i) the offence must carry 12 months' imprisonment or more; and *either* (ii) in corresponding circumstances equivalent conduct outside the U.K. would be an extraterritorial offence against the U.K., *or* (iii) the foreign State bases jurisdiction on the nationality of the offender, and the offence occurred outside the U.K. and would be an offence in U.K. law.

[99] ibid., s. 3(1).

[100] ibid., s. 7.

[101] ibid., s. 8. The High Court may order his discharge if it would be unjust or oppressive to return him by reason of the triviality of the offence, or the passage of time since the alleged offence, or if the accusation against him is not made in good faith: ibid., s. 8(3). He may waive the right to apply: ibid., s. 10.

[102] ibid., s. 9.

[103] ibid., s. 9.

[104] *R.* v. *Bow Street Magistrates, ex p. Mackeson* (1982) 75 Cr. App. R. 24.

[105] Extradition Act 1870, s. 3. It would seem that for extradition to be refused on this last ground the 'political' offence must have already been committed. See *R.* v. *Brixton Prison Governor, ex p. Keane* [1972] A.C. 204 (a case decided on the similar but not identical wording of section 2(2) of the Backing of Warrants (Republic of Ireland) Act 1965).

[106] *Atkinson* v. *United States Government* [1971] A.C. 197.

ground that the accused had been convicted by the foreign court without an opportunity to defend himself and hence in breach of natural justice;[107] it lies within the discretion of the Home Secretary[108] to decide whether, in all the circumstances, the extradition order should be enforced. The courts are also extremely reluctant to attribute ulterior motives to a foreign government with which the United Kingdom maintains diplomatic relations; consequently they will accept assurances that the accused will not be tried or detained for any other offence or on political grounds upon his surrender.[109] The Home Secretary may exercise a political discretion after the court proceedings have terminated.

The magistrate, or the court on a habeas corpus application, will direct the release of the accused if of the opinion that the offence with which he has been charged is of a political character. Indeed, the Home Secretary should refuse to proceed with a request for surrender in the first place if the offence is political. To this extent the law does recognize a right, and not merely a privilege, of political asylum.[110]

For a long time it was thought that an offence could not be political unless it was committed in pursuance of a struggle for power between contending factions within a State. The murder of a Swiss official in furtherance of an uprising was an offence of a political character;[111] a murder committed by a bomb-throwing anarchist whose destructive impulses were directed against organized society at large was not.[112] Up to a point this test is serviceable; thus, a family dispute about the religious education of children in Israel, leading to perjury, kidnapping and a national political controversy did not fall within the concept of a political offence.[113] But no all-inclusive test is acceptable. For example, a mutiny and assault on the high seas designed to enable the criminals to escape to the West from a communist régime – an offence which in Poland would have been regarded as treasonable – was held to be of a political character, although there was no element of a struggle for power.[114] The murder of Jews in a Nazi concentration camp was an act of State policy, but it was not a political offence because the offenders

---

[107] *R.* v. *Brixton Prison Governor, ex p. Kotronis* [1971] A.C. 250.

[108] Extradition Act 1870, s. 11.

[109] *R.* v. *Brixton Prison Governor, ex p. Kotronis* (see above). cf. the differences in approach to this question in the judgments in *R.* v. *Brixton Governor, ex p. Kolczynski* [1955] 1 Q.B. 540.

[110] cf. p. 445. But to be 'political', the offence must be directed against the requisitioning State, not a third State: *Cheng* v. *Governor of Pentonville Prison* [1973] A.C. 931.

[111] *Re Castioni* [1891] 1 Q.B. 149.

[112] *Re Meunier* [1894] 2 Q.B. 415.

[113] *R.* v. *Brixton Prison Governor, ex p. Schtraks* (see above).

[114] *R.* v. *Brixton Prison Governor, ex p. Kolczynski* [1955] 1 Q.B. 540, *per* Cassels J.

would not have been entitled to political asylum in Britain.[115] Genocide is now an extradition crime and is deemed not to be of a political character (Genocide Act 1969, s. 2). Hijacking aircraft and unlawful acts against the safety of aircraft are also extradition crimes, but the ordinary exception for political offences remains (Aviation Security Act 1982, s. 9).

In the eyes of the courts, the categories of offences of a political character have not been closed. In deciding whether an offence does fall within this general description, or within the list of extradition crimes, the courts are entitled to receive additional material and can review the determination of the magistrate *de novo*. If, of course, the offence (for example, espionage) is not one of the scheduled crimes, the question whether it is of a political character does not arise.

The combined effect of the Suppression of Terrorism Act 1978 and the European Convention on the Suppression of Terrorism[116] is to eliminate or restrict the possibility of terrorists evading extradition by pleading that their crimes are political offences. The listed offences include murder, kidnapping and use of imitation firearms. If the United Kingdom refuses to extradite in circumstances covered by the convention because the fugitive might suffer on account of his race, religion, nationality or political opinions, it can take jurisdiction itself to try the offence.[117]

The Fugitive Offenders Act 1967 falls into two main parts.[118] Rendition to designated independent Commonwealth countries is permissible only for offences listed in the schedule to the Act. Rendition must be refused if the offence is of a political character, or if the request has in fact been made for the purpose of prosecuting or punishing him on account of his race, religion or political opinions, or if the offender might[119] be prejudiced at his trial or detained on any of these grounds. References to offences of a political character do not include offences against the life or person of the Queen.[120]

For dependent territories there is no list of scheduled offences and

---

[115] *Re Extradition Act 1870, ex p. Treasury Solicitor* [1969] 1 W.L.R. 12.

[116] Cmnd 7031 (1977) ratified by the United Kingdom and in force since 21 August 1978.

[117] For a reasoned criticism of this Act, see Schiff [1979] *Public Law* 353. And see Taking of Hostages Act 1982.

[118] It is amended by the Criminal Justice Act 1988, Sched. 1, to allow a Commonwealth State to challenge in the High Court a refusal to commit an alleged offender to the Home Secretary's custody for his decision on rendition.

[119] If the apprehended prejudice is grave, it is enough for the applicant for habeas corpus to show that a serious possibility of its occurrence exists; he does not have to show that the degree of possibility exceeds 50 per cent: *R. v. Pentonville Prison Governor, ex p. Fernandez* [1971] 1 W.L.R. 987.

[120] 1967 Act, s. 4.

rendition is still permissible for any offence punishable with twelve months' imprisonment. Nor is the rendition of 'political' fugitives prohibited, though the Home Secretary has a discretionary power to refuse to return offenders on political grounds.[121]

In relation to requests for return of offenders by *any* Commonwealth country, the magistrate or court *may* order discharge, on committal proceedings or on an application for habeas corpus, if it would be unjust or oppressive to return an offender because of the triviality of the offence or the lapse of time since it was committed or because the accusation has not been made in good faith in the interests of justice.[122] The Home Secretary *must* refuse to surrender the prisoner to an independent Commonwealth country, and *may* refuse to surrender him to a dependent territory, if he is satisfied on these grounds that surrender would be unjust or oppressive; he *may* refuse surrender of an offender to any part of the Commonwealth where he faces the capital penalty for an offence not punishable with death in Britain.

Special arrangements between Northern Ireland and the Republic of Ireland exist under the Criminal Jurisdiction Act 1975 and equivalent Irish legislation. The 1975 Act allows Northern Ireland courts to try offenders in the province accused of serious crimes of violence committed in the Republic apparently with political motives. These extraterritorial offences are described in Schedule 1 to the Act. A person accused in Northern Ireland of such an offence may choose to be tried in the Republic, and vice versa.

[121] s. 9(3).
[122] s. 8. The High Court may receive additional evidence for this purpose or when determining whether there are 'political' reasons for discharging him within the meaning of section 4. The Home Secretary is not to surrender a 'political' offender even if the courts refuse to order his discharge.

Chapter 24

Personal Freedom

Legal restraints on the liberty of the person

A typical bill of rights in a Commonwealth country's constitution will provide that no person shall be deprived of his personal liberty save as authorized by law and on specified grounds: unfitness to plead on a criminal charge; sentence by a court for a criminal offence; committal for contempt of court; detention in pursuance of any other court order, or to bring him before a court, or on reasonable suspicion of having committed or being about to commit a crime; custody for care and protection, in the case of an infant; detention to prevent spread of certain diseases; detention for mental illness, drug addiction, alcoholism or vagrancy; detention for illegal immigration, or to secure deportation or extradition; or detention under a reasonably justifiable order restricting his movements or place of residence. With the exception of the last, these are roughly the grounds on which deprivation of personal liberty may be based in English law.

The constitution will go on to lay down minimum safeguards for persons detained, arrested or tried on criminal charges. They must be brought before a court without undue delay. If they are not going to be tried within a reasonable time, they must be released on bail. They and their property are not to be arbitrarily searched. Persons unlawfully detained are entitled to compensation. One charged with a criminal offence must be given a fair hearing before an impartial court. He is to be presumed innocent till proved guilty. He is to be informed as soon as is reasonably practicable of the offence with which he is charged; he must be given proper defence facilities, including the free assistance of an interpreter if needed. He cannot be subjected to retroactive, inhuman or degrading punishment. He cannot be compelled to give evidence at his trial; nor in general can he be tried twice for the same offence.

This is, in effect, an outline sketch of some basic principles of English criminal law and procedure, transposed into a constitutional text. In England the most important legal inhibitions on personal liberty consist in the powers and duties vested in those entrusted with the task of investigating and detecting crime. To these we shall give special attention, though other matters will also be introduced.

Powers of arrest

Unfortunately no branch of English law is more obscure or complex than that relating to powers of arrest.[1] The general common-law principles have been partly codified by the Police and Criminal Evidence Act 1984 but hardly clarified.[2]

To lay hands on another against his will and without lawful justification is an assault.[3] Unlawful detention (including arrest) is false imprisonment. Both are crimes and civil wrongs. In what circumstances, then, are the detention and arrest of suspected criminals justified by law?

The police have no general power to detain suspects for questioning unless they are arrested,[4] or even to require suspects or witnesses to accompany them to a police station or to give their names and addresses[5] or indeed to answer any questions, or to compel anyone to attend for an identity parade.[6] Apart from certain common-law powers, the police now have a general power, on reasonable suspicion, to search any person or vehicle for stolen or prohibited articles, and to detain a person or vehicle for that purpose.[7] If a police officer decides to arrest a person on a criminal charge, he must normally obtain an arrest warrant from a magistrate by information supported by a sworn

[1] For detailed analyses of powers of arrest, see Glanville Williams [1954] *Crim. L. Rev.* 6, 408, 508; [1959] *Crim. L. Rev.* 73, 155; Thomas [1962] *Crim. L. Rev.* 520, 597; [1966] *Crim. L. Rev.* 639; Lidstone [1978] *Crim. L. Rev.* 332.

[2] See ss 24, 25. On the Act generally see V. Bevan and K. Lidstone, *A Guide to the Police and Criminal Evidence Act 1984* (1985); M. Zander, *The Police and Criminal Evidence Act 1984* (1985); L. H. Leigh, *Police Powers in England and Wales* (2nd edn, 1985); St. J. Robilliard and J. McEwan, *Police Powers and the Individual* (1986).

[3] Though cf. *Donnelly* v. *Jackman* [1970] 1 W.L.R. 562 (see note 54, below).

[4] *R.* v. *Lemsatef* [1977] 1 W.L.R. 812; *R.* v. *Houghton and Franciosy* (1978) 68 Cr. App. R. 197.

[5] *Rice* v. *Connolly* [1966] 2 Q.B. 414; but see p. 464 how the general power of arrest may oblige a suspect to give his name and address.

[6] Sargant [1966] *Crim. L. Rev.* 485.

[7] Police and Criminal Evidence Act 1984, ss 1–3. Prohibited articles are defined (ibid.) as offensive weapons, articles to be used in specified offences under the Theft Act 1968, and now include articles with a blade or sharp point, as defined by the Criminal Justice Act 1988, s. 139.

statement. The warrant must specify the name of the person to be arrested and general particulars of the offence. A general warrant, not naming the person to be arrested or failing to give adequate particulars of the offence, is illegal at common law.[8] Arrest warrants are hardly ever issued to persons other than police officers; and they are issued only in respect of arrestable offences[9] punishable (subject to various statutory exceptions) with a maximum of at least five years' imprisonment. If the issue of the warrant is outside the magistrate's jurisdiction but is *prima facie* valid on its face, a constable executing it is protected from civil liability.[10]

An arrest involves an element of compulsion, though not necessarily physical seizure; a mere request by a constable that a person accompany him to a police station is not an arrest;[11] the arrest is not lawful unless the person arrested is informed that he is under arrest (even if the fact of arrest is obvious).[12] In effecting an arrest, no more physical force must be used that is reasonably required; otherwise the arrest becomes an actionable assault.

Special difficulties arise in ascertaining the legal grounds on which an arrest may be effected without a warrant.

Any member of the public may arrest without warrant:[13]

1 Anyone who is in the act of committing an arrestable offence.
2 Anyone whom he has reasonable grounds for suspecting to be committing such an offence.
3 Anyone who is, or whom he reasonably suspects to be, guilty of an arrestable offence, where such an arrestable offence has been committed.[14]

A *constable, in addition*, may arrest without warrant:

1 Anyone whom he has reasonable grounds for suspecting has

---

[8] *Leach* v. *Money* (1765) 3 Burr. 1692, 1742. See also *Wilkes* v. *Wood* (1769) 19 St. Tr. 1406 (search warrant); *Entick* v. *Carrington* (1765) 19 St. Tr. 1030.

[9] Police and Criminal Evidence Act 1984, s. 24(1), (2) (hereafter 'the 1984 Act'); both statutory and common-law offences are included under the Act.

[10] Constables' Protection Act 1750.

[11] *Alderson* v. *Booth* [1969] 2 Q.B. 216. See, however, *Wheatley* v. *Lodge* [1971] 1 W.L.R. 29 (defendant lawfully arrested although he failed to realize, because of deafness unknown to the police officer, that he was being required to go to police station under arrest). cf. *R.* v. *Inwood* [1973] 1 W.L.R. 647.

[12] 1984 Act, s. 28(1), (2).

[13] 1984 Act, s. 24(4), (5).

[14] If no arrestable offence exists, a private person (including a store detective) is liable in false imprisonment if he carries out an arrest, even if he reasonably believes that an arrestable offence has taken place: *Walters* v. *Smith (W.H.) and Son Ltd* [1914] 1 K.B. 595.

committed an arrestable offence – even though no such crime has been committed.[15]

2 Anyone who is about to commit an arrestable offence, or whom he has reasonable grounds for suspecting is about to commit such a crime.[16]

3 Any person, when the constable has reasonable grounds for suspecting that any offence which is not an arrestable offence is being or has been committed or attempted, provided that service of a summons is impracticable or inappropriate because any of the specified 'general arrest conditions' is satisfied.[17]

The conditions are (i) that the suspected person's name is unknown to, and cannot be readily ascertained by, the constable; or (ii) that the constable has reasonable grounds for doubting whether a name furnished is correct; or (iii) that the address furnished is unsatisfactory for service; or (iv) that the constable has reasonable grounds for believing that, unless he arrests the person, he may cause physical harm to himself or another, or he may suffer physical injury or cause loss of or damage to property, or commit an offence against public decency, or an unlawful obstruction of the highway; or (v) that the constable has reasonable grounds for believing that an arrest is necessary to protect a child or other vulnerable person from the suspected person.[18] A member of the public is entitled to use reasonable force 'in the prevention of crime', or in effecting or assisting in the 'lawful arrest' of offenders or suspected offenders.[19] Given the uncertainty about the degree of force justifiable to prevent crime and the meaning of a lawful arrest – this includes arrest for specified arrestable offences (but few members of the public will carry the list in their heads) and arrest for breaches of the peace committed in one's presence[20] (but even the term 'breach of the peace' has an uncertain meaning apart from acts of violence to the person) – it is obviously risky for the citizen to take a

[15] 1984 Act s. 24(6). See the consideration of common-law authority in *Barnard* v. *Gorman* [1941] A.C. 378 and *Wiltshire* v. *Barrett* [1966] 1 Q.B. 312. The question whether a constable has 'reasonable cause' to suspect that a person is guilty of an offence is to be determined objectively on the basis of the information available to him at the time of the arrest; the constable need not also have an honest belief in the suspect's guilt: *Castorina* v. *Chief Constable of Surrey*, *The Independent*, 16 June 1988.

[16] ibid., s. 24(7).

[17] This is a new general power conferred by the 1984 Act, s. 25.

[18] 1984 Act, s. 25(3).

[19] Criminal Law Act 1967, s. 3; or of persons 'unlawfully at large': this category includes not only escaped prisoners but detained mental patients.

[20] For the powers of the police and citizens to arrest for suspected breaches of the peace, see *R.* v. *Howell* [1982] Q.B. 416.

suspected offender into custody. To respond to the request of a police officer to help him apprehend a criminal may evince public spirit but does not confer immunity from liability if the arrest is unlawful. On the other hand, to refuse compliance with such a request without lawful excuse when two or more persons are actually committing a breach of the peace is an offence.[21]

If these prerequisites of a valid arrest are present, the arrest will still not be lawful unless, at the time of making the arrest, the person arrested is informed of the ground for the arrest, at that time or as soon as practicable afterwards – and if a constable makes the arrest, even if that ground is obvious, such as being caught red-handed.[22] He does not have to be told the technical name of the offence in question; nor is it necessary to say anything to him if it is reasonable to think that announcing one's presence before seizing him would cause him to run away from the scene; nor does one have to shout the reasons to a person who, unknown to oneself, is deaf. The purpose of requiring communication, where practicable, is to enable the person arrested to clear himself by explanation at the first opportunity.[23]

A person who is unlawfully arrested may use reasonable force to free himself.[24] But although passive submission may not be required by law, active resistance is apt to be perilous, because a court may hold that excessive force has been used, and not every mistaken arrest by the police is unlawful.

Since 1974, Prevention of Terrorism Acts have been in operation with the aims of banning the Irish Republican Army and allied organizations, and of excluding from Great Britain any terrorists who might use violence for political ends.[25] Police are empowered to arrest without warrant on reasonable suspicion of terrorism. They are given powers to detain suspects pending investigation for two days at their discretion. The Home Secretary may authorize a further five days' detention.

---

[21] *R.* v. *Brown* (1841) Car. & M. 314.

[22] 1984 Act, s. 28(3), (4).

[23] See *Christie* v. *Leachinsky* [1947] A.C. 573; *John Lewis & Co.* v. *Tims* [1952] A.C. 672; *D.P.P.* v. *Hawkins* [1988] 3 All E.R. 673. For a marginal case, where a person was held to have been lawfully arrested although he was given the wrong legal ground for his arrest, see *Gelberg* v. *Miller* [1961] 1 W.L.R. 138; the facts constituting the reason for his arrest were, however, apparent to the defendant, and he could have been arrested for an offence arising out of those facts. See also *R.* v. *Kulynycz* [1971] 1 Q.B. 367 (original arrest wrongful, no proper reason having been given, but error rectified while defendant still in custody). Contrast *R.* v. *Holah* [1973] 1 W.L.R. 127.

[24] As in *Kenlin* v. *Gardiner* [1967] 2 Q.B. 510.

[25] The current Act is the Prevention of Terrorism (Temporary Provisions) Act 1984.

Police detention

The powers of the police to detain a person after arrest and before charging him are now subject to the Police and Criminal Evidence Act 1984.[26] As soon as the police decide that there is sufficient evidence to support a charge the person must be charged. Otherwise he must be released, unless the police have reasonable grounds for believing that his detention without charge is necessary to secure or preserve or obtain evidence.[27] After being charged the arrested person may be released, but may instead be further detained if specified conditions are satisfied, such as police suspicion about any name and address furnished.[28] In any event the Act imposes time limits on the period of detention without charge.[29] From the time at which the arrested person arrives at the police station, the police have twenty-four hours in which to charge him, failing which he must be released;[30] but the police may themselves authorize his detention for a total of up to thirty-six hours, and a magistrates' court for up to a total of ninety-six hours, if this is necessary to obtain evidence of a 'serious arrestable offence'.[31] The arrested person must be released within these limits unless he is charged.[32] Detention for questioning for such long periods must, in practice, endanger the right to silence.

Bail

A person arrested and charged must be brought before a magistrates' court as soon as practicable and in any event not later than the first sitting after he is charged (which will usually be the following day).[33] He may be remanded in custody or on bail pending further proceedings by way of summary trial, preliminary hearing, committal for trial on indictment or appeal. Release on bail may be granted by a police sergeant following arrest without warrant,[34] or by magistrates or by a High Court or Circuit judge. The powers of magistrates and judges to

---

[26] 1984 Act, Part IV.
[27] ibid., s. 37.
[28] ibid., s. 38(1).
[29] ibid., ss 41–4.
[30] ibid., s. 41(1).
[31] ibid., ss 42, 43, 44; 'serious arrestable offence' is defined in s. 116 partly by reference to certain named crimes and partly by reference to other arrestable offences made serious by their consequences in the particular case.
[32] See below, under *Bail*.
[33] 1984 Act, s. 46.
[34] ibid., s. 47. For granting of bail by police to persons under 17, see Children and Young Persons Act 1969, s. 29; Bail Act 1976, s. 3(7).

refuse release on bail have been curtailed by the Bail Act 1976. There is a statutory presumption in favour of bail for an accused in custody who has not yet been convicted. He must be remanded on bail (whether or not he has applied for it) unless the court is satisfied that there is an unacceptable risk that if he were released on bail he would fail to surrender to custody or commit an offence while on bail, or interfere with witnesses or otherwise obstruct the course of justice.[35] Before being admitted to bail, the person arrested may be required to produce sureties for his appearance and other relevant conditions may be imposed. An accused can no longer be asked to provide a recognizance, to be forfeited should he not surrender for trial.[36] Instead the Act introduces a new offence of absconding while on bail.[37] If he is refused bail or objects to the conditions under which it is offered, he must be told the reasons, and of his right to apply to the Crown Court or a High Court judge, who have power to admit to bail or vary the conditions under which it has been offered.[38]

Binding over to be of good behaviour or to keep the peace[39]

A person convicted of crime may, instead of being sent to prison, be bound over. This power is ancillary to the exercise of criminal jurisdiction (Justices of the Peace Act 1968, s 1(7)) and does not presuppose the conviction of the person bound over. Alternatively, a bind-over order may be made by way of preventive justice. Under section 115 of the Magistrates' Courts Act 1980 the court may, on the complaint of X, bind Y over to enter into a recognizance, with or without sureties, to keep the peace or to be of good behaviour towards X. No such order may be made unless the complaint is properly proved. Magistrates also have a general power under the Justices of the Peace Act 1361 to bind persons over to be of good behaviour or to keep the peace; this power may be exercised without a formal complaint, and in the course of other proceedings, though if the order is to keep the peace, some threat to the peace must be disclosed by the

[35] Section 3.
[36] Section 3(2).
[37] Section 6.
[38] Criminal Justice Act 1967, s. 22; Supreme Court Act 1981, s. 81; Criminal Justice Act 1982, s. 60. The detainee cannot apply to successive judges in turn in the hope of obtaining bail: *R.* v. *Reading Crown Court, ex p. Malik* [1981] Q.B. 451.
[39] See generally Glanville Williams (1953) 16 *Mod. L. Rev.* 417; D. G. T. Williams, *Keeping the Peace*, ch. 4; [1970] *Camb. L.J.* at 103–6; [1963] *Public Law* 441; D. A. Thomas, *Principles of Sentencing* (2nd edn, 1979), pp. 228–9. See also Law Commission Working Paper No. 103 (1987) which has an excellent review of the law.

evidence adduced.[40] If the person against whom an order is made refuses to give the required undertaking, or refuses or is unable to offer sureties for his conduct, he can be sent to prison for a period of up to six months even though he has committed no crime. Because such an order is not a conviction, no appeal against the merits of the decision lay till one was provided by statute in 1956.[41] Binding-over orders have been used not only to restrain political agitators from repeating or encouraging violence or from inciting other persons to break the law[42] but also to prevent persons from behaving in a way likely (though not intended) to provoke others to commit breaches of the peace[43] and to inhibit the activities of transvestites, prostitutes, kerb-crawling motorists looking for prostitutes, protestors against nuclear weapons and increased car-parking charges, and gentlemen who peep into ladies' lavatories and bedrooms.

Obstructing the police in the execution of their duty

Under section 51(3) of the Police Act 1964 (substantially reproducing the wording of an Act of 1885) it is an offence, punishable with up to a month's imprisonment, wilfully to obstruct a constable in the execution of his duty.[44] It will be considered further in the context of the law of public meeting, but the case law tells us something, albeit in discordant language, about the duties of the police. The general duty of the police is to preserve public order and secure due observance of the criminal law; and they cannot divest themselves of these obligations.[45] They have other specified statutory duties and numerous powers. The courts have attempted to strike a balance between facilitating the proper discharge of the functions of the police on the one hand and the maintenance of individual liberty on the other. Police powers and

---

[40] See generally *R. v. Aubrey-Fletcher, ex p. Thompson* [1969] 1 W.L.R. 872. The party against whom an order is made must first be given an opportunity to argue against it: *Sheldon v. Bromfield JJ.* [1964] 2 Q.B. 573.

[41] Magistrates' Courts (Appeals from Binding-Over Orders) Act 1956 as amended by the Courts Act 1971 (appeal on the merits to the Crown Court). But a bind-over made without jurisdiction may be quashed at common law by the High Court on an application for certiorari (*R. v. Aubrey-Fletcher*, above) and appeal lies by case stated on a question of law to a Divisional Court of the Queen's Bench Division: see, for example, *Beattie v. Gillbanks* (1882) 9 Q.B.D. 308.

[42] For example, *Lansbury v. Riley* [1914] 3 K.B. 229.

[43] *Wilson v. Skeock* (1949) 65 T.L.R. 4128, approved in *Aubrey-Fletcher*'s case, above.

[44] See *Lewis v. Cox* [1984] 3 All E.R. 672 for a discussion of the offence, especially in relation to the defendant's motive.

[45] See generally *R. v. Metropolitan Police Commissioner, ex p. Blackburn* [1968] 2 Q.B. 118; ch. 20.

duties for securing public order have been widely interpreted; the police have a duty to break up public gatherings where serious disorders occur and to prevent reasonably apprehended breaches of the peace, and a refusal on the part of a member of the public to desist when called upon to do so is an obstruction of a constable in the execution of his duty.[46] Again, unreasonable use of the highway amounting to a public nuisance or wilful obstruction should be stopped by the police, and it will be an offence to refuse to comply with a police instruction to disperse.[47] In these circumstances the police have an implied power to arrest without warrant; but it would seem that there is no *general* power of arrest merely for wilful obstruction of the police,[48] though a summons may be issued. Obstruction of police investigations into suspected crimes is not necessarily an offence although the police may be acting in the general execution of their functions. Deliberately attempting to prevent the apprehension of one guilty of an arrestable offence, or wasting the time of the police by making allegations one knows to be false, are separate statutory offences.[49] To give other offenders prior warning of the approach of the police so as to enable them to escape detection is a wilful obstruction of a constable in the execution of his duty,[50] and the same is probably true of the deliberate destruction or removal of relevant evidence,[51] or having an extra drink in order to frustrate a breathalyser test that is about to be administered by a police officer to oneself,[52] or giving misleading statements while under police interrogation. But it has been held not to be an offence simply to refuse to answer police questions[53] or to resist with reasonable force detention for the purpose of being so questioned.[54] Nor do police officers have a general licence to enter upon private

---

[46] *Duncan* v. *Jones* [1936] 1 K.B. 218. See also *Piddington* v. Bates [1961] 1 W.L.R. 162.

[47] *Tynan* v. *Balmer* [1967] 1 Q.B. 91. See also *Gelberg* v. *Miller* [1961] 1 W.L.R. 153 (power to arrest for highway obstruction in the Metropolitan area), and see generally Highways Act 1980, s. 137.

[48] *Gelberg* v. *Miller* (see above); but see pp. 464–5.

[49] Criminal Law Act 1967, ss 4, 5(2).

[50] *Hinchliffe* v. *Sheldon* [1955] 1 W.L.R. 1207; *Betts* v. *Stevens* [1910] 1 K.B. 1; contrast *Bastable* v. *Little* [1907] 1. K.B. 59 (warning of speed trap).

[51] Though cf. *R.* v. *Waterfield and Lynn* [1964] 1 Q.B. 164 (attempt by police officers to prevent motor car suspected of involvement in serious offence from being driven off, held not part of their duties). See criticisms of that decision in *Ghani* v. *Jones* [1970] 1 Q.B. 693 at 707–8.

[52] *Dibble* v. *Ingleton* [1972] 1 Q.B. 480.

[53] *Rice* v. *Connolly* [1966] 2 Q.B. 414.

[54] *Kenlin* v. *Gardiner* [1967] 2 Q.B. 510 (a case of alleged assault on the police). Contrast *Donnelly* v. *Jackman* [1970] 1 W.L.R. 562 (where the police officer had merely touched his assailant on the shoulder with a view to questioning him).

premises without the occupier's permission in order to investigate suspected crime.[55] Even if they enter with permission, they become trespassers once consent is withdrawn,[56] unless they have entered in pursuance of a valid warrant or to effect a lawful arrest[57] or for the prevention of a reasonably apprehended breach of the peace[58] or under other, ill-defined, conditions furnishing justification for entry. The general duty to investigate suspected crime imports powers[59] limited in scope; and a member of the public is not inevitably guilty of an offence by deliberately making it more difficult for the police to exercise those powers or effectively to discharge this general duty.

Police interrogation

As has been noted, detention for questioning is generally unlawful except where it amounts to a lawful arrest; and a person interrogated by the police is not obliged to say anything. Moreover, confessions of guilt are inadmissible in evidence at a criminal trial if procured by oppression or in consequence of anything said or done which was likely to render them unreliable,[60] and other admissions detrimental to an accused are sparingly admitted. The accused is not required to give evidence at his trial.

The American constitutional Bill of Rights provides that no one shall be compelled to be a witness against himself, that an accused shall have the assistance of counsel, and generally that due process of law shall be observed. English law does not go so far as the law in the United States in restricting methods of police interrogation.[61] The procedure to be followed is prescribed partly by the exclusionary rules of evidence indicated above, and partly by the Police and Criminal Evidence Act 1984[62] and codes of practice made under it.

---

[55] For example, *Davis* v. *Lisle* [1936] 2 K.B. 434; p. 479, below. *Morris* v. *Beardsmore* [1980] 3 W.L.R. 283 (constable entering driver's home 1½ hours after accident to conduct a breathalyser test a trespasser).

[56] See the general discussion of legal principle in *Robson* v. *Hallett* [1967] 2 Q.B. 393.

[57] See Police and Criminal Evidence Act 1984, s. 17.

[58] *Thomas* v. *Sawkins* [1935] 2 K.B. 249; see pp. 514–15, below.

[59] *R.* v. *Prebble* (1858) 1 F. & F. 325 (constable turned persons out of public house at landlord's invitation; resistance to him held to be an assault, but not an assault committed while he was executing his *duty*, because there was no nuisance or danger of a breach of the peace).

[60] Police and Criminal Evidence Act 1984, s. 76.

[61] There is a valuable comparative study of American and Commonwealth (including English) law on these matters by H. J. Glasbeek and D. D. Prentice in (1968) 23 *Cornell L. Rev.* 473. And see Gooderson (1970) 48 *Can. Bar. Rev.* 270.

[62] 1984 Act, Parts V and VI.

The codes are not rules of strict law in the ordinary sense. Non-compliance does not render statements by an accused person inadmissible in evidence, but the provisions of the codes must be 'taken into account' by a court when deciding any question to which they are relevant.[63] The details of the codes need not be examined here, but they are designed to ensure first that interrogation shall not be oppressive, secondly that statements to the police shall be voluntary, and thirdly that a person shall be notified, by formal cautions, that he is not obliged to say anything in answer to questions. A person must be allowed access to a solicitor, as soon as is practicable if he so requests, and in any case within thirty-six hours of arrival at a police station.[64] The police have no positive duty to notify an arrested person that he is entitled to consult a solicitor. At least in form, the 'right to be silent' enjoys better protection under the American case law than under the 1984 Act and codes. A defence lawyer on the spot will tend to advise his client to say nothing to the police in the first instance. An arrested person has the right to have one person told, if he so requests, that he has been arrested. This must be done within thirty-six hours of arriving at the station,[65] but the police are under no legal duty to tell him of this right.

Habeas corpus[66] and other remedies

A person subjected to invalid or excessive physical restraint may exercise self-help, sue or prosecute for assault or false imprisonment. If he is prosecuted without reasonable or probable cause and for improper motives, he may sue for damages for malicious prosecution.

The most celebrated safeguard of the liberty of the subject is the prerogative writ[67] of habeas corpus. Traceable beyond Magna Carta, in the fourteenth century the modern function of the writ emerged: to require a person having custody of a prisoner to bring him before the court together with grounds for detention. The court could then test the legality of the detention and direct release if the imprisonment was found to be unlawful. The Habeas Corpus Act 1679 made the writ an

[63] ibid. s. 67(10), (11).
[64] ibid., s. 58. The right to consult a solicitor is 'fundamental', and may only be delayed under the exceptions in s. 58 in very limited circumstances: see *R.* v. *Samuel* (1988) 2 All E.R. 135.
[65] ibid., s. 56.
[66] The leading monograph is R. J. Sharpe, *The Law of Habeas Corpus* (1976).
[67] See de Smith, *Judicial Review of Administrative Action* (4th edn, 1980), Appendix 1, on the term 'prerogative' writ.

efficient remedy in criminal cases by providing stringent safeguards against lengthy imprisonment without trial. Time limits were laid down for entering a return to the writ, and for producing the prisoner before a superior court if there were *prima facie* grounds for supposing the imprisonment to be unlawful; the court was empowered or required to admit to bail or provide for speedy trial if detention were founded on a criminal charge; heavy financial penalties were imposed on judges wrongfully refusing to issue the writ,[68] on gaolers evading service or compliance with the writ (for example, by moving the prisoner from one gaol to another or overseas), and on persons recommitting a prisoner already discharged on an application for habeas corpus. An Act of 1816 extended some of these provisions to civil cases, and empowered the court to inquire into the truth of the return made to the writ.[69]

The modern law of habeas corpus[70] is governed partly by statute, partly by case law and partly by Rules of the Supreme Court.[71] An application is made to a Divisional Court of the Queen's Bench Division or, if no such court is then sitting, to a single judge of any division, even at his private house. Habeas corpus applications have priority over all other business. The application is to be made by or with the concurrence of the detainee unless he is incapable of consenting, in which case a relative, guardian or friend may apply on his behalf. It must be accompanied by an affidavit showing why his restraint is unlawful. If *prima facie* grounds are demonstrated, the person who ordered the detention or who has actual custody (for example, a prison governor, the Serjeant at Arms, the superintendent of a mental hospital, or a Minister) must then show cause, on a date fixed by the court, why the writ should not issue to release the detainee. Production of the record of an apparently valid conviction by a court places on the applicant the burden of proving that the court had exceeded its jurisdiction. On the other hand, in a case of private detention, or where a British citizen is being detained by the Executive, allegedly on grounds specified by statute, the onus of proving that there existed facts justifying the detention rests on the custodian.[72]

[68] s. 10. This section of the Act is still in force. Some of the other sections have been repealed, amended or indirectly superseded by new statutory provisions for the granting of bail and the expedition of trials, cf. *R.* v. *Campbell* [1959] 1 W.L.R. 646.

[69] The history of habeas corpus is traced by Holdsworth, *History of English Law*, vol. 10, pp. 108–25. See also Jenks (1902) 18 *L.Q.R.* 64.

[70] The only significant form of the writ now used is called *habeas corpus ad subjiciendum.*

[71] Especially R.S.C. Ord. 54.

[72] *R.* v. *Brixton Prison Governor, ex p Ahsan* [1969] 2 Q.B. 222. Contrast *Green* v. *Home Secretary* [1942] A.C. 284, a wartime preventive detention case.

In general, habeas corpus cannot be used as a device for impeaching the correctness of a determination made by a court of competent jurisdiction, the only appropriate means of redress being appeal;[73] though not all decisions on habeas corpus are reconcilable with this principle.[74] On habeas corpus applications made by persons committed by magistrates for extradition or rendition as fugitive offenders, the court did not substitute its own opinion for the magistrate's on the question whether there was a *prima facie* case, but it might award the writ if satisfied that his conclusion on the facts as found was such as no reasonable magistrate properly directing his mind to the issues could have reached[75] or if it disagreed with his finding that the offence was not of a political character.[76] The scope of review will in practice vary according to the context. The courts have given short shrift to wartime security suspects;[77] they have flinched from questioning the validity of a Speaker's warrant alleging contempt of the House of Commons in general terms, even though the inadequacy in law of the true grounds for commitment has been notorious.[78] The House of Lords held in 1983 that where an immigration officer has exercised his power to detain and remove an illegal immigrant, the court will have to be satisfied, on the civil standard of proof to a high degree of probability, that in fact the applicant was an illegal immigrant when the power was exercised.[79] This decision may herald a greater willingness on the part of the courts, whenever personal liberty is threatened by executive decision, to require the official to prove that the facts existed on which his power to detain depended.

Applicants for habeas corpus in recent years have mostly been persons in detention for the purpose of extradition, deportation or implementation of a refusal to admit as an immigrant.[80] The introduction of an immigration appeals system has stemmed[81] the flow by

---

[73] *Ex p. Hinds* [1961] 1 W.L.R. 325. The court may admit to bail on an application on a criminal matter.

[74] Amnon Rubinstein, *Jurisdiction and Illegality* (1965), pp. 105–16, 178–86.

[75] See *R. v. Brixton Governor, ex p. Armah* [1968] A.C. 192, especially at 229–35, *per* Lord Reid, conceding that the scope of review is not confined to strictly jurisdictional grounds.

[76] But see now pp. 455–60.

[77] For example, *Green's* case, note 72; and pp. 527–8.

[78] *Sheriff of Middlesex's* case (1840); p. 341.

[79] *R. v. Secretary of State for the Home Department, ex p. Khawaja* [1984] A.C. 74, overruling its own decision in *Zamir v. Home Secretary* [1980] A.C. 930.

[80] The writ was unsuccessfully sought in 1984 by a prisoner held on remand who had not been produced from prison to court at the time fixed because of an industrial dispute at the prison: *R. v. Brixton Prison Governor, ex p. Walsh* [1985] A.C. 154.

[81] See ch. 23.

providing an alternative remedy. The abolition of conscription for military service and the creation of a Courts-Martial Appeal Court have almost ended applications made by persons complaining that they are not subject to military law or that courts-martial have exceeded jurisdiction.[82] A new procedure for determining child custody cases has rendered habeas corpus applications almost superfluous. Alternative remedies do not necessarily exclude the right to apply for habeas corpus, but they make recourse to the writ less frequent. Unusual cases of paramount importance may yet arise; others have followed the 1974 example of Mr Milhench by seeking the writ to challenge the validity of the police detaining for questioning.[83] It was on a habeas corpus application that slavery was declared illegal in England.[84]

Successive applications and appeals

It used to be thought that an unsuccessful applicant could renew his application before each superior court and judge in turn till his funds ran out or he obtained a favourable ruling.[85] No appeal lay from a decision to *grant* habeas corpus except in cases of private civil detention (for example, child custody), or against a *refusal* of habeas corpus in a criminal cause or matter.

The Administration of Justice Act 1960 restated the law. No application for habeas corpus can be made on the same grounds to the same court or judge or any other court or judge unless fresh evidence is adduced.[86] The Act reformed the law relating to habeas corpus appeals. In civil matters the right of an unsuccessful applicant to appeal to the Court of Appeal and thence, with leave, to the House of Lords was retained, but the same rights were extended to the respondent where the application had been granted. In criminal matters (for example, extradition), a single judge may issue habeas corpus, but if minded to refuse he must refer the case for hearing by the Divisional Court. From a decision by the Divisional Court *to grant or refuse* an

---

[82] cf. pp. 212–13.

[83] The police eventually charged Milhench two hours before the time fixed by the judge for the police to show cause why he should not be released. Unfortunately the judge usually adjourns the application for at least 24 hours to enable the police to be represented; meanwhile police questioning during unlawful detention may continue. And see Gifford and O'Connor (1979), *Legal Action Group Bulletin* 182.

[84] *Somersett* v. *Stewart* (1772) 20 St. Tr. 1 (Negro slave brought to England; released though slavery still lawful in the territory from which he came).

[85] See especially *Eshugbayi Eleko* v. *Government of Nigeria* [1928] A.C. 459. This view was aptly criticized by R. F. V. Heuston (1950) 66 *L.Q.R.* 79.

[86] Administration of Justice Act 1960, s. 14(2). The fresh evidence must be relevant and admissible: *Ex p. Schtraks* [1964] 1 Q.B. 191.

application in a criminal matter[87] an appeal lies, with leave either of that court or of the House of Lords, direct to the Lords at the instance of the applicant or respondent.[88] A curious feature of this type of appeal is that if the detainee is discharged on his original application, and the respondent's appeal is successful, the former detainee is nevertheless immune from recommittal unless the court below, having been notified of the respondent's intention to appeal, makes an order for his remand in custody or temporary release on bail.

Territorial scope

Habeas corpus will not issue from the High Court to Scotland or Northern Ireland[89] or, in general, in respect of detention on foreign soil. It will not issue to a dependent territory where there is a court competent to award and supervise the execution of the writ.[90] Scots law has developed its own procedures to secure release from wrongful imprisonment.[91]

Emergency powers

In wartime there is provision for preventive detention of enemy aliens and security suspects. These powers will be briefly considered in a later chapter.[92] Powers of detention in Northern Ireland have been mentioned separately.[93]

Habeas corpus and damages

Unlawful detention is false imprisonment. Consequently a person released on habeas corpus will normally be entitled to recover damages in tort against the persons responsible for his detention. To the general rule there is a limited range of exceptions. For example, the custodian

[87] An application by a compulsorily detained mental patient is deemed to be in respect of a criminal matter.

[88] Possibly this change in the law is attributable to the problems created by the decision in *R. v. Board of Control, ex p. Rutty* [1956] 2 Q.B. 109. See Harry Street, *Freedom, the Individual and the Law* (5th edn, 1982), p. 45.

[89] *Re Keenan* [1972] 1 Q.B. 533. In this case the Court of Appeal assumed, it is thought erroneously, that habeas corpus was a discretionary remedy. cf. Yale [1972A] *Camb. L.J.* 4. But Northern Ireland courts have jurisdiction to award habeas corpus.

[90] Habeas Corpus Act 1862; Sir Kenneth Roberts-Wray, *Commonwealth and Colonial Law*, pp. 612–15.

[91] See J. D. B. Mitchell, *Constitutional Law* (2nd edn, 1968), pp. 339–41.

[92] ch. 27.

[93] ch. 3.

may have a special statutory defence to an action for damages if he acted in good faith. Moreover, a person whose initial arrest was wrongful may be entitled to nominal damages for false imprisonment although he is subsequently convicted and cannot obtain release on habeas corpus.

Privacy and search

Offensive invasion of personal privacy[94] is not yet recognized in English law as an independent tort.[95] An intrusion into one's private affairs may indeed constitute the torts of defamation, trespass, nuisance, conspiracy, injurious falsehood, breach of copyright or passing off, depending on the circumstances; or if it tends to prejudice the outcome of pending judicial proceedings it may be a contempt of court. Some intrusions on privacy are criminal offences – for example, using an electronic eavesdropping device in breach of the Wireless Telegraphy Act 1949; sending out unsolicited advertisements for sex manuals.[96] An injunction and possibly damages can be claimed for certain forms of breach of confidence[97] – a civil wrong which has a capacity for development. But there is no legal redress available to one whose past life is mercilessly publicized, or who is accurately photographed in embarrassing circumstances, or whose conversations are deliberately recorded by mechanical or electronic devices in the absence of conspiracy, trespass or breach of the 1949 Act. Moreover, evidence obtained by an eavesdropping device is admissible in criminal proceedings;[98] so, indeed, is evidence procured as a result of an unlawful search which is a trespass.[99]

[94] The primary source is now the Report of the Committee on Privacy (Cmnd 5012 (1972)). Appendixes I and J to the Report consider the law in England, Scotland and overseas countries. The text above is concerned only with English law.

[95] Because English law recognizes no general right of privacy there is no right to have a telephone conversation in one's home without interruption: *Malone* v. *Metropolitan Police Commissioner* [1979] Ch. 344.

[96] Unsolicited Goods and Services Act 1971, s. 4.

[97] For example, *Argyll* v. *Argyll* [1967] Ch. 602; *Schering Chemicals Ltd* v. *Falkman Ltd* [1982] Q.B. 1; *Att.-Gen.* v. *Jonathan Cape Ltd* [1976] Q.B. 752, Cmnd 5012 (1972). In *Att.-Gen.* v. *The Observer Ltd, Guardian Newspapers Ltd, Times Newspapers Ltd* [1988] 3 All E.R. 545, the House of Lords rejected the Government's claim for a permanent injunction to restrain the newspaper publication of parts of Mr Peter Wright's memoirs, *Spycatcher*. The Government had asserted that members of the Security Services owe a lifelong duty of confidentiality to the Crown. The House of Lords, however, noted that, as the book had been published in many other countries, secrecy had been destroyed, and the public interest in freedom of speech meant that permanent injunctions should not be granted. The House of Lords had upheld the granting of interim injunctions at [1987] 1 W.L.R. 1248. On the *Spycatcher* affair, see [1987] *Public Law* 626; D. G. T. Williams (1988) *Camb. L.J.* 1.

[98] *R.* v. *Maqsood Ali* [1966] 1 Q.B. 688. Contrast *Katz* v. *U.S.* 389 U.S. 347 (1967).

[99] *Kurama* v. *R.* [1955] A.C. 197; *King* v. *R.* [1969] 1 A.C. 304 (notwithstanding a

Parliament has intervened, however, to safeguard further the citizen's right not to have his telephone calls or mail interfered with, except according to the provisions of the Interception of Communications Act 1985.[100] It is an offence under that Act[101] to intercept unlawfully a communication sent by post or by means of a public telecommunications system, but it is a defence to show that such interception had been authorized by a warrant issued under the Act.[102] Such a warrant may only be issued by the Secretary of State[103] if he considers it to be necessary in the interests of national security, or for the purpose of preventing serious crime[104] or for the purpose of safeguarding the economic well-being of the United Kingdom.[105] Unusually, the Act requires the Secretary of State himself to sign the warrant, except in urgent cases. Anyone who thinks that his communications have been unlawfully intercepted may apply to the Tribunal established by the Act.[106] It will investigate whether a relevant warrant had been issued, and if so whether there had been any breach of the Act. If it discovers a breach, the Tribunal must inform the complainant and the Prime Minister, and it may order that the warrant be quashed, that any copies of intercepted material be destroyed, and it may also award compensation. If the Tribunal finds that no warrant had been issued, the

---

constitutional guarantee of freedom from unreasonable search). Contrast the position in the United States: *Mapp* v. *Ohio* 367 U.S. 643 (1961). But in *Lindley* v. *Rutter* [1981] 1 Q.B. 128 it was held unlawful to remove a woman's brassière by force.

[100] The interception of telephone calls and of the mails had been authorized before 1985 by the Secretary of State as an exercise of the prerogative: see Report of a Committee of Privy Councillors, Cmnd 283 (1957) (the Birkett Report). In practice the Home Secretary issued (and continues to issue) most warrants, and the Foreign and Commonwealth Secretary and the Secretary of State for Scotland issue some as well. In *Malone* v. *United Kingdom* (1985) 7 E.H.R.R. 14, the European Court had held that telephone tapping as authorized by the Home Secretary violated article 8 of the European Convention on Human Rights, because English law and practice contained inadequate safeguards for the individual. The Government then caused the 1985 Act to be passed, on which see Lloyd (1986) 49 *Mod. L. Rev.* 86; Prosser [1986] *Public Law* 8; Robilliard and McEwan, op. cit., pp. 31–6.

[101] 1985 Act, s. 1.

[102] ibid., ss 1(2), 2. See also Post Office Act 1953, s. 58(1) (as amended by the 1985 Act, s. 11(2)). The 1985 Act now covers the interception of overseas telegrams and cables, previously governed by the Official Secrets Act 1920, s. 4 (which is repealed: 1985 Act, s. 11(5)).

[103] Warrants are issued to the police, Customs and Excise, and the Security Service (MI5).

[104] Defined (ibid., s. 10(3)) as the use of violence, or resulting in substantial gain, or conduct by a large number of people; or an offence which in the circumstances could carry a sentence of 3 years' imprisonment.

[105] ibid., s. 4(1).

[106] ibid., s. 7 and sched. 1.

Tribunal must inform the complainant that there has been no breach of the Act [107] – a provision which amply shows that the Tribunal has no power over any interception conducted wholly unlawfully and without any attempt to stay within the law. A Commissioner holds office under the Act [108] to keep under review the Secretary of State's functions under the Act, and to assist the Tribunal. [109]

Powers of search and seizure ancillary to a valid arrest are exercisable by the police. Upon a person's arrest a constable can search him if he reasonably believes that he may present a danger to himself or others, or has on him anything which could help him escape, or has evidence relating to the suspected offence. He may also search any premises in which the arrest was carried out for evidence relating to the crime. [110] Reasonable force may be used for the purpose, [111] and the constable may detain anything for which the search was carried out. [112] An arrested person may be searched again at a police station to ascertain what property he has, and it may be retained if it could be used to cause injury, damage, interference with evidence or to help him escape. [113] He may also be subjected to an 'intimate search'. [114] After arrest the police may enter and search, without a warrant, any premises of the arrested person on reasonable suspicion that there is evidence there about the crime for which he has been arrested. [115]

A constable in uniform may enter and search any premises without a warrant, using reasonable force if necessary, to execute an arrest warrant, to arrest a person for an arrestable offence (and for other specified and limited offences), to recapture one who is unlawfully at large and whom he is chasing, or to save life and limb or to prevent serious damage. All the common-law rules about entry without a warrant (save in relation to breach of the peace) are abolished. [116] Police officers and immigration officers have certain exceptional

---

[107] The Tribunal's decisions cannot be questioned in any court, nor be subject to an appeal there: ibid., s. 7(8).

[108] ibid., s. 8. He must be a senior judge, and is currently Lloyd L.J.

[109] In his Report for 1987, Cm 351 (1988), the Commissioner reported that 3 telephones had been tapped other than those specified in warrants, the result of faulty British Telecom equipment or mistakes by B.T. engineers. Some 250 telephone taps were in force in December 1987, authorized either by the Home Secretary or by the Scottish Secretary; the number of taps authorized by the Foreign Secretary and by the Northern Ireland Secretary was not published by the Commissioner.

[110] Police and Criminal Evidence Act 1984, s. 32.

[111] ibid., s. 117.

[112] ibid., s. 32(8), (9).

[113] ibid., s. 54.

[114] ibid., s. 55.

[115] ibid., s. 18.

[116] ibid., s. 17(5), (6).

powers to stop and detain persons without effecting any arrest, for the purpose of search or examination.[117]

In the celebrated case of *Entick* v. *Carrington* (1765)[118] it was held that a general warrant issued by a Secretary of State to arrest a named person for sedition, and to search for and seize his papers, was illegal and could not be justified on the ground of State necessity[119] or reasonable suspicion. An Englishman's home was his castle. Indeed, the 'great end for which men entered into society was to secure their property. That right is preserved sacred . . . in all instances where it has not been abridged by some public law for the good of the whole.'[120] As Salmon L.J., a judge noted for robust assertions of individual rights, once observed, these words today have 'an odd ring – both archaic and incongruous'.

Here one moves from the theme of personal liberty to freedom of property – a topic with vast ramifications which will not be explored here. Powers of entry for the purpose of inspection, testing, survey, levying execution and distress, taking possession, destruction and demolition are vested by some 200 or so different statutory provisions in numerous officials.[121] Police powers of entry, like administrative powers, are not unfettered: there is, as we have seen, no general licence to enter or remain on private property in the investigation of a crime.[122] The police can enter premises without permission for the purpose of preventing or stopping a reasonably apprehended or actual breach of the peace[123] or for effecting an arrest for certain offences,[124] or for the execution of a search warrant. Search warrants may be issued by magistrates or judges under a number of statutes, some of them of constitutional importance (for example, the Official Secrets Acts, the Public Order Act); they do not invariably have to be ancillary to an arrest. The Police and Criminal Evidence Act 1984 is now the main

[117] See, for example, Misuse of Drugs Act 1971, s. 23 (police power to stop and search); Immigration Act 1971, s. 4; sched. 1, §§ 2, 16 (detention for examination or prior to removal). See also Customs and Excise Management Act 1979, s. 164.

[118] (1765) 19 St. Tr. 1030.

[119] A ground accepted as one justification for retention of papers seized in circumstances of doubtful legality in *Elias* v. *Pasmore* (above) at 173 (police entered premises to arrest H under warrant for a seditious offence; they had no search warrant, but impounded papers found there and used them in a successful prosecution of E for a similar offence).

[120] *Per* Lord Camden at 1066. See also *Wilkes* v. *Wood* (1763) 19 St. Tr. 1153.

[121] See generally R. Stone, *Entry, Search and Seizure* (1985)

[122] *Great Central Rly Co* v. *Bates* [1921] 3 K.B. 578; *Davis* v. *Lisle* [1936] 2 K.B. 434; *McArdle* v. *Wallace* (No. 2) (1964) 108 S.J. 483.

[123] As in *Thomas* v. *Sawkins* [1935] 2 K.B. 249, a power expressly preserved in the 1984 Act, s. 17(6).

[124] ibid., s. 17(1).

statute. A magistrate may issue a search warrant if, on an application by a constable, he is satisfied that there are reasonable grounds for believing that a serious arrestable offence[125] has been committed; that evidence likely to be of serious value to the investigation of that offence is on the premises; that it is not 'excluded' or 'special procedure' material[126] and that entry without such a warrant (that is, by consent) would not be practicable or possible.[127] A constable may use reasonable force, if necessary, in the execution of a search warrant.[128] Anything may be seized under the warrant, provided that it is not subject to legal privilege[129] and provided that the constable has reasonable grounds for believing that it is evidence about a crime he is investigating or any other crime, and that it is necessary to seize it to prevent its concealment, loss or destruction.[130] If premises are lawfully searched in pursuance of a warrant specifying stolen property to be seized, the taking of property not included in the warrant is normally unlawful; but it appears that reasonable mistake, and reasonable suspicion that goods not specified have been stolen and are evidence on a charge of stealing or receiving against the person in possession or his associates, may justify seizure. The common-law rule that the police, having lawfully obtained entry, are not entitled to conduct a search of private property, without a warrant, in order to fish hopefully for evidence of a crime, is preserved.[131]

The risk remains after the enactment of the Police and Criminal Evidence Act 1984 that the courts, having formerly leaned over backwards in their solicitude for private property, may give too much weight to the public interest in crime detection and too little to the

---

[125] Defined in the 1984 Act, s. 116.

[126] Defined ibid., ss 9–14, Sched. 1: such material requires a warrant from a Circuit judge to authorize search and seizure. For the procedure to be followed, see *R.* v. *Central Criminal Court, ex p. Adegbesan* [1986] 3 All E.R. 113.

[127] ibid., s. 8.

[128] ibid., s. 117.

[129] Defined ibid., ss 10, 19(6) and including communications between a legal adviser and his client. But items held with the intention of furthering a criminal purpose are not protected: see s. 10(2) and *R.* v. *Crown Court at Snaresbrook, ex p. D.P.P.* [1988] 1 All E.R. 315; *R.* v. *Central Criminal Court, ex. p. Francis and Francis*, the *Independent*, 4 November 1988 (H.L.).

[130] ibid., s. 19(3).

[131] ibid., s. 19;m *Ghani* v. *Jones* [1970] 1 Q.B. 693 at 706 (detention of Pakistani passports obtained in police search without warrant held unlawful in absence of reasonable grounds for believing plaintiffs to be implicated in a suspected murder or for believing the documents to be material evidence to prove the offence); *Reynolds* v. *Metropolitan Police Commissioner* [1985] Q.B. 881.

claims of personal privacy. That the apprehensions of the police must be shown to be reasonable is not much of a safeguard against abuse of powers given the notorious reluctance of magistrates[132] to reject assertions by the police as to the reasonableness of their own suspicions.

[132] And often superior judges: see *Piddington* v. *Bates* [1961] 1 W.L.R. 164 at 170. See also K. Lidstone [1984] *Crim. L. Rev.* 499.

Chapter 25

Freedom of Expression

In general

Bills of rights in modern Commonwealth constitutions include qualified guarantees of freedom of conscience and religion, freedom of speech and expression, and freedom of peaceable assembly and association. In practice these liberties are intimately related. If serious encroachments are made on any one of them, some or all will be diminished. Of all the basic freedoms in the world today the most precarious are the rights to express opinions and associate with like-minded persons for the purpose of opposing and eventually deposing the government in office. Fortunately in Britain these political rights, though not formally guaranteed, enjoy adequate protection in practice. In this chapter the outline of the law relating to freedom of expression will be considered.[1] In the next, aspects of the law of assembly and association will be dealt with. These areas of the law intersect but can be treated separately.

Freedom of conscience and religion does not call for an extensive discussion.[2] Freedom of conscience falls partly within the scope of freedom of expression, partly under freedom of assembly and association. The law does not concern itself with individual beliefs or disbeliefs unless a person propagates his views in scurrilous terms or in circumstances likely to give rise to a breach of the peace or in a place to which he is denied lawful access. There is no compulsory State religion, no obligation to submit to any form of religious instruction, no religious test for the tenure of public office save in the case of the monarch.[3] Religious disqualifications for the franchise and sitting in Parliament had been abolished by the end of the nineteenth century.

---

[1] See E. Barendt, *Freedom of Speech* (1985); H. Street, *Freedom, the Individual and the Law* (5th edn, 1985), chs 3–7; Boyle [1982] *Public Law* 574.

[2] See generally St. J. Robilliard, *Religion and the Law* (1984).

[3] See pp. 122–3. Section 1 of the Lord Chancellor (Tenure of Office and Discharge of

Not since the sixteenth century have men and women been burnt at the stake as heretics and the worst horrors of the Inquisition passed England by. No one has yet to be required to make a public affirmation of his devotion to the Party or to confess his political sins. Compassing or imagining the monarch's death is still a statutory offence, but treasonable conduct must be manifested by overt acts for a conviction to be obtained,[4] 'the devil himself knoweth not the thought of man',[5] and though a person's state of mind may be an essential ingredient of a specific criminal or civil wrong, the law refrains from imposing sanctions in the absence of a wrongful act or omission.[6] Potentially subversive political opinions may, however, be a ground for preventive detention in wartime,[7] and for dismissal from the civil service or removal to a non-sensitive post.[8]

Prior restraints

'Freedom of discussion', in Dicey's words, was 'in England little else than the right to write or say anything which a jury, consisting of twelve shopkeepers, think it expedient should be said or written.'[9] It was subject to no prior restraint. Press censorship had lapsed in 1695. Press libels, moreover, were triable according to the ordinary law of the land by the ordinary courts; the rule of law prevailed.

This simple picture, portraying the laws of defamation, sedition and blasphemy as the main restrictions of freedom of expression, needs to be modified today. The restrictions, though not oppressive, are multifarious. Trial of offenders is not always by jury. Moreover, restraints may operate before any legal wrong has been committed. These prior restraints are not neatly segregated from offences arising from dissemination. For example, one needs a licence to transmit a radio broadcast; if one broadcasts without such a licence, one incurs a criminal penalty. Obscene literature can be seized, condemned and

---

Ecclesiastical Functions) Act 1974 declares that for the avoidance of doubt, the office of Lord Chancellor is and shall be tenable by an adherent of the Roman Catholic faith.

[4] Statute of Treasons 1351; *R.* v. *Thistlewood* (1820) 33 St. Tr. 681; Treason Act 1795, s. 1; Treason Felony Act 1848, s. 3.

[5] *Per* Brian C.J. in 1477.

[6] Misprision (concealment) of treason is still a common-law offence, but misprision of another's felony has been superseded by section 5(1) of the Criminal Law Act 1967 which makes it an offence to accept a valuable consideration for concealment of an arrestable offence.

[7] See p. 526.

[8] See pp. 201–4.

[9] *Introduction to the Study of the Law of the Constitution* (10th edn), p. 246.

destroyed; if such literature escapes suppression it is still an offence to publish it. A public meeting held on private premises is a civil trespass if conducted without the occupier's permission and an injunction may be obtained to prevent it from being held.

Prior restraints are not all of the same kind. Some are strictly legal prohibitions coupled with a sanction; others are extra-legal and have to be analysed in different terms. If there is a sanction annexed to disregard of a prohibition, it may range from imprisonment to loss of a licence or of promotion prospects. Such restraints are more easily tabulated than classified.

Accessibility of media for publicity

I may be at liberty to express an opinion but unable to obtain an audience because nobody will let a hall to me for the conduct of a public meeting, or because the competent authority refuses me a permit to hold a meeting in a public place under its control, or because the police (if no prior authority is required by law) threaten to prosecute me for obstruction of the highway or a similar offence if I proceed; or the police may simply assert their power to stop me because they reasonably apprehend a breach of the peace,[10] though by participating in a mass demonstration I may at once achieve more publicity and gain a measure of safety in numbers. I cannot compel newspaper editors to publish my letters, or editors and publishers to accept my articles and books. If I have the money and persistence I can have my work printed privately and distributed by post. Provided that it does not contain offensive or obscene material and it is not prejudicial to public safety or security[11] it will be immune from interception and seizure in the mails. But booksellers and public libraries may refuse to purchase it, and indeed blacklist it.[12] I may offer to pay for or subscribe to the cost of an advertisement for the propagation of my opinions; newspapers may decline to print it and other bodies owning advertising space are not obliged to display it.[13] I cannot set up a private broadcasting station to air my opinions to the public at large within the United Kingdom unless I am awarded a programme contract by the Indepedent Broadcasting Authority or a licence by the Cable Authority.[14]

[10] See ch. 26.
[11] Post Office Act 1953, ss 11, 58, 66.
[12] See Harry Street, *Freedom, the Individual and the Law* (5th edn, 1982), p. 107.
[13] See ibid., 109, on informal regulation of advertising.
[14] See Wireless Telegraphy Act 1949; Marine etc. Broadcasting (Offences) Act 1967; Broadcasting Act 1981; Cable and Broadcasting Act 1984, and below, p. 486.

Censorship and suppression[15]

The Press. Executive censorship of the press ended in 1695, to be revived only in wartime. The legal requirements as to the registration of newspapers and the printing of the names of their publishers and printers in each issue are not substantial restraints.

Offences committed by the publication of material by reason of its content will be considered separately, but it may be noted at this point that it is unlawful for the press to publish the evidence (otherwise than such as is disclosed by the judge's summing up or judgment) in divorce and nullity proceedings, or any indecent matter disclosed in judicial proceedings,[16] or (subject to limited exceptions) information divulging the identity of juveniles involved in court proceedings,[17] or in general except at the defendant's request, a contemporaneous report of the evidence given at committal proceedings before magistrates.[18]

Reference can also be made here to the 'D' Notice system. There exists a non-statutory Defence, Press and Broadcasting Committee, with a senior civil servant as chairman; it includes other senior officials, but representatives of the press, press agencies and broadcasting services are in the majority among its members; it has a full-time secretary, a retired senior officer from the armed services. Its main function is to approve the issue of 'D' Notices, which are confidential letters initiated by government Departments and addressed to newspaper, periodical and news bulletin editors, requesting that material not be published because it would have an adverse effect on national defence or security.[19] Non-compliance with such a request is not an offence in itself, but it may result in a prosecution for a breach of the Official Secrets Acts,[20] compliance with the request being in practice a safeguard against a prosecution, though an assurance that an item of

[15] See generally Paul O'Higgins, *Censorship in Britain* (1972) for radical criticism of present law and practice.

[16] Judicial Proceedings (Regulation of Reports) Act 1926, s. 1. See also Domestic and Appellate Proceedings (Restriction of Publicity) Act 1968.

[17] R. M. Jackson, *The Machinery of Justice in England* (7th edn, 1977), p. 22.

[18] Criminal Justice Act 1967, s. 3, as amended by the Magistrates' Courts Act 1980, s. 8(2A) (see above, p. 361). The restrictions do not apply if the defendant is *not* committed for trial.

[19] See generally Cmnd 1681 (1962), ch. 9; Cmnd 3309, 3312 (1967); D. G. T. Williams, *Not in the Public Interest*, p. 80ff.; Marshall [1967] *Public Law* 261; Report of the (Franks) Committee on section 2 of the Official Secrets Act 1911 (Cmnd 5104 (1972), §65: Minutes of Evidence, vol. 2, pp. 241–5, vol. 3, pp. 51–68; Report from the Defence Committee, H.C. 773 (1979–80), and Jaconelli [1982] *Public Law* 37. 'D' Notices are also sent to book publishers from time to time, requesting non-publication of certain matters or the submission of manuscripts for security clearance.

[20] See pp. 493–7.

information is not covered by a 'D' Notice is not in itself such a safeguard.[21] Even if disclosure of the information is not a breach of the Acts, the news medium concerned may be publicly censured and may find that confidential information formerly supplied to it from official sources is thereafter withheld.

Broadcasting services. The British Broadcasting Corporation, constituted by royal charter in 1926, provides all non-commercial radio and television services. Its functions are prescribed by its charter, the current licence and agreement[22] under which it operates, and any directions issued to it by the Home Secretary in pursuance of powers conferred on him by the governing instruments. Under the agreement he is empowered to require the Corporation to refrain from broadcasting any matter or class of matter at any time. If the Corporation fails to comply with a valid direction he may revoke its licence.[23]

He enjoys statutory powers of direction in relation to the Independent Broadcasting Authority,[24] which regulates commercial services provided by programme contractors. A number of positive duties (for example, to broadcast Government announcements but to maintain political impartiality) are cast on the BBC and the IBA.

In what circumstances (if any) can a breach of such duties by the broadcasting authorities give rise to judicial proceedings? This question has come before the courts once, in the important case of *Attorney-General ex rel. McWhirter* v. *IBA*[25] concerning the duty of the IBA to satisfy themselves that so far as possible '. . . nothing is included in the programmes which offends against good taste or decency or is likely to . . . be offensive to public feeling'.[26] The court held that it could grant an injunction only if the decision of the Authority were wrong in law or one to which it could not reasonably have come. The Attorney-General seeks the injunction as guardian of the public interest, but a private citizen can do so only with the leave of the Attorney-General.[27] Whether breach of a particular duty is actionable depends on the

---

[21] This was the position in the *Sunday Telegraph* (or Biafra) case, 1970–71; see Jonathan Aitken, *Officially Secret* (1971).

[22] Cmnd 8233 (1981) sets out the present licence and agreement.

[23] Licence, clauses 13(4), 23. In 1985 the BBC board of governors at the Home Secretary's 'request' cancelled the broadcast of a programme which included an interview with the IRA chief of staff. The Home Secretary has issued a directive banning the broadcasting of interviews with supporters of terrorist organizations: see 139 H.C. Deb. *1075* (2 November 1988).

[24] Broadcasting Act 1981, s. 28; see also note 23.

[25] [1973] Q.B. 639.

[26] s. 4(1)(*a*).

[27] *Gouriet* v. *Union of Post Office Workers* [1978] A.C. 435. The House of Lords expressly

nature and wording of the duty. The duties of the BBC to send out broadcasts 'efficiently' and of the IBA to maintain a 'high quality' in programmes are so vague that a court would be reluctant to enforce them. (It is, of course, possible for the Minister to cancel the BBC's licence, or to initiate the dismissal of the Governors of the BBC by the Crown or himself to dismiss the members of the IBA. Such drastic action, however, would hardly be conceivable unless there was direct disobedience of a specific ministerial direction; in the Republic of Ireland in November 1972 the members of RTE, the equivalent body of the BBC, were dismissed *en bloc* for refusal to comply with a direction.) Duties to broadcast Government announcements and to maintain political impartiality[28] are potentially enforceable in judicial proceedings by an order of mandamus awarded by the High Court on the application of the Minister.

Technological development in cable and (particularly) in satellite broadcasting[29] led to the passage of the Cable and Broadcasting Act 1984. The Cable Authority operates under the Act to license the provision of programmes by cable, and the Satellite Broadcasting Board oversees programmes broadcast directly from satellites. Cable programmes must not be obscene;[30] direct satellite broadcasts are subject to similar standards imposed on the BBC and the IBA by the Broadcasting Act 1981.[31] Satellite broadcasting is likely to be much more popular than cable transmissions; it could also be much more difficult to censor.

The broadcasting authorities maintain their own standards, subject to formal obligations and ministerial directives, in the presentation of films and plays and other programmes.[32] As we have seen, they are also included within the ambit of the 'D' Notice system.

The Government has set up a Broadcasting Standards Council further to monitor programme standards.[33] The Council will draw up a code of practice on the portrayal of sex and violence, and on

---

disapproved dicta in the *McWhirter* case to the effect that a private individual could seek the injunction himself in circumstances of urgency or where the Attorney-General wrongly withheld his permission.

[28] In 1986 Ministers were critical of the BBC's coverage of the United States bombing of Libya, on the ground that it was not 'impartial'.

[29] See Cmnd 8679 (1982); Cmnd 8751 (1982); Cmnd 8866 (1983).

[30] 1984 Act, ss 25, 26. Other conditions are also imposed in licences.

[31] ibid., s. 44.

[32] See generally Street, op. cit., pp. 86–103. Anyone having a direct interest in a programme broadcast by either the BBC or IBA can complain about it to the Broadcasting Complaints Commission: Broadcasting Act 1981, Part III.

[33] See 133 H.C. Deb. 685–6 (16 May 1988).

standards of taste and decency; it will monitor the portrayal of sex and violence on television and radio, undertake research, and report annually. *Imported* fictional material will be *previewed* by the Commission – if the broadcasting authorities agree. The relationship between the Council and the Broadcasting Complaints Commission is unclear.

Theatres and plays. Till 1968, stage performances and theatres had to receive a licence from the Lord Chamberlain before they could lawfully be performed and used; it was a criminal offence to stage a play in an unapproved form. A private member's bill was introduced to abolish the Lord Chamberlain's powers; it became the Theatres Act 1968. Premises still require a local authority licence if they are to be used for the public performance of a play, but no condition may be imposed restricting the content of the 'plays' to be performed other than an exhibition of hypnotism.[34] The law relating to criminal offences and civil wrongs committed in the course of a stage performance has been redefined. The immediate practical effects of the Act were an increase in plays dealing with controversial topics such as homosexuality, the production of nude musicals, and the use of earthier language than the Lord Chamberlain would formerly have permitted.

Films.[35] Film censorship is a blend of statutory and non-statutory regulation. Cinemas are licensed[36] by local authorities. Conditions may be attached to the grant of licences, restricting the admission of children, prohibiting the exhibition of films likely to be injurious to morality, and so on. A condition commonly imposed is that no film not approved by the British Board of Film Classification shall be exhibited without the express consent of the licensing authority. The Board is a non-statutory body constituted by the film industry; the president is appointed by a committee representing the industry after consultation with the Home Office and the local authority associations, but he is independent of the industry. The full-time secretary of the Board has, in practice, been its most dominant figure. Films are classified as 'U' (suitable for universal exhibition), 'PG' (parental guidance; some scenes may be unsuitable for young children), '15' (no child under fifteen being permitted to be present), '18' (no person under eighteen being

[34] s. 1(2). Conditions may be imposed in the interests of physical safety and health. An appeal lies to a magistrates' court at the instance of a person aggrieved by a licensing decision (s. 14).
[35] Street, op. cit., pp. 73–83.
[36] Cinemas Act 1985.

permitted to be present) or 'RESTRICTED' (restricted distribution through segregated premises, 18 and over). The Board may refuse a film a certificate altogether, or grant one only if prescribed cuts are made. A licensing authority cannot validly fetter its discretion by automatically following the Board's decisions[37] though it may elect to follow them unless exceptional circumstances are present. There is nothing, apart from the sanctions of the criminal law which may be applied to an exhibitor, to prevent a local authority from allowing a film to be exhibited to which the Board has denied a certificate or from permitting the restoration of cuts made at the insistence of the Board. Nor is an authority obliged to permit the exhibition of a film passed by the Board. It is not uncommon for different authorities to adopt various attitudes towards a particularly controversial film.

Having regard to the higher attendance of children at cinemas than theatres, there is a stronger case for film censorship than for theatrical censorship. Accordingly the Departmental Committee on Obscenity and Film Censorship recommended in 1979 a statutory body for censoring films.[38]

The Video Recordings Act 1984 now provides for the censorship of video films before sale or hire to the public. It is an offence to supply an unclassified video cassette outside of the terms of the Act. The classification scheme is similar to that which applies to films, but there are complex definitions of 'exempted works'. The British Board of Film Classification is charged with the censorship of the thousands of different videos which were in circulation before the Act came into force, as well as new productions. The aim was to have all of the Act in force by the end of 1988. The hire and purchase of video films is extremely popular, and it is right that potential viewers (and their parents) be adequately warned of the contents of any given video cassette.[39]

Official documents and civil servants' publications. As has been indicated, State papers (including Cabinet documents) are made available to public scrutiny only after the lapse of thirty years. Records may still be withheld after that period by the Lord Chancellor, with the approval or at the request of the relevant Ministers, or if they embody information received under a pledge of confidence.[40]

---

[37] *Ellis* v. *Dubowski* [1972] 3 K.B. 621.

[38] Cmnd 7772 (1979). Under s. 2 of the Local Government (Miscellaneous Provisions) Act 1982 any district council or London borough council may resolve to introduce a licensing system for sex cinemas as set out in sched. 3 of that Act.

[39] For a critical view of such censorship, see Hunnings [1985] *Public Law* 214.

[40] Public Records Acts 1958 and 1967.

The former practice whereby whole classes of departmental documents relevant to judicial proceedings could be withheld from disclosure by virtue of a ministerial objection on the ground that their production would be injurious to the national interest has been substantially diminished in the last few years.[41] Moreover, departmental documents must be made available to the Parliamentary Commissioner for Administration for the purpose of his investigations.

Any student of central government administration in Britain will be aware of the difficulty experienced in persuading civil servants to divulge particulars of internal procedures or the undisclosed reasons for individual decisions if there is any likelihood of his publishing an account of his research. The ethos generated by the Official Secrets Act is still pervasive. Serving and retired civil servants must obtain official approval of the manuscript of any book they themselves write before it is published. A civil servant who writes a controversial letter to the press or gives a broadcast interview will be well advised to seek approval in advance; otherwise he risks contravening service regulations and earning the severe disapproval of his superiors.

Contempt of court. A news medium proposing to publish material which would tend to prejudice a fair trial may be restrained by an injunction in proceedings instituted by the Attorney-General.[42]

Miscellaneous. In 1971 leading American newspapers published extracts from the 'Pentagon papers', a record of top-secret policy discussions about Vietnam. An attempt by the United States Government to obtain an injunction to restrain further publication of the information was rejected by the United States Supreme Court.[43] This may be contrasted with the decision of Widgery L.C.J. in the *Crossman Diaries Case* that the publication of Cabinet memoirs is a breach of confidence, which may be stopped by injunction, when the public interest demands it.[44]

---

[41] See especially *Conway* v. *Rimmer* [1968] A.C. 910; and pp. 639–43.
[42] See Contempt of Court Act 1981, ss 1–7, Sched. 1, and above, pp. 377–9, and *Att.-Gen.* v. *Times Newspapers Ltd* [1974] A.C. 273.
[43] *New York Times Co.* v. *United States* 403 U.S. 713 (1971); *The Pentagon Papers* (Bantam Books, 1971); *Secrecy and Foreign Policy*, eds T. M. Franck and E. Weistrand, ch. 17. In *Secretary of State for Defence* v. *Guardian Newspapers Ltd.* [1985] A.C. 339 the Court of Appeal ordered the *Guardian* to return to the Minister a photocopy of a document leaked to it by a civil servant, on the ground that the Government had the copyright in the photocopy; see further above, p. 377.
[44] *Att.-Gen.* v. *Jonathan Cape Ltd* [1976] Q.B. 752; Hugo Young, *The Crossman Affair*.

Prior censorship, and the seizure and destruction of documents under legal powers, are the most obvious means of suppressing freedom of expression. The prospect of incurring penal sanctions *ex post facto* will also tend to inhibit free expression. So will the foreknowledge that one's communications may be intercepted and read or overheard.

Freedom of expression is not an end in itself. Doctrinaire absolutism is an inept instrument for evaluating the competing claims of the individual and society. John Stuart Mill, himself a powerful defender of human liberty, declared: 'The sole end for which mankind are warranted, individually or collectively, in interfering with the liberty of action of any of their number, is self-protection.' This grudging concession is a starting point, not the conclusion, of any attempt to define the proper limits of freedom of expression. But the onus to be discharged by one seeking to justify the stifling of opinion should be heavier than that cast upon one asserting the propriety of penalizing its expression after the event. History bears witness to the insidious effects of the suppression of dissent and the denial of free interchange of ideas. These effects are all the more insidious when the fact of suppression is itself suppressed or so concealed as not to be identifiable.

Crimes, torts and other wrongs

The following are the principal wrongs in English law that may be committed by words or pictorial demonstrations.

Treason and treason felony

These offences overlap. Treason is still punishable with death, treason felony with life imprisonment. It is treason to conspire or incite to kill or overthrow the monarch, to levy war against her by raising an insurrection, or to adhere to her enemies[45] in time of war (for example, by broadcasting propaganda for the enemy).[46] Incitement to rebellion against the Government in the United Kingdom, or a conspiracy to deprive the Queen of her sovereignty in any part of her dominions, or an invitation to a foreigner to invade any part of them, is also treason felony.[47]

---

[45] Within or without Her Majesty's dominions (*R.* v. *Casement* [1917] K.B. 98).
[46] To be guilty of treason the accused must be a person owing allegiance; on which see *Joyce* v. *D.P.P.* [1946] A.C. 347; and see p. 453. There must be overt acts of disloyalty.
[47] Treason Felony Act 1848. Again, only persons owing allegiance may commit the offence.

Seditious offences[48]

To publish spoken or written words with a seditious intention is a common-law misdemeanour. A seditious intention has been defined in very broad terms, including 'an intention to bring into hatred and contempt, or excite disaffection against ... the government and constitution ... either House of Parliament, or the administration of justice ... or to raise discontent or disaffection among Her Majesty's subjects, or to promote feelings of ill-will and hostility between different classes of such subjects'.[49] This could encompass any forceful criticism of the existing structure of authority within the State.

In this century prosecutions for sedition have been so few that the ingredients of the offence cannot be stated with assurance, but it would seem that there must now be an intent to incite to violence against the institutions and laws of the State[50] or a section of the community[51] for a conviction to be obtained. Nevertheless, in a modern case the Privy Council held that under the laws of a colony sedition could be committed without any incitement to violence,[52] and some of the successor governments to the colonial régimes have used the wide concept of sedition as an instrument for browbeating their opponents.[53]

There are several statutory offences akin to sedition in its broadest meaning. It is an offence to do any act 'calculated to cause disaffection' among the police.[54] Under the Incitement to Disaffection Act 1934,[55] it is an offence maliciously and advisedly to endeavour to seduce a member of the forces from his duty or allegiance to the Crown, or to have in one's possession, with intent to commit or counsel the offence, literature the dissemination of which would be such an offence. Prosecutions have been very rare, and leave of the Director of Public Prosecutions is required. A search warrant may be issued by a High

---

[48] For good synopses, see Smith and Hogan, *Criminal Law* (6th edn, 1988), pp. 837–8; Brownlie's *Law of Public Order and National Security* (2nd edn, 1981) pp. 234–44, and for proposals for reform, Law Commission Working Paper No. 72 (1977).

[49] Sir James Stephen, *Digest of the Criminal Law* (3rd edn), art. 93.

[50] *R.* v. *Burns* (1886) 16 Cox C.C. 355. See also *R.* v. *Aldred* (1909) 22 Cox C.C. 1, where the publication had been calculated to incite to violence but it was not made clear by the judge that an intent to provoke violence had to be established.

[51] *R.* v. *Caunt* (1947) (*An Editor on Trial*, an offensive attack on British Jewry; jury directed that an intent to excite violence had to be demonstrated). Such an attack might still be indictable as a public mischief.

[52] *R.* v. *Wallace-Johnson* [1940] A.C. 231 (Gold Coast).

[53] See, for example, G. Ezejiofor, *Protection of Human Rights under the Law*, pp. 194–8.

[54] Police Act 1964, s. 53, reproducing earlier legislation. See also Aliens Restriction (Amendment) Act 1919, penalizing forms of disaffection instigated by aliens.

[55] See also Incitement to Mutiny Act 1797; D. G. T. Williams, *Not in the Public Interest*, pp. 102–3, 113–14.

Court judge in respect of an offence under the Act. The Act could be used against persons distributing pacifist literature to members of the forces. In this area of the law, restraint in instituting prosecutions, the prospect of a restrictive direction by a judge and an acquittal by a jury are the effective safeguards for the expression of political dissent.[56]

Breaches of the Official Secrets Act[57]

Till 1889 there was no legislation making it an offence to disclose official secrets to foreign powers or to other unauthorized persons. The present law is contained in the Official Secrets Acts 1911, 1920 and 1939. The ambit of the Acts is by no means confined to espionage. The marginal note to section 1 of the 1911 Act reads 'Penalties against spying', and makes it an offence punishable with fourteen years' imprisonment for any person, 'for any purpose prejudicial to the safety or interests of the State', not only to engage in specified conduct calculated to be useful to an enemy but also to approach, inspect or enter a 'prohibited place'[58] within the meaning of the Act. Nuclear disarmers who approached a military airfield with the intention of immobilizing it were convicted under this section,[59] although their purpose was not espionage but non-violent sabotage; the fact that in their opinion they were acting in the true interests of the State was held to be irrelevant, inasmuch as they were intentionally engaging in conduct prohibited by the Act and the policy behind the disposition and use of the armed forces of the Crown fell within the scope of the royal prerogative and could not be a subject of independent judicial scrutiny. It is also an offence to refuse to supply information to a senior police officer as to the commission of an offence under this section.[60] In a prosecution for the principal offence, the prejudicial purpose may be inferred from the circumstances in the absence of an overt act; and if information about a prohibited place is proved to have been obtained or communicated without lawful authority, the onus of proving that the purpose was not

---

[56] The Law Commission has provisionally recommended the abolition of the crime of sedition: Working Paper No. 72 (1977), paras 76–8.

[57] The leading study is D. G. T. Williams, *Not in the Public Interest*. See now Report of the Committee on Section 2 of the Official Secrets Act 1911 (Cmnd 5104 (1972)) and Minutes of Evidence in three volumes; these contain a mine of information, much of it previously undisclosed.

[58] s. 3 (for example, defence establishments and places used by or belonging to the Crown and declared by a Secretary of State to be prohibited places).

[59] *Chandler* v. *D.P.P.* [1964] A.C. 763; criticized by Thompson [1963] *Public Law* 201; but see Smith and Hogan, *Criminal Law* (6th edn, 1988), p. 839.

[60] Official Secrets Act 1920, s. 6 (as amended by the Official Secrets Act 1939).

one prejudicial to the interests of the State is cast upon the accused.[61]

Under section 2 of the 1911 Act it is an offence punishable with up to two years' imprisonment to retain without permission, or fail to take reasonable care of, information obtained as a result of one's present or former employment under the Crown or a government contract; or to *communicate* information so obtained, or entrusted to one in confidence by a person holding office under Her Majesty,[62] or obtained in contravention of the Act, to anybody other than a person to whom one is authorized to convey it or to whom it is one's duty to impart it in the interests of the State; or to *receive* such information, knowing or having reasonable cause to believe it has been given in contravention of the Act. These are wide-ranging prohibitions. It may be an offence under section 2 for a civil servant to pass on, or for a research worker to acquire from him, information about internal departmental procedures although the material has no bearing on security and is not even classified as confidential. This section is indeed convoluted and abstruse. The Franks Committee which reported in 1972 described it as 'catch-all' and a 'mess'.[63] Yet who could malign a section which creates 2,324 separate offences?[64]

However, the section has undoubtedly many defects. For instance, it is not clear whether guilty knowledge (*mens rea*) has to be proved for unauthorized communication to be an offence.[65] When is communication authorized?[66] What of 'leaks' by Ministers?[67] According to official doctrine, Ministers 'authorize themselves' to convey information about matters of government and administration; civil servants have implied authorization depending on the nature of their job and the circumstances of the case. All this is very vague. And in the absence of authorization, when is it my duty or a journalist's duty 'in the

---

[61] 1911 Act, s. 1(2).

[62] This term includes a police officer: *Lewis* v. *Castle* [1938] 2 K.B. 454; and a civilian computer operator employed by a local authority but taking instructions from a police inspector at the police station where he operated it: *Loat* v. *Andrews* [1985] I.C.R. 679.

[63] Cmnd 5104 (1972), §§ 17, 88.

[64] Minutes of Evidence, vol. 2, p. 262 (Appendix to evidence of Bar Council).

[65] In the *Sunday Telegraph* case (1971, unreported; see Jonathan Aitken, *Officially Secret*) Caulfield J. directed the jury that *mens rea* on the part of all involved in the chain of communication had to be proved. This interpretation is not universally accepted: it was, for example, rejected by McCowan, J. in the course of the trial of Clive Ponting (who was nonetheless acquitted by the jury); see Clive Ponting, *The Right to Know* (1985) and *R.* v. *Ponting* [1985] *Crim. L. Rev.* 318.

[66] The burden is on the Crown to prove that the communicator had not been authorized: *R.* v. *Galvin* [1987] Q.B. 862.

[67] The Attorney-General did not prosecute the publishers of the Crossman Diaries under the Act, apparently because he concluded that the Act did not apply once Mr Crossman had died; Lord Lloyd of Hampstead (*semble*) took the opposite view: Young, op. cit., at pp. 21 and 33.

interests of the State' to publicize official information? No intelligible answer has yet been produced. What is the policy in instituting prosecutions? The Attorney-General has an absolute discretion in this matter; the criteria adopted in deciding whether to bring or authorize a prosecution are nebulous; there has been a marked rise in the number of prosecutions since 1979, although most (but by no means all) have involved elements of obvious impropriety.[68] But the deterrent effect of the Act on junior and middle-grade civil servants in particular may be considerable.

The Franks Committee made detailed proposals for replacing section 2 by a new Official Information Act. They would restrict criminal sanctions to defined areas of major importance: wrongful disclosures of (i) information of major national importance in the fields of defence, security, foreign relations, currency and the reserves; (ii) Cabinet documents; and (iii) information facilitating criminal activity or violating the confidentiality of information supplied to the Government by or about individuals; and the use of official information for private gain. Mere receipt of protected information would not be an offence under the Act, but communication by journalists and others would still be if the author or speaker had reasonable grounds for believing that it had been conveyed to him in breach of the Act. Only material classified as Top Secret or Secret (or Defence-Confidential) would be protected in category (i); and before a prosecution could be brought, the responsible Minister in person would have to certify that the information was properly so classified at the relevant time. Although the prosecution would have to prove that the information fell within the scope of a classified category in the first place, the Minister's certificate as to classification at the time of instituting proceedings would be binding on the court. There should be an advisory committee (similar to the 'D' Notice committee[69]) on matters relating to classification.

The proposals, outlined very briefly above, would restrict the ambit of the criminal law, but were not really radical. There would be no defence, for example, that the public interest was not in fact injured by a disclosure; the difficulties and uncertainty inherent in the concept of implied authorization would remain; over-classification of information might still occur; there was no recommendation about giving fuller publicity to official information along the lines of American or Swedish practice. But they were a careful attempt to draw lines in an area where cartography is extraordinarily difficult. They have not been implemented

[68] From 1978 to 1987 the Attorney-General authorized 23 prosecutions under s. 2: see 124 H.C. Deb. *606–9* (written answers 17 December 1987).
[69] See p. 485.

by legislation. The present Government introduced a Protection of Official Information Bill into the House of Lords in the 1979–80 session, but it was so heavily criticized (and faced almost certain defeat in Parliament) that it was withdrawn.[70] A backbench Conservative M.P., Mr Richard Shepherd, introduced a liberalizing bill with the same title in the 1987–8 session, but thanks to the imposition of a Government three-line whip against it – an unprecedent Government interference in the fortunes of a private Member's measure – the bill was denied a second reading.[71] The Home Secretary announced that the Government had been working for some months on its own replacement for section 2 (a section which he conceded had become virtually inoperable). The Government published a White Paper in 1988;[72] a Bill was introduced in the 1988–9 session of Parliament. The White Paper advocated the narrowing of the ambit of the criminal law, which in future might cover only four categories of official information. (1) Disclosures about defence, security and intelligence would be criminal, provided it was proved that a specified test of harm was passed to a court's satisfaction. (2) Disclosures in this country of information in category (1) (or about other matters, such as international relations or terrorism) already disclosed abroad, which had been supplied in confidence to another government, would be an offence. (3) Official information useful to criminals, and information obtained from telephone taps, would attract prosecution if disclosed. (4) It would be an offence for a present or former member of the Security Services to disclose information about security or intelligence. In categories (2) to (4), no test of harm beyond the fact of disclosure would be necessary. The White Paper rejected the introduction of other defences which had been mooted. The maximum penalty would be two years' imprisonment. Disclosure of other official information would cease to be a crime, although civil servants might face disciplinary proceedings for doing so.

Since the Franks Report there has been an unceasing pressure for more open government. Governments of the day pay lip-service to the idea[73] but their practice is otherwise.[74] They continue unnecessarily to

---

[70] The fact that the truth about the traitor Anthony Blunt could not have been revealed by the press had the bill been law became the bill's death blow.

[71] However, twenty Conservative M.P.s defied the whip to vote for the bill and others abstained: the Government's majority was cut to 37 despite an actual Commons majority of 101: see 125 H.C. Deb. 563–637 (15 January 1988).

[72] Cm 408 (1988); see also 137 H.C. Deb. 1412–81 (22 July 1988).

[73] e.g. Green Paper on Open Government, Cmnd 7520 (1979).

[74] See C. Bennett and P. Hennessy, *A Consumer's Guide to Open Government: Techniques for Penetrating Whitehall* (1980), which showed how inadequately a direction from the Head of the Civil Service, Lord Crohan, had been implemented.

withhold information from the media and the public; for example, the terms of reference and membership of Cabinet committees, internal guides to the exercise of those discretionary powers which affect private citizens, and the responsibilities of individual senior civil servants. Some well-documented proposals (utilizing American and Swedish experience) for legislative reform have been published,[75] but there is no prospect of their implementation. The present Act is seen to be so unreasonably wide in impact that all believe that Governments will not enforce it, whereas one which identified its targets with precision might well be rigorously enforced.

Blasphemy

It is an offence at common law to outrage the feelings of a Christian by abusing Christ or by denying and attacking the Christian religion. This crime is not obsolete[76] and in 1978 the House of Lords upheld a conviction and also ruled that it is unnecessary to prove an intention to blaspheme; the intention to publish is enough. The House of Lords also confirmed that there is no need to prove that the publication tended to lead to a breach of the peace.[77]

Defamation[78]

A defamatory statement is one which tends to expose another to hatred, ridicule or contempt or to cause him to be shunned by reasonable persons. Defamatory matter consisting of spoken words, or gestures, is slander; in permanent form it is libel. By statute,[79] words used in a broadcast or a public performance of a play are deemed to be libel. The distinction between slander and libel is of practical importance. In the first place although both slander and libel are torts, no action will lie for slander in the absence of proof of special pecuniary damage, save in a limited range of situations. Secondly, slander is not

---

[75] e.g. The Other Circle Policy Unit, *An Official Information Act* (1977); James Michael, *The Politics of Secrecy*.

[76] The Law Commission has recommended that the common-law offence of blasphemy be abolished, and that statutory offences be enacted of disrupting religious worship and of offensive behaviour in a place of worship: Law Com. No. 145 (1985).

[77] *R.* v. *Lemon* [1979] A.C. 617. 'Indecent' behaviour in a place of religious worship (an offence under s. 2 of the Ecclesiastical Courts Jurisdiction Act 1860) includes interrupting a service by shouting political slogans: *Abrahams* v. *Cavey* [1968] 1 Q.B. 479.

[78] For details, see the latest editions of *Gatley on Libel and Slander*, and the leading textbooks on the law of tort (*Clerk and Lindsell, Salmond, Street,* and *Winfield and Jolowicz*). Only a very brief outline of this complex branch of the law is presented here.

[79] Defamation Act 1952, s. 1; Theatres Act 1968, ss 4, 7.

of itself a criminal offence. A conviction for libel may be obtained even though the statement was published only to the person defamed and was true (unless publication was for the public benefit). A libel may also be indictable, though not actionable as a tort, if it relates to a class of persons, or if it relates to a dead person. No prosecution against a newspaper proprietor, publisher or editor may be brought except with leave of a judge in chambers.[80]

For a civil action to lie, the defamatory statement must have been published to a third party. It is a defence that the statement was true, or was a fair comment on a matter of public interest, or was uttered on a privileged occasion. No action will lie in respect of an absolutely privileged statement even if it is false and malicious. Absolute privilege attaches to statements made in the course of judicial proceedings, proceedings in Parliament, parliamentary papers, and to communications between high officers of State and to fair and accurate newspaper or broadcast reports of judicial proceedings. Qualified privilege is lost by proof of malice, which is not easily established. Among the numerous situations covered by qualified privilege are fair and accurate newspaper reports of parliamentary proceedings,[81] and of the proceedings of public meetings, local councils and administrative tribunals and inquiries;[82] and communications between members of the public and M.P.s and M.P.s and Ministers, on matters of public interest.[83] If a person is unintentionally defamed, the innocent publisher may defend himself successfully in an action by making an offer of amends (which means the publication of a correction and an apology) as soon as possible; he must also show that he had acted with reasonable care.[84]

The law of defamation still presents many hazards for the press; and

[80] Law of Libel Amendment Act 1888, s. 8 (permission was given for Mr Jimmy Goldsmith to prosecute the publishers of *Private Eye: Goldsmith* v. *Pressdram Ltd* [1977] Q.B. 83). Leave is not required to prosecute a television company or a journalist. The House of Lords has discouraged criminals from prosecuting by allowing the defence to adduce evidence of the general bad reputation of private prosecutors; *Gleaves* v. *Deakin* [1980] A.C. In the same case the House of Lords went out of its way to advocate that leave of the Attorney-General should be required for all prosecutions for this crime. See also Newspaper Libel and Registration Act 1881, s. 4 (certain newspaper libels are triable summarily before magistrates). The Law Commission has recommended that criminal libel be abolished and replaced by a statutory offence of publishing defamatory material knowing it to be seriously defamatory: see Law Com. No. 149 (1985).

[81] *Wason* v. *Walter* (1868) L.R. 4 Q.B. 73.

[82] See generally Defamation Act 1952, ss 7, 16, Schedule, extending the defence of qualified privilege in respect of libellous newspaper reports. In many of these situations qualified privilege will be a defence only if the newspaper has published, at the plaintiff's request, a reasonable statement by way of contradiction or explanation.

[83] See p. 314.

[84] ibid., s. 4.

juries are still apt to make heavy awards of compensatory damages to persons defamed by newspapers.[85] Many proprietors and editors of journals would doubtless welcome a judicial decision such as one delivered in 1964 by the United States Supreme Court, that false and defamatory press statements about the conduct of a holder of a public office were not actionable provided that the critic was acting in good faith.[86] Justice may have been done in the particular circumstances of that case, but it would be deplorable if English law gave a licence for character assassination of public figures. At the present time some journals achieve a mass circulation by 'shocking revelations' about the private lives of persons in the news. As was mentioned earlier,[87] there is in general no legal remedy for the improper but non-defamatory invasion of privacy. But a complaint may be made to the Press Council,[88] a non-statutory investigatory body with a legal chairman but composed largely of representatives of the press, and this Council can do no more than administer a public rebuke. When invoked, the sanctions of the law of defamation are quite severe, but they are not open to persons of modest means: actions for defamation cannot be brought in county courts, High Court costs may be extremely heavy and the legal aid scheme does not extend to such proceedings.

Contempt of court and of the Houses of Parliament[89]

In some respect these legal restrictions on free expression do bear harshly on journalists and broadcasters. Premature disclosure of the report of a parliamentary committee is a contempt of the House in question. The protection given to a journalist's sources by section 10 of the Contempt of Court Act 1981 is so set about with limitations that he may easily commit contempt by refusing to disclose his sources to a court.[90]

Miscellaneous wrongs involving speech or writing

A great number of criminal offences can be committed by the use of spoken words or writing. For example, it is an offence to incite another

---

[85] For example, the £½ m. awarded to Mr Jeffrey Archer in 1987. Exemplary damages in tort can only be awarded in a limited range of situations: *Broome* v. *Cassell & Co.* [1972] A.C. 1027.

[86] *New York Times Ltd* v. *Sullivan*, 376 U.S. 255 (1964).

[87] See p. 476.

[88] See H. Philip Levy, *The Press Council*; Report of the Committee on Privacy, Cmnd 5012 (1972), ch. 7, and G. Robertson, *The People Against the Press* (1983).

[89] See ch. 17 and pp. 377–9.

[90] See above, p. 377, note 98.

to commit a crime. A criminal conspiracy can hardly be effected without verbal communication. Intimidating words accompanied by threatening behaviour may be an assault although there is no physical contact with the person put in fear. Perjury, blackmail, fraud and attempting to pervert the course of justice by, for example, interfering with witnesses, all involve some form of verbal communication. It is an offence to waste the time of the police by knowingly making a false report;[91] or to pester people with false or offensive telephone calls;[92] or to publish a false description of articles and goods for sale.[93] Among torts, fraudulent misrepresentation, deceit, slander of title and passing off are essentially verbal misdeeds.[94]

Insulting words and behaviour [95]

Under a number of local Acts and by-laws it has long been an offence to use threatening, abusive or insulting words or behaviour in a public place with intent to provoke a breach of the peace or whereby a breach of the peace is likely to be occasioned.[96] Section 5 of the Public Order Act 1936 made this a general offence, and extended it to public meetings. In 1963 the maximum penalties for the offence were increased;[97] in 1965 the offence was extended to the distribution or display of written matter and signs;[98] and in 1968 to theatrical performances to which the public was admitted.[99] The Public Order Act 1986[100] altered the law further. Section 5 of the 1936 Act was repealed[101] and replaced by a new crime under section 4 of the 1986 Act. It is an offence (*a*) to use towards another person threatening, abusive or insulting words or behaviour; or (*b*) to distribute or display any writing, sign or visible representation which is threatening, abusive or insulting, in each case with intent to cause that other person to fear

[91] Criminal Law Act 1967, s. 5(2).
[92] Telecommunications Act 1984, s. 43.
[93] Trade Descriptions Act 1968.
[94] It is an offence under s. 1 of the Malicious Communications Act 1988 (which was based on Law Com. No. 147 (1985)) to send a letter or article conveying an indecent or grossly offensive message, or a threat, or information which the sender knows or believes to be false, with the intention of causing distress or anxiety.
[95] See D. G. T. Williams, *Keeping the Peace*, pp. 153–69; Brownlie, *The Law of Public Order and National Security* (2nd edn, 1981), pp. 3–15.
[96] See, for example, *Wise* v. *Dunning* [1902] 1 K.B. 167.
[97] Public Order Act 1963.
[98] Race Relations Act 1965, s. 7. This provision (restating section 5 of the 1936 Act) had no direct connection with race relations: see below.
[99] Theatres Act 1968, s.6.
[100] On which see generally below, pp. 512–14, 516–20.
[101] Public Order Act 1986, s. 9(2).

immediate unlawful violence, or to provoke such violence, or whereby that other person is likely to believe that such violence will be used or whereby it is likely to be provoked. The offence can be committed in a public[102] or private place, and it is potentially a much wider offence than the one which it replaced. The maximum penalty is six months' imprisonment and a fine of £2,000. Another crime was created by section 5 of the 1986 Act, that of using threatening, abusive or insulting words or behaviour, or displaying any writing, sign or other visible representation which is threatening, abusive or insulting, within the hearing or sight of a person likely to be caused harassment, alarm or distress thereby.[103] The maximum penalty is a £400 fine. The powers of the police at common law to deal with or prevent a breach of the peace are expressly preserved.[104]

The importance of the section 4 offence in the context of freedom of expression is that it restricts the freedom of speakers at political meetings. Judicial interpretation of some of the key words in that section is likely to be carried over from the 1936 Act provisions. So, the word 'insulting' is to be understood in its ordinary sense.[105] There need be no intention to insult: it is sufficient that an ordinary person might feel so insulted.[106] Putting one person in fear of unlawful violence is enough under s. 4 of the 1986 Act, as is conduct likely to provoke such violence. In deciding what is 'likely', a 1963 decision will probably be followed. So if a speaker deliberately insults a hostile audience with the result that they are likely to commit a breach of the peace, it is immaterial that he may not have intended to provoke them to acts of violence or that they would not have resorted to violence had they been reasonably phlegmatic or decorous persons. When Colin Jordan, the British Nazi, insulted a hostile audience in Trafalgar Square, calling them 'red rabble' and asserting that Britain had picked on the wrong enemy in 1939, that international Jewry was the real culprit and that 'Hitler was right', it was held that he had to take the audience as he found them; the gist of the offences was public insult, likely in the circumstances to give rise to a breach of the peace, and he was convicted.[107] The offence is not confined to political diatribes; it includes abusive language directed

---

[102] Defined (ibid., s. 16) as any highway, or any place to which at the material time the public has access, on payment or otherwise, as of right or by express or implied permission.

[103] Again, it can be committed in a public or private place: see note 101.

[104] ibid., s. 40(4).

[105] *Brutus* v. *Cozens* [1973] A.C. 854 (anti-apartheid demonstration on tennis court during Wimbledon championships not an offence, though spectators angered).

[106] *Parkin* v. *Norman* [1982] 3 W.L.R. 523.

[107] *Jordan* v. *Burgoyne* [1963] 2 Q.B. 744.

against a neighbour in public.[108] However, it is not enough to show that other people were annoyed or affronted.

Incitement to racial hatred

This was first made an offence in 1965; it was further refined by section 70 of the Race Relations Act 1976; it is now contained (with other offences) in the Public Order Act 1986, sections 17 to 23. 'Racial hatred' means hatred against a group of people in Great Britain defined by reference to colour, race, nationality or ethnic or national origins. It is an offence to use threatening, abusive or insulting words or behaviour, or to display any written material which is threatening, abusive or insulting, if done with intent to stir up racial hatred, or if in the circumstances racial hatred is likely to be stirred up.[109] Leave of the Attorney-General must be obtained before a prosecution can be instituted; the offences are triable summarily or on indictment, and if the defendant elects to be tried by jury on indictment, the possibility of acquittal or disagreement may be very real. The gist of these offences is the opprobrious nature of the words or conduct in question and the feelings of disgust they are likely to arouse. To this extent the offence is more akin to the old common law of obscenity than to other modern limitations imposed by the criminal law on freedom of expression.

Obscenity [110]

The law of obscenity is both complex and controversial. It encompasses a range of common-law offences, statutory offences, and provisions for search, forfeiture and destruction. And it bears on the limits of free expression and the relationship between the law and ideas about morality.

In 1663 indecent exposure, coupled with the projection of urine from a balcony upon an audience at Covent Garden, was held to be a common-law misdemeanour.[111] A common-law offence of obscene libel

---

[108] *Ward* v. *Holman* [1964] 2 Q.B. 580.

[109] 1986 Act, s. 18. Other offences include publishing or distributing written material with intent to stir up racial hatred or whereby racial hatred is likely to be stirred up (s. 19); to perform a public play, or distribute or play a recording, with similar intent or likelihood (ss 20, 21), and to possess racially inflammatory material (s. 23).

[110] The law is well reviewed by Smith and Hogan, op. cit., pp. 719–37, and Street, op. cit., pp. 118–46. The leading monograph is Robertson, *Obscenity*.

[111] *R.* v. *Sidley* (1663) I Siderfin 168; *sub nom. Sydlye*'s case (1663) 1 Keb. 620, stating the facts more fully. See also Vagrancy Act 1824, s, 4; Criminal Justice Act 1925, s. 42.

developed from this bizarre episode. The common-law crime appeared to have been largely superseded by statute, but in 1961 the House of Lords held that an obscene publication was also indictable as a common-law conspiracy to corrupt public morals[112] and in 1972 it reaffirmed this proposition in a case where a majority of their Lordships were also of the opinion that a conspiracy to outrage public decency was an offence.[113] The defences now provided by the Obscene Publications Acts do not apply to such charges.

Statutory obscenity. Under the Obscene Publication Acts 1959 and 1964 it is an offence to publish an obscene article, or to have an obscene article for gain. Authors, photographers, artists, publishers, booksellers and other distributors may find themselves prosecuted under the Acts. Similarly, it is an offence under the Theatres Act 1968 to direct or present an obscene theatrical performance. The Criminal Law Act 1977 has extended the 1959 Act to films.[114]

The test of obscenity under these Acts is similar to that laid down in a mid-Victorian case, where it was held to be whether the matter in question had a tendency to deprave and corrupt those who were open to such influences and into whose hands it might fall.[115] Under the recent Acts, the prosecution must prove that the matter, *taken as a whole*, would tend to deprave and corrupt persons likely to read or see or hear it; hence a book is not now obscene merely because it contains a few obscene words or sentences. However, a magazine or other publication consisting of a number of separate items may be obscene although only one item falls within that description.[116] A person may be convicted under the Acts even if he had no intention to deprave or corrupt;[117] though it is a defence[118] for him to prove that he had not

[112] *Shaw* v. *D.P.P.* [1962] A.C. 220 (the *Ladies' Directory* case; publication of a guide to specified prostitutes for prospective clients). There could be a criminal conspiracy without publication. No prosecution can be brought in respect of a theatrical performance: Theatres Act 1968, s. 2(4), or a film (Criminal Law Act 1977, s. 53(3)); for this offence or for conspiracy to outrage public morals, see next note.

[113] *Knuller Ltd* v. *D.P.P.* [1973] A.C. 435 (agreement to publish advertisements in the *International Times* by person seeking homosexual relationships, although such conduct between consenting adult males was no longer unlawful). Held, also, that there was an insufficient element of *publicity* for the offence of conspiracy to outrage public decency to be committed; but that the latter common-law offence could also be committed publicly by an individual in the absence of conspiracy.

[114] s. 53. The consent of the Director of Public Prosecutions is required for the prosecution of any feature film.

[115] *R.* v. *Hicklin* (1868) L.R. 3 Q.B. 360 (a seizure, not a prosecution).

[116] *R.* v. *Anderson* [1972] 1 Q.B. 304 (the *Oz* 'schoolkids' issue case).

[117] *R.* v. *Calder & Boyars Ltd* [1969] 1 Q.B. 151.

[118] Obscene Publications Act 1959, s. 2(5); Obscene Publications Act 1964, s. 1(3)(*a*).

examined the offending article and had no reasonable cause to believe that publication or possession would be an offence.

It is also a statutory defence to a prosecution under the Act of 1959 that the publication was for the public good in the interests of science, literature, art or learning [119] or other objects of public concern. [120] If a tendency to deprave and corrupt is proved, the defendant is entitled to acquittal if he can establish this defence on a balance of probabilities. [121] Expert opinion as to the scientific, literary or artistic merits of the book or article is admissible in evidence on both sides. However, such evidence is not admissible (save in highly exceptional circumstances [122]) on the primary issue of whether the article is obscene or not. [123]

What, then is meant by a tendency to deprave and corrupt? And deprave and corrupt whom? Judicial pronouncements on these matters have shown a conspicuous lack of uniformity. Depravity and corruption have generally been understood to imply the weakening of moral fibre. Nowadays a judge, magistrate or jury is unlikely to be persuaded that anything less than the explicit portrayal or description of sexual activity tending to evoke erotic desires and an inclination to imitate what has been described or depicted is obscene in this sense. Yet this approach raises many problems. It is almost impossible to establish a causal connection between an erotic book or film and subsequent conduct. [124] In the decisions of magistrates and juries, and the directions of judges, there have been elements of unpredictability amounting to caprice. In 1928 the *Well of Loneliness*, a discreetly written literary work dealing with a sad theme of female homosexuality, was condemned as obscene. In the 1960s *Fanny Hill*, a well-written and amusing eighteenth-century erotic work, was condemned, and the publishers of *Last Exit to Brooklyn*, a book containing descriptions of male homosexual intercourse and brutal violence but in a manner calculated to arouse feelings of pity and disgust, were held by a jury to be guilty of obscene

---

[119] In *Attorney-General's Reference (No. 3 of 1977)*[1978] 3 All E.R. 1166 it was held that 'learning' meant 'the product of scholarship' so that evidence of the educational effect of sexually explicit material was not admissible.

[120] 1959 Act, s. 4. In *R. v. Jordan* [1977] A.C. 699 the House of Lords held that these words meant the value inherent in obscene material, so that evidence was not admissible that it was of therapeutic benefit to some readers. See also Theatres Act 1968, s. 3, and Criminal Law Act 1977, s. 53 (films).

[121] See *R. v. Calder & Boyars Ltd*.

[122] As in *D.P.P. v. A. & B.C. Chewing Gum Ltd* [1968] 1 Q.B. 159 (expert evidence as to effect on children).

[123] *R. v. Anderson* [1972] 1 Q.B. 304; see also *R. v. Stamford* [1972] 2 Q.B. 391.

[124] See, for example, the Report of the Committe on Obscenity and Film Censorship, Cmnd 7772 (1979).

libel,[125] but the publishers of *Lady Chatterley's Lover* (a serious though unconsciously funny novel, liberally interspersed with four-letter words and descriptions of extra-marital intercourse) were acquitted,[126] and no proceedings had been taken in connection with a book such as *Portnoy's Complaint.* In the mid-seventies administrative and police practice had become more indulgent as society had become more permissive. Since 1977 enforcement action by the police has been much more vigorous, but the outcome of judicial proceedings remains a lottery.[127]

If the tendency of a book to deprave and corrupt is established, it is not refuted merely because the most likely purchasers would already be depraved; they may be capable of being further depraved by reading it.[128] If, on the other hand, the only person to whom it was shown, for example, a senior police officer, was unlikely to be depraved or corrupted, there should be no conviction unless there was an intention to publish to others.[129] It seems that only if a significant proportion of the persons into whose hands a book may fall (not merely well-brought-up fourteen-year-old girls[130]) are likely to be depraved or corrupted by it is the offence committed.[131] The circumstances of publication or offer for sale are therefore material. An expensive hardback book may not offend against the Acts, though a cheap and easily accessible paperback edition may. Erotic prints or sculpture in a shop window may offend against them though the same representations in an art gallery may not. But the matter may still be so pornographic (for example, photographs of sexually deviant conduct) that the Act will be contravened despite the fact that display and distribution have been carefully restricted. Yet if the matter is so disgusting as to cause aversion or revulsion rather than corruption or depravity, the Acts are not contravened.[132]

---

[125] The conviction was reversed because of a misdirection by the recorder (note 121, above).

[126] See C. H. Rolph, *The Trial of Lady Chatterley.*

[127] The problems of the police in enforcing the law against 'hard-core pornography' are well depicted in *R.* v. *Metropolitan Police Commissioner, ex p. Blackburn (No. 3)* [1973] A.C. 849.

[128] *D.P.P* v. *Whyte* [1972] A.C. 849.

[129] *R.* v. *Clayton and Halsey* [1963] 1 Q.B. 163; he had *mens rea* and might now be guilty of an offence under the Criminal Attempts Act 1981, s. 1(1); see also *R.* v. *Barker* [1962] 1 W.L.R. 349; 1964 Act, s. 1(3)(*b*).

[130] cf. *R.* v. *Martin Secker & Warburg Ltd* [1954] 1 W.L.R. 1138 at 1139. Read as a whole, the direction given by Stable J. to the jury in that case (a charge of obscene libel at common law) is remarkable for its eloquent common sense.

[131] *R.* v. *Calder & Boyars Ltd* (note 121, above).

[132] *R.* v. *Anderson* (note 116). Because the 'aversion' defence was not put properly to the jury, the conviction of the defendants under the Obscene Publications Acts (though not their conviction under the Post Office Act: see below) was quashed.

The Acts are not confined to matters of sexual morality. A book extolling the pleasures of drug-taking may be an 'obscene' publication.[133] So, it seems, may a publication tending to induce violent behaviour,[134] but the publication of horror comics is a separate statutory offence.[135]

General. To outrage decency in public is a common-law misdemeanour. The offence may be committed not only by conduct, but also, by words and pictures.[136] If the words or conduct are both insulting and likely to cause a breach of the peace, this is a separate statutory offence.[137] Under a number of local Acts and by-laws, the use of obscene language in public, the display of obscene signs and other reprehensible forms of public conduct are also offences.

Obscene articles reasonably suspected of being kept for publication for gain can be searched for and seized under a magistrate's warrant.[138] Forfeiture proceedings can then be brought before the magistrate; the occupier is entitled to appear and show cause why they should not be forfeited. The defence of public good is available, but there is no provision for trial by jury. The quantity of articles thus seized and condemned is very large; again, there is no uniformity of police or magisterial practice.

Indecent or obscene articles dispatched through the mails may be detained and destroyed. An article (for example a photograph) may be indecent for this purpose though not 'obscene'.[139] In this context

---

[133] *Calder (John) Publications Ltd* v. *Powell* [1965] 1 Q.B. 509.

[134] *D.P.P.* v. *A. & B.C. Chewing Gum Ltd* [1968] 1 Q.B. 159.

[135] Children and Young Persons (Harmful Publications) Act 1955. No prosecution under this Act can be commenced without the consent of the Director of Public Prosecutions. The Protection of Children Act 1978 makes it an offence to take indecent photographs of children under 16 or to distribute or exhibit such photographs.

[136] A London cinema proprietor was convicted for exhibiting *More About the Language of Love* even though the G.L.C. had given it an X certificate: *D.P.P.* v. *Jacey Ltd*; the *Guardian*, 6 June 1975.

[137] See pp. 500–502.

[138] Obscene Publications Act 1959, s. 3. The warrant may be obtained only on information laid by the Director of Public Prosecutions or a constable (Criminal Justice Act 1967, s. 25), and criminal proceedings must be conducted by the D.P.P. (Prosecution of Offences Act 1985, ss 3(2)(*d*), 15(5)). A *prosecution* under the 1959 Act can be brought by a member of the general public, but leave of the Attorney-General is required in respect of plays and of the Director of Public Prosecutions in respect of films.

[139] Post Office Act 1953, s. 11; *R.* v. *Stanley* [1965] 2 Q.B. 327, where the court quoted with approval (at 333) the following dictum in a Scottish case: 'For a male bather to enter the water nude in the presence of ladies would be indecent, but it would not necessarily be obscene. But if he directed the attention of a lady to a certain member of his body his conduct would certainly be obscene. The matter might perhaps be roughly expressed thus in the ascending scale: positive – immodest; comparative – indecent; superlative – obscene. These, however, are not rigid categories.' See also Unsolicited Goods and Services Act 1971, s. 4.

'obscene' is given its 'usual' meaning; an article may be obscene though repulsive, and there is no need to prove a tendency to deprave and corrupt, nor is the defence of public good available.[140] The importation of indecent or obscene works is prohibited under customs legislation and customs officers may seize them.[141] They are forfeited within a month unless the importer exercises his right of objection, in which case forfeiture can be ordered only by a magistrate; no defence of 'public good' is available in such a proceeding.

The Indecent Displays (Control) Act 1981 makes it an offence punishable by up to two years' imprisonment to display indecent material in public, so that, it is hoped, Soho and the like can be cleaned up. Shops can display such material inside in a separate section prominently identified and to which under-eighteens are refused admission.

Much dissatisfaction with the law of obscenity has persisted. The scope of the law is uncertain and juries seem increasingly reluctant to convict either on obscenity or indecency charges.[142] Police enforcement has lacked consistency. Consequently, a Departmental Committee on Obscenity and Film Censorship was set up; it reported in 1979.[143] Its finding was that 'the law in short, is a mess'. It proposed the replacement of the 'deprave and corrupt' test by what it called the 'harm condition', i.e. that no conduct should be suppressed by law unless it can be taken to harm someone. It also proposed prohibition in those limited circumstances where harm can be assumed, and a statutory board for film censorship.

[140] *R.* v. *Anderson* [1972] 1 Q.B. 304; *R.* v. *Stamford* [1972] 2 Q.B. 391.

[141] Customs Consolidation Act 1876, s. 42; Customs and Excise Management Act 1979, ss 139–44, Sched. 3. See also Post Office Act 1953, ss 16, 17, 26(6); Post Office Act 1969, s. 64; Street, op. cit., pp. 144–6; *Derrick* v. *Customs and Excise Commissioners* [1972] 2 Q.B. 28.

[142] e.g. the 1976 acquittals of an exhibition of *The Language of Love* and a publisher of *Inside Linda Lovelace*.

[143] Cmnd 7772.

Chapter 26

Freedom of Assembly and Association

Association

Freedom of political association in Britain is subject to two main limitations, neither of which affects movements seeking to operate within the framework of the existing constitutional order. In the first place, there is section 2 of the Public Order Act 1936, subheaded 'Prohibition of quasi-military organizations'. The Act was passed mainly to cope with the situation created by the activities of the British Union of Fascists in the 1930s. Under section 2, it is an offence to take part in the control, management, organization or training of a body which is *either* organized or trained or equipped for the purpose of enabling it to usurp the functions of the police or the armed forces; *or* organized or trained, or organized or equipped, for the use or display of force in promoting any political object.[1] The offence is punishable, upon conviction on indictment, with a maximum two years' imprisonment and an unlimited fine. No prosecution can be instituted without the Attorney-General's consent, which has been very sparingly granted. In the 1960s, leaders of Spearhead, a neo-Nazi organization, and of the Free Wales Army, were convicted under section 2.

The Prevention of Terrorism (Temporary Provisions) Act 1984[2] bans the IRA and the INLA altogether (other proscribed organizations may be added) and makes it an offence to belong to it or to invite

---

[1] For comment on this section, see Ian Brownlie, *The Law of Public Order and National Security* (2nd edn, 1981), pp. 184–6. This book and D. G. T. Williams's *Keeping the Peace* are the leading works on the topics covered by this chapter, although they pre-date the Public Order Act 1986, on which see Law Com. No. 123 (1983); Cmnd 9510 (1985); P. Thornton, *Public Order Law* (1987); R. Card, *Public Order: the New Law* (1987); A. T. H. Smith, *Offences Against Public Order* (1987).

[2] See Clive Walker, *The Prevention of Terrorism in British Law* (1986). The Act was last officially reviewed by Lord Colville: see Cm 264 (1987).

others to contribute to its finances or to make or receive such a contribution.[3] To arrange or address a meeting of three or more persons knowing that the meeting is in support of the IRA or other proscribed organization is also an offence.[4] It is also a crime for anyone in a public place to dress or wear, carry or display any article, so as to arouse reasonable apprehension that he is a member of the IRA or INLA.[5]

Meetings and processions: prior restraints and preventive measures

It is usually said that there is no 'right of public meeting', but that public processions are *prima facie* lawful.[6] These statements need to be explained and examined.[7]

Clearly there is no right to hold any kind of meeting on private premises without the consent of the owner or occupier; such conduct will be a trespass. A trespasser may be evicted by the use of such force as is reasonable in the circumstances. Police officers may render assistance, as private individuals, to the occupier, but they are not obliged to do so and will normally refuse, though they have a common-law duty to take such steps as are reasonably required to quell a breach of the peace and to prevent a reasonably apprehended breach of the peace. Trespass is a tort, for which nominal damages are recoverable; if the court considers that the case is serious enough and that repetition is likely, it may in its discretion award an injunction against the trespasser at the instance of the occupier. Disobedience to an injunction is a contempt of court. It is a crime to use or threaten violence for the purpose of securing entry into any premises.[8]

Does it make any difference if the premises are public buildings belonging to a local authority? Candidates at elections are entitled to have access to locally maintained schools and other public halls in order to hold campaign meetings.[9] For the rest, local authorities have an ostensibly free discretion whether to let premises to anybody wishing

---

[3] Section 1(1)(*a*) and (*b*), and sched. 1.

[4] Section 1(1)(*c*).

[5] Section 2.

[6] See, for example, Goodhart (1937) 6 *Camb. L.J.* 161; E. C. S. Wade (1939) 2 *Mod. L. Rev.* 177.

[7] See especially Brownlie, op. cit., ch. 2, for criticism of the usual analysis of the law relating to meetings in public places.

[8] s. 6(1) Criminal Law Act 1977.

[9] Representation of the People Act 1983, ss 95, 96, sched. 5. The courts will compel a local authority to make premises available: *Webster* v. *Southwark L.B.C.* [1983] Q.B. 698.

to hold a meeting there. Since, however, they are public bodies, the exercise of their discretionary powers is potentially subject to judicial review. A decision not to allow *any* political meeting, or a particular *class* of political meeting, to be held on any premises under their control might possibly be held to be an unlawful fetter on their own discretion. Again, the validity of a decision to refuse the promoters of a particular meeting permission to conduct it on such premises might conceivably be impugned as being based on legally irrelevant considerations or as being so arbitrary that no reasonable body of persons could have reached it.[10]

Is there a general right or liberty to hold demonstrations or meetings in public open spaces? To conduct such a meeting is not a criminal or civil wrong merely because a Minister, a local authority, a police officer or a magistrate purports to prohibit it[11] unless their prior permission is required by law. For example, the permission of the Secretary of State for the Environment has to be obtained before a meeting can be held in Trafalgar Square.[12] Provisions in local legislation requiring advance notice of processions are in effect in some 107 local authority areas in England and Wales. The right to hold meetings at Speakers' Corner in Hyde Park is conferred only by statutory regulations.[13] The mere fact that an open space is dedicated to the public use does not apparently entitle persons to use it for holding a public meeting.[14] There is no procedure for banning open air meetings as distinct from processions[15] even though serious disorder is feared – although as will be explained shortly the police may impose conditions on both assemblies and processions under the Public Order Act 1986, Part II so as to maintain public order.

The House of Commons regularly makes a sessional order instructing the police to keep the streets leading to the Houses of Parliament free from obstruction to members. This order can have no legal effect outside the precincts of the House,[16] but the Commissioner of Police

---

[10] cf. *Associated Provincial Picture Houses Ltd.* v. *Wednesbury Corporation* [1948] 1 K.B. 223. And see *Webster* v. *Newham London B.C.*, *The Times*, 22 November 1980.

[11] *Beatty* v. *Gillbanks* (1882) 9 Q.B.D. 308; *M'Ara* v. *Edinburgh Magistrates* 1913 S.C. 1059.

[12] Trafalgar Square Regulations 1952 (S.I. 1952, No. 776), r. 3. cf. *Ex p. Lewis* (1888) 21 Q.B.D. 191.

[13] It is not a common-law liberty: *Bailey* v. *Williamson* (1873) L.R. 8 Q.B. 118. See Royal Parks and Gardens Act 1872; Williams, op. cit., ch. 3.

[14] See *De Morgan* v. *Metropolitan Board of Works* (1880) 5 Q.B.D. 155. See also *Llandudno U.D.C.* v. *Woods* [1899] 2 Ch. 705 (religious services on the foreshore).

[15] See p. 512.

[16] *Papworth* v. *Coventry* [1967] 1 W.L.R. 663 at 669–70. See also p. 324.

has statutory power[17] to give directions for the prevention of obstruction by assemblies in that vicinity and in various other places in the police district. Not every direction given with those purposes in view for the dispersal of a public assembly is necessarily valid, but the power is a wide one.[18]

Stationary gatherings on highways are generally regarded as trespasses at common law against the person or body in whom the highway is vested, unless the consent of the owner has been obtained. This is because the primary purpose to which a highway is dedicated is passage and repassage.[19] And since a public procession involves people marching down a highway, participation is *prima facie* lawful except perhaps while the procession is assembling. But a procession may well constitute an unlawful obstruction of the highway or a public nuisance.

The general rule that meetings on highways are trespasses is derived from private law. It gives no weight to the public interest in freedom of expression, and it seems ripe for reconsideration by the courts. In any event, the principle of dedication to passage and repassage is subject to exceptions indeterminate in scope – ancillary activities such as holding private conversations and shopping are not trespasses, nor are brief stoppages by motor cars,[20] but what of distributing leaflets or soliciting answers from passers-by to questionnaires – and it would be sensible to replace the prevailing concept by one which equates trespass with unreasonable user.[21] Seldom would a large meeting in a public thoroughfare be a reasonable use.

If an employee attends at or near his place of work in contemplation of furtherance of a trade dispute for the purpose only of peacefully obtaining or communicating information or peacefully persuading any

---

[17] Metropolitan Police Act 1839, s. 52. It is an offence to contravene a valid direction (s. 54(9)).

[18] See *Papworth* v. *Coventry* (note 16). The assembly in question in *Papworth*'s case comprised only seven stationary protestors against the Vietnam War. Although they were standing at the corner of Downing Street, it is doubtful whether they were reasonably capable of causing obstruction or annoyance.

[19] See, for example, *ex p. Lewis* (1888) 21 Q.B.D. at 197; *Harrison* v. *Duke of Rutland* [1893] 1 Q.B. 142; *Hickman* v. *Maisey* [1900] 1 Q.B. 752. See also cases cited in note 14, and the Scottish cases *M'Ara* v. *Edinburgh Magistrates* 1913 S.C. 1059, and *Aldred* v. *Miller* 1924 S.C. (J.) 117. See, however, *Burden* v. *Rigler* [1911] 1 K. B. 337 where it was held that a meeting held on a highway was not necessarily unlawful.

[20] See *Iveagh* v. *Martin* [1961] 1 Q.B. 232 at 273; *Randall* v. *Tarrant* [1955] 1 W.L.R. 255.

[21] In *Hirst and Agu* v. *Chief Constable of West Yorkshire* (1987) 85 Cr. App. R. 143, the Divisional Court held that the reasonableness of user by protesters handing out leaflets in the street was a relevant consideration, such conduct not in itself being unlawful. See also the dissenting judgment of Lord Denning in *Hubbard* v. *Pitt* [1976] 1 Q.B. 142 for a passionate defence of constitutional freedom, and Wallington (1976) 35 *Camb. L.J.* 82.

person to work or abstain from working, his conduct is lawful.[22] That rule applies also to recently dismissed employees and to trade union officials accompanying and representing their members. Subject to those statutory provisions pickets have no immunity from the impact of the various laws examined in this chapter. The law recognizes no right to demonstrate in a trade dispute; the picketing provisions do not protect anyone who does not work at the place being picketed. There is no authority to obstruct the passage of vehicles to and from the work place.[23]

Of more practical importance than the law of trespass are the miscellany of local statutory restrictions already referred to, the law of obstruction and the regulatory powers of the police under the Public Order Act 1986, Part II. Wilfully to obstruct the free passage along a highway without lawful authority or excuse is a criminal offence.[24] If there has been an appreciable and unreasonable obstruction, it is no defence that a way round it could be found or that nobody was proved to have been obstructed,[25] nor is it a defence that a speaker holding a meeting did not wish to create an obstruction, or that other speakers holding meetings in the same place had not been prosecuted.[26] The prosecution must prove its case, but since the amount and duration of an obstruction that it needs to establish in order to obtain a conviction are slight, the police and the local authority have almost a *de facto* licensing power with regard to public meetings and even the distribution of leaflets in the streets. If they decide to take no action, their abstention from prosecution means that no proceedings are likely to be taken at all. If a police officer orders a speaker, distributor, vendor or audience to 'move along', non-compliance with this direction is likely to lead to a conviction for obstruction of the highway or obstruction of a constable in the execution of his duty.

Public processions were first made subject to general statutory powers of regulation by the Public Order Act 1936. Newer forms of public disorder over recent years, especially at some industrial disputes, riots in some cities and football hooliganism, gave an impetus for fresh and more effective preventative arrangements. These are contained in the

---

[22] s. 16 of the Employment Act 1980.
[23] *Thomas* v. *N.U.M.* (*South Wales*) [1986] 1 Ch. 20; see generally Carty [1984] *Public Law* 600; Bennion [1985] *Crim. L. Rev.* 64.
[24] Highways Act 1980, s. 137.
[25] See generally *Horner* v. *Cadman* (1886) 55 L.J.M.C. 110; *Nagy* v. *Weston* [1965] 1 W.L.R. 280.
[26] *Arrowsmith* v. *Jenkins* [1963] 2 Q.B. 561. Or that the local authority had acquiesced in the defendant's obstruction of the highway for a long period before deciding to prosecute: *Redbridge L.B.C.* v. *Jaques* [1970] 1 W.L.R. 1604.

Public Order Act 1986, Part II. First, advance written notice of a public procession[27] intended (*a*) to show support for (or opposition to) the views or actions of any person or body of persons, or (*b*) to publicize a cause or campaign, or (*c*) to mark or commemorate an event, must be given to the police.[28] That notice must be received by the police at least six clear days ahead, specifying the proposed date, route, time and the name and address of the organizer (or organizers). It is an offence for the organizers not to give such notice, punishable by a maximum fine of £400. Secondly, a senior police officer may give directions in relation to a planned or actual public procession if he reasonably believes that (*a*) the procession may result in serious public disorder, serious damage to property or serious disruption to the life of the community, or (*b*) the purpose of the organizers is to intimidate others.[29] The directions can be of any type which seem to him to be necessary to prevent his fears coming to fruition. Knowingly failing to comply with such directions is an offence,[30] and a constable in uniform may arrest anyone whom he reasonably believes is committing it. Organizers may well negotiate with the police (as was common before the 1986 Act) to get agreement about planned marches, rather than have conditions forced upon them. Thirdly, if a chief constable reasonably believes that his powers to impose conditions on a procession would not be enough to prevent serious public disorder, he may apply to the district council in whose area the procession would take place for an order prohibiting for a period up to three months the holding of all, or a specified class of, public processions in the area.[31] The council may make such an order with the Home Secretary's consent; it may be amended or revoked in the same way.[32] Knowingly contravening such an order is an offence,[33] and a constable in uniform may arrest for it. Fourthly, the police have a new power to give directions in relation to public assemblies.[34] If the senior police officer[35] has the same fears about an assembly as were set out above in relation to public processions, he

[27] i.e., a procession in a public place: 1986 Act, s. 16.

[28] 1986 Act, s. 11. If it is not reasonably practicable to do so (e.g. when a gathering is spontaneous), no such duty exists.

[29] ibid., s. 12. The 'senior police officer' is the chief constable (for planned processions), or the senior officer present (at an actual procession).

[30] The organizer, and an inciter, are liable to 3 months' imprisonment and a £1,000 fine; a participant to a £400 fine.

[31] ibid., s.13.

[32] In the City of London or the Metropolitan Police District the two chief officers may each make an equivalent order with the Home Secretary's consent.

[33] See note 30.

[34] 1986 Act, s. 14.

[35] See note 29.

may impose similar directions upon it – although he cannot ban it. A public assembly is one of twenty or more persons in a public place which is wholly or partly open to the air:[36] meetings inside buildings are excluded. Offences may be committed as for breach of conditions for public processions,[37] and the same power of arrest exists. All these powers seek to balance, on the one hand, the rights to process and to assemble against, on the other, the rights of those not involved to live peaceful lives which are not unreasonably disrupted. Although the validity of conditions imposed on the organizers of a procession might be challenged in court on various grounds, it would seem that a prohibitory order could be impugned only if it were perverse or singled out an individual procession as distinct from a class of processions; the court cannot review the merits of an order.

Preventive justice may be (and quite frequently is) involved by the police in bringing potentially disorderly demonstrators or other 'agitators' before local magistrates, who may bind them over to be of good behaviour or to keep the peace.[38] If they refuse to enter into a recognizance or are unable to find sureties, they may be sent to prison for up to six months. If they break the conditions set out in the recognizance they become liable to forfeiture of the sum there specified.

If the police reasonably apprehend that the holding of a gathering in a public place will give rise to a breach of the peace, they are under a common-law duty to take reasonable steps to prevent that gathering from taking place or to break it up. This power was used, for example, to prevent disorder during the miners' strike of 1984–5. In *Moss and Others* v. *McLachlan*[39] four would-be pickets ignored police requests to turn back from their intended picket site while still some few miles away from it. They were convicted of obstructing the police, who had ample evidence to fear a breach of the peace at the intended destination. The common-law powers of the police to deal with a breach of the peace are unaffected by the Public Order Act 1986 or by the arrest provisions of the Police and Criminal Evidence Act 1984. The problems caused by the ambit of *Duncan* v. *Jones*,[40] however, have been greatly reduced by the Public Order Act 1986.[41]

If a public meeting is held on private premises, and the police

---

[36] 1986 Act, s. 16.
[37] See note 30.
[38] Williams, op. cit., ch. 4; Law Com. No 103 (1987).
[39] [1985] I.R.L.R. 77.
[40] [1936] 1 K.B. 218.
[41] See below, p. 518.

reasonably apprehend that, should they not be present, a breach of the peace or an incitement to violence will occur, they are entitled to attend and insist on remaining in order to prevent such an occurrence. This is the narrowest possible *ratio decidendi* of *Thomas* v. *Sawkins*,[42] a decision that has been widely criticized, not least because the judgments included some unacceptably sweeping propositions aobut the extent of police powers.[43] Nevertheless, the principle set out above is reasonable, provided that it is confined to apprehended violence and the dissemination of incitements. The presence of a policeman on the spot can have a restraining influence at both indoor and outdoor meetings. An ordinary member of the public cannot claim a right to enter a meeting or to remain there after his invitation or licence to remain has been withdrawn, even though the meeting has been advertised as being open to the public.[44] But the police have special common-law responsibilities for the maintenance of public order, and it would be unreasonable to deny them a right of entry until a breach of the peace has actually occurred. It may be asked whether the same rule applies to private gatherings on private premises. One has to balance the public interest in the prevention of disorder against (i) the public interest in the maintenance of personal privacy against unsolicited intrusion, (ii) the possibility that a power to insist on entry might be abused, and (iii) the probability that, where incitements to violence are apprehended, the presence of police officers might not serve any useful purpose because

---

[42] [1935] 2 K.B. 249.

[43] See, for example, Goodhart (1936) 6 *Camb. L.J.* 22. A meeting was organized by the Communist Party to protest against the Incitement to Disaffection Bill, then before Parliament, and to demand the dismissal of the Chief Constable of Glamorgan. Uniformed police entered the meeting and refused to leave; the speaker laid hands on a police officer whom he wished to eject as a trespasser; the officer resisted; the speaker took out a summons against the police officer for assault; the magistrates dismissed the case, holding that the police officer was not a trespasser. The speaker appealed on a point of law by way of case stated to the Divisional Court. Some passages in Lord Hewart C.J.'s judgment were too loosely expressed. Avory J. held that the police were entitled to remain if they reasonably apprehended that if they were not present seditious speeches and/or breaches of the peace would occur. He observed (at 256): 'In principle I think there is no distinction between the duty of a police constable to prevent a breach of the peace and the power of a magistrate to bind a person over to prevent a breach of the peace.'

In the text above 'sedition' has been equated with an incitement to violence (see p. 492). It should be noted that the magistrates found as a fact that the police had reasonable grounds for thinking that if they were not present there would be incitements to violence and breaches of the peace.

[44] Subject to limited exceptions. Whether a person who has paid for admission to a public meeting can be ejected as a trespasser whenever the promoters think fit is questionable. A member of an organization may also have a legal right to attend a private meeting of that organization.

the group could quietly arrange another meeting at a different time and place. The point is not clearly covered by English authority, but it is thought that the powers of the police do extend to insistence on being present at such a meeting[45] where violence at or immediately after the gathering is reasonably apprehended.

Offences

We have seen how the mere holding of a public meeting or procession may be wrongful. It may be a trespass. It will be a criminal offence if it is held without the permission required by a local Act or by-law, or in breach of the provisions of Part II of the Public Order Act 1986. Organizers of a procession commit an offence if a ban on public processions in that area is in force, or if they infringe conditions lawfully imposed by the police. A meeting held in a public place may well constitute an obstruction of the highway. So may a public procession if it causes significant obstruction.

A demonstration, mobile or stationary, may also be a public nuisance if it entails an unreasonable use of the highway, causing obstruction or excessive noise. Prosecutions for public nuisance in this context have been uncommon,[46] but in 1963 the leader of a political demonstration in Central London was sentenced to eighteen months' imprisonment for inciting other persons to commit a nuisance. The conviction was quashed on appeal because the jury had not been directed to consider whether the obstruction caused was an unreasonable use of the highway.[47] In that case there was evidence of obstruction by a large crowd. The decision of the appellate court may indicate a benign attitude towards processions (as distinct from meetings) or a difference in the degrees of obstruction needed to obtain convictions for a public nuisance and for wilful obstruction under the Highways Act 1980.[48] In any event, the most remarkable feature of the case was the sentence imposed by the court of first instance.

It is an offence to use or threaten violence for the purpose of securing entry into any premises.[49] Squatters or other persons who occupy

---

[45] For example, a meeting of a student body on university premises. However, the possibility that the presence of police may provoke rather than dampen inflammatory statements is not to be disregarded.

[46] The Attorney-General, on behalf of the general public, may also sue for an injunction to restrain the continuance or repetition of a public nuisance; see pp. 588–91.

[47] *R.* v. *Clark* (No. 2) [1964] 2 Q.B. 315.

[48] On the question of unreasonable obstruction, the case-law does not point unambiguously to any such difference.

[49] S.6(1) Criminal Law Act 1977.

premises and refuse to leave at the request of a displaced residential occupier of the premises also commit a crime.[50]

There is an obvious danger that a large number of people in a mobile or static demonstration may be so stimulated by the fervour of their cause that serious public order crimes result. So, for example, about 140 charges of riot and over 500 of unlawful assembly were brought during the miners' strike of 1984–5.[51] The common-law offences of riot, rout, unlawful assembly and affray were, as the Law Commission concluded, unsatisfactory[52] and the law was modernized by the Public Order Act 1986, Part I. Those four common-law offences were abolished[53] and in their place statutory crimes of riot, violent disorder and affray were created; rout and unlawful assembly were not recreated (at least, not under those names).

Riot[54] is an offence in which twelve or more people who are present together use or threaten unlawful violence[55] for a common purpose,[56] and the conduct of them (taken together) is such as would cause a person of reasonable firmness present at the scene[57] to fear for his personal safety. That common purpose may be inferred from their conduct;[58] a riot may take place in a private or in a public place;[59] it carries a maximum penalty of ten years' imprisonment and a fine.[60] It is clearly the most serious public order offence, and the consent of the Director of Public Prosecutions is necessary for any prosecution of it.[61] Civil claims to compensation out of public funds under the Riot (Damages) Act 1886 will continue to be made for loss suffered by property-owners as a result of riots.

---

[50] S.7(1) Criminal Law Act. 1977.
[51] No evidence was offered, however, in a large number of cases, and there was a high rate of acquittals – partly as a result of the problems of establishing those offences, as Lord Scarman had warned in his report on the Brixton disorders would be the case: see Cmnd 8427 (1983).
[52] See Law Com. No. 123 (1983).
[53] 1986 Act, s. 9. See the commentaries on the Act cited above, p. 508, note 1.
[54] ibid., s. 1.
[55] 'Violence' for purposes of riot and violent disorder means (s. 8) any violent conduct including violence towards property.
[56] The mental element required is an intention to use violence, or that the accused is aware that his conduct may be violent: s. 6(1).
[57] No such person need actually be, or be likely to be, present at the scene: ibid., s. 1(4).
[58] ibid., s. 1(3).
[59] ibid., s. 1(5): for the definition, see s. 16.
[60] ibid., s. 1(6). It is therefore an arrestable offence under s. 24 of the Police and Criminal Evidence Act 1984. On the common-law offence, see *Field* v. *Metropolitan Police Receiver* [1921] 3 K.B. 334; *Munday* v. *Metropolitan Police District Receiver* [1949] 1 All E.R. 337.
[61] ibid., s. 7(1).

Violent disorder[62] is committed when three or more persons who are present together use or threaten unlawful violence[63] and the conduct of them (taken together) is such as would cause a person of reasonable firmness present at the scene to fear for his personal safety.[64] The maximum penalty on indictment is a five-year prison sentence and a fine, or on summary conviction six months' imprisonment or a fine of up to £2,000.[65] Violent disorder will be the usual charge following serious disorder. The crime replaces unlawful assembly, about which there was uncertainty as to its nature and scope: the Law Commission had identified no less than four ways of defining it.[66] Difficulties of interpretation existed about when an assembly became unlawful,[67] about what constituted a breach of the peace,[68] and about the liability of people in one group for unlawful acts which were likely to be provoked in or committed by others. That last problem was highlighted in the attempts to reconcile, in particular, *Beatty* v. *Gillbanks*,[69] *Wise* v. *Dunning*[70] and *Duncan* v. *Jones*.[71] No doubt the courts will find fresh problems in interpreting the Public Order Act 1986, although perhaps not of the some intellectual complexity.

Affray[72] is committed by one who uses unlawful violence towards another when his conduct is such as would cause a person present of reasonable firmness to fear for his personal safety. A threat cannot be made by words alone.[73] On indictment the maximum penalty is three years' imprisonment and a fine; summarily it is three months' imprisonment and a fine up to £2,000.[74] A constable may arrest without warrant anyone he reasonably suspects is committing an affray.[75]

---

[62] ibid., s. 2.

[63] An accused must intend to use or threaten violence, or be aware that his conduct may be violent or threaten violence: s. 6(2).

[64] Again, no such person need be, or be likely to be, present (s. 2(3)); it can be committed in public or private (s. 2(4)).

[65] ibid., s. 2(5). It is an arrestable offence under s. 24 of the Police and Criminal Evidence Act 1984.

[66] Law Commission Working Paper No. 82 (1982), paras 2.43–2.50.

[67] See *R.* v. *Caird* (1970) 50 Cr. App. R. 449.

[68] Contrast *R.* v. *Howell* [1982] Q.B. 416 and *R.* v. *Chief Constable of Devon and Cornwall, ex p. CEGB* [1982] Q.B. 458.

[69] (1889) 9 Q.B.D. 308.

[70] [1902] 1 K.B. 167.

[71] [1936] 1 K.B. 218. See the 5th edn, 1985, of this book, pp. 513–18.

[72] 1986 Act, s. 3. No such person need be present (s. 3(4)); it can be committed in public or private (s. 3(5)). If two or more people so act, it is their conduct taken together that must be considered: s. 3(2).

[73] ibid., s. 3(3).

[74] ibid., s. 3(7).

[75] ibid., s. 3(6). For the common-law offence, see *Button* v. *DPP* [1966] A.C. 591 and *Taylor* v. *DPP* [1973] A.C. 964 (H.L.); *Att.-Gen.'s Reference (No. 3 of 1983)* [1985] 1 Q.B. 24.

It should be remembered that if none of these offences can be proved prosecutions could succeed under the Public Order Act 1986, sections 4 and 5,[76] and for obstructing a police officer in the execution of his duty.[77]

In the exercise of their powers the police must be aware of the importance of the right of assembly so that those who are lawfully conducting themselves but who encounter opposition should receive police protection. Under the old common-law position, the police were occasionally too ready to move against those who were exercising their constitutional rights, rather than to act against others who threatened them or the public peace.[78] The offences in Parts I and II of the Public Order Act 1986 are, on the whole, constructed so as to redress the balance in favour of freedom of assembly.

Finally, there are three points of some importance in the conduct of public meetings but not directly associated with the foregoing discussion.

1 Section 2(6) of the Public Order Act 1936 recognized the legality of employing a reasonable number of stewards to assist in the maintenance of order in public meetings on private premises. However, they are not to be so organized as to usurp the functions of the police or to display force in the promotion of a political object.

2 It is an offence under section 1 of the Act punishable by three months' imprisonment and/or a fine up to £1,000 to wear a political uniform (except with the permission of the Home Secretary) in a public place or at a public meeting. Emblems, badges and armbands will not normally be understood to be uniforms, but a shirt with a colour signifying the wearer's political associations would be so regarded. Those who, in 1974, attended a London IRA funeral procession in black berets and dark glasses were convicted under the section.[79]

3 Under the Prevention of Crime Act 1953 it is an offence to have, without lawful authority or reasonable excuse, an offensive weapon

---

[76] See above, pp. 500–501.
[77] Police Act 1964, s. 51(3): see above, p. 468.
[78] The Public Meeting Act 1908, s. 1 (which remains in force) makes it an offence to act in a disorderly manner for the purpose of preventing the transaction of business at a lawful meeting. A constable may take the name and address of a suspect; if he refuses to give it, or if the constable believes it is false, he may arrest him under the Police and Criminal Evidence Act 1984, s. 25.
[79] *O'Moran v. D.P.P.* [1975] Q.B. 864. The Prevention of Terrorism (Temporary Provisions) Act 1984, s. 2 now makes it a specific offence for members of the IRA or other proscribed organizations to wear any item of dress or wear, carry or display any article in public support of that organization.

in a public place. For this purpose, a public place includes a public meeting on private premises. The burden of proving lawful authority or reasonable excuse will lie on the defendant. An offensive weapon is an article made or adapted for causing injury to the person, or alternatively one that is intended by the person having it with him to be used for that purpose; in the latter case the prosecution must prove intent.

The range of crimes and civil wrongs that may be committed by participants in public gatherings is therefore impressive. And the miscellany of crimes and torts described in the previous chapter may be committed on such occasions. The ample scope of punitive, preventive and repressive powers (which, as is to be expected, is far wider in Northern Ireland [80]) implies that considerable self-restraint must be shown by the police and magistrates if the spokesmen of unpopular or eccentric causes are to be allowed to ventilate their opinions.

[80] See Claire Palley, *The Evolution, Disintegration and Possible Reconstruction of the Northern Ireland Constitution*, pp. 400–404, 412–16, 434–40; Lord MacDermott (1972) 17 *Juridical Review* (N.S.) 1 and ch. 3.

Chapter 27

National Emergencies

Civil disorder [1]

The issues involved in civil emergencies in the 1980s have proved to be of a character different from that usually examined in constitutional law treatises. The sequence has not been mayor, magistrates and local police in action against local rioters, and then, if necessary, calling in soldiers to put down local insurrections. Public order is now subject to threats of a different type, especially attacks from political terrorists from overseas, and hijacking of aircraft. [2] Nor is it a case of invoking military aid if and only if the use of firearms is required. The police are now trained in handling firearms to deal with political terrorists, and their internal rules regulate the circumstances in which they may use them. And the sight of armed police patrolling airports is now commonplace. When a chief officer of police believes that his force can no longer deal with a threat to public order he will consult the Home Office. The Home Secretary and the Secretary of State for Defence and, if the matter is serious enough, the Prime Minister and Cabinet will decide whether to sanction the use of force by troops. A combined operation of police and military will then be put into effect. [3] This is the kind of plan for protecting airports such as Heathrow against terrorist attacks. Nonetheless, circumstances may arise where a military officer on the spot may have to make a snap decision whether to use force,

---

[1] See D. Bonner, *Emergency Powers in Peacetime* (1985); G. Marshall, *Constitutional Conventions* (1984), ch. 9.

[2] See above, p. 519.

[3] See Report of the Metropolitan Police Commissioner for 1975 (1976) Cmnd 1976, app. 9; 91 H.C. Deb. *317* (written answers 10 February 1986). The General Officer Commanding British troops in Northern Ireland has been subject to the political direction of the United Kingdom Government.

and if so, how much, to quell a riot.[4] It may be sufficient to use batons, tear gas, rubber bullets or water cannon. If such methods are ineffective in the circumstances, he must decide whether to order his men to open fire with lethal bullets. Failure to give an order may lead to the triumph of the rioters and perhaps the capture of arms, followed perhaps by his being court-martialled and cashiered,[5] or even indicted for a common-law offence,[6] in respect of his breach of duty. If he orders deadly violence to be used when this is not justified under the conditions, he (and possibly his subordinates)[7] may be convicted of murder or manslaughter.

The officer's predicament is made more acute by the obscurity of the legal principles governing the scope of his duties. Judges and writers have insisted many times over that soliders are entitled, indeed obliged at common law, to use all necessary force, including deadly violence in the last resort, to disperse rioters, who are doing serious and extensive damage to property – for example, demolishing and setting fire to colliery buildings.[8] Is this still the law? Section 3 of the Criminal Law Act 1967 provides that a person may use such force as is *reasonable* in the circumstances in the prevention of crime; and it expressly replaces the common-law rules on this matter. Referring to this section,[9] the authors of a leading textbook on criminal law assert that it can rarely, if ever, be justifiable to use deadly force merely for the protection of property.[10] What if skinheads try to burn down the National Gallery, or if revolutionaries try to demolish No. 10 Downing Street as the symbol of an immoral society? In the last analysis, answers to the questions whether it can be justifiable to use lethal weapons to prevent the destruction of property, in the absence of an immediate threat to human life, may depend on value judgements which may reasonably differ. Soldiers can be expected to be equipped with common sense. They can hardly be expected to make fundamental judgements about

---

[4] See the official *Manual of Military Law*. Relevant extracts are set out in Appendix 5 to Brownlie's *Law of Public Order and National Security* (2nd edn, 1981).

[5] See Professor Heuston's account of the sequel to the Bristol Riots of 1831 in *Essays in Constitutional Law* (2nd edn), pp. 137–8. For a fuller account of the use of troops in aid of the civil power at that time and in the preceding years, see L. Radzinowicz, *A History of English Criminal Law and its Administration*, vol. 4, pp. 141–52.

[6] cf. *R. v. Pinney* (1832) 3 B. & Ad. 947.

[7] Subject to the doubtful defence of superior orders; see pp. 211–12.

[8] See, for example, *Report of the Committee on the Featherstone Riots* (C. 7734 (1893)).

[9] For an interpretation of the corresponding provision in Northern Ireland law see *Devlin v. Armstrong* [1971] N.I. 13 (organization of petrol-bomb throwing by Miss Devlin not reasonable to prevent invasion of Bogside by constabulary and suspected Protestant mob).

[10] J. C. Smith and Brian Hogan, *Criminal Law* (6th edn, 1988), p. 246.

social institutions when they are under stress in the face of mob violence; and their oath of loyalty implies an obligation to do what appears necessary for the preservation of the existing order and its physical manifestations.[11]

It is possible to analyse the duties of soldiers to quell local riots as being the duties of the ordinary citizen writ large.[12] But when riot passes into rebellion or guerrilla warfare, emphases shift and other principles intrude. Levying 'war' against the Queen in her realm is both treason and treason felony. The civil power primarily responsible for containing and suppressing an uprising must be the Government in office. The military authorities will be obliged to act in its support. The Crown, acting through its advisers, has, moreover, a prerogative power to direct the disposition and use of the armed forces. The exact limits of this prerogative are far from clear;[13] but it cannot mean that troops can lawfully be ordered to do whatever the Crown thinks fit whenever it thinks fit to maintain internal security, irrespective of what necessity requires. However, it may well imply that the strict tests of legality applied to the conduct of those entrusted with the preservation of order in local disturbances[14] should be slightly relaxed in time of extensive turmoil.

If the situation moves a stage further and the civil authorities become incapable of governing because of a large-scale insurrection, powers to do whatever may be needed to restore peace may be handed over to (or assumed by) the military authorities. This is a new situation, different both in degree and kind. A state of martial law will then exist, and the powers of the General Officer Commanding the Forces will, so it is usually thought, become non-justiciable and, for the time being, absolute, subject only to consultation (if this is feasible) with the civil power.

Martial law has been aptly described as 'a peculiar system of legal

---

[11] However, the potentially grave social consequences of resorting to deadly violence, even in a situation where troops are being subjected to physical assault by riotous demonstrators, were vividly illustrated by the events of 'Bloody Sunday' in Londonderry (30 January 1972). See the Report of the Widgery Tribunal of Inquiry (H.C. 220 (1971–2)), where it seems to have been assumed that instructions to the troops to fire without warning only against persons endangering or about to endanger life (see paras 89 et seq.) were correct in law.

[12] In Reference under 48A of the Criminal Appeal (Northern Ireland) Act 1968 (No. 1 of 1975) [1977] A.C. 105 at 136 Lord Diplock said: '. . . when troops are called on to assist in controlling a riotous assembly . . . it may not be inaccurate to describe the legal rights and duties of a soldier as being no more than those of an ordinary citizen in uniform.'

[13] The common-law rules on the prerogative in emergencies falling short of war are remarkably abstruse; see the inconclusive comments in *Halsbury's Laws of England* (4th edn), vol. 8, pp. 625–6.

[14] See *Lynch* v. *Fitzgerald* [1938] I.R. 382; Kier and Lawson, *Cases* (6th edn, 1979) p. 206.

relations'[15] which arises in time of civil war or insurrection, or, it may be added, invasion. It is a state of affairs, not a settled body of rules, though rules and orders will be promulgated and enforced by the military authorities as they see fit. It must be sharply distinguished from military law, a settled body of rules applied in accordance with prescribed procedures to members of the armed forces and ancillary personnel. Military law is simply a specialized branch of United Kingdom law administered by military officers acting summarily or sitting in courts-martial, subject to the supervisory and appellate jurisdiction of the ordinary courts.[16] Courts-martial applying military law are regular courts. Courts-martial applying martial law are not: they are informal tribunals or committees of officers,[17] and appear to be no more subject to the supervisory jurisdiction of the superior courts than are 'drumhead courts' or soldiers meting out summary punishment to armed rebels, curfew-breakers or other supposed malefactors among the civil population.

Confusion of martial law and military law was far more common before a regular corpus of military law was introduced in the eighteenth century. In the Middle Ages the prerogative Court of the Constable and Marshal dispensed the 'law martial' against rebellious civilians as well as undisciplined soldiers; it lost most of its jurisdiction in 1640.[18] Under the Tudors and early Stuarts special commissions were issued from time to time under the prerogative for the trial by martial law of serious offenders against public order. The issue of such commissions was forbidden by the Petition of Right 1628. But the terminological confusion lingered on.

The term 'martial law' is also sometimes used to denote military rule over enemy territory occupied by British forces. Such a situation is regulated rather by the international law of war than by British municipal law.

Finally, 'martial law' can be used to describe an entirely different kind of situation – one where military officers overthrow the legitimate government, establish a new régime and proclaim a state of martial

---

[15] Keir and Lawson, op. cit., p. 217; also see generally pp. 217–50; Heuston, *Essays* (2nd edn, 1964), pp. 150–63; symposium in (1902) 18 L.Q.R. 117–58.

[16] See pp. 212–13.

[17] Hence the courts will not control them by issuing prerogative orders: *Re Clifford and O'Sullivan* [1921] 2 A.C. 570 (prohibition). This House of Lords decision skirted the main issue – whether the courts had any jurisdiction at all to interfere with the decisions of the military tribunals.

[18] However, the ancient Court of Chivalry retains a minor aspect of the jurisdiction: see *Manchester Corporation* v. *Manchester Palace of Varieties Ltd* [1955] P. 133 (right to use a coat of arms).

law. The phenomenon is all too familiar in many countries. It has not arisen in Britain in modern times and our constitutional law books are silent on its legal consequences. Briefly, one can say that the judges and officials are not obliged to recognize the validity of such a proclamation, any more than they are obliged to accept any other revolutionary *coup d'état*, but that if they defy the mailed fist, they cannot expect to retain office for long. If they do recognize the supersession of the old order as valid,[19] successful revolution has begotten its own legality.[20]

Propositions about martial law situations, as reviewed by the courts, are deducible from cases arising out of the Irish troubles and the Boer War. They presuppose (i) the existence of civil authorities who (ii) are unable to cope with widespread disorders or armed conflict and who therefore (iii) authorize or acquiesce in the imposition of military government upon civilians for the purpose of restoring order.

1 A state of martial law may be introduced by or without a proclamation. A proclamation purporting to introduce a state of martial law is of no legal effect in itself; martial law is justified only by paramount necessity.

2 If the ordinary courts are still sitting, it seems that they have jurisdiction to determine whether 'a state of war' (not necessarily war in the international sense, but a state of affairs requiring military 'pacification' by the imposition of martial law) exists in an area where they normally have jurisdiction. In determining this question, they will give heavy weight to the opinion of the local military commander, but his opinion is not binding on them.[21]

3 If they decide that a 'state of war' does exist, then (according to the present weight of legal opinion) they should decline to review the legality of anything done by the military authorities in the purported discharge of military responsibilities till, in their independent judgement, the 'state of war' has terminated.[22]

[19] As they did in Pakistan in 1958 (*The State* v. *Dosso* P.L.D. 1958 S.C. 533); though the prevailing conditions did not justify the initial proclamation of martial law in that year: see Alan Gledhill, *Pakistan: The Development of its Laws and Constitution* (2nd edn), p. 108. Martial law was again declared in Pakistan in 1969 during a widespread breakdown of law and order, but after the collapse of the régime early in 1972 following the defeat of the Pakistan army by India, the Pakistan Supreme Court held (*Jilani* v. *Government of the Punjab* P.L.D. 1972 S.C. 139; disapproving *Dosso*'s case) that the martial-law régime was unlawful.

[20] See pp. 67–70.

[21] See, for example, *R.* v. *Allen* [1921] 2 I.R. 241; *R. (Garde)* v. *Strickland* [1921] 2 I.R. 317; cf. the striking decision in *Egan* v. *Macready* (note 23, below).

[22] *Ex p. Marais* [1902] A.C. 109; *Tilonko* v. *Att.-Gen. of Natal* [1907] A.C. 93; cases cited in note 21, above, and note 23, below.

4   The non-justiciability of acts done by the military authorities during the 'state of war' seems to embrace situations where they have exceeded emergency powers conferred on them by statute.[23]

5   When ordinary civil proceedings can be resumed, proceedings may be brought against the military authorities by persons aggrieved by acts done during the state of martial law. According to one view, soldiers will be legally liable at common law in respect of any unnecessary use of force against persons or property.[24] A more realistic view is that liability should attach only to such conduct as was manifestly unreasonable in the circumstances.[25] In practice an Act of Indemnity is almost certain to be passed (assuming that the disturbances are quelled), exonerating from liability persons who were acting in good faith for the suppression of the uprising.[26]

War

The declaration and general conduct of war, as the term is understood in international law, are matters of prerogative. Among the specific prerogatives exercisable in time of war are powers to intern and deport enemy aliens,[27] to prohibit trading with the enemy except by licence, to requisition property (including land[28] and British ships[29]) for military purposes, to requisition neutral ships and chattels (the right of angary),[30] and to destroy property in order to impede, or deny facilities to, an advancing enemy.[31] Compensation is payable at common law

[23] *R.* v. *Allen* (above); but see *Egan* v. *Macready* [1921] I.R. 265, where the court held that the 'prerogative' powers exercised by the military authorities had been superseded by statute. See the valuable discussion of these cases in Keir and Lawson, op. cit., pp. 233–7. And note the courageous decision of a Pakistan court in *Mir Hasan* v. *The State* P.L.D. 1969 (2) Lahore 786, interpreting a martial-law regulation and holding an order made by a martial-law authority to be invalid; see Dias [1970] *Camb. L.J.* 49. It is arguable that public policy does not require a total abdication of judicial review during a state of martial law.

[24] Dicey, op. cit., pp. 289–91.

[25] Keir and Lawson, op. cit., pp. 224–5.

[26] For interpretation of such an Act, see *Wright* v. *Fitzgerald* (1798) 27 St. Tr. 759. But much will depend on the wording of the particular Act and a jury's view of the merits of the case: see O'Higgins (1962) 25 *Mod. L. Rev.* 413, discussing unreported Irish decisions on the activities of 'Flogger Fitzgerald'.

[27] *R.* v. *Bottrill, ex p. Kuechenmeister* [1947] K.B. 41.

[28] See discussion of the precedents in *Att.-Gen.* v. *De Keyser's Royal Hotel Ltd* [1920] A.C. 508.

[29] *The Broadmayne* [1916] P. 64.

[30] *Commercial & Estates Co. of Egypt* v. *Board of Trade* [1925] 1 K.B. 271.

[31] *Burmah Oil Co.* v. *Lord Advocate* [1965] A.C. 75 (destruction of British-owned oil installations in Burma in 1942, on orders of military commander, acting in pursuance of Government 'scorched earth' policy, so as to prevent Japanese army from taking them intact).

for requisitioning, damaging or destroying private property (except in battle);[32] but the War Damage Act 1965 abolished the duty to pay compensation for lawful *damage* to or *destruction* of property during, or in contemplation of the outbreak of, war.[33] The exact scope of the prerogative in time of war may never be exactly ascertained. Nor is it clear how far the war prerogatives extend to a state of immediately apprehended war. Again, some of the emergency powers exercisable by the Crown (for example, to enter upon private property and construct defence works to repel an invasion)[34] may be regarded as common-law powers exercisable by all citizens as a matter of necessity, and not peculiar to the Crown; hence they would not usually be classifiable as prerogatives. In practice most of the powers that the Crown is likely to exercise during war will be regulated by statute.

There seems to be no justification for the view that a state of martial law may be imposed within the realm whenever the Crown is at war; if the civil authorities are capable of governing, there is no legal warrant for the introduction of military rule by prerogative.

Reference has already been made to the vast powers conferred on the Crown in Council by the Defence of the Realm Acts 1914–15 and the Emergency Powers (Defence) Acts 1939–40.[35] The general words of the Defence of the Realm Acts, authorizing the making of regulations to secure the public safety and the defence of the realm, were construed as being wide enough to validate a regulation for the preventive detention of British subjects on security grounds.[36] The emergency legislation of the Second World War was more explicitly worded. It expressly saved the royal prerogative;[37] it authorized the sub-delegation of delegated powers and the imposition of charges on the subject,[38] and the making of regulations for the detention of persons on security grounds and for the amendment of any prior Act of Parliament.[39] The Emergency Powers (Defence) (No. 2) Act 1940 authorized the making of Defence Regulations for the trial of civilians by special courts if the military situation so required. No such regulation was in fact made. The Acts

[32] ibid.
[33] The Act was severely criticized in that it had retroactive effect, overruling the actual decisions of the House of Lords in the *Burmah Oil* case.
[34] *Case of the King's Prerogative in Saltpetre* (1606) 12 Co. Rep. 12.
[35] See above, p. 339.
[36] *R.* v. *Halliday, ex p. Zadig* [1917] A.C. 260 (Regulation 14B).
[37] Emergency Powers (Defence) Act 1939, s. 9.
[38] ibid., ss 1(3), 2; cf. *Att.-Gen.* v. *Wilts United Daries Ltd* (1921) 37 T.L.R. 884, where it was held that the Food Controller, purporting to act under emergency powers, could not validly require a milk purchaser to pay him 2d. a gallon as a condition of being granted a licence to purchase, since he had no express statutory authority to impose a charge.
[39] ibid., ss 1(2)(*a*), 1(4).

expired in 1946, but some of the Defence Regulations were continued in force and others were made under post-war emergency legislation. Those which had survived were placed on a permanent footing by statute in 1964. Regulation 18 B, authorizing the internment of security suspects, had been revoked immediately after the termination of armed hostilities with Germany.

It should be noted that in neither world war was the right to apply for the writ of habeas corpus against the Executive expressly suspended. However, regulations authorizing a Secretary of State to detain persons of hostile origins or associations were so broadly interpreted by the courts as to leave a detainee hardly any room for successfully challenging an internment order by habeas corpus or any other means.[40]

Disruption of essential services

Permanent legislation gives the Executive power to deal with dislocation caused by strikes in essential services and by natural catastrophes.[41] Under the Emergency Powers Acts 1920 and 1964 Her Majesty may proclaim a state of emergency if at any time it appears to her that there have occurred, or are about to occur, events of such a nature as to be calculated to deprive the community, or any substantial part of it, of the essentials of life by interference with the supply and distribution of food, water, fuel or light, or with the means of locomotion. If Parliament is not sitting when such a proclamation is issued, it has to meet within five days. The proclamation will be in force for one month but may be revoked before the expiry of that time or renewed after it.

During the state of emergency, such regulations may be made by Order in Council as are deemed necessary for securing and regulating the supply and distribution of the necessities of life, for preserving the peace and for other essential purposes and incidental matters.

---

[40] *R.* v. *Halliday* (note 36, above); *Liversidge* v. *Anderson* [1942] A.C. 206; *Greene* v. *Home Secretary* [1942] A.C. 284; cf. *R.* v. *Secretary of State for Home Affairs, ex p. Budd* [1942] 2 K.B. 14 (release by habeas corpus where detention order defective in form, followed by valid detention under detention order properly made out). For a hostile critique of the implementation of a policy of preventive detention of security suspects, see C. K. Allen, *Law and Orders* (3rd edn, 1965), Appendix 1. Earlier editions were even more critical.

[41] Local authorities may use Civil Defence resources in an emergency or disaster involving destruction of property or danger to life or property: Civil Protection in Peacetime Act 1986.

A court would probably hold the grounds for making the proclamation to be non-justiciable, and the power to make regulations is so widely drawn that it would be difficult to establish that any such regulation was *ultra vires*, though it might be less difficult to show acts done ostensibly in pursuance of a regulation were unlawful. Under a number of new Commonwealth constitutions which give power to the Executive to proclaim a state of emergency, derogation from certain guarantees of fundamental rights is permitted but only to the extent 'reasonably required' or 'reasonably justifiable' for the purposes of dealing with the emergency situation.[42]

In a state of emergency, troops may be employed on agricultural duties;[43] and there is a statutory power (not confined to formal states of emergency) vested in the Secretary of State to call out the reserve forces, if required, to assist the civil power in preserving public order.[44]

Several safeguards are provided against the serious abuse of statutory emergency powers. Regulations made under Acts of 1920 and 1964 must be laid before both Houses of Parliament as soon as may be, and expire seven days after being laid unless approved by affirmative resolutions of both Houses. They may create new criminal offences triable by magistrates' courts, but the maximum penalty is to be three months' imprisonment and a £2,000 fine and they cannot change existing criminal procedure or authorize punishment by imprisonment or the imposition of fines without trial.[45] Nor may any such regulation make it an offence to take part in a strike or peacefully to persuade others to take part in a strike or impose compulsory military service or industrial conscription.

States of emergency were proclaimed in 1921, 1924, and again in 1926 at a time of the General Strike followed by a miners' strike. From 1945 to the end of 1984 they were proclaimed on eight occasions, five of them under the Heath Government (arising from a dock strike and 'work to rule' at electricity power stations in 1970, a miners' strike and a dock strike in 1972 and a ban on overtime by miners and electric

---

[42] For reviews and critiques of 'emergency' powers in Northern Ireland, see Lord MacDermott (1972) 17 *Juridical Review* (N.S.) 1; Claire Palley, *The Evolution, Disintegration and Possible Reconstruction of the Northern Ireland Constitution* (reprinted from (1972) I *Anglo-American L. Rev.* 368–476); Fabian Soc., *Emergency Powers: A Fresh Start* (1972). See also the Northern Ireland (Emergency Provisions) Act 1978; Northern Ireland (Emergency Provisions) Act 1987 (see above, p. 55).

[43] Emergency Powers Act 1964, s. 2.

[44] Reserve Forces Act 1980, s. 23.

[45] The late Sir Carleton Allen's suggestion (*Law and Orders*, op. cit., p. 378) that preventive detention orders might be made under the Emergency Powers Act 1920 is sustainable only if such detention is differentiated from punishment.

power workers in 1973–4).[46] The content of the regulations has depended on the kind of emergency situation: wide powers to fix food prices, requisition property and prohibit public gatherings may be conferred, but in the periods of emergency since 1945 the action taken in pursuance of the regulations[47] has had only a mild impact on the ordinary citizen and the emergencies have not been accompanied by civil disturbances apart from some acts of mob violence and intimidation of non-strikers in 1972. Potentially, however, very extensive authority could be exercised by the police and the armed forces under the Acts,[48] quite apart from their common-law powers and duties to secure the maintenance of public order.

The miners' strike of 1984–5 is perhaps indicative of a change of tactics by the authorities faced by a major industrial dispute. There was widespread mob violence and intimidation especially at coalfields, involving in some instances thousands of miners and demonstrators, but the supply of coal was not disrupted to any significant extent and no state of emergency was declared: the police used their ordinary powers to the full to maintain public order and carry out arrests. And a 'national reporting centre' was set up at Scotland Yard to coordinate the necessary movements of large numbers of police from all over England and Wales, a development objected to by some as a blueprint for a national police force.

[46] See K. Jeffery and P. Hennessy, *States of Emergency: British Government and Strikebreaking Since 1919* (1983).

[47] In 1948 the strikers went back to work before any regulations had been issued. The proclamation of emergency had an immediate psychological effect.

[48] For critical comment, see Ronald Kidd, *British Liberty in Danger*, pp. 48–51.

Part Six

Administrative Law

In this Part there is an introduction to the most rapidly developing area of public law in this country – the law of public administration, or administrative law. The subject has vast ramifications; here the treatment is confined to those aspects which have general constitutional importance.

Chapter 28 explains what administrative law is about. It goes on to classify the different types and forms of decisions in the law of public administration and outlines their procedural characteristics. As will be seen, the picture is untidy.

Chapter 29 reflects the changing attitudes of the courts towards judicial review of administrative action and the flood of case law in a way which highlights the major principles and leaves sufficient detail to allow for wider reading. It deals with the general principles governing judicial review of administrative acts, orders, decisions and omissions. The principles are illustrated by a selection of judicial decisions. In the 1960s the courts became less reticent in reviewing administrative acts and decisions, laying down more exacting standards of legality and fair procedure to be observed by the Administration. In particular, the courts widened the scope of the duty to observe the rules of natural justice in the course of arriving at administrative decisions, and emphasized the importance of a more loosely formulated 'duty to act fairly'. The progress of the doctrine of legitimate expectation is noted.

Some of the principles applied by the courts have already been illustrated in earlier chapters, notably those on subordinate legislation (chapter 18) and local government (chapter 21).

In chapter 30 the main features of the more important remedies in administrative law are outlined. The changes brought about by the application for judicial review are explained and evaluated, together with the effect of the cases on the public law/private law divide. The restrictions placed on leave to apply for judicial review if alternative remedies have been exhausted are noted.

Chapter 31 examines the part played by special tribunals and statutory inquiries in the general scheme of administrative law. We note the work of the Committee on Ministers' Powers and the Franks Committee on Administrative Tribunals and Enquiries; the effect of the Tribunals and Inquiries Act 1958; and the functions and influence of the Council on Tribunals.

Chapter 32 is about civil proceedings for damages and other private law remedies by and against the Crown, with sidelong glances at proceedings against other public bodies. Here again the law has controversial features, and further developments in the operation of public interest immunity are traced.

The final chapter in this Part deals with redress of individual grievances outside the system of the courts, tribunals, formal inquiries, and proceedings in Parliament. In particular, it is concerned with the Parliamentary Commissioner for Administration (sometimes called the Ombudsman). This chapter links up with earlier chapters on ministerial responsibility and the functions of the House of Commons.

Chapter 28

Administrative Law: Introduction

Administrative law as part of constitutional law

Administrative law[1] is the branch of public law dealing with the actual operation of government, the administrative process. When the constitutional process has resulted in a duly elected Government which has determined its policies and enacted any necessary primary legislation, the administrative process begins. It concerns the day-to-day administration of the country at central and local level and putting into practice constitutionally decided policies. Administrative law regulates that process. It relates to the organization, composition, functions and procedures of public authorities and special statutory tribunals, their impact on the citizen and the legal restraints and liabilities to which they are subject. It controls the making of subordinate legislation by public authorities.[2] In essence administrative law is that part of constitutional law which reveals what tangible and enforceable limits can be placed on administrative action. Today, when administrative action and decisions impinge on so many areas of the citizen's life, certain topics in administrative law have developed special statutory and judge-made rules peculiar to themselves and which have become independent legal topics. Local government, tax law, social security law and immigration are but a few examples. The aim here is to introduce the basic framework of administrative law in the context of a study of constitutional law.

It is sometimes said that there is no developed system of English administrative law and that in its function of regulating the powers of

---

[1] The leading general works on administrative law are H. W. R. Wade, *Administrative Law* (6th edn, 1988); J. F. Garner, *Administrative Law* (6th edn, 1986 by Garner and B. L. Jones). A refreshingly new approach is taken by P. P. Craig, *Administrative Law* (1983). See also D. Foulkes, *Administrative Law* (6th edn, 1986).

[2] See ch. 18.

the Administration English administrative law compares unfavourably with France's *droit administratif*.[3] The French citizen personally aggrieved by an administrative decision simply submits his complaint to the nearest *Tribunal Administratif* who investigates the issue and then may quash the decision, and if necessary award compensation to the citizen. Appeal from the *Tribunal Administratif* lies to the source of French administrative law, the *Conseil d'État*. The French student simply applies himself diligently to the case-law developed by the *Conseil d'État* and will be able to deduce a set of coherent and logical principles determining the rights and duties of the state and the limits of its powers in its relationship with individuals. The English student is less fortunate. In the latter part of the last century Dicey's polemic[4] against the tyrannical nature of *droit administratif* prejudiced whole generations against administrative law in any form. For the French courts applying *droit administratif* are completely separate from the ordinary courts of law and staffed by judges with an administrative, not a legal, background. This, declared Dicey, was contrary to the rule of law, sacred to all Englishmen, which demanded that the conduct of the Administration and its officials be judged in the same common-law courts and governed by the same principles applied to ordinary citizens in private disputes. The problem is that the second part of Dicey's thesis is impossible. Once government vests wider discretionary powers in public authorities and creates special tribunals outside the ordinary court system there are no private law principles which can be applied when the powers or proceedings of an authority or tribunal are called in question. Like it or not, the common-law courts were forced to develop a system of principles of administrative law.[5] Nor can identical rules apply to the Government even where on the face of it proceedings by the citizen against a public authority resemble an ordinary contract or tort action. If a local council is empowered to keep roads free of ice and an individual slips on the ice the court, in determining whether the authority was negligent, cannot ignore the duty owed by the council to the whole community, the limited resources available to fulfil that duty and the consequent need for the council to determine priorities.[6]

Recent developments in relation to the remedies available in administrative law would probably cause Dicey to turn in his grave. Long

---

[3] See L. Neville Brown and J. F. Garner, *French Administrative Law* (3rd edn, 1983).

[4] *Introduction to the Study of the Law of the Constitution* (10th edn), chs 4 and 12.

[5] See Lord Denning M.R. in *Breen* v. *A.E.U.* [1971] 2 Q.B. 175 at p. 189: 'It may now truly be said that we have a developed system of administrative law.' See also *Mahon* v. *Air New Zealand* [1984] A.C. 808 at 816, *per* Lord Diplock.

[6] See *Haydon* v. *Kent C.C.* [1978] Q.B. 343.

overdue reform of the procedure for challenging administrative decisions[7] has caused the House of Lords to pronounce that public law rights are enforceable only through application for judicial review. The distinction between public and private law rights has resulted in no little difficulty for the courts. In France, where the distinction has been entrenched for over a century, a special court, the *Tribunal de Conflits*, is required to make a final decision in case of dispute. The conceptual basis of any such distinction in English law has been vigorously attacked.[8] But its emergence, at the same time as administrative changes, has led to the creation of a separate court list for administrative cases, the Crown Office List, all of which must lead us to speculate whether an Administrative Court has been smuggled into our legal system by the back door.[9]

In attempting a survey of English administrative law the tendency is to concentrate on the role of the Judiciary in controlling statutory powers, introducing the concept of natural justice into administrative decision-making and on certain occasions genuinely fulfilling the role allocated to them by Dicey of involving the common law as a bulwark against tyrany. Nevertheless, the bulk of English administrative law is statutory in origin. This is not simply because Acts of Parliament create public authorities and confer their powers on them. Very often today a statute which grants powers of a nature likely to affect individual interests also builds in safeguards for the individual. It may be only the right to complain to a Minister. But most statutes with a substantial impact on individual interests provide either for a special tribunal to hear disputes arising between the authority and the citizen, or make provision for holding a public inquiry prior to the final decision. Tribunals and inquiries were once condemned as kangaroo justice far removed from the judicial atmosphere of the courts. Now their procedure is usually controlled by statutory instrument and provides for a fair hearing without the awsome formality of the common-law courts. More and more provision is made for an appeals system in the case of tribunals, and access to the High Court to determine disputed points of law is generally allowed from both tribunal decisions and decisions made after an inquiry has been held.[10] The statutory safeguards are far from perfect. Property rights are better protected

---

[7] Supreme Court Act 1981, s. 31.

[8] See Cane [1984] *Public Law* 16, and *Davy* v. *Spelthorne B.C.* [1983] 2 All E.R. 278 at 284 (Lord Wilberforce). See also Wade (1983) 99 *L.Q.R.* 166; for a defence of the distinction, see Woolf, L. J. [1986] *Public Law* 220.

[9] See Blom-Cooper [1982] *Public Law* 250.

[10] Note particularly the Tribunals and Inquiries Act 1971.

than a man's legitimate right to or expectation of social security benefits. Immigrants get a raw deal, and once a murmur is raised about national security, safeguards against administrative abuse become minimal. It will be seen that the judges have similar priorities in their view of the protection of the citizen's interests.

The function of the judges is to invoke 'the justice of the common law to supply the omission of the legislature'.[11] The Judiciary first imposed elementary notions of justice on the proceedings of tribunals and inquiries using the remedies developed by their predecessors to curb over-mighty justices of the peace and inferior courts. They still intervene where no statutory rules exist or where those rules do not meet the judicial concept of natural justice. The courts, especially recently, have developed principles curbing the misuse of discretionary powers to a level equal to their French counterparts on the *Conseil d'État*. They do stand in a very real sense as the ultimate arbitrator of the balance between the demands of effective government and individual interests. In this capacity the judges wield political power, a feature of administrative law not to be overlooked by the constitutional law student. Whether they like it or not, a body of men with power to decide that the Secretary of State for Education may not intervene to prevent a local council reintroducing selective secondary education[12] and to ensure that, despite a new Government's opposition, Sir Freddie Laker's Skytrain takes off for New York,[13] and to declare valid although in breach of the rules of natural justice the Government's removal of trade union rights without prior consultation from civil servants at the Government Communications Headquarters at Cheltenham[14] are taking decisions of political significance. They cannot be surprised when some people question whether they have sufficient understanding of administrative problems to take such decisions,[15] and speculate whether in view of the predominantly upper middle-class background of most judges it is possible for judges to be completely impartial in essentially political controversies.[16]

Finally, the extent of the discretionary powers of the judges in administrative law is as important constitutionally as the extent of discretionary powers vested in public authorities. All remedies in administrative law are discretionary. The applicant may make out his

[11] *Cooper* v. *Wandsworth Board of Works* (1863) 14 C.B. (N.S.) 180.
[12] *Secretary of State for Education* v. *Tameside M.B.C.* [1977] A.C. 1014.
[13] *Laker Airways Ltd* v. *Department of Trade* [1977] Q.B. 643.
[14] *Council of Civil Service Unions* v. *Minister for the Civil Service* [1985] A.C. 374.
[15] See, e.g., J. A. G. Griffith [1985] *Public Law* 564.
[16] See generally J. A. G. Griffith, *The Politics of the Judiciary* (3rd edn, 1985).

case only to be told that he may have been prejudiced by lack of fairness but his own conduct was so deplorable he does not deserve any remedy.[17] The court may decide that this is an area of government into which they would rather not intervene save in the grossest case of abuse and so in its discretion refuse a remedy in the normal case.[18] The element of choice in judicial review is further developed in chapter 29 and is a vital feature of judicial review today.

Decision-making in the administrative process

The administrative process, and therefore administrative law, consists of the making of thousands of decisions each day. How far those decisions are open to challenge is a central issue in administrative law. Decisions are classified in various ways and the classification of a decision has an important effect on the degree to which it may be reviewed either as provided for in a statute or by the courts. The democratic nature of the constitution is tested by the extent to which an individual affected can challenge a decision and whether decision-making offers any real opportunity for the members of the public involved by the decision to participate in the process. Decisions in the administrative process can be classified in various ways. For example, is the decision legislative or non-legislative, judicial or non-judicial? Does the decision involve the exercise of a power or the performance of a duty? Which type of administrative authority makes the decision? Does it have to be made after a hearing, or is it subject to a subsequent hearing before it has final effect, or can it have effect without any hearing at all? Is it subject to appeal or review, and if so, what body is vested with the appellate or supervisory jurisdiction?

Classes of function[19]

Functions may be classified as legislative, administrative, judicial, quasi-judicial and ministerial. None of these terms is unambiguous or self-explanatory and there is often scope for appending two or more labels to a specific act or decision, to the confusion of all students. Briefly, the ingredients of a *typical* function belonging to the main classes can be stated.

[17] *Glynn* v. *University of Keele* [1971] W.L.R. 487.
[18] *R.* v. *Preston Supplementary Benefits Appeal Tribunal, ex p. Moore* [1975] 1 W.L.R. 624.
[19] For fuller analysis of the terminology used, see de Smith, *Judicial Review of Administrative Action* (4th edn, 1980), ch. 2.

1   A legislative function involves making rules of general application with prospective effect. Legislation is made by Acts of Parliament, statutory instruments, other regulations and by-laws.

2   An administrative (or executive) function may involve making policy or carrying out a policy or simply deciding what is the most appropriate thing to do in particular circumstances. Examples of administrative decisions are determining new standard terms of public contracts, placing public contracts, making decisions on public appointments, and allocating resources such as council houses.

3   A judicial function involves the determination of a question of law or fact by reference to pre-existing rules or standards.

4   A ministerial act is not normally something done by a Minister; it is the performance of a legal duty (for example, to refund overpaid income tax) into which no element of choice or discretion enters.

These terms have to be used because they are in common currency. The term 'legislative' does not give rise to a great deal of difficulty in practice, for most of us can recognize legislation when we see it; but we also know that legislative rules can have retrospective as well as prospective effect, that they may simply restate (by consolidation or codification) existing law, that the boundary line between a not very 'general' legislative rule and particular administrative decisions affecting many people can become so blurred as to be imperceptible, and that judges sometimes change the law under the guise of declaring or interpreting it.

Difficulties lurk in the term 'administrative', 'judicial' and 'quasi-judicial' when they are being contrasted with one another. 'Quasi-judicial' is, on the whole, a superfluous adjective which increases rather than diminishes confusion. Usually it means a discretionary (administrative-type) decision preceded by a judicial-type procedure (for example, confirming a compulsory purchase order after a local inquiry), but the term is also sometimes used to describe the final decision itself and sometimes to describe the preliminary procedure.

As we have seen, 'administrative' acts are what administrators *typically* do and 'judicial' acts are what judges typically do. This terminology does not preclude us from saying that officials (administrators) can perform analytically 'judicial' functions – for example, deciding (subject to appeal) that X is legally obliged to pay £100 in capital gains tax, or that publications imported by Y are obscene, or that Z is not legally entitled to unemployment benefit – or that judges, especially in administrative law, have to exercise wide discretionary powers. A law student's problem (sometimes so puzzling as to seem insoluble) lies in the fact that judges in the reported cases on administrative law use the terms inconsistently. A function that is judicial in one context is labelled 'administrative' in another context. Occasionally these discrepancies are nothing more than an inelegant use of language; occasionally they are attributable to the looseness of the concept of 'administrative' functions; more frequently they can be explained by looking for the legal *consequences* of calling a function 'judicial' or 'administrative' as the case may be.

Duty and discretion

The contrast between public duty and discretionary power is ostensibly clear cut. A duty is an act that *must* be performed; thus, a tribunal has a duty to entertain an application or appeal in a matter within its jurisidiction; a local authority has a duty to grant a rate rebate when prescribed conditions are satisfied. Performance of such a duty can normally be enforced in judicial proceedings.[20] Compliance with some of the statutory duties cast on local authorities is enforceable by Ministers exercising default powers.

A discretionary power implies freedom of choice; the competent authority *may* decide whether or not to act (for example, whether to order television sets for local schools) and, if so, how to act (for example, with whom should the order be placed; how many sets should be bought?). In practice, duties and powers tend to be interwoven. Seldom does a public body have no discretion at all as to the circumstances in which it is to perform a duty. Police officers, who have a general duty to enforce the law, have a limited discretion to abstain from reporting particular offences. And discretionary powers are normally accompanied by express or implied duties. For instance, a licensing authority may have a discretion to attach such conditions as it thinks fit when granting a licence; but it will be under a legal duty to exercise a genuine discretion in each individual case, and not fetter its choice by adopting rigid rules; and the conditions imposed must not be irrelevant to the purposes for which the power was conferred on it.

[20] See further pp. 548 and 588–91. But some public duties (for example, to provide 'a varied and comprehensive educational service') are so widely framed that no court will direct their enforcement at the suit of a member of the public; and others (for example, those imposed on certain public corporations administering the nationalized industries) are expressed to be unenforceable in any court; see pp. 32 and 221. Duties unenforceable by a court obviously resemble statutory powers in this context.

Decision-makers

Powers and duties to make decisions in public administration may be vested in the Crown, Ministers, government Departments, civil servants, public corporations and their officers, local authorities, local government officers, tribunals and courts. The distribution of functions among them is not predetermined by any grand design; it is a product of historical accident, tenacious tradition, experiment, and largely uncoordinated decisions about the most appropriate ways of handling individual problems. Patterns are irregular, reflecting the untidy structure of administrative authority in England. A few points should be noted; some have already been mentioned in earlier chapters.

1 Government Departments with ministerial heads did not assume an important role in the provision and regulation of social services till the late nineteenth and early twentieth centuries. Even today, the main providers of public services (for example, education, environmental planning, housing, public health) are the elected local authorities. They have been joined by semi-autonomous public corporations (for example, for broadcasting, hospitals, and the management of nationalized industries). The primary initiative in the direction of national policy, particularly in legislative change and the allocation of financial resources, rests with the central government, but the immediate impact of administrative decisions on the individual citizen generally occurs at a lower level.

2 Decisions by government Departments directly affecting individual rights are usually made by officials in the Minister's name. The courts recognize the reality of the situation by treating the Minister and his officials within the Department as one entity: thus the Minister may receive advice without having to disclose it to affected individuals in the same way as he would not have to disclose his own cerebral deliberations.[21] Powers are sometimes conferred by statute on specified classes of officials (for example, immigration officers, customs and excise officers, local authority auditors and inspectors conducting inquiries) to be exercised in their own official capacities.

3 Local authority decisions are usually taken by councils or committees of councils. Officials do not have a general power to act on the council's behalf, but very wide powers can be delegated to them. Some functions are vested by statute directly in specified officials (for example, medical officers of health).

[21] *Bushell* v. *Secretary of State for the Environment* [1981] A.C. 75.

4 Decision-making by tribunals in the sphere of public administration has a long history. For centuries the local government authorities in the counties were the justices of the peace, who granted licences, regulated taverns, enforced the poor law and the upkeep of highways and bridges, and so on, under judicial forms. Most of their administrative functions passed to elected local authorities in the nineteenth century, but some survive – for example, liquor licensing – and other administrative jurisdiction has been vested in magistrates' courts, notably the hearing of appeals from certain decisions by local authorities.

5 The justices of the peace and borough corporations were subject, during the Tudor and early Stuart periods, to control by the King's Council and the Star Chamber. This was replaced after 1650 by the supervisory jurisdiction of the Court of King's Bench. The basic features of this supervisory jurisdiction survived and have been extended to other types of decision-making bodies.

6 Particularly since the Second World War, power to determine a wide range of claims and controversies in administrative law has been vested in specialized 'administrative' tribunals.[22] The jurisdiction of these tribunals may be original or appellate. The High Court has powers to review their determinations.

7 The functions of the superior courts in administrative law are varied:[23] they include appellate and supervisory review of determinations by inferior tribunals, and affording legal redress for wrongful acts committed by other administrative bodies.

Decisions with or without a hearing

Obviously most decisions in the fields of government and administration have to be taken without a formal inquiry or hearing. If a Minister has to make a major policy decision, he will normally consult the main interest groups likely to be affected – and in some situations he will be under a statutory duty to do so – but government could not be carried on if every important decision had to await the outcome of a full-dress inquiry. Some policy decisions affecting a large number of private individuals in a locality – for example, a decision as to the route of a motorway, or whether to develop an area as a new town – will be preceded by a formal public inquiry. But a decision by a Minister to refuse an application for a passport, an export or import licence, an

[22] See ch. 31.
[23] See chs 29, 30, 32.

industrial grant or loan, can be made summarily, without any antecedent hearing, though informal representation before and after the decision may be entertained. And clearly decisions made on departmental initiative (for example, to vary rates of taxation) will not usually entail formal hearings either before or after the event.

Again, a great number of decisions made by other public bodies will be made without any formal hearing or inquiry – for example, decisions on the allocation of a council house or a place in an old people's home: or to place a contract with X rather than with Y or Z, or to promote P rather than Q or R. It does does not follow that such decisions will be capricious; they may be regulated or influenced by administrative precedent or general guiding principles; they may be preceded by thorough investigations and personal interviews even though these are not required by law; in some instances they will be subject to appeal.[24]

Nevertheless, the formal pre-decision hearing or inquiry is an important feature of the administrative process in England.[25] Thus, one who applies for a licence to operate a commercial air service or a betting shop, or who claims compensation for injuries sustained as a result of violent crime, will be entitled or may be required to appear before a board or tribunal which will make the decision. If there are objectors to his application, they too will, in some instances, be entitled to a hearing. Of more general importance is the statutory procedure followed where public authorities wish to take away or restrict the exercise of private rights in land. A person whose property is the subject of a compulsory purchase order is entitled to be heard at a formal local inquiry before the order can be confirmed; this safeguard is absent from the legal systems of many other developed countries. Again, a local inquiry must be held if objections are lodged against proposals to close an uneconomic railway line or to impose certain types of street restrictions, and conservation and local interest groups often make a substantial contribution to inquiries.

Appeals

More common than a statutory right to a prior hearing is a right to be heard on appeal against an administrative decision. Three preliminary points need to be made.

1   A right of appeal is the creature of statute and it can only be

[24] For example, under the Sex Discrimination Act 1975. See above pp. 437–9.
[25] See generally R. E. Wraith and G. B. Lamb, *Public Inquiries as an Instrument of Government* (1971).

conferred by express language. There is no such thing as an implied right of appeal to a court or any other body.

2 The absence of a right of appeal does not necessarily mean that a decision cannot be challenged at all in a court of law. The jurisdiction of the High Court in matters of administrative law is supervisory as well as appellate. This question will be examined in chapters 29 and 30.

3 There is no clear pattern of rights of appeal. This point emerges only too plainly from the following outline sketch.

Ministers and civil servants. In general, no appeal will be provided against discretionary decisions involving questions of national policy or the allocation of scarce resources. Reference was made earlier to discretionary decisions made without a prior hearing; no right of appeal is provided against any of the classes of decisions there illustrated. But there is no universal rule in this matter. The Immigration Appeals Act 1969 gave rights of appeal to adjudicators from discretionary decisions of immigration officers, and to an Immigration Appeal Tribunal from discretionary orders by the Secretary of State for the deportation of aliens. However, under the Immigration Act 1971 the more politically sensitive types of decision were removed from the scope of the appellate system.[26]

Where a decision by a Minister or a civil servant entails the determination of a question of law, appeal often lies to an independent tribunal or the superior courts; rights of appeal to the courts are usually confined to the legal issues. From decisions on liability to income tax, an appeal lies to the Commissioners of Income Tax (a special tribunal), and thence to the Chancery Division of the High Court. If a local planning authority considers that planning restrictions have been contravened, it may issue an enforcement notice; the person aggrieved may appeal to the Secretary of State against the notice, and if dissatisfied with the Secretary of State's decision he may appeal on a point of law to the Divisional Court of the Queen's Bench Division. A person dissatisfied with a decision of an officer of the Department of Social Security holding that he is not entitled to a social security benefit may appeal to a social security appeal tribunal and thence to a Social Security Commissioner.

Public corporations. Decisions made by bodies administering nationalized industries are seldom subject to appeal; they are on a similar footing to decisions by privately owned commercial and industrial undertakings.

[26] See pp. 449–52.

Local authorities. Here again, allocative decisions – decisions on the discretionary allocation of limited resources – are not, as a rule, appealable, but there are a number of exceptions. The statutory designation of appellate bodies can only be described as bizarre. For example, a full appeal lies to magistrates' courts against the merits of various kinds of licensing decisions (for example, the licensing of theatres, street traders, massage establishments); to the Crown Court against decisions on cinema licensing; and to a county court against a decision to make an order for the demolition of an individual insanitary house. Appeals against decisions to refuse planning permission (i.e. permission to 'develop' land by making a material change of use), or to grant such permission subject to conditions to which the applicant objects, lie to the Secretary of State for the Environment or, in cases of minor development raising no big policy issue, to an inspector exercising delegated powers.

Special tribunals

Some administrative tribunals exercise original jurisdiction; some are appellate bodies. There is usually (but not always) an appeal on the merits of the decisions from a tribunal exercising original jurisdiction to a superior tribunal; in a few cases the appellate authority is a Minister. Appeals lie on points of law to the superior courts from the decisions of a majority of tribunals of last instance. In most cases the appellate tribunal is the Divisional Court of the Queen's Bench Division, but even in this context there is no uniform pattern; appeals lie in income tax cases to a Chancery judge; from service pensions appeal tribunals to a Queen's Bench judge; from the Transport Tribunal, the Lands Tribunal and the Foreign Compensation Commission to the Court of Appeal; and from some professional disciplinary bodies to the Judicial Committee of the Privy Council.

In general

We appear to be losing ourselves in a labyrinth through which even the most expert guide could not be relied on to conduct us. Are there, then, no general principles of English administrative law? Is there but a wilderness of individual instances? An answer can be offered at two levels. In the first place, to achieve a full mastery of the subject one requires an encyclopaedic range of knowledge which is hardly worth while acquiring. So much depends on the wording of particular legislation, which is influenced by a motley array of policy considerations. Development of the law has been pragmatic, empirical, even adventitious; only occasionally do broad general principles intrude into the devising of a legislative scheme, and these intrusions tend to operate in the area of the *procedure* followed in decision-making rather than in the substantive structure and inter-relationship of authority. Secondly, if one concentrates on the part played by the *courts* in affording legal redress for grievances, the law is still complex and rather confusing, but it is possible to elicit general principles according to which the courts will afford remedies and redress to a person aggrieved by administrative action. These principles sometimes have to be stated at a high level of generality, but they are at least intelligible.

Chapter 29

Judicial Review of Administrative Action: Principles

This chapter is about the general principles applied by the superior courts in reviewing the validity or legality of the acts, decisions and omissions of administrative authorities, including statutory tribunals. In the chapters on delegated legislation and local authorities we have already been introduced to this subject.[1] In chapter 30 some special features of judicial remedies in administrative law will be considered. Actions for damages for civil wrongs committed by public authorities, particularly the Crown, will be considered in chapter 32.

Four preliminary words of warning are needed. First, this is an extremely complex subject with intricate ramifications.[2] Every aspect cannot be considered here, even in outline. And some matters will have to be oversimplified if they are to be explained at all. They may still seem rather mysterious. Secondly, a grasp of general principles is obviously important. But to apply these principles to concrete situations demands flexibility and subtlety. In approaching the solution to a particular case, the crucial questions will often be: What are the context and purpose of the legislation in question? What significance is to be attributed to the language in which a grant of statutory power is worded? To a large extent judicial review of administrative action is a specialized branch of statutory interpretation. Thirdly, administrative law is not very coherent. For example, the laws of town and country planning, social security and immigration have some points of contact but far more points of disimilarity. Precedents laid down in one area of the law may be treated by a court as irrelevant if cited as authorities in another area. One needs to be an expert forecaster to be able to predict

---

[1] Chs 18 and 21.
[2] See de Smith, *Judicial Review of Administrative Action* (4th edn, 1980); H. W. R. Wade, *Administrative Law* (6th edn, 1988); P. P. Craig, *Administrative Law* (1983); C. Emery and B. Smythe, *Judicial Review: Legal Limits of Official Power* (1986).

how a court will react to such citations in any given case. Fourthly, from time to time the courts shift their position, and they are apt not to be entirely consistent in their attitudes.

Hence, if one is asked what legal principles a public authority is obliged to observe when exercising a specific discretionary power, one's answer may often have to be hedged about by words like 'probably' and 'perhaps'. The state of the law is elusive and fluid.

One further point must always be borne in mind – a point more obvious to the uninstructed layman than to a law student grappling with an intractable body of legal material. In deciding individual cases the courts will try to do justice by balancing the needs of administration and the public interest against the claims of the private citizen to fair treatment. Some judges are prepared to 'bend' the law by manipulating precedent and principle in order to achieve and vindicate what appears to them a just solution to the case in hand. Judges exercise more freedom of manoeuvre than in most of the other branches of English law.

Going to court

Judicial review of administrative action may be invoked for a wide range of purposes by a person claiming to be aggrieved.

1 To obtain damages or another private law remedy (for example, an injunction) for a civil wrong, such as a breach of contract or a tort.
2 To have an order, act or decision of a public body quashed or declared invalid on the ground that it is *ultra vires* or outside jurisdiction. This purpose may be achieved by means of an appeal (if one is provided by statute), or a statutory application to quash (for example, a decision to confirm a compulsory purchase order), or an application to the High Court for judicial review and an order of certiorari to quash a decision, or a declaration that the act, order or decision is invalid. Already one sees that substantive administrative law is interwoven with the law of remedies.
3 To procure, on appeal, the reversal or variation of an order or determination for error of law. This overlaps with (2); the difference between *invalidity* and *error* will be explained shortly.
4 To restrain the performance or continuance of unlawful action. This may be achieved by an application for an order of prohibition or for an injunction or a declaration, or a statutory application to restrain (for example) the making of an invalid compulsory purchase order.

5   To obtain release from unlawful detention. The appropriate remedy will be either appeal or an application for habeas corpus.

6   To secure an authoritative statement of the law governing a specific legal dispute by means of a binding declaration awarded by the courts. Consequential relief (for example, damages) does not have to be claimable as well.

7   To secure the performance of a public duty (for example, to make reimbursement; to exercise a discretion according to law; to hear an application or appeal within a tribunal's jurisdiction). Normally the judicial remedy for a wrongful omission will be an order of mandamus; a declaration, or even a mandatory injunction, are possible remedies. Sometimes non-performance of a public duty will give rise to an action for damages.

8   To defend oneself in proceedings which rely on the validity of an administrative act or order. If, for example, one is prosecuted for breach of a by-law, one can set up the defence that the by-law is *ultra vires*.

Public authorities may appear in the courts for other reasons. For instance, many enforcement powers vested in public authorities (for example, to abate nuisances) are exercisable only with leave of a court or magistrate; and in most of these situations the prospective victim can be heard on his own behalf. Again, sometimes criminal proceedings can be brought *against* public authorities (for example, for breaches of the Public Health Acts).

Ultra vires and excess of jurisdiction

The starting point for judicial review of administrative action is that public authorities will be restrained from exceeding their powers (acting *ultra vires*) and inferior tribunals will be prevented from exceeding the limits of their jurisdiction. This important constitutional function of containing both the Executive and inferior tribunals within the limits of their authority has long been exercised by the courts. In the seventeenth century it was established that the Crown could not set itself above the law by a bare assertion of prerogative.[3] Today the *ultra vires* doctrine prevents public authorities from doing anything which the law forbids, or taking any action for which they have no statutory authority.

A dramatic example of the *ultra vires* rule in practice can be seen in

[3] See pp. 70–2, 127–8.

Laker Airways Ltd v. *Department of Trade*.[4] Freddie Laker wanted to operate his Skytrain service across the Atlantic. Two obstacles stood in his way. He had to obtain a licence for the service from the Civil Aviation Authority and he had to be accepted as a 'designated air-carrier' by the British and United States Governments in order to fly Skytrain into the U.S.A. The Civil Aviation Act 1971 empowered the Civil Aviation Authority to license air services and laid down criteria for them to follow in fulfilling this function. These included the principle that British Airways should not have a monopoly on any air route. The Act also empowered the Secretary of State for Trade to give guidance to the Authority. Any guidance had to be approved by both Houses of Parliament. Skytrain was granted a licence in 1972 to operate from Stansted to New York and the then British Government started the process to have Laker Airways accepted as a designated air-carrier by the United States Government. In 1975 a new British Government adopted a complete reversal of policy towards Skytrain. The Secretary of State for Trade subsequently issued guidance to the Civil Aviation Authority directing them in effect that British Airways were to retain a monopoly on scheduled transatlantic routes. Both Houses of Parliament gave their approval. Skytrain's licence was withdrawn by the Authority and the process to have Laker Airways accepted as a designated air-carrier by the U.S.A. was stopped. The Court of Appeal held that the Secretary of State had acted *ultra vires*. He had authority merely to guide the Authority, not to direct it. The guidance was itself unlawful in that it was directly contrary to the objectives set out in the Civil Aviation Act. The withdrawal of the designation might be the exercise of a prerogative power arising under a treaty with the U.S.A., but prerogative powers could not be used in order to deprive Laker Airways of rights which they were granted by statute. Prerogative powers were discretionary powers and subject to judicial control. The Secretary of State had exercised the power unlawfully in an attempt to do indirectly what he was unable to do directly, that is, prevent Laker Airways competing on the transatlantic route. So Laker Airways were successful in their action.

The general principle underlying the *ultra vires* doctrine is easy to illustrate. Acts reasonably incidental to powers expressly granted may be construed as falling within the grant of power. So when a local authority in the performance of its statutory duties regularly needed a certain amount of printing work done it did not exceed its powers by establishing its own printing machinery and personnel for internal

[4] [1977] Q.B. 643.

work.[5] But a local authority empowered to provide wash-houses where local people could bring their own washing and do it themselves acted *ultra vires* when it proceeded to open a laundry service trading for profit.[6] As far as local authorities are concerned the Local Government Act 1972 slightly enlarged their incidental powers.[7]

The problem of whether an act is reasonably incidental to the power granted is relatively easily solved by examination of the enabling statute. A more intractable problem is what effect should be given to an order which is partly *ultra vires* and partly lawful. An authority may lawfully issue a licence, or order, but attach to that licence conditions which it is not entitled to impose. Can the court sever the invalid conditions, leaving operative the grant of the licence?[8] If it is apparent that the invalid condition is peripheral to the grant of the licence, or that even in the absence of the *ultra vires* condition the licence would still have been granted by the licensing body, then this is the course which may be taken.[9] When the condition is part and parcel of the reasons for granting the licence then the court faces a dilemma. If it severs the invalid condition from the licence the result will be that the applicant obtains an unconditional licence which the authority entrusted with the power to license would never have given. If it strikes down the entire decision on the grounds of the unlawful nature of the attached conditions then the applicant has to start all over again before the licensing body. Nevertheless this last course has more than once commended itself to the Court of Appeal[10] and has the attraction that it does not detract from the powers conferred on the licensing body; the price is no more than inconvenience and delay to the applicant.

Action taken by a public authority not only runs the risk of being *ultra vires* in substance but may in certain cases be *ultra vires* in form. Certain powers are exercisable only subject to procedural safeguards enshrined in the enabling statute. The relevant Act may require that some person or organization be consulted before action is taken or an order made. Notice of intention to act may have to be given in a particular form or by a specified date. What happens if the procedure laid down is not complied with by the authority? First the courts will classify the procedural or formal requirement as *mandatory* or *directory*.

[5] *Att.-Gen.* v. *Smethwick Corporation* [1932] 1 Ch. 562.
[6] *Att.-Gen.* v. *Fulham Corporation* [1921] 1 Ch. 440.
[7] See p. 415.
[8] See *R.* v. *Secretary of State for Transport, ex p. GLC* [1986] Q.B. 556.
[9] *See Kingsway Investments (Kent) Ltd* v. *Kent* C.C. [1971] A.C. 72, and see de Smith, op. cit., p. 105.
[10] *Hall & Co.* v. *Shoreham-by-Sea U.D.C.* [1964] 1 W.L.R. 240; *R.* v. *Hillingdon L.B.C., ex p. Royco Homes Ltd* [1974] Q.B. 720.

If a requirement is merely directory then substantial compliance with the procedure laid down will suffice to validate the action; and in some cases even total non-compliance will not affect the validity of what has been done. If a mandatory requirement is not observed then the act or decision will be vitiated by the non-compliance with the statute. This does not mean that the act or decision has no legal effect and can be ignored or treated as void. The House of Lords has stressed that the use of such terms as void and voidable has little practical meaning in administrative law where the supervisory jurisdiction of the High Court operates to ensure the proper exercise of powers by public authorities. Non-compliance with a mandatory procedural requirement results in the act or decision being susceptible to being quashed by the High Court which will then make whatever order to the public authority it sees as appropriate to remedy the unlawful action taken.[11]

Determining whether a requirement is mandatory or directory is not simple. Where the impact of the action taken on private rights is material then an ostensibly small deviation from statutory requirements may render the action invalid. And where the procedural requirement can be seen to be intended to assist the citizen in enforcing his rights, then it is likely to be regarded as mandatory. Examples of procedural requirements which have been held to be mandatory include failure to give notice of a right to appeal within a specified period,[12] failure to give the address to which an appeal must be lodged,[13] failure to notify persons affected by a proposed administrative order *in due time*,[14] and where a person aggrieved is substantially prejudiced by non-compliance with a requirement to give adequate, proper, clear and intelligible reasons for a decision where reasoned decisions are required by statute.[15] The aim of the courts is to try to deduce (a) what Parliament intended in instituting a particular procedural requirement, and (b) what effect on the validity of the process Parliament would have desired to result from non-compliance.[16] Consequently the practical results of holding compliance to be mandatory will be weighed in the balance. In an extreme example, when the Governor-General of New Zealand issued his warrant for the holding of a General Election at a

---

[11] *London & Clydeside Estates Ltd.* v. *Aberdeen D.C.* [1980] 1 W.L.R. 182.
[12] ibid.
[13] *Agricultural etc. Training Board* v. *Kent* [1970] 2 Q.B. 18.
[14] *Lee* v. *Department of Education and Science* (1967) 66 L.G.R. 211.
[15] *Givaudan & Co.* v. *Minister of Housing and Local Government* [1967] 1 W.L.R. 250; *French Kier Developments Ltd* v. *Secretary of State for the Environment* [1977] 1 All E. R. 296.
[16] *London & Clydeside Estates Ltd* v. *Aberdeen D.C.* [1979] 3 All E.R. 876, *per* Lord Hailsham at p. 881].

later date than the law prescribed it was contended that the ensuing General Election was therefore invalid. Not surprisingly the courts held that the rules about time were only directory. For if they had held otherwise there would have been a legal vacuum which nobody within New Zealand could have filled, for no Parliament could lawfully have been summoned and the administration of the country might have ground to a halt.[17] And no sane Parliament would have intended or desired this result.

When no question of any statutory provision excluding judicial review arises the narrow and literal view of *ultra vires* adopted by some of their Lordships in *Smith* v. *East Elloe R.D.C.*[18] would now appear obsolete. In that case a property-owner challenged a compulsory purchase order confirmed by a Minister on the grounds that it had been procured by fraud. The enabling statute permitted the confirmation of the order to be challenged in the High Court within six weeks of it being made on the grounds that the authorization of the order 'was not empowered to be granted under the Act'. The House of Lords held that any form of judicial review was precluded once the prescribed six weeks had elapsed. Certain Law Lords also expressed the view that even within the six weeks allowed the order could be challenged only if it was *ultra vires* in the sense that it was an order outside the competence of the Minister to confirm, and that irregularities in the decision-making process culminating in the confirmation of the order did not render it *ultra vires*. The views of Lord Radcliffe and Lord Reid that powers abused or misused are powers exercised *ultra vires* now prevail. But the narrow view of *ultra vires* cannot be relegated to history because it may be that in some later case a return to the narrow construction of *ultra vires* will be invoked as a device to determine a case in favour of the public authority when a court feels that the merits of the dispute lie on the government side. And it is clear that the distinction between acts entirely outside the authority of the relevant body and acts founded on a misuse of power within that authority is still crucial in some instances when a statutory provision excluding judicial review is in question. This problem is dealt with in the penultimate section of this chapter.[19]

Discussion so far has been generally in terms of *vires* or powers. When considering judicial control of tribunals and similar bodies whose function is to decide the outcome of a dispute, rather than

---

[17] *Simpson* v. *Att.-Gen.* [1955] N.Z.L.R. 271.
[18] [1956] A.C. 736.
[19] At pp. 579–83.

exercise a specific power, it is more appropriate to talk in terms of jurisdiction. All inferior tribunals (magistrates' courts, county courts, special tribunals, professional disciplinary bodies, committees of clubs and trade unions, Ministers determining legal disputes) have a limited jurisdiction. Since the end of the seventeenth century certiorari could be issued to quash a decision of an inferior tribunal outside its jurisdiction and the writ of prohibition lay to prevent an anticipated departure by the tribunal from its proper jurisdiction. Jurisdiction might be exceeded if the tribunal tried a case outside its competence, for example because it had no authority to deal with the subject-matter of the dispute, or no authority over the particular persons before it, or tried a case beyond its territorial jurisdiction. Failure to comply with essential procedural steps in instituting the hearing, or incorrect composition, or grave defects in the manner of the hearing, or a final order which the tribunal was not empowered to make – all such errors resulted in the decision of the tribunal being quashed as being in excess of its jurisdiction. But mistakes made within the jurisdiction whether of fact or law did not lay the tribunal open to certiorari for excess of jurisdiction. Jurisdiction to determine a dispute necessarily includes the authority to determine the merits of the dispute. If every error in assessing the arguments presented to the tribunal were to be subject to review by the High Court the intention of Parliament to create the tribunal as the decision-making body in a particular field would be frustrated. For example, the membership of rent assessment committees is balanced so as to combine lay and expert opinion. This is the kind of body to which Parliament has chosen to entrust rent disputes. Unlimited access to the High Court for the disappointed party would result in effective jurisdiction being transferred to that institution.

Yet equally judicial review which operated only a narrow view of the jurisdiction of the tribunal, considering only whether the tribunal was properly constituted, complied with the proper procedure and began its inquiry into the correct matter, would be inadequate. The supervisory jurisdiction of the High Court over tribunals has been extended in the following ways.

1   From most inferior tribunals an appeal on points of law lies to the High Court.[20]
2   Certiorari will issue not only for excess of jurisdiction but also in respect of an 'error of law on the face of the record'.[21] The 'record'

[20] See especially the Tribunals and Inquiries Act 1971, s. 13.
[21] *R.* v. *Northumberland Compensation Appeal Tribunal, ex p. Shaw* [1951] 1 K.B. 711; affirmed [1952] 1 K.B. 338, C.A. See Emery and Smythe (1984) 100 *L.Q.R.* 612.

consists of the written statement of the tribunal's decision, read in conjunction with relevant statutory provisions. If the decision sets out reasons for the decision, or findings and inferences of fact, these form part of the 'record' and so do any documents referred to in the statement of the decision.[22] Since the Tribunals and Inquiries Act of 1958 the giving of reasons has been required from many tribunals if requested by the parties[23] and the reasons given, whether orally or in writing, form part of the record and an important means of ensuring that tribunals do not err on questions of law.[24]

3   Provided no statutory provision excluding judicial review is operative the extension of the *ultra vires* doctrine to include any misuse of the power has been applied to jurisdiction to determine disputes or appeals. In the case of Ministers deciding planning appeals and other disputed issues in relation to the control of land use, the statutory rights of challenge on the grounds that the Minister's order is outside the powers conferred by the enabling Act, or that some procedural requirement has not been observed, has been interpreted by the courts to mean that any decision *erroneous in law* is a decision taken in excess of his jurisdiction.[25] The Minister's jurisdiction is to determine the dispute on the correct legal basis only.

4   Allied to this last extension of the powers of the High Court to superintend the jurisdiction of inferior tribunals is the view of jurisdictional error taken by the House of Lords in *Anisminic* v. *Foreign Compensation Commission*.[26] It was held that even when a tribunal had engaged within the limits of its jurisdiction on a proper inquiry into the dispute before it, its decision could be quashed and regarded as a nullity if in the course of its deliberations the tribunal deviated from the rules of natural justice, or asked itself the wrong questions, or took into account irrelevant matters. Parliament conferred jurisdiction on the tribunal to consider the dispute in a fair and proper manner and act on relevant and material considerations. Departure from these conditions would take the tribunal outside its jurisdiction for it would cease to be making the inquiry directed and intended by Parliament.

---

[22] *See R.* v. *Southampton JJ., ex p. Green* [1976] Q.B. 11, C.A., as to when the 'record' may be supplemented by affidavits disclosing errors of law on the part of the tribunal.

[23] See now the Tribunals and Inquiries Act 1971, s. 12.

[24] And see *R.* v. *Knightsbridge Crown Court, ex p. International Sporting Club (London) Ltd* [1982] Q.B. 304.

[25] *Ashbridge Investments Ltd.* v. *Minister of Housing and Local Government* [1965] 1 W.L.R. 1320.

[26] [1969] 2 A.C. 147.

The distinction between jurisdictional and non-jurisdictional error has lost some of its importance in modern times. Its relevance lies mainly in relation to statutory exclusion of judicial review which is discussed later and as a possible means of retreat from extending judicial control of administrative action and adjudication when a particular area of the administrative process is one where judges fear to tread.

Law and fact

Although the distinction between jurisdictional and non-jurisdictional matters is so hard to draw or define, perhaps we can hope to explain the important distinction between matters of law and matters of fact more easily. Unfortunately this is not so: the latter distinction is fiendishly difficult to define or even to illustrate at all clearly.

The superior courts will afford redress for errors of fact in two main situations: first, in those rare circumstances where rights of appeal are not restricted to questions of law; and secondly, where a factual error causes a tribunal to step outside its jurisdiction. The courts will be somewhat reluctant to make an independent determination of a question of pure fact if the issue turns upon conflicting evidence and they have not heard the oral testimony themselves.

Whether X hit Y on the head is a question of fact. The state of X's mind at the time is also a question of fact (or of opinion). These questions will be left to the jury to answer. Whether X's conduct is *capable* of being construed as maliciously causing grievous bodily harm to Y[27] is a question of law on which the judge directs the jury; the words 'maliciously' and 'grievous bodily harm' have acquired technical legal meanings. We can describe the whole issue as one of mixed law and fact.

Decisions by special tribunals and public authorities are made without juries; so one convenient line of demarcation is absent. Still, administrative law controversies may sometimes be compartmentalized as questions partly of law and partly of fact for the purposes of judicial review. Other approaches to analysis may be adopted. An entire question may be characterized as one of law, or as one of fact (or fact and degree, which means 'fact'). The technical meaning of a term used in a public contract may be a pure question of law, because only a trained lawyer could be expected to understand it in the light of

[27] Offences against the Person Act 1861, ss 18, 20, as amended by the Criminal Law Act 1967.

principle and decided authority. If a tribunal is obliged to observe the rules of evidence or specified statutory procedures, and there is no dispute as to what actually took place, a question whether the rules were duly observed is again purely one of law. But suppose that the question is whether a building is a dwelling-house, or 'of special architectural or historic interest', or is 'unfit for human habitation', or whether an industrial injury arose 'out of or in the course of employment', or whether consent to a particular act was 'unreasonably withheld', or whether there was a 'material change in the use' of land for which planning permission was required. The tribunal or other deciding body finds the basic or primary facts (for example, who did which and with what and to whom?); it may draw inferences from the facts; it has to go on to decide whether the facts as found *fall within the ambit of the statutory description.* A court, on review or appeal, can choose whether to characterize the conclusion as one of fact or as one of law; either form of characterization is possible, for here we are in a 'grey zone'. Generally speaking, the following are categorized as questions of fact: questions decided by specialized expert tribunals in which the courts repose confidence; questions on which reasonable persons might arrive at divergent conclusions; questions which the courts consider to have been correctly decided; questions on which the courts would find it very difficult to form an independent judgment without hearing all the evidence. But where the crux of the issue is a question of the interpretation of the language adopted in a statute or statutory instrument the courts reserve the final say in the matter to themselves. So the Court of Appeal held that it was entitled to overrule the Price Commission on the meaning of the term 'costs' in the Price Code.[28]

Findings of fact may still be held to embody reviewable errors of *law* if they are made without any supporting evidence at all, or if the conclusions drawn from them are perverse (in that the facts as found point unmistakably the other way) or are based on the application of a wrong legal test or if the reasons given for the findings or conclusions are unintelligible or inadequate in law; in these cases the tribunal will be held to have misdirected itself in law. Nevertheless, the courts will be slow to interfere with erroneous findings, inferences or conclusions of fact. For instance, in one case the question was whether land had been developed without planning permission; the central issue was whether the change of use to which it had been put was 'material'. The only change was the installation of an automatic egg-vending machine in the

[28] *H.T.V.* v. *Price Commission* [1976] I.C.R. 170.

forecourt of a petrol-filling station. The court held[29] that whether a change of use was 'material' was a question of 'fact and degree',[30] not a question of law; the local planning authority's decision that there had been a material change of use was surprising, but it was not so perverse as to justify the court's interference. If the question had been categorized as one of law, the court could have substituted its own opinion. Now, if the court had adopted a slightly different approach – if it had applied the following test: there is an error of law if the inference or conclusion drawn from the facts found could not *reasonably* have been arrived at[31] – it might possibly have set the decision aside. Sometimes the courts do apply this broader test to conclusions of fact.

Natural justice

The rules of natural justice are minimum standards of fair decision-making, imposed by the common law on persons or bodies who are under a duty to 'act judicially'. They were applied originally to courts of justice and now extend to any person or body deciding issues affecting the right or interests of individuals where a reasonable citizen would have a legitimate expectation that the decision-making process would be subject to some rules of fair procedure. The content of natural justice is therefore flexible and variable. All that is fundamentally demanded of the decision-maker is that his decision in its own context be made with due regard for the affected parties' interests and accordingly be reached without bias and after giving the party or parties a chance to put his or their case. Nevertheless some judges now prefer to speak of a duty to act fairly rather than a duty to observe the rules of natural justice. Often the terms are interchangeable. But it is perhaps now the case that while a duty to act fairly is incumbent on every decision-maker within the administrative process whose decision will affect individual interests, the rules of natural justice apply only when some sort of definite code of procedure must be adopted, however flexible that code may be and however much the decision-maker is said to be master of his own procedure. The rules of natural justice are

[29] *Bendles Motors Ltd* v. *Bristol Corporation* [1963] 1 W.L.R. 247 (enforcement notice) an appeal on a question of law.

[30] See the valuable articles by Wilson in (1963) 26 *Mod. L. Rev.* 609; (1969) 32 *Mod L. Rev.* 361.

[31] See *Ashbridge Investments Ltd* v. *Minister of Housing and Local Government* [1965] 1 W.L.R. 1320 at 1326 *per* Lord Denning, M.R.; adopted in *British Dredging (Services) Ltd* v. *Secretary of State for Wales* [1975] 1 W.L.R. 687.

generally formulated as the rule against bias (*nemo judex in causa sua*) and the right to a fair hearing (*audi alteram partem*). They will be examined first and then a brief explanation of the duty to act fairly, inasmuch as it has a separate existence from natural justice, will be considered.

Rule against bias (Nemo judex in causa sua) [32]

The rule has two main aspects. First, an adjudicator must not have any direct financial or proprietary interest in the outcome of the proceedings. Secondly, he must not be reasonably suspected, or show a real likelihood, of bias.

In its first aspect, the rule is very strict. No matter how small the adjudicator's pecuniary interest may be, no matter how unlikely it is to affect his judgment, he is disqualified from acting and the decision in which he has participated will be set aside,[33] unless (i) the parties are made fully aware of his interest in the proceedings and clearly waive their right to object to his participation, or (ii) he is empowered to sit (or the validity of the proceedings is preserved if he does sit) by a special statutory dispensation or (iii) in very exceptional circumstances, all the available adjudicators are affected by a disqualifying interest, in which case they may have to sit as a matter of *necessity*. Perhaps we should classify under the same heading the rule that nobody should act as both judge and prosecutor, plantiff or advocate in a controversy. But here we begin to move towards the second aspect of the rule.

If an adjudicator is likely to be biased he is also disqualified from acting. Likelihood of bias may arise from a number of causes: membership of an organization or authority that is a party to the proceedings; partisanship expressed in extra-judicial pronouncements; the fact of appearing as a witness for a party to the proceedings; personal animosity or friendship towards a party; family relationship with a party; professional or commercial relationships with a party; and so on. The categories of situations potentially giving rise to a likelihood of bias are not closed.

The test of likelihood of bias must be applied realistically. If a controversy has aroused strong local passions, one cannot reasonably demand that every member of a local bench of magistrates deciding the issue must have maintained a total and lofty detachment from the

---

[32]   de Smith, op. cit., ch. 5. See also Paul Jackson, *Natural Justice* (2nd edn, 1979).
[33]   In *Dimes* v. *Grand Junction Canal Proprietors* (1852) 3 H.L.C. 759 a decree made by the Lord Chancellor was set aside because he was a shareholder in the company which was a party to the proceedings.

controversy from the time when it first arose. When a Minister (like the Minister in the *Stevenage* case) is placed by a statute in a position where he must inevitably incline toward confirming his own provisional decision notwithstanding the force of objections subsequently expressed, he cannot be subjected to the rigorous standards of impartiality rightly imposed on a superior judge or indeed on a member of an independent statutory tribunal.[34]

How should the test of disqualification for likelihood of bias be formulated? The strict test of disqualification for personal interest is based on the principle that public confidence in the administration of justice must not be impaired by even the smallest suspicion of judicial impropriety; the rule looks to the *appearance* of the matter to an outsider. Occasionally the courts have adopted a similarly exacting approach to the 'likelihood of bias' test. A magistrates' clerk retired with the bench while they were considering their verdict in a case of dangerous driving; the defendant was convicted; he applied, successfully, for certiorari to quash the conviction, on the ground that the clerk belonged to a firm of solicitors acting in civil proceedings on behalf of the other party to the accident out of which the criminal proceedings arose. It was 'of fundamental importance that justice should not only be done, but should manifestly and undoubtedly be seen to be done'.[35] Yet in that case there was no evidence at all that the clerk had influenced or attempted to influence the decision. A more common formulation of the test is: Would a member of the public, looking at the situation as a whole, *reasonably suspect* that a member of the adjudicating body would be biased? Another common formulation is: Is there in fact a *real likelihood* of bias?[36] There is no need, on either formulation, to prove *actual* bias; indeed, the courts may refuse to entertain submissions designed to establish the actual bias of a member of an independent tribunal, on the ground that such an inquiry would be unseemly. In practice the tests of 'reasonable suspicion' and 'real likelihood' of bias will generally lead to the same result. Seldom indeed will one find a situation in which reasonable persons adequately apprised of the facts will reasonably suspect bias but a court reviewing the facts will hold that there was no real likelihood of bias. Neither formulation is concerned wholly with appearances or wholly with objective reality. In ninety-nine cases out of a hundred it is enough for

---

[34] *Franklin* v. *Minister of Town and Country Planning* [1948] A.C. 87.

[35] *R.* v. *Sussex JJ., ex p. McCarthy* [1924] 1 K.B. 256 at 259, *per* Lord Hewart C.J.

[36] *R.* v. *Camborne JJ., ex p. Pearce* [1955] 1 Q.B. 41 and 51. It has been doubted, however, whether there is any distinction between those two tests: see *R.* v. *St Edmondsbury B.C., ex p. Investors in Industry Ltd* [1985] 1 W.L.R. 1168.

the court to ask itself whether a reasonable person viewing the facts would think that there was a substantial possibility of bias. So the decision of a rent assessment committee was quashed because the chairman, a solicitor, was acting for his father and other tenants in a separate dispute with the landlords. Reasonable people would have seen his conduct as unwise and unjudicial.[37]

Clearly the nature of these criteria offers scope for the exercise of judicial discretion. In *Hannam* v. *Bradford Corporation*[38] it was held that it was contrary to natural justice for school governors to sit as members of a local education authority's sub-committee which had to decide whether to confirm a decision of the governors to dismiss a teacher. This was so even though the relevant governors had been absent from the meeting of governors which took the decision to dismiss. But in *Ward* v. *Bradford Corporation*[39] the court refused to interfere with the decision of the governors of a teachers' training college to expel a girl student who had had a man in her room for several weeks, despite the fact that the same body instituted the disciplinary proceedings against the girl. The court's disapproval of the applicant's conduct was unveiled. Nevertheless it seems better to regard *Hannam* as the rule and *Ward* as the exception. The Divisional Court in 1978 quashed a decision of the Leicestershire Fire Authority reducing an officer to the ranks after evidence that the Chief Fire Officer, who had brought the disciplinary charge, had spent five minutes or so with the committee after they had retired. Justice, said the court, must be seen to be done and it was inevitable that the applicant would infer that the Chief Fire Officer had influenced the committee. There was no reason to treat the case as one of those exceptional instances requiring some degree of flexibility in the rule against the likelihood or suspicion of bias.[40]

Subject to the qualifications already indicated, the principles apply to the conduct of all statutory tribunals, to bodies other than tribunals deciding matters analogous to the judicial (for example, local authorities deciding whether to grant a permit after objections have been lodged, or to revoke a licence[41]) and to Ministers deciding disputes between parties. If the deciding body is a large one (for example, a local

[37] See *Metropolitan Properties Co. (F.G.C.) Ltd* v. *Lannon* [1969] 1 Q.B. 577.
[38] [1970] 1 W.L.R. 937.
[39] (1971) 70 L.G.R. 27.
[40] *R.* v. *Leicestershire Fire Authority, ex p. Thompson* (1978) 77 L.G.R. 375. Constrast *R.* v. *Board of Visitors of Frankland Prison, ex p. Lewis* [1986] 1 W.L.R. 130 (Board member not disqualified from adjudicating despite knowledge of prisoner's previous criminal record: such knowledge is common in such members).
[41] *R.* v. *Barnsley M.B.C., ex p. Hook* [1976] 1 W.L.R. 1052, C.A.

council), the pecuniary interest of a single member will disqualify[42] although it may be that likelihood of his being biased will not be material unless he took an active part in influencing the decision. This is still a doubtful point.

The right to a fair hearing (audi alteram partem)[43]

The right to a fair hearing requires at least that nobody be penalized by a decision affecting his rights or legitimate expectations unless he has been given (a) notice of the case he has to meet and (b) a fair opportunity to answer the case against him and put his own case. The enforcement of this right has a long and chequered history. In 1723 a Dr Bentley obtained an order of mandamus to secure his reinstatement to degrees of which he had been deprived by the University of Cambridge without notice or hearing.[44] When a local authority exercised a statutory power to demolish a house without giving the owner notice or an opportunity to make representations on his own behalf he was awarded damages for trespass, for the authority had failed to observe a rule 'of universal application and founded on the plaincst principles of justice'. The court claimed that it 'invoked the justice of the common law to supply the omission of the legislature' which had failed to give the property-owner any right to be heard. So in *Cooper* v. *Wandsworth Board of Works* the foundations of the rules of natural justice were laid.[45]

Natural justice binds Ministers and officials in departmental adjudication. They must 'act in good faith and fairly listen to both sides, for that is a duty lying upon anyone who decides anything'.[46] Did the rules of natural justice then bind all decision-makers? The authoritative statement is to be found in the judgment of Atkin L. J. in *R.* v. *Electricity Commissioners*.[47] Certiorari, the remedy used to correct a breach of the rules of natural justice, lay to 'any body of persons having legal authority to determine questions affecting the rights of subjects, and having the duty to act judicially'. From 1920 to 1960 this much quoted passage was used to limit the application of natural

[42] *R.* v. *Hendon R.D.C., ex p. Chorley* [1933] 2 K.B. 696 (unanimous decision by council on application to change use of land quashed because one councillor was an estate agent acting for an interested party).
[43] de Smith, op. cit., ch. 4.
[44] *R.* v. *Chancellor of the University of Cambridge* (1723) 1 Str. 557.
[45] (1863) 14 C.B. (N.S.) 180.
[46] *Board of Education* v. *Rice* [1911] A.C. 179.
[47] [1924] 1 K.B. 171 at p. 205.

justice to the extent that the rules of natural justice almost faded into obscurity. A series of decisions held that only if the decision-making body was similar in nature to a court of law or obliged to follow a judicial procedure was there any duty to 'act judicially'. To take one example, the Commissioner of Metropolitan Police had a discretionary power to cancel taxi-drivers' licences. The Divisional Court held that he was not obliged to observe the rules of natural justice because his powers were of an administrative and disciplinary nature.[48] In no sense did the deprivation of a licence by the Commissioner resemble proceedings in court – that is, judicial proceedings. Effectively, only if the decision-making body was required to determine a dispute between parties independent of itself did any question of granting a fair hearing arise.

The House of Lords in *Ridge* v. *Baldwin*[49] breathed new life into natural justice. They held that the Chief Constable of Brighton, who held an office from which by statutory regulations he could only be removed on grounds of neglect of duty or inability, could not validly be dismissed in the absence of notification of the charge and an opportunity to be heard in his defence. The duty to act judicially could be inferred from the nature of the decision to be taken and was not dependent on the nature of the decision-making body.

Since *Ridge* v. *Baldwin* the general trend has been to extend the application of the rules of natural justice to any decision-maker who determines questions affecting the rights or legitimate expectations of individuals. The content of the rules has been adapted and rendered sufficiently flexible to meet the needs of the wide spectrum of decision-making now subject to natural justice. Public policy is openly considered in determining whether the rules should apply to a body and what constitutes a fair hearing in a particular instance.[50] And as the remedies available to those who allege a breach of natural justice are discretionary, the courts may refuse a remedy despite a breach of natural justice, because in the circumstances it is felt that there is no merit in the applicant's case or it is clear that even if natural justice had been scrupulously observed the applicant would still have met the same fate.[51]

A few examples will illustrate the general trend of extending the scope of natural justice. The right to a hearing was said by the Privy Council to apply to the dissolution of a local council for incompetence

[48] R. v. *Metropolitan Police Commissioner, ex p. Parker* [1953] 1 W.L.R. 1150.
[49] [1964] A.C. 40.
[50] R. v. *Hull Prison Board of Visitors, ex p. St Germain* [1978] Q.B. 678, C.A.
[51] *Glynn* v. *University of Keele* [1971] 1 W.L.R. 487.

by the Minister of Local Government in Ceylon.[52] Three matters were important in determining whether a right to be heard must be granted: the nature of the benefit of which the applicant was deprived by the decision, the circumstances in which the decision-making body could intervene, and the severity and effect of the sanction which could be imposed. So a Scottish schoolteacher dismissible at pleasure had to be afforded an opportunity to be heard before dismissal.[53] A local constituency party was entitled to a hearing before final suspension or disaffiliation from the party organization.[54] Before it was held that exclusive jurisdiction over university students as members of the university vested in the Visitor,[55] students were said to be entitled to a hearing before being sent down either on academic or disciplinary grounds.[56] In *R.* v. *Hull Prison Board of Visitors*[57] the Court of Appeal found that prisoners appearing before the Board of Visitors to answer serious disciplinary charges which could result in severe punishment had the right to a proper hearing. Despite their deprivation of general liberty the prisoners retained rights which the Board of Visitors had power to affect materially either by punishment within the prison through solitary confinement or loss of privileges, or by effectively extending their period of incarceration through loss of remission.[58] The Board's power to intervene was in cases of gravity where judicial conduct would be expected of a decision-making body and the sanctions at their disposal were severe. Nor did their Lordships see that the extension of natural justice to the deliberations of Boards of Visitors would disrupt the efficiency of the prison service, although they admitted that demanding the same standards from the governor in his day-to-day disciplinary role might do so.[59] In *Hone* v. *Maze Prison Board of Visitors*[60] the House of Lords held, however, that this does not imply an absolute right to legal representation before the Board, and that such representation would never be required on a charge heard by the governor of a prison. The rigid application of pre-

---

[52] *Durayappah* v. *Fernando* [1967] 2. A.C. 337.
[53] *Malloch* v. *Aberdeen Corporation* [1971] 1 W.L.R. 1578, H.L.
[54] *John* v. *Rees* [1970] Ch. 345.
[55] See *Thomas* v. *University of Bradford* [1987] 1 All E.R. 834.
[56] *R.* v. *Aston University Senate, ex p. Roffey* [1969] 2. Q.B. 538.
[57] [1978] Q.B. 678.
[58] See also *Raymond* v. *Honey* [1983] A.C. 1.
[59] That qualification was subsequently accepted in *R.* v. *Deputy Governor of Camphill Prison, ex p. King* [1985] Q.B. 735, but that case was later overruled by the House of Lords in *Leech* v. *Parkhurst Prison Deputy Governor* [1988] 1 All E.R. 485, the House refusing to give special immunity to a prison governor's 'management function'. See further [1988] *Public Law* 183.
[60] [1988] 1 All E.R. 321.

determined policy without allowing representations for a change in the policy may be a breach of the rules of natural justice.[61]

Natural justice is not confined to decisions depriving citizens of existing rights. Dicta suggest that when a citizen has a legitimate expectation that his application for a discretionary benefit such as a licence or permit will not be refused without a chance for him to put his case then he is entitled to some sort of hearing.[62] Where he already enjoys the benefit, the expectation that he should not be deprived of it arbitrarily and unheard by the decision-maker makes his case morally and legally stronger.[63] But this is an area where judges tend to speak in terms of the duty to act fairly, a more fluid and less formalized duty than the duty to observe the rules of natural justice.

While finding against the trade union members of G.C.H.Q. who had been deprived by the Government of their right to belong to their unions on the grounds of national security, some at least of their Lordships held that, but for national security, the trade unionists would have had a legitimate expectation of consultation before the ban was imposed.[64] The G.C.H.Q. case illustrates two important trends in judicial attitudes towards the expectation of a fair hearing. First, it may open the door to a wider practice of requiring consultations with groups rather than with individuals. Secondly, once again the courts have shown a great unwillingness to go behind the Government's view of what national security requires.[65]

Today it can be assumed that the rules of natural justice will apply in the following cases.

1   Where the decision-making body is a court or tribunal. Such a body may nevertheless be empowered or required to act *ex parte* (hearing one side only) in special circumstances – for example, to order that a person suffering from a prescribed infectious disease be detained in hospital.

2   Where the decision-making body has as its functions the holding

---

[61]   *R.* v. *Secretary of State for the Environment, ex p. Brent L.B.C.* [1983] 3 All E.R. 321.

[62]   *McInnes* v. *Onslow-Fane* [1978] 1 W.L.R. 1520; *O'Reilly* v. *Mackman* [1983] A.C. 237.

[63]   *Schmidt* v. *Home Secretary* [1969] 2 Ch. 149 at p. 170; *R.* v. *Gaming Board, ex p. Benaim and Khaida* [1970] 2. Q.B. 417, at p. 430; *Att.-Gen. of Hong Kong* v. *Ng Yuen Shiu* [1983] 2 A.C. 829.

[64]   *Council of Civil Service Unions* v. *Minister for the Civil Service* [1985] A.C. 374, applied on the legitimate expectation point in *R.* v. *Secretary of State for Transport, ex p. GLC* [1986] Q.B. 556.

[65]   But in *R.* v. *Secretary of State for the Home Department, ex p. Ruddock* [1987] 2 All E.R. 518, Taylor J. held that the courts would not decline to intervene merely because a Minister asserted that national security would be prejudiced if there were a hearing, and that the doctrine of legitimate expectation imposed a duty to act fairly.

and hearing of inquiries, or the determination of disputes between parties.

3 In any case where a decision-making body is required to determine questions of law or fact in individual cases and its decisions will have a direct impact on the interests of the individuals concerned.

4 When a decision-making body vested with discretionary powers in the exercise of those powers will take a decision seriously impinging on individual rights and expectations. But it may well be that today such bodies will be characterized as under a duty to act fairly rather than observe the rules of natural justice.

So wide is the class of cases when it will be presumed that the rules of natural justice apply that it is the exceptions which repay more careful attention and analysis.

1 Where a body conducts an investigation but has no power to decide,[66] providing that the investigation is truly only a preliminary fact-finding exercise and there are no circumstances to suggest that it would be unfair to prevent the aggrieved individual putting his case at this stage. But a duty to act fairly will attach to such bodies.[67] The stringency and content of this duty will depend to what degree the preliminary investigation is of a kind where some degree of disclosure of the case against him and opportunity to put his case would reasonably be expected by the person under investigation. So if the investigation exposes a person to legal hazard and is a necessary prelude to other proceedings which may seriously affect the person's rights or interests then the investigator must at least inform the person of adverse imputations against him and give him an opportunity to reply.[68] The requirements of 'fairness' will depend on the circumstances of each case. Where the function of the investigating authority is akin to that of the police gathering evidence in order to determine whether further proceedings are necessary, even a suspicion of bias may not affect the validity of the action taken.[69] The duty to act fairly in such circumstances is a duty not to misuse the discretionary powers vested in the investigating body, not a duty to attempt to achieve a fair procedure.

2 Where an exhaustive statutory procedural code has been

[66] *Herring* v. *Templeman* [1973] 3 All E.R. 569.
[67] *Norwest Holst Ltd* v. *Department of Trade* [1978] Ch. 201, C.A.; *Lewis* v. *Heffer* [1978] 1 W.L.R. 1601, C.A.
[68] *Re Pergamon Press* [1971] Ch. 388; *Maxwell* v. *Department of Trade and Industry* [1974] Q.B. 523.
[69] *R.* v. *Secretary of State for Trade, ex p. Perestrello* [1980] 1 All E.R. 28.

prescribed.[70] Since the establishment of the Council on Tribunals, such codes have proliferated. But the courts may hold that an ostensibly exhaustive code imports further duties to act fairly in accordance with natural justice.

3   Where a decision affects so many people that it is really a legislative act;[71] or where the range of public policy considerations that the deciding body can legitimately take into account is very wide.[72] This proposition has to be expressed guardedly, for the idea of procedural fairness is not necessarily thus restricted, and in such cases judges will often state that there is a duty to act fairly even though the rules of natural justice are not applicable.

4   Where an employer decides to dismiss an employee. Unless contractual or statutory procedural duties are cast on the employer, the courts may confine the employee to damages for breach of contract if the dismissal is wrongful.[73] But there are now large exceptions to the general rule,[74] particularly since the concept of 'unfair dismissal' was introduced by the Industrial Relations Act 1971 and preserved by subsequent employment legislation.

5   Where a decision entails the allocation of scarce resources – for example, university places, council houses, industrial grants, certain discretionary licences – for which there are numerous competitors. But withdrawal or non-renewal of any such advantage *may*, in justice, have to be preceded by notice and an opportunity to make representations.[75]

In addition, as we have seen, factors such as urgency or an overriding need for confidentiality or national security may negative the existence of a *prima facie* duty to observe the rule or aspects of the rule. Nor need the rule be observed in the exercise of those prerogative powers which are not justiciable.

---

[70] *Wiseman* v. *Borneman* [1971] A.C. 297; *Pearlberg* v. *Varty* [1972] 1 W.L.R. 534; *Furnell* v. *Whangarei High Schools Board* [1973] A.C. 660.

[71] See, for example, *Essex C.C.* v. *Ministry of Housing and Local Government* (1967) 66 L.G.R. 23 (designation of third London airport); *Bates* v. *Lord Hailsham* [1972] 1 W.L.R. 1373 (making statutory rules for solicitors' charges).

[72] *Schmidt* v. *Home Secretary* [1969] 2 Ch. 149 (non-renewal of entry permits for alien scientology students).

[73] See, for example, *Vidyodaya University Council* v. *Silva* [1965] 1 W.L.R. 77; *Pillai* v. *Singapore City Council* [1968] 1 W.L.R. 1728. The decision in *Ridge* v. *Baldwin* [1964] A.C. 40 is not inconsistent with the principle; a chief constable is nobody's servant and enjoys a special legal *status*.

[74] See *Malloch*'s case (note 53): *Hill* v. *Parsons* (*C.A.*) & *Co.* [1972] Ch. 305 (injunction to restrain wrongful dismissal).

[75] See notes 62 and 63. See also *R.* v. *East Berkshire Health Authority, ex p. Walsh* [1985] Q.B. 152; C.A., and *R.* v. *BBC, ex p. Lavelle* [1983] 1 W.L.R. 23.

6 Where the conduct of the person claiming to be affected by the denial of a hearing was such that he could have 'no legitimate expectation of a hearing'. Mini-cab drivers who had persistently flouted the law and regulations concerning touting for custom at London Airport were found to have only themselves to blame when they were denied any opportunity to make representations to the authority when it acted to exclude all persons from the airport who were not bona fide passengers.[76]

What is a fair hearing?

When a person has a right to a hearing he must know what evidence has been given and what statements made against him and he must be given a fair opportunity to correct or contradict them.[77] There is no fixed rule that the right to be heard means a right to be heard orally; in some situations a case can fairly be concluded in writing.[78] But there is a rebuttable presumption in favour of the duty to afford an oral hearing if one is requested. All relevant information, including information gathered by the decision-maker on his own initiative or as a result of his own expertise or consideration of the case,[79] must be disclosed to persons likely to be affected by its concealment, except when full disclosure may injure the individual affected or the public interest.[80] The Gaming Board was not required to disclose its sources of information suggesting that applicants for gaming licences had underworld connections.[81] And in *R.* v. *Secretary of State for Home Affairs, ex p. Hosenball,*[82] when a young American journalist sought to have a deportation order quashed on the grounds that his presence in the United Kingdom was not prejudicial to national security, Cumming Bruce L. J. said, '. . . the field of judicial scrutiny by reference to the enforcement of the rules of common fairness is an extremely restricted

---

[76] *Cinnamond* v. *British Airports Authority* 190] 1 W.L.R. 582; and see *Lovelock* v. *Secretary of State for Transport* [1979] .

[77] *Kanda* v. *Government of Malaya* [1962] A.C. 322 at pp. 337–8.

[78] *Local Government Board* v. *Arlidge* [1915] A.C. 120; *Brighton Corporation* v. *Parry* (1972) 70 L.G.R. 576.

[79] *Sabey* v. *Secretary of State for the Environment* [1978] 1 All E.R. 586 (refusal of permission to extract gravel based on conclusions reached by the inspector at the inquiry which he had never put to the applicants for their consideration).

[80] *R.* v. *Kent Police Authority, ex p. Godden* [1971] 2 Q.B. 662 (distressing medical report disclosed to the applicant's medical adviser only and withheld from him); *Re WLW* [1972] 1 Ch. 456 (psychiatric reports held back in a case where an infant would suffer if published).

[81] *R.* v. *Gaming Board, ex p. Banaim and Khaida* [1970] 2 Q.B. 417.

[82] [1977] 1 W.L.R. 766.

field in the sphere of operations necessary to protect the security of the state'. So Mr Hosenball was deported, despite the fact that when he was afforded an opportunity of appearing before a panel advising the Home Secretary on his decision to deport, he was given totally inadequate information on which to answer the general charge against him.

Generally when an oral hearing is granted parties must be allowed to call witnesses and make submissions. They must have a fair chance to put their case and an adjournment of the hearing should be granted if necessary to prevent a party being taken by surprise,[83] but where there are a large number of parties (as in a public inquiry) the prejudice to one party must be weighed against the inconvenience to everyone else.[84] Cross-examination of witnesses should generally not be prevented[85] and hearsay evidence should not be allowed if it results in a person being effectively disabled from answering the points made against him in the hearsay testimony.[86] There are no hard and fast rules either on cross-examination or hearsay. The crucial factors are the nature of the decision and process challenged and whether at the end of the day the persons affected did have a proper opportunity to put their case. A refusal by the inspector at a public inquiry to allow cross-examination of departmental witnesses giving evidence on national road policies did not result in a breach of natural justice.[87] But prisoners appearing on disciplinary charges before a Board of Visitors should be allowed to cross-examine any witness the reliability of whose evidence is material to the case against them.[88]

It has been said that a party who is entitled to be heard is *prima facie* entitled to be legally represented.[89] The number of circumstances in which this implied right can be excluded[90] makes it more accurate to say now that there is probably a right to be legally represented when a fair hearing is not possible without legal representation. The more that the person affected has at stake and the more severe the potential sanction then the more likely it is that legal representation may become a right enforced by the rules of natural justice.[91] And so where

[83] *R.* v. *Thames Magistrates, ex p. Polemis* [1974] 1 W.L.R. 1371.
[84] *Ostreicher* v. *Secretary of State for the Environment* [1978] 1 W.L.R. 810.
[85] *Ceylon University* v. *Fernando* [1960] 1 W.L.R. 223.
[86] *R.* v. *Hull Prison Board of Visitors, ex p. St Germain* (*No. 2*) [1979] 1 W.L.R 1401.
[87] *Bushell* v. *Secretary of State for the Environment* [1980] 2 All E.R. 608.
[88] *R.* v. *Hull Prison Board of Visitors* (*No. 2*) [1979] 1. W.L.R. 1401.
[89] *R.* v. *Assessment Committee of St Mary Abbots, Kensington* [1891] 1 Q.B. 378.
[90] See *Enderby Town F.C. Ltd* v. *Football Association Ltd* [1971] Ch. 591; *Fraser* v. *Mudge* [1975] 1 W.L.R. 1132; *Hone* v. *Maze Prison Board of Visitors* (1988) 1 All E.R. 321 (prisoners on disciplinary charges).
[91] *Pett* v. *Greyhound Racing Association Ltd* [1969] 1 Q.B. 125; (*No. 2*) [1970] 1 Q.B. 46.

prisoners faced charges of mutiny before the prison Board of Visitors, the Board was held to have acted wrongly in refusing them legal representation. The requirements of a fair hearing demand that the tribunal exercise its discretion over the issue of representation. No reasonable Board could refuse legal representation to men facing charges of such gravity and complexity.[92]

In some situations there is an oral hearing conducted by a small committee or tribunal but the decision is made by a larger body. The general rule is that he who decides must also hear.[93] This requires that those who listen to the evidence and make recommendations must deliver to the deciding body an adequate report on which that body can discharge its obligation to hear as well as decide. The stringency with which this requirement is enforced will depend on the nature of the decision-making process under review. The more closely it resembles proceedings in the ordinary courts then the more strictly the rule will apply.[94] Departmental adjudication, where it is obvious that the Minister cannot hear and decide every case remitted to him, has always been outside the scope of the rule.[95] With the decision the fair hearing is complete. The common law has not as yet enforced any general rule that fairness demands that those affected be told the reasons for the decision, nor did it oblige Ministers to disclose the reports of inspectors at public inquiries.[96] In the case of the decisions of most special statutory tribunals, and of Ministers reaching decisions after the holding of inquiries, statute has filled the gap.[97] The courts enforce the giving of reasons when required by statute but the full rigour of the statutory rule is not always brought to bear on public authorities. For example, in one case concerning an application that the plaintiff's houses be rehabilitated rather than demolished a statement of reasons read: 'for the reason that the premises should be demolished and the site used for the erection of new housing accommodation'. The Court of Appeal held this to be sufficient although the Court also said that their finding did not mean that such a formula would always fulfil the duty to give reasons.[98]

In making sense of the inconsistencies in the application of the rules of natural justice it should never be forgotten that natural justice is not

---

[92] *R.* v. *Secretary of State for the Home Department, ex p. Tarrant* [1985] Q.B. 251; but see *Hone* v. *Maze Prison Board of Visitors* (above, p. 563, note 60).

[93] *Jeffs* v. *New Zealand Dairy Production & Marketing Board* [1967] 1 A.C. 551.

[94] *R.* v. *Race Relations Board, ex p. Selvarajan* [1975] 1 W.L.R. 1986. And see *Chief Constable of the North Wales Police* v. *Evans* [1982] 1 W.L.R. 1155, H.L.

[95] *Local Government Board* v. *Arlidge* [1915] A.C. 120.

[96] ibid.

[97] Tribunals and Inquiries Act 1971, s. 12.

[98] *Elliot* v. *Southwark L.B.C.* [1976] 1 W.L.R. 499.

and is not intended to be a precise and uniform code of procedure. What the courts seek to enforce is substantial justice. The whole of the decision-making process under review is examined. In *Calvin* v. *Carr*[99] the appellant had been accused of being a party with his jockey to stopping his horse running a fair race. It was assumed that he had been denied a fair hearing by the course stewards but his appeal to the Australian Jockey Club was conducted with scrupulous fairness. The Privy Council held that the unfairness of the first hearing did not necessarily vitiate the entire decision-making process.

Duty to act fairly

The duty to act fairly is not rationally distinguishable from the duty to observe the rules of natural justice. Judges on occasion use the terms interchangeably. Examples have been noted in which it has been suggested that although there is no right to a hearing, in the sense discussed in the previous section, the decision-maker is still bound to act fairly. This duty to act fairly prohibits the decision-maker from acting capriciously and here it merges with principles preventing misuse of discretionary powers. But it is in the area of decisions which either (1) affect large groups rather than individuals, or (2) appear to be part and parcel of everyday administration, or (3) are made by bodies so very different in form and functions from those usually subject to natural justice, that the courts appear happier to use the flexible notions of fairness rather than stretch the rules of natural justice even further.

In *R.* v. *Liverpool Corporation, ex p. Liverpool Taxi Fleet Operators' Association*[100] the town clerk of Liverpool assured bodies representing taxi drivers that no increase in the number of taxi licences would be made without consulting them. A sub-committee of the council recommended graduated increases after hearing representations from lawyers representing the taxi drivers. An undertaking was given in the council that there would be no increases made until forthcoming legislation was passed. The council was then advised that this restriction acted as an improper fetter on their discretion and the numbers of taxi-licences increased. The Court of Appeal held that although the council was indubitably exercising an administrative function in determining the number of taxi-licences to be allocated in the city the court should not hesitate in a suitable case to intervene to ensure fairness. A similar

<hr/>

[99] [1979] 2 W.L.R. 755.
[100] [1972] 2 Q.B. 299.

attitude has been taken to the functions of an immigration officer determining whether an immigrant in front of him is truly under sixteen and entitled to enter the United Kingdom as a dependant;[101] and to a magistrate condemning potatoes as unfit for human consumption.[102] In *H.T.V.* v. *Price Commission*[103] the Commission had regularly treated payments made by commercial television companies to the Exchequer as part of their total costs even though the scale of the payments was calculated as a percentage of advertising profits. In 1975 the Commission changed its mind and in determining an application for a price increase calculated H.T.V.'s profits as including those payments, refusing to treat them as costs. The Court of Appeal held that the Commission was obliged to act consistently and fairly and, having regularly interpreted costs in one manner, must allow representations from the affected company before reversing their policy.

These examples, and those cited earlier where 'the duty to act fairly' was preferred to the rules of natural justice as a tool of judicial control, illustrate the three points made at the beginning of the section. They are examples of decision-making processes so far removed from the original sphere of natural justice that even after *Ridge* v. *Baldwin* it would stretch the English language to say that the decision-makers must 'act judicially'. Additionally they are decisions taken in a context where the effect of requiring fairness to one group or individual must be considered in the light of the administration's general policy and conduct. Speaking of a duty to act fairly frees the judge to consider whether his decision will result in a general improvement in standards of fairness in that area of government without causing inefficiency, or delay, or insuperable administrative difficulties. Only if he is satisfied that this is so will the individual be afforded a remedy.

Discretionary powers

General

Discretion implies power to choose between alternative courses of action. If X applies to a London borough council for a licence to open a massage establishment, the council may grant the licence unconditionally or subject to such conditions as it thinks fit to impose, or

---

[101] *Re H.K.* [1967] 2 Q.B. 617.
[102] *R.* v. *Birmingham City Justice, ex p. Chris Foreign Foods (Wholesalers) Ltd* [1970] 1 W.L.R. 1428.
[103] (1976) I.C.R. 170.

refuse the application. But its discretion is not unlimited; and it must exercise a genuine discretion in each individual case. Thus, it has an implied duty not to refuse the application on legally irrelevant grounds (for example, that X is a Jehovah's Witness) or to attach legally irrelevant conditions to the grant of a licence (for example, that X shall employ only persons resident in the borough); nor must it adopt a rigid rule not to grant any new applications for licences irrespective of the merits of the individual case. If no appeal lay from its decisions, X would be entitled to go to the High Court for an order of mandamus to compel it to perform its public duty. Mandamus would lie not to compel the council to give him a licence but to exercise its discretion according to law.

In fact mandamus is unnecessary, for an appeal against the merits of the decision lies to a magistrates' court. If the magistrate wrongfully refuses to entertain the appeal at all, he has declined jurisdiction in breach of his public duty and mandamus will issue to him. If he listens to submissions and then erroneously dismisses the appeal, the question might arise on an application for mandamus whether he had wrongfully declined jurisdiction or made an error of law on a matter within his jurisdiction; in this context the answer is unimportant, for an appeal will lie to the Divisional Court by case stated. In arriving at his decision, he can substitute his own opinion for that of the local authority, giving due weight to the council's knowledge of local conditions. Indeed, he has a legally enforceable duty to exercise an independent discretion.[104]

It is fairly unusual to provide a full right of appeal to a court against the merits of a statutory discretionary decision. Judicial control of the exercise of discretion is normally limited to two questions: Has the discretion been exercised at all? If so, has it been exercised according to law?

Failure to exercise a discretion

1   The general rule is that, unless expressly authorized to do so, an authority cannot sub-delegate its powers to another person or body: *delegatus non potest delegare*. Application of this principle gives rise to a number of difficult problems – for example, what exactly is meant by 'delegation'? – which we need not pursue. But it is not hard to illustrate the application of the general rule. A local authority empowered to issue cinema licences subject to conditions cannot validly impose a condition that *no* film shall be exhibited

---

[104] *Sagnata Improvements Ltd* v. *Norwich Corporation* [1971] 2 Q.B. 614. The same principles apply to the Crown Court hearing an appeal from a magistrates' court.

unless approved by the British Board of Film Classification;[105] it must preserve a residual discretion to override the rulings of the Board in an individual case; otherwise it will be held to have abdicated from its statutory duty to exercise its own discretion.[106] Again, in deciding an appeal, Minister X must not dispose of the matter solely on the basis of Minister Y's policy; otherwise the decision becomes Minister Y's.[107]

2   One authority cannot lawfully act under the dictation of another unless the other is a superior in the administrative hierarchy or is empowered by law to give instructions to it.[108]

3   An authority must not so fetter its own discretion by self-created rules as to preclude itself from applying its mind to the merits of an individual case before it. The borough council, in our hypothetical illustration, could, however, adopt a general policy of not granting any further massage establishment licences for the time being (because, for example, some of these establishments had been improperly conducted), provided that it was prepared to make an exception in a particular case.[109] It must keep its mind ajar. But an authority entitled to take general considerations of national policy into account may be entitled to refuse to consider any application belonging to a particular class. For example, the Home Secretary may validly instruct immigration officers not to admit any alien wishing to enter the country as a student member of a cult which he deems to be harmful to the public welfare.[110]

4   An authority cannot validly bargain away, or otherwise undertake not to exercise, powers vested in it for the purpose of fulfilling an important public purpose. As has been noted,[111] a local authority cannot disable itself from making a particular by-law or revoking a grant of planning permission; and in general public bodies cannot

[105] *Ellis* v. *Dubowski* [1921] 3 K.B. 621. But see *R.* v. *Greater London Council, ex p. Blackburn* [1976] 1 W.L.R. 550 (authority may adopt policy of approving all films passed by the British Board of Film Censors unless a specific objection is made).

[106] *Mills* v. *L.C.C.* [1925] 1 K.B. 213.

[107] *Lavender (H.) and Son Ltd* v. *Minister of Housing and Local Government* [1970] 1 W.L.R. 1231 (planning appeal dismissed because Minister of Agriculture always opposed such development).

[108] See *Laker Airways Ltd* v. *Department of Trade* above, p. 549, and *R* v. *Secretary of State for the Environment and Cheshire County Council, ex p. Halton D.C. The Times,* 14 July 1983.

[109] See, for example, *Cumings* v. *Birkenhead Corporation* [1972] Ch. 12 (allocation of pupils to denominational schools); *British Oxygen Co.* v. *Board of Trade* [1971] A.C. 610 (policy on investment grants).

[110] See *Schmidt* v. *Home Secretary* [1969] 2 Ch. 149.

[111] pp. 415–16.

be estopped from exercising their powers by erroneous assurances given to members of the public.[112] In matters of national policy, the Crown cannot fetter its own freedom to act for the public good.[113] But these rules are easier to formulate than to apply in practice.

Misuse of discretion

Today the courts have demonstrated that they can if they wish review the legality of the exercise of virtually any discretionary power. That a power derives from the prerogative or is subject to the approval of Parliament will not deter judicial examination of the propriety of the decision to act and the action taken.[114] The Judiciary choose not to intervene on occasion. This is especially the case when the statutory power challenged concerns national security or the operation of the immigration rules. In times of emergency the ordinary rules of judicial review are naturally modified, and in some sensitive political areas such as industrial relations the courts will back away from intervening in controversy. Unfortunately, rather than stating clearly that their view of public policy inhibits them from investigating certain areas of government, judges too often fall back on earlier notions of the limited power to review administrative acts or the presumption that an authority granted powers in subjective terms has satisfied itself of the necessary conditions for the lawful exercise of its discretion.

How far may the courts go in examining the exercise of discretionary power? All statutory powers must be exercised in good faith and to promote the objects of the enabling Act. Statutory discretions are potentially reviewable on these grounds at the instance of a person aggrieved by their exercise. Bad faith – the intentional abuse of power for extraneous motives – may be virtually impossible to prove. Misuse of powers in good faith – by using them for an unauthorized purpose or without regard to legally relevant considerations or on the basis of legally irrelevant considerations – need not be so difficult to establish. If a power expressly granted for one purpose is in fact used for a different purpose the administrative act is invalid.[115] If such a power is used to achieve its proper purpose and another unauthorized purpose the court must consider what was the 'dominant' purpose of the action

---

[112] On assurances given by Crown servants, see *Howell* v. *Falmouth Boat Construction Co.* [1951] A.C. 837 at 845, 849 (contrast *Robertson* v. *Minister of Pensions* [1949] 1 K.B. 227). For local authorities, see now pp. 405–9.

[113] *Rederiaktiebolaget Amphitrite* v. *R.* [1921] 3 K.B. 500; and see pp. 629–30.

[114] *Laker Airways Ltd* v. *Department of Trade* [1977] Q.B. 643.

[115] *Congreve* v. *Home Office* [1976] Q.B. 629.

taken.[116] Was the exercise of the power a colourable sham or has the purpose for which the power was granted been substantially fulfilled?[117] If the statutory purpose has not been spelt out, the courts may read implied limitations into an ostensibly unfettered grant of power.[118] As was pointed out in an earlier chapter, the courts are nowadays reluctant to hold that an administrative authority is the sole judge of the legality of the purpose for which it exercises a discretionary power. They may interpret a statute restrictively, relying if necessary on common-law presumptions of legislative intent; and they may draw adverse inferences from the conduct of the administrative authority.[119]

Perhaps the most outstanding recent example of judicial activism in this field of the law was the decision of the House of Lords in *Padfield* v. *Minister of Agriculture* (1968).[120] Under a statutory marketing scheme, the Milk Marketing Board fixed prices to be paid to producers in each of eleven regions in England and Wales. Producers from the south-east region wanted an increase in the basic price paid to them by the Board. They could not get a majority on the Board for their view. But under the Act they could, and did, make a complaint to the Minister. The Act provided that, 'if the Minister ... so directs', a committee was to be appointed to investigate and report on such a complaint. The Minister refused to appoint a committee. He claimed that he had a free discretion to do as he thought fit. But he was induced to give reasons for his refusal: the complaint raised issues affecting other regions; he would be expected to implement the report of such a committee, and this could lead to political difficulties. The House of Lords held that the Minister had had regard to irrelevant considerations and had failed to promote the implied purposes of the Act; and an order of mandamus was issued to direct him to consider the appellants' complaint according to law.[121]

---

[116] *Westminster Corporation* v. *L. & N. W. Railway Co.* [1905] A.C. 426. See also *R.* v. *Inner London Education Authority, ex p. Westminster City Council* [1986] 2 W.L.R. 28 (purpose of the exercise of a power held improper so irrelevant that a proper purpose had been achieved as well).

[117] *Asher* v. *Secretary of State for the Environment* [1974] Ch. 208.

[118] *R.* v. *Barnet & Camden Rent Tribunal, ex p. Frey Investments Ltd* [1972] 2 Q.B. 372 (local council could not use its power to refer contracts of letting to a rent tribunal for the purpose of using the tribunal as a general rent-fixing agency irrespective of the circumstances of individual cases).

[119] *Congreve* v. *Home Office* [1976] Q.B. 629 (and note the effect of a finding of maladministration by the Parliamentary Commissioner for Administration in proving the invalidity of an administrative act).

[120] [1968] A.C. 997.

[121] The Minister then set up the committee; the committee reported in favour of the south-eastern producers; the Minister rejected the report.

Thus the House of Lords subjected a wide executive discretion to judicial standards. *Padfield* was hailed as the dawn of a new era of judicial review, showing that English administrative law did recognize a principle akin to the French *détournement de pouvoir*, or misuse of administrative power. Moreover, misuse of power might be inferred from inadequate reasons or, so the Law Lords observed *obiter*, from the absence of any reason given in rebuttal when an aggrieved person had established a *prima facie* case. Alas, once again the courts failed to demonstrate a consistent policy. In the years that followed *Padfield* there appeared to be a retreat from the implications of that decision. Either the terms in which the discretion was granted or the circumstances of its exercise were held to preclude the rigours of the *Padfield* approach [122] or the complainant was required to establish that the authority was motivated by an improper purpose. [123]

In 1976 in *Congreve* v. *Home Office* [124] and in the *Tameside* case [125] the courts re-asserted judicial willingness to examine the reasons advanced in support of an exercise of discretion and to infer misuse of discretion in the absence of good reasons to support a decision. Mr Congreve, anticipating a price rise in colour television licences, renewed the licence before the date on which renewal was due in order to avoid paying the increased charge. The Home Secretary, after Mr Congreve had refused to pay an additional sum equivalent to the increase, revoked his television licence. The Court of Appeal held that the Minister's reasons – loss of revenue, dissatisfaction on the part of licence holders less financially astute than Mr Congreve – were quite insufficient and the revocation consequently unlawful. More important, the court reiterated that had the Minister hidden behind a refusal to give reasons, then they would have been prepared to infer that his reasons were inadequate.

The *Tameside* decision reduced the efficacy of the device of excluding judicial review by granting a discretion in subjective terms, which apparently requires only that the Minister, or other authority, be satisfied, or form an opinion and so at first sight exclude judicial review. Framing a power in subjective terms will no longer prevent judicial examination of the exercise of that power. The 1944 Education Act authorizes the Secretary of State for Education to intervene and give directions to a local education authority if he 'is satisfied' that the

---

[122] See *Secretary of State for Employment* v. *ASLEF* [1972] 2 Q.B. 455.
[123] See *Asher* v. *Secretary of State for the Environment* [1974] Ch. 208; and see *Hoveringham Gravels Ltd* v. *Secretary of State for the Environment* [1975] Q.B. 754.
[124] [1976] Q.B. 629.
[125] *Secretary of State for Education and Science* v. *Tameside M.B.C.* [1977] A.C. 1014.

authority has acted or proposes to act 'unreasonably'. In 1976 the Secretary of State for Education applied for an order of mandamus to enforce directions which he had given to the newly-elected Conservative council for Tameside requiring them to go ahead with comprehensive plans scheduled to come into effect that September, and not to continue with the eleventh-hour re-introduction of selection. Counsel for the Secretary of State argued that the opinion of the Secretary of State was conclusive as to whether Tameside's action was unreasonable. All Parliament demanded for the lawful exercise of this power granted in subjective terms was that the Secretary of State himself form a judgment. The House of Lords rejected this argument. They held that when the exercise of a power requires the formation of a judgment which depends on the existence of certain facts, then although the evaluation of those facts is a matter for the relevant authority, the courts are entitled to inquire whether the facts exist and whether the authority in reaching its judgment has done so in accordance with the usual principles governing the exercise of discretionary powers. In the *Tameside* case the Secretary of State lost because he was unable to show that a reasonable Minister, applying the proper criteria to the circumstances, and disregarding any irrelevant considerations, would have been satisfied that Tameside were acting unreasonably.

The Courts have at their disposal a formidable armoury for investigating and controlling administrative action. When they choose not to unleash their weapons they may take three courses of action. The Court of Appeal in the *Hosenball*[126] deportation appeal frankly admitted that judicial scrutiny of matters touching on national security was extremely limited and no assistance would be given to the applicant in proving his case that the Home Secretary had misused his discretion. The Minister would not be required to disclose his reasons and no inferences would be drawn from his silence. Less admirably the court may state that although it is open to the courts to review the exercise of a subjectively framed decision there are no grounds for them to do so unless the applicant for review can advance positive evidence that the Minister did not have proper grounds to be satisfied, or form an opinion, that he was entitled to exercise his discretion.[127] The *Tameside* case was unusual because it was the Minister who applied to the court seeking aid to enforce his statutory powers. When a citizen alleges that powers have been misused the court may decide to presume that the Minister has acted properly until the contrary is proved. This attitude

[126] *R.* v. *Secretary of State for Home Affairs, ex p. Hosenball* [1977] 1 W.L.R. 766.
[127] See note 122, above.

frustrates any coherent growth in judicial enforcement of reasoned decision-making and in the absence of reasons the task of determining whether a power has been exercised lawfully is very much a matter of guesswork. Where an immigration officer's power to detain depends on the existence of certain facts, even though he had reasonable grounds for believing that the facts existed the court will, on challenge of the detention by habeas corpus or judicial review, uphold the detention only if it is satisfied that the facts did exist.[128]

If a statutory power is expressed to be exercisable only where there exist 'reasonable grounds', 'reasonable cause' or 'reasonable suspicion', the courts can properly inquire independently whether these conditions precedent were satisfied.[129] And when the Secretary of State for Education purported to give directions to a local authority in the exercise of his power to intervene if the authority had acted 'unreasonably' the House of Lords held that the courts could inquire whether there was evidence to support the Minister's finding of unreasonableness.[130]

If there is no express statutory obligation cast on the competent authority to act reasonably, the courts may nevertheless impose minimum standards of reasonableness. The Poplar councillors who voted to pay unskilled employees a minimum wage of £4 a week in the early 1920s were held to have exercised their discretion unlawfully by taking irrelevant considerations into account and failing to have regard to relevant considerations.[131] To say that they had acted unreasonably would come to the same thing. But suppose that an authority vested with a wide discretion is not deflected into the paths of irrelevancy; instead, it gives too much weight to one relevant factor and too little to others, and ends by coming to an unreasonable decision. In the *Wednesbury Corporation* case[132] a local authority, empowered to attach such conditions as it thought fit to the grant of a permit for Sunday cinema opening, imposed a condition that no child under fifteen should be admitted to a Sunday performance at all. The condition was attacked as being void for unreasonableness. The Court

---

[128]   *R.* v. *Secretary of State for the Home Department, ex p. Khawaja* [1984] A.C. 74, H.L. overruling *Zamir* v. *Secretary of State for the Home Department* [1980] A.C. 934, H.L.

[129]   *Nakkuda Ali* v. *Jayaratne* [1951] A.C. 66 at 76–7, distinguishing *Liversidge* v. *Anderson* [1942] A.C. 206.

[130]   *Secretary of State for Education and Science* v. *Tameside M.B.C.* [1977] A.C. 1014, H.L. cf. *Luby* v. *Newcastle-under-Lyme Corporation* [1965] 1 Q.B. 214.

[131]   *Roberts* v. *Hopwood* [1925] A.C. 578. See p. 413. And see *Pickwell* v. *Camden L.B.C.* [1983] 1 All E.R. 602; *R.* v. *London Transport Executive, ex p. G.L.C.* [1983] 2 All E.R. 262.

[132]   *Associated Provincial Picture Houses Ltd* v. *Wednesbury Corporation* [1948] 1 K.B. 223.

of Appeal held that it was valid; the courts should be slow to substitute their own opinion for that of the competent authority, and only if the condition were such as no reasonable body of persons could have imposed should they be prepared to pronounce it invalid. This seems to suggest that only a preposterous decision ('something overwhelming') could be successfully impugned on its merits; and a preposterous decision would in any event probably be characterized as having been made in bad faith or for an improper purpose. The test thus formulated appeared to be every bit as narrow as that adopted to determine the validity of by-laws alleged to be void for manifest unreasonableness.[133] However, cases of conditions annexed to grants of planning permission and caravan site licences show that the *Wednesbury* test of unreasonableness need not be a formality, and it has been invoked to strike down clearly unreasonable conditions.[134] But the courts are, on the whole, still chary of holding the exercise of local authority discretionary powers to be void for unreasonableness *per se*, especially if they contain a significant policy element.[135]

In *Council for Civil Service Unions* v. *Minister for the Civil Service*[136] Lord Diplock suggested that judicial review could be said to be available on three grounds (while not denying that there might be others). These were 'illegality', 'irrationality' and 'procedural impropriety'. He saw irrationality as a more appropriate term for '*Wednesbury* unreasonableness' – 'a decision which is so outrageous in its defiance of logic or of accepted moral standards that no sensible person . . . could have arrived at it'.[137]

---

[133] *Kruse* v. *Johnson* [1898] 2 Q.B. 91 at 99–100. From time to time local authority by-laws have been held invalid for manifest unreasonableness, though the test of validity may appear similar to the *Wednesbury* test. See, for example, *Parker* v. *Bournemouth Corporation* (1902) 66 J.P. 440; *Repton School Governors* v. *Repton R.D.C.* [1918] 2 K.B. 133.

[134] *Mixnam's Properties Ltd* v. *Chertsey U.D.C.* [1965] A.C. 735; *Hartnell* v. *Minister of Housing and Local Government* [1965] A.C. 1134.

[135] See, for example, *R.* v. *Barnet & Camden Rent Tribunal, ex p. Frey Investments Ltd* [1972] 2 Q.B. 372 (power to refer private tenancies to rent tribunal); *Cumings* v. *Birkenhead Corporation* [1972] Ch. 12 (allocation of pupils to secondary schools). The courts will not review the reasonableness of a Minister's decision if it requires and receives the approval of the Commons, unless both Minister and House misconstrue the Act under which it was made, or unless he deceived the House: *R.* v. *Secretary of State for the Environment, ex p. Nottinghamshire County Council* [1986] A.C. 560. But in *Tower Hamlets LBC* v. *Chetnik Developments Ltd* [1988] 1 All E.R. 961, the House of Lords held that a local authority's statutory discretion to refund overpaid rates was a power which had to be exercised according to the purpose for which it had been conferred.

[136] [1985] A.C. 374 at 410.

[137] His classification is being used in judgments: see, e.g., *R.* v. *Secretary of State for Social Services, ex p. Association of Metropolitan Authorities* [1986] 1 All E.R. 164 at 169.

Statutory exclusion of judicial control

The gradual extension of judicial control over administrative action has been demonstrated in the preceding pages. How far can Parliament limit judicial intervention in government? We are concerned in this section with direct exclusionary formulae which are generally worded 'The decision of X shall not be called into question in any court of law.' The courts will normally construe very strictly any statutory provision ousting or restricting their ordinary jurisdiction. If such a provision is reasonably capable of having more than one meaning, the meaning preserving the courts' ordinary jurisdiction will be adopted.[138] But the presumption against judicial review does not apply where the tribunal vested with exclusive jurisdiction is itself a court of law, albeit an inferior court.[139]

To some extent excluding judicial review has ceased to be a burning issue. The Tribunals and Inquiries Act 1971, s. 14, provides that with one exception any provision in an Act passed before 1 August 1958 seeking to oust the jurisdiction of the courts shall not prevent the removal of proceedings to the High Court by way of certiorari or mandamus. But by section 14(3) this provision has no effect on statutes providing for access to the High Court for a limited period (usually six weeks), and thereafter excluding judicial review. What we must consider is the potential effect of any new attempt to oust the courts' jurisdiction altogether, and whether there are any circumstances in which a decision can be challenged after a limited period of access to the High Court which had been permitted by statute had expired. A series of judicial decisions has to be analysed.

In 1956, in *Smith* v. *East Elloe R.D.C.*,[140] the House of Lords refused to allow the validity of a compulsory purchase order to be challenged when the applicant alleged bad faith in the procuring of the order. Their Lordships gave literal effect to the statutory provision that once the six weeks allowed to challenge the confirmation of the order by the Minister had expired the decision could not be questioned in any legal proceedings whatsoever. Twelve years later the House of Lords considered the case of *Anisminic Ltd* v. *Foreign Compensation Commission*.[141] The dispute arose from the agreement between the Governments of Egypt and the United Kingdom that a sum paid by Egypt to

---

[138] *Anisminic Ltd* v. *Foreign Compensation Commission* [1969] 2 A.C. 147, at p. 170.
[139] *Re Racal Communications Ltd* [1980] 2 All E.R. 634.
[140] [1956] A.C. 736.
[141] [1969] 2 A.C. 147.

provide compensation for those British companies and persons whose property had been lost or damaged in the 1956 Suez incident, and subsequent expropriations of British property by the Egyptian Government. The United Kingdom Government entrusted the distribution of compensation to the Foreign Compensation Commission and s. 4(4) of the Foreign Compensation Act provided that 'The determination by the Commission of any application made to them under this Act shall not be called into question in any court of law.'

The statutory instrument defining the powers of the Commission in relation to applications arising out of the Suez incident contained complicated and obscure provisions as to the nationality of applicants for compensation. The object was to ensure that only those of British nationality received compensation, be they the original owners of the property lost or damaged, or their successors in title. Anisminic was a British company but its property had been first sequestrated and then sold to an Egyptian organization. The Commission interpreted the statutory instrument defining proper applicants for compensation as excluding Anisminic because their successor in title was of Egyptian nationality. The House of Lords held that the Commission had misconstrued the instrument because where the original owner of the property claimed he was British the nationality of his successor in title was irrelevant. The Commission had considered a matter totally irrelevant to the questions which they had been granted jurisdiction to determine. They had embarked on an inquiry beyond the limited inquiry directed by Parliament. Accordingly they had exceeded their jurisdiction and their purported determination was invalid and not protected by the provision preventing proper determination of the Commission being questioned in the courts.

Anisminic established the basic principle that if an authority or tribunal exceeds its jurisdiction then its decision is regarded by the courts as invalid and beyond the protection of any exclusionary formula yet devised by Parliamentary draftsmen. It reinforces the importance of the distinction between error depriving a tribunal of jurisdiction and errors within the jurisdiction. Lord Denning's suggestion in *Pearlman* v. *Keepers and Governors of Harrow School*[142] that the distinction be disregarded has been firmly rejected by the Privy Council.[143] The Malaysian Industrial Relations Act 1967 provided that awards of the Industrial Court should be 'final and conclusive, and no award shall be

---

[142] [1979] Q.B. 56, at p. 70.
[143] *South East Asia Fire Bricks* v. *Non-Metallic Mineral Products Manufacturing Union* [1981] A.C. 363.

challenged, appealed against, reviewed, quashed or called into question in any court of law'. The Industrial Court's original award depended on a finding that a strike by employees did not terminate their contracts of employment. This was clearly a question which the Industrial Court had jurisdiction to determine. The Privy Council held that they had no jurisdiction to review the Industrial Court's decision on the grounds of an error of law within the jurisdiction in the face of the clear and express exclusionary formula in the governing statute.

More common now than a complete ouster of the courts' jurisdiction is the provison of a short time in which a decision may be challenged on the expiry of which the courts are excluded from reviewing the decision. In *R.* v. *Secretary of State for the Environment, ex p. Ostler*[144] there was a proposal to build an inner relief road in Boston. An inquiry took place to consider the new road in the course of which it was alleged that a secret promise had been made to an objector that access to his business would be ensured by widening a subsidiary road, Craythorn Lane. The general scheme for the trunk road was approved by the Secretary of State and a second inquiry into consequent changes to subsidiary roads was held. Mr Ostler objected because his business would be badly affected by the widening of Craythorn Lane. Later he found out about the alleged promise made at the first inquiry and sought to challenge the order concerning the trunk road made nearly two years earlier. But the Highways Act of 1959 provided that such schemes might be questioned in the High Court within six weeks of being made and thereafter should not be questioned in any legal proceedings whatsover. The Court of Appeal dismissed Mr Ostler's application for certiorari. They held that *Smith* v. *East Elloe R.D.C.* was still a good authority. *Anisminic* was distinguished on the following grounds. (1) The confirmation of a compulsory purchase order was an administrative decision, not a genuinely judicial decision as was the case in *Anisminic*. It followed that the public interest in swift and conclusive decision-making had to be considered. Six weeks were allowed to challenge the decision and, after that, action in the form of acquiring land, demolishing buildings and erecting others should not be left at the mercy of some later judicial intervention. (2) What was impugned by Mr Ostler was not the jurisdiction of the Minister to make the order but the alleged fraud or unfairness which procured the order. Lord Denning also considered it relevant that the jurisdiction of the courts was limited to six weeks and not ousted altogether.

From this survey of case-law the following guidelines can be put

[144] [1977] Q.B. 122.

forward. When a statutory provision excludes the ordinary jurisdiction of the courts it will prevent judicial review of errors of law within the jurisdiction of the authority or tribunal. If a tribunal has considered the questions entrusted to it by Parliament, and not embarked on consideration of matters outside its authority, then a mistake in its evaluation of those questions cannot be reviewed or corrected when an authority in the exercise of an administrative power, requiring swift and irrevocable action, has exercised that power within the limits set by Parliament, and its decision cannot be challenged on the grounds that the process leading up to the decision was affected by bad faith or want of natural justice. Two questions remain and allow the courts room to enlarge their jurisdiction in the face of exclusionary formulae. First, exactly what type of error deprives an authority or tribunal of jurisdiction to make a valid decision has not been conclusively decided. For example, certain judges in *Anisminic* thought a decision procured by fraud or want of natural justice was a decision outside jurisdiction. Jurisdiction was not limited simply by what matters an authority had power to decide but by an implied requirement to follow a proper procedure and to conduct oneself lawfully in exercising jurisdiction. Secondly, the well-tried device of characterizing a power as administrative or judicial enables the judges to juggle terms in order to arrive at a decision which they believe to be fair and in the public interest.

Compensation for unlawful administrative action

When an unlawful administrative decision results in the commission of an actionable wrong, a citizen suffering loss as a result of that decision may be able to claim damages[145] as well as obtaining an order to quash or declare the decision invalid. But if the decision or action taken does not fall into any category of actionable wrong recognized at common law, then no compensation is payable even though the decision may be found to be invalid and to have resulted in financial loss to individual citizens.[146] The absence of a logical theory of compensation for unlawful administrative action is one of the main defects of English administrative law.[147]

[145] See above, p. 417 and below, p. 634.
[146] See *Dunlop* v. *Woolahra Municipal Council* [1982] A.C. 158 (P.C.).
[147] See Craig (1980) 96 *L.Q.R.* 413.

Chapter 30

Judicial Review of Administrative Action: Remedies

This chapter attempts no more than a preliminary survey of the judicial remedies available against administrative bodies.[1] Remedies may be statutory or non-statutory and the practical importance of the former should not be ignored, despite the fact that only a brief mention of statutory remedies will be made in the following pages.

Statutory remedies

1   Rights of appeal to the courts. From most statutory tribunals appeals lie to the High Court (normally the Divisional Court of the Queen's Bench Division) or the Court of Appeal on points of law.
2   Statutory applications to quash, or restrain the making of, compulsory purchase and similar orders, and decisions on planning appeals, on the ground that the order or decision is *ultra vires* or that the applicant has been substantially prejudiced by non-compliance with a procedural or formal requirement on the part of the competent authorities. Applications lie to a single judge of the High Court,[2] and must be brought within a brief period, normally six weeks. The statutory procedure excludes the non-statutory grounds for challenge.

Sometimes the classes of persons and bodies entitled to lodge an appeal or bring an application to quash are specified by the Act. Unfortunately, it is more common for the Act merely to afford these rights to a 'person aggrieved', leaving it to the courts to interpret what this expression means. Until recently the courts tended to adopt a restrictive interpretation requiring that a 'person

[1] de Smith, *Judicial Review of Administrative Action* (4th edn, 1980), Part III.
[2] In practice in the Queen's Bench Division. See further, Order 94 of the Rules of the Supreme Court.

aggrieved' be some person or body whose existing legal rights had been interfered with or upon whom a new legal obligation was to be imposed.[3] Now the trend seems to be towards a more liberal policy. Loss of amenity has been held to render a householder a 'person aggrieved'.[4] An amenity society which was *permitted* by the inspector in his discretion to make representations at a public inquiry has been found to have a sufficient interest to qualify as a 'person aggrieved'.[5] In some statutory contexts, a 'person aggrieved' must clearly be given a wider meaning than usual: if a right of appeal lies from decisions of a licensing body, an unsuccessful applicant must obviously be a person aggrieved and entitled to appeal although he has not been deprived of existing legal rights by the adverse decision.[6]

3   In some contexts statutory default powers, exercisable by Ministers to enforce compliance with public duties, particularly duties imposed on local authorities, may involve applications to the courts.[7]

Application for judicial review

The main non-statutory remedies in administrative law are the prerogative writ of habeas corpus, the prerogative orders of certiorari, prohibition and mandamus,[8] the injunction, the declaration and damages. Actions for damages are touched on in the next chapter. The prerogative writ of habeas corpus remains subject to its own procedure. Until 1978 applications for the other remedies also had their own and diverse procedural rules. Combining proceedings for more than one form of relief and claiming damages in addition to the desired remedy was not always possible and was always fraught with technical hazard. Nor was the discovery of documents in the possession of a public authority available. Cross-examination of witnesses was not provided for, and if the aggrieved citizen sought compensation he was forced to institute a separate claim for damages by writ. Important reforms,

---

[3]   *Ealing Corporation* v. *Jones* [1959] 1 Q.B. 884; *Buxton* v. *Minister of Housing and Local Government* [1961] 1 Q.B. 278.

[4]   *Maurice* v. *L.C.C.* [1964] 2 Q.B. 362 (and hence entitled to lodge an appeal). See also *Att.-Gen. of the Gambia* v. *N'jie* [1961] A.C. 617 at 634; *Arsenal Football Club* v. *Smith* (*Valuation Officer*) [1979] A.C. 1, at p. 17.

[5]   *Turner* v. *Secretary of State for the Environment* (1973) 72 L.G.R. 380.

[6]   *Stepney B.C.* v. *Joffe* [1949] 1 K.B. 509.

[7]   For example, for an order of mandamus or a declaration against the defaulter. But such proceedings are rare. On the effect of default powers on the rights of *individuals* to go to court, see pp. 598–60.

[8]   On which see de Smith (1951) 11 *Camb. L.J.* 40, and op cit., App. 1.

introduced in 1978 and now embodied in section 31 of the Supreme Court Act 1981 and a revised Order 53 of the Supreme Court, provide at last for the common procedure for instituting claims for relief against public authorities.[9] An application for mandamus, prohibition or certiorari, or for a declaration or injunction in relation to public law rights, is to be made by way of an application to the High Court for judicial review.[10] The rules provide for discovery to be ordered, for cross-examination to be permitted and most importantly for a claim for compensation to be annexed to the application for review. Where a claim for damages is joined with the application for judicial review the court may award damages if satisfied that a separate claim for damages would have succeeded had it been instituted.[11] The applicant still has to establish a common-law claim for damages. The Supreme Court Act introduces no new principle of compensation for unlawful administrative action. But the applicant is at least spared the expense of two distinct sets of proceedings. The procedure also provides for substantial safeguards for the administration. Leave of the High Court must be sought before the application can proceed. The applicant must show a sufficient interest in the matter to which the application relates.[12] And he must act with speed. The Act provides that where the court considers that there has been undue delay in making an application, it may refuse to grant leave for the making of the application, or any relief sought under the application, if it considers that the granting of the relief sought would be likely to cause substantial hardship to, or substantially prejudice the rights of, any person, or if to do so would be detrimental to good administration.[13] Order 53 provides that applications have to be made promptly and in any event within *three* months from the date when the grounds for the application first arose, unless the court considers that there is a good reason for extending that period.

Finally, the award of any of the remedies to be discussed below is discretionary and the applicant must show that he has a moral as well as a legal case to be granted relief.

The reformed procedure has led to a profound change of direction in administrative law in England. The House of Lords has interpreted the provisions of Order 53 and of the Act as meaning that a claim which

[9] See generally R. J. F. Gordon, *Judicial Review: Law and Procedure* (1985); G. Aldous and J. Alder, *Applications for Judicial Review: Law and Practice* (1985).
[10] Supreme Court Act 1981, s. 31(1), (2).
[11] ibid., s. 31(4).
[12] ibid., s. 31(3).
[13] ibid., s. 31(6).

relates solely to public law rights may be pursued only by way of an application for judicial review: the general power to apply to the courts for a declaration or injunction by way of ordinary proceedings instituted by a writ is no longer available in public law claims. In *O'Reilly* v. *Mackman*[14] some prisoners alleged that they had lost remission after a disciplinary hearing which had failed to comply with the rules of natural justice. The started a claim for a declaration by way of service of writ. Proceeding by writ had two major advantages for them. First, they would not be subject to a three-month time limit, but rather the usual six-year limitation period; and secondly they would not need leave to start their action. The House of Lords struck out the action as an abuse of the process of the court. Lord Diplock said that, *as a general rule*, where a claim related to the infringement of rights protected exclusively by public law, then that claim must be brought by way of an application for judicial review. Lord Diplock said that the disadvantages to the claimant which encumbered the pre-1978 procedure for application for the prerogative orders had been swept away by the reforms of 1978 and 1981. The safeguards for good administration, particularly in relation to the need for leave, the short time limit and the discretionary nature of the availability of remedies embodied in the new procedures were not to be circumvented by claimants bringing their actions via a different route.

But what are rights protected exclusively by public law? In *O'Reilly* v. *Mackman* the claimants' rights depended entirely on the principles related to fair hearings developed in the public law domain: it was most unlikely that those rights could be asserted through actions in contract or tort. In *Cocks* v. *Thanet D.C.*[15] the plaintiff brought an action for breach of statutory duty in relation to the defendant council's failure to house him as a homeless person. His action, too, was struck out. His private law remedy for breach of statutory rights would succeed only if he could successfully challenge the refusal of the council to house him as being *ultra vires*. His claim related essentially to his right to require a discretionary decision of a public authority to be taken lawfully according to the principles developed, once again, in the public law domain. The claim for damages was subsidiary. But once the claimant is asserting essentially private rights, arising from the general law of, say, tort or contract, the fact that a public authority is the defendant will not force the claimant to rely on an application for judicial review.

[14] [1983] 2 A.C. 237; and see [1983] *Public Law* 190.
[15] [1983] 2 A.C. 286.

So in *Davy* v. *Spelthorne D.C.*[16] the plaintiff sued the defendant council for negligence. He alleged that he had suffered loss because he had relied on misleading advice from the council's planning officers in not appealing against an enforcement order in respect of the use of his premises. He did not challenge the validity of the order. The House of Lords refused to strike out his claim. They held that he did not seek to impugn any decision of the council. None of the traditional public law remedies would help him. His claim purely and simply related to the alleged negligence of the officers for whom the council was vicariously liable, and was founded in the general law of negligence. Lord Wilberforce in a forceful judgment made two points. First, a claimant could not be required to proceed by application for judicial review where none of the prerogative orders was appropriate to enforce his rights. Secondly, he stressed that, even where a public law remedy was available to the claimant, Lord Diplock in *O'Reilly* v. *Mackman* had expressed a general rule to prevent plaintiffs improperly and flagrantly evading the safeguards for good administration embodied in the procedure for judicial review. Exceptions are available to the general rule. Where issues of private rights arise and when the procedure for judicial review would cause serious procedural obstacles to the claimant, exceptions will be made.[17]

Mandamus

Mandamus, to compel the performance of a public duty, was evolved by the King's Bench early in the seventeenth century to restore persons to public offices of which they had been unlawfully deprived.[18] For the next two hundred years or more it enjoyed vast popularity as a means of prodding inert and inept officials, magistrates and borough corporations into fulfilment of their public obligations. A synopsis of the case law, published in 1848, ran to 252 pages. But its importance was already dwindling as local government was reformed; and it shrivelled as new statutory remedies by way of appeal, complaint or objection to government Departments, tribunals or courts, were introduced. For mandamus was always an 'extraordinary' remedy, awarded only if no alternative remedy was equally convenient or effective.

However, it will still lie in quite a wide range of situations. It may be

---

[16] [1984] A.C. 262; see [1984] *Public Law* 16, and *Wandsworth L.B.C.* v. *Winder* [1985] A.C. 461; *An Bord Bainne Co-operative Ltd* (*Irish Dairy Board*) v. *Milk Marketing Board, The Times*, 22 May 1984. C.A.

[17] See *Wandsworth L.B.C.* v. *Winder* [1985] A.C. 461.

[18] The leading case is *Bagg*'s case (1615) 11 Co. Rep. 93b.

issued to compel a tribunal or a Minister or a local authority to entertain an appeal or application in respect of which they have wrongfully declined jurisdiction. It will lie to compel a body to carry out a duty to give reasons for a decision or to give adequate reasons; and to require a local authority to produce minutes and accounts for inspection. If an authority required to exercise a discretion in a matter fails to consider it on its merits because it has improperly sub-delegated its powers or acted under dictation or fettered its own discretion by unauthorized promises or a rigid self-imposed rule, mandamus will lie. It will also lie to order an authority which has abused its statutory discretion (for example, by rejecting an application on the basis of legally irrelevant considerations) to hear and determine the matter according to law: see *Padfield*'s case.[19] Although on an application for mandamus, the courts are not supposed to direct the competent authority *how* to exercise its jurisdiction or discretion (for example, to issue a licence to X), they may in effect achieve this result by holding that only one avenue of approach to a particular case is legally permissible.[20]

Mandamus will not lie against the Crown, nor will it lie to a Crown servant to order the performance of a duty owed *only* to the Crown; but it will lie to a Minister to carry out a duty in the performance of which a member of the public has a substantial personal interest.

There are important limitations on its availability. It cannot be obtained (except in some instances on the application of a Minister) to compel a local authority to provide a public service or a board running a nationalized industry to discharge its primary duties. The courts might refuse to issue such an order on a number of different grounds – that enforcement could not be adequately supervised; that the matter is non-justiciable because judicial review has been expressly excluded or because the duty is merely descriptive of a general administrative function; that there are adequate alternative remedies.

Who may apply for mandamus? In other words, who has *locus standi*? Section 31(3) of the Supreme Court Act 1981 enacts that the court shall not grant leave to make an application for judicial review unless it considers that the applicant has a sufficient interest in the matter to which the application relates. *Locus standi* to apply for mandamus has been equated with *locus standi* to apply for certiorari and prohibition in *R.* v. *I.R.C., ex p. National Federation of Self-*

[19] *Padfield* v. *Minister of Agriculture* [1968] A.C. 997; see above, p. 575.
[20] See *R.* v. *Derby JJ., ex p. Kooner* [1971] 1 Q.B. 147 (where 'may' was treated as meaning 'must'). See also *R.* v. *Home Secretary, ex p. Phansopkar* [1976] Q.B. 606 (effect of court's order was to force the Home Office to reconsider procedure concerning the admission to the United Kingdom of wives of patrials).

Employed and Small Businesses Ltd.[21] The Revenue reached an agreement with casual workers on Fleet Street that they would be granted an amnesty in respect of past tax avoidance in return for agreement to arrangements to ensure that tax could be properly collected from them in the future. The National Federation of the Self- Employed objected to such preferential treatment and in an application for judicial review sought a declaration that the Revenue had acted unlawfully and mandamus to compel the Revenue to do their duty according to law and collect the tax owing. The Court of Appeal (Lawton L.J. dissenting) held that as taxpayers the Federation had a genuine grievance in the unfairness to them caused by the Revenue allowing other taxpayers to be free of part of the normal burden of taxation. The House of Lords held that no taxpayer or group of taxpayers had *locus standi* to ask the court to investigate the affairs of other taxpayers or to complain that other taxpayers had been over or under assessed. The existence of sufficient interest to apply for mandamus depended on evidence of an alleged breach of duty or illegality which when related to the position of the claimant made it clear that he had an *individual* interest to pursue and protect. This test is wider than that laid down in some earlier cases that the applicant must have a specific legal right to the performance of the duty. It may be assumed that all earlier cases accepting *locus standi* remain authoritative, but some denying it may have to be reconsidered in the light of the House of Lords' decision. The House of Lords agreed that on all applications for judicial review standing and merits may have to be considered together. Under the Supreme Court Act, the court will ordinarily hear applications for leave *ex parte*. The applicant may make a *prima facie* case for leave. At the later hearing the court will consider the whole legal and factual context, including the nature of the duty and the breach in order to decide whether the applicant has a sufficient interest in the matter.

The applicant for mandamus must have demanded performance and been met by a wrongful refusal, communicated directly or by conduct evincing an intention not to comply or a failure to understand what compliance means.

There are several discretionary bars to the award of the order. Alternative remedies, unreasonable delay in making an application, the absence of any useful purpose in issuing a judicial command, and the unacceptable motives of the applicant are among the most common. For example, the Commissioners of Customs and Excise had allowed

---

[21] [1982] A.C. 617.

bookmakers to pay a new and heavy licensing duty on betting premises by monthly instalments. But the Finance Act 1969 had provided that the tax was to be paid in one sum or by two half-yearly instalments. There was no statutory authority for the concession made by the Commissioners acting under the responsible Minister's instructions. Two bookmakers who had paid their duties in accordance with the Act applied for mandamus to compel the Commissioners to administer the Act according to law. The court dismissed the application.[22] Even assuming that the applicants had *prima facie* a sufficient legal interest to maintain the proceedings, their ulterior purpose was to put less affluent competitors out of business, and this was not a purpose for which mandamus should be granted for non-compliance with this statutory obligation.

Certiorari and prohibition

Certiorari will issue to quash, and prohibition to prevent, an order or decision on any of the following grounds.

1 Excess or want of jurisdiction. If part of an impugned order is quite distinct and severable from the rest of the order, the invalid part may be quashed, leaving the remainder intact.
2 Breach of the rules of natural justice or of the duty to act fairly.
3 Error of law on the face of the record.
4 Fraud, perjury or duress in procuring a decision.

Certiorari has become less important in administrative law because of the extension of alternative remedies. But within its own field it has been fortified by the revival of the concept of review for error of law on the face of the record, by the statutory enlargement of the 'record', by the extension of duties to give reasons for decisions and by the nullification of statutory formulae purporting to exclude judicial review.

In the *Electricity Commissioners* case Atkin L.J. said[23] that certiorari and prohibition may issue to 'any body of persons having legal authority to determine questions affecting the rights of subjects, and having the duty to act judicially . . .'

A 'body of persons' included one person – for example, a Minister. 'Legal authority' was generally understood to mean authority derived from statute or royal charter. In 1967, however, it was held[24] that

---

[22] *R. v. Customs and Excise Commissioners, ex p. Cook* [1970] 1 W.L.R. 450.
[23] *R. v. Electricity Commissioners* [1924] 1 K.B. 171 at 204–5.
[24] *R. v. Criminal Injuries Compensation Board, ex p. Lain* [1967] 2 Q.B. 864.

certiorari would lie to a judicial-type body (the Criminal Injuries Compensation Board) fulfilling public functions but created by purely administrative action.[25] Decisions by a *private* non-statutory tribunal (for example, the committee of a club or trade union) are challengeable not by certiorari but by injunctions and declarations.[26]

The courts in the past sometimes refused to award certiorari and prohibition against bodies with no power to make a final decision; such bodies are not 'determining questions'.[27] And a narrow view of questions 'affecting rights' was taken. A licence was not a right even though its revocation resulted in a man losing his livelihood.[28] The qualification that the body must be under a duty to 'act judicially' was used to exclude decisions characterized as administrative in nature.[29] The modern approach is to examine the decision-making process and determine whether the body deciding any question, even a preliminary matter,[30] which affects the rights, legitimate interests or expectations of citizens is required to act fairly in their dealings with affected persons.[31] If they are so required and fail to meet the requisite standard of fairness which their kind of decision-making of its nature demands, then certiorari will issue to quash their decision. The duty to act fairly as much as the rules of natural justice is now enforced by the orders of certiorari and prohibition.[32]

The requirement to 'act judicially' is no longer a prerequiaite to control of an authority by certiorari. In *Ridge* v. *Baldwin*[33] Lord Reid found that the inclusion of a duty to 'act judicially' in the conditions precedent for the award of the order of certiorari was itself devoid of authority. Excess of jurisdiction, error of law on the face of the record or improper procuration of a decision may form grounds for an order of certiorari against any public authority determining questions affecting the rights of subjects. Certiorari lay to quash a decision of a local authority attaching *ultra vires* conditions to a grant of planning

---

[25] Though the Board is financed out of moneys provided by Parliament under the Appropriation Act. It was placed on a statutory basis by the Criminal Justice Act 1988, Part VII.

[26] See, e.g. *R.* v. *City Takeover Panel, ex p. Datafin plc* [1987] 2 W.L.R. 699.

[27] *Jayawardne* v. *Silva* [1970] 1 W.L.R. 1365.

[28] *Nakudda Ali* v. *Jayaratne* [1951] A.C. 66 at p. 78.

[29] *R.* v. *Metropolitan Police Commissioner, ex p. Parker* [1953] 1 W.L.R. 1150.

[30] See *R.* v. *Kent Police Authority, ex p. Godden* [1971] 2 Q.B. 662.

[31] *R.* v *Hull Prison Board of Visitors, ex p. St Germain* [1979] Q.B. 425; *O'Reilly* v. *Mackman* [1983] 2 A.C. 237, H.L.; *Att.-Gen. of Hong Kong* v. *Ng Yuen Shiu* [1983] 2 A.C. 629 (P.C.); *R.* v. *Greater Manchester Coroner, ex p. Tal* [1985] Q.B. 67.

[32] *R.* v. *Birmingham City Justice* [1970] 1 W.L.R. 1428; *R.* v. *Liverpool Corporation, ex p. Liverpool Taxi Fleet Operators' Association* [1972] 2 Q.B. 299.

[33] [1964] A.C. 40, at pp. 71–9.

permission.[34] In that case Lord Widgery C.J. went so far as to say that he saw 'no general legal inhibition on the use of such orders, although no doubt they must be exercised only in the clearest cases and with a good deal of care on the part of the court'.[35] Whether public policy will be served by making an order of certiorari to control the proceedings of a particular authority is expressly considered by judges dealing with applications for certiorari.[36] It is to be hoped that if a case arises when certiorari should *not* issue on the grounds that it is inappropriate to extend judicial intervention into the relevant part of the administrative process, this will be openly admitted and the subterfuge of retreating back to a narrow interpretation of the governing dictum of Atkin L.J. in the *Electricity Commissioners* case be avoided.

The courts, before application for judicial review was introduced, took a liberal view of *locus standi* in relation to certiorari. Any person with a substantial personal interest to vindicate, and members of a local community who have a special grievance by virtue of their membership of that community, had a sufficient interest to challenge a decision affecting them by way of certiorari. In *R. v. G.L.C., ex p. Blackburn*[37] the Court of Appeal held that Mr and Mrs Blackburn had a sufficient interest as citizens of London and ratepayers to apply for prohibition to prevent the exhibition of allegedly pornographic films. Lord Denning M.R. seemed to abandon any precise definition of *locus standi* in favour of the principle that any person offended or injured by a decision on the part of a public authority should have access to the courts who 'in their discretion can grant whatever remedy is appropriate'. With the enactment of the Supreme Court Act 1981, standing for certiorari will be affected only to the extent mentioned when considering *locus standi* for mandamus.[38]

The principles governing the discretion of the court to award certiorari have partly crystallized. The courts exercise discretion in practice when deciding whether the applicant had *locus standi*. An application may be refused for waiver of or acquiescence in an excess of jurisdiction or a breach of natural justice; or (exceptionally) because there is a more appropriate alternative remedy; or because the applicant had delayed unreasonably before instituting the proceedings, the normal time limit being three months. The Aston University students who had been denied natural justice lost their case on the

[34] *R. v. Hillingdon L.B.C., ex p. Royco Homes Ltd* [1974] Q.B. 720, at p. 728.
[35] Ibid., at p. 728.
[36] *R. v. Hull Prison Board of Visitors* (note 31, above).
[37] [1976] 1 W.L.R. 550.
[38] See p. 589, above.

ground of delay.[39] Certiorari may also be refused because to award it would serve no useful purpose, or because of the applicant's unreasonable behaviour.[40]

Prohibition does not call for special discussion. In administrative law it will lie to the same bodies as certiorari, and on similar grounds,[41] though a case for prohibition for error of law on the face of the record could hardly ever arise because by the time the error had become apparent the order would nearly always be final. Occasionally certiorari and prohibition may be awarded in conjunction – certiorari to quash a decision already taken by a tribunal and prohibition to prevent the tribunal from proceeding or continuing to entertain other like cases outside its jurisdiction.[42]

Injunction

Injunctions may be prohibitory (to restrain the commission or continuance of unlawful conduct) or mandatory (to compel the performance of a duty). Mandatory injunctions are granted sparingly; and in administrative law they are of little practical importance.[43] An interim or interlocutory injunction may be awarded as a matter of urgency *ex parte* (on the strength of the plaintiff's representation alone) to restrain the commission or repetition of an allegedly wrongful act which is liable to do very serious harm, pending a full hearing of the case.

The injunction is essentially a discretionary private law remedy, awarded where damages would not be a sufficient form of redress. It is also obtainable against public authorities and officials, other than the Crown and Crown servants acting in that behalf,[44] not only for actionable wrongs (such as trespasses or nuisances) but also to restrain acts which are *ultra vires* but give no right of action for damages. Who may sue? Local authorities are now entitled to take proceedings on behalf of the local community.[45] A private individual can sue to

---

[39] R. v. *Aston University Senate, ex p. Roffey* [1969] 2 Q.B. 538. And see R. v. *Herrod, ex p. Leeds City Council* [1976] Q.B. 540.

[40] *Glynn* v. *University of Keele* [1971] 1 W.L.R. 223.

[41] See especially the *Godden* case, note 30; R. v. *Board of Visitors of Dartmoor Prison, ex p. Smith* [1987] Q.B. 106 (appeal dismissed).

[42] R. v. *Paddington & St Marylebone Rent Tribunal* [1949] 1 K.B. 666.

[43] See, for example, *Att.-Gen.* v. *Colchester Corporation* [1955] 2 Q.B. 207 (no mandatory injunction to compel continued operation of ferry service); and see generally *Glossop* v. *Heston and Isleworth Local Board* (1879) 12 Ch. D. 102. See, however, *Ghani* v. *Jones* [1970] 1 Q.B. 693 (mandatory order to police to return wrongfully detained Pakistani passports).

[44] See Crown Proceedings Act 1947, s. 21, for this exception; pp. 634–6, below.

[45] Local Government Act 1972, s. 222, and see *Solihull M.B.C.* v. *Maxfern Ltd* [1977] 1 W.L.R. 127; *Stoke-on-Trent City Council* v. *B & Q Ltd* [1984] A.C. 754.

restrain 'a public wrong' if his own legal rights have been encroached upon, or are threatened by the defendant, and perhaps in exceptional circumstances when the individual is threatened with special damage over and above that which the 'wrong' inflicts on the rest of the public.[46] In all other cases only the Attorney-General acting in his sole discretion can institute proceedings to vindicate public rights. The citizen aggrieved by a public wrong must seek the Attorney-General's consent, obtain his *fiat*, to the proceedings which are then conducted in the Attorney-General's name. These actions are known as 'relator' actions and effectively the citizen, the 'relator', is in control of the proceedings, for having given his consent the Attorney-General takes little active part in the proceedings. Nevertheless if he refuses to consent to a 'relator' action the citizen cannot proceed. In *Gouriet* v. *Union of Post Office Workers*[47] Mr Gouriet had sought the Attorney-General's consent to proceedings for an injunction to restrain the Union of Post Office Workers from breaking the law by blacking mail from this country to South Africa. The Attorney-General refused. Mr Gouriet went to court asserting that the Attorney-General had acted unlawfully in refusing his consent and/or he was entitled to proceed for an injunction in his own right. There was never any suggestion that Mr Gouriet had any special interest in the free passage of mail or would suffer any special damage by the blacking. In the Court of Appeal Mr Gouriet was triumphant. The House of Lords threw out his case. Their decision established that (1) the courts would not question the discretionary decision of the Attorney-General whether or not to consent to a 'relator' action, and (2) in no circumstances could a citizen whose sole standing in the matter was his concern as a member of the public that a breach of the criminal law was threatened proceed with an action for an injunction except by way of a 'relator' action.

The Attorney-General himself may sue for an injunction to restrain repeated breaches of regulatory legislation where the sanctions of the criminal law have proved inadequate.[48] He has also been awarded injunctions against individuals breaking or proposing to break the criminal law where the matter is very urgent, notwithstanding that the criminal courts have not yet dealt with the issue.[49] The House of Lords in *Gouriet* said that this was a power which should be exercised only in exceptional cases and for this reason was entrusted to the Attorney-

[46] *Boyce* v. *Paddington Corporation* [1903] 1 Ch. 109.
[47] [1978] A.C. 435.
[48] *Att.-Gen.* v. *Harris* [1961] 1 Q.B. 74 (Manchester flower-seller repeatedly breaking local Act but preferring to pay fines rather than desisting).
[49] *Att.-Gen.* v. *Chaudry* [1971] 1 W.L.R. 1614 (breach of fire safety law).

General, who was obliged to consider the public interest as a whole, and would not be afforded to individuals who might have genuine grievance at the prospect of criminal behaviour by others but be unable to judge what action would best serve the national interest. *Gouriet* was decided before application for judicial review was introduced. The effect of the Supreme Court Act 1981 will be examined in the next section on the declaration.

Declaration [50]

The declaratory judgment is basically a twentieth-century judicial remedy and has come to be used for a great variety of purposes in public and private law.[51] Declarations can be awarded in almost every situation where an injunction will lie – the most important exception is that interim relief cannot be granted by way of a declaration – and they extend to a number of situations where an injunction would be inappropriate (for example, because there is nothing to prohibit) or could not be obtained for other reasons (for example, because the prospective defendant was the Crown).

Where civil proceedings in private law for a declaration (or an injunction) are appropriately brought without the need to apply for judicial review under the Supreme Court Act 1981,[52] the pre-Act rules about *locus standi* will continue to apply. Infringement of a private right or special damage flowing from the infringement of a public right has to be proved.[53] Those rules are of greatly reduced importance in administrative law now that application for judicial review is normally required in public law, even where an injunction or declaration is sought.[54] In the *I.R.C.* case the House of Lords interpreted the *Gouriet* case as one solely in private law, so that it was not binding in the *I.R.C.* case, where an application for judicial review was required. In effect the *I.R.C.* case must be taken as deciding that on an application for judicial review, if the applicant proves sufficient interest to seek a prerogative order then an injunction or declaration may be granted even though the common-law requirements about standing for an injunction or declaration would not have been met.

The declaration is also a discretionary remedy; thus, the courts may

[50] See de Smith, op. cit., ch. 10.
[51] See I. Zamir, *The Declaratory Judgment* (1962).
[52] See p. 585, above.
[53] *Gouriet* v. *Union of Post Office Workers* [1978] A.C. 435; *Barrs* v. *Bethell* [1982] 1 All E.R. 186.
[54] See p. 586, above.

refuse a declaration if its award would serve no useful purpose or if there are more appropriate alternative remedies.[55] Subject to those cautionary reservations, there are few limits to the potential scope of declaratory relief in public law. For example, declarations can be obtained that administrative orders or notices directly affecting the plaintiff are invalid;[56] that conditions annexed to a grant of planning permission are invalid;[57] that one's products are exempt from tax;[58] that one enjoying a special statutory or public[59] status has been invalidly dismissed[60] or suspended[61] (though the courts will be very reluctant to make a declaration entitling an ordinary employee to reinstatement[62]); and that the decision of a tribunal is invalid for excess of jurisdiction[63] or breach of natural justice[64] or (possibly) that it is wrong in law, provided at least that the error is patent and the tribunal has power to rescind its determination.[65] A bare declaration that natural justice had not been observed where no other relief is asked for, and no decision exists to be quashed, will be granted only in the most exceptional circumstances.[66] The declaration does not, however, have to be accompanied by a claim for consequential relief (for example damages), nor is it necessary that such relief be claimable at all. Indeed, it does not have to be a declaration of invalidity. A person may obtain a declaration as to his nationality or marital status. Declarations may be sought by one public authority to resolve a legal dispute with another (for example, as to financial obligations), or by a

---

[55] See *Maxwell* v. *Department of Trade and Industry* [1974] Q.B. 523.

[56] *Dyson* v. *Att.-Gen.* [1911] 1 K.B. 410 (court had jurisdiction to declare that a tax form requiring submission of certain particulars under threat of a penalty was *ultra vires*). This was the effective starting-point for the rise of the declaratory judgment in administrative law. *Gillick* v. *West Norfolk and Wisbech A.H.A.* [1986] A.C. 112 (departmental circular based on incorrect interpretation of the law).

[57] *Hall & Co.* v. *Shoreham-by-Sea U.D.C.* [1964] 1 W.L.R. 240.

[58] *Sebel Products Ltd* v. *Customs and Excise Commissioners* [1949] Ch. 409.

[59] *Ridge* v. *Baldwin* [1964] A.C. 40 (chief constable); *Malloch* v. *Aberdeen Corporation* [1971] 1 W.L.R. 1578.

[60] *Vine* v. *National Dock Labour Board* [1957] A.C. 488 (dock labourer); *Hanson* v. *Radcliffe U.D.C.* [1922] 2 Ch. 490 (schoolteacher).

[61] *Barnard* v. *National Dock Labour Board* [1953] 2 Q.B. 18.

[62] See, for example, *Pillai* v. *Singapore City Council* [1968] 1 W.L.R. 1278. For an exceptional case, see *Hill* v. *Parsons (C.A.) & Co.* [1972] Ch. 305.

[63] For example, *Anisminic Ltd* v. *Foreign Compensation Commission* [1969] 2 A.C. 147.

[64] For example, *Cooper* v. *Wilson* [1937] 2 K.B. 309. Many decisions of non-statutory domestic tribunals have been declared invalid on this ground.

[65] This is a difficult question, still unresolved. See especially *Healey* v. *Minister of Health* [1955] 1 Q.B. 221. The main difficulty lies in the principle that an erroneous determination *within* jurisdiction is *not* invalid but binding till properly set aside. See also *Punton* v. *Ministry of Pensions and National Insurance* (No. 2) [1964] 1 W.L.R. 226.

[66] See *Maxwell*'s case (note 55, above).

public authority wishing to obtain a judicial pronouncement as to the scope of its own powers or duties before it acts in relation to a specific matter.[67] And a declaration may be awarded as to the true construction of a statute or other legal document which is the subject of a controversy between parties.

Declarations granted by the courts may be formulated in a number of different ways to meet the particular circumstances of a case. This is yet another characteristic of the flexibility of declaratory judgments. Where a declaration is sought that a tribunal has as a result of an error of law made a perverse determination of the question entrusted to its jurisdiction, the court has a discretionary power to do more than quash the determination as a nullity: it may issue a positive declaration of the applicant's rights. This power is only to be exercised in the clearest of cases as the courts are wary of cutting down the jurisdiction of inferior tribunals.[68]

Effect of alternative remedies

Reference has been made to the exclusion of judicial remedies in the High Court by special statutory formulae or the provision of alternative remedies. The latter type of exclusion is still important. Despite the presumption against excluding the right of access to the courts for the determination of civil rights and obligations, there is a well-known principle that the *original* jurisdiction of the superior courts is ousted where a statute creates a *new* legal right or obligation and *that same Act* prescribes a specific method for its enforcement.[69] The method of enforcement may be by taking proceedings in an inferior court or tribunal[70] or by complaint or appeal to an administrative authority or by the potential exercise of administrative default powers.[71] Particularly in declaratory proceedings or on applications for mandamus, persons attempting to obtain judicial declarations of their rights or the

---

[67] See, for example, *Central Electricity Generating Board* v. *Jennaway* [1959] 1 W.L.R. 937, where the Board obtained a ruling on the question whether it had power (disputed by the landowner) to erect lines over private property. See also *C.E.G.B.* v. *Dunning* [1970] Ch. 643.

[68] *Barty-King* v. *Ministry of Defence* [1979] 2 All E.R. 80.

[69] *Barraclough* v. *Brown* [1897] A.C. 615.

[70] For example, an income tax tribunal (*Inland Revenue Commissioners* v. *Pearlberg* [1953] 1 W.L.R. 331), or an industrial tribunal (*Road Transport Industry Board* v. *Wyatt (Haulage) Ltd* [1972] 3 All E.R. 913). See also *Department of Health and Social Security* v. *Walker Dean Walker Ltd* [1970] 2 Q.B. 74.

[71] For example, complaints about alleged breaches of duty by education authorities: *Cumings* v. *Birkenhead Corporation* [1972] Ch. 12.

enforcement of public duties have often found the courts refusing to entertain their claims for these reasons. (In Scots law it seems that the courts are more resistant to this kind of argument.) But if it is possible to hold that the alternative remedy is only optional – for example, because *pre-existing* legal rights are in issue [72] or because the prescribed remedy is inadequate or less convenient [73] or if there is inordinate delay in the domestic disciplinary process [74] or if the interests of justice call for intervention by the High Court [75] – the result may be different. Moreover, even if the courts hold that their *original* jurisdiction to determine the issue in the first instance has been excluded, they can still exercise a *supervisory* jurisdiction after the appointed body or tribunal has acted, so as to see that the law has been duly observed. In exercising that supervisory jurisdiction the court will sometimes go on to declare what the correct decision is or should have been.[76] The courts will intervene in appropriate cases to quash decisions taken *ultra vires* by the original authority even though an alternative remedy exists to correct mistaken decisions taken within the limits of that authority's powers. Certiorari, for example, lay to quash a decision of a planning authority to grant planning permission subject to invalid conditions despite the statutory system of appeals in the Town and Country Planning Act 1971.[77] On the other hand the existence of a comprehensive appeals system provided by statute has led the courts to declare that judicial review should not be available to immigrants [78] or to applicants for social security [79] who had exhausted their statutory rights of appeal. The existence of such rights will, therefore, usually preclude judicial review.[80] And the House of Lords has said that leave to apply for judicial review should be granted only sparingly when Parliament has intended that a public body be the judge of matters of

[72] *Pyx Granite Co.* v. *Ministry of Housing and Local Government* [1960] A.C. 260 (property rights affected by planning legislation).

[73] *Ealing L.B.C.* v. *Race Relations Board* [1972] A.C. 342 (council could test legality of its housing policies in High Court instead of waiting to be sued by Race Relations Board in county court).

[74] *R.* v. *Chief Constable of Merseyside Police, ex p. Calveley* [1986] Q.B. 424.

[75] *Enderby Town F.C. Ltd* v. *Football Association Ltd* [1971] Ch. 591 (dicta) (High Court could give ruling on difficult and important point of law).

[76] *Cooper* v. *Wilson* [1937] 2 K.B. 309 and the *Anisminic* case [1969] 2 A.C. 147 (declarations as to plaintiff's rights consequential on declaration that decision of tribunal was void); *Barty-King* v. *Ministry of Defence* (above). And see *R.* v. *Sheffield C.C.* (1978) 77 L.G.R. 26; *Meade* v. *Haringey L.B.C.* [1979] 1 W.L.R. 637.

[77] *R.* v. *Hillingdon L.B.C.* [1974] Q.B. 720.

[78] *R.* v. *Secretary of State for the Home Department, ex p. Swati* [1986] 1 W.L.R. 477.

[79] *R.* v. *Secretary of State for Social Services, ex p. Connolly* [1986] 1 W.L.R. 421.

[80] *R.* v. *Inland Revenue Commissioners, ex p. Preston* [1985] A.C. 835.

fact, for to do otherwise could lead to the courts' usurpation of that function. So, in *R.* v. *Secretary of State for the Environment, ex p. Puhlhofer* [81] the applicants were denied leave as the local authority had properly decided that the applicants were not homeless. (The sympathy expressed by the courts for would-be immigrants, seekers after social security and of homes does not detract from the fact that it is precisely such groups who need the greatest measure of protection which the courts can allow.)

[81] [1986] A.C. 484.

Chapter 31

Tribunals and Inquiries

In general [1]

In 1957 the Report of the Franks Committee on Administrative
Tribunals and Enquiries went a long way to remove certain misconcep-
tions contained in the Report of the Committee on Ministers' Powers
which had been published twenty-five years earlier.[2] By 1957 statutory
tribunals appointed by Ministers had proliferated. The Committee like
its predecessor did indeed prefer to see judicial functions vested in the
courts rather than special tribunals, and in special tribunals rather than
in Ministers. However, it did not label special tribunals as 'Ministerial
tribunals'. It insisted that tribunals were not 'appendages of Government Departments'. It considered that tribunals 'should properly be
regarded as machinery provided by Parliament for adjudication rather
than as part of the machinery of administration',[3] and it made detailed
proposals designed to integrate them more closely with the general
judicial system of the country. It drew a sharp distinction between
'administrative' adjudication, on the one hand, and discretionary
decisions reached by Ministers following a local inquiry, on the other.
Its proposals for reforming procedures involving inquiries in matters
affecting the regulation of land use were radical but far better informed

[1] The best general review is R. M. Jackson's *Machinery of Justice in England* (7th edn,
1977), ch. 6. The Report of the Committee on Administrative Tribunals and Enquiries
(the Franks Committee (Cmnd 218 (1957)), is prescribed reading. The published Minutes
of Evidence of the Committee also contain a wealth of information. See also the
Tribunals and Inquiries Act 1971 and any of the Annual Reports of the Council on
Tribunals (HMSO). See further R. E. Wraith and P. G. Hutchesson, *Administrative
Tribunals* (1973); G. Ganz, *Administrative Procedures* (1974), ch. 4; J. A. Farmer,
Tribunals and Government (1974); J. Bowers (ed.), *Tribunals: Practice and Procedure*
(1985).
[2] Cmd 4060 (1932).
[3] Cmnd 218 (1957), § 40.

and more realistic than those of the 1932 Committee. Its detailed recommendations were too persuasive to be ignored, and most of them have been implemented. Today no reasonably well-read student has any excuse for confusing tribunals with inquiries. Whitehall's terrible twins are neither terrible nor twins.

The Franks Committee itself was an outstanding example of a particular type of public inquiry. Its members were appointed by the Lord Chancellor, not under statutory authority but in virtue of the prerogative. They were judges, former high-ranking civil servants, practising lawyers, leading academics, trade unionists, elder statesmen, active politicians. It was directed to inquire into and make recommendations on matters raising broad issues of public policy. It sat in public to receive oral evidence from officials and others; it obtained a number of written memoranda; it accumulated and published a mass of factual information, much of which had not previously been divulged to the public; it was a new clearing-house for informed opinion and original ideas. Its reports stimulated public debate and refertilized official thinking. In substance it fulfilled the role of a Royal Commission (the members of which are appointed by Her Majesty on the Prime Minister's advice) and unlike so many Royal Commissions, its recommendations were not disregarded.[4]

Public inquiries are basically instruments of government[5] (using the term 'government' in the broadest sense) or Parliament. As instruments of Parliament, or a House of Parliament, their role may be to investigate an alleged public scandal, or a national disaster such as the Aberfan catastrophe. Upon a resolution of both Houses, a 'tribunal' headed by a superior judge may be appointed under the Tribunals of Inquiry (Evidence) Act 1921.[6] The practice of setting up a select committee of the House of Commons to inquire into such a matter fell into disuse after the partisan report and debate on the Marconi scandal in 1913.

---

[4] The appointment of a Royal Commission is sometimes prompted by a Government's desire to avoid making a decision on an awkward question. The matter can be shelved till the Commission has reported; the Government may then spend several months formulating its own reactions to the recommendations, and may find itself supplied with new reasons why nothing of importance should or could be done. See T. J. Cartwright, *Royal Commissions and Departmental Committees in Britain* (1975).

[5] See R. E. Wraith and G. B. Lamb, *Public Inquiries as an Instrument of Government* (1971) – the fullest study of the subject.

[6] cf. G. W. Keeton, *Trial by Tribunal* (1960); and the report of the Royal Commission on Tribunals of Inquiry, Cmnd 3121 (1966) suggesting procedural reforms, which the Government accepted: Cmnd 5313 (1973). So far no such reforms have been enacted. For the controversial Vehicle and General Inquiry (Report, H.C. 133 (1971–2)) see p. 186. These tribunals (unlike most of the other types of inquisitorial bodies) have powers to subpoena witnesses and to require the production of documents.

There are other alternatives. Covert official telephone tapping, security leaks, 'D' Notices, interrogation techniques in Northern Ireland, the use made by former Ministers of 'confidential' information for their memoirs and the lessons to be drawn from the Falklands conflict have all led to the appointment by the Prime Minister of *ad hoc* committees of Privy Councillors to inquire and report; the outcome has sometimes been embarrassing to the Government. Lord Denning investigated aspects of the Profumo affair.[7] Major security leaks are now referred to a Security Commission under a superior judge. Another non-statutory technique, commonly employed, is for Ministers to appoint a departmental or interdepartmental committee of inquiry into a particular issue – for example, section 2 of the Official Secrets Act 1911,[8] and the fertilization of human embryos.[9] Again, a Minister may appoint a committee or an independent person to inquire into serious complaints about the conduct of officials. The Crichel Down inquiry, conducted by a Q.C., was such a case.[10] The publication of the Report led to the censure and transfer of some officials, to the resignation of the Minister of Agriculture on his own initiative, and indirectly to the appointment of the Franks Committee (from whose terms of reference the Crichel Down type of situation was, nevertheless, excluded).

Other types of formal inquiry may be held under statutory authority to investigate allegations of suspicions of malpractice or culpable negligence or organizational deficiencies – for example, an inquiry by Department of Trade and Industry inspectors into the affairs of a company; or an inquiry into the causes of an aircraft, shipping, railway or mine disaster or a factory accident; or a military 'court of inquiry' into an untoward incident that requires special investigation; or an inquiry into complaints against police officers.

The common features of these inquiries are (i) that the persons

---

[7] For his report, see Cmnd 2152 (1963).

[8] For the second Franks Report (Cmnd 5104 (1972)), see ch. 25. The first Franks Committee was also, in a sense, a departmental committee, though the Lord Chancellor, who appointed it, occupies a kind of 'crossbench' position.

[9] The Warnock Committee: see Cmnd 9314 (1984).

[10] See Cmnd 9176, 9220 (1954); Griffith (1955) 18 *Mod. L. Rev.* 557, (1987) 1 *Contemporary Record* 35; Chester (1954) 32 *Public Administration* 389. Crichel Down had been compulsorily acquired by the Air Ministry as a bombing range. After the war it was handed back to the civil authorities. Lieut.-Commander Marten, the son-in-law of the former owner, wished to buy it or alternatively to become the tenant farmer of the area. The civil servants concerned decided to re-equip the estate, to let it to another tenant, and not to accede to Marten's requests, but failed to keep him properly informed and created false impressions in his mind. Marten pursued his grievance through political channels. The procedure for dealing with the disposition of such land was not regulated by statutory rules.

conducting them are expected to hold hearings and ascertain facts about specified matters of public concern and (ii) that they do not make *decisions*, though their findings and recommendations may be a foundation for decisions by others, including decisions to institute legal proceedings. Indeed, in some situations a finding of culpability, or of a *prima facie* case of culpability, may be a necessary condition for the institution or continuance of such proceedings. But the fact that the investigating body may be called a 'court' or 'tribunal' does not endow it with the characteristic power of a judicial body to make decisions. On the other hand, an inquisitorial body may exceptionally be endowed with such powers. The verdict of a coroner's inquest in a case of homicide may assert that X was legally culpable but does not amount to a conviction though it may be the foundation of criminal proceedings against X; a verdict that Y committed suicide does, however, have binding legal effect; and so does a verdict that Z, who has found ancient precious coins, is legally entitled to them because they do not come within the definition of treasure trove.[11] Inspectors conducting inquiries in town planning law are generally restricted to finding and reporting on facts, and recommending a decision to be taken by or on behalf of the Minister; since 1968, however, power to make decisions in consequence of certain types of inquiries has been delegated by the Minister to the inspectors themselves.[12] In these few intermediate zones the distinction between tribunals and inquiries disappears; the investigator *is* the tribunal.

The typical inquiry – one which does not culminate in a binding decision by the person who presides at the hearing – may be directed to a very wide range of public purposes. The point is well illustrated by an Order made in 1967,[13] bringing within the purview of the Council on Tribunals no fewer than sixty-five types of discretionary inquiries held in pursuance of statutory powers. They ranged from inquiries held in pursuance of section 5 of the renowned Fisheries (Oyster, Crab, and Lobster) Act 1877 to the committee of inquiry appointed by the Home Secretary to advise him before he decides whether to deprive a naturalized or registered citizen of his citizenship.[14] And they included inquiries that may be held by a person appointed by a Secretary of State for a large number of administrative purposes in local government

---

[11] Treasure trove is hidden (as distinct from abandoned) treasure, and belongs to the Crown in virtue of the prerogative: see *Att.-Gen. of the Duchy of Lancaster* v. *G. E. Overton (Farms) Ltd* [1982] Ch. 277.

[12] See now Local Government Act 1972, s. 101.

[13] S.I. 1967, No. 451.

[14] British Nationality Act 1981, s. 40(7).

law – for example, before the Secretary of State confirms various statutory schemes. Add to these all the sundry types of inquiries which a Minister *must* cause to be held when a prescribed state of affairs exists (for example, when he entertains an appeal against certain administrative decisions taken at a lower level), and the indeterminate miscellany of situations in which a discretionary inquiry may be set up *without* statutory authority,[15] and one has a very mixed bag. One finds, for example, Acts providing that before certain kinds of subordinate legislation can be made or confirmed a statutory inquiry may or must be held.[16] If one can offer any useful generalizations in this variegated field of public law, they ought to be focused rather on the public local inquiry. Local inquiries are used for three main purposes.[17]

1   As a means of consulting and informing local opinion, and gleaning local information as to the likely impact of a proposed administrative decision (for example, to alter constituency or local boundaries, or to amalgamate police forces) affecting the interests of persons and bodies in that locality. This slows down the pace of decision-making but provides the decision-maker with a better fund of knowledge.

2   As a means of giving those whose interests will be most directly affected by a proposed or provisional decision (for example, to make an order for the compulsory purchase of their land or to designate an area as the site of a new town) the legal right to put their objections orally, and through legal representatives, to a person appointed by the Minister or another competent authority before a final decision is made. Other points of view may be expressed at the inquiry, and the outcome should (as in (1)) be conducive to better decision-making. Purposes (1) and (2) are complementary. In some cases the scope of inquiry will be confined to the objections and not directed to the general merits of the proposed order.

3   As a stage in the process of determining appeals against an administrative decision that has already been taken. The best-known examples arise in planning law.

For instance, X applies to his local planning authority for

---

[15] In general, persons conducting inquiries in pursuance of statutory powers have authority to compel the attendance of witnesses and the production of documents, and those conducting non-statutory inquiries have not.

[16] See, for example, Radioactive Substances Act 1948, s. 9; Griffith and Street, *Principles of Administrative Law* (5th edn, 1973), p. 127ff.

[17] 'Neat classification is impossible. See Wraith and Lamb, op. cit., chs 3, 4, 8.

permission to make a material change in the use of his land; planning permission is refused, or is granted subject to conditions that X dislikes; X is entitled to appeal to the Secretary of State for the Environment; the Secretary of State causes a local inquiry to be held through an inspector; the inspector makes a report and the Secretary of State (or a civil servant on his behalf) decides.[18]

In situations (1) and (2) one can speak of judicialized administration; in the third type of situation, judicialized administration merges into administrative adjudication.

Special tribunals [19]

One tends to use the terms 'special tribunals', 'administrative tribunals' and 'statutory tribunals' interchangeably. Terminological inexactitude does not matter much in this field, because no single term could be all-embracing; but a few preliminary points should be borne in mind.

1 Some tribunals that are commonly called 'administrative' deal with disputes between private landlords and tenants. These tribunals are the rent assessment committees and agricultural land tribunals.[20]

2 A small number of tribunals which can well be described as 'administrative' (in the sense that they deal with claims and controversies involving public authorities) are non-statutory. But the most important of them – the Criminal Injuries Compensation Board (which makes discretionary awards out of funds provided by Parliament to claimants who are victims of criminal violence) – has now been placed on a statutory basis.[21]

3 Not all 'special' tribunals are in any conceivable sense 'administrative'. Commercial and industrial arbitrators, the disciplinary committees of trades unions and clubs, professional statutory disciplinary bodies,[22] the stewards of the Jockey Club and the Greyhound Racing Association are obviously not 'administrative'; the disciplinary committees of private organizations are called *domestic* tribunals.

4 Tribunals exercising functions in administrative law may be designated as tribunals, courts, boards, committees, commissioners,

[18] Unless the power of decision has been delegated to the inspector; see note 12, above.
[19] The body of literature on this subject is now extensive. W. A. Robson, *Justice and Administrative Law* (3rd edn, 1951) is the classic pioneering work.
[20] The Lands Tribunal (see below) also has a private law jurisdiction to vary restrictive covenants.
[21] Criminal Justice Act 1988, Part VII. It had operated for 20 years without such a footing.
[22] See, e.g., *R.* v. *General Medical Council, ex p. Gee* [1986] 1 W.L.R. 1247.

referees, umpires; the name is unimportant. The Lands Tribunal is more court-like than the local valuation courts from which it entertains appeals.

5   Tribunals dispensing 'administrative justice' may in substance be doing exactly the same kind of work, in a specialized field, as an ordinary court of law, and doing it with the same degree of freedom from political pressure and influence.

Neither the creation of specialized courts nor the hostility of the legal profession to them need cause any surprise. And any new specialized tribunal, set up to serve a general public purpose, could be assured of an ample measure of initial hostility following the struggle against the Star Chamber, especially if it neither looked nor functioned like a court of common law. Military courts-martial, professional disciplinary bodies and commercial arbitrators could be tolerated. Tribunals adjudicating informally in disputes arising out of social welfare legislation were another matter. The rules they applied interfered with freedom of property and contract; their members were appointed and removable by Ministers; often they exercised discretionary powers which could only be reposed with safety in the hands of Chancery or Circuit judges; if lawyers appeared before them at all, everyone tended to be ill at ease. To some, their very existence was a slur upon the legal profession and a constructive contempt of court. Dicey and Hewart were right: the rule of law was in jeopardy. So ran the train of thought – one that the Committee on Ministers' Powers did little to disturb. Nevertheless, the Committee grudgingly conceded[23] that 'Ministerial tribunals' might, in exceptional circumstances, be preferred to the ordinary courts on five grounds: cheapness, accessibility to the parties, freedom from technicality, speed, and expert knowledge of their particular subject-matter.

The climate of opinion has now changed. No longer must exceptional circumstances be present to justify the establishment of a special tribunal to determine controversies arising under regulatory or welfare legislation. We have about fifty different *types* of these tribunals and some 2,000 tribunals altogether. If, for instance, the question of how disputes about the entitlement of dismissed workers to redundancy payments from their employers ought to be decided under a new Act, there is an *expectation* that the deciding body will be a special tribunal. The alternatives would be (1) a Minister, (2) one of the ordinary courts,

---

[23] Cmd 4060 (1932), p. 97. See also the Franks Report, Cmnd 218 (1957), § 38, making the same point in less grudging terms.

(3) a specially constituted court, and (4) an independent arbitrator. Giving the power of decision to a Minister means in practice that the parties may not know who takes the decision in the Minister's name and will not be entitled to be heard before that person;[24] and they will not usually feel confident that departmental adjudication is justice according to law. There is, therefore, a presumption in favour of vesting the power of decision in a person or body conducting oral hearings; this presumption may be rebutted only if considerations of national or regional policy, for which the Minister is responsible, will often condition the manner in which an individual issue ought to be determined, or if uniformity of decision is of primary importance. A possible compromise – and not a very satisfactory one – is to set up an independent tribunal with an appeal to the Minister.[25] Setting up a specialized court, rather than a tribunal, may be to make heavy weather of small issues. The outstanding modern example of a specialized court in the strict sense is the Restrictive Practices Court; this is a court because it is expressed to be a superior court of record and is presided over by a superior judge (though it includes expert laymen); its jurisdiction (to nullify restrictive trading agreements which are contrary to the public interest) *could* have been vested in a body styled as a tribunal, and when it was first constituted there are many who would have preferred to see that course adopted.[26] Committing issues to independent arbitrators – the last alternative – is most appropriate where the number of issues arising is relatively small and a high level of expertise, likely to be found only among specialists willing to act as part-time adjudicators, is required.

The grounds, already indicated, for giving jurisdiction to tribunals rather than courts are sometimes overstated. Certainly it would be absurd to make applicants for sickness benefit or supplementary benefits go before a High Court judge; the cost, delay and formality would thwart the objectives of social security schemes and would clog up the general administration of justice. These considerations do not apply with anything like the same force to the county courts, which are more accessible and expeditious than some special tribunals and hardly more expensive. County courts do, moreover, have jurisdiction in some matters of administrative law. Where the county courts have been by-

---

[24] They will have no such entitlement at common law: *Local Government Board* v. *Arlidge* [1915] A.C. 120 (housing appeal). But they may be entitled to be heard before a person appointed by the Minister to report to him.

[25] For example, the Civil Aviation Authority, from which an appeal lies to the Secretary of State for Trade and Industry.

[26] See R. B. Stevens and B. S. Yamey, *The Restrictive Practices Court* (1965).

passed and new statutory tribunals established instead, the reasons have generally been as follows.

1   Circuit judges and registrars are generalists, not specialists. There is no reason to expect them to be experts in transport licensing or the rating of property or to be familiar with the problems of the sick and needy or to have the time and opportunity to acquire the necessary expertise or familiarity. A special statutory tribunal may include persons with the desired initial qualifications and others who will acquire them through specialization and experience.

2   Courts are formal. The kind of person who is aggrieved by refusal of a social security benefit or who wants to make a complaint arising out of the administration of the National Health Service may be overawed by the atmosphere of a judicial proceeding and reduced to incoherence or silence if he is precluded by the rules of evidence from telling his story in his own way. In some situations justice can be dispensed only in an informal environment. Special tribunals can be very informal. And none of them is obliged to follow all the strict rules of evidence and procedure of a court of law.

3   Tribunals usually take an active part in finding the facts for themselves; they may adopt 'inquisitorial' procedures, probing away with questions, not acting as detached umpires who rely almost entirely on the material as presented to them by the parties or their advocates. Some of them (for example, valuation courts) regularly conduct site inspections. And though they must observe those minimum requirements of procedural fair play called the rules of natural justice they can draw on their own expert and acquired knowledge in drawing inferences from the facts found.

4   Courts are bound by precedent. Tribunals, though bound by judicial precedents laid down in their own field of the law, and capable of evolving a body of 'case law' themselves, can be more flexible in formulating standards (for example, what is reasonable under local conditions; whether premises are educationally suitable) and departing from them when the circumstances of a case warrant relaxation.[27] Indeed, one of the more formal special tribunals was warned by the Court of Appeal that it ought *not* to adopt a rigid body of case law.[28]

---

[27] A point well made by H. Street, *Justice in the Welfare State* (2nd edn, 1975), pp. 6–9.
[28] *Merchandise Transport Co.* v. *British Transport Commission* [1962] 2 Q.B. 173 at 186, 192–3.

One of the most significant legal developments in the immediate post-war period was the replacement of the Workmen's Compensation Act by the national insurance (industrial injuries) scheme.[29] Not only was private insurance replaced by public social insurance; the tribunals constituted to administer the new scheme were special tribunals before which legal representation was at first excluded; such representation is now allowed. The jurisdiction of county court judges was ousted and the massive body of case law evolved in the many legal battles fought as far as the House of Lords was deprived of binding authority. This was a drastic repudiation of technical legalism in which social justice had too often been overlooked.

Types of tribunals[30]

No attempt will here be made to present a full synopsis. Only a broad outline under general headings will be offered.

Fiscal liability and claims, property and land. Appeals against administrative assessments to income tax, corporation tax and capital gains tax are heard either by special commissioners of income tax (who are civil servants) or by general commissioners (who are not).[31] Appeals against value added tax assessments by the Customs and Excise lie to special value added tax tribunals. Persons aggrieved by rating assessments made by valuation officers (who are civil servants) may object before a local valuation court, which is composed largely of unpaid local councillors and magistrates. Appeal lies to the Lands Tribunal, a body which could easily be styled an administrative court; its members are professional lawyers and surveyors appointed by the Lord Chancellor; its procedure is fairly informal but its judgments are often reported. The jurisdiction of the Tribunal also includes the assessment of compensation for compulsory acquisition of land where this is not agreed between the acquiring authority and the property-owner.

Industrial tribunals are possibly the most important group of tribunals today. They have jurisdiction over a wide range of questions, including claims to compensation for unfair dismissal, disputes concern-

---

[29] W. A. Robson, *Justice and Administrative Law* (3rd edn, 1951), pp. 209–22.

[30] There is a good classification and synopsis in J. F. Garner's *Administrative Law* (6th edn by J. F. Garner and B. L. Jones), ch. 10. Figures of cases heard by most of the various tribunals are supplied in an Appendix to the Annual Report of the Council on Tribunals.

[31] Appeals concerning capital transfer tax are heard only by the special commissioners or by the High Court.

ing redundancy payments, appeals against assessments to the industrial training levy and appeals for compensation for loss of public office under statutory reorganization schemes. They sit in London and over sixty other centres in England and Wales, and in 1985 they disposed of some 34,000 cases, in many of which there was no hearing.[32]

The Foreign Compensation Commission entertains claims to the award of compensation out of funds received by the British Government from foreign Governments for the expropriation or destruction of British-owned property overseas, and allocates the money to successful claimants on a discretionary basis. The Criminal Injuries Compensation Board makes discretionary awards to claimants who are victims of criminal violence.

The informal rent assessment committees fix fair rents between private landlords and tenants; they are appellate bodies, an initial determination having already been made by a rent officer. Reasonable rents for council tenants under the Housing Rents and Subsidies Act 1975 are determined not by tribunals but by the local authorities themselves. Agricultural land tribunals deal with disputes between landlords and tenant farmers about notices to quit.

Social welfare. Post-war legislation has substantially enlarged the number and jurisdiction of such tribunals. Most are appellate bodies hearing appeals lodged by persons aggrieved by initial administrative decisions; and in most of the cases before them the monetary sums in issue are small, though often of major importance to the poor and disabled. There are the social security appeal tribunals (dealing with claims to unemployment benefit, sickness benefit, industrial injuries benefit, retirement pensions, child benefit and so on), and medical appeal tribunals on industrial injuries claims.[33] Appeals in respect of disability pensions claimed by ex-servicemen lie to separate pensions appeal tribunals. From the social security appeal and medical appeal tribunals, appeals lie to senior full-time lawyers, the social security commissioners. A complex network of tribunals (including the Secretary of State for Health and the Health Service Commissioners) exists to hear complaints and allegations against practitioners in the National Health Service and to entertain appeals. Persons compulsorily committed to a mental hospital can seek their release from custody by application to a mental

---

[32] See Annual Report of the Council on Tribunals for 1982–3 (H.C. 129 (1982–3)), Appendix C.

[33] Between them they disposed of some 117,000 cases in 1982. For a good critique of the social security tribunals see Street, op. cit., pp. 10–32.

health review tribunal; these tribunals heard nearly 2,500 cases in 1985.

Among other tribunals concerned with social welfare in a broad sense are the industrial tribunals, rent assessment committees, agricultural land tribunals, the Criminal Injuries Compensation Board, independent schools tribunals (which determine whether a private school or its proprietor or any of its teachers ought to be struck off the official register or disqualified as the case may be) and tribunals exercising roughly similar functions with regard to voluntary children's homes.

Regulatory. Regulation by licensing, normally coupled with powers of inspection, is a familiar feature of public supervision of private activity. Powers to grant licences will be accompanied by powers to impose conditions, to refuse renewal of a licence, and to revoke a licence when prescribed violations of the terms of the licence are established: powers to revoke in the absolute discretion of the licensing authority are rarely conferred today. Licensing powers may be vested in government Departments, public corporations or local authorities.[34] Aspects of the regulation of transport communications have been committed, for reasons of practical convenience, to independent tribunals. For example, applications for licences to operate commercial air routes are heard by the Civil Aviation Authority; objectors have a right to be heard in opposition; an appeal lies to the Secretary of State for Trade and Industry. Regulation of carriage of goods and passengers by road follows a curious pattern. There are area licensing authorities. Appeal lies from decisions on passenger road services to the Secretary of State for Transport, on goods carriers' licences to the Transport Tribunal. The latter is an anomalous body; till 1969 it also heard applications for variations of railway passenger charges in the London transport area. It is a court with judicial trappings and procedure; its rate-functions (still exercisable for limited purposes) are successors to the jurisdiction exercised from 1921 by the Railway Rates Tribunal, the antecedents of which can be traced to the Railway and Canal Commission, a superior court and an arbitral body, set up in 1873.

Among other regulatory bodies are the Comptroller-General of Patents, Designs and Trade Marks (from which an appeal lies to the Patents Court), the Plant Variety Rights Tribunal exercising similar functions, the Performing Right Tribunal, the tribunal appointed to consider alleged violations of the Prevention of Fraud (Investments) Act 1958 by dealers in securities, and the Wireless Telegraphy Appeal

[34] Street, op. cit., ch. 4.

Tribunal set up to consider complaints of undue interference with radio broadcasts on the part of private operators.

Tribunals to consider complaints about the conduct of voluntary schools and children's homes are also regulatory bodies. Perhaps one should include the immigration appellate bodies (over 7,000 cases in 1985) in this category too. The Gaming Board for Great Britain, which decides on the basis of police reports and other information whether to grant a certificate of consent to gaming-club proprietors, thus enabling them to apply for a local licence, is a regulatory body which may be regarded as a kind of informal tribunal.

This is not a complete list,[35] and some classes of tribunals defy classification. Informal adjudication within government Departments is also of practical importance. Civil servants in Britain are more accessible to informal interviews than in many foreign countries.

Franks and after

The Franks Committee found nothing fundamentally wrong with the system and working of statutory tribunals, and it did not seek to put tribunals into a strait-jacket. But its bias in favour of judicialization led it to make a number of recommendations designed to assimilate tribunals more closely to specialized courts. For example, it deprecated undue informality, and stressed the need for settled rules of procedure, reasons for decisions, rights to legal representation, proper channels of appeal and the removal of any suspicion of political dictation of or influence over decisions. The procedures of tribunals ought to be characterized by 'openness, fairness and impartiality'.[36] Openness implied not only reasoned decisions but also public hearings (except where the interests of the public – for example, in security – or the parties demanded privacy, as in potentially embarrassing social security appeals and complaints against National Health Service practitioners), with evidence given orally. Fairness demanded that the parties knew their rights in advance, had proper notice of the case they had to meet, an adequate opportunity to put their own case in person or through their representatives, and rights to appeal against and obtain review of decisions. Impartiality required new safeguards for the appointment and tenure of members, and to preserve the appearance of impartiality, independent tribunals ought not to sit in departmental premises. To maintain some degree of coherence and surveillance over

[35] The latest Annual Report of the Council on Tribunals gives a full list.
[36] Cmnd 217 (1957), § 23.

the tribunal system, there should be a standing Council on Tribunals.

The Tribunals and Inquiries Act 1958 provided for the establishment of the Council on Tribunals, to keep under review the constitution and working of specified tribunals; other tribunals have been added to the list. The current Act is the Tribunals and Inquiries Act 1971. The Council[37] consists of up to fifteen members appointed by the Lord Chancellor and the Secretary of State for Scotland, and the Parliamentary Commissioner for Administration *ex officio*. The chairman is salaried; the other appointed members receive fees; but the Council is essentially a part-time supervisory body with a minute official staff. It meets once a month. Members of the Council and its Scottish Committee attended 17 hearings by tribunals in 1985. More specifically, the functions of the Council in respect of tribunals – it has powers in connection with inquiries too[38] – are as follows.

1   To consider and report on the statutory tribunals under its supervision, and on such particular matters concerning these and other tribunals as may be referred to it by the Lord Chancellor and the Secretary of State.

    Within the limited scope of its resources, it has attempted to conduct general reviews of specific classes of tribunals and has reported on special matters such as the power to award costs and the law of defamation. It organizes conferences with tribunal chairmen.

2   To receive and investigate complaints about tribunals made by members of the public.

    In its first ten years the Council received only 242 complaints relating to tribunals. This small figure probably indicates a widespread ignorance of the Council's very existence or whereabouts rather than a general satisfaction of consumers with the work of tribunals. The Council has no power to alter a tribunal's decision and in most cases the tribunal would have no jurisdiction to rescind its own decision even if it wished to do so. However, individual complaints may lead to further investigations and recommendations for reform. The Council can get to know where the shoe pinches.

3   To make an annual report to the Lord Chancellor and the Secretary of State. The Report is laid before Parliament and is now published as a House of Commons paper. It attracts little public comment but is a very useful source of information.

[37] See Bernard Schwartz and H. W. R. Wade, *Legal Control of Government* (1972), pp. 179–80; D. G. T. Williams [1984] *Public Law* 73.
[38] See pp. 624–5.

4   To be consulted by the responsible Minister before procedural rules for tribunals and inquiries are made.

This is probably its most important function – one in which the minority of lawyers on the Council play a leading role. It has helped to promote a higher degree of uniformity in tribunal procedures, and in particular to instil the essentials of judicial fairness into procedural regulations – for example, adequate notification of rights of appeal, proper notice of hearings and disclosure of the case to be answered; rights of cross-examination; rights to legal representation at oral hearings.

The Council is also consulted by the Department sponsoring legislation under which a new tribunal is to be constituted or an existing one abolished or reorganized. It has complained that in these matters it is sometimes consulted too late for its representations to have any effect, and has urged that more thought be given to coordinated rationalization of the tribunal system, involving the amalgamation of some types of tribunals and reallocations of jurisdiction.[39] The Council has asked for statutory provision to be made to give it the right to be consulted whenever legislation is being drafted affecting its jurisdiction and, if the Council's opinion were not accepted by the Minister, the new statutory provision should oblige him to disclose the Council's view when introducing the legislation.[40]

5   To make *general* recommendations to the appropriate Minister as to the appointment of members of tribunals.

In practice this has not been an important function of the Council. However, the Franks recommendations have had a significant effect on appointments and tenure. The chairmen of certain tribunals have to be legally qualified, and appointed either by the Lord Chancellor or by the Minister generally concerned with the area of administration in question from a panel maintained by the Lord Chancellor. Members of most tribunals cannot be removed except with the Lord Chancellor's concurrence;[41] they may, however, be refused reappointment after their term of office has expired.

Tribunals are not cast in a common mould, but some general points are important.

(i) Most tribunals are not composed of officials,[42] though there are

---

[39] Annual Report for 1969–70 (H.C. 72 (1970–71), pp. 10–11, 29–32; and for 1973–4 (H.C. 289 (1974–5)), pp. 4–5, 6, 18–19.

[40] Council on Tribunals Special Report on Functions, Cmnd 7805 (1980).

[41] See Tribunals and Inquiries Act 1971, ss 5, 7–9. For the Franks recommendations on these matters, see Cmnd 218, ch. 5.

[42] See further R. E. Wraith and P. G. Hutchesson, op. cit.; H. W. R. Wade, op. cit., ch. 23.

some exceptions – for example, Ministry inspectors deciding planning appeals, special commissioners of income tax, the Comptroller-General of Patents, Designs and Trade Marks; these officers nevertheless act independently.

(ii) A fairly typical tribunal is composed of a legally qualified chairman, appointed by one of the procedures indicated above, and two lay members, one of whom will perhaps be an employer and another a trade union official; or both may be independent specialists or local worthies.

(iii) They are bound by regulations made by the Minister, but only in highly exceptional circumstances defined by legislation will the Minister be legally entitled to give them specific directions for the determination of a particular case.

(iv) For a variety of reasons the position of a legally qualified chairman may be of crucial importance. The legislation which a tribunal has to interpret and apply may be just as complicated as law in the courts. Although the parties will nearly always be *entitled* to legal representation,[43] they will seldom be so represented before tribunals like social security tribunals dealing with small matters. Unfortunately, the legal aid and advice scheme has not been applied to proceedings before tribunals except the Lands Tribunal, the Commons Commissioners and the Employment Appeal Tribunal.[44] If one party is legally represented, the chairman will have to do his best to help the unrepresented party put his case without shedding his own impartiality as a fact-finder and adjudicator. Obviously this is a difficult task.

Before some tribunals legal representation may, however, be a mixed blessing to a party. Clearly, such representation is important if a party is accused of culpability or if his vital interests are in serious jeopardy. But advocates appearing before tribunals can also sow confusion and protract the proceedings unnecessarily by reading documents at length, conducting long examinations and cross-examinations of witnesses, making elaborate submissions and generally frustrating the object of an informal hearing. Few practising lawyers appear regularly before the minor tribunals, and unfamiliarity with the atmosphere can be a serious disadvantage. There

---

[43] The Franks Report (§ 87) recommended that the right to legal representation be curtailed only in the most exceptional circumstances.

[44] The Lord Chancellor's Legal Aid Advisory Committee has recommended that legal aid be extended to all tribunals at present within the supervision of the Council on Tribunals in which representation is permitted. Twenty-fourth Annual Report, H.C. 20 (1974–5).

is a real dilemma: in certain cases it is very desirable for all interested parties to have the right kind of legal representation; that kind of representation may simply not be available, and the chairman has to do his best to supply the omission or remedy the deficiency.

6 The last function of the Council on Tribunals in this context is concerned with reasons for decisions. Under section 12 of the Tribunals and Inquiries Act 1971, tribunals under the superintendence of the Council are required, when requested, to supply oral or written reasons for their decisions when giving or notifying their decision, unless exempted by order made by the Lord Chancellor after consultation with the Council. Only one class of tribunal has been accorded exemption.

The general statutory duty to give reasons[45] is, however, subject to qualifications. The tribunals in question are not obliged to volunteer reasons or to inform the parties of their right to request them. Some tribunals interpret their statutory duty literally and, in the absence of a request, simply do not give reasons.[46] Moreover, the duty to give reasons does not import a duty to summarize the evidence or state findings of fact. Reasons may properly be withheld on grounds of national security, or if they are asked for by somebody not primarily concerned with the decision and it would be contrary to the interest of any of the parties to supply them.[47]

Appeal and review

There is no common appellate structure. From most tribunals of last resort an appeal lies to the superior courts on questions of law,[48] but there is no such appeal from determinations by, for example, the social security commissioners or the immigration appeal tribunal. On questions of fact and discretion the pattern is irregular. Appeal may lie to a superior tribunal or to a Minister, or there may be no appeal on the merits at all; there is no such appeal, for instance, from decisions of mental health review tribunals or the Foreign Compensation Commission.

Judicial review may be exercisable although no appeal is provided by statute or in addition to appellate review. A determination by a

---

[45] Some tribunals were already under a duty to give reasons for decisions and they cannot be exempted from this duty. Their duty was not subject to all the qualifications mentioned in the text below.

[46] See Street, op. cit., pp. 67–9.

[47] 1971 Act, s. 12(2).

[48] See p. 544, and Tribunals and Inquiries Act 1971, s. 13.

tribunal may be quashed if it is made without jurisdiction or in breach of the rules of natural justice, or if it exhibits an error of law on the face of the 'record'. A tribunal may be restrained from exceeding its jurisdiction or commanded to hear a case within its jurisdiction; it can also be ordered to perform a duty to give reasons for its decision. These matters were discussed in chapter 29.

Inquiries and land use

The Franks Committee emphasized the need for openness and fairness in inquiries held on behalf of a Minister, but it recognized that a procedure culminating in a discretionary decision by a Minister responsible for national policy could not be expected to exhibit the same degree of impartiality as proceedings before an independent tribunal.[49]

The difference is best illustrated by situations where the purpose of the inquiry is to investigate, for the information of the Minister, objections to the Minister's own proposals.[50] The New Towns Act 1946 provided for the establishment of new towns to attract population and industry from the metropolis. Before the bill had been introduced, the Minister had already provisionally decided, as a matter of policy, to designate Stevenage as the site of a new town. While the bill was before Parliament, he imprudently made a speech in Stevenage, proclaiming that he intended to carry out a daring exercise in town planning there, and affirming (amid hostile interruptions . . . 'Gestapo' . . .) that the project would go forward. Subsequently a draft order was made, designating Stevenage; objections were lodged; a public local inquiry into the objections was held by a Ministry inspector; the Minister, having received the report on the inquiry and considered the objections, finally made the order. In *Franklin* v. *Minister of Town and Country Planning*[51] objectors challenged the validity of the order in the courts, claiming that the Minister had failed to act judicially. He had manifested bias or a real likelihood of bias in favour of his proposal from the outset; and the fact that he had made the final order while important technical problems (water supply and sewage disposal) remained unsolved showed that his bias had continued to the end. The House of Lords held that the standard of impartiality imposed on an

---

[49] Cmnd 218 (1957), § 25.

[50] On the difficulty in applying judicial standards to procedures involving public inquiries held as part of a process in arriving at a discretionary decision, see *Wednesbury Corporation* v. *Ministry of Housing and Local Government* (No. 2) [1966] 2 Q.B. 275; and *Essex C.C.* v. *Ministry of Housing and Local Government* (1967) 66 L.G.R. 23.

[51] [1948] A.C. 87.

independent tribunal was inapplicable to this type of situation; the Minister's role made it inevitable that he would incline in favour of his own scheme. The only duties cast upon him were to cause a properly conducted inquiry to be held and to consider the objections and the report fairly, with a mind not closed to argument. The Minister's functions were 'purely administrative'.

The decision in this case was sensible, though the term 'purely administrative' may have been unfortunate. A duty to act fairly may imply a duty to behave like an adjudicator *for certain purposes* – for example, in ensuring that everyone directly concerned is adequately informed of his rights, knows the case he has to meet and has a proper chance to put his case, and that reasons are given for decisions.[52]

A more typical situation in administrative law is where a Minister, X, has to decide a dispute between Y, a local authority, and Z, a property-owner.[53] This 'triangular' situation may arise where Y makes an order for the compulsory purchase of Z's property and Z objects; or where Z applies to Y for permission to make a material change in the use of his land or premises (planning permission), Y refuses, or consents subject to conditions, and Z appeals to the Minister, X, against the refusal or the conditions. In certain respects the Minister resembles an adjudicator determining a *lis inter partes*, a dispute between parties. Long before the Franks Committee had ever been thought of, the courts had recognized that certain *implied* duties ought to be cast on the Minister when deciding whether or not to confirm a compulsory purchase order initiated by a local authority in so far as his role was analogous to the judicial. They divided his functions into three stages. First, before objections were lodged, he had no duty to 'act judicially'; thus, if relevant communications were made to him by the local authority, he had no obligation to divulge them to the objectors; he was acting in an 'administrative' capacity.[54] Secondly, after objections had been lodged and up to the time of the final decision, he had to 'act judicially' in accordance with the minimum standards of natural justice; hence, the inspector conducting the public local inquiry had to behave impartially, and the Minister could not communicate with one party behind the other's back (for example, by viewing the site, through his officials, in company with representatives of the local authority, without giving the

---

[52] See now Compulsory Purchase by Ministers (Inquiries Procedure) Rules 1967 (S.I. 1967, No. 720).
[53] Z may also be a public authority.
[54] *Johnson (B.) & Co. (Builders) Ltd* v. *Minister of Health* [1947] 2 All E.R. 395. The leading judgment by Lord Greene M.R. contains the fullest review of the case law up to that time.

objectors the opportunity to be present) on evidential matters raised at the inquiry.[55] In making his final decision the Minister cannot be regarded as separate and distinct from his Department. He is entitled to consult his officials, and advice (including technical advice), tendered to him within the Department is not new evidence of the kind which he would be required to disclose to the objectors had he received it from sources outside his Department.[56]

The courts recognize that over-judicialization of the procedure at inquiries will lead to delay and unnecessary technical fetters on the inspector's conduct of the inquiry. Their aim is to ensure that objectors at an inquiry are able to take 'an active, intelligent and informed part in the decision-making process'.[57] In putting their case and answering the points made on behalf of the public authority, objectors must be given 'a fair crack of the whip'.[58] When an inspector based his recommendations on a substantial matter which, although it had been mentioned at the inquiry, had not been treated as part of the case for denying the applicants permission to extract gravel, so that they had not had a chance to deal with the question, the Minister's decision, based on the inspector's findings, was quashed.[59] But the Court of Appeal refused to treat the inclusion of the inspector's own opinion of the architectural value of a house as new evidence which should have been disclosed at the inquiry or which should have caused the inquiry to be re-opened.[60] Any sensible person would have expected the inspector to form an opinion based on such a fact. Considering the effect of refusal by an inspector to adjourn an inquiry, that same court took into account the multiplicity of parties at an inquiry and found that the inspector must be allowed to weigh the possible unfairness to one objector against the delay to the inquiry and consequent inconvenience to all the other parties.[61] The inspector is master of the procedure at an inquiry. While actual prejudice need not always be proved for an objector to succeed in getting an order consequent upon an inquiry quashed for lack of natural justice,[62]

---

[55] *Errington* v. *Minister of Health* [1935] 1 K.B. 249 (a slum clearance case; the same principles applied). For an acute analysis see Griffith and Street, *Principles of Administrative Law*, op. cit., pp. 171–5.

[56] *Bushell* v. *Secretary of State for the Environment* [1981] A.C. 75; *R.* v. *Secretary of State for Transport, ex. p. Gwent County Council* [1987] 1 All E.R. 161.

[57] *Nicholson* v. *Secretary of State for Energy* (1977) 76 L.G.R. 693.

[58] *Fairmount Investments Ltd* v. *Secretary of State for the Environment* [1976] 1 W.L.R. 1255.

[59] *Sabey* v. *Secretary of State for the Environment* [1978] 1 All E.R. 586.

[60] *Winchester C.C.* v. *Secretary of State for the Environment* (1979) 77 L.G.R. 715.

[61] *Ostreicher* v. *Secretary of State for the Environment* [1978] 1 W.L.R. 810.

[62] *Hibernian Property Co. Ltd* v. *Secretary of State for the Environment* (1973) 72 L.G.R. 350.

absence of any real prejudice to the objector may be used as a ground for denying him relief.[63]

Judge-made safeguards left some gaps in the protection afforded to the citizen. The House of Lords had held that even while the Minister was acting 'judicially', he did not have to disclose the inspector's report.[64] The Franks Committee recommended disclosure of the fact-finding sections of inspectors' reports before they were submitted to the Minister, so as to enable the parties to propose corrections of fact; and full disclosure of the report with the Minister's reasoned letter of decision.[65] The recommendation for disclosure *prior* to the decision has not been implemented by legislation because it would lead to too much delay in decision-making, but subsequent disclosure must now be made on request. Most of the other Franks recommendations have been implemented. For instance, an acquiring authority must give advance particulars of its case; if a Department has expressed a view in support of the local authority's proposal or decision and this fact is stated in the local authority's submissions, a representative of the Department must be available at the inquiry to give evidence, in the absence of special statutory rules, but natural justice does not require that objectors be permitted to cross-examine him on questions of national policy, or on the accuracy of the material on which the policy is based. The inspector has a discretion to determine whether cross-examination serves any useful purpose.[66] There are statutory codes for the conduct of inquiries, specifying who has a right to be heard and who may be heard, embodying rules of procedure analogous to those for a judicial-type proceeding, and dealing with the procedure before and after the hearing.[67]

All this seemed eminently reasonable; and it was. But in practice judicialization tended to slow down the process of making decisions. Inspectors' reports, for example, and reasoned letters of decision setting out the inspectors' main findings had to be carefully composed;

[63] *George* v. *Secretary of State for the Environment* (1979) 77 L.G.R. 689.

[64] *Local Government Board* v. *Arlidge* [1915] A.C. 120.

[65] Cmnd 218 (1957) §§ 343–5. Partial disclosure of reports prior to the decision is the practice followed in Scotland. The rules governing reasoned decisions by the tribunals named in the Tribunals and Inquiries Act were applied to decisions in pursuance of mandatory statutory inquiries (1971 Act, ss 12(1), 19(1)) and to a number of voluntary inquiries held on behalf of a Minister.

[66] *Bushell* v. *Secretary of State for the Environment* [1981] A.C. 75.

[67] See, for example, Compulsory Purchase by Local Authorities (Inquiry Procedure) Rules 1965 (S.I. 1965, No. 473), and S.I. 1976, No. 746; and see S.I. 1967, No. 720 (note 52), Town and Planning (Inquiries Procedure) Rules 1974 (S.I. 1974, No. 419); and cf. S.I. 1974, No. 420 (procedure on planning appeals where the inspector makes the decision).

otherwise the decisions might be struck down in the courts for failure to comply with the requirements of the legislation.[68] This could be quite serious in the case of compulsory purchase orders, because judicial review meant uncertainty, and the work of building roads, schools or houses could not safely be begun while judicial proceedings were pending (though they had to be instituted within a few weeks of the confirmation of the order).

For a different reason, delay was serious in the context of planning appeals; they were very numerous, and private development of property was held up while a backlog piled up in the Ministry. In 1967 it was taking an average of nine months to determine those planning appeals where the appellant had asked for an oral hearing.[69] One answer to the latter problem was decentralization of decision-making; hence power to decide minor appeals has been delegated to inspectors, who do not have to make a full-scale report but can simply issue a short letter of decision containing reasons.[70] Another device was to encourage appellants to agree to having the matter decided by written representations coupled with an unaccompanied site inspection. There have been other reforms in planning procedure.[71] Instead of having area planning policy settled by a development plan to which hundreds of objections could be entertained at a massive public inquiry, the larger planning authorities now prepare outline structure plans subject to ministerial approval. The Secretary of State can decide which aspects of the plan shall be considered at 'an examination in public' and whom to invite to be heard; and he has a free discretion whom to consult when he is considering the plan.[72]

In some respects implementation of the Franks recommendations did not go far enough. For example, the Government refused to carry out the proposals that there should be an express duty to acquaint the parties with relevant statements of policy and changes in policy prior to

[68] See *Givaudan & Co.* v. *Minister of Housing and Local Government* [1967] 1 W.L.R. 250 (decision quashed because the reasons given in the letter of decision, read together with extracts from the inspector's report, were unintelligible).

[69] Cmnd 3333 (1967), p. 7. In 1982 the average times taken for planning appeals in England decided after a local inquiry were 46 weeks for appeals decided by the Secretary of State and 27 weeks for those decided by inspectors.

[70] See notes 12 and 67.

[71] Richard Buxton, *Local Government* (2nd edn, 1973), ch. 7.

[72] Town and Country Planning (Amendment) Act 1972, s. 3(1) modifying section 9 of the Town and Country Planning Act 1971. *Local* plans do not necessarily have to be confirmed by the Secretary of State at all (1971 Act, ss 11, 14), unless the Secretary of State so directs, in which case he is free to consult with any interested party without having to go back to the others (1972 Act, s. 3(2)); cf. *Errington*'s case, note 55. See also S.I. 1974, No. 1486. The 1971 Act provides for local publicity and participation in the preparation of structure and local plans (ss 8, 12).

the decision. Again, at first nothing was done to implement recommendations about re-opening the inquiry where the Minister proposed to disagree with the inspector's recommendations. The latter issue came to a head in the Saffron Walden chalkpit case.[73] A company sought permission to quarry chalk in a pit. Neighbouring farmers claimed that these operations would seriously damage their land and livestock. The local planning authority refused the application for planning permission; the company appealed, and an inspector, having conducted a local inquiry on behalf of the Minister and heard expert evidence, recommended that the appeal be dismissed. The Minister overruled the inspector and allowed the appeal, having consulted other experts. Naturally this created a bad impression in so far as an open inquiry had been followed first by closed consultations behind the back of the parties and then by a decision overruling the weight of the body of expert opinion already tested by public interrogation. A neighbouring landowner, Major Buxton, challenged the Minister's decision in the High Court; he failed on the technical ground that he was not a person aggrieved by the decision,[74] though certainly he thought he had a legitimate grievance. The Council on Tribunals took up the issue with the Lord Chancellor and the Minister. Eventually new rules were laid down to be applied in the future. Major Buxton had lost his private battle, but he triumphed in defeat. Now, if the Minister is minded to disagree with an inspector's recommendation on a planning appeal, he must normally notify the applicant, the local planning authority, and any other person with a direct interest in the land who gave evidence at the inquiry, and must give them an opportunity of making fresh representations to him.[75] If, moreover, the reason for the proposed disagreement is that the Minister has received new evidence, including expert opinion on a matter of fact, or has considered any new issue of fact (not being a new issue of government policy) which was not raised at the inquiry, he must be prepared to reopen the inquiry if requested to do so.[76] This change could, of course, slow down decision-making

[73] See J. A. G. Griffith and H. Street, *A Casebook of Administrative Law* (1964), pp. 142–92.

[74] *Buxton* v. *Minister of Housing and Local Government* [1961] 1 Q.B. 278 (B was only a 'third party' in the appeal to the Minister).

[75] If the Minister simply disagrees with the inspector's views about what planning policy *is*, or how that policy should be *applied* to the facts found at an inquiry, or on a matter of aesthetic taste, this decision is final: *Luke of Pavenham* v. *Minister of Housing and Local Government* [1968] 1 Q.B. 172; *Vale Estates (Acton) Ltd* v. *Secretary of State for the Environment* (1970) 69 L.G.R. 543. If there is disagreement between the Minister and inspector on a material *finding of fact*, an opportunity to make further written representations must be afforded.

[76] See, for example, S.I. 1974, No. 420, r. 12.

still further. In practice it has not been particularly important.[77] A White Paper stated that the Minister agreed with thirty-nine out of forty recommendations by inspectors.[78]

Not many people had suggested that under the old procedure decisions were in fact unfair. Now they *look* fairer. Furthermore, the liberalization in the procedure of inquiries, in particular the discretion given to the inspector to hear anyone with a genuine grievance, has led to a corresponding liberalization in the attitude of the courts to the issue of who is entitled to challenge a decision before them. Any person appearing at the inquiry, whether by right or at the discretion of the inspector, may now seek a final ruling from the courts on the legality of the decision.[79]

Scrutiny of inquiries

The functions of the Council on Tribunals are of some importance. It considers and reports on such matters as the Lord Chancellor or the Secretary of State may refer to it; on its own initiative it may also raise particular questions affecting inquiries; it has to be consulted before procedural rules are made for inquiries; it receives complaints from members of the public. It is not entrusted with the task of keeping the general working of statutory inquiries under review, nor is it empowered to make recommendations as to the kind of person who should be appointed to conduct them; in these respects its functions are narrower than its functions relating to tribunals, but the impediment is not a serious one.

Its tendency to emphasize the need for procedural safeguards, particularly after the termination of an inquiry,[80] and its criticisms of the procedure adopted in two controversial cases,[81] brought it into

[77] It has led to several unsuccessful applications to the courts to quash Ministers' decisions for refusing to re-open an inquiry; see *Luke*'s and *Vale*'s cases; *Continental Sprays Ltd* v. *Minister of Housing and Local Government* (1968) 67 L.G.R. 147, 19 P. & C.R. 774; *Boyer (William) & Sons Ltd* v. *Minister of Housing and Local Government* (1968) 67 L.G.R. 374; 20 P. & C.R. 176 (complaints of inadequate findings of fact in inspectors' reports).

[78] Cmnd 3333 (1967), §§ 33, 34.

[79] See *Turner* v. *Secretary of State for the Environment* (1973) 72 L.G.R. 380 and S.I. 1974, No. 420, r. 7. (What would be the position of a person with a substantial grievance who had not appeared at the inquiry? Would the *Buxton* decision still bar him from the courts?)

[80] It was instrumental in securing a more satisfactory final draft of the procedural rules for planning appeals and compulsory purchase order inquiries in 1962.

[81] The Saffron Walden Chalkpit case (p. 623) and the Packington Estate case [1966] *Public Law* 1; Annual Report of the Council on Tribunals for 1965, §§ 77–82.

intermittent conflict with Ministers of Housing and Local Government; the Lord Chancellor, more sympathetic to its objectives, was at times hard pressed to maintain the principle of collective ministerial responsibility. Procedures involving inquiries held on behalf of Ministers tend to evoke stronger feelings than matters affecting tribunals, not only among local inhabitants but also in the Departments concerned. The potential conflict between the needs for affording fair play to individuals and for speedy implementation of policy decisions in compulsory purchase cases is apt to develop into a heated battle in which an independent scrutineer can hardly fail to earn obloquy as a busybody, a nonentity or a supposed partisan. Relations between the Council and the Departments are not generally hostile, and Departments voluntarily consult the Council when introducing bills providing for new inquiry procedures. But when conflicts arise the Council is handicapped by its lack of a political powerbase.

The Parliamentary Commissioner for Administration[82] can also entertain complaints about injustice caused by maladministration in connection with procedures involving inquiries held on behalf of a Minister; and because of the jurisdictional overlap he has been made an *ex officio* member of the Council. However, he cannot investigate a complaint unless it is addressed to him through a member of Paraliament.[83] He has no power to investigate complaints of decisions by tribunals or by Ministers acting in a judicial capacity,[84] but may, in his discretion, investigate a complaint of departmental 'administrative' maladministration in presenting or otherwise handling the matter.

[82] See ch. 33.
[83] But for an amendment to this procedure, see below, p. 648. For the procedure adopted for passing on to him complaints addressed to the Council and vice versa, see Annual Report of the Council for 1968 (H.C. 272 (1968–9)), § 2.
[84] Parliamentary Commissioner Act 1967, s. 5(2). He is concerned only with the 'administrative' functions of Ministers and officials. Determination of a planning appeal or confirmation of a compulsory purchase order is to be regarded as 'administrative' for this purpose.

Chapter 32

Crown Proceedings

Aspects of civil proceedings to which the Crown is a party have been referred to earlier in this book. The Crown Proceedings Act 1947 made substantial changes in the law. Archaic forms of proceedings advantageous to the Crown were abolished;[1] various privileges and immunities of the Crown were abridged; the Crown was at last made liable in tort. But on a number of issues we have to look at the common-law and equitable principles evolved before the Act and left unaltered by it. Some of these principles are still remarkably obscure. New puzzles have been added by the wording of certain provisions of the Act; some of these are highly technical, and we shall not trouble to examine them in any detail[2] except where they are of general practical importance.

Contracts[3]

Before the Crown Proceedings Act, claims against the Crown for breach of contract had to be brought by way of petition of right[4] in the High Court. The plaintiff was a 'suppliant'; the procedure was unsatisfactory – for example, the Home Secretary's fiat had to be granted before proceedings could be commenced – and too favourable to the Crown. The 1947 Act repealed the Petitions of Right Act 1860 and provided that claims formerly brought by petitions of right (with the exception of proceedings against Her Majesty in her private

---

[1] In particular by section 13 of the Act and the First Schedule to the Act.

[2] The leading works are Glanville Williams, *Crown Proceedings* (1948), P. W. Hogg, *Liability of the Crown* (1971), and Harry Street, *Governmental Liability* (1953). H. W. R. Wade, *Administrative Law* (6th edn, 1988), ch. 21, offers a lucid review of the main features of the law.

[3] Colin Turpin, *Government Contracts* (1972).

[4] Petitions of right also lay for recovery of land and chattels, for compensation due under a statute (for example, the *De Keyser* case [1920] A.C. 508) and in quasi-contract, but not for pure torts.

capacity)[5] were to be enforceable through ordinary civil proceedings against the Crown. These proceedings could be instituted in county courts; this was perhaps the most salutary innovation introduced by the Act. The substantive law of Crown liability in contract was left unchanged.

How far does Crown liability in this sphere differ from that of local authorities or private persons?

1 The Crown, as a corporation sole at common law, has a potentially unrestricted competence to enter into contracts, save in so far as it is disabled from so doing by the terms of a statute or an overriding common-law principle. Statutory corporations can contract only for purposes within the defined scope of their authority.

2 If the Crown is to be able to discharge its obligations under a contract, funds for this purpose must have been appropriated by Parliament. It is sometimes said that the Crown is under no contractual liability at all in the absence of such an appropriation.[6] This view seems to be correct only where a statute or the terms of a contract have expressly provided that the supply of parliamentary funds shall be a condition precedent to the validity of a contract with the Crown.[7] Normally there is, of course, no such provision. The proper analysis of the normal situation appears to be that if money is not made available to meet the Crown's obligations, the contract is not void but unenforceable against the Crown.[8]

3 Crown contracts are made by agents acting on its behalf. The agent cannot be sued on the contract; only the Crown, as principal, is

[5] Which are maintainable only by petition of right and in respect of matters for which petitions of right could be brought. Section 39(1) and the Second Schedule having repealed the Petitions of Right Act 1860, it is arguable that such petitions must now be brought under the still more archaic pre-1860 procedure. However, section 40(1) of the 1947 Act provides that *nothing* in the Act shall apply to proceedings against the Sovereign in his or her private capacity. This may well be understood to mean that the repeal of the 1860 Act does not include such proceedings. A petition of right under the pre-1860 procedure may still be brought under the Colonial Stock Act 1877 to sue for interest due from the Crown: *Franklin* v. *Att.-Gen.* [1974] 2 Q.B. 185, 205.

[6] See especially *Churchward* v. *R.* (1865) L.R. 1 Q.B. 173 at 209; cf. *Commercial Cable Co.* v. *Government of Newfoundland* [1916] 2 A.C. 610 at 617.

[7] As was the position in *Churchward*'s case, where a long-term government contract for the carriage of mails was discontinued; the annual Appropriation Act indeed expressly stated that no more money was to be applied towards payments to Churchward. S.O. No. 55 of the House of Commons now expressly provides that in government contracts for the carriage of mails by sea, extending over a period of years, there shall be inserted the condition that the contract shall not be binding till approved by a resolution of the House.

[8] See *New South Wales* v. *Bardolph* (1934) 52 C. L. R. 455 (Australia); Wilson, *Cases and Materials*, p. 626. For an incisive analysis, see Street, op. cit., pp. 85–92. It is still not clear whether 'unenforceable' means unenforceable by the other party in an action or merely that judgment against the Crown could be awarded but not executed; if the latter is the

liable.[9] The agent's authority to bind the Crown, may be express or implied. But what if the agent has no such authority? In private law the principal will still be liable if he has held the agent out as having the authority he lacks; this is called 'ostensible' authority. In certain situations a principal will also be liable if the agent was acting in the course of his 'usual' authority although that authority was neither implied nor ostensible. It is still unclear whether, and if so when, the Crown is bound in such cases. Possibly the Crown will be estopped from denying that its servant or agent has authority to bind it in these situations, provided that (i) the other party could not reasonably have been expected to know the limits of the agent's authority;[10] (ii) the limits of the agent's authority were not defined by legislation[11] and (iii) the Crown itself was not precluded from entering into the contract.[12] But nobody can be sure of the legal position at the present time. It has been held that if a Crown agent exceeds his authority and the Crown is not bound, the other party to the 'contract' cannot recover damages against the agent for breach of warranty of authority,[13] though the agent would be so liable in private law.

4   As has been seen,[14] the Crown is in a different legal position from other employers. The common-law rule is that civil servants hold office at the pleasure of the Crown and cannot sue for damages for wrongful dismissal, though they are legally entitled to be paid for

---

correct interpretation, the position is the same as with any other contract with the Crown; see p. 635, below.

[9]   *Macbeath* v. *Haldimand* (1786) 1 T.R. 172.

[10]   In *Robertson* v. *Minister of Pensions* [1949] 1 K.B. 227 (not a case of contract) the Crown was held to be estopped from denying through one Department the binding force of assurances (about entitlement to a service pension) which another Department had given without authority but on which the other party had relied to its detriment. (Followed in *Re L (An Infant)* [1971] 3 All E.R. 743.) Even today the authority of this proposition is uncertain (cf. *Howell* v. *Falmouth Boat Construction Co.* [1951] A.C. 837).

[11]   *Att.-Gen. for Ceylon* v. *Silva* [1953] A.C. 461 (Crown not bound). In that case the agent had held *himself* out as having the authority he lacked; the principal would therefore not have been bound in private law according to the doctrine of ostensible authority. It has nevertheless been suggested that the Crown might have been bound if a superior officer had held the agent out as having authority; or alternatively that the Crown should have been bound according to the doctrine of 'usual' authority. See further Treitel [1957] *Public Law* 321 at 335–9, J. A. G. Griffith and H. Street, *Principles of Administrative Law* (5th edn, 1973), p. 261, note 2. Turpin, *Government Contracts* (1972), pp. 34–6; Hogg, *Liability of the Crown* (1971), pp. 125–9. There are wide differences of opinion among commentators.

[12]   For example, because of a statutory restriction or the *Amphitrite* principle; see below.

[13]   *Dunn* v. *Macdonald* [1897] 1 Q.B. 401, 555, a much criticized decision, but applied in *The Prometheus* (1949) 82 Ll.L. Rep. 859.

[14]   pp. 199–200 and 206–7.

the work they have done and they can obtain a statutory order for reinstatement or re-engagement and an award of compensation for unfair dismissal.[15] Military servants of the Crown cannot even sue for their pay.

5   In the *Amphitrite* case the rule that Crown servants are dismissible at pleasure was ascribed to a general principle of law that the Crown 'cannot by contract hamper its freedom of action in matters which concern the welfare of the State'.[16] In that case, which arose during the First World War, the Crown had assured the owners of a neutral ship that if it put into a British port with cargo, it would be given a clearance and allowed to depart. The ship was nevertheless detained and the owners brought a petition of right for breach of contract. It was held that there was no contract, first because the assurance given by the Crown was to be construed as no more than a statement of intent,[17] and secondly, because the Crown was incapacitated from binding itself in the manner contended by the suppliants, though it could have bound itself to perform an ordinary commercial contract. The decision raises a number of problems, and some critics have denied that any principle of law precluding a Government from fettering its future executive action exists. Nevertheless, there is no doubt that such a principle does exist;[18] the question is how to formulate it and determine its scope. The Crown, like other public authorities, ought not to be able to bind itself to abstain from exercising discretionary powers or performing public duties in matters of primary importance.[19] If it were to purport to bind itself in such ways, then the undertaking should be either of no legal effect at all or capable of being repudiated by the Crown when the national interest so demanded. But the courts must retain power to determine when, for example, executive necessity justifies the Crown in repudiating an ostensibly binding contract. It is not reasonable to insist that engagements with established civil servants must be subject to the *Amphitrite*

[15] Employment Protection (Consolidation) Act 1978, ss 67–79, 138. See above, p. 200.

[16] *Rederiaktiebolaget Amphitrite* v. *R.* [1921] 3 K.B. 500 at 503–4.

[17] See also *Australian Woollen Mills Ltd* v. *Commonwealth of Australia* [1956] 1 W.L.R. 11. But in *Amphitrite* the ingredients of a contract were present.

[18] It has seldom been relied on by the Crown in reported cases, and in *Robertson*'s case (see above) Denning J. held that it was applicable only where there was an implied term introducing it, but the principle was both recognized and applied in *Board of Trade* v. *Temperley Steam Shipping Co.* (1927) 27 Ll.L. R. 230 (charterparty of a ship to the Government) and *Crown Lands Commissioners* v. *Page* [1960] 2 Q.B. 274 (requisitioning of land in wartime and for some years after the end of the war): see especially Devlin L.J.'s judgment at 291–4.

[19] See pp. 415, 573; and J. D. B. Mitchell, *The Contracts of Public Authorities* (1954).

principle – a point originally (and albeit indirectly) conceded by the Industrial Relations Act 1971 [20] – nor, on the other hand, does it follow that all commercial contracts are excluded from its scope (for example, in time of grave emergency). Where the principle does apply, the other party to the 'contract' has no right to damages or compensation. It would be a useful law reform to give the courts jurisdiction to award compensation (but not an injunction or a decree of specific performance) to a party damnified by the repudiation of a contract by the Crown on the grounds of executive necessity in cases where the Crown was initially bound by the agreement.

6   The Government is a large-scale purchaser and is often able to impose its own terms on a contractor. There is no special body of case law governing the standard term contract; the quasi-legislative character of such contracts should be recognized and their terms subject to a measure of judicial review.

Tort

Before the Crown Proceedings Act, the individual Crown servant was personally liable as a tortfeasor even though he was purporting to act in the execution of his official functions. But if sued he might not be able to pay the damages or indeed the costs. The Crown was immune from liability; the King could do no wrong and hence was immune from liability for the wrongful acts of his servants although in the same circumstances other employers (including autonomous public authorities) would have been liable. Ministers and superior officials were not legally liable either,[21] unless they had authorized or otherwise participated in the wrongdoing, in which case they were personally liable as joint tortfeasors in their private capacities.

The Crown would often pay damages awarded against its servants for torts committed in the general course of their employment. It would submit some claims to arbitration and abide by the result. If liability were disputed, it would sometimes put up a Crown servant as a nominated defendant though the real defendant should have been the Crown, and it would stand behind him. In two cases, where no legal duty towards the plaintiff had been owed by the nominated defendant, the courts disapproved of this convenient practice;[22] these strictures expedited the introduction of the Crown Proceedings Bill.

[20] See now the Employment Protection (Consolidation) Act 1978, s. 138.
[21] *Bainbridge* v. *Postmaster-General* [1906] 1 K.B. 178.
[22] *Royster* v. *Cavey* [1947] K.B. 204; *Adams* v. *Naylor* [1946] A.C. 543.

The Act preserved the personal immunity of the Sovereign. It did not state in general terms that the Crown was to be liable in tort; instead, it made the Crown liable in the same manner as a private person of full age and capacity for specified classes of torts which, subject to certain exceptions, cover the general field.[23] The Crown is now liable for torts committed by its servants or agents[24] acting in the general course of their functions, and for breach of the common-law duties owed by employers and those owed by owners or occupiers of property. In cases of vicarious liability (liability for acts of a servant or agent) there must also be a right of action against the servant himself. Are public corporations administering nationalized industries servants or agents of the Crown? Almost certainly none of them is; the point is now usually made clear by statute, but even if it is not, they have the requisite degree of autonomy in relation to Ministers for them to be excluded from the category of Crown servants.[25] Certain public corporations providing social services may be in a more ambiguous position. So may incorporated bodies promoting or regulating economic activity as instruments of the central government. The Act providing for their constitution and functions is not always clear on this matter; a corporation may be a Crown servant or agent for certain purposes but not others. The question may assume practical importance only if the corporation is sued and claims a special Crown immunity (for example, from injunctions) or if the Crown is sued instead of the corporation because the latter lacks adequate funds. In determining whether a corporation is a Crown servant the court will scrutinize not only the constitutent instrument but also the degree of ministerial control over the corporation.[26]

Section 2(6) has a curious look about it. It renders the Crown liable for the Acts or omissions only of such of its officers as are (i) appointed, directly or indirectly, by the Crown and (ii) paid wholly out of central government funds. The main practical effect of this subsection was to exempt the Crown from liability for acts of the police.[27] Under the Police Act 1964, chief constables are now vicariously liable for the torts of police officers.[28] But section 2(6) leaves the Crown immune from liability for the torts of borrowed 'servants'.

The Crown is liable in tort for breaches of statutory duty in

---

[23] Crown Proceedings Act 1947, s. 2. Detailed analysis is not included in the text below.
[24] 'Agent' was defined (s. 38(2)) as including an independent contractor (i.e. one who was doing the work for the Crown otherwise than as a servant). The term 'officer' of the Crown includes a Crown servant.
[25] See especially *Tamlin* v. *Hannaford* [1950] 1 K.B. 18.
[26] See generally pp. 135–6 and 220.
[27] Assuming, of course, that they were officers of the Crown. See ch. 20.
[28] s. 48. They are indemnified out of local funds.

situations where breach gives rise to a right of civil action.[29] However, its position is not quite the same as that of other public authorities on this matter. A statutory duty will not be held to bind the Crown unless it does so expressly or by a very necessary implication.[30] Moreover, the Crown will not be liable unless the statute is also binding on persons *other* than the Crown and its officers; there seems to be no good reason for this limitation. On the other hand, the Crown is liable for breaches of statutory duties imposed on its servants; this goes beyond the liability of other public bodies.

The Crown is not, of course, liable in respect of acts of State or acts done by virtue of the royal prerogative.[31] Section 11(2) of the Act provides that where, in proceedings under the Act, it is material to determine whether anything was properly done (or left undone) in the exercise of the prerogative, a certificate given by the responsible Minister that the act or omission was necessary for the defence of the realm or for training or maintaining the efficiency of the armed forces shall be conclusive. The exact effect of this provision, like so many other matters touching the prerogative, is obscure; the certificate will be conclusive of the facts stated but cannot conclusively determine, as a matter of law, whether the act or omission in question fell within the scope of the prerogative.

Under section 10 of the Act, no action in tort lay against a member of the armed forces, who, while on duty, caused death or injury to another member of the forces on duty or on land, premises or transport being used for the purposes of the forces, provided that the responsible Minister certified that the death or injury was attributable to service for entitlement to a pension. Nor was the Crown liable in these circumstances. Similarly, no action would lie against the Crown for death or personal injury suffered by a member of the forces as a result of the condition of such land, premises or transport, or equipment or supplies (for example, through the crash of a defective transport plane or the premature explosion of a shell or food-poisoning in the cookhouse), provided that the appropriate certificate of pensionability was awarded. The right of civil action was barred even though in the end no pension was in fact awarded to the claimant.[32] In recent years it became generally accepted that section 10 could cause injustice: for example, pension payments and disability allowances for members of the armed forces no

---

[29] For those situations a student should consult a textbook on the law of tort. For a brief synopsis see de Smith, op. cit. (4th edn, 1980), pp. 530–36.

[30] See pp. 132–6.

[31] See ch. 7.

[32] *Adams* v. *War Office* [1955] 1 W.L.R. 1116.

longer compared favourably with the levels of damages recoverable in civil actions. The courts showed some subtlety in interpreting the section so as to restrict its scope,[33] and the Government supported a private Member's bill which became the Crown Proceedings (Armed Forces) Act 1987. Under it section 10 was repealed[34] except in relation to anything suffered by a person in consequence of an act or omission before the date on which the Act was passed: the 1987 Act is therefore not retrospective.[35] Section 10 may, however, be revived by the Secretary of State by statutory instrument, either generally or for such purposes as the instrument may describe; it must, in any case, be expedient to revive it by reason of imminent national danger or great emergency or warlike preparations outside the United Kingdom.[36]

Section 9 excluded liability of the Crown and its officers in tort for any default in connection with postal, telephone or telegraphic services, apart from a limited financial liability for wrongful loss or damage to registered inland postal packets.[37] This immunity was justifiable on grounds of public policy; to introduce the principle of liability would probably encourage a great number of unmeritorious claims. When the Post Office ceased to be a government Department and became a public corporation, section 9 was replaced by sections 29 and 30 of the Post Office Act 1969 which reproduced similar immunities. Immunities in favour of British Telecom have since been repealed.[38]

The Crown is also exempt from liability for the acts or omissions of persons discharging or purporting to discharge responsibilities of a judicial nature or in connection with judicial process (section 2(5)). But for this subsection (which is presumably intended to emphasize the independence of the judicial function), interesting problems would arise in determining whether a person performing judicial functions was a Crown servant.[39] Individual liability is not affected.[40]

---

[33] See *Bell* v. *Secretary of State for Defence* [1986] Q.B. 322; *Pearce* v. *Secretary of State for Defence* [1988] 2 All E.R. 348.

[34] 1987 Act, s. 1.

[35] The Government agreed, however, to make ex gratia payments relating to claims made during the few months before its enactment.

[36] 1987 Act, ss. 2(1), (5), 2(2). The instrument is subject to parliamentary approval.

[37] On the interpretation of this section, see *Triefus* v. *Post Office* [1957] 2 Q.B. 352; *Building & Civil Engineering Holidays Scheme Management Ltd* v. *Post Office* [1966] 1 Q.B. 247.

[38] Telecommunications Act 1984, s. 109 and Sched. 7.

[39] cf. *Ranaweera* v. *Ramachandran* [1970] A.C. 962 (P.C.). Clearly officers sitting as members of a court-martial administering military law, and Crown servants such as the special commissioners of income tax, are officers of the Crown exercising judicial functions. Are judges officers of the Crown? And which (if any) licensing authorities exercise functions of a 'judicial' nature?

[40] See p. 376.

Subject to these exceptions, the tortious liability of the Crown is much the same as that of local authorities[41] and other public bodies. In other words, it is not set apart from the private law of tort. The doctrine of 'sovereign immunity', which in American law exempts governmental bodies from civil liability for discretionary acts, forms no part of English law. And, although in particular classes of situations liability without fault may be attributed,[42] there is as yet no *general* principle of English law that public authorities are liable without fault (as they are in France) for damage caused by an exceptional risk created by a public activity.

Reasonable care has to be exercised in the discharge of statutory powers and duties so as to prevent the occurrence of reasonably foreseeable damage to private rights or unnecessary aggravation of such damage as must inevitably be caused. But this general principle cannot be applied mechanically without reference to the context. For example, it would be futile for a farmer, whose fertile land had been compulsorily acquired under statutory powers, to claim damages for trespass against the acquiring authority on the ground that it was unreasonable to take his land. Even if the jurisdiction of the courts to entertain such a claim were not ousted by the provision of an exclusive alternative remedy (a statutory application to quash the order within a limited period), he would still have to show that the order was not merely unreasonable but tainted with a vitiating defect.

Liability in negligence for the careless exercise of, or failure to exercise, discretionary powers is still in an embryonic stage. The basic principle emerging from *Dorset Yacht Co. Ltd* v. *Home Office*[43] and *Anns* v. *Merton L.B.C.*[44] is that an individual claiming damages for loss sustained as a result of the negligent operation of a discretionary power, or failure to exercise such a power at all, must prove that the conduct of the public authority was not simply negligent but amounted to a misuse of the relevant discretionary powers.

Procedure and evidence

Crown proceedings must be brought by or against an 'authorized Department' – the Department concerned with the general field of

[41] cf. pp. 414, 416–17.
[42] For example, under the rule in *Rylands* v. *Fletcher* (1866) L.R. 1 Ex. 265 and in certain cases of breach of statutory duty.
[43] [1970] A.C. 1004.
[44] [1978] A.C. 882, and see above, p. 417.

conduct in issue; or if none of the authorized Departments is appropriate or if it is not clear which is appropriate, proceedings must be brought against the Attorney-General. A list of authorized Departments is published by the Cabinet Office (section 17).

In general, the same periods of limitation apply to proceedings against the Crown as against other persons. Damages and costs may likewise be awarded against the Crown. However, execution of a judgment cannot be levied against Crown property; this is not a matter of any consequence, for the Crown does comply with judgments against it. Coercive orders – for the specific restitution of land and property, for the specific performance of contracts, and injunctions – cannot issue against the Crown; instead, the court may make an order declaratory of the plaintiff's rights (section 21(1)).[45] Moreover, the court cannot grant an injunction against an officer of the Crown if the effect of granting it would be to give relief against the Crown which could not have obtained in proceedings against the Crown itself (section 21(2)).[46] Interpretation of the latter subsection presents difficulties. It appears to preclude the award of an injunction against government Departments, those public corporations which are Crown servants, Ministers and other officers of the Crown for acts done in the purported exercise of their statutory functions,[47] save perhaps where the unlawful act is not merely *ultra vires* but also a tort, in which case an injunction might be awarded against an offending Crown officer in his *personal* capacity if the act was far removed from his field of lawful authority. More liberal interpretations are possible. So in a High Court action it was held that an injunction may be granted against the Crown or a Crown servant in proceedings brought by way of an application for judicial review.[48] The state of the law before the Act was by no means crystal clear. What is clear, unfortunately, is that where the courts have no jurisdiction to issue a final injunction, they have no jurisdiction to issue an interim injunction either; and although a declaration may be an effective substitute for a final injunction (because the Crown will comply with it) the courts do not issue interim

---

[45] See, e.g., *R.* v. *Secretary of State for the Home Department, ex p. McAvoy* [1984] 1 W.L.R. 408.

[46] See, e.g., *R.* v. *Secretary of State for the Home Department, ex p. Kirkwood* [1984] 1 W.L.R. 913; *R.* v. *Secretary of State for the Home Department, ex p. Yaqood* [1984] 1 W.L.R. 920.

[47] *Merricks* v. *Heathcoat-Amory* [1955] Ch. 567. See also *Harper* v. *Home Secretary* [1955] Ch. 238, where the question was not firmly decided. cf. Hogg, op. cit., pp. 24–6, putting the case for a more restrictive interpretation of section 21(2).

[48] *R.* v. *Governor of Pentonville Prison, ex p. Herbage* [1987] Q.B. 872 (but relief was refused on the facts).

declarations.[49] It would seem that unless the Crown consents to a specially expedited hearing of a declaratory action,[50] a person aggrieved may be unable to invoke the jurisdiction of the courts as a matter of urgency to restrain the Crown or its officers from inflicting irreparable damage on private rights by unlawful conduct.

A blanket exclusion of injunctive relief against the Crown and its servants is hard to justify. Mandamus (also a coercive remedy, disobedience to which is likewise a contempt of court) will lie against a Minister in his official capacity on the application of a person with a sufficient interest in the performance of the duty. So will an order of prohibition, and a statutory order to restrain the making or confirmation of a compulsory purchase order; these remedies are closely analogous to injunctions. The arguments against giving the courts a general jurisdiction to award injunctions seem to be (i) that injunctions cover a wider field than these classes of orders and (ii) that the Crown through its servants might find it necessary to disobey the strict letter of the law in an unpredictable emergency and ought not to be impeded or embarrassed by an adverse court order. But injunctions are discretionary and judges are not in the habit of ignoring the existence of a grave national emergency. In several other Commonwealth countries, injunctions can be awarded against governments and their officers in their public capacities.

Public interest immunity

By section 28 of the 1947 Act the courts could make an order for discovery of documents against the Crown and require the Crown to answer interrogatories, but this new power was subject to important qualifications. It was not to affect any rule of law about the withholding of any document or refusal to answer any question on the ground that disclosures or answers would be injurious to the public interest; nor was it to affect any rules made to secure non-disclosure of the very existence of a document if in the opinion of a Minister it would be injurious to disclose its existence.[51]

The first proviso referred to the broad rule laid down in *Duncan* v.

---

[49] *Underhill* v. *Ministry of Food* [1950] 1 All E.R. 591; *International General Electric Co. of New York* v. *Customs and Excise Commissioners* [1962] Ch. 784.

[50] In *Marsh (Wholesale) Ltd* v. *Customs and Excise Commissioners* [1970] 2 Q.B. 206, where final declarations were claimed, the case was tried only three weeks after the issue arose. In *Lee* v. *Department of Education and Science* (1967) 66 L.G.R. 211, judgment was delivered within three *days* of the institution of proceedings.

[51] See now Rules of the Supreme Court, Order 77, r. 12(2).

Cammell, Laird & Co.,[52] propounding the common-law doctrine of Crown privilege. The rule was not confined to proceedings to which the Crown was a party. In *Duncan*'s case dependants of men lost when the submarine *Thetis* sank on its trials sued the shipbuilders for negligence. The plaintiffs sought production of various documents in the possession of the defendants. Some of these would in fact have revealed unique features of the submarine which would, if openly divulged, have been of considerable advantage to the enemy; the proceedings were brought during the Second World War. The defendants, under Government instructions, objected to their production, and the First Lord of the Admiralty swore an affidavit to the effect that he had considered the documents and had formed the opinion that their disclosure to anybody would be injurious to the public interest. All the courts upheld this objection and declined even to inspect the documents. Viscount Simon L.C., speaking for a unanimous House of Lords, stated the principle at a high level of generality. Documents otherwise relevant and liable to production in judicial proceedings were not to be produced if the public interest required that they be withheld. The objection to production should be taken personally by the Minister in charge of the Department, or, if he were unavailable, by the permanent head of the Department. An objection properly taken should be accepted by the courts as conclusive. The test of injury to the public interest might be satisfied by reference either to the contents of the particular document or to the fact that the document belonged to a class which, as a class, had to be withheld from production. Examples of classes of documents which could properly be withheld were those where disclosure would be injurious to national defence, good diplomatic relations or the proper functioning of the public service. The public interest might well require 'a particular class of communication with, or within, a public department to be protected from production on the ground that the candour and completeness of such communications might be prejudiced if they were ever liable to be disclosed in subsequent litigation . . .'[53] The same consideration applied to oral evidence of the contents of such documents,[54] but they did not necessarily apply to criminal proceedings.

It will be noted that 'Crown privilege', as thus formulated, was not confined to those proceedings to which the Crown was a party. Indeed, the principle was not so much a privilege of the Crown as an

[52] [1942] A.C. 624.
[53] At 635.
[54] *Gain* v. *Gain* [1962] 1 W.L.R. 1469.

exclusionary rule of evidence based on the public interest, of which the Minister was deemed to be the sole judge if he expressed a view in the appropriate form; but if the Minister did not object, the judge himself ought to exclude evidence contrary to the national interest.

Probably no modern rule of English law has attracted so much criticism.[55] The courts had abdicated in favour of the Executive at the expense of the interests of litigants and the public interest in the due administration of justice. And privilege was claimed as a matter of principle for most classes of communications within and between central government Departments and many types of communications between Departments and outside bodies. In *Ellis* v. *Home Office* (1953), where a prisoner on remand, who had been assaulted and severely injured by a mentally disturbed patient in the prison hospital, sued the Crown for negligence, privilege was successfully claimed for prison medical reports on the assailant;[56] the action had to fail, and doubts were expressed by judges themselves whether justice had in fact been done.

In 1956, and again in 1962 and 1964, administrative concessions were announced: privilege would no longer be claimed for various classes of documents, including those in issue in *Ellis*'s case. The law was not modified, but the basis of the broad rule in *Duncan*'s case was being questioned. Critics harked back to a Privy Council decision (disapproved in *Duncan*'s case) where it had been held that the courts had an inherent power, exercisable in exceptional circumstances, to inspect documents for which privilege had been claimed and to disallow the claim altogether if it were clearly unreasonable.[57] The Scottish courts reasserted a somewhat similar residuary power (denied in *Duncan*'s case) to overrule a claim to privilege if the interests of the administration of justice so demanded.[58] In the mid-1960s, courts in some Commonwealth countries rejected the general rule laid down in *Duncan*'s case. And the Court of Appeal in three cases decided in 1964,[59] began to undermine the authority of the rule in English law, declining to

---

[55] One of the best critiques is by Clark (1967) 30 *Mod. L. Rev.* 489.

[56] [1953] 2 Q.B. 135. Privilege was also successfully claimed for documents affecting international relations on an application for habeas corpus: *Soblen*'s case [1963] 2 Q.B. 243.

[57] *Robinson* v. *South Australia* (No. 2) [1931] A.C. 704, applied in *Burmah Oil Co. Ltd* v. *Bank of England* [1980] A.C. 1090.

[58] *Glasgow Corporation* v. *Central Land Board* 1956 S.C. (H.L.) I; *Whitehall* v. *Whitehall* 1957 S.C. 30.

[59] *Re Grosvenor Hotel, London (No. 2)* [1965] Ch. 1210; *Merricks* v. *Nott-Bower* [1965] 1 Q.B. 57; *Wednesbury Corporation* v. *Ministry of Housing and Local Government* [1965] 1 W.L.R. 261.

accept 'the proper functioning of the public service' as a sufficient reason for withholding disclosure and affirming that the court did have a reserve power, if dissatisfied with the Minister's reasons, to inspect and order disclosure. But the court refrained from overruling the Minister's claim in any of these cases.

In *Conway* v. *Rimmer* (1968) a probationary police constable had been prosecuted for theft; the charge was dismissed, but he was dismissed from his post soon afterwards. He brought an action for malicious prosecution against his former superintendent, and in the course of preliminary proceedings for discovery the Home Secretary objected to the disclosure of certain reports relevant to the case. His objection was made in proper form, particularizing the classes of documents into which they fell (confidential reports on police officers and reports concerning investigation into crime) and specifying that in his opinion the production of documents of each class would be injurious to the public interest. The House of Lords held [60] unanimously that the Minister's assertion as to the effect of disclosure was not to be accepted as conclusive; that although *Duncan*'s case was rightly decided on its own facts, the broader propositions for which that case had been regarded as an authority were wrong;[61] that the courts had a residuary power to inspect the documents in question privately in order to determine whether the public interest in suppressing them outweighed the interests of parties to proceedings and the general public in the unfettered administration of justice; and this power should be exercised in the instant case. Having inspected the documents, their Lordships overruled the Minister's claim of Crown privilege and ordered disclosure.

This important decision – the most striking example of judicial activism in administrative law since the war – left some questions unanswered. Five separate judgments seldom elicit a clear-cut *ratio decidendi*. Opinions differed on the criteria to be adopted by courts in evaluating claims to Crown privilege, but it can be inferred that judges ought not even to call for inspection of documents described as belonging to certain classes (for example Cabinet papers, and documents concerned with national security or diplomatic relations). Documents belonging to other classes (for example, concerning the formation of policy, or methods used in the investigation of crime) might be

---

[60] [1968] A.C. 910.
[61] If these propositions are to be regarded as part of the *ratio decidendi* in *Duncan*'s case, then the House of Lords was exercising its newly asserted power to overrule its own binding precedents. Some judges and commentators have regarded those propositions merely as *obiter dicta*. I prefer the first of these opinions.

inspected but should not normally be disclosed.[62] Official documents of a more routine nature would be inspected and, if relevant, normally disclosed. It was still not clear what standards judges should apply in balancing the possible injury to the public interest caused by disclosure (or the prospect of disclosure) against the claims of the administration of justice in an individual case; or what criteria or procedure should be used if a claim for privilege were to be raised before an inferior court.[63] But there was no obvious reason for differentiating claims on a 'class' basis from claims for privilege based on the *contents* of a particular document. It had already been held[64] that a claim to exclude a subpoenaed witness from giving any *oral* evidence at all should be disallowed; objection should be taken to individual questions and answers on behalf of a Minister at the hearing.

Conway v. *Rimmer* has substituted absolute judicial discretion for absolute executive discretion. There was no obvious reason why judicial wisdom and experience should be surer guides to the public interest on these matters than the judgments formed by the Executive. That Ministers and civil servants have tended to give far too much weight to the interests of secrecy and confidentiality and too little weight to the hardship caused to individual litigants can at once be conceded. On the other hand, the implementation of judicial policy is now unpredictable, whereas executive policy in relation to the withholding of relevant evidence was at least regulated by intelligible principles. Consistency is not an end in itself, but problems of such public importance ought not to be left to be dealt with merely on a case-to-case basis. A primary purpose of Crown privilege was to maintain the efficient conduct of affairs or 'the proper functioning of the public service'. Some important information cannot be obtained at all except under a pledge of secrecy. Many persons will not write completely candid appreciations if they have reason to think that their comments may be subsequently divulged.[65] To some people, including judges, who ought to know better, the latter statement is apparently incredible, at any rate when it

[62] Though disclosure of a report concerned with an investigation of a particular suspected crime was ordered in *Conway* v. *Rimmer*.

[63] Clearly there ought to be a right of appeal or reference on this issue to a superior court before a decision to overrule the claim to privilege from disclosure is final.

[64] *Broome* v. *Broome* [1955] P. 190.

[65] This point emerges in the selection of candidates for university places. Head teachers' confidential assessments are occasionally wrong-headed, but they are usually quite frank. Disclosure of such assessments would probably be self-defeating while we maintain a system of selective admissions, because some head teachers would 'pull their punches'. Testimonials for graduate students coming from certain countries where 'open testimonials' are the rule (and actions for libel against the authors of testimonials have not been uncommon) are seldom worth the paper they are written on.

is made with reference to civil servants. One can only reply by dogmatic assertions.

1 If, for example, a Department is to place a contract worth £10 millions, it must have the fullest possible information about the standing of potential contractors and any personal characteristics of their directors and managers which cast doubt on their suitability to be entrusted with a major project.

2 Similarly, if a Minister has to conduct personal negotiations with a group of people with whom he is unacquainted, he ought to be briefed by frank appreciations prepared by his advisers.

3 These comments will sometimes be disparaging and defamatory.[66]

4 They ought to be put in writing, not left to oral communication. Memory fades and Ministers change.

5 Senior civil servants do in fact express themselves on paper far more fully and bluntly on 'personnel' matters than, for example, local government officers or most university teachers.

6 The prospect of disclosure to the persons disparaged will tend to transfer comments from the departmental file to private conversations in the office or the club.

7 This tendency is not limited to a handful of moral cowards: many of us are afflicted with this foible.

And why do defamatory comments by judges in court, and M.P.s in parliamentary proceedings, need to be protected by absolute privilege?

Developments in the courts since *Conway* v. *Rimmer* have been surprising. In 1972 the Law Lords described the very term 'Crown privilege' as 'wrong', 'misleading', 'not accurate' and 'a misnomer'.[67] The courts now prefer the term public interest immunity. But in the case in question they were unanimously upholding a claim by the Home Secretary and the Gaming Board to set aside a witness summons obtained by a gaming club proprietor for the purpose of procuring disclosure of a confidential police report on him to the Gaming Board so as to enable him to prosecute a police officer for libel.[68] What they were trying to emphasize was that the withholding of evidence on

---

[66] There is admittedly a risk that disparaging comments will be unfair, irrelevant or founded on inadequate information.

[67] *R.* v. *Lewes JJ., ex p. Home Secretary* [1973] A.C. 388 at 400, 406, 412.

[68] There had been doubts whether 'Crown privilege' applied to criminal proceedings. See also *Rogers* v. *Home Secretary* [1973] A.C. 388. For the approach of the Australian courts on this point, see *Sankey* v. *Whitlam and others* (1978) 53 A.L.J.R. 11, and of the New Zealand Court of Appeal see *Environmental Defence Society* v. *South Pacific Aluminium Ltd* [1981] N.Z.L.R. 146, 153.

grounds of public interest was not really a 'privilege' of the Crown at all. Two revenue cases in the Lords have touched on some especially awkward problems about the scope of 'public interest'.[69] There has been a belated acknowledgement that what used to be called Crown privilege can be justified in some circumstances on the grounds indicated above – that if certain communications were thought to be likely to be revealed, they would either not be made candidly or not be made at all – and that this might be a very undesirable state of affairs. Recognition of these elementary facts has also been shown in other contexts.[70] But prediction of how the courts will react to claims of public interest immunity is not easy. So, for example, in *Peach* v. *Commissioner of Police for the Metropolis*[71] the Court of Appeal decided that documents must be admitted in a civil action in which it was alleged that a policeman had unlawfully killed the deceased, for the public interest in establishing the cause of a violent death outweighed the claim to confidentiality. And in *Conerney* v. *Jacklin*[72] the immunity was held not to attach to a complaint made against a police officer when he wished to sue the complainant in libel. Information obtained by an adoption society about the child of an unmarried couple was held admissible in affiliation proceedings against them in *R.* v. *Bournemouth Justices, ex p. Grey*.[73] On the other hand, in *Evans* v. *Chief Constable of Surrey*[74] a report sent by the chief constable to the Director of Public Prosecutions in the course of a murder investigation was held to be covered by public interest immunity and so could not be disclosed in a

---

[69] *Crompton (Alfred) Amusement Machines Ltd* v. *Customs & Excise Commissioners* (No. 2) [1974] A.C. 405. (Court of Appeal overruled: disclosure of the documents asked for considered contrary to public interest). *Norwich Pharmacal Co.* v. *Customs and Excise Commissioners* [1974] A.C. 133 (discovery allowed: documents not highly confidential and would relate to persons who were probably tortfeasors). *Inspection* of documents was allowed in *Burmah Oil Co Ltd* v. *Bank of England* [1980] A.C. 1090 because it was considered that the documents, although containing confidential information about the Bank's financial dealings, would not, if disclosed, be 'prejudicial to state policy'. On inspection, however, discovery was refused: the documents did not contain material necessary to dispose fairly of the case.

[70] See *R.* v. *Gaming Board, ex p. Benaim and Khaida* [1970] 2 Q.B. 417 (p. 567, above); *Collymore* v. *Att.-Gen.* [1970] A.C. 538 at 549–51 (confidential information about industrial disputes); *Re D (infants)* [1970] 1 W.L.R. 599 (local authority case records of children under care).

In *Blackpool Corporation* v. *Locker* [1948] 1 K.B. 349 it was held that Crown privilege could not be claimed by local authorities. Now it seems that a local authority may object to the production of evidence on grounds of public interest and that the material excluded does not even have to emanate from the central government (*Re D*, above).

[71] [1986] Q.B. 1064.

[72] [1985] *Crim. L. Rev.* 234.

[73] *The Times*, 31 May 1986.

[74] *The Independent*, 21 January 1988.

later civil action for damages against the police for false imprisonment.

The way ahead is uncertain. The problems of public policy involved are still fundamental and complex. It is easier to take refuge in platitudes such as these than to formulate clear-cut criteria for the regulation of judicial discretion. But sooner or later that task will have to be attempted.

Chapter 33

Redress of Grievances: The Ombudsman and Others

Forms of redress against official conduct

Judicial redress

The main features of judicial review have been outlined in the last four chapters and need not be recited again. The most obvious defects are: (*a*) the centralization of the main forms of proceedings (other than actions for damages) in the High Court; this conduces to delay and expense; (*b*) the still quite wide range of unreviewable administrative action; (*c*) the difficulty in penetrating to the merits of an administrative decision; challenges to validity often have to be based on a technical, procedural or formal flaw; it is very hard to impugn an act or decision for unreasonableness or even for an error of fact; the procedure of the courts is not well adapted to finding out the facts of a case, particularly where relevant material is in departmental files; (*d*) the limited scope of duties to give reasons for administrative decisions; (*e*) various gaps in the law governing the civil liability of public authorities; (*f*) perhaps above all, the fact that a successful challenge to an invalid order or decision may prove a Pyrrhic victory; the winner may find himself back in 'square one', with a heavy bill of costs and no statutory entitlement to any form of compensation.[1]

Some defects have been eliminated or diminished since 1958 by statutory reform, and as has been seen, the Judiciary in recent years has once again shown itself to be willing to adapt the limited methods available to exercise where possible effective review of administrative

---

[1] For imaginative proposals for reform, see *Administration under Law* (Justice, 1971). For the doubtful blessings of victory in the courts, see, for example, *Hall & Co.* v. *Shoreham-by-Sea U.D.C.* [1964] 1 W.L.R. 240 (plaintiff obtained declaration that conditions annexed to grant of planning permission were void; but the court refused to sever the conditions and the grant fell with them).

action. There is still room for much improvement. There is also strong resistance to significant change, as was shown when the Law Commission's attempt[2] to instigate widespread reform was resisted by the Government. Proponents of larger changes fall into two main groups. First, there are those who think in terms of reform within the framework of the existing legal system; they may advocate amalgamation or simplification of judicial remedies, some extension of the scope of review and of administrative liability to pay damages and compensation, and the creation of a special Administrative Division of the High Court, which might include members or assessors with experience in public administration.[3] Secondly, there is a more radical school of thought, consisting mainly of admirers of the French *Conseil d'État*, who despair of piecemeal reform within the existing system and urge the creation of a separate administrative court staffed by members with specialized qualifications in law and administration and applying a separate body of administrative law. Only thus, so they claim,[4] can the law free itself from superficiality, burdensome precedent and inadequate fact-finding techniques and develop rules of administrative justice consonant with the needs of public authorities as well as the citizen. Their point of view has, however, made little headway during the last few years.

Appeals to tribunals and Ministers

These have been considered in chapter 31.

Parliamentary safeguards

The various opportunities to ventilate individual grievances in Parliament, and in particular in the House of Commons, by invoking the doctrine of individual ministerial responsibility at question time and in debate, have also been considered. Departmental select committees concern themselves only incidentally with *individual* grievances. Occasionally a parliamentary storm over an alleged scandal leads to the appointment of a special tribunal or committee of inquiry, but sledgehammers have too often been used to crack nuts.

---

[2] *Administrative Law* (Law Com. No. 20, 1969).

[3] See note 1.

[4] The most eloquent exponent of this point of view is Professor J. D. B. Mitchell. See his articles in [1965] *Public Law* 95; (1966) 15 *I.C.L.Q.* 95; (1967) 38 *Political Quarterly* 360; [1967] *Camb. L.J.* 46. See also *Let Right be Done* (Inns of Court Conservative and Unionist Society, 1966), pp. 16–23.

Commissioners for Local Administration

These have been considered in chapter 21.

Other safeguards

Letters to M.P.s [5] (which may result in informal written questions to Ministers and, if satisfaction is not obtained, a question in the House), complaints to local councillors, to consumers' and consultative councils and committees linked with the work of nationalized industries, to the Office of Telecommunications and to the Director-General of Gas Supply, and to the Council on Tribunals; rights of objection at formal statutory inquiries to proposed administrative orders; opportunities to make informal representations against departmental decisions and proposals where no statutory machinery has been provided – these are among the media for voicing protest and, from time to time, securing redress in respect of administrative acts and omissions. The activities of national and local opposition political parties, of pressure groups agitating on behalf of their members, of the press and broadcasting media and of a body such as the National Council for Civil Liberties, and, at a different level, the work of the Citizens' Advice Bureaux, impose constraints on the exercise of public power and afford prospects of redress by a person injured by its abuse.

Nevertheless, in the early 1960s a widespread body of opinion had been converted to the view that a new institutional safeguard was needed. This development sprang from at least six sources. First, the report of the Franks Committee, and the detailed implementation of its recommendations, showed that a good deal of valuable work could be done in improving the facilities already provided in the area covered by statutory tribunals and inquiries. Secondly, it was noted that no comparable review had been undertaken of situations typified by the Crichel Down affair, where there was no machinery at all for statutory appeal against or review of discretionary decisions. Thirdly, there was a feeling in some quarters that Crichel Down was but the tip of an iceberg; horrendous things were being done to the detriment of the little man by faceless bureaucrats. To put the matter more conservatively, there had been an increase in State control and regulation of national resources and economic activity since 1939; the State had become a massive provider of social services and financial benefits; these develop-

[5] See Page [1985] *Public Law* 1.

ments seemed to be irreversible, and many cases of injustice arising from maladministration would surely occur. Fourthly, disenchantment with judicial and parliamentary methods of redress had grown. A new phase of judicial activism was about to begin, but commentators were more conscious of the long period of judicial self-restraint, particularly in relation to acts done by Ministers. Parliamentary questions and the like were of limited efficacy; it was noted that Commander Marten of Crichel Down was wealthy, well connected and tenacious, but that even so he did not get his wrong redressed. Fifthly, the Danish Ombudsman, Professor Hurwitz, made a lecture tour in this country in 1958. Publicity was gradually built up; perhaps a cure-all would emerge from Scandinavia? Sixthly, the Labour Party was eventually persuaded to incorporate a version of the Ombudsman idea in its electoral programme.

The Parliamentary Commissioner for Administration [6]

In 1965 the Labour Government, rejecting the view of its Conservative predecessor, published a White Paper proposing the appointment of a Parliamentary Commissioner for Administration.[7] The Parliamentary Commissioner Act 1967 was the outcome.

The Commissioner (hereinafter called the P.C.A.) is appointed by the Crown on the Prime Minister's advice; his salary is charged on the Consolidated Fund; he holds office during good behaviour, subject to a retiring age of sixty-five and a power of removal on addresses from both Houses of Parliament. The first P.C.A. was the retiring Comptroller and Auditor-General, Sir Edmund Compton.[8] He has his own Office, and appoints his own staff subject to Treasury approval. He has a staff of about thirty, drawn from the civil service; none of them, astonishingly, is a professional lawyer.

His terms of reference are to investigate complaints by individuals and bodies corporate (other than local authorities and other public corporations) who claim to have 'sustained injustice in consequence of maladministration', while they were in the United Kingdom, at the hands of scheduled central government Departments or persons or bodies acting on their behalf, performing or failing to perform

---

[6] For the background to the establishment of this office, see R. Gregory and P. G. Hutchesson, *The Paraliamentary Ombudsman* (1975).
[7] Cmnd 2767 (1965).
[8] His two immediate successors were also civil servants; but the fourth Commissioner was, and the current Commissioner (A. R. Barrowclough) is, a Q.C.

administrative [9] functions, or at the hands of specified non-departmental public bodies ('quangos').[10]

He cannot act on his own initiative, nor can he be approached directly by a member of the public. But since 1978 the P.C.A. has adopted the practice of forwarding any letter sent by a citizen straight to him to an M.P., stating that he is willing to investigate. The citizen's consent to this is still necessary. His investigations must be conducted in private, and the official head of the Department concerned and any other official implicated in the complaint must be notified and given the opportunity of commenting on the allegations. No set form of inquiry is prescribed, but the P.C.A. has adequate powers to investigate a complaint thoroughly. He can administer oaths and compel the attendance of witnesses and documents. Wilful obstruction of his investigations is punishable as if it were a contempt of court. His reports on investigations, and communications with M.P.s on the subject-matter of a complaint, are protected by absolute privilege in the law of defamation.[11] Irrespective of the Official Secrets Acts and the law relating to Crown privilege, he must be allowed access to any relevant document other than one relating to the proceedings of the Cabinet and its committees (section 8),[12] though public interest immunity may be asserted to prevent the P.C.A. and his officers from *disclosing* information thus obtained (section 11(3)), and the Official Secrets Acts apply to disclosures other than for the purposes of investigations and reports (sections 11(1), (2)).

The P.C.A. has no power to alter or rescind decisions. His statutory powers are confined to making reports on his investigations, or giving to the M.P. who referred the complaint his reasons for not investigating. Reports on investigations go to the M.P. who referred the complaint, and the official against whom the allegations were made and his departmental head. If it appears to the P.C.A. that an injustice has been caused by maladministration and has not been rectified, he may make a special report to both Houses; he may make other special reports, and must make an Annual Report, to each House. His Special and Annual Reports are considered by a small Select Committee of the House of Commons on the

---

[9] As distinct from judicial or legislative. See pp. 336, 537–9.

[10] 1967 Act, s. 4 and Sched. 2, as substituted by the Parliamentary and Health Service Commissioners Act 1987, s. 1 and Sched. 1.

[11] s. 10(5). The M.P. also enjoys absolute privilege in respect of such communications and in the communication of the P.C.A.'s report to the complainant.

[12] It has, however, been recommended that he should have access to Cabinet and Cabinet committee papers, but Parliament has not yet given such authority: see *Fourth Report from the Select Committee on the P.C.A.* (H.C. 444 and 615 (1977–8)).

Parliamentary Commissioner for Administration. Occasionally his special reports have been debated on the floor of the House. A considerable quantity of published material about his work is now available.

Jurisdictional limitations

'Injustice' and 'maladministration' were deliberately left undefined.[13] 'Injustice' means something wider than legally redressible damage; it includes hardship and a sense of grievance which ought not to have arisen. 'Maladministration' covers a multitude of administrative sins, sins of commission and omission – corruption, bias, unfair discrimination, harshness, misleading a member of the public as to his rights, failing to notify him properly of his rights or to explain the reasons for a decision, general high-handedness, using powers for a wrong purpose, failing to consider relevant materials, taking irrelevant material into account, losing or failing to reply to correspondence, delaying unreasonably before making a tax refund or presenting a tax demand or dealing with an application for a grant or licence, and so on. The Commissioner is not allowed to question 'the merits of a decision taken without maladministration . . . in the exercise of a discretion . . .' (section 12(3)). He interpreted this limitation as meaning that he could not consider whether a decision was manifestly unreasonable or even, apparently, based on a clear mistake of fact, if the appropriate procedures had been followed and there was no evidence of impropriety. He was persuaded by the Select Committee that in an extreme case he ought to infer maladministration from the 'thoroughly bad' *quality* of a decision;[14] but he has shown extreme circumspection in this matter. The Committee also persuaded him to consider the 'bad rule' – an internal departmental rule which caused undue hardship to individuals – and to find maladministration if hardship had arisen in a subsequent case arising under the same rule where it had not been properly reviewed by the Department. There are indications that his activities in this area have induced some Departments to re-examine their rules and give them better publicity. The P.C.A. has also accepted that he can investigate the administrative procedures attendant on the making and review of statutory orders other than statutory instruments.

Until 1973 the P.C.A. had no jurisdiction to investigate complaints

---

[13] See *R.* v. *Local Commissioner for Administration, ex p. Bradford City Council* [1979] Q.B. 287, especially Lord Denning M.R.'s judgment, for an attempt to give a judicial definition of maladministration.
[14] H.C. 350 (1967–8), 11–14.

about the National Health Service. The National Health Service Reorganization Act 1973, Part III[15] provided for the appointment of a Health Service Commissioner for England and one for Wales, and the P.C.A. was given these additional posts on 1 October 1973. The relevant statute is now the consolidating National Health Service Act 1977, section 106 of which governs his appointment. The procedures are broadly similar to those under the 1967 Act, although an improvement is that a complaint may be made direct to the Commissioner (section 111). Subject to exceptions in sections 110 and 116, he may investigate an alleged failure in a service, or failure to supply a service provided by specified National Health Service bodies, or any other action taken by or on behalf of such bodies (sections 109 and 115). The 1977 Act, like its predecessor, does not go as far as some might have wished; schedule 13, paragraph 19 lists several matters not subject to investigation, the most important being action which, in the Commissioner's opinion, was taken solely in consequence of clinical judgement.[16]

Among the matters excluded from his jurisdiction under the Third Schedule to the Parliamentary Commissioner Act 1967 are matters arising in external relations and overseas territories (except for complaints against consular officials[17]), extradition, action taken for the investigation of crime or the protection of national security (including the withholding or impounding of passports), judicial proceedings, the prerogative of mercy, government contractual and commercial transactions (subject to limited exceptions), personnel matters in the armed forces and the civil service, the award of honours and the granting of royal charters. Nor can he investigate complaints against local authorities, public corporations (other than instruments of the Crown) or the police. These are very big exclusions. If the subject-matter of a complaint lies within the jurisdiction of a special tribunal or a court of law, the P.C.A. has a discretion: normally he should abstain from investigating the matter, but he may waive the rule if it is unreasonable in the particular circumstances to expect the complainant to resort or to have resorted to the tribunal or court (section 5(2)). We cannot all be experts in administrative law. In practice, wittingly or otherwise, he has

---

[15] See also Cmnd 5055 (1972), pp. 44–5, 55–6; National Health Service (Scotland) Act 1972, Part VII, and the current National Health Service (Scotland) Act 1978, Part VI.

[16] But see *Report from the Select Committee on the P.C.A.: Independent review of hospital complaints in the National Health Service* (H.C. 45 (1977–8)), in which the Committee urged that complaints based on a doctor's clinical judgement should be reviewable by the Commissioner. No legislative action has been forthcoming.

[17] Parliamentary Commissioner (Consular Complaints) Act 1981.

frequently investigated complaints of procedural maladministration which would have been judicially reviewable. This makes it all the more incongruous that he should be so averse from treating manifest unreasonableness as maladministration. There is no bar to investigating matters that could be or have been raised at a statutory inquiry held on behalf of a Minister, provided that the inquiry leads to an 'administrative' type of decision.

In 1986 the P.C.A. received 719 complaints via M.P.s. Of those 719, 549 were rejected and 168 full investigations were completed. The P.C.A. found that 153 cases were wholly or partly justified. The pattern of the year was typical: the Department of Health and Social Security and the Inland Revenue together accounted for 50 per cent of the total number of complaints.[18] Of such dry statistics it is indeed worth quoting the P.C.A.:[19] 'The complaints which I have had to consider (in 1979) scarcely attained a national dimension . . . But to the complainants the grievance of each was important: and it is the mark of a great civilization that it believes in the importance of the individual and finds time for his concerns.'

Evaluation[20]

The Ombudsman was greeted by the sceptics as an Ombudsmouse. Following his special report on the Sachsenhausen case late in 1967,[21] when he found that Foreign Office officials had been guilty of procedural maladministration in dealing with an application by ex-prisoners-of-war for discretionary compensation for suffering caused by incarceration in a Nazi concentration camp, the ranks of Tuscany were cheering. The Foreign Secretary strenuously defended his officials and complained of an encroachment on the principle of ministerial responsibility, but still agreed to pay up.[22]

From him there have come no sensational exposures of bureaucratic turpitude or gross abuses of power. The general picture emerging from his reports is one of a high level of integrity (not to be confused with

---

[18] Annual Report for 1986, H.C. 248 (1986–7), ch. IV.

[19] Annual Report for 1979, H.C. 402 (1979–80), para. 4.

[20] See Marshall [1973] *Public Law* 32; Sir Kenneth Wheare, *Maladministration and its Remedies* (1973), ch. 5; JUSTICE, *Our Fettered Ombudsman* (1977); Frank Stacey, *Ombudsmen Compared* (1978); R. Gregory and P. G. Hutchesson, *The Parliamentary Ombudsman* (1975); Gregory [1982] *Public Law* 49; G. Marshall, *Constitutional Conventions* (1984), ch. V.

[21] H.C. 54 (1967 8).

[22] 758 H.C. Deb. 107–70 (5 February 1968); Fry [1970] *Public Law* 336.

efficiency) in British central government administration.[23] There are other factors impossible to quantify. The Select Committee has asked whether, if the P.C.A. is to be appointed from the civil service, a period of 'quarantine' between leaving the service and taking up office should be introduced, and also is strongly of the view that the House of Commons should be consulted before an appointment is made.[24] With the appointment of Mr Anthony Barrowclough the Government for the second time appointed to the office a person who had not previously been a full-time public official. The 'M.P. filter' has not worked well. The P.C.A. has placed a very high priority on cultivating good relations with heads of Departments, so as to obtain their cooperation in his investigations, but he is little known to the general public. He is a remote figure, neither seeking nor. being accorded publicity.[25] His terms of reference are fairly narrow and have, on the whole, been conservatively interpreted,[26] despite the prodding by the Select Committee. Another possible reason for disillusionment or tepid enthusiasm is that a finding of maladministration does not necessarily lead to anything more than an expression of official regret or an undertaking that the Department will take another look at its procedures.

On the credit side of the balance, it is apparent that the P.C.A.'s investigations are extremely thorough. Departments have often re-scinded decisions, made *ex gratia* payments or refunds, waived or modified tax claims in response to his adverse findings; they have been made more aware of the need for giving adequate and prompt explanations in response to requests and inquiries from members of the public. The Select Committee on the Parliamentary Commissioner,

[23] This is not to say that official turpitude is non-existent. Occasional prosecutions, and revelations of financial malversation in reports of the Comptroller and Auditor-General, show that it does exist; but all the available evidence suggests that it exists only on a very small scale at the central government level. cf. Report of the Royal Commission on Standards of Conduct in Public Life, Cmnd 6524 (1976).

[24] *Second Report from the Select Committee of the Parliamentary Commissioner for Administration, 1975–76* (H.C. 480 (1975–6)).

[25] His reports on investigations go to M.P.s; he does not give them any publicity himself, except in special reports and his Annual Report. Lack of publicity for the office probably tends to cause fewer complainants to *take the initiative in asking* M.P.s to bring their own cases before him. But note the P.C.A.'s views on publicity in his Annual Report for 1975 (H.C. 141 (1975–6)), paras 38–9, and for 1979 (H.C. 402 (1979–80)), paras 11–12.

[26] Subject to exceptions, some of which (the 'bad rule' and the type of case where there might also be a successful invocation of judicial review) are mentioned below. There are others – cases where an action for negligent misstatements might have been brought (but the law on this matter is still developing), and cases where the complainant shows a *prima facie* case of injustice but cannot point to an act of maladministration, in which event the P.C.A. will often begin an investigation.

which has acquired a good deal of information about administrative procedures by considering his reports and examining senior departmental witnesses, has not been as inhibited as the P.C.A. in passing judgment on the merits of a rule or decision. It has been instrumental in securing a relaxation in the Inland Revenue rules for remission of tax arrears in cases of hardship,[27] though it has been unsuccessful in persuading the Government to sponsor legislation enlarging the Commissioner's terms of reference.[28] This is quite undramatic stuff, but those who would write the experiment off as a failure would do well to read his Annual Reports and the Reports (with Minutes of Evidence) of the Select Committee. Some people have obtained redress which they would almost certainly have been denied had these institutions not existed.

To assess the impact of his work on civil service efficiency is impracticable. As he cannot deal with personnel matters or the most politically sensitive issues, there is no obvious reason why the knowledge that he has access to files should inhibit civil servants in expressing their opinions. There have been isolated complaints that he has made officers in some departments too non-committal. Complaints that he has heavily increased departmental workloads are unsubstantiated. Civil Service morale does not appear to have suffered from his activities. He has been careful, as far as possible, to avoid identifying individual culprits in his reports, and in general he has shielded the service against sweeping and unwarranted aspersions. (This has indeed been the experience of Ombudsmen in several other countries.) Senior departmental officers, and Ministers, have been given a better idea of personal, organizational and procedural deficiencies at a lower level.

Although Departments cease to be monolithic under the P.C.A.'s scrutiny, the concept of individual ministerial responsibility to Parliament has not been undermined. The P.C.A.'s criticisms are indeed directed almost exclusively against officials, but the Minister remains politically vulnerable within the limits already explained;[29] and he is supplied with ample material for the meaningful discharge of his responsibility. There is no evidence at all that the P.C.A. has detracted from the traditional functions of M.P.s in procuring the redress of individual grievances. M.P.s have a wide discretion whether or not to pass a complaint on to him for investigation, as has unfortunately been

[27] See Cmnd 4729 (1971).
[28] Cmnd 4661 (1971), where the Government rejected its recommendations for an extension of the P.C.A.'s jurisdiction to include various personnel matters in the public service and the forces.
[29] See pp. 181–6.

demonstrated. He is able to obtain access to materials closed to M.P.s and has coercive powers that they lack. His criticisms of individual administrative decisions cannot be brushed aside as superficial or politically motivated. They have provided opportunities for well-informed parliamentary questions and some well-informed debates.

When a government of this country seriously addresses itself to administrative law reform, a primary source of information will be the reports of the Parliamentary Commissioner for Administration. In particular, he has exposed a number of situations in which administrative ineptitude has led to loss or hardship for which no legal redress may yet be obtainable as of right. Where it is proper to make an *ex gratia* award, it is often unjust that a remedy in the courts should be denied.

Part Seven

Commonwealth Affairs

This Part is devoted entirely to the Commonwealth. Although it would now be absurd to compare the United Kingdom's relationship with the Commonwealth to that of the European Communities, we shall see that the Commonwealth dimension is one which can undoubtedly remain of mutual benefit to Britain and the other members and dependencies. The rise and fall of the 'associated statehood' experiment needs to be mentioned. And the coming to lawful independence of Southern Rhodesia as Zimbabwe deserves to be described in these pages.

Relations between the United Kingdom and the independent members of the Commonwealth are regulated less by strict law than by constitutional convention and political practice. Indeed, the Commonwealth has become so loose an international association that it is doubtful whether one could reasonably speak of its 'constitutional structure'. Constitutional rules in Commonwealth relations are mainly about how membership is acquired and lost; there are few rules saying what members ought to do.

No attempt is made to survey the internal constitutional laws of individual Commonwealth countries, save to the extent that they have a residual impact on United Kingdom constitutional law. Such a task could only be undertaken properly in a different and very large book; and it would have to be rewritten every few months if it were to be kept up to date.

Chapter 34

The Commonwealth

Terminology

The term 'Commonwealth' has no single fixed meaning. It is used in two main senses: first, to denote an association of independent member States; secondly, to include territories which are in various ways dependent on those independent members. The Commonwealth evolved from the British Empire, which came to be called the British Commonwealth of Nations in the 1920s; the latter designation was also ambiguous, usually (though not always) referring to the United Kingdom and the self-governing Dominions. In the late 1940s, after the independent membership of the Commonwealth had been broadened to include three Asian countries, the adjective 'British' was dropped from the semi-official name of the association; and the term 'Dominion' also passed into disuse,[1] the Secretary of State for Dominion Affairs being redesignated Secretary of State for Commonwealth Relations. In the late 1960s the Colonial Office was merged with the Commonwealth Office, and then the Commonwealth Office was merged with the Foreign Office under the Secretary of State for Foreign and Commonwealth Affairs.

Status [2]

The countries or territories of the Commonwealth (using the term in the broadest sense) fall into the following categories.

---

[1] de Smith, *The Vocabulary of Commonwealth Relations* (1954).
[2] The leading work on all legal matters concerning the Commonwealth is Sir Kenneth Roberts-Wray's *Commonwealth and Colonial Law* (1966), although many changes have taken place in the Commonwealth since that date. See also Sir William Dale, *The Modern Commonwealth* (1983).

Full Members. These are independent countries, equal in status with one another in Commonwealth affairs. They are the United Kingdom, Canada, the Commonwealth of Australia,³ New Zealand, Antigua and Barbuda, Bahamas, Bangladesh, Barbados, Belize (formerly British Honduras), Botswana (formerly Bechuanaland), Brunei, Cyprus, Dominica, The Gambia, Ghana, Grenada, Guyana (formerly British Guiana), India, Jamaica, Kenya, Kiribati (formerly the Gilbert Islands), Lesotho (formerly Basutoland), Malawi (formerly Nyasaland), Malaysia, Maldives, Malta, Mauritius, Nauru, Nigeria, Papua New Guinea, St Kitts-Nevis, St Lucia, St Vincent and the Grenadines, Seychelles, Sierra Leone, Singapore, Solomon Islands, Sri Lanka (formerly Ceylon), Swaziland, Tanzania (formerly Tanganyika and Zanzibar), Tonga, Trinidad and Tobago, Tuvalu, Uganda, Vanuatu (formerly the New Hebrides), Western Samoa, Zambia (formerly Northern Rhodesia) and Zimbabwe (formerly Southern Rhodesia).

Condominia. Sovereignty in the Canton and Enderbury Islands is shared between the United Kingdom and the United States.

Colonies. All the remaining colonies are islands or island groups, except Gibraltar and the British Antarctic Territory. With the exception of Hong Kong (to be retroceded to China in 1997: see the Hong Kong Act 1985) none has a population as high as 200,000.

Trust territory. Under the Covenant of the League of Nations, dependencies detached from the countries defeated in the First World War were placed under the administration of developed countries as mandated territories. The United Kingdom, Australia, New Zealand and South Africa became mandatories. After the Second World War, the mandated territories that had not yet achieved independence were brought under the United National trusteeship system, with the sole exception of South West Africa which has been in substance (though not in form) annexed by South Africa. South Africa is now negotiating for South West Africa to become independent as 'Namibia'. South Africa arranged elections for a constituent assembly in South West Africa in 1978, which was transformed into a National Assembly with legislative powers in 1979. But SWAPO, a liberation movement, continues to contest the validity of these moves and seeks genuine

---

³ In Australia the term 'the Commonwealth' usually means the central or federal government of Australia, as opposed to the states.

independence for the area from South Africa.[4] The United Kingdom's other trust territories have all attained to independence in one manifestation or another.

Miscellaneous. Australia and New Zealand have several small dependencies.[5]

Constitutional aspects of dependence

The large corpus of constitutional law relating to British dependent territories has dwindled in practical importance. Here it will be dealt with only in outline or selectively.

At several points in this book, reference has been made to protected states, protectorates and the status of British protected persons.[6] Only two matters need to be emphasized. First, the legislative, executive and judicial powers of the Crown in protected states and protectorates were exercised by virtue of the royal prerogative as regulated by the Foreign Jurisdiction Acts 1890 and 1913. Secondly, since the authority claimed and exercised by the Crown in relation to *protected states* was often very restricted, a protected state could accede to independence merely by an agreement between the Crown and the local ruler that protection be removed, though consequential legislation might have been needed to modify some rules of English law. No protectorates or protected states remain today.[7]

Colonies have traditionally been classified, for the purposes of both public and private law, according to the methods by which they were acquired. Settled colonies were territories without a regular 'civilized' system of government when occupied by British settlers and annexed by the Crown; they included a number of territories in Australia, North America and the Caribbean. The prerogative powers of the Crown in a settled colony are narrowly circumscribed,[8] but legislative power over a settled colony which did not receive a representative legislature under the prerogative can be exercised under

---

[4] For a decision of the South African courts on some of the powers of South Africa in relation to Namibia, see *Beukes* v. *Administrator-General of South West Africa* 1980 (2) S.A. 664.

[5] Roberts-Wray, op. cit., p. 88.

[6] For example, pp. 139, 453.

[7] Brunei (in Borneo) was the last protected state to become independent and the Solomon Islands was the last protectorate.

[8] They are usually stated as covering power to appoint a Governor, an Executive Council and officials and to provide for the establishment of courts to administer the common law (but not another system of law – for example, ecclesiastical law: *Re Lord Bishop of Natal* (1864) 3 Moo, P.C.C. (N.S.) (115)) and a representative legislature.

the British Settlements Acts 1887 and 1945.[9] The general rule is that the settlers carried the common law of England with them.

Conquered or ceded colonies were territories taken from another metropolitan power or an indigenous ruler and placed under the sovereignty of the Crown. The terms of a treaty of cession are not legally binding on the Crown unless incorporated in legislation. The Crown has plenary prerogative legislative powers with respect to such a colony, subject to the rule in *Campbell* v. *Hall* (1774)[10] – that if it grants a representative legislature to the colony (i.e., one in which at least half the members of one House are elected)[11] it cannot derogate from that grant and thus loses that prerogative power unless (as is usually the case) it has expressly reserved the power when granting the constitution. If the prerogative power has been lost but representative institutions are later revoked by statutory authority, the prerogative revives.[12] In conquered or ceded colonies, the basis of the pre-existing legal system usually survived; hence, for example, the retention of Roman–Dutch law in Ceylon and French law in Quebec and Mauritius.

There is also a residual category of colonies which were merely annexed without settlement, conquest or cession. To this class belong the Falkland Islands and the British Antarctic Territory.

Constitutional changes in dependent territories are normally made by Orders in Council – under statutory powers in settled colonies and under prerogative powers in conquered and ceded colonies. If a colony with a representative legislature has power to alter the composition, powers and procedure of that legislature, the amendments must be made in the manner and form required by existing law.[13] In practice, major constitutional changes are made by agreement after discussions or a conference with the United Kingdom Government.

There is no set pattern of constitutional evolution towards internal self-government. Trends of development have varied a great deal according to changing ideas at different periods of imperial history and the particular circumstances of individual territories.[14] Of more prac-

---

[9] See further *Sabally and N'Jie* v. *Att.-Gen.* [1965] 1 Q.B. 273 (Orders in Council made thereunder may be given retroactive effect; validation of elections in Gambia).

[10] 1 Cowp. 204.

[11] This is the definition for the purposes of the Colonial Laws Validity Act 1865. In other contexts the meaning is not necessarily uniform.

[12] *Sammut* v. *Strickland* [1938] A.C. 678.

[13] Colonial Laws Validity Act 1865, s. 5; see *Att.-Gen. for N.S.W.* v. *Trethowan* [1932] A.C. 526, and the analysis of the scope of section 5 by Roberts-Wray, op. cit., pp. 403–5.

[14] See further de Smith, *The New Commonwealth and its Constitutions* (1964), ch. 2; Sir Ivor Jennings, *The Approach to Self-Government*; H. V. Wiseman, *The Cabinet in the Commonwealth*.

tical importance today is how independence is achieved by an internally self-governing colony.

Independence and Dominion status

The following is a description of the typical mechanism for the attainment of independence by an internally self-governing colony.

1 An independence conference is held in London, to determine the date of independence, the content of the independence constitution (which is likely to bear a close similarity to the self-government constitution) and consequential matters – for example, questions of nationality and citizenship.

2 A public officers' agreement, *inter alia*, facilitating the retirement, with special compensation, of expatriate officers serving locally who do not wish to continue under the new régime,[15] and an agreement for state succession to existing international obligations, will be negotiated after the introduction of self-government, to come into effect upon the date of independence.

3 An independence Act will be passed by the United Kingdom Parliament. This will be brought into effect on the 'appointed day' (independence day). It will include the following provisions:

(i) Termination of all authority and responsibility of the United Kingdom Government for the affairs of the territory.

(ii) Total abrogation of the power of the United Kingdom Parliament to make laws for the territory.[16]

(iii) Adaptations of United Kingdom law relating to nationality, citizenship and certain other matters.

(iv) Exclusion of the territory from the expression 'colony' used in United Kingdom legislation.

(v) A schedule providing for

(a) repeal of the Colonial Laws Validity Act 1865 in relation to the territory;

(b) abolition of the doctrine of repugnancy to United Kingdom legislation, and conferment of authority on the local Legislature to make laws (subject to the constitution) inconsistent with

---

[15] Roberts-Wray, op. cit., pp. 287–8. The agreement will deal with other questions and may be given legal effect under the independence constitution.

[16] See pp. 77–8. The power of the United Kingdom Parliament to alter the law of the territory at its request and with its consent does not appear in any *independence* Act since 1957, cf., however, the West Indies Act 1967, pp. 665–6, below.

United Kingdom legislation extending to the territory, including the Independence Act itself;

(c) conferment of full power to make laws with extraterritorial effect.

4   An independence Order, to which the independence constitution will be scheduled, will be made before independence by Her Majesty in Council. This Order will be made under existing statutory or prerogative powers, hardly ever under the Independence Act, but will likewise have effect on the date of independence. The Governor will become a Governor-General unless the territory becomes a republic or has a separate monarch. The Governor-General will be a constitutional representative of the Queen with very limited personal discretionary powers; in no sense will he now be a representative of the United Kingdom Government. It is open to the local Government to advise the appointment of the last colonial Governor or another person to the office. The constitution will include no provision for disallowance of legislation.

Equality of status with the United Kingdom and sovereignty in international law are thus achieved in one bound.

The development of Dominion status is a tortuous, oft-told tale.[17] By 1926 the following Commonwealth countries were called self-governing Dominions: Canada, Australia, New Zealand, South Africa (which left the Commonwealth in 1961),[18] the Irish Free State (which became known as Eire in 1937 and seceded from the Commonwealth under the name of the Republic of Ireland, in 1949)[19] and New-foundland (which relinquished its self-governing institutions after a financial collapse in 1933 and joined Canada as its tenth province in 1949).[20] In the Report of the Inter-Imperial Relations Committee (the Balfour Report) of the Imperial Conference held in 1926, it was declared that the United Kingdom and the Dominions were 'equal in status, in no way subordinate one to another in any aspect of their domestic or external affairs, though united by a common allegiance to the Crown, and freely associated as members of the British Commonwealth of Nations'.[21]

---

[17] See especially Sir Kenneth Wheare, *The Statute of Westminster and Dominion Status* (5th edn, 1953); R. McG. Dawson, *The Development of Dominion Status, 1900–1936* (1937); Sir Ivor Jennings, *Constitutional Laws of the Commonwealth* (3rd edn), vol. I, chs 1–3.

[18] See p. 671.

[19] Ireland Act 1949. For many years before this, Eire had regarded itself as being 'externally associated' with the Commonwealth. For the position in United Kingdom law, see *Murray* v. *Parkes* [1942] 2 K.B. 126.

[20] Newfoundland Act 1949. This followed a referendum in Newfoundland.

[21] Cmnd 2768 (1926), p. 14.

This affirmation was not quite an accurate reflection of the constitutional position of the Dominions at that time. There remained matters in which they were less than equal in status to the United Kingdom. Yet the declaration was substantially correct. The Dominions were more than internally self-governing colonies. They had acquired independent international personalities. Some of their governments had successfully asserted, in the early 1920s, the rights to conclude political treaties in their own names and to be represented separately in foreign capitals. In effect they were sovereign states in international law. But their status had evolved by constitutional convention and usage, not by virtue of statutory change; and no precise moment could be pinpointed as the date of their accession to independence. The term 'independence' was not as fashionable then as it is now; and appeals to the 'unity of the Empire' still evoked some response.

Some surviving elements of formal inequality with the United Kingdom were removed by the enunciation of constitutional conventions at Imperial Conferences held in 1926, 1929 and 1930. The ambiguous status of a Governor-General was resolved; he was to be the representative of the monarch, not of the United Kingdom Government; the United Kingdom Government could not properly give him any instructions in relation to a Dominion's affairs; his appointment (and by implication, his dismissal) was a matter for the Dominion Government alone, tendering direct advice to the monarch. These conventions apply to the newly independent members of the Commonwealth unless varied by agreement.

Other conventions were adopted, reducing provisions for the reservation of bills under Dominion constitutions to empty shells, and providing that it would be improper for the United Kingdom Government to advise that a Dominion Act be disallowed except for the protection of Dominion stockholders.

As was indicated in chapter 2,[22] some elements of inequality could be eliminated only by imperial legislation. It was necessary to pass the Statute of Westminster 1931 in order to remove the Dominions from the definition of 'colony' (section 11), to abolish the doctrine of legislative repugnancy and to exclude Dominion Parliaments from the restrictive operation of the Colonial Laws Validity Act 1865 (section 2),[23] to declare that Dominion Parliaments had full extraterritorial

---

[22] pp. 29–30.

[23] Section 2 (possibly coupled with section 3) of the Statute of Westminster also made it possible for Dominion Parliaments to abolish all appeals from Dominion courts to the Judicial Committee of the Privy Council, including the appeal by special leave, which was a prerogative power placed on a statutory footing by United Kingdom legislation

powers (section 3) and to provide that no future United Kingdom Act was to extend or be deemed to extend to a Dominion as part of its law unless the request and consent of the Dominion concerned were expressly recited in the Act in question.[24] In 1931 Australia and New Zealand, averse from legalistic formulas, were expressly excluded from the main provisions of the Statute; but these provisions were adopted by Australia in 1942 (with retroactive effect to September 1939) and by New Zealand in 1947. (New Zealand repealed the adoption in 1987.[25]) They were never adopted by Newfoundland.

The Statute preserved the method of amending the British North America Acts 1867 to 1930, which were the basis of the Canadian constitution.[26] Most of the provisions of those Acts could be amended only by the United Kingdom Parliament at the request of the Canadian Parliament.[27] The legal position was made to accord with the reality of Canadian independence by the Canada Act 1982, passed at Westminster, which put the constitution and its amendment entirely in Canadian hands.[28]

The position in Australia was more complicated. There too the *status quo* was preserved.[29] But the Australian states were not even excluded from the operation of the Colonial Laws Validity Act 1865,[30] so that they were unable to legislate repugnantly to United Kingdom legislation extending to them as part of their law, and they lacked general extra-territorial powers. They could not abolish appeals on matters of state law from their own Supreme Courts to the Judicial Committee; nor could the Parliament of the Commonwealth of Australia. Moreover, they had certain direct relationships with the United Kingdom Government. They could request the enactment of legislation at Westminster on matters falling within their exclusive sphere without the concurrence of the Commonwealth Government of Parliament; the appointment of a State Governor was made on the advice of the United Kingdom Government on local initiative; the state governments submit their own proposals to London for the award of honours.[31] It might have been

---

(see *British Coal Corporation* v. *R.* [1935] A.C. 500); this accession of power was, however, subject to any impediment that might be imposed by the Dominion constitution itself.

[24] For the possible effect of this section, see pp. 76–8.

[25] Constitution Act 1986 (N.Z.), s. 26.

[26] Section 7. For an excellent general textbook, see P. W. Hogg, *Constitutional Law of Canada* (2nd edn, 1985).

[27] See Scott (1979) 57 *Canadian Bar Review* 587 for a good summary of the position.

[28] See above, p. 31.

[29] Statute of Westminster 1931, ss 8, 9; Wheare, op. cit., ch. 8.

[30] But they were excluded from the definition of 'colony' (Statute, s. 11).

[31] See further, Castles [1962] *Public Law* 175; R. D. Lumb, *The Constitutions of the*

very difficult fo the United Kingdom to remove some of these anomalies merely at the request of the Commonwealth Government and Parliament. However, any such difficulty was avoided by the British Government acceding to the Australia (Request and Consent) Act 1985, to which all the Australian states and the Commonwealth Parliament and Government subscribed, and causing the Australia Act 1986[32] to be enacted at Westminster. That Act ended the power of the United Kingdom Parliament to legislate for Australia.[33] It gave the state Parliaments the same power to legislate for the peace, order and good government of the states as the United Kingdom Parliament had before the Act was passed,[34] including the power to legislate with extra-territorial effect.[35] The application of the Colonial Laws Validity Act 1865 to the states was abolished.[36] State laws are no longer subject to disallowance or suspension by Her Majesty,[37] nor to the withholding of assent by a state Governor from any law passed in the manner and form required by law.[38] State Governors are appointed and dismissed on the recommendation of state Premiers.[39] No appeals from Australian courts lie to the Privy Council.[40] In those ways was the previous anomalous position of the Australian states removed, and the residual Westminster powers over the Commonwealth of Australia abolished.

Associated statehood

Although smallness in size and population, and poverty of resources, are not absolute bars to the attainment of sovereign independence, it is sensible for a small dependent territory to achieve self-determination by means of federation or association with a larger country. A system of 'associated statehood' was devised by the British Government in 1965,[41] and it came into being in the Eastern Caribbean in 1967,[42] without the

---

Australian States (4th edn. 1977). In practice the United Kingdom Parliament hardly ever legislated for the states. The United Kingdom would refuse a state request for the enactment of U.K. legislation to enable it to secede from the Commonwealth of Australia: see H.C. 88 (1934–5), the case of Western Australia.

[32] See Goldring [1986] *Public Law* 192.
[33] Australia Act 1986, s. 1.
[34] ibid., s. 2(2).
[35] ibid., s. 2(1).
[36] ibid., s. 3.
[37] ibid., ss 8, 9(2).
[38] ibid., s. 9(1).
[39] ibid., s. 7(5).
[40] ibid., s. 11. See above, p. 156.
[41] Cmnd 2865 (1965). See generally Sir Fred Phillips, *Freedom in the Caribbean* (1977).
[42] See Broderick (1968) 17 *I.C.L.Q.* 368.

blessing of the United Nations but by agreement with the territories concerned following constitutional conferences in London. In pursuance of the West Indies Act 1967, new constitutions were brought into force for Antigua, Dominica, Grenada, St Kitts-Nevis-Anguilla and St Lucia, which became associated states; St Vincent joined them in 1969. Broadly, the West Indies Act excluded these territories from the definition of 'colony' and conferred on them 'Statute of Westminster powers', with certain exceptions. The Legislature of an associated state could not make laws repugnant to the West Indies Act itself,[43] or United Kingdom legislation relating to nationality, citizenship, the royal style and titles, the succession to the throne, defence or external affairs; nor could it encroach on the United Kingdom Government's retained responsibilities for defence or external affairs.[44] The United Kingdom had positive powers to implement its responsibilities in the associated states. Thus, an Order in Council relating to defence or the external affairs of an associated state could be made with *or without* the consent of the Government of the associated state and could contain 'such provision as appears to Her Majesty to be appropriate' for changing the law of that state.[45] But the Act did not permit the merger or dismemberment of an associated state except at the request and with the consent of the state concerned.

All the original six associated states have now become fully independent.[46] The mechanism of associated statehood remains as a potential model for other small dependencies who might wish to reach a measure of self-determination.

Zimbabwe: a note[47]

It would be inappropriate for any current textbook dealing with Commonwealth matters to fail to record the settlement in 1979-80 of the apparently intractable Southern Rhodesian problem. Rhodesia is

---

[43] They could, however, amend their own constitutions in the manner there prescribed (see, for example, Antigua Constitution Order 1967 (S.I. 1967, No. 225) Sched. 2, s.38), and they could abolish appeals from their own courts to the West Indies Associated States Supreme Court (from which appeals lay to the Judicial Committee of the Privy Council).

[44] West Indies Act 1967, ss 2–4, Sched. 1.

[45] Including derogations from constitutional guarantees of fundamental rights (s. 7). The question whether legislation is in fact required for the discharge of the United Kingdom's responsibilities for defence or external affairs is non-justiciable (ss 2(1) (*a*), 3(2), 7(2), 18).

[46] See Sir Fred Phillips, *West Indian Constitutions: Post-Independence Reforms* (1985).

[47] See Claire Palley, *The Constitutional History and Law of Southern Rhodesia 1888–1965* (1966) for a full analysis up to 1965.

now the independent republican State of Zimbabwe and a member of the Commonwealth.

Following the illegal unilateral declaration of independence of 1965,[48] several unsuccessful attempts were made to negotiate a settlement. Ian Smith's white minority 'Government' refused to bow to mandatory United Nations sanctions; indeed, in 1969 a republican constitution was adopted. Thus far the revolution had been bloodless,[49] but in the early 1970s a guerrilla war began and grew in intensity. The whites reluctantly accepted a degree of power-sharing under Bishop Abel Muzorewa as Prime Minister in 1979, and in the same year a constitutional conference of all sides was held at Lancaster House under the chairmanship of the Foreign and Commonwealth Secretary, Lord Carrington. To the surprise of many, the conference succeeded.[50] An independence constitution was agreed; Lord Soames (Lord President of the Council in the British Cabinet) went to Salisbury as Governor with (on paper) sweeping powers, and on his arrival the rebellion, by consent, ended. The cease-fire broadly held; sanctions were lifted, and an amnesty was granted to wipe the entire U.D.I. slate clean in respect of what had happened between 1965 and 1979.[51]

Elections supervised by a Commonwealth monitoring force resulted in Mr Robert Mugabe's ZANU (PF) party winning an absolute majority of seats. He formed a Government which included members of other parties, and two were whites. Lord Soames returned to London – and a well-earned C.H. Independence day was on 18 April 1980.[52] So ended one of the unhappiest periods in Commonwealth history – but with an enormous task ahead of reconstruction, reconciliation and reform.

Rules of the Commonwealth association today [53]

Relationships between the United Kingdom and its dependencies are governed by detailed rules. Relations between independent

---

[48] See *Madzimbamuto* v. *Lardner-Burke* [1969] 1 A.C. 645 (H.L.). For possible treasonable actions connected with U.D.I., see Hepple, O'Higgins and Turpin [1966] *Criminal L. Rev.* 5 and Wharam [1967] *Camb. L. J.* 189.

[49] Save for some judicial executions carried out despite the exercise by the Queen of the prerogative of mercy on the advice of the British Government.

[50] For a summary of the agreement, see Cmnd 7758 (1979). Immunity from arrest and prosecution was granted to participants at the conference under S.I. 1979, No. 1374.

[51] Zimbabwe Act 1979, s. 3.

[52] For the main instruments which brought about lawful independence, see the Southern Rhodesia Act 1979, the Zimbabwe Act 1979 and the Zimbabwe Constitution Order 1979, S.I. 1979, No. 1600.

[53] See Wheare, op. cit.; de Smith, *The New Commonwealth and its Constitutions* (1964), ch. 1.

Commonwealth countries are not; the Commonwealth in this sense is almost a lawless association. It does not act as an international entity. It has no legislative, executive or judicial organ of government. Meetings of Commonwealth heads of government are in the nature of informal international conferences; they make few decisions, and members are not obliged in strict law to implement such decisions as may be made. The Commonwealth Secretariat, set up in 1965,[54] has no executive powers; it services Commonwealth conferences, acts as a clearing-house for furnishing information to Commonwealth countries, and assists in coordinating Commonwealth activities. The Judicial Committee of the Privy Council has jurisdiction to entertain certain appeals from the courts of Bahamas, Barbados, Belize, the Gambia, Jamaica, Malaysia, Mauritius, New Zealand, Singapore, and Trinidad and Tobago. Britain has a constitution in the sense of rules regulating a coherent government structure; the Commonwealth has not. The old fundamental rules of the British Commonwealth – the sovereignty of the Imperial Parliament and common allegiance to the Crown – have gone.[55]

Most of the rules of the Commonwealth association today are about the methods of acquiring and relinquishing membership. The rules relating to the incidents of membership are few: they emphasize equality of status, but the conventional obligations attached to membership are blurred, indeed scarcely tangible.

Acquisition of membership

To become a full member of the Commonwealth, a country must (*a*) be independent, (*b*) be accepted by the existing full members and (*c*) recognize the Queen as Head of the Commonwealth. A dependent territory which is about to achieve independence may obtain approval of an application for full membership in advance of independence day; accession to full membership then takes effect on independence. It is possible for a country outside the Commonwealth to become a full member: Cyprus left the Commonwealth in 1960 when it became independent, but re-entered as a full member in 1961. Western Samoa joined the Commonwealth in August 1970. Consultations on applications with other members are now made through the Com-

---

[54] Cmnd 2713 (1965). The Secretariat has its headquarters in London but is not in any sense an organ of the British Government. The quarterly *Commonwealth Law Bulletin* published by the Secretariat is very valuable. The present Secretary-General is Guyanese.

[55] cf. R. T. E. Latham, *The Law and the Commonwealth* (1949), for a brilliant jurisprudential essay on the Commonwealth shortly before the Second World War. The author was killed in action in the Royal Air Force during the war.

monwealth Secretariat. The need for the concurrence of existing full members is implicit in the concept of equality of status. There is no settled rule that consent must be unanimous. When Bangladesh was admitted to membership in April 1972 it appears that no opposition was expressed, but several Commonwealth members had not recognized the independence of Bangladesh at that time. If there were to be substantial opposition to an application – for example, if the United Kingdom had been prepared to advance Southern Rhodesia, a colony with a white minority régime, to independence in (say) 1964 and to propose that country's admission to full membership – then either the application would be rejected or withdrawn, or a dissenting minority might choose to secede from the Commonwealth or refuse to participate in aspects of Commonwealth affairs.

The Queen's status as Head of the Commonwealth flows directly from the London Declaration of April 1949. India had achieved Dominion status and independence in 1947, and wished to adopt a republican constitution but remain within the Commonwealth. At a meeting of Commonwealth Prime Ministers, a formula was devised whereby (i) India proclaimed its desire to continue as a full member of the Commonwealth and its acceptance of the King as the symbol of the free association of its independent member nations, and, as such, Head of the Commonwealth, and (ii) the other members recorded their acceptance and recognition of India's continuing membership as a republic on this basis. India became a republic within the Commonwealth in January 1950.

At the time it was envisaged that India would be a special case. Inevitably, however, it set a precedent: what had been granted to India could hardly be denied to others. In 1957 Malaya (now Malaysia) became independent with its own monarch, the Yang di-Pertuan Agong, elected from among the hereditary Malay rulers. In 1964 Zambia became independent as a republic. Many others followed suit. Today only a minority of Commonwealth countries have the Queen as their head of State.[56] Following a military coup in Fiji in 1987 the country was declared to be a republic by the military régime. The Queen, as Queen of Fiji, eventually accepted the fact of republican status and consented to the Governor-General's resignation.[57] At the Commonwealth Conference later in that year the members confirmed that Fiji's membership of the Commonwealth had automatically lapsed with the declaration of a republic.

In her capacity as Head of the Commonwealth she performs no

[56] See p. 112.
[57] See above, p. 112.

constitutional function. Controversy over her Christmas Day broadcast to the Commonwealth in 1983 (which some people in Britain criticized for concentrating on other members of the Commonwealth to the detriment of Britain) produced statements from Buckingham Palace and from the Prime Minister that, in the exercise of her role as Head of the Commonwealth, the Queen is not obliged to take or act on advice from British or any other Ministers.[58]

There is no other formal qualification (for example, size, ideology) for admission to full membership.

Incidents of membership. The governments of full members of the Commonwealth are entitled to be represented at heads of government meetings, which are held at irregular intervals – roughly every two years. These used invariably to be held in London, but since 1966 other Commonwealth capitals have been chosen as well. These governments are also entitled to take part, on an equal footing, in other Commonwealth activities – for example, meetings of Finance Ministers, educational programmes, and so on. It can hardly be said that there is a clearly defined *obligation* to participate in any particular activity; though a country which decided not to cooperate in Commonwealth affairs at all would (unless it was making a temporary gesture of protest) probably withdraw from the Commonwealth altogether. The conventional duty to consult other Commonwealth members or to keep them informed on matters directly affecting their interests is ill-defined and loosely interpreted. Members have indeed broken off diplomatic relations with one another,[59] even gone to war with one another (India and Pakistan) and still remained in the Commonwealth. Pakistan left the Commonwealth only when recognition of the independence of Bangladesh by the older States was imminent.

It is to be inferred that most of the conventions relating to equality of status (for example, regarding the constitutional position of a Governor-General) formulated in the era of Dominion status apply to the new members as well.

Retention of membership. If a member which has the Queen as head of State wishes to become a republic or separate monarchy and remain within the Commonwealth, it must obtain the concurrence of existing members. The rationale of this rule, adopted when severance of

[58] Blackburn [1985] *Public Law* 361.
[59] The United Kingdom severed diplomatic relations with Uganda in 1976, but renewed them in 1979 following the overthrow of Idi Amin's dictatorship.

allegiance to the Crown was thought of as a serious step to take, has disappeared, but the practice has survived. It was used as a means of driving South Africa out of the Commonwealth in 1961. The Union wished, like India, to become a republic and to retain its place in the Commonwealth. Opposition developed among other Commonwealth members who objected strongly to South Africa's racial policies; and there was so much dissension at the meeting of Commonwealth Prime Ministers at which South Africa's application for continuance of membership on the new basis was discussed, that the Union Government withdrew its application, choosing the least of evils. Subsequently, in May 1961, South Africa became a republic and its membership of the Commonwealth automatically lapsed.[60]

Termination of membership. This may occur in four ways: by loss of independence, by voluntary secession, by lapse (on failing to seek, or failing to obtain, the concurrence of the other members on becoming a republic or a separate monarchy), and (probably) by expulsion. The only instances of voluntary secession by countries already independent members of the Commonwealth were the withdrawal of Eire (the Republic of Ireland) in 1949 and of Pakistan in January 1972.[61] Lapse of membership had occurred only in the case of South Africa. There was no precedent for expulsion and there are still no accepted rules governing such a matter, but South Africa had in effect been forced out of the Commonwealth by a procedural device, and even if it had abandoned the idea of adopting a republican constitution there can be little doubt that it would have been evicted by a majority decision soon afterwards.[62]

Commonwealth relations[63]

Over-enthusiastic descriptions of the Commonwealth – 'a family of

[60] For Fiji, see above, p. 669.
[61] There have been other cases (for example, Burma in 1948) where a territory ceased to be part of the Commonwealth *on attaining independence.*
[62] The following countries have left (or, when eligible for membership, have failed to join) the Commonwealth: Burma, Palestine (1948); Eire (1949); Sudan (1956); British Somaliland (1960); South Africa, Southern Cameroons (1961); Maldive Islands (1963); Yemen (1967); Pakistan (1972).
[63] For a very useful short survey, see Derek Ingram, *The Commonwealth at Work* (1969). See also P. N. S. Mansergh, *Survey of British Commonwealth Affairs*, vols 3 and 4; *The Commonwealth Experience* (1969); J. D. B. Miller, *The Commonwealth in the World* (3rd edn, 1965). A mass of factual information is digested in the *Year Book of the Commonwealth* published annually by the Foreign and Commonwealth Office in London.

like-minded nations, speaking the same political language and voluntarily co-operating on matters of common concern . . .' – have led to a reaction. Nowadays the Commonwealth is apt to be dismissed as a gigantic farce, as the emperor who had no clothes, as the disembodied grin on the face of the Cheshire Cat. Relations between Commonwealth countries are indeed often disharmonious; conflicts of interest and differences of approach may run deep. In international affairs the Commonwealth now bears comparison with the United Nations writ small. And it is not and cannot be an independent power factor in the modern world. As an entity, it suffers from special disadvantages. For too many members, Commonwealth relations have meant relations with the United Kingdom; [64] and for too many people in the United Kingdom the Commonwealth ought to behave like a grateful Empire. Unrealistic expectations have been unfulfilled. Racial discord and restrictions in Commonwealth immigration into the United Kingdom, Britain's refusal to use force in order to quell the Rhodesian rebellion and Britain's entry into the EEC in pursuit of its own interests have imposed severe stresses on the Commonwealth relationships. The unsuccessful search for a common course of action against South African apartheid has caused major rifts between members, the worst of which occurred in 1986 after South Africa had declared a state of emergency in response to rising violence. At a meeting in London the Commonwealth agreed on substantial economic sanctions against South Africa, but the British Government refused to implement them on the grounds that they would not work and would hit black South Africans hardest.

The Commonwealth, as at present constituted, has no prospect of developing supranational organs qualifying the sovereignty of its members. The small Commonwealth Secretariat, treading warily so as not to risk causing any affront to any members, symbolizes some of the weaknesses of the Commonwealth. The Secretariat, incarnated by the Secretary-General, is also a symbol that the Commonwealth exists and that its members want it to be a useful organization – the Secretariat is financed by agreed contributions from individual members – serving a limited range of agreed purposes. The Commonwealth is in fact a minor consultative and cooperative international body, whose members have certain special relationships with one another. These special relationships are not easy to define at all precisely. The representatives of Commonwealth governments in Commonwealth capitals are called

---

[64] The grounds on which Pakistan withdrew from membership in January 1972 (see p. 670) are significant.

High Commissioners, not Ambassadors of Ministers, and some have direct access to government Departments other than the Foreign Office. But if we search for a distinct body of Commonwealth law, we shall find only a miscellany of statutory provisions, lacking in uniformity, dealing with such matters as the rendition of fugitive offenders, reciprocal recognition of professional qualifications, grants of probate and so on; and differentiating, for some purposes, the status of citizens of other Commonwealth countries from that of aliens. Even before the United Kingdom joined the European Communities and thereby became obliged to replace Commonwealth preference by Community preference, Commonwealth preference was not offered by all Commonwealth countries to imports from all other Commonwealth countries. The concept of the Commonwealth as an economic, political or legal unit is illusory.

Yet the Commonwealth survives and is unlikely to suffer total disintegration in the near future. Since not a single full member seceded voluntarily for over forty years following 1949 (and eighteen new full members joined in 1970–85), there were surely advantages, tangible or intangible, in belonging to such an organization. Or perhaps the matter should be phrased more negatively; the obligations imposed by membership are slight, and reasons offered for withdrawal are seldom, on balance, convincing. Few members, however, would give an identical set of reasons for wishing to remain. For a newly independent small country, the advantages of membership may be considerable. Membership offers these countries new windows on the world; a large fund of factual information; an opportunity to reduce their sense of isolation and to resist the gravitational pull of intrusive and powerful neighbours; prospects of a helping hand from friendly countries in various parts of the world if they are in political, administrative or economic difficulties; and readier access to the London money market, technical assistance and special financial aid. Mauritius, a small, overpopulated sugar island in the Indian Ocean, a strategically important area, had the benefits of a defence agreement with Britain, British diplomatic protection for its citizens in countries where Mauritius had no representative of its own, a relatively high guaranteed price under the Commonwealth Sugar Agreement for much of its export crop, Commonwealth preference for most of the rest of its exports, and development and budgetary aid from Britain. This is, perhaps, an extreme example – and Mauritius was able to negotiate a reasonably advantageous association agreement with the EEC when the support for its sugar exports was jeopardized by Britain's accession – but the

Commonwealth had become increasingly an organization attractive to small States. Of the large members, Canada, Australia and New Zealand, still felt a certain sense of affinity with Britain and one another, they appreciated the importance of cultivating good relations with developing countries. For some of the African and large Asian members, the benefits of membership were becoming more problematical; one of them might be the possibility of influencing the external policies of the 'western' members; another, a feeling that withdrawal would place them at a disadvantage *vis-à-vis* rivals who remained within the organization.

The attitudes struck at plenary sessions of meetings of Commonwealth heads of government are not characteristic of the general pattern of Commonwealth relations. Functional cooperation and interchange at official and unofficial levels are less conspicuous but more impressive. Commonwealth activities at the official level range over a very wide field – from occasional conferences of Finance Ministers or Law Ministers to the work of specialized operational, consultative or advisory bodies such as the Commonwealth Telecommunications Organization, the Commonwealth Agricultural Bureaux and the Commonwealth War Graves Commission. Educational cooperation, illustrated by the recruitment of university teachers through the Inter-University Council, the Association of Commonwealth Universities, the schemes for the interchange of teachers, the award of Commonwealth fellowships and scholarships and the training of Zimbabwean Africans abroad, has been an asset to nearly every Commonwealth country. At the semi-official and unofficial levels, there are the numerous conferences organized by the Commonwealth Parliamentary Association; Commonwealth Legal Conferences; arrangements for professional conferences and exchanges of personnel, now promoted or subsidized by the Commonwealth Foundation (established in 1966); and the work of a host of voluntary bodies, mainly in the United Kingdom, which diffuse information and goodwill and sometimes perform services of a more practical utility to Commonwealth countries and their citizens.

Table of Cases

Table of Statutes

Index

FOR THE BEST IN PAPERBACKS, LOOK FOR THE 🐧

In every corner of the world, on every subject under the sun, Penguin represents quality and variety – the very best in publishing today.

For complete information about books available from Penguin – including Puffins, Penguin Classics and Arkana – and how to order them, write to us at the appropriate address below. Please note that for copyright reasons the selection of books varies from country to country.

In the United Kingdom: Please write to *Dept JC, Penguin Books Ltd, FREEPOST, West Drayton, Middlesex, UB7 0BR.*

If you have any difficulty in obtaining a title, please send your order with the correct money, plus ten per cent for postage and packaging, to *PO Box No 11, West Drayton, Middlesex*

In the United States: Please write to *Dept BA, Penguin, 299 Murray Hill Parkway, East Rutherford, New Jersey 07073*

In Canada: Please write to *Penguin Books Canada Ltd, 2801 John Street, Markham, Ontario L3R 1B4*

In Australia: Please write to the *Marketing Department, Penguin Books Australia Ltd, P.O. Box 257, Ringwood, Victoria 3134*

In New Zealand: Please write to the *Marketing Department, Penguin Books (NZ) Ltd, Private Bag, Takapuna, Auckland 9*

In India: Please write to *Penguin Overseas Ltd, 706 Eros Apartments, 56 Nehru Place, New Delhi, 110019*

In the Netherlands: Please write to *Penguin Books Netherlands B.V., Postbus 3507, NL–1001 AH, Amsterdam*

In West Germany: Please write to *Penguin Books Ltd, Friedrichstrasse 10–12, D–6000 Frankfurt/Main 1*

In Spain: Please write to *Alhambra Longman S.A., Fernandez de la Hoz 9, E–28010 Madrid*

In Italy: Please write to *Penguin Italia s.r.l., Via Como 4, I-20096 Pioltello (Milano)*

In France: Please write to *Penguin France S.A., 17 rue Lejeune, F-31000 Toulouse*

In Japan: Please write to *Longman Penguin Japan Co Ltd, Yamaguchi Building, 2–12–9 Kanda Jimbocho, Chiyoda-Ku, Tokyo 101*

FOR THE BEST IN PAPERBACKS, LOOK FOR THE 🐧

PENGUIN BUSINESS AND ECONOMICS

Almost Everyone's Guide to Economics
J. K. Galbraith and Nicole Salinger

This instructive and entertaining dialogue provides a step-by-step explanation of 'the state of economics in general and the reasons for its present failure in particular in simple, accurate language that everyone could understand and that a perverse few might conceivably enjoy'.

The Rise and Fall of Monetarism   David Smith

Now that even Conservatives have consigned monetarism to the scrapheap of history, David Smith draws out the unhappy lessons of a fundamentally flawed economic experiment, driven by a doctrine that for years had been regarded as outmoded and irrelevant.

Atlas of Management Thinking   Edward de Bono

This fascinating book provides a vital repertoire of non-verbal images that will help activate the right side of any manager's brain.

The Economist Economics   Rupert Pennant-Rea and Clive Crook

Based on a series of 'briefs' published in *The Economist*, this is a clear and accessible guide to the key issues of today's economics for the general reader.

Understanding Organizations   Charles B. Handy

Of practical as well as theoretical interest, this book shows how general concepts can help solve specific organizational problems.

The Winning Streak   Walter Goldsmith and David Clutterbuck

A brilliant analysis of what Britain's best-run and most successful companies have in common – a must for all managers.

FOR THE BEST IN PAPERBACKS, LOOK FOR THE 🐧

PENGUIN BUSINESS AND ECONOMICS

Lateral Thinking for Management Edward de Bono

Creativity and lateral thinking can work together for managers in developing new products or ideas; Edward de Bono shows how.

Understanding the British Economy Peter Donaldson and John Farquhar

A comprehensive and well signposted tour of the British economy today; a sound introduction to elements of economic theory; and a balanced account of recent policies are provided by this bestselling text.

A Question of Economics Peter Donaldson

Twenty key issues – the City, trade unions, 'free market forces' and many others – are presented clearly and fully in this major book based on a television series.

The Economics of the Common Market Dennis Swann

From the CAP to the EMS, this internationally recognized book on the Common Market – now substantially revised – is essential reading in the run-up to 1992.

The Money Machine How the City Works Philip Coggan

How are the big deals made? Which are the institutions that really matter? What causes the pound to rise or interest rates to fall? This book provides clear and concise answers to these and many other money-related questions.

Parkinson's Law C. Northcote Parkinson

'Work expands so as to fill the time available for its completion': that law underlies this 'extraordinarily funny and witty book' (Stephen Potter in the *Sunday Times*) which also makes some painfully serious points about those in business or the Civil Service.

PENGUIN HISTORY

Modern Ireland 1600–1972   R. F. Foster

'Takes its place with the finest historical writing of the twentieth century, whether about Ireland or anywhere else' – Conor Cruise O'Brien in the *Sunday Times*

Death in Hamburg   Society and Politics in the Cholera Years 1830–1910 Richard J. Evans

Why did the cholera epidemic of 1892 kill nearly 10,000 people in six weeks in Hamburg, while most of Europe was left almost unscathed? The answers put forward in this 'tremendous book' (Roy Porter in the *London Review of Books*) offer a wealth of insights into the inner life of a great – and uniquely anomalous – European city at the height of an industrial age.

British Society 1914–1945   John Stevenson

A major contribution to the *Penguin Social History of Britain*, which 'will undoubtedly be the standard work for students of modern Britain for many years to come' – *The Times Educational Supplement*

A History of Christianity   Paul Johnson

'Masterly … a cosmic soap opera involving kings and beggars, philosophers and crackpots, scholars and illiterate *exaltés*, popes and pilgrims and wild anchorites in the wilderness' – Malcolm Muggeridge

The Penguin History of Greece   A. R. Burn

Readable, erudite, enthusiastic and balanced, this one-volume history of Hellas sweeps the reader along from the days of Mycenae and the splendours of Athens to the conquests of Alexander and the final dark decades.

Battle Cry of Freedom   The American Civil War James M. McPherson

'Compellingly readable … It is the best one-volume treatment of its subject I have come across. It may be the best ever published … This is magic' – Hugh Brogan in *The New York Times Book Review*

FOR THE BEST IN PAPERBACKS, LOOK FOR THE 🐧

PENGUIN HISTORY

The Penguin History of the United States   Hugh Brogan

'An extraordinarily engaging book' – *The Times Literary Supplement*.
'Compelling reading ... Hugh Brogan's book will delight the general
reader as much as the student' – *The Times Educational Supplement*. 'He
will be welcomed by American readers no less than those in his own
country' – J. K. Galbraith

The Making of the English Working Class   E. P. Thompson

Probably the most imaginative – and the most famous – post-war work of
English social history.

The Waning of the Middle Ages   Johan Huizinga

A magnificent study of life, thought and art in 14th- and 15th-century
France and the Netherlands, long established as a classic.

The City in History   Lewis Mumford

Often prophetic in tone and containing a wealth of photographs, *The City
in History* is among the most deeply learned and warmly human studies of
man as a social creature.

The Habsburg Monarchy 1809–1918   A. J. P. Taylor

Dissolved in 1918, the Habsburg Empire 'had a unique character, out of
time and out of place'. Scholarly and vividly accessible, this 'very good
book indeed' (*Spectator*) elucidates the problems always inherent in the
attempt to give peace, stability and a common loyalty to a heterogeneous
population.

Inside Nazi Germany   Conformity, Opposition and Racism in Everyday Life
Detlev J. K. Peukert

An authoritative study – and a challenging and original analysis – of the
realities of daily existence under the Third Reich. 'A fascinating study ...
captures the whole range of popular attitudes and the complexity of their
relationship with the Nazi state' – Richard Geary

FOR THE BEST IN PAPERBACKS, LOOK FOR THE

PENGUIN HISTORY

The Victorian Underworld Kellow Chesney

A superbly evocative survey of the vast substratum of vice that lay below the respectable surface of Victorian England – the showmen, religious fakes, pickpockets and prostitutes – and of the penal methods of that 'most enlightened age'. 'Charged with nightmare detail' – *Sunday Times*

Citizens Simon Schama

The award-winning chronicle of the French Revolution. 'The most marvellous book I have read about the French Revolution in the last fifty years' – Richard Cobb in *The Times*. 'He has chronicled the vicissitudes of that world with matchless understanding, wisdom, pity and truth, in the pages of this huge and marvellous book' – *Sunday Times*

Stalin Isaac Deutscher

'The Greatest Genius in History' and the 'Life-Giving Force of Socialism'? Or a tyrant more ruthless than Ivan the Terrible whose policies facilitated the rise of Nazism? An outstanding biographical study of a revolutionary despot by a great historian.

Jasmin's Witch Emmanuel Le Roy Ladurie

An investigation into witchcraft and magic in south-west France during the seventeenth century – a masterpiece of historical detective work by the bestselling author of *Montaillou*.

The Second World War A J P Taylor

A brilliant and detailed illustrated history, enlivened by all Professor Taylor's customary iconoclasm and wit.

Industry and Empire E. J. Hobsbawm

Volume 3 of the *Penguin Economic History of Britain* covers the period of the Industrial Revolution: 'the most fundamental transformation in the history of the world recorded in written documents.' 'A book that attracts and deserves attention ... by far the most gifted historian now writing' – John Vaizey in the *Listener*

FOR THE BEST IN PAPERBACKS, LOOK FOR THE

PENGUIN ARCHAEOLOGY

Archaeology and Language The Puzzle of Indo-European Origins
Colin Renfrew

'His most important and far-reaching book: the pace is exhilarating, the issues are momentous ... *Archaeology and Language* breaks new ground by bringing the findings of the two sciences back into relationship more successfully than any other scholar in this century ... We have come a long step closer towards understanding human origins' – Peter Levi in the *Independent*

The Dead Sea Scrolls in English G. Vermes

This established and authoritative English translation of the non-biblical Qumran scrolls – offering a revolutionary insight into Palestinian Jewish life and ideology at a crucial period in the development of Jewish and Christian religious thought – now includes the Temple Scroll, the most voluminous scroll of them all.

Hadrian's Wall David J. Breeze and Brian Dobson

A penetrating history of the best-known, best-preserved and most spectacular monument to the Roman Empire in Britain. 'A masterpiece of the controlled use of archaeological and epigraphical evidence in a fluent narrative that will satisfy any level of interest' – *The Times Educational Supplement*

Before Civilization The Radiocarbon Revolution and Prehistoric Europe
Colin Renfrew

'I have little doubt that this is one of the most important archaeological books for a very long time' – Barry Cunliffe in the *New Scientist*. 'Pure stimulation from beginning to end ... a book which provokes thought, aids understanding, and above all is immensely enjoyable' – *Scotsman*

The Ancient Civilizations of Peru J. Alden Mason

The archaeological, historical, artistic, geographical and ethnographical discoveries that have resurrected the rich variety of Inca and pre-Inca culture and civilization – wiped out by the Spanish Conquest – are surveyed in this now classic work.

PENGUIN RELIGION

Adam, Eve and the Serpent   Elaine Pagels

How is it that the early Church, advocate of individual free will, came to preach the doctrine of original sin and to regard sexual desire as the inherent and shameful enslavement of humanity? This paradox is explored by the author of *The Gnostic Gospels*.

Islam in the World   Malise Ruthven

This informed and informative book places the contemporary Islamic revival in context, providing a fascinating introduction – the first of its kind – to Islamic origins, beliefs, history, geography, politics and society.

The Orthodox Church   Timothy Ware

In response to increasing interest among western Christians, and believing that a thorough understanding of Orthodoxy is necessary if the Roman Catholic and Protestant Churches are to be reunited, Timothy Ware explains Orthodox views on a vast range of matters from Free Will to the Papacy.

Judaism   Isidore Epstein

The comprehensive account of Judaism as a religion and as a distinctive way of life, presented against a background of 4,000 years of Jewish history.

Mysticism   F. C. Happold

What is mysticism? This simple and illuminating book combines a study of mysticism with an illustrative anthology of mystical writings, ranging from Plato and Plotinus to Dante.

The Penguin History of the Church: 4   Gerald R. Cragg
The Church and the Age of Reason

Gerald Cragg's elegant and stimulating assessment of the era from the Peace of Westphalia to the French Revolution – a formative period in the Church's history – ranges from the Church life of France under Louis XIV to the high noon of rationalism and beyond.

FOR THE BEST IN PAPERBACKS, LOOK FOR THE

PENGUIN REFERENCE BOOKS

The New Penguin English Dictionary

Over 1,000 pages long and with over 68,000 definitions, this cheap, compact and totally up-to-date book is ideal for today's needs. It includes many technical and colloquial terms, guides to pronunciation and common abbreviations.

The Penguin Spelling Dictionary

What are the plurals of *octopus* and *rhinoceros*? What is the difference between *stationary* and *stationery*? And how about *annex* and *annexe*, *agape* and *Agape*? This comprehensive new book, the fullest spelling dictionary now available, provides the answers.

Roget's Thesaurus of English Words and Phrases   Betty Kirkpatrick (ed.)

This new edition of Roget's classic work, now brought up to date for the nineties, will increase anyone's command of the English language. Fully cross-referenced, it includes synonyms of every kind (formal or colloquial, idiomatic and figurative) for almost 900 headings. It is a must for writers and utterly fascinating for any English speaker.

The Penguin Dictionary of Quotations

A treasure-trove of over 12,000 new gems and old favourites, from Aesop and Matthew Arnold to Xenophon and Zola.

The Penguin Wordmaster Dictionary
Martin H. Manser and Nigel D. Turton

This dictionary puts the pleasure back into word-seeking. Every time you look at a page you get a bonus – a panel telling you everything about a particular word or expression. It is, therefore, a dictionary to be read as well as used for its concise and up-to-date definitions.

FOR THE BEST IN PAPERBACKS, LOOK FOR THE

PENGUIN REFERENCE BOOKS

The Penguin Guide to the Law

This acclaimed reference book is designed for everyday use and forms the most comprehensive handbook ever published on the law as it affects the individual.

The Penguin Medical Encyclopedia

Covers the body and mind in sickness and in health, including drugs, surgery, medical history, medical vocabulary and many other aspects. 'Highly commendable' – *Journal of the Institute of Health Education*

The Slang Thesaurus

Do you make the public bar sound like a gentleman's club? Do you need help in understanding *Minder*? The miraculous *Slang Thesaurus* will liven up your language in no time. You won't Adam and Eve it! A mine of funny, witty, acid and vulgar synonyms for the words you use every day.

The Penguin Dictionary of Troublesome Words   Bill Bryson

Why should you avoid discussing the *weather conditions*? Can a married woman be *celibate*? Why is it eccentric to talk about the *aroma* of a cowshed? A straightforward guide to the pitfalls and hotly disputed issues in standard written English.

The Penguin Spanish Dictionary   James R. Jump

Detailed, comprehensive and, above all, modern, *The Penguin Spanish Dictionary* offers a complete picture of the language of ordinary Spaniards – the words used at home and at work, in bars and discos, at cafés and in the street, including full and unsqueamish coverage of common slang and colloquialisms.

The New Penguin Dictionary of Geography

From *aa* and *ablation* to *zinc* and *zonal soils*, this succinct dictionary is unique in covering in one volume the main terms now in use in the diverse areas – physical and human geography, geology and climatology, ecology and economics – that make up geography today.

FOR THE BEST IN PAPERBACKS, LOOK FOR THE 🐧

PENGUIN DICTIONARIES

Abbreviations

Archaeology

Architecture

Art and Artists

Biology

Botany

Building

Business

Chemistry

Civil Engineering

Computers

Curious and Interesting
  Words

Curious and Interesting
  Numbers

Design and Designers

Economics

Electronics

English and European
  History

English Idioms

French

Geography

German

Historical Slang

Human Geography

Literary Terms

Mathematics

Modern History 1789--1945

Modern Quotations

Music

Physical Geography

Physics

Politics

Proverbs

Psychology

Quotations

Religions

Rhyming Dictionary

Saints

Science

Sociology

Spanish

Surnames

Telecommunications

Troublesome Words

Twentieth-Century History

FOR THE BEST IN PAPERBACKS, LOOK FOR THE

PENGUIN POLITICS AND SOCIAL SCIENCES

Political Ideas David Thomson (ed.)

From Machiavelli to Marx – a stimulating and informative introduction to the last 500 years of European political thinkers and political thought.

On Revolution Hannah Arendt

Arendt's classic analysis of a relatively recent political phenomenon examines the underlying principles common to all revolutions, and the evolution of revolutionary theory and practice. 'Never dull, enormously erudite, always imaginative' – *Sunday Times*

Ill Fares the Land Susan George

These twelve essays expand on one of the major themes of Susan George's work: the role of power in perpetuating world hunger. With characteristic commitment and conviction, the author of *A Fate Worse than Debt* and *How the Other Half Dies* demonstrates that just as poverty lies behind hunger, so injustice and inequality lie behind poverty.

The Social Construction of Reality Peter Berger and Thomas Luckmann

Concerned with the sociology of 'everything that passes for knowledge in society' and particularly with that which passes for common sense, this is 'a serious, open-minded book, upon a serious subject' – *Listener*

The Care of the Self Michel Foucault
The History of Sexuality Vol 3

Foucault examines the transformation of sexual discourse from the Hellenistic to the Roman world in an inquiry which 'bristles with provocative insights into the tangled liaison of sex and self' – *The Times Higher Education Supplement*

Silent Spring Rachel Carson

'What we have to face is not an occasional dose of poison which has accidentally got into some article of food, but a persistent and continuous poisoning of the whole human environment.' First published in 1962, *Silent Spring* remains the classic environmental statement which founded an entire movement.

PENGUIN POLITICS AND SOCIAL SCIENCES

Comparative Government S. E. Finer

'A considerable *tour de force* ... few teachers of politics in Britain would fail to learn a great deal from it ... Above all, it is the work of a great teacher who breathes into every page his own enthusiasm for the discipline' – Anthony King in *New Society*

Karl Marx: Selected Writings in Sociology and Social Philosophy
T. B. Bottomore and Maximilien Rubel (eds.)

'It makes available, in coherent form and lucid English, some of Marx's most important ideas. As an introduction to Marx's thought, it has very few rivals indeed' – *British Journal of Sociology*

Post-War Britain A Political History Alan Sked and Chris Cook

Major political figures from Attlee to Thatcher, the aims and achievements of governments and the changing fortunes of Britain in the period since 1945 are thoroughly scrutinized in this readable history.

Inside the Third World Paul Harrison

From climate and colonialism to land hunger, exploding cities and illiteracy, this comprehensive book brings home a wealth of facts and analysis on the often tragic realities of life for the poor people and communities of Asia, Africa and Latin America.

Housewife Ann Oakley

'A fresh and challenging account' – *Economist*. 'Informative and rational enough to deserve a serious place in any discussion on the position of women in modern society' – *The Times Educational Supplement*

The Raw and the Cooked Claude Lévi-Strauss

Deliberately, brilliantly and inimitably challenging, Lévi-Strauss's seminal work of structural anthropology cuts wide and deep into the mind of mankind, as he finds in the myths of the South American Indians a comprehensible psychological pattern.